THE ROUGH GUIDE TO
SCOTLAND

rough GUIDES

This thirteenth edition updated by
Norm Longley

Contents

A NOTE TO READERS

At Rough Guides, we always strive to bring you the most up-to-date information. This book was produced during a period of continuing uncertainty caused by the Covid-19 pandemic, so please note that content is more subject to change than usual. We recommend checking the latest restrictions and official guidance.

Introduction to
Scotland

Clichéd images of Scotland abound – postcards of wee Highland terriers, glittering lochs, infinite variations on tartan and whisky – and they drive many Scots apoplectic. Yet Scotland has a habit of delivering on its classic images. In some parts ruined castles really do perch on every other hilltop, in summer the glens do indeed turn purple with heather, and you'll be unlucky not to catch sight of a breathless bagpiper while you're up here. Sure, the roads can be wiggly and the drizzle can be oppressive. But there's something intoxicating about these patriotic, Tolkienesque lands that will have you yearning for more.

The complexity of Scotland can be hard to unravel: somewhere deep in its genes a generous dose of romantic **Celtic** hedonism blends (somehow) with stern **Calvinist** prudence. It's a country where the losers of battles (and football games) are more romanticized than the winners. Scotland has given the world steam power, the television and penicillin. Chefs throughout Europe rhapsodize over Scottish langoustine and Aberdeen Angus beef, while back at home there is still a solid market for deep-fried pizza.

Naturally, the tourist industry tends to play up the heritage, but beyond the nostalgia lies a modern, dynamic nation. **Oil** and **nanotechnology** now matter more to the Scottish economy than fishing or Harris tweed, and the **video gaming** industry continues to prosper. Edinburgh's medieval Royal Mile still pulls a crowd, but just as many are drawn by its **nightclubs** and modern **restaurants**, while out in the Hebrides, the locals are more likely to be building websites than shearing sheep. Even the Highland huntin' shootin' fishin' set are outnumbered these days by **mountain bikers** and wide-eyed whale-watchers. The ceilidh remains an important part of the Highlands social scene, although large-scale **outdoor music festivals** draw in revellers from around the world.

Scotland will never be able to cut its geographical and historic ties with England, the 'auld enemy' south of the border, and relations between the two are as complicated as ever. Although, Scots voted to remain part of the United Kingdom by a margin of 55.3 percent to 44.7 percent in the 2014 **Scottish independence referendum,** the nationalist movement continued to build momentum and the SNP recorded a historic landslide victory in the **2015 UK general election**, taking 56 of 59 seats; they had won just four in 2010. In **2017,** the SNP's lost 21 seats, but staged a comeback in the **2019 UK general election** and won 48 seats.

In contrast, thanks to ancient links with Ireland, Scandinavia, France and the Netherlands, Scots are generally enthusiastic about the **European Union**, which – up until the 2016 **EU membership referendum** – had poured large sums of money into infrastructure and cultural projects, particularly in the Highlands and Islands. While the UK as a whole defied pollsters by voting to leave the EU, 62 percent of Scottish voters and all 32 councils opted to remain. Whether this will eventually lead to a second Scottish independence referendum, as First Minister **Nicola Sturgeon** desires, remains to be seen.

Where to go

Even if you're planning a short visit, it's perfectly possible to combine a stay in either Edinburgh or Glasgow with a brief foray into the Highlands. With more time, a greater variety of **landscapes** in Scotland is available, but there's no escaping the fact that travel in the more remote regions of Scotland takes time and money, even with your own transport. If you plan to spend most of your time in the countryside, concentrate on just one or two areas for a more rewarding visit.

The initial focus for many visitors to Scotland is the capital, **Edinburgh**, a dramatically handsome and engaging city famous for its castle and historic Old Town. Come in August and you'll find the city transformed by the Edinburgh Festival, the largest arts festival in the world. An hour's travel to the west, the country's biggest city, **Glasgow**, is quite different in character. Once a sprawling industrial metropolis, it now has a lively social and cultural life to match its impressive architectural heritage. Other urban centres are inevitably overshadowed by the big two, although the transformation from industrial grey to cultural colour is injecting life into **Dundee**, while there's a defiant separateness to **Aberdeen**, with its silvery granite architecture and port. Other centres serve more as transport or service hubs to the emptier landscapes beyond, though some contain compelling attractions such as the wonderful castle in **Stirling** or the Burns' monuments in **Ayr**.

You don't have to travel far north of the Glasgow–Edinburgh axis to find the first hints of **Highland** landscape, a divide marked by the Highland Boundary Fault, which cuts across central Scotland. The lochs, hills and wooded glens of the **Trossachs** and **Loch Lomond** are the most easily reached and correspondingly busier. Further north, **Perthshire** and the Grampian hills of **Angus** and **Deeside** show the Scottish countryside at its richest, with colourful woodlands and long glens rising up to distinctive mountain peaks. South of Inverness the **Cairngorm** massif hints at the raw wilderness Scotland still provides, which is at its most spectacular in the north and western Highlands. To get to the far north you'll have to cross the **Great Glen**, an ancient geological fissure which cuts right across the country from Ben Nevis to **Loch Ness**, a moody stretch of water rather choked with tourists hoping for a glimpse of its monster. Arguably, Scotland's most memorable scenery is to be found on the jagged

EILEAN DONAN CASTLE ON LOCH DUICH

west coast, stretching from **Argyll** all the way north to **Wester Ross** and the sugarloaf hills of **Assynt**.

Not all of central and northern Scotland is rugged Highlands, however. The east coast in particular mixes fertile farmland with pretty stone-built fishing villages and golf courses – none more famous than that at the university town of **St Andrews**, the spiritual home of the game. Elsewhere, the whisky trail of **Speyside** and the castles and Pictish stones of the **northeast** provide themes for exploration, while in the southern part of the country, the rolling hills and ruined abbeys of the **Borders** offer a refreshingly untouristy vision of rural Scotland.

The splendour of the Highlands would be bare without the **islands** off the west and north coasts. Assorted in size, flavour and accessibility, the long chain of rocky Hebrides which necklace Scotland's Atlantic shoreline includes **Mull** and its nearby pilgrimage centre of **Iona**; **Islay** and **Jura**, famous for their wildlife and whisky; **Skye**, the most visited of the Hebrides, where the snow-tipped peaks of the Cuillin rise above deep sea lochs; and the **Western Isles**, an elongated archipelago that is the country's last bastion of Gaelic language and culture. Off the north coast, **Orkney** and **Shetland**, both with a rich Norse heritage, differ both from each other and quite distinctly from mainland Scotland in dialect and culture – far-flung islands buffeted by wind

MUNRO-BAGGING

As the Inuit have dozens of words for snow, so a **hill** is rarely just a hill in Scotland. Depending on where you are, what it's shaped like and how high it is, a hill might be a ben, a mount, a law, a pen, a brae or even a pap (and that's without talking about the Gaelic *beinn*, *cnoc*, *creag*, *meall*, *sgurr* or *stob*). Even more confusing are **Munros**. These are Scottish hills over 3000ft high, defined by a list first drawn up by one Sir Hugh Munro in 1891. You 'bag' a Munro by walking to the top of it, and once you've bagged all **284** you can call yourself a Munroist. Actually, Munro-bagging at heart is less about conquering than appreciating the great Scottish outdoors. And if you do meet Sir Hugh's challenge, you can then start on the Corbetts (hills 2500–2999ft high) and the Donalds (hills 2000–2499ft high).

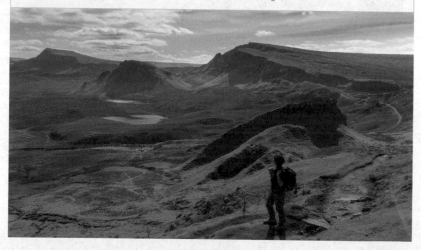

THE WEATHER

When asked why he liked holidaying on Scotland's west coast, the late poet laureate, Ted Hughes is alleged to have replied that 'there's no such thing as bad weather, only inadequate clothing'. For those who don't share Hughes' attitude, the **weather** is probably the single biggest factor to put you off visiting Scotland. It's not that it's always bad, it's just that it is **unpredictable**: you could just as easily enjoy a week of fabulous sunshine in early April while the rest of the UK was sodden as suffer a week of low-lying fog and drizzle in high summer.

No surprise then that six of the ten wettest counties in the UK are here. The reason is location: almost every **low pressure system** that barrels east out of the North Atlantic passes over Scotland, often forced north by the Azores' high pressure system. The good news is that such systems tend to blow over rapidly. Out in the islands, they say you can get all four seasons in a day. And even if the weather's not necessarily good, it's generally interesting – often exhilarating or dramatic, and certainly photogenic. And when the **sun** finally comes out all is forgiven. A week spent in thick mist is transformed when the clouds lift to reveal a majestic mountain range or a group of islands far offshore.

and sea that offer some of the country's wildest scenery, finest bird-watching and best archaeological sites.

When to go

Scottish comedian Billy Connolly once said that 'there are two seasons in Scotland: June and winter'. While the country is partial to a spot of unseasonal drizzle, the busy **summer** months – June, July and August – are generally warm and, most importantly, long, with daylight lingering until 9pm or till 10pm further north. **August** in Edinburgh is Festival time, which dominates everything in the city and means accommodation gets booked up very early. Elsewhere, events such as Highland Games, folk festivals or sporting events – most of which take place in the summer months – can tie up accommodation, though normally only in a fairly concentrated local area. If you're out and about in the countryside throughout the summer, you won't be able to avoid the clouds of small biting **midges**, which can be a real annoyance on still days, particularly around dusk.

AVERAGE DAILY TEMPERATURES AND MONTHLY RAINFALL

	Jan	Feb	March	April	May	June	July	Aug	Sept	Oct	Nov	Dec
EDINBURGH												
Max/min (°C)	7/1	8/1	10/3	12/4	15/7	17/10	19/12	19/11	17/9	13/7	10/4	7/1
Max/min (°F)	45/34	46/34	50/37	53/39	59/44	63/50	66/53	66/52	63/48	55/44	50/39	45/34
Rainfall (mm)	68	47	52	41	49	61	65	60	64	76	62	61
FORT WILLIAM												
Max/min (°C)	6/0	6/-1	7/1	10/2	14/4	16/7	17/10	17/9	15/7	11/5	8/2	6/1
Max/min (°F)	42/32	42/30	45/34	50/36	57/40	60/45	63/49	62/49	59/45	52/41	46/36	52/34
Rainfall (mm)	248	175	184	97	85	77	89	107	140	202	206	201
LERWICK												
Max/min (°C)	6/2	6/2	6/2	8/4	10/5	12/8	14/10	14/10	13/9	10/6	8/4	6/2
Max/min (°F)	43/35	43/35	43/35	46/38	51/42	54/46	58/40	58/50	55/48	51/43	46/39	43/35
Rainfall (mm)	143	121	125	71	53	58	67	84	106	142	146	143
TIREE												
Max/min (°C)	8/3	8/3	9/4	10/5	13/7	15/10	16/11	16/11	15/10	13/8	10/6	8/4
Max/min (°F)	46/38	46/38	48/39	51/41	55/45	59/49	61/52	61/52	59/49	55/46	49/43	46/39
Rainfall (mm)	138	101	103	73	60	66	80	107	112	150	136	132
WICK												
Max/min (°C)	6/1	6/1	8/2	10/4	11/5	14/8	16/10	16/10	14/9	12/6	9/4	7/1
Max/min (°F)	43/34	43/34	46/36	49/38	53/42	57/46	60/50	60/50	57/47	53/43	47/38	44/34
Rainfall (mm)	72	64	67	50	49	53	62	65	74	95	90	75

May and **September** throw up weather every bit as good as, if not better than, the months of high summer. You're less likely to encounter crowds or struggle to find somewhere to stay, and the mild temperatures combined with the changing colours of nature mean both are great for outdoor activities, particularly hiking. The caveat is that September is prime **stalking season** for deer, which can affect access to some parts of the Highlands for hiking, fishing or riding a mountain bike.

The **spring** and **autumn** months of April and October bracket the tourist season for many parts of rural Scotland. A large number of attractions, tourist offices and guesthouses often open for business on the Easter weekend and shut up shop after the school half-term in mid-October. If places do stay open through the winter, it's normally with reduced opening hours; this is the best time to pick up deals at hotels and guesthouses. Note too that in more remote spots public transport will often operate on a reduced winter timetable.

Winter days, from November to March, occasionally crisp and bright, are often cold, gloomy and all too short, although Hogmanay and New Year has traditionally been a time to visit Scotland for partying and warm hospitality – something which improves as the weather worsens. While even tourist hotspots such as Edinburgh are notably quieter during winter, a fall of snow in the Highlands will prompt plenty of activity around the ski resorts.

Author picks

Scotland has its poster places: Edinburgh's Royal Mile or Eilean Donan castle, for example. But the cherished memories of a country are usually more personal discoveries. Here are those of Rough Guides' authors as they travelled down every lane and supped in every pub in the cause of researching this Guide.

Mill on the Clyde Glasgow's prosperity wasn't just built on iron and ships. In the late eighteenth century, the utopian mill village of New Lanark (see page 211) inspired the Cooperative movement and introduced adult education.

Seafood sensation Look for the wooden shack in Crail harbour (see page 300), select your lobster (caught that day), and have it cooked to order. Seafood doesn't get fresher than this.

Subculture Release your inner bohemian in the caverns beneath Edinburgh's South Bridge, rediscovered after two hundred lost years and turned into entertainment venue *The Caves* (see page 97).

Skye crafts The mountains are marvellous, but Skye also appeals for its crafts; tanneries, weavers, brewers and all (see page 465).

Stonehaven This coastal town (see page 359), best known for its annual folk festival, is also near Scotland's finest medieval ruin, Dunnottar Castle.

North Coast 500 This road trip around the northernmost reaches of Scotland covers some of the most spectacularly rugged scenery in the British Isles (see page 420).

Beavers Back in Scotland after a four-hundred-year absence, seek out these hard-working creatures in Knapdale, Argyll (see page 250) – the 60ft-long dam is a feat of engineering.

Flying visit The trip in an eight-seater plane to North Ronaldsay, Orkney (see page 532), is worth it to see seaweed-eating sheep, even without a night at the ecofriendly bird observatory.

Our author recommendations don't end here. We've flagged up our favourite places – a perfectly sited hotel, an atmospheric café, a special restaurant – throughout the Guide, highlighted with the ★ symbol.

PITTENWEEM
NORTH RONALDSAY LIGHTHOUSE

30

things not to miss

It's not possible to see everything that Scotland has to offer on a short trip – and we don't suggest you try. What follows, in no particular order, is a selective taste of the country's highlights: compelling sights, vibrant festivals and some of the most spectacular scenic wonders in Europe. All highlights have a page reference to take you straight into the Guide, where you can find out more.

1

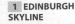

1 EDINBURGH SKYLINE
See page 80
From Calton Hill, the Old Town appears as an unforgettable vista of tightly packed tenements and spires that rise to the immense castle.

2 HOGMANAY
See page 41
New Year celebrations, with whisky, dancing and fireworks staving off the midwinter chill.

3 CALEDONIAN FOREST
See page 405
Among the gnarled survivors of the great ancient forests you'll find one of Scotland's largest populations of the elusive red squirrel.

4 LOCH NESS
See page 391
Take the old road around the east shores to escape the caravanning crowds, and find tiny lochans and pretty pubs like the *Dores Inn*.

5 WHISKY
See page 38
Single malts have never been more varied or so innovative, and you'll find hundreds of varieties in Scotland's pubs. Good luck.

6 RHINNS OF GALLOWAY
See page 149
Famous for its balmy gulf-stream-fed microclimate, the southwest is a sanctuary for exotic plants, with six botanic gardens to discover.

7 ROSSLYN CHAPEL
See page 106
This richly decorated cathedral-like masterpiece is a testament to the skills of its medieval sculptors.

8 ISLAY
See page 257
Endless pretty villages and bays, wonderfully varied wildlife, and no fewer than nine whisky distilleries.

9 AILSA CRAIG
See page 163
Conspicuous, muffin-shaped hump just off the Ayrshire coast that's home to one of the world's largest colonies of gannets.

10 EIGG
See page 476
Perfect example of a tiny Hebridean island with a golden beach to lie on, a hill to climb and stunning views across to Rùm.

11 KNOYDART PENINSULA

See page 426

No matter whether you arrive by boat or on foot, the sense of dropping off the radar is the same in one of Britain's last wilderness regions.

12 BIKING AT GLENTRESS

See page 127

7stanes has seven forest centres with adrenaline-pumping downhill biking for all levels.

13 THE CUILLIN RANGE

See page 467

The most spectacular mountain range on the west coast: superb to see, breathtaking (literally) to climb.

14 THE CAIRNGORM MOUNTAINS

See page 405

Natural splendour and terrific outdoor activities abound here.

15 STAFFA AND THE TRESHNISH ISLES

See page 235

View the basalt columns of Fingal's Cave from the sea, then picnic beside the puffins on the Isle of Lunga.

11

12

24

21 WHALE-WATCHING, MULL
See page 233
Look out for minke and killer whales in the abundant waters around Mull.

22 AUGUST FESTIVALS IN EDINBURGH
See page 100
Actors, comedians, artists, writers and celebs converge en masse for the world's biggest arts gathering.

23 IONA
See page 238
The cradle of Christianity in Scotland, an island of pilgrimage today as in antiquity.

24 FOOD ON SKYE
See pages 469 and 471
Skye is Scotland's foodie capital, from slap-up lobster and chips at *The Oyster Shed* to dining in the kitchen at *The Three Chimneys*.

25 CRAIL
See page 299
Fife's picture-perfect harbour town, home to small fishing vessels, caught-that-morning seafood and easel-toting artists.

25

26 STIRLING CASTLE

See page 272
The grandest castle in Scotland, with a commanding outlook over the Highlands and Lowlands.

27 GLEN COE

See page 388
Scotland's most spectacular glen puts Munro summits, glacial valleys and cool waterfalls within day-trip distance of Fort William.

28 CALLANISH, LEWIS

See page 491
Prehistoric standing stones that occupy a serene setting in the Western Isles.

29 CEILIDHS

See page 439
The ultimate Highland get-together, full of music, singing and dancing like there's no tomorrow.

30 WEST HIGHLAND RAILWAY

See page 424
From Glasgow to Mallaig, this is one of the great railway journeys of the world – 264 miles of ever-more spectacular scenery, with steam trains in the summer.

29

30

Itineraries

The following routes celebrate Scotland in all its variety, from the royal castles of Edinburgh to the black houses of the Western Isles, the putting greens of St Andrews and the Cuillin mountains' jagged ridges. Whether you're after a whistle-stop week, a fortnight of utter escapism or you're looking for an excuse to discover some of the finest tastes in Scotland, they will point the way. The trips below give a flavour of what the country has to offer, and what we can plan and book for you at ⓦroughguides.com/trips.

A SCOTLAND PRIMER

Ten days isn't enough time to do the entire nation justice, yet this tour offers tasters of contemporary culture, heritage, Highland scenery and even island life.

❶ **Edinburgh** The capital deserves two days of any visit. Must-sees include the cobbled streets and castle of the Old Town, the view from Calton Hill, and perhaps the Museum of Scotland, or a pub like *Bow Bar* if it rains. See page 54

❷ **Fife** So close to Edinburgh, so different in atmosphere, Fife has some highlights of Scottish culture: lovely Culross village; a novice-friendly putting green at St Andrews; and fresh lobster for lunch in Crail. See page 292

❸ **Stirling and the Trossachs** One of Scotland's most iconic castles is reason enough to visit Stirling. It's also the gateway for walks and bike rides in the Trossachs, a sort of Highlands-lite, and beyond them, the much-mythologized Loch Lomond. See page 268

❹ **Gigha** Subtropical gardens, golden beaches and life in the slow lane – Gigha is the perfect island introduction to the Hebrides. See page 253

❺ **Glasgow** We bookend the route with the great rival to Edinburgh. Vibrant, modern Glasgow is all about the architecture – especially Mackintosh's masterpieces – and nightlife that is glam and gritty by turns. See page 174

A TASTE OF SCOTLAND

A whistle-stop tour around the regional culinary highlights of Scotland – you'll have no trouble

---

Create your own itinerary with Rough Guides. Whether you're after adventure or a family-friendly holiday, we have a trip for you, with all the activities you enjoy doing and the sights you want to see. All our trips are devised by local experts who get the most out of the destination. Visit **www.roughguides.com/trips** to chat with one of our travel agents.

finding porridge, broth, Cullen skink, haggis and neeps and tatties wherever you go.

❶ Edinburgh With Michelin-starred restaurants and fine old drinking holes, foodies have never had it so good here. Highlights include *Wedgwood* and *The Kitchin*. See page 54

❷ Arbroath 'A world-class delicacy' is how chef and writer Rick Stein describes the humble haddock after it's been smoke-cured here, and who are we to argue? Head to the harbour and take your pick from the family-run smokehouses. See page 338

❸ Speyside Welcome to the heartland of whisky country, nurtured by pure cold water and a gentle climate. Of the fifty distilleries in the area, eight are on an official Malt Whisky Trail, from famous names like Glenfiddich and Glenlivet to wee distilleries like Strathisla. See page 410

❹ Skye Small gourmet restaurants like *Three Chimneys* and *Loch Bay* are reason enough to visit Skye. Expect innovative menus of super-fresh produce. See page 462

❺ Islay Peat and smoke define Islay single malts, heavy pungent whiskies compared to the lighter honeys and vanilla in Speyside. Laphroaig, Lagavulin and Bowmore are the big hitters, and all nine offer tours. See page 257

❻ Loch Fyne Fine dining without the fuss in the most famous seafood restaurant in Scotland, the *Loch Fyne Oyster Bar and Restaurant*. Expect local oysters, langoustine, scallops and superb fish. See page 223

TWO WEEKS ON THE ISLANDS

While Orkney and Shetland deserve a dedicated trip, the west coast islands seem tailor-made to explore by ferry. Who needs Greece?

❶ Mull Embark from one of the Highlands' loveliest fishing ports, Tobermory, for one of its best wildlife adventures – whale-watching – and visit nearby Iona, its atmosphere steeped in thousands of years as a pilgrimage destination. See page 229

❷ Barra A pipsqueak among the Western Isles where clear bays, white

beaches and impressive mountains deliver a concentrated dose of Hebridean magic. See page 503

❸ The Uists Trout fishing doesn't get much more fun than in the half-drowned lochs of North Uist. See page 496

❹ Lewis and Harris The conjoined twins of the Hebrides deserve several days of a trip. Visit for astonishing beaches like Luskentyre, mysterious standing stones at Callanish and to journey back a century in the restored village of Garenin. See pages 485 and 494

❺ Skye Skip back to Skye to tackle the Cuillin ridge, the must-do mountain route of any trail-junkie, or discover Loch Coruisk by boat, then settle into one of the island's many excellent hotels. See page 462

❻ The Small Isles So, what do you feel like doing today: sampling genuine island life on Eigg; discovering a barmy baronial manor on Rum; or spotting birdlife on strolls around tiny Muck? From Mallaig they're all just across the water. See page 474

A SCOTLAND PRIMER

A TASTE OF SCOTLAND

TWO WEEKS ON THE ISLANDS

ATLANTIC OCEAN

NORTH SEA

NORTHERN IRELAND

ENGLAND

Basics

Getting there

The quickest, easiest and cheapest way to get to Scotland is by plane. Scotland has four main international airports: Glasgow, Glasgow Prestwick (a hub for the budget airline Ryanair), Edinburgh, and Aberdeen. Glasgow and Edinburgh handle most long-haul flights, and all four have a reasonable spread of European connections.

With most airlines nowadays, how much you pay depends on how far in advance you book and how much **demand** there is during that period – generally speaking, the earlier you book, the cheaper the fare. That said, it's worth looking out for sales, which often start ten to twelve weeks before the departure date.

If you're coming from elsewhere in Britain, from Ireland or even northwest Europe, you can reach Scotland easily enough by **train**, **bus** or **ferry** – it probably won't work out cheaper or faster than flying, but it's undoubtedly better for the environment.

From England and Wales

If you're ultimately heading out to the Highlands and Islands, **flying** is the quickest way to travel. The main airlines with domestic routes within the UK are British Airways (ⓦbritishairways.com), Ryanair (ⓦryanair.com) easyJet (ⓦeasyjet.com) and Loganair (ⓦloganair.co.uk). Airfares are most competitive on popular routes such as London or Birmingham to Edinburgh and Glasgow, which can cost as little as £40 return (journey time around 1hr). However, once you add on the cost of transport to the airport and flying with checked **baggage** (most budget airlines charge for all but the smallest carry-on bag), the savings compared with doing the same journey overland can be minimal.

Train and coach (long-distance bus) fares can be pretty competitive if you book in advance. Return **train** fares to Glasgow can cost as little as £30 from Manchester (3hr 30min) or £60 from London (4hr 45min), with the very cheapest tickets going on sale twelve weeks in advance. A more flexible or last-minute fare will cost two or three times the amount. Another option is the overnight **Caledonian Sleeper** (ⓦsleeper.scot) service from London Euston (Mon–Fri & Sun; journey time to Glasgow around 7hr 30min); again, if you book in advance (up to twelve months), single overnight fares cost around £45 for a reclining seat, with no saving on return fares. The Caledonian Sleeper also goes to Aberdeen, Edinburgh, Fort William and Inverness. The **coach** takes much longer than the train (around 9hr one-way), but can cost significantly less, with a London or Birmingham to Glasgow return starting for as little as £20.

From Ireland

Travel from Ireland is quickest by plane, with **airfares** from either Belfast or Dublin to Glasgow from as little as €45 return; try Aer Lingus (ⓦaerlingus.com) and Ryanair (ⓦryanair.com), both based in Ireland. There are good **ferry** links with Northern Ireland via Cairnryan, near Stranraer, with P&O operating up to seven sea crossings daily from Larne (2hr; single passenger without car from £27; with car from £114), and Stena Line operating up to six services daily from Belfast (2hr 15min; single passenger without car from £31; with car from £139).

From mainland Europe

Ferries run by DFDS Seaways (ⓦdfds.com) sail overnight from Amsterdam to Newcastle (daily; 16–17hr), less than an hour's drive south of the Scottish border. Return fares for single passengers start at £130, which includes an overnight berth (around £150 extra with a small car). A much quicker (and usually cheaper) alternative is to fly with one of Europe's big budget carriers, such as easyJet (ⓦeasyjet.com), Ryanair (ⓦryanair.com) and Norwegian (ⓦnorwegian.com).

From the US and Canada

If you fly nonstop to Scotland from **North America**, you'll arrive in either Glasgow or Edinburgh. The

---

A BETTER KIND OF TRAVEL

At Rough Guides we are passionately committed to travel. We believe it helps us understand the world we live in and the people we share it with – and of course tourism is vital to many developing economies. But the scale of modern tourism has also damaged some places irreparably, and climate change is accelerated by most forms of transport, especially flying. We encourage all our authors to consider the carbon footprint of the journeys they make in the course of researching our guides.

majority of cheap fares, however, route through Amsterdam, London, Manchester, Dublin or Paris. To reach any other Scottish airport, you'll most likely need to go via London, Glasgow or Edinburgh.

Figure on six to seven hours' flight time nonstop from the **east coast** of the US to Glasgow, or seven hours to London plus an extra hour and a quarter from London to Glasgow or Edinburgh (not including stopover time). Add three or four hours more for travel from the **west coast**.

United (Ⓦunited.com) flies direct from Newark Liberty International Airport in New York to Glasgow, with return fares (including taxes) from around US$950. Air Canada (Ⓦaircanada.com) has direct flights to Edinburgh from Toronto; return fares for nonstop flights (including taxes) cost around CA$800.

From Australia and New Zealand

Flight time from **Australia** and **New Zealand** to Scotland is at least 22 hours. There is a wide variety of routes, with those touching down in Southeast Asia the quickest and cheapest on average. To reach Scotland, you usually have to change planes either in **London** – the most popular choice – or in another European gateway such as Paris or Amsterdam. Given the length of the journey involved, you might be better off including a night's stopover in your itinerary.

The cheapest scheduled flights to London are usually to be found on one of the Asian airlines, such as Malaysia Airlines (Ⓦmalaysiaairlines.com) or Thai Airways (Ⓦthaiairways.com). Average **return fares** (including taxes) from eastern Australian cities to London are around AU$1500–2000. Fares from Perth or Darwin cost around AU$100 less. Return fares from Auckland to London range between NZ$2000 and NZ$3000 depending on the season, route and carrier.

From South Africa

There are **no direct flights** from South Africa to Scotland, so you must change planes en route. The quickest and cheapest route to take is via **London**, with flight time around eleven hours, usually overnight. **Return fares** from Cape Town to London are around ZAR10,000; try British Airways (Ⓦbritishairways.com), South African Airways (Ⓦflysaa.com) or Virgin Atlantic (Ⓦvirginatlantic.com). You'll save money if you buy the next leg of your journey to Scotland separately, through one of the budget airlines.

AGENTS AND OPERATORS

Travel agencies

North South Travel UK ☎01245 608291, Ⓦnorthsouthtravel.co.uk. Friendly, competitive travel agency, offering discounted fares worldwide. Profits are used to support projects in the developing world, especially the promotion of sustainable tourism.

Trailfinders UK ☎020 70846500, Ireland ☎021 4648800 Ⓦtrailfinders.com. One of the best-informed and most efficient agents for independent travellers.

Travel CUTS Canada ☎1800 6672887, US ☎1800 5922887, Ⓦtravelcuts.com. Canadian youth and student travel firm.

Rail and bus operators and resources

Avanti West Coast Ⓦavantiwestcoast.co.uk. Main operator from London to Scotland on both the East and West Coast routes.

Caledonian Sleeper Ⓦsleeper.scot. Overnight train to Glasgow, Edinburgh, Aberdeen, Inverness and Fort William.

The Man in Seat Sixty-One Ⓦseat61.com. The best train information website on the internet.

National Express Ⓦnationalexpress.com. Coaches to Scotland.

ScotRail Ⓦscotrail.co.uk. Scotland's principal domestic operator, with full route and timetable info.

Trainline Ⓦtrainline.com. The best site for cheap tickets, with popular mobile app.

Traveline Scotland Ⓦtravelinescotland.com. Excellent Scotland-wide journey planner, connected to the latest bus and train timetables.

Ferry companies

DFDS Seaways UK ☎0871 5229955, International ☎+44 330 3330245, Ⓦdfds.com.

P&O Ferries UK 0800 1300030, Ireland ☎+353 1 6869467, Ⓦpoferries.com.

Stena Line UK ☎0844 7707070, Ⓦstenaline.co.uk.

Getting around

The majority of Scots live in the central belt, with Glasgow in the west and Edinburgh in the east. Public transport in this region is efficient and most places are easily accessible by train and bus. Further south and north it can be a different story: off the main routes, public transport services are few and far between, particularly in more remote parts of the Highlands and Islands. With careful planning, however, practically everywhere is accessible, and the scenery is usually adequate compensation for a long journey.

By train

Scotland has a modest **rail network**, at its densest in the central belt, skeletal in the Highlands, and non-existent in the Islands. However, the successful 2015 reopening of part of the historic Waverley Route

MINIBUS TOURS

Minibus tours that operate out of Edinburgh (and Glasgow) and head off into the Highlands are popular with backpackers who want a quick taste of Scotland. Aimed at the youth market, they adopt an upbeat and irreverent approach to sightseeing, as well as offering a good opportunity to get to know fellow travellers.

The current leading operator, **Haggis** (☎0131 5579393, ⓦhaggisadventures.com), has bright yellow minibuses setting off daily on whistle-stop tours lasting between one and ten days, in the company of a live-wire guide. A three-day trip from Edinburgh to Skye via Loch Ness costs £135 (food and accommodation not included).

Several other companies offer similar packages, including **Macbackpackers** (☎0131 2201869, ⓦmacbackpackers.com), which runs tours linking up with their own hostels round the country. The popular **Rabbie's** tours (☎0131 2263133, ⓦrabbies.com) don't aim quite so squarely at the backpacker market and have a mellower outlook.

---

to the Borders (known as the Borders Railway) proves that there's both the political will and public appetite for full-scale reversals of the infamous Beeching closures of the 1960s, and reopening the whole line (as far as Carlisle) hasn't been ruled out. ScotRail (ⓦscotrail.co.uk) runs the majority of train services, reaching all the major towns – sometimes on lines rated among the great scenic routes of the world.

You can buy train **tickets** at most stations, but if the ticket office is closed, or the automatic machine isn't working, you may buy your ticket on board from the inspector using cash or card. Those eligible for a national railcard (ⓦrailcard.co.uk; £30) can obtain discounted tickets, with up to a third off most fares. These include the **16–25 Railcard**, for full-time students and those aged between 16 and 25, the **Two Together Railcard** for two named people aged over 16 travelling together, and the **Senior Railcard** for people over 60. Alternatively, a **Family & Friends Railcard** entitles up to four adults and up to four children to a reduction.

ScotRail's Club 50 (£15) membership club offers discounted travel for those aged 50 and over. In addition, ScotRail offers several regional passes. The most flexible is the **Spirit of Scotland Travelpass**, which gives unlimited train travel within Scotland. It's also valid on all Caledonian MacBrayne (aka CalMac) ferries and on various buses in the remoter regions. The pass costs £149 for four days' travel in an eight-day period, or £189 for eight days' travel in a fifteen-day period. The **Highland Rover** allows unlimited train travel within the Highlands; it costs £95 for four out of eight consecutive days. Lastly, there's a **Central Scotland Rover**, which gives unlimited train travel on lines between Glasgow and Edinburgh; it costs £55 for three days' consecutive travel.

On most ScotRail routes **bicycles** are carried free, but since there are only between two and six bike spaces available, it's a good idea to reserve ahead, and this is a requirement on longer journeys.

By coach and bus

All of Scotland's major towns and cities are served by a few long-distance bus services, known across Britain as **coaches**. Scotland's main long-distance operator is **Scottish Citylink** (ⓦcitylink.co.uk). On the whole, coaches are cheaper than trains and, as a result, are very popular, so for longer journeys it's advisable to book ahead.

There are various **discounts** on offer for those with children, those under 26 or over 60, and full-time students (contact Scottish Citylink for more details), and you can also buy an **Explorer Pass**, which gives unlimited travel throughout Scotland (£49 for three days out of five; £74 for five days out of ten; £99 for eight days out of sixteen). **Local bus services** are run by a bewildering array of companies, many of which change routes and timetables frequently. Local tourist offices can provide free timetables or you can contact **Traveline Scotland** (☎0871 2002233, ⓦtravelinescotland.com), which provides a reliable service both online and by phone. There is also a free app available for download.

By car

In order to **drive** in Scotland you need a current full driving licence. If you're bringing your own vehicle into the country you should also carry your vehicle registration, insurance and ownership documents at all times.

In Scotland, as in the rest of the UK, you **drive on the left**. Speed limits are 20–40mph in built-up areas, 70mph on motorways and dual carriageways (freeways) and 60mph on most other roads. Though many built-up areas (including Edinburgh) are increasingly moving towards 20mph, with speed bumps popping up all over the place, as a rule, assume that in any area with street lighting the limit is 30mph.

In the Highlands and Islands, there are still plenty of **single-track roads** with passing places; in addition to allowing oncoming traffic to pass at these points, you should also let cars behind you overtake. These roads can be frustrating but take care and stay alert for vehicles coming in the opposite direction, which may have been hidden by bends or dips in the road. In more remote regions, the roads are dotted with sheep (and occasionally even cattle), which are entirely oblivious to cars, so slow down and edge your way past; should you kill or injure one, it is your duty to inform the local farmer.

The AA (☎ 0800 887766, ⓦ theaa.com), RAC (☎ 0330 2000999, ⓦ rac.co.uk) and Green Flag (☎ 0800 400600, ⓦ greenflag.com) all operate 24-hour **emergency breakdown** services. You may be entitled to free assistance through a reciprocal arrangement with a motoring organization in your home country. If not, you can make use of these emergency services by joining at the roadside, but you will incur a hefty surcharge. In remote areas, you may have a long wait for assistance.

The drink driving limit is 50mg of alcohol per 100ml of blood, meaning that even one pint of beer or a glass of wine could leave you on the wrong side of the law.

Car rental

Car rental in Scotland is cheaper than it used to be thanks to online advance deals with comparison sites such as ⓦ holidayautos.co.uk. The most economical cars can be rented for as little as £110 a week. Walk-in prices are more expensive at £20–50 per day, or around £130–200 a week. The major chains are confined mostly to the big cities, so it may be cheaper to use small **local agencies** – we've highlighted some in the Guide. With all rentals it's worth checking the terms and conditions carefully; some rentals only allow you to drive a limited number of miles before paying extra.

Automatics are rare at the lower end of the price scale – if you want one, you should book well ahead. **Campervans** are another option, offering a wonderful sense of freedom and of course allowing you to save money on accommodation; in high season, rates start at around £650 a week for a VW Campervan and £850 for a four-berth campervan. One excellent company is Bunk Campers (ⓦ bunkcampers.com), who have depots in Edinburgh and London Heathrow. Few companies will rent to drivers with less than one

year's experience and most will only rent to people over 21 or 25 and under 70 or 75 years of age.

At the time of writing, petrol (gasoline) and diesel were priced at around £1.35 per litre, though with such a volatile market prices are likely to continue fluctuating wildly. Note also that prices increase the further you travel from the central belt, with the Highlands and Islands being considerably more expensive, albeit offset to some degree by government subsidies.

By ferry

Scotland has more than ninety inhabited islands, and nearly fifty of them have scheduled **ferry** links. Most ferries carry cars and vans, and, if you're driving, the vast majority can – and should – be booked in advance; there's usually a window of four to six months. There's no need to book if you're travelling on foot; simply buy your ticket at the port office or on board.

CalMac has a virtual monopoly on services on the River Clyde and to the Hebrides, sailing to over twenty islands and four peninsulas. They aren't quick – no catamarans or fast ferries – but they are reasonably priced due to the Scottish Government-sponsored RET (Road Equivalent Tariff). The ferry from Mallaig to Skye, for example, costs £3.20 for foot passengers and £10.65 for cars. If you're taking more than one ferry, or aiming for a specific island grouping, you can also make significant savings with an **Island Hopscotch** ticket (there are thirty different variations to choose between). Given the notoriously fickle west coast weather, especially in winter, it's probably worth downloading the CalMac Service Status app.

Car ferries to **Orkney and Shetland** are run by NorthLink Ferries. Pentland Ferries also run a car ferry to Orkney, and John O'Groats Ferries run a summer-only passenger service to Orkney. The various Orkney islands are linked to each other by Orkney Ferries; Shetland's inter-island ferries are mostly council-run so the local tourist board (ⓦ shetland.gov.uk/ferries) is your best bet for information. There are also numerous **small operators** round the Scottish coast that run fast RIB taxi services, day-excursion trips, and even the odd scheduled service; their contact details are given in the relevant chapters of this Guide.

FERRY COMPANIES

CalMac ☎ 0800 0665000, ⓦ calmac.co.uk.
John O'Groats Ferries ☎ 01955 611353, ⓦ jogferry.co.uk.
NorthLink Ferries ☎ 08456 000449, ⓦ northlinkferries.co.uk.
Orkney Ferries ☎ 01856 872044, ⓦ orkneyferries.co.uk.
Pentland Ferries ☎ 0800 6888998, ⓦ pentlandferries.co.uk.

By plane

Apart from the four main **airports** of Glasgow, Glasgow Prestwick, Edinburgh and Aberdeen, Scotland has numerous minor airports around the Scottish Highlands and Islands, some of which are little more than gravel airstrips. Airfares fluctuate enormously depending on demand, but are generally expensive – if you book early enough you can fly from Glasgow to Islay for £54 one-way, but leave it to the last minute and it could cost you more than twice that. Most flights within Scotland are operated by **Loganair** (Ⓦloganair.co.uk). For inter-island flights in Shetland, you need to book through **Airtask** (Ⓦairtask.com/shetland-islands-inter-island-service). Competition emerges from time to time, with **Eastern Airways** (Ⓦeasternairways.com) currently offering flights from Aberdeen to Wick.

> ## ACCOMMODATION ALTERNATIVES
>
> Useful websites that provide alternatives to standard hotel and hostel accommodation.
> **CouchSurfing** Ⓦcouchsurfing.com.
> **Vacation Rentals by Owner** Ⓦvrbo.com.
> **Airbnb** Ⓦairbnb.co.uk.
> **onefinestay** Ⓦonefinestay.com.

If you take advantage of this service, it's worth being clear as to what kind of place you'd prefer, as the tourist office quite often selects something quite randomly across the whole range of their membership. Bear in mind, too, that outside the main towns and cities many places are only open for the **tourist season** (Easter to Oct): you'll always find somewhere to stay outside this period, but the choice may be limited.

Accommodation

In common with the rest of Britain, Scotland is expensive, but in terms of accommodation, budget travellers are relatively well catered for, with numerous hostels, campsites and bunkhouses. Those with money to spend will relish the more expensive country house hotels. In the middle ground, however, the standard of many B&Bs, guesthouses and hotels can be disappointing. Welcoming, comfortable, well-run places do, of course, exist in all parts of the country – and you'll find the best ones listed in this Guide.

Star ratings

VisitScotland, the country's tourist board, operates a system for grading accommodation, which is updated annually. However, not every establishment participates, and you shouldn't assume that a particular B&B is no good simply because it's not on VisitScotland's lists. The tourist board uses star awards, from one to five, which are supposed to reflect the quality of welcome, service and hospitality – though it's pretty clear that places without en-suite facilities, a TV in every room, matching fabrics or packets of shortbread on the sideboard are likely to be marked down.

Booking accommodation

If you decide not to book online, most **tourist offices** will help you find accommodation and **book a room** directly, for which they normally charge a small fee.

Hotels

Hotels come in all shapes and sizes. At the **upper end** of the market, they can be huge country houses and converted castles offering a very exclusive and opulent experience. Most will have a licensed bar and offer both breakfast and dinner, and often lunch as well. In the cities the increasing prevalence of modern **budget hotels** run by national (and international) chains may not win any prizes for aesthetics or variety, but they are competitively priced and for the most part meet criteria for clean, smart, serviceable accommodation.

Guesthouses and B&Bs

Guesthouses and B&Bs offer the widest and most diverse range of accommodation. VisitScotland uses the term **guesthouse** for a commercial venture that has four or more rooms, at least some of which are en suite, reserving **B&B** for a predominantly private family home that has only a few rooms to let. In reality, however, most places offer en-suite facilities, and the different names often reflect the pretensions of the owners and the cost of the rooms more than differences in service: in general, guesthouses cost more than B&Bs.

Inns (in other words, pubs), or their modern equivalent, 'restaurants with rooms' are similarly priced. These will often have only a handful of rooms, but their emphasis on creating an all-round convivial atmosphere as well as serving top-quality food often makes them worth seeking out.

A surprising number of guesthouses and B&Bs still have decor that consists of heavy chintz and floral

FIVE CAMPSITES NOT TO MISS

Comrie Croft Near Crieff. See page 316.
Red Squirrel Glen Coe. See page 390.
Ardnamurchan Campsite Ormsaigbeg.
See page 422.
Badrallach Badrallach. See page 437.
Camusdarach Campsite Camusdarach.
See page 425.

designs, but a good location, and the chance to get an insight into the local way of life, can be some compensation. Many B&Bs, even the pricier ones, have only a few rooms, so **advance booking** is recommended, whatever the season, especially in the Islands.

Hostels

There's an ever-increasing number of **hostels** in Scotland to cater for travellers – youthful or otherwise – who are unable or unwilling to pay the rates charged by hotels, guesthouses and B&Bs. Most hostels are clean and comfortable, and some offer **doubles** and **singles** as well as **dormitory accommodation**. Others concentrate more on keeping the price as low as possible, simply providing a roof over your head and a few basic facilities. Whatever type of hostel you stay in, expect to pay £8–20 per night.

Hostelling Scotland (☎0345 2937373; ⓦhostellingscotland.org.uk) – formerly The Scottish Youth Hostels Association – run the longest-established hostels in the Highlands and Islands. While these places sometimes occupy handsome buildings, many retain an institutionalized air. Bunk bed accommodation in single-sex dormitories, lights out before midnight and no smoking and no alcohol policies are the norm outside the big cities. Breakfast is not normally included in the price, though most hostels have self-catering facilities.

If you're not a **member** of one of the hostelling organizations affiliated to **Hostelling International** (HI), you can pay your £15 joining fee (£6 for under-25s) at most hostels. **Advance booking** is recommended, and essential at Easter, Christmas and from May to August. You can book online, in person or by phone.

There are also loads of **independent hostels** (sometimes known as 'bunkhouses') across Scotland. These are usually laid-back places with no membership, fewer rules, mixed dorms and no curfew. You can find most of them in the annually updated *Independent Hostel Guide* (ⓦindependenthostels.co.uk). Many of them are also affiliated to Scottish Independent Hostels

(ⓦhostel-scotland.co.uk), which has a programme of inspection and lists members on its website.

Camping

There are hundreds of **caravan and camping parks** around Scotland, most of which are open from April to October. The majority of sites charge about £10–15 for two people with a car to pitch a tent, and are usually well equipped, with shops, a restaurant, a bar and, occasionally, sports facilities. Most of these, however, are aimed principally at **caravans**, trailers and motorhomes, and generally don't offer the tranquil atmosphere and independence that those travelling with just a tent are seeking.

That said, peaceful and **informal sites** do exist, and are described throughout this Guide, though they are few and far between. Many **hostels** allow camping, and farmers will usually let tourists camp on their land for free or for a nominal sum. In this Guide, we've listed **the price for a pitch** (one tent for two people, plus a car) wherever possible. Where campsites charge per person, we've listed prices in that format instead.

Scotland's relaxed land access laws allow **wild camping** in open country. The basic rule is 'leave no trace' – visit ⓦwww.outdooraccess-scotland.scot for guidance on good practice. The great majority of **caravans** are permanently moored nose to tail in the vicinity of some of Scotland's finest scenery; others are positioned singly in back gardens or amid farmland. Some can be booked for self-catering, and with prices starting at around £100 a week, this can work out as one of the cheapest options if you're travelling with kids. If travelling by **campervan**, ⓦcampa.org.uk is a really useful website.

If you're planning to do a lot of camping at official camping and caravanning sites, it might be worthwhile joining the **Camping and Caravanning Club** (CCC; ⓦcampingandcaravanningclub.co.uk). Membership costs £42 for the digital option and £46 for paper (with hard copies of the monthly magazine and campsite directory), entitling you to up to thirty percent discount at CCC sites. Those coming from abroad can get the same benefits by buying a Camping Card International (aka CARNET), available from home motoring organizations or a CCC equivalent.

Self-catering accommodation

A huge proportion of visitors to Scotland opt for **self-catering** accommodation, booking a cottage or apartment for a week and often saving themselves a considerable amount of money by doing so. In many cases, the minimum rental period is still one week, and therefore not a valid option if you're aiming to tour round the country, though increasingly, with the rise of websites like ⓦ airbnb.co.uk, owners are becoming more flexible. The least you can expect to pay in the high season is around £250 per week for a place sleeping four, but something special, or somewhere in a popular tourist area, might cost £500 or more. Such is the number and variety of self-catering places on offer that we've mentioned very few in the Guide. A good source of information is **VisitScotland**'s self-catering website (ⓦ visitscotland.com/accommo-dation/self-catering), updated frequently and listing thousands of properties. Alternatively, you could try holiday rental agencies.

HOLIDAY RENTAL AGENCIES

Cottages and Castles ☏ 01738 451610, ⓦ cottages-and-castles.co.uk. A range of self-catering properties, mostly in mainland Scotland.

cottages.com ☏ 0345 2680766, ⓦ cottages.com. Hundreds of reasonably priced properties all over Scotland.

Landmark Trust ☏ 01628 825925, ⓦ landmarktrust.org.uk. A very select number of historical properties, often in prime locations.

LHH ☏ 01381 610496, ⓦ lhhscotland.com. Attractive homes across Scotland, including mansions, castles and villas.

National Trust for Scotland ☏ 01314 580200, ⓦ nts.org.uk/holiday-accommodation. The NTS lets around forty of its converted historic cottages and houses, and also offers working conservation holidays.

Scottish Country Cottages ☏ 0345 2680801, ⓦ scottish-country-cottages.co.uk. Superior cottages with lots of character, scattered across the Scottish mainland plus some of the Inner Hebrides.

Unique Cottages ☏ 01835 822277, ⓦ uniques-cottages.co.uk. Carefully selected cottages across mainland Scotland, plus a few in the Hebrides and Orkney.

Campus accommodation

A different and generally cheaper self-catering option, especially if you're staying a week or more in one of the cities, is **campus accommodation**. The universities of Glasgow, Strathclyde, Edinburgh, Stirling, St Andrews and Dundee all open their halls of residence to short-term visitors during the summer break, and some also offer rooms during the Easter and Christmas holidays.

ACCOMMODATION PRICE CODES

To give you an idea of prices we have used the following symbols:

£	under £75
££	£75–120
£££	£120–175
££££	over £175

Accommodation varies from tiny single rooms in long, lonely corridors to relatively comfortable places in small, shared apartments. Prices start at around £30 per night for a single room, not always including breakfast. All the useful university details are given in the Guide.

Food and drink

While Scotland isn't exactly known for its culinary heritage, the country's eating habits are changing, and from the cities to some of the furthest islands, you can often eat extremely well, with a strong emphasis on fresh, local and organic produce.

Scottish **fish and shellfish** is the envy of Europe, with a vast array of different types of fish, prawns, lobsters, mussels, oysters, crabs and scallops found around the extensive coastline. The prevalence of fish-farming, now a significant industry in the Highlands and Islands, means that the once-treasured salmon is now widespread and relatively inexpensive. Both salmon and trout, another commonly farmed fish, are frequently served cold with bread and butter.

Scottish-reared **beef** is often delicious, especially the Aberdeen Angus breed, though Highland cattle are also rated for their depth of flavour. **Venison**, the meat of the red deer, is also popular – low in choles-terol and very tasty, it's served roasted or in casseroles, and is often cooked with juniper and red wine. Other forms of **game** include grouse, which when cooked properly is strong, dark and succulent; pheasant, a lighter meat; and the less commonly served, but still tasty, pigeon and rabbit.

In rural Scotland, attitudes towards **vegetarianism** are still some way behind the big cities. While almost all pubs and restaurants will have at least one or two vegetarian options on their menus, they're too often lazily predictable and overpriced. Veggies – and vegans for that matter – will nevertheless find plenty of great food on offer in Edinburgh and Glasgow.

Breakfast

In most hotels and B&Bs you'll be offered a full **Scottish breakfast** – Lorne sausage or beef links, bacon and egg, black pudding (blood sausage) and potato scones. Porridge is another likely option, as is fish in the form of kippers, smoked haddock or even kedgeree. Scotland's staple drink, like England's, is **tea**, though **coffee** is just as readily available everywhere. However, while smart coffee shops are now a familiar feature in the cities, execrable versions of espresso and cappuc-cino, as well as instant coffee, are still all too familiar.

CLASSIC SCOTTISH DISHES

Arbroath smokies Powerful smoked haddock (see page 338).
Cullen skink Rich soup made from smoked haddock, potatoes and cream (see page 369).
Haggis Flavoursome sausage meat (spiced liver, offal, oatmeal and onion) cooked inside a bag made from a sheep's stomach. Tasty and satisfying, particularly when eaten with its traditional accompaniments, 'bashed neeps' (mashed turnips) and 'chappit tatties' (mashed potatoes).
Porridge A breakfast staple, this is properly made with oatmeal and water, and cooked with a pinch of salt. Some prefer to add milk and honey, fruit or sugar to sweeten.
Scots broth Hearty soup made with stock (usually mutton), vegetables and barley.

Lunches and snacks

The most common lunchtime fare in Scotland remains the **sandwich**. A bowl or cup of hearty **soup** is a typical accompaniment, particularly in winter. A **pub lunch** is often an attractive alternative. Bar menus generally have filling but unambitious options such as soup, sandwiches, scampi and chips, or steak pie and chips, with vegetarians suffering from a paucity of choice. That said, some bar food is freshly prepared and rivals the a la carte dishes served in adjacent hotel restaurants. Pubs or hotel bars are among the cheapest options when it comes to eating out – in the smallest villages, these might be your only option.

Restaurants are often, though not always, open at lunchtimes, when they tend to be less busy and generally offer a shorter and cheaper menu compared with their evening service. For morning or afternoon snacks, as well as light lunches, **tearooms** are a common feature; you will often find decent home baking on offer.

As for **fast food**, chip shops, or **chippies**, abound, the best often found in coastal towns within sight of the fishing boats. Deep-fried battered fish is the standard choice – when served with chips it's known as a 'fish supper', even if eaten at lunchtime – though everything from hamburgers to haggis suppers is normally on offer, all deep-fried, of course. Scotland is even credited with inventing the **deep-fried Mars bar**, the definitive badge of a nation with the worst heart disease statistics in Western Europe. For alternative fast food, major towns feature all the usual pizza, burger and baked potato outlets, as well as Chinese, Mexican and Indian takeaways.

Evening meals

There's no doubt that, as with the rest of the UK, eating out in Scotland is **expensive**; our restaurant listings include a mix of high-end and budget establishments. Wine in restaurants is marked up strongly, so you'll often pay £15 for a bottle selling for £5 in the shops; house wines generally start around the £10 mark.

If you're travelling in more remote parts of Scotland, or staying at a B&B or guesthouse in the countryside, ask advice about nearby options for your **evening meal**. Many B&Bs and guesthouses will cook you dinner, but you must book ahead and indicate any dietary requirements.

As for **restaurants**, standards vary enormously, but independent restaurants using good-quality local produce are now found all over Scotland. Less predictable are hotel restaurants, many of which also serve non-residents. Some can be very ordinary despite the highfalutin descriptions on the a la carte menu. You could easily end up paying £30–40 a head for a meal with wine.

In central Scotland (particularly in Edinburgh and Glasgow), and increasingly beyond, you'll find a range of **international cuisines** including Japanese, Thai, Caribbean and Turkish, as well as the more ubiquitous Indian, Chinese and Italian establishments. Glasgow is one of Britain's curry capitals, while Edinburgh's restaurant scene is consistently lively, its seafood and vegetarian restaurants a particular strength.

Among traditional **desserts**, clootie dumpling is a sweet, stodgy fruit pudding bound in a cloth and cooked for hours, while cranachan, made with toasted oatmeal steeped in whisky and folded into whipped cream flavoured with fresh raspberries, or the similar Atholl brose, are considered more refined.

Food shopping

Most Scots get their supplies from supermarkets, but you're increasingly likely to come across good delis, farm shops and specialist **food shops**. Many stock local produce alongside imported delicacies, as well as organic fruit and veg, specialist drinks such as locally brewed beer, freshly baked bread, and sandwiches and other snacks to take away. Look out too for **farmers' markets** (🔊 taste-of-scotland.com/farmers-markets-in-scotland), which generally take

MEALTIMES

In many parts of Scotland outside the cities, inflexible **mealtimes** mean that you'll have to keep an eye on your watch if you don't want to miss out on eating. B&Bs and hotels frequently serve breakfast only until 9am, lunch is usually over by 2pm, and, despite the long summer evenings, pub and hotel kitchens often stop serving dinner as early as 8pm.

place on Saturday mornings; local farmers and small producers, from pig farmers to cheesemakers and small smokeries, set up stalls to sell their specialist lines.

Scotland is notorious for its sweet tooth, and **cakes and puddings** are taken very seriously. Bakers with extensive displays of iced buns, cakes and cream-filled pastries are a typical feature of any Scottish high street, while home-made shortbread, scones or tablet (a hard, crystalline form of fudge) are considered great treats. In the summer, Scottish berries, in particular raspberries and strawberries, are particularly tasty.

You'll also find a number of specialist cheesemongers. Many restaurants serve only **Scottish cheese** after dinner. Look out for Isle of Mull, a tangy farmhouse cheddar; Dunsyre Blue, a Scottish Dolcelatte; or farmhouse Dunlop, the local version of cheddar.

Drinking

As in the rest of Britain, Scottish **pubs**, which originated as travellers' hostelries and coaching inns, are the main social focal points of any community. Pubs in Scotland vary hugely, from old-fashioned inns with open fires and a convivial atmosphere, to raucous theme pubs with loud music and satellite TV. Out in the islands, pubs are few and far between, with most drinking taking place in the local hotel bar. In Edinburgh and Glasgow you'll find traditional pubs supplemented by upbeat, trendy café-bars.

Pub **opening hours** are generally 11am to 11pm, but in the cities and towns, or anywhere where there is demand, places stay open much later. Whatever time the pub closes, last orders will be called by the bar staff about fifteen minutes before closing time to allow for drinking-up time. In general, you have to be 16 to enter a pub unaccompanied, though some places are relaxed about people bringing children in, or have special family rooms and beer gardens where the kids can run free. The legal drinking age is 18. As with the rest of the UK, **smoking** is not allowed in any pubs, bars or restaurants. Note that often-restrictive local by-laws govern alcohol consumption in public places, though enforcement varies.

MAKING MALT WHISKY

Malt whisky is made by soaking barley in **steeps** (water cisterns) for two or three days until it swells, after which it is left to germinate for around seven days, during which the starch in the barley seed is converted into soluble sugars – this process is known as **malting**. The malted barley or green malt is then dried in a **kiln** over a furnace, which can be oil-fired, peat-fired or, more often than not, a combination of the two.

Only a few distilleries still do their own malting and kilning in the traditional pagoda-style kilns, three of which are on Islay, including Laphroaig; the rest simply have their malted barley delivered from industrial maltings. The first process in most distilleries is therefore **milling**, which grinds the malted barley into grist. Next comes the **mashing**, during which the grist is infused in hot water in mash tuns, producing a sugary concoction called wort. After cooling, the wort passes into the washbacks, traditionally made of wood, where it is fermented with yeast for two to three days. During **fermentation**, the sugar is converted into alcohol, producing a brown foaming liquid known as wash.

Distillation now takes place, not once but twice: the wash is steam-heated, and the vapours siphoned off and condensed as a spirit. This is the point at which the whisky is poured into oak casks – usually ones which have already been used to store bourbon or sherry – and left to age for a minimum of three years.

The average **maturation** period for a single malt whisky, however, is ten years; and the longer it matures, the more expensive it is, because two percent evaporates each year. Unlike wine, as soon as the whisky is bottled, maturation ceases.

Whisky

Whisky – *uisge beatha*, the 'water of life' in Gaelic – has been produced in Scotland since the fifteenth century, but only really took off after the 1780 tax on claret made wine too expensive for most people. The taxman soon caught up with whisky, however, and drove the stills underground. Today, many distilleries operate on the site of simple cottages that once distilled the stuff illegally.

Despite the dominance of blended whiskies such as Johnnie Walker, Bell's, Teacher's and The Famous Grouse, **single malt whisky** is infinitely superior and, as a result, a great deal more expensive. Single malts vary in character enormously depending on the amount of peat used for drying the barley, the water used for mashing and the type of oak cask used in the maturing process. Malt whisky is best drunk with a splash of water to release its distinctive flavours. The greatest concentrations of distilleries are on Speyside and on Islay (whose whiskies are renowned for their smoky character), though there are distilleries popping up all over the place. Between 2018 and 2022, over a dozen new ones entered the market.

Beer

Traditional Scottish beer is a thick, dark ale known as **heavy**, served at room temperature in pints or half-pints, with a full head. Quite different in taste from English 'bitter', heavy is a more robust, sweeter beer with less of an edge. All of the big-name breweries – McEwan's, Tennent's, Bellhaven and Caledonian – produce a reasonable selection of heavies. However, if you really want to discover Scottish beer, look out for the products of small **local breweries** such as Cairngorm, Cromarty, the Black Isle, Isle of Arran, Fyne Ales, Isle of Skye, and Orkney. Look out, too, for Fraoch, available mostly in bottles, a delicious, lighter-coloured ale made from heather according to an ancient recipe. The big guns at present though are the Aberdeenshire-based **Brewdog**, who have taken both the Scottish and international markets by storm in recent years with hard-nosed marketing and an ever-expanding range of often eye-wateringly strong concoctions; they've now got in excess of fifty bars across Britain.

Water and soft drinks

Scotland produces a prodigious amount of **mineral water**, much of which is exported – tap water is chill, clean and perfectly palatable in most parts of the country, including the areas of the Highlands and Islands where it's tinged the colour of weak tea by peat in the ground. Locally produced **Irn-Bru**, a fizzy orange, sickly sweet concoction, has been known to outsell Coke and Pepsi in Scotland.

The media

Many Scots see the UK's national media as London-based and London-biased, and prefer to listen to Scottish radio programmes, read Scottish newspapers, and – albeit to a much lesser extent – watch Scottish TV. Local papers are also avidly consumed, with the weekly papers in places like Orkney and Shetland read by virtually the entire adult population.

The press

The Scottish press has traditionally centred on two serious **daily newspapers** – *The Scotsman*, now published in tabloid format and based in Edinburgh, and *The Herald*, a broadsheet published in Glasgow; founded in 1783, it's one of the longest running national papers in the world. Both offer good coverage of the current issues affecting Scotland, along with British and foreign news, sport, arts and lifestyle pages. They've recently been joined by *The National*, a serious, low-priced left-wing and pro-independence daily launched in 2014. A rare success in an era of dwindling circulations, the paper has filled a glaring gap in the market and provided an alternative voice for just under half of the population who voted in favour of independence in the referendum. However, Scotland's biggest-selling daily newspapers remain the downmarket *Daily Record*, a tabloid from the same stable as the *Daily Mirror*, and the local edition of *The Sun*. Most of the main UK newspapers produce specific Scottish editions, although the 'quality press', ranging from the right-wing *Daily Telegraph* to the left-of-centre *Guardian*, are justifiably seen in Scotland as being London papers.

The provincial daily press in Scotland is more widely read than its English counterpart, with the two biggest-selling **regional titles** being Aberdeen's famously parochial *Press and Journal*, read in the northeast, Orkney and Shetland, and the right-wing *Dundee Courier*, mostly sold in Perth, Angus, Tayside and Fife. The weekly *Oban Times* gives an insight into

---

EATING PRICE CODES

To give you an idea of prices we have used the following symbols:

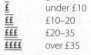

£	under £10
££	£10–20
£££	£20–35
££££	over £35

BURNS NIGHT

To celebrate the birthday of the country's best-known poet, Robert 'Rabbie' Burns (1759–96), Scots all over the world gather together for a **Burns Supper** on 25 January. Strictly speaking, a piper should greet the guests until everyone is seated, ready to hear the 'Selkirk Grace'.

At this point the star attraction of the evening, the **haggis**, is piped in on a silver platter, after which someone reads out Burns's *'Address to a Haggis'*, beginning with the immortal line, *'Fair fa' your honest, sonsie face, / Great chieftain o' the pudding-race!'*. During the **recitation**, the reader raises a knife (*'His knife see Rustic labour dight'*), pierces the haggis (*'trenching your gushing entrails bright'*), and then toasts the haggis with the final line, *'Gie her a Haggis!'*. After everyone has tucked into their **haggis**, **neeps** and **tatties**, someone gives a paean to the life of Burns along with more of his poetry. A male guest then has to give a speech in which women are praised (often ironically) through selective quotations from Burns, ending in a Toast to the Lassies. This is followed by a (usually scathing) reply from one of the lassies, again through judicious use of Burns's quotes. Finally, there's a stirring rendition of Burns''*Auld Lang Syne'* to the familiar tune.

life in the Highlands and Islands, but is staid compared with the radical, campaigning weekly *West Highland Free Press*, printed on Skye; both carry articles in Gaelic as well as English. Further north, the lively *Shetland Times* and sedate *Orcadian* are essential weekly reads.

Many national **Sunday newspapers** have a Scottish edition, although Scotland has its own offerings – *Scotland on Sunday*, from the *Scotsman* stable, and the *Sunday Herald* (the only newspaper to come out in support of independence prior to the referendum), complementing its eponymous daily. Far more fun and widely read is the anachronistic *Sunday Post*, published by Dundee's D.C. Thomson Media. It's a wholesome paper, uniquely Scottish, and has changed little since the 1950s, since which time its two long-running cartoon strips, *Oor Wullie* and *The Broons*, have acquired cult status.

TV and radio

In Scotland there are six main (sometimes called 'terrestrial') **TV channels**: state-owned BBC1, BBC2 and the Gaelic-language BBC Alba, and three commercial channels: STV, Channel 4 and Channel 5. **BBC Scotland** produces news programmes and a regular crop of local-interest lifestyle, current affairs, drama and comedy shows which slot into the schedules of the BBC channels. The vast majority of homes receive dozens of additional TV channels and radio stations through digital services like Freeview and Sky.

The **BBC radio** network broadcasts six main FM stations in Scotland, five of which are national stations originating largely from London: Radio 1 (youth-focused, playing pop and dance music), Radio 2 (mainstream pop, rock and light music), Radio 3 (classical music), Radio 4 (current affairs, arts and drama) and Radio 5 Live (sports, news, live

discussions and phone-ins). Only the award-winning BBC Radio Scotland offers a Scottish perspective on news, politics, arts, music, travel and sport, as well as providing a Gaelic network in the Highlands with local programmes in Shetland, Orkney and the Borders. Note that in large areas of the Highlands and Islands, some or all of these stations are impossible to receive.

A web of local **commercial radio** stations helps to fill in the gaps, mostly mixing rock and pop music with news bulletins, but a few tiny community-based stations such as Lochbroom FM in Ullapool – a place famed for its daily midge count – transmit documentaries and discussions on local issues. The most populated areas of Scotland also receive UK-wide commercial stations such as Classic FM, Virgin Radio and TalkSport. With a DAB **digital radio**, you can get all the main stations crackle-free, along with special interest and smaller-scale stations.

Events and spectator sports

Scotland offers a huge range of cultural and heritage-themed events as well as a packed sporting calendar. Many tourists will home straight in on the Highland Games and other tartan-draped theatricals, but there's more to Scotland than this: numerous regional celebrations perpetuate ancient customs, and the Edinburgh Festival is an arts celebration unrivalled in size and variety in the world. A few of the smaller, more obscure events (particularly those with a pagan bent) do not always welcome the casual visitor. The

tourist board publishes a weighty list of all Scottish events on its website (W visitscotland.com).

Events calendar

DEC–JAN

31 Dec and 1 Jan Hogmanay and Ne'er Day. Traditionally more important to the Scots than Christmas, the occasion is known for the custom of 'first-footing' (see page 41). More popular these days are huge and highly organized street parties, most notably in Edinburgh (W edinburghshogmanay.com), but also in Aberdeen, Glasgow and other centres.

1 Jan Stonehaven Fireball Ceremony. Locals swing fireballs on long sticks to welcome New Year and ward off evil spirits. Also Kirkwall Boys' and Men's Ba' Games, Orkney: mass, drunken football game through the streets of the town, with the castle and the harbour the respective goals. As a grand finale the players jump into the harbour.

11 Jan Burning of the Clavie, Burghead, Moray W burghhead.com/clavie. A burning tar barrel is carried through the town and then rolled down Doorie Hill. Charred fragments of the Clavie offer protection against the evil eye.

Mid- to late Jan Celtic Connections, Glasgow W celticconnections.com. A major celebration of Celtic, folk, country and world music held in venues across the city.

Last Tues in Jan Up-Helly-Aa, Lerwick, Shetland W uphellyaa.org. Norse fire festival culminating in the burning of a specially built Viking longship. Visitors will need an invite from one of the locals, or you can buy a ticket for the Town Hall celebrations.

25 Jan Burns Night. Scots worldwide get stuck into haggis, whisky and vowel-grinding poetry to commemorate Scotland's greatest poet, Robert Burns (see pages 39 and 161).

FEB–MARCH

Feb Scottish Curling Championship W scottishcurling.org. Held in a different (indoor) venue each year.

Feb–March Six Nations W sixnationsrugby.com. Rugby tournament between Scotland, England, Wales, Ireland, France and Italy. Scotland's home games are played at Murrayfield Stadium in Edinburgh.

1 March Whuppity Scourie, Lanark. Local children race round the church beating each other with home-made paper weapons in a representation (it's thought) of the chasing away of winter or the warding off of evil spirits.

APRIL–MAY

April Scottish Grand National, Ayr W ayr-racecourse.co.uk. Not quite as testing as the English equivalent steeplechase, but an important event in the Scottish racing calendar. Also, Rugby Sevens (seven-a-side tournaments; W melrose7s.co.uk) in the Borders and the entertaining and inclusive Edinburgh Science Festival (W sciencefestival.co.uk).

6 April Tartan Day. Over-hyped celebration of ancestry by North Americans of Scottish descent on the anniversary of the Declaration of Arbroath in 1320. Ignored by most Scots in Scotland, other than journalists.

Early May Spirit of Speyside Scotch Whisky Festival W spiritofspeyside.com. Six-day binge with pipe bands, gigs and dancing as well as distillery crawls. The Shetland Folk Festival (W shetlandfolkfestival.com) is one of the liveliest and most entertaining of Scotland's round of folk festivals.

Late May Atholl Highlanders Parade at Blair Castle, Perthshire W blair-castle.co.uk. The annual parade and inspection of Britain's last private army by their colonel-in-chief, the Duke of Atholl, on the eve of their Highland Games. Also Burns an' a' That (W burnsfestival.com), a modern celebration of Robert Burns, including gigs by contemporary pop acts.

JUNE–JULY

June–Aug Riding of the Marches in border towns such as Hawick, Selkirk, Jedburgh, Langholm and Lauder. The Ridings originated to check the boundaries of common land owned by the town and also to commemorate warfare between the Scots and the English.

June Beginning of the Highland Games season across the Highlands, north-east and Argyll. Also, the St Magnus Festival, Orkney (W stmagnusfestival.com), a classical and folk music, drama, dance and literature festival celebrating the islands. The Edinburgh International Film Festival (W edfilmfest.org.uk) runs from mid-June for ten days.

Late June Royal Highland Agricultural Show, at Ingliston near Edinburgh W royalhighlandshow.org. Old wooden boats and fishing craft gather for the Traditional Boat Festival at Portsoy on the Moray Firth coast (W stbfportsoy.org). Glasgow Jazz Festival (W jazzfest.co.uk).

Early July Kelburn Garden Party (W kelburngardenparty.com) is an intimate boutique affair in gorgeous surroundings near Largs featuring some wonderful alternative and underground music. The Scottish Open Golf Championship is held just before the British Open tournament, which is played in Scotland at least every alternate year.

AUG–SEPT

Early Aug Belladrum Tartan Heart Festival, near Inverness W tartanheartfestival.co.uk. One of Scotland's most scenic and fastest-growing music shindigs; family friendly as well.

Aug Edinburgh Festival W eif.co.uk. One of the world's great arts jamborees (see page 100). The Edinburgh Military Tattoo (W edintattoo.co.uk) features floodlit massed pipe bands and drums on the castle esplanade. There's also the World Pipe Band Championship in Glasgow (W theworlds.co.uk), and plenty more Highland Games.

Early Sept Shinty's Camanachd Cup Final W shinty.com. The climax of the season for Scotland's own stick-and-ball game, normally held in one of the main Highland towns. Also, various food festivals and events under the banner of Scottish Food and Drink Fortnight (W fooddrinkfort.scot).

Late Sept Doors Open Day Ⓦ doorsopendays.org.uk. The one weekend a year when many public and private buildings are open to the public; actual dates vary. Also, the Scottish Book Town Festival in Wigtown (Ⓦ wigtown-booktown.co.uk).

OCT–NOV

Oct Tiree Wave Classic Ⓦ tireewaveclassic.co.uk. Annual event attracting windsurfers from around the world to the breezy Hebridean island.

Mid-Oct The National Mod Ⓦ ancomunn.co.uk/nationalmod. Held over nine days at a different venue each year, the Mod is a competitive festival and features all aspects of Gaelic performing arts.

30 Nov St Andrew's Day. Celebrating Scotland's patron saint. The town of St Andrews hosts a week of events leading up to it (Ⓦ standrewsweek.co.uk).

Highland Games

Despite their name, **Highland Games** are held all over Scotland between May and mid-September, varying in size and in the range of events they offer. The Games probably originated in the fourteenth century as a means of recruiting the best fighting men for the clan chiefs, and were popularized by **Queen Victoria** to encourage the traditional dress, music, games and dance of the Highlands; indeed, various royals still attend the Games at Braemar.

Apart from **Braemar**, the most famous games take place at **Oban** and **Cowal**, but the smaller events are often more fun – like a sort of Highland version of a school sports day. There's money to be won, too, so the Games are usually pretty competitive. The most distinctive events are known as the 'heavies' – tossing the caber (pronounced 'kabber'), putting the stone, and tossing the weight over the bar – all of which require prodigious strength and skill, and the wearing of a kilt. Tossing the caber is the most

spectacular, when the athlete must lift an entire tree trunk up, cupping it in his hands, before running with it and attempting to heave it end over end. Just as important as the sporting events are the **piping** competitions – for individuals and bands – and **dancing** competitions, where you'll see girls as young as 3 tripping the quick, intricate steps of dances such as the Highland Fling.

Football

Football (soccer) is far and away Scotland's most popular spectator sport. The national team (accompanied by its distinctive and vocal supporters, known as the 'Tartan Army') is a source of pride and frustration for Scots everywhere. Once a regular at World Cups where they were involved in some memorable matches against the likes of Holland and Brazil, Scotland have failed to qualify for the tournament since 1998, though they did qualify for the 2020 European Championships.

The national domestic league established in 1874 is one of the oldest in the world and holds many European attendance records (with attendances still among the highest per head of population in Europe), but sadly today most of the teams that play in it are little known beyond the boundaries of Scotland. The exceptions are the two massive Glasgow teams that have long dominated the Scottish scene, **Rangers** and **Celtic** (see page 197) – known collectively as the 'Old Firm'. The infamous, sectarian-tainted, and occasionally violent, rivalry between these two is one of the least attractive aspects of Scottish life. Rangers were also at the heart of one of the biggest news stories of 2012 when labyrinthine financial problems ultimately led to their liquidation, with the business and assets sold to a new company and the remains of the team forced to climb their way back from the

---

HOGMANAY

When hardline Scottish Protestant clerics in the sixteenth century abolished Christmas for being a Catholic mass, the Scots, not wanting to miss out on a mid-winter knees-up, instead put their energy into greeting the New Year, or **Hogmanay**. Houses were cleaned from top to bottom, debts were paid and quarrels made up, and, after the bells of midnight were rung, great store was laid by welcoming good luck into your house. Though it's a dying custom, this still takes the form of the tradition of '**first-footing**' – visiting your neighbours and bearing gifts. The ideal first-foot is a tall dark-haired male carrying a bottle of whisky; women or redheads, on the other hand, bring bad luck – though, to be honest, no one carrying a bottle of whisky tends to be turned away these days, whatever the colour of their hair. All this neighbourly greeting means a fair bit of partying, and no one is expected to go to work the next day, or, indeed, the day after that. Even today, 1 January is a public holiday in the rest of the UK, but only in Scotland does the holiday extend to the next day too.

former Third Division. Now finally back in the Premiership (Ⓦ spfl.co.uk), they're sure to make coming seasons slightly less predictable than of late.

Moreover, with Scottish football now operating in a severely restricted financial environment, the balance is increasingly tipping back in favour of home-grown young players over expensive imports, which should, in the long run, benefit the national team.

The **season** begins in early August and ends in mid-May, with matches on Saturday afternoons at 3pm (noon–1pm for televised games), and also often on Sunday afternoons and Tuesday or Wednesday evenings. Standard tickets cost around £25 for big games and can be purchased from club websites.

Rugby

Although **rugby** has always lived under the shadow of football in Scotland, it ranks as one of the country's major sports. Weekends when the national team is playing a home international at Murrayfield Stadium in Edinburgh are colourful occasions, with kilted masses filling the capital's pubs and lining the streets leading to the ground. Internationals take place in late winter, when Scotland takes on the other 'home nations', along with France and Italy, in the annual **Six Nations** tournament (see page 40), although there are always fixtures in the autumn against international touring teams such as New Zealand, Australia and South Africa. Tickets for big games are hard to come by; contact the **Scottish Rugby Union** (Ⓦ scottishrugby.org).

Scotland's two professional clubs are Glasgow Warriors and Edinburgh, both of whom play in the United Rugby Championship (made of up of Welsh, Irish and South African clubs); both clubs regularly qualify for the European Rugby Champions Cup, though as yet neither has made it beyond the quarter final stage. However, the area where the **domestic rugby** tradition runs deepest is in the Borders, where towns such as Hawick, Kelso, Melrose and Gala can be gripped by the fortunes of their local team on a Saturday afternoon; all these teams play in either the Scottish League Championship or Borders League. The Borders are also the home of **seven-a-side rugby**, an abridged version of the game that was invented in Melrose in the 1890s and is now played around the world, most notably at the glamorous annual event in Hong Kong. The **Melrose Sevens** is still the biggest tournament of the year in Scotland (see page 121), although you'll find events at one or other of the Border towns through the spring, most going on right through an afternoon and invoking a festival atmosphere in the large crowd.

Shinty

Played throughout Scotland but with particular strongholds in the West Highlands and Strathspey, the game of **shinty** (the Gaelic *sinteag* means 'leap') arrived from Ireland around 1,500 years ago. Until the latter part of the nineteenth century, it was played on an informal basis and teams from neighbouring villages had to come to an agreement about rules before matches could begin. However, in 1893, the **Camanachd Association** – the Gaelic word for shinty is *camanachd* – was set up to formalize the rules, and the first Camanachd Cup Final was held in Inverness in 1896. Shinty, still fairly close to its Gaelic roots, is similar to the Irish game of hurling. Teams have twelve players including a goalkeeper and each goal counts for a point. The game, which can be likened to an undisciplined version of hockey, isn't for the faint-hearted; it's played at a furious pace, with sticks – called camans or cammocks – flying alarmingly in all directions. Support is enthusiastic and vocal, and if you're in the Highlands during the season, which runs from March to October, it's well worth trying to catch a match: check with tourist offices or the local paper, or go to Ⓦ shinty.com.

Curling

The one winter sport which enjoys a strong Scottish identity is **curling** (Ⓦ scottishcurling.org), occasionally still played on a frozen outdoor rink, or 'pond', though most commonly these days seen at indoor ice rinks. The game, which involves gently sliding smooth-bottomed 18kg discs of granite called 'stones' across the ice towards a target circle, is said to have been invented in Scotland, although its earliest representation is in a sixteenth-century Flemish painting. Played by two teams of four, it's a highly tactical and skilful sport, enlivened by team members using brushes to sweep the ice furiously in front of a moving stone to help it travel further and straighter. If you're interested in seeing curling being played, go along to the ice rink in places such as Perth, Pitlochry or Inverness on a winter evening.

Outdoor activities

Scotland boasts a landscape that, weather conditions apart, is extremely attractive for outdoor pursuits at all levels of fitness and ambition, and legislation enacted by the Scottish Parliament has ensured a right of access to hills, mountains, lochs and rivers. Within striking distance of

its cities are two national parks, remote wilderness areas and vast stretches of glens and moorland, while sea-kayakers, sailors and surfers can enjoy excellent conditions along the rugged but beautiful coastline.

Walking and climbing

The whole of Scotland offers superb opportunities for **walking**, with some of the finest areas in the ownership of bodies such as the National Trust for Scotland (NTS) and the John Muir Trust (W johnmuir-trust.org); both permit year-round access. Bear in mind, though, that restrictions may be in place during lambing and deerstalking seasons. See W www.outdooraccess-scotland.scot for information about **hiking safely** during the stalking season. In addition, the green signposts of the Scottish Rights of Way Society point to established paths and routes all over the country.

There are several **long-distance footpaths**, such as the well-known West Highland Way (see page 384), which take between three and seven days to walk, though you can, of course, just do a section of them. Paths are generally well signposted and well supported, with a range of services from bunkhouses to baggage carrying services.

Numerous short walks (from accessible towns and villages) and several major walks are touched on in this Guide. However, you should only use our notes as general outlines, and always in conjunction with a good map. Where possible, we have given details of the best maps to use – in most cases one of the excellent and reliable **Ordnance Survey** (OS) series (see page 49), usually available from local tourist offices, which, along with outdoor shops, can also supply other local maps, safety advice and guidebooks/leaflets.

For relatively gentle walking in the company of knowledgeable locals, look out for guided walks offered by rangers at many National Trust for Scotland, Forestry Commission and Scottish Natural Heritage sites. These often focus on local **wildlife**, and the best can lead to some special sightings, such as a badger's sett or a golden eagle's eyrie.

MIDGES AND TICKS

Despite being only a fraction of an inch long, and enjoying a life span on the wing of just a few weeks, the **midge** (genus: *Culicoides*) – a tiny biting fly prevalent in the Highlands (mainly the west coast) and Islands – is considered to be second only to the weather as the major deterrent to tourism in Scotland. There are more than thirty varieties of midge, though only half of these bite humans. Ninety percent of all midge bites are down to the female *Culicoides impunctatus* or **Highland midge** (the male does not bite), which has two sets of jaws sporting twenty teeth each; she needs a good meal of blood in order to produce eggs.

These persistent creatures can be a nuisance, but some people also have a violent allergic reaction to midge bites. The easiest way to avoid midges is to visit in the winter, since they only appear between April and October. Midges also favour still, damp, overcast or shady conditions and are at their meanest around sunrise and sunset, when clouds of them can descend on an otherwise idyllic spot. Direct sunlight, heavy rain, noise and smoke discourage them to some degree, though wind is the most effective means of dispersing them. If they appear, cover up exposed skin and get your hands on some kind of repellent. Recommendations include Autan, Eureka!, Jungle Formula (widely available from pharmacists) and the herbal remedy citronella. An alternative to repellents for protecting your face, especially if you're walking or camping, is a **midge net**, which is a little like a beekeeper's hat; though they appear ridiculous at first, you're unlikely to care as long as they work. The latest deployment in the battle against the midge is a gas-powered machine called a 'midge magnet' which sucks up the wee beasties and is supposed to be able to clear up to an acre; the most basic unit costs between £400 and £500, but there's been a healthy take-up by pubs with beer gardens and by campsite owners.

A huge rise in confirmed cases of Lyme disease in recent years means that extra care should be taken to avoid **ticks** if you're walking through long grass or bracken. These tiny parasites, no bigger than a pin head, bury themselves into your skin; the medically favoured way of extracting them is to pull them out carefully with small tweezers or a tick removal device. If flu-like symptoms persist after a tick bite, you should see a doctor immediately.

WALKING INFORMATION

W **www.outdooraccess-scotland.scot** All you need to know about the Scottish Outdoor Access Code, plus daily information for hill walkers about deerstalking activities (July–Oct).

W **visitscotland.com/see-do/active/walking** Official site from VisitScotland, with good lists of operators, information on long-distance footpaths, and details of deerstalking restrictions and contact phone numbers.

W **wildlife.visitscotland.com/see-do/wildlife** Highlights the fauna and flora you may spot on a walk.

Walking clubs and associations

Mountain Bothies Association W mountainbothies.org.uk. Charity dedicated to maintaining huts and shelters in the Scottish Highlands.

Mountaineering Council of Scotland W mountaineering.scot. The representative body for all mountain activities, with detailed information on access and conservation issues.

Ramblers Association Scotland W ramblers.org.uk/scotland. Campaigning organization with network of local groups, and news on events and issues.

Scottish Mountaineering Club W smc.org.uk. The largest mountaineering club in the country. A well-respected organization which publishes a popular series of mountain guidebooks.

WALKING TOUR OPERATORS

Activity Scotland W activityscotland.com. Highly experienced Perthshire-based operator providing a wide range of adventures and activities, from horse riding and abseiling to kayaking and biking.

Easyways Scotland W easyways.com.com. Scotland's longest-established operator, offering Munro-bagging for novices and experts with qualified leaders.

G2 Outdoor W g2outdoor.co.uk. Personable, highly qualified adventure specialists offering gorge scrambling, hillwalking, rock climbing, canoeing and telemark skiing in the Cairngorms.

Glenmore Lodge W glenmorelodge.org.uk. Based within the Cairngorm National Park, and internationally recognized as a leader in outdoor skills and leadership training.

Hebridean Pursuits W hebrideanpursuits.org. Offers hillwalking and rock climbing in the Hebrides and West Highlands, as well as surf-kayaking and sailing trips.

Nae Limits W naelimits.co.uk. This excellent Perthshire-based operator offers everything from wet 'n' wild rafting to bug canyoning and cliff jumping.

North-West Frontiers W nwfrontiers.com. Based in Ullapool, offering guided mountain trips with small groups in the northwest Highlands, Hebrides and even the Shetland Islands.

Vertical Descents W verticaldescents.com. Ideally located for the Glencoe and Fort William area. Activities and courses include canyoning, 'funyakking' (a type of rafting) and climbing.

Walkabout Scotland W walkaboutscotland.com. A great way to get a taste of hiking in Scotland, from exploring Ben Lomond to the Isle of Arran. Guided day and weekend walking trips from Edinburgh with all transport included.

Wilderness Scotland W wildernessscotland.com. Guided, self-guided and customized adventure holidays that focus on exploring the remote and unspoiled parts of Scotland by foot, bike, sea-kayak, yacht and even on skis.

Winter sports

Skiing and **snowboarding** take place at five different locations in Scotland – Glen Coe, the Nevis Range beside Fort William, Glenshee, the Lecht and the Cairngorms near Aviemore. The resorts can go for months on end through the winter with insufficient snow, then see the approach roads suddenly made impassable by a glut of the stuff. When the conditions are good, Scotland's **ski resorts** have piste and off-piste areas that will challenge even the most accomplished alpine or cross-country skier.

Expect to pay up to £35 for a standard day-pass at one of the resorts, around £25 for a half-day pass (usually available from noon) or around £110 for a four-day pass; rental of skis or snowboard comes in at around £30 per day, with reductions for multi-day rentals. At weekends, in good weather with decent snow, expect the slopes to be packed with trippers from the central belt, although midweek usually sees queues dissolving. For a comprehensive rundown of all the resorts, including ticket prices and conditions, visit W visitscotland.com/see-do/active/skiing-snowsports.

Cross-country skiing (along with the related telemark or Nordic skiing) is becoming increasingly popular in the hills around Braemar near Glenshee and the Cairngorms. The best way to get started or to find out about good routes is to contact an outdoor pursuits company that offers telemark or Nordic rental and instruction; in the Aviemore area try G2 Outdoor (see page 44). Also check out the Huntly Nordic and Outdoor Centre in Huntly, Aberdeenshire (W huntly-nordicandoutdoorcentre.com).

Pony trekking and horse riding

There are approximately sixty pony trekking or riding centres across the country, most approved by either the Trekking and Riding Society of Scotland (TRSS; W ridinginscotland.com) or the British Horse Society (BHS; W bhs.org.uk). As a rule, any centre will offer the option of **pony trekking**, **hacking** and **trail riding**. In addition, a network of special horse-and-rider B&Bs means you can ride independently on your own horse. The **Buccleuch Country Ride**, a three- to four-day, 57-mile-long route using private tracks, open country and quiet bridleways was the first route of its kind to be opened in Scotland. For more information about this, and the B&B network for riders, contact the Scottish Borders Tourist Board, or visit ⓦ southofscotlandcountrysidetrails.co.uk/buccleuch.php, where you'll find a link to an OS-based route map.

Cycling and mountain biking

Cycle touring is a great way to see some of the remoter parts of Scotland and navigate city streets (especially in Edinburgh). You'll find cycle shops in towns but few dedicated cycle lanes. In the country-side it can be tricky finding spare parts unless you are near one of Scotland's purpose-built mountain-bike trail centres.

Scotland is now regarded as one of the world's top destinations for **off-road mountain biking**. The Forestry Commission has established more than 1150 miles of excellent off-road routes. These are detailed in numerous 'Cycling in the Forest' leaflets, available from the Commission's Forest Enterprise offices. Alternatively, get hold of the *Scottish Mountain Biking Guide* from tourist information centres. Some of the tougher routes are best attempted on full suspension mountain bikes, although the easier (blue/green) trails can be ridden on a standard mountain or road bike. Pocket Mountains also publish a series of compact cycling guides to the country (ⓦ pocketmountains.com).

For up-to-date information on long-distance routes, including **The Great Glen Cycle Way**, along with a list of publications detailing specific routes, contact the cyclists' campaigning group Sustrans (ⓦ sustrans.co.uk), as well as the other organizations listed here.

Another option is to shell out on a cycling holiday package. Britain's biggest cycling organization, Cycling UK (formerly the **Cycle Touring Club**; ⓦ cyclinguk.org), provides lists of tour operators and

rental outlets in Scotland, and supplies members with touring and technical advice, as well as insurance. Visit Scotland's 'Cycling in Scotland' brochure is worth getting hold of, with practical advice and suggestions for itineraries around the country. The tourist board's 'Cyclists Welcome' scheme gives guesthouses and B&Bs around the country a chance to advertise that they're cyclist-friendly, and able to provide an overnight laundry service, a late meal or a packed lunch.

Transporting your bike **by train** is a good way of getting to the interesting parts of Scotland without a lot of hard pedalling. Bikes are allowed free on mainline East Coast and ScotRail trains, but you need to book the space as far in advance as possible. Train stations in all of Scotland's cities and many large towns have now signed up to the Bike & Go scheme (ⓦ bikeandgo.co.uk), whereby, for an annual membership fee of £10, you can simply jump off the train and rent a bike (£3.80/24hr; up to 72hr). Bus and coach companies, including National Express and Scottish Citylink, rarely accept cycles unless they are dismantled and boxed. You'll find **bike rental** facilities in large towns and tourist centres; expect to pay around £20 per day, or more for top-notch mountain bikes. Most outlets also give good discounts for multi-day rents.

CYCLING INFORMATION

Cycle Scotland ⓦ cyclescotland.co.uk. Fully customized cycle tours at all levels, with accommodation ranging from campsites to country-house hotels, and a good range of bikes available for rent, from tandems to children's bikes.

Cycling UK ⓦ cyclinguk.org. Britain's largest cycling organization, and a good source of general advice; their handbook has lists of cyclist-friendly B&Bs and cafés in Scotland. Annual membership £46.50.

STAYING SAFE IN THE HILLS

Due to rapid weather changes, the **mountains** are potentially extremely **dangerous** and should be treated with respect. Every year, in every season, climbers and walkers lose their lives in the Scottish hills.

• Wear sturdy, ankle-supporting **footwear** and wear or carry with you warm, brightly coloured and **waterproof** layered clothing, even for what appears to be an easy expedition in apparently settled weather.

• Always carry adequate **maps**, a **compass** (which you should know how to use), food, water and a whistle. If it's sunny, make sure you use **sun protection**.

• Check the **weather forecast** before you go. If the weather looks as if it's closing in, get down from the mountain fast.

• Always **leave word** with someone of your route and what time you expect to return, and remember to contact the person again to let them know that you are back.

• In an emergency, call **mountain rescue** on ☎ 999.

Forestry and Land Scotland W forestryandland.gov.scot/visit/activities/mountain-biking. The best source of information on Scotland's extensive network of forest trails – ideal for mountain biking at all levels of ability.

Full On Adventure W fullonadventure.co.uk. Specialists in fully guided mountain-bike tours of the Cairngorms and Strathspey.

Highland Wildcat Trails W highlandwildcat.com. Scotland's most northerly dedicated mountain-bike centre, complete with one of the country's longest downhill tracks.

Nevis Range W ridefortwilliam.co.uk. Information on all the trails around Fort William, including the home of Scotland's World Cup downhill and cross-country tracks at Nevis Range.

Spokes W spokes.org.uk. Active Edinburgh cycle campaign group with plenty of good links, and news on events and cycle-friendly developments.

WolfTrax Mountain Bike Centre W forestryandland.gov.scot/visit/lagan-wolftrax. This Central Highland bike centre near Newtonmore has almost 22 miles of routes for every standard of rider.

Air sports

Scotland has its fair share of fine sunny days, when it's hard to beat scanning majestic mountain peaks, lochs and endless forests from the air. Whether you're a willing novice or an expert **paraglider** or **skydiver**, there are centres just outside Glasgow, Edinburgh and Perth that will cater to your needs. There are also opportunities to try ballooning and gliding.

AIR SPORTS INFORMATION

British Gliding Association W gliding.co.uk. Governing body for gliding enthusiasts and schools across the UK with information on where to find clubs in Scotland.

Cloudbusters W cloudbusters.co.uk. Highly reputable paragliding school that runs taster and fully accredited paragliding courses in the Lanarkshire hills outside Glasgow every weekend. Full day's training £130.

Flying Fever W flyingfever.net. Based on the stunning Isle of Arran, forty miles southwest of Glasgow. From March to October, fully accredited paragliding courses and tandem flights cost £150.

Skydive St Andrews W skydivestandrews.co.uk. Year-round, highly professional, fully accredited parachute school that offers tandem, solo "static" line and "accelerated free-fall courses" over the Fife countryside. Tandem jump £270.

Skydive Strathallan W skydivestrathallan.co.uk. Located just outside Auchterarder, this non-commercial school operates year-round. Tandem jump £270.

Golf

There are more than four hundred golf courses in Scotland, where the game is less elitist and more accessible than anywhere else in the world. **Golf** in its present form took shape in the fifteenth century on the dunes of Scotland's east coast, and today you'll find some of the oldest courses in the world on these coastal sites, known as 'links'. It's often possible to turn up and play, though it's sensible to phone ahead; booking is essential for the championship courses.

Public courses are owned by the local council, while **private courses** belong to a club. You can play on both – occasionally the private courses require that you are a **member** of another club, however, and the odd one asks for introductions from a member, but these rules are often waived for overseas visitors and all you need to do is pay a one-off fee. The cost of a round will set you back around £20 on a small nine-hole course, around £70 on many good-quality eighteen-hole courses, and well into three figures on the championship courses.

St Andrews is the top destination for golfers: it's the home of the Royal and Ancient Golf Club, the body that regulates the rules of the game. Go to W scottish-golfcourses.com for contacts, scorecards and maps of signature holes for most of the main courses. If you're coming to Scotland primarily to play golf, it's worth shelling out for one of the various multi-course passes or packages available, which gives you access to a number of courses in any one region. There's more information at W visitscotlandgolf.com and W visitscotland.com/see-do/active/golf.

Fishing

Scotland's serrated **coastline** – with the deep sea lochs of the west, the firths of the east and the myriad offshore islands – ranks among the cleanest coasts in Europe. Combine this with an abundance of salmon, sea trout, brown trout and pike, acres of open space and easy access, and you have a wonderful location for game-, coarse- or sea-fishing.

No licence is needed to fish in Scotland, although nearly all land is privately owned and its fishing therefore controlled by a landlord/lady or his/her agent. Permission, however, is usually easy to obtain: permits can be bought at local tackle shops, rural post offices or through fishing clubs in the area – if in doubt, ask at the nearest tourist office. Salmon and sea trout have strict **seasons**, which usually stretch from late August to late February. Individual tourist offices will know the precise dates, or see the information and booking website W fishpal.com.

Watersports

Opportunities for **sailing** around Scotland are outstanding. However, even in summer the full force of the North Atlantic can be felt, and changeable conditions combined with tricky tides and rocky shores demand good sailing and navigational skills. Yacht charters are available from various ports, either bareboat or in yachts run by a skipper and crew; contact Sail Scotland (Ⓦ sailscotland.co.uk) or the Association of Scottish Yacht Charterers (Ⓦ asyc.co.uk). An alternative way to enjoy Scotland under sail is to spend a week at a sailing school. Many schools, as well as small boat rental operations dotted along the coast, will rent sailing dinghies by the hour or day, as well as **windsurfing boards**.

Scotland's top spots for windsurfing and **kitesurfing** are Troon on the Ayrshire coast, St Andrews and Tiree. The latter is renowned for its beaches and waves and has an excellent surf, windsurfing and kitesurfing school, Suds Surf (Ⓦ surfschoolscotland.co.uk).

In recent years **sea-kayaking** has witnessed an explosion in popularity, with a host of operators offering sea-kayaking lessons and expeditions across the country. Canoe Scotland (Ⓦ canoescotland.org) offers useful advice, while Glenmore Lodge (Ⓦ glenmorelodge.org.uk), and Skyak Adventures (Ⓦ skyakadventures.com) are highly reputable for training and tours.

Surfing

In addition to sea-kayaking, Scotland is fast gaining a reputation as a **surfing** destination. However, the northern coastline lies on the same latitude as Alaska, so the water temperature is very low: even in midsummer it rarely exceeds 15°C, and in winter can drop to as low as 7°C. The one vital accessory, therefore, is a good **wet suit** (ideally a 5/3mm steamer), wet-suit boots and, outside summer, gloves and a hood, too.

Many of the best surf spots – such as Thurso, Tiree and the Isle of Lewis – are surrounded by stunning scenery, and you'd be unlucky to share the waves with other surfers. However, this isolation – combined with the cold water and big, powerful waves – means that many of the best locations can only be enjoyed by experienced surfers. Surf shops rent or sell equipment and provide good information about local breaks and events on the surfing scene.

SURF SHOPS AND SCHOOLS

Coast to Coast Surf School Station Rd, Dunbar Ⓦ c2csurfschool.com. Year-round surfing lessons and surf safaris across Scotland.
Clan 45 Hyndland St, Partick, Glasgow Ⓦ clanskates.co.uk. Combined surf, skate and snowboard shop. Lessons also available.
Suds Surf School Isle of Tiree Ⓦ surfschoolscotland.co.uk. Professional instruction and rental for surfing, windsurfing, kitesurfing and kayaking.

Travel essentials

Costs

Scotland is a relatively **expensive** place to visit, with travel, food and accommodation costs higher than the EU average, though this has been balanced out with a plunging pound in the wake of the Brexit vote. Given Scotland's – and the UK's – unstable political and economic climate, costs are likely to continue fluctuating for the foreseeable future. The minimum expenditure for a couple travelling on public transport, self-catering and camping, is in the region of £35 each a day, rising to around £60 per person a day if you're staying at hostels and eating the odd meal out. Staying at budget B&Bs, eating at unpretentious restaurants and visiting the odd tourist attraction, means spending at least £75 per person per day. If you're renting a car, staying in comfortable B&Bs or hotels and eating well, you should reckon on at least £100 a day per person.

Crime and personal safety

For the most part the Scottish **police** are approachable and helpful to visitors. If you're lost in a major town, asking a police officer is generally the quickest way to get help. As with any country, Scotland's major towns and cities have their danger spots, but these tend to be inner-city housing estates where no tourist has any reason to roam. The chief urban risk is **pickpocketing**, so carry only as much money as you need, and keep all bags and pockets fastened. Out in the Highlands and Islands, crime levels are very low. Should you have anything stolen or be involved in some incident that requires reporting, contact the local police station (dial ☎ 101 from any location); ☎ 999 (or ☎ 112) should only be used in emergencies – in other words, if someone is in immediate danger or a crime is taking place.

Discounts

Most attractions in Scotland offer **concessions** for senior citizens, the unemployed, full-time students and children under 16, with under-5s being admitted free almost everywhere – proof of eligibility will be required in most cases. Family tickets are often available for those travelling with kids.

Once obtained, **youth/student ID cards** soon pay for themselves in savings. Full-time students are eligible for an International Student Identity Card (**ISIC;** Ⓦ isic.org), which costs £12 and entitles the bearer to special air, rail and bus fares, and discounts at museums, theatres and other attractions. If you're not a student, but you're 25 or younger, you can get an International Youth Travel Card (**IYTC**), which costs the same as the ISIC and carries the same benefits.

Electricity

The current in Scotland is the **EU standard** of approximately 230v AC. All sockets are designed for British three-pin plugs, which are totally different from the rest of the EU. Adaptors are widely available at airports and electronics stores.

Emergencies

For **police**, **fire** and **ambulance** services phone ☎ 999.

Entry requirements

EU, EEA and Swiss nationals, Americans, Canadians, Australians, New Zealanders and citizens of some Latin American and Caribbean countries can enter the UK visa-free with a valid passport and stay as a tourist for up to six months provided they meet Standard Visitor eligibility requirements such as proof of adequate funds for return or onward journey and to cover stay. Irish citizens can travel freely in the UK via the Common Travel Area (CTA) arrangement between the UK and Ireland. Citizens of most other countries require a **visa**, obtainable from the British consulate or mission office in the country of application.

Note that visa regulations are subject to frequent changes. Visit Ⓦ ukvisas.gov.uk, to check online if you need a visa, download the full range of **application forms** and information leaflets, and find out the contact details of your nearest embassy or consulate, as well as the rules regarding visa extensions. In addition, an independent charity, the Immigration Advisory Service or IAS (Ⓦ iasservices.org.uk), offers free and confidential advice to anyone applying for entry clearance into the UK.

LGBTQ travellers

Both Glasgow and Edinburgh have reasonably prominent **LGBTQ** communities, with a well-established network of bars, cafés, nightclubs, support groups and events. In **Edinburgh**, the area around Broughton Street is the heart of the city's 'pink triangle', while in **Glasgow** the scene is mostly found in the Merchant City area; our entertainment listings for both cities include a number of gay bars and clubs. Elsewhere in Scotland, there are one or two gay bars in both Aberdeen and Dundee, and support and advice groups dotted around the country. Details for these, and many other aspects of the LGBTQ scene in Scotland, can be found in the monthly *Scotsgay* newspaper, versions of which can be downloaded for free online (Ⓦ scotsgay.co.uk).

Health

Pharmacists can dispense only a limited range of drugs without a doctor's prescription. Most pharmacies (aka chemists) are open standard shop hours, though there are also late-night branches in large cities and at 24-hour supermarkets.

If your condition is serious enough, you can turn up at the Accident and Emergency (A&E) department of local **hospitals** for complaints that require immediate attention. Obviously, if it's an absolute emergency, ring for an ambulance (☎ 999). These services are free to all.

Scotland, like the rest of the world, was hit hard by the Covid-19 pandemic, with more cases and deaths in the second wave of the virus. Check www.gov.scot for the latest updates and requirements regarding the pandemic such as mask-wearing.

Insurance

Even though, European Health Insurance Cards (EHICs) are valid in Scotland, it's still a good idea to take out **travel insurance** before travelling to cover

---

HISTORIC ENVIRONMENT SCOTLAND AND NATIONAL TRUST FOR SCOTLAND

Many of Scotland's most treasured sights – from castles and country houses to islands, gardens and tracts of protected landscape – come under the control of the privately-run **National Trust for Scotland** (Ⓦ nts.org.uk) or the state-run **Historic Environment Scotland** (Ⓦ historicenvironment.scot); we've quoted **NTS** or **HES** respectively for each site reviewed in this Guide. Both organizations generally charge an admission fee, these can be quite high, especially for the more grandiose NTS estates.

If you think you'll be visiting more than half a dozen NTS properties, or more than a dozen HES ones, it's worth taking an **annual membership**, which costs around £52 (HES) or £60 (NTS), and allows free admission to their properties. In addition, HES offers an **Explorer Pass**, which is valid for either five (£35 adult, £70 family) or fourteen (£45 adult, £90 family) consecutive days.

ROUGH GUIDES TRAVEL INSURANCE

Rough Guides has teamed up with **World Nomads** (Ⓦworldnomads.com) to offer great travel insurance deals. Policies are available to residents of over 150 countries, with cover for a wide range of adventure sports, 24hr emergency assistance, high levels of medical and evacuation cover, and a stream of travel safety information. **roughguides.com** users can take advantage of their policies online 24/7, from anywhere in the world – even if you're already travelling. And since plans often change when you're on the road, you can extend your policy and even claim online. roughguides.com users who buy travel insurance with World Nomads can also leave a positive footprint and donate to a community development project. For more information, go to Ⓦroughguides.com/travel-insurance.

against theft, loss and illness or injury. For non-EU citizens, it's worth checking whether you are already covered before you buy a new policy. If you need to take out insurance, you might want to consider the travel insurance deal we offer (see box, above).

Internet

Wi-fi is available at most B&Bs and hostels, even in the Highlands and Islands. If you don't have your own smartphone, laptop or tablet, the tourist office should be able to help – sometimes they will have an access point – and public libraries often provide cheap or free access. Network coverage for 3G and 4G is good in cities and the central belt but patchy to non-existent in the Highlands, Islands and Borders.

Laundry

Coin-operated **laundries** are still found in a few Scottish cities and towns, but are becoming less and less common. A wash followed by a spin or tumble dry costs about £3.50; a service wash (having your laundry done for you in a few hours) costs about £2 extra. In the more remote regions of Scotland, you'll have to rely on hostel and campsite laundry facilities.

Mail

A stamp for a **first-class letter** to anywhere in the British Isles currently costs 85p and should arrive the next day; second-class letters cost 66p, taking three days. Note that there are now size restrictions: letters over 240 x 165 x 5mm are designated as 'Large letters' and are correspondingly more expensive to send. Prices to Europe and the rest of the world vary depending on the size of the item and how quickly you would like it delivered. To get an idea of how much you'll need to spend, or for general postal info, check the Royal Mail website (Ⓦroyalmail.com/price-finder).

Note that in many parts of the Highlands and Islands there will only be one or two mail collections each day, often at lunchtime or even earlier. **Stamps** can be bought at post office counters or from newsagents, supermarkets and local shops, although they usually only sell books of four, ten or twelve stamps.

Most **post offices** are open Monday to Friday 9am–5.30pm and Saturday 9am–12.30pm. In small communities you'll find post office counters operating out of a shop, shed or even a private house, and these will often keep extremely **restricted hours**.

Maps

The most comprehensive maps of Scotland are produced by the **Ordnance Survey** or OS (Ⓦordnancesurvey.co.uk), renowned for their accuracy and clarity. If you're planning a walk of more than a couple of hours in duration, or intend to walk in the Scottish hills at all, it is strongly recommended that you carry the relevant OS map and familiarize yourself with how to navigate using it. Scotland is covered by 85 maps in the 1:50,000 (pink) **Landranger** series which shows enough detail to be useful for most walkers and cyclists. There's more detail still in the full-colour 1:25,000 (orange) **Explorer** series, which covers Scotland in around 170 maps. All OS maps come with a smartphone download. The full range is only available at a few big-city shops or online, although in any walking district of Scotland you'll find the relevant maps in local shops or tourist offices.

Virtually every service station in Scotland stocks at least one large-format **road atlas**, covering all of Britain at around three miles to one inch, and generally including larger-scale plans of major towns. For getting between major towns and cities a satnav or GPS-enabled smartphone is hard to beat, but you'll have less luck in rural areas, where landmarks and even entire roads can be positioned incorrectly, leading to long and sometimes expensive detours.

PUBLIC HOLIDAYS

Official **bank holidays** in Scotland operate on: 1 and 2 January; Good Friday; the first and last Monday in May; the last Monday in August; St Andrew's Day (30 Nov), Christmas Day (25 Dec); and Boxing Day (26 Dec). In addition, all Scottish towns have one-day holidays in spring, summer and autumn – dates vary from place to place but normally fall on a Monday. While many local shops and businesses close on these days, few tourist-related businesses observe the holidays, particularly in summer.

Money

The basic unit of **currency** in the UK is the pound sterling (£), divided into 100 pence (p). Coins come in denominations of 1p, 2p, 5p, 10p, 20p, 50p, £1 and £2. Bank of England £5, £10, £20 and £50 banknotes are legal tender in Scotland; in addition, the **Bank of Scotland**, the **Royal Bank of Scotland** and the **Clydesdale Bank** issue their own banknotes in all the same denominations, plus a £100 note. All Scottish notes are legal tender throughout the UK, no matter what shopkeepers south of the border might say. In general, few people use £50 or £100 notes, and shopkeepers are likely to treat them with suspicion; fear of forgeries is widespread. At the time of writing, £1 was worth around €1.19, US$1.35, CA$1.70, AU$1.85 and NZ$1.95. For the most up-to-date exchange rates, check the useful website ⓦxe.com.

Credit/debit cards are by far the most convenient way to carry your money, and most hotels, shops and restaurants in Scotland accept the major brand cards. In every sizeable town in Scotland, and in some surprisingly small places too, you'll find a branch of at least one of the big Scottish high-street **banks**, usually with an **ATM** attached. However, on some islands, and in remoter parts, you may find there is only a **mobile bank** that runs to a timetable (usually available from the local post office). General **banking hours** are Monday to Friday from 9 or 9.30am to 4 or 5pm, though some branches are open until slightly later on Thursdays. Post offices charge **no commission**, have longer opening hours, and are therefore often a good place to change money and cheques. Lost or stolen credit/debit cards should be reported to the police and the following numbers: MasterCard ☎0800 964767; Visa ☎0800 891725.

Opening hours and public holidays

Traditional **shop hours** in Scotland are Monday to Saturday 9am to 5.30 or 6pm. In the bigger towns and cities, many places now stay open on Sundays and late at night on Thursdays or Fridays. Large supermarkets typically stay open till 8pm or 10pm and a few manage 24-hour opening (excluding Sunday). However, there are also plenty of towns and villages where you'll find precious little open on a Sunday, with many small towns also retaining an '**early closing day**' – often Wednesday – when shops close at 1pm. In the Highlands and Islands you'll find precious few attractions open outside the tourist season (Easter to Oct), though ruins, parks and gardens are normally accessible year-round. Note that last entry can be an hour (or more) before the published closing time.

Phones

Public **payphones** are still occasionally found in the Highlands and Islands, though with the ubiquity of mobile phones, they're seldom used.

If you're taking your **mobile phone/cell phone** with you to Scotland, check with your service provider whether your phone will work abroad and what the call charges will be. The cost of calls within the EU has decreased significantly within recent years, and roaming charges within the EU have been abolished. Again, though, the Brexit vote has thrown into doubt how any new law in this regard will affect the UK. Calls to destinations further afield, however, are still unregulated and can be prohibitively expensive. Unless you have a tri-band phone, it's unlikely that a mobile bought for use in the **US** will work outside the States and vice versa. Mobiles in **Australia** and **New Zealand** generally use the same system as the UK so should work fine. All the main UK networks cover the Highlands and Islands, though you'll still find many places in among the hills or out on the islands where there's no signal at all. If you're having trouble with **reception**, ask a local where the strongest signals are.

Beware of premium-rate numbers, which are common for pre-recorded information services – and usually have the prefix ☎09.

Time

Greenwich Mean Time (GMT) – equivalent to Co-ordinated Universal Time (UTC) – is used from the end of October to the end of March; for the rest of the year the country switches to **British Summer Time** (BST), one hour ahead of GMT.

Tipping

There are no fixed rules for **tipping**. If you think you've received good service, particularly in restaurants or cafés, you may want to leave a tip of ten percent of the total bill (unless service has already been included). It's not normal, however, to leave tips in pubs, although bar staff are sometimes offered drinks, which they may accept in the form of money. The only other occasions when you'll be expected to tip are in hairdressers, taxis and smart hotels, where porters and table waiters rely on being tipped to bump up often dismal wages.

Tourist information

The official tourist board, **VisitScotland** (Ⓦ visitscotland.com), operates 26 iCentres. These are effectively regional visitor centres that dispense information on the surrounding area (and invariably beyond). Opening hours are often fiendishly complex, but have been listed throughout the guide; however, these hours are subject to change.

As well as being stacked full of souvenirs and other gifts, most centres have a decent selection of leaflets, displays, maps and books relating to the local area. The staff are usually helpful and will do their best to help with enquiries about accommodation, local transport, attractions and restaurants, although it's worth being aware that they're sometimes reluctant to divulge information about local attractions or accommodation options that are not paid-up members of the Tourist Board, and a number of perfectly decent guesthouses and the like choose not to pay the fees.

Travellers with disabilities

Scottish attitudes towards **travellers with disabilities** still lag behind advances towards independence made in North America and Australia. Access to many public buildings has improved, with legislation ensuring that all new buildings have appropriate facilities. Some hotels and a handful of B&Bs have one or two adapted rooms, usually on the ground floor, with step-free showers, grab rails and wider doorways. It's worth keeping in mind, however, that installing ramps, lifts, wide doorways and disabled toilets is impossible in many of Scotland's older and historic buildings.

Most **trains** in Scotland have wheelchair lifts, and assistance is, in theory, available at all manned stations – see Ⓦ scotrail.co.uk/plan-your-journey/accessible-travel. Wheelchair-users (alone or with a companion) and blind or partially sighted people (with a companion only) are automatically given thirty to fifty percent reductions on train fares (though there are usually no facilities for wheelchairs in first class), and people with other disabilities are eligible for the **Disabled Persons Railcard** (£20/year; Ⓦ disabledpersons-railcard.co.uk), which gives a third off most tickets. There are no bus discounts for disabled tourists. **Car rental** firm Avis will fit their cars (generally automatics only) with hand controls for free as long as you give them a few days' notice.

For more information and advice contact the disability charity Capability Scotland (☎0131 3379876, Ⓦ capability.scot).

Working in Scotland

Irish citizens via the Common Travel Area (CTA) arrangement and nonnationals with settled or pre-settled status have the right to work in Scotland. Other nonnationals must apply for short- or long-term work visas to legally work in the UK. Visit Ⓦ gov.uk/government/organisations/uk-visas-and-immigration for further information.

CALLING HOME FROM ABROAD

To make an international call, dial the international access code (in Scotland it's 00), then the destination's country code, before the rest of the number. Note that the initial zero is omitted from the area code when dialling Ireland, Australia and New Zealand from abroad.

Australia international access code + 61
New Zealand international access code + 64
US and Canada international access code + 1
Ireland international access code + 353
South Africa international access code + 27

Edinburgh and the Lothians

SCOTTISH PARLIAMENT

1 Edinburgh and the Lothians

Venerable, dramatic Edinburgh, the showcase capital of Scotland, is a historic, cosmopolitan and cultured city. The setting is wonderfully striking: perched on a series of extinct volcanoes and rocky crags which rise from the generally flat landscape of the Lothians, with the sheltered shoreline of the Firth of Forth to the north. 'Mine own romantic town', Sir Walter Scott called it, although it was another native author, Robert Louis Stevenson, who perhaps best captured the feel of this 'precipitous city', declaring that 'No situation could be more commanding for the head city of a kingdom; none better chosen for noble prospects'.

The centre has two distinct parts: the unrelentingly medieval **Old Town**, with its tortuous alleys and tightly packed closes, and the dignified, eighteenth-century Grecian-style **New Town**. Dividing the two are **Princes Street Gardens**, which run roughly east to west under the shadow of **Edinburgh Castle**.

Set on the hill that rolls down from the fairy-tale castle to the royal **Palace of Holyroodhouse**, the Old Town preserves all the key landmarks from its role as a historic capital, augmented by the dramatic and unusual **Scottish Parliament building**, opposite the palace. A few hundred yards away, a tantalizing glimpse of the wild beauty of Scotland's scenery can be had in **Holyrood Park**, an extensive area of open countryside dominated by **Arthur's Seat**, the largest and most impressive of the city's volcanoes.

Among Edinburgh's many museums, the exciting **National Museum of Scotland** houses ten thousand of Scotland's most precious artefacts, while the **Scottish National Gallery** and its offshoot, the **Scottish National Gallery of Modern Art**, have two of Britain's finest collections of paintings.

In August, around a million visitors flock to the city for the **Edinburgh Festival**, a series of separate festivals that make up the largest arts extravaganza in the world. On a less elevated theme, the city's distinctive pubs, allied to its brewing and distilling traditions, make it a great **drinking** city. Its four **universities**, plus several colleges, mean that there is a youthful presence for most of the year. Beyond the city centre, the liveliest area is **Leith**, the city's medieval port, now a culinary hotspot with a series of great bars and upmarket seafood restaurants.

The wider rural hinterland of Edinburgh, known as the **Lothians**, mixes rolling countryside and attractive country towns with some impressive historic ruins. In East Lothian, blustery clifftop paths lead to the romantic battlements of **Tantallon Castle**, while nearby North Berwick, home of the **Scottish Seabird Centre**, looks out to the gannet-covered Bass Rock. The most famous sight in Midlothian is the mysterious fifteenth-century **Rosslyn Chapel**, while West Lothian boasts the towering, roofless **Linlithgow Palace**, thirty minutes from Edinburgh by train. To the northwest of the city, the dramatic steel geometry of the Forth Rail Bridge is best seen by walking across the parallel road bridge, starting at **South Queensferry**.

Brief history

It was during the **Dark Ages** that the name Edinburgh – at least in its early form of Dunedin or Din Eidyn (fort of Eidyn) – first appeared. The strategic fort atop the Castle Rock volcano served as Scotland's **southernmost border post** until c. 1018, when King Malcolm II established the River Tweed as the permanent frontier. In the late eleventh century, during the reign of Malcolm Canmore, the castle became one of the main seats of the court, and the town, which was given privileged status as a **royal burgh**, began to grow.

Highlights

❶ The Old Town The evocative heart of the historic city, with its tenements, closes, courtyards, ghosts and catacombs cheek by jowl with many of Scotland's most important buildings. See page 60

❷ Edinburgh Castle Vertiginously sited upon an imposing volcanic plug, the Castle dominates Scotland's capital, its ancient battlements protecting the Scottish Crown Jewels. See page 60

❸ Scottish Parliament Enric Miralles' quirky yet thrilling design is a dramatic modern presence in Holyrood's historic royal precinct. See page 72

❹ Holyrood Park Wild moors, sheer cliffs and an 823ft-high peak (Arthur's Seat), all slap in the middle of the city. See page 72

❺ Café Royal Circle Bar In a city filled with fine drinking spots, there are few finer pubs in which to sample a pint of 'Heavy' – a medium-strength Scottish cask ale; order six oysters (once the city's staple food) to complete the experience. See page 95

❻ The Edinburgh Festival The world's biggest arts gathering transforms the city every August: bewildering, inspiring, exhausting and endlessly entertaining. See page 100

❼ Rosslyn Chapel This impeccably preserved, cathedral-like Gothic masterwork boasts some of the finest examples of medieval stone craft in the world. See page 106

HIGHLIGHTS ARE MARKED ON THE MAPS ON PAGES 56 & 62

Scotland's new capital

Robert the Bruce granted Edinburgh a **new charter** in 1329, giving it jurisdiction over the nearby port of Leith, and during the following century the prosperity brought by foreign trade enabled the newly fortified city to establish itself as the permanent **capital of Scotland**.

Under King James IV, the city enjoyed a short but brilliant **Renaissance era**, which saw not only the construction of a new palace alongside Holyrood Abbey, but also the granting of a **royal charter** to the College of Surgeons, the earliest in the city's long line of academic and professional bodies.

Turbulent Age of Reformation

Edinburgh's Renaissance period came to an abrupt end in 1513 with the calamitous defeat by the English at the **Battle of Flodden**, which led to several decades of political instability. In the 1540s, King Henry VIII's attempt to force a royal union with Scotland led to the sack of Edinburgh, prompting the Scots to turn to France: French troops arrived to defend the city, while the young queen, Mary, was dispatched to Paris as the promised bride of the dauphin, later (briefly) François II of France. While the French occupiers succeeded in removing the English threat, they themselves antagonized the locals, who had become increasingly sympathetic to the ideals of the **Reformation**. When the radical preacher **John Knox** (see page 69) returned from exile in 1555, he quickly won over the city to his Calvinist message.

James VI's rule saw the foundation of the University of Edinburgh in 1582, but following the **Union of the Crowns** in 1603 the city was totally upstaged by London. In 1633, Charles I visited Edinburgh for his coronation, but soon afterwards precipitated a crisis by introducing episcopacy to the Church of Scotland, in the process making Edinburgh a bishopric for the first time. Fifty years of religious turmoil followed, culminating in the triumph of **Presbyterianism**.

Acts of Union

The **Union of the Parliaments** of 1707 dealt a further blow to Edinburgh's political prestige, though by guaranteeing the preservation of the Church of Scotland and the legal and educational systems the acts ensured that the city was never relegated to a purely provincial role. Indeed, the second half of the eighteenth century saw Edinburgh achieve the height of its intellectual influence, led by natives such as David Hume and Adam Smith. Around the same time, the city began to expand beyond its medieval boundaries, laying out the **New Town**, a masterpiece of the Neoclassical style.

Victorian Edinburgh

Industrialization affected Edinburgh less than any other major city in the nation, and it never lost its white-collar character. Through the Victorian era Edinburgh cemented its role as a conservative bastion of the establishment, controlling Scotland's legal, ecclesiastical and education systems. Indeed, the city underwent an enormous **urban expansion** in the course of the nineteenth century, annexing, among many other small burghs, the large port of Leith.

The twentieth century and beyond

In 1947, Edinburgh was chosen to host the great **International Festival** which served as a symbol of the new peaceful European order; despite some hiccups, it has flourished ever since, in the process helping to make tourism a mainstay of the local economy. During the 1980s, Glasgow, previously the poor relation but always a tenacious rival, began to challenge the city's status as a cultural centre, and it took the re-establishment of a devolved Scottish **Parliament** in 1999 for Edinburgh to reassert its status in a meaningful way. With debates, decisions and demonstrations about crucial aspects of the government of Scotland taking place in Edinburgh, there was a marked upturn

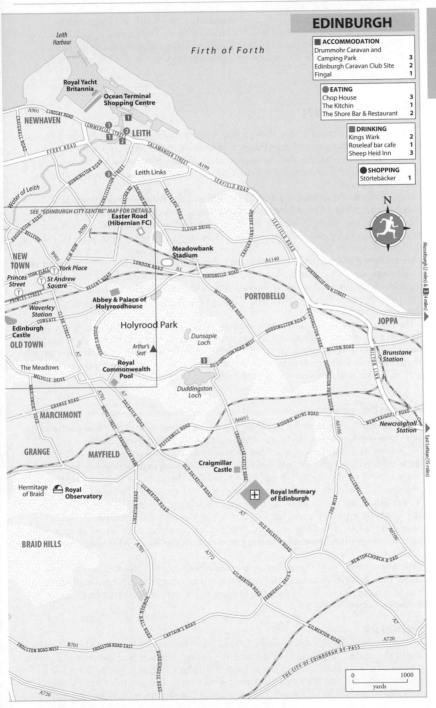

EDINBURGH

1

■ **ACCOMMODATION**
Drummohr Caravan and Camping Park	3
Edinburgh Caravan Club Site	2
Fingal	1

● **EATING**
Chop House	3
The Kitchin	1
The Shore Bar & Restaurant	2

■ **DRINKING**
Kings Wark	2
Roseleaf bar cafe	1
Sheep Heid Inn	3

● **SHOPPING**
Störtebäcker	1

in the perceived importance of the city, augmented by notable achievements in scientific research and the arts. The city's financial sector burgeoned up until the Global Financial Crisis; in the wake of Lehman Brothers 2008 collapse, the Royal Bank of Scotland group, formerly the second-largest banking group in the UK, required a £45bn taxpayer bailout.

The Old Town

The **OLD TOWN**, although only about a mile long and 400yd wide, represented the total extent of the twin burghs of Edinburgh and Canongate for over six hundred years, and its general appearance and character remain indubitably medieval. Containing the majority of the city's most famous tourist sights, it makes the best starting point for your explorations.

In addition to the obvious goals of the **castle** and the **Palace of Holyroodhouse** at either end of the famous **Royal Mile**, you'll find scores of historic buildings along the length of the street. Inevitably, much of the Old Town is sacrificed to hard-sell tourism, and can be uncomfortably crowded throughout the summer, especially during the festival. Yet the area remains at the heart of Edinburgh, with important daily business being conducted in the law courts, city chambers and, of course, the **Scottish Parliament**, which is housed in a radical and controversial collection of buildings at the foot of the Royal Mile. It's well worth extending your explorations to the area immediately to the south of the Royal Mile, and in particular to the engaging **National Museum of Scotland**.

The Old Town is compact enough to allow a brief glance at the highlights in a single day, but a thorough visit requires several days. Be sure to spare time for the wonderfully varied scenery and breathtaking vantage points of **Holyrood Park**, an extensive tract of open countryside on the eastern edge of the Old Town that includes Arthur's Seat, the peak of which rises so distinctively in the midst of the city.

The castle

Castlehill • Daily April–Sept 9.30am–6pm; Oct–March 9.30am–5pm; last entry 1hr before closing • Charge (cheaper tickets are available online) • Guided tours daily April–Sept; every 30min; Oct–March; every 60min • Charge • HES • ⓦ edinburghcastle.scot

The history of Edinburgh, and indeed of Scotland, is tightly wrapped up with this **castle**, which dominates the city from a lofty seat atop an extinct volcanic rock. It requires no great imaginative feat to comprehend the strategic importance that underpinned the castle's, and hence Edinburgh's, pre-eminence in Scotland. From Princes Street, the north side rears high above an almost sheer rock face; the southern side is equally formidable and the western, where the rock rises in terraces, only marginally less so. Would-be attackers, like modern tourists, were forced to approach the castle from the narrow ridge to the east on which the Royal Mile runs down to Holyrood.

The disparate styles of the architecture reflect the change in its role from defensive citadel to national monument, and today, as well as attracting more paying visitors than anywhere else in the country, the castle is still a **military barracks** and home to Scotland's **Crown Jewels**.

Brief history

Although this rocky outcrop has been settled since the Bronze Age, the oldest surviving part of the castle complex is from the twelfth century. Nothing remains from its period as a seat of the Scottish court in the reign of Malcolm Canmore, having been lost to (and recaptured from) the English on several occasions. The return of King David II from captivity introduced a modicum of political stability and thereafter it gradually

THE STONE OF DESTINY

Legend has it that the **Stone of Destiny** (also called the Stone of Scone) was 'Jacob's Pillow', on which he dreamed of the ladder of angels from earth to heaven. Its real history is obscure, but it is known to have been moved from Ireland to Dunadd by missionaries, and thence to Dunstaffnage, from where Kenneth MacAlpine, the king of Alba, brought it to Scone, near Perth, in AD 838. It remained in Perthshire for almost five hundred years, the **coronation throne** on which all kings of Scotland were crowned.

In 1296, Edward I stole what he believed to be the Stone from Scone Abbey and installed it at **Westminster Abbey**, where, apart from a brief interlude in 1950 when it was removed by Scottish nationalists and hidden in Arbroath for several months, it remained for seven hundred years. All this changed in December 1996 when, after a ceremony-laden journey from London, the Stone returned to Scotland. Much to the annoyance of the people of Perth and the curators of Scone Palace (see page 312), and the general indifference of the people of Scotland, the Stone was placed in **Edinburgh Castle**. In 2024, the Stone will be relocated to a new museum in Perthshire.

However, speculation surrounds the **authenticity** of the Stone, for the original is said to have been intricately carved, while the one seen today is a plain block of sandstone. Many believe that the canny monks at Scone palmed this off onto the English king (some say that it's nothing more sacred than the cover for a medieval septic tank), and that the real Stone of Destiny lies hidden in an underground chamber, its whereabouts a mystery to all but the chosen few.

developed into Scotland's premier castle, with the dual function of fortress and royal palace. It last saw siege action in 1745, when Bonnie Prince Charlie's forces, fresh from their victory at Prestonpans, made a half-hearted attempt to storm it. Subsequent advances in weapon technology diminished the castle's importance, but under the influence of the Romantic Movement it came to be seen as a great national monument.

The Esplanade

Castlehill, top end of the Royal Mile • Free

The castle is entered via the **Esplanade**, a parade ground laid out in the eighteenth century and enclosed a hundred years later by ornamental walls. In the summer months huge grandstands are erected for the Royal Edinburgh Military Tattoo (see page 101), which takes place for three weeks (Mon–Sat) in August, coinciding with the Edinburgh Festival. A shameless and spectacular pageant of swinging kilts and massed pipe bands, the tattoo makes full use of its dramatic setting.

Various memorials are dotted around the Esplanade, including the Art Nouveau Witches' Fountain which commemorates those burnt at this spot, on charges of sorcery. Rising up to one side of the Esplanade are the higgledy-piggledy pink-and-white turrets and high gables of **Ramsay Gardens**, surely some of the most picturesque city-centre apartment buildings in the world. Most date from the 1890s and are the vision of Patrick Geddes, a pioneer of the modern town-planning movement.

The defences

Edinburgh Castle has a single entrance, a 10ft-wide opening in the **gatehouse**, one of many Romantic-style additions made in the 1880s. Rearing up behind is the most distinctive and impressive feature of the Castle's silhouette, the sixteenth-century **Half Moon Battery**. Once through the gatehouse, you'll find the main ticket office on your right, with an information centre alongside. Continue uphill along Lower Ward, showing your ticket at the **Portcullis Gate**, a handsome Renaissance gateway of the same period as the battery above, with a nineteenth-century upper storey equipped with anachronistic arrow slits. Beyond this the wide main path is known as Middle

1

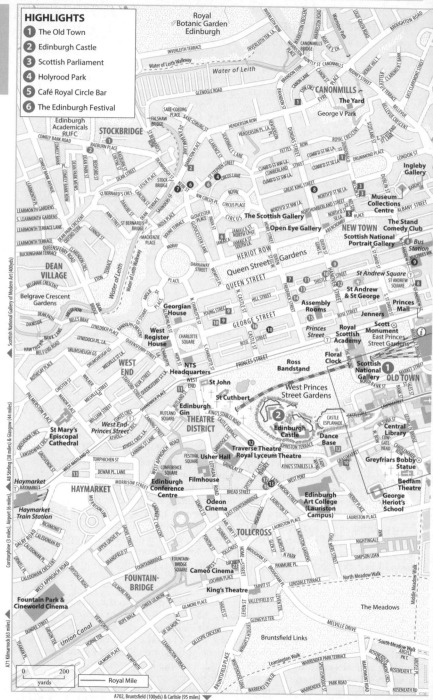

HIGHLIGHTS

1. The Old Town
2. Edinburgh Castle
3. Scottish Parliament
4. Holyrood Park
5. Café Royal Circle Bar
6. The Edinburgh Festival

EDINBURGH CITY CENTRE

● **SHOPPING**

Archipelago Bakery	8
Edinburgh Books	13
Edinburgh Farmers' Market	12
Golden Hare Books	4
Harvey Nichols	9
I.J. Mellis	6
McNaughtan's Bookshop	2
Sicilian Pastry Shop	1
Stockbridge Market	7
Tiso	10
Valvona & Crolla	3
Vinyl Villains	5
W. Armstrong & Son	11/14

● **EATING**

Artisan Roast	1/5
Chaophraya	16
Chez Jules	9
Dusit	11
El Cartel Casera Mexicana	13/19
Eteaket	14
Fortitude	8
The Gardener's Cottage	7
Hanedan	25
Henderson's	10
Indaba	23
Kalpna	22
L'Escargot Bleu	3
Lian Pu	21
Lovecrumbs	18
Mussel Inn	15
Saboteur	20
The Scran & Scallie	2
The Stockbridge Restaurant	6
Tanjore	24
Timberyard	17
Valvona & Crolla	4
Yeni Meze Bar	12

■ **NIGHTLIFE**

CC Bloom's	5
Ghillie-Dhu	11
Lulu's	10
The Queen's Hall	15

■ **DRINKING**

Beehive Inn	12
Café Royal	7
Cumberland Bar	1
The Jolly Botanist	13
Kays Bar	6
Oxford Bar	9
Pear Tree House	14
Planet	4
Smith & Gertrude	2
Star Bar	3
The Voodoo Rooms	8

■ **ACCOMMODATION**

Apex Grassmarket Hotel	10
Ardenlee Guest House	1
Cheval the Edinburgh Grand	8
Edinburgh Central Youth Hostel	2
Gerald's Place	5
The Glasshouse	6
The Guest Room	3
Regent House	4
Rabble	7
Ten Hill Place	11
Tigerlily	9
University of Edinburgh, Pollock Halls of Residence	12

1

Ward, with the six-gun **Argyle Battery** to the right. Further west on **Mill's Mount Battery**, a well-known Edinburgh ritual takes place – the firing of the **one o'clock gun** (except Sun, Good Friday & Christmas). Originally designed for the benefit of ships in the Firth of Forth, these days it's an enjoyable ceremony for visitors to watch and a useful time signal for city-centre office workers. There's an interesting little exhibition about the history of the firing of the gun in a room immediately below Mill's Mount Battery.

National War Museum

Hospital Square • Daily April–Sept 9.45am–5.45pm; Oct–March 9.45am–4.45pm; last entry 15min before closing • Free • ⓦ nms.ac.uk

Located in the old military hospital buildings, down the hill between the café-restaurant and the Governor's House, the **National War Museum** covers the last four hundred years of Scottish military history. While the various rooms are packed with uniforms, medals, paintings of heroic actions and plenty of interesting memorabilia, the museum manages to convey a reflective, human tone. Just as delicate is the job of showing no favouritism to any of the Scottish regiments, each of which has strong traditions more forcefully paraded in the various regimental museums found in regions of Scotland – the Royal Scots and the Scots Dragoon Guards, for instance, both have displays in other parts of Edinburgh Castle.

St Margaret's Chapel

Near the highest point of the citadel is tiny **St Margaret's Chapel**, the oldest surviving building in the Castle, and probably in Edinburgh. Although once believed to have been built by the saint herself, and mooted as the site of her death in 1093, its architectural style suggests that it actually dates from about forty years later.

Mons Meg

The battlements in front of the chapel offer the best of all the Castle's panoramic views. Here you'll see the famous fifteenth-century siege gun, **Mons Meg**, which could fire a 300lb stone nearly two miles. It last saw active service in the 1570s, and was thereafter used occasionally as a ceremonial saluting gun before being moved to the Tower of London in 1754. Such was Meg's emblematic value that Sir Walter Scott campaigned for its return; though Scott was unsuccessful, she was eventually returned by military escort in 1829.

Continuing eastwards, you skirt the top of the Forewall and Half Moon Batteries, passing the 110ft-deep **Castle Well** en route to Crown Square.

Crown Square

Crown Square, the historic heart of the Castle, is the most important and secure section of the entire complex. The square's eastern side is occupied by the **Palace**, a surprisingly unassuming edifice begun in the 1430s which owes its present appearance to King James VI who had it remodelled ahead of celebrations for his Golden Jubilee in 1617. It is embellished with details that celebrate his ancestry – above the entrance you can see the entwined initials MAH together with the date 1566, honouring his mother Mary, Queen of Scots, his father Henry, Lord Darnley, and the year he was born. This gives access to a few historic rooms, the most interesting of which is the tiny panelled bedchamber at the extreme southeastern corner, where Mary gave birth to James VI.

A section of the Palace houses a detailed audio-visual presentation on the nation's **Crown Jewels**, properly known as the **Honours of Scotland** and one of the most potent images of Scotland's nationhood; the originals are housed in the Crown Room at the very end of the display. James V's jewel-encrusted **crown** incorporates gold from an earlier crown and is topped by an enamelled orb and cross. The glass case containing the Honours has been rearranged to create space for the incongruously plain **Stone of Destiny** (see page 61).

On the south side of Crown Square is James IV's **Great Hall**. Much of what you see today is a romantic recreation of Victorian date, but the impressive hammer-beam roof and corbels are original. On the north side is the **Scottish National War Memorial**, created in 1927 by the architect Sir Robert Lorimer and two hundred Scottish artists and craftsmen.

The rest of the complex

There are a series of cavernous chambers erected by James IV to provide a level surface for the buildings above. They were later used as a prison for captured foreign nationals, who bequeathed a rich legacy of graffiti. Directly opposite the entrance to the Vaults is the **Military Prison**, built in 1842, when the design and function of jails was a major topic of public debate. The cells, designed for solitary confinement, are less forbidding than might be expected. The Fight for the Castle exhibition tells the story of Edinburgh Castle in the Wars of Independence, and is located in the Argyle Tower, directly above the gateway that was fought over in 1341 during the final siege of the castle in the wars. It features animations, a huge sculptural trebuchet and many medieval objects, including a stone ball that may have been fired by the English in the siege of 1296.

The Royal Mile

The **Royal Mile**, the main thoroughfare linking the Castle to Holyrood Palace, was described by Daniel Defoe in 1724, as 'the largest, longest, and finest street for buildings and number of inhabitants, not in Britain only, but in the world'. It is divided into five separate streets (**Castlehill**, **Lawnmarket**, **High Street**, **Canongate and Abbey Strand**, west to east respectively) – from which, branching out in a herringbone pattern, is a series of tightly packed **closes** and steep **lanes** entered via archways known as 'pends'. Hosting an architectural feast of styles from lofty rubblestone tenements and merchant houses to grand post-sixteenth-century sandstone structures built on medieval foundations – often resulting in hidden subterranean vaults and closes – The Royal Mile caters well to the hordes of tourists who gravitate towards it.

Scotch Whisky Experience

354 Castlehill • **Gold** (70–90min) and **Silver** (50min) **tours** Sun–Thurs 11am–5pm, Fri & Sat until 5.45pm; **Tasting Tales** (60 min) Sat 4.30pm; **Platinum Tour** (90min) and **Taste of Scotland** (3hr) Sun–Thurs 5.15pm, Fri & Sat 6pm & 6.30pm; with exceptions; unavailable during Royal Edinburgh Military Tattoo in Aug • Charge • ⓦ scotchwhiskyexperience.co.uk

The **Scotch Whisky Experience** mimics the kind of tours offered at distilleries in the Highlands, and while it can't match the authenticity of the real thing, the centre does offer a thorough introduction to the 'water of life' (*uisge beatha* in Gaelic), with tours featuring an entertaining tutorial on the specialized art of whisky 'nosing', a gimmicky ride in a moving 'barrel' car, a peek at the world's largest whisky collection and a tasting. On the ground floor, a well-stocked shop gives an idea of the sheer range and diversity of the drink, while downstairs there's a pleasant whisky bar and restaurant, *Amber*.

Camera Obscura and World of Illusions

549 Castlehill • Mon–Thurs 9.30am–7pm, Fri until 9, Sat 9am–9.30pm, Sun 9am–9pm; with exceptions • Charge • ⓦ camera-obscura.co.uk

Edinburgh's **Camera Obscura** is the city's oldest visitor attraction, established in 1853. Housed in the domed black-and-white turret on the roof, the 'camera' consists of a small, darkened room with a white wooden table onto which a periscope reflects live images of prominent buildings and people walking on the streets below. Today, you can also experience the **World of Illusions**, a five-floor labyrinth of family-friendly exhibits of visual trickery – many of them playfully interactive – in the floors below.

The Hub

348 Castlehill • Mon–Fri 9.30am–5.30pm; box office Mon–Sat 10am–5pm • Tickets ☎ 0131 4732000 • ⓦ thehub-edinburgh.com; ⓦ eif.co.uk

The imposing black church at the foot of Castlehill is **The Hub**, also known as 'Edinburgh's Festival Centre'. It's open year-round, providing performance, rehearsal and exhibition space, a ticket centre and a café. The building itself was constructed in 1845 to designs by James Gillespie Graham and Augustus Pugin, the latter one of the architects of the Houses of Parliament in London – a connection obvious from the superb neo-Gothic detailing and the sheer presence of the building, whose spire is the highest in Edinburgh.

Gladstone's Land

477B Lawnmarket • Early Jan–late Dec daily 10am–3pm; last entry 30min before closing • Charge • Guided tour 3pm; 50mins • Charge • NTS • ⓦ nts.org.uk

Doing its best to maintain its dignity among a sea of cheap tartan gifts and discounted woolly jumpers, **Gladstone's Land** is the Royal Mile's best surviving example of a typical seventeenth-century tenement. The tall, narrow building would have been home to various families: the well-to-do Gladstones, who extended it between 1619–20, are thought to have occupied the fourth and fifth floors. The National Trust for Scotland has carefully restored the rooms, filling them with period furnishings and fittings, giving you a sense of what life was like in Edinburgh 400 years ago. Enter through the arcaded ground floor, then climb the narrow turnpike stair to explore the first and second floors, richly decorated with 400-year-old paintings.

Writers' Museum

Lady Stairs Close, Lawnmarket • Daily 10am–5pm • Free • ⓦ edinburghmuseums.org.uk

Situated within the seventeenth-century Lady Stair's House, the **Writers' Museum** is dedicated to Scotland's three greatest literary lions: Sir Walter Scott, Robert Louis

■ ACCOMMODATION	
a&o Edinburgh	6
Castle Rock Hostel	3
Cheval Old Town Chambers	1
High Street Hostel	5
Ibis Edinburgh Centre	4
Stay Central Hotel	7
The Witchery Apartments	2

● EATING	
Chop House	1
Colonnades at The	
Signet Library	6
David Banns Vegetarian	
Restaurant & Bar	10
The Edinburgh Larder	5
The Grain Store	8
La Garrigue	2
Mother India's Café	11
Ondine	7
The Outsider	9
Wedgwood the Restaurant	3
The Witchery by the Castle	4

● SHOPPING	
Blackwell's	4
I.J. Mellis	2
Underground Solu'shun	1
W. Armstrong & Son	3

Stevenson and Robert Burns. The house itself holds as much interest as the slightly lacklustre collection of portraits, manuscripts and knick-knacks that make up the museum, its tight, winding stairs and poky, wood-panelled rooms offering a flavour of the medieval Old Town.

The Heart of Midlothian
Parliament Square, High St

The pattern set in the cobblestones near the main entrance to St Giles is known as the **Heart of Midlothian**, a nickname for the Edinburgh Tolbooth, which stood on this spot and was regarded as the heart of the city. The prison attached to the Tolbooth was immortalized in Sir Walter Scott's novel *Heart of Midlothian*, and you may still see locals spitting on the cobblestone heart, a continuation of the tradition of spitting on the door of the prison to ward off the evil contained therein.

High Kirk of St Giles
High St • Mon–Fri 10am–6pm, Sat 9am–5pm, Sun 1–5pm • Free • Guided tours Mon–Sat 10.30am & 2.30pm; 45min • Free • ⓦ stgilescathedral.org.uk

The **High Kirk of St Giles** is the original parish church of medieval Edinburgh, from where John Knox (see page 69) launched and directed the Scottish Reformation. St Giles is often referred to as a cathedral, and in fact the official name is St Giles Cathedral so the term has been somewhat grandfathered in. According to one of the city's best-known legends, the attempt in 1637 to introduce the English Prayer Book, and thus episcopal government, so incensed a humble stallholder named Jenny Geddes that she hurled her stool at the preacher, prompting the rest of the congregation to chase the offending clergy out of the building. It's said that a tablet in the north aisle marks the spot from where she let rip. Free, thirty minutes guided tours around the cathedral take place each day at 10.30am and 2.30pm.

1

The spire and interior

The resplendent **crown spire** of the kirk is formed from eight flying buttresses and dates back to 1485, while **inside**, the four massive piers supporting the tower date back to the fourteenth century. In the nineteenth century, St Giles was adorned with a whole series of funerary monuments on the model of London's Westminster Abbey; around the same time it acquired several attractive Pre-Raphaelite stained-glass windows designed by Edward Burne-Jones and William Morris. A more recent addition was the great **west window**, dedicated to Robert Burns in 1985. Look out for an elegant bronze relief of Robert Louis Stevenson on the south side of the church.

Thistle Chapel

At the southeastern corner of St Giles, the **Thistle Chapel** was built by Sir Robert Lorimer in 1911 as the private chapel of the sixteen knights of the Most Noble Order of the Thistle, the highest chivalric order in Scotland. Based on St George's Chapel in Windsor, it's an exquisite piece of craftsmanship, with an elaborate ribbed vault, huge drooping bosses and extravagantly ornate stalls showing off Lorimer's bold Arts and Crafts styling.

Mary King's Close

2 Warriston's Close, High St • Daily April–Oct first tour 10am; last tour 9pm; Nov–March times vary; every 15min; 1hr • Charge; advance booking required • Ⓦ realmarykingsclose.com

When work on the Royal Exchange, known as the City Chambers, began in 1753, the existing tenements that overlooked **Mary King's Close** were only partially demolished to make way for the new building being constructed on top of them. The process left large sections of the houses, together with the old closes that ran alongside them, intact but entirely enclosed within the basement and cellars of the City Chambers. You can visit this rather spooky subterranean 'lost city' on **tours** led by costumed actors, who take you round the cold stone shells of the houses where various scenes from the close's history have been re-created. As you'd expect, blood, plague, pestilence and ghostly apparitions are to the fore, though there is an acknowledgement of the more prosaic side of medieval life in the archaeological evidence of an urban cow byre. The tour ends with a stroll up the remarkably well-preserved close itself.

Museum of Childhood

42 High St • Daily 10am–5pm • Free • Ⓦ edinburghmuseums.org.uk

Harking back to simpler times, the **Museum of Childhood** was the first museum in the world dedicated to the history of childhood, displaying toys and games from across the generations. The museum also explores other aspects of growing up, from schooldays to clothing and holidays.

The Scottish Storytelling Centre and John Knox House

43–45 High St • Thurs–Tues 10am–6pm • **Storytelling Centre** • Free; charge for some events • John Knox House; last entry 1hr before closing • Charge • Ⓦ scottishstorytellingcentre.com

The **Scottish Storytelling Centre** is a stylish contemporary development containing a café, the Netherbow Theatre and an airy **Storytelling Court**, with a small permanent exhibition about Scottish stories through history. The centre hosts regular events and even scooped up the accolade 'Best Performing Arts Venue' at the 2018 Scottish Culture Awards. By contrast, the adjacent **John Knox House** is a fifteenth-century stone-and-timber building which, with its overhanging upper storeys and busy pantile roof, is a classic example of the Royal Mile in its medieval heyday. The interior of the house is steeped in history with its low doorways, uneven floors and ornate panelling. Inside, a series of displays explore one of Scotland's most turbulent times in history – the Scottish Reformation – with information about John Knox, the minister who led the Reformation, Mary, Queen of Scots who clashed with Knox and James Mosman, goldsmith to the Queen. To get to the lovely, quiet **garden** behind the centre, head down Trunk's Close, a few doors uphill from John Knox House.

The People's Story Museum

Canongate Tolbooth, 163 Canongate · Daily 10am–5pm · Free · ⓦ edinburghmuseums.org.uk

Dominated by a turreted steeple and an odd external box clock, the late sixteenth-century **Canongate Tolbooth** has served both as the headquarters of the burgh administration and as a prison. It now houses **The People's Story Museum**, which contains a series of display cases, dense information boards and rather old-fashioned tableaux dedicated to the everyday life and work of Edinburgh's population down the centuries. This isn't one of Edinburgh's essential museums, but it does have a down-to-earth reality often missing from places dedicated to high culture or famous historical characters.

Museum of Edinburgh

142–146 Canongate · Daily 10am–5pm; last entry 45min before closing · Free · ⓦ edinburghmuseums.org.uk

The **Museum of Edinburgh** houses the city's principal collection devoted to local history, though the museum is as interesting for the labyrinthine network of wood-panelled rooms within as for its rather quirky array of artefacts. These do, however, include a

---

JOHN KNOX

Protestant reformer **John Knox** has been credited with, or blamed for, the distinctive national characteristic of rather gloomy reserve that emerged from the Calvinist Reformation and which has cast its shadow right up to the present. Little is known about Knox's early years: he was born between 1505 and 1514 in East Lothian, and trained for the priesthood at St Andrews University. Ordained in 1540, Knox then served as a private tutor, in league with Scotland's first significant Protestant leader, **George Wishart**. After Wishart was burnt at the stake for heresy in 1546, Knox became involved with the group who had carried out the revenge murder of the Scottish primate, Cardinal David Beaton, subsequently taking over his castle in St Andrews. The following year this was captured by the French, and Knox was carted off to work as a galley slave.

He was freed in 1548, as a result of the intervention of the English, who invited him to play an evangelizing role in the spread of their own Reformation. When Mary Tudor, a Catholic, acceded to the English throne in 1553, Knox fled to the Continent to avoid becoming embroiled in the religious turmoil, ending up as minister to the English-speaking community in Geneva, which was then in the grip of the theocratic government of the Frenchman **Jean Calvin**.

When Knox was allowed to return to Scotland in 1555, he took over as spiritual leader of the Reformation, becoming minister of St Giles in Edinburgh, where he gained a reputation as a charismatic preacher. The establishment of Protestantism as the official religion of Scotland in 1560 was dependent on the forging of an alliance with **Elizabeth I**, which Knox himself rigorously championed: the swift deployment of English troops against the French garrison in Edinburgh dealt a fatal blow to Franco–Spanish hopes of re-establishing Catholicism in both Scotland and England. Although the return of **Mary, Queen of Scots** the following year placed a Catholic monarch on the Scottish throne, Knox was reputedly always able to retain the upper hand in his famous disputes with her.

Before his death in 1572, Knox began mapping out the organization of the **Scots Kirk**, sweeping away all vestiges of episcopal control and giving lay people a role of unprecedented importance. He also proposed a nationwide education system, to be compulsory for the very young and free for the poor, though lack of funds meant this could not be implemented in full. His final legacy was the posthumously published *History of the Reformation of Religion Within the Realm of Scotland*, a justification of his life's work.

1

number of items of real historical significance, in particular the **National Convention**, the petition for religious freedom drawn up on a deerskin parchment in 1638, and the original plans for the layout of the New Town drawn by James Craig (see page 76), chosen by the city council after a competition in 1767.

Scottish Poetry Library

5 Crichton's Close, Canongate • Mon–Fri 10am–2pm • Free • Ⓦ scottishpoetrylibrary.org.uk

A small island of modern architectural eloquence amid a cacophony of large-scale developments, the **Scottish Poetry Library**'s attractive design harmoniously combines brick, oak, glass, Caithness stone and blue ceramic tiles while incorporating a section of an old city wall. Inside you'll encounter Scotland's most comprehensive collection of native poetry, and visitors are free to read the books, periodicals and leaflets found on the shelves, or listen to recordings of poetry in the nation's three tongues, Lowland Scots, Scots Gaelic and English. The library is also home to five of the Mystery Book Sculptures: a series of miniature sculptures made from books and left anonymously in cultural centres across Edinburgh.

Holyrood

At the foot of Canongate lies the last leg of the Royal Mile, Abbey Strand, and **Holyrood**, for centuries known as Edinburgh's royal quarter, with its ruined thirteenth-century **abbey** and the **Palace of Holyroodhouse**, the Queen's official Edinburgh residence. In recent times, however, the area has been transformed by the addition of Enric Miralles' dazzling but highly controversial new **Scottish Parliament**, which was designed to mimic the cliffs and ridges of Edinburgh's most dramatic natural feature, the nearby **Holyrood Park**, and its slumbering peak, Arthur's Seat.

The Palace of Holyroodhouse

Canongate • Thurs–Mon April–Oct 9.30am–6pm; last entry 90 min before closing; Nov–March 9.30am–4.30pm; last entry 75min before closing; closed to visitors when the Queen is in residence • Charge; includes multimedia tour; discounted rate for joint entry with the Queen's Gallery • HES • Ⓦ rct.uk

In its present form, the **Palace of Holyroodhouse** is largely a seventeenth-century creation, planned for Charles II. However, the tower house of the old palace (the sole survivor of a fire during Oliver Cromwell's occupation) built for James V in 1532 was skilfully incorporated to form the northwestern block of today's building, with a virtual mirror image of it erected as a counterbalance at the other end.

Tours of the palace move through a series of royal **reception rooms** featuring some outstanding encrusted plasterwork, each more impressive than the last – an idea Charles II had picked up from his cousin Louis XIV's Versailles – while on the northern side of the internal quadrangle, the **Great Gallery** extends almost the full length of the palace and is dominated by portraits of 96 Scottish kings, painted by Jacob de Wet in 1684 to illustrate the lineage of Stewart royalty. The result is unintentionally hilarious, as it is clear that the artist's imagination was taxed to bursting point by the need to paint so many different facial types without having an inkling as to what the subjects actually looked like.

THE WORLD'S END BURGH

Canongate was for over seven hundred years a burgh in its own right that was entered through the now demolished gatehouse known as **Netherbow Port**. Some of the town's poorer residents couldn't afford the toll to pass through and spent their whole lives in Edinburgh – inspiration for the name of the *World's End* pub found by the site. Look for the brass plates – sunk into the road outside the pub – that mark the outline of the old gatehouse.

EDINBURGH'S CONTROVERSIAL PARLIAMENT

Made up of various linked elements rather than one single building, the unique design of the new **Scottish Parliament** complex was the vision of Catalan architect **Enric Miralles**, whose death in 2000, halfway through the building process, caused more than a few ripples of uncertainty as to whether the famously whimsical designer had in fact set down his final draft. Initial estimates for the cost of the building were tentatively put at £40 million; by the time the Queen cut the ribbon in October 2004, the final bill was over £400 million. A major public inquiry into the overspend blamed costing failures early in the project and criticized the spendthrift attitude of politicians and civil servants alike, yet the building is still an impressive – if imperfect – testament to the ambition of Miralles. While locals still mutter over the cost and the oddness of the design, the building has won over the majority of the architectural community, scooping numerous prizes including, in 2005, the most prestigious in Britain, the Royal Institute of British Architects (RIBA) **Stirling Prize**. Among the most memorable features of the building are the fanciful motifs and odd architectural signatures running through the design, including the anvil-shaped panels which clad the exterior and the extraordinary windows of the offices shaped like the profile of a mountain or a section of the Forth Rail Bridge.

The stark concrete of the building's interior may not be to all tastes, but while some parts of the design are undoubtedly experimental and over-elaborate, there are moments where grace and boldness convene, exemplified by the **Garden Lobby**: an airy, bright meeting place in the heart of the campus with a fascinating roof of glass panels forming the shape of an upturned boat.

As you move into the oldest part of the palace, known as **James V's tower**, the formal, ceremonial tone gives way to dark medieval history, with a tight spiral staircase leading to the chambers used by **Mary, Queen of Scots**. These contain various relics, including jewellery, associated with the queen, though the most compelling viewing is a tiny supper room, from where, in 1566, Mary's Italian secretary, **David Rizzio**, was dragged by conspirators – including her jealous husband, Lord Darnley – to the outer chamber and stabbed 56 times; a brass plaque on the wall points out what are rather optimistically identified as the 'bloodstains' on the wooden floor.

Holyrood Abbey

Free as part of palace tour

Standing beside the palace are the evocative ruins of **Holyrood Abbey**, some of which date back to the thirteenth century. Various invading armies paid little respect to the building over the years, and although it was patched up for Charles I's coronation in 1633, it was gutted in 1688 by an anti-Catholic mob. The roof finally tumbled down in 1768, but the melancholy scene has inspired artists down the years, among them Felix Mendelssohn, who in 1829 wrote: 'Everything around is broken and mouldering, … I believe I found today in that old chapel the beginning of my Scottish Symphony'. Adjacent to the abbey are the formal palace gardens, open to visitors during the summer months and during the Christmas period (otherwise open at weekends only in the winter) and offering some pleasant strolls.

Queen's Gallery

Canongate • Thurs–Mon April–Oct 9.30am–6pm; Nov–March 9.30am–4.30pm; last entry 1hr before closing • Charge; discounted rate for joint entry with Holyroodhouse • ⓦ rct.uk

Essentially an adjunct to the Palace of Holyroodhouse, the **Queen's Gallery** is located in the shell of a former church directly between the palace and the Parliament. With just two principal viewing rooms, it's a compact space, but has an appealing contemporary style which manages to remain sympathetic to the older elements of the building.

1

It's used to display changing exhibitions from the **Royal Collection**, a vast array of art treasures held by the Queen on behalf of the British nation. Displays have included Charles II: Art & Power, Canaletto & the Art of Venice, and Splendours of the Subcontinent: A Prince's Tour of India 1875–6.

The Scottish Parliament

Horse Wynd • Mon, Fri & Sat 10am–5pm; Tues, Wed & Thurs 9am–6.30pm; last entry 30min before closing • Free • Guided tours; 1hr; advance booking recommended; self-guided tours are limited to the lobby and debating chamber • Free • Crèche • Free • Ⓦ visitparliament.scot

For all its grandeur, Holyrood Palace is in danger of being upstaged by the striking buildings that make up the new **Scottish Parliament**. The most controversial public building to be erected in Scotland since World War II, it houses the country's directly elected assembly, which was reintroduced into the British political scene in 1999 – Scotland's parliament was abolished in 1707, when it joined the English assembly at Westminster under the Act of Union.

There's free access into the building's **entrance lobby**, where you'll find a small exhibition providing some historical, political and architectural background. If Parliament is in session, it's normally possible to watch proceedings in the **debating chamber** from the public gallery or committee meetings, though you have to get a free pass from the front desk in the lobby. To see the rest of the interior properly you'll need to join one of the regular **guided tours**, highly recommended to better appreciate the quality, detailed features and unique vision of the building's design. Special tours include those focused on the building's architecture, its collection of contemporary Scottish art, as well as photography-focused tours – however these take place much less frequently, check the website for details.

Our Dynamic Earth

112 Holyrood Rd • Thurs & Fri 10am–4.30pm, Sat & Sun until 5.30pm; last entry 90min before closing • Charge; advance booking required • Ⓦ dynamicearth.co.uk

Beneath a pincushion of white metal struts that make it look like a miniature version of London's Millennium Dome, **Our Dynamic Earth** is a hi-tech attraction based on the wonders of the natural world and aimed at families with kids between 5 and 15. Although James Hutton, the Edinburgh-born 'Father of Geology', lived nearby in the eighteenth century, there are few specific links to Edinburgh or Scotland. Galleries cover the formation of the earth and continents with crashing sound effects and a shaking floor, while the calmer grandeur of glaciers and oceans is explored through magnificent large-screen landscape footage; further on, the polar regions – complete with a real iceberg – and tropical jungles are imaginatively re-created, with interactive computer screens and special effects at every turn. The tour is rounded off with a 'smellivized' 4D cinema experience complete with moving furniture, a chilly blast of snow and a whiff of rhino poo. Another highlight is the ShowDome, a 360-degree planetarium cinema that gives a stunningly immersive film experience.

Holyrood Park

Queen's Drive • 24hr year-round • Free • HES • Ⓦ historicenvironment.scot/visit-a-place/places/holyrood-park

A natural wilderness in the very heart of the modern city, **Holyrood Park** is one of Edinburgh's greatest assets. Packed into an area no more than five miles in diameter is an amazing variety of landscapes – hills, crags, moorland, marshes, glens, lochs and fields – representing something of a microcosm of Scotland's scenery. While old photographs of the park show crops growing and sheep grazing, it's now used mostly by walkers, joggers, cyclists and other outdoor enthusiasts. A single tarred road, **Queen's Drive**, loops through the park, enabling many of its features to be seen by car, although you need to get out and stroll around to fully appreciate it.

THE CONNOLLY CONNECTION

Among Edinburgh's multitude of famous and infamous sons is James Connolly, commandant-general of the Dublin forces in the 1916 Easter Rising, which eventually led to the formation of the Irish Free State. With no monument save for a small plaque at the foot of George IV Bridge in the Cowgate, few among Edinburgh's tourist hordes are likely aware that Connolly was born and raised there in the bowels of Edinburgh's Old Town. A pivotal figure in emerging socialist and trade union movements in Scotland, Ireland and beyond, including Keir Hardie's Independent Labour Party (a forerunner of the contemporary Labour Party), Connolly came to believe that armed insurrection was the only way to free Ireland from the British Empire, and his prominent role in the rising ultimately led to execution by firing squad (infamously while badly wounded and tied to a chair). While the uprising resulted in heavy casualties on both sides, as well as many civilian deaths, and the independent state that eventually emerged wasn't the socialist utopia he'd dreamed of, his vision of freedom and equality for all has remained an inspiration to many.

Salisbury Crags

The amber hue of the setting sun's reflection on **Salisbury Crags**' sheer cliff face makes an enticing backdrop to an evening stroll. An easy hour-long circular route begins across the road from Holyroodhouse; the path – nicknamed the 'Radical Road' – winds southwards around the foot of the crags for a little under a mile before you have the opportunity to hike north through the glen separating the Salisbury Crags and Arthur's Seat and back to your starting point.

Arthur's Seat

The usual starting point for the ascent of **Arthur's Seat**, which at 823ft above sea level towers over Edinburgh's numerous high points, is Dunsapie Loch, reached by following the tarred Queen's Drive in a clockwise direction from the palace gates (30–40min walk). Part of a volcano which last saw action 350 million years ago, its connections to the legendary king are fairly sketchy: the name is likely to be a corruption of the Gaelic *Ard-na-said*, or 'height of arrows'. From Dunsapie Loch it's a twenty-minute climb up grassy slopes to the rocky summit. On a clear day, the views might just stretch to the English border and the Atlantic Ocean; more realistically, the landmarks that dominate are Fife, a few Highland peaks and, of course, Edinburgh laid out on all sides.

The Grassmarket

South of the Castle

Used as the city's cattle market from 1477 to 1911, the **Grassmarket** is an open, partly cobbled area, which despite being girdled by tall tenements offers an unexpected view up to the precipitous Castle walls. Come springtime, café tables often spill out onto the pavement; however, such Continental aspirations are a bit of a diversion as the Grassmarket is best remembered as the location of Edinburgh's public gallows – the spot is marked by a tiny garden. The notorious serial killers William Burke and William Hare had their lair in a now-vanished close just off the western end of the Grassmarket, and for a long time before its relatively recent gentrification there was a seamy edge to the place, with brothels, drinking dens and homeless shelters.

The Grassmarket's two-sided character is still on view, with stag and hen parties carousing between the area's pubs by night, while by day you can admire the architectural quirks and a series of interesting shops, in particular the string of independent boutiques on curving **Victoria Street**, an unusual two-tier thoroughfare, with arcaded shops below and a pedestrian terrace above.

GREYFRIARS BOBBY

The small statue of **Greyfriars Bobby** at the junction of George IV Bridge and Candlemaker Row is one of Edinburgh's more mawkish tourist attractions. Bobby was a **Skye terrier** acquired as a working dog by a police constable named John Gray. When Gray died in 1858, Bobby was found a few days later sitting on his grave, a vigil he maintained until his death fourteen years later. In the process, he became an Edinburgh celebrity, fed and cared for by locals who gave him a special collar to prevent him being impounded as a stray. The statue was modelled from life and erected soon after his death. Bobby's legendary dedication easily lent itself to children's books and was eventually picked up by Disney, whose 1960 feature film hammed up the story and ensured that streams of tourists have paid their respects ever since.

The Bridges

Leading eastwards from the Grassmarket is the **Cowgate**, one of Edinburgh's oldest surviving streets. It was also once one of the city's most prestigious addresses, but the construction of the great **viaducts** of George IV Bridge and South Bridge entombed it below street level, condemning it to decay and neglect and leading the nineteenth-century poet and essayist, Alexander Smith, to write: 'the condition of the inhabitants is as little known to respectable Edinburgh as are the habits of moles, earthworms, and the mining population'. Various nightclubs and Festival venues have established themselves here – on Friday and Saturday nights the street heaves with revellers – but it remains a slightly insalubrious spot.

High above the crestfallen Cowgate, both bridges give the curious impression that you're on ground level thanks to the terraced buildings that rise up in line with the elevated streets. The lowermost **South Bridge**, leading off from halfway down the High Street, is congested with buses, garish retailers and cheap cafés.

By contrast, **George IV Bridge** to the west – built in the 1830s – boasts an appealing melange of neo-French Renaissance and Neoclassical architecture.

At the southern end of the bridge, tourists invariably cluster around the tiny bronze statue of a Skye terrier called Greyfriars Bobby (see box, above), while across the road, Chambers Street links the southernmost ends of the two bridges where you'll find the unmissable National Museum of Scotland (see page 75).

Greyfriars Kirk

Greyfriars Place • April–Oct Mon–Fri 10.30am–4.30pm, Sat noon–4pm; Nov–March Thurs 10.30am–3.30pm; occasionally closed for events, check before visiting • Free • Ⓦ greyfriarskirk.com

Greyfriars Kirk was built in 1620 on land that had belonged to a Franciscan convent, though little of the original late Gothic-style building remains. A fire in the mid-nineteenth century led to significant rebuilding and the installation of the first **organ** in a Presbyterian church in Scotland; today's magnificent instrument, by Peter Collins, arrived in 1990.

Outside, the kirkyard has a fine collection of seventeenth-century gravestones and mausoleums set against a backdrop of the Old Town. The graves here include the one mourned over by the world-famous canine, Greyfriars Bobby (see page 74). Visited regularly by ghost tours (see page 89), the kirkyard was known for **grave-robbing** as freshly interred bodies were exhumed and sold to the nearby medical school (a crime taken to a higher level by the notorious Burke and Hare, who bypassed the graveyards by simply murdering the victims they'd then sell on for dissection). More significantly, the kirkyard was the setting, in 1638, for the signing of the **National Covenant**, a dramatic act of defiance by the Presbyterian Scots against the attempts of Charles I to impose an episcopal form of worship on the country. In an undemocratic age, thousands of townsfolk as well as important nobles signed the original at Greyfriars;

copies were then made and sent around the country, with some three hundred thousand names being added.

National Museum of Scotland

Chambers St • Daily 10am–5pm • Free • Guided tours 11am, 1pm & 3pm; 1hr • Free • ⓦ nms.ac.uk

The **National Museum of Scotland** is essentially two distinct museums, internally connected to each other: the unorthodox **modern sandstone building** on the corner of George IV Bridge houses collections of Scottish heritage, while the much older **Venetian-style palace** offers a more global perspective. Inside, the wealth of exhibits is enough to occupy days of your time, dip in and out at leisure or during rain showers. Parents will also find the place a useful sanctuary since there are numerous child-friendly rooms, interactive exhibits and cafés.

The old building

Modelled on the former Crystal Palace in London, and with a spectacular cast-iron interior, the old building packs in a bedazzling array of artefacts, covering natural history, world culture, geology and technology. The exhibits are housed over three levels surrounding the **Grand Gallery**, a huge central atrium whose beautiful limestone floor turns out to be teeming with fossils, predominantly ammonites. One stand-out exhibit, by the main concourse, is the gruesome **Millennium Clock Tower**, a jumble of cogs, chains and wheels modelled in the form of a Gothic cathedral, with gargoyles and sinister-looking figurines representing characters from twentieth-century politics.

The museum's areas are grouped into: Natural World; World Cultures; Art, Design and Fashion; and Science and Technology. The **Natural World gallery** is particularly fine, inhabiting all tiers of the museum's eastern end with numerous re-created animals hanging top to bottom from the rafters and a fearsome T-rex skeleton at the entrance.

A 10-year refurbishment has also brought three new galleries to the old building's collection: Ancient Egypt, East Asia, and Ceramics.

The new building

Given its confusing and unconventional layout, you might want to pick up a free map before tackling the new building's **Scottish galleries**, which detail the history and culture of Scotland from its geological formation through to the present day. Kicking off with **Beginnings and Early People**, the chronology moves into a wealth of remarkably well-preserved medieval exhibits – religious, regal and day-to-day objects – on display in the **Kingdom of the Scots**, including the exquisitely idiosyncratic **Lewis chessmen**. Moving forward in time, **Scotland Transformed** offers an insight into the Union of Crowns and the crushed Jacobite rebellion, leading up to the Industrial Revolution – evoked by an unmissable life-size working model of a steam-driven Newcomen Atmospheric Engine. Designed in 1712, it foreshadows Scotland's role as covered in the next section, **Industry and Empire**, where you can see a full-size steam locomotive, the *Ellesmere*, highlighting the fact that in the nineteenth century Scotland was building more railway engines than anywhere else in the world. The final stage, **Scotland: A Changing Nation** takes visitors up to the twentieth century.

Surgeons' Hall Museum

Nicolson St • Daily 10am–5pm; last entry 30min before closing • Charge • ⓦ museum.rcsed.ac.uk

Surgeons' Hall, the former headquarters of the Royal College of Surgeons, is a handsome iconic temple with a stately columned facade, built by William Playfair (1789–1857), one of Edinburgh's greatest architects. Housed round the back is one of the city's most unusual and morbidly compelling museums. In the eighteenth and nineteenth centuries, Edinburgh was a leading centre of medical and anatomical

1

research, nurturing world-famous pioneers such as James Young Simpson, founder of anaesthesia, and Joseph Lister, the father of modern surgery. The **history of surgery** takes up one part of the museum, with intriguing exhibits ranging from early surgical tools to a pocketbook covered with the leathered skin of serial killer William Burke (see page 73). Another room has an array of gruesome instruments illustrating the history of dentistry, while the third and most remarkable part of the museum, the Wohl Pathology Museum is located in the elegant **Playfair Hall** and contains an array of specimens and jars from the college's anatomical and pathological collections dating back to the eighteenth century.

The New Town

The **NEW TOWN**, itself well over two hundred years old, stands in contrast to the Old Town: the layout is symmetrical, the streets are broad and straight, and most of the buildings are Neoclassical. Originally intended to be residential, the entire area, right down to the names of its streets, is something of a celebration of the Union, which was then generally regarded as a proud development in Scotland's history. Today, the New Town's main streets form the bustling hub of the city's commercial, retail and business life, dominated by shops, banks and offices.

In many ways, the layout of the greater New Town is its own most remarkable sight, an extraordinary grouping of squares, circuses, terraces, crescents and parks with a few set pieces such as **Register House**, the north frontage of **Charlotte Square** and the assemblage of curiosities on and around **Calton Hill**. However, it also contains assorted Victorian additions, notably the **Scott Monument** on Princes Street, the **Royal Botanic Garden** on its northern fringe, as well as two of the city's most important public collections – the **Scottish National Gallery** and the **Scottish National Gallery of Modern Art**.

Brief history

The existence of the New Town is chiefly due to the vision of **George Drummond**, who made schemes for the expansion of the city soon after becoming Lord Provost in 1725. Work began on the draining of the Nor' Loch below the castle in 1759, a task that lasted some sixty years. The North Bridge, linking the Old Town with the main road leading to the port of Leith, was built between 1763 and 1772 and, in 1766, following a public competition, a plan for the New Town by 22-year-old architect **James Craig** was chosen. Its gridiron pattern was perfectly matched to the site: central **George Street**, flanked by showpiece squares, was laid out along the main ridge, with parallel **Princes Street** and **Queen Street** on either side below, and two smaller streets, Thistle Street and Rose Street, in between the three major thoroughfares providing coach houses, artisans' dwellings and shops. Princes and Queen streets were built up on one side only, so as not to block the spectacular views of the Old Town and Fife respectively. Architects were accordingly afforded a wonderful opportunity to play with vistas and spatial relationships, particularly well exploited by Robert Adam, who contributed extensively to the later phases of the work. The First New Town, as the area covered by Craig's plan came to be known, received a series of extensions in the early decades of the nineteenth century, all carefully in harmony with the Neoclassical idiom.

Princes Street

Although only allocated a subsidiary role in the original plan of the New Town, **Princes Street** had developed into Edinburgh's principal thoroughfare by the middle of the nineteenth century, a role it has retained ever since. Its unobstructed **views** across to the Castle and the Old Town are undeniably magnificent. Indeed, without the views, Princes Street would lose much of its appeal; its northern side, dominated by large chain stores, is almost always crowded with shoppers, and few of the original eighteenth-century buildings remain. Across the road, the southern side looks down onto the basin of Princes Street Gardens which is bisected midway by a direct route into the heart of the Old Town known as the **Mound**, formed in the 1780s by dumping piles of earth and other waste brought from the New Town's building plots.

General Register House

2 Princes St • Mon–Fri 9am–4.30pm • Charge; day pass • ⓦ nrscotland.gov.uk

Designed by Robert Adam and opened to the public in 1789, the **General Register House** is the most distinguished building on Princes Street. Today it is home to Scotland's national archives, free to access through the Historical Search Room, and the **ScotlandsPeople Centre**, a dedicated family history unit for those researching genealogical records. Visitors can pore over a huge archive of records ranging from national censuses, criminal records and, stretching back to 1553, old parish registers of births, marriages and deaths. Part of the appeal of embarking on some research is the opportunity to spend time in the elegant interior, centred on a glorious rotunda, lavishly decorated with plasterwork and antique-style medallions.

Princes Street Gardens

Dawn to dusk • Free

It's hard to imagine that the Princes Street Gardens which flank nearly the entire length of Princes Street were once the stagnant, foul-smelling Nor' Loch into which the effluent of the Old Town flowed for centuries. The railway has since replaced the water and today a sunken cutting carries the main lines out of Waverley Station to the west and north. The gardens, split into east and west sections, were originally the private domain of Princes Street residents and their well-placed acquaintances, only becoming a public park in 1876. These days, the swathes of green lawn, colourful flower beds and mature trees are a green lung for the city centre: on sunny days office workers appear in their droves at lunchtime, while in the run-up to Christmas the gardens' eastern section is home to a German Market, a towering Ferris wheel and a number of rides. The larger and more verdant western section has a floral clock and the Ross Bandstand, a popular Festival venue.

Scott Monument

East Princes Street Gardens • Daily Oct–April 10am–4pm; May & Sept until 7pm; June–Aug until 9pm; last entry 30min before closing • Charge • ⓦ edinburghmuseums.org.uk

Facing the Victorian shopping emporium Jenners, and set within East Princes Street Gardens, the 200ft high **Scott Monument** was erected in memory of prolific author and patriot Sir Walter Scott within a few years of his death. The largest monument in the world to a man of letters, the architecture is closely modelled on Scott's beloved Melrose Abbey (see page 120), and the rich sculptural decoration shows sixteen Scottish writers and 64 characters from Scott's famous *Waverley* novels. On the central plinth at the base of the monument is a **statue** of Scott with his deerhound Maida, carved from a thirty-ton block of Carrara marble.

Inside, a tightly winding spiral staircase climbs 287 steps to a narrow platform near the top: from here, you can enjoy some inspiring – if vertiginous – vistas of the city below and hills and firths beyond.

Scottish National Gallery

The Mound, Princes St • Daily 10am–5pm • Free; charge for some temporary exhibitions • ⓦ nationalgalleries.org

Built as a 'temple to the fine arts' in 1850, the **Scottish National Gallery** houses Scotland's premier collection of pre-twentieth-century **European art** in the larger of the two grand Neoclassical buildings found at the foot of the Mound (the other houses the **Royal Scottish Academy**, which mostly shows temporary exhibitions).

Though by no means as vast as national collections found elsewhere in Europe, it does include a clutch of exquisite Old Masters and some superb Impressionist works. Benefiting greatly from being a manageable size, its series of elegant octagonal rooms is enlivened by imaginative displays and a pleasantly unrushed atmosphere.

On the ground floor the rooms have been restored to their 1850s appearance with pictures hung closely together on claret-coloured walls, often on two levels, and intermingled with sculptures and objets d'art to produce a deliberately cluttered effect. As a result some lesser works, which would otherwise languish in the vaults, are on display, a good 15ft up. The **layout** is broadly chronological, starting in the upper rooms above the gallery's entrance on the Mound and continuing clockwise around the ground floor.

Early works

Among the Gallery's most valuable treasures are **Hugo van der Goes'** *Trinity Altarpiece*, on a long-term loan from the Queen. Painted in the mid-fifteenth century, they were commissioned by Provost Edward Bonkil for the Holy Trinity Collegiate Church, which was later demolished to make way for Edinburgh's Waverley Station. Bonkil can be seen amid the company of organ-playing angels in the finest and best preserved of the four panels, while on the reverse sides are portraits of James III, his son (the future James IV) and Queen Margaret of Denmark. The panels are turned by the gallery every half-hour.

European highlights

Poussin's *Seven Sacraments* are proudly displayed in their own room, the floor and central octagonal bench of which repeat some of the works' motifs. The series marks the first attempt to portray scenes from the life of Jesus realistically, rather than through images dictated by artistic conventions. **Rubens'** *The Feast of Herod* (in storage at the time of writing), enlivened by meticulous restoration, is an archetypal example of his sumptuously grand manner, its gory subject matter overshadowed by the gaudy depiction of the delights of the table. Among the canvases by **Rembrandt** are a poignant *Self-Portrait Aged 51* and the ripely suggestive *Woman in Bed*, which is thought to represent the biblical figure of Sarah on her wedding night, waiting for her husband Tobias to put the devil to flight. *Christ in the House of Martha and Mary* is the largest and probably the earliest of the thirty or so surviving paintings by **Vermeer**.

Scottish and English works

On the face of it, the gallery's Scottish collection, ambitiously covering the entire gamut from seventeenth-century portraiture to the Arts and Crafts movement, is a bit of an anticlimax. There are, however, a few significant works displayed within a broad European context. Both **Gavin Hamilton's** *Achilles Lamenting the Death of Patroclus*,

---

THE NATIONAL GALLERIES' COLLECTION

The **Scottish National Gallery** is just one part of the national art collection housed around Edinburgh. Other works of the **National Galleries' collection** are on display at the **Scottish National Portrait Gallery** (see page 80) and the **Scottish National Gallery of Modern Art** (see page 81), housed in two neighbouring buildings, Modern One and Modern Two.

A **free bus service** shuttles between the three gallery sites, starting and finishing at Modern One (outbound: daily 11am–4pm, every hour on the hour except 1pm; return: 11.45am–4.45pm, hourly except 1.45pm).

painted in Rome, and Arts and Crafts painter **Robert Burns**' *The Hunt* (in storage at the time of writing) are finer examples of arresting Scottish art.

One of the most popular portraits in the gallery is the immediately recognizable painting of a lesser-known pastor, *Reverend Robert Walker Skating on Duddingston Loch*, by Sir Henry Raeburn.

George Street

Running parallel to Princes Street, **George Street** was designed to be the centrepiece of the First New Town, joining two grand squares (St Andrew Square and Charlotte Square). These days, the street is rapidly changing its role from a thoroughfare of august financial institutions to a highbrow version of Princes Street, where the big deals are done in designer-label shops.

St Andrew Square

Lying at the eastern end of George Street is the smartly landscaped **St Andrew Square**, whose centre is marked by the **Melville Monument**, a towering column topped by a statue of Lord Melville, Pitt the Younger's Navy Treasurer. Around the edge of the square you'll find Edinburgh's bus station, Multrees Walk – the city's swankiest shopping arcade – and a handsome eighteenth-century townhouse, designed by Sir William Chambers. Still the ceremonial headquarters of the Royal Bank of Scotland, the palatial mid-nineteenth-century banking hall is a symbol of the success of the New Town.

Charlotte Square

At the western end of George Street is **Charlotte Square**, designed by Robert Adam in 1791, a year before his death. For the most part, his plans were faithfully implemented, an exception being the domed and porticoed church of St George, simplified on grounds of expense. Generally regarded as the epitome of the New Town's elegant simplicity, the square was once the most exclusive residential address in Edinburgh, and though much of it is now occupied by offices, the imperious dignity of the architecture is still clear to see. Indeed, the north side, the finest of Adam's designs, is once again the city's premier address, with the official residence of the First Minister of the Scottish Government at No. 6 (Bute House), the Edinburgh equivalent of 10 Downing Street.

Georgian House

7 Charlotte Square • March–Oct daily 10am–5pm; last entry 45min before closing • Charge • NTS • ⓦ nts.org.uk

Restored by the National Trust for Scotland, the interior of this residential townhouse provides a revealing sense of well-to-do New Town living in the early nineteenth century. Though a little stuffy and lifeless, the rooms are impressively decked out in period **furniture** – look for the working barrel organ which plays a selection of Scottish airs – and hung with fine **paintings**, including portraits by Ramsay and Raeburn, seventeenth-century Dutch cabinet pictures and the beautiful *Marriage of the Virgin* by El Greco's teacher, the Italian miniaturist Giulio Clovio. In the basement you can see the original wine cellar, lined with roughly made bins, and a **kitchen** complete with an open fire for roasting and a separate oven for baking; video reconstructions of life below and above stairs are shown on the second floor.

Queen Street

The last of the New Town's three main streets and the least tarnished by post Georgian development. **Queen Street**'s southern side is occupied mostly by offices, while across the road there's a huge private residents' garden. There are few individual attractions

1

here, with the exception of the **Scottish National Portrait Gallery** at the eastern end, just to the north of St Andrew Square.

Scottish National Portrait Gallery

1 Queen St • Daily 10am–5pm • Free; charge for some exhibitions • ⓦ nationalgalleries.org

Housed in a fantastic Gothic Revival palace in red sandstone, the **Scottish National Portrait Gallery** makes an extravagant contrast to the New Town's prevailing Neoclassicism. The exterior of the building is encrusted with statues of national heroes, a theme reiterated in the stunning two-storey entrance hall by William Hole's tapestry-like **frieze** and **mural**, carefully restored in the building's revamp.

The gallery's **collection** extends to over thirty thousand images with seventeen exhibition spaces exploring the differing characteristics of Scotland as a nation and a people. Inevitably oil paintings of the likes of Mary, Queen of Scots and Robert Burns form the backbone of the collection, but there's a lot to be said for the contemporary portraits that often show a country in cultural flux.

Past exhibitions have included ARTIST ROOMS Self Evidence, which celebrated the work of three of the twentieth century's most influential photographers: Francesca Woodman, Diane Arbus and Robert Mapplethorpe.

Calton Hill

Edinburgh's enduring tag as the 'Athens of the North' is nowhere better earned than on **Calton Hill**, the volcanic crag which rises up above the eastern end of Princes Street. Numerous architects homed in on it as a showcase for their most ambitious and grandiose buildings and monuments, the presence of which emphasizes Calton's aloof air and sense of detachment. It's also one of the best viewpoints from which to appreciate the city as a whole, with its tightly knitted suburbs, landmark Old and New Town buildings and the sea beyond.

Calton Gaol

Waterloo Place • No public access

Many visitors arriving into Waverley Station at Calton Hill's southern drop imagine the picturesque castellated building hard up against rock to be Edinburgh Castle itself. In fact, it's the only surviving part of **Calton Gaol**, once Edinburgh's main prison where former serial killer William Burke spent his final hours before being executed on Lawnmarket. Most of the prison was demolished in the 1930s to make way for the looming Art Deco St Andrew's House, which is today occupied by civil servants.

Old Calton Burial Ground

Waterloo Place • 24hr year-round • Free

On Calton Hill's southern slopes, tucked behind a line of high, dark, forbidding walls, the picturesque assembly of mausoleums and gravestones of **Old Calton Burial Ground**, some at a jaunty angle and others weathered with age, makes for an absorbing wander. Notable among the monuments are the cylindrical memorial by Robert Adam to the philosopher David Hume, one of Edinburgh's greatest sons, and a piercing obelisk commemorating various political martyrs.

Nelson Monument

Calton Hill • Daily Oct–April 10am–4pm; May & Sept until 7pm; June–Aug until 9pm; last entry 30min before closing • Museum • Free • Tower climb • Charge • ⓦ edinburghmuseums.org.uk

Robert Louis Stevenson reckoned that Calton Hill was the best place to view Edinburgh, 'since you can see the Castle, which you lose from the Castle, and Arthur's Seat, which you cannot see from Arthur's Seat'. Though the panoramas from ground level are spectacular enough, those from the top of the **Nelson Monument**, perched near the summit of Calton Hill, are even better. Each day at 1pm a white ball drops down a mast at the top of the monument; this, together with the one o'clock gun fired from the Castle battlements (see page 64), once provided a daily check for the mariners of Leith, who needed accurate chronometers to ensure reliable navigation at sea.

National Monument
Summit of Calton Hill

The **National Monument** is often referred to as 'Edinburgh's Disgrace', yet many locals admire this unfinished and somewhat ungainly attempt to replicate the Parthenon atop Calton Hill. Begun as a memorial to the dead of the Napoleonic Wars, the project's shortage of funds led architect William Playfair to ensure that even with just twelve of the massive columns completed, the folly would still serve as a striking landmark.

Collective at the City Observatory
Summit of Calton Hill • Tues–Sun 10am–5pm • Free • ⓦ collective-edinburgh.art

Designed by William Playfair in 1818, the **City Observatory** has for many years stood as an abandoned ruin. Once the city's astronomical base, due to pollution and the advent of street lighting, which impaired views of the stars, the observatory proper had to be relocated to Blackford Hill before the end of the nineteenth century. However, arts group, Collective, has now given the monument a new lease of life, restoring and transforming it – alongside a new purpose-built exhibition space – into a spectacular gallery.

The Water of Leith

Slicing a diagonal cleft from the Pentland hills southwest of town, the **Water of Leith** twists and churns, carrying its peaty, golden-brown burden towards The Shore, Leith's (and now Edinburgh's) attractive old harbour. En route, although comfortably bypassing the city's Old Town, the river trundles by old villages that once depended on its power to drive mills. Nature abounds: swans and mallards are commonly sighted, while otters, mink and kingfishers make sporadic appearances. The satellite attractions of the **Scottish National Gallery of Modern Art** near Dean Village and the **Royal Botanic Gardens** beside Stockbridge make a good draw from the river's edge. Downstream, the river's final twist opens wide as the boats and restaurants of Leith's harbour come into view. **The Shore** possesses two of Edinburgh's three Michelin-starred establishments while the wealth of quaint traditional pubs, cafés and floating restaurants on offer makes this the ideal finishing point for a **walk** along the river.

Scottish National Gallery of Modern Art
75 Belford Rd • Daily 10am–5pm • Free; charge for some temporary exhibitions • ⓦ nationalgalleries.org • A free shuttle service connects the Scottish National Gallery & Scottish National Portrait Gallery with Modern One and Two (see page 78)

Set in spacious parkland at the far northwestern fringe of the New Town, just west of quaint, riverside Dean Village, the **Scottish National Gallery of Modern Art** was the first

---

WATER OF LEITH WALKWAY

The Water of Leith flows in a northeasterly direction from the Pentland Hills to The Shore in Leith, over a distance of 24 miles. Following the final twelve miles of the river's course is the **Water of Leith Walkway**, making for a lovely riverside walk – a popular seven-mile stretch is from Colinton Village in the southwest (bus No. 10 from Princes St) to The Shore. For more information or to download a map, see ⓦ www.waterofleith.org.uk.

1

collection in Britain devoted solely to post nineteenth-century painting and sculpture. The Gallery is housed in two impressive Neoclassical buildings – **Modern One** and **Modern Two** – while its grounds serve as a **sculpture park**, featuring works by Richard Long, Henry Moore, Rachel Whiteread and, most strikingly, Charles Jencks, whose prize-winning *Landform*, a swirling mix of ponds and grassy mounds, dominates the area in front of Modern One.

The art collection here has a strong Scottish contingent, with a particularly fine body of works from the early twentieth-century **Colourists** – a term attributed to the Scots-born painters of the era who spent enough time in France to soak up some post-Impressionist ideas and blend them with Scottish painting traditions. Fluid paint handling and vivid colours characterize the works you're likely to encounter from the leading figures of the movement, such as Samuel Peploe, John Duncan Fergusson and Leslie Hunter. The collection's **international works** from the same period feature crowd-pleasing names like Matisse and Picasso, while Hockney, Warhol and Freud form the backbone of a solid postwar catalogue.

The gallery has also picked up a considerable collection of **contemporary** material from living British exponents of modern art such as Damien Hirst and Tracey Emin.

Modern One

The more cutting-edge of the two sister galleries, **Modern One** draws on the Gallery's enviable collection to bolster the themes of the temporary exhibits on show.

The building is divided into 22 exhibition spaces spread over two floors, with a good mix of audio-visual and sculpture art complementing the main exhibition, while on the ground floor there's a café with sun terrace and a well-stocked book and gift shop.

Modern Two

Just across Belford Road from Modern One, **Modern Two**, originally an orphanage, has been dramatically refurbished specifically to make room for the work of Edinburgh-born sculptor **Sir Eduardo Paolozzi**, described by some as the father of Pop Art. The collection, partly a gift from the artist himself, who died in 2005, includes some three thousand sculptures, two thousand prints and drawings and three thousand books.

There's an awesome introduction to Paolozzi's work in the form of the huge *Vulcan*, a half-man, half-machine which squeezes into the Great Hall immediately opposite the main entrance – view it both from ground level and the head-height balcony to appreciate the sheer scale of the piece. No less indicative of Paolozzi's dynamic creative talents are the rooms to the right of the main entrance, where his London studio has been expertly re-created, right down to the clutter of half-finished casts, toys and empty pots of glue. Elsewhere in the gallery, a selection of his sculptures and drawings is exhibited in a more traditional manner. The rooms upstairs are normally given over to special and touring exhibitions, which usually carry an entrance charge.

Dean Village

From Princes St, take bus Nos 19, 37 or 113 and alight before Dean Bridge; Dean Village is a 10min walk down Miller Row, the lane immediately before the bridge

Less than half a mile from Princes Street's west end is the old milling community of **Dean Village**, one of central Edinburgh's most picturesque yet unexpected corners, its atmosphere of decay arrested by the conversion of numerous granaries and tall mill buildings into designer flats. Nestling close to the river, with steep banks rising up on both sides, the Victorian community has a self-contained air, its surviving features including a school, clock tower and communal drying green. High above Dean Village, **Dean Bridge**, a bravura feat of 1830s engineering by Thomas Telford, carries the main road over 100ft above the river.

Stockbridge

Bus Nos 24, 29 or 42 from Princes St

Between the New Town and the Botanic Gardens, the busy suburb of **Stockbridge** grew up around the Water of Leith ford (and its seventeenth-century bridge) over which cattle were driven to market in Edinburgh. The hamlet was essentially gobbled up in the expansion of the New Town, but a few charming buildings and an independent character prevail today. The area is a popular quarter for young professionals who can't afford the property prices in New Town proper, and as a result there's a good crop of bars, boutiques and places to eat along both Raeburn Place, the main road, and St Stephen's Street, one of Edinburgh's more offbeat side streets.

The Royal Botanic Garden Edinburgh

Arboretum Place • Daily Nov–Jan 10am–4pm; Feb & Oct until 5pm; March–Sept until 6pm; last entry 45min before closing • Free • Guided tours April–Oct 11am & 2pm; 1hr; from John Hope Gateway • Charge • ⓦ rbge.org.uk • Take bus Nos 23, 27 or 29 from The Mound

Just beyond the northern boundaries of the New Town is the seventy-acre **Royal Botanic Garden**. Filled with mature trees and a huge variety of native and exotic plants, the 'Botanics' (as they're commonly called) are most popular simply as a place to stroll and lounge around. The main entrance is the West Gate on Arboretum Place, through the contemporary, eco-designed John Hope Gateway, where you'll find interpretation areas, information, exhibitions, a shop and restaurant. Towards the eastern side of the gardens, a series of ten **glasshouses**, including a soaring 1850s **Palm House**, shows off a steamy array of palms, ferns, orchids, cycads and aquatic plants, including some huge circular water lilies. Elsewhere, different themes are highlighted: the large Chinese-style garden, for example, has a bubbling waterfall and the world's biggest collection of Asian wild plants outside China, while in the northwest corner there's a Scottish native woodland which evokes the wild unkemptness of parts of the Scottish Highlands and west coast. **Art** is also a strong theme within the Botanics, with a gallery showing changing contemporary exhibitions in the attractive eighteenth-century **Inverleith House** at the centre of the gardens. Scattered all around are outdoor sculptures, including a giant pine cone by landscape artist Andy Goldsworthy and the striking stainless-steel east gate, designed in the form of stylized rhododendrons. Parts of the garden are also notable for their great vistas: the lawns near Inverleith House offer one of the city's best views of the Castle and Old Town.

Leith

Bus Nos 16 or 22 eastbound from Princes St

Although **LEITH** is generally known as the port of Edinburgh, it developed independently of the city up the hill, its history bound up in fishing, shipbuilding and trade. The presence of sailors, merchants and continental traders also gave the place a cosmopolitan – if slightly rough – edge, which is still obvious today. While specific attractions are few, Leith is an intriguing place to explore, worth visiting not just for the contrasts to central Edinburgh, but also for its nautical air and the excellent eating and drinking scene, which majors on seafood but also includes haute cuisine and well-worn, friendly pubs.

Leith's initial revival from down-and-out port to upscale waterfront began in the 1980s around the area known as The Shore, the old harbour at the mouth of the Water of Leith. Until recently, the massive dock areas beyond were being transformed at a rate of knots, with landmark developments including a vast building to house civil servants from the Scottish Executive, and Ocean Terminal, a shopping and entertainment complex, beside which the former **Royal Yacht Britannia** has settled into her retirement.

1

The Shore

The best way to absorb Leith's history and seafaring connections is to take a stroll along **The Shore**, a tenement-lined road running alongside the Water of Leith. Until the mid-nineteenth century this was a bustling, cosmopolitan **harbour**, visited by ships from all over the world, but as vessels became increasingly large, they moored up at custom-built docks built beyond the original quays; these days, only a handful of boats are permanently moored here. Instead, the focus is on the numerous **pubs and restaurants** that line the street, many of which spill tables out onto the cobbled pavement on sunny days. And the dining here is good; within a few hundred yards of each other Leith has two Michelin-starred restaurants: *The Kitchin* (see page 94) and *Martin Wishart*. The historic buildings along this stretch include the imposing Neoclassical **Custom House**, still used as offices by the harbour authority (and not open to the public); the round **signal tower**, which was originally constructed as a windmill; and the turrets and towers of the **Sailors' Home** – now a *Malmaison* hotel – built in Scots Baronial–style in the 1880s as a dosshouse (lodging house) for seafarers.

Royal Yacht Britannia

Ocean Terminal • Daily April–June 9.30am–6pm; July & Aug until 6.30pm; Sept–Oct 10am–6pm; Nov–March 10am–5pm; last entry 2hr before closing • Charge • Ⓦ royalyachtbritannia.co.uk • Bus Nos 11, 22 or 34 from Princes St; otherwise jump on one of the tour buses that leave from Waverley Bridge

A little to the west of The Shore, moored alongside **Ocean Terminal**, a huge shopping and entertainment centre designed by Terence Conran, is one of the world's most famous ships, the **Royal Yacht Britannia**. Launched in 1953 at John Brown's shipyard on Clydeside, *Britannia* was used by the royal family for 44 years for state visits, diplomatic functions and royal holidays. Leith acquired the vessel following decommission in 1997, against the wishes of many of the royal family, who felt that scuttling would have been a more dignified end. Alongside *Britannia*, the sleek former royal sailing yacht, *Bloodhound*, is also on view (Sept–June).

Visits to *Britannia* begin in the **visitor centre**, on the second floor of Ocean Terminal, where royal holiday snaps and video clips of the ship's most famous moments, which included the 1983 evacuation of Aden, and the British handover of Hong Kong in 1997, are shown. An audio handset is then handed out and you're allowed to roam around the yacht: the **bridge**, the **engine room**, the **officers' mess** and a large part of the **state apartments**, including the cabins used by the Queen and the Duke of Edinburgh. The ship has been kept largely as it was when in royal service, with a well-preserved 1950s dowdiness that the audio guide loyally attributes to the Queen's good taste and astute frugality in the lean postwar years. Certainly, the atmosphere is a far cry from the opulent splendour that many expect.

The guide's commentary also reveals quirkier aspects of *Britannia*'s history: a full Marine Band was always part of the three-hundred-strong crew; hand signals were used by the sailors to communicate orders as shouting was forbidden; and a special solid mahogany rail was built onto the royal bridge to allow the Queen to stand on deck as the ship came into port, without fear of a gust of wind lifting the royal skirt.

Greater Edinburgh

Beyond the compact city centre, there's a great deal to be discovered in **Greater Edinburgh**. The attractive coastal suburbs of **Cramond**, **Newhaven** and **Portobello** are all popular at weekends when the sun shines. The pick of the historical destinations includes the imposing fifteenth-century **Craigmillar Castle** on the south side of the city and the sleepy medieval village of **Duddingston**, with its ancient pub, on the far side of Arthur's Seat. On the opposite side of town is **Edinburgh Zoo**, one of the city's best-loved attractions and home to the UK's only giant pandas.

Newhaven

2 miles north of the centre of town • Bus Nos 10, 11 or 16 eastbound from Princes St

The old village (now suburb) of **Newhaven** was established by James IV at the start of the sixteenth century as an alternative shipbuilding centre to Leith: his massive warship, the *Great Michael*, capable of carrying a hundred and twenty gunners, three hundred mariners and a thousand troops, and said to have used up all the trees in Fife, was built here. Newhaven has also been a ferry station and an important fishing centre, landing some six million oysters a year in its 1860s heyday. Today, the chief pleasure is a stroll around the stone **harbour**, which still has a pleasantly salty feel, with a handful of boats tied up alongside or resting gently on the tidal mud.

ROBERT LOUIS STEVENSON

Though **Robert Louis Stevenson** (1850–94) is sometimes dismissed for his straight-up writing style, he was one of the best-loved writers of his generation, and one whose novels, short stories, travelogues and essays remain enormously popular over a century after his death.

Born in Edinburgh into a distinguished family of lighthouse engineers, Stevenson was a sickly child, with a solitary childhood dominated by his governess, Alison 'Cummy' Cunningham, who regaled him with tales drawn from Calvinist folklore. Sent to the university to study engineering, Stevenson rebelled against his upbringing by spending much of his time in the city's lowlife howffs (haunts) and brothels. He later switched his studies to law, and although called to the bar in 1875, by then he had decided to channel his energies into literature. While still a student, he had already made his mark as an **essayist**, and eventually had more than a hundred essays published, ranging from light-hearted whimsy to trenchant political analysis.

Stevenson's other early successes included the **travelogue** *Travels with a Donkey in the Cevennes*, kaleidoscopic jottings based on his journeys in France, where he went to escape Scotland's weather, which was damaging his health. It was there that he met Fanny Osbourne, an American ten years his senior, who was estranged from her husband and had two children in tow. His voyage to join her in San Francisco formed the basis for his most important factual work, *The Amateur Emigrant*, a vivid firsthand account of the great nineteenth-century European migration to the United States. Having married the now-divorced Fanny, Stevenson began an elusive search for an agreeable climate that led to Switzerland, the French Riviera and the Scottish Highlands.

He belatedly turned to the novel, achieving immediate acclaim in 1881 for **Treasure Island**, a moralistic adventure yarn that began as an entertainment for his stepson and future collaborator, Lloyd Osbourne. In 1886, his most famous short story, **Strange Case of Dr Jekyll and Mr Hyde** (despite its nominal London setting) offered a vivid evocation of Edinburgh's Old Town: an allegory of its dual personality of prosperity and squalor, and an analysis of its Calvinistic preoccupations with guilt and damnation. The same year saw the publication of the historical romance **Kidnapped**, an adventure novel which exemplified Stevenson's view that literature should seek above all to entertain.

In 1887, Stevenson left Britain for good, travelling first to the United States where he began one of his most ambitious novels, *The Master of Ballantrae*. A year later, he set sail for the South Seas, and eventually settled in **Samoa**; his last works include a number of stories with a local setting, such as the grimly realistic *The Ebb Tide* and *The Beach of Falesà*. However, Scotland continued to be his main inspiration: he wrote *Catriona* as a sequel to *Kidnapped*, and was at work on two more novels with Scottish settings, *St Ives* and *Weir of Hermiston*, a dark story of father and son confrontation, at the time of his sudden death from a brain haemorrhage in 1894. He was buried on the top of Mount Vaea overlooking the Pacific Ocean.

1

1

Portobello

3 miles east of the centre of town • Bus Nos 26, 44, 113 or 124 eastbound from Princes St

Among Edinburgh's least expected assets is its **beach**, a mile-long stretch of golden sand, most of which falls within **Portobello**, the suburb to the east of Arthur's Seat. Seeing a bit of a resurgence following the removal of some down-at-heel amusement arcades, it retains a certain faded charm from its heyday thanks to some attractive Victorian buildings and its delightful promenade. On hot summer weekends the beach can be a mass of swimmers, sunbathers, surfers and pleasure boats, while the rest of the year it makes for a pleasant stroll in between café stops.

Edinburgh Zoo

134 Corstorphine Rd, 3 miles west of the centre of town • Daily Nov–Feb 10am–4pm; March & Oct until 5pm; April–Sept until 6pm • Charge; cheaper rates online • ⓦ edinburghzoo.org.uk • Bus Nos 12, 26 & 31 all run from the city centre

Set on an eighty-acre site on the slopes of Corstorphine Hill, **Edinburgh Zoo** is a modern and highly successful conservation and recreation park – one of the city's most popular attractions. Appealingly set in the midst of a botanic garden, the enclosures offer plenty of opportunities for up-close animal encounters, and the heralded arrival of two **giant pandas** in 2012 bolstered the zoo's already impressive collection. Other highlights include the 2.15pm **Penguin Parade**, the **Budongo Trail** – a huge chimpanzee enclosure with intimate viewing positions – and the several walk-through enclosures where you might come face to face with a curious Saki monkey or a wallaby. Given the zoo's steep incline, you may want to hop on the regular free Hilltop Safari bus to the top of the hill and work your way back down. The zoo is big enough to warrant a full day's exploration so you may want to pick up a picnic from the nearby artisan German baker shop, *Störtebäcker* (see page 99), prior to entry.

Duddingston

2.5 miles southeast of the centre of town • Bus Nos 4, 42 or 104 south from Waverley Bridge

The beautiful conservation village of **Duddingston**, at the opposite end of Arthur's Seat from the centre, is attractively set on the shores of **Duddingston Loch** – best known as the setting for Henry Raeburn's *Reverend Robert Walker Skating on Duddingston Loch*, on show at the National Gallery (see page 77). Most visitors come here for a stiff drink at the *Sheep Heid Inn* (see page 96) after a hike over Arthur's Seat.

Cramond

5 miles northwest of the centre of town • Bus Nos 41 or 43 westbound from central Princes St • For tide times, check the notice board on shore or look for tide times for Leith on the BBC weather website

The enduring image of **Cramond** – a picturesque village by the Firth of Forth – is of step-gabled whitewashed houses rising uphill from the waterfront, though it also has the foundations of a Roman fort, as well as a tower house, church, inn and mansion, all from the seventeenth century. The best reason to come here is to enjoy a stroll around and a bit of fresh air. The **walk** along the wide promenade that follows the shoreline offers great views of the Forth; or head out across the causeway to the uninhabited bird sanctuary of **Cramond Island** – though be aware that the causeway disappears as high tide approaches and can leave you stranded if you get your timings wrong. Aim to get to and from the island in the two hours either side of low tide. Inland of Cramond, there's another pleasant walk along a tree-lined path leading upstream along the River Almond, past former mills and their adjoining cottages towards the sixteenth-century Old Cramond Bridge. These walks should take around an hour each.

Craigmillar Castle

1

Craigmillar Castle Rd, 5 miles southeast of the centre • Daily 10am–4pm; last entry 30min before closing • Charge • HES • ⓦ historicenvironment.scot • Take bus Nos 8, 33 or 49 from North Bridge to Edinburgh Royal Infirmary, from where the castle is a 10min walk along a signposted footpath

Situated amid a small tranche of green belt, **Craigmillar Castle** offers an atmospheric, untrammelled contrast to packed Edinburgh Castle in the city centre. Before Queen Victoria set her heart on Balmoral, Craigmillar was considered her royal castle north of the border – which is hard to imagine now, given its proximity to the ugly council housing scheme of Craigmillar, one of Edinburgh's most deprived districts. That said, the immediate setting feels very rural and Craigmillar Castle enjoys splendid views back to Arthur's Seat and Edinburgh Castle. The oldest part of the complex is the L-shaped **tower house**, which dates back to the early 1400s – this remains substantially intact, and the **great hall**, with its resplendent late Gothic chimneypiece, is in good enough shape to be rented out for functions. The tower house was surrounded in the 1500s by a quadrangular wall with cylindrical corner towers and was used on occasion by Mary, Queen of Scots. It was abandoned to its picturesque decay in the mid-eighteenth century, and today the peaceful ruins and their adjoining grassy lawns make a great place to explore – and kids, in particular, love having the run of their very own castle.

The Pentland Hills

For Hillend, 6 miles south of the centre, take bus Nos 4 or 15 westbound from Princes St; to get to Swanston, 5 miles south of the centre, take bus No.16 westbound from Princes St or No. 27 southbound from The Mound to Oxgangs Rd, from where you can walk along Swanston Rd

The **Pentland Hills**, a chain some eighteen miles long and five wide, dominate most views south of Edinburgh and offer walkers and mountain bikers a thrilling taste of wild Scottish countryside just beyond the suburbs.

The simplest way to get a taste of the scenery of the Pentlands is to set off from the car park by the ski centre at **Hillend**, at the northeast end of the range; take the path up the right-hand side of the dry ski slopes, turning left shortly after crossing a stile to reach a prominent point with outstanding views over Edinburgh and Fife. If you're feeling energetic, go higher up where the vistas get even better. An alternative entry point to the Pentland Hills is **Swanston**, a short distance northwest of Hillend. It's an unspoiled, highly exclusive hamlet of whitewashed thatched-roof dwellings separated from the rest of the city by almost a mile of farmland; **Robert Louis Stevenson** (see page 85) spent his boyhood summers in Swanston Cottage, the largest of the houses, immortalizing it in the novel *St. Ives*.

ARRIVAL AND DEPARTURE   EDINBURGH

BY PLANE
Edinburgh International Airport Edinburgh's airport (ⓦ edinburghairport.com) is at Turnhouse, about eight miles west of the city centre, just off the A8.

Getting to/from the city centre Airlink No.100 shuttle buses connect the airport with St Andrew Square in the centre of town (30min; ⓦ lothianbuses.com), with daily 24hr services, running every 15min during the day and 30min at night; a night bus No. N22 also runs. The tram service also goes to the centre of town every 7–10min, running between 6am and 11pm and stopping at Murrayfield Stadium en route (38min; ⓦ edinburghtrams.com). Otherwise, a metered taxi will charge around £20–24 to go between the airport and the town centre, while fixed-

price taxis (£44 to the city centre) are offered by Airport Transfers Direct (ⓦ airport-transfers-direct.com) – you can pre-book larger vehicles if required.

BY TRAIN
Conveniently situated at the eastern end of Princes St, right in the heart of the city, Waverley Station (ⓦ nationalrail. co.uk) is the arrival point for all mainline trains. There's a second mainline train stop, Haymarket Station, just under two miles west on the lines from Waverley to Glasgow, Fife and the Highlands, although this is only really of use if you're staying nearby.

Destinations Aberdeen (hourly; 2hr 20min–2hr 40min); Birmingham (hourly; 4hr 15min–5hr); Dunbar (hourly;

1

20–35min); Dundee (every 30min; 1hr 15min–1hr 30min); Falkirk (every 5–10min; 30min); Fort William (2–3 daily, change at Glasgow; 4hr 55min); Galashiels (every 30min; 50min); Glasgow (every 5min; 50min–1hr 15min); Inverness (2–6 daily direct; 3hr 35min); London (every 30min; 4hr 20min–5hr 40min); Manchester (every 30min; 3hr 15min–4hr); Newcastle upon Tyne (every 30min; 1hr 30min); North Berwick (hourly; 30min); Oban (2–3 daily, change at Glasgow; 4hr 10min–5hr); Perth (every 30min– 1hr; 1hr 15min–1hr 45min); Stirling (every 30min; 50min); York (every 30min; 2hr 30min).

BY BUS

The bus and coach terminal for intercity services is located on the east side of St Andrew Square, a 2min walk from Waverley Station.

Destinations Aberdeen (7 daily direct; 3hr–3hr 30min); Birmingham (4 daily direct; 8hr 10min–10hr); Dundee (hourly; 1hr 30min–2hr); Glasgow (every 15min; 1hr 25min); Inverness (hourly; 3hr 45min–4hr 30min); London (4 daily; 8hr 30min–11hr); Newcastle upon Tyne (8 daily direct; 4hr); Perth (hourly; 1hr 15min–1hr 30min).

GETTING AROUND

Although Edinburgh occupies a large area relative to its population – fewer than half a million people – most places worth visiting lie within the compact city centre, which is easily explored **on foot**. Most public transport services terminate on or pass through or near **Princes St**, the city's main thoroughfare, which divides the Old Town from the New Town, with the main **bus station** located just north of here on St Andrew Square.

BY BUS AND TRAM

Transport for Edinburgh The city is generally well served by buses; the white and maroon ones operated by Lothian Buses (Waverley Bridge TravelHub, 31 Waverley Bridge; Mon–Sat 8.30am–5.30pm; ⓦ lothianbuses.com) and one solitary tram line connecting the airport with the centre via a few key stops. Note that all buses referred to in the text are run by Lothian unless otherwise stated. Usefully, every bus stop displays diagrams indicating which services pass by and the routes they take. A good investment, especially if you're staying away from the centre or want to explore the suburbs, is the £20 'Ridacard' pass allowing a week's unlimited travel on Lothian and tram services (including airport services). Lothian also offer a day ticket allowing unlimited travel on bus or tram for £4.50, or you can pay £1.80 for any single journey. Tickets can be bought as you board the bus (exact change needed), whereas tram tickets must be purchased from the ticket machines prior to boarding.

First Edinburgh The predominantly white, single-decker buses of First Edinburgh (ⓦ firstgroup.com) run services on a number of the main routes through town, but are better for outlying towns and villages. They have their own system of tickets and day tickets, similar in structure to Lothian Buses. Most services depart from or near the main bus station at St Andrew Square.

Art Gallery Bus A free shuttle service (see page 78) connects the Scottish National Gallery with the Modern One and Two galleries.

BY TAXI

Edinburgh is well endowed with taxi ranks, and you can also hail black cabs on the street. Costs are reasonable – from the city centre to Leith, for example, costs around £8. All taxis are metered and the price structure is set by the council with evening and weekend rides costing £1 more than during the week. Companies include Central Taxis (ⓦ taxis-edinburgh. co.uk) and City Cabs (ⓦ citycabs.co.uk). Uber users will have little trouble finding a ride as the city is comprehensively covered.

BY CAR

Edinburgh is a relatively uncongested city (except during the August festivals) with just a few traffic jam hot spots, namely the main arterial routes to the centre and also the city bypass, particularly at the A7 intersection. Parking is very expensive and controlled areas stretch far out into the suburbs. Most on-street parking regulations don't apply on Sundays or after 6.30pm Mon–Sat and after 5.30pm Mon– Fri a little further out from the centre.

Car rental There are a few car rental desks in Waverley train station which arrange for customers to be shuttled to collect cars from nearby depots. Also, in the centre of town, try Hertz at 10 Picardy Place (ⓦ hertz.co.uk), or Avis, 24 East London St (ⓦ avis.co.uk). In addition, all the main rental companies have desks at the airport.

BY BIKE

Although hilly, Edinburgh is a reasonably bike-friendly city, with several cycle paths, particularly in the university areas south of the centre. The local cycling action group, Spokes (ⓦ spokes.org.uk), publishes an excellent map of the city with recommended cycle routes; pick up a copy at the tourist office.

Bike rental Available from Biketrax, 11–13 Lochrin Place, Tollcross (£20/day then £15 for additional days; ⓦ biketrax. co.uk), and Edinburgh Cycle Hire, 29 Blackfriars St (from £25/day; ⓦ cyclescotland.co.uk).

INFORMATION

Edinburgh iCentre, 249 High St (July–Aug Mon–Sat 9.30am–7.30pm; Sun 10am–6pm; April–June & Sept Mon– Sat 9.30am–5.30pm, Sun 10am–5pm; Oct–Mar Mon–Sat 9.30am–5.30pm, Sun 10am–4pm; ⓦ visitscotland.com).

Although inevitably hectic at the height of the season, it's reasonably efficient, with scores of free leaflets and a bank of computers available for free web surfing.

TOURS

BUS TOURS

Open-top, hop-on, hop-off bus tours are big business in Edinburgh. All cost the same (£16 per person) and depart from Waverley Bridge; see ⓦ edinburghtour.com for more info. Recommended companies include Majestic Tour, which is ideal for seeing the harder-to-reach sites like the Royal Yacht Britannia (see page 84) and the Royal Botanic Garden Edinburgh (see page 83).

WALKING TOURS

Several companies offer walking tours, many of which depart from the central section of the Royal Mile near the High Kirk of St Giles, or further uphill on the High Street's Mercat Cross. Advance booking is recommended during peak season. The following companies are worth singling out.

Auld Reekie Tours 45 Niddry St, ☎0131 5574700, ⓦ auldreekietours.com. Departs from 300 Lawnmarket daily at noon, 1.30pm, 3pm, 4.30pm, 6pm, 8pm & 10pm, also Fri & Sat at 5pm, 7pm & 9pm; fewer tours outside high season (£14–18). With a friendly mixture of ghost stories, town history and other jovial banter, the tours focus on Edinburgh's narrow closes and vaults, one of which contains a torture exhibition.

Edinburgh Literary Pub Tour ☎0800 1697410, ⓦ edinburghliterarypubtour.co.uk. Mixing a pub crawl with extracts from local authors acted out along the way, this tour is a fun way to explore Edinburgh's fine drinking establishments. While being introduced to the scenes, characters and words of the major figures of Scottish literature, including Burns, Scott, and MacDiarmid, you'll have the opportunity to nip in for a swift ale at each stop. Tours depart from outside the *Beehive Inn*, Grassmarket (see page 95), at 7.30pm (Jan–March Fri & Sun; April & Oct Thurs–Sun; May–Sept daily; Nov & Dec Fri; £16, or £14 online).

Mercat Tours ☎0131 2255445, ⓦ mercattours.com. Offers a wide range of history and ghost tours from Mercat Cross, High St (£13–17); some depart late in the evening and include a candlelit exploration of the underground vaults of Blair St. They also run tours to Edinburgh Castle, the Palace of Holyroodhouse and the National Museum of Scotland.

ACCOMMODATION SEE MAPS PAGES 58, 62 AND 66

As befits its status as a busy tourist city and important commercial centre, Edinburgh has a greater choice of **accommodation** than anywhere in Britain outside London. Hotels, hostels and rental apartments are essentially the only options you'll find right in the heart of the city, but within relatively easy reach of the centre the choice of guesthouses, B&Bs, campus accommodation and even **campsites** broadens considerably.

ESSENTIALS

Rates Room rates are significantly higher in Edinburgh than elsewhere in Scotland, with double rooms starting at around £80 a night. Budget hotel chains offer the best value if you want basic accommodation right in the centre, while £120–150 will get you something more stylish. The prices listed here are for high season (July & Aug) but excluding the 'super peak' prices that come into play during the Festival. Self-catering apartments – of which there are many in Edinburgh – are often the most economical option, especially if you're travelling in a group.

Reservations It's worth making advance reservations at any time of year, and is essential for stays during the Festival and around Hogmanay, when places can get booked out months in advance. Note that Visit Scotland (ⓦ visitscotland.com) operates a booking centre for accommodation in Edinburgh (and the rest of Scotland).

Access Bear in mind that many of the guesthouses and small hotels are located in Georgian and Victorian townhouses, over three or more floors, and usually have no lift, so are not ideal for those with restricted mobility.

OLD TOWN

The Old Town offers a well-balanced mix to cater for all budgets, although in recent years the number of five-star hotels being built has rapidly increased. There's a choice of hostels tucked in among the gloomier alleys, while mid-range accommodation sits just off the main drag.

HOTELS

Apex Grassmarket Hotel 31–35 Grassmarket

TOP 5 BUDGET ACCOMMODATION OPTIONS
Castle Rock Hostel See page 90
Gerald's Place See page 91
High Street Hostel See page 90
Ibis Edinburgh Centre See page 90
Stay Central Hotel See page 90

Ⓦapexhotels.co.uk. This ex-university building turned 169-bed hotel has comfortable rooms, some with unencumbered views to the Castle and balconies that peer down onto the happening Grassmarket below. There's an on-site restaurant, as well as a small pool and gym. It's worth noting that a two- or three-night minimum stay kicks in during peak times. ££££

Cheval Old Town Chambers Roxburgh's Court, 329 High St Ⓦchevalcollections.com. Enviably sited in the heart of the Old Town – tucked down a narrow passageway off the High Street – these luxury serviced apartments are set in a restored fifteenth-century building enlivened with contemporary touches from Nespresso machines and an on-site gym to a concierge team. ££££

Ibis Edinburgh Centre 6 Hunter Square Ⓦibis.accor.com. Probably the best-located chain hotel cheapie in the Old Town, within sight of the Royal Mile; rooms are modern and comfortable, but there are few facilities other than the restaurant and bar. It's not really a problem with so many bars and cafés directly outside. £££

Stay Central Hotel 139 Cowgate Ⓦstaycentral.co.uk. An economical option if you are travelling in a large group, this neoteric hotel has lots of rooms that sleep up to six – as well as a number of double rooms. Be sure to ask for a room at the back to avoid the noise of the revellers rising up from the late-opening pub next door. Doubles ££; whole dorm room ££££

Ten Hill Place 10 Hill Place Ⓦtenhillplace.com. A contemporary hotel owned by the historic Royal College of Surgeons, with 129 sleek and smartly styled bedrooms in six different categories and all run according to an environmentally conscious policy. The upper floors have a great view of the Salisbury Crags and Arthur's Seat. Breakfast not included. £££

GUESTHOUSES

★ **The Witchery Apartments** 352 Castlehill Ⓦthewitchery.com. Nine riotously indulgent suites grouped around the famously spooky restaurant just downhill from the Castle; expect antique furniture, big leather armchairs, tapestry-draped beds, oak panelling and huge roll-top baths, as well as ultra-modern sound systems and complimentary bottles of champagne. Top of the range, unique and memorable. ££££

HOSTELS

a&o Edinburgh 50 Blackfriars St Ⓦaohostels.com. An upmarket hostel just off the Royal Mile, with private rooms (sleeping two to four people) or dorms accommodating up to ten guests. The bar/restaurant (also open to the public) serves good-value food and breakfasts, and has a little courtyard with tables. Breakfast not included. Doubles ££; dorms £

★ **Castle Rock Hostel** 15 Johnston Terrace Ⓦcastlerockedinburgh.com. Located just beside the Castle, with almost three hundred beds arranged in large, bright dorms, as well as triple and quad rooms and some doubles. There's a large kitchen and a number of spacious communal areas. £

High Street Hostel 8 Blackfriars St Ⓦhighstreethostel.com. Lively and popular hostel in an attractive sixteenth-century building just off the Royal Mile with dorms of up to eighteen beds and doubles. The communal facilities include a kitchen, a quiet room and a large party dining lounge with piano and pool table. Continental breakfast extra charge. £

CAMPUS ACCOMMODATION

★ **University of Edinburgh, Pollock Halls of Residence** 18 Holyrood Park Rd, Newington Ⓦedinburghfirst.com. Unquestionably the best setting of any of the city's university accommodation, right beside Holyrood Park, just southeast of the Old Town. It provides bed and breakfast with en-suite single rooms, doubles and self-catering flats, during the university's summer vacation from the end of May to the beginning of September. Singles £; doubles ££; flats per week ££££

NEW TOWN

Most of the New Town's accommodation is made up of townhouses converted into independent guesthouses and boutique hotels, with Georgian architecture meaning elegant large rooms, high ceilings and loftier prices.

HOTELS

★ **Cheval The Edinburgh Grand** 42 St. Andrew's Sq Ⓦchevalcollection.com. Fantastically located with the best of the New Town on its doorstep and the Old Town just a short stroll away, *The Edinburgh Grand* inhabits the elegant former Royal Bank of Scotland's headquarters. Fifty luxury serviced apartments, ranging from one-bed Grand Studios to the three-bed rooftop Penthouse, combine touches of the building's heritage with modern luxuries. Grand studio ££££

★ **The Glasshouse** 2 Greenside Place, Broughton Ⓦtheglasshousehotel.co.uk. Incorporating the castellated facade of the former Lady Glenorchy's Church, this ultra-hip hotel has 77 chichi rooms with floor to ceiling windows, push-button curtains and sliding doors opening onto private terraces or the huge, lush roof garden scattered with Philippe Starck furniture. Perfect if you're in town for an indulgent weekend. ££££

Regent House 3–5 Forth St, Broughton Ⓦregenthousehotel.co.uk. A good-value small hotel over four floors (there is no lift) that makes up for its lack of glamour with a great location, right in the heart of Broughton on a quiet side street. There are singles and doubles, with some rooms big enough to accommodate three to five people. They also have a nearby apartment that can sleep six people. Singles ££, doubles ££, apartment ££££

GUESTHOUSES

Ardenlee Guest House 9 Eyre Place ⓦardenlee-guest-house.edinburgh-hotel.org. Welcoming guesthouse at the foot of the New Town, with original Victorian features and ten reasonably spacious rooms – singles, doubles and triples – seven of which are en suite, some are suitable for families. **£££**

★**Gerald's Place** 21b Abercromby Place ⓦgeraldsplace.com. A homely taste of New Town life at an upmarket but wonderfully hospitable and comfy basement B&B. The rustic decor is tasteful, with some fine artwork and old books to catch your eye, while the breakfasts are generous, with many home-made components. A good location for transport links and events. Breakfast not included. **££**

★**The Guest Room** 31a Nelson St ⓦtheguestroom.co.uk. A notably unobtrusive B&B offering two spacious rooms with a choice of courtyard or garden views. Start the day with a breakfast tray of berries, porridge and freshly squeezed orange. **£££**

Rabble 55a Frederick St ⓦrabbleedinburgh.co.uk. Ten much-sought-after rooms at the back of the popular New Town Rabble Taphouse & Grill. Beautifully styled with beds fitted with walnut headboards and plush fabrics, they look out onto a cobbled lane behind. **££££**

Tigerlily 125 George St ⓦtigerlilyedinburgh.co.uk. A glitzy boutique hotel, bar and restaurant that epitomizes the excess of twenty-first-century George St. A classic Georgian townhouse transformed into a flamboyant design extravaganza; indulgent pink or black bedroom suites are kitted out with Bluetooth speakers, decadent fabrics, and some even have a gas fireplace. **££££**

HOSTELS

Edinburgh Central Youth Hostel 9 Haddington Place ⓦhostellingscotland.org.uk. In a handy location at the top of Leith Walk (a 5min stroll from the centre), this five-star hostel has single, double and triple private rooms as well as four- and six-bed dorms with en-suite facilities. There is a reasonably priced bistro/restaurant in addition to self-catering kitchen facilities. Doubles **££**; dorms **££**

LEITH AND THE SHORE

With its charming nautical air, fantastic dining scene and scattering of good accommodation options Leith makes for an alternative experience to staying in Edinburgh's city centre.

★**Fingal** Alexandra Dock ⓦfingal.co.uk. Edinburgh's most unique stay, this luxury floating hotel was once a working ship that serviced lighthouses around Scotland's west coast. Each of the 23 cabins has been woven with thoughtful touches like compasses above the bed showing the direction you are sleeping in, while some rooms feature roll-top baths and spiral staircases. There's an on-site restaurant/bar, plus being berthed at The Shore, you've got Leith's food scene on your doorstep. **££££**

CAMPING

Drummohr Caravan and Camping Park Levenhall, Musselburgh, on the B1348 ⓦdrummohr.org. A large, pleasant site on the eastern edge of Musselburgh, a coastal satellite town to the east of Edinburgh, with excellent transport connections to the city centre. As well as the usual pitches, there are a few pods and bothies (sleeping between two and four), and more luxurious lodges that sleep up to six. Bothies **£**; pods **££**; lodges **£££**; camping per pitch **£**

Edinburgh Caravan Club Site 35–37 Marine Drive, Silverknowes, 5 miles northwest of the centre ⓦcaravanclub.co.uk. Caravan-dominated site in a pleasant location close to the shoreline, though there's little else here. Cramond village is a 10min walk west along the shore and has a pub and cafés. Per pitch **£**

EATING

SEE MAPS PAGES 58, 62 AND 66

Café culture has hit the city centre and this has been matched by the rise of original, upmarket and stylish **restaurants**, many identifying their cuisine as modern Scottish and championing top-quality local meat, game and fish. With three establishments holding **Michelin stars**, Edinburgh can justifiably claim third place behind London and Birmingham in the UK's fine-dining pecking order. There are some great **neighbourhood** restaurants and cafés outside the centre in **Stockbridge**, **Southside** and particularly in the **Shore of Leith**, the city's most inviting gastro hub.

THE OLD TOWN

There's a wide choice of restaurants to suit all budgets and it doesn't take too much investigative work to track down places of character tucked away down the Old Town's lanes.

In summer, it's advisable to book a table for an evening meal.

CAFÉS

Colonnades at The Signet Library Parliament Square ⓦthesignetlibrary.co.uk. Eye-wateringly expensive afternoon teas with mouth-wateringly tasty cakes and savoury bites. A giant gourmet leap above the egg and cress sandwiches of norm, here it's the likes of winter berry macarons, smoked salmon and poppy seed meringues and, naturally, scones. Silver service in these prestigious surroundings comes at a price. **££££**

★**The Edinburgh Larder** 15 Blackfriars St ⓦedinburghlarder.co.uk. Just off the Royal Mile, this overwhelmingly popular café dishes up top-quality breakfasts, cream teas and lunches if you can get a seat.

1

TOP FIVE MUST-TRY RESTAURANTS

Lian Pu See page 94
The Outsider See page 92
Tanjore See page 94
Timberyard See page 94
Wedgwood the Restaurant See page 92

Care is taken to ensure ingredients are in season and sourced from local producers. Begin with the veggie breakfast with haggis, home-made beans, blistered tomatoes, roasted mushroom and egg and return later for a soup and sandwich combo. ££

Fruitmarket Gallery, 45 Market St ⓦ fruitmarket.co.uk. This attractive café feels like an extension of the gallery space, its airy, reflective ambience enhanced by the wall of glass onto the street. Lots of colourful, modern and healthy brunch options here like smashed avocado and za'atar with poached egg on toast. Nice cakes and good coffee too. £

RESTAURANTS

★ **David Banns Vegetarian Restaurant & Bar** 56–58 St Mary's St ⓦ davidbann.com. Fine dining, vegetarian style, with a tried and tested menu. There are a few unconventional dishes offered here, such as their mushroom, goat's cheese and Heather Ale strudel. ££

The Grain Store 30 Victoria St ⓦ grainstore-restaurant. co.uk. This unpretentious restaurant is a relaxing haven amid the bustle of the Old Town, combining top-quality modern Scottish and French cuisines. Lunches offer the likes of seared fish of the day with broccoli, garlic and chorizo, while the evening's polenta with butternut squash and parmesan foam is a great option on the a la carte menu. £££

La Garrigue 31 Jeffrey St ⓦ lagarrigue.co.uk. A double AA rosette-awarded bistro, with a menu and wine list dedicated to the produce and traditions of the Languedoc region of France. Dishes such as the casserole of confit duck, Toulouse sausage, pork belly and lingot beans are unmistakably authentic and delivered with a high degree of finesse. The lunch and early dinner menus (two courses and three courses) offer consistent quality and value for money. £££

Mother India's Cafe 3–5 Infirmary St ⓦ motherindia. co.uk. Tapas with a twist, so the restaurant slogan goes; the twist being that the food is Indian not Spanish. There's plenty to please seasoned curry connoisseurs, with classics like daal makhni and chicken tikka on offer. ££

Ondine 2 George IV Bridge ⓦ ondinerestaurant.co.uk. Dedicated seafood restaurant from Edinburgh-born Roy

Brett, once Rick Stein's main chef in Padstow, turning out sublime dishes using native shellfish and fish from sustainable sources, such as monkfish chop with bharta aubergine and spiced cashew. ££££

★ **The Outsider** 15–16 George IV Bridge ⓦ theoutsiderrestaurant.com. Gorgeous split-level space with tall windows affording jaw-dropping views of the castle looming over the city rooftops. While it makes for an atmospheric choice in the evening, the lunchtime prices are a steal with large portions of mains like steamed mussels with basil cream, bacon, pine nuts and parmesan with a side of chips. £££

★ **Wedgwood the Restaurant** 267 Canongate ⓦ wedgwoodtherestaurant.co.uk. This small but reputable fine-dining restaurant, with an in-house forager, creatively plates all the best of Scotland's land, rivers and seas. There's so much choice on the a la carte menu they offer 'deciding time' – canapés and champagne – while you peruse the menu. The mains here might include the likes of Ayrshire partridge with barley, parsnip, mushroom and tarragon jus, though the lunch deal is the best value, with seasonal freshness guaranteed. £££

The Witchery by the Castle 352 Castlehill ⓦ thewitchery.com. An upmarket restaurant that only Edinburgh could create, set in magnificently over-the-top medieval surroundings full of Gothic wood panelling and heavy stonework, all a mere broomstick-hop from the Castle. There's even a 'secret garden' dining area. The a la carte menu is as ostentatious as the surroundings with wallet-draining lamb Wellington and cote de boeuf on offer; however, there are good-value weekday three course lunch set menus. ££££

NEW TOWN

For the flashier end of the restaurant scene, the New Town and its western fringe, known as the West End, are the happening parts of town. Many chains restaurants centre on Princes and George streets but explore a little further afield to areas such as Broughton Street for find more home-grown places.

CAFÉS

★ **Artisan Roast** 57 Broughton St; 100a Raeburn Place, Stockbridge; ⓦ artisanroast.co.uk. If you're into the black stuff, this is the must-visit coffee shop in Edinburgh. A seemingly unstoppable force in the connoisseur coffee roasters' market, Artisan Roast's sweet, nutty brews are found in independent cafés all over town these days, but this narrow, cosy shop with obligatorily bearded baristas is where their revolution started. ££

Eteaket 41 Frederick St ⓦ eteaket.co.uk. The best of the tea boutiques in the city centre, with a restrained but contemporary decor scheme and tables outside. There's an extensive menu of good-quality loose-leaf teas, some

1

decent nibbles plus, for the adventurous, tea cocktails such as Earl Grey G&T. They also do afternoon tea menus. ££

Fortitude 3c York Place ⓦfortitudecoffee.com. Small but friendly coffee bar where the baristas really know their beans: single origin coffee straight from their roastery. There's a great selection of cakes too – with gluten free and vegan options – as well as some brunch dishes like avocado on sourdough toast. £

Valvona & Crolla 19 Elm Row, Leith Walk ⓦvalvonacrolla.co.uk. The café-bistro hidden at the back of what is arguably Britain's finest Italian deli serves authentic Italian pizzas and seasonal, traditional dishes such as pasta with tomato sauce and their own sausages, alongside a cracking selection of wines. There's a two-course menu and a three-course option too. The best advert for the café is the walk through the shop (see page 99) – which has food stacked from floor to ceiling with the best Italian produce and display cabinets full of sublime olives, meats and cheese. £££

RESTAURANTS

Chaophraya 4th floor, 33 Castle St (between George & Princess St) ⓦchaophraya.co.uk. Thai restaurant housed in one of Edinburgh's most glamorous dining spaces with a rooftop location that gives diners who sit in the 'Glassbox' section a near 360-degree view of the city. The menu is stunning too, go veggie or try the crispy pork belly or pass on the food altogether and have a drink on the convivial roof terrace. £££

Chez Jules 109 Hanover St ⓦchezjulesbistro.com. Run by the former boss of the once mighty Pierre Victoire bistro chain, the formula here is much the same: cheap and generous set menus, good table wine and an informal, atmospheric setting (checked tablecloths, walls covered in chalk writing, and candles even at lunchtime). Your two-course lunch might include French onion soup and *moules frites* with aioli. ££

Dusit 49a Thistle St ⓦdusit.co.uk. Bold Thai flavours delivered with uncustomary refinement, it's little wonder this wee restaurant is consistently the talk of the town. There are many of the usual suspects on the menu like Thai green curry, but the overriding genius of this place is its adventurous spirit and local leanings such as the Pattaya local favourite dish *hor mok* (fish in spicy coconut cream soufflé). The two-course lunch is a steal. £££

★ **El Cartel Casera Mexicana** 64 Thistle St; 15–16 Teviot Place ⓦelcartelmexicana.co.uk. Mexican *antojitos* (tapas-sized street food) served with funky margaritas in a cool setting that draws heavily from the Día de los Muertos festival. Tacos, street corn and quesadillas feature on the menu as you might expect, but there are some more unusual options too like baby back pork ribs with a cumin, garlic and pineapple glaze. ££

★ **The Gardener's Cottage** 1 Royal Terrace Gardens,

London Rd ⓦthegardenerscottage.co. In an achingly beautiful little cottage, uniquely located in a strip of parkland. Dining is intimate, in two small rooms with communal long tables, while the open kitchen is stamp sized. Menus feature seasonal ingredients such as wild garlic or rhubarb in spring or chanterelles in autumn. ££££

Henderson's 7–13 Barclay Place ⓦhendersons restaurant.com. Born out of the original Henderson's, which closed in 2020, this new venture retains all the hallmarks of its predecessor, namely top draw vegetarian and vegan food with locally sourced, organic and seasonal produce at its heart; expect tasty treats like wild mushroom cobbler, and haggis with root mash and whisky tarragon cream. £££

L'Escargot Bleu 56 Broughton St ⓦlescargotbleu. co.uk. A big step on from the rustic, no-frills French bistro of yesteryear, here classic French country cooking is brought to bear on a range of locally sourced produce, as in the pan-fried venison with its own pie, braised red cabbage and apple sauce. £££

Mussel Inn 61–65 Rose St ⓦmussel-inn.com. With an honest lunchtime offering of a bowl of mussels or seafood chowder with a salad or fries for £7.95 it's no surprise there's a demand to get in here. Their close ties to west-coast shellfish farmers help ensure that the journey from sea to plate is short and swift. £££

Yeni Meze Bar 73 Hanover St ⓦyenirestaurant. com. Specializing in lamb kofte and *imam bayildi* (baked aubergine dish), this is ultimately a Turkish restaurant that draws in additional dishes from around the Med like their Italian *arancini*. The best way to tackle the vast menu is to go for the banquet (min two people) and see the delights that keep arriving. There are good lunch and early evening offers. £££

STOCKBRIDGE AND AROUND

Stockbridge is home to many of the city's young professionals and consequently has plenty fine cafés and restaurants.

RESTAURANTS

The Scran & Scallie 1 Comely Bank Rd ⓦscranandscallie.com. This Tom Kitchin restaurant's laidback vibe belies the quality of food on offer. Inspired by traditional Scottish menus, expect twists on pub grub with steak pies and fish pies, as well as the likes of Jerusalem artichoke and pearl barley risotto. £££

The Stockbridge Restaurant 54 St Stephen St ⓦthestockbridgerestaurant.co.uk. It's hard to believe swanky St Stephen's St used to be one of Edinburgh's worst slums. This basement restaurant sums up how far things have come with its fine linen, silverware and fancy platters, while the blackened stone walls and candlelit hearth give it a slightly bohemian atmosphere. The quality is exceptional and food affordable, with a menu that is meat, game and fish all the way. ££££

LOTHIAN ROAD AND TOLLCROSS
Lothian Road's twin role as Edinburgh's theatre and financial districts has seen money pour into the area in recent times. It still has a rough element on a Friday night, however, gentrification is in full swing and consequently there's a decent selection of sophisticated places to eat and drink, plus good-value pre- and post-theatre deals.

CAFÉS
Lovecrumbs 155 West Port ⓦlovecrumbs.co.uk. Buzzy café in a gorgeously dilapidated space: chipped plaster ceilings, worn-wooden floors and draped foliage. There's a communal vibe, great coffee and locally baked cakes. There's always a vegan baked option, plus a little shop in the corner sells local produce. £̄

RESTAURANTS
★**Indaba** 3 Lochrin Terrace ⓦedindaba.co.uk. An unlikely combination of South African and northern Spanish cuisine, this modest side-street restaurant delivers some of the best tapas in town. The South African contributions are predominantly meaty, like the dried boerewors, a thin chewy sausage with spices, while the Spanish plates are vibrantly colourful. £££
★**Timberyard** 10 Lady Lawson St ⓦtimberyard.co. This gorgeously rustic old workshop makes for a special place to dine with exposed ceiling beams, suspended bulb lighting and plenty of wooden touches from the candlelit mini indoor benches to the small tree stumps that hold the wine bottles beside each table. There's also a lovely courtyard out the back. The food focuses on high-quality Scottish produce, some of it home-grown or smoked on site; much of the rest is sourced from local foragers or farmers directly. As a result, unlikely bedfellows like halibut, wild leeks and elderberries come together harmoniously on one plate as part of a four-dinner menu. ££££

SOUTHSIDE
As the student quarter of the city, the Southside boasts plenty of good value eating, but it's also an area where more progressive restaurants can establish themselves.

RESTAURANTS
Hanedan 41 West Preston St ⓦhanedan.co.uk. Not the roomiest of restaurants but that's partly down to the unrelenting popularity of this authentic Turkish gem. There are plenty of the usual meze choices and skewered meats on offer, but the charcoal grilled sardines are not to be missed when available. ££
Kalpna 2–3 St Patrick Square ⓦkalpnarestaurant. com. Outstanding vegetarian family restaurant that's been serving authentic Gujarati dishes in town for over 25 years. Four *thaalis*, including a vegan option, stand alongside the main menu for those keen to sample a range of dishes, while the lunch buffet is outstanding value. £££
★**Lian Pu** 14 Marshall St ⓦlianpu.co.uk. Very popular restaurant with Edinburgh's surging Chinese community, thanks to its true home-from-home cooking and palatable prices. The place retains a canteen, fast-food atmosphere despite the addition of contemporary soft furnishings and some interesting pictures of old China. The beef flank ramen soup is a popular choice. ££
Saboteur 19–20 Teviot Place ⓦsaboteurrestaurant. com. Relaxed place with a buzzy atmosphere and a cool industrial-leaning interior. The delicious Vietnamese street food and good prices make it popular with a young, student crowd. There's plenty of *pho* on the menu as well as more unusual options like pan-fried sea bass with chilli jam, coriander, mint and lime; the crispy fried tofu will even impress tofu-haters. £̄
★**Tanjore** 6–8 Clerk St ⓦtanjore.co.uk. South Indian cuisine's finest ambassador on these shores, drawing in all the regional standards including *vadai* (crunchy lentil doughnuts), *idli* (rice and lentil cake) and *sambar* – a distinctly rich, savoury curry with fragrant, bitter-sweet curry leaves. The freshly made *dosai* (lentil and rice crêpes) are among the lightest and crispiest you'll ever taste and come with a wide variety of fillings. ££

LEITH AND THE SHORE
The area around the cobbled Shore of Leith, along the edge of the Water of Leith just as it reaches the sea, is the best-known dining quarter in Edinburgh, and lives up to its billing with good-quality, laidback seafood bistros and a concentration of Michelin stars.

RESTAURANTS
★**Chop House** 102 Constitution St; Arch 15, 29 East Market St ⓦchophousesteak.co.uk. First established on Constitution Street – with its cool interior of charcoal hues – *Chop House* has become the go-to place for steak lovers: dry aged and butchered in house (there are vast hunks of it displayed in a glass cabinet), cooked over coals and best enjoyed as large sharing cuts such as the porter house (price by weight). £££
★**The Kitchin** 78 Commercial Quay ⓦthekitchin. com. Opened in 2006 by celebrity chef Tom Kitchin, and the winner – less than six months later – of a Michelin star, the motto here is 'from nature to plate', a philosophy that ensures the freshest ingredients, particularly well demonstrated on their 'Celebration of the Season' menu that might include hand-dived Orkney scallops or roast Highland wagyu beef. Menus range from a two-course a la carte menu to a surprise tasting menu. Closed Sun & Mon. ££££
★**The Shore Bar & Restaurant** 3 The Shore

ⓦ fishersrestaurants.co.uk. Part of the Fishers' family of restaurants, this tasteful, well-lived-in bar/restaurant has huge mirrors, wood panelling and good sea and land food such as their own fish pie. Live jazz (Tues–Thurs 8.30– 10pm & Sun 2–5pm) and hubbub float through from the adjoining bar where you'll find a wide selection of snacks on offer, including deep fried calamari with coriander yoghurt. **££**

DRINKING

SEE MAPS PAGES 58, 62 AND 66

Many of Edinburgh's **pubs**, especially in the Old Town, have histories that stretch back centuries, while others, particularly in the New Town, are unaltered Victorian or Edwardian period pieces. Add a plentiful supply of trendy, modern **bars**, and there's enough to cater for all tastes. The standard licensing hours are 11am–11pm (noon–11pm on Sun), but many places stay open later and, during the Festival especially, you won't have a problem finding a bar open till at least 1am. Edinburgh has a long history of beer-making, though only one significant working brewery remains in the city itself, the small **Caledonian Brewery** in the western reaches of town. Owned by multinational Scottish & Newcastle, it still uses old techniques and equipment to produce some of the best specialist beers in Britain, including its popular Deuchars IPA. If you fancy a pub crawl, a fun option is the **Literary Pub Tour** (see page 89).

THE ROYAL MILE AND AROUND

Beehive Inn 18–20 Grassmarket ⓦ belhavenpubs. co.uk. One of the few family-friendly pubs in the centre with an even scarcer beer garden out back. Inside it's an early Victorian building with high-backed red leather seating and corniced ceilings in each of its three rooms. Out front is the regular starting point for the Literary Pub Tour.
Bow Bar 80 West Bow ⓦ thebowbar.co.uk. Wonderful old wood-panelled bar and one of the nicest, most convivial drinking spots in the city centre, although it can get uncomfortably busy at weekends. Choose from among nearly four hundred whiskies or a changing selection of first-rate Scottish and English cask beers.
Halfway House 24 Fleshmarket Close ☎ 0131 225 7101. Edinburgh's smallest pub, found halfway up the steep, narrow close between the train station and the Royal Mile, is a good place to stop and catch your breath. Lots of real ales and a few simple bar meals such as Cullen skink.
★ **Jolly Judge** 7 James Court ⓦ jollyjudge.co.uk. Atmospheric, low-ceilinged bar in a close just down from the Castle which features in the Literary Pub Crawl. Cosy with a warming fireplace in winter and pleasant outside in summer.

NEW TOWN

Café Royal 19 West Register St ⓦ caferoyal.org. uk. Worth a visit just for its Victorian decor, notably the huge elliptical island bar and tiled portraits of renowned inventors. The menu is appropriately swanky too, with a wide choice of champagnes and oysters, while real ale fans will not be disappointed by the native selection.
★ **Cumberland Bar** 1–3 Cumberland St ⓦ cumberlandbar.co.uk. This lovely old pub is just far enough off the beaten track to remain off the radar to the weekend's pub-crawling masses – a bonus when you're after their Sunday roast. Its other great assets are its willow-shaded beer garden, fantastic assortment of cask ales and dog-friendly attitude. It's worth noting they don't have a licence for children under 5 years.
★ **Kays Bar** 39 Jamaica St ⓦ kaysbar.co.uk. Tucked away in a New Town side street, this former Georgian coaching house was remodelled in the Victorian era as a wine and spirit merchant. Thankfully it has retained its Victorian charm and now operates as a cosy little pub serving real ale and plenty of whiskies.
Oxford Bar 8 Young St ⓦ oxfordbar.co.uk. This is an unpretentious, unspoilt, no-nonsense city bar – which is why local crime writer Ian Rankin and his 'Inspector Rebus' like it so much. Fans duly make the pilgrimage, but fortunately not all the regulars have been scared off.
Star Bar 1 Northumberland Pl ⓦ starbar.business. site. A veritable antidote to the smart cocktail purveyors that comprise much of the New Town's drinking scene. Reassuringly down to earth and so well hidden it's seldom stumbled upon by tourists. A dark, unpretentiously decorated pub with a dartboard, pool table and well stocked juke box, its greatest asset, however, is its south-facing beer garden.
The Voodoo Rooms 19a West Register St ⓦ thevoodoorooms.com. Glamorous gilt and plush booths attract a dressed-up crowd, especially at the weekend, to this cocktail bar, restaurant and venue. There's frequent live music and club nights.

LGBTQ BARS
Planet 6 Baxter's Place, New Town, ⓦ planetbaredinburgh.co.uk. Loud and outrageous bar beside the Playhouse Theatre, with DJs at weekends and regular drinks promotions making it a popular meeting point.

OUTSIDE THE CITY CENTRE
Smith & Gertrude 26 Hamilton Place, Stockbridge ⓦ smithandgertrude.com. Run by a friendly husband and wife team, this wine and cheese bar has fast become a local favourite. There's a welcoming atmosphere and cool interior with blackboards, a bring-your-own record player, and a colour-dashed wooden floor. The wine flight of three

small glasses with a cheese pairing is a good place to start, plus there's usually something going on from tastings to live music events.

The Jolly Botanist 256–260 Morrison St, Haymarket ⓦ thejollybotanist.co.uk. Riding on the back of gin drinking's phenomenal comeback, this bar has made a name for itself for its range of eclectic liquor sourced from micro-distilleries around the globe. The neo-Victorian decor completes the vibe if you can ignore the flat-screen TV on the wall.

Kings Wark 36 Shore, Leith ⓦ thekingswarkpub.com. Real ale in a restored fifteenth-century pub and restaurant right in the heart of Leith's old port. Its picturesque interior of stone walls and corniced ceilings – with a roaring fire in the winter – that gives an ambience that harks back to the days when old sea dogs would tell tales at the bar.

Pear Tree House 36 West Nicolson St, Southside ⓦ peartreeedinburgh.co.uk. Fine bar in an eighteenth-century house with two beautiful old pear trees trained on its west wall. Its greatest asset, however, is its large courtyard – one of central Edinburgh's very few beer gardens. In summer there are live bands and barbecues outside, weather permitting.

Roseleaf bar cafe 23–24 Sandport Place, Leith ⓦ roseleaf.co.uk. Chintzy-cool local that's a little off the beaten track but worth the trip for the pot-tails alone – funky cocktails served in vintage teapots.

Sheep Heid Inn 43–45 The Causeway, Duddingston ⓦ thesheepheidedinburgh.co.uk. Laying claim to be the city's oldest licensed premise and one-time rural watering hole to Bonnie Prince Charlie, this pub retains many of its historical charms, including an antique skittle alley (rentable for £20) through the back. In winter there are open fires and comfy chairs, while in summer, punters gravitate to the courtyard garden.

NIGHTLIFE

SEE MAPS PAGES 58, 62 AND 66

Inevitably, Edinburgh's **nightlife** is at its best during the Festival (see page 100), which can make the other 48 weeks of the year seem like an anticlimax. However, while it lacks Glasgow's clout, Edinburgh's **club scene** can be enormously enjoyable, with a mix of mainstream discos and left-field clubs with a dressed-down vibe and a wide range of themed nights. Most of the city-centre clubs stay open till around 3am. Meanwhile, you can normally hear **live jazz**, **folk** and **rock** in one or other of the city's pubs. For really big events, ad hoc places – such as the Castle Esplanade or Murrayfield Stadium – are pressed into service.

LISTINGS INFO

The best way to find out about clubs, music and anything else that's going on is to pick up a copy of *The List* (ⓦ list. co.uk), a fortnightly magazine covering Edinburgh and Glasgow. Alternatively, get hold of *The Skinny* (ⓦ theskinny. co.uk), a free culture magazine with frequent arts, music and events listings found in trendy bars and cafés around town.

CLUBS

The Bongo Club 66 Cowgate, Old Town ⓦ thebongoclub. co.uk. Legendary Edinburgh club and arts venue; its line-up is eclectic but always worth checking out. Look out for the monthly dub and reggae Messenger Sound System. Entry prices vary depending on events.

Cabaret Voltaire 36 Blair St, Old Town ⓦ thecabaretvoltaire.com. Atmospheric nightclub in the Old Town's subterranean vaults, playing host to some of the city's best underground electronic music, showcasing local and International DJ talent, as well as early evening live

---

HOGMANAY

Hogmanay's meaning is, put simply, the last day of the year, but in reality it's all about celebrating the beginning of a new one. The best way to do so is to join one of the street parties that are held in the middle of towns and cities, often centred around a prominent clock face which rings out 'the bells' at midnight. These days, the largest New Year's Eve street party in Europe takes place in Edinburgh, with around eighty thousand people enjoying the culmination of a week-long series of events. On the night itself, stages are set up in different parts of the city centre, with big-name rock groups and local ceilidh bands playing to the increasingly inebriated masses. The high point of the evening is, of course, midnight, when hundreds of tons of fireworks are let off into the night sky above the castle, and revellers begin to chorus '**Auld Lang Syne**', an old Scottish tune with lyrics by Robert Burns, Scotland's national poet. For information about celebrations in Edinburgh, and how to get hold of **tickets** for the street party, visit the Edinburgh's Hogmanay Box Office on Bristo Square (☎0131 510 0395; tickets go on sale in July) or go to ⓦ edinburghshogmanay.com.

music events.

Lulu's 125b George St, New Town Ⓦ luluedinburgh. co.uk. Sultry subterranean nightspot beneath restaurant *Tigerlily*. A place to see and be seen; Monaco's Prince Albert and Zara Phillips are among the A-listers who have pulled shapes on the sound-responsive disco light floor.

LGBTQ CLUBS

Edinburgh has a dynamic LGBTQ culture, for years centred round the top of Leith Walk and Broughton Street, where the first gay and lesbian centre appeared in the 1970s. Since the early 1990s, more and more LGBTQ enterprises, especially cafés and nightclubs, have moved into this area, now dubbed the 'Pink Triangle'.

CC Bloom's 23–24 Greenside Place, New Town Ⓦ ccblooms.co.uk. Edinburgh's most enduring LGBTQ bar, with a big dancefloor, stonking rhythms, a young, friendly crowd and free entry all night.

LIVE MUSIC VENUES

Bannerman's 212 Cowgate, Old Town Ⓦ bannermanslive.co.uk. A subterranean labyrinth of caves and musky warrens located at the base of South Bridge; the most atmospheric joint in town in which to discover local rock and indie bands hoping for a big break.

★ The Caves 8–12 Niddry St, Old Town Ⓦ unusualvenuesedinburgh.com. Housed in a labyrinth of arches underneath Edinburgh's South Bridge, this historical multi-functional venue has the city's most staggeringly atmospheric setting. The venue hosts weddings and private

events, as well as live music and occasional club nights. Consequently, there's little consistency as to when public nights are on.

Ghillie-Dhu 2 Rutland Place, New Town Ⓦ ghillie-dhu.co.uk. Housed in a rather fancy auditorium just off Princes St, Ghillie-Dhu (a male fairy from Scottish folklore) wholeheartedly embraces Scotland's traditional musical heritage. There's live music on weeknights, culminating in Friday and Saturday's jovial ceilidh nights.

The Liquid Room 9c Victoria St, Old Town Ⓦ liquidroom. com. Open every evening, this small venue is frequented by local acts and touring indie bands as well as a variety of alternating club nights geared towards student patronage.

The Queen's Hall 85–89 Clerk St, Southside Ⓦ thequeenshall.net. Converted Georgian church which has been an intimate live music and performance venue for more than forty years. There's a jam-packed programme with more than two hundred events each year, ranging from comedy and spoken word to gigs across all music genres.

Royal Oak 1 Infirmary St, Old Town Ⓦ royal-oak-folk. com. Traditional Scottish pub hosting daily informal folk sessions performed by locals. On Sunday evenings there's the 'Wee Folk Club' where they bring in soloists or groups from around the country and beyond.

Whistlebinkies 4–6 South Bridge, Old Town Ⓦ whistlebinkies.com. One of the most reliable places to find live music every night of the week. On the whole it's local indie bands or rock and pop covers, though there are some folk evenings as well.

ENTERTAINMENT

Edinburgh has permanent venues large enough to host touring **orchestras** and **ballet** companies, while elsewhere you can uncover a lively **comedy** club and a couple of excellent art-house **cinemas**.

THEATRE, DANCE AND CONCERTS

Assembly Rooms 54 George St, New Town Ⓦ assemblyroomsedinburgh.com. Provides a slick, grand setting for top-of-the-range drama and big-name music and comedy acts. Crowds spill out of here onto the temporarily pedestrianized George St to enjoy refreshments in the beer garden.

Edinburgh Playhouse 18–22 Greenside Place Ⓦ atgtickets.com/venues/Edinburgh-playhouse. The largest theatre in Britain with a capacity of over three thousand. Opened in the 1920s as a cinema, it's now used largely for extended runs of popular musicals and occasional music concerts.

Festival Theatre 13–29 Nicolson St, Southside Ⓦ capitaltheatres.com. The largest stage in Scotland, home to world-class dance, opera, musicals, comedy, live music and event theatre.

King's Theatre 2 Leven St, Tollcross Ⓦ capitaltheatres. com. One of the UK's most opulent theatre venues, this stately Edwardian civic theatre, with its bold neoclassical frontage, hosts quality touring drama, children's shows, the city's amateur theatre productions and Scotland's biggest festive pantomime.

Royal Lyceum Theatre 30 Grindlay St, Lothian Rd Ⓦ lyceum.org.uk. A fine, moderately compact, Victorian civic theatre with its stage overlooked by three curved tiers orbiting the ornate ceiling's glittering chandelier. The leading venue for mainstream drama, the theatre commissions around seven plays annually as well as hosting travelling productions.

Traverse Theatre 10 Cambridge St, Lothian Rd Ⓦ traverse.co.uk. Next to the Usher Hall, Scotland's foremost theatre company is dedicated to new writing from Scotland and around the world, producing and programming diverse work. It also has a lively café-bar.

Usher Hall Lothian Rd Ⓦ usherhall.co.uk. Boasting a strikingly contemporary extension, Edinburgh's main civic concert hall frequently features choral and symphony concerts, as well as country, jazz, world and pop legends.

1

The upper-circle seats are cheapest and have the best acoustics.

COMEDY

The Stand Comedy Club 5 York Place, New Town ⓦ thestand.co.uk. The city's undisputed top comedy spot, with different acts on every night and some of the UK's top comics headlining at the weekends. Be sure to arrive early to secure a good table for the evening; there's a free show every Sunday afternoon.

CINEMAS

Cameo 38 Home St, Tollcross ⓦ picturehouses.com. A treasure of an art-house cinema with a cosy wee bar – opened by the late Sean Connery – attached; screens more challenging mainstream releases and cult late-nighters in its traditional and intimate auditoria. Tarantino's been here and thinks it's great.

Dominion Cinema Newbattle Terrace ⓦ dominioncinema.co.uk. Just south of the centre, this lovely Art Deco cinema generally sticks to the blockbusters. Screen One has reclining leather sofas and side tables for your snacks.

Filmhouse 88 Lothian Rd ⓦ filmhousecinema. com. Three screens showing an eclectic programme of independent, art-house and classic films. The box office doubles as a DVD shop with an excellent range of arty titles, while through the back the café-bar is a hangout for the city's film buffs and serves healthy, light meals too.

Odeon 118 Lothian Rd ⓦ odeon.co.uk. This central four-screen cinema shows the latest Hollywood releases, including those available in 3D. It sells the same average food as the multiplexes but with fewer films on offer.

Vue Omni Centre, Greenside Row, New Town ⓦ myvue. com. The most central of the big multiscreen venues, this modern glass-fronted cinema shows all the latest mainstream releases including the 3D ones. On Saturday and Sunday mornings they do a Mini Mornings showing – usually a kids' film released a few months prior.

SHOPPING

SEE MAPS PAGES 58, 62 AND 66

Despite the relentless advance of the big chains – especially on **Princes Street**, one of Britain's most famous shopping streets – it's still possible to track down some unusual shops in central Edinburgh. More upmarket shops and boutiques are to be found on and around **George Street**, including an upscale shopping area on the east side of St Andrew Square. For more original outlets, head for **Cockburn Street**, south of Waverley Station, a hub for trendy clothes and record shops, while on **Victoria Street** and in and around the **Grassmarket** you'll find an eclectic range of antiques, crafts, food and bookshops. Along and around the **Royal Mile**, meanwhile, several offbeat places sit among the tacky souvenir sellers.

BOOKS

Blackwell's 53–62 South Bridge, Southside ⓦ blackwells.co.uk. Sited near the university, this rambling, multi-floored bookseller has a strong – although far from exclusive – focus on academic tomes. You'll also find many volumes and travel guides relating to Scotland.

Edinburgh Books 145–147 West Port, Old Town ⓦ edinburghbooks.net. Edinburgh's largest second-hand bookseller is a quirky place: overlooked by a bust of a water buffalo, patrons shuffle through the narrow corridors of teetering bookcases unnervingly stuffed to the ceiling. Just when you think you've seen it all you find a further warren of rooms downstairs in the basement.

Golden Hare Books 68 St Stephen's St, Stockbridge ⓦ goldenharebooks.com. A gorgeously laid-out space, this bookshop is a pleasure to browse through. Three light-filled rooms beautifully display a fantastic selection of books – the little room at the back is a playfully decorated space for children

– and in winter a roaring wood burner warms the space.

McNaughton's Bookshop 3a–4a Haddington Place, Leith Walk ⓦ mcnaughtans.co.uk. Probably Edinburgh's oldest purveyor of antiquarian literature, this shop aims for quality over quantity, consequently feeling more spacious than its counterparts. Housed in a beautiful old basement, there's also a contemporary gallery space that's home to Typewronger Books – a business that sells new books and old typewriters –and also hosts a variety of literary and artistic events.

CLOTHES

In the town centre, Princes Street – particularly its east end and the Princes Mall next to Waverley train station – are where you'll find the biggest names in clothing retail. For more exclusive retailers and expensive designer labels aim for George Street and Multrees Walk next to the bus station.

W. Armstrong & Son 83 Grassmarket, Old Town; 64–66 Clerk St; 14 Teviot Place; ⓦ armstrongsvintage.co.uk. A real treasure trove of vintage and retro fashion, this small chain is like a museum; stuffed to the gunwales with items encompassing everything from prewar civvies to the static-inducing nylon-wear of the 1970s.

FOOD SHOPS

Edinburgh has plenty of good delis and specialist food retailers, particularly down Broughton Street or through the main parts of Stockbridge or Bruntsfield, where you're most likely to find small artisan shops, good delis and traditional butchers and fishmongers.

Archipelago Bakery 39 Dundas St, New Town ⓦ archipelagobakery.co.uk. Serving up some of

Edinburgh's crustiest loaves, you can sit and drink coffee here while marvelling at the freshly baked organic loaves, savoury tarts and other tasty morsels like *spanakopita* (a spinach-based Greek savoury pastry) as they come straight out of the oven. There's a vegan-friendly focus and it makes for a good lunch stop too.

Harvey Nichols 30–34 St Andrew Square, New Town ⓦ harveynichols.com. Harvey Nichols' top-floor food hall is at the cutting edge of foodie fads with a mind-numbing array of ingredients you never thought you needed, but do now, like black Venus rice or lobster oil. Don't miss the 'chocolate lounge', a revolving belt of grabbable treats that's perfect for a mid-afternoon sugar hit.

I.J. Mellis 30a Victoria St, Old Town; 6 Bakers Place, Stockbridge; ⓦ mellischeese.net. Founded in 1993, Mellis' Old Town shop on Victoria Street is charmingly kitted out in a Victorian style and well stocked with expertly conditioned farmhouse and artisan cheese from Britain, Ireland and, to a lesser extent, the Continent. They also have a good selection of organic wines. The Mellis brand is expanding fast, with a branch in Stockbridge and on Morningside Rd, as well as outlets in St Andrews and Glasgow.

Sicilian Pastry Shop 14–16 Albert St, Leith ☎0131 554 7417. A brilliant little family shop selling sweet and colourful cakes, mostly Sicilian in style – featuring lots of cream. Not really a café but they do sell a good strong espresso here, too.

★ **Störtebäcker** 38 St John's Rd, Corstorphine, 3 miles west of the centre ⓦ stortebacker.co.uk. Surely the world's smallest bakery, housed in 'The Wee Shop' with standing room for just two people and a veritable bounty of outstanding home-made sourdoughs, cakes, pastries and tarts. Loosely translated as 'harassed baker', this is the brainchild of two German friends with a passion for pastries and the recipes from their native country.

Valvona & Crolla 19 Elm Row, Leith Walk ⓦ valvonacrolla.com. Open the door to this most venerated of Edinburgh's delis – with its on-site restaurant (see page 93) and you're instantly welcomed by a glorious odour reminiscent of Italian markets. It's a wonder to behold: shelves stacked floor to ceiling with the best Italian produce, vast legs of ham and strings of dried chillies hanging from the ceiling, and a large room at the back dedicated to wine.

MARKETS

Edinburgh Farmers' Market Castle Terrace, Lothian Rd ⓦ edinburghfarmersmarket.co.uk. Run by the council, the majority of this market's stallholders must be primary producers, selling what they grow. The rigidity of

---

THE FRINGE

In the wake of World War II, a few wise civic leaders were offered an opportunity to create a festival that would celebrate diversity and 'provide a platform for the flowering of the human spirit'. When a handful of theatre companies turned up uninvited to the International Festival's 1947 inauguration, the seeds of the Fringe Festival were unintentionally sown. In the following years, more and more performers began showing up, culminating in the formation of the **Festival Fringe Society** in 1958.

A charitable union, it provided unbiased assistance to artists and companies who wished to perform in Edinburgh during August. Today, it still provides the same service, but on a much grander scale. Even standing alone, the **Edinburgh Festival Fringe** is now easily the world's largest arts gathering. Each year sees over thirty thousand performances from some seven hundred companies, with more than twelve thousand participants from all over the world. There's something in the region of 1,500 shows every day, round the clock, in two hundred venues around the city. While the headlining names at the International Festival reinforce the festival's cultural credibility, it is the dynamism, spontaneity and sheer exuberance of the Fringe that dominate Edinburgh every August, giving the city its unique atmosphere. The most prominent and ubiquitous aspect of the Fringe is **comedy**, having overtaken theatre as the largest genre in 2008. As well as sell-out audiences and quotable reviews, most of the comedy acts are chasing the **Edinburgh Comedy Award**, given to the most outstanding stand-up or comedy cabaret.

At the same time, the Fringe's **theatre** programme shows no signs of dying out, with hundreds of brand-new works airing alongside offbeat classics and familiar Shakespearean tragedies. The venues are often as imaginative as the shows themselves – playgrounds, restaurants and even parked cars have all been used to stage plays. The Fringe also offers fine musicals, dance, children's shows, exhibitions, lectures and music.

1

this policy may have somewhat stifled its success as there's an oversupply of vacuum-packed meat and fish; however, you'll always find some interesting cottage-industry produce here. Sat 9am–2pm.

Stockbridge Market Saunders St, Stockbridge ⓦ stockbridgemarket.com. The capital's favourite foodie market, Stockbridge Market was the first in this family of markets that has now expanded to Grassmarket (Sat) and Leith (Sat). Even with the belligerent Scottish climate, there's somehow an international buzz as scores of locals and tourists dine out on paella or African samosas, or wash a German pastry down with a coffee served out of the back of a VW camper. Sun 10am–5pm.

MUSIC

Underground Solu'shun 9 Cockburn St, Old Town ⓦ undergroundsolushn.com. The only surviving dance and electronic music specialist in town, selling records

mostly in vinyl format and DJ-oriented hardware. There's a lot of house and techno here, but also a wide variety of genres from electronica to funk and soul.

Vinyl Villains 5 Elm Row, Leith Walk ⓦ vinylvillains. co.uk. This ancient Edinburgh institution, with a grungy vibe and packed floor to ceiling with records, sells some new but mostly second-hand records. The racks are mostly filled with Sixties and Seventies rock LPs and singles, but no genre or era is excluded entirely.

OUTDOOR GEAR

There's a concentration of useful stores specializing in outdoor gear on Rose St in the New Town and round the corner on Frederick St.

Tiso 123–125 Rose St ⓦ tiso.com. A department store for the outdoors; spread over four floors, with maps, knowledgeable staff and all you could need to explore Scotland's vast wilderness.

THE EDINBURGH FESTIVAL

August's **Edinburgh Festival** is actually an umbrella term encompassing several different festivals taking place at around the same time in the city. The principal events are the **Edinburgh International Festival** and the much larger **Edinburgh Festival Fringe**, but there are also **Book, Jazz and Blues** and **Art** festivals, among others, as well as the **Military Tattoo** on the Esplanade.

PROGRAMMES, LISTINGS AND INFORMATION

As well as the official Edinburgh Festivals website (ⓦ edinburghfestivals.co.uk), each festival produces its own programme well in advance. During August, various publications give information about what's on and what's good – best of these is *The Scotsman* newspaper's daily supplement, but also worthwhile are *The Guide*, published daily by the Fringe Office; weekly *The List*; and *Fest*, best of the freebie newspapers available around town.

THE EDINBURGH INTERNATIONAL FESTIVAL

The original Edinburgh Festival, sometimes called the 'Official Festival', was conceived in 1947 as a celebration of Pan-European culture in the postwar era. Initially dominated by opera, other elements such as top-grade theatre, ballet, dance and classical music were gradually introduced, and it's still very much a highbrow event, its high production values and serious approach offering an antidote to the Fringe's slapdash vigour.

International Festival Box Office The Hub, Castlehill, Old Town ⓦ eif.co.uk. This is the year-round headquarters and box office for the Edinburgh International Festival, which generally runs for most of August, culminating in a ticketed Fireworks Concert based in Princes Street Gardens

but visible from all over the city. Performances take place at the city's larger venues such as the Usher Hall and the Festival Theatre, and, while ticket prices can run to over £90, it is possible to see even the big productions for as little as £10 if you're prepared to sit at the back.

The Fireworks Concert Princes Street Gardens ⓦ eif. co.uk. Tickets for the Fireworks Concert (£15.50 standing, £36 seated) sell out well in advance; however, a few extra tickets are released for sale at 10am at the Hub, Castlehill, on the day before the show. The concert begins on the last day of the festival at 9pm.

THE EDINBURGH FESTIVAL FRINGE

The Edinburgh Festival Fringe is easily the world's largest arts gathering, and dealing with the logistics of it all can be bewildering. We set out the basics below, but as dates, venues and acts change from one year to the next, be prepared for the unexpected. The Fringe starts and finishes on the same days as the International Festival, kicking off in early August and ending on the last weekend of the month.

BOOKING TICKETS FOR THE FRINGE

Festival Fringe Office 180 High St, Old Town ⓦ edfringe.com. The full Fringe programme is usually available in June from the Festival Fringe Office. Online and telephone bookings for shows can be made immediately after its release, while during the Festival, tickets are sold at the Fringe Office, as well as online or at venues. Advance ticket prices – and therefore guaranteed entry – for most Fringe shows start at £6, and average from £10 to £15 at the main venues, with the best-known acts going for even more; there are often cheap deals on the opening weekend. A number of shows are free,

while others operate a Pay What You Want at the end of the show option – there's no guarantee you'll get in though. Performances are staged around the clock, with most scheduled to run for an hour. A downloadable app is available from ⓦ edfringe.com where you can find shows and book tickets, including those from the Half Price Hut (see below). During the Festival daily 10am–9pm.
Half Price Hut Mound Precinct, beside the Scottish National Gallery. This is the place to head for bargains, where Fringe shows cut their prices in half. There's a downloadable app available from iTunes linked from the edfringe.com website. During the Festival daily 10am–9pm.

FRINGE VENUES

While the Fringe is famous for its tiny and unexpected auditoria – there are more than 300 venues across the city – the most visible venues are the four dominant Fringe companies (Assembly, Pleasance, Gilded Balloon and Underbelly). If you're new to the Fringe, these are all safe bets for decent shows and a bit of star-spotting.
The Assembly Rooms 54 George St, New Town ⓦ assemblyroomsedinburgh.co.uk. Provides a slick, grand setting for top-of-the-range drama and big-name music and comedy acts. Crowds spill out of here onto the temporarily pedestrianized George St where there are makeshift beer gardens.
Gilded Balloon Teviot Row House, Bristo Square, Southside ⓦ gildedballoon.co.uk. Basing its operations in a Fringe hot-spot housed in a beautiful Victorian building designed to look like a sixteenth-century palace, this is the most elegant of the main Old Town venues. It's predominantly mainstream comedy here, although they don't shy away from championing emerging talent. Shows continue into the wee small hours with their raucous Late n Live show from 1am to 5am.
Pleasance Courtyard 60 Pleasance, Old Town ⓦ pleasance.co.uk. The atmosphere in the courtyard surrounded by the sixteen auditoria here has a slightly chaotic feel thanks to its busy courtyard bars and kids' zone. Indoors you'll find offbeat comedy mixing with whimsical appearances by panellists on Radio 4 game shows.
Pleasance Dome Potterrow, 1 Bristo Square, Southside ⓦ pleasance.co.uk. Located in one of Edinburgh University's student unions, there are four small auditoria here, all accessed from the skylit dome room.
The Underbelly Bristo Square, Southside ⓦ underbelly. co.uk. Underbelly's giant, inflatable upside-down cow – the Udderbelly – is a makeshift performance space that is one of the Fringe's most unusual and eye-catching venues. The company provides further shows down in their labyrinthine Cowgate building and have also expanded to George Square, Circus Hub and Bristo Square.

EDINBURGH INTERNATIONAL BOOK FESTIVAL

Edinburgh International Book Festival Ticket office at Charlotte Square, New Town ⓦ edbookfest.co.uk. The world's largest celebration of the written word is held in a tented village in Charlotte Square during the last two weeks of August. It offers talks, readings and signings by a star-studded line-up of visiting authors, as well as panel discussions and workshops. Well-known Scottish authors such as Ian Rankin and Alexander McCall-Smith are good for an appearance most years, while visitors from a bit further afield have included Paul Merton, Louis de Bernières, Marilynne Robinson, George Monbiot and Salman Rushdie. In addition, there's a dedicated programme of children's activities, debates, writing workshops and book-related events, an on-site café and, of course, a bookshop.

EDINBURGH JAZZ AND BLUES FESTIVAL

The Edinburgh Jazz and Blues Festival Ticket office at Hub Tickets, 348 Castlehill, Old Town ⓦ edinburghjazzfestival.com. Easing the city into the festival spirit, the Edinburgh Jazz and Blues Festival runs for two weeks from mid-July with a full programme of gigs in many different locations. Scotland's own varied and vibrant jazz scene is always fully represented, and atmospheric late-night clubs complement major concerts given by international stars. Past visitors have included B.B. King, Bill Wyman, Dizzy Gillespie, Dave Brubeck, Van Morrison, Carol Kidd and The Blues Band. Highlights include the nightly Jam Sessions and a colourful New Orleans–style Mardi Gras and street parade. Tickets range in price from £5 for small pub gigs to £30 for a seat in a big venue.

EDINBURGH ART FESTIVAL

Edinburgh Art Festival ⓦ edinburghartfestival.com or ⓦ nationalgalleries.org. Founded in 2004, August's Edinburgh Art Festival has established itself as an important addition to the festivals portfolio. This is due, in large part, to the ambition and diversity of its programme, which has included high-profile exhibitions by internationally renowned contemporary artists such as Tracey Emin, Douglas Gordon and Ron Mueck, as well as retrospectives of work by pioneering twentieth-century artists including sculptor Eva Hesse, photographer Robert Mapplethorpe, pop artists Gilbert and George and elder statesmen of Scottish painting Alan Davie and John Bellany. Virtually every art gallery in the city participates in the festival, from small private concerns to blockbuster shows at the National Galleries of Scotland's venues. Most exhibitions are free, though entry to the National Galleries' exhibitions is charged.

THE MILITARY TATTOO

The Military Tattoo The Tattoo Office, 1–3 Cockburn St, Old Town ⓦ edintattoo.co.uk. Staged in the spectacular stadium of the Edinburgh Castle Esplanade, the Military Tattoo is an unashamed display of pomp and military pride. The programme of choreographed drills, massed pipe bands, historical tableaux, energetic battle reenactments, national dancing and pyrotechnics has been a feature of the Festival for over half a century, its emotional climax provided by a lone piper on the Castle battlements. Followed by a quick fireworks display, it's a successful formula barely tampered with over the years. Tickets (£30–95 depending on seat location, plus a £6.50 booking fee if bought online) need to be booked well in advance, and it's advisable to take a cushion and rainwear.

EDINBURGH'S OTHER FESTIVALS AND EVENTS

Science Festival Two weeks in April ⓦ sciencefestival. co.uk. Incorporates hands-on children's events as well as numerous lectures on a vast array of subjects.

Beltane Night of April 30 ⓦ beltane.org. An ancient Celtic fire festival, held on Calton Hill, celebrating the arrival of spring. Has a New Age feel to it, with lots of painted flesh, beating drums and huge bonfires. Tickets cost £10.

Imaginate Festival Mid-May ⓦ imaginate.org.uk. Low-key children's festival with readings, magicians, drama and puppetry.

International Film Festival Second half of June ⓦ edfilmfest.org.uk. With a programme crammed with premieres, film shorts and retrospectives, this is the perfect Hollywood antidote. That said, you still see the occasional film star getting the red carpet treatment outside the festival's main hub at The Filmhouse on Lothian Rd.

Edinburgh's Christmas Mid-Nov until early Jan ⓦ edinburghschristmas.com. Growing exponentially every year, Edinburgh's Christmas draws together various seasonal events, most prominently the installation of a huge Ferris wheel beside the Scott Monument and the 60,000-bulb Street of Lights – a free, synchronized light show – on the Royal Mile. There's also outdoor skating, fairground rides and a German Christmas market.

Edinburgh's Hogmanay The Festival Fringe Office, 180 High St ⓦ edinburghshogmanay.com. One of the world's largest New Year street parties, involving torchlight processions, folk and rock concerts, ceilidhs and fireworks galore (see page 41). Box office opens early December.

SPORTS

SPECTATOR SPORTS

FOOTBALL

Heart of Midlothian FC McLeod St, off Gorgie Rd ⓦ heartsfc.co.uk. Edinburgh's oldest football club dating back to 1874, Heart of Midlothian or 'Hearts' play in the west of Edinburgh in their 19,850-capacity Tynecastle Stadium.

Hibernian FC 12 Albion Place, off Easter Rd ⓦ hibernianfc. co.uk. Hearts arch rivals Hibernian FC or 'Hibs' was founded in 1875 by Irish immigrants. Based at the 20,000-capacity Easter Road Stadium, northeast of the centre, their support tends to come from Leith and its surrounding areas.

RUGBY

Murrayfield Roseburn St ⓦ scottishrugby.org. The home of Scottish rugby, this huge stadium plays host to Six Nations games in February and March and occasional friendlies, plus the odd rock concert.

SPORTS FACILITIES

CLIMBING

Edinburgh International Climbing Arena South Platt Hill, Ratho ⓦ edinburghleisure.co.uk. Immense indoor climbing facility built into the shell of an old quarry just west of the city beyond the airport. There's a huge choice of climbs to challenge climbers of all levels, plus bouldering practice and a vertiginous aerial assault challenge. Prices start at £9.60 plus equipment rental.

SNOWSPORTS

Midlothian Snowsports Biggar Rd (buses Nos 4 & 15 from Princes St) ⓦ midlothian.gov.uk. Sited just south of the city limits in the Pentland Hills (see page 87), the extensive dry slope here makes for an excellent year-round ski and snowboard facility; you can also do tubing here. Skiing and snowboarding costs £15 for the first hour then £8 per hour plus equipment rental.

SWIMMING

Royal Commonwealth Pool 21 Dalkeith Rd ⓦ edinburghleisure.co.uk. Huge facility with three pools: for diving, for kids and a 50m pool for general swimming.

TENNIS

There are tennis courts available at The Meadows (free at certain times) near Buccleuch St and in Inverleith Park across the road from the Royal Botanic Gardens Edinburgh (see page 83).

DIRECTORY

Banks and exchange All the major UK banks have branches in central Edinburgh, with ATMs and currency exchange; the main concentrations are in the area between Hanover St and St Andrew Square in the east end of the central New Town. Post offices will exchange currency and there are also currency exchange outlets in Waverley Station. To change money after hours, try one of the upmarket hotels – but expect a hefty commission charge.

Hospitals and clinics Royal Infirmary of Edinburgh, 21 Little France Crescent (☎0131 536 1000), has a 24hr casualty department, while the new Royal Hospital for Children and Young People, 50 Little France Crescent (☎0131 536 1000), has a casualty department for children. Western General, Crewe Rd South (☎0131 537 1000), provides a minor injuries clinic 8am–9pm. NHS24 (☎111,

ⓦnhs24.scot) offers 24hr health advice and clinical assessment over the phone or online.

Left luggage Waverley train station has a counter charging £12.50 per item per day (daily 8am–9pm; ☎0208 090 9937). The Bus Station is far more reasonable, at £8 to £12 per day depending on bag size (daily 24hr ☎0131 555 6363).

Police Lothian and Borders Police (☎999, or ☎101 for non-emergencies) have a station at 2 Gayfield Square.

Post office 33 Forrest Rd (Mon–Fri 8.30am–6pm, Sat 9am–5.30pm); 46 St Mary's St (Mon–Fri 9am–5.30pm, Sat 9am–4pm).

East Lothian

East Lothian consists of the coastal strip and hinterland immediately east of Edinburgh, bounded by the Firth of Forth to the north and the Lammermuir Hills to the south. All of it is within easy day-trip range from the capital, though there are places you can stay overnight if you're keen to explore it properly. Often mocked as the 'home counties' of Edinburgh, there's no denying its well-ordered feel, with prosperous farms and large estate houses dominating the scenery.

The most immediately attractive part of the area is the coastline, extending from the town of Musselburgh, all but joined onto Edinburgh, round to the harbour town of **Dunbar**, birthplace of the famous naturalist John Muir. There's something for most tastes here, including wide sandy beaches, the enjoyable Seabird Centre at **North Berwick** and the nearby castles of **Dirleton** and **Tantallon**, the latter set in a vertiginous clifftop location. Inland, at the foot of the Lammermuirs, is the county town of **Haddington**, a pleasant enough place, though the attraction nearby of **Glenkinchie**, Edinburgh's 'local' whisky distillery by Pentcaitland, is likely to be a stronger draw.

North Berwick and around

NORTH BERWICK, 25 miles east of Edinburgh, has a great deal of charm and a somewhat faded, old-fashioned air, its guesthouses and hotels extending along the shore in all their Victorian and Edwardian sobriety. The town's small harbour is set on a headland which cleaves two crescents of sand, providing the town with an attractive coastal setting, though it is the two nearby volcanic heaps, the offshore **Bass Rock** and 613ft-high **North Berwick Law**, which are the town's defining physical features.

Scottish Seabird Centre

The Harbour • Daily Feb, March, Sept & Oct 10am–5pm; April–Aug 10am–6pm; Nov–Jan 10am–4pm • Charge • Boat trips April–early Oct daily • Charge • ⓦseabird.org

Housed in an attractively designed new building by the harbour, the **Scottish Seabird Centre** offers access to the gannets and puffins that thrive on the rocky outcrops in the Firth of Forth before North Berwick. There are live links from the centre to cameras mounted on the islands which show close-up pictures of the birds in their nesting grounds. At the risk of getting wet, you can hop aboard one of the thrilling fast RIB rides to the islands – weather permitting. Trips range from an hour-long Seabird Catamaran cruise, to a two-hour-plus trip to (and landing on) Bass Rock. Contact the Seabird Centre to find out what boat tours are available on any given day.

1

Dirleton Castle

2.5 miles west of North Berwick, signposted off the A198 • Daily April–Sept 9.30am–5.30pm; Oct–March 10am–4pm; last entry 30min before closing • Charge • HES • ⓦ historicenvironment.scot • Reached in 15min from North Berwick on the Edinburgh bus (First Bus No. 124; every 30min)

The genteel hamlet of Dirleton huddles around the romantic thirteenth-century ruins of **Dirleton Castle**, which saw action in the Wars of Scottish Independence. It was later rendered militarily defunct after a besiegement by Oliver Cromwell's army to flush out bandits. Today, it's an attractive relic, largely intact, with restored Victorian gardens making for a popular wedding venue.

Tantallon Castle

3 miles east of North Berwick on the A198 • Daily April–Sept 9.30am–5.30pm; Oct–March 10am–4pm; last entry 30min before closing • Charge • HES • ⓦ historicenvironment.scot • From North Berwick take the Dunbar bus (Eves Coaches No. 120; Mon–Sat six per day, two on Sun; 6min), or you can walk there from town along the cliffs in around an hour

The melodramatic ruins of **Tantallon Castle** stand on the precipitous cliffs facing the Bass Rock. With a sheer drop down to the sea on three sides and a sequence of moats and ditches on the fourth, the desolate invincibility of this fourteenth-century stronghold is daunting, especially when the wind howls over the remaining battlements and the surf crashes on the rocks far below.

ARRIVAL AND DEPARTURE   NORTH BERWICK AND AROUND

By train North Berwick is served by an hourly train from Edinburgh Waverley (33min). From the station it's a 10min walk east to the town centre.

By bus First Group Nos 124 and X24 from Edinburgh's bus station (every 30min; 1hr 35min) run along the coast and stop on High St, North Berwick.

By car From Edinburgh take the A1 (London Rd) and turn onto the A198 at Tranent. From here, it's a further thirteen miles to North Berwick.

ACCOMMODATION AND EATING

The Glebe House B&B 4 Law Rd, North Berwick ⓦ glebehouse-nb.co.uk. A grand eighteenth-century manse in secluded grounds 100yd inland but still overlooking the sea. With decor befitting of its period, the three rooms (including one with a four-poster bed) are spacious yet homely, and at breakfast you can opt for a Scottish fry-up – although there are healthier choices too. They also offer cheaper rates for single occupancy. **£££**

★ **Osteria** 71 High St, North Berwick ⓦ osteria-no1. co.uk. Run by a highly successful father and daughter team; this is one of the country's top Italian restaurants. Expect bold flavours, vibrant colours and a level of finesse little seen outside the main cities. **£££**

Dunbar

Thirty miles east of Edinburgh lies the coastal town of **DUNBAR**, with its delightfully intricate double harbour set beside the shattered remains of a once-mighty castle. Its local industry is fishing but the more affluent residents are commuters who take advantage of the town's station on the main London to Edinburgh train line. Dunbar's High Street is graced by several grand old stone buildings, one of which is the birthplace of nineteenth-century explorer and naturalist, **John Muir**, whose name is also given to the attractive **country park** neighbouring the town. You can get to the park on an easy three-mile walk west of the harbour, along a rugged stretch of coast to the sands of Belhaven Bay.

John Muir Birthplace

126 High St • April–Oct Mon–Sat 10am–5pm, Sun 1–5pm; Nov–March Wed–Sat 10am–5pm, Sun 1–5pm; last entry 45min before closing • Free • ⓦ jmbt.org.uk

More famous abroad than in his native Scotland, John Muir (1838–1914) was a tireless campaigner for the protection of the natural world and played an integral role in the creation of the United States' national parks system. The **John Muir Birthplace** was born out of demand from the many Americans visiting Dunbar in the hope of learning more about Muir's early life and childhood inspirations. The three-storey whitewashed tenement describes itself as an interpretative centre rather than a museum, and while it engagingly tells the story of Muir's passage from childhood to pioneer, there are few historical artefacts on show.

ARRIVAL AND DEPARTURE
DUNBAR

By train Dunbar is served by trains from Edinburgh Waverley (hourly; 25min). From the station it's a 5min walk north to the high street.

By bus For Dunbar the bus No. X7 runs from Edinburgh Waverley (every 30min), while bus No. 253 departs from Edinburgh's bus station (hourly).

By car From Edinburgh take the A1 (London Rd) and turn onto the A199 three miles after East Linton, after which Dunbar is a 5min drive.

EATING

The Creel Restaurant 25 Lamer St, near the old harbour ⓦ creelrestaurant.co.uk. Run by a former chef to Rick Stein, this restaurant knows a thing or two about seafood. Championing locally sourced food, this is a great place to tuck into posh fish (battered using the local Belhaven beer) and chips or, if you prefer something more exotic, lemon sole with a spicy Spanish-influenced salsa. The lunch menu is best value for two courses.

Haddington and around

Sitting on the banks of the River Tyne with the hulking mass of **St Mary's Church**, Scotland's largest parish church, rising tall near its centre, this is one of Scotland's most respectable county towns. Other than a stroll along the riverbank or through the seventeenth-century medicinal gardens of **St Mary's Pleasance** on Sidegate, there's not much to detain you in the town unless you arrive on the last Saturday of the month for the **farmers' market**.

Just four miles south of town, the pretty hamlet of **Gifford**, with its eighteenth-century estate cottages flanked by a trim whitewashed church and a couple of pleasant pubs, makes for a good last stop before the wilderness of the Lammermuir Hills.

Glenkinchie Distillery
7 miles southwest of Haddington on the A6093 • Daily 10am–5pm; last tour 1hr before closing • Charge • ⓦ malts.com

Home of The Edinburgh Malt, **Glenkinchie Distillery** is the closest place to Scotland's capital city where malt whisky is made. Here, of course, they emphasize the qualities that set Glenkinchie, a lighter, drier malt, apart from the peaty, smoky whiskies of the north and west. On display is a pleasant little exhibition showing how the Water of Life is made, featuring some quaint distilling relics, which enhance the factory tour experience almost as much as the free dram at the end.

Midlothian

Immediately south of Edinburgh lies the old county of **Midlothian**, once called Edinburghshire. It's one of the hilliest parts of the Central Lowlands, with the Pentland chain running down its western side and the Moorfoots defining its boundary with the Borders to the south. Though predominantly rural, it contains a belt of former mining communities that are still struggling to come to terms with the industry's decline. An otherwise nondescript place, the village has two unusual claims to fame: it was near here, at the Roslin Institute, that the **world's first cloned sheep**, Dolly, was created in 1997; and it is home to the mysterious, richly decorated late Gothic **Rosslyn Chapel**.

1

LEGENDS OF ROSSLYN CHAPEL

Rosslyn Chapel is famous for its exquisite carvings – but almost as compelling are the fascinating **legends** associated with this mysterious building, and the many secrets said to lurk within the cracks and crannies of its skilfully engraved stone.

The greatest and most original carving to grace Rosslyn Chapel is the extraordinary knotted **Apprentice Pillar** at the southeastern corner of the Lady Chapel. According to local legend, the pillar was carved by an apprentice during the absence of the master mason, who **killed** him in a fit of jealousy on seeing the finished work. A tiny head of a man with a slashed forehead, set at the apex of the ceiling at the far northwestern corner of the building, is popularly supposed to represent the apprentice, his murderer the corresponding head at the opposite side.

The imagery of carvings such as the floriated **cross and five-pointed star**, together with the history of the family, the St Clairs of Rosslyn, who own the chapel, leaves little doubt about its links to the **Knights Templar** and **Freemasonry**. Two members of the St Clair family, for example, were allegedly grand masters of the Prieuré de Sion, the shadowy order linked to the Templars, while the Masonic connection was said to have saved the chapel from the armies of Oliver Cromwell, himself a Freemason, which destroyed the surrounding area but spared Rosslyn.

More intriguing still are claims that, because of such connections, Rosslyn Chapel has been the repository for items such as the lost Scrolls of Solomon's Temple in Jerusalem, the true Stone of Scone and, most famously, the **Holy Grail**.

The chapel is regularly drawn into conspiracy theories on these themes, most famously through Dan Brown's 2003 bestseller **The Da Vinci Code**; the chapel's appearance in the film of the same name precipitated a huge surge in visitor numbers, detracting a little from the mysterious air of the place.

Rosslyn Chapel

Chapel Loan, Roslin, 7 miles south of Edinburgh just off the A701 • Jan–May & Sept–Dec Mon–Sat 9.30am–5pm, Sun noon–4.45pm; June–Aug Mon–Sat 9.30am–6pm, Sun noon–4.45pm; last entry 30min before closing • Charge • ⍟ rosslynchapel.com • Bus No. 37 (every 30min; 40–60min) westbound from Princes St in Edinburgh

Revered for its sublime **stone carvings** – some of the finest in the world – and subject of intrigue and mystery with its alleged Crusader connections, Rosslyn is more like a cathedral than a chapel in its dimensions. It was intended to be a huge collegiate church dedicated to St Matthew, but construction halted soon after the founder's death in 1484, and the vestry built onto the facade nearly four hundred years later is the sole subsequent addition. After a long period of neglect, a massive fifteen-year restoration project has been completed.

Rosslyn's **exterior** bristles with pinnacles, gargoyles, flying buttresses and canopies, while **inside** the stonework is, if anything, even more intricate. The **foliage carving** is particularly outstanding, with botanically accurate depictions of over a dozen different leaves and plants. Among them are cacti and Indian corn, compounding the legend that the founder's grandfather, the daring sea adventurer Prince Henry of Orkney, did indeed set foot in the New World a century before Columbus. The rich and subtle **figurative sculptures** have given Rosslyn the nickname of 'a Bible in stone', though they're more allegorical than literal, with portrayals of the Dance of Death, the Seven Acts of Mercy and the Seven Deadly Sins.

West Lothian

To many, **West Lothian** is a poor relative to the rich, rolling farmland of East and Midlothian, with a landscape dominated by motorways, industrial estates and giant hillocks of ochre-coloured mine waste called 'bings'. However, in the ruined royal palace at **Linlithgow**, the area boasts one of Scotland's more magnificent ruins. Not too far away, the village of **South Queensferry** lies under the considerable shadow of the Forth rail and road bridges, though it's an interesting enough place in its own right, with a historic high street and the notable stately homes **Dalmeny** and **Hopetoun** nearby. It's also the starting point for boat trips out to **Inchcolm Island**, home to a beautifully preserved medieval abbey.

Linlithgow

Roughly equidistant between Falkirk and the outskirts of Edinburgh, the ancient burgh of **Linlithgow** has largely kept its medieval layout. Sadly, development since the 1960s has stripped it of some fine buildings, in particular close to the **Town Hall** and **Cross** (the former marketplace) on the long High Street – the town does, however, preserve some notable gems, including a ruined palace and an ancient church.

Linlithgow Palace

Kirkgate • Tues–Sat 10am–4pm • Charge • HES • ⓦ historicenvironment.scot

Hidden from the main road, **Linlithgow Palace** is a splendid fifteenth-century ruin romantically set on the edge of Linlithgow Loch. The pile is associated with some of Scotland's best-known historical figures, including **Mary, Queen of Scots** who was born here on December 8, 1542 and became queen six days later. A royal manor house is believed to have existed on this site since the time of David I, though James I began construction of the present palace, a process that continued through two centuries and the reign of no fewer than eight monarchs. From the top of the northwest tower, Queen Margaret looked out in vain for the return of James IV from the field of Flodden in 1513 – indeed, the views from her bower, six giddy storeys up from the ground, are exceptional. The ornate octagonal **fountain** in the inner courtyard, with its wonderfully intricate figures and medallion heads, flowed with wine for the wedding of James V and Mary of Guise.

This is a great place to take children: the elegant, bare rooms echo with footsteps and there's a labyrinthine network of spiral staircases and endless nooks and crannies. The galleried **Great Hall** is magnificent, as is the adjoining kitchen, which has a truly cavernous fireplace.

St Michael's Church

The Cross • Daily May–Sept 10.30am–4pm; Oct–April 10.30am–1pm • Free • ⓦ stmichaelsparish.org.uk

St Michael's Church, adjacent to Linlithgow Palace, is one of Scotland's largest pre-Reformation churches, consecrated in the thirteenth century. The present building was completed two hundred years later, with the exception of the hugely incongruous aluminium spire, tacked on in 1964. Inside, it's a soaring Gothic masterwork with a layout typical of the time; huge stone arches and pillars combine to divide the outer aisles from the nave, above which the impressive vaulted ceiling draws the eye forward to the chancel.

Linlithgow Canal Centre

Manse Rd Basin, 100yd southwest of Linlithgow's train station • Early April–late Sept Sat & Sun 1.30–4.30pm; late June–mid-Aug Mon–Fri 1.30–4pm • Town Boat Trips every 30min • Charge • Aqueduct Cruises Sat & Sun 2pm • Charge • ⓦ lucs.org.uk

The **Linlithgow Canal Centre** sits on the banks of the tranquil **Union Canal**, the 31-mile-long waterway that runs from Fountainbridge, near the heart of Edinburgh, through Linlithgow and west to Falkirk, where it meets the Forth and Clyde Canal linking the capital with Glasgow – the two canals are connected by the Falkirk Wheel (see page 280). The Canal Centre runs a couple of regular **narrow-boat trips** through town or east towards the Avon Aqueduct – Scotland's largest – as well as the occasional foray

1

onto the Forth and Clyde via the Falkirk Wheel. Along the way, the guide will tell of the near two-hundred-year history of the canals and serve tea and biscuits too.

ARRIVAL AND DEPARTURE

LINLITHGOW

By train Linlithgow is on the main train routes from Edinburgh to both Glasgow Queen St (4 trains hourly) and Stirling (2 trains hourly); the journey from Edinburgh takes 20min and the train station lies at the southern end of town. **By car** 19 miles west of Edinburgh, Linlithgow is just off the M9 road to Stirling.

South Queensferry

Eight miles northwest of Edinburgh city centre, the small town of **South Queensferry** (also known as Queensferry) is best known today for its location at the southern end of the three mighty **Forth bridges** (see page 304). Named after the saintly wife of Malcolm Canmore, Margaret, who would often use the ferry here to travel between the royal palaces in Dunfermline and Edinburgh, it's an attractive settlement tightly packed with old buildings, most of which date from the seventeenth and eighteenth centuries. Only one row of houses separates the cobbled High Street from the water; through the gaps there's a great perspective of the bridges, an old stone harbour and a curved, pebbly beach, the scene each New Year's Day of the teeth-chattering 'Loony Dook', when a gaggle of hungover locals charge into the sea for the quickest of dips.

Queensferry Museum

53 High St • Daily 10am–1pm & 2.15–5pm • Free • ⓦ edinburghmuseums.org.uk

The tiny **Queensferry Museum** contains photos and relics of the town's history showing its importance as a ferry port. The most interesting item on show is the **Burry Man costume**, part of a unique Queensferry tradition designed to ward off evil spirits. Still worn around town on the first Friday of August every year, the Burry man suits are cotton with over ten thousand sticky 'burrs' – burdock seed cases – attached from head to toe. You'll also find details on the building of the first two bridges.

ARRIVAL AND DEPARTURE

SOUTH QUEENSFERRY

By train From Edinburgh Waverley take the train to Dalmeny (every 20min; 15min). From there it's a mile to town: head west on Station Rd then turn right on The Loan. **By bus** Regular buses (3 hourly) connect Edinburgh's bus station with Hopetoun Rd at the heart of South Queensferry within 40min. **By car** South Queensferry is signposted off the M90 motorway on the south end of the Forth Rd Bridge.

EATING AND DRINKING

The Boathouse 22 High St ⓦ theboathouse.online. With incredible views of the Forth Rail Bridge and River Forth it's little wonder this bistro wine bar is so popular. They specialise in fresh fish and seafood, with the likes of pan-seared coley on a Shetland mussel stew with parmesan ham garnish and chunky fries on the menu. There's always a catch of the day too. £££

Dalmeny House

Dalmeny Estate, 3 miles east of South Queensferry • June & July Mon–Wed & Sun; guided tours 2.15pm & 3.30pm • Charge • ⓦ roseberyestates.co.uk • Arriving on foot from South Queensferry, follow the High St eastwards for 1.5 miles until you reach the estate entrance; by car follow signposts from the A90 near South Queensferry

Set on a two-thousand-acre estate, **Dalmeny House** may not be the prettiest mansion you'll encounter in Scotland, but the quality of the items on show within makes it a fascinating place to visit. As well as some of the finest Baroque and Neoclassical **furniture** produced for Louis XIV, Louis XV and Louis XVI in the hundred years before the French Revolution, there's also a valuable selection of memorabilia relating to Napoleon Bonaparte. The **art** collection is surprisingly strong too, with a very rare set of **tapestries** made from cartoons by Goya, and portraits by Raeburn, Reynolds, Gainsborough and Lawrence.

Hopetoun House

3 miles west of South Queensferry • Mid-April–late Sept Thurs–Mon 11am–5pm (last entry 1hr before closing) • Charge • ⓦ hopetoun. co.uk • Arriving on foot from South Queensferry, follow the coastline westwards for 3 miles; by car take the M90 turn-off onto the A904, from where it's signposted

Sitting in its own extensive estate on the south shore of the Forth, **Hopetoun House** is one of the most impressive stately homes in Scotland. The original house was built at the turn of the eighteenth century for the first earl of Hopetoun by Sir William Bruce, the architect of Edinburgh's Holyroodhouse. A couple of decades later, William Adam carried out an enormous extension, engulfing the structure with a curvaceous main facade and two projecting wings – superb examples of Roman Baroque pomp and swagger. Hopetoun's **architecture** is undoubtedly its most compelling feature, but the **furnishings** aren't completely overwhelmed, with some impressive seventeenth-century tapestries, Meissen porcelain and portraits by Gainsborough, Ramsay and Raeburn. The house's **grounds** include a regal driveway and some lovely walks along woodland trails and the banks of the Forth.

Inchcolm Island

From South Queensferry's Hawes Pier, just west of the rail bridge, a couple of ferry services head out to **Inchcolm Island**, located about five miles northeast of South Queensferry near the Fife shore. The island is home to the best-preserved medieval **abbey** in Scotland, founded in 1235 after King Alexander I was storm-bound on the island and took refuge in a hermit's cell. Although the structure as a whole is half-ruined, the tower, octagonal chapterhouse and echoing cloisters are intact and well worth exploring. The hour and a half you're given ashore by the boat timetables also allows time for a picnic on the abbey's lawns or the chance to explore Inchcolm's old military fortifications and extensive bird-nesting grounds.

ARRIVAL AND DEPARTURE	**INCHCOLM ISLAND**

BY BOAT
From South Queensferry The *Maid of the Forth* runs 3hr trips from Hawes Pier with landings on Inchcolm Island between April and Oct (times vary, more regular in high season; ⓦ maidoftheforth.co.uk).

From Edinburgh From Waverley Bridge, *Forth Belle* runs a 'Three bridges and Inchcolm Island' trip mid-Feb and Oct (£18 boat trip, landing fee on the island £7 extra; 3hr boat tour; ⓦ forthtours.com).

The Borders

TRAQUAIR HOUSE

The Borders

Sandwiched between the Cheviot Hills on the English border and the Pentland, Moorfoot and Lammermuir hills south of Edinburgh, the Borders is a region made up of the old shire counties of Berwick, Roxburgh, Selkirk and Peebles. Travelling from the bleak moorland of neighbouring Northumberland, you'll be struck by the green lushness of Tweeddale, whose river is the pivotal feature of the region's geography. Yet the Borders also incorporate some of the barren stretches of the Southern Uplands, with their bare, rounded peaks and weather-beaten heathery hills.

Tweeddale is the Borders at its best, with the finest section between **Melrose** and **Peebles**, where you'll find a string of attractions, from the eccentricities of Sir Walter Scott's mansion at **Abbotsford** to the intriguing Jacobite past of **Traquair House**, plus a clutch of ruined abbeys. The valley widens to the east to form the **Merse** basin, an area of rich arable lands that features a series of grand stately homes, principally **Floors Castle**, **Manderston**, **Paxton** and **Mellerstain House**, all featuring the Neoclassical work of the Adam family.

To the west, the Borders have a wilder aspect, where a series of four narrow valleys lead, up to the border with Dumfriesshire. North of the Tweed, the bleak **Lammermuir Hills** form the southern edge of Lothian and are a favourite haunt of Edinburgh-based ramblers, while further east in **Berwickshire**, especially around **St Abb's Head**, the coastline becomes more rugged, its dramatic cliffs and rocky outcrops harbouring a series of desolate ruined castles.

Brief history

The Borders' most famous sights are its **ruined abbeys**, founded under King David I (1124–53), whose policy of encouraging the monastic orders had little to do with spirituality. The monks of Kelso, Melrose, Jedburgh and Dryburgh were the frontiersmen of David's kingdom, helping advance his authority in areas of doubtful allegiance. This period of relative stability was interrupted in 1296 by the Wars of Independence with England.

From the first half of the sixteenth century until the Act of Union, the Borders again experienced turbulent times, bloodily fought over by the English and the Scots, and plagued by endless clan warfare and Reivers' raids (see page 120). Consequently, the countryside is strewn with ruined castles and keeps, while each major town celebrates its agitated past in the **Common Ridings**, when locals – especially the 'callants' (young men) – dressed in period costume ride out to check the burgh boundaries. It's a boisterous, macho business, performed with pride and matched only by the local love of **rugby union**, which reaches a crescendo with the **Melrose Sevens** tournament in April.

GETTING AROUND AND INFORMATION   THE BORDERS

By bus and train There are two train lines in the Borders: one follows the A7 southeast from Edinburgh to Galashiels; the other runs along the east coast between Edinburgh and Berwick-upon-Tweed without stopping in the Borders at all. | Travelling around by bus can take some planning, although there is a good network of bus routes linking the key towns and smaller villages – pick up timetables from the local tourist offices or consult ⓦ borderbuses.co.uk.

Eyemouth and around

The history of **EYEMOUTH**, the only settlement of any size on the Borders' coastline, is forever tied up with the sea. Its long, slender harbour remains very much the focus

MELROSE ABBEY

Highlights

❶ St Abb's Head Easily accessible, spectacular coastal scenery with sea stacks, sheer cliffs and nesting seabirds galore, all found at the point where Scotland collided with its southern neighbour over four hundred million years ago. See page 115

❷ Melrose Abbey The vast Border abbey with the best-preserved sculptural detail set within the most charming of the Border towns. Look out for the burial plot of Robert the Bruce's heart. See page 120

❸ Dawyck Botanic Garden Take an exotic hike around one of the world's finest arboreta, with

seventeenth-century origins and links to the great, global plant-hunting expeditions. See page 126

❹ Walking around Peebles The banks of the Tweed are at their most scenic around Peebles, and you can walk to medieval Neidpath Castle or the lovely Kailzie Gardens. See page 125

❺ Traquair House A romantic, castellated former hunting lodge of royalty dating back to the eleventh century. Explore the house and extensive grounds then sink a dark and spicy Jacobite ale made at the in-house brewery. See page 126

❻ Biking at Glentress and Innerleithen Eight adrenaline-pumping downhill trails through thick forest. See page 127

HIGHLIGHTS ARE MARKED ON THE MAP ON PAGE 114

of activity, its waters packed with deep-sea and inshore fleets and its quay strewn with tatters of old net, discarded fish and fish crates.

Eyemouth Museum

Auld Kirk, Manse Rd · April–Oct Mon–Sat 11am–4pm · Charge · ⓦ eyemouthmuseum.co.uk

Documenting the life and times of this small fishing community, the **Eyemouth Museum** focuses in particular on the 1881 disaster when a freak storm took the lives of 189 men, including 129 from Eyemouth, a tragedy of extraordinary proportions for a place of this size. A 15ft tapestry commemorating the event hangs in the museum along with old social and industrial memorabilia relating to farming and fishing. Regularly changing exhibitions can be found on the first floor.

Gunsgreen House

Gunsgreen Quay · April–Oct daily 11am–5pm · Charge · ⓦ gunsgreenhouse.org

Built for local merchant and smuggler John Nesbit in 1753 and styled by John Adams, this fine house contains a museum dedicated to smuggling on the first two

THE BORDERS

HIGHLIGHTS

1. St Abb's Head
2. Melrose Abbey
3. Dawyck Botanic Garden
4. Walking around Peebles
5. Traquair House
6. Biking at Glentress and Innerleithen

floors. Throughout the house are several hiding places for contraband, including the vaulted cellars and the 'tea chute' where smuggled tea was kept away from prying eyes. Gunsgreen House is at the centre of a smugglers' trail along the Berwickshire Coastal Path.

St Abb's Head

4 miles northwest of Eyemouth • Reserve year-round • Nature Centre April–Oct daily 9am–4pm • Parking charge • NTS • ⓦ nts.org.uk • From just outside the village of St Abbs, take the only single-track north and continue to the end of the road

Perhaps not suited for those without a head for heights, **St Abb's Head** rises 300ft out of the sea, its sheer cliffs providing a nesting place for great numbers of kittiwakes, guillemots, razorbills and other seabirds. Either side of the small valley you'll see different coloured rock marking a geological divide: grey sedimentary to the west and red volcanic to the east. From the car park, an easily followed, mile-long walking trail ends at a Stevenson-designed lighthouse, but you only need to take it for half a mile before being rewarded with a spectacular view of the Berwickshire coast.

Paxton House

10 miles south of Eyemouth; 5 miles west of Berwick-upon-Tweed on the B6461 • **House** April–Oct daily 1–5pm; tours 1pm, 2pm, 3pm & 4pm; 1hr • Charge • **Grounds and gardens** daily 10am–5pm • Charge • ⓦ paxtonhouse.co.uk • No. 32 bus (Mon–Fri 4 daily, Sat 3 buses; 17min) from Berwick-upon-Tweed

Overlooking the River Tweed, **Paxton House** is a perfectly proportioned Palladian mansion built for Patrick Home of Billie. It was a desperate and unsuccessful attempt to woo his Prussian lover, Sophie de Brandt, lady-in-waiting to Queen Elizabeth Christine, wife of Frederick the Great. He returned home when his mother was murdered – apparently, the butler did it – and began building Paxton in 1758 but lost interest in the project when Sophie died in the late 1760s. Patrick never moved in and sold the house unfinished to his cousin for £15,000.

The interior features a stunning collection of Chippendale furniture, commissioned by Ninian Home. The other highlight is the **Picture Gallery**, designed in 1810, with its rich Neoclassical plasterwork and changing display of works from the National Gallery of Scotland. The **grounds**, laid out by an assistant of Capability Brown, include gentle footpaths, a croquet lawn, an army-built adventure playground, a tearoom, Highland cattle, Shetland ponies, a Victorian boathouse housing a salmon-netting museum, and a hide, from where you can spy on red squirrels and woodpeckers.

Manderston House

1 mile east of Duns, signposted off the A6105 • **House** early April–late April & July–early Aug daily 1.30–5.30pm; tours 1.30pm & 3pm • Charge • **Gardens** 11.30am–dusk • Charge • ⓦ manderston.com • Bus No. 60 from Galashiels, Melrose, Berwick-upon-Tweed and Tweedmouth (Mon–Fri 9 daily; Sat–Sun 6 daily)

Manderston House encapsulates high-class living in late Victorian and Edwardian Britain. Between 1871 and 1905, the Miller family spent most of their herring and hemp fortune on turning their Georgian home into a prestigious country house. It's certainly a staggering sight, from the intricate plasterwork ceilings to the inlaid marble floor in the hall and the extravagant silver staircase. The whole is sumptuously furnished with trappings worthy of a man who had just married into the aristocracy: James Miller married Eveline Curzon, the daughter of Lord Scarsdale, in 1893. Manderston is currently the home of Lord and Lady Palmer, of Huntley & Palmers biscuits fame – hence the Biscuit Tin Museum in the house. The extensive **gardens** are noted for their courtyard stables (where the café is situated), cloistered marble dairy, mock tower house, rhododendrons and azaleas.

2

By bus Buses to Eyemouth stop in Albert St, one block south of the main shopping thoroughfare.
Destinations Berwick-upon-Tweed (every 90min, Sun 2 buses; 20min); Edinburgh (Mon–Sat 6 buses, Sun 2 buses;

2hr); St Abbs (hourly; 15min; Sun 7 buses).
Tourist information There is a visitor information centre in Eyemouth Museum, Auld Kirk, Manse Rd (April–Oct Mon–Sat 11am–4pm; ☎01890 751701).

ACCOMMODATION AND EATING

★ **Giacopazzi's** 20 Harbour Rd ⓦ giacopazzis.co.uk. There's no mistaking from the man-sized ice-cream models outside this shop that Giacopazzi's are tremendously proud of their gelati. Made daily, the ice cream is, for many, reason alone to come to Eyemouth; they also do a good fish dinner. £︎£︎

The Glenerne Guest House Albert Road ⓦ theglenerne.com. Located next to the harbour, this attractively decorated guest house offers six well-furnished rooms, one with a four-poster bed. There are lovely mature gardens and a particularly good breakfast is served. £︎£︎

The Tweed Valley

Rising in the hills far to the west, the **River Tweed** snakes its way across the Borders until it reaches the North Sea at Berwick-upon-Tweed, most of its final stretch forming the boundary between Scotland and England. This is the area known as the **Merse** (from the Old English for marsh), a flat landscape of rich farmland and wooded riverbanks where the occasional military ruin serves as a reminder of more violent days. The **Border abbeys** – perhaps the best reason for visiting the region – also lie in ruins, not because of the Reformation, but because they were burnt to the ground by the English, for whom the lower Tweed was the obvious point at which to cross the border into Scotland.

The lower Tweed has just one town of note, **Kelso**, a busy agricultural centre, with a couple of stately homes close by and a ruined abbey, the latter easily upstaged by those at **Melrose** and **Dryburgh**, further upstream. Melrose makes a great base for exploring the middle reaches of the Tweed valley. The rich, forested scenery inspired Sir Walter Scott, whose own purpose-built creation, **Abbotsford**, stands a few miles outside

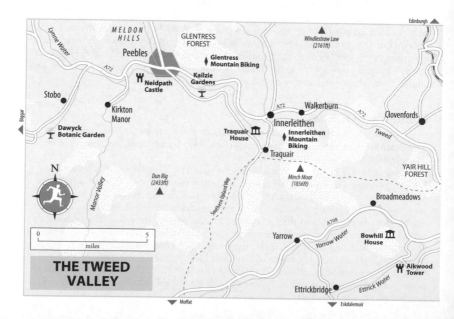

Melrose. Perhaps fortunately, Scott died before the textile boom turned his beloved **Selkirk** and **Galashiels** into mill towns. The Tweed is at its most beguiling in the stretch between Melrose and the pleasant country town of **Peebles**, when it winds through the hills past numerous stately homes, most notably **Traquair House**. Public transport is no problem, with frequent buses travelling along the valley. Just west of Peebles, the Tweed curves south towards Tweedsmuir, from where it's just a few miles further to Moffat in Dumfries and Galloway.

Kelso and around

Sir Walter Scott (see page 124) once referred to **KELSO** as the 'the most beautiful, if not the most romantic village in Scotland'. While its aesthetic powers may have diminished somewhat since Scott's days, this place retains a somewhat jaded charm thanks to its historical buildings and its position at the confluence of the Tweed and Teviot. Today's Kelso grew up in the shadow of its now-ruined Benedictine abbey, which had brought prosperity to the town until the Reformation. The town is now centred on **The Square**, an unusually large cobbled expanse a short distance from the abbey and presided over by the elegant honey-hued **Town Hall**. To one side stands the imposing *Cross Keys Hotel*, with its distinctive rooftop balustrade, and a supporting chorus of three-storey eighteenth- and nineteenth-century pastel buildings on every side. Leaving The Square along Roxburgh Street, take the alley down to the **Cobby Riverside Walk**, where a brief stroll leads to Floors Castle.

Kelso Abbey

Bridge St • April–Sept daily 9.30am–5.30pm; Oct–March Sat–Wed 10am–4pm; last entry 30min before closing • Free • HES • ⓦ historicenvironment.scot

Once the richest and most powerful abbey in the Borders, **Kelso Abbey** was savaged by the English three times in the sixteenth century: the last (and by far the worst) assault was part of the 'Rough Wooing' (see page 563). Such was the extent of the devastation – further compounded by the Reformation – that less survives of

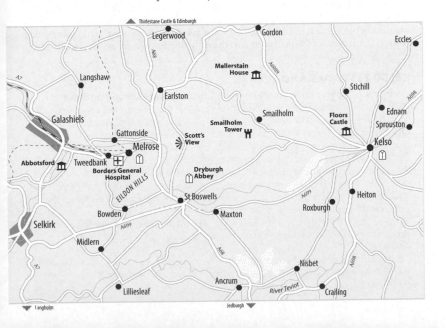

Kelso than any of the other Border abbeys. Nevertheless, at first sight it looks pretty impressive, with the heavy Norman west end of the abbey church almost entirely intact. Beyond, little remains, though it is possible to make out the two transepts and towers that gave the abbey the shape of a double cross, unique in Scotland.

Floors Castle

One mile northwest of Kelso; • **Castle** April–Sept daily 10.30am–5pm; last entry 1hr before closing • Charge • **Gardens and grounds** daily April–Sept 10.30am–5pm; Oct–March 10.30am–4pm • Charge • Ⓦ floorscastle.com • From The Square, follow Roxburgh St to the entrance gate on the outskirts of town, or walk from town centre along Cobby Riverside Walk

From Kelso's handsome bridge over the Tweed, you can easily make out the pepper-pot turrets and castellations of **Floors Castle**, the country's largest inhabited building. Designed by William Adam in the 1720s for the first Duke of Roxburghe, the interior still demonstrates his uncluttered style, despite some Victorian modifications, while the superb views from the windows give the place an airy feel. Floors remains the home of the Duke of Roxburghe – his imperious features can be seen in a variety of portraits and photos around the house – so you get to see only ten rooms and the basement. In 1903, the eighth duke married Mary Goelet, the wealthiest heiress in America at the time, and the **paintings**, by Matisse, Augustus John and Odilon Redon, as well as the Brussels and Gobelin **tapestries** she carried off from her family home, are now the castle's highlights. There's an above-average **café**, and you can wander down to the Tweed and see the holly tree that marks the spot where James II was killed by an exploding cannon during the siege of Roxburgh Castle. His son, also James, was crowned James III at the age of 9 at Kelso Abbey.

Mellerstain House

6 miles northwest of Kelso, signposted off the A6089 • May–Sept Fri–Mon 11am–4pm • Charge • Ⓦ mellerstain.com

Mellerstain House represents the very finest of the Adam family's work: William designed the wings in 1725, and his son Robert the main mansion house fifty years later. Inside, it has an elegant, domestic air, lacking in pomposity. Robert Adam's love of columns, delicate roundels and friezes culminates in a stunning sequence of plaster-moulded, pastel-shaded ceilings, which still preserve the original colours; the **library** is the architectural highlight, with four unusual long panels in plaster relief of classical scenes relegating the books to second place. Perhaps the most intriguing Adam creation is the bathroom in the basement, the only one known to have been designed

---

KELSO FESTIVALS AND EVENTS

In Springwood Park during one weekend in mid-June, the **Border Union Dog Show** (Ⓦ borderunion.co.uk), a canine festival and Crufts qualifier, takes place. Over a hundred horse riders in period regalia canter cross-country from Kelso to Yetholm and back for the **Civic Week Sat** (Ⓦ kelsocivicweek.co.uk), a Borders tradition in mid-July. Prior to the ride there are week-long festivities including a ceilidh, fireworks and a torch-lit procession. Also held annually in Springwood Park on the last Friday and Saturday in July is the Border Union Show, a genuine traditional agricultural show that features all manner of livestock from horses and ponies, sheep and cattle to donkeys, goats, poultry and rabbits. There are stands for machinery, crafts, gifts and country clothing; some fifty stands showcase produce from the Borders and beyond, plus there's a children's fun fair.

During September to May at Golf Course Road just north of town, the **Kelso Races** (Ⓦ kelso-races.co.uk) feature a small-jump horse racing circuit with race meets mostly at weekends.

On the last Saturday of each month Kelso hosts a small but appealing farmers' market in the main square with a range of stalls selling fantastic picnic food, like artisan goat's cheese and crusty bread.

by him. Notable among the paintings are works by Constable, Gainsborough, Ramsay and Veronese. The house remains the home of the Earl of Haddington, descendant of the Baillie family who acquired the estate in 1642. After the tour you can wander the formal Edwardian gardens, which slope down to the lake, or venture further afield to the Fairy Glen. There's also a children's play area and an excellent café.

Smailholm Tower

Sandyknowe Farm; signposted from Smailholm village and 7 miles west of Kelso • April–Sept daily 9.30am–5.30pm; last entry 30min before closing • Charge • HES • ⓦ historicenvironment.scot

Perched alone on a remote rocky outcrop, craggy and evocative **Smailholm Tower** inspired Walter Scott, and conjures up the era of Reivers' raids and border skirmishes. The fifteenth-century tower was designed to withstand sudden attack: the rough rubble walls are 6ft thick and both the entrance – once guarded by a heavy door plus an iron yett (gate) – and the windows are disproportionately small. Inside, make your way up to the roof, where two narrow **wall-walks**, jammed against the barrel-vaulted roof and the crow-stepped gables, provide panoramic views. On the north side, the watchman's seat has also survived, stuck against the chimney stack for warmth and with a recess for a lantern.

2

ARRIVAL AND INFORMATION   KELSO AND AROUND

By bus Buses arrive at the covered stop on Horsemarket, the road leading off from The Square.

Destinations Berwick-upon-Tweed (Mon–Sat 8 daily, 5 on Sun; 50min); Galashiels (Mon–Sat 8 daily, 5 on Sun; 50min); Hawick (Mon–Fri 5 daily, 3 on Sat, 4 on Sun; 55min); Jedburgh (Mon–Fri 8 daily, 3 on Sat, 4 on Sun; 25min); Melrose (Mon–Sat 8 daily; 5 on Sun; 30min).

Tourist Information There is no longer a tourist office in Kelso but ⓦ visitkelso.com is a good online resource.

ACCOMMODATION, EATING AND DRINKING

The Central Guesthouse 51 The Square ⓦ thecentralguesthousekelso.co.uk. Excellent, self-catering accommodation in the shape of a mix of double and twin en-suite rooms contained within one flat, so can be rented whole if desired; some rooms have basic kitchen facilities such as kettle, toaster and fridge. **££**

Cobbles Inn 7 Bowmont St ⓦ cobbleskelso.co.uk. This pub has a formidable reputation locally, not just for real ales (supplied by the proprietor's own brewery, Tempest) but also for its top-notch gastro-cuisine. The dinner menu reflects the produce of the region, with dishes like wild wood pigeon, rabbit and the well-loved fish soup, Cullen skink. Less formal bar meals are also available, including fish and chips. **££**

★ **The Old Priory** Woodmarket ⓦ theoldpriorykelso. com. Just off The Square, this is a beautifully furnished Georgian townhouse, full of lived-in character, and with a lush garden out back. There are two double rooms, the best of which overlooks the garden, as well as a two-room connected family suite. **££**

★ **Rutherfords Micropub** 38 The Square ⓦ rutherfords-micropub.co.uk. Fiercely proud of its status as Scotland's 'first micropub', the ethos here is all about back-to-basics drinking. No TVs or fruit machines (slot machines) here; just quality craft ales poured straight from the cask, artisan gin on tap and handmade pork pies.

SHOPPING

Kelso Pottery The Knowes; across the graveyard from Kelso Abbey to the east ☎ 01573 224027. Run by Ian and Elizabeth Hird, who use differing colours of local clay to make a variety of objects, including 'Time Tablets', using patterns from other countries, all wrapped in dried local vegetation and fired in their large outdoor pit kiln.

Melrose and around

Tucked in between the Tweed and the gorse-backed Eildon Hills, minuscule **MELROSE** is one of the most appealing towns in the Borders. Centred on its busy little market square, its narrow streets are trimmed by a harmonious ensemble of styles, from pretty little cottages and tweedy shops to high-standing Georgian and Victorian facades. Its chief draw is its ruined **abbey**, by far the finest of the Border abbeys, but it's also perfectly positioned for exploring the Tweed valley. Most of the year it's a sleepy little town, but as the birthplace in 1883 of the **Rugby Sevens** (seven-a-side games; see page

121), it swarms during Sevens Week (second week in April) and during the **Borders Book Festival** in mid-June.

Melrose Abbey

Abbey St • Daily April–Sept 10am–5pm; Oct–March 10am–4pm • Charge • HES • Ⓦ historicenvironment.scot

The pink- and red-tinted stone ruins of **Melrose Abbey** soar above their riverside surroundings. Founded in 1136 by King David I, Melrose was the first Cistercian settlement in Scotland and grew rich selling wool and hides to Flanders. However, its prosperity was fragile, the English repeatedly razed Melrose, most viciously under Richard II in 1385 and the Earl of Hertford in 1545. Most of the present remains date from the intervening period, when extensive rebuilding abandoned the original Cistercian austerity for an elaborate, Gothic-style inspired by the abbeys of northern England.

The site is dominated by the **Abbey Church**, which has lost its west front, and whose nave is reduced to the elegant window arches and chapels of the south aisle. Amazingly, the stone **pulpitum** (screen), separating the choir monks from their lay brothers, is preserved. Beyond, the **presbytery** has its magnificent perpendicular window, lierne vaulting and ceiling bosses intact, with the most intricate of curly kale carving on the supporting columns, while in the **south transept**, another fine fifteenth-century window sprouts yet more delicate, foliate tracery. This kind of finely carved detail is repeated everywhere you look. Outside, the exterior sculpture is even more impressive: crouching figures holding scrolls bearing inscriptions such as 'He suffered because he willed it'. Elsewhere, look for the numerous mischievous **gargoyles**, from peculiar crouching beasts to the pig playing the bagpipes on the roof on the south side of the nave. The abbey's greatest claim to fame, however, is that this is where the heart of Robert the Bruce is held (see page 122).

Commendator's House

The paltry ruins of Melrose's abbey continue across Cloisters Road where they edge on to the **Commendator's House** (same hours as the abbey), a lovely red-sandstone

---

THE BORDER REIVERS

From the thirteenth to the early seventeenth centuries, the wild, inhospitable border country stretching from the Solway Firth in the west to the Tweed valley in the east, well away from the power bases of both the Scottish and English monarchs, was overrun by outlaws known as the **Border Reivers**, *reive* being a Scots word for plunder. As George MacDonald Fraser put it in his book *The Steel Bonnets*, 'The great border tribes of both Scotland and England feuded continuously among themselves. Robbery and blackmail were everyday professions; raiding, arson, kidnapping, murder and extortion were an accepted part of the social system'. This, then, was no cross-border dispute, but an open struggle for power among Borders folk. Those who 'shook loose the Border' included people from all walks of life – agricultural labourers, gentleman farmers, smallholders, even peers of the realm – for whom theft, raiding, tracking and ambush became second nature.

The source of this behaviour was the destruction and devastation wrought upon the region by virtually continual warfare between England and Scotland, and the 'slash and burn' policy of the era. With many residents no longer able to find sustenance from the land, crime became the only way to survive. Cattle-rustling, blackmail and kidnapping led to an anarchical mindset, where feuding families would habitually wreak havoc and devastation on each other.

The legacy of the Border Reivers can still be seen today in the region's fortified farms and churches; in the **Common Riding** traditions of many border towns; in the great family names such as Armstrong, Graham, Kerr and Nixon, which once filled the hearts of Borderers with dread; and in the language – the words 'blackmail' (first used to describe the protection money paid by farmers to the local clan chiefs) and 'bereaved' (originally referred to being robbed) have their roots in the mayhem of this period.

RUGBY SEVENS

With a surprisingly long lineage, **seven-a-side rugby** was initially conceived by a pair of Melrose butchers in 1883 as a fundraiser for their local club and quickly became a regional obsession. Nowadays, all the main Borders towns (and a few beyond) take on a kind of carnival atmosphere as they take turns to host one of ten all-day **tournaments** between April and May, with twelve teams competing for the 'Kings of the Sevens' crown. See Ⓦ K7s.co.uk.

2

building converted into a private house in 1590 by the abbey's last commendator, and now housing a modest collection of ecclesiastical bric-a-brac. Beyond the house is the mill lade, where water used to flow in order to power the abbey's mills; it was also diverted to flush the monks' latrines.

Priorwood Garden

Abbey St • April–Oct daily 10am–5pm • Free • NTS • Ⓦ nts.org.uk

As well as the kempt flower and herb borders, **Priorwood Garden** features a heritage apple orchard, beautifully set within the garden's walled confines with Melrose Abbey standing tall beyond. Unique for its focus on growing flowers for drying, the shop here sells some of the produce that you'll see in the drying area en route to the garden.

Harmony Garden

St Mary's Rd • April–Oct daily 10am–5pm • Free • NTS • Ⓦ nts.org.uk

More of a pleasant picnic spot than an exotic botanical experience, **Harmony Garden** is as memorable for its setting as for its plants. Its roomy croquet lawn lies before the garden's Georgian villa while the borders and vegetable plots form a seductive foreground to the abbey and Eildon Hills, which rise beyond the garden walls.

Dryburgh Abbey

Dryburgh village, 6 miles southeast of Melrose, off the B6356 • daily 10am–4pm • Charge • HFS • Ⓦ historicenvironment.scot

Hidden away in a u-shaped bend in the Tweed, the remains of **Dryburgh Abbey** occupy an idyllic position against a hilly backdrop, with ancient cedars, redwoods, beech and lime trees and wide lawns flattering the pinkish-red hues of the stonework. The Premonstratensians, or White Canons, founded the abbey in the twelfth century, but they were never as successful – or apparently as devout – as their Cistercian neighbours in Melrose. Their chronicles detail interminable disputes about land and money: one story relates how a fourteenth-century canon called Marcus flattened the abbot with his fist.

The romantic setting is second to none, but the ruins of the **Abbey Church** are much less substantial than, say, at Melrose or Jedburgh. Virtually nothing survives of the nave, but the transepts have fared better, their chapels now serving as private burial grounds for, among others, **Sir Walter Scott** and Field Marshal Haig.

Scott's View

Drivers and cyclists should approach the abbey via the much-visited **Scott's View**, to the north on the B6356, overlooking the Tweed valley, where the writer and his friends often picnicked and where Scott's horse stopped out of habit during the writer's own funeral procession. The scene inspired J.M.W. Turner's *Melrose* (1831), now on display in the National Gallery of Scotland (see page 77).

Abbotsford

B6360, 2 miles west of Melrose • Daily April–Oct 10am–5pm; Nov & March 10am–4pm • **House, Chapel & Gardens or Gardens** only • Charge • Ⓦ scottsabbotsford.com

A stately home designed to satisfy the romantic inclinations of Sir Walter Scott, **Abbotsford** was home to the writer from 1812 until his death twenty years later. Built

2

THE HEART OF ROBERT THE BRUCE

Legend has it that the heart of **Robert I** is buried at Melrose Abbey (his body having been buried at Dunfermline Abbey), and in 1997, when a heart cask was publicly exhumed, this theory received an unexpected boost. However, the burial location was not in accordance with Bruce's own wishes. In 1329, the dying king told his friend, Sir James Douglas, to carry his heart on a Crusade to the Holy Land in fulfilment of an old vow: 'Seeing therefore, that my body cannot go to achieve what my heart desires, I will send my heart instead of my body, to accomplish my vow'. Douglas tried his best, but was killed fighting the Moors in Spain – and Bruce's heart ended up in Melrose. A commemorative stone laid in 1998 marks its current resting place in the chapterhouse, north of the sacristy.

on the site of a farmhouse Scott bought and subsequently demolished, Abbotsford (as Scott chose to call it) took twelve years to evolve, with the fanciful turrets and castellations of the Scots Baronial exterior incorporating copies of medieval originals: the entrance porch imitates that of Linlithgow Palace and the screen wall in the garden echoes Melrose Abbey's cloister. Scott was proud of his *folie de grandeur*, writing to a friend, 'It is a kind of Conundrum Castle to be sure, … it pleases a fantastic person in the style and manner of its architecture and decoration'. That said, it was undoubtedly one of the chief causes of Scott's subsequent bankruptcy.

Despite all the exterior pomp, the interior is surprisingly small and poky, with just six rooms open for viewing on the upper floor. Visitors start in the wood-panelled **study**, with its small writing desk made of salvage from the Spanish Armada at which Scott churned out the Waverley novels at a furious rate. The heavy wood-panelled **library** contains Scott's collection of more than nine thousand rare books and an extraordinary assortment of memorabilia, the centrepiece of which is Napoleon's pen case and blotting book. Also here are Rob Roy's purse and *skene dhu* (knife), a lock of Nelson's hair – and of Bonnie Prince Charlie's – plus the latter's *quaich* (drinking cup), Flora Macdonald's pocketbook, the inlaid pearl crucifix that accompanied Mary, Queen of Scots, to the scaffold and even a piece of oatcake found in the pocket of a dead Highlander at Culloden. You can also see Henry Raeburn's famous portrait of Scott in the **drawing room**, and all sorts of weapons – notably Rob Roy's sword, dagger and gun – in the **armoury**. In the barbaric-looking **entrance hall**, hung with elk and wild cattle skulls, and spoils gathered from the battlefield of Waterloo by Scott himself, is a model of the skull of Robert the Bruce and some of Scott's dandyish clothes.

Thirlestane Castle

B6362, Lauder • May–Sept Tues–Sun 10am–4pm • Charge • **Tours** 10.30am, 12.30pm & 2.30pm; 90min • Charge • Ⓦ thirlestanecastle. co.uk • Take the signposted footpath from the main square in Lauder

Located ten miles north of Melrose is **Thirlestane Castle**, an imposing Scots Baronial pile with reddish turrets and castellated towers. Begun by John Maitland in the late sixteenth century, when he became Lord Chancellor of Scotland, and still owned by the family, the castle's somewhat undistinguished interior is redeemed by the extravagant plasterwork of the Restoration ceilings and a wealth of domestic detail from the Victorian period, including a wonderland of children's toys. There's also an adventure playground for those with children, and a woodland walk.

ARRIVAL AND INFORMATION
MELROSE AND AROUND

By bus Buses to Melrose stop in Buccleuch St, a few paces from the abbey ruins.

Destinations Berwick-upon-Tweed (Mon–Fri 8 daily, 7 on Sat, 5 on Sun; 1hr 10min); Duns (Mon–Fri 8 daily, 6 on Sat, 5 on Sun; 50min); Edinburgh (Mon–Sat every 30min, Sun hourly; 2hr 20min); Galashiels (Mon–Sat every 30min, Sun hourly; 20min); Kelso (Mon–Sat 8 daily, 5 on Sun; 30min); Jedburgh (Mon–Sat 8 daily, 1 on Sun; 40min); Peebles (Mon–Sat every 30min, Sun hourly; 1hr 10min).

Tourist information There is no tourist office in town

but several local attractions belong to the VisitScotland Information Partner (VIP) programme including Melrose Abbey and Abbotsford House where leaflets are available.

ACCOMMODATION

Gibson Caravan Park Gibson Park; off the B6374 just west of the centre ⓦcaravanclub.co.uk. This lovely, central little campsite opposite the rugby ground caters mostly to caravans although tents are welcome too. **£**

Harleyburn Coach House Chiefswood Rd ⓦharleyburn.com. Super high-quality B&B with two spotless modern bedrooms and en suites, recommended for its warm hospitality and first-class breakfasts, served on the terrace in summer. They've also got two cosy, very reasonably priced cottages, sleeping three and five. It's in a good location for walkers and cyclists. **££**

Townhouse Market Square ⓦthetownhousemelrose. co.uk. Upmarket, central hotel with tasteful, modern decor and generously proportioned en-suite rooms that come in single, double and family sizes. Avoid the street-facing suites to ensure a peaceful night's sleep. **£££**

EATING AND DRINKING

★**Abbey Fine Wines** 17 Market Square ⓦabbeyfinewines.co.uk. Stocking the finest range of wines and spirits in the Borders, there are always bottles opened and ready for sampling here. You can pick any bottle you fancy and enjoy it in the café at the back of the shop with a cheese platter.

The Hoebridge Hoebridge Rd East, Gattonside; 500yd past Melrose Abbey and across the old suspension bridge ⓦthehoebridge.com. Once a bobbin mill, this restaurant retains a timeless charm thanks to its deep rubble walls and simple furnishings. Its menu offers some European-style choices using Scots produce such as roast lamb rump, polenta fries, cauliflower with mint and caper dressing. **£££**

Marmion's Brasserie Buccleuch St ⓦmarmionsbrasserie.co.uk. While this popular all-day bistro might have overdone it a bit with pine cladding, it still manages to conjure up a peppy atmosphere of an evening. The menu offers plenty of choice: dependable meat dishes as well as a surprisingly adventurous selection of vegetarian mains like the Mediterranean vegetables and stuffed baked aubergine. **£££**

Ship Inn East Port ⓦshipinnmelrose.co.uk. The liveliest pub in town, especially on certain Saturday afternoons when Melrose rugby supporters file in before and after the games. While it could certainly do with some redecoration, its saving grace is the beer garden out back. **££**

ENTERTAINMENT

The Wynd 7 The Wynd, Buccleuch St ⓦsites.google. com/site/thewyndtheatre. Melrose's very own pint-sized theatre, tucked away down an alleyway, north off the main square, shows films and puts on classic, jazz and folk concerts as well as live drama.

WALKING IN THE EILDON HILLS

Ordnance Survey Explorer map 338

From the centre of Melrose, it's a vigorous three-mile walk to the top of the **Eildon Hills**, whose triple volcanic peaks are the Central Borders' most distinctive landmark. You can download a map detailing the hike, which begins about 90yd south of, and up the hill from, the Market Square, along the B6359 to Lilliesleaf (ⓦwalkscottishborders.com/route/eildon-hills-path).

The hills have been associated with all sorts of legends, beginning with tales of their creation by the wizard-cum-alchemist Michael Scott (1175–1230) who, in the words of Sir Walter Scott, 'cleft Eildon hills in three'. It was here that the mystic **Thomas the Rhymer** received the gift of prophecy from the Faerie Queen, and Arthur and his knights are reckoned to lie asleep deep within the hills, victims of a powerful spell. The ancient Celts, who revered the number three, also considered the site a holy place and maintained their settlements on the slopes long after the Romans' departure.

Melrose is also the starting point for the popular **St Cuthbert's Way**, a sixty-mile walk which finishes at Lindisfarne (Holy Island) on the Northumbrian coast. The trail is well marked by yellow arrows from the abbey up over the Eildons to the pretty village of **Bowden**, where you can make a detour to see a twelfth-century kirk, half a mile down the hill from the square, and browse second-hand books and get a fine home-made tea at *The Old School*.

SIR WALTER SCOTT

Walter Scott (1771–1832) was born to a solidly bourgeois family in Edinburgh. Crippled by polio, he was sent by his parents to recuperate at his grandfather's farm in Smailholm, where the boy's imagination was fired by his relatives' tales of derring-do, the violent history of the Borders retold amid the rugged landscape that he spent long summer days exploring. Throughout the 1790s he transcribed hundreds of old Border ballads, publishing a three-volume collection entitled *Minstrelsy of the Scottish Borders* in 1802. An instant success, *Minstrelsy* was followed by Scott's own *Lay of the Last Minstrel*, a narrative poem whose strong story and rose-tinted regionalism proved very popular.

More **poetry** was to come, most successfully *Marmion* (1808) and *The Lady of the Lake* (1810), not to mention an eighteen-volume edition of the works of John Dryden and nineteen volumes of Jonathan Swift. However, despite having two paid jobs, one as **Sheriff-Depute** of Selkirkshire, the other as clerk to the Court of Session in Edinburgh, his finances remained shaky.

From 1813, Scott was writing to pay the bills and poured out a veritable flood of **historical novels** using his extensive knowledge of Scottish history and folklore. He produced his best work within the space of ten years: *Waverley* (1814), *The Antiquary* (1816), *Rob Roy* and *The Heart of Midlothian* (both 1818), as well as two notable novels set in England, *Ivanhoe* (1819) and *Kenilworth* (1821). In 1824, he returned to Scottish tales with *Redgauntlet*, the last of his quality work. As Scott's financial problems increased, the quality of his writing deteriorated, and the effort broke his health. His last years were plagued by illness, and in 1832 he died at Abbotsford and was buried at Dryburgh Abbey (see page 121).

Although Scott's interests were diverse, his historical novels focused mostly on the Jacobites, whose loyalty to the Stewarts had riven Scotland since the 'Glorious Revolution' of 1688. That the nation was prepared to be entertained by such tales was essentially a matter of timing: by the 1760s it was clear that the Jacobite cause was lost for good and Scotland, emerging from its isolated medievalism, had been firmly welded into the United Kingdom. Thus its turbulent history and independent spirit were safely in the past, and ripe for romancing – as shown by the arrival of King George IV in Edinburgh during 1822 decked out in Highland dress. Yet for Sir Walter the romance was tinged with a genuine sense of loss. Loyal to the Hanoverians, he still grieved for Bonnie Prince Charlie; he welcomed a commercial Scotland but lamented the passing of feudal ties, and so his heroes are transitional, fighting men of action superseded by bourgeois figures searching for a clear identity.

Galashiels

In a tour of the region, it's hard to avoid going through 'Gala', a hard-working textile town four miles west of Melrose whose grey-green workers' terraces spread along the valley of the Gala Water near its junction with the Tweed. Hopes for a return to prosperous times were given a much-needed boost after the 2015 opening of the Borders Railway, re-linking Gala with Edinburgh after a 45-year hiatus. Its main street runs parallel with the river, the southern end cheered by a melodramatic equestrian statue of a Border Reiver above the town's war memorial. The long-demolished New Gala House, a mansion that stood at the top of the town, was taken over during World War II by Edinburgh girls' school, **St Trinnean's**; the artist Ronald Searle met two of the pupils in 1941, inspiration for the unruly schoolgirls in his St Trinian's novels.

ARRIVAL AND INFORMATION   GALASHIELS

By train The train station is just east of the town centre, across the river beside the A7.

Destination Edinburgh (Mon–Sat every 30min, Sun 1 hourly; 50min).

By bus The region's principal bus station is just east of the town centre, across the river and near the train station.

Destinations Edinburgh (Mon–Sat every 30min, Sun 1 hourly; 2hr); Peebles (Mon–Sat 2 hourly, 1 on Sun; 40min); Hawick (Mon–Sat 2 hourly, 1 on Sun; 35min); Jedburgh (Mon–Sat 8 daily, 1 on Sun; 50min); Kelso (Mon–Sat 8 daily,

5 on Sun; 55min); Langholm (Mon–Sat 1 hourly, 4 on Sun; 1hr 15min); Melrose (Mon–Sat 2 hourly, 1 on Sun; 20min); Selkirk (Mon–Sat 2 hourly, 1 on Sun; 15min).
Tourist information There's no tourist office in town, but there are plenty of leaflets at the library (Lawyers Brae, south of the river; Mon & Fri 9.30am–5pm, Tues 9.30am–6pm, Wed 9.30am–4pm; ☎ 01896 664170).

Peebles and around

Fast, wide, tree-lined and fringed with grassy banks, the Tweed looks at its best at **PEEBLES**, a handsome royal burgh that sits on the north bank, 22 miles due south of the capital. The town has a genteel, relaxed air, its wide, handsome High Street bordered by houses in a medley of architectural styles, mostly dating from Victorian times. A steady stream of day-trippers from the capital, as well as the large population of commuter locals, makes this an affluent place; consequently, there are plenty of enticing shops, restaurants and tearooms.

Nearby, hills, drove roads and a disused railway line make this a perfect starting point for easy-going treks into the lush green landscape. Upstream from Peebles the Tweed gradually narrows as the hills tighten up on either side and settlements become small and sparse. Lush fields and deciduous trees thrive in the valley floor while the surrounding high peaks offer a foreboding blanket of heather interrupted frequently by over-regular spruce plantations.

Old Parish Church

High St • Daily 10am–4pm • Free • ⓦ topcop.org.uk

The soaring crown spire of the **Old Parish Church** rises up at the western end of the High Street and, inside, the church has some unusual features such as the elegant oak, bronze and engraved-glass entrance screen and 22 modern oil paintings illustrating the Scriptures. Suspended from the ceiling are tattered Napoleonic flags, emblems of 1816, the year the Peebleshire Militia disbanded.

Tweeddale Museum and Gallery

Chambers Institute, High St • Mon, Tues, Fri & Sat 10am–3pm, Thurs 10am–5pm • Free • ⓦ liveborders.org.uk

Housed in the Chambers Institute, presented to the town by local worthy William Chambers in 1859, the **Tweeddale Museum and Gallery** is dedicated to the enlightenment of his neighbours. The benefactor stuffed the place with casts of the world's most famous sculptures and, although most were lost long ago, today's 'Secret Room', once the Museum Room, contains two handsome friezes: one a copy of the Elgin marbles taken from the Parthenon; the other of the Triumph of Alexander, originally cast in 1812 to honour Napoleon.

WALKS AROUND PEEBLES

Ordnance Survey Explorer maps 337 and 338

A series of footpaths snakes through the rough-edged burns, bare peaks and deep wooded hills of the surrounding Peebles. The five-mile **Sware Trail** is one of the easiest and most scenic, weaving west along the north bank of the river and looping back to the south. On the way, it passes **Neidpath Castle**, a gaunt medieval tower house perched high above the river on a rocky bluff. The walk also goes by the splendid skew rail bridge, part of the Glasgow line, which was finished in 1850 and closed in 1969. Other, longer footpaths follow the old drove roads, like the thirteen-mile haul to **St Mary's Loch** or the fourteen-mile route to Selkirk via Traquair House (see page 126). For either of these, you'll need an Ordnance Survey map, a compass and proper hiking gear, while for a gentler stroll there's a three-mile amble downstream on the Tweed's southern banks which takes you to the privately owned **Kailzie Gardens**.

2

Dawyck Botanic Garden

Stobo, 8 miles southwest of Peebles on the B712 • Daily Feb, March & Nov 10am–4pm; April–Oct until 5pm • Charge • Ⓦ rbge.org.uk

An outstation of the Royal Botanic Garden in Edinburgh, the masterpiece of seventeenth-century horticultural passion and creativity that is **Dawyck Botanic Garden** ranks among the world's finest arboreta. Hosting species from climatically similar corners of the globe, the 65-acre garden was the culmination of early plant-hunting expeditions, particularly those by David Douglas (of Douglas fir fame). One of the best times to visit is in spring, when, as you enter the garden through the ultra-modern visitor centre, you're welcomed by the feast that is the Azalea Walk in full bloom. Over the brow of the hill, 300-year-old redwoods tower over a gushing burn that feeds the roots of gigantic gunnera plants. In autumn, sorbis and acers mount a flaring foliage of reds, oranges and yellows.

Kailzie Gardens

3 miles east of Peebles on the B7062 • Daily April–Oct 10am–5pm; Nov–March dawn–dusk • Charge • Ⓦ kailziegardens.com

Kailzie Gardens encompasses fifteen acres of pleasant, partly formal gardens including a burnside walk, a fishable pond, a delightful walled garden (not open in winter), and a pleasant wood-panelled tearoom. In the dedicated viewing hut, you can watch live CCTV pictures of the ospreys (£1.50) that have been successfully introduced into the nearby forest.

Robert Smail's Printing Works

High St, Innerleithen, 7 miles east of Peebles on the A72 • April–Oct Fri–Mon 10.30am–5pm; tours 1hr • Charge • NTS • Ⓦ nts.org.uk

Little changed since its establishment in 1866, **Robert Smail's Printing Works** is now a living, working museum, offering an enjoyable insight into the world of Victorian printing. Originally powered by watermill, the great machines' huge belts and flywheels are now electrically powered, about the only concession to progress here. Tours also take in the case room upstairs where you get the chance to set and print your own block. Most fascinating of all, however, is the archive of every single job the Smails printed for nearly a hundred years as well as wage books, ledgers and other ephemera.

Traquair House

7 miles southeast of Peebles on the B7062 • Daily April–Sept 11am–5pm; July & Aug 10am–5pm; Oct 11am–4pm; Nov Sat & Sun 11am–3pm • Charge • Ⓦ traquair.co.uk

Peeping out from the trees just south of Innerleithen, **Traquair House** is the oldest continuously inhabited house in Scotland, with the present line of owners – the Maxwell Stuarts – having lived here since 1491. The first laird of Traquair inherited an elementary fortified tower, which his powerful descendants gradually converted into a mansion that was visited, it is said, by 27 monarchs, including Mary, Queen of Scots.

Traquair's main appeal is in its ancient shape and structure. The whitewashed facade is strikingly handsome, with narrow windows and trim turrets surrounding the tiniest of front doors. Inside, you can see the original vaulted cellars, where locals once hid their cattle from raiders, and the twisting main staircase as well as the earlier medieval version, later a secret escape route for persecuted Catholics until the Emancipation Act freed things up in 1829. Of the furniture and fittings, it's not any particular piece that impresses, but rather the accumulation of family possessions and revealing letters that give a real insight into the Maxwell Stuarts' revolving-door fortunes and eccentricities. In the **museum room** is a wealth of treasures, including a rosary and crucifix owned by Mary, Queen of Scots and the cloak worn by the Earl of Nithsdale during his dramatic escape from the Tower of London, where he was under sentence of death for his part in the Jacobite Rising of 1715. The earl was saved by his wife who got his jailers drunk and smuggled him out disguised as a maid in spite of his red beard.

It's worth sparing time for the surrounding **gardens**, where you'll find a **hedge maze**, several craft workshops and the **Traquair House Brewery** dating back to 1566, which was revived in 1965 and claims to be the only British brewery that still ferments totally in oak. You can learn about the brewery and taste the ales in the Brewery Shop.

There's also an attractive café serving above-average snacks in an estate cottage on the redundant avenue, which leads to the locked **Bear Gates**; Bonnie Prince Charlie departed the house through the gates, and the then-owner promised to keep them locked until a Stuart should ascend the throne.

ARRIVAL AND DEPARTURE

By bus The bus terminal is next to the main car park just north of the eastern end of the main shopping street.

Destinations Edinburgh (2 hourly, 1 on Sun; 1hr); Galashiels (2 hourly, 1 on Sun; 40min); Melrose (2 hourly, 1 on Sun; 1hr).

2

ACCOMMODATION

Glentress Forest Lodges The Peel Gateway, entrance to Glentress, 2 miles east of Peebles on the A72 ⓦ glentressforestlodges.co.uk. Like sections of upturned boat hulls, these simple but attractive wooden huts are arranged in clusters, somehow resembling a prehistoric settlement. The accommodation is basic; some benches to sit/sleep on, a door and a window, but there's also a communal kitchen and a generous firewood supply. They all sleep three comfortably, five at a push. Tents and motorhomes welcome too. **£**

Green Tree Hotel 41 Eastgate ☎ 01721 720582. An economical option in the heart of town, between the bus station and the High St, with a choice of singles, doubles and family rooms. All are perfectly comfortable with simple decor and come with en suite and breakfast included. **££**

Kingsmuir House Springhill Rd ⓦ kingsmuirhouse. co.uk. Dating from the 1850s, this generously proportioned villa offers two exemplary guest rooms with well-coordinated decor and traditional furnishings; just 2min from the main drag and overlooking Victoria Park across the Tweed from the centre. **£££**

Rosetta Holiday Park Rosetta Rd ⓦ www. rosettaholidaypark.com. The only campsite in Peebles not next to a main road, it's peacefully set on the northwest edge of town, surrounded by mature woods, with hikeable drove roads up the Meldon Hills starting almost from the site entrance. There's a bar that serves food in the evenings, and, for kids, a TV/pool room as well as a walled playground. **£**

Traquair 7 miles east of Peebles, on the B7062 ⓦ traquair.co.uk. Most visitors come here as a day-trip from Peebles, but if you're really taken by the place, you can stay in one of its three double guest rooms (blue, pink and white), exquisitely decked out with antiques and four-posters, on a bed-and-breakfast basis. **££££**

EATING AND DRINKING

★ **Bridge Inn** 72 Port Brae ⓦ thebridgeinnpeebles. co.uk. With its attractive mock-Tudor, dormer frontage, this traditional pub cuts a fine figure in the Peebles skyline. Inside, its classic decor and cosy seating arrangements complement the wide range of real ales and whiskies on offer while out back there's a sunny terrace looking on to the river. **££**

★ **Cocoa Black Chocolate Shop and Café** 1–3 Cuddybridge ⓦ cocoablack.com. This is the place for chocoholics but also for lovers of coffee, tea, cakes and

---

MOUNTAIN BIKING IN GLENTRESS FOREST AND INNERLEITHEN

Glentress Forest, two miles east of Peebles on the A72, has some of the best opportunities for mountain biking in Scotland. Not only are there five superb, carefully crafted, purpose-built trails, colour-coded for difficulty, there's a fantastic bike centre at the entrance to the forest called the **Peel Gateway**. This is a great place for mountain bikers, with changing rooms and showers, a café and a shop filled with spares as well as bike rental from Alpine Bikes. If you fancy staying several days it's worth checking out the timber wigwams near the entrance. There are more trails just a few miles southeast of Glentress near **Innerleithen**, geared towards more advanced riders. Glentress and Innerleithen are collectively one of eight forest biking centres in southern Scotland, known collectively as the **7stanes** (ⓦ forestryandland. gov.scot).

BIKE RENTAL

Bike hire can be pricey hereabouts, ranging from £30 to £100 per day for an e-bike although child bikes are just £20. Alpine Bikes has a centre at the entrance to **Glentress Forest**, two miles east of Peebles on the A72 (Daily 9am–5pm; ⓦ tweedvalleybikehire.com).

2

pastries, overseen by master chocolatier Ruth Hinks who also runs chocolate and pastry masterclasses. It's great for chocolate gifts too. ££
Coltman's Deli & Kitchen 71–73 High St ⓦcoltmans. co.uk. Passing through the narrow alley next to their immaculate deli, you'll find yourself at *Coltman's*, Peebles' most sophisticated dining experience. While most of the ingredients are seasonal and sourced locally, the cuisine thinks globally with imagination and originality. Fish enthusiasts might try the loin of cod with mussel and saffron broth then move on to the marmalade bread-and-butter pudding with orange custard, which is much nicer than it sounds. £££

Osso 1 Innerleithen Rd ⓦossorestaurant.com. Contemporary restaurant, just east of the Eastgate theatre, with a sharing style menu of small to medium sized plates, and very creative they are too; for example whipped salt cod mousse with toasted sourdough, and beef shin croquettes with chilli slaw. £££
The Prince of India 84–86 High St ⓦprinceofindiarestaurant.com. Long-established and thriving Indian restaurant with a wide choice of robust curries, many with unashamedly liberal spicing. It's a tad more expensive than your average curry house but well worth forking out for. £££

ENTERTAINMENT

Eastgate Theatre and Arts Centre Eastgate ⓦeastgatearts.com. This former church east of High St has been converted into a modern arts space with an eclectic programme of world, folk and light orchestral music as well as theatre, dance and cinema performances. Art exhibitions are, naturally, here too, sited beside the in-house café.

Yarrow Valley

Cutting through the hills southeast of Peebles is the **Yarrow Water**, a river system that, along with the Ettrick Water, fed the once prosperous mills of Selkirk. First stop upstream is **Bowhill House**, a part Georgian, part Victorian stately home with one of the finest private art collections in the county and a pleasant lakeside walk. For more strenuous exercise, head three miles west on the A708 to the parking area at Yarrowford, a starting point for some of the Borders' finest hikes. From here, you can reach the hilltop cairns of **The Three Brethren** (1530ft), whose summit offers excellent views over this remote corner of the Borders. You can also link up with stretches of the Southern Upland Way by heading east down through Yair Hill Forest, or by following an old drove road west to the Cheese Well at Minch Moor and ending up at Traquair House near Innerleithen (see page 126).

St Mary's Loch and Loch of the Lowes

Sixteen miles west of Selkirk on the A708 lies the Yarrow's source, a pair of icy lakes: **St Mary's Loch**, and its diminutive neighbour, **Loch of the Lowes**, separated by a slender isthmus – home to the Tibbie Shiels Inn (currently closed to the public) – and magnificently set beneath the surrounding hills. This spot was popular with the nineteenth-century Scottish literati, especially Walter Scott and James Hogg, the 'Shepherd Poet of Ettrick', who eulogized 'the bosom of the lonely Lowes' in *The Queen's Wake*.

For a short and enjoyable walk, follow the path from the inn along the east side of St Mary's Loch into the forest. Eventually this meets up with the Southern Upland Way from where you can head across the moors north to Traquair House or south to the valley of the **Ettrick Water**, both strenuous hikes that require an Ordnance Survey map, a compass and proper clothing.

Grey Mare's Tail Waterfall

If you're continuing west along the A708 into Dumfries and Galloway, don't miss the 200ft **Grey Mare's Tail Waterfall** (NTS), four miles southwest of Loch of the Lowes, which tumbles down a rocky crevasse as you descend into Dumfriesshire. The base of the falls is approached by a precipitous footpath along the left side of the stream, a ten-minute clamber each way from the road.

Bowhill House

3 miles west of Selkirk on the A708 · **House** May bank holiday, Aug and last weekend Oct; tours noon, 1pm, 2pm & 3pm · Charge · **Estate** Easter–June & Sept Fri–Sun 10am–5pm, July–Aug daily 10am–5pm · ⓦ bowhillhouse.co.uk

The property of the Duke of Buccleuch, a seriously wealthy man, the fine part Georgian, part Victorian mansion **Bowhill House** is well known for its art collection and connections to Sir Walter Scott, who visited regularly. There's a room dedicated to the writer, with Henry Raeburn's 1826 portrait of Scott on display alongside various artefacts relating to the author. Other famous painters' works are on display here too, including portraits by Reynolds, Gainsborough and a Canaletto cityscape, while the drawing room has Boulle furniture, Meissen tableware plus paintings by Ruysdael, Leandro Bassano and Claude Lorraine.

The adjoining estate is criss-crossed by scenic paths that loop around a pair of forest-fringed lakes. The grounds also shelter the Bowhill Theatre, a seventy-seat auditorium housed in what was once the estate's cold storage larder with productions ranging from musical comedies to children's fables. Details of plays are listed on the website.

Jedburgh

Just ten miles north of the English border, **JEDBURGH** nestles in the lush valley of Jed Water near its confluence with the Teviot out on the edge of the wild Cheviot Hills. During the interminable wars between England and Scotland, Jedburgh was the quintessential frontier town, a heavily garrisoned royal burgh incorporating a mighty castle and abbey. Though the castle was destroyed by the Scots in 1409 to keep it out of the hands of the English, its memory has been kept alive by stories. In 1285, for example, King Alexander III was celebrating his wedding feast in the great hall when a ghostly apparition predicted his untimely death and a bloody civil war; sure enough, he died in a hunting accident shortly afterwards and chaos ensued. Today, Jedburgh is the first place of any size that you come to on the A68 if crossing over Carter Bar from England, and as such gets quite a bit of passing tourist trade. The ruined **abbey** is the main event, though a stroll round the old town centre is a pleasant way to while away an hour or so.

Jedburgh Abbey

Abbey Bridge End · Daily April–Sept 10am–5pm, Oct–March 10am–4pm · Charge · HES · ⓦ historicenvironment.scot

Despite its ruinous state, **Jedburgh Abbey** still dominates the town, particularly when approached from the south. Founded in the twelfth century as an Augustinian priory by King David I, it's the best preserved of all the Border abbeys, its vast church towering over a sloping site right in the centre of town, beside Jed Water. The abbey was burnt and badly damaged on a number of occasions, but by far the worst destruction was inflicted by the English in the 1540s. By this time, the contemplative way of life had already fallen prey to corruption and only a few canons remained living in the ruins of the abbey, until it was finally closed in 1560. The abbey church remained the parish kirk for another three centuries and as a result has survived particularly intact.

All that remains of the conventual buildings where the canons lived are the foundations and basic ground plan, but then Jedburgh's chief glory is really its **Abbey Church**, which remains splendidly preserved. As you enter via the west door, the three-storey nave's perfectly proportioned parade of columns and arches lies before you, a fine example of the transition from Romanesque to Gothic design, with pointed window

2

JEDBURGH FESTIVALS

Jedburgh is at its busiest during the town's two main festivals. The **Common Riding**, or Jethart Callant's Festival, takes place from late June to early July, when the young people of the town mount up and ride out to check the burgh boundaries, a reminder of more troubled days when Jedburgh was subject to English raids. In similar spirit, early February sees the day-long **Jedburgh Hand Ba'** game, an all-male affair between the 'Uppies' (those born above Market Place) and the 'Doonies' (those born below). The aim of the game is to get a hay-stuffed leather ball – originally representing the head of an Englishman – from one end of town to the other.

arches surmounted by the round-headed arches of the triforium, which, in turn, support the lancet windows of the clerestory. Be sure you climb up the narrow staircase in the west front to the balcony overlooking the nave, where you can contemplate how the place must have looked all decked out for the marriage of Alexander III to Yolande de Dreux in 1285.

Jedburgh Castle Jail

Castlegate • April–Oct Mon–Sat 10am–4pm, Sun 10–3pm • Free • ⓦ liveborders.org.uk • 5min walk (signposted) from the main square

An impressive castellated nineteenth-century pile, **Jedburgh Castle Jail**, as its name suggests, was built on the site of the old royal castle. As well as detailed information about Jedburgh's history, there's a fascinating insight into conditions in jail, deportations, crime and punishment. The cells themselves are, for the period, remarkably comfortable, reflecting the influence of reformer John Howard.

Mary, Queen of Scots House

Queen St • April–Oct Mon–Sat 10am–4pm, Sun 10am–3pm; Nov daily 10am–3pm • Free • ⓦ liveborders.org.uk

Despite the name, it's unlikely that Mary actually stayed in the sixteenth-century house known as **Mary, Queen of Scots House**, though she did visit the town in 1566 for the Assizes. The attempt to unravel her complex life is cursory, the redeeming features being a copy of her death mask and one of the few surviving portraits of the Earl of Bothwell, her third husband.

ARRIVAL AND INFORMATION   JEDBURGH

By bus Buses pick up and drop off by the car park on Canongate near the town centre.

Destinations Edinburgh (Mon–Sat 6 daily, 7 on Sun; 1hr 50min); Galashiels (Mon–Sat 8 daily, 1 on Sun; 45min); Hawick (Mon–Fri 8 daily, 7 on Sat, 5 on Sun; 25min); Kelso (Mon–Fri 8 daily, 3 on Sat, 4 on Sun; 25min); Melrose (Mon–Sat 8 daily, 1 on Sun; 30min).

Tourist office The Jedburgh iCentre on Murray's Green, across the road from the Abbey, stocks the Jedburgh Town Trail leaflet (April to mid-June & Sept–Oct Mon–Sat 9am–5pm, Sun 10am–4pm; mid-June to Aug Mon–Sat 9am–5.30pm, Sun 10am–5pm; Nov to March Mon–Sat 10am–4pm; ⓦ jedburgh.org.uk).

ACCOMMODATION

The Capon Tree Town House 61–63 High St ⓦ thecapontree.com. You'll find first-class accommodation at this lovely restaurant with rooms. Decorated to a very high standard all rooms come with en-suite showers and a nice range of toiletries. ££

Jedwater Caravan Park 4 miles south of Jedburgh, signposted off the A68 ⓦ jedwater.co.uk. The cheaper and more secluded choice of two campsites nearby, with

a pleasant riverside setting. It's a family-orientated site, sizeable enough to have a shop, a decent play park and a few cute farm animals. £

Meadhon House 48 Castlegate ⓦ meadhon.co.uk. Pronounced 'mawn', this is the finest of several B&Bs among Castlegate's pleasant and antique row of houses, with tasteful en-suite rooms, including some family rooms. ££

EATING AND DRINKING

Border Meringues Unit 1, Old Station Yard, Edinburgh Rd; 0.5 mile north of the Abbey opposite the Shell garage ☎01835 863383. An unlikely setting for a café/cake shop in an anonymous industrial estate building on the outskirts of town, but locals go out of their way for this place. There is all manner of cakes and tray bakes here. ̲£

★ **The Capon Tree Town House** 61 High St

ⓦthecapontree.com. Part fine dining restaurant, part wine bar, this place conjures up the best plates in the dinner-only menu, which plays around with the classics like roast salmon with butter samphire, crayfish and smoked salmon cream and black caviar. Starters may include such delights as *moules marinière* or classic French onion soup. ̲£̲£̲£

2

Hawick and around

Despite being a busy, working mill town, **HAWICK** (pronounced 'hoyk') has a surprising number of visitors, the majority of whom come in search of bargains from its woollen knitwear factory outlets. Its textiles industry has been the mainstay of the economy for the last few hundred years, but the town's true heyday came with the advent of steam power which saw a rapid expansion from the town's fifty or so watermills and the formation of knitwear brands like Pringle, Lyle & Scott, and Peter Scott. Much of the Victorian architecture here reflects the prosperity of this period, particularly the Scots Baronial- style town hall halfway down the high street. The town's pre-industrial fortunes were not so good, though one exception is a skirmish in 1514 when the local Hawick callants (boys) defeated a small English force and captured their banner, an event immortalized by the statue at the end of the high street.

Hermitage Castle

16 miles south of Hawick, signposted off the B6399 • April–Sept daily 9.30am–5.30pm; last entry 30min before closing • Charge • HES • ⓦhistoricenvironment.scot

Bleak and forbidding, **Hermitage Castle** is bedevilled by all sorts of horrifying legends: one owner, William Douglas, starved his prisoners to death, while Lord de Soulis, another occupant, engaged the help of demons to fortify the castle in defiance of Robert the Bruce, who had him boiled to death. From the outside, the castle remains an imposing structure, its heavy walls topped by stepped gables and a tidy corbelled parapet. However, the apparent homogeneity is deceptive: certain features were invented during a Victorian restoration, a confusing supplement to the ad hoc alterations that had already transformed the fourteenth-century original. The ruinous interior is a bit of a letdown; look out for the tight Gothic doorways and gruesome dungeon though.

ARRIVAL AND INFORMATION   HAWICK AND AROUND

By bus The main bus stand is just north of the centre in Mart St. Destinations Edinburgh (Mon–Sat half-hourly, Sun hourly; 2hr 5min); Galashiels (Mon–Sat half-hourly, Sun hourly; 40min); Jedburgh (Mon–Fri 8 daily, 7 on Sat, 5 on Sun; 25min); Kelso (Mon–Fri 8 daily, 3 on Sat, 4 on Sun; 25min); Langholm (Mon–Sat hourly, 4 on Sun; 40min); Selkirk

(Mon–Sat half-hourly, Sun hourly; 20min).
Tourist information There is no tourist office in Hawick but leaflets and helpful staff can be found in the Heritage Hub and the adjacent Borders Textile Towerhouse in Kirkstile. Welcome hosts can be found in the streets of the town in summer to help with local information.

EATING

The Nightsafe 12 High St ☎01450 377045. A popular venue serving coffees, lunches, teas and dinner. Light bites are available at lunchtime with substantial sandwiches

but there is a full menu too. Mains include dishes such as slow cooked ox cheek with red wine jus and pan-fried Gressingham duck with Jerusalem artichoke fondant. ̲£̲£̲£

Dumfries and Galloway

CAERLAVEROCK CASTLE

Dumfries and Galloway

Scotland's southwest corner, now known as Dumfries and Galloway, is a region set apart, with few people bothering to exit the main Carlisle–Glasgow motorway that runs through the county. Yet the area has stately homes, deserted hills and ruined abbeys to compete with the best of the Borders. It also has something the Borders don't have, and that's the Solway Coast, a long, indented coastline of sheltered sandy coves that's been dubbed the 'Scottish Riviera' – an exaggeration perhaps, but it's certainly Scotland's warmest, southernmost stretch of coastline.

3

Dumfries is the region's main settlement, a market town by the **River Nith** originally founded as a royal burgh in 1186. Today, it's a must for those on the trail of **Robert Burns**, who spent the last part of his life here. More compelling is the nearby coast, overlooking the Solway Firth, the shallow estuary wedged between Scotland and England, famed for its wildlife and for the nearby red-sandstone ruins of **Caerlaverock Castle** and **Sweetheart Abbey**. Edged by tidal marsh and mudbank, much of the Solway shoreline is flat and eerily remote, but there are also some fine rocky bays sheltering beneath wooded hills, most notably along the **Colvend Coast**. Further along the coast is **Kirkcudbright**, once a bustling port thronged with sailing ships, later an artists' retreat and now a tranquil, well-preserved, little eighteenth- and early nineteenth-century town. Like Kirkcudbright, **Threave Garden** and **Threave Castle**, just outside Castle Douglas, are popular with – but not crowded by – tourists.

Contrasting with the essentially gentle landscape of the Solway coast is the brooding presence of the **Galloway Hills** to the north, their beautiful moors, mountains, lakes and rivers centred on the 235 square miles of the **Galloway Forest Park**, a hillwalking and mountain biking paradise that deserves to be better known than it is. As you continue west into what used to be Wigtownshire, the landscape becomes flatter and more relentlessly agricultural. The main points of interest here are the attractive seaport of **Portpatrick** on the hammer-headed Rhinns of Galloway and the **Mull of Galloway**, Scotland's southernmost point and a nesting site for thousands of seabirds.

The combination of rolling landscape and quiet back roads makes the region good for **cyclists**: five of the **7stanes** (ⓦforestryandland.gov.scot/visit/activities) purpose-built mountain bike routes are in the forested hills of Dumfries and Galloway. This is also rewarding **walking** country, featuring the **Southern Upland Way** (ⓦdgtrails.org/southern-upland-way/route), a 214-mile coast-to-coast hike from Portpatrick in the west to Cockburnspath in the east. And, in a riposte to the North Coast 500, there's now the **South West Coastal 300** (ⓦvisitsouthwestscotland.com), a scenic (though much gentler) 300-mile-long circular touring route around Dumfries and Galloway.

Brief history

The region has a fascinatingly diverse heritage. Originally inhabited by southern Picts, it has at various times been overrun by Romans, Anglo-Saxons from Northumberland and Gaels from the north of Ireland: the name Galloway means the 'land of the stranger Gaels'. It was an unruly land, where independent chieftains maintained close contacts with the Vikings rather than the Scots, right up until medieval times. Gradually, this autonomy was whittled away, and the area was swallowed up by the Scottish Crown, though Galloway continued to be a fiercely independent region, typified by local hero Robert the Bruce. Later, it became a stronghold of the Covenanters, and suffered terribly during the 'Killing Times' following the Restoration, when the government forces came to impose Episcopalianism. From around the

Highlights

❶ Caerlaverock Castle One of Scotland's most photogenic moated castles, beside a superb site for waterfowl and waders. See page 141

❷ Crawick Multiverse Charles Jencks's otherworldly landscape of sculptured hills and standing stones, representing humanity's connection with the Universe. See page 143

❸ Kirkcudbright One-time artists' colony, and the best-looking town in the 'Scottish Riviera'. See page 144

❹ Threave Garden and Threave Castle The perfect day-trip from Castle Douglas: azaleas

and rhododendrons to die for and a medieval castle on an island. See page 146

❺ Galloway Forest Park Go mountain biking along remote forest tracks, or hiking on the Southern Upland Way. See page 148

❻ Logan Botanic Garden Scotland's most exotic garden, where tree ferns, palms and eucalyptus flourish in the southwest's balmy climate. See page 150

❼ Mull of Galloway Picture-postcard headland, with a Stevenson lighthouse, cliffs full of seabirds and views across the Irish Sea. See page 151

HIGHLIGHTS ARE MARKED ON THE MAP ON PAGE 136

DUMFRIES & GALLOWAY

HIGHLIGHTS

1. Caerlaverock Castle
2. Crawick Multiverse
3. Kirkcudbright
4. Threave Garden and Threave Castle
5. Galloway Forest Park
6. Logan Botanic Garden
7. Mull of Galloway

ENGLAND

CUMBRIA

ESKDALE

ANNANDALE

NITHSDALE

FOREST OF AE

GLENKENS

GALLOWAY FOREST PARK

The Machars

Wigtown Bay

Luce Bay

The Rhinns of Galloway

Firth of Clyde

Solway Firth

Grey Mare's Tail

Langholm

Gretna Green

Annan

Eskdalemuir

Lockerbie

Ecclefechan

Moffat

Ruthwell

Caerlaverock Castle

Dumfries

Sweetheart Abbey

New Abbey

Criffel (1864ft)

Southerness

Sandyhills

Kippford

Rockcliffe

Leadhills

Wanlockhead

Crawick Multiverse

Sanquhar

Drumlanrig Castle

Thornhill

Penpont

Moniaive

Glenkiln Reservoir

Dalbeattie

Castle Douglas

Threave Garden

Threave Castle

Kirkcudbright

Dundrennan Abbey

Cumnock

Kilmarnock

Dalmellington

Carsphairn

St John's Town of Dalry

Parton

Loch Ken

New Galloway

Southern Upland Way

Corserine (2670ft)

Clatteringshaws Loch

Cairnsmore of Fleet (2330ft)

Gatehouse of Fleet

Merrick (2746ft)

Glentrool

Kirroughtree

Newton Stewart

Wigtown

Whithorn

Isle of Whithorn

Ayr

Girvan

Port William

Glenluce

Scares

Castle Kennedy Gardens

Cairnryan

Stranraer

Drummore

Mull of Galloway

Corsewall Point

Belfast & Larne

Dunskey Gardens

Dunskey Castle

Portpatrick

Logan Botanic Garden

Port Logan

Arran

Pladda

Ailsa Craig

Workington

N

0   miles   10

GRETNA GREEN MARRIAGES

Up until 1754 English couples could buy a quick and secret wedding at London's Fleet Prison, bribing imprisoned clerics with small amounts of money. The **Hardwicke Marriage Act** brought an end to this seedy wheeze, enforcing the requirement of a licence and a church ceremony. However, in Scotland, a marriage declaration made before two witnesses remained legal. The consequences of this difference in the law verged on farce: hundreds of runaway couples dashed north to Scotland, their weddings witnessed by just about anyone who came to hand – ferrymen, farmers, tollgate keepers and even self-styled 'priests' who set up their own 'marriage houses'.

Gretna Green, due to its position beside the border on the main turnpike road to Edinburgh, became the most popular destination for the fugitives. In their rush, many people tied the knot at the first place to hand after dismounting from the stagecoach, which happened to be a **blacksmith's shop** situated at the crossroads, though the better-off maintained class distinctions, heading for the staging post at Gretna Hall. The association with blacksmiths was strengthened by one of the first 'priests', the redoubtable Joseph Paisley, a 25-stone Goliath who – in business from 1754 to 1812 – gave a certain style to the ceremony by straightening a horseshoe, a show of strength rather than a symbolic act. His melodramatic feat led to stories of Gretna Green weddings being performed over the blacksmith's **anvil**, and later 'priests' were more than happy to act out the rumour. Gretna Green boomed until the marriage laws were further amended in 1856, but some businesses continued right up to 1940, when marriage by declaration was made illegal.

The only marriages that take place in Gretna Green nowadays, however, are for couples taken in by the 'romance' of the name – more than 4,000 annually – and English couples under 18, who want to get married without the permission of their parents.

seventeenth century, the ports of the Solway Coast prospered with the expansion of local shipping routes over to Ireland. The region subsequently experienced economic decline as trade routes changed, turning busy ports into sleepy backwaters.

ARRIVAL AND DEPARTURE

By train Three train lines run through Dumfries and Galloway. One tracks the A74 motorway between Carlisle and Glasgow, while another heads up Nithsdale via Dumfries and a third stretches from Glasgow to Stranraer in the far southwest.

By ferry Two companies provide services between

DUMFRIES AND GALLOWAY

Northern Ireland and Cairnryan, six miles north of Stranraer with 4–8 daily bus connections from Cairnryan to Stranraer and Ayr. Stena Line serves Belfast (6 crossings daily; 2hr 15min; ⓦ stenaline.co.uk) and P&O Ferries has services to Larne (5–7 crossings daily; 2hr; ⓦ poferries.com).

GETTING AROUND AND INFORMATION

By bus The main bus company for the region is Stagecoach West Scot (ⓦ stagecoachbus.com), servicing all the main towns and villages but of little use for the Galloway Forest Park.

Tourist information The website ⓦ visitsouthwest scotland.com is a good resource for in-depth information and ideas, particularly for families and walking enthusiasts.

Dumfries

Situated on the wide banks of the River Nith, a short distance inland from the Solway Firth, **DUMFRIES** is by far the largest town in southwest Scotland, with a population of more than thirty thousand. Long known as the 'Queen of the South' (as is its football club), it flourished as a medieval seaport and trading centre, its success attracting the attention of many English armies. Despite this, it went on to prosper, with its light industries and port supplying the agricultural hinterland. The town planners of the

1960s badly damaged its appearance, but many of the warm red-sandstone buildings that distinguish Dumfries from other places in the southwest survive. The town is second only to Ayr for its associations with **Robert Burns** (see page 161), who spent the last five years of his life here employed as an excise man. Consequently, a number of sights in Dumfries pay homage to the great poet, including his home, his statue, Burns House, his pub, the *Globe Inn*, and his final resting place in a mausoleum beside St Michael's Church.

Globe Inn

56 High St • Mon–Sat 11am–11pm, Sun 11.30am–9pm • Globes Burns Room Wed–Sat 4pm, Fri & Sat 11am; 45min • Charge • ⓦ globeinndumfries.co.uk

If you're on Burns' trail, make sure you duck down the alleyway to the seventeenth-century **Globe Inn**, just past the ornate but badly fading red and gold Victorian fountain. Burns had a fling with Annie Park, a barmaid in this pub, and the resultant child was taken into the Burns household by his long-suffering wife, Jean Armour. Beyond the main bar you can enter the beautifully panelled snug and sit in the very chair used by the poet – although if you do, by tradition you'll be expected to recite a Burns poem or else buy everyone in the bar a drink.

Robert Burns House

Burns St • April–Sept Mon–Sat 10am–5pm, Sun 2–5pm; Oct–March Tues–Sat 10am–1pm & 1.30–4pm • Free • ⓦ dgculture.co.uk/venue/Robert-burns-house

In the simple sandstone building now known as Robert **Burns House**, Robert Burns died of rheumatic heart disease in 1796 aged 37, a few days before the birth of his last son, Maxwell. He lived here for his last three years, though his wife, Jean Armour, stayed on until her own death, some 38 years later – indeed, there's a fine collection of some of her personal effects, including a pair of spectacles, a gold ring and a signed bible. Otherwise, the rooms are packed with Burns memorabilia: manuscripts and first editions, letters, numerous items from when he was an excise officer, and, unsurprisingly, lots of drink-related paraphernalia such as drinking horns and his toddy ladle. There are some remarkable photos, too, not least one of his granddaughters, Jane Emma Burns Brown, standing next to his great granddaughter, Jean Armour Burns Brown. Meanwhile, one of the bedroom windows bears his signature, scratched with his diamond ring.

St Michael's Church

As a member of the Dumfries Volunteers, Burns was given a military funeral, before being buried nearby in a simple grave by **St Michael's Church**, a large red-sandstone church on St Michael's Street, built in 1745. In 1815, his body was dug up (the original resting place is denoted by a plaque in the back left corner of the graveyard) and moved across to a purpose-built **mausoleum**, a bright white Neoclassical eyesore that houses a statue of him being accosted by his poetic muse; buried alongside him is his wife and two sons. Otherwise, the graveyard features many ostentatious tombstones of the poet's friends, a number of them inscribed with wonderfully verbose epitaphs. In the church itself, a brass plaque on the back pillar to the right as you enter denotes the spot where Burns and his wife sat during services. Across the busy main road from the church is an oversized statue of Jean Armour.

Robert Burns Centre

Mill Rd • April–Sept Mon–Sat 10am–5pm, Sun 2–5pm; Oct–March Tues–Sat 10am–1pm & 1.30–4pm • Free • ⓦ rbcft.co.uk

In a converted watermill on the western banks of the Nith, the **Robert Burns Centre** (RBC) has an exhibition on the poet that – although much smaller – is more than a match for anything on display at Robert Burns House. Among the many outstanding items here are manuscripts, excise permits, his sword, and a slice of bark from a tree felled at Ellisland Farm into which Burns carved his name. More movingly, there's a funeral invitation typed out by Burns' then 9-year-old son, also called Robert, following his father's death. Take time to cast your eye over the scale model of the town from the 1790s. The centre otherwise shows predominantly art-house films in the evenings.

Dumfries Museum and Camera Obscura

The Observatory, Rotchell Rd • April–Sept Mon–Sat 10am–5pm, Sun 2–5pm; Oct–March Tues–Sat 10am–1pm & 1.30–4pm • Free • ⓦ dgculture.co.uk/venue/Dumfries-museum

On the hill west of the Nith stands the **Dumfries Museum**, from which there are great views over the town. The museum is housed partly in an eighteenth-century windmill, which was converted into the town's observatory in the 1830s and features the world's oldest working **camera obscura** on its top floor, well worth a visit on a clear day when the views are projected inside to maximum effect; note that if there is even the slightest hint of rain, the camera is not operational. On the floors below, the focus is on local history and prehistory, with a good collection of tools and weaponry from the region's earliest peoples as well as some impressive carved masonry from the era of the first Christians.

Devorgilla Bridge and Old Bridge House Museum

Old Bridge House Museum, Mill Rd, • April–Sept Mon–Sat 10am–5pm, Sun 2–5pm • Free • ⓦ dgculture.co.uk/venue/old-bridge-house-museum

Spanning the wide River Nith at the northern end of Whitesands, the elegant **Devorgilla Bridge** – named after the noblewoman of Sweetheart Abbey fame (see page 141) – was originally constructed in 1430, making it one of Scotland's oldest multi-spanned bridges, though at one stage it possessed nine arches as opposed to the six it has now. On the western bank stands the delightful **Old Bridge House**, which is not, as is often thought, the former customs house. It is in fact the town's oldest domestic building (dating from around 1660), though it served various purposes – including, at one time, as an inn (probably frequented by Burns) – before being converted into a couple of council flats, one of which was inhabited by a certain Granny Black (quite a character hereabouts apparently) until 1955. Its numerous rooms, spread over two floors, now display items pertaining to a particular theme, for example, childhood and, somewhat more bizarrely, dentistry. Walking along the riverside, look out for some surprisingly varied birdlife – it's not unusual, for example, to see a heron or two patiently waiting for some supper.

ARRIVAL AND INFORMATION

DUMFRIES

By train Dumfries train station is a 5min walk east of the town centre.

Destinations Carlisle (Mon–Sat every 1–2hr, 5 on Sun; 40min); Glasgow Central (Mon–Sat every 1–2hr, 2 on Sun; 1hr 45min); Sanquhar (Mon–Sat every 1–2hr, 2 on Sun; 25min).

By bus Most buses stop off at Whitesands beside the River Nith.

Destinations Kirkcudbright, with a coordinated change at Castle Douglas (Mon–Sat hourly, 3 on Sun; 1hr 20min), Moffat (Mon–Sat hourly, Sun every 1–2hr; 40min); New Abbey (Mon–Sat hourly, 6 on Sun; 15min).

Tourist office Dumfries iCentre, 64 Whitesands (April–mid-June & Sept–Oct Mon–Sat 9.30am–5pm, Sun 11am–4pm; mid-June–Aug Mon–Sat 9.30am–5.30pm, Sun 11am–4pm; Nov–March Mon–Sat 9.30am–4.30pm; ☏01387 253862).

ACCOMMODATION

SEE MAP PAGE 138

Cairndale Hotel English Street ⓦ cairndalehotel.co.uk. Large, centrally located hotel, with a warren of solidly furnished rooms, some with four-poster beds and gleaming marble bathrooms. Additional facilities include a sauna, steam room and pool. **£££**

Glenaldor House 5 Victoria Terrace ⓦ glenaldorhouse. co.uk. A light and bright Victorian house near the station with four comfortably spacious en-suite bedrooms. Wake up to a customized cooked breakfast offered alongside a buffet with healthy cereal options, pastries and jams. **££**

EATING

SEE MAP PAGE 138

★ **Frothy Coffee** 77–79 Whitesands ⓦ thefrothybikeco.com. Run by a couple of hardcore cycling enthusiasts, this fabulous café should be your first (and only) port of call here in Dumfries; not only is the coffee far and away the best in town (the food's not bad either) but the place looks great too, with huge floor-to-ceiling windows, hand-crafted tables and chairs and chipboard-walls; best of all, for cyclists at least, there's an indoor bike parking area and they offer servicing and repairs. **£**

Home 92 Whitesands ☏ 07896 355074. One of only two places in town worth eating at, this terrific place offers a short, concise menu that may feature inventively crafted dishes like caponata, whipped feta and lemon polenta or venison loin with truffle mash and mushroom *bon bons*, while the locally-sourced steaks are always a good bet. Booking advisable. **£££**

DRINKING

SEE MAP PAGE 138

Globe Inn 56 High St ⓦ globeinndumfries.co.uk. The Robert Burns connection certainly pulls in the punters in this pub, but is by no means the only reason to visit. It's a rare example of traditional pub authenticity with its attractive wood panelling and ornate cornices. The food is top draw too, the chefs here conjuring up clever, classy plates like curried John Dory with mussels and leeks. **£££**

Around Dumfries

Southeast of Dumfries, the medieval ruins of **Caerlaverock Castle** are simply magnificent, as is the adjacent nature reserve and the early Christian cross at nearby

Ruthwell. On the west bank of the Nith estuary, the star attraction is **Sweetheart Abbey**, the best preserved of the trio of Cistercian abbeys in Dumfries and Galloway.

Caerlaverock Castle

8 miles southeast of Dumfries along the B725 • Daily April–Sept 9.30am–5.30pm; Oct–March 10am–4pm • Charge • HES • ⓦ historicenvironment.scot • No. D6A bus from Great King St in Dumfries (5 daily Mon–Sat; 30min)

Picture-perfect **Caerlaverock Castle**, a moated ruin, was built in the late thirteenth century out of the rich local red sandstone and is unique for being one of the very few triangular fortresses anywhere in the world; indeed, during the siege of 1300 by Edward I, a contemporary bard wrote: 'Its shape was like that of a shield, for it had only three sides, all round, with a tower on each angle'. Caerlaverock sustained further damage in 1312, this time from the Scots, and again in 1356–57 from the English, forcing numerous rebuilding programmes. Beyond the mighty double-towered gatehouse, you're confronted by the ornate Renaissance facade of the **Nithsdale Lodging**, erected in the 1630s by the first earl of Nithsdale, Robert Maxwell. Just six years later Maxwell and his garrison were forced to surrender after a thirteen-week siege and bombardment by the Covenanters, who proceeded to wreck the place. It was never inhabited again. The facade retains some exquisite architectural detail, not least the various coats-of-arms and allegorical scenes above each window; above the top right-hand corner window, you can quite clearly make out Neptune being drawn by a sea creature in a chariot. Rounding off the visit, there's an exhibition and video on the siege of 1300, where kids can create their own heraldry, a small play area and tearoom.

Caerlaverock Wetland Centre

Eastpark Farm, 9 miles southeast of Dumfries along the B725 • Daily 10am–5pm • Charge • ⓦ wwt.org.uk/wetland-centres/caerlaverock

The perfect complement to a visit to Caerlaverock Castle is the **Caerlaverock Wetland Centre**, just a couple of miles away. An area of salt marsh and mud flats abutting the Solway Firth, this is the only Wildfowl and Wetland Trust reserve in Scotland, and one of only ten in the UK. To this end, Caerlaverock is one of the most rewarding wildlife watching areas in the country, and among its many seasonal highlights is the arrival of thousands of barnacle geese in October (who usually stay here until March) and ospreys in April. Throughout the reserve, there are numerous walking trails, hides and observation towers, and if you haven't got your own binoculars, these can be hired from the admissions desk.

Ruthwell Church

7 miles east of Caerlaverock

The modest country church at **RUTHWELL** houses the remarkable 18ft **Ruthwell Cross**, an extraordinary early Christian monument from the early or mid-eighth century when Galloway was ruled by the Northumbrians. The cross was considered idolatrous during the Reformation, smashed and buried, and only reassembled in the nineteenth century. The decoration reveals a strikingly sophisticated style and iconography, probably derived from the eastern Mediterranean. The main inscriptions are in Latin; but running around the edge is a poem written in the Northumbrian dialect in runic figures. However, it's the biblical carvings on the main face that really catch the eye – notably Mary Magdalene washing the feet of Jesus.

Sweetheart Abbey

Main St, New Abbey • April–Sept daily 9.30am–5.30pm; Oct–March Sat–Wed 10am–4pm • Charge • HES • ⓦ historicenvironment.scot • Bus No. 372 from Dumfries every 2hr Mon–Sat, 3 on Sun; 15min

The last of the Cistercian abbeys to be founded in Scotland, in 1273, **Sweetheart Abbey** is dominated by the red-sandstone abbey church, intact minus its roof. Standing in the grassy nave, flanked by giant compound piers supporting early Gothic arches, and above them a triforium, it's easy to imagine what the completed church must have looked like. The central square tower is a massive, brutal structure, but the elaborate tracery in some of the windows and flamboyant corbelling below the central tower clearly mark a change from the austere simplicity of earlier Cistercian foundations. For the foreseeable future, however, this central part of the complex is enveloped in scaffolding, pending the shoring up of what has become, in places, a rather fragile structure. Sweetheart Abbey takes its unusual name from its founder, Devorgilla de Balliol, Lady of Galloway. She carried the embalmed heart of her husband, John Balliol (after whom Balliol College, Oxford, is named) around with her for the remaining 22 years of her life – she is buried, with the casket, in the presbytery.

ACCOMMODATION AND EATING   **DUMFRIES AND AROUND**

Abbey Cottage 26 Main St, New Abbey ⓦ abbeycottagetearoom.com. Enjoying an unrivalled view over Sweetheart Abbey, this tearoom with terrace is renowned for its quality home-made cakes and even sells its own cake-related cookbook. If you're stopping for lunch, expect to pay around £5 for soup or a smoked salmon and cream cheese bagel. £̲

★ **Marthrown of Mabie** Mabie Forest, ⓦ marthrownofmabie.com. Deep in the heart of the forest this remote encampment offers tipis and yurts (each sleeping four), a bunkhouse and, most magical of all, a beautifully thatched, replica Iron Age roundhouse with a central log fire for cooking and warmth. There's a wood-fired hot tub and sauna as well as meals provided at the bunkhouse. Also in the forest are superb purpose-built mountain biking trails run by the 7stanes (see ⓦ forestryandland.gov.scot). £̲–£££̲

Nithsdale

North of Dumfries, the A76 and the railway line to Kilmarnock travel the length of **Nithsdale**, whose gentle slopes and old forests hide one major attraction: the many-turreted seventeenth-century mansion of **Drumlanrig Castle** near **Thornhill**, just one of three substantial country seats owned by the duke of Buccleuch. At the opposite end of the class system were the miners who worked the lead mines in the neighbouring Lowther Hills, to the east, now commemorated in the intriguing **Museum of Lead Mining** in Wanlockhead.

Wanlockhead

From the Nith Valley 24 miles north of Dumfries, **WANLOCKHEAD** is six miles northeast up the striking Mennock Pass. Exposed in its remote and windswept position at a lofty 1500ft, this is the highest village in Scotland, or so it's claimed.

Museum of Lead Mining

Toll Brae, Wanlockhead • Daily Easter–June & Sept 11am–4.30pm, July & Aug 10am–4.30pm • Charge • ⓦ leadminingmuseum.co.uk

A visit to the **Museum of Lead Mining** starts with a brief foray into the main exhibition where the miners' lives and working conditions are described with the aid of a few mannequin-enhanced historic scenes. From there you don a hard hat and go on a guided tour of the underground **Lochnell Mine**, a tour that now extends to some 300 metres and is relatively flat throughout. Resurfacing, you then take a tour of a **miner's cottage** from the 1740s and then one from a hundred years or so later. Also well worth a look is the remarkable eighteenth-century **Miners' Library**, whose 3,000-plus volumes were purchased from the voluntary subscriptions of its members; indeed, it's Europe's second oldest subscription library. At the end of the visit you can try your hand at gold panning – a sure-fire hit if you have children in tow, though it does cost extra. In fact,

Wanlockhead has become something of a gold-panning mecca (for wont of a better description), with the British Championships held here at the end of May each year.

ARRIVAL AND DEPARTURE	**WANLOCKHEAD**

By bus Buses run from Sanquhar (4 daily: Mon–Sat; 15min), which is well served by buses from Dumfries.

Crawick Multiverse

Sanquhar, 27 miles north of Dumfries, signposted from the A76 • Daily Sept–June 10am–4pm; July–Aug until 6pm • Charge • Ⓦ crawickmultiverse.co.uk • Regular trains between Dumfries and Glasgow Central stop at Sanquhar, 1 mile south of the park, and the No. 246 bus from Dumfries

Renowned landscape artist Charles Jencks' tangible vision of the Universe – or indeed multiverse – is splayed across the site of a 55-acre former coal pit. Hike up sculptured hills that spiral up to giant standing stones – representing the Milky Way's destined collision with Andromeda – or follow the Comet Walk that elliptically surrounds the main amphitheatre. While Jencks' subject matter may have been otherworldly, there's an unmistakable familiarity to the place, like a homage to those paganistic cultures that looked up into space and were inspired to build Stonehenge and the like. Indeed, the summer solstice is celebrated here with a festival featuring fire displays, music and arts performances.

Drumlanrig Castle

Thornhill, 18 miles north of Dumfries, signposted from the A76 • **House** July–Aug daily; Easter & early May bank holiday weekend; tours 11am, 12.30pm, 2pm & 3.30pm; 1h • Charge • **Gardens** April–Sept daily 11am–4pm • Charge • Ⓦ drumlanrigcastle.co.uk • Bus stop 1.5 miles' walk; services from Dumfries (every 1 to 2hr; 45min) and from Ayr (Mon–Sat 5 daily; 1hr 20min)

Stately **Drumlanrig Castle** is not a true castle but the grandiose home of the supremely wealthy Duke of Buccleuch and Queensberry. Approached by an impressive, arrow straight driveway that sweeps along an avenue of lime trees (built in anticipation of a visit by Queen Victoria, though in the end she never came), the perfectly symmetrical, seventeenth-century sandstone 'Pink Palace' bristles with cupolas, turrets and towers. Lively, hour-long tours take in a dozen or so of the lavishly furnished, yet surprisingly homely, rooms, each with its own particular point of interest and, invariably, a distinguished painting or two – by far the most famous is Rembrandt's *An Old Woman Reading*, though the likes of Reynolds and Gainsborough are also represented here. The castle has had its fair share of distinguished (and occasionally infamous) guests too, including Bonnie Prince Charlie, who stopped over at (and then pillaged) Drumlanrig during his northward retreat in 1745; in his haste, however, he inadvertently left his safe box behind, which remains on display in the bedroom. Meanwhile, in 1971 the astronaut Neil Armstrong overnighted here, and apparently tried to sleep in Charlie's bed, until he realised how uncomfortable it was.

The formal **gardens** and a forested **country park** are not to be missed, the latter contains some of the region's most exciting mountain biking trails; **bike hire** is available (£10 per hour) from an outlet in the old stable yard. There are also four waymarked walks, ranging from one to three miles.

The Colvend Coast

The **Colvend Coast**, twenty miles or so southwest of Dumfries, is probably one of the finest stretches of coastline along the so-called 'Scottish Riviera'. The best approach is via the A710, which heads south through New Abbey, before cutting across a handsome landscape of rolling farmland to the aptly named **Sandyhills**. A scenic five-mile coastal path runs from there past the cliffs of Castlehill Point and through the pleasant estuary villages of **Rockcliffe** and **Kippford**.

Sandyhills

Little more than a scattering of houses dotted around a wide, sandy bay, **SANDYHILLS**, eighteen miles southwest of Dumfries, looks across the tidal mud flats of the Solway Firth to the Lake District beyond. There are some dramatic coves a short walk west of the bay, while inland the hills undulate gently with farmland interspersed with clutches of forest and small lochs.

ARRIVAL AND DEPARTURE   SANDYHILLS

By bus Buses from Dumfries (6 daily, Mon–Sat, 4 on Sun; 55min) and Rockcliffe (5 daily, Mon–Sat, 4 on Sun; 10min).

Rockcliffe and Kippford

A village on the Urr estuary twenty miles southwest of Dumfries, **ROCKCLIFFE** shelters peacefully between wooded hills and its beautiful rocky, sand and shell bay. For vehicles, Rockcliffe is a dead end, but it's the start of a pleasant half-hour walk along the Jubilee Path to neighbouring **KIPPFORD**, a tiny, lively yachting centre strung out along the east bank of the estuary. En route, the path passes the ancient hillfort of the **Mote of Mark**, a useful craggy viewpoint. At low tide you can walk over the Rough Firth causeway from the shore below across the mud flats to **Rough Island**, a humpy bird sanctuary owned by the National Trust for Scotland – it's out of bounds in May and June when terns and oystercatchers are nesting.

ARRIVAL AND DEPARTURE   ROCKCLIFFE AND KIPPFORD

By bus Buses stop at the road's end next to the bay and serve Dumfries (Mon–Sat 3 daily, 4 on Sun; 1hr 5min) and Kippford (Mon–Sat 5 daily, 4 on Sun; 10min).

ACCOMMODATION AND EATING

The Mariner Hotel Opposite Kippford harbour ☎ 01556 620206. With its greatest asset being the large beer garden overlooking the harbour, this is the best place in town to sink a cold one. The food is nothing special – typical pub grub like fish and chips – but it is available all day at weekends and for lunch and dinner daily midweek. **££**

Roughfirth House Roughfirth, Kippford ⓦ kippford. co.uk. Halfway between Kippford and Rockcliffe accessed by a private cul-de-sac from Kippford, this B&B has an en-suite double and a two-bedroomed family suite with sun lounge overlooking the waterfront. Double **££**; family suite **£££**

Kirkcudbright and around

Hugging the muddy banks of the River Dee ten miles southwest of Castle Douglas, **KIRKCUDBRIGHT** – pronounced 'kir-coo-bree' – is the only major town along the Solway Coast to have retained a working harbour. In addition, it has a ruined castle and the most attractive of town centres, a charming medley of simple two-storey cottages with medieval pends, Georgian villas and Victorian townhouses, all built in a mixture of sandstone, granite and brick, and attractively painted. Not surprisingly, Kirkcudbright became something of a magnet for Scottish artists from the late nineteenth century onwards, including Edward Hornel who cofounded the Kirkcudbrightshire Fine Art Association in 1886, and it has remained that way ever since. The Kirkcudbright Art Map outlines studios, galleries and workshops that are open year-round.

MacLellan's Castle

Castle St • April–Sept Mon–Sat 9.30am–5.30pm • Charge • HES • ⓦ historicenvironment.scot

The most striking sight in Kirkcudbright is **MacLellan's Castle**, a pink-flecked sixteenth-century tower house that sits at one end of the High Street, by the harbourside. Part fortified keep and part spacious mansion, the castle was built in the 1570s for the Provost of Kirkcudbright, Sir Thomas MacLellan of Bombie, when a degree of law and order permitted the aristocracy to relax its defensive preoccupations and satisfy its desire for comfort. As a consequence, chimneys replaced battlements and windows begin at the ground floor. Nevertheless, the walls remain impressively thick and there is a handful of wide-mouthed gun loops. The interior is well preserved, from the kitchen and vaulted storerooms in the basement, to the warren of well-appointed domestic apartments above. MacLellan's son, Robert, amassed so many debts that on his death in 1639, the house had to be sold off, and from then on it was more or less abandoned.

Broughton House

12 High St • April–late June & Sept–Oct Thurs–Mon 10am–4pm; late June–Aug daily 10am–5pm • Charge • NTS • Ⓦ nts.org.uk

This smart Georgian townhouse, set back from, and elevated above, the surrounding terraces, is the former home of the artist **Edward Hornel** (1863–1933). An important member of the late nineteenth-century Scottish art scene, he spent his childhood a few doors down the street, and returned in 1900 to establish an artists' colony in Kirkcudbright with some of the 'Glasgow Boys' (see page 190). Hornel bought Broughton House in 1901 and added a studio and a glass-roofed, mahogany-panelled gallery at the back of the house; his old studio now hosts an artist in residence, who usually remains *in situ* for around six months – you can see them at work. The gallery,

3

now filled with the mannered and rather formulaic paintings of girls at play that he churned out in the latter part of his career, is far less interesting than the upstairs rooms, which offer up numerous personal effects, including several items Hornel returned home with following his many foreign expeditions, for example cloisonné dishes from China and a snake charmer basket from Myanmar (Burma) – his well-travelled suitcase is also here.

Broughton's real triumph, however, is its wonderful jewel-box **gardens**, whose strong Japanese influence – particularly the water features –owes much to trips Hornel made to the country in 1893 and 1921. Other glorious highlights include snowdrops in February, wisteria in May, and a year-round kitchen garden packed with goodies; there are fabulous views of the garden from the upstairs library.

Stewartry Museum

6 St Mary St • Mon–Sat 11am–1pm & 1.30–4pm • Free • ☏ 01557 331643

An extraordinary collection not to be missed, the **Stewartry Museum** has cabinets crammed with everything from glass bottles, weaving equipment, pipes, pictures and postcards to stuffed birds, pickled fish and the tricorn hats once worn by town officials. There are also examples of book jackets designed by Jessie M. King and E.A. Taylor. By far its most prestigious item, however, is a model 'siller' gun (used as a prize in shooting competitions), which was given to the town by James VI in 1587.

Dundrennan Abbey

Dundrennan, 6 miles southeast of Kirkcudbright • April–Sept daily 9.30am–5.30pm • Charge • HES • ⊕ historicenvironment.scot • Bus No. 505 connects Dundrennan with Kirkcudbright (Mon–Sat 6 daily; 10min)

Founded in 1142, Dundrennan was the mother house of the local Cistercian abbeys of Sweetheart and Glenluce, and was clearly the grandest of the lot, even though it's now reduced to just its transepts. The chief treasures of the abbey are the chapterhouse's finely carved cusped portal, and the medieval effigy of a tonsured abbot in the northwest corner of the nave; he was murdered – hence the faded dagger in his chest – and the figure being trampled at his feet is thought to be his assassin, in the process of being disembowelled.

Threave Garden

2 miles southwest of Castle Douglas • Garden daily Nov–late Dec; mid-Feb–late March 10am–4pm; late March–Oct until 5pm • Charge • Nature Reserve year-round • Free • NTS • ⊕ nts.org.uk

The premier horticultural sight in Dumfries and Galloway, **Threave Garden** is a pleasant mile-long walk or cycle south of Castle Douglas, along the shores of Loch Carlingwark. The garden features a magnificent spread of flowers and woodland across sixty acres, subdivided into more than a dozen areas, from the old-fashioned herbaceous borders of

---

KIRKCUDBRIGHT'S FESTIVALS

The town's big music event of the year is the four-day **jazz festival** (⊕ kirkcudbrightjazzfestival.co.uk) in mid-June, with a strong emphasis on Dixieland. The town's artistic renown is showcased to wonderful effect during the **Kirkcudbright Arts & Crafts Trail** (late July–early Aug; ⊕ artsandcraftstrail.com), when local artists and crafts people throw open their doors for the public to view (and potentially buy) their work. Late August sees the colourful **Kirkcudbright Tattoo and Fireworks Display** on Cuthbert Street, which pretty much does what it says on the tin. Finally, at the end of October, there's the **Kirkcudbright Food Festival**, with tastings, demonstrations and talks throughout town.

the Walled Garden to the brilliant banks of rhododendrons in the Woodland Garden and the ranks of primula, astilbe and gentian in the Peat Garden. In springtime, thousands of visitors turn up for the flowering of more than two hundred types of daffodil.

Threave is also home to the School of Practical Gardening, whose postgraduate students occupy one floor of **Threave House**, a hulking Scots Baronial–style mansion built by the Gordon family in 1872, and now restored to its 1938 condition.

Threave Castle

2 miles west of Castle Douglas, off the A75 • Daily April–Sept 10am–4.30pm, Oct 10am–3.30pm • Charge • HES • ⓦ historicenvironment.scot

A visit to **Threave Castle** begins with a ten-minute walk from the car park to the River Dee, where you ring a brass bell for the boat to take you over to the flat and grassy island on which the stern-looking castle stands.

Built in around 1370 for one of the 'Black Douglases', Archibald the Grim, first Lord of Galloway and third Earl of Douglas, the fortress was among the first of its kind, a sturdy, rectangular structure completed shortly after the War of Independence. The rickety curtain wall to the south and east is all that remains of the **artillery fortifications**, hurriedly constructed in the 1450s by the ninth earl in a desperate – and unsuccessful – attempt to defend the castle against James II's newfangled cannon. The castle was partially dismantled in the 1640s, but enough remains of the interior to make out its general plan. In recent years, the castle has become a big attraction for very different reasons; firstly, in 2009, a pair of **ospreys** arrived – their nest is some two hundred metres from the castle, and can be viewed from a dedicated hide – and then, in 2016, a couple of **peregrine falcons** pitched up and took it upon themselves to occupy the upper floors of the castle itself. For this reason, this area is closed off between April and July, though the very real possibility of seeing these magnificent birds is more than ample compensation.

ARRIVAL AND INFORMATION

KIRKCUDBRIGHT AND AROUND

By bus Buses to Kirkcudbright stop by the harbour car park, near the tourist office.

Destinations Dumfries, with a coordinated change at Castle Douglas (Mon–Sat hourly, 3 on Sun; 1hr 20min); Gatehouse of Fleet (Mon–Sat 8 buses; 17min).

Information Kirkcudbright Visitor Centre (daily 10am–4pm; ⓦ kirkcudbright.town).

ACCOMMODATION

SEE MAP PAGE 145

Selkirk Arms 125 High St ⓦ selkirkarmshotel.co.uk. This erstwhile eighteenth-century coaching inn is now a welcoming, cyclist friendly hotel offering sixteen bright en-suite rooms decorated in pleasing pastel colours; they've also got a very accomplished restaurant and bar (see below). Two-night minimum stay April–Oct. **££**

Silvercraig Caravan and Camping Site Silvercraigs Rd ⓦ silvercraigscaravanpark.co.uk. Centrally located overlooking town, this small, community-run site mostly caters to caravans and motorhomes but it's possible to pitch a tent here too. The facilities on offer include shower blocks, electric connection, a playground and self-service laundry. **£**

EATING

SEE MAP PAGE 145

Castle Street Bistro 5 Castle St ⓦ castlestreetbistro. co.uk. An intimate contribution to Kirkcudbright's restaurant scene, offering Scots-French cuisine in tasteful, homely surroundings overlooking the castle. The changing menu offers generally good value, with dishes like tomato and red pepper hummus with toast and duck breast with orange and Cointreau – although the wine list is less palatably priced. Occasional music nights. Book ahead. Evenings only. **£££**

Selkirk Arms 125 High St ⓦ selkirkarmshotel.co.uk. One of the town's more worthwhile dining options, the Selkirk boasts both a bar lounge/bistro and a handsome-looking restaurant. A wide-ranging menu covers the likes of beer-battered haddock and chips, and whisky-baked salmon with purple potatoes and fennel; to their credit they also have an extensive Green (vegetarian and vegan) menu. **£££**

Galloway Forest Park and around

The strange thing about Galloway is that, while the area around the coast is all rolling farmland, stately homes, sandy coves and estuarine mud flats, you only have to head north ten or twenty miles and you're transported to the entirely different landscape of the Galloway Hills, an environment of glassy lochs, wooded hills and bare, rounded peaks. Much of this landscape is now incorporated into the **Galloway Forest Park**, Britain's largest forest park, which stretches all the way from the southern part of Ayrshire right down to Gatehouse of Fleet, laid out on land owned by Forest and Land Scotland (formerly the Forestry Commission). Few people live here, but the park is a major draw for hikers and mountain bikers. Accommodation is sparse in the park itself: use **Newton Stewart**, to the southwest, as a base.

ARRIVAL AND DEPARTURE

By bus No buses run along the park's only road (the Queen's Way/A712), so if you don't have transport you either need to approach the park from New Galloway to the east or Newton Stewart to the southwest.

Destinations from New Galloway Castle Douglas (Mon– Sat 6 daily; 30min); Dumfries (Mon–Sat 2 daily; 1hr).

Destinations from Newton Stewart Dumfries (Mon–Sat every 1–2hr, 2 on Sun; 1hr 30min); Stranraer (Mon–Sat hourly, 4 on Sun; 45min); Wigtown (Mon–Sat hourly, 6 on Sun; 15min).

INFORMATION

Visitor centres Kirroughtree Forest (April–Oct daily 10am–5pm, Nov–March Mon–Fri 11am–2.30pm, Sat &

HIKING, BIKING AND STARGAZING: GALLOWAY FOREST PARK

Both Glentrool and Kirroughtree have mountain bike trails, which form part of southern Scotland's outstanding mountain biking facilities, known as the **7stanes** (⊕ forestryandland. gov.scot). Of the two, **Kirroughtree**, three miles east of Newton Stewart, is by far the most varied and fun, with four exciting single-track trails ranging from four to ten miles, suitable for all abilities, as well as excellent facilities, including showers and jet washes, and bike rental courtesy of **The Breakpad** (⊕ thebreakpad.com), which is located next to the **Kirroughtree Visitor Centre** (see page 148).

Hikers are better off heading for **Glentrool**, at the western edge of the park, about ten miles north of Newton Stewart, where a narrow lane twists the five miles over to **Loch Trool**. On the north side of the loch the **Bruce Stone**, near the lovely Buchan Waterfall, marks the spot where Robert the Bruce ambushed an English force in 1307 after routing the main body of the army at Solway Moss. From here, you can follow the Garland Burn to Loch Neldricken and Loch Enoch, with their silver granite sands, and then on to the Devil's Bowling Green, strewn with hundreds of erratic boulders left by the retreating glaciers. Alternatively, you can head for the Range of the Awful Hand, whose five peaks include the **Merrick** (2746ft), the highest hill in southern Scotland.

The only surfaced road to cross the park is the desolate twenty-mile stretch of the A712 between Newton Stewart and New Galloway, known as the **Queen's Way**. About seven miles east of Newton Stewart, at the **Grey Mare's Tail Bridge**, there are various forest trails, all delving into the pine forests beside the road, crossing gorges, waterfalls and burns. There's also a **Wild Goat Park** (actually just a large pen) and, a mile or so further up the road, a **Red Deer Range**. A few more miles on, you'll come to **Clatteringshaws Loch**, a reservoir surrounded by pine forest, and connected with the Southern Upland Way (see page 134) on its north side. Heading southeast from Clatteringshaws is the **Raiders Road**, a ten-mile-long toll road that shadows the River Dee, with some great waterfalls and pools for swimming in.

In 2009, the park was the first in the UK to be formally designated a **Dark Sky Park**, with designated spots for astronomy (see ⊕ forestryandland.gov.scot/visit/forest-parks/Galloway-forest-park/dark-skies).

Sun 10am–4pm; ☎01671 402615), three miles east of Newton Stewart just off the A75, is the best of the park's three visitor centres; there's also Glentrool (April–Oct daily 10.30am–4.30pm, Nov–March Sat & Sun 10.30am–3pm; ☎01671 840745), and one by Clatteringshaws Loch (same times as Glentrool; ☎01644 420221). Each has a tearoom, several waymarked walks and lots of information on activities and events.

ACCOMMODATION AND EATING

Wild camping is permitted within the Galloway Forest Park but otherwise most accommodation options are limited to in and around Newton Stewart and New Galloway on the park's western and eastern fringes.

Creebridge House Hotel Creebridge, Newton Stewart ⓦcreebridge.co.uk. The town's most luxurious hotel is this eighteenth-century former hunting lodge, with extensive grounds. It's also a welcoming spot for a pint of local real ale; the chef's signature dish is the bitter-sweet barbary duck breast, which comes with ratatouille fondant potato. **££**

Galloway Activity Centre Loch Ken, on the A713, near New Galloway ⓦlochken.co.uk. As well as hosting a wide variety of land- and water-based activities, this company also offers a terrific range of accommodation, including camping, loch-side cabins with heating and electricity, a Mongolian yurt, tipi and dome, all with a central wood stove, and bunkhouse with shower rooms and lounge/ diner. The café caters for non-residents and sells cakes, tray bakes and light lunches, while set meals are also available in the evening, though these must be booked in advance. Camping, cabins and bunkhouse **£**, yurt, tipi and dome **££**

Wigtown

Seven miles south of Newton Stewart, **WIGTOWN** is tiny yet was once the county town of Wigtownshire. Despite its modest size, it has a remarkable main square, a vast, triangular-shaped affair, its layout unchanged since medieval times. Over the last twenty years or so Wigtown has reinvented itself as 'Scotland's National Book Town', with around a dozen, mostly second-hand, **bookshops** occupying some of the houses lining the square. A couple worth investigating are Foggie Toddle Books, a dedicated children's bookshop at 18 North Main Street (ⓦfoggietoddlebooks.co.uk), and Beltie Books at 6 Bank Street (ⓦbeltiebooks. co.uk), an eccentric little lair that also boasts a fabulous café offering scrummy home baked treats. At the end of September, the town hosts a prestigious ten-day-long book festival (ⓦwigtownbookfestival.com), which draws a good number of high-profile authors.

ARRIVAL AND DEPARTURE
WIGTOWN

By bus Buses stop on the main square and services run to   Newton Stewart (Mon–Sat hourly, 4 on Sun; 15min).

EATING AND DRINKING

ReadingLasses 17 South Main St ☎01988 403266. Although first and foremost a book shop – note the cunningly disguised name – this is also the best place for a bite to eat, whether that's one of their delicious muffins together with a cup of coffee or something more substantial like home-made sausage rolls with salad; and you can read until your heart's content whilst munching away. **££**

The Rhinns of Galloway

The hilly, hammer-shaped peninsula at the westernmost point of the Solway Coast, known as the **Rhinns of Galloway**, encompasses two contrasting towns: the old seafaring port of **Portpatrick** and the dishevelled port of **Stranraer**, which is struggling since the loss of its regular ferry services to Northern Ireland in 2011 (these now depart from Cairnryan seven miles north). At either end of the peninsula are two lighthouses: one stands above **Corsewall Point**, and now houses a luxury hotel, the other stands on the **Mull of Galloway**, a windswept headland at the southwest tip of Scotland, which is home to a vast array of nesting seabirds.

The Gulf Stream dominates the climate here and subtropical plants grow in abundance throughout the area's gardens, linked by the signposted official garden route. Each has its own personality, with colourful seasonal displays and palm trees, and many have coastal views. If you only have time to visit two, aim for Castle Kennedy and Logan gardens.

Castle Kennedy Gardens

Castle Kennedy, 3 miles east of Stranraer • Feb–March Sat–Sun 10am–5pm; April–Oct daily 10am–5pm • Charge • Ⓦ castlekennedygardens.com

The approach to **Castle Kennedy Gardens** passes along a tree-lined avenue that frames the ruined medieval fortress of Castle Kennedy beyond, and then across a palm-fringed canal. The castle forms the centrepiece of the gardens, on a hill squeezed between two lochs, though its ruins can no longer be visited. The 75-acre landscaped gardens stretch west as far as nearby Lochinch Castle, seat of the earls of Stair (and also inaccessible), via a giant lily pond and a stupendous avenue of monkey puzzle trees.

Portpatrick

Situated roughly halfway along the west shore of the Rhinns, **PORTPATRICK** has an attractive pastel-painted seafront wrapped around a small rocky bay, sheltered by cliffs. Until the mid-nineteenth century Portpatrick was a thriving seaport, serving as a major embarkation point for Ireland, with coal, cotton and British troops heading in one direction, Ulster cattle and linen in the other. Nowadays, minus its railway, it's a quiet, comely resort enjoyed for its rugged scenery, sea angling and gentle hikes.

ARRIVAL AND DEPARTURE

PORTPATRICK

By bus Buses leave from South Crescent next to the sandy bay for Ayr (8 daily, 4 on Sun; 1hr 30min) and Stranraer (hourly; 25min).

ACCOMMODATION

Castle Bay Holiday Park 0.5 miles south of Portpatrick Ⓦ castlebayholidaypark.co.uk. Near the cliff's edge next to Dunskey Castle a short walk south of town, with camping space and two-bedroom static homes available to rent by the week. The caravans are reasonably well equipped and there's a little playground in the grounds. Camping £; caravans per week ££££

★ **Rickwood House Hotel** Heugh Rd Ⓦ portpatrick. me.uk. Set back from the harbour, with six contemporarily furnished en-suite rooms with views of the sea and, weather permitting, the sunset. Guests can take a drink in the conservatory where there's a small library of books, or have a good soak in the garden hot tub. ££

EATING AND DRINKING

Connor's Restaurant 1 South Crescent ☎ 01776 810314. Pleasantly located overlooking the town's crescent-shaped sandy bay, this modern bistro churns out some superb seafood dishes, for example sticky honey and garlic salmon, pan-fried seabass with Provençal puy lentils, or you could just stick with the catch of the day. £££

The Crown 9 North Crescent Ⓦ crownhotelportpatrick. com. Right on the seafront, this cosy inn is a good bet for fresh seafood, hand-pulled ales and live music in front of an open fire. For a light lunch try the Cullen skink (smoked haddock soup) or the delightful seafood pancake gratin. £££

Logan Botanic Garden

2 miles north of Port Logan • Feb Sun 10am–4pm; March–mid-Nov daily 10am–5pm • Charge • Ⓦ rbge.org.uk • Bus No. 407 from Stranraer stops at Port Logan (Mon–Sat 6 daily; 30min), then a 2-mile walk north

An outpost of Edinburgh's Royal Botanic Garden, **Logan Botanic Garden** is a marvellously exotic place where the mild air brought by the Gulf Stream supports an

WALKS AROUND PORTPATRICK

Ordnance Survey Explorer map 309

For a spectacular one-mile circular stroll from Portpatrick along the sea cliffs to the shattered ruins of **Dunskey Castle**, follow the coastline south from the harbour until you reach the steps leading up to the cliffs. The route up to the castle, a sixteenth-century L-shaped tower house, is vertiginous in places, but the way back via the disused railway is less hair-raising.

An easy four-mile circular walk takes you north from Main Street to **Dunskey Gardens**. From there head southwest following the stream down Dunskey Glen to the coast to link up with the **Southern Upland Way** (see page 134), which takes you back to the quayside.

eye-opening abundance of tree ferns and palm trees. Check out the primeval giant Brazilian rhubarb in the Gunnera Bog, take a wander in the woods to the south, and head for the enormous walled gardens, where you'll find a water garden, the first ever peat garden, and a massive 20ft-high beech hedge.

Mull of Galloway

Right at the southern tip of the Rhinns peninsula, the isolated **MULL OF GALLOWAY** is well worth the ride and really feels like the end of the road. From this precipitous headland on a clear day you can see the Isle of Man and the coasts of Ireland and England. The southernmost point in Scotland, it's a favourite nesting spot for guillemots, razorbills, kittiwakes, shags, fulmars and even a few puffins; skeins of gannets fish here, too, from their gannetry on the Scares, clearly visible to the east. The headland is also an RSPB reserve – good for spotting linnets and twite – with a **visitor centre** in a building near the **lighthouse**.

Mull of Galloway Lighthouse

Mull of Galloway • **Tower** Easter June & Sept Oct Sat–Sun 11am–5pm; July & Aug daily 11am–5pm • Charge • **Exhibition** Easter–Oct daily 10am–5pm • Charge • ⓦ mull-of-galloway.co.uk

Sited 325ft above sea level at the southern end of the Rhinns peninsula, the **Mull of Galloway Lighthouse**, built by Robert Stevenson, was manned from 1830 up until 1988; it's now operated remotely from headquarters in Edinburgh. It's possible to visit the lighthouse on a guided tour, but otherwise, there's an illuminating exhibition documenting its history. Better still are the spectacular views, on a clear day it's possible to see as far as Cumbria, the Isle of Man and Ireland.

ARRIVAL AND INFORMATION   MULL OF GALLOWAY

By bus The nearest bus stop is four miles north at Drummore, with services to Port Logan (Mon–Sat 5 daily; 10min) and Stranraer (Mon–Sat 6 daily; 40min).

Information Next to the lighthouse, the RSPB Visitor Centre (April–Oct daily 10am–4pm; ⓦ rspb.org.uk) provides a wealth of material about local bird, plant and marine life, and has live images of bird colonies nesting on the cliffs. Outside there's a couple of short nature trails.

EATING

Gallie Craig Just south of the lighthouse ⓦ galliecraig. co.uk. Perched on the cliff edge, roofed with turf and with a panoramic glass wall and terrace looking out to the sea, Scotland's most southerly building provides armchair birdwatching while you enjoy some coffee and cake. If you're stopping for lunch there are also some reasonably priced light meals here too like soups, toasties and burgers. £

Ayrshire
and Arran

DUMFRIES HOUSE, AYRSHIRE

Ayrshire and Arran

The rolling hills and rich soil of Ayrshire make for prime farming country, etched with a patchwork of lush fields and hedgerows. The region's real draw, however, is its coastline, thanks to its wide, flat, sandy beaches, while its endless, fantastic golfing possibilities (including several championship links courses) attract golfers from all over the world. The county town is Ayr, which draws a healthy number of visitors thanks to its associations with Robert Burns, who was born in nearby Alloway. The real highlight here, though, is Arran, often described as 'Scotland in miniature', thanks to its highland/lowland divide and abundance of man-made and natural heritage.

Fifty miles from top to bottom, the largely unblemished **South Ayrshire coastline**, between Ayr and Stranraer, offers several appealing possibilities: notably **Culzean Castle**, Robert Adam's cliffside Neoclassical mansion, and the little-visited but wonderful medieval ruins of **Crossraguel Abbey**. Out in the Firth of Clyde stands **Ailsa Craig**, the giant muffin-shaped island, which is home to the world's second-largest gannetry. Back inland, **Dumfries House** is one of the finest eighteenth-century stately homes in Britain.

The disparate **North Ayrshire coastline**, whose towns once benefited from the industrialization of Glasgow, offers fewer incentives to visit. That said, **Irvine**, home to the terrific Scottish Maritime Museum, and **Largs**, the area's liveliest seaside resort, from where you can catch a ferry across to **Great Cumbrae**, both merit a portion of your time.

Without doubt the most alluring destination in Ayrshire is the **Isle of Arran**, its jagged outline visible across the Firth of Clyde from the entire length of the Ayrshire coast. The beautiful, barren north of the island is a great place to get a quick taste of the Highlands, while the southern half contains the island's largest settlements, including the capital, **Brodick**, and bulk of attractions.

GETTING AROUND
AYRSHIRE AND ARRAN

By bus All the towns along the coast are well served by buses from Glasgow, with a regular express service (No. X77) to Ayr.

By train Ayr, Largs and Irvine are all served by frequent trains from Glasgow Central; the line to Ayr continues down the coast to Stranraer.

By ferry to Arran CalMac (⦿ calmac.co.uk) operate ferries to Brodick, on Arran (5–10 daily; 55min), from Ardrossan, 23 miles north of Ayr.

Ayr and around

With a population of around fifty thousand, **AYR** is by far the largest town on the Firth of Clyde coast. It was an important seaport and trading centre for many centuries, rivalling Glasgow in size and significance right up until the late seventeenth century. In recognition, Cromwell made it a centre for his administration and built an enormous fortress here, long since destroyed. With the relative decline of its seaborne trade, Ayr reinvented itself in the nineteenth century as an administrative centre and a popular resort for middle-class Victorians – aided by the opening of the Glasgow-to-Ayr train line in 1840, which brought in the first major influx of holiday-makers. While there are few real sights in town to detain you, its prestigious **racecourse** pulls in huge crowds, there's superb **golf** all around, and the local tourist industry continues to do steady business out of the fact that Robert Burns was born in the neighbouring village of **Alloway** (see page 159).

CULZEAN CASTLE

Highlights

❶ Alloway The village where poet Robert Burns was born, and the best of many Burns pilgrimage spots in the region. See page 159

❷ Dumfries House An eighteenth-century architectural masterpiece, designed by the Adam brothers and decked out by Thomas Chippendale. See page 161

❸ Culzean Castle Stately home with a fabulous cliff-edge setting, surrounded by acres of gardens and woods reaching down to the shore. See page 163

❹ Ailsa Craig Watch baby gannets learn the art of flying and diving for fish on this distinctive island mountain some nine miles offshore. See page 163

❺ Goat Fell, Arran Spectacular views over north Arran's craggy mountain range and the Firth of Clyde. See page 169

❻ Isle of Arran Distillery, Lochranza Take a tour and have a dram at one of Scotland's smallest distilleries. See page 171

HIGHLIGHTS ARE MARKED ON THE MAP ON PAGE 156

Auld Brig and Auld Kirk

Auld Kirk, Blackfriars Walk • Feb–June & Sept–Nov Tues 1–2pm; July & Aug Sat 10.30am–12.30pm • Free • Ⓦ auldkirk.org

One of the oldest stone bridges in Scotland, Ayr's wonderfully crooked, four-arched **Auld Brig** was built during the reign of James IV (1488–1513), having replaced an earlier, thirteenth-century wooden one. Thankfully, it survived the threat of demolition in the early twentieth century, thanks largely to Burns' poem '*The Brigs of Ayr*', as the plaque halfway along the bridge acknowledges.

HIGHLIGHTS

1. Alloway
2. Dumfries House
3. Culzean Castle
4. Ailsa Craig
5. Goat Fell, Arran
6. Isle of Arran Distillery, Lochranza

AYRSHIRE & ARRAN

A short stroll upstream from the Auld Brig stands the town's much-restored **Auld Kirk**, which Burns attended as a young boy. At the lych gate, look out for the coffin-shaped mortsafe (heavy grating) on the walls; placed over newly dug graves, these mortsafes were an early nineteenth-century security system, meant to deter body snatchers at a time when bodies were swiftly bought up by medical schools, with no questions asked.

Citadel and St John's Tower

All you can see of Cromwell's zigzag **Citadel**, built to the west of the town centre in the 1650s, is a small section of the old walls – the area was built over, for the most part, in Victorian times, but is still known locally as 'the Fort'. The best-preserved section of the fortifications lies on South Harbour Street, though the one surviving corbelled corner turret is, in fact, a Victorian addition known as **Miller's Folly** after its eccentric former owner.

Another survivor from the distant past is **St John's Tower**, near Bruce Crescent, which stands on its own in a well-kept walled garden at the heart of the old citadel, and is all that remains of the medieval church where the Scottish parliament met after the Battle of Bannockburn in 1315 to decide the royal succession. Although a spiral staircase links the five floors (vault, three rooms and bell chamber), it's only possible to visit the tower on Doors Open Day in mid-September each year.

Wellington Square and Esplanade

The epitome of Ayr's main Georgian and Regency residential development, and the town's showpiece, is **Wellington Square**, whose first occupants were 'Gentlemen of Rich Fortune and Retired Army Officers'; its trim gardens and terraces are overlooked by the **County Buildings**, a vast, imposing Palladian pile from 1820.

Esplanade and Low Green

Unless the weather's fantastic, you'll find only the hardiest types taking a stroll along Ayr's bleak, long **Esplanade** and beach, which look out to the Isle of Arran. The one building of note is the distinctive whitewashed **Ayr Pavilion**, built in 1911, with its four tall corner towers; it's known locally as 'the Piv' and now houses the suitably tacky Pirate Pete's Family Entertainment Centre. You're far better off directing the kids to the superb adventure playground next door.

The pavilion sits on the edge of **Low Green**, a lovely expanse of grass that was originally used as common grazing land. As well as being a great spot for a bracing walk, and, if it's not too windy, a picnic, it's also where tens of thousands of people congregate in early September for the **Scottish International Airshow** (@ tsia.scot), with spectacular flying displays along the seafront; this isn't held every year, so check the website for the latest details.

ARRIVAL AND INFORMATION

AYR AND AROUND

By train Ayr train station is 10min walk southeast of the town centre on Station Rd.

Destinations Girvan (Mon–Sat hourly, 5 on Sun; 25min); Glasgow Central (every 20min; 50min–1hr 15min); Irvine (every 20min; 20min); Stranraer (Mon–Sat 8 daily, 5 on Sun; 1hr 25min).

By bus The bus station is smack-bang in the centre of town at the corner of Sandgate and Fullarton St.

Destinations Ardrossan (Mon–Sat every 30min, Sun 6; 55min); Culzean Castle (Mon–Sat hourly, Sun every 2hr; 30min); Girvan, for Ailsa Craig (Mon–Sat every 30min, Sun hourly; 1hr); Glasgow (Mon–Sat every 30min, Sun hourly; 55min); Irvine (Mon–Sat every 30min, Sun hourly; 35min); Largs (Mon–Sat every 30min, 5 on Sun; 1hr 40min); Stranraer (Mon–Sat 7 daily, 4 on Sun; 2hr); Wemyss Bay (Mon–Sat every 30min, 5 on Sun; 2hr).

ACCOMMODATION

SEE MAP PAGE 158

Guesthouses dominate in Ayr, with plenty clustered in the streets between the town centre and the Esplanade, and a few smarter places to be found in the leafy streets to the south of the town centre. There are no hostels in town, though there are a couple of **campsites** in the vicinity.

Burnside Guest House 14 Queen's Terrace ⓦ theburnsideguesthouse.co.uk. The pick of the many guesthouses along this street, the six extremely comfortable, tastefully designed rooms (including a single and a family room) come with restored wooden furnishings, wicker chairs and old-fashioned clocks and lamps. ££

The Crescent 26 Bellevue Crescent ☏ 01292 287329. Spacious and cosy Victorian house with five distinctively furnished rooms (one a four-poster suite), though Laura Ashley-style wallpaper, curtains and the like dominate. A

cracking breakfast is served in the elegant dining room. ££

Heads of Ayr Caravan Park Dunure Rd ⓦ headsofayr-caravanpark.co.uk. Some three miles south of town along the coastal A719, beside the popular Heads of Ayr Farm Park, this caravan site also has pitches for tents. £

Savoy Park Hotel 16 Racecourse Rd ⓦ savoypark.com. A splendid red sandstone Scots Baronial building which, though a little lacking in atmosphere (and often geared towards weddings), does possess extremely well-appointed rooms. The public rooms are suitably grand, too, and there's a lovely garden complete with gazebo and swings. ££

EATING

SEE MAP PAGE 158

Cecchini's 72 Fort St ⓦ cecchinisayr.co.uk. A cut above your average pizza and pasta joint, cool *Cecchini's* has an enticing range of mains, such as borlotti casserole (beans with thickly chopped Italian sausage on a bed of mash), and *spezzatino* (Scotch beef cooked with red wine and tomatoes), as well as any number of terrific value daily deals. ££

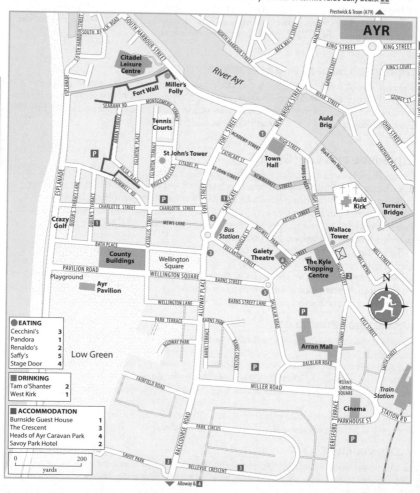

AYR

EATING
Cecchini's	3
Pandora	1
Renaldo's	2
Saffy's	5
Stage Door	4

DRINKING
| Tam o'Shanter | 2 |
| West Kirk | 1 |

ACCOMMODATION
Burnside Guest House	1
The Crescent	3
Heads of Ayr Caravan Park	4
Savoy Park Hotel	2

0   200
yards

HORSE RACING IN AYR

Horse racing in Ayr dates back to the seventeenth century, though Ayr's present **racecourse** (ⓦ ayr-racecourse.co.uk) only staged its first race in 1907. Today, it ranks as Scotland's premier course, staging both flat and national hunt (jump) races, including Scotland's two most prestigious outings; the **Scottish Grand National** in April and the **Gold Cup** in September.

Pandora 32 New Bridge St ☎ 01292 289919. Stylish, dark wood-panelled coffee house offering great caffeine fixes alongside light snacks like soups, baguettes and crêpes. The poached egg and toasted bagel breakfasts (served until noon) are a good shout too. £

Renaldo's 98 Sandgate ⓦ renaldosayr.co.uk. Cheery *Renaldo's* is renowned for its authentic Italian ice cream, all of which is made on the premises, with flavours (36 of them) ranging from the sublime (pistachio, strawberries and cream) to the ridiculous (Irn-Bru). £

Saffy's 2 Dalblair Rd ⓦ saffys-ayr.com. There's certainly nothing fancy about the exterior, but the interior – mixed-up furniture and wall-mounted artwork – is most comforting, as is the food; the specials are more appealing than the regular menu, so expect fish stew with tomato, orange and chilli, or spiced Shetland salmon with curry cream. Well-priced two- and three-course lunches. ££

Stage Door 12 Carrick St ⓦ stagedoorcafe.co.uk. Sharing the same space as the theatre box office, this simple but perennially busy restaurant offers favourably priced dishes like pan-fried chicken and haggis in a pepper sauce to tempt you in. The two-course express lunch menu is particularly good value. ££

DRINKING
SEE MAP PAGE 158

Tam o' Shanter 230 High St ☎ 01292 611684. So-named after the eponymous Burns character, this cosy, thatched inn, dating from 1749, receives a steady flow of locals throughout the day, here for a bit of banter while supping on a pint of the local real ale, from the Ayr Brewing Company. Open mic night on Fridays.

West Kirk 58a Sandgate ☎ 01292 880416. For a quiet pint of real ale, or a craft beer, head to this music-free Wetherspoon church-to-pub conversion, with wooden balconies held up by pistachio-coloured fluted pillars.

Alloway

ALLOWAY, formerly a small village but now on the southern outskirts of Ayr, is the birthplace of Robert Burns (1759–96), Scotland's national poet. Today it is totally dominated by all things Burnsiana, all of which is gathered under the umbrella of the **Robert Burns Birthplace Museum**. Note that the entrance fee applies only to the museum and cottage, and tickets are valid for three consecutive days meaning you can visit as many times as you wish during this period; the other sights are free to visit and have no set opening times.

Robert Burns Birthplace Museum

Murdoch's Lone • Daily Nov–Mar 10am–4.30pm; April–Oct until 5pm; last entry 30min before closing • Charge; includes entry to Burns Cottage • NTS • ⓦ burnsmuseum.org.uk

The centrepiece of the Birthplace Museum is the **museum** itself, a voluminous and illuminating exhibition that should satisfy even the most ardent Burns fan. Inevitably, the main focus is on his extraordinary literary accomplishments – look out for four skilfully carved wooden friezes depicting the key scenes in '*Tam o' Shanter*', and a marvellous chair made from the Kilmarnock printing press, which produced the first edition of *Poems, Chiefly in the Scottish Dialect* in 1786; it, too, features some wonderful carvings, including a bas-relief of the Brig o' Doon and, on the armrest, two dogs (Luath and Caesar from *The Twa Dogs*); above is a photo of Muhammad Ali (a man who wasn't averse to a rhyme or two himself) sitting in this very chair in 1965. Elsewhere, the beautifully presented glass cabinets are stuffed with memorabilia pertaining to other, lesser known, aspects of his life, such as the pistol he used as an exciseman, and the apron he wore at Masonic meetings in Dumfries. In addition, you can view his parlour chair and desk, the wedding

ON THE BURNS TRAIL

As well as the numerous attractions associated with Robert Burns in **Alloway**, two more places that resonate with Burns fans can be found not too far from Ayr; six miles northeast of Ayr is **The Bachelors' Club** (Easter–Sept Thurs–Mon noon–4pm; charge; NTS; ☎01292 541940), a wee thatched house in the tiny village of Tarbolton. It was here in the upstairs room that the 20-year-old Burns attended dancing classes, set up a debating society and became a Freemason. In Kirkoswald, fourteen miles southwest of Ayr, is **Souter Johnnie's Cottage** (Easter–Sept Thurs–Mon 11am–4pm; free; NTS; ☎01655 760603), once the home of John Davidson, Burns' boon companion and the original inspiration for Souter (Cobbler) Johnnie in 'Tam o' Shanter'. The main building is now an art gallery, while the restored alehouse to the rear houses brilliant, life-size sandstone figures of Johnnie, Tam, the innkeeper and his wife. In the graveyard across the road are the graves of John Davidson and Tam, as well as those of Burns' grandparents and his headmaster; a plate on the gate denotes their whereabouts. Inside the roofless kirk is the font reputedly used for the christening of Robert the Bruce in 1274, though the event itself actually took place at Crossraguel (see page 162).

ring belonging to his wife, Jean Armour, and dozens of books and letters dedicated to friends and family.

Burns Monument and Brig o' Doon

Heading through the carefully manicured garden behind the museum, you can't miss the **Burns Monument**, a striking, slightly ludicrous Neoclassical rotunda, topped by a scalloped cornice and a miniature copper-gilt baldachin. Climb to the top for views over to the **Brig o' Doon**, the picturesque thirteenth-century hump-backed bridge over which Tam is forced to flee for his life. In the nearby **Statue House**, admire some eighteenth-century stone statues of Tam, Souter and Nance, which are, in fact, portraits of Burns' friends.

Alloway Kirk

Across the road from the museum is the plain, roofless ruin of the sixteenth-century **Alloway Kirk**, setting for much of 'Tam o' Shanter'; Tam, having got drunk in Ayr, passes 'by Alloway's auld haunted kirk' and stumbles across a riotous witches' dance. All that remains inside are a pair of iron mortsafes. The kirk is also where Robert's father, William, and his sister, Isabella Burns Begg, are buried. His father's grave is prominently located at the entrance to the church; the mournful epitaph on the back of the headstone was penned by Burns.

Burns Cottage

Greenfield Avenue · Daily 11am–15.30pm; last entry 30min before closing · Charge; includes entry to RBBM · NTS · 🌐 burnsmuseum. org.uk

Standing opposite the village post office is the **Burns Cottage**, birthplace of the poet and his home for the first seven years of his life. Built by his father, William, the low, whitewashed, thatched cottage was where animals and people lived under the same roof, with a separate section for grain storage – something that was quite modern in its day. Much altered over the years, there's not an awful lot to see inside, but you can nevertheless gain an impression of what the place must have been like when Burns, the first of seven children, was born in the box bed in the only room in the house.

ARRIVAL AND DEPARTURE   ALLOWAY

By bus The No. X77 from Glasgow (via Ayr) drops off at the museum (2–3 daily), while bus No. 361 (hourly) departs from Carrick St in Ayr and drops off at Burns Cottage.

Dumfries House

Outside Cumnock, 14 miles east of Ayr off the A70 • April–Oct Sun–Fri first tour at 10.45am, last tour 3.30pm, Sat 10.45am & noon; Nov–March Sat 10.45 & noon, Sun first tour 10.45am, last tour 3.30pm; pre-booking advised • Charge • Ⓦ dumfries-house.org.uk • Bus No. 42 (hourly) from Ayr to Cumnock

A handsome Palladian villa, **Dumfries House** was commissioned by the fifth Earl of Dumfries, a widower who wanted to remarry and ensure that he had an heir for the family estate. The house, the first major early commission for the Adam brothers, was conceived as a honey trap to lure a potential wife, and, judging by the portrait of the ageing, gouty Earl in the Pink Drawing Room, he needed all the help he could get. Such was the Earl's urgency, the house was built and decked out relatively

ROBERT BURNS

The first of seven children, **Robert Burns**, the national poet of Scotland, was born in Alloway on 25 January 1759. His father, William, was a tenant farmer at Mount Oliphant, near Alloway, moving to Lochlea Farm, Tarbolton, eleven years later. A series of bad harvests and the demands of the landlord's estate manager bankrupted the family, and William died almost penniless in 1784. These events had a profound effect on Robert, leaving him with an antipathy towards political authority and a hatred of the land-owning classes.

With the death of his father, Robert became head of the family and they moved again, this time to a farm at Mossgiel, near Mauchline. Burns had already begun writing **poetry** and **prose** at Lochlea, recording incidental thoughts in his *First Commonplace Book*, but it was here at Mossgiel that he began to write in earnest, and his first volume, *Poems, Chiefly in the Scottish Dialect*, was published in Kilmarnock in 1786. The book proved immensely popular, with the satirical trilogy 'Holy Willie's Prayer', 'The Holy Fair' and 'Address to the Devil' attracting particular attention. The object of Burns' poetic scorn was the kirk, whose ministers had obliged him to appear in church to be publicly condemned for **fornication**.

Burns spent the winter of 1786–87 in the capital, lionized by the literary establishment. Despite his success, however, he felt trapped, unable to make enough money from writing to leave **farming**. He was also in a political snare, fraternizing with the elite, but with radical views and pseudo-Jacobite nationalist sympathies that constantly landed him in trouble. His frequent recourse was to play the part of the unlettered ploughman-poet, the noble savage who might be excused his impetuous outbursts and hectic womanizing.

He had, however, made useful contacts in **Edinburgh** and as a consequence was recruited to collect, write and rearrange two volumes of songs set to traditional Scottish tunes. These volumes, James Johnson's *Scots Musical Museum* and George Thomson's *Select Scottish Airs*, contain the bulk of his **songwriting**, and it's on them that Burns' international reputation rests, with works like 'Auld Lang Syne', 'Scots', 'Wha Hae', 'Coming Through the Rye' and 'Green Grow the Rushes, O'. At this time, too, though **poetry** now took second place, he produced two excellent poems: 'Tam o' Shanter' and a republican tract, 'A Man's a Man for a' That'.

Burns often boasted of his sexual conquests, and he fathered several illegitimate children, but in 1788, he eventually married **Jean Armour**, a stonemason's daughter from Mauchline, with whom he already had two children, and moved to Ellisland Farm, near Dumfries. The following year he was appointed excise officer and could at last leave farming, moving to Dumfries in 1791. Burns' years of comfort were short-lived, however. His years of labour on the farm, allied to a rheumatic fever, damaged his heart, and he died in Dumfries on 21 July 1796, aged 37.

Burns' work, inspired by a **romantic nationalism** and tinged with a wry wit, has made him a potent symbol of 'Scottishness'. Ignoring the anglophile preferences of the Edinburgh elite, he wrote in Scots vernacular about the country he loved: an exuberant celebration that filled a need in a nation culturally colonized by England. Today, Burns Clubs all over the world mark every anniversary of the poet's birthday with the **Burns Supper**, complete with Scottish totems – haggis, piper and whisky bottle – and a ritual recital of Burns' *Address to a Haggis*.

4

GOLF IN AYR

Few parts of Scotland can boast as many world-class **golf courses** as this stretch of the Ayrshire coast, with two in particular – **Royal Troon** (ⓦ royaltroon.co.uk), ten miles north of Ayr, and **Turnberry** (ⓦ turnberry.co.uk), sixteen miles south of Ayr – ranking among the world's most prestigious. Both courses are on the British Open roster, with Troon the last of these two great courses to stage the event, in 2016. A round at either course will cost you a small fortune (upwards of £175), but there are half a dozen or so far more affordable places to play throughout the region; check out ⓦ golfsouthayrshire.com.

swiftly – between 1756 and 1760 – meaning its Rococo decorative scheme is in perfect harmony with the graceful sandstone exterior. The Earl secured a wife but died without producing an heir; the family subsequently turned their attention to creating **Mount Stuart** (see page 221), leaving Dumfries House to be looked after by a series of housekeepers. The recent story of the house is as remarkable as its past: the building and its contents were all up for sale in 2007, and some of the furniture had begun its journey south to Christie's when Prince Charles and a hastily assembled trust intervened to make a heritage 'save'.

Chief among the treasures is an outstanding collection of **Chippendale furniture**, some ordered direct from Thomas himself, and some created from his 'Director' (book of designs) and augmented by local craftsmen with Scottish saltires. Among the 57 Chippendale pieces on display (which amounts to around ten percent of his entire oeuvre) is a truly spectacular, one-of-a-kind rosewood bookcase, reputedly now worth around £20 million; elsewhere, card tables, gilded mirrors, a study table with drawers on all four sides, and a gorgeous, blue stretch silk bed lie in wait. Otherwise, the family symbols of the wyvern (small dragon) and the thistle recur in inventive and playful touches, and exotic Oriental motifs crop up in the fanciful Adam plasterwork ceilings, tapestry fire screens and gilded pier glasses. Among the many other highlights is a rare, eighteenth-century Grand Orrery, a mechanical model of the solar system, this one featuring an exquisite ivory globe. Note that visits to the house are by guided tour only.

The grounds

Following Prince Charles' intervention, the whole estate, with its sweet-smelling pines, ponds and streams, has continued to undergo a remarkable transformation; a few paces from the house is the Adam-designed **Avenue Bridge**, an elegant, triple-arched structure, across which lies a beautifully landscaped **arboretum**, lined with red gravel walkways and an abundance of woodland flowers and shrubs. Completing this fabulous ensemble is a five-acre **walled garden**, with neatly laid out plots of flowers, herbs and vegetables, stepped terraces and greenhouses.

Crossraguel Abbey

A77, 2 miles south of Maybole • April–Sept Sun–Wed 9.30am–5.30pm • Charge • HES • ⓦ historicenvironment.scot

The substantial remains of **Crossraguel Abbey** provide a lovely antidote to the hordes that pile into Culzean. A Cluniac monastery – one of only two in Scotland – it was founded in 1250, though most of what you see here dates from the late fourteenth century following extensive damage during the wars with England.

At the heart of the complex is the **abbey church**, which has ornate carvings over the piscina and sedilia, though it's not as impressive as the fifteenth-century **sacristy**, which has kept its vaulted ceiling and its decorative capitals, corbels and bosses, embellished with squirrels, lions, a triple-faced head and a green man. Next door, off the cloisters, is the similarly intact, though less decorative, **chapterhouse**. The **tower house**, tacked onto the eastern end of the complex, was built in the early sixteenth century as luxury accommodation for William Kennedy, the last abbot to reside here, between 1520 and 1547; in keeping with the abbot's high status in the outside world, it clearly illustrates the corruption of the monastic ideal that spurred the Reformation. On the opposite side of the abbey, the **gatehouse** is equally grand, and has been restored so that you can climb right up to the cap house and walk out onto the battlements.

Visible in one corner of the complex is a beehive-shaped **dovecote**, complete with well-preserved nesting boxes. This was a crucial part of the abbey's economy, as the monks not only ate the doves but also relied on them for eggs.

Culzean Castle

A719, 2.5 miles west of Maybole • **Castle** April–Oct daily 10.30am–4.30pm; last entry 30min before closing • Charge • **Country Park** daily Jan–March & Nov–Dec 10am–4pm; April–Oct until 5pm • Charge • NTS • ⊕ nts.org.uk/visit/places/culzean • Bus No. 60 from Ayr

Sitting on the edge of a sheer cliff, looking out over the Firth of Clyde to Arran, **Culzean Castle** couldn't have a more impressive situation. Given its strategic position, it's hardly surprising that the Kennedy family maintained a castle at Culzean (pronounced 'cullane') from the twelfth century onwards. The current castle is actually a grand, late eighteenth-century stately home, designed by the Scottish Neoclassical architect **Robert Adam** for the tenth Earl of Cassillis (pronounced 'cassles'), as the Kennedys had by then become.

From the **visitor centre** in the modernized Home Farm buildings, where you can watch an audio-visual show on the house, it's a few minutes' walk through Adam's mock-ruined arch to the **castle** itself, which overlooks the pristine lawn and herbaceous borders of the Fountain Court on one side, with the high sea cliffs on the other. Begun in 1777, Culzean's exterior preserves a medieval aspect, with its arrow slits and battlements; the interior, however, exemplifies the delicate, harmonious Neoclassical designs that Adam loved – look out for the dolphins and swans (emblems of the Kennedy family) and the rams' heads (Adam's own favourite motif). The most brilliantly conceived work by Adam is the **Oval Staircase**, where tiers of classical columns lead up to a huge glazed cupola allowing light to stream down. After admiring the portrait of Napoleon by Lefèvre, you pass through to the impressive circular **Saloon**, whose symmetrical flourishes deliberately contrast with the natural land and seascapes dramatically on view through the windows. One of the last rooms you come to (though it's closed off by Perspex) is the still fully furnished office used by General Eisenhower (including a beaten leather chair, his phone and some family photos); one of the conditions stipulated by the Kennedys before handing over the castle to the National Trust in 1945 was that Eisenhower be gifted use of the top-floor apartments, in recognition of America's support during World War II; in the event, he visited Culzean four times, including once during his second term of presidency.

It's worth leaving enough time for an exploration of the 500-acre **country park**, the highlights of which are the walled garden, with its stone and glass orangery, stone grotto and fruit houses, and the Swan Pond, abundant with waterfowl. Close by is Adventure Cove, a vast wooden playground with all manner of climbing equipment for kids to get lost in.

Ailsa Craig

As you travel along the South Ayrshire coast, the giant muffin-shaped island of **Ailsa Craig** is an intriguing presence on the horizon, stranded as it is in the middle of the Firth of Clyde. The island's name means 'Fairy Rock' in Gaelic, though it was a less than enchanting place for the persecuted Catholics who escaped here during the Reformation. The island's granite has long been used for making what many consider

BATTLE OF LARGS

Largs' chief historical claim to fame is the **Battle of Largs**, which took place in 1263. The battle was forced on King Haakon's Vikings when their longships were blown ashore by a gale. The invaders were attacked by the Scots and, although both sides claimed victory, the Norwegians retreated north and abandoned their territorial claims to the Hebrides three years later. The battle is celebrated in a hugely entertaining, week-long **Viking Festival** (late Aug–early Sept; Ⓦ largsvikingfestival.co.uk), with music, dancing and fireworks. The highlights are the burning of the Viking Longship and a re-enactment of the famous skirmish.

to be the finest curling stones – a company in nearby Mauchline still has exclusive rights and sporadically collects a few boulders. In the late nineteenth century, 29 people lived on the island, either working in the quarry or at the Stevenson lighthouse.

With its volcanic, columnar cliffs and 1114ft summit, Ailsa Craig is now a **bird sanctuary** that's home to some 40,000 gannets, plus thousands of other seabirds. Trips to the island depart from **Girvan**, 21 miles south of Ayr. The best time to make the trip is at the end of May and in June when the fledglings are trying to fly. It takes about an hour to reach the island, after which you get enough time to walk up to the summit of the rock and watch the birds, weather permitting.

TOURS   AILSA CRAIG

Boat tours Several companies in Girvan offer cruises round the island, but only Mark McCrindle is licensed to land (Ⓦ ailsacraig.org.uk). The exact timings and prices depend on the length of trip, tides and weather, but, generally speaking, these take place between April and September with either one or two trips each day (£20/3hr). Booking ahead is essential.

Irvine

IRVINE, twelve miles north of Ayr, was once the principal port for trade between Glasgow and Ireland, and later for coal from Kilmarnock. Those halcyon days are long gone, and the town, sadly, has little now to commend it. That said, it does possess one of the region's finest museums, and for that reason alone, it is worth a visit.

Scottish Maritime Museum

6 Gottries Rd • Daily 10am–5pm • Charge • Ⓦ scottishmaritimemuseum.org

Irvine's one major draw is the **Scottish Maritime Museum**, which is spread across several locations down at the town's carefully restored old harbour. The main exhibition is held inside the **Linthouse Engine Shop**, a magnificent late nineteenth-century hangar-like building held up with massive iron girders, moved here brick by brick from Govan in 1991. As well as superbly documenting the many marvellous feats of engineering, courtesy of engines and turbines galore, it's the spectacular array of vessels that really catches the eye, such as the rusting hull (minus bow) of the **SS Rifle**, the earliest surviving example of a pre-fabricated screw steamer; this one was laid up in 1930, before sinking and then being raised in 1990. There's also an ingeniously crafted parachuted airborne lifeboat – named the **Uffa Fox** after its creator – designed to be dropped close to airmen forced to ditch at sea. Inevitably though, some vessels recall tales of disaster, such as the **RNLI TGB**, which capsized in 1969 while attempting a rescue at Longhope in the Orkneys, leading to the loss of all eight crew members. More mysterious is the story of Kenneth Kerr and his 13ft glass-fibre dinghy, **Bass Conqueror**. In October 1980, while on his second attempt to row across the Atlantic in the smallest ever boat, Kerr ran into difficulties somewhere off the Irish coast and all radio contact was lost. The dinghy was found near Stavanger several months later, but Kerr was never found.

Moored at the **pontoons** on Harbour Street is the **MV Kyles**, a coaster built in 1872, which you can board, alongside a couple of other vessels, namely the **MV Spartan**, a 'puffer' boat, and the **SY Carola**, the oldest seagoing steam yacht in the country – though these last two are due to be moved to the car park. Three times a day there are free guided tours of MV *Kyles*, in conjunction with the nearby **Shipyard Worker's Tenement Flat**, which has been restored to something like its appearance in 1910, when a family of six to eight would have occupied its two rooms and scullery.

Largs

Nineteen miles north of Irvine, tucked in between the hills and the sea, **LARGS** remains the most traditional of Ayrshire's family resorts, its guesthouses and B&Bs spreading out behind an elongated seaside promenade. Despite the obvious tack along parts of the seafront, the town does have a couple of worthwhile sites, and is also where ferries depart for the short hop across the water to Great Cumbrae.

Skelmorlie Aisle

Manse Court • May–Aug Thurs–Sun 1.30–4.30pm; keys available from the museum next door • Free • HES • ⓦ historicenvironment.scot

Largs' one real gem is **Skelmorlie Aisle**, a slice of the Renaissance hidden away beside the old graveyard off Main Street – to get there, enter the yard opposite WHSmith. Once the north transept of a larger church (long since gone), and now standing alone in the graveyard, the aisle was converted in 1636 into a **mausoleum** by Sir Robert Montgomerie, a local bigwig, in memory of his wife who died in a horse riding accident. Carved by Scottish masons following Italian patterns, the tomb is decorated with Montgomerie's coat of arms as well as symbols of mortality such as the skull, winged hourglass and inverted torch. Up above, the intricate paintwork of the barrel-vaulted ceiling includes the signs of the zodiac, biblical figures and texts.

Vikingar!

Greenock Rd, 5min walk north of the pier • Feb & Nov Sat & Sun 11.30am, 12.30pm, 1.30pm & 2.30pm; March Sat & Sun 11.30am, 12.30pm & 13.30pm; April–June daily 10.30am, 11.30am, 12.30pm, 1.30pm & 2.30pm; July–Aug Mon–Fri 10.30am, 11.30am, 12.30pm, 1.30pm, 2.30pm & 3.30pm, Sat & Sun 11.30am, 12.30pm, 1.30pm, 2.30pm, 14.30pm & 3.30pm; Sept & Oct daily 10.30am, 11.30am, 12.30pm, 1.30pm & 2.30pm • Charge • ⓦ kaleisure.com

The Battle of Largs provides a historical link for **Vikingar!**, a light-hearted Viking-themed museum housed, slightly oddly, in a purpose-built leisure complex that also includes a swimming pool and theatre. Led by your very own Viking (in a manner of sorts), you first enter a mock-up Norwegian longhouse, which variously functioned as a living space, bedroom, kitchen and barn – you get to try on various bits of armoury too, if you so wish; thereafter you head into the Hall of the Gods (or Valhalla), featuring impressively carved wooden friezes of four of the gods, before finishing with a big-screen presentation re-creating the famous battle.

Kelburn Castle and Estate

Fairlie, 2 miles south of Largs • Grounds April–Oct daily 10am–6pm • Free; parking charge • Castle July & Aug daily 1.30pm & 2.30pm • Charge • ⓦ kelburnestate.com

The Battle of Largs is commemorated by the distinctive **Pencil Monument** in Fairlie, a modern obelisk a mile south of town, close to the marina, and opposite the **Kelburn Castle and Estate**, seat of the earls of Glasgow (aka the Boyle family) since the twelfth century. The castle itself is no great shakes inside and can only be seen by guided tour. Much more enticing are the **grounds**, which feature a steep gorge and waterfall, 1000-year-old yew trees, an Adam monument and some lovely gardens. There's also plenty for kids to do, including a small adventure course, a secret forest playground, animal farm and pets' corner, a playbarn, and pony rides in the paddock.

ARRIVAL AND DEPARTURE

By train The train station is on Main St, from where it's a 5min walk to the pier and seafront.

Destinations Glasgow Central (hourly; 1hr).

By bus The bus station is on Main St, next door to the train station.

Destinations Ayr (Mon–Sat every 30min, 5 on Sun; 1hr 25min); Glasgow (every 20–30min; 1hr 30min).

ACCOMMODATION AND EATING

Nardini's 2 Greenock Rd ⓦnardinis.co.uk. Locally renowned Italian restaurant and ice-cream parlour housed in a wonderful L-shaped Art Deco building on the Promenade, just north of the pier. The freshly caught fish and home-made pasta are terrific, though the Tea-Time Special (fish and chips, ice cream and a pot of tea; 5–7pm) is a real steal. ££

Old Rectory 2 Aubery Crescent ☎01475 674405. Formerly the home of the ministers of the neighbouring Episcopal Church, this accomplished seafront guesthouse at the northern end of town has five rooms (four doubles and a twin), all of which are exquisitely furnished with period pieces

and have excellent views over to Cumbrae and Arran. ££

South Whittlieburn Farm Brisbane Glen Rd ⓦwhittlieburn.co.uk. Situated on a working sheep farm in a peaceful glen about 3 miles northeast of town, this is a great option if you're up for a genuine rural retreat; although primarily a (small) caravan and camping site, they also do excellent B&B in the farmhouse. Camping £; B&B ££

St Leonard's Guest House 9 Irvine Rd ☎01475 673318. Located just down the hill as you come into Largs on the road from Ayr, this comely guesthouse offers six modestly sized but extremely comfortable rooms (doubles and twins), and a cracking breakfast. ££

Great Cumbrae

Immediately offshore from Largs lies **GREAT CUMBRAE**, a plump, hilly and wonderfully peaceful little island roughly four miles long and half as wide. The most popular activity here is **cycling**, a circuit of the island taking no more than two hours even at a very leisurely pace, while there are a couple of good red sandstone beaches on the west coast overlooking Bute. The only settlement of any size is **Millport**, which curves around a lovely wide bay on the south coast, overlooking the privately-owned neighbouring island of Wee Cumbrae.

Garrison House and the Museum of the Cumbraes

Glasgow St • Mon 1–5pm, Tues 1–7.30pm, Fri 10am–1pm & 2–5pm, Sat 10am–noon • Free • ⓦ garrisonhousecumbrae.com

Millport's seafront is one long parade of Victorian seaside villas and terraces, interrupted only by **The Garrison**, a distinctive old barracks building with castellated gables, and the one-time summer retreat of the earls of Glasgow. Although its main function is now as a library, it also houses the small but illuminating **Museum of the Cumbraes**, which documents life on Cumbrae through the years; the main focus is on some of the characters who have shaped the island's development, such as G.F. Boyle, provost of Millport for 22 years, and local entrepreneur John Kennedy, who ran a highly successful lemonade business in Fintry Bay in the early twentieth century. The exhibition also recalls how smuggling and tourism have influenced island life, though the most prominent exhibit here is the lamp and dick from the Wee Cumbrae lighthouse, the first one to be built on the Clyde, in 1757, and where it remains to this day. There's a delightful courtyard café here, too.

Cathedral of Argyll & the Isles

College St • Daily 8.30am–6pm • Concerts July–Sept Sun 3pm • Free

Hidden from view in the woods above the town is the Episcopal **Cathedral of Argyll & the Isles**, completed in 1851 to a design by William Butterfield, one of the leading High Victorian Gothic architects. The cathedral's most striking feature is a stone screen with cross supported by chunky granite pillars, but otherwise it's pretty modest by Butterfield standards, with only the polychromatic tiling in the chancel giving any hint of his usual exuberance. However, it does have the distinction of being Britain's smallest cathedral, with seating for just a hundred or so worshippers.

Robertson Museum & Aquarium

Near Millport • July–Sept Mon–Fri 9am–4.30pm, Sat 10am–4pm; Oct–June Mon–Fri 9am–12.15pm & 2–4.15pm • Charge • ☎ 01475 530581

Just out of Millport, to the east, overlooking the Hunterston nuclear power station and iron-ore terminal back on the mainland, is the Field Studies Council, one part of which contains the **Robertson Museum & Aquarium**; so-named after the esteemed nineteenth-century naturalist, David Robertson, it holds a laudably ecological exhibition on the local marine environment, a mock-up of the Ark (Millport's original marine station), and an aquarium displaying all manner of local marine life. On the waterfront opposite the museum, a plaque on a large stone marks the spot where the *Scotia* landed upon the return of the 1902–04 Scottish National Antarctic Expedition.

ARRIVAL AND GETTING AROUND

GREAT CUMBRAE

By ferry The CalMac ferry from Largs (every 15min in summer; £3.60 return/person, £13.90/car) takes just 10min to reach the island's northeast tip, with a connecting bus to Millport.

Bike rental On Your Bike, 27 Stuart St (ⓦ onyourbikemillport.com; £10/day), also does repairs and rents out single and double kayaks (£12/hr; £20/hr).

ACCOMMODATION AND EATING

College of the Holy Spirit College St ⓦ cumbraeguesthouse.co.uk. If you fancy stopping over, make a beeline for the delightfully tranquil Anglican retreat house adjacent to the cathedral, which has a mix of twins, double and family rooms, some en suite. The library and common rooms are available to guests too. £̲£̲

Ritz Café 26 Stuart St ☎ 01475 530459. If you don't fancy fish and chips, head to the fabulous *Ritz Café*, which has been in business since 1906, doling out home-made ice cream, marshmallow ices, toasties and Millport Rock, among other goodies. £̲

Isle of Arran

Shaped like a kidney bean and occupying centre stage in the Firth of Clyde, **ARRAN** is the most southerly (and therefore the most accessible) of all the Scottish islands. The Highland–Lowland dividing line passes right through its centre – hence the cliché about it being like 'Scotland in miniature' – leaving the northern half sparsely populated, mountainous and bleak, while the lush southern half enjoys a much milder climate. The population of around five thousand tends to stick to the southeastern quarter of the island, leaving the west and the north relatively undisturbed.

There are two big crowd-pullers on Arran: **geology** and **golf**. The former has fascinated rock-obsessed students since Sir James Hutton came here in the late eighteenth century to confirm his theories of uniformitarianism. A hundred years later, Sir Archibald Geikie's investigations were a landmark in the study of Arran's geology,

ARRAN GOLF PASS

The **Arran Golf Pass** (ⓦ golfonarran.com) currently costs £120, which is remarkable value given that it entitles you to a round on each of the island's seven courses; three 18-hole, two 9-hole courses, an 11-hole course, and the superb 12-hole course at Shiskine. You can buy the pass online or at any of the seven clubs and it's valid for one year meaning that you can come back and play any course that you didn't have time to on a previous visit.

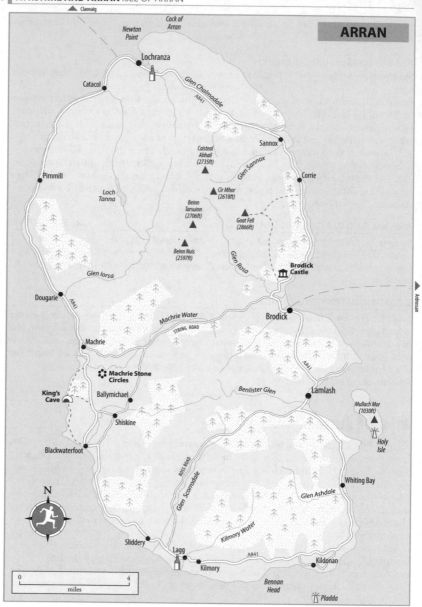

ARRAN

Claonaig

Cock of Arran

Newton Point

Lochranza

Catacol

Glen Chalmadale

A841

Pirnmill

Loch Tanna

Sannox

Caisteal Abhail (2735ft)

Glen Sannox

Corrie

Cir Mhor (2618ft)

Beinn Tarsuinn (2706ft)

Goat Fell (2866ft)

Glen Rosa

Beinn Nuis (2597ft)

Brodick Castle

Glen Iorsa

Dougarie

A841

Machrie Water

STRING ROAD

Brodick

Ardrossan

Machrie

Machrie Stone Circles

Ballymichael

King's Cave

Shiskine

Benlister Glen

Lamlash

Mullach Mor (1030ft)

Holy Isle

Blackwaterfoot

ROSS ROAD

Glen Scorrodale

Glen Ashdale

Whiting Bay

N

Sliddery

Lagg

Kilmory

A841

Kilmory Water

Kildonan

Bennan Head

Pladda

0   4
miles

and the island remains a popular destination for university and school field trips. As for golf, Arran boasts seven courses, including three of the eighteen-hole variety at Brodick, Lamlash and Whiting Bay, and a unique twelve-hole course at Shiskine, near Blackwaterfoot.

Although **tourism** is now by far its most important industry, Arran, at twenty miles in length, is large enough to have a life of its own. While the island's post-1745 history, including the Clearances (set in motion by the local lairds, the Hamiltons), is as depressing as elsewhere in the Highlands, in recent years Arran's population has actually increased, in contrast with more remote islands.

| ARRIVAL AND GETTING AROUND | ISLE OF ARRAN |

By ferry CalMac (Ⓦ calmac.co.uk) operate two year-round ferry services: one from Ardrossan in Ayrshire to Brodick (May–Sept 6–10 daily, Oct–April 4–6 daily; 55min), and a smaller ferry from Claonaig on the Kintyre peninsula to Lochranza in the north (8–9 daily; 30min).

By bus Transport on Arran itself is pretty good: daily buses circle the island (Brodick tourist office has timetables) while the Arran Day Rider (£6) allows you to hop on and off as you please. Buses also link in with the two ferry services.

Brodick

The resort of **BRODICK** (from the Norse *breidr vik*, 'broad bay') is a place of only moderate charm, but it does have a grand setting in a wide, sandy bay set against a backdrop of granite mountains. Its development as a tourist resort was held back for a long time by its elitist owners, the dukes of Hamilton, though nowadays, as the island's capital and main communication hub, Brodick is by far the busiest town on Arran.

The town's shops and guesthouses are spread out along the south side of the bay, along with the tourist office and the CalMac pier. Its tourist sights, meanwhile, are clustered on the west and north side of the bay, a couple of miles from the ferry terminal.

4

Arran Heritage Museum

Rosaburn • April–Oct daily 10.30am–4.30pm • Charge • Ⓦ arranmuseum.co.uk

Up along the road to the castle, the intermittently interesting **Arran Heritage Museum** is housed in a whitewashed eighteenth-century crofter's farm, and contains an old smiddy and a twee Victorian cottage with box bed and range. In the old stables, the main exhibition considers the island's intriguing geological and archaeological heritage – the most notable exhibit is an incredibly well-preserved early Bronze Age cist grave, complete with intact food vessel – while another section recalls the island's prominent wartime role, as testified by the dozen or so air crashes here during the course of World War II.

Brodick Castle

2.5 miles north of town, just off the A841 • **Castle** early April–Oct daily 10.30am–5pm; last entry 90min before closing • Charge • **Gardens** & Country Park year-round 10am–5pm • Charge • NTS • Ⓦ nts.org.uk/visit/places/brodick-castle-garden-country-park

Former seat of the Duke of Hamilton, **Brodick Castle** is set on a steep bank on the north side of Brodick Bay. The bulk of the castle was built in the nineteenth century, giving it a domestic rather than a military look, and the interior is decidedly dour in tone, though there are a few gems to look out for. Don't miss the portrait of the eleventh Duke's faithful piper, who injured his throat on a grouse bone, was warned never to pipe again, but did so and died. There are also a handful of sketches by **Gainsborough** in the boudoir. Probably the most atmospheric room is the copper-filled Victorian kitchen, which conjures up a vision of the sweated and sweating labour required to feed the folk upstairs.

GOAT FELL

Arran's most accessible peak is also the island's highest, **Goat Fell** (2866ft) – take your pick from the Gaelic, *goath*, meaning 'windy', or the Norse, *geit-fjall*, 'goat mountain' – which can be ascended in around four hours from Brodick or around five hours from Corrie, though it's a strenuous hike whichever way you do it; the latter route is, though, tougher.

Much more attractive are the walled **gardens** and extensive grounds, a treasury of exotic plants, trees and rhododendrons, which command a superb view across the bay. There's an adventure playground for kids, but the whole area is a natural playground, with waterfalls, a giant pitcher plant that swallows thousands of midges daily, and a maze of paths. Buried in the grounds is a bizarre Bavarian-style **summerhouse** lined entirely with pine cones; it's one of three built by the eleventh Duke to make his wife, Princess Marie of Baden, feel at home.

ARRIVAL AND INFORMATION

BRODICK

By bus The main bus station is by the ferry terminal. Destinations Blackwaterfoot (bus No. 322: Mon–Sat 7–10 daily, 4 on Sun; 30min); Lamlash (bus No. 323; Mon–Sat hourly, 4 on Sun; 10–15min); Lochranza (bus No. 324; Mon–Sat 5–7 daily, 4 on Sun; 45min).

Tourist office By the CalMac pier (April & Oct Mon–Sat 9am–5pm; May–Sept Mon–Sat 9am–5pm, Sun 10am–5pm; Nov–March Mon–Sat 10am–4pm; ⓦ visitarran.com).

ACCOMMODATION

★ **Brodick Bunkhouse** Shore Rd ⓦ brodickbunkhouse. co.uk. Sparkling bunkhouse offering brightly painted six-bed mixed dorms each with spacious triple height bunks made from wood sourced from the local sawmill; all rooms have sinks, though the wet rooms are as stylish as the dorms, and there's an honesty breakfast bar. There's no reception; you'll be emailed the code to let yourself in. £

Douglas Hotel Shore Rd ⓦ thedouglashotel.co.uk. Virtually opposite the ferry terminal, this large and handsome sandstone building offers some of the most comfortable accommodation on the island, with a selection of bright, modern and tidily furnished rooms, in a mostly grey-checked tartan flavour, many of which have sea-facing views. ££

Glen Rosa 2 miles from town off the B880 to Blackwaterfoot ☎ 07985 566004. Very basic, almost wild, campsite (no showers and cold water only) enjoys a wonderful setting beside a burn, with superb views across the glen. Campfires are allowed too. There's no reception; the owner will pitch up at some point and collect your money. £

Glenartney Guest House Mayish Rd ⓦ glenartney-arran.co.uk. Tucked away just uphill from the post office, this is the pick of the town's guesthouses, with ten immaculately presented, albeit not overly spacious, rooms. Two homely lounges enhance the Glenartney's charms, while you can expect a spectacular breakfast to see you on your way. ££

EATING AND DRINKING

Brodick Bar and Brasserie Alma Rd ⓦ brodickbar. co.uk. There's decent fare on offer at this big, family-orientated restaurant opposite the post office. Chalked up on a huge board, the diverse menu features lots of fish and meaty treats (baked halibut with asparagus, honey-glazed belly of pork and bean casserole), while the home-made thin-crust pizzas are worth a punt. Closed Sun & Mon. ££

Crofters Shore Rd ⓦ croftersarran.com. The fabulous music bar, with acoustic performances Mon, Wed, Fri & Sat at 7.30pm (1pm on Sundays), is actually more restaurant than drinking den, offering succulent dishes like chargrilled tuna loin with red pesto chilli, and steak burger with a blue cheese sauce. Diners are given preference (and keep their table for the evening), but if you just fancy a pint, pop along after 9.30pm. ££

Lamlash and around

With its distinctive Edwardian architecture and mild climate, **LAMLASH**, four miles south of Brodick, epitomizes the sedate charm of southeast Arran. Lamlash Bay has, in its time, sheltered King Haakon's fleet, in 1263, and, more recently, served as a naval base during both world wars.

Holy Isle

The Holy Island boat runs April–Oct daily and more or less hourly, though it's subject to cancellations in windy weather • Charge • ⓦ holyisle.org and ⓦ lamlashcruises.org.uk

The best reason for coming to Lamlash is to visit the slug-shaped hump of **Holy Island**, where a group of **Tibetan Buddhists** have established a retreat. Whilst the retreat is reserved for people staying the night, it is possible to visit the organic garden and have a (free) cup of tea in the information centre, while volunteer residents are happy to advise on local walks. Providing you don't dawdle, it's possible to scramble up to the top of Mullach Mòr (1030ft), the island's highest point, and still catch the last boat back. En route, you might well bump into the island's most numerous residents: feral goats, Eriskay ponies, Soay sheep and rabbits.

ACCOMMODATION AND EATING
LAMLASH AND AROUND

Drift Inn Shore Rd ⓦ driftinnarran.com. Ignore the undistinguished exterior: the food at this seafront pub – home-made fishcakes or braised beef cheek in Loch Fyne ale gravy – make it worth a visit. The convivial beer garden is a lovely spot to eat with its stunning views across to Holy Isle. **£££**

Glenisle Hotel Shore Rd ⓦ glenislehotel.com. High-end, if slightly overpriced, option, with thirteen gorgeous rooms, each painted and furnished in colours that reflect those of the island itself; around half the rooms have a sea view. Terrific bistro too. **£££**

Lilybank Shore Rd ☎ 01770 600230. This sunny roadside B&B is a typically welcoming island guesthouse, offering six floral, pastel-coloured rooms, four of which overlook the bay. Two-night minimum stay. **££**

Lochranza

The ruined castle that occupies the mud flats of the surrounding bay and the brooding north-facing slopes of the mountains that frame it make for one of the most spectacular ensembles on the island, yet **LOCHRANZA**, despite being the only place of any size in this sparsely populated area, attracts far fewer visitors than Arran's southern resorts.

Arran distillery

South end of the village • Daily March–Oct 10am–5.15pm, Nov–Feb 10am–4pm; first tour 10am (11am in winter), then hourly except 1pm • Charge • ⓦ arranwhisky.com

One of the island's most popular tourist attractions these days is the **Arran distillery**, distinguished by its pagoda-style roofs at the south end of the village. Established as recently as 1995 – the first on the island since 1837 – this modern distillery produces the relatively little-known, fourteen-year-old single Arran malt. The tour itself is an entertaining and slick affair, beginning with an audio-visual presentation in a mock-up crofter's cottage, before you are led through the distillery; two tastings are included. In 2019, the company opened a second distillery, Lagg, in Kilmory on the southern tip of the island, where a heavily peated malt is currently in production. Tours are available here too (Tues–Sat 10am–4.30pm), while there's also a fabulous on site café-cum-bistro.

ACCOMMODATION
LOCHRANZA

Lochranza Camping By the golf course ⓦ arrancampsite.com. Relaxed and scenically placed campsite where red deer come to graze in the early evening. Aside from pitches, there are four pods sleeping two- to four, each with heating and lighting, while facilities include modern shower blocks, laundry and a camper's lounge. Camping **£**; pods **££**

Lochranza Youth Hostel Near the castle, en route to the ferry terminal ⓦ hostellingscotland.org.uk. Friendly and well-equipped hostel with three- to eight-bed dorms, plus doubles, most of which overlook the bay. Two lounges, kitchen and laundry facilities also available. Breakfast and packed lunches available too. **£**

EATING AND DRINKING

Sandwich Station Opposite the CalMac slipway ⓦ thesandwichstation.weebly.com. Long-standing favourite that rustles up some of the best snacks in Scotland, no exaggeration: hot breakfast rolls, sandwiches (hot, smoked Skipness salmon with cream cheese), paninis and soups, plus hot drinks and smoothies. Perfect if you need a bite before hopping aboard the ferry. **£**

Stags Pavilion ⓦ stagspavilion.com. Warm, family-run restaurant set in an attractive pavilion at the entrance to the campsite, with sumptuous dishes like slow-roasted honey and rosemary Arran lamb, and blackberry crème brûlée. No licence but bring your own bottle (no corkage fee). Reservations advised. **£££**

4

Glasgow and the Clyde

THE FINNIESTON BRIDGE OVER THE RIVER CLYDE

5 | Glasgow and the Clyde

Rejuvenated, upbeat Glasgow, Scotland's largest city, changed irrevocably in 1990 when it energetically embraced its status as European City of Culture. Set on the banks of the mighty River Clyde, this former industrial giant can seem less than enticing as you approach, and many of its outer suburbs remain seriously deprived. However, after a little time exploring, visitors will find a city that is, in its own idiosyncratic way, a cultured and dynamic place well worth getting to know.

GLASGOW has much to offer, including some of the most imaginative museums and galleries in Britain – among them the voluminous **Kelvingrove Art Gallery and Museum**, and the Zaha Hadid-designed **Riverside Museum** – nearly all of which are free. Glasgow's **architecture** is some of the most striking in the UK, from the restored eighteenth-century warehouses of the **Merchant City** to the hulking Victorian prosperity of **George Square**. Most distinctive of all is the work of local luminary Charles Rennie Mackintosh, whose elegantly streamlined Art Nouveau designs appear all over the city, reaching their apotheosis in the stunning **Glasgow School of Art**, currently being restored after two devastating fires. Development of the old shipyards of the Clyde, notably in the space-age shapes of the **Glasgow Science Centre**, hint at yet another string to the city's bow: combining design with innovation. The metropolis also boasts thriving live-music venues, busy theatres, concert halls and an opera house. Moreover, Glasgow has undergone a dramatic culinary renaissance in recent years, and eating out here is a real joy, as is frequenting one of the city's many new craft coffee houses. Above all, the feature that best defines the individualism and peculiar attraction of the city is its **people** – something acknowledged in the city's marketing slogan, 'Glasgow Makes People' – whether rough-edged comedians on the football terraces or style-obsessed youth hitting the designer bars.

Despite all the upbeat hype, Glasgow's gentrification has passed by deprived inner-city areas including much of the **East End**, home of the **Barras market** and some staunchly change-resistant pubs. Indeed, even in the more fashionable quarters of Glasgow, there's a gritty edge that's never far away, reinforcing a peculiar mix of grime and glitz that the city seems to have patented.

Glasgow is the obvious base from which to explore the **Clyde Valley and coast**, made easily accessible by a reliable train service. Chief among the draws is the remarkable eighteenth-century **New Lanark** mills and workers' village, a UNESCO World Heritage Site, while other day-trips might take you to Charles Rennie Mackintosh's **Hill House** in Helensburgh or on a boat heading 'doon the watter' towards the scenic Argyll **sea lochs**, past the old shipbuilding centres on the Clyde estuary.

Brief history

Glasgow's earliest history is obscured in a swirl of myth. The city's name is said to derive from the Brythonic *Glas-cu*, which loosely translates as 'green hollow' – a name quite contrary to the sooty images of popular imagination. It is generally agreed that the first settlers arrived in the sixth century to join Christian missionary **Kentigern** – later to become St Mungo – in his newly founded monastery on the banks of the tiny Molendinar Burn.

The growth of the city

William the Lionheart gave the town an official charter in 1175, after which it continued to grow in importance, peaking in the mid-fifteenth century when the **university** – the

Highlights

❶ Necropolis Elegantly crumbling graveyard on a city-centre hill behind the ancient cathedral, with great views. See page 186

❷ Rennie Mackintosh architecture The visionary architect left an extraordinary legacy, manifest in masterpieces such as the Glasgow School of Art and Scotland Street School. See pages 187 and 195

❸ Kelvingrove Art Gallery and Museum Splendid civic collection of art and artefacts in a Gothic red-sandstone palace in the city's lively West End. See page 190

❹ Clydeside The river that made Glasgow: walk or cycle along it, take a boat on it, cross a

bridge over it, or get a view of it from the superb Riverside Museum. See page 193

❺ Craft coffee Get your caffeine kicks with a double shot of espresso in one of the city's cool artisan coffee houses, such as *Laboratorio* or *Spitfire Espresso*. See page 201

❻ 'Glesga' nightlife Glasgow is home to one of the best clubbing and music scenes in the UK, so don't miss a chance to sample the city's grit and glamour, which is especially thriving in the lively West End. See page 205

❼ New Lanark A fascinating eighteenth-century planned mill village set in a dramatic gorge. See page 211

HIGHLIGHTS ARE MARKED ON THE MAPS ON PAGES 176, 180 AND 184

GLASGOW & THE CLYDE

HIGHLIGHT
7 New Lanark

IRISH SEA

0   miles   10

5

second in Scotland after St Andrews – was founded on Kentigern's site. This led to the establishment of an archbishopric, and city status, in 1492, and, due to its situation on a large, navigable river, Glasgow soon expanded into a major industrial **port**.

The first cargo of tobacco from Virginia offloaded in Glasgow in 1674, and the 1707 Act of Union between Scotland and England – despite demonstrations against it in Glasgow – led to a boom in trade with the colonies until American independence. Following the **Industrial Revolution** and James Watt's innovations in steam power, coal from the abundant seams of Lanarkshire fuelled the ironworks all around the Clyde, which were worked by the cheap hands of the Highlanders and, later, those fleeing the Irish potato famine of the 1840s.

Victorian Glasgow

The **Victorian age** transformed Glasgow beyond recognition. The population mushroomed from 77,000 in 1801 to nearly 800,000 at the end of the century, and new tenement blocks swept into the suburbs in an attempt to cope with the influxes of people. Two vast and stately **International Exhibitions** were held in 1888 and 1901 to showcase the city and its industries to the outside world, necessitating the construction of huge civic monoliths such as the Kelvingrove Art Gallery and the Council Chambers in George Square. At this time Glasgow revelled in the title of the 'Second City of the Empire', an unexpected epithet for a place that rarely acknowledges second place in anything.

The shipbuilding era

By the turn of the twentieth century, Glasgow's industries had been honed into one massive **shipbuilding** culture. Everything from tugboats to transatlantic liners was fashioned out of sheet metal in the yards that straddled the Clyde from Gourock to Rutherglen.

In the harsh economic climate of the 1930s, however, unemployment spiralled, and Glasgow could do little to counter its popular image as a city dominated by inebriate violence and (having absorbed vast numbers of Irish emigrants) sectarian tensions. The **Gorbals** area in particular became notorious as one of the worst slums in Europe.

Renaissance

Shipbuilding, and many associated industries, died away almost completely in the 1960s and 1970s, leaving the city depressed, jobless and directionless. Then, in the 1980s, the self-promotion began, starting with the upbeat 'Glasgow's Miles Better' campaign in 1983, and snowballing towards the 1988 Garden Festival and the year-long party as European City of Culture in 1990. Further prestige came in 1999 when Glasgow was designated UK City of Architecture and Design. Glasgow has since gone on to host a number of big events: the 2002 **Champions' League Final**, the 2014 **Commonwealth Games** and the 2019 European **Athletics Indoor Championships**. These various titles have helped to reinforce the impression that Glasgow, despite its many problems, has successfully broken the industrial shackles of the past and evolved into a city of stature and confidence.

George Square and around

The imposing architecture of **George Square** reflects the confidence of Glasgow's Victorian age. The wide-open plaza almost has a continental airiness about it, at its centre rises an 80ft column topped by a statue of Sir Walter Scott. Haphazardly dotted around the great writer's plinth are statues of assorted luminaries, ranging from Queen Victoria to Scots heroes such as James Watt and Rabbie Burns.

City Chambers

George Square • Guided tours Mon–Fri 10.30am & 2.30pm; 45min • Free • ⓦ glasgow.gov.uk • Buchanan Street subway

5

The florid splendour of the **City Chambers**, opened by Queen Victoria in 1888, occupies the entire eastern end of George Square. Built from wealth gained by colonial trade and heavy industry, it epitomizes the aspirations and optimism of late Victorian city elders. Its intricately detailed facade includes high-minded **friezes** typical of the era: the four nations which then comprised the United Kingdom at the feet of the throned queen, the British colonies and allegorical figures representing Religion, Virtue and Knowledge. The only way to see the labyrinthine interior is to join a **guided tour**, which begins at the bottom of a magnificent Italian marble stairwell; the highlight of the tour (which may be restricted owing to council business) is a visit to the council chamber, richly furnished in Spanish dark mahogany and embossed leather.

GREATER GLASGOW

If you want to see the chamber in full swing, it's possible to attend one of the council meetings, which are held roughly every six weeks on a Thursday.

The Gallery of Modern Art

Royal Exchange Square • Mon–Thurs & Sat 10am–5pm, Fri & Sun 11am–5pm • Free • ⓦ glasgowlife.org.uk • Buchanan Street subway

The focal point of **Royal Exchange Square** is the graceful mansion built in 1775 for tobacco lord William Cunninghame. This was the most ostentatious of the Glasgow merchants' homes and, having served as the city's Royal Exchange and central library, it now houses the **Gallery of Modern Art** (GoMA). Alas, GoMA hasn't really lived up to the potential of the building itself, or the location, though as it's free it does merit a quick visit. The mirrored reception area leads you straight into the spacious ground-floor gallery, a striking room with rows of Corinthian pillars and huge windows. This is one of the four galleries housed here, each one typically staging two or three exhibitions a year; the basement, meanwhile, is home to a library and a café.

Buchanan Street

Buchanan Street runs north–south one block west of George Square, defining Glasgow's main shopping district. At the southern end lies the **Princes Square** shopping centre, hollowed out of a sandstone building the interior is all recherché Art Deco and ornate ironwork, filled with high-end fashion stores. Glaswegians' voracious appetite for shopping is fed further at the northern end of Buchanan Street in the vast **Buchanan Galleries** shopping centre, stuffed with a raft of chain stores. Just below the Royal Concert Hall is a statue of **Donald Dewar**, Scotland's First Minister until his untimely death in 2000.

The Lighthouse

11 Mitchell Lane • Mon–Sat 10.30am–5pm, Sun noon–5pm • Free • Guided tours Sat 1pm • Charge • ⓦ thelighthouse.co.uk • St Enoch subway

A spectacularly converted Charles Rennie Mackintosh building, **the Lighthouse** has found new life as Scotland's **Centre for Design and Architecture**. The 1895 building was Mackintosh's first public commission, and housed the offices of the *Glasgow Herald* newspaper until 1980, before remaining derelict until 1999; despite glass and sandstone additions, it retains many original features, including its namesake tower.

The building's star attraction is the superb **Mackintosh Interpretation Centre** up on the third floor. It's an illuminating trawl through the great man's work, with plans, photographs, models and video displays exploring the themes behind his buildings and interiors; here too are some original items, including an armchair designed for the director's room at the School of Art and a gorgeous cabinet for the manager's office at the *Herald*. Elsewhere, paintings and book cover designs further demonstrate Mackintosh's outstanding versatility. There's also a varied programme of temporary exhibitions relating to architecture and design. Don't miss catching a free view of Glasgow: there's a viewing platform on the sixth floor, although the best city views are from the Water Tower. There's also a fifth-floor café and a ground-floor shop (see page 207), while guided tours (£5) of the building are offered every Saturday at 1pm.

The Merchant City

The grid of streets that lie immediately east of the City Chambers is known as the **Merchant City**, an area of eighteenth-century warehouses and homes once bustling with cotton, tobacco and sugar traders. In the last two decades the area has been sandblasted and swabbed clean with greater enthusiasm and municipal money than any other part of Glasgow in an attempt to bring residents back into the city centre; the resulting designer shops, stylish bars and cafés give the area a pervasive air of sophistication. It is a fantastic area of the city to explore and makes for a great afternoon.

Trades Hall

85 Glassford St • Often hosts events so check if open • Free • **W** tradeshallglasgow.co.uk • St Enoch subway

Passing the delicate white spire of **Hutcheson Hall**, an early nineteenth-century building designed by Scottish architect David Hamilton, you come to the Robert Adam-designed **Trades Hall**, easily distinguished by its green copper dome. Purpose-built in 1794, it still functions as the headquarters of the Glasgow trade guilds. These include

5

HIGHLIGHTS

1. Necropolis
2. Rennie Mackintosh architecture
3. Kelvingrove Art Gallery and Museum
4. Clydeside
6. "Glesga" nightlife

● SHOPPING

Barras market	8
De Courcy's Arcade	2
Mansfield Park Farmers' Market	7
Glickman's	9
I.J. Mellis	1
Lupe Pintos Chili & Spice Shop	5
Roots, Fruits & Flowers	4
Starry Starry Night	3
Voltaire & Rousseau Books	6

■ ACCOMMODATION

Alamo Guest House	3
Glasgow Youth Hostel	2
Queensgate Apartments	1

● EATING

Ashoka	5
Balbir's	13
The Bothy	3
Cail Bruich	1
Crabshakk	15
Dockyard Social	16
Eusebi	9
The Finnieston	17
The Hanoi Bike Shop	4
Kember & Jones	7
The Left Bank	10
La Fiorentina	20
MOoD Food	19
Mother India	14
Number 16	12
Paesano	2
Stravaigin	8
Two Fat Ladies	18
The Ubiquitous Chip	6
University Café	11

5

corporations of Bakers, Hammermen, Gardeners and Weavers, among others, although today they have limited connections to their respective trades and act as charitably minded associations. The former civic pride and status of the guilds is still evident, however, from the rich assortment of carvings and stained-glass windows, with a lively representation of the different trades in the silk frieze around the walls of the first-floor grand hall. Visitors are free to look around the building, and access is only restricted if there is a function.

Trongate 103

Trongate 103 • Mon & Fri 9.30am–5.30pm, Tues & Wed until 6.30pm, Thurs until 8.30pm, Sat until 7.30pm, Sun noon–6.30pm (galleries closed Mon; entry times vary) • Free • ⓦ facebook.com/trongate103 • St Enoch subway

Behind a sleek glass frontage among otherwise nondescript and downmarket shops on Trongate you'll find **Trongate 103**, a sparkling, six-storey arts hub housing a range of organisations across various art forms and exhibiting printmaking, contemporary photography, video work and ceramics in airy light-filled spaces. Formerly a tannery, clothes factory and air-raid shelter, among other things, this B-listed Edwardian building dating from 1902 today houses a number of organizations, including the Glasgow Print Studio (ⓦ glasgowprintstudio.co.uk), Street Level Photoworks (ⓦ streetlevelphotoworks.org) and Project Ability (ⓦ project-ability.co.uk).

Sharmanka Kinetic Gallery

Trongate 103 • Shows Wed 3.30pm, Thurs 3.30pm, 5pm & 7pm, Fri 2.30pm & 4pm, Sat 2.30pm, 4pm & 6pm, Sun 1.30pm, 3pm & 5pm • Charge • ⓦ sharmanka.com • St Enoch subway

Trongate 103 is home to Glasgow's most unusual attraction. Founded by Russian émigrés Eduard Bersudsky and Tatyana Jakovskaya, the **Sharmanka Kinetic Gallery** is like a mad inventor's magical workshop, with dozens of allegorical contraptions made from old wheels, levers, lights, carved wooden figures and scrap metal that spark into life during performances. A unique art form, Sharmanka (Russian for 'barrel organ' or 'hurdy-gurdy') is at once hypnotic, playful and deeply poignant, with its mechanical sculptures, or 'kinemats', imprisoned in their relentless routine, while choreographed lighting draws you from one part of the show to the next and rather sinister fairground-style music plays in the background.

The East End

East of Glasgow Cross, down Gallowgate beyond the train lines, lies the **East End**, the district that perhaps most closely corresponds to the old perception of Glasgow. Hemmed in by Glasgow Green to the south and the old university to the west, this densely packed industrial area essentially created the city's wealth. The Depression caused the closure of many factories, leaving communities stranded in an industrial wasteland. Today, isolated pubs, tatty shops and cafés stand in contrast to the glossy Merchant City only a few blocks to the west. You're definitely off the tourist trail, but unless you're here after dark it's not threatening, and there's no doubt that the area offers a rich flavour of working-class Glasgow. In recent years, regeneration has filtered through to some parts of the East End with openings such as Barras Art and Design (BAaD), a striking events and gig venue that's also home to the *A'Challtainn* restaurant (see page 204).

Glasgow Green

Between London Road and the River Clyde are the wide, tree-lined spaces of **Glasgow Green**. Reputedly Britain's oldest public park, the Green has been common land since at least 1480, when it was first mentioned in records. Glaswegians hold it very dear, considering it to be an immortal link between themselves and their ancestors, for whom a stroll on the Green was a favourite Sunday afternoon jaunt. Various memorials are dotted around the lawns: an Adams triumphant arch rescued from the demolished Assembly Rooms on Ingram Street, with panels featuring the three Graces and Apollo with his lyre; the 146ft-high **Nelson Monument**; and a stern monument extolling the evils of drink and the glory of God that was erected by the nineteenth-century **Temperance movement**.

The People's Palace

Glasgow Green • Mon–Thurs & Sat 10am–5pm, Fri & Sun 11am–5pm • Free • ⓦ glasgowlife.org.uk • St Enoch subway

Glasgow Green's most conspicuous building, **The People's Palace** houses a wonderfully haphazard evocation of the city's history. This squat, red sandstone Victorian building was purpose-built as a museum in 1898 – almost a century before the rest of the country caught on to the fashion for social history collections. Many of the displays are designed to instil a warm glow in the memories of locals: indeed, the museum is refreshingly unpretentious, even if a little tired.

Throughout, various themes with a particular resonance in Glasgow are explored, including alcohol – look out for the Drunk's Barrow in which the most inebriated were carted off to jail for the night – and crime and punishment, where you'll find the bell from the notorious Duke Street Prison, which rang when someone was hanged on the Green. On a more cheerful note, the section on the Barras recalls evenings of dancing and merriment at the nearby Barrowland Ballroom and there's some guidance to understanding 'the Patter' – Glaswegians' idiosyncratic version of the Queen's English. There's also a reconstruction of a 'single-end' or one-roomed house, a typical setting for daily life for many Glaswegians through the years. For all this, though, the star exhibit is Billy Connolly's pair of big banana boots.

The Victorian glasshouse at the back of the palace was home to the **Winter Gardens**, but the building itself is now in a parlous state with little sign that the gardens will return to their former glory anytime soon.

Templeton's Carpet Factory

On the northeast side of the Green, just beyond the People's Palace, it's worth taking a look at the extraordinary **Templeton's Carpet Factory**, a massive brick and moulded terracotta edifice of turrets, arched windows, mosaic-style patterns and castellated grandeur designed in the style of the Doge's Palace in Venice and built in 1892. It has been converted into apartments, but also houses the West Brewery's excellent *bier halle* and microbrewery (see page 204). Opposite the factory, you can still see lines of **Victorian washing poles**, recalling the days when the Green was very much a public space in daily use.

Glasgow Cathedral and around

Castle St • Mon–Sat 10am–noon & 1pm–4pm, Sun 1–4pm • Free • HES • ⓦ glasgowcathedral.org.uk • Buchanan Street subway

Built in 1136, destroyed in 1192 and partially rebuilt soon after, stumpy-spired **Glasgow Cathedral** was not completed until the late fifteenth century, with the final reconstruction of the chapterhouse and the aisle commissioned by Robert Blacader, the city's first archbishop. Thanks to the intervention of the city guilds, it is the only Scottish mainland cathedral to have escaped the hands of religious reformers in the sixteenth century. The cathedral is dedicated to the city's patron saint and founder, St Kentigern, otherwise known as St Mungo.

Because of the sloping ground on which it is built, at its east end the cathedral is effectively on two levels, the crypt being part of the lower church. Either side of the nave, the narrow **aisles** are illuminated by vivid stained-glass windows from the nineteenth and twentieth centuries, with two twenty-first century additions, The Millennium Window and The Tree of Jesse. Beyond the nave, there's a view of the **choir** ceiling. In the choir's northeastern corner, a small door leads into the **sacristy**, in which

Glasgow University was founded over five hundred years ago. Wooden boards mounted on the walls detail the clergy of the cathedral in a linear progression from Catholic to Protestant and finally the Church of Scotland.

Two sets of steps from the nave lead down into the **lower church**, where you'll see the dark and musty **chapel** surrounding the tomb of St Mungo, though the saint's relics were removed in the late Middle Ages, their whereabouts unknown. The chapel itself is

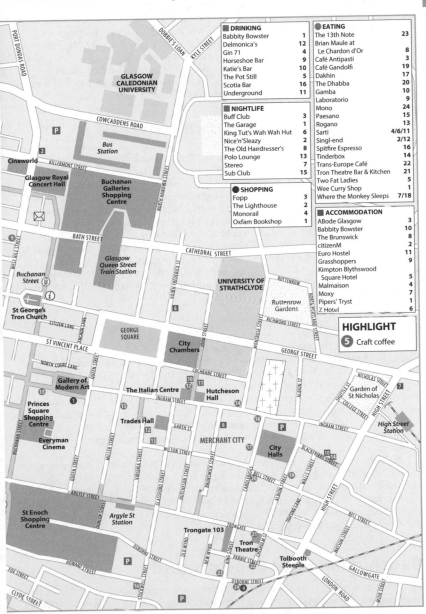

■ **DRINKING**

Babbity Bowster	1
Delmonica's	12
Gin 71	4
Horseshoe Bar	9
Katie's Bar	10
The Pot Still	5
Scotia Bar	16
Underground	11

■ **NIGHTLIFE**

Buff Club	3
The Garage	1
King Tut's Wah Wah Hut	6
Nice'n'Sleazy	2
The Old Hairdresser's	8
Polo Lounge	13
Stereo	7
Sub Club	15

● **SHOPPING**

Fopp	3
The Lighthouse	2
Monorail	4
Oxfam Bookshop	1

● **EATING**

The 13th Note	23
Brian Maule at Le Chardon d'Or	8
Café Antipasti	3
Café Gandolfi	19
Dakhin	17
The Dhabba	20
Gamba	10
Laboratorio	9
Mono	24
Paesano	15
Rogano	13
Sarti	4/6/11
Singl-end	2/12
Spitfire Espresso	16
Tinderbox	14
Trans-Europe Café	22
Tron Theatre Bar & Kitchen	21
Two Fat Ladies	5
Wee Curry Shop	1
Where the Monkey Sleeps	7/18

■ **ACCOMMODATION**

ABode Glasgow	3
Babbity Bowster	10
The Brunswick	8
citizenM	2
Euro Hostel	11
Grasshoppers	9
Kimpton Blythswood Square Hotel	5
Malmaison	4
Moxy	7
Pipers' Tryst	1
Z Hotel	6

HIGHLIGHT

5 Craft coffee

5

one of the most glorious examples of medieval architecture in Scotland, best seen in the delicate fan vaulting rising up from the thicket of cool stone columns.

The Necropolis

Rising up behind the cathedral, the atmospheric **Necropolis** is a grassy mound covered in a fantastic assortment of crumbling and tumbling gravestones, ornate urns, gloomy catacombs and Neoclassical temples. Inspired by the Père Lachaise cemetery in Paris, this garden of death was established in 1832, and it quickly became a fitting spot for the great and the good of wealthy nineteenth-century Glasgow to indulge their vanity; some 50,000 burials have taken place since the first one, and there are 3,500 monuments. Various paths lead through the rows of eroding, neglected graves, and from the summit, next to the column topped with an indignant John Knox, there are superb **views** of the cathedral below and the city beyond.

St Mungo Museum of Religious Life and Art

2 Castle St • Tues–Thurs & Sat 10am–5pm, Fri & Sun 11am–5pm • Free • ⓦ glasgowlife.org.uk • Buchanan Street subway

The **St Mungo Museum of Religious Life and Art**, housed in a late twentieth-century pastiche of a Scots medieval townhouse, is not nearly as bland as its title might suggest. Focusing on objects, beliefs and art from Christianity, Buddhism, Judaism, Islam, Hinduism and Sikhism, the most enlightening of the museum's three galleries is the Gallery of Religious Art, whose stand-out objects are a rare Kalabari screen – an ancestral funerary screen from Nigeria comprising three wood-carved figures – and a fabulous bronze sculpture of a dancing Shiva, the Hindu god. The Religion in Scotland Gallery offers up a rich collection of photographs, papers and archive material looking at religion in Glasgow, the zealotry of the nineteenth-century Temperance movement and Christian missionaries, notably local boy David Livingstone, whose telescope, map and bible used on expeditions in Africa are exhibited here. Outside there's a dry-stone Zen Buddhist garden.

Provand's Lordship

3 Castle St • Tues–Thurs & Sat 10am–5pm, Fri & Sun 11am–5pm • Free • ⓦ glasgowlife.org.uk • Buchanan Street subway

The oldest house in the city, the **Provand's Lordship** dates from 1471 and has been used as an ecclesiastical residence and an inn, among other things. A warren of rooms, the house is of more appeal from an architectural perspective, unless you've an interest in seventeenth-century period furniture, that is. As a reminder of the manse's earthier history, the upper floor contains pictures of assorted low-life characters such as the notorious drunkards and prostitutes of eighteenth- and nineteenth-century Glasgow; one of the most infamous being Hawkie, a street beggar and political street entertainer.

Behind the Provand's Lordship lies the small **Garden of St Nicholas**, a herb garden contrasting medieval and Renaissance aesthetics and approaches to medicine. The cloistered walkway that surrounds it is an unattractive feature, save for the so-called Tontine heads, thirteen keystones removed from the old, eighteenth-century *Tontine Hotel* which once stood in Trongate; carved in wonderfully expressive poses, they remain remarkably well preserved given their age.

Sauchiehall Street and around

Glasgow's most famous street, **Sauchiehall Street**, runs in a straight-line west from the northern end of Buchanan Street, past some unexciting shopping malls to a few of the city's most interesting sights, including Mackintosh's reconstructed **Willow Tea Rooms** and his masterpiece, the **Glasgow School of Art**. Close by, the touching **Tenement House** is well worth a visit.

Mackintosh at the Willow

215–217 Sauchiehall St • The Main Tearooms daily 11am–5pm • Free • Exhibition daily 10am–5pm; last entry 30 min before closing • Charge • Tours daily 10am & 11am; 45min • Charge • ⓦ mackintoshatthewillow.com • Cowcaddens subway

Charles Rennie Mackintosh fans should head for the **Mackintosh at the Willow** (previously referred to as the **Willow Tea Rooms**), which were originally created for Kate Cranston – one of the architect's few contemporary supporters in the city – in 1903. Closed for more than fifty years, the faithfully re-created tearooms reopened in 1983, before shutting again in 2016 for a major refurbishment; today, under its new name, the building has been handsomely restored to its former glory.

Taking inspiration from the word *Sauchiehall*, which means 'avenue of willow', Mackintosh chose the willow leaf as a theme to unify the whole structure, from the tables to the mirrors and the ironwork. The motif is most apparent in the stylized linear panels of the bow window, which continues into the intimate dining room as if to surround the sitter, like a willow grove. These elongated forms were used to enhance the small space and demonstrate Mackintosh's superb ability to fuse function with decoration. As well as sampling the tea rooms themselves, there's an exhibition to nose around as well as guided tours for those really keen to learn more about the history of the building – tours must be pre-booked.

The Glasgow School of Art

167 Renfrew St • ⓦ www.gsa.ac.uk • Cowcaddens subway

Rising above Sauchiehall Street to the north is one of the city centre's steepest hills, with Dalhousie and Scott streets veering up to Renfrew Street, where you'll find Charles Rennie Mackintosh's **Glasgow School of Art** at No. 167 – one of the most prestigious art schools in the UK. Tragically, in May 2014, a fire – which started in the basement – took hold in the west wing, destroying studios, archival stores and, worst of all, the library. The restoration work, which was expected to cost anything up to £40 million, was ongoing when, incredibly, another fire broke out in June 2018. At the time of writing, the visitor centre, shop and exhibition spaces in the Reid building were all closed and tours were not running, which us likely to remain the case for time yet.

The Glasgow School of Art was actually founded in 1845, occupying two previous sites before moving here in 1897. Widely considered to be the pinnacle of Mackintosh's work, the school is a characteristically angular building of warm sandstone that, due to financial constraints, had to be constructed in two stretches (1897–99 and 1907–09). There's a clear change in the architect's style from the mock-Baronial east wing to the softer lines of the western half.

Previously, student-led **guided tours** began inside the big glass **Reid Building** directly opposite the Art School, which, ironically, was finished just one month prior to the first fire. The tours concentrated on the exterior, and in particular the east and north facades, the latter distinguished by beautiful wrought-iron brackets and railings, and the iconic square light box above the entrance. Back over in the Reid building, the tour concluded in the **Furniture Gallery**, an Aladdin's cave of Mackintosh's original designs – numerous tall-backed chairs, a semi-circular settle designed for the Willow Tea Rooms, a chest of drawers with highlighted silver panels, and a fine Kimono-shaped bookcase from Windyhill; and a couple of pieces by his wife, Margaret, notably a magnificent gesso panel.

Venue for the school's design courses, the Reid Building is also home to the **Window on Mackintosh Visitor Centre**, an enlightening timeline tracing the work of the school's

5

students, featuring many original items such as a copper mantel clock, and a canvas skirt with block pattern print, plus drawers stuffed with plans, programmes and flyers.

The Tenement House

145 Buccleuch St • March–Oct Thurs–Mon 10am–5pm; Nov–Feb Fri–Sun 10am–5pm; last entry 1hr before closing • Charge • NTS • Ⓦ nts. org.uk • Cowcaddens subway

For a snapshot of life in Glasgow in the late nineteenth and early twentieth centuries, pay a visit to the fascinating **Tenement House**. Glasgow's tenements were originally conceived as a convenient way to house the influx of workers to the city in the late 1800s, though it didn't take long for the wealthy middle classes to realize their potential. Rising three to five storeys, they have two or three apartments per floor; important rooms are picked out with bay windows, middle storeys are emphasized by architraves or decorated panels below sill or above lintel, and street junctions are given importance by swelling bay windows, turrets and domes. Indeed, tenement flats were home for the vast majority of Glaswegians for much of

---

CHARLES RENNIE MACKINTOSH

The work of the architect **Charles Rennie Mackintosh** (1868–1928) has come to be synonymous with the image of Glasgow. Historians may disagree over whether his work was a forerunner of the modernist movement or merely the sunset of Victorianism, but he undoubtedly created buildings of great beauty, idiosyncratically fusing Scots Baronial with Gothic, Art Nouveau and modern design. Though the bulk of his work was conceived at the turn of the twentieth century, since the 1970s Mackintosh's ideas have become particularly fashionable, giving rise to a certain amount of ersatz '**Mockintosh**' in his home city, with his distinctive lettering and design features used by shops, pubs and businesses. Fortunately, there are also plenty of examples of the genuine article, making Glasgow a pilgrimage centre for art and design students from across the world.

Mackintosh's big break came in 1896, when he won the competition to design a new home for the **Glasgow School of Art** (see page 187). This is his most famous work, but a number of smaller buildings created during his tenure with the architects Honeyman and Keppie, which began in 1889, document the development of his style. One of his earliest commissions was for a new building to house the *Glasgow Herald* on Mitchell Lane, off Argyle Street. A massive tower rises up from the corner, giving the building its popular name of **The Lighthouse**; it now houses the Mackintosh Interpretation Centre (see page 179).

In the 1890s Glasgow went wild for tearooms, where the middle classes could play billiards and chess, read in the library or merely chat. Miss Cranston, who dominated the Glasgow teashop scene, commissioned Mackintosh to plan the interiors for her growing business. Over the next twenty years he designed articles from teaspoons to furniture and, finally, as in the case of the **Mackintosh at the Willow** (see page 187), the structure itself.

The spectre of limited budgets was to haunt Mackintosh throughout his career, and he never had the chance to design with complete freedom. However, these constraints didn't dull his creativity, as demonstrated by the **Scotland Street School** of 1904, just south of the river (see page 195). It is his most symmetrical work, with a whimsical nod to history in the Scots Baronial conical tower roofs and sandstone building material. Mackintosh's forceful personality and originality did not endear him to construction workers: he would frequently change his mind or add last minute details, often overstretching a budget. This lost him the support of local builders and architects and prompted him to move to Suffolk in 1914 to escape the 'philistines' of Glasgow. Indeed, the building that arguably displays Mackintosh at his most flamboyant was one he never saw built, the **House for an Art Lover** (see page 195), constructed in Bellahouston Park in 1996, 95 years after the plans were submitted to a German architectural competition.

the twentieth century, and as such developed a culture and vocabulary all of their own: the 'hurley', for example, was the bed on castors which was kept below the box bed in an alcove off the kitchen.

This is a typical tenement block still lived in on most floors, except for the ground and first floors, where you can see the respectable if cramped home of **Agnes Toward**, who moved here with her mother in 1911, changing nothing and throwing very little out until she was hospitalized in 1965, where she remained until her death in 1975. Thereafter, it was inhabited for seven years by Anne Davidson, niece of Sam Davidson, Miss Toward's church elder.

On the ground floor, there's a fascinating display on the development of the humble tenement block as the bedrock of urban Scottish housing, with a poignant display of relics – ration books, letters, bills, holiday snaps and so forth – from Miss Toward's life. The ground floor is also home to a visitor centre with an exhibition space and a shop, while the opposite ground-floor flat hosts temporary exhibitions about life in old Glasgow.

Upstairs, you have to ring the doorbell to enter the flat, whose four rooms give every impression of still being inhabited; the cluttered kitchen features a superb cast-iron range, cupboards crammed with utensils (one has a full jar of jam from 1929) and a box bed, which would sleep up to five children. Elsewhere, there are framed religious tracts, a sewing machine and a walnut and rose piano, which it is believed both Miss Toward and her mother played. The only major change since Miss Toward left has been the reinstallation of the flickering **gas lamps** she would have used in the early days.

National Piping Centre

30–34 McPhater St • Museum Mon–Fri 9am–5pm • Charge • ⓦ thepipingcentre.co.uk • Cowcaddens subway

Equipped with rehearsal rooms, performance halls, a conference centre, accommodation (see page 200), a museum and a café, the **National Piping Centre** prides itself on being an international centre for the promotion of the bagpipe. For the casual visitor, the single-room **museum** is of most interest, with a fascinating collection of instruments and related artefacts. The museum features Highland pipes from the eighteenth century through to the present day, as well as instruments from the European bagpipe tradition such as the Hungarian duda, Spanish gaita and Italian zampogna. You can even have a go yourself on the bagpipes and a chanter (a practice pipe).

The West End

The urbane **West End** seems a world away from Glasgow's industrial image. In the 1800s the city's wealthy merchants established huge estates away from the soot and grime of city life, and in 1870, the ancient university was moved from its cramped home near the cathedral to a spacious new site overlooking the River Kelvin. Elegant housing swiftly followed, the Kelvingrove Art Gallery and Museum was built to house the 1888 International Exhibition, and, in 1896, the Glasgow District Subway – today's underground metro – started its shuffle from here to the city centre.

The hub of life in this part of Glasgow is **Byres Road**, running between Great Western Road and Dumbarton Road past Hillhead subway station. Shops, restaurants, cafés, pubs and hordes of roving young people, including thousands of students, lend a buzz to the area. Glowing red-sandstone tenements and graceful terraces provide a suitably stylish backdrop to this cosmopolitan district.

The main sights straddle the banks of the River Kelvin, which meanders through the gracious acres of the **Botanic Gardens** and the slopes, trees and statues of

5

Kelvingrove Park. Overlooked by the Gothic towers and turrets of the University of Glasgow, which also houses the marvellous **Hunterian Museum**, Kelvingrove Park is home to the pride of Glasgow's civic collection of art and artefacts, **Kelvingrove Art Gallery and Museum.**

Kelvingrove Art Gallery and Museum

Argyle St • Mon–Thurs & Sat 10am–5pm, Fri & Sun 11am–5pm • Free • ⓦ glasgowlife.org.uk • Kelvin Hall subway

Founded on donations from the city's Victorian industrialists and opened at an international fair held in 1901, the huge, red sandstone fantasy castle of **Kelvingrove Art Gallery and Museum** is a brash statement of Glasgow's nineteenth-century self-confidence. Intricate both in its riotous outside detailing and within, where a superb galleried main hall running the length of the building gives way to attractive upper

---

THE GLASGOW BOYS AND THE COLOURISTS

In the 1870s, a group of Glasgow-based painters formed a loose association that was to imbue Scottish art with a contemporary European flavour far ahead of the rest of Britain. Dominated by five men – Guthrie, Lavery, Henry, Hornel and Crawhall – **The Glasgow Boys** came from very different backgrounds, but all violently rejected the eighteenth-century sentimental renditions of Scottish history peopled by 'poor but happy' families. They began to experiment with colour, liberally splashing paint across the canvas. The content of the paintings, often showing peasant life and work, were as offensive to the art establishment as their style.

Sir James Guthrie, taking inspiration from the *plein-air* painting of the Impressionists, spent his summers in the countryside. Typical of his finest work during the 1880s, *A Highland Funeral* (in the Kelvingrove collection, see page 190) was hugely influential for the rest of the group, who found inspiration in its restrained emotional content, colour and unaffected realism. It persuaded **Sir John Lavery**, then studying in France, to return to Glasgow. Lavery was eventually to become an internationally popular society portraitist, his subtle use of paint revealing his debt to Whistler, but his earlier work, depicting the middle class at play, is filled with fresh colour and figures in motion.

Rather than a realistic aesthetic, an interest in colour and decoration united the work of friends **George Henry** and **E.A. Hornel**. The predominance of colour, pattern and design in Henry's *Galloway Landscape*, for example, is remarkable, while their joint work *The Druids*, in thickly applied impasto, is full of Celtic symbolism; both are part of the Kelvingrove collection. In 1893, the two artists set off for Japan, funded by Alexander Reid and later William Burrell, where their vibrant tone and texture took Scottish painting to the forefront of European trends.

Newcastle-born **Joseph Crawhall** combined superb draughtsmanship and simplicity of line with a photographic memory to create watercolours of an outstanding naturalism and freshness.

THE SCOTTISH COLOURISTS

The Glasgow Boys school had reached its height by 1900 and did not outlast World War I, but they inspired the next generation of Edinburgh painters, who became known as the 'Colourists'. Samuel John Peploe, John Duncan Fergusson, George Leslie Hunter and Francis Cadell shared an understanding that the manipulation of colour was the heart and soul of a good painting. All took inspiration from the avant-garde of late nineteenth-century Paris as well as the landscapes of southern France. **J.D. Fergusson**, in particular, immersed himself in the progressive Parisian scene, rubbing shoulders with writers and artists including Picasso. The influence of **post-Impressionists** such as Matisse and Cézanne is obvious in the work of all four, with their seascapes, society portraits and still lifes bursting with fluidity, unconventionality and a manipulation of colour and shape.

balconies and small, interlinked display galleries, Kelvingrove offers an impressive setting for the engaging display of art and artefacts within. There are recitals on the giant organ in the Centre Hall at 1pm (3pm on Sundays).

The displays are organized under two principal headings: **Life**, in the western half of the building, encompassing archaeology, local history and stuffed animals – of which the ancient Egyptian relics and a logboat from Loch Glashan are highlights – and **Expression**, in the eastern half, which houses much of the superb art collection. However, it does occasionally feel a little muddled – in any case, there's much to absorb, and a repeat visit may be in order.

Inevitably though, it's the **paintings** that draw the biggest crowds, the most famous of which is Salvador Dalí's radically foreshortened *Christ of St John of the Cross*, located on the South Balcony. The focus of huge controversy when it was purchased by the city in 1952 for what was regarded as the vast sum of £8,200, it has become an icon of the collection and essential viewing on any visit. Other favourites include Rembrandt's calm *A Man in Armour*, Van Gogh's *The Blute-Fin Windmill*, and a portrait of Glasgow art dealer Alexander Reid (with whom he once briefly shared a flat in Paris), and a very strong French presence, with at least one painting apiece by Monet, Gauguin, Pissarro, Cézanne and Renoir. You can also acquaint yourself with significant **Scottish art** including works by the Glasgow Boys and the Scottish Colourists, the latter heavily influenced by the French school, as demonstrated in wildly colourful pieces like *Landscape* and *Laggan Farm Buildings near Dalbeattie* by Peploe. There's also a special section of paintings, furniture and murals devoted to Charles Rennie Mackintosh and the '**Glasgow Style**' that he and his contemporaries inspired.

University of Glasgow

University Ave • University Visitor Centre & Shop Mon–Fri 9.30am–5pm • Guided tours Tues–Sun April–Oct 11am & 2pm; Nov–March 2pm; 1hr • Charge • Ⓦ gla.ac.uk • Kelvin Hall or Hillhead subways

Dominating the West End skyline, the turreted tower of the **University of Glasgow**, designed by Sir George Gilbert Scott in the mid-nineteenth century, overlooks the glades edging the River Kelvin; the university itself was founded in 1451, which ranks it as the fourth oldest in the English-speaking world, and was originally located near the cathedral on High Street. Access to the main buildings and museums is from University Avenue, running east from Byres Road. In the dark neo-Gothic pile under the tower you'll find the **University Visitor Centre & Shop** which is where student-led tours of the campus begin; no buildings are entered; instead the tour focuses on the university's history, taking in the grounds, statues, tombstones and the like.

Hunterian Museum

University Ave • Tues–Sun 10am–5pm • Free • Ⓦ gla.ac.uk/hunterian • Kelvin Hall or Hillhead subways

Located in the university's main building, The Gilbert Scott Building, is the **Hunterian Museum**, Scotland's oldest public museum, dating back to 1807. The collection was donated to the university by ex-student William Hunter (1718–83), a pathologist and anatomist, whose eclectic tastes form the basis of a diverting zoological and archaeological jaunt. The most fascinating – and gruesome – exhibits pertain to obstetrics, a discipline in which Hunter was pre-eminent, having published, in 1774, *The Anatomy of the Human Gravid Uterus*, an illustrated text on pregnancy; alongside the book is a womb with a foetus that died at five months, as well as a crude-looking assortment of implements, including wooden forceps. On a lighter note, keep an eye out for a superb ceremonial Maori knife inlaid with shark's teeth from Captain Cook's third voyage, and the world's smallest dinosaur footprint. Upstairs is Lord Kelvin's exhaustive collection of scientific instruments, one of the

5

most notable objects being a gas discharge tube presented to him by Nikola Tesla, the leading physicist of the time.

The Hunterian's most outstanding spectacle, however, is the exhibition entitled *The Antonine Wall: Rome's Final Frontier*; the shorter counterpart to Hadrian's Wall further south, this highly developed wall was built around AD 142 and ran from the Firth of the Clyde to the Firth of Forth (see page 279). On display are sixteen distance slabs (it's thought that there were nineteen), carved stones that document the work of the legions, alongside funerary monuments and sculptural stones, a quite unique ensemble from the Roman Empire.

The Hunterian Art Gallery

82 Hillhead St • Tues–Sun 10am–5pm • Free; charge for some special exhibitions • Ⓦ gla.ac.uk/hunterian • Kelvin Hall or Hillhead subways.

Across University Avenue is Hunter's more frequently visited bequest, the **Hunterian Art Gallery**, best known for its wonderful works by **James Abbott McNeill Whistler**: only Washington DC has a larger collection. Whistler's portraits of women give his subjects a resolute strength in addition to their occasionally winsome qualities: look out especially for the trio of full-length portraits, *Harmony of Flesh Colour*; *Black, Pink and Gold: The Tulip* and *Red and Black: The Fan*, as well as his dreamy night-time visions of the Thames. Whistler's most important piece, however, is *The Rich and Poor Peacock*, a decorative mural designed for Frederick Leyland's Peacock Room in London, which supposedly symbolized the fractious relationship between artist and client.

The gallery has some exceptional Old Master works here: there are oil sketches by Rubens and Rembrandt, paintings by Chardin and Stubbs, as well as eighteenth-century British portraits by Reynolds and Ramsay. Scottish artists are well represented, including the quasi-Impressionist landscapes of **William McTaggart**, a forerunner of the **Glasgow Boys** movement, itself represented here by Hornel, Henry (keep an eye out for the striking *The Hedge Cutter*) and Paterson, whose lovely *Morning in Glencairn* is suggestive of southern France but is in fact south of Glasgow near Dumfries. Taking the aims of this group one step further were the **Scottish Colourists**; the monumental dancing figures of J.D. Fergusson's *Les Eus* preside over a small collection of work by this group, including Hunter, Peploe and Cadell, who left a vibrant legacy of thickly textured, colourful landscapes and portraits, a fine example being Hunter's bold *Houseboats: Loch Lomond*.

A small selection of **French Impressionism** includes works by Boudin and Pissarro, with Corot's soothing *Distant View of Corbeil* being a highlight from the Barbizon school.

Mackintosh House

82 Hillhead St • Tues–Sun 10am–5pm • Charge • Ⓦ gla.ac.uk/hunterian

A side gallery off the Hunterian leads to the **Mackintosh House**, an assemblage of the interior of the now-demolished Glasgow home of Margaret MacDonald and Charles Rennie Mackintosh. Passing the original front door, which was deliberately placed ten feet off the ground for maximum light effect, you are led into an exquisitely cool interior that contains more than sixty pieces of Mackintosh furniture on three floors, many featuring his signature leaf and rose motifs. The first room is the dining room, complete with three-dimensional fireplace and a half a dozen chairs considered so futuristic that they have been used in episodes of *Babylon 5* and *Dr Who*. The studio drawing room – a startlingly modern design for that period – contains Mackintosh's ebony writing desk, while the standout items in the white-painted oak bedroom are a pair of stunning dove wardrobes and a slimming mirror. There are also plenty of contributions from his wife.

The Botanic Gardens

730 Great Western Rd • Grounds daily 7am–dusk • Glasshouses daily April–Sept 10am–6pm; Oct–March 10am–4.15pm • Tearooms daily April–Sept 10am–6pm; Oct–March 10am–4pm • Free • ⓦ glasgowbotanicgardens.com • Hillhead subway

For a spot of peace and tranquillity, pop into Glasgow's lush **Botanic Gardens**, which date back to 1817. The best-known glasshouse here, the hulking, domed **Kibble Palace**, was built in 1863 for wealthy landowner John Kibble's estate on the shores of Loch Long, where it stood for ten years before he decided to transport it up the Clyde into Glasgow on a vast raft pulled by a steamer. For over two decades, it was used not as a greenhouse but as a Victorian pleasure palace, before the gardens' owners put a stop to the drunken revels. Today, the palace is more sedate, housing the magnificent **National Collection of Ferns** with samples from around the world. Nearby, the **Main Range Glasshouse** is home to lurid flowers and plants luxuriating in the humidity, including orchids, cacti, palms and tropical fruit; the annual Orchid Fair is held in mid-May.

In addition to the area around the main glasshouses, there are some beautifully remote paths in the gardens that weave along the wooded banks of the River Kelvin, linking up with the walkway that runs alongside the river all the way down to Dumbarton Road, near its confluence with the Clyde; en route you'll find a rose garden and a children's garden and, beyond here, the **arboretum**, replete with birch, fir and pine trees.

Clydeside

'The **Clyde** made Glasgow and Glasgow made the Clyde' runs an old saw, full of sentimentality for the days when the river was the world's premier shipbuilding centre, and when its industry lent a confidence that made Glasgow the second city of the British Empire. Despite the hardships that heavy industry brought, Glaswegians would follow the progress of the skeleton ships under construction in the riverside yards, cheering them on their way down the Clyde as they were launched. The last of the great liners to be built on **Clydeside** was the *QE2* in 1967, yet such events are hard to visualize today, with the banks of the river all but devoid of any industry: shipbuilding is now restricted to a couple of barely viable yards, as derelict warehouses, crumbling docks and wastelands crowd the river's flanks.

Following a flurry of construction in the last few years, Clydeside has once again become a focus of attention. Striking constructions such as the titanium-clad SEC Armadillo auditorium, the creatively lit **Clyde Arc** (known as 'the squinty bridge') and the enormous **OVO Hydro** centre (sadly without a nickname), have become icons of the city's forward-thinking image. On the opposite side stands the box-like home of **BBC Scotland** and the curvaceous **Glasgow Science Centre.**

Its shipbuilding heritage has not been forgotten though, with the **Tall Ship Glenlee**, located next to the superb **Riverside Museum**, and the **Finnieston Crane**, retained as an icon of shipbuilding days.

THE WAVERLEY

One of Glasgow's best-loved treasures is the **Waverley**, the world's last seagoing passenger-carrying paddle steamer, which spends the summer cruising to various ports on the Firth of Clyde and the Ayrshire coast from its base at the Glasgow Science Centre. Built on Clydeside in 1947 to replace the previous steamer lost at Dunkirk in World War II, she's an elegant vessel to look at, not least when she's thrashing away at full steam with the hills of Argyll or Arran in the background. The booking office (ⓦ waverleyexcursions.co.uk) has information on sailing times and the itinerary.

5

The Riverside Museum

Riverside Museum 100 Pointhouse Place • Mon–Thurs & Sat 10am–5pm, Fri & Sun 11am–5pm • Free • ⓦ glasgowlife.org.uk • **Tall Ship** daily winter 10am–3.30pm; summer 10am–4.30pm; last entry 30min before closing • Free • ⓦ thetallship.com • Partick subway; the No. 100 Riversider bus runs every 30min from George Square via the Kelvingrove Art Gallery

The wave-like titanium-clad building on the north bank of the river houses the **Riverside Museum**, Scotland's old Museum of Transport and Travel. Designed by the late Zaha Hadid, and a past winner of the European Museum of the Year Award, its cathedral-like interior is home to a dramatically displayed collection of trains, boats, trams, bikes and cars, and the intricate models on which full-scale ships were based. Of the many fine trams on show, look out for the No. 1088, boasting a beautiful, upholstered leather interior, brass fittings and stained-glass windows, though for sheer spectacle, nothing comes close to the formidable South African Class 15F locomotive, which is testament to the engineering prowess of the North British Locomotive Company in Glasgow, once the largest loco manufacturer in Europe.

On the two-wheeled front, there's the bike that Graham Obree twice broke the one-hour world record on, plus his skins from the 1996 Olympics; a speedway bike belonging to World War II pilot George Pinkerton (who, allegedly, got the first kill in the Battle of Britain); and the motorbike ridden by Ewan McGregor during his 22,000-mile road trip through eighteen countries in 2004, recorded in the television documentary *Long Way Round*. The one disappointment is the Wall of Cars, the vehicles are mounted on shelves several levels high, meaning that you don't actually get to see them properly. Elsewhere, interactive exhibits provide engaging background on the city's social fabric, with walk-through streets incorporating real interiors from Glasgow shops and cafés.

Berthed alongside the museum is **The Tall Ship**, a square-rigger called *Glenlee*. A 245ft-long, three-masted barque launched on the river in 1896, she circumnavigated the globe four times before being put to use as a sail training vessel – it's now one of only five large sailing vessels built on Clydeside that are still afloat. Here too is the **Clyde Ride**, a rigid inflatable that offers breakneck trips along the river (ⓦ seaforcepowerboats.co.uk).

The Glasgow Science Centre

Science Mall 50 Pacific Quay • April–Oct daily 10am–5pm; Nov–March Sat & Sun 10am–5pm • Charge • **Glasgow Tower** April–Nov 11am–5pm • Charge • ⓦ glasgowsciencecentre.org • Cessnock or Ibrox subways; Exhibition Centre railway station

The south bank of the river is dominated by three space-age constructions which make up the **Glasgow Science Centre**, the largest of which is the curvaceous, wedge-shaped **Science Mall**. Inside are four floors of interactive exhibits ranging from lift-your-own-weight pulleys to high-tech thermograms. Described as 'hands-on info-tainment for the genome generation', it's like all your most enjoyable school science experiments packed into one building, with in-house boffins demonstrating chemical reactions, and pensioners and toddlers alike captivated by cockroach colonies and jigsaw puzzles of human organs. The centre covers almost every aspect of science, from simple optical illusions to cutting-edge computer technology, including a section on moral and environmental issues. Within the mall, an impressive planetarium and 3D virtual science theatre put on shows throughout the day. Alongside the Science Mall is the bubble-like **IMAX theatre** (see page 207).

Also on-site is the 417ft-high **Glasgow Tower**, the tallest freestanding structure in Scotland, built with an aerofoil-like construction to allow it to rotate to face into the prevailing wind. Glass lifts ascend to the viewing cabin, which offers terrific panoramic views of central Glasgow. The centre makes for a great afternoon so make sure to visit.

The Southside

The section of Glasgow south of the Clyde is generally described as the **Southside**, though within this area there are a number of districts with recognizable names, including the notoriously deprived **Gorbals** and **Govan**, which are sprinkled with new developments but still obviously derelict in many parts. There's little reason to venture here unless you're making your way to one of the revived architectural gems of Charles Rennie Mackintosh – the **Scotland Street School** and the **House for an Art Lover**, or the famously innovative **Citizens' Theatre** (see page 206).

As you move further south, inner-city decay fades into more salubrious suburbs, including **Queen's Park**, home to Scotland's national football stadium, **Hampden Park**; Pollokshaws and the rural landscape of **Pollok Park**, which contains two of Glasgow's major museums, the **Burrell Collection** and **Pollok House**; and Cathcart, location of Alexander 'Greek' Thomson's **Holmwood House**.

Scotland Street School Museum

225 Scotland St • Tues–Thurs & Sat 10am–5pm, Fri & Sun 11am–5pm • Free • ⓦ glasgowlife.org.uk • Shields Road subway

The wonderfully designed **Scotland Street School Museum** is another of the city's Mackintosh treasures, and the one to head for if time is limited. This was Mackintosh's second commission for the School Board and the last individual building he designed in Glasgow. The school opened in 1906, before closing in 1979. Throughout its period of construction, there were frequent clashes between Mackintosh and the governors, the former favouring a distinctly more ornamental style; in the event, Mackintosh was forced to back down. The most immediately striking elements are the twin towers (one of Mackintosh's favoured design features), one an entrance for boys, the other for girls. Entering via the light-filled Drill Hall and its superb geometrically patterned, green- and white-tiled columns, you continue up to the mezzanine, where blue tiles are employed along with leaded pane windows.

There are reconstructed classrooms from the Victorian era – which would cater for up to seventy pupils – and World War II, the 1950s and 1960s, when forty-five pupils was the norm; indeed, if you visit on a weekday during termtime, you're quite likely to stumble on a period lesson, local schoolkids struggling with their ink blotters, gas masks and archly unsympathetic teachers. One room is given over to exhibiting Mackintosh's designs, while another fondly recalls the school's history, with books, photos, and a rather grand roll-top desk belonging to William Davidson, the first headmaster. In addition, there are changing rooms, a primitive domestic science room and re-creations of the school matron's sanatorium and a janitor's lair.

House for an Art Lover

10 Dumbreck Rd, Bellahouston Park • Daily 10am–4pm, though it's best to call ahead as the building is often used for private functions • Charge • ☎ 0141 4831600; ⓦ houseforanartlover.co.uk • Dumbreck Station

Tucked just inside Bellahouston Park is Charles Rennie Mackintosh's **House for an Art Lover**. Designed in 1901 for a German competition, it wasn't until 1987 that civil engineer Graham Roxburgh conceived the idea of building the house (he just happened to be running past the site one day), and it eventually opened in 1996; however, few original drawings for the house remained, so its design was largely based on other Mackintosh buildings. It's all quintessential Mackintosh, the exquisitely stylish and original nature of the design making it hard to imagine it suffering the wear and tear of day-to-day life.

The house is entered via the **Main Hall**, a deliberately grand space with massive windows designed for large parties. In the **Margaret Macdonald Room**, there's a film

5

giving a detailed account of the building's history, before you pass into the delicate **Oval Room**, intended for women to retire to after dinner; not only is the room itself oval, but so is everything within it: the windows, stained-glass ceiling light, the chair motifs. Next door, the dazzling white **Music Room** has bow windows opening out to a large balcony, though the garden view is marred by an artificial ski slope; designed to symbolize a forest glade, features here include floor-to-ceiling pillars, teardrop leaves, clusters of lanterns, and rose stencils above the hearth – the room's most theatrical piece, though, is a wonderfully encased piano. In complete contrast, the **Dining Room** is decorated with stained wood and enhanced by beautiful gesso tiles. While here, it'd be remiss not to have a bite to eat in the lovely ground-floor **café** (see page 204).

Hampden Park

Mount Florida • Museum Mon–Sat 10am–5pm, Sun 11am–5pm • Charge • Stadium Tour 11am, 12.30pm, 2pm & 3pm; 45–60min • Charge • ⓦ scottishfootballmuseum.org.uk • Trains from Central station to Mount Florida

Just east of leafy Queen's Park, the floodlights and giant stands of Scotland's national football stadium, **Hampden Park**, loom over the surrounding suburban tenements. Home of Queen's Park Football Club, the fact that it's the venue for Scotland's international fixtures and major cup finals makes it a place of pilgrimage for the country's football fans. Regular **guided tours** offer the chance to see the changing rooms and warm-up areas before climbing the stairs for the obligatory lifting of the cup.

The engaging **Scottish Football Museum** has extensive collections of memorabilia, video clips and displays. While the standard of Scottish football might not be up to much these days, it has rated some fine players over the years, as demonstrated in the **Hall of Fame**, which honours the likes of Denis Law, Jimmy Johnstone and Kenny Dalglish.

Pollok House

2060 Pollokshaws Rd • House mid-March–late March Thurs–Mon 10am–4pm; April–Oct daily 10am–4.30pm; Nov–late Dec & early Jan–early March Fri–Sun 10am–4pm; last entry 30min before closing • Charge • Garden & County Park year-round • Free • NTS • ⓦ nts.org.uk/visit/places/pollok-house • Train to Pollokshaws West (not to be confused with Pollokshields West)

Lovely eighteenth-century **Pollok House** was the manor of the Pollok Park estate and once home of the Maxwell family, local lords and owners of most of southern Glasgow until well into the last century. Designed by **William Adam** in the mid-1700s, the house is typical of its age: graciously light and sturdily built, it looks out onto pristine raked and parterre gardens. Appropriately, the house is now under the management of the National Trust for Scotland, as it was in the upstairs smoking room in 1931 that the then-owner, Sir John Stirling Maxwell, held the first meetings with the Eighth Duke of Atholl and Lord Colquhoun of Luss that led to the formation of the NTS. The Trust has made a deliberate effort to return the house to the layout and style it enjoyed when the Stirling Maxwells were living here in the 1920s and 1930s. As a result, the **paintings** range from Spanish masterpieces – among them two El Greco portraits and works by Murillo and Goya – in the morning room and some splendid Dutch hunting scenes in the dining room to Sir John's own worthy but noticeably amateur efforts, which line the upstairs corridors.

Generally, though, the rooms have the flavour of a well-to-do but unstuffy country house, with the odd piece of attractive furniture and some pleasant rooms, but little that can be described as outstanding. The servants' quarters downstairs, however, do capture the imagination – the virtually untouched labyrinth of tiled Victorian parlours and corridors includes a **tearoom** in the old kitchen. Free tours of the house are available from the front desk, or you can wander around at your own pace.

Holmwood House

5

61–63 Netherlee Rd • House March–Oct Thurs–Sun 10am–5pm; last entry 1hr before closing • Charge • Grounds • Free • NTS • ⓦ nts.org.
uk/visit/places/holmwood • Train to Cathcart station, from where it's a 15min walk, or buses Nos 4 and 6

Holmwood House is the finest domestic design by rediscovered Glasgow architect Alexander 'Greek' Thomson. A commission by James Couper, co-owner of a paper mill on the nearby River Cart, the house shows off Thomson's bold classical concepts, with exterior pillars on two levels and a raised main door, as well as his detailed and highly imaginative interiors. One room upstairs is given over to a series of displays about Thomson and the history of the house. Also on the upper floor is the **drawing room** – look for the white marble fireplace and the night-time star decorations on the ceiling, which contrast with a black marble fireplace and sunburst decorations in the **parlour** immediately underneath on the downstairs level, which also features a delightful round bay window. Across the corridor, the **dining room** has a frieze of scenes from the *Iliad*, along with a skylight at the back of the room designed to allow the Greek gods to peer down on the feasts being consumed inside. One unusual feature not designed by Thomson is the small hatch cut in the interconnecting door between the dining room and the butler's pantry; the house was last occupied by a sisterhood of nuns, who used the dining room as a chapel and created the small hatch for use as a confessional.

ARRIVAL AND DEPARTURE

GLASGOW

BY PLANE
Glasgow International Airport Abbotsinch, eight miles

southwest of the city (ⓦ glasgowairport.com).
Getting to/from the city centre The Glasgow Airport

FOOTBALL IN GLASGOW

Football is one of Glasgow's great passions – and one of its great blights. While the city can claim to be one of Europe's premier footballing centres, it's known above all for one of the most bitter rivalries in any sport, that between **Celtic** and **Rangers**. The latter climbed back to the premiership in 2016, four years after being demoted to the fourth (bottom) tier following liquidation. Two of the largest clubs in Britain, with weekly crowds regularly topping 50,000, the Old Firm, as they're collectively known, have dominated Scottish football for a century, lavishing vast sums of money on foreign talent (albeit much less so in recent years) in an often frantic effort both to outdo each other and to keep up with the top English and European teams.

The roots of Celtic, who play at **Celtic Park** in the eastern district of Parkhead, lie in the city's immigrant Irish and Catholic population, while Rangers, based at **Ibrox Park** in Govan on the Southside, have traditionally drawn support from local Protestants. As a result, sporting rivalries have been enmeshed in a sectarian divide that many argue would not have remained so long, nor so deep, had it been divorced from the footballing scene. While large-scale violence on the terraces and streets has not been seen for some time – thanks in large measure to canny policing – Old Firm matches often seethe with bitter passions, and sectarian-related assaults do still occur in parts of the city.

However, there is a less intense side to the game in Glasgow, and watching one of the smaller clubs – who actively distance themselves from the Old Firm – offers the best chances of experiencing the more down-to-earth side of Glaswegian football. The three other Glasgow clubs are **St Mirren**, from Paisley, the third of the city's premiership clubs; **Partick Thistle**, who play at Firhill Stadium in the West End and compete in the championship (the second tier); and **Queen's Park**, residents of Hampden who currently play in League 1 (the third tier).

THE TEAMS
Celtic Celtic Park, Parkhead (ⓦ celticfc.com).
Partick Thistle Firhill Stadium (ⓦ ptfc.co.uk).
Queen's Park Hampden (ⓦ queensparkfc.co.uk).
Rangers Ibrox Park, Govan (ⓦ rangers.co.uk).
St Mirren Paisley (ⓦ stmirren.com).

5

Express bus (daily 5am–11pm, every 15–30min; £9, open return £14.80) runs to the Buchanan St bus station, also stopping at Bothwell St, Hope St and Queen St train station; tickets can be purchased on the bus or online (ⓦ firstglasgow.com). Taxis charge around £22 to the city centre.

BY TRAIN

Central station Above Argyle St, one of the city's main shopping thoroughfares, Central station (ⓦ nationalrail. co.uk) is the terminus for trains to Ayrshire and the Clyde coast, as well as nearly all trains from England. The walk between Glasgow Central and Queen St station takes less than 10min; otherwise, bus No. 398 from the front entrance on Gordon St shuttles every 10min to Queen St.

Destinations Ardrossan for Arran ferry (every 30min–1hr; 45–50min); Ayr (every 20–30min; 50min); Birmingham (two per hour; 4–6hr); Blantyre (every 10–30min; 20min); Carlisle (every 15–30min; 1hr 10min–2hr 25min); East Kilbride (every 30min; 30min); Gourock (every 20min; 45min); Greenock (every 20min; 30–45min); Lanark (every 20–30min; 45–50min); Largs (hourly; 1hr); London Euston (once or twice per hr; 4hr 30min–5hr 30min); Paisley (every 5–10min; 10min–20min); Queens Park (every 15min; 6min); Wemyss Bay (hourly; 50min–1hr).

Queen Street Station Corner of George Square. Terminus for trains serving Edinburgh and the north.

Destinations Aberdeen (once or twice per hr; 2hr 30min–3hr 30min); Aviemore (hourly; 2hr 30min–3hr); Balloch (every 30min; 48min); Dumbarton (every 10–20min; 35min); Dundee (hourly; 1hr 20min–1hr 50min); Edinburgh (every 5–10min; 55min–1hr 30min); Fort William (Mon–Sat 3 daily, 1 on Sun; 3hr 50min); Helensburgh (every 30min; 45min); Inverness (Mon–Sat 11 daily, 7 on Sun; 3hr 15min–3hr 35min); Mallaig (Mon–Sat 3 daily, 2 on Sun; 5hr 15min); Milngavie (every 20min; 25min); Oban (Mon–Sat 6 daily, 3 on Sun; 3hr 10min); Perth every 30 min; 1hr); Stirling (every 10–20min; 25–35min).

BY BUS

Buchanan Street Station This is the arrival point for regional and intercity coaches.

Citylink coaches Connects major Scottish cities including Aberdeen, Dundee, Edinburgh, Fort William, Inverness, Oban and Perth (ⓦ www.citylink.co.uk).

Destinations Aberdeen (once or twice per hr; 3hr); Campbeltown (4 daily; 4hr–4hr 15min); Dundee (once or twice hourly; 1hr 50min–2hr 30min); Edinburgh (every 15min; 1hr 30min); Fort William (4 daily; 3hr–3hr 15min); Glen Coe (4 daily; 2hr 30min); Inverness (almost hourly; 3hr 20min–3hr 40min); Kyle of Lochalsh (3 daily; 5–6hr); Loch Lomond (9 daily; 50min); Oban (3 daily; 3hr); Perth (every 1–2hr; 1hr 25min–1hr 40min); Portree (3 daily; 6hr 15min–7hr 15min); Stirling (hourly; 45min).

GETTING AROUND

ON FOOT

Walking is the best way of exploring any one part of the city. However, as the main sights are scattered – the West End, for example, is a good 30min walk from the centre – you'll probably need to use the comprehensive public transport system, which includes an underground network. If you're travelling beyond the city centre or the West End, or to the main sights on the Southside, you may need to use the bus and train networks. For information on all transport within the city and further afield, call Traveline or check online (ⓦ travelinescotland.com); otherwise, you can get information and pick up timetables at the Travel Centre (daily 9am–5pm) in Buchanan St bus station.

PASSES

Various public transport passes are available if you plan to do lots of travelling on one day or are in the city for more than a few days. See ⓦ spt.co.uk for more information.

Roundabout Glasgow For train and subway travel the Roundabout Glasgow ticket gives unlimited travel for a day (Mon–Fri after 9am, all day Sat & Sun; £7.40).

ZoneCard The ZoneCard, covers travel by train, subway, most buses and some ferries, and costs around £20.90 and gives travel for a week in central Glasgow, including all the

attractions on the Southside.

BY SUBWAY

The best way to get between the city centre and the West End is to use the subway (Mon–Sat 6.30am–11.30pm, Sun 10am–6pm), whose stations are marked with a large orange S. Affectionately known as the 'Clockwork Orange' (there's only one, circular, route and the trains are a garish bright orange), the service is extremely easy to use. There's a flat fare of £1.75, or you can buy a day ticket for £4.20.

Stations The main stations are Buchanan St, near George Square and connected to Queen St train station by a moving walkway, and St Enoch, at the junction of Buchanan St pedestrian precinct and Argyle St. Hillhead station is bang in the heart of the West End, near the university.

BY TRAIN

Suburban trains The suburban train network is swift and convenient. Suburbs south of the Clyde are connected to Central station, either at the mainline station or the subterranean low-level station, while trains from Queen St (which also has mainline and low-level stations) head into the northeast suburbs.

Cross-city lines There are two functional cross-city

lines: the one running through Central station connects to southeastern districts as far out as Lanark, while the Queen St line links to the East End and points east. Trains on both lines go through Partick station, near the West End, which is also an underground stop; beyond Partick, the trains are an excellent way to link to points west and northwest of Glasgow, including Milngavie (for the start of the West Highland Way), Dumbarton and Helensburgh.

BY BUS
Buchanan Street bus station Glasgow's main bus terminus (station open 24hr; concourse open daily 6am–11pm; ☎0141 333 3708), north of Sauchiehall St and opposite the Royal Concert Hall. As well as intercity buses, this is where local city services depart from.

First Glasgow Serves Glasgow, Edinburgh, central Scotland, the Borders and Aberdeen (ⓦfirstbus.co.uk/greater-glasgow). A flat fare costs £2 and a FirstDay pass, allowing unlimited travel throughout Glasgow, costs £4.70; tickets can be purchased on the bus (have the exact change ready) or online.

BY TAXI
You can hail a black taxi from anywhere in the city centre, day or night. There are also taxi ranks at Central and Queen St train stations and Buchanan St bus station. Expect to pay around £7 for a journey from the city centre to the West End. Uber users will have little trouble finding a ride as the city is comprehensively covered.

Taxis Glasgow Taxi Ltd (ⓦglasgowtaxis.co.uk), GlasGo Cabs (ⓦglasgocabs.co.uk), West End Radio Cars (ⓦwestendradiocars.co.uk).

BY CAR
The M8 motorway runs right through the heart of Glasgow, making the city centre very accessible by car; once you're there, however, the grid of one-way streets and pedestrian precincts can be frustrating to navigate. You'll find plenty of parking meters as well as car parks dotted all around the centre.

Car rental Arnold Clark, multiple branches (ⓦarnoldclarkrental.com); Avis, 70 Lancefield St (ⓦavis.co.uk); Budget, Glasgow Airport (ⓦbudget.co.uk); Hertz, various branches including 200 Argyle St (ⓦhertz.co.uk). All the main rental companies have desks at the airport.

BY FERRY
Govan Ferry The Govan ferry (June–Sept; free) runs between the pontoon at Water Row and the Kelvin Harbour landing stage linking the Riverside Museum with Govan. Note, though, that this service is likely to stop once the Govan to Partick bridge is complete, either in 2023 or 2024.

INFORMATION AND TOURS

Tourist office There's a VisitScotland iCentre at 156a/158 Buchanan St (May & June Mon–Wed, Fri & Sat 9am–6pm, Thurs 9.30am–6pm, Sun 10am–4pm; July & Aug Mon–Wed, Fri & Sat 9am–7pm, Thurs 9.30am–7pm, Sun 10am–5pm; Sept–April Mon–Sat 9am–5pm, Sun 10am–4pm, Thurs open from 9.30am Nov–April; ⓦvisitscotland.com) and ⓦpeoplemakeglasgow.com is a useful online resource.

City Sightseeing Open-top, hop-on, hop-off bus tours (daily late May–Sept 9.30am–6.30pm, Oct–late May 9.30am–4.30pm; one day £16, two days £17; ⓦwww.citysightseeingglasgow.co.uk) leave every 10min (every 30mins in winter) from George Square on a continuous circuit of all the major attractions in the city centre and West End, allowing you to get on and off as you please.

ACCOMMODATION

SEE MAPS PAGES 178, 180 AND 184

Glasgow has plentiful accommodation, and while many hotels are business-oriented, this means that you can often negotiate good deals at weekends. There are an increasing number of fashionable (though fairly priced) design hotels, while the majority of the best guesthouses and B&Bs can be found in the **West End**. There's also a reasonable, though not particularly exciting, spread of hostels across the city.

CITY CENTRE

HOTELS AND GUESTHOUSES
ABode Glasgow 129 Bath St ⓦabodeglasgow.co.uk. A classy hotel that delights on many levels, from the warm welcome and original cage lift, to the rooms themselves, of which there are four categories, ranging from 'Comfortable' to 'Fabulous'; the main difference between them is size and the odd extra (for example, Nespresso machines), though nearly all feature black and white, or colour, print wallpaper, picture frame headboards and tartan spreads, while a few rooms retain the original wood-panelled walls and stained-glass windows. **££**

Babbity Bowster 16–18 Blackfriars St, off High St ⓦbabbitybowster.com. Best known as a pub (see page 204), *Babbity Bowster* also features five plain but serviceable rooms (singles and doubles) that provide visitors with a great, and decently priced, Merchant City location; a simple breakfast is included. **££**

The Brunswick 106–108 Brunswick St ⓦbrunswickhotel.co.uk. A small, independent hotel in the heart of the Merchant City offering twenty-seven fashionable rooms with minimalist furniture; the 'Compact' rooms (which really are compact) are a bargain, while those standard rooms on the higher levels are less prone to the traffic noise; there's a restaurant/bar to boot. Standard rooms **££**

5

TOP 5 BOUTIQUE HOTELS

ABode Glasgow See page 199
citizenM See page 200
Hotel du Vin See page 200
Kimpton Blythswood Square Hotel See page 200
Z Hotel See page 200

---

citizenM 60 Renfrew St ⓦcitizenm.com. This modern European chain offers a luxury experience that won't break the bank; check in via computer then head to your room to enjoy the innovative mood lighting, hip decor and rain shower. After that, you could do a lot worse than hang around in the cool canteenM, a homely breakfast bar-meets-lounge area that's open round the clock – indeed, you're quite likely to spend more time in this hotel than out of it. Breakfast can be added on. **££**

★ **Grasshoppers** 87 Union St ⓦgrasshoppersglasgow. com. Occupying the sixth (top) floor of the former Caledonian Railway Company building, the ground-floor entrance is somewhat unprepossessing, but don't let that put you off. This medium-sized hotel is a real gem, from the artwork-lined corridors to the rooms themselves, which manifest an understatedly cool, urban feel: oak flooring, bespoke, Scandinavian-style furnishings and pod-like bathrooms. The service, meanwhile, is second to none. **££**

Kimpton Blythswood Square Hotel 11 Blythswood Square ⓦkimptonblythswoodsquare.com. Luxury hotel boasting gorgeous Georgian architecture, with smartly renovated rooms and an on-site spa, plus a top-notch seafood restaurant, iasg (pronounced 'ee-usk') and posh cocktail bar. **££££**

Malmaison 278 West George St ⓦmalmaison.com. At Glasgow's version of this sleek, chic hotel group, the austere Grecian-temple frontage masks a superbly comfortable designer hotel whose rooms are dominated by various shades of greys and purples, and come with deep, inviting beds and big fluffy pillows. Breakfast can be added on. **££**

Moxy 210 High St ⓦmoxy-hotels.marriott.com. Playful and energetic, this place would score highly on a budget-savvy millennial-traveller's checklist: flat-screen TVs, ultrafast wi-fi and an edgy, urban location – it's just east of the city centre. The rooms are compact but the communal space is where the action is: a buzzing area with a central bar, long communal tables dotted with coffee table books, and a pool and table football table. **££**

Pipers' Tryst 30–34 McPhater St ⓦthepipingcentre. co.uk. Attached to the National Piping Centre (see page 189), set back from the main road in the heart of Glasgow, the eight decently sized rooms feature decor that is firmly on the side of cheery tartan. There are cheaper rates for single occupancy, tremendously helpful staff and a wholesome breakfast to see you on your way. **£££**

★ **Z Hotel** 36 North Frederick St ⓦthezhotels.com. The handsome, sandstone facade of this former printworks conceals compact but fabulously sleek rooms, minimally furnished (there are few tables and chairs to speak of, and TVs are embedded in the wall), with sparkling wet rooms boxed off by glass partitions; each evening between 5 and 8pm there's a free wine and cheese buffet (which includes a selection of four cheeses and a glass of wine), while the good-humoured, unfailingly helpful staff conspire to make this a terrific place to spend a night or two. Breakfast not included. **££**

HOSTELS AND CAMPUS ACCOMMODATION

Euro Hostel 318 Clyde St ⓦeurohostels.co.uk. This enormous, seven-storey hostel can feel a bit impersonal given its size, though its location facing the Clyde means that many rooms have great views. A mix of en-suite rooms (sleeping anything from two to fourteen) and suites, the latter with a small lounge/TV area; all beds are fitted with a shelf station complete with LED light, USB port, and plug socket. There's also a self-catering kitchen, laundry and adjoining bar, which is where breakfast is taken. Dorms **£**, suites per person **££**, doubles **£**

THE WEST END

HOTELS AND GUESTHOUSES

Alamo Guest House 46 Gray St ⓦalamoguesthouse. com. Good-value, family-run boarding house next to Kelvingrove Park, with ten rooms, each one completely different in size and character, variously featuring stucco plasterwork, French oak beds, slate-tile sinks and cast-iron chandeliers, or perhaps a freestanding tub. **££**

Hotel du Vin 1 Devonshire Gardens, Great Western Rd ⓦhotelduvin.com. Glasgow's most exclusive and exquisite small hotel, set in a handsome row of converted townhouses a 10min walk up the Great Western Rd from the Botanic Gardens; rooms typically feature large open-plan seating areas, Bose sound systems and monsoon power showers, and there's further decadence courtesy of the glamorous bar. **£££**

HOSTEL

Glasgow Youth Hostel 8 Park Terrace

TOP 5 BUDGET STAYS

Alamo Guest House See page 200
Babbity Bowster See page 199
Glasgow Youth Hotel See page 200
Grasshoppers See page 200
Moxy See page 200

ⓦ hostellingscotland.org.uk. Popular but surprisingly low-key hostel located in a wonderful townhouse in one of the West End's grandest terraces. All the dorms (singles up to eight-bed shared rooms) are en suite, while other facilities include common area, self-catering kitchen and laundry. It's a 10min walk south of Kelvinbridge subway station, while bus Nos 4 or 4A from the city centre leaves you with a short stroll west up Woodlands Rd. Dorms **£**, doubles **££**

EATING

Glasgow's restaurant scene has improved dramatically and can now hold its own with the best cities in Britain. Originally brought up on the culinary skills of the long-established **Italian** community and later waves of **Indian** and **Chinese** immigrants – indeed, its home to some of the UK's best Indian restaurants – there's been a move towards celebrating great **Scottish produce**. Although there's a decent spread of cafés and restaurants throughout the city centre, there's a fantastic concentration of places in the West End, particularly along Argyle St, Byres Rd and Gibson St. Many restaurants have excellent **set lunch**, pre-theatre or early dining deals.

CITY CENTRE AND THE MERCHANT CITY

CAFÉS

★ **Laboratorio** 93 West Nile St ⓦ labespr.tumblr. com. The 'Lab', as it's more popularly known, is a terrific little bolthole with cement board walls and recycled wood panelling, and super-friendly baristas who really know their beans; there's typically a single-origin espresso and a guest espresso on the go at any one time. You can perch inside, takeaway or grab one of the sought-after pavement tables. **££**

Singl-end 263 Renfrew St ⓦ thesingl-end.co.uk. An engaging, below-street-level café and bakehouse with pretty, blue shuttered windows and, inside, blue-painted steel girders and glass-topped tables laden with postcards and photos of Glasgow. This is a great spot to kick back with a cup of coffee and a slice of apple and olive oil cake, or something more substantial like baked eggs with pork and fennel sausage or halloumi and spinach. Also, at 15 John St. **££**

Spitfire Espresso 127 Candleriggs St ⓦ spitfireespresso. com. Another fine addition to the city's roster of artisan coffee houses, this light and airy space, with turquoise painted window frames set against cream walls and a scattering of tables outside facing a street art mural, offers a short but enticing coffee menu, using Gunnerbean coffee from Colombia and Brazil. There's a friendly atmosphere, a delicious all-day egg menu and a good sandwich selection. **££**

Tinderbox 118 Ingram St ⓦ tinderboxespresso.com.

SELF-CATERING

Queensgate Apartments 107 Dowanhill St ⓦ queensgateapartments.com. An attractive and cosy apartment, a short walk from cosmopolitan Byres Road and Glasgow University, with its own private entrance to an Edwardian West End townhouse. It sleeps four in two large double bedrooms and has a spacious dining kitchen. Four-person apartment per week **££££**

SEE MAPS PAGES 178, 180 AND 184

Split-level coffee house serving half a dozen varieties of strong espressos, as well as good fresh sandwiches and cakes. **££**

★ **Trans-Europe Café** 25 Parnie St ☎ 0141 552 7999, ⓦ transeuropecafe.co.uk. Named after the legendary Kraftwerk album, this fun, railway-style diner – with 80s-style bus seating – takes culinary inspiration from various European capitals, hence gourmet sandwiches like the Madrid (chorizo sausage, pesto and mozzarella) and the Monte Carlo (tuna melt with cheddar and mayonnaise). **£**

Tron Theatre Bar & Kitchen Tron Theatre, 63 Trongate ⓦ tron.co.uk. Arty hangout of this well-respected theatre (see page 206) that's especially popular with writers and theatrical types. A great place for a pre-show fuel up, with a range of small plates as well as a more-in depth pre-theatre menu. **££**

Where the Monkey Sleeps 182 West Regent St; 340 Argyle St ⓦ monkeysleeps.com. Originally owned by graduates of the nearby Glasgow School of Art who acquired their barista skills between classes, this hip home-grown café features freshly prepared sandwiches, bagels, salads and a range of breakfast dishes, and the espressos are superb. **££**

RESTAURANTS

The 13th Note 50–60 King St ⓦ 13thnote.co.uk. Vegetarian and vegan food with Greek and other Mediterranean influences in one of Glasgow's hipper restaurants and experimental indie music haunts on arty King St. Mains include delights like pan-fried lemongrass and ginger rice cakes in red Thai curry sauce. Terrific selection of vegan wines and beers too. **££**

Brian Maule at Le Chardon d'Or 176 West Regent St ⓦ brianmaule.com. Owner-chef Maule, who worked with

---

TOP 5 BUDGET EATS

The 13th Note See page 201
The Hanoi Bike Shop See page 203
Paesano See page 202
University Café See page 202
Wee Curry Shop See page 202

the Roux brothers at *Le Gavroche* in London, turns out fancy but unpretentious French-influenced food along the lines of assiette of pork with creamed potatoes and truffle jus. Good value three-course lunch and pre-theatre menu. **££££**

Café Antipasti 305 Sauchiehall St ⓦantipasti.co.uk. A busy and bright Italian bistro with a handsome wood interior, serving tasty and well-priced stone-baked pizzas and pasta dishes; with a two-course pre-theatre menu. **££**

Café Gandolfi 64 Albion St ⓦcafegandolfi.com. Designed with distinctive wooden furniture from the Tim Stead workshop, *Café Gandolfi* serves up a wonderful selection of Scottish-inspired dishes, such as Stornoway black pudding, peat-smoked salmon and seared Barra scallops with Stornoway black pudding. The snappy little attic bar offers the same food daily plus a cracking little pizza menu; great gin card too. **£££**

Dakhin 89 Candleriggs, ⓦdakhin.com. Roomy first-floor restaurant specializing in South Indian cuisine – you won't find *naan* here, but instead lots of clean and fresh-tasting dishes like flame-cooked jumbo prawns in a ginger, garlic and cumin marinade, though the *dosas* are well worth considering – and the entire menu is gluten-free. **£££**

The Dhabba 44 Candleriggs ⓦthedhabba.com. Sister restaurant to *Dakhin*, this is not your typical Glasgow curry house. Prices are higher and portions are smaller, but the menu has some truly interesting options and uses fresh ingredients that place it steps above most others. The tandoor dishes are cooked with North Indian spices in a clay oven, for example whole black bream laced with tandoori masalas. **£££**

★**Gamba** 225a West George St ⓦgamba.co.uk. Continental contemporary sophistication prevails in this super basement restaurant where fish is king: once you've devoured the signature fish soup – a delicious mix with Portland crabmeat and prawn dumplings – perhaps try some seared king scallops with creamed celeriac and black pudding. A beautifully refined interior and outstanding service. Both the weekday two-course lunch menu and Saturday three-course menu are good value, and there's a pre-theatre deal too. **££££**

Mono 12 Kings Court ⓦmonocafebar.com. This unassuming, multi-functional venue combines a fully vegan restaurant, bar and indie CD shop (see page 208) all within an airy space. Mains include tofu, beansprout and tenderstem broccoli noodles with *gado gado* dressing, and there's a superb selection of craft beers and organic wines. Regular gigs (alternative, rock) too. **££**

★**Paesano** 94 Miller St; 417 Great Western Road; ⓦpaesanopizza.co.uk. In a city bursting with great Italian restaurants, this authentic, hugely popular Neapolitan pizzeria is a real standout. Rustled up in wood-fired ovens made in Naples, there are nine different pizzas to choose from, each one made using a hybrid yeast and sourdough recipe and with the freshest Italian ingredients. **££**

Rogano 11 Exchange Place ⓦroganoglasgow.com. A Glasgow institution since 1935, this Art Deco fish restaurant replicates the style of the Queen Mary ocean liner, which was launched that same year. It's wearing its age well and the food is still top drawer, from the legendary fish soup to dishes like hand-dived Barra scallops with braised fennel and saffron potatoes; *Café Rogano*, in the basement, is slightly cheaper, but, better still, park yourself down at the bar and indulge in some oysters. **££££**

Sarti 133 Wellington St; 121 Bath St; 42 Renfield St ⓦsarti.co.uk. The Sarti brothers' flagship Italian café and restaurant – at Wellington St – remains as authentic and as popular as ever, with pizzas and *primi* piatti; the breakfast club (8–11am) is great fun. The slightly more formal dining space is accessed from the Bath St entrance. **£££**

Wee Curry Shop 7 Buccleuch St; 29 Ashton Lane ⓦweecurryshop.co.uk. Tiny but welcoming place near the Glasgow Film Theatre and Sauchiehall St shops, serving home-made bargain meals to compete with the best in town. Expect the likes of chicken curry and smoked aubergines with potatoes and okra – to have in or takeaway. A speedy two-course lunch menu is served from noon until 2pm. **££**

THE WEST END

CAFÉS

Kember & Jones 134 Byres Rd ☎0141 337 3851. This stylish café and deli more than holds its own in the ultra-competitive Byres Rd area, thanks to its freshly made salads, sandwiches, and irresistible cakes and pastries. Better still, they roast their own coffee, most enjoyable with a warm waffle breakfast. **£**

University Café 87 Byres Rd ☎0141 339 5217. This charming institution dates from the 1910s and has been adored by several generations of students and West End residents, with its Formica tables in snug booths, etched glass partitions and cinema-style pull-down seating. The favourites here are fish'n'chips or mince'n'tatties, rounded off with an ice-cream wafer sandwich. **£**

RESTAURANTS

Ashoka 19 Ashton Lane ⓦashokarestaurants.com. Lively and moderately priced curry house which has

---

TOP 5 FINE DINING

Brian Maule at Le Chardon d'Or see page 201

Crabshakk see page 203

Gamba see page 202

Stravaigin see page 203

The Ubiquitous Chip see page 203

franchises across the west of Scotland; all offer consistent quality. **££**

Balbir's 7 Church St ⓦ balbirs.co.uk. Owner Balbir Singh Sumal is one of the city's long-standing curry kings, and this quite startling-looking restaurant – with its capacious, darkened interior – features his wholesome approach to affordable Indian cuisine. The menu features dishes such as lamb *karahi* and okra fries. **££**

The Bothy 11 Ruthven Lane ⓦ bothyglasgow.co.uk. Set in a lovely 1870s stone mansion, cosy inside and with bench seating in the cobbled yard outside. The emphasis here is firmly on Scottish flavours, for example Isle of Arran haggis and beer-battered Scrabster haddock with hand-cut chips and mushy peas. **£££**

★ **Cail Bruich** 725 Great Western Rd ⓦ cailbruich. co.uk. Under the helm of Lorna McNee, a protégé of Andrew Fairlie, this is Glasgow's first Michelin-starred restaurant for aeons, and McNee is also currently the only female chef to hold a star. Five- and seven-course tasting menus dazzle with plates like Gigha halibut with Jerusalem artichoke and beurre noisette, and Orkney scallops with creme fraiche and sauce albuféra. The restaurant itself looks gorgeous. **££££**

★ **Crabshakk** 1114 Argyle St ⓦ crabshakk.com. Fantastic little restaurant serving up an array of superb Scottish seafood. There's an ever-changing line-up of specials, as well as some unmissable stalwarts such as scallops served in a sizzling, caramelised anchovy sauce. If you're feeling flush (and hungry), the shellfish platter is recommended. **££££**

★ **Dockyard Social** 95–107 Haugh Rd, ⓦ dockyardsocial.com. Taking over a vast warehouse in Finnieston, this street food hub has the local community at its heart with an inspiring three-pronged ambition to showcase the best of Glasgow's food scene, give a leg-up to start-up food businesses, and support Glasgow's most disadvantaged people through a professional culinary training school. **£**

★ **Eusebi** 152 Park Rd ⓦ eusebideli.com. Cheery, family-run enterprise that has been doling out a veritable cornucopia of foodie treats for forty years: hand-made pasta straight out of the *pastaficio*, cured meats from the *salumeria* and delectable-looking cannoli in the cabinets; the venison *ragu* pappardelle shouldn't be missed. With its floor-to-ceiling windows and bold red and white livery, *Eusebi* has a great feel to it too. **£££**

The Finnieston 1125 Argyle St ⓦ thefinniestonbar. com. The West End's burgeoning culinary reputation has been further enhanced by this snappy neighbourhood restaurant where fish and seafood reigns supreme – indeed, you could do a lot worse than opt for the Shetland grey sole or the fish of the day, perhaps with a side of garlic-fried potatoes. Even if you're not eating here, the gin cocktail bar is worth rolling up for. **£££**

The Hanoi Bike Shop 8 Ruthven Lane ⓦ hanoibikeshop.

co.uk. This colourful place just off the busy Byres Rd might not have much to do with bicycles (though there are wheels on the walls), but it is just the ticket for a quick hit of Vietnamese street food from salt and chilli squid, to steaming bowls of *pho*. There's a vegan menu and lots of gluten free options. **££**

The Left Bank 33–35 Gibson St ⓦ theleftbank.co.uk. Part bar and part bistro, this neighbourhood gaff, adjacent to the university, dishes up wholesome, rustic food in a chic modern setting; the brunch and breakfast menus are firm favourites, especially the Lebanese breakfast, a delicious combination of halloumi, chickpea *shakshuka* and garlic sautéed potatoes. **£££**

The Marlborough 340 Crow Rd ⓦ marlborough broomhill.com. Taking over the premises of the once much loved Wee Lochan, this easy-going café/restaurant offers the full gamut of breakfast, brunches, lunches and dinners, including a cracking Sunday roast. **£££**

Mother India 28 Westminster Terrace, off Sauchiehall St ⓦ motherindia.co.uk. Still setting the standard for Indian cuisine in Glasgow, there's fine home cooking to be enjoyed here, with some original starters (ginger crab and prawn *dosa*) alongside mains like slow-cooked chicken curry. Surroundings are elegant but laidback. **£££**

Number 16 16 Byres Rd ⓦ number16.co.uk. Intimate, wood-beamed establishment covering two floors, daily changing menus and a set three-course lunch menu reflect the best Scottish produce. Mains might include the likes of pork belly with Hispi cabbage and heritage carrots. **£££**

★ **Stravaigin** 28 Gibson St ⓦ stravaigin.co.uk. This gorgeous basement restaurant and hip street-level café-bar combination offers exciting dining utilizing a host of unexpected ingredients, resulting in unusual and wildly inventive combinations such as ox tongue, *baba ganoush*, cracked-wheat risotto and shallot crisp to start, followed by truffled celeriac and potato gratin with wild mushrooms, shaved chestnut and fermented cabbage. Look out, too, for the occasional 'wild food' night. **£££**

Two Fat Ladies 652–654 Argyle St ☎ 0141 221 8188; 118A Blythswood St ⓦ twofatladiesrestaurant.com. The *Two Fat Ladies* has been in business for over twenty-five years and their two restaurants have stayed in the hearts of Glasgow's fish lovers. Heavy on fresh Scottish seafood, there are daily changing fish platters alongside regulars like flash-fried West Coast scallops, crispy gnocchi, wild mushrooms and cheddar cream. **££££**

The Ubiquitous Chip 12 Ashton Lane ⓦ ubiquitouschip. co.uk. Opened in 1971, the *Chip* led the way in headlining high-end modern Scottish cuisine, and it's still going strong today. There's fine dining in the foliage-entwined courtyard or more informal brasserie food upstairs, but either way, expect mouth-watering plates like guinea fowl breast with bulgur wheat and merguez and barberry juice, in the brasserie the Aberdeen Angus Scotch rib eye with roast

5

garlic butter and hand-cut chips is unmissable. **££££**

THE EAST END

RESTAURANTS

MOoD Food BAaD, 54 Calton Entry Ⓦ baadglasgow. com. Set in BAaD's airy atrium, this ace restaurant boasts a beautiful plant-strewn interior of wood floors and muted greys. The food focuses on sustainable Scottish seafood with mains like Shetland *moules marinière* and Scottish lobster with garlic butter and seaweed fries. **£££**

THE SOUTHSIDE

RESTAURANTS

Art Lovers' Café House for an Art Lover (see page 195), Bellahouston Park Ⓦ houseforanartlover.co.uk. Whether you're visiting the house or not, the dining room in this showcase house is well worth making the effort to get to; both light lunches and full meals are served, for example smoked haddock rarebit on toasted sourdough with leeks and poached eggs and chargrilled flat iron steak on toasted ciabatta; afternoon tea (book in advance) is served 2–4pm. Lovely garden views too. **££**

La Fiorentina 1 Paisley Rd West Ⓦ la-fiorentina.com. A critics' favourite that also tops popular surveys, this Tuscan-oriented restaurant has become an institution. The highly creditable, and lengthy, menu features the like of pan-fried veal medallions with a white wine sauce and Parma ham. **£££**

DRINKING

SEE MAP PAGES 180 AND 184

Many drinking dens in Glasgow's city centre, the adjoining Merchant City and buzzy West End are places to experience real local bonhomie. The city's mythical tough-guy image was once linked to its **pubs**, mistakenly believed by a few to be no-go areas for visitors. Today, however, the city is much changed, and windowless, nicotine-stained working-men's taverns are much harder to find than airy modern **bars** (except in neighbourhoods that you're unlikely to visit). If you tire of trendy bars, set out for the slightly edgier district near the Clyde and Glasgow Green, where the local spit-and-sawdust establishments offer a welcome change. A **pub crawl** through either the West End or city centre is easily done; decent pubs are more widely scattered across the Southside, but you'll still find a handful of pleasant spots.

CITY CENTRE AND MERCHANT CITY

Babbity Bowster 16–18 Blackfriars St, off High St Ⓦ babbitybowster.com. Named after an eighteenth-century wedding dance, this lively, fuss-free pub offers an assortment of colourful local characters, and features traditional live music on Wednesdays and Saturdays, from mid-afternoon onwards, as well as spontaneous folk sessions at other times.

Clutha Bar 167 Stockwell St ☎ 0141 552 7400. The scene of a tragic helicopter accident in 2013, the original part of this iconic live music venue remains closed, but is operating out of the (now covered) beer garden; there's still live music most nights.

Drygate 85 Drygate Ⓦ drygate.com. Injecting a welcome dollop of life into the East End, this small but progressive brewery is housed in a converted box factory that is a nod to Glasgow's industrial past. There's a ground-floor brasserie and an upstairs beer hall (Peaks Bar) leading to a rooftop terrace. The twenty-three rotating taps include many of their own craft beers, plus there's a specially curated bottle selection and a programme of live events. Well worth the short trek out from the city centre.

★ **Gin 71** 71 Renfield St Ⓦ gin71.com. The night-time incarnation of *Cup Tea Lounge*, this gorgeous, glamorous gin bar occupies the old Bank of India building, hence the lavishly coloured tiles and dazzling mosaic flooring. There are gins of every persuasion here – 71 in fact: fruity, floral, citrus, spiced, you name it, and all with superb tasting notes. But if it's all still too confusing, have a cheeky bash at a gin flight.

Horseshoe Bar 17–21 Drury St Ⓦ thehorseshoebar glasgow.co.uk. A must for pub aficionados, this original 'Gin Palace', from 1894, has the longest continuous bar in the UK (and possibly the longest in Europe too); it's no less renowned for its nightly karaoke sessions, which take place upstairs.

The Pot Still 154 Hope St Ⓦ thepotstill.co.uk. Whisky galore! Nearly 750 different single malts are to be found in this warm and very traditional pub, which also offers a decent real ale selection.

Scotia Bar 112 Stockwell St ☎ 0141 552 8681. Dating from 1792, which (allegedly) makes it the city's oldest pub, this happily careworn place has a cracking atmosphere, thanks in no small part to its programme of semi-pro live folk, blues and rock sessions.

West Brewery Templeton Building, Glasgow Green Ⓦ westbeer.com. Housed inside the old Templeton building, this place is fashioned after a Bavarian beer hall and brews its own excellent Munich-style lager, free of additives and preservatives, the most popular of which is the cool and crisp St Mungo.

LGBTQ BARS

Delmonica's 68 Virginia St Ⓦ delmonicas.co.uk. One of Glasgow's liveliest and largest LGBTQ bars, in a popular area with a mixed, hedonistic crowd, and nightly entertainment and events from karaoke and bingo nights to quizzes and

DJ sets.

Katie's Bar 17 John St ⓦkatiesbar.co.uk. The city's hottest LGBTQ bar, with an easy-going vibe and staging an event most nights.

Underground 6a John St ☏0141 553 2456. This welcoming, low-key basement bar is geared more towards the art of conversation than dance, but they run some fun events from karaoke (Tues, Sat & Sun) to bigger event nights on Sat; welcomes men and women.

THE WEST END

Bon Accord 153 North St ⓦbonaccordpub.com. Located at the eastern edge of the West End, this pub began the real-ale revival in Glasgow, though it can also boast in excess of five hundred malt whiskies. Often hosts beer festivals too.

★ **Brewdog** 1397 Argyle St ⓦbrewdog.com. Dedicated, and quite brilliant, craft beer bar with typically twenty or so beers on tap (over half of which are Brewdog's own creations), plus dozens more bottled possibilities; tricky choices await, therefore, but if you're completely stumped, try guzzling a beer flight. There's a terrific punk-ethos about the place and it's popular with all-comers.

The Clydeside Distillery The Old Pumphouse, Queen's Dock, 100 Stobcross Rd ⓦtheclydeside.com. An urban single malt whisky distiller that's made itself home in an old pumphouse offering a fantastic selection of drams and whisky flights (and, somewhat improbably, doughnuts). Tours available too (Wed–Sun; charge).

Dram! 232–246 Woodlands Rd ⓦdramglasgow.co.uk. The name suggests whisky, and indeed that's one of this big bar's main draws, but there's much more besides, including a healthy selection of craft beers, great food and a regular programme of events from folk music to quiz nights.

Lismore Bar 206 Dumbarton Rd ☏0141 576 0102. Decorated with specially commissioned stained-glass panels depicting the Highland Clearances, this bar is a meeting point for the local Gaels, who come here to chat, relax and listen to live music sessions (folk music on Mon & Tues; acoustic sessions on Sun; open mic last Thurs of every month).

★ **Òran Mór** Top of Byres Rd, at Great Western Rd ⓦoran-mor.co.uk. Multi-purpose arts venue that comprises a bar with over 250 malt whiskies, two restaurants, a club and a private event space, all within the beautifully restored Kelvinside Parish Church. Perhaps the best reason to visit, though, is for the perennially popular *A Play, A Pie and A Pint* lunchtime theatre programme (Mon–Sat; charge).

Stravaigin 28 Gibson St ⓦstravaigin.co.uk. Above the expensive restaurant of the same name (see page 203) is this lively and amiable café-cum-bar, harbouring decent ales, an extensive wine selection and top-notch food.

NIGHTLIFE

SEE MAPS PAGES 180 AND 184

The liveliest area for nightlife remains the **West End**, with students mixing with locals around Byres Rd, as well as in the nearby Woodlands and Kelvingrove districts. The city's **clubbing** scene is rated among the best in the UK, attracting top international DJs and breeding a good deal of local talent. There's a thriving **underground scene**, while some mega-clubs in this designer-label-conscious city insist on **dress codes**. Opening hours hover between 11pm to 3am, though some stay open until 5am. **Cover charges** vary from around £5 during the week up to £25 at the weekend. Glasgow has long had one of the UK's most exciting **music** scenes – indeed, it has produced some of the finest UK bands, such as Franz Ferdinand, Primal Scream and Mogwai – and on any given night you can catch a raft of top-class gigs.

INFORMATION AND TICKETS

For detailed listings on what's on, check out *The List* (ⓦlist.co.uk) or visit ⓦtheskinny.co.uk, both of which also cover Edinburgh.

Tickets Scotland 237 Argyle St, under Central station's platforms ⓦtickets-scotland.com. Sells tickets for theatre productions and big concerts.

CLUBS

Buff Club 142 Bath Lane ⓦthebuffclub.com. The playlist of vintage disco, funk and northern soul here draws an eclectic crowd of clubbers.

The Garage 490 Sauchiehall St ⓦgarageglasgow.co.uk. Medium-sized, multi-purpose gig and club venue hosting a range of DJs, artists and touring acts.

Nice'n'Sleazy 421 Sauchiehall St ⓦnicensleazy.com. Don't be put off by the name – this fiercely individual, great Glasgow institution is the city's longest running independent venue. There are gigs on every night (Mon is electric open mic) with bands of all genres kicking off at 7.30pm, after which DJs take over the fab sound system, playing everything from garage and punk to indie and techno.

Polo Lounge 84 Wilson St, off Glassford St ⓦpologlasgow.co.uk. LGBTQ venue with original Victorian decor – think marble tiles and open fires – and a dark, pounding nightclub underneath that attracts a fun crowd.

Sub Club 22 Jamaica St ⓦsubclub.co.uk. Legendary venue and base for some first-rate club nights, not least Saturdays Subculture, this is the home for house and techno lovers in the west of Scotland.

LIVE MUSIC VENUES

Barrowland Ballroom 244 Gallowgate ⓦbarrowland-ballroom.com. Legendary East End ballroom accommodating around two thousand people, it hosts big-time acts who return to it as their favourite venue in

5

Scotland, as well as bands on the rise.

King Tut's Wah Wah Hut 272a St Vincent St ⓦ kingtuts. co.uk. Renowned as the place where Oasis were discovered, and still with one of the city's best live music programmes, with a mix of established and upcoming bands. Also has a good bar that serves pub grub style food.

O2 Academy 121 Eglinton St ⓦ academymusicgroup. com. With a capacity for 2,500, the city's principal mid-sized venue is much like any other in this chain – though there's always a cracking atmosphere.

The Old Hairdresser's 23–27 Renfield Lane ⓦ theoldhairdressers.com. Once a hairdresser's, obviously, this place is now a bar, exhibition space and intimate gig venue. It's a gorgeous space with high ceilings,

dilapidated walls and a twisted central staircase leading to the mezzanine level where everything from film screenings to live gigs takes place.

Queen Margaret Union 22 University Gardens ⓦ qmunion.org.uk. This fifty-year old venue hosts a mix of international touring artists, local talent and the indie club-night Propaganda (Fri).

Stereo 22–28 Renfield Lane ⓦ stereocafebar.com. Housed inside the Mackintosh-designed former *Daily Record* office, this cool vegan café/bar/gig venue is now the place to track down up-and-coming local bands and catch international touring artists. It's also a lovely place to hang out, even when there are no gigs on, with its long drinks list chalked up on the boards, great pizzas and a laidback vibe.

ENTERTAINMENT

Glasgow is no slouch when it comes to performing arts: it is home to the Scottish Opera, Scottish Ballet, Royal Scottish National Orchestra, and the BBC Scottish Symphony Orchestra. The city's cultural programme offers a range of **music**, from contemporary to heavyweight classical, plus **dance** and **theatre**. Most of the larger theatres, cinema multiplexes and concert halls are in the city centre; the West End is home to one or two venues, while the Southside has the Citizens', a much-loved theatre noted for cutting-edge drama.

is a superb contemporary art, theatre and dance space; its lofty proportions qualified it as the only suitable UK venue for Peter Brook's famous production of the *Mahabharata* in 1998, while in 2015 it hosted the Turner Prize.

Tron Theatre 63 Trongate ⓦ tron.co.uk. Critically acclaimed venue staging a varied repertoire of some mainstream, as well as more challenging, productions from leading local companies. Hosts jazz performances once a month and sometimes other live music events.

CONCERT HALLS

City Halls Candleriggs ⓦ glasgowconcerthalls.com. Completely renovated Victorian halls, this Merchant City venue is home to the BBC Scottish Symphony Orchestra and hosts many of the annual Celtic Connections concerts. The adjoining Old Fruitmarket, with its cast-iron columns and balcony, is a fabulously atmospheric space, hosting mainly jazz and contemporary music events.

THEATRES AND COMEDY VENUES

Citizens' Theatre 119 Gorbals St ⓦ citz.co.uk. The 'Citz' has evolved from its 1960s working-class roots into one of the most respected and innovative contemporary theatres in Britain; it's also home to the well-regarded Vanishing Point theatre company. Offers three stages, concession rates for students and free preview nights.

Cottier Theatre 93–95 Hyndland St ⓦ cottiers.com. This performance space in the old Dowanhill church hosts touring shows, dance performances, comedy shows and gigs. An adjoining bar with beer garden is a favourite on warm summer evenings.

King's Theatre 297 Bath St ⓦ atgtickets.com. This theatre has gorgeous interiors within an imposing red-sandstone Victorian building; the programme is good quality, if safely mainstream.

The Stand 333 Woodlands Rd ⓦ thestand.co.uk. Sister to the first-rate comedy club in Edinburgh, booking local, national and international acts, with gigs on most nights of the week.

Theatre Royal 282 Hope St ⓦ www.glasgowtheatreroyal. org.uk. Glasgow's oldest playhouse, dating from 1867, is the opulent home of the Scottish Opera and Scottish Ballet. It also plays regular host to visiting theatre groups, including the Royal Shakespeare Company, as well as orchestras.

Tramway 25 Albert Drive, off Pollokshaws Rd ⓦ tramway.org. Based in a converted tram terminus, this

Glasgow Royal Concert Hall 2 Sauchiehall St ⓦ glasgowconcerthalls.com. One of Glasgow's less memorable modern buildings, though with great acoustics, this is the venue for big-name touring orchestras and the home of the Royal Scottish National Orchestra. Also features major rock and R'n'B stars.

OVO Hydro SEC ⓦ ovohydro.com. Part of the Scottish Exhibition and Conference centre, this vast 12,500-capacity arena, which opened in 2013, is Glasgow's – and Scotland's – premier concert venue, hosting the very biggest names in the world.

CINEMAS

Cineworld 7 Renfrew St ⓦ cineworld.co.uk. Gigantic multi-storey cinema with first-run Hollywood mainstream movies, plus a few art and independent films.

Glasgow Film Theatre 12 Rose St ⓦ glasgowfilm.org. Dedicated art, independent and repertory cinema house in an Art Deco building; it's also home to the Glasgow Film Festival in February.

GLASGOW'S FESTIVAL YEAR

Glasgow offers a terrific year-round roster of festivals: kicking things off in early March is the **Glasgow Film Festival** (Ⓦ glasgowfilm.org) offering up premieres of both mainstream and independent movies from both home and abroad. That same month is the three-week-long **Glasgow International Comedy Festival** (Ⓦ glasgowcomedyfestival.com), one of Europe's largest, while April and May see the biennial **Glasgow International Festival** (Ⓦ glasgowinternational.org), which brings together local and international artists in dozens of city-wide spaces, from shop fronts to market stands. Music takes over in June with the **Glasgow International Jazz Festival** (Ⓦ jazzfest.co.uk) at various venues including the Old Fruitmarket in Merchant City. This area is also the location for the eponymous **Merchant City Festival** (Ⓦ merchantcityfestival.com) in July, four days of colourful street art, music, theatre, food and drink and loads more. The year's major rock/indie gathering is the four-day TRNSMT Festival (Ⓦ trnsmtfest.com) on Glasgow Green in mid-July; with a line up that's invariably excellent, bands that played in 2022 included The Strokes, Foals and Wolf Alice.

Grosvenor 24 Ashton Lane Ⓦ grosvenorwestend.co.uk. Renovated two-screen West End film house with a bar, and sofas you can reserve for screenings of mostly mainstream films.

IMAX Theatre Glasgow Science Centre, 50 Pacific Quay Ⓦ imax.com. Shows 3D and super-screen documentaries and features.

Everyman Unit 3–5, Princes Sq, Buchanan St Ⓦ everymancinema.com. Three-screen cinema from the Everyman boutique cinema chain, known for its mix of mainstream and independent film programmes, special events and good food and drink offerings.

SHOPPING

SEE MAPS PAGES 180 AND 184

Glasgow's **shopping** is among the best in the UK. The main area for spending in the city centre is formed by the Z-shaped and mostly pedestrianized route of **Argyle**, **Buchanan** and **Sauchiehall streets**. Along the way you'll find **Princes Square**, the city's poshest mall (see page 179), plus major department stores and branches of high-end chains. **The Buchanan Galleries**, a bland complex which features some high-fashion budget stores; more interesting is the Parisian-style Victorian **Argyll Arcade**, specializing in antique and contemporary jewellery. Fashionistas should make for the **Merchant City's** pricey Italian Centre, while the **West End** features quirky vintage and one-off boutiques – specifically along Byres Rd and the vintage stores on Ruthven Lane – and is the only district with antiquarian **bookshops**.

ARTS AND CRAFTS

The Lighthouse 11 Mitchell Lane Ⓦ thelighthouse. co.uk. Well stocked with tasteful gifts and original design items, from furniture to lighting and accessories, much of it Mackintosh-inspired.

BOOKS

Oxfam Bookshop 5 Royal Exchange Square ☎ 0141 248 9176. Small, but incredibly well-stocked second-hand bookshop near the GoMA, with fiction, crime, history, cookery and Scottish sections.

Voltaire & Rousseau Books 12 Otago Lane Ⓦ voltaireandrousseaubooks.com. This bookshop, which has been going for more than forty years, really has to be seen to be believed; second-hand books of every persuasion, including many rare titles, piled high on shelves and floors with barely an inch to move.

VINTAGE FASHION

De Courcy's Arcade 5 Cresswell Lane ☎ 0141 334 8211. This little shopping arcade features an appealing collection of cute boutiques and vintage stores selling upcycled and preloved furniture, clothing and accessories; there's also a vinyl shop and a wonderful retro teashop serving tea and cupcakes.

Starry Starry Night 19 Dowanside Lane, near Byres Rd Ⓦ starrystarrynightvintage.co.uk. Stocks all sorts of vintage items: clothing, costume jewellery, textiles and accessories, including some antique pieces such as top hats.

FOOD AND DRINK

Glickman's 157 London Rd Ⓦ glickmans.co.uk. Fulfil all your sweet-toothed fantasies in this wonderfully old-fashioned East End confectioner's that's been around since 1903; specialities are cream tablets and macaroon cakes, but there's loads more to feast on.

I.J. Mellis 492 Great Western Rd Ⓦ mellischeese.net. Superb cheesemonger specializing in farmhouse cheese from the British Isles, though they also stock a selection of the best from the Continent; there's also a terrific charcuterie.

Lupe Pintos Chili & Spice Shop 313 Great Western Rd

Ⓦlupepintos.com. Those looking for Mexican, Spanish, American and Asian treats shouldn't miss this crazily colourful store.

Roots, Fruits & Flowers 451–457 Great Western Rd Ⓦrootsfruitsandflowers.com. Fabulous fruit and veg merchant with shelves piled high with breads, jams and olives, among other things; they also specialize in products for vegans, vegetarians and coeliacs. On-site deli and florist's too.

MARKETS

Barras market 244 Gallowgate Ⓦtheglasgowbarras. com. Red iron gates announce the official entrance, but boundaries are breached as the stalls – selling household goods, bric-a-brac, second-hand clothes and records (none of it of particularly high quality) – spill out into the surrounding streets. This weekend market is a little tired these days, but the fast-talking traders and entertaining vignettes of Glasgow life make it an offbeat diversion from shopping-mall banality.

Mansfield Park Farmers' Market Just off Dumbarton Rd. The countryside comes to Glasgow every second and fourth Saturday, with more than forty vendors selling fine Scottish produce and tempting snacks.

MUSIC

Fopp 19 Union St Ⓦfopp.com. This small UK-wide chain (now part of Sunrise Records-owned HMV) really is the business when it comes to cheap CDs, but they've also got a fantastic collection of vinyl.

Monorail Inside Mono café bar (see page 202), 97 King St, Kings Court Ⓦmonorailmusic.com. Indie record store with close links to the local music community, offering a big range of contemporary CDs, eclectic vinyl, second-hand stock and reissues; good choice of world music too.

DIRECTORY

Hospital There is a 24hr A&E at the Royal Infirmary, 84 Castle St near Glasgow Cathedral (Ⓣ0141 211 4000).
Left luggage Buchanan St bus station has left-luggage facilities (£5–7 depending on bag size/24hr), there are also left-luggage facilities at Central and Queen St train stations.
Police Police Scotland, Glasgow City Centre Office, 50 Stewart St. For emergencies, dial Ⓣ999.
Post office General information (Ⓣ0345 6112970). 136 West Nile St (Mon & Wed–Sat 9am–5.30pm, Tues 9.30am–5.30pm); 177 Sauchiehall St (Mon–Sat 9am–5.30pm, Sun 10.30am–2.30pm); 59 Glassford St (Mon–Sat 8.30am–5.30pm).

The Clyde

The **RIVER CLYDE** is the dominant physical feature of Glasgow and its environs, an area that comprises the largest urban concentration in Scotland, with almost two million people living in a hinterland of satellite towns. West of the city, regular trains and the M8 motorway dip down from the southern bank of the Clyde to **Paisley**, where the distinctive cloth pattern gained its name, before heading back up to the edge of the river again as it broadens into the **Firth of Clyde**. Here you have **Wemyss Bay**, jumping-off point for the lochs and hills of Argyll, and Helensburgh, birthplace of architect Charles Rennie Mackintosh and the site of one of his greatest buildings, the **Hill House**.

As you head southeast out of Glasgow, the industrial landscape of the **Clyde Valley** eventually gives way to far more attractive scenery of gorges and towering castles, and is also home to a couple of interesting museums. Here eighteenth-century philanthropists built their model workers' community around the mills of **New Lanark**, and the spectacular Falls of Clyde, a mile upstream.

Paisley

Founded in the twelfth century as a monastic settlement around an abbey, **PAISLEY** expanded rapidly after the eighteenth century as a linen-manufacturing town, specializing in the production of highly fashionable imitation Kashmiri shawls. The town quickly eclipsed other British centres producing the cloth, eventually lending its name to the swirling pine-cone design; these days, it more than merits a visit, courtesy of its quite superb abbey. At the time of writing, the Paisley Museum and Art Gallery was undergoing a major redevelopment, and is expected to reopen in 2023.

Paisley Abbey

Abbey Close • Wed–Fri 10.30am–2.30pm • Free • Guided tours Tues & Thurs • Free • ⓦ paisleyabbey.org.uk

Established by Cluniac monks in 1163, **Paisley Abbey** became an abbey in 1219, before being massively overhauled in the Victorian age. Inside the squat grey building, the elongated choir – the longest of any medieval abbey in Scotland – is illuminated by jewel-coloured stained glass from a variety of ages and styles. Elsewhere, take a look inside the St Mirin chapel, whose superb, though incomplete, frieze depicts the life of the saint, to whom the original priory was dedicated. The abbey's oldest monument, meanwhile, is the tenth-century Celtic cross of St Barochan, located under the Wallace Memorial window. Finally, don't miss the exhibition in the sacristy, which displays finds from a section of the monastery's **Medieval Drain**, an arched tunnel dating from the fourteenth century that was discovered in 1990; among the extraordinary items recovered are copper alloy tweezers, a bone die, and a fragment of lead slate with script.

ARRIVAL AND DEPARTURE   PAISLEY

By train Regular trains from Glasgow Central run to Paisley's Gilmour St station in the centre of town, and they're a faster, more convenient option than buses.

By bus McGills bus No. 38 departs from Renfield St in Glasgow every 5min. Bus No. 757 departs from Paisley's Gilmour St every 15min for Glasgow International Airport, two miles north of the town.

Greenock and around

Newark Castle, Castle Rd • April–Sept daily 9.30am–5.30pm; last entry 30min before closing • Charge • HES • ⓦ historicenvironment.scot

Twenty-five miles west of Glasgow, **GREENOCK** was the site of the first dock on the Clyde, founded in 1711, and the community has grown on the back of shipping ever since. To get there, you'll pass through **Port Glasgow**, a small fishing village until 1688, when the burghers of Glasgow bought it and developed it as their main harbour. On the banks of the river stands the sturdy fifteenth-century **Newark Castle**, which originally dates from 1478 and the time of the Maxwells; its present, largely Renaissance, form was implemented by Sir Peter Maxwell just over a century later.

In Greenock itself, the finest building is the Neoclassical **Custom House** on the dockside, splendidly located looking out over the river. It was from here that tens of thousands of nineteenth-century emigrants departed for the New World.

McLean Museum and Art Gallery

15 Kelly St • Mon–Sat 10am–5pm • Free • ☎ 01475 715624

The **McLean Museum and Art Gallery** contains pictures and contemporary records of the life and achievements of Greenock-born James Watt, a prominent eighteenth-century inventor and pioneer of steam power, as well as featuring exhibits on the shipbuilding industry and other local trades. The **art gallery** on the upper floor contains a range of works including maritime paintings plus works by Scottish Colourists Fergusson, Cadell and Peploe (see page 190).

ARRIVAL AND DEPARTURE   GREENOCK AND AROUND

By train Trains run from Glasgow Central to Greenock Central (every 10–20min; 30–45min).

By bus Served by regular McGill's buses (Nos 901 & 906) from Glasgow's Buchanan St station.

By ferry CalMac (ⓦ calmac.co.uk) and the more frequent Western Ferries (ⓦ western-ferries.co.uk) ply the 25min route across the Firth of Clyde from Gourock (two miles west of Greenock) to Dunoon on the Cowal peninsula (£5; car plus passenger £19). CalMac also run a passenger-only ferry from Gourock to Kilcreggan on the north bank of the Clyde (Mon–Sat 12–13 daily; £3.80 single).

5

Hill House

Upper Colquhoun St, Helensburgh, 20 miles northwest of Glasgow • Daily 10am–5pm; last entry 1hr before closing • Charge • NTS • ⓦ nts.
org.uk • Train to Helensburgh Central, from where it's a 20min uphill walk; alternatively, take a taxi from the station

In 1902, Charles Rennie Mackintosh was commissioned by the Glaswegian publisher Walter Blackie to design the **Hill House** in Helensburgh. The best surviving example of Mackintosh's domestic architecture, the house is stamped with his personal, elegant interpretation of Art Nouveau – right down to the light fittings and fire irons. Various upstairs rooms are given over to interpretative displays on the architect's use of light, colour, form and texture, while changing exhibitions on contemporary domestic design from around Britain are a testament to Mackintosh's ongoing influence. After exploring the house, head for the **tearoom and** wander round the beautiful **gardens**.

The Clyde Valley

The journey southeast of Glasgow into Lanarkshire, while mostly following the course of the **CLYDE VALLEY** upstream, is dominated by endless suburbs, industrial parks and concrete highway. The principal road here is the M74, though you'll have to get off the motorway to find the main points of interest. Less than ten miles from central Glasgow, **Bothwell Castle** lies about a mile north of Blantyre, and five miles west of here, on the outskirts of the new town of East Kilbride, the **National Museum of Rural Life** offers an in-depth look at the history of agriculture in Scotland.

From here, the Clyde winds through market gardens and orchards before passing beneath the sturdy little town of Lanark, the best base from which to explore the valley; **New Lanark**, on the riverbank, is a remarkable eighteenth-century planned village.

Bothwell Castle

Castle Ave, Uddingston; a mile or so north of Blantyre • April–Sept daily 9.30am–5.30pm; Oct–March Thurs–Sat 10am–4pm; last
entry 30min before closing • Charge • HES • First Bus No. 255 from Glasgow (Buchanan St) will drop you off on the Bothwell Rd near the
entrance; by car, approach from the B7071 Bothwell–Uddingston Rd

Bothwell Castle is one of Scotland's most dramatic citadels, its great red sandstone bulk looming high above a loop in the Clyde. The oldest, and most impressive, section is the solid cylindrical donjon built by the Moray family in the late thirteenth century to protect themselves against the English king, Edward I, during the Scottish Wars of Independence; Edward only succeeded in capturing it after ordering the construction of a massive siege engine. Elsewhere throughout the stronghold, you can explore the prison tower and peek inside the fourteenth-century chapel.

National Museum of Rural Life

East Kilbride, 7 miles southeast of Glasgow • Daily 10am–5pm • Charge • NTS • ⓦ nms.ac.uk • First Bus No. 31 from Glasgow's St Enoch
Centre to East Kilbride takes you past the museum (Stewartfield Way bus stop is 200yd from the museum); you can also get a train from
Glasgow Central, and then take a taxi or bus for the final 3 miles

An unexpected union of historic farm and modern museum, the **National Museum of Rural Life** documents some three centuries of farming life. From the museum, a tractor and trailer shuttles visitors the half-mile up to the eighteenth-century **farmhouse**, which is furnished as it would have been in the 1950s. As a working farm, there's plenty to entertain the kids, including cattle, sheep, pigs and hens, while harvesting and haymaking are further activities, depending upon the season.

New Lanark

1 mile below Lanark town on Braxfield Rd

The first sight of **NEW LANARK**, hidden away down in the gorge, is unforgettable: large broken curving walls of honeyed warehouses and tenements, built in Palladian style, are lined up along the turbulent river's edge. The community was founded by David Dale and Richard Arkwright in 1785 to harness the power of the Clyde waterfalls in their **cotton-spinning industry**, but it was Dale's son-in-law, Robert Owen, who revolutionized the social side of the experiment in 1798, creating a 'village of unity'. Believing the welfare of the workers to be crucial to industrial success, Owen built adult educational facilities, the world's first day nursery and playground, and schools in which dancing and music were obligatory and there was no punishment or reward. The spinning centre closed in 1968, before the whole site was granted UNESCO World Heritage status in 2001.

New Lanark Visitor Centre

New Lanark • April–Oct daily 10am–5pm; Nov–March 10am–4pm • Guided tours daily 10.30am & 4pm; book at Visitor Centre reception in advance • Charge; passport ticket includes entrance to all attractions and two guided tours • ⓦ newlanark.org

While you're free to wander around the village, which is still partially residential, to get into any of the **exhibitions** you need to buy a passport ticket. The Neoclassical building that now houses the visitor reception was opened by Owen in 1816 under the utopian title of **The Institute for the Formation of Character**. The multitude of fascinating on-site attractions includes the **Annie McLeod Experience Ride**, an 'immersive' ride which whisks visitors on a chairlift through a social history of the village through the eyes of the eponymous millworker, reconstructed **Millworker's Houses** from both the 1820s and the 1930s, the **Historic Classroom**, and the stunningly designed **Roof Garden**, complete with water features and animal sculptures. You can also poke around the domestic kitchen, study and living areas of **Robert Owen's House**, which contains his desk.

Beyond the visitor centre, a riverside path leads you the mile or so to the **Falls of the Clyde**, where the river plunges 90ft in three tumultuous stages.

ARRIVAL AND INFORMATION
NEW LANARK

By train Trains run from Glasgow Central to Lanark (every 20–30min; 45–50min); from there either walk (it's 1.5 miles away) or take one of the hourly buses, which depart from next to the train station.

Accommodation and eating

New Lanark Mill Mill 1, New Lanark Mills ⓦ newlanarkhotel.co.uk. A four-star hotel converted from an eighteenth-century mill building, holding accomplished rooms with lovely views and bags of character; there's also a heated indoor swimming pool and sauna, as well as the very creditable *Mill One* restaurant (£££), where you can expect the likes of steak and haggis pie or braised shoulder of lamb with a Mediterranean vegetable cassoulet. £̄£̄

Wee Row Hostel Wee Row ⓦ newlanarkhotel.co.uk. At the heart of the New Lanark complex, this lovely hostel is located within a restored mill-workers' tenement row, with two-, three- and four-bed rooms, all with river views; self-catering kitchen and laundry available, as well as bike storage and a drying room. Doubles £̄

Argyll and Bute

IONA BEACH

Argyll and Bute

Cut off for centuries from the rest of Scotland by the mountains and sea lochs that characterize the region, Argyll remains remote, its scatter of offshore islands forming part of the Inner Hebridean archipelago (the remaining Hebrides are dealt with in Chapters 13 & 14). Geographically as well as culturally, this is a transitional area between Highland and Lowland, boasting a rich variety of scenery, from lush, subtropical gardens warmed by the Gulf Stream to flat and treeless islands on the edge of the Atlantic; it's these islands that are the real magnet here, with their magnificent wildlife, endless walking possibilities and some of the world's finest whiskies. It's in the folds and twists of the countryside, the interplay of land and water and the views out to the islands that the strengths and beauties of mainland Argyll lie, though there is also one area of man-made sights you shouldn't miss, which is the cluster of Celtic and prehistoric relics in mid-Argyll near Kilmartin.

Much of mainland Argyll is comprised of remote peninsulas separated by a series of long sea lochs. The first peninsula you come to from Glasgow is **Cowal**, cut off from the rest of Argyll by a set of mountains including the Arrochar Alps. Nestling in one of Cowal's sea lochs is the **Isle of Bute**, whose capital, Rothesay, is probably the most appealing of the old Clyde steamer resorts. **Kintyre**, the long finger of land that stretches south towards Ireland, is less visually dramatic than Cowal, though it does provide a stepping stone for several Hebridean islands, as well as Arran (see page 167). North of here, **Inveraray**, picturesquely set upon the shores of Loch Fyne, has a superb jail museum to detain you, while further north still, **Oban** is comfortably the largest town in Argyll, as well as its chief ferry port.

Of the islands covered in this chapter, mountainous **Mull** is the most visited, though it is large enough to absorb the crowds, many of whom are only passing through en route to the tiny isle of **Iona**, a centre of Christian culture since the sixth century, or to visit **Tobermory**, the island's impossibly picturesque port (aka 'Balamory'). **Islay**, best known for its distinctive malt whiskies, is fairly quiet even in the height of summer, as is neighbouring **Jura**, which offers excellent walking opportunities. And, for those seeking further solitude, there's the island of **Colonsay**, with its beautiful golden sands, and the windswept islands of **Tiree** and **Coll**, which also have great beaches and enjoy more sunny days than anywhere else in Scotland.

ARRIVAL AND GETTING AROUND
ARGYLL AND BUTE

By train The one main train line in the region runs from Glasgow up to Oban, though it takes in very few places covered in this chapter.

By bus Buses serve most major mainland settlements, with fairly regular services on weekdays, though usually a much-reduced service at weekends. There's a good service from Glasgow down to Campbeltown via Arrochar, Inveraray and Tarbert. Most of the islands have at least a handful of daily buses too.

By car If you're planning to take a car across to one of the islands, it's essential that you book both your outward and return journeys as early as possible, as the ferries get booked up early, especially in summer.

By ferry CalMac (⊕ calmac.co.uk) operates a comprehensive timetable of ferries between the islands, though this is reduced during the winter months; information on individual ferry crossings is given in the relevant town accounts.

Highlights

❶ Mount Stuart, Bute Explore this architecturally overblown mansion set in magnificent grounds. See page 221

❷ Tobermory, Mull Archetypal picturesque fishing village, with colourful houses arranged around a sheltered harbour. See page 231

❸ Boat trip to Staffa and the Treshnish Isles Take the boat to see the 'basalt cathedral' of Fingal's Cave, and then picnic amid the puffins on Lunga. See page 233

❹ Golden beaches Kiloran Bay on Colonsay is one of the most perfect sandy beaches in Argyll,

but there are plenty more on Islay, Coll and Tiree. See page 244

❺ Knapdale Explore ancient Atlantic woodland, lochs and coastline in one of Scotland's least-known but most alluring spots. See page 250

❻ Whisky distilleries, Islay With eight beautifully sited distilleries to choose from, Islay is the ultimate whisky lover's destination. See page 258

❼ Corryvreckan Whirlpool Get rocking and rolling in one of the UK's great natural phenomena. See page 264

HIGHLIGHTS ARE MARKED ON THE MAP ON PAGE 216

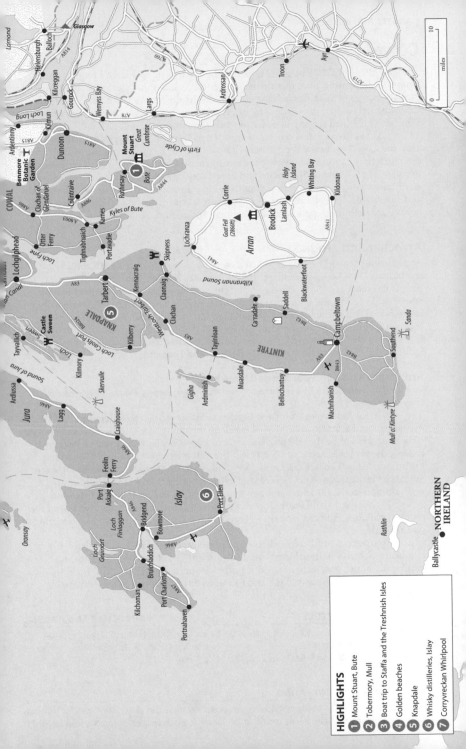

6

Cowal

The claw-shaped **COWAL** peninsula, formed by Loch Fyne and Loch Long, has been a popular destination since the nineteenth century when rapid steamer connections brought hordes of Glaswegian holidaymakers to its shores. It's still quickest to reach Cowal by ferry across the Clyde – by car, it's a long, though exhilarating, drive through some rich Highland scenery in order to reach the same spot.

Beyond the old-fashioned coastal towns such as **Dunoon**, the largest settlement in the area, the Cowal landscape is extremely rich and varied, ranging from the Munros of the north to the gentle, low-lying coastline of the southwest. One way to explore it is to follow the 57-mile **Loch Lomond and Cowal Way** (ⓦlochlomondandcowalway.org), a terrifically scenic, often rugged, waymarked long-distance footpath between Portavadie and Inveruglas. The western edge of Cowal is marked by the long, narrow Loch Fyne, famous for both its kippers (smoked herrings) and oysters.

Arrochar and around

Approaching by road from Glasgow, the entry point to Cowal is **ARROCHAR**, at the head of Loch Long. The village itself is ordinary enough, but the area has the peninsula's most grandiose scenery, including the ambitiously named **Arrochar Alps**, whose peaks offer some of the best climbing in Argyll: Ben Ime (3318ft) is the tallest range, while Ben Arthur or '**The Cobbler'** (2891ft), named after the anvil-like rock formation at its summit, is the most distinctive. If you head west from Arrochar to Inveraray or the rest of Cowal, you can climb **Glen Croe**, a strategic hill pass whose saddle is called – for obvious reasons – **Rest-and-be-Thankful**.

Ardkinglas Woodland Garden and House

Just off the A83, behind the village of Cairndow • **Garden** Daily dawn–dusk • Charge • **House** April–Oct Fri 2pm; guided tour only • Charge • ⓦ ardkinglas.com

The wonderful **Ardkinglas Woodland Garden** contains exotic rhododendrons, azaleas, hydrangeas and a superb collection of conifers, including five so-called Champion Trees – those deemed to be the tallest or broadest examples of their kind within Britain; indeed, the garden is home to what is still the tallest tree in the British Isles, a Grand Fir introduced by David Douglas in 1830 and now standing at a mighty 210ft. Look out, too, for the magnificent Silver Fir (159ft), typically found in Central Europe. A new addition to the gardens – and one that will appeal to kids first and foremost – is a cleverly conceived Gruffalo Trail, complete with galvanized steel characters from the much-loved book. You can pick up a *Woodland Garden Map* at the entrance to guide you around.

In the southern part of the gardens stands **Ardkinglas House**, a particularly handsome Scottish Baronial mansion, built in 1907 by Robert Lorimer for the Noble family; the house was, technologically, fairly advanced for its time, and included a goods lift, central heating and the latest sanitary fittings, much of which remains unaltered to this day.

ARRIVAL AND DEPARTURE ARROCHAR AND AROUND

By train Arrochar and Tarbet train station is a mile or so east of town, just off the A83 to Tarbet.
Destinations Glasgow (Mon–Sat 5–6 daily, Sun 3 daily; 1hr 20min).

By bus Buses stop just on the A814 near Church Rd.
Destinations Glasgow (6 daily; 1hr 10min); Inveraray (6 daily; 35min).

ACCOMMODATION AND EATING

Fascadail House Church Rd, Arrochar ⓦ fascadail.com. A Victorian guesthouse set within its own grounds in the quieter southern part of the village, with five colourfully furnished and superbly equipped rooms. Enjoy breakfast in the dining room with glorious views across the garden. **££** **Village Inn** Shore Rd, Arrochar ☎01301 702279. If you need a bite to eat, or just fancy a pint, head for this delightful hostelry a short walk south of the Fascadail, which has tables outside overlooking the loch as well as a cosy real-ale bar.

Benmore Botanic Garden

A815, 6 miles north of Dunoon • March–Oct daily 10am–5pm • Charge • Ⓦ rbge.org.uk • Buses Nos 484 and 486 from Dunoon

Serenely pitched amid lush mountain scenery at the foot of Loch Eck, **Benmore Botanic Garden** is an offshoot of Edinburgh's Royal Botanic Garden. It's a beautifully laid-out garden occupying 120 acres of hillside, the mild, moist climate allowing a vast range of unusual plants to grow here, with different sections devoted to rainforest species native to places as exotic as China, Chile and Bhutan. The garden boasts three hundred species of rhododendron and a memorably striking avenue of great redwoods, planted in 1863 and now over 150ft high. You can also wander through a Victorian **fernery**, as impressive for its architectural features – notably a fine vaulted entrance, grotto and pool – as for the plants housed within. And look out, too, for 'Puck's Hut', designed by the prolific Scottish architect Sir Robert Lorimer, in honour of Sir Isaac Bayley Balfour, who did much to raise awareness of the Royal Botanic Garden Edinburgh. Clad in various timbers and tiled with red cedar, it originally stood in Puck's Glen in the Eachaig Valley, hence the name.

Isle of Bute

The island of **BUTE** is in many ways simply an extension of the Cowal peninsula, from which it is separated by the narrow Kyles of Bute. Thanks to its mild climate and its ferry link with Wemyss Bay, Bute has been a popular holiday and convalescence spot for Clydesiders for over a century. In its heyday in the 1880s, thirty steamers a day would call in at the island's capital, **Rothesay**, which still rates as the most attractive seaside resort on the Clyde, although it does feel a little weary in places these days. The most compelling reason to visit Bute, however, is the chance to amble around **Mount Stuart**, one of Scotland's most singular aristocratic piles.

Bute's inhabitants live around the two wide bays on the island's east coast, which resembles one long seaside promenade. To escape the crowds head for the sparsely populated west coast, which, in any case, has the sandiest beaches. The best of these, six miles south of Rothesay, are **Kilchattan Bay**, which has a lovely arc of sand overlooked by a row of grand Victorian houses and, further up the west coast, **Ettrick Bay**.

ARRIVAL AND DEPARTURE	ISLE OF BUTE
By ferry Two CalMac ferry services operate from the mainland to Bute; the main crossing is from Wemyss Bay to Rothesay, and the other is the very short crossing at the northern tip of the island, from Colintraive, in Cowal, to	Rhubodach. Destinations Colintraive–Rhubodach (every 30min; 5min); Wemyss Bay–Rothesay (every 45–60min; 35min).

Rothesay

Bute's only town, **ROTHESAY** is a handsome Victorian resort, set in a wide, sweeping bay, backed by green hills, with a classic palm-tree promenade and 1930s pagoda-style pavilion originally built to house the Winter Gardens; the long awaited refurbishment and reopening of this Art Deco beauty remains on hold owing to lack of funds. Elsewhere, many of the buildings could use a lick of paint or two, but despite this, the town retains a certain well-worn charm.

6

BUTE FESTIVALS

Bute stages a trio of terrific annual events; namely, the long-standing **Bute Jazz Festival** (ⓦ butejazz.com) over the May bank holiday, which always draws some class international artists; **Bute Fest** (ⓦ butefest.co.uk) on the last weekend of July, featuring well-established pop, rock and folk acts; and finally, its own **Highland Games** (ⓦ butehighlandgames.org) on the third Saturday of August – this ends in a grand parade through town.

Pavilion toilets

The Pier • Daily Easter–Sept 8am–7.45pm; Oct–Easter 9am–4.45pm • Charge

Rothesay's **Victorian toilets**, built in 1899 by Twyfords, are a feast of marble, ceramics and brass so ornate that they're now one of the town's most celebrated sights. The Victorians didn't make provision for ladies' conveniences, so the women's half is a modern add-on, but if the coast is clear the attendant (attired in a neat burgundy waistcoat) will allow ladies a tour of the gents; it's clad in colourfully painted ceramic tiles and mosaics, and stars an impressive central stand with six urinals – never has the call of nature seemed so attractive.

Rothesay Castle

Castle Hill St • April–Sept daily 9.30am–5.30pm; Oct–March Mon–Wed, Sat & Sun 10am–4pm • Charge • HES • ⓦ historicenvironment.scot

Incongruously located amid the town's backstreets stand the militarily useless, but architecturally impressive, moated ruins of **Rothesay Castle**. Built around the twelfth century, it was twice captured by the Norwegians, firstly in 1230, then in 1263; such vulnerability was the reasoning behind the unusual, almost circular, curtain wall, with its four big drum towers, only one of which remains fully intact. Look upwards inside the tower and you'll see a superbly preserved dovecot (with nesting boxes), which was a seventeenth-century addition. The wall was actually heightened in the early sixteenth century – the line is clearly identifiable in the stonework; the earlier, lower half comprises light ashlar, the upper half is darker and of rougher hew.

Ascog Hall Gardens

Ascog, a mile or so east of Rothesay • Easter–Oct daily 10am–5pm • Charge • ⓦ ascogfernery.com

The **Ascog Hall Gardens** is chiefly notable for its highly unusual **Victorian fernery**, a beautiful, dank place, sunk into the ground, and featuring ferns from all over the world. This one fairly recently replaced the original fernery dating from around 1870, its red, weathered sandstone walls, shade and humidity ideal conditions for cultivating these plants. The gardens themselves are a delight, featuring a truly exotic array of flowers, such as rhododendrons, wild orchids and a stunning array of blue poppies; look out, too, for the magnificent Chilean firetree. The best time to visit is spring when the aforementioned flowers are in full bloom.

ARRIVAL AND DEPARTURE
ROTHESAY

By ferry The CalMac terminal is smack-bang in the middle of the esplanade.

Destinations Wemyss Bay (every 45–60min; 35min).

By bus The main point for bus departures and arrivals is Guildford Square, opposite the ferry terminal.

Destinations Kilchattan Bay (Mon–Sat hourly, 6 on Sun; 30min); Mount Stuart (Mon–Sat hourly, Sun 8; 15min); Rhubodach (Mon–Sat 2–3 daily; 20min).

ACTIVITIES AND INFORMATION

Tourist office Inside the Winter Gardens on Victoria St (April–May & Oct daily 10am–5pm, June & Sept daily 9.30am–5pm, July & Aug daily 9.30am–5.30pm, Nov– March Mon–Sat 10am–4pm, Sun 11am–3pm; ⓦ visitbute. com). Also located here is the 'Discovery Centre', which has some well-presented displays on the life and times of Bute.

ACCOMMODATION

Boat House 15 Battery Place ⓦtheboathouse-bute. co.uk. Chic and utterly contemporary guesthouse with five self-contained suites furnished in cool pinks, greys and blacks and offering all the modern conveniences you could wish for. Each suite – all of which have sea views – sleeps between two and four and offers a kitchen-cum-dining room; breakfast ingredients (bread, jam, coffee, cereal) are also provided. Three-night minimum stay. £̲£̲

Bute Backpackers 36 Argyle St, ⓦbutebackpackers. co.uk. Conveniently located a 5min walk along the seafront towards Port Bannatyne, the island's sole hostel offers reasonably furnished two- to six-bed rooms, with shared shower facilities. Breakfast is not included but there's a large kitchen for general use. Dorm £̲; Double £̲£̲

EATING

Harry Haws 23–25 High St ⓦharryhawsbute.co.uk. Wholesome, warming food is the deal here, such as stone-baked pizzas, steaks and slow-cooked leg of lamb with buckwheat. The interior, meanwhile, offers up some lovely, homely touches, notably framed black-and-white photos of locals and visitors to Rothesay over the years. £̲£̲£̲

Musicker 11 High St ⓦmusicker.co.uk. Funky café-cum-music retailer just across from the castle, with delicious coffee and cakes, decent veggie snacks and even better music, courtesy of the rather ace jukebox and occasional jam session. They've also got some wall-bound instruments for sale. £̲£̲

6

Mount Stuart

4 miles south of Rothesay · **Grounds** daily 10am–6pm · Charge · **House and grounds** April–Oct daily noon–4pm · Charge · ⓦmountstuart.com

Bute's most compelling sight is **Mount Stuart**, a huge, fantasy Gothic mansion set amid acres of lush woodland gardens overlooking the Firth of Clyde, and ancestral home of the Eighth Marquess of Bute, also known as John Bryson Bute (or Jack Dumfries), who assumed the seat in 2021 following the death of his father, Johnny (who once raced in Formula One as Johnny Dumfries). The building was created by the marvellously eccentric third marquess and architect Robert Rowand Anderson after a fire in 1877 destroyed the family seat. With little regard for expense, the Marquess shipped in tons of Italian marble, built a railway line to transport it down the coast and employed craftsmen who had worked with William Burges on the Marquess's other medieval concoction, Cardiff Castle.

The *pièce de resistance* is the columned **Marble Hall**, its vaulted ceiling and twelve stained-glass windows decorated with the signs of the zodiac, reflecting the Marquess's taste for mysticism; during World War I, the hall was used as a makeshift medical centre, some lovely photos of which you can see in the courtyard toilets. He was equally fond of animal and plant imagery; hence you'll find birds feeding on berries in the dining-room frieze and monkeys reading (and tearing up) books and scrolls in the library. Look out also for the unusual heraldic ceiling in the drawing room. After all the heavy furnishings, there's aesthetic relief in the vast **Marble Chapel**, built entirely out of dazzling white Carrara marble, with a magnificent Cosmati floor pattern. Upstairs, the highlight is the **Horoscope Room**, so named after the fine astrological ceiling, though do seek out the wall panels carved with occasionally amusing friezes, such as a frog playing a lute.

There are a number of fine **walks** to be had within the vast grounds, ranging from a 45-minute stroll down through the woods to the seashore, to a more vigorous, two-hour walk taking in the **Wee Garden** and **Calvary Pond** (the latter located at the head of a small burn).

| EATING | MOUNT STUART |

Courtyard Café Main House courtyard Mount Stuart ⓦmountstuart.com. Mount Stuart's on-site café is certainly worth making a trek to even if you're not visiting the estate. All ingredients are sourced from the island, including many from Mount Stuart's own kitchen garden, resulting in simple but scrumptious dishes like smoked salmon fishcakes with charred lemon and aioli and handmade haggis sausage roll with caramelised onion chutney. £̲£̲

Inveraray

The traditional county town of Argyll, and a classic example of an eighteenth-century planned town, **INVERARAY** was built in the 1770s by the Duke of Argyll in order to distance his newly rebuilt castle from the hoi polloi in the town, and to establish a commercial and legal centre for the region. Inveraray has changed very little since and remains an absolute set piece of Scottish Georgian architecture, with a truly memorable setting, the brilliant white arches of Front Street reflected in the still waters of Loch Fyne.

Despite its picture-book location, there's not much more to Inveraray than its distinctive **Main Street** (perpendicular to Front Street), flanked by whitewashed terraces, which are characterized by black window casements. At the top of the street, the road divides to circumnavigate the town's Neoclassical **church**: originally the southern half served the Gaelic-speaking community, while the northern half served those who spoke English.

Inveraray Jail

Church Square • Daily April–Oct 9.30am–6pm; Nov–March 10am–5pm • Charge • ⓦ inverarayjail.co.uk

Inveraray's most enjoyable attraction is **Inveraray Jail**, comprising an attractive Georgian courthouse and two grim prison blocks that, in their day, were the principal ones in Argyll. Originally built in 1820, the prison blocks ceased to function in 1889, though the courthouse continued in one form or another until 1954. The jail is now a thoroughly enjoyable museum, which graphically recounts prison conditions from medieval times to the twentieth century.

Following a trawl through some of the region's most notorious crimes, you get to listen to a **re-enactment** of a trial of the period, staged in the original semi-circular courthouse. More fascinating, though, are the prisons themselves; the Old Prison housed all convicts – men, women, children, the insane – until 1849 when the New Prison was built, whose twelve cells held male prisoners only. In the courtyard stands the minute **Airing Yards**, two caged cells where the prisoners got to exercise for an hour a day, though they were forbidden to talk to each other.

Inveraray Castle

North of Main Street • April–Oct daily 10am–5.45pm • Charge • ⓦ inveraray-castle.com • 10min walk

Inveraray Castle remains the family home of the Duke of Argyll, the present (thirteenth) incumbent being Torquhil Ian Campbell. Built in 1745, it was given a touch of the Loire in the nineteenth century with the addition of dormer windows and conical corner spires. In truth, the interior is fairly dull, save for a pair of Beauvais tapestries in the drawing room, and the armoury hall, whose displays of weaponry – supplied to the Campbells by the British government to put down the Jacobites – rise through several storeys. Otherwise, look out for the small exhibition on Rob Roy, complete with his belt, sporran and dirk handle.

ARRIVAL AND INFORMATION   INVERARAY

By bus Buses stop on Front St.
Destinations Campbeltown (4–5 daily; 2hr 20min);

Dunoon (3 daily; 1hr 10min); Glasgow (4–6 daily; 2hr); Oban (4 daily; 1hr 5min); Tarbert (4–5 daily; 1hr 20min).

ACCOMMODATION

Inveraray Hostel Dalmally Rd ⓦ inveraryhostel.co.uk. Small, low-key hostel in a low, wood-and-stone chalet-type building a short walk up the A819 to Oban (just beyond the petrol station). Single, double, twin, triple and quad rooms,

all with shared shower facilities, as well as a lounge and kitchen for communal use. Breakfast costs extra. Easter–Oct. Dorms £̄, doubles £̄£̄

Loch Fyne Hotel Shore Rd ⓦ crerahotels.com. Refined

spa hotel out on the road to Lochgilphead offering the full complement of spa facilities (pool, hot tub, steam room and Jacuzzi), in addition to a supremely comfortable range of rooms, many with a tartan theme. **£££**

Newton Hall Shore Rd ⓦ newtonhallguesthouse.co.uk. This former church now accommodates an outstanding ensemble of six rooms. Each one is named after an Argyll Island and has been conceived in a completely different style, though they're all possessed of strikingly bold colours and cool, modern furnishings; a couple of rooms have even retained Gothic-style church windows, through which there are splendid views across the loch. **££**

EATING AND DRINKING

Fyne Ales Brewery Achadunan, 1.5 miles north of Cairndow and 8.5 miles east of Inveraray ⓦ fyneales. com. Friendly, family-run farm brewery superbly located in a lush valley at the head of Loch Fyne where you can sample a wide range of ales – cask, keg and bottled – in their welcoming tap room, while munching on a sausage roll; core range ales include Jarl (a former British Champion ale), Highlander and the splendidly named Hurricane Jack.

George Hotel Main St East ⓦ thegeorgehotel.co.uk. The rambling, and very convivial, restaurant/bar of the *George* feels like a proper pub with its flagstone flooring, log fires, and dimly lit nooks and crannies in which to linger over a pint; the food is surprisingly accomplished too, such as pork belly cured in Loch Fyne whisky with pickled cabbage, though there are of course the classic pub standards. **£££**

★ **Loch Fyne Oyster Bar and Shop** On the A83, 2 miles north of Cairndow and 8 miles east of Inveraray ⓦ lochfyne.com. On the shores of Loch Fyne is the famous *Loch Fyne Oyster Bar*, which spawned the Loch Fyne chain of restaurants. The food is utterly delicious and beautifully thought out, from smoked haddock and bacon chowder to salmon fillet with smoked paprika cream and spring onions. The restaurant itself oozes class, though it's anything but stuffy, but more fun is the superb marble-topped oyster bar where you can tuck into oysters, clams, cockles and heaps of other tasty wet stuff. The gorgeous on-site shop/deli is a great place to assemble a gourmet picnic. Reservations advised. **££££**

Samphire 6a Arkland ⓦ samphireseafood.com. Smart yet informal restaurant whose dazzling seafood menu features flamboyantly prepared dishes like pancetta-wrapped loin of cod with roasted pepper butter bean and chorizo ragout, or you might just like to plump for some poached Isle of Mull scallops in a white wine and parsley sauce. **£££**

Oban and around

The solidly Victorian resort of **OBAN** enjoys a superb setting – the island of Kerrera to the southwest providing its bay with a natural shelter – distinguished by a bizarre granite amphitheatre, dramatically lit at night, on the hilltop above the town. Despite a population of just 8,000, it's by far the largest port in northwest Scotland, the second-largest town in Argyll and the main departure point for ferries to the Hebrides. Although Oban is not blessed with a particularly stunning array of sights, there's more than enough to keep you entertained for a day or so, and it's one of the best places in Scotland to eat fresh seafood.

McCaig's Tower

Apart from the setting and views, the only truly remarkable sight in Oban is the town's landmark, **McCaig's Tower**, a stiff 10min climb from the quayside. Built in imitation of Rome's Colosseum, it was the brainchild of a local businessman a century ago, who had the twin aims of alleviating off-season unemployment among the local stonemasons and creating a museum, art gallery and chapel. Originally, the plan was to add a 95ft central tower, but work never progressed further than the exterior granite walls before McCaig died. In his will, McCaig gave instructions for the lancet windows to be filled with bronze statues of the family, though no such work was ever undertaken. Instead, the folly has been turned into a sort of walled garden, which is a popular rendezvous for Oban's youth after dark, but for the rest of the time simply provides a wonderful seaward panorama, particularly at sunset. It's a fantastic place to explore towards the end of the day.

Oban Distillery

Stafford St • Daily Jan–Feb & Dec noon–4.30pm; March–April & Oct–Nov 9.30am–5pm; May–Sept 9.30am–7.30pm; last tour 75min before closing • Charge • Ⓦ malts.com; Ⓦ obanwhisky.com

Oban Distillery is one of Scotland's oldest, founded in 1794 by the Stevenson brothers, and today it produces in excess of a million bottles a year of its lightly peaty malt, which is acknowledged to be a touch easier on the palate than many other whiskies produced hereabouts. The excellent 45-minute guided tours take in the Mash House, with four massive Scandinavian larch washbacks, and the Still House, with its beautifully proportioned copper stills – the tours ends, as is the custom, with a generous dram.

DRINKING
The Corryvreckan — 1

EATING
Coast — 2
Ee-Usk — 4
Julie's Coffee House — 3
Oban Fish and Chips — 1
Original Green Shack — 5
Waterfront Fishouse Restaurant — 6

ACCOMMODATION
Cologin Country Chalets — 6
Hawthornbank Guest House — 3
Kilchrenan House — 1
Oban Backpackers — 4
Oban Caravan & Camping Park — 5
Oban Youth Hostel — 2

Oban War and Peace Exhibition

Corran Esplanade • May–Oct Mon–Thurs 10am–6pm, Fri–Sun 10am–4pm; March, April & Nov daily 10am–4pm • Free • ⓦ obanmuseum.org.uk

Housed in the old *Oban Times* building beside the Art Deco *Regent Hotel* on the Esplanade, the charming **War and Peace Exhibition** is stuffed full of local (and not so local) memorabilia – bizarrely, even a chunk of the Berlin Wall has ended up here. Overall though, the emphasis is on the wartime role of the area around Oban, when it operated as a flying-boat base, mustering point for Atlantic convoys, and as a training centre for the D-Day landings. Also on display are bits of cargo (including a ladder) washed ashore from the Dutch cargo steamer, the *Breda*, which was attacked in nearby Ardmucknish Bay in 1940. It's now a popular site for wreck diving.

6

ARRIVAL AND DEPARTURE

OBAN AND AROUND

By plane Tiny Oban Airport is six miles north of town in North Connel (ⓦ obanandtheislesairports.com); the nearest train station to the airport is Connel Ferry, or take bus No. 405 from Oban to Barcaldine.

Destinations Coll (Wed 2 daily, Fri & Sun 1 daily; 30min); Colonsay (Thurs 2 daily); Islay (Thurs 2 daily; 40min); Tiree (Wed 2 daily; 1hr).

By train The train station is on Railway Pier.

Destinations Glasgow, Queen St (4 daily; 3hr 15min).

By bus On Station Rd, adjacent to the train station.

Destinations Appin (Mon–Sat 2–3 daily; 45min); Connel (daily hourly; 10–15min); Cruachan (5 daily; 30min); Fort William (3 daily; 1hr 30min); Glasgow (5 daily; 3hr); Inveraray (4 daily; 1hr 10min); Kilmartin (Mon–Fri 6 daily, Sat 2 daily; 1hr 15min).

By ferry The CalMac terminal (ⓦ calmac.co.uk) is on Railway Pier, close to both the train and bus stations.

Destinations Achnacroish, Lismore (Mon–Sat 4 daily, 2 on Sun; 55min); Castlebay, Barra (Thurs–Tues daily; 4hr 45min); Coll (Sat–Tues & Thurs daily; 2hr 40min); Colonsay (daily; 2hr 15min); Craignure, Mull (9 daily; 50min); Tiree (1 daily; 3hr 40min).

INFORMATION, ACTIVITIES AND TOURS

Tourist office 3 North Pier (April, May, Sept & Oct Mon–Sat 9am–5pm, Sun 10am–5pm; June Mon–Sat 9am–6pm, Sun 10am–5pm; July & Aug Mon–Sat 9am–7pm, Sun 10am–5pm; Nov–March Mon–Sat 10am–5pm, Sun 11am–4pm; ⓦ oban.org.uk).

Bike rental Oban Cycles, 87 George St (Tues–Sat 10am–5pm; ⓦ obancyclescotland.com), rents bikes (£30/day) and also does repairs and servicing.

Diving If you fancy something a little more vigorous, head to the Puffin Dive Centre, based a mile south of Oban at Port Gallanach (ⓦ puffin.org.uk), where you can take the plunge with a fully qualified instructor (£95/2hr).

Wildlife-watching tours The best of the wildlife-watching companies hereabouts is Coastal Connection, based on Oban Pier (ⓦ coastal-connection.co.uk), who offer 2–5hr trips (£30–45) spotting bird and sea life.

ACCOMMODATION

SEE MAP PAGE 224

Oban is positively heaving with **hotels** and **B&Bs**, most of them reasonably priced and many within easy walking distance of the quayside. Unlikely as it is, if you're struggling to find a place, note that there are stacks more guesthouses in Connel, five miles north.

Cologin Country Chalets 2.5 miles south of town in Lerags Glen ⓦ cologin.co.uk. Secreted away in a lush glen, this fabulous mix of one-and two-bedroom self-catering lodges and cabins provide some respite from the relative hubbub of Oban; the popular on-site Barn Bar (March–Oct) serves excellent bar meals, and breakfast if you can't be bothered to do your own. £££/night; ££££/week

Hawthornbank Guest House Dalriach Rd ⓦ hawthornbank.co.uk. Decent, traditional guesthouse in the lower backstreets of Oban, just across the road from the leisure centre. Its seven immaculately kept rooms, one of which has a four-poster bed, come complete with mahogany antique furnishings and a small seating area with coffee table. No children under 14. ££

Kilchrenan House Corran Esplanade ⓦ kilchrenanhouse.co.uk. A bright and hospitable home located near the cathedral, with sixteen rooms, variously furnished with antique furnishings, leather armchairs and tartan sofas to go alongside the tremendous sea views. ££

Oban Backpackers Breadalbane St ⓦ obanbackpackers.com. Large, friendly and colourful hostel with a range of differently sized dorms, the largest accommodating twelve beds. The big, open lounge-dining area has mismatched sofas, a pool table and a real fire. Breakfast not included. Dorms £

Oban Youth Hostel Corran Esplanade ⓦ hostellingscotland.org.uk. Occupying a super seafront position in a converted Victorian house, this hostel hardly sparkles with character, but the two- to six-bed en-suite rooms are kept to a very high standard. The only downside is that it's a fair trek with a backpack from the ferry terminal. Breakfast not included. Doubles ££; dorms £

6

CAMPSITE

Oban Caravan & Camping Park Gallanach Rd ⓦobancaravanpark.com. Two miles southwest of Oban up a pretty glen, this is a huge, well-equipped site with lots of camping space and great views across to Kerrera, with a good chance of a breeze to blow the midges away; there are also a handful of cool pods, with a small kitchen area, that sleep two to four people. Facilities include a self-catering kitchen, TV/games lounge, BBQs and on-site shop. Per pitch $\overline{\underline{£}}$; pods $\overline{\underline{£}}$

EATING

SEE MAP PAGE 224

Oban rates as one of the finest places in Scotland to eat **fresh seafood**, with a handful of highly commendable seafood **restaurants** to choose from, not to mention several superb fish-and-chip shops. Moreover, if you're on the go, or just need a quick bite while waiting for the ferry, you'll find a cluster of excellent seafood **stalls** down by the harbour.

Coast 104 George St ⓦcoastoban.co.uk. A slick place with a metropolitan atmosphere, serving acclaimed and original fish dishes like pan-fried fillet of hake with sea vegetables and fresh crab broth. As you'd expect from one of the town's classiest outfits, the atmosphere and service are first-rate. $\overline{\underline{£££}}$

Ee-Usk North Pier ⓦeeusk.com. Salmon mousse, sea bass with creamed leeks and savoury mash, and glistening seafood platters are typical offerings in this bright and breezy waterfront restaurant that makes the most of the uninterrupted harbour views. Children under twelve not allowed in the evenings. $\overline{\underline{£££}}$

Julie's Coffee House 33 Stafford St, ⓦjuliescoffeehouse. co.uk. The pick of the many cafés hereabouts, this is a warm, friendly local with super home-baked treats – from panini to peanut butter and chocolate cheesecake – and tasty coffee. $\overline{\underline{££}}$

★**Oban Fish and Chips** 116 George St ⓦobanfishandchipshop.co.uk. A cut above your average chippie, with some surprisingly sophisticated food like battered salt and pepper squid with chilli jam to go alongside the stock fish and chips; good ice cream too, and there's indoor seating available. $\overline{\underline{££}}$

Original Green Shack Railway Pier. Long-standing and hugely popular seafood shack serving langoustine sandwiches, scallops in hot garlic butter, mussels in white wine, oysters, prawns, cockles and much, much more. Wooden benches available for seating. $\overline{\underline{£}}$

Waterfront Fishouse Restaurant 1 Railway Pier ⓦwaterfrontfishouse.co.uk. Despite the unprepossessing exterior, this is a great place rustling up impressive dishes primarily using scallops (Isle of Mull scallops with smoked salmon and leek risotto), langoustine (crispy tails) and the best of the daily catch; alternatively, have some oysters (natural, grilled or deep-fried) with a choice of dressings. The two-course lunch and early evening menu is a steal. Try and bag a sea-facing table. $\overline{\underline{£££}}$

DRINKING

SEE MAP PAGE 224

The Corryvreckan The Waterfront Centre ☎01631 568910. Although it looks and feels just like the Wetherspoons it is, this barn of a place is the town's social hub and occupies a terrific harbourfront spot; the £1.50 coffee (free refills) is just the job before a ferry crossing.

Isle of Kerrera

One of the best places to escape from the crowds in Oban is the low-lying island of **KERRERA**, which shelters Oban Bay from the worst of the westerly winds. Measuring just five miles by two, the island is easily explored on foot. The island's most prominent landmark is the **Hutcheson's Monument**, commemorating David Hutcheson, one of the Victorian founders of what is now Caledonian MacBrayne. The most appealing vistas, however, are from Kerrera's highest point, **Càrn Breugach** (620ft), over to Mull, the Slate Islands, Lismore, Jura and beyond.

The ferry lands roughly halfway down the east coast, at the north end of **Horseshoe Bay**, where King Alexander II died in 1249. If the weather's good and you feel like lazing by the sea, head for the island's finest sandy beach, **Slatrach Bay**, on the west coast, one mile northwest of the ferry jetty. Otherwise, there's a very rewarding trail down to the clifftop ruin of **Gylen Castle** and back to the ferry via Drove Road.

ARRIVAL AND DEPARTURE

ISLE OF KERRERA

By ferry The passenger and bicycle ferry crosses regularly (summer 8.45am & 10.05am, then every 30min until the last crossing at 6.05pm; winter every 90min; ⓦcalmac. co.uk; £3.40 return) through the day from the mainland

2miles down the Gallanach road from Oban. In summer, bus No. 431 from Oban train station connects with the ferry

once a day.
Destinations Gallanach (every 30min; 10min).

ACCOMMODATION AND EATING

Kerrera Bunkhouse Lower Gylen ⓦ kerrerabunkhouse. co.uk. Located in a lovely spot a 45min walk from the ferry, this converted eighteenth-century stable building has seven beds, a bell tent with double bed and wood-burning stove, and a cowshed living space for rent by the evening.

Next to the bunkhouse, the delightful tea garden (April–Sept) – which is the island's only refreshment option – offers home-made veggie snacks, cakes and coffee. Bed per person $\overline{\underline{\texttt{£}}}$; bell tent (June–Sept) $\overline{\underline{\texttt{£}}}$

6

Appin

Seventeen miles north of Oban is **APPIN**, best known as the setting for Robert Louis Stevenson's *Kidnapped*, a fictionalized account of the 'Appin Murder' of 1752, when Colin Campbell was shot in the back, allegedly by one of the disenfranchised Stewart clan. The name Appin derives from the Gaelic *abthaine*, meaning 'lands belonging to the abbey', in this case the one on the island of Lismore, which is linked to the peninsula by passenger ferry from **Port Appin**.

Port Appin and Castle Stalker

Castle Stalker A828, near Port Appin • Tours April–Sept • Charge • ⓦ castlestalker.com

One of Argyll's most picturesque spots, **Port Appin** is a pretty little fishing village at the peninsula's westernmost tip, overlooking a host of tiny little islands dotted around Loch Linnhe, with Lismore and the mountains of Morvern and Mull in the background.

Framed magnificently as you wind along the single-track road to Port Appin is one of Argyll's most romantic ruined castles, the much-photographed sixteenth-century ruins of **Castle Stalker**. Privately owned, the castle can only be visited on a pre-booked tour, which departs from the boathouse and lasts for around two hours. Otherwise, there is a footpath from the *Castle Stalker View* café that winds down to a point some 200yards from the castle, affording some cracking photo opportunities.

ARRIVAL AND DEPARTURE   PORT APPIN

By ferry Ferries to Lismore depart from a small jetty at the southernmost point of the village, by the *Pierhouse Hotel*.

Destinations Lismore (hourly; 10min).

ACCOMMODATION AND EATING

Castle Stalker View Overlooking Castle Stalker ⓦ castlestalkerview.co.uk. In a tiptop position overlooking Castle Stalker, this large, light-filled café makes for a super little pit stop, serving up, among other things, fluffy jacket spuds with unusual fillings like crayfish tails or haggis and cheddar, and a mouthwatering selection of baked goodies. $\overline{\underline{\texttt{££}}}$

Pierhouse Hotel Just a few paces from the jetty ⓦ pierhousehotel.co.uk. Perched on the waterfront, the whitewashed Pierhouse has twelve sumptuously furnished, though very pricey, rooms decorated in cool beige and mocha tones, half of which have unrivalled loch views; the others have cliff views but are cheaper. The hotel's sparkling seafood restaurant is highly rated in these parts too. $\overline{\underline{\texttt{£££}}}$

Isle of Lismore

Lying in the middle of Loch Linnhe, to the north of Oban, and barely rising above a hillock, the narrow island of **LISMORE** (around ten miles long and a mile wide) offers wonderful gentle walking and cycling opportunities, with unrivalled views – in fine weather – across to the mountains of Morvern, Lochaber and Mull. Legend has it that saints Columba and Moluag both fancied the skinny island as a **missionary base**, but as they raced towards it Moluag cut off his finger and threw it ashore ahead of Columba, claiming the land for himself. Of Moluag's sixth-century foundation nothing remains, but from 1236 until 1507 the island served as the seat of the **bishop of Argyll**. Lismore is one of the most fertile of the Inner Hebrides – its name derives from the Gaelic *lios mór*, meaning 'great garden' – and before the Clearances (see page 569) it supported nearly 1,400 inhabitants; the population today is around 170. The island's main settlement, and landing spot for the ferry, is Achnacroish.

Ionad Naomh Moluag

500yd west of Achnacroish • April–Oct daily 11am–4pm • Charge • ⓦ lismoregaelicheritagecentre.org

To get to grips with the history of the island and its Gaelic culture, follow the signs to the Heritage Centre, **Ionad Naomh Moluag**, a turf-roofed, timber-clad building with a permanent exhibition on Lismore, a reference library, a gift shop and a café with an outdoor terrace. Your ticket also covers entry to the nearby restored nineteenth-century cottar's (landless tenant's) cottage, **Taigh Iseabal Dhaibh**, with its traditionally built stone walls, birch roof timbers and thatched roof.

Cathedral of Moluag and around

In **CLACHAN**, two and a half miles north of Achnacroish, you'll find the diminutive, whitewashed fourteenth-century **Cathedral of St Moluag**, whose choir was reduced in height and converted into the parish church in 1749. Due east of the church – head north up the road and take the turning signposted on the right – the circular **Tirefour Broch**, over two thousand years old, occupies a commanding position and has walls almost 10ft thick in places.

ARRIVAL AND DEPARTURE   ISLE OF LISMORE

By ferry Two ferries serve Lismore: a small CalMac car ferry from Oban to Achnacroish (Mon–Sat 4 daily, 2 on Sun; 55min), roughly halfway along the eastern coastline; and a shorter passenger- and bicycle-only crossing from Port Appin to Point, the island's north point (hourly; 10min).

GETTING AROUND AND INFORMATION

Bike rental Bike rental is available from Lismore Bikes (ⓣ 07376 425996; £20/day), who will deliver to the ferry upon request.

Information In the absence of a tourist office, the website ⓦ isleoflismore.com has some useful information.

ACCOMMODATION AND EATING

Lismore bunkhouse and campsite Baleveolan Croft ⓣ 07720 975433. Welcoming and very cosy bunkhouse with accommodation in both dorm and private rooms, all en suite, up to a maximum of twelve people; space, too, for tents and a couple of campervans. **£**

Loch Awe

Legend has it that **Loch Awe**, twenty miles east of Oban, was created by a witch and inhabited by a monster even more gruesome than the one at Loch Ness. At more than 25 miles in length, Loch Awe is actually the longest stretch of fresh water in the country, but most travellers only encounter the loch's north end as they speed along its shores by car or train on the way to or from Oban.

Kilchurn Castle

Several tiny islands on the loch sport picturesque ruins, none more so than the fifteenth-century ruins of **Kilchurn Castle**, strategically situated on a rocky spit (once an island) at the head of Loch Awe; although essentially just a shell, its watery setting and imposing outlines make it well worth a detour. There is no signposting, but to reach the castle, there's a car park just off the A85 around two miles east of Lochawe village, from where it's a pleasant five-minute walk to the ruins.

6

MULL FESTIVALS

Mull stages a terrific triple-header of festivals, the first of which is the **Mendelssohn on Mull Festival** (ⓦsoundwavesscio.org.uk) at the beginning of September, a week of world-class chamber music commemorating the composer's visit here in 1829. Also, in July (usually the third weekend) is the **Mull Highland Games** (ⓦmullhighlandgames.com), and then, in October, the three-day **Mull Rally** (ⓦmullrally.org), a major racing event around the island's fantastically winding roads.

Cruachan Power Station

A85, 19 miles east of Oban • April–Oct: Mon–Fri 9.15am–4.45pm; Nov–March: Mon–Fri 9.15am–3.45pm • charge for tours • ⓦ visitcruachan.co.uk

Constructed inside mighty Ben Cruachan (3693ft), which looms over the head of Loch Awe, **Cruachan Power Station** was built in 1965 as part of the hydroelectric network that generates around ten percent of Scotland's electricity. Thirty-minute guided tours set off every half-hour from the **visitor centre** by the loch, taking you to a viewing platform above the generating room deep inside the 'hollow mountain', a 91-yard-long cavern big enough to contain the Tower of London. The whole experience of visiting an industrial complex hidden within a mountain is very James Bond. Even if you don't partake in a tour, the visitor centre offers thorough and interesting explanations of the workings of the power station and renewable energy projects, and an interactive play area for kids, while the adjoining café has marvellous loch views.

ACCOMMODATION AND EATING

Ben Cruachan Inn ⓦ bencruachaninn.com. In the tiny village (hamlet really) of Lochawe, this superbly renovated inn, has a selection of colourful, tidily furnished rooms in the main building and, better still, four self-catering garden suites (sleeping up to four) in a neighbouring building. The modern bar/restaurant offers an accomplished menu. **£££**

Isle of Mull and around

The second largest of the Inner Hebrides, **MULL** is by far the most accessible: just forty minutes from Oban by ferry. As so often, first impressions largely depend on the weather – it is the wettest of the Hebrides (and that's saying something) – for without the sun the large tracts of moorland, particularly around the island's highest peak, Ben More (3169ft), can appear bleak and unwelcoming. There are, however, areas of more gentle pastoral scenery around **Dervaig** in the north, and the indented west coast varies from the sandy beaches around **Calgary** to the cliffs of Loch na Keal. The most common mistake is to try and 'do' the island in a day or two: flogging up the main road to the picturesque capital of **Tobermory**, then covering the fifty-odd miles between there and Fionnphort, in order to visit **Iona**. Mull is a place that will grow on you only if you have the time and patience to explore; try to spend a couple of nights here at least.

Historically, crofting, whisky distilling and fishing supported the islanders (*Muileachs*), but the population – which peaked at 10,000 – decreased dramatically in the late nineteenth century due to the Clearances and the 1846 potato famine. On Mull, it is a trend that has been reversed, mostly owing to the large influx of settlers from elsewhere in the country, which has brought the current population up to more than 2,800. One of the main reasons for this resurgence is, of course, tourism – more than half a million visitors come here each year. As good a reason as any to visit Mull, and one of the main reasons why many do so, is to view the abundant **wildlife**, with the magnificent white-tailed eagles the major draw, followed by whale and dolphin watching.

ARRIVAL AND DEPARTURE

By ferry Craignure is the main ferry terminal, with a frequent daily car ferry link to Oban, though booking ahead on this route is strongly advised. A smaller and less expensive car ferry crosses daily from Lochaline on the Morvern peninsula (see page 420) to Fishnish, six miles northwest of Craignure. Another even smaller car ferry connects Kilchoan on the Ardnamurchan peninsula (see page 421) with Tobermory, the island's capital.

GETTING AROUND

By bus The two main bus routes are the No. 95 (No.495) between Craignure and Tobermory, and the No. 96 (No.496) between Craignure and Fionnphort, with a third route (No. 494) from Tobermory to Dervaig and Calgary.

By car The majority of the island's roads are single-track, with passing places, which can slow journeys down considerably – hence patience and concentration is required when driving here.

By bike There's excellent bike hire courtesy of Cycle Mull, located on Pier Road in Salen, roughly midway between Craignure and Tobermory (April–Oct daily 9am–5pm; ⓦ cycle-mull.co.uk); they have both mountain bikes (£20 per day) and e-bikes (£35).

Craignure and around

CRAIGNURE is little more than a scattering of cottages, though there is a small shop, a bar, some toilets and a CalMac ticket and **tourist office** situated opposite the pier. However, there is plenty of accommodation here, as well as a few places to eat and drink, so it is a useful place to base yourself, particularly with an early ferry to catch.

Duart Castle

A848, 3 miles south of Craignure • Daily April 11am–4pm; May–mid-Oct 10.30am–5pm • Charge • ⓦ duartcastle.com

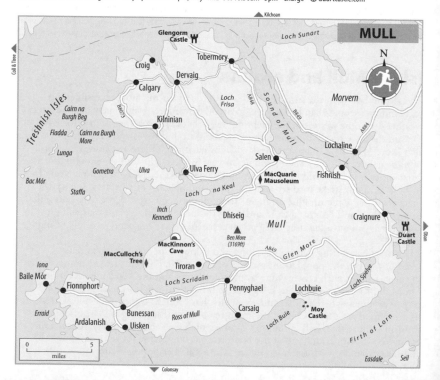

Perched on a rocky promontory sticking out into the Sound of Mull, and buffeted by winds and weather, **Duart Castle** makes for a striking landmark viewed from the Oban–Craignure ferry. Duart was headquarters of the once-powerful MacLean clan from the thirteenth century, but was burnt down by the Campbells and confiscated after the 1745 rebellion. In 1911, the 26th clan chief, Fitzroy MacLean – not to be confused with the Scottish writer of the same name – managed to buy it back and restore it, and he remained here until his death, in 1936, at the ripe old age of 101 – look out for the wonderful black-and-white photos of MacLean on his 100th birthday, still looking remarkably fit even then. The banqueting room showcases some superb exhibits, particularly items belonging to Fitzroy from his time serving in the 13th Light Dragoons and 13th Hussars; keep an eye out for his dirk, passport and fob watch used during the Crimean War. Among the many gifts on display is a dazzling silver cup presented to Fitzroy from the former French president Giscard d'Estaing.

In the upstairs exhibition room you can also learn about the world scout movement; in 1959, Charles MacLean (the 27th clan chief) became Chief Scout, a role he performed with some distinction until 1971. From here, climb up to the ramparts for superlative views of the island and beyond; on a clear day, you can just make out the summit of Ben Nevis. Sir Lachlan, the current clan chief, lives in the castle annexe and you're quite likely to see him mingling among visitors. After your visit, head to the castle's pretty, barn-like tearoom, where there's an impressive array of home-made cakes on offer.

ARRIVAL AND INFORMATION

CRAIGNURE AND AROUND

By ferry The ferry terminal dominates the centre of the village, with the CalMac office located directly opposite, in the same building as the tourist office.

Destinations Oban (9 daily; 50min).

By bus Buses pick up and drop off by the main road by the ferry terminal.

Destinations Fionnphort (Mon–Sat 3–5 daily, 1 on Sun; 1hr 15min); Fishnish (4–5 daily; 15min); Salen (5–6 daily; 25min); Tobermory (5–6 daily; 50min).

Tourist office Opposite the ferry terminal in shared premises with CalMac (April–June, Sept & Oct Mon 9am–5pm, Tues–Sat 8.15am–5pm, Sun 10am–5pm; July & Aug Mon 9am–6.15pm, Tues–Sat 8.15am–6.15pm, Sun 10am–6.15pm; Nov–March Mon 9am–5pm, Tues–Sat 8.30am–5pm, Sun 10am–5pm; ☎ 01680 812377).

ACCOMMODATION AND EATING

★ **Craignure Bunkhouse** 350yd up the road towards Fionnphort ⓦ craignure-bunkhouse.co.uk. Super-smart eco-designed hostel accommodating four en-suite bunk rooms, each with four or six beds (with own reading light and USB), plus a large, homely lounge with wood burner, sofas and a library of books. A self-catering kitchen, laundry and drying room complete this excellent ensemble. Reception closed 10.30am–4pm. £

Craignure Inn 400yd up the road towards Fionnphort ⓦ craignure-inn.co.uk. Right next to *Craignure Bunkhouse*, this eighteenth-century whitewashed inn, frequented by locals and tourists alike, is a snug little place to hole up in, be it for a pint in the bar or a meal in the adjoining restaurant; Scotch steak and ale pie is a popular dish. ££

Shieling Holidays Half a mile from the ferry terminal on the road to Fionnphort ⓦ shielingholidays.co.uk. Set above a shingle beach, this tidy campsite also offers cool accommodation in the form of 'shielings' – large, hard-top tents with en-suite facilities and a basic inside cooking area – sleeping between two and six people; these now include shared hostel shielings (male or female tents sleeping six). Cooking and eating equipment can be hired and there are bikes for rent too. Per pitch £; shielings ££

Tobermory

Mull's chief town, **TOBERMORY**, at the northern tip of the island, is easily the most attractive fishing port on the west coast of Scotland, its clusters of brightly coloured houses and boats sheltering in a bay backed by a steep bluff. Founded in 1788 by the British Society for Encouraging Fisheries, it never really took off as a fishing port and only survived due to the steady influx of crofters evicted from other parts of the island during the Clearances. It is now the most important, and by far the most vibrant, settlement on Mull, and if you've got young kids, you'll instantly recognize it as the place where *Balamory* was filmed.

The harbour – known as **Main Street** – is one long parade of multicoloured hotels, guesthouses, restaurants and shops, and you could happily spend an hour or so meandering around. The rest of the upper town, laid out on a classic grid plan, merits a stroll too, if only for the great views over the bay.

Mull Museum

Main St • Easter–mid-Oct Mon–Fri 11am–3pm • Free • Ⓦ mullmuseum.org.uk

A good wet-weather retreat is the **Mull Museum**, essentially a tiny room packed with fascinating local information and artefacts. Among these is a handful of objects salvaged from the *San Juan de Sicilia*, a ship from the Spanish Armada which sank in 1588 and now lies at the bottom of Tobermory harbour; even today, it remains subject to repeated salvage attempts by locals still, somewhat optimistically, seeking gold. During World War II, Tobermory was an important naval base, in particular as a centre for the training of Escort vessels, whose job it was to protect convoy ships from being attacked by U-boats. Leading the training was one Vice Admiral Gilbert Stephenson, whose prolific and strict regime (he trained up over nine hundred ships in just four years) earned him the moniker, 'The Terror of Tobermory'. Such was the Admiral's notoriety that he even had a beer named after him.

Tobermory Distillery

Ledaig car park • Mon–Sat 11am–4pm, Sun noon–4pm • **Warehouse Experience**; 45min • Charge • **Whisky tastings**; 30min • Charge • **Gin tastings**; 30min • Charge • Ⓦ tobermorydistillery.com

Founded in 1798, the minuscule **Tobermory Distillery** has had a chequered history, closing down three times since then, though today it's back in business and thriving thanks to its signature fifteen-year-old Tobermory and ten-year-old Ledaig malts. Although its tour is rather drab compared to most distilleries, you do get to see the four magnificent copper stills, as well as try a dram or two at the end. As is the vogue, they've now also started producing their own gin, a rather sumptuous affair called Tobermory Hebridean Gin, concocted from local botanicals including elderflower and wild heather.

Mull Aquarium

Harbour Building, Ledaig car park • April–Oct Mon–Thurs 10am–4.30pm, Sun 12.30am–4.30pm • Charge • Ⓦ mullaquarium.co.uk

An absolute delight, the small, community-owned **Mull Aquarium** is the first catch-and-release aquarium in Europe, meaning that all marine life – caught by local divers, fishermen and anyone else willing to head out to sea – is released back into the waters within four weeks. So, for example, you might get to see dogfish, jellyfish, sea scorpions, velvet swimming crabs or curled octopus in the half a dozen or so tanks, alongside all manner of other weird and wonderful creatures. There are touchpool stations, too, where demonstrations are given and visitors are encouraged to handle the creatures.

Glengorm Castle

5 miles northwest of Tobermory • Easter–Oct daily 10am–5pm • Ⓦ glengormcastle.co.uk

Dramatically overlooking the sea along a dead-end single-track road, **Glengorm Castle** is a Scots Baronial pile that's now a small luxury hotel (see page 233). Although the castle is not open to the public (unless you're staying there), you can walk around their attractive walled garden or make for the longer forest, archaeological and coastal trails; they also offer guided walks of varying lengths, though you need to book in advance. Here too is an attractively converted steading, housing a wildlife visitor centre, café and farm shop, and art gallery.

WILDLIFE-WATCHING TRIPS FROM TOBERMORY

Although boat trips leave from several different places around Mull, Tobermory is as good a place as any from which to begin a **wildlife-watching tour**. The best company is **Staffa Tours** (Easter–Oct; ⓦstaffatours.com), who focus on seeking out the whales (minke and killer whales are the most common), porpoises, dolphins and basking sharks that spend time in the waters around the Hebrides; their standard tour is a four-hour whale-watch trip (adult £60, child £30), though they also offer other wildlife trips to Staffa and Fingal's Cave (£55/4hr), and Staff and the Treshnish Isles (£70/6hr). For more information on the local wildlife, pop into the **Hebridean Whale and Dolphin Trust discovery centre** at 28 Main St (April–Sept daily 10.30am–4.30pm; ⓦhwdt.org), where you can also view a small exhibition. The HWDT have also launched the **Hebridean Whale Trail**, a series of land-based whale watching sites along the west coast of Scotland; one of these is at Glengorm, and during the summer they run a Headland Watch excursion from here on Thursdays at 10am (£6).

6

ARRIVAL AND INFORMATION

TOBERMORY

By ferry The CalMac terminal is at the far end of Main St, in the northernmost part of the bay.

Destinations Kilchoan (5–7 daily; 35min).

By bus The bus station is in the town's main Ledaig car park, by the distillery.

Destinations Calgary (Mon–Fri 4 daily, Sat 2 daily; 45min);

Craignure (4–6 daily; 45min); Dervaig (Mon–Fri 4 daily, Sat 2 daily; 25min); Fishnish (2–4 daily; 40min).

Tourist information Privately run Explore Mull, located in a cabin in the Ledaig car park (April–Oct daily 9am–5pm; ⓦisle-of-mull.net), has tons of information, and also arranges accommodation and wildlife tours.

ACCOMMODATION

Glengorm Castle 5 miles northwest of Tobermory ⓦglengormcastle.co.uk. Fairy-tale, rambling Baronial mansion in a superb, secluded setting, with incredible coastal views, lovely gardens and local walks. Guests get use of the castle's wood-panelled whisky library and snooker lounge, the five large bedrooms are full of splendid features and there are self-catering cottages available too. £££

★ **Highland Cottage** Breadalbane St ⓦhighlandcottage.co.uk. Super-luxurious B&B run by a very welcoming couple in a quiet street high above the harbour; the six modestly sized but gorgeously furnished rooms, each one named after an Argyll island, are fashioned with home comforts firmly in mind, such as shelves rammed with books. ££££

Tobermory Hotel 53 Main St ⓦthetobermoryhotel. com. Smallish, fairly smart hotel converted from three fishermen's cottages, hence the maze-like warren of variously configured, extremely cosy, rooms, some with

coved ceilings, others with window seats, though most with a smattering of light tartan. £££

Tobermory Youth Hostel Main St ⓦhostellingscotland. org.uk. Small, friendly and superbly located on the harbourfront, with two- to- five-bed rooms all with shared shower facilities, plus a very well-equipped kitchen, TV lounge and laundry facilities. Groups only Oct–March. Doubles ££; dorms £

CAMPSITE

Tobermory Camping 1.5 miles uphill from Tobermory on the B8073 to Dervaig ⓦtobermory-campsite.co.uk. Small, spruce campsite serenely situated in woodland; tents are pitched alongside the burn and there are seven sweet little shepherd's huts, sleeping either two or four, with cooking facilities (though you do need to bring your own bedding). Buses from Tobermory to Calgary stop here. Pitch £, shepherd's huts £

EATING

An Tobar Argyll Terrace ⓦcomar.co.uk. Housed in a converted Victorian schoolhouse at the top of Back Brae, this small but attractive café doubles up as the town's principal arts centre, with a strong and imaginative programme of visual art and live music, often attracting some stellar names. The café can also be accessed via a very steep path from Main St. £

Café Fish The Pier ⓦthecafefish.com. Stylish harbourfront restaurant above the CalMac office sporting an all-glass frontage with superb views. Fresh from their

own boat, the day's catch is prominently displayed in a large glass cabinet, which could mean anything from whole creel caught langoustines with herb garlic butter to miso and sesame glazed Mull scallops. £££

Fisherman's Pier Fish & Chip Van Fisherman's Pier ☎01688 301109. The friendly proprietors of this venerable takeaway van serve up all the traditional fish suppers (cod and chips), though most venture here for their scrumptious scallops and chips. £

Hebridean Lodge Baliscate W hebrideanlodge.co.uk. Admittedly it doesn't look like the most enticing venue – right by the road as you enter Tobermory – and the interior, above a shop, is a little bland, but the food is beautifully cooked and tastes terrific: for example, Tobermory smoked trout with beetroot jelly and fennel butter, or spinach, goat's cheese and mushroom Wellington. Reservations advised. £££

Tobermory Hotel 53 Main St W thetobermoryhotel.com. The *Tobermory Hotel*'s highly creditable restaurant conjures up tempting seafood dishes like Croig crab cannon balls with Thai red mayo, and pan-seared seabass with grilled asparagus and lemon and chive hollandaise. There's a pleasant, warming atmosphere about the place and the service is first-rate. £££

DRINKING

MacGochan's Ledaig car park W macgochans-tobermory.co.uk. Heaving, hugely popular harbourside pub just a few paces from the distillery, with a terrific beer garden (albeit facing a car park), well-frequented restaurant-bar and occasional live music to liven things up further.

Mishnish Main St T 01688 302500, W themishnish.co.uk. Inside the hotel of the same name, the 'Mish' has been the town's most popular local watering hole for aeons, with a couple of superb snugs rammed with maritime and musical paraphernalia, and regular evenings of live music, quizzes and loads of other happenings.

Dervaig

The gently undulating countryside west of Tobermory, beyond the freshwater Mishnish lochs, provides some of the most beguiling scenery on the island. Added to this, the road out west, the B8073, is exceptionally dramatic. The only village of any size on this side of the island is **DERVAIG**, which nestles beside narrow Loch a' Chumhainn, just eight miles southwest of Tobermory, distinguished by its unusual pencil-shaped church spire and single street of dinky whitewashed cottages and old corrugated-iron shacks. Dervaig has a shop, a bookshop/café and a number of places to stay, eat and drink.

ACCOMMODATION AND EATING   DERVAIG

Am Birlinn Penmore W ambirlinn.com. The cross-country road from Dervaig takes you through Penmore where you'll find this striking wood-and-glass-clad building serving up meat and seafood of the highest order: pan seared guinea fowl on puy lentils with tarragon, sherry, bacon and confit potatoes is one of the restaurant's typically flamboyant dishes. £££

The Bellachroy Centre of village W thebellachroy.co.uk. Rugged early seventeenth-century inn with an attractive whitewashed interior, whose pull is its local real ales; the food is comforting rather than being anything particularly sophisticated, for example shepherd's pie with parsley mash. ££

Dervaig Village Hall Hostel Centre of village W dervaigbunkrooms.co.uk. Somewhat peculiarly located inside the village hall, though certainly none the worse for it, this clean and welcoming bunkhouse offers two bunkrooms, one sleeping six, the other four, each of which has its own wet room. Bedding is provided. There's also a self-catering kitchen, sitting room and washing machine. Breakfast not included. £

Druimnacroish Hotel 2 miles out on the Salen road W druimnacroish.co.uk. Erstwhile farmhouse and mill, this lovely country house, pleasantly secreted away, has six amply sized and very reasonably priced rooms. Breakfast is taken in the conservatory overlooking the gardens and glen, and there's also a cosy lounge with an honesty bar. ££

Calgary

Some five miles beyond Dervaig is **CALGARY**, once a thriving crofting community, now a quiet glen which opens out onto Mull's finest sandy bay, backed by low-lying dunes and machair, with wonderful views over to Coll and Tiree. Aside from the beach, there's a super **woodland sculpture walk** entitled Calgary Art in Nature that begins at the *Calgary Farmhouse* and winds gently down through the woods. It encompasses some 24 cleverly constructed pieces of artwork hewn from various materials; bronze, copper, steel, willow and so on – a little map (£2) outlining the trail is available from the farmhouse. For the record, the city of Calgary in Canada does indeed take its name from this little village, though it was not so named by Mull emigrants, but instead by one Colonel McLeod of the North West Mounted Police, who once holidayed here. In the car park there's a super little ice cream hut (an upturned hull on stilts), which opens between April and October (noon–4pm or 5pm).

ACCOMMODATION AND EATING CALGARY

Calgary Farmhouse Back up the road from the beach Ⓦ calgary.co.uk. The owners here have scaled down operations so that there is now just one self-catering cottage (sleeping four) and a two-person wooden hut complete with woodburning stove. They have also retained their on-site art gallery, which is well worth a nose. Three-day minimum stay. **££££**

Camping Down by the beach itself, there's a spectacular and very popular spot for camping rough; the only facilities are the basic public toilets.

Isle of Ulva

ULVA's population peaked in the nineteenth century at a staggering 850, sustained by the huge quantities of kelp that were exported for glass and soap production. That was before the market for kelp collapsed and the 1846 potato famine hit, after which the remaining population was brutally evicted. In 2018, Ulva was subject to a community buyout – the third Hebridean Island buyout after Eigg in 1997 and Ghiga in 2002. Purchased in somewhat controversial circumstances from the aristocrat, James Howard – whose family had owned Ulva since 1946 – the intention is, over time, to repopulate the island (there are currently eleven residents) and regenerate the local economy by opening up new facilities. Littered with ruined crofts, it is great walking country, with several clearly marked paths crisscrossing the native woodland and the rocky heather moorland interior – and you're almost guaranteed to spot some of the abundant wildlife, particularly red deer, mountain hares and seals.

Heritage Centre and Sheila's Cottage

You can learn more about the history of the island from the exhibition inside the **Heritage Centre** (just up from the pier on Ulva) and, nearby, the thatched smiddy housing **Sheila's Cottage**, which has been restored to the period when islander Sheila MacFadyen lived there in the first half of the last century. Originally a milkmaid, Sheila later made her living by gathering and selling winkles to locals and visitors to the island.

ARRIVAL AND INFORMATION ISLE OF ULVA

By car To get to Ulva, which lies just a hundred yards or so off the west coast of Mull, follow the signs for 'Ulva Ferry' west from Salen or south from Calgary.

By bus From April to October, the Ulva Ferry Community Bus runs a twice-daily service on Fridays, Saturdays and Sundays between Calgary and Salen, stopping at Ulva Ferry en route; this is, though, a request service so you must phone or text by 4pm the day before (☏ 07775 531301; Ⓦ ufct.co.uk).

By ferry From Ulva Ferry, a small bicycle/passenger-only ferry (£5 return; bike 50p) is available on demand (Mon–Fri 9am–5pm; June–Aug also Sun; at other times by arrangement on ☏ 01688 500226).

ACCOMMODATION AND EATING

The Boathouse Near the ferry slip on the Ulva side Ⓦ theboathouseulva.co.uk. The island's sole catering establishment, this cheery, licensed tearoom serves a mouthwatering selection of seafood tempters like smoked mackerel pâté, potted crab and Ulva oysters, alongside home-baked cakes and coffee. **££**

Camping There's no accommodation here, but wild camping is permitted on the island, so long as it's not within sight of any dwelling and you stay no longer than one night in the same place.

Isle of Staffa and around

Five miles southwest of Ulva, **STAFFA** is one of the most romantic and dramatic of Scotland's many uninhabited islands. On its south side, the perpendicular rock face features an imposing series of black basalt columns, known as the Colonnade, which

6

have been cut by the sea into cathedral-esque caverns – most notably **Fingal's Cave**. The Vikings knew about the island – the name derives from their word for 'Island of Pillars' – but it wasn't until 1772 that it was 'discovered' by the world. Turner painted it, Wordsworth explored it, but Mendelssohn's *Die Fingalshöhle* (the lovely '*Hebrides Overture*'), inspired by the sounds of the sea-wracked caves he heard on a visit here in 1829, did most to popularize the place – after which Queen Victoria gave her blessing, too. The polygonal basalt organ-pipes were created some sixty million years ago when a huge mass of molten basalt burst forth onto land and, as it cooled, solidified into hexagonal crystals. The same phenomenon produced the Giant's Causeway in Northern Ireland, and folk tales often link the two with rival giants Fionn Mac Cumhail (Irish) and Fingal (Scottish) throwing rocks at each other across the Irish Sea.

Treshnish Isles

Northwest of Staffa lie the **Treshnish Isles**, an archipelago of uninhabited volcanic islets, none more than a mile or two across. The most distinctive is **Bac Mór**, shaped like a Puritan's hat and popularly dubbed the Dutchman's Cap. **Lunga**, the largest island, is a summer nesting place for hundreds of seabirds, in particular guillemots, razorbills and puffins; the last of these are far and away the star attraction and, for many, the main reason for visiting. It's also a major breeding ground for seals. The two most northerly islands, **Cairn na Burgh More** and **Cairn na Burgh Beg**, have remains of ruined castles, the first of which served as a lookout post for the Lords of the Isles and was last garrisoned in the Civil War; Cairn na Burgh Beg hasn't been occupied since the 1715 Jacobite uprising.

TOURS

ISLE OF STAFFA AND AROUND

Boat tours From April to October several operators offer boat trips to Staffa and the Treshnish Isles. Long-established Turus Mara, based in Penmore (ⓦturusmara.com), sets out from Ulva Ferry and charges £70 for a 6hr round trip to Staffa and the Treshnish Isles – typically including 1hr on Staff and 2hr on Lunga; as well as a 3.5hr trip just to Staffa (£35). Another good outfit offering the same 6hr trip to Staffa and the Treshnish Isles is **Staffa Tours** (ⓦstaffatours.com) though their boats depart from Tobermory. There's also Staffa Trips (ⓦstaffatrips.co.uk), who charge £35 for passage from Iona and Fionnphort to Staffa on the *Iolaire of Iona*.

Ben More and around

From the southern shores of Loch na Keal, which almost splits Mull in two, rise the terraced slopes of **Ben More** (3169ft) – literally 'big mountain' – a mighty extinct volcano, and the only Munro in the Hebrides outside of Skye. It is most easily climbed from Dhiseig, halfway along the loch's southern shores, though an alternative route is to climb up to the col between Beinn Fhada and A'Chioch, and approach via the mountain's eastern ridge. Further west along the shore the road carves through spectacular overhanging cliffs before heading south past the Gribun rocks, which face the tiny island of **Inch Kenneth**, where Unity Mitford lived until her death in 1948. There are great views out to Staffa and the Treshnish Isles as the road leaves the coast behind, climbing over the pass to Loch Scridain, where it eventually joins the equally dramatic Glen More road (A849) from Craignure.

If you're properly equipped for walking, you can also explore the **Ardmeanach peninsula**, to the west of the road. The area, which features a large sea cave and a fossilized tree, is NTS-owned, and there is a car park just before *Tiroran House*.

Mull Eagle Watch

April–Sept Sun–Fri 11am & 2pm, booking required · Charge · ⓦ mulleaglewatch.com

The largest and heaviest bird of prey, the **white-tailed eagle** (or sea eagle) became an extinct species in the British Isles in 1916, but since a successful reintroduction programme from Norway in the late 1970s, the population has thrived, and today there are currently around twenty pairs of breeding eagles on Mull. In association with the RSPB, ranger-led tours currently take place at two sites: the first is the Glen Seilisdeir hide, located a short way north of Loch Scridain in the Tiroran forest, with another at West Ardhu near Dervaig – the rendezvous point is arranged at the time of booking and tours last around two hours. While a sighting is by no means guaranteed, the chances of seeing one, or more, of these magnificent birds are usually pretty good; eaglets typically hatch at the beginning of May, before fledging in August.

The Ross of Mull

Stretching for twenty miles west as far as Iona is Mull's rocky southernmost peninsula, the **Ross of Mull**, which, like much of Scotland, appears blissfully tranquil in good weather, and desolate and bleak in bad climes. Most visitors simply drive through the Ross en route to Iona, but if you have the time it's definitely worth considering exploring, or even staying in, this little-visited part of Mull.

Bunessan

BUNESSAN is the largest village on the peninsula, roughly two-thirds of the way along the Ross. Just before the *Argyll Arms Hotel*, a road leads up to **Ardalanish Weavers** (April–Oct daily 10am–5pm, Nov–March Mon–Fri 10am–4pm; free; ⓦardalanish. com), where beautiful durable organic tweed is produced on Victorian looms originally from Torosay Castle. The tweed is snapped up by high-street stores, and is used for the elegant couture collection displayed in the small shop; you can also buy other beautiful items here, such as scarves, rugs, wraps and blankets, though they don't come cheap. Otherwise, on weekdays, you're quite welcome to watch the girls at work in the mill. A couple of miles out of Bunessan is the wide expanse of **Ardalanish Bay**.

Fionnphort and around

The road along the Ross of Mull ends at **FIONNPHORT**, a small, not especially attractive settlement, but it does offer some handy accommodation as well as several places to eat, including the island's best restaurant; it's also where ferries ply the short route across to Iona. Around a mile and a half south of Fionnphort are the golden sands of **Fidden beach**, which looks out to the **Isle of Erraid**, where Robert Louis Stevenson is believed to have written *Kidnapped* while staying in one of the island's cottages; the book's hero, David Balfour, is shipwrecked on the Torran Rocks, out to sea to the south of Erraid, beyond which lies the remarkable, stripy **Dubh Artach Lighthouse** (meaning 'black stony ground' in Gaelic), built by Stevenson's father in 1867. In the book, Balfour spends a miserable time convinced that he's stranded on Erraid, which can, in fact, be reached across the sands on its eastern side at low tide.

ARRIVAL AND DEPARTURE   THE ROSS OF MULL

By bus Craignure, via Bunessan (Mon–Sat 4–5 daily, 1 on Sun; 1hr 10min).

By ferry The CalMac passenger ferry from Fionnphort to Iona is very frequent and takes just 10min (£3.70 return, bicycles free).

ACCOMMODATION AND EATING

UISKEN

Camping Uisken beach, two miles south of Bunessan, is a wonderful spot for wild camping, but ask permission first at *Uisken Croft* (ⓣ 01681 700307), just up the hill. £

FIONNPHORT

Fidden Farm Campsite Knockvologan Rd, Fidden

ⓣ 01681 700427. This simple, getting away from it all campsite has a wonderful location, with direct access to Fidden beach. There's a shower block, and although campfires are not allowed on site, they are allowed on the beach. £

★ **Ninth Wave** Bruach Mhor ⓦ ninthwaverestaurant. co.uk. For something a little special, head to this fabulous

6

restaurant – in a renovated 200-year-old bothy – secreted away in wonderful rural isolation about a mile north of the village (it's well signposted). The owner catches and then serves up crab, lobster and other fishy treats, while the veg is supplied from their own kitchen garden, resulting in fantastic dishes like miso salt cod *brandade* with garden fennel slaw and fried garlic shallots. The wines (mostly organic), gins and cocktails are something special too. Reservations required. **££££**

Seaview About 200yd up from the ferry terminal Ⓦ iona-bed-breakfast-mull.com. This conscientiously run

sandstone Victorian villa has five somewhat boxy, but pretty and well-equipped, rooms (with either sea or garden views) adorned with splashes of artwork. **££**

Staffa House 300yd up from the ferry terminal Ⓦ staffahouse.co.uk. Handsome whitewashed building, with four light and immaculately presented rooms, and a lovely glass conservatory where breakfast is taken around a communal table looking out to the Sound of Iona. Two-night minimum stay in high season. They also offer evening dinner on Tues, Thurs & Sat. **££**

Isle of Iona

Less than a mile off the southwest tip of Mull, **IONA** – just three miles long and not much more than a mile wide – has been a place of pilgrimage for several centuries, and a place of Christian worship for more than 1,400 years. For it was to this flat Hebridean island that St Columba fled from Ireland in 563 and established a monastery which was responsible for the conversion of more or less all of pagan Scotland as well as much of northern England. This history and the island's splendid isolation have lent it a peculiar religiosity; in the much-quoted words of Dr Johnson, who visited in 1773, 'That man is little to be envied … whose piety would not grow warmer among the ruins of Iona'.

Few of Iona's many day visitors get further than Baile Mór, the island's village, and the abbey, but it's perfectly possible to walk to the stunning sandy beaches and turquoise seas at the **north end** of the island, or up to the highest point, **Dún I**, a mere 328ft above sea level but with views on a clear day to Skye, Tiree and Jura. Alternatively, it takes about half an hour to walk over to the **machair**, or common grazing land, on the west side of Iona, which lies adjacent to the evocatively named Bay at the Back of the Ocean, a crescent of pebble and shell-strewn sand with a spouting cave to the south. Those with more time (2–3hr) might hike over to the **south** of the island, where Port a' Churaich ('Bay of the Coracle', also known as St Columba's Bay), the saint's traditional landing place on Iona, is filled with smooth round rocks and multicoloured pebbles and stones.

Baile Mór

The passenger ferry from Fionnphort drops you off at **BAILE MÓR** (literally 'Large Village'), which is in fact little more than a single terrace of cottages facing the sea. You will, though, find the island's main hotel, restaurant and shop.

Augustinian nunnery

A short walk up from the jetty lie the extensive pink-granite ruins of the fourteenth-century **Augustinian nunnery**, disused since the Reformation, though it did continue to be used as a place of burial for women. A beautifully maintained garden now occupies the cloisters, and if nothing else the complex gives you an idea of the state of the present-day abbey before it was restored.

Iona Heritage Centre

North of the Augustinian nunnery • Easter–Oct Mon–Sat 10am–5pm • Charge • Ⓦ ionaheritage.co.uk

In the island's former manse is the **Iona Heritage Centre**, with displays on the social history of the island over the last 200 years, including the Clearances, which nearly halved the island's population of 500 in the mid-nineteenth century. One of the more intriguing exhibits is part of the stern belonging to the *Guy Mannering*, a sailing packet

Dún I & the north end beaches

BAILE MÓR

ACCOMMODATION
Argyll 2
Iona Camping 3
The Green Shed 1

EATING
Martyr's Bay Restaurant 1

MacLeod Centre
Shop
Abbey Museum
The Abbey
Ticket Office
St Oran's Chapel
Reilig Odhráin
Bishop's House
Iona Heritage Centre
MacLean's Cross
Cottages
School
Augustinian nunnery
Library
Cottages
Village Hall
Shops
Post Office
St Ronans Bay
Finlay Ross General Store
Toilets

Machair & Port a'Churraich

Fionnphort (hull)

0   100
yards

N

on the New York to Liverpool route which sank in machair in 1865 – indeed, it was just one of twenty or so vessels believed to have been lost in waters hereabouts around that time. At a bend in the road, just south of the manse, stands the slender, fifteenth-century **MacLean's Cross**, a fine, late medieval example of the distinctive, flowing, three-leaved foliage of the Iona school.

Iona Abbey

A 5min walk up the road from the Heritage Centre • **Abbey** Mon–Sat 10am–4pm, Sun 1–4pm; Nov–late Dec & early Jan–March Mon–Sat 10am–4pm • Charge • **Tours**; times posted up at the ticket office • Free • HES • ⓦ historicenvironment.scot

Although no buildings remain from Columba's time, the present **Iona Abbey** dates from the arrival of the Benedictines in around 1200, though it was extensively rebuilt in the fifteenth and sixteenth centuries, and restored virtually wholesale last century.

St Oran's Chapel

Iona's oldest building, the plain-looking eleventh-century **St Oran's Chapel**, lies south of the abbey, on the right. Legend has it that the original chapel could only be

6

ST COLUMBA AND IONA

Legend has it that **St Columba** (Columcille), born in Donegal sometime around 521, was a direct descendant of the semi-legendary Irish king, Niall of the Nine Hostages. A scholar and soldier priest, who founded numerous monasteries in Ireland, he is thought to have become involved in a bloody dispute with the king when he refused to hand over a copy of *St Jerome's Psalter*, copied illegally from the original owned by St Finian of Moville. This, in turn, provoked the Battle of Cúl Dreimhne (Cooldrumman) – also known as the **Battle of the Book** – at which Columba's forces won, though with the loss of over 3,000 lives.

The story goes that, repenting this bloodshed, Columba went into exile with twelve other monks, eventually settling on **Iona** in 563, allegedly because it was the first island he encountered from which he couldn't see his homeland. The bottom line, however, is that we know very little about Columba, though he undoubtedly became something of a cult figure after his death in 597. He was posthumously credited with miraculous feats such as defeating the Loch Ness monster – it only had to hear his voice and it recoiled in terror – and casting out snakes (and, some say, frogs) from the island. He is also famously alleged to have banned women and cows from Iona, exiling them to **Eilean nam Ban** (Woman's Island), just north of Fionnphort, for, as he believed, 'Where there is a cow there is a woman, and where there is a woman there is mischief'.

completed through human sacrifice. Oran apparently volunteered to be buried alive, and was found to have survived the ordeal when the grave was opened a few days later. Declaring that he had seen hell and it wasn't all bad, he was promptly reinterred for blasphemy.

Reilig Odhráin

Oran's Chapel stands at the centre of Iona's sacred burial ground, **Reilig Odhráin** (Oran's Cemetery), which is said to contain the graves of sixty kings of Norway, Ireland, France and Scotland, including Duncan and Macbeth. The best of the early Christian gravestones and medieval effigies that once lay in the Reilig Odhráin have been removed to the Abbey Museum and to various other locations within the complex.

Street of the Dead

Approaching the abbey from the ticket office, you cross an exposed section of the evocative medieval **Street of the Dead**, whose giant pink-granite cobbles once stretched from the abbey, past St Oran's Chapel, to the village. Beside the road stands the most impressive of Iona's Celtic high crosses, the eighth-century **St Martin's Cross**, smothered with figural scenes – the Virgin and Child at the centre, Daniel in the lions' den, Abraham sacrificing Isaac, and David with musicians in the shaft below. The reverse side features Pictish serpent-and-boss decoration. Standing directly in front of the abbey is the base of **St Matthew's Cross** (the rest of which is in the Abbey Museum) and, to the left, a concrete cast of the eighth-century **St John's Cross**, decorated with serpent-and-boss and Celtic spiral ornamental panels. Before you enter the abbey, take a look inside **St Columba's Shrine**, a small steep-roofed chamber to the left of the main entrance. Columba is believed to have been buried either here or under the rocky mound to the west of the abbey, known as Tórr an Aba.

The Abbey

The **Abbey** itself has been simply and sensitively restored to incorporate the original elements. You can spot many of the medieval capitals in the south aisle of the choir and in the south transept, where the white marble effigies of the Eighth Duke of Argyll and his wife, Ina, lie in a side chapel – an incongruous piece of Victorian pomp in an otherwise modest and tranquil place. The finest pre-Reformation effigy is that of John

MacKinnon, the last abbot of Iona, who died around 1500, and now lies on the south side of the choir steps. For reasons of sanitation, the **cloisters** were placed, contrary to the norm, on the north side of the church (where running water was available); entirely reconstructed in the late 1950s, they now shelter lots of medieval grave slabs.

ARRIVAL, INFORMATION AND TOURS ISLE OF IONA

By ferry The CalMac passenger ferry from Fionnphort is very frequent and takes just 10min (£3.70 return, bicycles free).

Information In the absence of a tourist office, ⓦ welcometoiona.com is a useful resource.

Boat tours Mark Jardine's Alternative Boat Hire is based at Lovedale Cottage, near the *Argyll Hotel* (ⓦ boattripsiona. com). The owner takes the lovely wooden gaff-rigged sailing boat *Birthe Marie* on short trips to some of the less-visited spots around the Sound of Iona and Erraid (Easter–Oct; 3hr trip £35). For details of trips across to Staffa, see page 235.

ACCOMMODATION AND EATING SEE MAP PAGE 239

Argyll ⓦ argyllhoteliona.co.uk. Inviting, stone-built hotel in the village's terrace of cottages overlooking the Sound of Iona, with sixteen sweet, though somewhat boxy, rooms spread throughout a maze of corridors. The restaurant (£££) is first-class and serves dishes such as haunch of venison with roast Portobello mushrooms and venison and red wine *ragu*; or you can just sup a pint out on the trim, sea-facing lawn. **££**

The Green Shed Lagandorain; follow the road past the abbey for half a mile ⓦ greenshediona.co.uk. Located to the north of the island, the former hostel boasts impeccable green credentials; its self-catering suites comprise two apartments sleeping two, one sleeping eight, and a delightful shepherd's bothy tucked away on a rocky outcrop just behind the main building. Three-night minimum stay. **££**

Iona Camping Cnoc-Oran ⓦ ionacampsite.co.uk. Turn left at the jetty and it's a 20min walk to this super little campsite, which has a couple of showers and toilets, fire pits and BBQs. You can also rent sleeping bags. **£**

Martyr's Bay Restaurant ⓦ martyrsbay.co.uk. A self-service canteen by day, a fully-fledged restaurant come evening; either way, the tourist hordes invariably pack this place out for steaks and seafood. Lunch meals like haddock and chips and baked potato with haggis are worth a punt too. **££**

Isle of Coll

Roughly thirteen miles long and three miles wide, the fish-shaped rocky island of **COLL**, with a population of around a hundred, lies less than seven miles off the coast of Mull. For the most part, this remote island is low lying, treeless and exceptionally windy, with white sandy beaches and the highest sunshine records in Scotland. The majority of visitors to Coll (and Tiree) stay for a week in self-catering accommodation, though there are hotels and B&Bs on the islands, which should be booked in advance – as should the ferries.

Arinagour

The ferry docks at Coll's only real village, **ARINAGOUR**, whose whitewashed cottages line the western shore of Loch Eatharna, a popular safe anchorage for boats. Half the island's population lives in the village, and it's here you'll find the island's hotel and pub, post office, churches and a couple of shops. The island's petrol pump is also in Arinagour, and is run on a volunteer basis – effectively it's open when the ferry arrives.

The Breachacha castles

On the southwest coast there are two edifices, both confusingly known as **Breachacha Castle**, and both built by the MacLeans. The older, at the head of Loch Breachacha, is a fifteenth-century tower house with an additional curtain wall, now used by Project Trust overseas aid volunteers as a training centre. The less attractive 'new castle', to the northwest, is made up of a central block built around 1750 and two side pavilions added a century later, now converted into holiday cottages. It was here that Dr Johnson and Boswell stayed in 1773 after a storm forced them to take refuge en route to Mull.

Much of the surrounding area is now owned by the RSPB, in the hope of protecting the island's corncrakes, of which there are currently around 66 calling males; you're also likely to see white-fronted and barnacle geese, lapwing and redshank.

ARRIVAL AND INFORMATION   ISLE OF COLL

By ferry Throughout the summer, the CalMac ferry from Oban calls daily at Coll (2hr 40min) and Tiree (3hr 40min). Destinations Barra (Wed 1 daily; 4hr); Oban (daily except Tues & Wed; 2hr 40min).

Information In the absence of a tourist office, ⓦ visitcoll. co.uk is a useful and up-to-date resource.

ACCOMMODATION AND EATING

Coll Hotel Arinagour ⓦ collhotel.com. Small, family-run hotel providing refined accommodation in six rooms, four of which overlook the bay; among the many lovely touches offered is a goodie basket with biscuits, tea, coffee and water. Wild camping is also possible on the hill behind the hotel, but you should contact the hotel first – and it is free, though a three-night maximum stay. Creel-caught seafood forms the mainstay of a mouthwatering menu. £££

Garden House Down a track on the left before the turn-off for the castle ☎ 01879 230374, ✉ collcampsite@ hotmail.com. There's very basic camping at this working farm in the shelter of what was formerly a walled garden, with showers, toilets and a campers' room. Closed Nov–

March. £

Island Café Shore St ⓦ theislandcafe.business.site. In the old harbour stores overlooking the bay, offering hot meals all day, plus an excellent pizza menu (including takeaway), as well as top draw cakes and coffee. ££

Tigh-na-Mara Arinagour Bay ⓦ tnmcoll.com. The 'House by the Sea' is a modern guesthouse near the pier, with a selection of shared bathroom and en-suite rooms, the latter being £10 more expensive. Such is its location that there's a good chance you'll see some great wildlife while eating your breakfast. Evening meals are also served Tues–Fri between April and October. ££

Isle of Tiree

TIREE, as its Gaelic name *tir-iodh* (land of corn) suggests, was once known as the breadbasket of the Inner Hebrides, thanks to its acres of rich machair. Nowadays, crofting and tourism are the main sources of income for the resident population of around 750. One of the most distinctive features of Tiree is its architecture, in particular the large numbers of 'pudding' or 'spotty' houses, where only the mortar is painted white. In addition, there are numerous 'white houses' (*tigh geal*) and traditional 'black houses' (*tigh dubh*). With no shortage of wind, Tiree's sandy beaches attract large numbers of windsurfers for the Tiree Wave Classic (ⓦ tireewaveclassic.co.uk) every October.

An Turas and Scarinish

An Iodhlann July & Aug Mon–Fri 10am–4pm; Sept–June Mon, Wed & Thurs 10am–1pm • Free • ⓦ aniodhlann.org.uk

The ferry calls at Gott Bay Pier, now best known for **An Turas** (The Journey), Tiree's award-winning 'shelter', a structure that consists of two parallel white walls connected via a black felt section to a glass box which punctures a stone dyke and frames a sea view. Just up the road from the pier is the village of **SCARINISH**, home to a post office, a supermarket, the butcher's and the bank, with a petrol pump back at the pier. You'll also find **An Iodhlann** – 'haystack' in Gaelic – the island's two-roomed archive, which has an enlightening exhibition on the islands' history, covering everything from the sea and settlers to saints and Vikings.

Hynish

The island's most intriguing sights lie in the bulging western half of the island, where Tiree's two landmark hills rise up. Below the higher of the two is **HYNISH** whose **harbour** was designed by Alan Stevenson – uncle of Robert Louis Stevenson – in the 1830s to transport building materials for the magnificent 157ft-tall **Skerryvore Lighthouse**, the tallest in the UK, which lies on a sea-swept reef some twelve miles southwest of Tiree. Up on the hill behind the harbour, beside the row of lighthouse keepers' houses, stands a stumpy granite signal tower, whose signals used to be the only contact the lighthouse keepers had with civilization.

Skerryvore Lighthouse Exhibition and the Treshnish Isles Exhibition
Lower Square • Daily 9am–5pm • Free • Ⓦ hebrideantrust.org

6

Occupying a converted smithy, the **Skerryvore Lighthouse Exhibition** recalls the Herculean effort required to erect the lighthouse, alongside many intriguing items gathered along the way. A few paces along, in some converted cowsheds, the **Treshnish Isles Exhibition** documents the wonderfully diverse array of flora and fauna to be found on the Hebridean Trust-owned islands.

Ceann a' Mhara and around

A mile or so across the golden sands of Balephuil Bay is the spectacular headland of **Ceann a' Mhara** (pronounced 'kenavara'), home to thousands of seabirds, including fulmars, kittiwakes, guillemots, razorbills, shags and cormorants, with gannets and terns feeding offshore.

Taigh Iain Mhoir
Taigh Iain Mhoir Sandaig • June–Sept Mon–Fri 2–4pm • Free

In the scattered west coast settlement of **SANDAIG**, to the north of Ceann a' Mhara, three thatched white houses in a row have been turned into the **Taigh Iain Mhoir**, which gives an insight into how the majority of islanders lived in the nineteenth century, thanks to a collection of old photographs and other memorabilia.

ARRIVAL AND DEPARTURE   ISLE OF TIREE

By plane Tiree Airport (Ⓦ hial.co.uk) is around three miles west of Scarinish. Most hosts are happy to collect you upon arrival.
Destinations Coll (Wed 1 daily; 15min); Glasgow (2 daily; 1hr); Oban (Wed 2 daily; 1hr).
By ferry Throughout the summer, the CalMac ferry from

Oban calls daily at Coll (2hr 40min) and Tiree (3hr 40min). On Wednesdays (though the day may change) the ferry continues to Barra in the Western Isles, and calls in at Tiree on the way back, making a day-trip from Oban possible.
Destinations Castlebay, Barra (Wed 1 daily; 2hr 45min); Oban (1 daily; 3hr 40min).

GETTING AROUND AND INFORMATION

By minibus Tiree has a Ring'n'Ride minibus service (Mon–Sat 8.30am–6pm, plus Tues 8.30am–10pm in summer; ☎ 01879 220419) that will take you anywhere on the island, though you should book in advance; costs vary between £1.25 and £3.

Car rental Based at Scarinish Pier, Tiree Car Hire (Ⓦ tireecarhire.com) offers car (£50/day); they can also drop cars at the airport.
Information In the absence of a tourist office, Ⓦ isleoftiree.com is a useful resource.

ACCOMMODATION

Balinoe Camping Balinoe Ⓦ tireecampsite.co.uk. Located in the southwest of the island, six miles from Scarinish, the island's only formal campsite is well equipped with showers, toilets, a self-catering kitchen and washing/drying facilities; they've also got two, two-person pods with floor mattresses and a bothy with three single beds. £̄
Millhouse Hostel Near Loch Bhasapol, in the northwest of the island Ⓦ tireemillhouse.co.uk. This superbly converted early twentieth-century barn now accommodates a colourful hostel, with two dorms each

sleeping six, a couple of doubles and a triple. The excellent open-plan kitchen/lounge opens up onto a patio where you can kick back with a beer and listen to corncrakes while watching the sunset. Doubles £̄£̄; dorms £̄
Scarinish Hotel Scarinish Ⓦ tireescarinishhotel.com. Super location overlooking the old harbour offering eight pristine rooms (a couple with shared bathroom facilities), furnished in solid, if not spectacular, fashion. The Upper Deck lounge is a lovely spot to watch the comings and goings around the harbour. £̄£̄

Isle of Colonsay and around

Isolated between Mull and Islay, **COLONSAY** – measuring just eight miles by three – is nothing like as bleak and windswept as Coll or Tiree. Its craggy, heather-backed hills even support the occasional patch of woodland, plus a bewildering array of plant and birdlife, including wild goats and rabbits, and a very fine quasi-tropical garden. The current population of around a hundred and thirty is down from a pre-Clearance peak of nearly a thousand. With only one hotel and infrequent ferry links with the mainland, there's no fear of mass tourism taking over any time soon, though you can expect a discernible rise in visitor numbers during the island's three excellent festivals: the Colonsay Book Festival (⑩colonsaybookfestival.com) at the end of April; the Ceol Cholasa Folk Festival (⑩ceolcholasa.co.uk) in mid-September; and the two-week long Colonsay Food Festival (⑩colonsayfoodfest.co.uk) in October, featuring, among other things, guided walks and foraging, baking and craft workshops, and whisky tasting, naturally. The ferry terminal is at **SCALASAIG**, on the east coast, where there's a post office/shop, a petrol pump, a brewery, a café and the island's hotel.

Colonsay House

Two miles north of Scalasaig • Gardens April–Sept Tues & Thurs noon–5pm; Oct Tues & Thurs noon–4.30pm; the house itself is closed to the public • Charge • ⑩ colonsayholidays.co.uk

Colonsay House was built in 1722 by Malcolm MacNeil, but in 1904 the island and house were bought by Lord Strathcona, who made his fortune building the Canadian Pacific Railway (and whose descendants still own the island). He was also responsible for the house's romantically dilapidated woodland **gardens**, home to one of the most extensive rhododendron collections anywhere in Scotland. The gardens also shelter the strange eighth-century **Riasg Buidhe Cross**, which is decorated with an unusually lifelike mug shot (possibly of a monk) – ask for directions from the tearoom.

The beaches

To the north of Colonsay House is the island's finest sandy beach, the breathtaking **Kiloran Bay**, where the breakers roll in from the Atlantic. There's another unspoilt sandy beach backed by dunes at Balnahard, two miles northeast along a rough track; en route, you might spot wild goats, choughs and even a golden eagle.

Isle of Oronsay

While on Colonsay, it's worth taking a day out to visit the **ISLE OF ORONSAY**, half a mile to the south, with its ruined Augustinian priory. The two islands are separated by 'The Strand', a stretch of tidal mud flats, which act as a causeway for two hours either side of low tide (check locally for timings); you can drive over to the island at low tide, though most people park their cars and walk across. Legends (and etymology) link saints Columba and Oran with Colonsay and Oronsay, although the ruins only date back to the fourteenth century. You can, nevertheless, still make out the original church and tiny cloisters, abandoned since the Reformation and now roofless. The highlight, though, is the **Oronsay Cross**, a superb example of late medieval artistry from Iona which, along with thirty or so beautifully carved grave slabs, can be found in the restored side chapel. It takes about an hour to walk from the tip of Colonsay across The Strand to the priory (Wellington boots are a good idea).

ARRIVAL AND DEPARTURE	ISLE OF COLONSAY AND AROUND
By plane Colonsay airport is three miles west of Scalasaig (⑩ hebrideanair.co.uk).	Destinations Islay (Tues & Thurs 1 daily; 20min); Oban (Tues & Thurs 2 daily; 25min).

By ferry CalMac ferries run from Oban and once a week from Kennacraig via Islay, when a day-trip is possible, giving you around six hours on the island. Ferries also make the trip from Port Askaig on Islay.

Destinations Kennacraig (Wed 1 daily; 3hr 40min); Oban (daily except Wed & Sat; 2hr 15min); Port Askaig (Wed & Sat 1 daily; 1hr 10min).

GETTING AROUND AND INFORMATION

By minibus There's no public transport, but a minibus meets the Wednesday ferry and takes people on a tour of the island.

Bike rental Colonsay Bikes and Boards (ⓦ colonsaybikesandboards.co.uk) rents bikes (£15/day) and can also deliver (for £5) to your accommodation.

Website In the absence of a tourist office, ⓦ colonsay.org. uk and ⓦ visitcolonsay.co.uk are useful resources.

ACCOMMODATION AND EATING

There are a couple of modern **B&Bs** to choose from, though most visitors rent **self-catering accommodation**, the majority of which is run by the estate. **Wild camping** is, of course, an option.

Backpacker's Lodge Overlooking Loch Fada about 2 miles from the ferry terminal ⓦ colonsayholidays.co.uk. The Colonsay Estate's very comfortable hostel consists of the house itself (a former gamekeeper's lodge), with twin rooms, lounge and real fire, and a bothy with three cabins, each sleeping two people and with a shower block outside. There's a well-equipped dining bothy too. £

The Colonsay Scalasaig ⓦ colonsayholidays.co.uk. A cosy eighteenth-century inn at heart, and a short stroll from the pier, the island's only hotel, with just nine rooms, has transformed itself into a really stylish, comfortable place to stay; handily, it also has a restaurant serving decent food and a convivial bar, which acts as the island's social centre. ££

★ **The Colonsay Pantry** Above the pier in Scalasaig ⓦ thecolonsaypantry.co.uk. Delightful seafood restaurant and bistro offering both light refreshments (tea, coffee and cake) alongside substantial and scrumptious home cooking, such as smoked haddock scramble with chips; Wednesdays and Saturday are seafood nights, but in any case, you must phone ahead for any evening meals. £££

Mid-Argyll

MID-ARGYLL loosely describes the central wedge of land south of Oban and north of Kintyre. The highlights of this gently undulating scenery lie along the sharply indented and remote western coastline. Closest to Oban are the former slate mining settlements of Seil, Easdale and Luing, known collectively as the **Slate Islands**. Further south, the rich Bronze Age and Neolithic remains in the **Kilmartin Glen** comprise one of the most important prehistoric sites in Scotland. Separating Kilmartin Glen from the **Knapdale** peninsula is the **Crinan Canal**, a short cut for boats disinclined to round the Mull of Kintyre, which ends in the pint-sized, picturesque port of **Crinan**.

The Slate Islands

Eight miles south of Oban, a road heads off the A816 west to the minuscule **SLATE ISLANDS**, which at their peak in the mid-nineteenth century quarried over nine million slates annually. Today the old slate villages are sparsely populated, and an air of melancholy hangs over them, but their dramatic setting amid crashing waves makes for a rewarding day-trip.

Isle of Seil

The most northerly of the Slate Islands is **Seil**, a lush island separated from the mainland only by the thinnest of sea channels, which is spanned by the elegant single-arched humpback **Clachan Bridge**, built in 1793 and popularly known as the 'Bridge over the Atlantic'. In spring, the bridge sprouts a splendid flourish of purple fairy foxglove, which makes for a quite lovely sight.

The main village on Seil is **ELLENABEICH**, its neat white terraces of workers' cottages crouching below black cliffs on the westernmost tip of the island. This was once the

6

tiny island of Eilean a' Beithich (hence Ellenabeich), separated from the mainland by a slim sea channel until the intensive slate quarrying succeeded in silting it up. Confusingly, the village is often referred to by the same name as the nearby island of Easdale, since they formed an interdependent community based exclusively around the slate industry.

Slate Islands Heritage Centre

Ellenabeich • April–Oct daily 11am–4pm • Free • ⓦ slateislands.org.uk

The **Slate Islands Heritage Centre**, in one of the village's little white cottages, documents the lives and times of island people in the form of old photographs and artefacts, though mostly the emphasis is inevitably on the local quarry workings, including a model of the slate quarry as it would have been in its heyday. Moreover, and in common with many of Argyll's heritage centres, there's a dedicated genealogical department here.

Isle of Easdale

ⓦ easdale.org

Easdale remains an island, though the few hundred yards that separate it from Ellenabeich have to be dredged to keep the channel open. Up until the eve of a great storm in 1881, Easdale supported an incredible 452 inhabitants, despite being less than a mile across at any one point. That night, waves engulfed the island and flooded the quarries and the island never really recovered.

With lots of wonderfully flat stones freely available, Easdale makes the perfect venue for the annual **World Stone Skimming Championships** (ⓦ stoneskimming.com), held on the last Sunday of September. Just for the record, a legal skim qualifies as a stone that bounces twice – and if you fancy having a go, you can, as it's open to anyone.

Easdale Folk Museum

Near the main square, Easdale • April–Oct 11am–4pm • Charge • ⓦ easdalemuseum.org

Many of the village's old workers' cottages now serve as holiday homes, and one is home to the interesting **Easdale Folk Museum**, near the main square, which has surprisingly expansive collections covering not just the local slate industry but also the island's social and military associations. It also sells a useful historical map of the island, and you can buy some interesting slate souvenirs in the shop.

Isle of Luing

ⓦ isleofluing.org

South of Seil, across the narrow, treacherous Cuan Sound, lies **Luing** – pronounced 'Ling' – the largest of the Slate Islands, a long, thin, fertile island which once supported more than six hundred people, but now has a third of that. During the Clearances, the population was drastically reduced to make way for cattle; Luing is still renowned for its beef and for the chocolate-brown crossbreed named after it.

Cullipool, a mile or so southwest of the ferry slipway, is the main village, its whitewashed cottages (mostly built by the slate company) dotted along the shore facing Scarba and Mull. Luing's only other village, **Toberonochy**, lies on the more sheltered east coast, three miles southeast, and boasts the same distinctive white cottages, with red- or blue-painted door and window frames.

Atlantic Islands Centre

Cullipool • Easter–Oct Mon–Fri 10am–5pm, Sat 10am–10pm, Sun 11am–4pm; Nov–Easter Fri–Sun 11am–3pm • Free • ☎ 01852 314096

Positioned near the waterfront, the **Atlantic Islands Centre** is a superb heritage centre comprising a couple of engaging exhibitions, art space and a terrific café (see page 247). On the ground floor, a series of colourful and informative wall panels documents the forces that have shaped life on this side of the Atlantic; here too is the original lens from the Fladda Lighthouse, which was used from its inception in 1860 until 1956, when it became one of the first lighthouses in Scotland to be automated. Upstairs, the **Living History Exhibition** traces the development of the island in tandem with the local slate industry; better still are the marvellous views of Scarba, the Garvellachs and the lighthouses on Fladda and Belnahua.

GETTING AROUND AND TOURS   THE SLATE ISLANDS

By ferry The Cuan Ferry runs from Seil to Luing (every 30min; 5min; £2.10 return, car £9.20 return). The passenger-only ferry from Ellenabeich to the Isle of Easdale runs more or less on demand (press the buttons in the ferry shed or phone ☎ 01852 300559).

Boat tours Three, four- and five-hour wildlife and whale-watching cruises (£66–109), as well as high-adrenaline boat trips to the Corryvreckan Whirlpool, are offered by Sealife Adventures (⊛ sealife-adventures.com), whose pontoon is located just across the Clachan Bridge on Seil; depending upon the time of year, expect to see gannets, shags, kittiwakes, seals, dolphins, porpoises and sea eagles.

EATING AND DRINKING

Atlantic Islands Centre Café Cullipool ☎ 01852 314096. Lovely, airy café offering both great views and great food, for example a hot smoked salmon panini or some homemade stilton and walnut pate with warm toast and butter; or you could just opt for a cuppa and a chunk of home-made chocolate cake. Meals are also served on Saturday evenings, for which booking is advised. £̄

Oyster Bar and Restaurant Ellenabeich ⊛ oysterbareasdale.com. For delicious seafood – mussels in white wine, king prawns and sweet chilli – or just a pint of real ale, pop inside the snug wood-panelled bar of the *Oyster* on the way to or from the ferry. £̄£̄£̄

Puffer Bar 200yd from the Folk Museum ⊛ pufferbarandrestaurant.co.uk. Should you wish to hang about, then you could do worse than visit the terrific *Puffer* restaurant and bar; the former serves the best of the day's fresh catch, while the latter is a convivial spot for a drink.

Arduaine Garden

A816, 10 miles north Kilmartin • April–Sept 9.30am–dusk • Charge • NTS • ☎ 01852 200366

A great spot at which to stop and have a picnic on the A816 from Oban to Lochgilphead is **Arduaine Garden**, overlooking Asknish Bay and the islands of Shuna, Luing, Scarba and Jura. The gardens, whose original foundations were laid in 1898, are stupendous, particularly in May and June, and have the feel of an intimate private garden, with immaculately mown lawns, lily-strewn ponds, mature woods and spectacular rhododendrons, azaleas and magnolias. In late spring, meanwhile, the wild meadow comes alive with orchids. You can follow several pathways through the gardens, one of which is the woodland walk, which leads down to the lakeshore, where there's a good chance of spotting otters, sea eagles and hen harriers.

ACCOMMODATION AND EATING   ARDUAINE GARDEN

★ **Loch Melfort Hotel** Adjacent to Arduaine Garden ⊛ lochmelfort.co.uk. This fine, privately run country-house hotel overlooking Asknish Bay offers a selection of beautifully appointed rooms, both in the main house and the adjoining Seaview Lodge, each with its own private patio or balcony; best of all, though, are the views, which are some of the finest in Scotland. The hotel's restaurant is outstanding (Argyll lamb with sweetbread and walnut jus, while their sparky *Bistro* next door has cheaper alternatives, for example Loch Melfort fishcakes and homemade burgers; you can also eat off the terrace here. Moreover, every first and third Friday evening of the month, the bistro has live music. £̄£̄£̄

Kilmartin Glen and around

The chief sight on the road from Oban to Lochgilphead is **KILMARTIN GLEN**, the most important prehistoric site on the Scottish mainland. The most remarkable relic is the **linear cemetery**, where several cairns are aligned for more than two miles to the south of the village of Kilmartin. These are thought to represent the successive burials of a

6

ruling family or chieftains, but nobody can be sure. The best view of the cemetery's configuration is from the Bronze Age **Mid-Cairn**, but the Neolithic **South Cairn**, dating from around 3000 BC, is by far the oldest and the most impressive, with its large chambered tomb roofed by giant slabs.

Close to the South Cairn, the two **Temple Wood stone circles** appear to have been the architectural focus of burials in the area from Neolithic times to the Bronze Age. Visible to the south are the impressively cup-marked **Nether Largie standing stones** (no public access), the largest of which looms over 10ft high.

Cup- and ring-marked rocks are a recurrent feature of prehistoric sites in Kilmartin Glen and elsewhere in Argyll. There are many theories as to their origin: some see them as Pictish symbols, others as primitive solar calendars. The most extensive markings in the entire country are at **Achnabreck**, off the A816 towards Lochgilphead.

Kilmartin Museum

Kilmartin village • Daily March–Oct 10am–5.30pm; Nov–late Dec 11am–4pm • Charge • Ⓦ kilmartin.org

Situated on high ground to the north of the Kilmartin cairns is the tiny village of **KILMARTIN**, an unremarkable place but home to the superb **Kilmartin Museum**, housed in the old manse adjacent to the village church; note though, that a long-awaited redevelopment of the museum finally got underway in 2021, and is not expected to reopen until 2023 When it does, you'll be able to learn about the various theories concerning prehistoric crannogs, henges and cairns, practise polishing an axe, examine different types of wood, and listen to a variety of weird and wonderful sounds (check out the Gaelic bird imitations). Among the many remarkable exhibits on display will be an eagle bone flute, a bronze sword from Shuna, a carved slab from the Nether Largie north cairn, and decorated querns (stones used for making flour from grain) from Barnluasgan. At 1.30pm on Wednesdays between April and October, museum staff run a superb (free) two-hour guided walk of the cairns; these are still taking place despite the museum's closure.

Carnasserie Castle

Commanding a high ridge a mile up the road towards Oban are the ruins of **Carnasserie Castle**. Built in the 1560s by Protestant reformer John Carswell – who published the first book to be printed in Scottish Gaelic (a translation of John Knox's *Book of Common Order*) – the castle is a good example of the transition between fully fortified castles and later mansion houses, and has several original finely carved stone fireplaces and doorways, as well as numerous gun-loops and shot holes. The reward for climbing the five-storey structure is a wonderful view of Kilmartin Glen dead straight ahead.

Moine Mhór and Dunadd

To the south of Kilmartin, beyond the linear cemetery, lies the raised peat bog of **Moine Mhór** (Great Moss), now a nature reserve and home to remarkable plant, insect and birdlife. To get a close look at the sphagnum moss and wetlands, head for the Tileworks Walk, just off the A816, which includes a short boardwalk over the bog.

Moine Mhór is best known as home to the Iron Age fort of **Dunadd**, one of Scotland's most important Celtic sites, occupying a distinctive 176ft-high rocky knoll once surrounded by the sea but currently stranded beside the winding River Add. It was here that Fergus, the first king of Dalriada – which embraced much of what is now Argyll – established his royal seat, having arrived from Ireland in around 500 AD. Its strategic position, the craggy defences and the view from the top are all impressive, but it's the **stone carvings** (albeit now fibreglass copies) between the twin summits which make Dunadd so remarkable: several lines of inscription in Ogham (an ancient alphabet of Irish origin), the faint outline of a boar, a hollowed-out footprint and a small basin. The boar and the inscriptions are probably **Pictish**, since the fort was clearly occupied long before Fergus got there, but the footprint and basin have been interpreted as being part of the royal coronation rituals of the kings of Dalriada. It is thought that the Stone of Destiny was used at Dunadd before being moved to Scone Palace (see page 61). From the car park (well signposted from the main road), it's a fabulous little scramble to the top of the fort, whereupon you'll be rewarded with sparkling views of the Glen and Knapdale Forest.

ACCOMMODATION AND EATING   KILMARTIN GLEN; SEE MAP PAGE 248

Dunchraigaig House 1 mile south of Kilmartin ⓦ dunchraigaig.co.uk. This large detached Victorian house situated opposite the Ballymeanoch standing stones offers five spotless en-suite rooms with either woodland or Jura Island views, though its star attraction is the local pine marten, which appears at the feeding table most mornings for a bite to eat. You'll enjoy your breakfast too, while packed lunches are available upon request. **££**

Kilmartin Museum Café Kilmartin Museum ⓦ kilmartin.org. Looking out across to Glebe Cairn, this is a lovely spot at which to refuel after examining the local treasures, with the likes of wild venison burger and smoked salmon hoagies to feast on, as well as lots of delicious home-baked fare, not least a divine selection of cakes and buns. Note, though, that the café will remain closed until work on the museum is complete. **££**

Kings Reach B&B Dunadd View, Kilmichael Glassary, ⓦ kingsreachbedandbreakfast.co.uk. Warm and welcoming vegan guesthouse whose three large, light and impeccably kept rooms offer gorgeous views of Dunadd, as well as some fabulous sunsets; breakfast might consist of stacked pancakes, scrambled tofu on toast, or chia pudding alongside fresh fruit and yoghurts; they've also got two very well-equipped self-catering cottages each sleeping four (5-night minimum stay). **££**

6

ARGYLL BEAVERS

In 2009, a colony of beavers from Norway was introduced to Knapdale Forest as part of a five-year project by the **Scottish Beaver Trial**. The first beavers in the wilds of Scotland for over four hundred years, their arrival met with a rather mixed reaction, though their effect on the environment (and to a lesser degree the local economy) was closely monitored by an independent project team; following the end of the trial phase in 2016, a decision was made by the Scottish government to keep the beavers, and in the process they were granted both legal protection and native species status.

From the Argyll Beaver Centre (seasonal opening times; Wargyllbeavercentre.co.uk) at **Barnluasgan** (four miles west of Cairnbaan), it's a twenty-minute walk to Dubh Loch, where most of the beaver activity takes place. Here, there's a viewing platform and another rough path that cuts through to Loch Coille Bharr, the two lochs separated by an 60ft-long dam that took the beavers around four to five months to build – a quite remarkable feat of engineering. Either side of these two lochs, you'll also see their lodges, large and impressive tangles of severed branches, wood and mud. The best time to see these fascinating creatures is either at dawn or dusk, and though sightings are by no means guaranteed, there is a strong possibility that you will witness some beaver activity. Take along some binoculars, midge repellent and refreshments (you could be waiting a while), and don't bring dogs. You can follow the trail yourself or, alternatively, join one of the **guided tours** (£10) that take place on Wednesday evenings at 6pm between April and September.

Knapdale and around

Forested **Knapdale** – from the Gaelic *cnap* (hill) and *dall* (field) – forms a buffer zone between the Kintyre peninsula and the rest of Argyll, bounded to the north by the Crinan Canal and to the south by West Loch Tarbert, and consisting of three progressively fatter fingers of land, separated by Loch Sween and Loch Caolisport. Knapdale is a little-visited area, which is surprising, as the ancient wooded landscape is among some of the most beautiful, and unique, in the country. Not only that, but there is some spectacular wildlife to observe here as well, not least thanks to the recent reintroduction of beavers to the area (see box, above).

Crinan Canal

The nine-mile-long **Crinan Canal** opened in 1801, linking Loch Fyne, at Ardrishaig south of Lochgilphead, with the Sound of Jura, thus cutting out the long and treacherous journey around the Mull of Kintyre. John Rennie's original design, although an impressive engineering feat, had numerous faults, and by 1816 Thomas Telford was called in to take charge of the renovations. The canal runs parallel to the sea for quite some way before cutting across the bottom of Moine Mhór and hitting a flight of locks either side of **CAIRNBAAN** (there are fifteen in total). The walk along the towpath is utterly delightful (both picturesque and not too strenuous), though you could, of course, cycle too.

The most relaxing place from which to view the canal in action is **CRINAN**, the pretty little fishing port at the canal's western end. Crinan's tiny harbour is, for the moment at least, still home to a small fishing fleet; a quick burst up through Crinan Wood to the hill above the village will give you a bird's-eye view of the sea lock and its setting.

ACCOMMODATION AND EATING   **CRINAN CANAL**

CAIRNBAAN

Cairnbaan Hotel By lock no. 5 on the canal ⓦ cairnbaan. com. Eighteenth-century coaching inn built at the same time as the canal, which it overlooks, with twelve very accomplished and well-designed rooms. The lively restaurant-cum-bar deservedly does well from lots of passing trade from the canal, with dishes such as steamed mussels in white wine and garlic, and smoked haddock on chive mash with Kintyre cheddar; they also do takeaways, including pizzas. Otherwise, just grab a pint and watch the boats pass by. **££**

CRINAN

Crinan Hotel ⓦ crinanhotel.com. Occupying an enviable position overlooking the harbour, this mildly eccentric family-run hotel has twenty superbly conceived rooms (indeed, the hotel has its own gallery), each one named after a Scottish artist and featuring an original piece of work by that artist. All offer splendid loch views, though you're certainly paying for the privilege. **££££**

Crinan Seafood Bar Crinan Hotel ⓦ crinanhotel.com. Reward yourself after the long canal-side walk with some steamed mussels or an Arbroath smokie washed down with a pint, at the same time as enjoying one of the most beautiful views in Scotland – especially at sunset, when the myriad islets and the distinctive Paps of Jura are reflected in the waters of the loch. Occupying the adjacent horse stables is the hotel's cheery coffee shop, serving bacon rolls, home-baked cakes, tea and coffee. **£££**

Kintyre

But for the mile-long isthmus between West Loch Tarbert and the much smaller East Loch Tarbert, the little-visited, sparsely populated peninsula of **KINTYRE** – from the Gaelic *ceann tire*, 'land's end' – would be an island. Indeed, in the eleventh century, when the Scottish king, Malcolm Canmore, allowed Magnus Barefoot, King of Norway, to lay claim to any island he could circumnavigate by boat, Magnus dragged his boat across the Tarbert isthmus and added the peninsula to his Hebridean kingdom. Despite its relative proximity to Scotland's central belt, Kintyre remains quiet and unfashionable; its main towns of **Tarbert** and **Campbeltown** have few obvious attractions, but that's part of their appeal.

Kintyre's bleak but often beautiful **west coast** ranks among the most exposed stretches of coastline in Argyll. Atlantic breakers pound the rocky shoreline, while the persistent westerly wind forces the trees against the hillside. However, when the weather's fine and the wind not too fierce, there are numerous deserted sandy beaches to enjoy, with great views over to Gigha, Islay, Jura and even Ireland. By way of contrast, the **east coast** of Kintyre is gentler than the west, sheltered from the Atlantic winds and in parts strikingly beautiful, with stunning views across to Arran.

ARRIVAL AND DEPARTURE   KINTYRE

By plane Campbeltown has an airport, with flights to and from Glasgow.

By bus There are regular daily buses from Glasgow to Campbeltown, via Tarbert and the west coast. Note that the bus service from Campbeltown only reaches as far as the fishing village of Carradale, some 13 miles up the coast.

By ferry Kintyre is well served with ferries: the main port is at Kennacraig, five miles south of Tarbert on the west coast, with ferries serving Port Askaig and Port Ellen on Islay. There are also ferries from Tarbert to Portavadie on the Cowal peninsula, from Claonaig to Lochranza on Arran, and a summer-only one from Campbeltown to Ardrossan.

Tarbert

A distinctive rocket-like church steeple heralds the fishing port of **TARBERT** (in Gaelic *An Tairbeart*, meaning 'isthmus'), sheltering an attractive little bay backed by rugged hills. Tarbert's **herring industry** was mentioned in the Annals of Ulster as far back as AD 836, though right now the local fishing industry is down to its lowest level ever. Ironically, it was local Tarbert fishermen who, in the 1830s, pioneered the method of herring fishing known as trawling, seining or ring-netting, which eventually wiped out the Loch Fyne herring stocks.

Tourism is now an increasingly important source of income, and though there's little of substance to see in Tarbert itself, it's a good hub, with excellent transport links, a decent stock of accommodation, and some highly commendable seafood restaurants. Moreover, it stages two prestigious annual events: the Scottish Series yacht races in late May, and the Tarbert Seafood Festival in early July when traditional boats also hit town.

KINTYRE WAY

The best way to really appreciate Kintyre's remote but beguiling landscape is to tackle the hundred-mile long **Kintyre Way** Wthekintyreway.com), which begins in Tarbert and zigzags its way down and across the peninsula to Southend with a final section heading northwest to Machrihanish. There are seven stages in all, mostly with moderate walking (one or two sections are more demanding), comprising hill paths, moorland, forest trails and coast. The website also has suggestions for accommodation at the end of each stage.

ARRIVAL AND DEPARTURE   TARBERT

By bus Buses stop in the centre of town on Campbeltown Rd and Barmore Rd.

Destinations Campbeltown (5 daily; 1hr 15min); Claonaig (Mon–Sat 3 daily; 30min); Glasgow (5 daily; 3hr 10min); Kennacraig (5 daily; 15min); Kilberry (2 daily termtime;

40min); Skipness (Mon–Sat 3 daily; 35min); Tayinloan (Mon–Fri 3 daily; 30min).

By ferry The ferry terminal is on Pier Rd, a 10min walk along Harbour St.

Destinations Portavadie (hourly; 25min).

ACCOMMODATION

★**Anchor Hotel** Harbour St Ⓦlochfyne-scotland. co.uk. While this smart, harbour-facing hotel itself has thirteen perfectly accomplished rooms, it's the barge across the road that you should be heading for; brilliantly converted into four luxury cabins, you wouldn't even know you were on the water were it not for the occasional gentle bob and swans gliding past your window at eye level. Cool, relaxing and a lot of fun. Rooms **££**; cabins **££££**

Knap Guest House Campbeltown Rd Ⓦknap guesthouse.co.uk. Handsome Victorian townhouse with four pristine rooms leading off a beautifully appointed

lounge; each room manifests a curious mixture of traditional Scottish and Asian furnishings, which somehow works very well. A little tricky to find, it's opposite the Co-op. **££**

Struan House Harbour St Ⓦstruan-house-lochfyne. co.uk. Built in 1846 as a small hotel, this is now a charming six-roomed guesthouse (singles, twins and doubles) with bespoke furnishings, grand wooden bedsteads, and some sweet little touches like bedside lamps, books and wall-mounted artwork. It's opposite the Harbour Authority building up towards the ferry terminal. **££**

EATING AND DRINKING

Ca'Dora Harbour St ☎01880 820258. The pick of several cafés ranged along the seafront which, despite looking rather dull from the outside, pulls in the punters for its comfort food such as cottage pie, and battered haddock and chips, though it's renowned, above all, for its ice cream. **£**

Seabed Restaurant Harbour St Ⓦlochfyne-scotland. co.uk. Complement your stay on the barge with dinner in the *Anchor Hotel's* inviting, cheerily staffed restaurant,

which offers up comforting dishes such as Cullen skink risotto and seafood linguine. **£££**

★**Starfish** Castle St Ⓦstarfishtarbert.com. Sparkling, informally run seafood restaurant where scallops are king, literally – a plate of these will set you back £19, as will the seafood stroganoff, comprising mussels, queen scallops, salmon, and smoked and fresh haddock in a paprika sauce. Complete your meal with a classic crème caramel. **£££**

Carradale and around

The village of **CARRADALE** itself is rather drab, but the tiny, very pretty harbour with its small fishing fleet, and the wide, sandy beach to the south, make up for it, while there is a handful of lovely places to stay and eat here too. On the road into town, the small **Network Centre** has bikes and all-terrain electric buggies to rent (daily 10am–4pm; ☎01583 431296; £14/5hr, £20/day), and there's good home baking to be had in the tearoom. The B842 ends fourteen miles north of Carradale at **CLAONAIG**, little more than a slipway for the small summer car ferry to Arran.

ARRIVAL AND DEPARTURE   CARRADALE AND AROUND

By ferry The ferry terminal is at Claonaig, fourteen miles north of Carradale.

Destinations Lochranza, Arran (8–9 daily; 30min).

6

ACCOMMODATION AND EATING

Ashbank Hotel Centre of village ⓦ ashbankhotel.com. A dinky little place in the heart of the village, with five boxy but comfy en-suite rooms – three with a sea view – and the Egyptian cotton bedding is something to savour. Breakfast is taken in the sweet little downstairs bar. **££**

Carradale Bay Caravan Park Outside Carradale village ⓦ carradalebay.com. The nearest campsite to town is the superbly equipped and well-sheltered Carradale Bay Caravan Park, right by, and with great access to, the sandy beach. Although it's predominantly a caravan site, there is a separate area to pitch tents. **£**

Skipness

Heading north of the Claonaig ferry terminal, a dead-end road winds its way along the shore a few miles further north to the tiny village of **SKIPNESS** and the considerable ruins of the thirteenth-century **Skipness Castle** (open access; free). The castle's two surviving rooms form the base of the sixteenth-century tower; from here a slender spiral staircase leads to the roof and glorious views across the Kilbrannan Sound to Arran. To the right as you enter, the old latrine was converted into a dovecote, as evidenced by the holes in the walls on all sides.

There are also several gentle **walks** laid out in the nearby mixed woodland, up the glen, but the main reason people make the effort to visit Skipness is the wonderful *Skipness Seafood Cabin*. Here, too, is the **Skipness Smokehouse** (ⓦ creelers.co.uk), where you can watch all manner of foodstuffs (including salmon, kippers, duck, venison) being smoked, after which you can of course make some purchases if so desired.

ARRIVAL AND EATING   SKIPNESS

By bus Buses run between Skipness and Kennacraig via the ferry terminal at Claonaig (Mon–Sat 3 daily; 20min).

Skipness Seafood Cabin Below the castle ⓦ skipnessseafoodcabin.co.uk. Little more than a hut, the Cabin has been doling out fresh local seafood for years:

hot smoked salmon or crab rolls, fresh oysters, grilled queen scallops, langoustine, mussels and home-baked cakes are just some of the treats. There are wooden tables and bench seating from which to admire the splendid views across to Arran. **£**

Isle of Gigha

Just six miles by one mile, **GIGHA** – pronounced 'Geeya', with a hard 'g' – is a low-lying, fertile island, with a population of around 150, just three miles off the west coast of Kintyre. The island's Ayrshire cattle produce over a quarter of a million gallons of milk a year to produce the island's distinctive (occasionally fruit-shaped) cheese. Like many of the smaller Hebrides, Gigha was bought and sold numerous times after its original lairds, the MacNeils, sold up, and was finally bought by the islanders themselves in 2002.

The real draw of Gigha, apart from the peace and quiet, is the white sandy beaches – including one at Ardminish, the island's only village – that dot the coastline. The ferry from Tayinloan deposits you at **ARDMINISH**, where you'll find the post office and shop, and the all-denomination island church, which has some interesting stained-glass windows. Although most visitors come to Gigha for the day, it's a great place to stay.

Achamore Gardens

1.5 miles south of Ardminish • Daily dusk–dawn • Charge • ☎ 01583 505390

The main attraction on Gigha is the **Achamore Gardens**, established by the first postwar owner, Sir James Horlick of hot-drink fame. Its spectacularly colourful displays of azaleas are best seen in early summer, but elsewhere, the rhododendrons merit seeking out, as does the walled garden, with its hugely diverse collection of plants, a bamboo maze, and a superb panorama across the island's west coast and beyond to Islay and

Jura. At the heart of the complex stands Achamore House itself, though this is now privately owned and off-limits to visitors.

To the southwest of the gardens, the ruins of the thirteenth-century **St Catan's Chapel** are floored with weathered medieval gravestones; the ogham stone nearby is the only one of its kind in the west of Scotland.

ARRIVAL AND INFORMATION   ISLE OF GIGHA

By ferry CalMac ferries depart more or less hourly from Tayinloan, 23 miles south of Tarbert, for the 20min crossing to Ardminish.

Gigha Activity Centre Ardminish Bay (Easter–Sept daily 10am–6pm; ☎07516 709249). Next to the ferry slip, this is effectively the island's information point, but is mainly concerned with renting out bikes (£10/half day, £16/day), kayaks (£10/1hr), stand-up paddle-boards (£10/1hr) and rowing boats (£20/1hr). The website, ⓦgigha.org.uk, is also a useful resource.

ACCOMMODATION AND EATING

The Boathouse Ardminish Bay ⓦboathouseongigha.com. Inside this low dark-stone building, perched above a white sandy bay, is a gorgeous little restaurant rustling up treats like potted brown shrimp with smoked onion relish and poached Gigha halibut with chorizo and saffron potato. **£££**

Gigha Hotel ⓦgighahotel.com. Just 200yd from the ferry terminal, this is the island's social hub and a very welcoming place to stay. Its twelve, largely pinewood-furnished rooms are inviting and spotlessly clean without being particularly exciting. Restaurant, bar and café too. **££**

Machrihanish and around

The only major development along the entire west coast of Kintyre is **MACHRIHANISH**, at the southern end of Machrihanish Bay, the longest continuous stretch of sand in Argyll. There are two approaches to the **beach**: from Machrihanish itself, or from Westport, at the north end of the bay, where the A83 swings east towards Campbeltown; either way, the sea here is too dangerous for swimming. Machrihanish itself was once a thriving salt-producing and coal-mining centre – you can still see the miners' cottages at neighbouring Drumlemble – but now survives solely on tourism, in particular golf.

Machrihanish Golf Club and Machrihanish Dunes Golf Club

Machrihanish Golf Club Between the beach and Campbeltown Airport • April–Oct £75 per round; Oct & March £55; Nov–Feb £35 • ⓦmachgolf.com **Machrihanish Dunes Golf Club** East of Campbeltown Airport • April–Oct £75 per round; Nov–March £40 • ⓦmachrihanishdunes.com

Dominating the village of Machrihanish is the exposed 18-hole championship course of the **Machrihanish Golf Club**, between the beach and Campbeltown Airport on the nearby flat and fertile swathe of land known as the Laggan. One of Scotland's finest links courses (established in 1876), it plays out on a quite spectacular landscape, and is particularly notable for its first hole, which cuts across the Atlantic in dramatic fashion.

Established as recently as 2009, the sister course of Machrihanish golf course, the 18-hole **Machrihanish Dunes**, on the other side of the airport, is perhaps even more impressive. The course layout, including the tee and green positions, is dictated solely by the lie of the land.

ARRIVAL AND INFORMATION   MACHRIHANISH

By bus Buses stop in the centre of the village near the golf club.

Destinations Campbeltown (Mon–Sat 7 daily; 20min).

ACCOMMODATION AND EATING

Machrihanish Holiday Park Machrihanish Village ⓦcampkintyre.co.uk. Superbly located next to the fairways and with direct sea views, this large, fully equipped, family-run campsite has a terrific mix of caravan and tent space, as well as heated wooden wigwams (sleeping three people) and fully fitted bell tents (sleeping two adults and two children). Per pitch £; wigwams £; bell tents (July & Aug only) ££

Old Clubhouse Pub Machrihanish Village

ⓦmachrihanishdunes.com. Overlooking the first tee, the erstwhile clubhouse is now a very agreeable village pub, frequented by golfers and locals alike, which means it's not nearly as pretentious as it might be. Good bar food and decent ales. ££

Campbeltown

6

Set within a deep bay, sheltered by Davaar Island and the surrounding hills, **CAMPBELTOWN** is Kintyre's largest town with a population of around 5,000. Originally known as Kinlochkilkerran (Ceann Loch Cill Chiaran), the town was renamed in the seventeenth century by the Earl of Argyll – a Campbell – when it became one of the main points for immigration from the Lowlands. As is evident from the architecture, Campbeltown's heyday was the Victorian era, when shipbuilding was going strong, coal was shipped by canal from Drumlemble, the fishing fleet was vast and Campbeltown Loch was said to be made of whisky. Nineteenth-century visitors to Campbeltown frequently found the place engulfed in a thick fog of pungent peat smoke from the town's 34 whisky distilleries. Today, only three distilleries are left to maintain this regional subgroup of single-malt whiskies.

If you're here on the third weekend of August, be prepared for the **Mull of Kintyre Music Festival** (ⓦmokfest.com), which pulls in some big-name rock bands, plus some good traditional Irish and Scottish ones.

Springbank distillery

55 Longrow • Mon–Sat 10am, 11.30am, 1.30pm & 3pm • Charge • ⓦ springbank.scot

Whisky-lovers shouldn't miss a visit to the **Springbank distillery**, a deeply traditional, family-owned business (founded in 1828) that produces three different single malts; indeed, it's the only distillery in Scotland to carry out the full production process on one site, from the malting to the bottling. You first get to see the malting floor (Springbank is now one of only half a dozen or so distilleries in Scotland that still does its own malting), before continuing down to the peat stacks and kiln, which again is not something you normally see on a distillery tour. Having viewed the magnificent copper stills, the tour winds up inside the capacious warehouse, which stretches for 100yd or so. The tour ends, as is customary, with a small tasting, but here you also get a free miniature and a glass to take away.

Burnet Building

St John St • Mon–Fri 9am–5pm • Free • ☎ 01586 559017

Built as the town library in 1897, the **Burnett Building** is crowned by a distinctive lantern and decorated with four relief panels depicting the town's main industries at the time. The building harbours a very old-fashioned one-room local **museum**, with some intriguing finds such as a gold Viking arm ring and a gorgeous jet necklace, as well as a few pieces by the acclaimed landscape painter William McTaggart. Most people, though, are drawn to the **Linda McCartney Memorial Garden**, which you should approach from Shore Street. Here, you'll find a slightly ludicrous bronze statue of Linda holding a lamb, a piece commissioned by Paul McCartney, who spent many happy times with Linda and the kids on the farm he owns near Campbeltown.

Campbeltown Heritage Centre

Big Kiln St • April–Oct Mon–Fri 11am–4pm • Donation • ⓦ campbeltownheritagecentre.co.uk

The former Lorne Street Church, with its stripy bell-cote and pinnacles, has been cleverly converted into the intermittently interesting **Campbeltown Heritage**

6

Centre. Due prominence is given to the town's once glittering industrial heritage, in particular the local fishing and whisky industries; going hand in hand with local malt production was a significant coopering industry, and at one stage there were more than sixty coopers in Campbeltown. By far the most prominent exhibit here, however, and occupying the spot where the main altar once stood, is a beautiful wooden skiff called 'Yerda', dating from 1906. Look out, too, for the model of the Victorian harbourfront with the light railway running along Hall Street.

ARRIVAL AND INFORMATION   CAMPBELTOWN

By plane Campbeltown Airport (ⓦ hial.co.uk) lies three miles west, towards Machrihanish.
Destinations Glasgow (Mon–Fri 2 daily, Sun 1; 40min).
By bus The town's main bus terminal is in front of the swimming pool on the Esplanade.
Destinations Carradale (Mon–Fri 5 daily, 4 on Sat; 45min); Glasgow (5 daily; 4hr 15min); Machrihanish (Mon–Sat 9

daily; 20min); Southend (Mon–Sat 6 daily, 25min); Tarbert (5 daily; 1hr 10min).
By ferry The ferry terminal is on the south side of the harbour, from where it's a 5min walk into the centre.
Destinations Ardrossan (Thurs, Fri & Sun 1 daily; 2hr 40min).

ACCOMMODATION

Ardshiel Hotel Kilkerran Rd ⓦ ardshiel.co.uk. A former whisky distiller's Victorian mansion situated on a lovely leafy square just a block or so back from the harbour front. The rooms are functional more than anything else. More impressive is the hotel's glamorous, grown-up whisky bar, stocking in excess of 700 malts, well worth a visit even if you're not staying here. **£££**

Campbeltown Backpackers Big Kiln ⓦ campbeltownbackpackers.co.uk. Occupying the old school house in the courtyard across from the heritage centre, this community-trust-run bunkhouse has sixteen firm, pine beds in two dormitories, a self-catering kitchen and small lounge. Cycle storage and drying room too. There's no reception as such, so if there's no one there, pop into the heritage centre; when that's closed just call the number on

the door. **£**
Oatfield House 3 miles down the B842 ⓦ oatfield.org. A beautifully renovated whitewashed laird's house set in its own grounds on the road to Southend, retaining three rooms of some character and distinction. Guests are also free to avail themselves of the panelled dining room and parlour. **££**
Royal Hotel Main St ⓦ machrihanishdunes.com. Owned by the golf club, this high-end hotel sits well with the redevelopment of the harbourfront area, and injects a big dollop of colour into this otherwise dull street. The supremely comfortable rooms are mostly furnished in bold tartan colour schemes, with deep armchairs, big beds with thick duvets and fluffy pillows, and a host of other neat touches. **£££**

EATING AND DRINKING

Black Sheep Pub Main St ⓦ machrihanishdunes.com. The *Royal Hotel*'s pub is by far the most enjoyable watering hole in town, with seating arranged around a shiny, semi-circular bar, in addition to some outdoor tables overlooking the harbour. Some decent cask ales too.

Café Bluebell 6 Hall St ☏ 01586 552800. Simple-looking but warm and welcoming café opposite the tourist office offering a terrific selection of light snacks (soups, sandwiches, sausage rolls), as well as a gut-busting all-day breakfast. **£**

Mull of Kintyre

Most people venture south of Campbeltown to make a pilgrimage to the **Mull of Kintyre**, made famous by the mawkish number-one hit by one time local resident Paul McCartney, with the help of the Campbeltown Pipe Band. It's also infamous as the site of the RAF's worst peacetime accident when, on 2 June 1994, a Chinook helicopter on its way from Belfast to Inverness crashed, killing all 29 on board. A small memorial can be found on the hillside, not far from the **Gap** (1150ft) – after which no vehicles are allowed. The Mull is the nearest Britain gets to Ireland, just twelve miles away, and the Irish coastline appears remarkably close on fine days. There's nothing specifically to see, but the trek down to the lighthouse, itself 300ft above the ocean waves, is challengingly tortuous.

Isle of Islay

The fertile, largely treeless island of **ISLAY** (pronounced 'eye-la') is famous for one thing – single-malt **whisky**. The smoky, peaty, pungent quality of Islay whisky is unique, recognizable even to the untutored palate, and all nine of the island's distilleries will happily take visitors on a guided tour, ending with the customary tipple. Yet, despite the fame of its whiskies, Islay still remains relatively undiscovered, especially when compared with Arran, Mull or Skye, partly, perhaps, because of the two-hour ferry journey from Kennacraig on Kintyre. If you do make the effort, however, you'll be rewarded with a genuinely friendly welcome from islanders proud of their history, landscape and Gaelic culture.

In medieval times, Islay was the political centre of the Hebrides, with **Finlaggan**, near Port Askaig, the seat of the MacDonalds, Lords of the Isles. The picturesque, whitewashed villages you see on Islay today, however, date from the planned settlements founded by the Campbells in the late eighteenth and early nineteenth centuries. Apart from whisky and solitude, the other great draw is the **birdlife** – there's a real possibility of spotting a golden eagle, or the rare crow-like chough, and

6

no chance of missing the white-fronted and barnacle geese that winter here in their thousands.

A great time to visit is late May for the ten-day **Feis Ile**, or Islay Festival of Malt and Music (ⓦfeisile.com), with whisky tasting, piping recitals, folk dancing and other events celebrating the island's Gaelic roots; you will, though, have to book accommodation months in advance.

ARRIVAL AND DEPARTURE
ISLE OF ISLAY

By plane Islay's airport (ⓦhial.co.uk) is five miles north of Port Ellen on the A846.

Destinations Colonsay (Thurs 1 daily; 20min); Glasgow (Mon–Fri 2 daily, Sat & Sun 1 daily; 40min); Oban (Thurs 2 daily; 35min).

By ferry CalMac ferries from Kennacraig on Kintyre connect with both Port Ellen and Port Askaig. There's also a ferry that makes the short trip across to Jura, and, between April and September, a passenger-only ferry between Craighouse and Tayvallich on the mainland.

ISLAY WHISKY DISTILLERIES

It goes without saying that Islay's **whisky distilleries** are a major tourist attraction. Nowadays, every distillery offers guided tours, which usually last an hour and traditionally end with a generous dram, and occasionally a free glass. Most also offer more comprehensive tours with more tastings, and some even do warehouse tours. Phone ahead to make sure there's a tour running, as times do change frequently.

Ardbeg Port Ellen ⓦardbeg.com. Ardbeg is traditionally considered the saltiest, peatiest malt on Islay, and that's saying something. Thoroughly overhauled and restored following its acquisition by Glenmorangie in 1997, it's a relatively small distillery by Islay's standards yet it has bags of character inside and the tour is one of the best. Tours £10; April–Oct 11am & 3pm; Feb–March & Nov–mid-Dec Mon–Fri 11am & 3pm.

Bowmore School St ⓦbowmore.com. Bowmore is the most touristy of the Islay distilleries, but it is by far the most central (with unrivalled disabled access), and also one of the few still doing its own malting and kilning. Tours £10; March–Oct Mon–Sat 10, 11, 2.30 & 3.30pm, Sun 12.30 & 2pm; Nov–Feb Mon–Sat 10.30am & 2pm.

Bruichladdich Bruichladdich ⓦbruichladdich. com. In the centre of the village of the same name, this independent distillery was rescued in 2001 by a group of whisky fanatics, but was bought out by Remy-Cointreau in 2012. Progressive and innovative, this is one distinctly cool distillery; moreover, they also produce the scrumptious Botanist Gin. Tours £5; April–Oct Mon–Fri 10am, 1 & 4pm, Sat 10am, 1 & 3pm, Sun 11am, 1 & 2pm; Nov–March Mon–Fri 10am & 1pm, Sat 10am & 2pm.

Bunnahabhain 4 miles north of Port Askaig ⓦbunnahabhain.com. A visit to Bunnahabhain (pronounced 'Bunna-have-in') is really only for whisky obsessives. The road from Port Askaig is windy, the whisky the least characteristically Islay and the distillery itself only in production for a few months each year. Tours £7; April–Oct Mon–Sat 9.30am & 3.30pm;

Nov–March Mon–Sat 10am & 2pm, Sun noon & 2pm.

Caol Ila Port Askaig ⓦmalts.com. Caol Ila (pronounced 'Cull-eela'), just north of Port Askaig, is a modern distillery, the majority of whose lightly peaty malt goes into blended whiskies. Tours £7; March–Oct Mon–Fri 9.30am & 12.30 & 3.30pm, Sat 9.30am, Sun 10.30am; Nov–Feb Tues–Sat 10.30am.

Kilchoman Rockside Farm, Bruichladdich ⓦkilchomandistillery.com. Established in 2005 as the first new distillery on Islay for over a century, Kilchoman is a very welcoming, tiny, farm-based enterprise that grows its own barley, as well as distilling, maturing and bottling its whisky on site. They've also got a terrific café here, serving good coffee, plus home-made soup and baked goodies. Tours £10; Tues–Sat 10am 2 & 3pm.

Lagavulin Port Ellen ⓦmalts.com. Enjoying a fabulous setting in the bay of the same name, Lagavulin – which marked two hundred years of production in 2016 – is probably the classic, all-round Islay malt, with lots of smoke and peat. Tours £8; April–Sept daily 9.30 & 11.30am & 3.30pm; March & Oct Mon–Fri 9.30am & 12.30pm, Sat & Sun 12.30pm; Nov–Feb daily 12.30pm.

Laphroaig Port Ellen ⓦlaphroaig.com. This famous distillery, in another wonderful setting, celebrated its two-hundredth anniversary in 2015, and is another classic smoky, peaty Islay malt. The third of the island's distilleries to do its own malting, it also has a great little museum. Tours £10; March–Oct daily 10.30 & 11.30am & 2, 2.30 & 3pm; Nov–Feb daily 11.30am & 2, & 3pm.

GETTING AROUND

By bus The island's main bus route links Port Askaig with Bridgend, from where buses continue down to Port Ellen, via Bowmore, and Portnahaven, via Port Charlotte. There is no service in Sundays.

Car rental To save on ferry fares, it's worth considering car rental on the island itself – Islay Car Hire (ⓦislaycarhire. com; from around £45/day) will deliver to both ferry terminals and the airport. If driving, there are filling stations at Port Askaig, Bowmore and Bridgend.

Port Ellen and around

6

Laid out as a planned village in 1821 by Walter Frederick Campbell, and named after his wife, **PORT ELLEN** is the chief port on Islay, with the island's largest fishing fleet, and main CalMac ferry terminal. The neat, whitewashed terraces that overlook the town's bay of golden sand are strikingly pretty, but the view is dominated by the village's modern maltings, whose powerful odours waft across the town.

The distilleries

As you head east out of Port Ellen, a dead-end road passes three **distilleries** in as many miles; however, a more relaxing – indeed, sensible – way of visiting them is to walk the **three distilleries path**, which begins just outside Port Ellen and links all three. First up is **Laphroaig**, which, as every bottle tells you, is Gaelic for 'the beautiful hollow by the bay', and, true enough, the whitewashed distillery is indeed in a gorgeous setting by the sea. Laphroaig also has the stamp of approval from Prince Charles, who famously paid a flying visit to the island in 1994, crashing an airplane of the Queen's Flight in the process.

A mile down the road lies **Lagavulin** distillery, beyond which stands **Dunyvaig Castle**, a romantic ruin on a promontory looking out to the tiny isle of Texa. Another mile further on, the traditional pagoda-style kiln roofs of **Ardbeg** distillery hove into view – in common with all Islay's distilleries, all three offer guided tours (see page 258).

Kildalton Chapel

Two miles down the track from Ardbeg and you eventually come to the simple thirteenth-century **Kildalton Chapel**, which has a wonderful eighth-century Celtic ringed cross made from the local 'bluestone'. The quality of the scenes matches any to be found on the crosses carved by the monks in Iona: the Virgin and Child are on the east face, with Cain murdering Abel to the left, David fighting the lion on the top, and Abraham sacrificing Isaac on the right; on the west side amid the serpent-and-boss work are four elephant-like beasts.

ARRIVAL AND DEPARTURE · PORT ELLEN AND AROUND

By ferry The ferry terminal is a 2min walk from the village's main through roads.
Destinations Kennacraig (3–4 daily; 2hr 20min).

By bus Buses pick up and drop off on Charlotte St in the centre of the village.
Destinations Bowmore (Mon–Sat 8 daily; 25min); Port Askaig (Mon–Sat 3 daily; 50min).

ACCOMMODATION AND EATING

Islay Hotel 18 Charlotte St ⓦtheislayhotel.com. One of the finest hotels on the island, with thoroughly modern, sharp-looking rooms, and superbly equipped and very large bathrooms (two with whirlpool bathtub). The *Islay* is also Port Ellen's social hub, with a fine restaurant and a buzzy, more informal whisky bar. The former rustles up sublime dishes like pan-fried Ghigha halibut with leek risotto and brown crab fritter, while at the latter you can grab a steak pie with creamy mash washed down with a micro-brewed beer. Live music every Thurs & Sat in summer. **£££**

★ **Kintra Farm campsite** 3 miles northwest of Port Ellen ⓦkintrafarm-islay.co.uk. Enjoying a stunning situation at the southern tip of sandy Laggan Bay among the grassy dunes, this is not far off wild camping at its best. Facilities are basic, but there are showers and running water as well as laundry. Once settled in, you're unlikely to bother exploring anywhere else. Bookings not required. $\underline{\overline{E}}$

★ **Machrie Hotel** Port Ellen ⓦ campbellgrayhotels. com. Following a long-awaited refurbishment, the *Machrie* golf hotel is now once again Islay's classiest outfit; its chic, light-filled rooms and suites, boasting thick warm carpets and capacious beds with the finest linen, all have superb views, typically of the Oa Peninsula or of the course itself. The hotel's first-rate facilities also include spa, sauna and gym, and a top draw restaurant. If you have neither the time nor the energy for a full-blown round on the historic main course, there's the fabulous wee course. $\underline{\underline{\underline{EEE}}}$

6 Bowmore

On the north side of the monotonous peat bog of Duich Moss, and the south shore of the tidal Loch Indaal, lies **BOWMORE**, Islay's administrative capital, with a population of around 800. Dominated by the distillery, it's a striking place, laid out in 1768 on a grid plan rather like Inveraray, with the whitewashed terraces of Main Street climbing up the hill in a straight line from the loch to the town's crowning landmark, the **Round Church**, whose central tower looks uncannily like a lighthouse. Built in the round, so that the devil would have no corners in which to hide, it has a plain, wood-panelled interior, with a lovely tiered balcony and a big central mushroom pillar.

ARRIVAL AND DEPARTURE
BOWMORE

By bus Buses stop on the main square, which, strangely enough, is called The Square.
Destinations Port Askaig (Mon–Sat 5–6 daily; 25min); Port Charlotte (Mon–Sat 6 daily; 25min); Port Ellen (Mon–Sat 9 daily; 25min); Portnahaven (Mon–Sat 6 daily; 50min).

GETTING AROUND AND INFORMATION

Bike rental Bike rental is available from the post office at the top of Main St (Mon–Fri 9am–5.30pm, Sat 9am–12.30pm; £10/day; ☏ 01496 850232).
Tourist office The Square, Main St (April–June Mon– Sat 10am–5pm, Sun noon–3pm; July & Aug Mon–Sat 9.30am–5.30pm, Sun noon–3pm; Sept & Oct Mon–Sat 10am–5pm; Nov–March Mon–Fri 10am–3pm; ☏ 01496 305165, ⓦ islayinfo.com).

ACCOMMODATION AND EATING

Bowmore House Shore St ⓦ thebowmorehouse.co.uk. This grand-looking house, positioned on the main road entering the village, has five fabulous rooms exquisitely furnished in different styles, but all with plush carpets and plump beds, as well as sparkling bathrooms replete with luxury toiletries. There's a complimentary laundry service too. $\underline{\underline{\underline{EEE}}}$
Harbour Inn The Square ⓦ bowmore.com/harbour-inn. Smart, if unadventurously decorated, harbourside restaurant with lovely views, and serving sumptuous plates of food like black squid ink risotto with pickled crab meat; scrummy oyster menu too. Alternatively, you can warm yourself by a peat fire in the adjoining pub, where they also do lunchtime bar snacks. $\underline{\underline{\underline{EEE}}}$
Lambeth Guesthouse Jamieson St ⓦ lambeth-guesthouse.co.uk. Just off Main St, this is a jovially run guesthouse with six modestly sized but impeccably prepared en-suite rooms. A little tricky to find: it's next to the tiny filling station, the door being around to the side. $\underline{\underline{EE}}$
Peatzeria 22 Shore St ⓦ peatzeria.com. The most enjoyable place to eat in Bowmore, if not the island, this cleverly titled restaurant rustles up a terrific selection of handmade stone baked pizzas (including some extravagantly priced seafood ones such as Islay Scallops) alongside genuinely exciting Italian dishes like Fiorelli pasta stuffed with salmon and crayfish; the space is great too, with ground floor and mezzanine seating as well as both covered and uncovered outdoor seating overlooking the water. $\underline{\underline{EE}}$

Loch Gruinart

Between October and mid-April, it's impossible to miss the island's staggeringly large wintering population of **Greenland barnacle** and **white-fronted geese**. You can see the geese just about anywhere on the island – there are an estimated 5,000 white-fronted and 40,000 barnacles here (and rising) – with the largest concentrations in the fields between Bridgend and Ballygrant, and on the tidal mud flats and fields around **Loch Gruinart**. There's an RSPB-run **visitor centre** (seven miles north of Bridgend on the B8017; daily 10am–5pm; free; Ⓦrspb.org. uk/lochgruinart) at the nearby farm of Aoradh (pronounced 'oorig'), with a scale model of the reserve and a sightings board, but you're better off getting yourself down to one of the two hides (both open access), just a couple of hundred yards apart from each other overlooking the salt flats and marshes at the head of the loch. The RSPB run two-hour guided walks (£5) through the reserve at 2pm on Thursdays between April and October.

6

Kilchoman

Without doubt the best sandy beaches on Islay are to be found on the isolated northwest coast near the village of **KILCHOMAN**, in particular, the lovely golden beach of **Machir Bay** which is backed by great white-sand dunes. The sea here has dangerous undercurrents, however, and is not safe to swim in (the same goes for the much smaller Saligo Bay, to the north), but the beaches are still lovely to walk across.

Port Charlotte

Founded in 1828 by Walter Frederick Campbell, and named after his mother, **PORT CHARLOTTE** was originally set up to provide housing facilities for the workers of the former Lochindaal distillery, which eventually closed in 1929. It's generally agreed to be Islay's prettiest village, its immaculate whitewashed cottages clustered round a sandy cove overlooking Loch Indaal.

Museum of Islay Life
Daal Terrace • April & Oct Mon–Fri 10.30am–4.30pm; May–Sept Mon–Sat 10.30am–4.30pm, Sun 1–4.30pm • Charge • Ⓦ islaymuseum. org

On the northern fringe of the village, in a whitewashed former chapel, the engaging **Museum of Islay Life** is crammed to bursting with local memorabilia. As well as tantalizing snippets about eighteenth-century illegal whisky distillers, there are some terrific photos and a good library of books about the island. Best of all, though, are the displays on the SS *Tuscania* and HMS *Otranto*, both of which were sunk in the waters hereabouts during World War I. Among the exhibits from the *Tuscania* is its bell, a bunk-side cabinet, and the notebook belonging to Sergeant Malcolm McNeill, in which he records the names and conditions of those who perished, including one, he writes rather grimly, 'whose body is so much decayed that it is crumbling to pieces'.

Islay Natural History Trust Visitor Centre
Main St • April–Sept Mon–Fri 10am–4pm • Charge • ☏ 01496 850288

The **Islay Natural History Trust Visitor Centre**, housed in the former distillery warehouse, is well worth a visit for anyone interested in the island's fauna and flora. As well as an extensive library to browse, there's lots of hands-on stuff for kids: microscopes, a touch table full of natural goodies, a sea-water aquarium, a bug world and owl pellets to examine. Tickets are valid for a week, allowing you to go back and identify things you've seen on your travels. They also organize weekly nature rambles at 2pm each Sunday between July and September (£4), as well as wildlife adventures at 2pm on Thursdays, which could be anything from rock-pooling to beachcombing.

ARRIVAL AND DEPARTURE	**PORT CHARLOTTE**
By bus Buses stop just outside the *Port Charlotte Hotel*. **Destinations** Bowmore (Mon–Sat 6 daily; 25min); Port	Wemyss (Mon–Sat 6 daily; 15min).

ACCOMMODATION AND EATING

Port Charlotte Hotel Main St ⓦportcharlottehotel. co.uk. Beautifully appointed whitewashed stone hotel right in the heart of the village overlooking the beach. A handful of the ten rooms have retained their original exposed stone walls, but they're all thoughtfully designed and decorated in bold but beautiful colours. The hotel restaurant is of a similarly high order, though it's much more fun to tuck into one of their seafood lunches out on the patio, for example pan-seared Islay scallops with apple puree and black pudding crumble. There's usually live music on Wednesday and Sunday evenings in the bar. ££££

Port Charlotte Youth Hostel Main St

ⓦhostellingscotland.org.uk. Next door to the Natural History Trust Visitor Centre, Islay's only hostel is housed in an old bonded warehouse by the sea. It possesses a handy mix of doubles and triples all the way up to six-bed dorms, and each with shared bathroom facilities; there's also a large kitchen and common room. Breakfast costs extra. Doubles ££; dorms £

Port Mòr Campsite Just outside the village out on the road to Portnahaven ⓦislandofislay.co.uk. A community-run campsite with glorious sea views and tip-top facilities: modern shower block, laundry, café and a brilliant playground for the kids. £

Portnahaven and Port Wemyss

The main coastal road on Islay culminates seven miles south of Port Charlotte at **PORTNAHAVEN**, a fishing and crofting community since the early nineteenth century. The familiar whitewashed cottages wrap themselves prettily around the steep banks of a deep bay where seals bask on the rocks in considerable numbers; in the distance, you can see Portnahaven's twin settlement, **PORT WEMYSS**, a mile south. The communities share a little whitewashed church, located above the bay in Portnahaven, with separate doors for residents of each village.

ARRIVAL AND DEPARTURE   **PORTNAHAVEN AND PORT WEMYSS**

By bus Buses make their way into the centre of both villages, dropping off first at Portnahaven.

Destinations Bowmore (Mon–Sat 6 daily; 50min); Port Charlotte (Mon–Sat 6 daily; 15min).

ACCOMMODATION AND EATING

Burnside B&B Shore St, Port Wemyss ⓦburnsidelodge. co.uk. Located just off the coastal path, this sweet little place offers two en-suite rooms of modest but tidy proportions. The friendly owner here also rustles up delectable home-baked goodies, including cupcakes and muffins, which are

left in a self-service cupboard (payment via an honesty box) just outside the house, alongside hot drinks, which can be enjoyed on one of the barrel seats looking across to Rhinns Point, below which seals bask on the shore. On Wednesdays, she serves up a wonderful selection of pies. ££

Loch Finlaggan

Just beyond Ballygrant, on the road to Port Askaig midway between Ballygrant and Port Askaig, a narrow road leads off north to **Loch Finlaggan**, site of a number of **prehistoric crannogs** (artificial islands) and, for four hundred years from the twelfth century, headquarters of the 'Lords of the Isles', semi-autonomous rulers of the Hebrides and Kintyre. The site is evocative enough, but there are, in truth, very few remains beyond the foundations. Remarkably, the palace that stood here appears to have been unfortified, a testament perhaps to the prosperity and stability of the islands in those days.

To the northeast of the loch, the **information centre** (April–Oct Mon–Sat 10.30am–4.15pm; charge; ⓦfinlaggan.org) exhibits a number of extraordinary finds uncovered on the site, notably some twelfth-century leather soles and uppers, and a thirteenth-century cast bronze figure of Christ. From the centre, a path heads down to the site itself, which is dotted with interpretive panels. Duckboards allow you to walk out across the reed beds of the loch and explore the main crannog, **Eilean Mòr**, where several carved gravestones are displayed under cover in the chapel, all of which seem to support the theory that the Lords of the Isles buried their wives and children there, while having themselves interred on Iona. Further out into the loch is another smaller crannog, **Eilean na Comhairle**, originally connected to Eilean Mòr by a causeway, where the Lords of the Isles are thought to have held meetings of the Council of the Isles.

Port Askaig

Islay's other ferry connection with the mainland, and its sole link with Colonsay and Jura, is from **PORT ASKAIG**, a scattering of buildings which tumbles down a little cove by the narrowest section of the Sound of Islay or Caol Ila. There's next to nothing here, save for a hotel, shop and post office.

6

ARRIVAL AND TOURS   PORT ASKAIG

By ferry After Port Ellen, Port Askaig is the second of the island's main ferry terminals.
Destinations Colonsay (Wed & Sat 1 daily; 1hr 10min); Feolin ferry to Jura (Mon–Sat hourly, Sun 7 daily; 5min); Kennacraig (3–4 daily; 2hr 5min).
By bus Buses depart from a spot just up from the ferry

terminal.
Destinations Bowmore (Mon–Sat 5–6 daily; 25min); Port Ellen (Mon–Sat 3 daily; 50min).
Boat tours Based in Port Askaig, Islay Sea Safari (ⓦ islayseasafari.co.uk) offers high-adrenaline boat trips round the distilleries in a rigid inflatable (£25/1hr, £40/2hr).

ACCOMMODATION AND EATING

★ **Ballygrant Inn** Ballygrant ⓦ ballygrant-inn. com. Incredibly hospitable, family-run affair, with seven immaculately kept rooms. Its restaurant is top notch, serving the likes of Islay venison and red wine casserole, though it's the brilliant bar, stocking some 400 whiskies and voted Scotland's Whisky Bar of 2015, that's the real draw; the half a dozen tasting menus are far superior to anything offered in the distilleries, so a visit is very much the order of the day. Look out, too, for their excellent curry and a pint night on Thursdays. **£££**
Kilmeny Farmhouse Ballygrant ⓦ kilmeny.co.uk. Three miles south of Port Askaig, this whitewashed farmhouse is a place that richly deserves all the superlatives it regularly receives. Antique furnishings, locally made

fabrics and slipper baths feature in some or all of the four colour-coordinated rooms. You can expect to be well pampered for the duration of your stay, and the gourmet breakfast is a real treat, comprising, among other things, poached plums, Scottish pancake stack, and smoked Argyll salmon and scrambled eggs. **£££**
Persabus Farm 1.5km inland from Port Askaig ⓦ persabus.co.uk. Out on the road to Bunnahabhain, one of the farm's outbuildings is now a delightful café-cum-pottery, where everything is handcrafted and fired on site – you can even have a go yourself, and while you're waiting for it to be set, partake in a fresh cup of coffee with a slice of scrummy home-made cake. **£**

Isle of Jura

Twenty-eight miles long and eight miles wide, the long whale-shaped island of **JURA** is one of the wildest and most mountainous of the Inner Hebrides, its entire west coast uninhabited and inaccessible except to the dedicated walker. The distinctive **Paps of Jura**, so-called because of their smooth breast-like shape, seem to dominate every view off the west coast of Argyll, their glacial rounded tops covered in a light dusting of quartzite scree. The island's name is commonly thought to derive from the Norse *dyr-oe* (deer island) and, appropriately enough, the current deer population of 6,000 outnumbers the 190 or so humans 33 to 1; other wildlife to look out for include mountain hares and eagles. With just one road, which sticks to the more sheltered eastern coast of the island, and only one hotel, a couple of B&Bs and some self-catering cottages, Jura is an ideal place to go for peace and quiet, and some great walking.

Craighouse

Anything that happens on Jura happens in the island's only real village, **CRAIGHOUSE**, eight miles up the road from Feolin Ferry. The village enjoys a sheltered setting,

6

GEORGE ORWELL ON JURA

In April 1946, Eric Blair (better known by his pen name of **George Orwell**), intending to give himself 'six months' quiet' in which to complete his latest novel, moved to a remote farmhouse called **Barnhill**, at the northern end of Jura, which he had visited for the first time the previous year. He appears to have relished the challenge of a spartan existence here with his adopted 3-year-old son Richard, and later his sister Avril; fishing almost every night, shooting rabbits, laying lobster pots and even attempting a little farming. The book Orwell was writing, under the working title *The Last Man in Europe*, was to become *1984* (the title was arrived at by simply reversing the last two digits of the year in which it was finished – 1948). During his time on Jura, however, Orwell was suffering badly from tuberculosis, and eventually he was forced to return to London, where he died in January 1950.

Barnhill, 23 miles north of Craighouse, is as remote today as it was in Orwell's day. The road deteriorates rapidly beyond Lealt, where vehicles must be left, leaving pilgrims a four-mile walk to the house itself. Orwell wrote most of the book in the bedroom (top left window as you look at the house); the place is now a self-catering cottage (☎01786 850274). If you're keen on making the journey out to Barnhill, you might as well combine it with a trip to the nearby **Corryvreckan Whirlpool**, which lies between Jura and Scarba, to the north. Orwell nearly drowned in the whirlpool during a fishing trip in August 1947, along with his three companions (including Richard): the outboard motor was washed away, and they had to row to a nearby island and wait for several hours before being rescued by a passing fisherman.

overlooking Knapdale on the mainland – so sheltered, in fact, that there are even a few palm trees thriving on the seafront. In terms of facilities, and things to see and do, there's a shop/post office, hotel and tearoom, plus the tiny **Isle of Jura distillery**.

Isle of Jura distillery

Opposite the Jura Hotel · Jan–April Mon–Fri 10am–4pm; May–Oct Mon–Sat 10am–4pm · **Distillery tours** 11am & 2pm · Charge · ⓦ jurawhisky.com

Established in 1810 by the Campbells, the **Isle of Jura distillery** has endured a somewhat chequered history. It went out of business in the early 1900s, before reopening in 1963 on the premises of the then derelict distillery. It now produces four distinctive single malts, with two notable success stories, the 10-year-old 'Origin', and the 16-year-old 'Diurachs' Own' – you'll get to sample one or both of these on one of the guided tours.

Corryvreckan Whirlpool

Between the islands of Scarba and Jura is the raging **Corryvreckan Whirlpool** (ⓦ whirlpool-scotland.co.uk), one of the world's most spectacular whirlpools – and supposedly the third largest – thought to be caused by a rocky pinnacle some 100ft below the sea. Exactly how the whirlpool appears depends on the tide and wind, but there's a potential tidal flow of over eight knots, which, when accompanied by gale-force winds, can create standing waves up to 15ft high. Inevitably there are numerous legends about the place – known as *An Coire Bhreacain* (speckled cauldron) in Gaelic – concerning *Cailleach* (Hag), the Celtic storm goddess. From the land, the best place from which to view it is Carraig Mhor on the northern tip of Jura, though the best trips to the whirlpool – which can be quite spectacular, and hair-raising – depart from Seil (see page 245).

ARRIVAL AND DEPARTURE   ISLE OF JURA

By ferry The Feolin ferry from Port Askaig will not run if there's a strong northerly or southerly wind, so bring your toothbrush if you're coming for a day-trip. Roughly six times a day, the Jura minibus (☎01496 820314) meets

the car ferry from Port Askaig and goes up to Inverlussa via Craighouse – phone ahead to check times.
Destinations Port Askaig (Mon–Sat every 45–60min, Sun 6 daily; 5min; £3.60 return, car £18.90 return).
By passenger ferry Between the end of May and the end of October, there's also a passenger ferry service (wjurapassengerferry.com; £20 single) from Tayvallich, on the Argyll mainland, to Craighouse; bikes can be carried too.
Destinations Tayvallich (Mon & Wed–Sat 2 daily, Sun 1 daily; 50min).

ACCOMMODATION AND EATING

The Antlers 100yd north of the distillery ☎01496 820496. Delightful bistro restaurant that serves up burgers, sandwiches and salads for lunch, and beautifully presented Jura lamb on the one evening it's open, booking is essential. It is unlicensed, but you're welcome to bring your own (corkage £3). <u>££</u>

Jura Hotel Craighouse wjurahotel.co.uk. The island's one and only hotel is not much to look at from the outside, but it's warm and friendly within and the rooms are right up to the mark. Campers are welcome to pitch tents (£) in the field fronting the hotel, and there's a shower block and laundry facilities round the back. Unsurprisingly, it's also the centre of the island's social scene, with a restaurant, lounge-bar and pub. <u>£££</u>

6

Stirling, Loch Lomond and the Trossachs

LOCH ARD

Stirling, Loch Lomond and the Trossachs

The central lowlands of Scotland were, for several centuries, the most strategically important area in the country. In 1250, a map of Britain was compiled by a monk of St Albans, which depicted Scotland as two separate land masses connected only by the thin band of Stirling Bridge; although this was a figurative interpretation, it is true that Stirling was once the only gateway from the fertile central belt to the rugged, mountainous north. For long periods of Scotland's history kings, queens, nobles, clan chiefs and soldiers wrestled for control of the area, and it's no surprise that today the landscape is littered with remnants of the past – well-preserved medieval towns and castles, royal residences and battle sites.

Lying at the heart of Scotland, **Stirling** and its fine **castle**, from where you can see both snowcapped Highland peaks and Edinburgh, are unmissable for anyone wanting to grasp the complexities of Scottish history. The castle esplanade commands an impressive view of the surrounding area, including the rocket-like **National Wallace Monument**, a Victorian homage to a local hero.

To the south of the city, on the road to Edinburgh, lies **Falkirk**, its industrial heritage enlivened by the intriguing Falkirk Wheel; to the east, the gentle Ochil Hills run towards Fife. The highlight of the string of mostly drab towns at the foot of the Ochils is handsome **Dollar**, from where a path leads up the steep glen to dramatically perched Castle Campbell. The flat plain extending west, the **Carse of Stirling**, has the little-visited **Campsie Fells** on its southern edge and the fabled mountains, glens, lochs and forests of the **Trossachs**, stretching west from **Callander** to Loch Lomond, to the north. Here you'll find abundant opportunities for hiking and mountain biking, as well as sublime mountain scenery.

On the western side of the region, **Loch Lomond** is the largest – and most romanticized – stretch of fresh water in Scotland. At the heart of Loch Lomond and the Trossachs National Park, the peerless scenery of the loch can be tainted by the sheer numbers of tourists and day-trippers who flock here in summer. It can get similarly clogged in parts of the neighbouring Trossachs, although there's much to appreciate once you break away from the main routes. The area is particularly good for **outdoor activities**: it's traversed by the **Glasgow–Loch Lomond–Killin cycleway**; the forest tracks are ideal for mountain biking; the mountains of the Trossachs provide great hiking; and the **West Highland Way**, Scotland's premier long-distance footpath, winds along the length of Loch Lomond up to Fort William in the Highlands.

GETTING AROUND AND INFORMATION
CENTRAL SCOTLAND

By train, bus, car or bike While Stirling, Falkirk and Perth are well served by trains from all over Scotland, the rest of the region is only accessible on sporadic local bus services so you may find it easier to have your own transport. Many people opt to explore the Trossachs by mountain bike. For a bus network map see ⓦ firstbus.co.uk.

Stirling

Straddling the River Forth a few miles upstream from the estuary at Kincardine, **STIRLING** appears at first glance like a smaller version of Edinburgh. With its crag-top

THE FALKIRK WHEEL

Highlights

❶ **Stirling Castle** Impregnable, impressive and resonant with history. If you see only one castle in Scotland, make it this one. See page 272

❷ **A dram at Deanston Distillery** Deanston produce a relatively new, non-peaty whisky, which you can sample in the beautiful surroundings of a former mill village. See page 279

❸ **Falkirk Wheel** The most remarkable piece of modern engineering in Britain, this fascinating contraption lifts boats 100ft between two canals. See page 280

❹ **Inchcailloch** Putter out on a Loch Lomond mail boat to this tranquil wooded island at

the heart of Scotland's first national park. See page 283

❺ **Mountain biking in the Trossachs** Cycle along a loch, ride a forest path or travel the National Cycle Network from Loch Lomond to Killin. See page 286

❻ **The Lake of Menteith** One of the loveliest stretches of water in the country, with fishing, swimming and boat trips to an island with a romantic ruined abbey. See page 286

❼ **Food at Brig o'Turk** This tiny Trossachs village has two enticing eating options: a wood-lined tearoom serving great cakes, and a gastro pub set in a rugged stone barn. See page 288

HIGHLIGHTS ARE MARKED ON THE MAP ON PAGE 270

castle, steep, cobbled streets and mixed community of locals, students and tourists, it's a fairly appealing city, though it definitely lacks the cosmopolitan edge of its near neighbours Edinburgh and Glasgow.

Stirling was the scene of some of the most significant developments in the evolution of the Scottish nation. It was here in 1297 that the Scots, under William Wallace, defeated the English at the **Battle of Stirling Bridge**, only to fight – and win again – under Robert the Bruce just a couple of miles away at the

STIRLING, LOCH LOMOND & THE TROSSACHS

Battle of Bannockburn in 1314. Stirling enjoyed its golden age in the fifteenth to seventeenth centuries, most notably when its castle was the favoured residence of the Stuart monarchy and the setting for the coronation of Mary, Queen of Scots in 1543.

Today the city is best known for the **castle** and the lofty **National Wallace Monument**, a mammoth Victorian monolith high on Abbey Craig to the northeast, though there is much else to enjoy besides.

HIGHLIGHTS

1. Stirling Castle
2. A dram at Deanston Distillery
3. Falkirk Wheel
4. Inchcailloch
5. Mountain biking in the Trossachs
6. The Lake of Menteith
7. Food at Brig o'Turk

Stirling Castle

Old Town • Daily: April–Sept 9.30am–6pm; Oct–March 9.30am–5pm • Charge; ticket includes free entry to Argyll's Lodging (see page 274); additional charges for audio-guide and parking; HES • ⓦ stirlingcastle.scot

Stirling Castle presented would-be invaders with a formidable challenge. Its impregnability is most daunting when you approach the town from the west, from where the sheer 250ft drop down the side of the crag is most obvious. The rock was first fortified during the Iron Age, though what you see now dates largely from the fifteenth and sixteenth centuries. On many levels, the main buildings are interspersed with delightful gardens and patches of lawn, while endless battlements, cannon ports, hidden staircases and other nooks and crannies make it thoroughly explorable and inspiring.

For the chance to see the castle at night, look out for special **events** such as the Hogmanay (new year) party and concerts in the atmospheric Great Hall by luminaries such as the Scottish Chamber Orchestra. Before exploring the castle further, take time to enjoy the illuminating exhibition housed inside the **Casemates**, a series of deep vaults built as part of the castle's overall defences, and which run alongside the lovely **Queen Anne Garden**, itself the ideal spot to escape the crowds.

The Great Hall
In the central part of the castle, the **Outer Close** is the first of two main courtyard areas. Looming over it is the magnificently restored **Great Hall**, dating from 1501–03 and used as a barracks by the British army until 1964. The building stands out across Stirling for its controversially bright, creamy yellow cladding, added in the 1990s after the discovery during renovations of a stretch of the original sixteenth-century limewash behind a bricked-up doorway. Inside, the hall has been restored to its original state as the finest medieval secular building in Scotland, complete with five gaping fireplaces and an impressive hammer beam ceiling of rough-hewn wood created from 35 oak trees.

The Palace
The exterior of the **Palace**, the largest building in the castle, dates from 1540–42 and is richly decorated with grotesque carved figures and Renaissance sculpture, including, in the left-hand corner, the glaring bearded figure of James V in the dress of a commoner. Now costumed actors play the role of various nobles, while specially commissioned furniture and tapestries – the result of an impressive fourteen-year research and weaving project – have returned the rooms to something like their appearance in the mid-sixteenth century. The real highlight, however, is the room containing the **Stirling Heads**, elegantly carved oak medallions that once comprised the ceiling of the Presence Chamber, where visitors were presented to royalty. It's not entirely clear how many there were in total, but what is known is that two were burnt (most likely broken down for kindling), three are currently in the National Museum of Scotland in Edinburgh, and there are 31 here. Unique pieces of art, these variously represent kings, queens, emperors, and biblical and mythological figures – four are thought to depict Hercules.

Chapel Royal and the King's Old Building
On one side of the Inner Close, the steeply sloping upper courtyard of the castle, is the **Chapel Royal**, built in 1594 by James VI for the baptism of his son. Otherwise rather dull, it's worth a fleeting glance for the colourful frieze completed by Valentine Jenkin in 1629 that frames the upper section of the four walls. Alongside, the **King's Old Building**, at the highest point in the castle, houses the museum of the Argyll and Sutherland Highlanders regiment, with its collection of well-polished silver and memorabilia.

The Old Town
Stirling evolved from its castle, gradually spreading south and east onto the low-lying flood plain. At the centre of the original **Old Town**, Broad Street was the main thoroughfare, with St John Street running more or less parallel, and St Mary's Wynd forming part of the original route to Stirling Bridge below. Because Stirling is a compact town, sightseeing in the Old Town is best done on foot.

Town Walls
The old centre of Stirling is fortified behind the massive, whinstone boulders of the **town walls**, built in the mid-sixteenth century and intended to ward off the advances of Henry VIII, who had set his sights on the young Mary, Queen of Scots as a wife for his son, Edward. The walls now constitute some of the best-preserved town defences in Scotland, and can be traced by following the path known as **Back Walk**. This walkway was built in the eighteenth century and in the upper reaches leads right under the castle, taut along the edge of the crag. It's a great way to take in the castle's setting, and gives panoramic views of the countryside.

Argyll's Lodging

At the top of Castle Wynd • Guided tour only; book on ☎ 01786 450000 • Entry included with ticket to Stirling Castle

Argyll's Lodging is a romantic Renaissance townhouse built by Sir William Alexander of Menstrie in the seventeenth century. Once the home of Alexander, the First Earl of Stirling, it was later used as a military hospital and youth hostel. The oldest part of the building, with its low ceilings and tiny windows, is the Great Kitchen, whose enormous fireplace comes complete with a special recess for salt, while the Drawing Room, hung with lavishly decorated purple tapestries, contains the Ninth Earl's imposing chair of state.

Mar's Wark and Church of the Holy Rude

Church of the Holy Rude St John St • May–Sept daily 11am–4pm • ⓦ holyrude.org

Down Castle Wynd and at the top of Broad Street, a richly decorated facade is about all that survives of **Mar's Wark**, a would-be palace that the First Earl of Mar, regent of Scotland and hereditary Keeper of Stirling Castle, started in 1570. His dream house was never to be realized, however, for he died two years later and what had been built was left to ruin, its degeneration speeded up by extensive damage during the 1745 Jacobite rebellion.

Behind here is the **Church of the Holy Rude**, the oldest parts of which, including the impressive oak hammer beam ceiling, date from the early fifteenth century. Otherwise unornamented, this capacious church is famed, above all else, for being the place where the infant James VI, son of Mary Queen of Scots, was proclaimed king in 1567; indeed, it's the only surviving Scottish church to have witnessed a coronation. A floor plaque marks the spot.

John Cowane's Hospital

49 St John St • Thurs–Sun 10am–4pm • Free • ⓦ cowanes.org.uk

Near the Church of the Holy Rude and on the edge of the crag, the rugged, whitewashed **John Cowane's Hospital** was built in 1649 as an almshouse for, at its founder John Cowane's request, 'decayed [unsuccessful] members of the Guild of Merchants'. Above the entrance, Cowane, a wealthy merchant himself, is commemorated in a painted statue that, it is said, comes alive at Hogmanay. The hospital reopened in 2021, following a superb renovation, central to which is an exhibition on the history of the building and its eponymous founder; there's a fabulous onsite café too.

Old Town Jail

St John St • July–Sept daily 10.15am–6pm plus some holidays • Charge • ⓦ oldtownjail.co.uk

A sweeping driveway leads from St John Street and up to the impressive **Old Town Jail**, built by Victorian prison reformers as an alternative to the depravity of the nearby medieval Tolbooth, which was deemed so bad (reputedly the worst in Britain) that it closed in 1840. Upon its construction in 1847, the Old Town Jail was one of the most progressive in the system, its 57 cells each occupied by one inmate only, with men and women located on separate floors and proper sanitation. It functioned as the county jail until 1888, before it was requisitioned by the Scottish Regiment for military purposes, remaining as such until 1935. Rescued from dereliction in 1994, part of the building was turned into offices and a substantial section used to create this visitor attraction. Telling the history of the building and prisons in general, tours are taken by actors, who enthusiastically change costumes and character a number of times; it's fabulously entertaining and a far cry from your average tour. Among the features of the jail they'll introduce you to is a working example of the dreaded crank, a lever that prisoners had to turn 14,400 times a day; look out, too, for the graffiti etched into the prison doors. You'll also be taken up in the glass lift to the prison roof to admire spectacular **views** across Stirling and the Forth Valley; the gallery here is also where inmates would take it in turns to exercise for thirty minutes each day.

Opposite and just uphill from the entrance to the Old Town Jail on St John Street, look out for the **Boys' Club**, a 1929 conversion of the town's old butter market, with its encouraging little mottoes engraved above the door such as 'Keep smiling' and 'Quarrelling is taboo'.

Tolbooth

Jail Wynd • Tues–Sat 10am–6pm • See website for admission charges • W stirlingevents.org/tollbooth-event

The town's original medieval prison is the **Tolbooth**, now an innovative music and arts centre. Originally built in 1705, the striking modern redevelopment received an architectural award as the UK's best public building. During the renovations a secret staircase was discovered, as was a complete skeleton, thought to have been that of the last man publicly hanged in Stirling. Inside there's access to a top-floor viewing platform looking out over the Old Town rooftops and a box office where you can find out about the centre's programme, which mostly centres on modern folk music (see page 277).

Mercat Cross and Darnley's House

On Broad Street, the town's former marketplace, the various historical buildings and monuments include the stone **Mercat Cross** (the unicorn on top is known, inexplicably, as 'the puggy') and **Darnley's House**, where Mary, Queen of Scots' husband is believed to have lodged while she lorded it up in the castle; it now houses a coffee shop (see page 276).

7

The Lower Town and around

In the eighteenth and nineteenth centuries, as the threat of attack on Stirling decreased, the centre of commercial life crept down towards the River Forth, with the modern town growing on the edge of the plain over which the castle stands guard. By the time the two main streets of the Old Town merge into King Street, austere Victorian facades block the sun from the cobbled road. The fifteenth-century **Old Bridge** over the Forth lies to the north on the edge of the town centre. Although once the most important river crossing in Scotland, it now stands virtually forgotten, an incidental reminder of Stirling's former importance.

Smith Art Gallery and Museum

Dumbarton Rd • Tues–Sat 10.30am–5pm, Sun 2–5pm • Free • W smithartgalleryandmuseum.co.uk

Founded in 1874 with a legacy from local painter and collector Thomas Stuart Smith, the **Smith Art Gallery and Museum** comprises two parts. The first room exhibits a selection of paintings by Smith himself and many more he collected; his most striking pieces are landscapes, such as *On the Forth* and *Bay of Naples* – his European sojourns influenced much of his work – while others, such as the wonderful *Pipe of Freedom*, is Smith at his radical best.

The larger room to the rear holds lots of dusty cabinets crammed with all manner of fascinating bits and bobs; among the most intriguing items is the world's oldest curling stone, and the world's oldest known football, made out of a pig's bladder; found in the rafters of the Queen's Chamber in the castle, it is thought to date from the 1540s.

The National Wallace Monument

1.5 miles north of the Old Town • Daily March 10am–5pm; April–June & Sept–Oct 9.30am–5pm • July & Aug 9.30am–6pm; Nov–Feb 10am–4pm • Charge • W yourstirling.com• Served by numerous local buses including No. 63 from Murray Place

A mile and a half north of the Old Town, the prominent **National Wallace Monument** is a freestanding, five-storey tower built in the 1860s as a tribute to Sir William Wallace, the freedom fighter who led Scottish resistance to Edward I, the 'Hammer of the Scots', in the late thirteenth century. Abbey Craig, the crag on which the monument is set, was the scene of Wallace's greatest victory, when he sent his troops charging down the hillside onto the plain to defeat the English at the Battle of Stirling Bridge in 1297. Inside the splendidly refurbished tower you can find the Hall of Arms, featuring (what is allegedly) Wallace's long steel sword, the Hall of (Scottish) Heroes, a row of stern white marble busts featuring, among others, Robert Burns, John Knox and Adam Smith, and the Royal Chamber, with explains the tactics employed during the Battle. If you can manage the climb – up 246 spiral steps – to the top of the 220ft **tower**, you'll be rewarded with superb views across to Fife and Ben Lomond. From the ticket office – where there's an excellent coffee shop serving light lunches – the steepish walk up to the monument takes about ten minutes, but there is a shuttle bus if that's not manageable.

ARRIVAL AND INFORMATION
STIRLING

By train The train station is near the centre of town on Station Rd, a 2min walk from the bus station and a 5min walk from the town centre.
Destinations Aberdeen (hourly; 2hr 5min); Dundee (hourly; 55min); Edinburgh (every 30min; 1hr); Falkirk (every 30min; 30min); Glasgow Queen Street (every 20min; 25–40min); Inverness (3–5 daily; 2hr 55min); Perth (hourly; 30min).

By bus The bus station is on Goosecroft Rd, within easy walking distance of the centre.
Destinations Aberfoyle (4 daily; 45min); Callander (every

40min–1hr; 45min); Dollar (every 2hr; 35min); Doune (every 40min–1hr; 25min); Dunblane (hourly; 20min); Dundee (hourly; 1hr 30min); Edinburgh (hourly; 1hr); Falkirk (hourly; 30min); Glasgow (hourly; 50min); Inverness (every 2hr; 3hr 20min); Perth (hourly; 40min); St Andrews (every 2hr; 1hr 55min).

Tourist office The tourist office is in the Old Town Jail, towards the castle, on St John St (daily 9.30am–4.30pm; ⊛ yourstirlng.com).

ACCOMMODATION
SEE MAP PAGE 272

Castlecroft Ballengeich Rd ⊛ castlecroft-uk.co.uk. Modern guesthouse with five en-suite rooms on the site of the King's Stables just beneath the castle rock, with terrific views north and west, and a very friendly welcome. There's also a warming guest lounge and rear deck where you can soak up more views with a complimentary drink. £££

Colessio 33 Spittal St ⊛ hotelcolessio.com. Superbly positioned in the heart of the Old Town, this magnificent Georgian building was formerly a bank and then the city's Royal Infirmary. But don't let the fact that this is a wedding-oriented hotel put you off; the rooms here – which come in four different categories – ooze class, and there's a better than average restaurant to boot. £££

Friars Wynd 17 Friars St St ⊛ friarswynd.co.uk. Decently located within earshot of the stations and the city centre, this handsomely renovated Victorian townhouse accommodates eight smoothly furnished rooms, each one named after a Scottish island or loch. Breakfast is a fulsome affair and they've also got a very creditable restaurant. ££

The Old Tram House 42 Causewayhead Rd ⊛ theoldtramhouse.com. Located near the Wallace Monument, this Victorian stone house offers two very spacious, good quality self-catering apartments, each with two double bedrooms; two-night minimum stay. £££

Stirling Highland Hotel Spittal St ⊛ stirlinghighlandhotel.co.uk. Somewhat pretentiously genteel hotel in a handsome Victorian Gothic building that

once housed Stirling High School and still maintains an observatory on the top floor. It is just 500yd from the castle and features comfortable, if unspectacular, rooms and leisure facilities. Room only rates available too. ££

Stirling Youth Hostel St John St, ⊛ hostellingscotland. org.uk. Situated at the top of the town (a strenuous trek with a backpack), in a converted church with an impressive 1824 Palladian facade. The small four-and six-bed dorms, plus twin rooms, are all en suite; facilities include a games room, kitchen, laundry and café. Dorms £; doubles ££

SELF-CATERING

Stirling University Bridge of Allan ⊛ stirlingvenues. com/accommodation. Campus accommodation in halls of residence, wooden chalets and self-catering flats a couple of miles north of the town centre. The famously leafy and beautiful campus is served by regular buses from Murray Place in the town centre. Accommodation is available June to early Sept. £

CAMPING

★ **Witches Craig Caravan & Camping Park** Blairlogie, 3 miles east of the centre off the A91 to St Andrews ⊛ witchescraig.co.uk. A very attractive and multi-award-winning site tucked under the Ochil Hills with every conceivable facility available – yep, they've previously won Loo of the Year among others. Take No. 62 bus from Stirling. £

EATING
SEE MAP PAGE 272

Darnley Coffee House 18 Bow St (the continuation of Broad St) ☎ 01786 474468. A bit old-fashioned but with plenty of Old Town atmosphere and serving reasonably priced lunches, teas and home-made cakes in an impressive sixteenth-century barrel-vaulted interior. £

★ **HBW Coffee** 54/56 Barnton St ⊛ hbwcoffeee.co.uk. Stirling's finest caffeine fix is to be found here in this superb

coffee house run by a young, enthusiastic barista who will happily chat all day long about the origin of his beans. And if you're feeling peckish, tuck into a wodge of cake or a sourdough sandwich. Somewhat misleadingly, it's in the building with an opticians sign above it. £

★ **Hermann's** Mar Place House, 58 Broad St ⊛ hermanns.co.uk. The classiest option in Stirling,

Hermann's is set in the historic and stately Mar Place House towards the top of the Old Town with views of the Church of the Holy Rude. It operates brasserie-style at lunchtime and offers upmarket Austrian-Scottish dining such as Tyrolean smoked ham and melon, and *jäger schnitzel* (veal) in the evening. Fantastic three-course lunches. **£££**

Mamma Mia 52 Spittal St ⓦ mammamiastirling.com. Set in an Old Town mansion, this is an irrepressibly friendly southern Italian restaurant, run by some boys from Bari. They specialize in seafood dishes such as *spaghetti alla pescatora* as well as Italian standards. **£££**

Mediterránea 4 Viewfield Place ⓦ mediterranea restaurant.co.uk. Spanish tapas (cured serrano ham with manchego cheese, prawns in chilli and garlic oil) and moderately priced pan-Mediterranean dishes (such as moussaka and paella) in an upbeat atmosphere. **££**

The Pend Café 81 Port St ☎ 01786 479159. A handy coffee or lunch stop, this lively deli/café tucked down a pend (passageway) in the centre of town serves delicious home-made soups, plus sharing platters, hearty sandwiches, scones and cakes. **£**

NIGHTLIFE AND ENTERTAINMENT

SEE MAP PAGE 272

MacRobert Arts Centre On the university campus at Bridge of Allan ⓦ macrobertartscentre.org. Shows mainstream and art-house films, and hosts theatre, music and dance events. The campus itself is regularly voted the most beautiful in Scotland.

★ **Tolbooth** Jail Wynd ⓦ stirlingevents.org/tollbooth-event. By far the best option for a night out, the Tolbooth has a glamorous high-ceilinged bar (open only when there's an event on) and a folk-orientated live music programme, with occasional classical and jazz concerts, plus comedy.

Around Stirling

Just on the outskirts of town is **Bannockburn**, one of the country's most significant battlefields, while the satellite town of **Bridge of Allan** offers more sedate attractions. North and west of Stirling are the historic draws of the cathedral at **Dunblane**, the imposing castle at **Doune** and the attractive settlements of the **Carse of Stirling**, while, on either side of the Forth, the county of **Clackmannanshire** lies at the foot of the **Ochil Hills**. A highlight of the semi-industrial hinterland to the east and south of the city is the massive **Falkirk Wheel**, a spectacular feat of modern engineering. Rugged ruined castles are the draw at both **Dollar** and **Loch Leven**.

Bannockburn Heritage Centre

A872, 2 miles south of Stirling city centre • Daily April–Sept 9.30am–6pm; Oct–March 10.30am–5pm • Charge • NTS • ⓦ nts.org.uk • Nos 24, 52 or 57 buses from Stirling bus station or Murray Place

A couple of miles south of Stirling, all but surrounded by drab suburban housing, the **Bannockburn Heritage Centre** commemorates the most famous battle in Scottish history, when King Robert the Bruce won his mighty victory over the English at the **Battle of Bannockburn** on June 24, 1314. It was this battle, the climax of the Wars of Independence, which united the Scots under Bruce and led to independence from England, sealed by the Declaration of Arbroath (1320) and the Treaty of Northampton (1328).

The main focus of the visitor centre is a **3-D military game** for kids, and there is interactive material where you can listen to a range of accounts of the proceedings. The whole affair is over-reliant on digital technology, impressive though that is, and lacks the emotional punch of an actual site: most experts agree that the location of the visitor centre is not that of the real-life battle.

Dunblane

Small, attractive **DUNBLANE** has been an important ecclesiastical centre since the seventh century, when the Celts founded the church of St Blane here. The cathedral, praised in the highest terms by John Ruskin, stands serenely amid a clutch of old buildings.

Dunblane Cathedral

The Cross • April–Sept Mon–Sat 9.30am–5.30pm, Sun 2–5.30pm; Oct–March Mon–Sat 10am–4pm, Sun 2–4pm • Free • HES • Ⓦ historicenvironment.scot

Dunblane Cathedral dates mainly from the thirteenth century, and restoration work carried out a century ago returned it to its Gothic splendour. Inside, note the delicate blue-purple stained glass, and the exquisitely carved pews, screen and choir stalls, all crafted in the early twentieth century. Memorials include a tenth-century Celtic cross-slab standing stone and a modern, four-sided standing stone commemorating the tragic shooting in 1996 of sixteen Dunblane schoolchildren and their teacher.

Dunblane Museum

The Cross • Easter–mid-Oct Mon–Sat 10.30am–4.30pm • Free • Ⓦ dunblanemuseum.org.uk

The seventeenth-century Dean's House contains the small **Dunblane Museum**, which has exhibits on local history, memorabilia from the battle of Sheriffmuir, medieval coins and suchlike. Of greater interest to most visitors, however, is the display on Dunblane's favourite son, **Andy Murray**, who triumphantly won the men's singles at Wimbledon in 2013 and 2016, as well as Olympic gold medals in London 2012 and Rio 2016: you can see a signed tennis racquet, plus his Olympic cap and jacket from the London 2012 Olympics. Not forgetting his very successful doubles playing brother, Jamie, who has also donated a few items to the permanent display. Andy's 2012 Olympic victory is further commemorated just a few paces away on the High Street, courtesy of a gold-painted post box.

Leighton Library

61 High St • May–Sept Mon–Sat 11am–1pm, other times by arrangement • Donation requested • Ⓦ leightonlibrary.org.uk

The crow-stepped and whitewashed **Leighton Library**, established in 1684, is the oldest private lending library in Scotland and houses 4500 books in ninety languages, printed between 1500 and 1840. Visitors can browse through some of the country's rarest books, including a first edition of Sir Walter Scott's *Lady of the Lake*.

ARRIVAL AND DEPARTURE
DUNBLANE

By train Frequent trains connect Stirling with Dunblane (every 20min; 13min); the station is a 10min walk south of the city centre.

By bus Occasional buses (Nos 47 and C48 from Stirling bus station) make the journey five miles north of Stirling to Dunblane train station.

ACCOMMODATION AND DRINKING

Old Churches House Hotel Kirk St Ⓦ oldchurcheshouse. com. Ranged along nearly the whole side of this cathedral-facing street is a neat row of whitewashed cottages that now conceal nine snug rooms manifesting the odd splash of tartan, as well as a self-catering apartment (The Chimes)

and an accomplished brasserie. ££

Tappit Hen Kirk St Ⓦ belhavenpubs.co.uk. This trad flower-bedecked pub right by the cathedral is a good place for a pint of real ale, and hosts regular folk music nights. £

Doune

DOUNE, eight miles northwest of Stirling and three miles due west of Dunblane, is a sleepy village surrounding a medieval **castle**, a marvellous semi-ruin standing on a small hill in a bend of the River Teith.

Doune castle

A 5min walk south of Main St • Daily: April–Sept 9.30am–5.30pm; Oct–March 10am–4pm • Charge • HES • Ⓦ historicenvironment.scot

Built in the fourteenth century by Robert, Duke of Albany, **Doune Castle** ended up in the hands of the Second Earl of Moray, James Stewart – son of James V and half-brother of Mary, Queen of Scots – who was murdered in 1592 and immortalized in the ballad *The Bonnie Earl of Moray*; it was also used as a prison by Bonnie Prince Charlie's army after the battle of Falkirk. The castle's greatest claim to fame today, however, is as the setting for the

1970s movie *Monty Python and the Holy Grail*, which attracts legions of Python fans. More recently it has been used as one of the key locations in the popular TV drama *Outlander*.

The castle's most prominent features are its mighty 95ft high **gatehouse** and the adjacent Great Hall, which is where many of the scenes for the *Holy Grail* were shot; seek out, too, the kitchens, complete with medieval rubbish chute. The audio guide is narrated, entertainingly, by Terry Jones of Monty Python fame.

Deanston Distillery

A84, 1 mile south of Doune • Daily 10am–4pm • Tours and **tastings**; contact for times • Charge • ⓦ deanstonmalt.com

In the eighteenth-century **Deanston** was a cotton mill staffed by Gaelic-speaking victims of the Clearances and featured the biggest water wheel in Europe. Following the decline of the British cotton industry, the mill finally closed in 1965, but swiftly reopened as a **distillery**; the first single malt was created in 1982. True to its water-powered origins, Deanston is self-sufficient in hydroelectricity and even supplies a surplus to the national grid. The distillery is notable for its gleaming brass stills as well as for its non-peaty whisky, with notes of vanilla and honey. Barrels are stored in the vast 1825 weaving shed, and the old mill clock still keeps time. A range of **tours** is on offer; afterwards, take a short stroll up the road from the distillery to see the attractive purpose-built **mill village**.

7

ACCOMMODATION AND EATING
DOUNE

Buttercup Café 7 Main St ☎ 01786 842511. This bright and inviting village café does breakfast (9–11.30am), lunches (everything from light salads to hearty steak sandwiches) and afternoon tea served on a tiered stand. They offer a good selection of cakes and bakes, including gluten-free options. £

Glenardoch House Castle Rd ☎ 01786 841489. An excellent eighteenth-century country house B&B near the castle, which has two comfortable en-suite rooms (the Grey Room and the Blue Room) and a beautiful riverside garden. ££

L'Angolino 47 Main St ⓦ langolino.co.uk. This little corner (*angolino*) of Doune is home to a rustic family-run Italian restaurant, dishing up home-made pizza and pasta (wild boar ravioli with pecorino cheese). Welcoming and unpretentious vibe. Cash only. Closed Mon & Tues. ££

SHOPPING

Scottish Antique & Arts Centre 1 mile west of Doune on the A84 ⓦ scottish-antiques.com. Just outside the village of Doune, the 'antiques village', as it's known locally, is a vast covered market with around a hundred dealers selling high-quality memorabilia and furniture, notably some stunning Arts and Crafts pieces. There's a reasonable on-site café.

The Carse of Stirling

West of Stirling, the wide flood plain of the Forth River is known as the Carse of Forth, or **Carse of Stirling**. This is beautifully lush farmland dramatically bounded on the south by the **Gargunnock** and **Fintry hills**, which gradually blend into the **Campsie Fells**. **Kippen**, a scenic village with strong Rob Roy associations, has a couple of good eating options. To the north, the Trossachs inevitably draw many visitors.

THE ANTONINE WALL

Rough Castle, signposted off the B816 just west of Falkirk, is one of the forts set up at two-mile intervals to defend the entire length of the Roman **Antonine Wall**. The most northerly frontier of the Roman Empire, the wall was built in AD 142, of turf rather than stone, and stretched for 37 miles right across the country from the Forth to the Clyde. Assailed by skirmishing Picts and the grim Scottish weather, it didn't take long for the Romans to abandon the wall and retreat to Hadrian's Wall, just south of Scotland's present border with England. The signposted site lies along the potholed back road, and though little more than a large grassy mound interpreted by a couple of information boards, the remains at Rough Castle are the best-preserved part of the wall, and have UNESCO World Heritage Site status.

Flanders Moss nature reserve

24hr year-round • Free • Turn north off the A811 on the B822 towards Callander, and follow the signs

You can find out about the rich ecology and history of the carse's reclaimed marshland at the **Flanders Moss** nature reserve, where you walk through the peat bog on raised boardwalks, spotting dragonflies, damselflies, pond-skaters and green tiger beetles among the sphagnum moss, heather, cotton grass and bog rosemary. A 23ft timber viewing tower allows you to survey it all from above.

Drymen

At the western end of the Campsie Fells, all roads, including the West Highland Way (see page 384), meet at the small village of **DRYMEN**, an ancient ecclesiastical centre and stopover point for Highland drovers, which sits peacefully in the hills overlooking the winding Endrick Water as it nears Loch Lomond.

Glengoyne Distillery

Dumgoyne • Daily 10am–5pm • **Tours** and **tastings**; contact for times • Charge • ⓦ glengoyne.com

South of Drymen and not far from Killearn, picturesque **Glengoyne Distillery** features a pagoda roof and whitewashed buildings. Tours range from explorations of the building, or classes on matching whisky with chocolate, to a five-hour masterclass.

ARRIVAL AND DEPARTURE   CARSE OF STIRLING

By bus The hourly bus No. 12 from Stirling to Balfron goes   through Gargunnock and Kippen.

ACCOMMODATION AND EATING

KIPPEN

★ **Inn at Kippen** Fore Rd ⓦ theinnatkippen.co.uk. A long, whitewashed sixteenth-century former coaching house, now housing a bar and an excellent restaurant. They dish up fabulous home-cooked dishes, many adaptable as dairy- and gluten-free; the land (meat and seafood) and earth (veg) platters are superb. There are four boutique-style en-suite rooms. **££**

Woodhouse Just off the roundabout outside Kippen on the A811 ⓦ thewoodhousekippen.co.uk. Buzzy, bright and irresistible self-styled diner with a wood-fired stove and an attached farm shop. Excellent soups, sandwiches, toasties and platters, in addition to some scrumptious homemade baked treats. **££**

DRYMEN

Clachan Inn Drymen Square ⓦ clachaninndrymen. co.uk. Dating back to 1734, the inn – a popular first night stop off point for walkers on the West Highland Way – is an atmospheric spot for a pint and offers a range of great simple pub grub such as scampi and burgers, as well as stone baked pizzas to eat in or takeaway. They've also got four twin rooms, ideal for walkers, though breakfast costs extra. **££**

Winnock Hotel The Square ⓦ winnockhotel.com. In the village square, this flower-bedecked eighteenth-century coaching inn has comfortable, if expensive, en-suite rooms in one of two styles: Heritage or Elegance, though both are similarly priced. **££££**

The Falkirk Wheel

Lime Rd, Tamfourhill • **Visitor centre** daily 10am–4pm • Free • **Boat tours** 11.10am, 12.20pm, 1.30pm, 2.40pm & 3.50pm • Charge • ⓦ scottishcanals.co.uk/falkirk-wheel • Bus No. 3 from Falkirk town centre or walk along the Union Canal from Falkirk High train station (2.5 miles to the east)

The icon of an ambitious project to link Falkirk's two long-neglected canals is the remarkable **Falkirk Wheel**, opened in 2002 two miles west of Falkirk town centre. Looking more like a giant metal claw than a wheel, it was designed to solve the problem of the 115ft gap between the Union and Forth and Clyde canals. Back in the 1930s, before the canals went to rack and ruin, barges had to spend a day passing though eleven locks. To solve the problem, engineers designed the giant lift, which scoops a boat in one claw and an equal weight of water in the other. The simple process of rotating the perfectly weighted claws 180 degrees and depositing the boat in the other canal (which takes four minutes) is said to use only the same energy that it takes to boil eight kettles. It's the only structure of its kind anywhere in the world.

Boat tours – either the *Archimedes* or *Antonine* – take you from the visitor centre on a one-hour journey from the lower basin into the wheel, along the Union Canal for a short distance through a reinforced concrete tunnel, then back down to the basin again via the wheel. On a clear day the views from the upper canal are stupendous. The boat trip isn't essential if you just want to see the wheel in action, which can be done by **walking** around the basin and adjoining towpaths. There's much more besides, especially if you've got kids, including splash and activity zones, bumper and peddle boats, and a water-themed mini-golf. There's an excellent café too.

Dollar

Nestling in a fold of the Ochils on the northern bank of the small River Devon, where mountain waters rush off the hills, affluent, and appropriately named, **DOLLAR** is known for its Academy, founded in 1820 with a substantial bequest from local lad John McNabb; its pupils and staff account for around a third of the town's population. The walk from town up the glen to moody Castle Campbell makes for a dramatic approach.

Castle Campbell

Castle Rd • April–Sept daily 9.30am–5.30pm; Oct–March Mon–Wed, Sat & Sun 10am–4pm • Charge • HES • ⓦ historicenvironment.scot

Above Dollar, the steep ravine of **Dollar Glen** is commanded by **Castle Campbell**, formerly, and unofficially, known as Castle Gloom – a fine and evocative tag but, prosaically, a derivation of 'Gloume', an old Gaelic name. Dating back to the early fifteenth century, the most intact part of the castle – which was torched in 1654 and never recovered – is its chunky **Tower Hall**. Its four floors still manifest some splendid architectural detail, not least the Green Chamber on the third floor, whose superb stone-vaulted ceiling is guarded by a pair of open-mouthed 'Green Men', Renaissance-style motifs popular during that time; these were probably used to hang oil chains. The views, from both the top of the tower and from the terraced gardens below, are superb.

Note that access is quite tricky. From Dollar's main street, a one-and-a-half-mile-long road climbs steeply, becoming narrower as you reach the first car park (about 800 yards shy of the castle), before continuing for another 400 yards or so to another smaller car park. From here, it's a demanding 300-yard walk to the castle entrance. A series of marked **walks** leads up the glen, taking in mossy crags, rushing streams and, if you strike out on the three-hour hike to the top of Dollar Hill, great views.

ARRIVAL AND ACTIVITIES	DOLLAR
By bus The Stagecoach bus service No. 23 between Stirling and St Andrews (Mon–Sat 4 daily) travels along the A91 through the Hillfoot villages to Dollar.	**Walking** A map shows the walks on a board on the way up to the castle, though it's advisable to buy the relevant OS map (Explorer 366) if you're setting off for the longer hike.

ACCOMMODATION AND EATING

Bridge Street Kitchen 24 Bridge St ⓦ bridgestreetkitchen.co.uk. Cool contemporary restaurant featuring different menus between Wednesday and Saturday – with dishes like harissa spice chicken tagliatelle – before a gut-busting brunch offering on Sundays. A few paces down the road, they've got a funky little bar. **£££**

★ **Kennels Cottage** Dollarbeg ⓦ guesthousescotland. co.uk. A great, vegetarian-oriented B&B with four rooms located in an attractive whitewashed former gamekeeper's cottage at Dollarbeg, just south of Dollar. Their own chickens provide the breakfast eggs. They can arrange classic car rental as part of the deal. **££**

Loch Leven

Without doubt the biggest attraction of **Kinross**, ten miles east of Dollar, is trout-filled **LOCH LEVEN**, signposted from the main street. The whole loch is a National Nature Reserve; it's a good place to see visiting geese. There's a reasonable **café** by the ferry ticket office.

7

Loch Leven Castle

Loch Leven • Daily April–Sept 10am–4.15pm; Oct 10am–3.15pm • Charge including ferry trip • HES • ⓦ historicenvironment.scot

From the shore a small ferry chugs over to an island on which stands the ruined fourteenth-century **Loch Leven Castle**, where Robert the Bruce established his exchequer and where Mary, Queen of Scots was imprisoned for eleven months in 1567–68. This isn't the only island fortress Mary spent time in; it's easy to imagine the isolation of the tragic queen, who is believed to have miscarried twins while here. She managed to charm the 18-year-old brother of the castle's owner, Sir William Douglas, into helping her escape: he stole the castle keys, secured a boat in which to row ashore, locked the castle gates behind them and threw the keys into the loch – from where they were retrieved three centuries later.

The classically proportioned pile you'll see on the boat trip is late seventeenth-century **Kinross House**, which was designed by Sir William Bruce, the architect of Holyroodhouse in Edinburgh.

ARRIVAL AND DEPARTURE   LOCH LEVEN

By bus Bus No. 23 from Stirling stops in the centre of Kinross (6 daily; 55min); from here, it is a 15min walk to the loch shore.

Loch Lomond

The largest stretch of fresh water in Britain (23 miles long and up to five miles wide), **Loch Lomond** is the epitome of Scottish scenic splendour, thanks in large part to the ballad that fondly recalls its 'bonnie, bonnie banks'. The song was said to have been written by a Jacobite prisoner captured by the English, who, sure of his fate, wrote that his spirit would return to Scotland on the low road much faster than his living compatriots on the high road.

The **Loch Lomond and the Trossachs National Park** covers over seven hundred square miles of scenic territory from the shores of Loch Long in Cowal to Loch Earn and Loch Tay, on the southwest fringes of Perthshire. The centrepiece is undoubtedly Loch Lomond, and the most popular gateway is **Balloch**, the town at the loch's southern tip; with Glasgow city centre just nineteen miles away, both Balloch and the southwest side of the loch around **Luss** are often packed with day-trippers and tour coaches. Many of these continue up the **western side** of the loch, though the fast A82 road isn't ideal for tourists who wish to enjoy a leisurely drive.

Very different in tone, the verdant **eastern side** of the loch, abutting the Trossachs, operates at a different pace, with wooden ferryboats puttering out to a scattering of tree-covered islands off the village of **Balmaha**. If you're looking for a relatively easy climb with an impressive view over Loch Lomond, start at Balmaha for the ascent of **Conic Hill** (1175ft), a two- to three-hour round-trip through forest and open hillside. Much of the eastern shore can only be reached by boat or on foot, although the West Highland Way long-distance footpath (see page 384) and the distinctive peak of **Ben Lomond** ensure that even these parts are well traversed.

Balloch

The main settlement by Loch Lomond is **BALLOCH**, at the southwestern corner of the loch, where the water channels into the River Leven for its short journey south to the sea in the Firth of Clyde. Balloch has few redeeming features and is little more than a suburb of the factory town of Alexandria, however, there are a couple of worthwhile attractions, and you can also take various loch trips from here. Across the river in the extensive mature grounds of **Balloch Castle Country Park**, there are shoreside and sylvan walks.

Loch Lomond Bird of Prey Centre

Ben Lomond Way • Daily April–Sept 10am–5pm; Nov–March 10am–4pm • Charge • ⓦ llbopc.co.uk

By far the best reason to visit Balloch is the Loch Lomond Bird of Prey Centre, whose high standards of animal welfare and conservation are among the best in Scotland. There's a fantastic display of owls (barn, tawny, eagle, great grey among them) alongside hawks, falcons and kestrels, and a majestic golden eagle, many of which are tethered on the lawn, allowing visitors to get much closer to the birds than would otherwise be the case. Better still, regular flying displays are held in the adjacent field, and there's also an informative little exhibition in a small wooden cabin.

ARRIVAL AND DEPARTURE · BALLOCH

By train Balloch has a direct train connection with Glasgow Queen Street (every 30min; 50min). The station sits between the loch and the town centre.

By bus Regular buses connect Balloch with Balmaha (every 2hr; 25min) and Luss (hourly; 15min).

INFORMATION AND ACTIVITIES

Tourist office The Old Station Building opposite the modern train station contains the tourist office (daily April–June & Sept 9.30am–5.30pm; July & Aug 9.30am–6pm; Oct–March 10am–5pm; ⓦ lochlomond-trossachs.org).

Loch trips Sweeney's Cruises, in the centre of town near the bridge (ⓦ sweeneyscruiseco.com), offers a choice of loch trips including a 1hr Experience Cruise of the South basin (£14), and a 2hr Island Discovery Cruise (£20).

ACCOMMODATION

Dumbain Farm Off Dumbain Crescent ⓦ dumbainfarm. co.uk. Rambling whitewashed farm with converted outbuildings, containing bright and elegant rooms with TVs

and tea- and coffee-making facilities. Traditional Scottish breakfast, cooked on an Aga, with home-made jams and baking. **££**

The eastern shore

The loch's tranquil **eastern shore** is far better for walking and appreciating its natural beauty than the overcrowded western side. It's the access point for climbing **Ben Lomond** and visiting **Inchcailloch** island, and where the minor road peters out at **Rowardennan** you can continue on foot to the village of **Inversnaid**.

Balmaha and Rowardennan

The tiny lochside settlement of **BALMAHA** stands on the Highland Boundary Fault: if you stand on the viewpoint above the pier, you can see the fault line clearly marked by the series of woody islands – many now privately owned – that form giant stepping stones across the loch. Balmaha gets very busy in summer, not least with day-trippers on the West Highland Way. Public transport ends at Balmaha, but another seven miles north through the woods brings you to the end of the road at **ROWARDENNAN**, a scattered settlement below Ben Lomond.

Inchcailloch

Ferries from Balmaha (ⓦ balmahaboatyard.co.uk) operate daily 9.30am–5pm, with departures on demand; the journey takes 5min and costs £7.50 return

Owned by Scottish Natural Heritage, **Inchcailloch** is the closest island to Balmaha. A signposted two-mile **nature trail** loops around the island, which was extensively planted with oaks to provide bark for the local tanning industry. Along the way you'll encounter the ruins of a fourteenth-century nunnery and associated burial ground, and there's a picnic and camping site at Port Bawn on the southwestern side of the island, near a sandy beach. Until the mid-seventeenth century parishioners on the far (western) shore of Loch Lomond used to row across to Inchcailloch for Sunday services at the church linked to the nunnery.

Ben Lomond

Ben Lomond (3192ft) is the most southerly of the Munros (see page 10) and one of the most popular mountains in Scotland, its commanding position above Loch

Lomond affording amazing views of both the Highlands and Lowlands. The well-signposted route to the summit and back from Rowardennan takes five to six hours.

Inversnaid

Only walkers can continue north up the lochside from Rowardennan, where the only other settlement is seven miles north at **INVERSNAID**, made famous by a poem of the same name by Gerard Manley Hopkins about a frothing waterfall nearby ('This darksome burn, horseback brown, / His rollrock highroad roaring down').

ARRIVAL AND INFORMATION

THE EASTERN SHORE

By car or bus The dead-end B837 from Drymen (see page 280) will take you halfway up the east bank to Rowardennan, as far as you can get by car or bus (No. 309 from Balloch and Drymen runs to Balmaha every 2hr), while the West Highland Way sticks close to the shore for the entire length of the loch.

Ferry to Rowardennan Passenger ferries (Easter–Sept 2 daily; ⓦ cruiselochlomond.co.uk) cross from Tarbert, on the west shore.

Ferry to Inversnaid It's also possible to get to or from Inversnaid by ferry (£4 one-way/£5 return), which crosses from Inveruglas, directly opposite on the western shore. You'll have to phone the *Inversnaid Hotel* (☎ 01887 386223) to make arrangements.

National Park Centre The national park visitor centre is located beside the large car park in Balmaha (April–Sept daily 9.30am–4pm; ⓦ lochlomond-trossachs.org), though it's more geared to illustrating the region's natural history than offering information.

ACCOMMODATION AND EATING

BALMAHA

Oak Tree Inn ⓦ theoaktreeinn.co.uk. Set back from the boatyard, this upscale inn offers smartly furnished doubles as well as quad rooms and a couple of two-person pods There's also a convivial pub, where food is served all day, plus the neighbouring *St Mocha* café, which, alongside superb coffee and ice cream, functions as a pop-up fish and chip shop on Friday and Saturday evenings. £££; pods £££

ROWARDENNAN

Cashel 3 miles south of Rowardennan ⓦ campingintheforest.co.uk A lovely, secluded Forestry and Land Scotland campsite on the loch shore with a decent loo block. Campers can launch craft from here onto the loch, and Ben Lomond is just four miles away. £

Clansman Bar Rowardennan Hotel, on the lake shore ⓦ rowardennanhotel.co.uk. Nightlife in the area centres on this hotel's bar, which features open fires, a beer garden and weekend live music.

Rowardennan Lodge Youth Hostel A 15min walk north of the Rowardennan Hotel ⓦ hostellingscotland.org.uk. A wonderfully situated hostel in a classic turreted Scots Baronial lodge with lawns running down to the shore. Four- to eight bed dorms plus twins and a double. Dorms £; doubles ££

The western shore

Despite the roar of traffic hurtling along the upgraded A82, the **west shore** of Loch Lomond is an undeniably beautiful stretch of water. Ten miles north of attractive **Luss** is the small settlement of **TARBET**, where the West Highland **train** reaches the shoreline. North of Tarbet, the A82 turns back into the narrow, winding road of old, making for slower but much more interesting driving. There's one more **train station** on Loch Lomond at Ardlui, at the mountain-framed head of the loch, but most travellers continue a couple of miles further north to **INVERARNAN**, where you'll find the *Drovers Inn*, possibly the most idiosyncratic hotel in Scotland.

Luss

LUSS is the prettiest village in the region, with its prim, identical sandstone and slate cottages garlanded in rambling roses, and its narrow sand and pebble strand. However, its charms are no secret and its streets and beach can become crowded in summer. If you want to escape the hordes, pop into the parish **church**, a haven of peace with some fine Victorian stained-glass windows and a lovely ceiling made from Scots pine rafters.

ARRIVAL AND DEPARTURE

By bus Buses run from Tarbet to Loch Lomond's western shore (hourly; 10min).

By ferry Between May and September, Sweeney's Cruise Co. (ⓦsweeneyscruisesco.com) operates waterbus services

THE WESTERN SHORE

between Luss and Balmaha on the eastern shore (4–5 daily; 30min), and Luss and Balloch (2–3 daily). From Tarbet there are ferries to Inversnaid (May–Oct 5 daily; 30min).

TOURS

Boat tours At the pier over the road from the prominent *Tarbet Hotel* you can hop on an hour-long loch cruise run by Cruise Loch Lomond (ⓦcruiselochlomond.co.uk). The same

operator also offers trips to Inversnaid and Rowardennan on the eastern side.

ACCOMMODATION AND EATING

LUSS
Coach House Loch Lomond Trading Company Ltd, Church Rd ☎01436 653186. A spruce and lively little tearoom with friendly tartan-wearing staff, serving a range of teas, cakes, ciabattas, Orkney ice cream and their own take on haggis. £

Loch Lomond Arms Main Road Wlochlomondarmshotel. com. Graceful seventeenth-century coaching inn possessing a stock of handsome-looking rooms named after Scottish clans and furnished in muted tartan colours; some have loch views. The warming bar/restaurant is a great spot to chow

down on the likes of haggis and black pudding scotch egg, and venison pie with horseradish mash. £££

INVERARNAN
Drovers Inn By Ardlui, North Loch Lomond ⓦdroversinn.co.uk. The bar (self-proclaimed 'pub of the year 1705') features a roaring fire, barmen dressed in kilts, weary hillwalkers sipping pints, and bearded musicians banging out folk songs. Down the creaking corridors, past moth-eaten stuffed animals, are a number of resolutely old-fashioned rooms. ££

Crianlarich and Tyndrum

CRIANLARICH, some eight miles north of the head of Loch Lomond, is an important staging post on various transport routes, including the West Highland Railway which divides here, one branch heading due west towards Oban, the other continuing north over Rannoch Moor to Fort William. The West Highland Way long-distance footpath (see page 384) passes by. Otherwise, there's little reason to stop here, unless you're keen on tackling some of the steep-sided hills that rise up from the glen.

Five miles further north from here on the A82/A85, the village of **TYNDRUM** owes its existence to a minor (and very short-lived) nineteenth-century gold rush, but today supports little more than a busy service station and several characterless hotels.

ARRIVAL AND DEPARTURE

By train Crianlarich is well served by regular trains. Tyndrum has two train stations: the upper station serves the scenic West Highland Line, while the lower has services to and from Crianlarich and the south.
Destinations from Crianlarich Fort William (3–4 daily Mon–Sat, 1–3 on Sun; 1hr 50min); Glasgow Queen Street (6–8 daily Mon–Sat, 1–3 on Sun; 1hr 50min); Oban (3–4

CRIANLARICH AND TYNDRUM

daily Mon–Sat, 1–3 on Sun; 1hr 15min).
Destinations from Tyndrum Fort William (upper station 3–4 daily; 1hr 35min); Crianlarich (lower station 5 daily; 8min); Glasgow Queen Street (lower station 5 daily Mon–Sat, 1 on Sun; 2hr 5min).
By car At Tyndrum the road divides, with the A85 heading west to Oban, and the A82 heading for Fort William via Glen Coe.

ACCOMMODATION AND EATING

By The Way Hostel and Campsite Lower Station Rd, Tyndrum ⓦtyndrumbytheway.com. Right beside Tyndrum Lower railway station is a good campsite and small purpose-built bunkhouse; they've also got a self-catering posh pod and glamping hut, both sleeping two, and cute wooden 'hobbit houses' sleeping four. £; pods and huts ££

Real Food Café Main St, Tyndrum ⓦtherealfoodcafe. com. For a refreshingly different roadside dining experience, it's well worth trying the airy café on the main road serving fresh, fast food that's locally sourced and cooked to order, including fish and chips; they've got terrific coffee and cakes too. ££

7

The Trossachs

Often described as the Highlands in miniature, the **Trossachs** area boasts a magnificent diversity of scenery, with distinctive peaks, silvery lochs and mysterious, forest-covered slopes. Strictly speaking, the name 'Trossachs', normally translated as either 'bristly country' or 'crossing place', originally referred only to the wooded glen between **Loch Katrine** and Loch Achray, but today it is usually taken as being the whole area from **Callander** right up to the eastern banks of Loch Lomond, with which it has been grouped as one of Scotland's national parks.

The Trossachs' high tourist profile was largely attributable in the early days to Sir Walter Scott, whose novels *Lady of the Lake* and *Rob Roy* were set in and around the area. According to one contemporary account, after Scott's *Lady of the Lake* was published in 1810, the number of carriages passing Loch Katrine rose from fifty the previous year to 270. Since then, neither the popularity nor beauty of the region has waned, and in high season it can be jam-packed. Autumn is a better time to come, when the hills are blanketed in rich, rusty colours and the crowds are thinner. In terms of where to stay, **Aberfoyle** has a rather dowdy air while **Callander** feels somewhat overrun, and you're often better off seeking out one of the guesthouses or B&Bs tucked away in secluded corners of the region.

GETTING AROUND   THE TROSSACHS

By bus First Group (ⓦfirstbus.co.uk) operates between Callander and Stirling; reduced service at weekends.
By bike Wheels Cycling Centre on Invertrossachs Rd, 1.5 miles southwest of Callander (ⓦscottish-cycling.com) has excellent bike hire (£15/4hr; £25/day), and also does servicing and repairs.

Aberfoyle and around

Each summer the sleepy little town of **ABERFOYLE**, twenty miles west of Stirling, dusts itself down for its annual influx of tourists. Though of little appeal itself, Aberfoyle has an ideal position in the heart of the Trossachs, with **Loch Ard Forest** and **Queen Elizabeth Forest Park** stretching across to Ben Lomond and Loch Lomond to the west, Loch Katrine and Ben Venue to the northwest, and Ben Ledi to the northeast. Don't come here for lively nightlife or entertainment, but for a good, healthy blast of the outdoors.

Lake of Menteith
About 4 miles east of Aberfoyle towards Doune

HIKING AND BIKING IN THE TROSSACHS

The Trossachs are ideal for exploring on **foot** or on a **mountain bike**. This is partly because the terrain is slightly more benign than the Highlands proper, but much is due to the excellent management of the **Queen Elizabeth Forest Park**, a huge chunk of the national park that lies between Loch Lomond and Loch Lubnaig. Located a mile or so south of Aberfoyle, **The Lodge** (see page 287) is the main visitor centre for the area, and is well worth a visit.

For **hillwalkers**, as far as height goes, the prize peak is Ben Lomond (3192ft), best accessed from Rowardennan (see page 283). Other highlights include Ben Venue (2370ft) and Ben A'an (1520ft) on the shores of Loch Katrine, as well as Ben Ledi (2857ft), just northwest of Callander, which all offer relatively straightforward but very rewarding climbs and, on clear days, stunning views.

Walkers can also choose from any number of waymarked routes through the forests and along lochsides; pick up a map of these at the visitor centre. A great long-distance option is the thirty-mile **Great Trossachs Path**, a series of linked routes along the lochs between Callander and Inversnaid: it can also be cycled. **Bikers** are served by a network of forest paths and one of the more impressive stretches of the National Cycle Network cuts through the region from Loch Lomond to Killin.

ROB ROY

A member of the outlawed MacGregor clan, **Rob Roy** was born in 1671 in Glengyle, just north of Loch Katrine, and lived for some time as a respectable cattle farmer and trader, supported by the powerful Duke of Montrose. In 1712, Rob Roy absconded with £1000, some of it belonging to the duke. He took to the hills to live as a brigand, his feud with Montrose escalating after the Duke repossessed Rob Roy's land and drove his wife from their house. He was present at the Battle of Sheriffmuir during the Jacobite uprising of 1715, ostensibly supporting the Jacobites but probably as an opportunist: the chaos would have made cattle-raiding easier. Eventually captured and sentenced to transportation, Rob Roy was pardoned and returned to **Balquhidder** (see page 289), where he remained until his death in 1734. His status as a local hero in the mould of Robin Hood should be tempered with the fact that he was without doubt a bandit and blackmailer. His life has been much romanticized, from Sir Walter Scott's 1818 novel **Rob Roy** to the 1995 film starring Liam Neeson, although the tale does serve well to dramatize the clash between the doomed clan culture of the Gaelic-speaking Highlanders and the organized feudal culture of lowland Scots, which effectively ended with the defeat of the Jacobites at Culloden in 1746. His **grave** in Balquhidder, a simple affair behind the ruined church, is mercifully free of the tartan trappings that plague parts of the Trossachs, predictably dubbed 'Rob Roy Country' by the tourist board.

The **Lake of Menteith** is Scotland's premier fly-fishing centre, and its only lake (as opposed to loch), so-named due to a historic mix-up with the word *laigh*, Scots for 'low-lying ground', which applied to the whole area. Abundant with pike and brown and rainbow trout, the lake attracts anglers from all over the world, especially during the National Fly Fishing Championships each May or June. But if fishing's not your thing, there are also some secluded spots along the shore for picnics and swims. To rent fishing gear, contact the Lake of Menteith Fisheries (ⓦmenteith-fisheries.co.uk; mid-March–mid-Nov).

Inchmahome Priory

Lake of Menteith • Daily April–Sept 10am–4.30pm; Oct 10am–3.30pm • Charge, including ferry • HES • ⓦ historicenvironment.scot

From the northern shore of the Lake of Menteith, you can take a little ferry out to the **Island of Inchmahome** to explore the ruined Augustinian abbey. Founded in 1238, **Inchmahome Priory** is the most beautiful island monastery in Scotland, its remains rising tall and graceful above the trees. The masons employed to build the priory are thought to be those who built Dunblane Cathedral (see page 278); certainly the western entrance there resembles that at Inchmahome. The nave of the church is roofless, but in the choir are preserved the graves of important families from the surrounding area. Most touching is a late thirteenth-century double effigy depicting Walter Stewart, First Earl of Menteith, and his wife Countess Mary, who, feet resting on lion-like animals, turn towards each other and embrace.

Mary, Queen of Scots was hidden at Inchmahome in 1547 before being taken to France, and there's a formal garden in the west of the island, known as Queen Mary's Bower, where she played, according to legend. Visible on a nearby but inaccessible islet is the ruined castle of **Inchtalla**, the home of the earls of Menteith in the sixteenth and seventeenth centuries.

Queen Elizabeth Forest Park

The Lodge Forest Visitor Centre • Daily Feb–Dec 10am–4pm; Jan 10am–3pm • Free; car parking charge • ⓦ forestryandland.gov.scot

North of Aberfoyle, the A821 road to Loch Katrine winds its way into the **Queen Elizabeth Forest Park**, snaking up **Duke's Pass** (so-called because it once belonged to the Duke of Montrose). You can walk or drive the short distance from Aberfoyle to the park's excellent **Lodge visitor centre**, where you can pick up maps of the walks and cycle routes in the forest, get background information on the area's flora and fauna or settle into the **café** with its splendid views out over the tree tops.

7

ABERFOYLE

By bus Regular buses from Stirling pull into the car park on Aberfoyle's Main St.

Destinations Callander (late June–mid-Oct 4 Thurs–Tues; 25min); Port of Menteith (late June–mid-Oct 4 Thurs–Tues; 10min).

Tourist office The very helpful tourist office on Main Street

(Daily April–Oct 10am–5pm; Nov–March 10am–4pm; ☎ 01877 381221) has full details of local accommodation, sights and outdoor activities.

LAKE OF MENTEITH

By bus Take First Edinburgh bus No. 11 from Stirling to the Lake of Menteith (5 daily; 50min).

ACCOMMODATION AND EATING

ABERFOYLE

Trossachs Holiday Park 3 miles south of Aberfoyle ⓦ trossachsholidays.co.uk. This excellent family-run 40-acre holiday park is fringed by oak and bluebell woods, and as well as excellent camping has basically furnished, four-man pods. Facilities include laundry, shop, games rooms and a play park, plus bikes for rent. £; pods ££

★ **Wee Blether Tea Room** 4 miles west of Aberfoyle on the shores of Loch Ard ⓦ weeblethertearoom.co.uk. Excellent home baking and an idyllic loch location make this

homely place a winner. Soups, toasties, pies, 'jacket tatties' and lots of cakes. £

LAKE OF MENTEITH

Karma Lake of Menteith Hotel Port of Menteith ⓦ karmagroup.com. Recently acquired by the Karma group, this resort hotel is a beautiful place to stay, with an idyllic waterfront setting next to Port of Menteith's Victorian Gothic parish church. The rooms are as plush as you'd expect at this price and it also has a classy restaurant. ££££

Loch Katrine

Heading down the northern side of the Duke's Pass, you come first to **Loch Achray**, tucked under Ben A'an. Look out across the loch for the small **Callander Kirk** in a lovely setting alone on a promontory. At the head of the loch a road follows the short distance through to the southern end of **Loch Katrine** at the foot of Ben Venue (2370ft).

Brig o' Turk and Loch Venachar

From Loch Katrine the A821 heads due east past the tiny village of **Brig o' Turk**, where there are a couple of excellent eating options. From here, carry on along the shores of **Loch Venachar**, where *Venachar Lochside* houses an attractive café and a **fishing centre** offering boat rental and fly-fishing tuition.

ACCOMMODATION AND EATING

★ **Byre Inn** Just east of Brig o' Turk ⓦ byreinn.co.uk. A tiny country pub set in an old stone barn with wooden pews; it's the starting point for waymarked walks to lochs Achray, Drunkie and Venachar. Food comprises good old

fashioned fish'n'chips alongside a terrific burger menu plus a few other delicious morsels. There's a boules/petanque piste outside too if you get bored. ££

★ **Loch Katrine Eco Lodges** Trossachs Pier Loch

CRUISES ON LOCH KATRINE

The elegant Victorian **passenger steamer**, the SS *Sir Walter Scott* (April–Oct daily; £18 return; ⓦ lochkatrine.com), has been plying the waters of Loch Katrine since 1900, chugging up to the wild country of Glengyle. It makes various **cruises** each day, stopping off at Stronachlachar; the shorter hour-long cruises (£15 return) don't make any stops. The much smaller, and far less glamorous *Lady of the Lake* and *Rob Roy III* cruisers make similar trips but are cheaper (£15.50/2hr, £12.50/1hr). A popular combination is to rent a bike from the Katrinewheelz hut by the pier (Easter–Oct; £25/4hr, £30/day; ⓦ katrinewheelz.co.uk), take the steamer up to Stronachlachar, where the waterside *Pier Café* is an excellent place for refreshments, then **cycle** back by way of the road around the north side of the loch.

Katrine ⓦ lochkatrine,com. Overlooking the water are ten brilliantly-designed lodges, sleeping two- to four people, and equipped with kitchenette, toilet/shower, underfloor heating and outside decking; some will take dogs. There are also a few pitches here for tents and campervans. The Steamship Café is open for breakfast from 9am. Two-night minimum stay. **££**

Callander and around

CALLANDER, on the eastern edge of the Trossachs, sits on the banks of the River Teith at the southern end of the **Pass of Leny**, one of the key routes into the Highlands. Significantly larger than Aberfoyle, it suffers in high season for being right on the main tourist trail from Stirling through to the west Highlands, meaning the plethora of restaurants, tearooms and gift shops is always well served. Callander first came to fame during the 'Scottish Enlightenment' of the eighteenth and nineteenth centuries, with the glowing reports of the Trossachs given by Sir Walter Scott and William Wordsworth. Development was given a further boost when Queen Victoria chose to visit, and then by the arrival of the train line – long since closed – in the 1860s.

North of Callander, you can walk or ride the scenic six-mile **Callander to Strathyre Cycleway** (Route 7), which forms part of the network of cycleways between the Highlands and Glasgow.

7

ARRIVAL AND INFORMATION

CALLANDER AND AROUND

By bus Callander has bus connections with Loch Katrine (late June to mid-Oct 4 daily Thurs–Tues; 55min).
Tourist office The regional Loch Lomond and Trossachs visitor centre is at 55 Main St (ⓦ visitcallander.uk; April to mid-Oct daily 9.30am–4.30pm).

ACCOMMODATION

Arden House Bracklinn Rd ⓦ ardenhouse.org.uk. A grand Victorian guesthouse in its own gardens with three period furnished rooms, good views and woodland walks from the back door. They've even got a snooker room and putting green. There's also a self-catering studio in the grounds. **£££**
Callander Hostel 6 Bridgend ⓦ cyp.org.uk. Swish hostel in a distinctive timbered building, with mountain views, a bistro, self-catering facilities and a BBQ area. Twin and family rooms (all en suite) are complemented by four cosy, fully-equipped two-berth pods (two-night minimum stay), one of which is fully accessible. Dorms **£**; doubles **££**; pods **££**

Callander Meadows 24 Main St ⓦ callandermeadows. co.uk. Centrally located accommodation in an attractive townhouse with a selection of comfortable en-suite rooms and a very good restaurant. **££**
Roman Camp Country House Hotel 182 Main St ⓦ romancamphotel.co.uk. The town's most upmarket, albeit overpriced, option is this turreted seventeenth-century hunting lodge set in riverside gardens; you could also spend hours enjoying the rambling public areas, like the library, lounge and conservatory, with a drink or two. **£££**

EATING AND DRINKING

Lade Inn Kilmahog, 1 mile west of Callander ⓦ theladeinn.com. Pub food such as beer-battered chicken goujons can be had at this convivial inn where the owners are keen on real ales; an on-site shop sells bottled beers. Regular live folk music too. **££**

★ **Mhor Fish** 75–77 Main St ⓦ mhorfish.net. Sit-down or takeaway restaurant with an impressive sustainable fish policy offering delicious meals like seafood chowder and salt and pepper squid alongside your more traditional fish and chip suppers. Licenced too. **£**

Balquhidder

Beyond the northern end of Loch Lubnaig is tiny **BALQUHIDDER**, famed as the site of the **grave of Rob Roy** (see page 287), which is just in front of the ruined church. Framed by a low black iron fence, his grave is marked by a rough stone carved with a sword, cross and a man with a dog. Buried here too is his wife, Mary, and two sons, Coll and Robert.

ACCOMMODATION AND EATING

BALQUHIDDER

★ **Monachyle Mhor** Loch Voil, 6 miles west of Balquhidder ⓦ monachylemhor.net. This eighteenth-century farmhouse features chic rooms and a terrific restaurant with much of the food sourced from the family's farm and bakery. Lovely, tranquil views over Loch Voil. **££££**

Fife

THE FORTH RAIL BRIDGE

Fife

Barely fifty miles at its widest point, the ancient Kingdom of Fife, designated as such by the Picts in the fourth century, is a small area but one which has a distinct identity. It is inextricably linked with the waters that surround it on three sides – the Tay to the north, the Forth to the south, and the cold North Sea to the east. One of its most striking aspects is how it changes in character within a few miles, with a marked difference between the rural north and the semi-industrial south. Tourism and agriculture are the economic mainstays of the northeast corner of Fife, where the landscape varies from gentle hills in the rural hinterland to windswept cliffs, rocky bays and sandy beaches. Fishing still has a role, but ultimately it is to St Andrews, Scotland's oldest university town and the home of the world-famous Royal and Ancient Golf Club, that most visitors are drawn. Development here has been cautious, and both the town itself and the surrounding area retain an appealing and old-fashioned feel. South of St Andrews, the tiny stone harbours of the East Neuk fishing villages are a deeply appealing extension to any visit to this part of Fife.

8

Inland from St Andrews, the central Fife settlements of **Glenrothes**, an unremarkable post-war new town, and **Cupar**, a more interesting market town, are overshadowed by the absorbing village of **Falkland** with its impressive ruined palace. In the **south**, the closure of the coal mines over the last thirty years has left local communities floundering to regain a foothold, and the squeeze on the fishing industry may well lead to further decline. In the meantime, a number of the villages have capitalized on their appeal and welcomed tourism in a way that has enhanced rather than degraded their natural assets. The perfectly preserved town of **Culross** is the most notable of these; once a lively port that enjoyed a thriving trade with Holland, the Dutch influence is obvious in the striking crow-step gabled houses that line the cobbled lanes. Otherwise, southern Fife is dominated by the town of **Dunfermline**, a former capital of Scotland, and industrial **Kirkcaldy**, with the Forth rail and road bridges the most memorable sights on this stretch of coastline.

GETTING AROUND

FIFE

By train The train line follows the coast as far north as Kirkcaldy where you can change for East Neuk bus connections. It then cuts inland towards Dundee, stopping en route at Cupar and Leuchars (from where buses run to St Andrews).

By bus The main bus operator in Fife is Stagecoach (ⓦstagecoachbus.com), with a fleet servicing St Andrews, East Neuk and the rest of the coast as well as the interior, with train connections at Kirkcaldy and Leuchars.

By car The main road into the region is the M90, which links the Forth Road Bridge northwest of Edinburgh with Perth. From just north of the bridge, you can join the 85-mile semicircular Coastal Tourist Route (signposted), taking in many of the highlights from the Forth to the Tay estuaries.

St Andrews

Confident, poised and well groomed, if a little snooty, **ST ANDREWS** is Scotland's oldest **university town** and a pilgrimage centre for **golfers** from the world over, situated on a wide bay on the northeastern coast of Fife. Of all Scotland's universities, St Andrews is the one most often compared to Oxford or Cambridge, both for the dominance of gown over

CULROSS PALACE

Highlights

❶ Himalayas putting green, St Andrews The world's finest putting course right beside the world's finest golf course. See page 298

❷ The East Neuk After a bracing walk along the Fife Coastal Path, try freshly cooked crab or lobster from the wooden shack at Crail's historic stone harbour, or dine in style at one of the excellent seafood restaurants in the nearby fishing towns. See page 299

❸ Falkland Palace Beautifully placed in a well-preserved village beneath the Lomond Hills, the former hunting retreat of the Stuart kings is an atmospheric semi-ruin in gracious gardens. See page 303

❹ Forth Rail Bridge One of the great engineering wonders of the Victorian age, a huge cantilever structure spanning the Firth of Forth, floodlit to stunning effect at night. See page 304

❺ Culross Scotland's best-preserved historic village, all pantile roofs and cobbled wynds, with its own palace and ruined medieval abbey. See page 304

❻ Dunfermline Abbey and Palace Vast, dramatic ruins of the former seat of the kings of Scotland and burial site of the legendary Robert the Bruce. See page 305

HIGHLIGHTS ARE MARKED ON THE MAP ON PAGE 294

town and for the intimate, collegiate feel of the place. The university attracts a significant proportion of English students including, famously, Prince William, who spent four years studying here and met his wife, Kate Middleton. There's an open, airy feel here, encouraged by the long stretches of sand on either side of town and the acreage of golf links all around.

St Andrews is compact and easy to walk around. With its medieval layout intact, its three main streets, almost entirely consisting of listed buildings, run west to east past several of the original fifteenth-century university campuses towards the heavily ruined Gothic **cathedral**. There's little left of the town's **castle**, which sits on the promontory further north.

St Andrews Cathedral

North St · Daily April–Sept 9.30am–5.30pm; Oct–March 10am–4pm · Charge; joint ticket available with castle · Grounds year-round 9am–5.30pm · Free · HES · ⓦ historicenvironment.scot

The ruin of the once-great **St Andrews Cathedral** gives only an idea of the importance of what was once the largest cathedral in Scotland. Though founded in 1160, it was not finished and consecrated until 1318, in the presence of Robert the Bruce. On 5 June 1559, the Reformation took its toll, and supporters of John Knox, fresh from a rousing meeting, plundered the cathedral and left it to ruin. Stone was still being taken from the building for various local projects as late as the 1820s.

The cathedral site, above the harbour where the land drops to the sea, can be a blustery place, with the wind whistling through the great east window and down the stretch of turf that was once the central aisle. In front of the window a slab is all that remains of the high altar, where the relics of St Andrew were once enshrined. From the top of the **St Rule's Tower** (a climb of 150-odd steps), built as part of an abbey in 1130,

HIGHLIGHTS

1. Himalayas putting green, St Andrews
2. The East Neuk
3. Falkland Palace
4. Forth Rail Bridge
5. Culross
6. Dunfermline Abbey and Palace

GOLF IN ST ANDREWS

St Andrews **Royal and Ancient Golf Club** (R&A) is the international governing body for golf, and dates back to a meeting of 22 of the local gentry in 1754, who founded the Society of St Andrews Golfers, being 'admirers of the ancient and healthful exercise of golf'. The game itself has been played here since the fifteenth century. Those early days – highlighted in the British Golf Museum (see page 297) – were instrumental in establishing Scotland as the home of golf, for the rules were distinguished from those of the French game by the fact that participants had to manoeuvre the ball into a hole, rather than hit an above-ground target. It was not without its opponents, however – James II banned his subjects from playing in 1457 as it was distracting them from archery practice.

The approach to St Andrews from the west runs adjacent to the famous **Old Course**, one of seven courses in the immediate vicinity of the town. The R&A's strictly private **clubhouse**, a solid, square building dating from 1854, is at the eastern end of the Old Course overlooking both the eighteenth green and the long strand of the West Sands. The British Open Championship was first held here in 1873, having been inaugurated in 1860 at Prestwick in Ayrshire, and since then it has been held at St Andrews regularly, pulling in enormous crowds. Fittingly, in 2022, it staged the 150th playing of the Open Championship. Guided walks of the Old Course are available (see page 297), though any golf aficionado will savour a stroll around the immediate environs of the golf courses, where there are numerous golf shops, including a couple selling and repairing old-fashioned hickory-shafted clubs.

there's a good view of the town and surroundings, and of the remains of the monastic buildings that made up the priory. Around the entire complex is a sturdy wall dating from the sixteenth century, over half a mile long and with three gateways.

Southwest of the cathedral enclosure lies **The Pends**, a huge fourteenth-century vaulted gatehouse that marked the main entrance to the priory, and from where the road leads down to the harbour.

St Andrews Castle

The Scores • Daily April–Sept 9.30am–5.30pm; Oct–March 10am–4pm • Charge, joint ticket available with cathedral • HES • Ⓦ historicenvironment.scot

With a drop to the sea on two sides and a moat on the inland side, **St Andrews Castle**, founded around 1200, was built as part of the palace of the bishops and archbishops of St Andrews. During the Reformation, it was the scene of some fairly grim incidents. There's not a great deal left, since the castle fell into ruin in the seventeenth century – most of what can be seen dates from a century earlier, apart from the fourteenth-century Fore Tower.

St Andrews Heritage Museum and Garden

12 North St • Wed–Sun noon–4pm • Free; charge for some exhibitions • Ⓦ standrewsmuseum.com

A compact museum housed in a picturesque sixteenth-century cottage with a low wooden door and rubble stone facade, the **St Andrews Heritage Museum** was originally home to four fishermen's families. Today, you'll encounter a mock-up vintage grocer's, a chemist and a gratifyingly generous array of antiquarian bric-a-brac.

St Andrews University

Ⓦ st-andrews.ac.uk

Scattered around the town centre, **St Andrews University** is the oldest in Scotland. Founded in 1410 by Bishop Henry Wardlaw, the original building was on the site of the Old University Library and by the end of the Middle Ages three colleges had been

ST ANDREWS

ACCOMMODATION
Castlemount	1
Craigtoun Meadows Holiday Park	5
Old Fishergate House	3
St Andrews Country Lodges	2
St Andrews Tourist Hostel	4

● EATING
Balgove Steak Barn	1
The Doll's House	4
Little Italy	3
The Peat Inn	5
The Tailend	2

DRINKING
The Criterion	1
The Rule	2

NORTH SEA

West Sands

Castle Sands

East Sands

St Andrews Castle

Cathedral

St Rule's Tower

St Leonard's School

Queen Mary's House

Byre Theatre

St Mary's College

Holy Trinity

St Salvator's College

St Andrews Heritage Museum

Spokes

New Picture House

St Andrews Aquarium

British Golf Museum

The Royal & Ancient Golf Club of St Andrews

The Old Course

The New Course

St Andrews Himalayas Putting Green

St Andrews Ladies' Putting Club

Jubilee Course

St Andrews Links Trust clubhouse

Bus Station

West Port

UNIVERSITY OF ST ANDREWS

Long Pier

Harbour

THE SHORE

SHOREHEAD

THE PENDS

THE SCORES

GREGORY PLACE

NORTH CASTLE STREET

NORTH STREET

MARKET STREET

SOUTH STREET

ABBEY STREET

WESTBURN LANE

BAKER LANE

UNION STREET

COLLEGE STREET

CRAILS LANE

CHURCH STREET

LOGIES LANE

MUTTOES LANE

BUTTS WYND

QUEEN'S GARDENS

Lade Braes Lane

BELL STREET

GREYFRIARS GARDEN

MURRAY PARK

MURRAY PLACE

ST MARY'S PLACE

HOPE STREET

ALEXANDRA PLACE

BRIDGE STREET

CITY ROAD

GOLF PLACE

THE LINKS

WEST SANDS ROAD

GIBSON PLACE

GRANNIE CLARK'S WYND

PILMOUR LINKS

Swilken Burn

WINDMILL ROAD

STATION ROAD

OLD STATION ROAD

ABBOTSFORD CRES

HOWARD PLACE

ARGYLE STREET

DOUBLEDYKES ROAD

LINKS CRESCENT

WARDLAW GARDENS

LANGLANDS ROAD

KENNEDY GARDENS

HEPBURN GARDENS

200 yards

N

▲ The Balgove Course, Leuchars & Dundee

▶ The Castle Course & Crail

▶ (6 miles) & St Andrews Botanic Gardens

8

built: **St Salvador's** (1450), **St Leonard's** (1512) on Pends Road and **St Mary's** (1538) on South Street. At the time of the Reformation, St Mary's became a seminary of Protestant theology, and today it houses the university's Faculty of Divinity.

R&A World Golf Museum

Bruce Embankment • April–Oct Mon–Sat 9.30am–5pm, Sun 10am–5pm; Nov–March daily 10am–4pm • Charge • ⓦ worldgolfmuseum.co.uk

A collection of national importance, the renovated and rebranded **R&A World Golf Museum** has pictures of golfing greats from Tom Morris to Tiger Woods, along with clubs, trophies and a variety of paraphernalia from the seventeenth century onwards. There are plenty of interactive digital experiences too, including learning how to play with leading Scottish golfer Catriona Matthews, and having a go at putting under pressure. It's predominantly an attraction for golfing obsessives, but the museum is designed to be family friendly.

East and West Sands

St Andrews has two great beaches: the vast expanse of **West Sands**, just north of town, and the more compact **East Sands**, beside the harbour. The West Sands are best known from the opening sequences of the Oscar-winning film *Chariots of Fire*, and while they're still used by budding athletes, less energetic activities include sandcastle competitions, breathtaking dips in the North Sea, and bird-watching at the lonely north end. The blustery winds that are the scourge of golfers and walkers alike do at least make the beach a great place to fly a kite.

8

ARRIVAL AND DEPARTURE   ST ANDREWS

By train The nearest train station is at Leuchars on the Edinburgh–Dundee line, five miles northwest across the River Eden, from where regular buses make the 15min trip into town. When you buy your rail ticket to Leuchars, ask for a St Andrews rail-bus ticket that includes the bus fare.
Destinations Aberdeen (1–2 hourly; 1hr 30min); Dundee

(1–2 hourly; 15min); Edinburgh (1–2 hourly; 1hr).
By bus The bus station is on City Rd at the west end of Market St.
Destinations Anstruther (hourly; 20–25min); Dundee (1–2 hourly; 35min); Edinburgh (1–2 hourly; 1hr 30min); Leuchars (3–4 hourly; 10min).

GETTING AROUND AND INFORMATION

Bike rental Spokes (37 South St; Mon–Sat 8.45am–5.30pm; ⓦ spokescycles.net) offers bike rental for £20/day including locks and helmets.
Tourist office The good-sized tourist office is at 70 Market

St (April–June & Sept–Oct Mon–Sat 9.15am–5pm, Sun 10am–5pm; Nov–March Mon–Sat 9.30am–5pm; July–Aug Mon–Sat 9.15am–6pm, Sun 10am–5pm; ☏ 01382 472021).

TOURS AND ACTIVITIES

TOURS
Golf tours For a bracing introduction to the importance of golf to the town, the St Andrews Links Trust runs 50min

guided walking tours of the Old Course before handing out a complimentary golf ball and novelty scorecard. The tours depart from outside the golf shop at the eighteenth hole of

---

THE VISION OF ST RULE

According to legend, St Andrews was founded, pretty much by accident, in the fourth century. **St Rule** – or Regulus – a custodian of the bones of St Andrew in Patras in southwestern Greece, had a vision in which an angel ordered him to carry five of the saint's bones to the western edge of the world, where he was to build a city in his honour. The conscientious courier set off, but was shipwrecked on the rocks close to the present harbour. Struggling ashore with his precious burden, he built a shrine to the saint on what subsequently became the site of the **cathedral**; St Andrew became Scotland's patron saint and the town its ecclesiastical capital.

8

the Old Course, north of town (April–mid-Sept daily 11am & 2pm, Oct daily 11am; £15; ⓦ standrews.com).

GOLF

You can play any of the town's courses, all of which are administered by the St Andrews Links Trust. With the exception of the Balgove Course and Ladies Putting Club, all of the town's courses must be booked; this can be done online at ⓦ standrews.com. The main courses are on the north side of St Andrews; follow the brown 'Golf' signposts off the A91.

Balgove Course The only nine-hole course in St Andrews is designed for families and beginners, and, unlike the others, you can just turn up and play. Green fees £8–15

Castle Course Built in 2008, the newest addition to the St Andrews Links has already gained a positive following in part thanks to its clifftop position and views to the town. However, putting here can be a bit frustrating as the greens are not as flat as you might expect for a modern course, and even experienced golfers can be heard cursing the design. Green fees £65–140. Course open March–Nov.

The Himalayas (Ladies Putting Club) Officially named the Ladies Putting Club but more commonly referred to as The Himalayas, this course is open to the public without booking, and offers arguably the best golfing experience in St Andrews. Even if you can't tell a birdie from a bogey, it's a fantastically lumpy eighteen-holer in an ideal setting right next to the Old Course and the sea. You can have all the thrill of sinking a six-footer in golf's most famous location for a bargain price. Green fees £3.

New Course Designed in 1895, this has some pretty bumpy putting greens and the fairways have hard ground and plenty of ball-swallowing bunkers to test any well-seasoned pro. Green fees £45–120.

Old Course The oldest course in the world offers the amateur the chance to pit their game against the generations of golfing legends that have birdied and bogeyed their way round the eighteen windswept greens. Its popularity is unrelenting; to play here you must have a handicap certificate (24 for men/36 for women) and enter a ballot at least two days in advance. Course closed on Sundays. Green fees £100–270.

ACCOMMODATION
SEE MAP PAGE 296

There's no shortage of accommodation both in town and around, although average **prices** in all categories vie with Edinburgh's as the highest in Scotland. **Upmarket hotels** are thick on the ground, notably around the golf courses. There are plenty of **guesthouses**, though rooms often get booked up in the summer, you should definitely book in advance.

Castlemount 2 The Scores ⓦ castlemount.net. Charming old B&B romantically set overlooking the castle ruins and to the sea beyond. Within, there's a patchwork of bygone furniture and fabrics throughout, and en-suite rooms, some with four-poster beds. £££

Craigtoun Meadows Holiday Park 2 miles southwest of town signposted off the A915 ⓦ craigtounmeadows. co.uk. Reasonably convenient for the centre of town, this site is well run and has a surprisingly good range of facilities, particularly for children. Camping per pitch £; static caravan rental per week (mid-March to Oct) ££££

★ **Old Fishergate House** 35 North Castle St

ⓦ oldfishergatehouse.co.uk. Entered via a quaint cobbled pavement, this seventeenth-century townhouse is one of the more personal places to stay in town, with its books, pictures and antique furniture including an old piano. Just two rooms (red and yellow), both with fridges and a private sitting area. The obvious choice for traditionalists. £££

St Andrews Country Lodges Cuplahills Farm, 7 miles northwest of St Andrews, off the A914 ⓦ standrewscountrylodges.co.uk. A surprisingly luxurious option for families and groups, these superb eco-lodges sleep six in three contemporary bedrooms. There's a kitchen and lounge as well as an exterior deck and site playground. Minimum stay three nights. Per night up to six guests ££££

St Andrews Tourist Hostel Inchcape House, St Mary's Place ☎ 01334 479911. Handily placed backpacker hostel in a converted townhouse right above *The Grill House* restaurant, with plenty of dorm beds, but no doubles. The cheapest option in town, but not the quietest. Dorms £

EATING
SEE MAP PAGE 296

St Andrews has no shortage of restaurants and cafés. Most are found on Market St, South St and the interlinking closes between the two.

★ **Balgove Steak Barn** 1 mile northwest of St Andrews on the A91 ⓦ balgove.com. Sited in an open former sawmill, mostly enclosed by stacked potato boxes and climbing plants, this ingenious fair-weather restaurant does a roaring trade thanks to its unorthodox set-up and gourmet comfort food. Beefburgers and mushroom burgers are grilled before your eyes on the huge cast-iron barbecue.

Wash them down with local draught ales before visiting their fantastic sister farm shop/deli next door. ££

The Doll's House 3 Church Square ⓦ dollshousestandrews.co.uk. Stylish comfort food based around Scottish meat and fish, with a continental feel to the outdoor tables. There are several nice pies such as steak and ale, fisherman's with smoked haddock or chestnut mushroom bourguignon – as well as lighter options like classic Caesar salad. Great brunch is served from 10am until midday too. £££

THE FIFE COASTAL PATH

Taking in the East Neuk villages, The **Fife Coastal Path** (⨂ fifecoastandcountrysidetrust.co.uk)
follows the shoreline for 117 miles between the Forth and Tay bridges, with useful bus services
covering some sections. To sample Fife's remoter seafront try the five-mile tranche between Crail
and Kingsbarns rounding the headland of Fife Ness. Buses between St Andrews and Crail stop at
Kingsbarns, from where the path is well signposted. Another interesting section is from St Andrews
south to Boarhills, just past the town's golf courses. It's an easy three-mile stretch passing by rocky
bays where you'll see the Rock and Spindle, a twisting volcanic sea stack by the water's edge.

Little Italy 2 Logies Lane ⨂ littleitaly.cc. Ticks every
cliché in the book from the Marlon Brando pictures on the
wall to the gaudy red and green decor, but the food and wine
are reliably great and the atmosphere is always lively. **££**

The Peat Inn 6 miles southwest of St Andrews, on the
junction of the B940 and B941 ⨂ thepeatinn.co.uk. With
a reputation as one of Scotland's gourmet hot spots for the
past thirty years, *The Peat Inn* offers Michelin star-quality
fine dining featuring top local produce in an intimate dining
room. Menus range from a three-course set dinner to a six-
course tasting menu, with dishes like wood pigeon salad or
poached skate wing. **££££**

The Tailend 130 Market St ⨂ thetailend.co.uk. A terrific
and popular restaurant/takeaway dishing up fresh fish
sourced from nearby Arbroath. Treat yourself to the famous
– and now EU-protected – Arbroath Smokie, a pungent
haddock smoked in the traditional way, over hardwood
chips. **££**

DRINKING

SEE MAP PAGE 296

★ **The Criterion** 99 South St ⨂ criterionstandrews.
co.uk. One of the town's more charming pubs; it's a
sensitively preserved Victorian relic – well illuminated by its
lofty windows – with good beers and whiskies and a vibrant
atmosphere, particularly on live music nights. South-facing
in aspect, the pavement tables are a particular draw on
sunny afternoons and, for the peckish, they sell a range of
'Cri pies' throughout the day.

The Rule 116 South St ⨂ craft-pubs.co.uk/the-rule.
A large, modern pub-diner with cheap grub and a strong
focus on noisy sports screenings. The one redeeming feature
here is the generous sun-trapping beer garden to the rear.

8

The East Neuk

Extending south of St Andrews as far as Largo Bay, the **East Neuk** ('neuk' is Scots for
'corner') is famous for its series of quaint fishing villages. Old cottages and merchants'
houses huddle round stone-built harbours in groupings that are fallen upon with joy
by artists and photographers. Their Flemish-influenced crow-stepped gables and red
pantile roofs indicate a history of strong trading links with the Low Countries. Inland,
gently rolling fields provide some of the best farmland in Scotland, with quiet country
lanes more redolent of parts of southern England than north of the border, although,
not surprisingly, the area is dotted with windy **golf courses**.

Well patronized by holiday-makers and weekenders from the central belt, the East Neuk
is particularly regarded for its arts and crafts and good food; the **restaurants** are well known
for serving fresh seafood, often complemented by produce from the fertile Fife farmland.

Crail

CRAIL is the archetypally photogenic East Neuk fishing village, its maze of rough cobbled
streets leading steeply down to a tiny stone-built harbour surrounded by piles of lobster
creels, with fishermen's cottages tucked into every nook and cranny in the cliff. Beyond
the harbour is a sand beach, and above are perched the grander merchants' houses, as
well as the twelfth-century church, where John Knox (see page 69) once delivered a
damning sermon rallying against the local fishermen for working on Sundays.

The village still has a working harbour, and if the boats have been out you can often buy
fresh lobster and crab cooked to order from a small wooden shack right on the harbour edge.

Kingsbarns Distillery

2 miles north of Crail just off the A917 • Daily Nov–Feb 11am–4pm; March & Oct 10am–5pm; April–Sept 10am–6pm • Tours; contact for times • Charge • ⓦ kingsbarnsdistillery.com

Set in a converted farm steading, the **Kingsbarns Distillery** opened for business in 2015 with its first drops of single malt flowing in December 2018. The tour guides proudly show off the beautiful hand-forged copper stills containing the spirit made from locally grown barley and the water pumped up from the aquifer below. The basic, one-hour tour ends, as always, with a whisky tasting; the quality will improve over time as the spirit ages. There are two further tours for those with a deeper interest in whisky and its production. Gin tours are also available at Darnley's Distillery on the Kingsbarns site.

ARRIVAL AND INFORMATION   CRAIL

By bus Stopping on the High St, bus No. 95 runs hourly to St Andrews (25min) and Leven (for bus connection to Edinburgh; 1hr 40mins).

Tourist information Leaflets, maps and information about local attractions can be found in the Crail Museum and Heritage Centre (62–64 Marketgate South; April–May & Oct Sat 11am–4pm, Sun 1.30–4pm; June–Sept Mon–Sat 11am–4pm, Sun 1.30–4pm; ⓦ crailmuseum.uk), which is a free village museum with displays on the village's close ties to the sea, farming and golf, as well as the local contribution to war efforts.

ACCOMMODATION

The Hazelton 29 Marketgate North, ⓦ thehazelton. co.uk. A pleasant and reasonably priced B&B peacefully located just off the High St. Rooms are well proportioned with high ceilings, en-suite shower rooms and a hospitality tray that includes home-made shortbread. ££

The Sauchope Links Park Balcomie Rd, on Crail's eastern fringe ⓦ largoleisureholidays.co.uk. A very pleasant caravan site on the coast with caravans, lodges and more basic beach huts, glamping pods and domes for rent. No tents. There's a grocery shop on site and recreation facilities include a heated outdoor pool (June–Sept) and a games room. Lodges ££££; Huts, glamping domes and pods ££

EATING

With a notable lack of places to sit down and eat, particularly in comparison with what's on offer elsewhere in the East Neuk, the village's businesses cater mostly for day-trippers. It's still possible to enjoy a good cooked lunch, usually involving seafood, but in the evening you'll be restricted to bar meals at one of the hotels.

Crail Harbour Gallery and Tearoom Shoregate ⓦ crailharbourgallery.co.uk. Discreet café/gallery tucked into a cottage on the way down to the harbour, with low timbers, rough stone flooring and a terrace overlooking the Isle of May. Serves fresh coffee and tea, cakes, soups, toasted panini also hot smoked salmon, herring and dressed crab. £

★ **Reilly Shellfish** 34 Shoregate ☎ 01333 450476. The little wooden shack down at the harbour cooks the freshest takeaway lobster you're ever likely to find. Take your pick from the condemned crustaceans scuttling around the tank next to the shack. ££

SHOPPING

Crail Pottery 75 Nethergate, ⓦ crailpottery.com. An unmissable stop for its wide range of stoneware, terracotta pots and painted earthenware, hand-thrown on the wheel in the workshop.

Anstruther and around

The largest of the East Neuk fishing harbours, **ANSTRUTHER** retains an attractively old-fashioned air and no shortage of character in its houses and narrow streets. Life here mostly centres on or around its part-cobbled promenade, which separates the fish and chip shops, cafés and ice creameries of the cheerful Shore Street from the old harbour where small pleasure yachts vie for limited mooring space.

Scottish Fisheries Museum

East Shore, harbour • Daily 10am–4pm • Charge • ⓦ scotfishmuseum.org

Set in an atmospheric complex of sixteenth- to nineteenth-century buildings with timber ceilings and wooden floors, the wonderfully unpretentious **Scottish Fisheries Museum** chronicles the history of the Scottish fishing and whaling industries with ingenious displays, including a whole series of exquisite model ships, built on site by a resident model-maker.

Isle of May
Anstruther Harbour · **Boat trips** April–Sept daily; contact for times; 50min each way; 2hr 30min on island · Charge · ⓦ isleofmayferry.com

Located on the rugged **Isle of May**, several miles offshore from Anstruther, is a lighthouse erected in 1816 by Robert Louis Stevenson's grandfather, as well as the remains of Scotland's first lighthouse, built in 1636, which burnt coals as a beacon. The island is now a nature reserve and bird sanctuary. Between April and July the dramatic sea cliffs are covered with breeding kittiwakes, razorbills, guillemots and shags, while inland there are thousands of puffins and eider ducks. Boat-trippers should bring warm waterproof clothing and a picnic.

Scotland's Secret Bunker
4 miles north of Anstruther on the B940 signposted from the St Andrews road (B9131) · March–Oct daily 10am–5pm · Charge · ⓦ secretbunker.co.uk

Scotland's Secret Bunker is as idiosyncratic a tourist attraction as you are likely to find. Long a top-secret part of the military establishment, the bunker was opened to the public in 1994 following its decommissioning at the end of the Cold War. Above ground is an innocent-looking farmhouse, although the various pieces of military hardware parked outside and the rows of barbed wire fencing hint that something more sinister is afoot. From the farmhouse, you walk down a long ramp to the bunker, which comprises a vast subterranean complex of operations rooms 100ft below ground and encased in 15ft of reinforced concrete. In the event of a nuclear war this was to have become Scotland's new administrative centre, with room for three hundred people; it has not been spruced up for tourists, and remains uncompromisingly spartan, with various rooms showing dormitories, radio rooms and James Bond-like control centres.

8

ARRIVAL AND DEPARTURE ANSTRUTHER AND AROUND

By bus Buses stop at the harbour and serve Edinburgh (1–2 hourly; 2hr 30min) and St Andrews (hourly; 25min).

ACCOMMODATION AND EATING

★ **Anstruther Fish Bar and Restaurant** 42–44 Shore St, ⓦ anstrutherfishbar.co.uk. There's nowhere in Fife better to tuck into a haddock and chips (takeaway or eat-in) than Anstruther. The reputation of this restaurant has for years been far-reaching thanks to a close relationship between the shop and the quayside fish sellers. £
The Waterfront 20 Shore St ⓦ anstruther-waterfront. co.uk. Overlooking the harbour, this restaurant with ten rooms offers modern and spacious en-suite comfort with a cooked breakfast included; only the superior rooms come with a view. The restaurant spills out onto the pavement on balmier days and serves all meals from breakfast to dinner, with cream teas in between. From the wide seafood menu, go for the Fisherman's Pie. £££

Pittenweem and around

Despite its steady tourist influx, the pretty East Neuk village of **PITTENWEEM** thrives, as it always has done, on fishing, thanks to its deep harbour and busy fish market. With its sandy bay west of the port and fishermen's cottages lining the seafront and up into the high street, the village has become something of an artists' colony. An arts festival takes place every year in early August (ⓦ pittenweemartsfestival.co.uk), with dozens of locals turning their houses into temporary galleries for the week.

Kellie Castle
3 miles northwest of Pittenweem on the B9171 · **Castle tours** April–Oct daily; **guided** 11am & 12.15pm; open guiding 1–5pm · Charge · Garden April–Oct daily 10.30am–5pm · Charge · **Estate** year-round dawn–dusk · NTS · ⓦ nts.org.uk

Kellie Castle has an unusual but harmonious mix of twin sixteenth-century towers linked by a seventeenth-century building. Abandoned in the early nineteenth century, it was rediscovered in 1878 by Professor James Lorimer, a distinguished political philosopher, who took on the castle as an 'improving tenant'. The wonderful, under-manicured **gardens**, where space is broken up by arches, alcoves and paths that weave between profuse herbaceous borders, were designed by the professor's son Robert, aged just 16.

ARRIVAL AND DEPARTURE

By bus Buses stop at Viewforth Place (on the main road through town) for Edinburgh (1–2 hourly; 2hr 15min) and St Andrews (2 hourly; 25–30min).

ACCOMMODATION AND EATING

Albert Cottage 15 Viewforth Place ⓦ albertcottagefife. co.uk. Offering the best value for money in town, this welcoming B&B on the main thoroughfare has one en-suite double and one twin room with private bathroom. Guests can also make use of the sitting room and the pleasant rear garden. **££**

West End Bar 30–32 South Loan ⓦ westendbar pittenweem.co.uk. Great draught beers, locally brewed ale, over twenty excellent wines, and a fine selection of whiskies, gins and other spirits. Delicious home-cooked traditional dishes including seafood chowder, beer-battered haddock and chips and Fife steak pie. The pub is dog friendly. **££**

Elie

Gathered round a curve of golden-brown sand twelve miles south of St Andrews, **ELIE** is a popular escape for middle-class Edinburgh families who come for the bracing air and golf courses. This was once a popular bathing spot; east of Elie bay stands a tower built as a summerhouse for Lady Janet Anstruther in the late eighteenth century, with a changing room to allow her to bathe in a pool in the rocks below.

ARRIVAL AND DEPARTURE

By bus Buses stop on the High St for Edinburgh (1–2 hourly; 1hr 55min) and St Andrews (2 hourly; 35–40min).

ACTIVITIES

Elie Watersports Elie Harbour ⓦ eliewatersports. co.uk. Elie's sheltered bay is understandably popular for watersports, and this is the place to come if you fancy a spin on a windsurfer (£25/hr), canoe/kayak (£20), sailing boat (£30), paddle board (£20) or even a fun pedal boat (£12/30min). Bikes too (£15/3hr).

ACCOMMODATION AND EATING

Ship Inn The Toft, by the harbour ⓦ shipinn.scot. The essential (and child-friendly) pub stop in Elie, the *Ship* has low timber ceilings and real fires, while the beer garden to the rear offers sweeping views over the golden sandy bay near the harbour. The meals offered here range from smoked salmon sandwiches to a local Scottish fillet steak. The pub also provides tasteful rooms, the best with views over the bay. **£££**

Central Fife

With its undulating landscape of fertile arable land, **central Fife** has markedly fewer settlements than its coastline and consequently sees less of the region's tourism. Notable exceptions to this are **Hill of Tarvit**, one of the country's finest Edwardian mansion houses, and **Falkland Palace**, a medieval gem in the heart of Scotland's first conservation village. **Falkland** sits at the foot of the twin-peaked, heather-swathed **Lomond Hills** that provide a grandstand view of the region from the easily walked ridge between West Lomond (1696ft) and East Lomond (1378ft).

Falkland

On the eastern margins of the Lomond Hills regional park, ten miles north of Kirkcaldy, the conspicuously handsome small town of **FALKLAND** is a popular day-tripping destination thanks to its grand, medieval palace and narrow streets lined with well-preserved historic buildings.

Falkland Palace

East Port, Falkland • March–Oct daily 11am–5pm • Charge • NTS • ⓦ nts.org.uk

A hunting retreat to the Stewart kings for two hundred years, the construction of **Falkland Palace** began at the behest of James IV in 1500, and was completed and embellished by James V. Charles II stayed here in 1650 when he was in Scotland for his coronation, but after the Jacobite rising of 1715 and temporary occupation by Rob Roy the palace was abandoned, remaining so until the late nineteenth century when the keepership was acquired by the Third Marquess of Bute. He completely restored the palace, and today it is a stunning example of early Renaissance architecture, complete with corbelled parapet, mullioned windows, round towers and massive walls. Inside there's a stately drawing room, a Chapel Royal (still used for Mass) and a Tapestry Gallery, swathed with seventeenth-century Flemish hangings. Outside, the **gardens** have well-stocked herbaceous borders lining a pristine lawn. Look out for the high walls of the oldest real (or royal) tennis court in Britain – built in 1539 for James V and still in use.

ARRIVAL AND DEPARTURE   FALKLAND

By bus Buses stop on New Rd, a few paces east of the palace.

Destinations Glenrothes (Mon–Sat 2 hourly; 15min); Perth (Mon–Sat hourly, 4 on Sun; 1hr)

ACCOMMODATION AND EATING

Covenanter Hotel The Square ⓦ covenanterfalkland. com. This traditional hotel at the heart of the village has a cosy wine bar and a good-value restaurant serving unpretentious food from its all-day menu. The evening a la carte options include roast vegetable lasagne or herb roasted chicken with mash. If you're staying over, the hotel offers wide en-suite rooms, big comfy beds and a full Scottish breakfast. **££**

Hill of Tarvit

Just off the A916, 2 miles south of the A91 at Cupar • **Mansion** April–Oct Sat–Sun 11am–5pm; last entry 1hr before closing • Charge • **Gardens** year-round 9am–6pm or dusk • Charge • NTS • ⓦ nts.org.uk • **Scotstarvit Tower** April–Sept daily 9.30am–5pm; call 01334 653127 to arrange access to the parapet • Free • HES • ⓦ historicenvironment.scot

Remodelled in 1906 by Sir Robert Lorimer from a late seventeenth-century building, **Hill of Tarvit** offers a rare insight into the lives of the wealthy from the turn of the twentieth century, with its central heating, telephones, plumbing and lighting – all state of the art at the time. This Edwardian mansion – formerly the home of the geographer and cartographer Sir John Scott – also contains an impressive collection of eighteenth-century Chippendale and French furniture, Dutch paintings, Chinese porcelain and a restored Edwardian laundry.

Three-quarters of a mile west of the present house and also on the estate, you can visit the five-storey, late sixteenth-century **Scotstarvit Tower**, a fine example of a Scots tower house.

ARRIVAL AND DEPARTURE   HILL OF TARVIT

By bus There are regular daily buses to Cupar from St Andrews and Glenrothes; from there it is three miles to Hill of Tarvit, taxis available in Cupar.

Western Fife

Fife's **south coast** curves sharply north at the mouth of the Firth of Forth, exposing the towns and villages to an icy east wind that somewhat undermines the sunshine image of the beaches. The highlight of the coast is one of the largest man-made structures in Scotland, the impressive **Forth Rail Bridge**, which joins Fife at **North Queensferry**.

East from here you'll find a straggle of Fife fishing communities such as **Aberdour** and **Kinghorn** which have depended on the sea for centuries, and now make popular, although not especially attractive, holiday spots as well as being part of Edinburgh's commuter belt.

To the west of the bridge, the shorefront, blighted by industry and docklands, has one great surprise in the time-capsule village of **Culross**, with links from the sixth century to the dawn of the industrial revolution.

Inland, just north from the bridge, lies **Dunfermline**, Scotland's capital until the Union of the Crowns in 1603. This 'auld, grey toun' is built on a hill, dominated by its abbey and ruined palace at the top.

The Forth Bridges

The cantilevered **Forth Rail Bridge**, built from 1883 to 1890 by Sir John Fowler and Benjamin Baker, ranks among the supreme achievements of Victorian engineering. Some fifty thousand tons of steel were used in the construction of a design that manages to express grace as well as might. Just upriver, the **Forth Road Bridge** is a suspension bridge that strikingly complements the older structure. Erected between 1958 and 1964, it finally killed off a 900-year-old route, and now attracts a heavy volume of traffic. A little further west is the **Queensferry Crossing**, opened in 2017 and the world's longest cable-stayed bridge. For the best **view** of the rail bridge, make use of the pedestrian and cycle lane on the east side of the road bridge. For more on the bridge, head to the museum in South Queensferry (see page 108).

ARRIVAL AND DEPARTURE   THE FORTH BRIDGES

By train: Trains from Edinburgh cross the rail bridge, stopping a short walk from the bridge at North Queensferry (every 10min; 20min).

By car The A90 crosses the road bridge 10 miles west of Edinburgh. Exit the dual carriageway at North Queensferry.

Culross

CULROSS (pronounced 'Coorus'), is the best-preserved seventeenth-century village in Scotland, thanks in large part to the work of the National Trust for Scotland, which has been renovating its palace and whitewashed buildings since 1932. All cobbled streets and squat cottages with crow-stepped gables, as well as crooked passageways with names such as 'Wee Causeway' and 'Stinking Wynd', the royal burgh was first developed in the fifth century with the arrival of St Serf on the northern side of the Forth at Cuileann Ros. By the sixteenth and seventeenth centuries Culross was at the centre of the coal industry and operated the world's first below-sea extractions via an Egyptian wheel system driven by horses. The village's time-warp character brings in plentiful visitors, but its popularity by no means detracts from its charms.

Culross Palace

West Green • Palace & Gardens daily April–Sept 10am–5pm; Oct 10am–4pm; last entry 1hr before closing • Charge • NTS • ⓦ nts.org.uk

The most impressive building in the village, the ochre-coloured **Culross Palace** was built by wealthy coal merchant George Bruce in the late sixteenth century. It is not a true palace at all, but a grand and impressive house with lots of small rooms and connecting passageways. Inside, you follow a fixed route, taking in wonderful painted ceilings, pine panelling, antique furniture and curios, while outside, dormer windows and crow-stepped gables dominate the walled court in which the house stands. The garden is planted with grasses, herbs and vegetables of the period (some on sale), carefully grown from seed, while Dumpy hens roam free.

Culross Abbey

Kirk St, beyond Back Causeway, which is signposted from the main road • Year-round • Free • ⓦ historicenvironment.scot

Founded by Cistercian monks on land given to the Church in 1217 by the earl of Fife, the nave of the original building of **Culross Abbey** is a ruin – a lawn studded with great stumps of columns. The choir of the abbey became the **parish church** in 1633; inside, wooden panels detail the donations given by eighteenth-century worthies to the parish poor, and a tenth-century Celtic cross in the north transept is a reminder of the abbey's origins. Many of the stones in the **graveyard** are eighteenth century, with symbols depicting the occupation of the person who is buried; the gravestone of a gardener has a crossed spade and rake as well as an hourglass with the sand run out.

ARRIVAL AND DEPARTURE
CULROSS

By bus Buses stop outside the palace for Dunfermline (Mon–Sat 1–2 hourly, 2 on Sun; 30min).

EATING AND DRINKING

Red Lion Inn Low Causeway @ redlionculross.co.uk. The only pub in the village and the only place for miles to serve food into the evening. Expect your standard pub menu with lots of meaty choices from sausages to steak pies. If you fancy something lighter, there are a few appealing vegetarian and salad dishes. ££

Dunfermline

The former de facto capital of Scotland and royal seat of power established by Malcolm III in the mid-eleventh century, **DUNFERMLINE** made a significant contribution to medieval Scots politics until it was abandoned by James VI after the 1603 Union of the Crowns. Today, the town's charm has been considerably eroded by twentieth-century development and few visitors venture further than the outstanding ruined abbey and the small old town.

Dunfermline Abbey and Palace
Monastery St • April–Sept daily 9.30am–5.30pm; Oct–March Sat–Wed 10am–4pm • Charge • HES • @ historicenvironment.scot • 10min walk west of Dunfermline train station

Dunfermline Abbey is a monolithic demonstration of stone workmanship from the Middle Ages. The oldest part is attributable to Queen Margaret, who began building a Benedictine priory in 1072 (still visible beneath the nave of the present church). Her son, **David I**, raised the priory to the rank of abbey in the following century. In 1303, during the first of the **Wars of Independence**, most of the monastic buildings were destroyed by Edward I's troops, who occupied the palace and had the church roof stripped of lead to provide ammunition for his army's catapults. **Robert the Bruce** helped rebuild the abbey and when he died was buried here minus his heart, which was sent, unsuccessfully, on a pilgrimage to the Holy Land, only to be buried at Melrose Abbey (see page 120). Inside, the stained glass is impressive, and the thick columns are artfully carved with chevrons, spirals and arrowheads.

The guesthouse of Queen Margaret's Benedictine monastery, south of the abbey, became the **palace** in the sixteenth century under James VI, who gave both it and the abbey to his consort, Queen Anne of Denmark. Charles I, the last monarch to be born in Scotland, entered the world here in 1600. Today, all that is left of the palace is a long sandstone facade, especially impressive when silhouetted against the evening sky.

ARRIVAL AND INFORMATION
DUNFERMLINE

By train Trains stop at Dunfermline's train station, halfway down the long hill of St Margaret's Drive, southeast of the centre, with services to Edinburgh (every 30min; 30min).
By bus The bus station is on Queen Anne St, a block north of High St.
Destinations Culross (Mon–Sat 1–2 hourly, 2 on Sun; 30min); Edinburgh (2 hourly; 1hr).
Tourist information Leaflets and maps are available from many public venues throughout the town including the Dunfermline Carnegie Library and Galleries, an excellent complex with its award-winning building containing a museum and gallery space (see @ onfife.com).

EATING AND DRINKING

★ **Khushi's** 1 Canmore St @ khushis.com/dunfermline. Dunfermline branch of the Edinburgh-based restaurant charged with introducing curry to Scotland back in the 1940s. Today, the family still keep a watchful eye on the quality. All the favourites are on the menu, from chicken tikka to Goan fish curry. ££

8

Perthshire

RANNOCH MOOR

9 Perthshire

Genteel, attractive Perthshire is, in many ways, the epitome of well-groomed rural Scotland. An area of gentle glens, mature woodland, rushing rivers and peaceful lochs, it's the long-established domain of Scotland's well-to-do country set. First settled over eight thousand years ago, it was ruled by the Romans and then the Picts before Celtic missionaries established themselves here, enjoying the amenable climate, fertile soil, and ideal location for defence and trade.

Occupying a strategic position at the mouth of the River Tay, the ancient town of **Perth** has as much claim as Stirling to be the gateway to the Highlands. Salmon, wool and, by the nineteenth century, whisky – Bell's, Dewar's and the Famous Grouse brands all hail from this area – were all exported from here. At nearby **Scone**, Kenneth MacAlpine established the capital of the kingdom of Alba in 846. When this settlement was washed away by floods in 1210, William the Lion founded Perth as a royal burgh, and it stood as Scotland's capital until the mid-fifteenth century.

Rural Perthshire is dominated by the gathering mountains of the Highlands, topography that tolerates little development. There's plenty of good agricultural land, however, and the area is dotted with neat, confident towns and villages like **Crieff**, at the heart of the rolling Strathearn Valley, ancient **Dunkeld**, with its independent cafés and craft shops, and lovely ruined cathedral, and **Aberfeldy**, set deep amid farmland east of Loch Tay. Among the wealth of historical sites in Perthshire are splendid Baronial **Blair Castle**, north of Pitlochry, and the impressive Italianate gardens at **Drummond Castle** near Crieff.

North and west of Perth, **Highland Perthshire** begins to weave its charms: mighty woodlands blend with glassy waterways, most notably the River Tay, overlooked by **Ben Lawers**, the area's tallest peak. Further north, the countryside becomes more sparsely populated and ever more spectacular, and there is some wonderful walking country around **Pitlochry**, **Blair Atholl** and the wild expanses of **Rannoch Moor** to the west.

GETTING AROUND

PERTHSHIRE

By train The Perth to Inverness train line hugs the A9 road. There are also train services connecting Perth with Dundee and, in the south, Stirling.

By bus Direct, long-distance buses link Perthshire with Dundee, Inverness and Aberdeen. Local buses – albeit often infrequent – connect towns like Perth with more remote areas.

By car Perthshire's most useful road is the A9, which cuts a line north from Perth to Inverness, passing Dunkeld and Pitlochry.

Perth and around

Surrounded by fertile agricultural land and beautiful scenery, the market town of **PERTH** was Scotland's capital for several centuries. It has a long history of **livestock trading**, a tradition continued throughout the year, with regular Aberdeen Angus shows and sales from June to September, while its position at the heart of one of Scotland's richest food-production areas encouraged a regular **farmers' market** (see page 314).

Perth's compact **centre** occupies a small patch on the west bank of the River Tay, flanked by two large areas of green parkland, known as the North and South Inch. The main shopping areas are **High Street** and **South Street**, as well as St John's shopping

BLAIR CASTLE

Highlights

❶ The Fergusson Gallery A touch of Antibes in Perthshire: this Perth gallery celebrates the vibrant work of J.D. Fergusson and his dancer wife Margaret Morris. See page 311

❷ Drummond Castle Gardens These terraced gardens near Crieff are a symmetrical marvel, leading into spacious parkland beyond. See page 315

❸ Folk music Join in a session at the bar of *The Taybank* in the gorgeously preserved town of Dunkeld. See page 317

❹ Pitlochry Festival Theatre A gleaming glassy building on the banks of the Tummel

River, home to a long-established repertory company. See page 323

❺ Blair Castle Observe the grand life of the Highland nobility, along with extensive parkland and the country's only private army. See page 323

❻ Schiehallion Scale Perthshire's 'fairy mountain' for the views over lochs, hills, glens and moors. See page 324

❼ Rannoch Moor One of the most inaccessible places in Scotland, where hikers can discover a true sense of remote emptiness. See page 325

HIGHLIGHTS ARE MARKED ON THE MAP ON PAGE 310

9

centre on King Edward Street. Opposite the entrance to the centre is the imposing **City Hall**, used by Scotland's politicians for party conferences. Perth is at its most attractive along **Tay Street**, with a succession of increasingly grand buildings along one side and the attractively landscaped riverside embankment on the other.

Brief history

During the reign of James I, Parliament met in Perth on several occasions, but its glory was short-lived: the king was murdered in the town's Dominican priory in 1437 by Sir Robert Graham, who was captured in the Highlands and tortured to death in Stirling. In May 1559, during the Reformation, John Knox preached a rousing sermon in St John's Kirk, which led to the destruction (by those Knox later condemned as 'the rascal multitude') of the town's four monasteries – an event that quickened the pace of reform in Scotland. Despite decline in the seventeenth century, the community expanded in the eighteenth century and has prospered ever since; today the whisky and insurance trades employ significant numbers.

St John's Kirk

31 St John St • May–Sept daily 10am–4pm; Sunday service 9.30am • Free • ⓦ st-johns-kirk.co.uk

---

OUT AND ABOUT IN PERTHSHIRE

To many, Perthshire means a celebration of the great outdoors, with **activities** from gentle strolls through ancient oak forests to white-knuckle rides down frothing waterfalls. The variety of landscapes and their relative accessibility from the central belt has led to a significant number of operators being based in the area.

Rafting and other water activities Nae Limits, based in Ballinluig, near Pitlochry (ⓦ naelimits. co.uk), runs a varied programme of canyoning, white water rafting, river tubing and cliff-jumping that's sure to satisfy adrenaline junkies. Splash, in Aberfeldy (ⓦ rafting.co.uk), offers rafting sessions on larger craft through the best rapids on the Tay at Grandtully, as well as accredited rafting courses.

Paintballing and quad biking As well as white water rafting, Splash can arrange other activities including paintballing and quad biking.

Safaris In Dull, near Aberfeldy, Highland Safaris (ⓦ highlandsafaris.net) are a good bet if you'd like an introduction to wild Scotland, in which you're taken by four-wheel-drive vehicle to search for golden eagle eyries, stags and pine martens.

Solid and attractive **St John's Kirk**, surrounded by cobbled lanes and cafés, was founded by David I in 1126. The present building dates from the fifteenth century and was restored in 1923–28 to house a war memorial chapel designed by Robert Lorimer. Perth was once known as 'St John's Town', and the local football team takes the name **St Johnstone** rather than that of Perth.

The Fergusson Gallery

Marshall Place • Thurs–Sat & Mon 10am–4.30pm, Sun 10am–4pm • Free • ⓦ culturepk.org.uk/museums-and-galleries/the-fergusson-gallery

On the corner of Tay Street and Marshall Place, the **Fergusson Gallery** is the town's one essential place to visit, located in a striking round Victorian water tower with a cast-iron dome. The gallery is home to an extensive collection of work by **J.D. Fergusson**, the foremost artist of the Scottish Colourist movement (see page 190). Born in Leith, he lived and worked for long periods in France, where he was greatly influenced by Impressionist and post-Impressionist artists. At the beginning of the twentieth century, Fergusson developed a more radical technique to paint some dramatic nudes such as the Matisse-inspired *At My Studio Window*, which mixes elements of an illuminated Celtic manuscript with his confident understanding of the female form. Look out, too, for *Eástre: Hymn to the Sun*, an exotic and radiant brass head inspired by his dancer wife and collaborator Margaret Morris.

Perth Museum and Art Gallery

78 George St • Thurs–Sat & Mon 10am–5pm, Sun 10am–4pm • Free • ⓦ culturepk.org.uk/museums-and-galleries/perth-museum-and-art-gallery

Housed in one of Perth's grandest buildings, the **Museum and Art Gallery** has exhibits on local history, art, natural history, archaeology, glass and whisky, and gives a good overview of local life through the centuries. Among the exhibits is a Pictish cross slab, and there's a display on the discoveries at prehistoric Forteviot, including a rare dagger burial.

Black Watch Castle and Museum

Hay St • Daily April–Oct 9.30am–4.30pm, Nov–March 10am–4pm • Free • ⓦ theblackwatch.co.uk

North of the town centre, just off Hay Street and adjacent to the North Inch, fifteenth-century Balhousie Castle is home to the headquarters of the Black Watch regiment and the **Black Watch Museum**. The Black Watch – whose name refers to the dark colour of

9

their tartan – was the local regiment until it was merged with other Scottish infantry battalions in 2006. The museum chronicles its history, dating back to 1740, through a good display of paintings, uniforms, documents, weapons and photographs.

Scone Palace

2 miles north of Perth on the A93 • Feb, March & Oct Fri–Sun 10am–4pm; April–Sept 9.30am–5pm; last entry 1 hr before closing • Charge • ⓦ scone-palace.co.uk • Take the No. 58 bus from Perth bus station, or bus No. 3 from South St

Almost as well-known as Perth itself is **Scone** (pronounced 'skoon'), one-time home of the Stone of Destiny and the first capital of a united Scotland. **Scone Palace** exudes graceful Scottish country living and there are some pleasant walks in the grounds that surround it. Owned and occupied by the Earl and Countess of Mansfield, whose family has held it for almost four centuries, the two-storey building on the eastern side of the Tay is more a home than a monument: the rooms, although full of antiques and lavish furnishings, feel lived-in and used.

Scone was once the capital of Pictavia, and it was here that Kenneth MacAlpine, first king of a united Scotland, brought the famous Coronation **Stone of Destiny**, or Stone of Scone, which is now to be found in Edinburgh Castle (see page 61). A replica of the (surprisingly small) stone can be found on Moot Hill, immediately opposite the palace. **Moot Hill**, as its name suggests, was the place where Scottish earls came to swear loyalty to their king and discuss

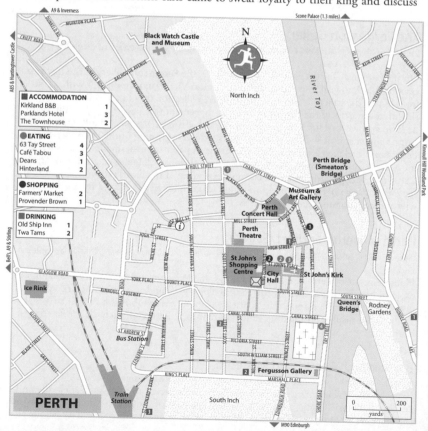

the affairs of state in an early form of national parliament. In a symbolic gesture, oak trees from the estate were used in the construction of Scotland's parliament at Holyrood in Edinburgh.

Inside the palace, the library houses one of the foremost collections of **porcelain** in the world, with items by Meissen, Sèvres, Chelsea, Derby and Worcester.

Huntingtower Castle

3 miles northwest of Perth on the A85 • April–Oct daily 10am–4pm; Nov–March Mon–Wed, Sat & Sun 10am–4pm • Charge • HES • Ⓦ historicenvironment.scot • Catch bus No. 13 from South St to Perth Mart

Nothing like as grand as Scone Palace, but intriguing for its historical connections, is **Huntingtower Castle**. Two three-storey towers formed the original fifteenth- and sixteenth-century tower house, linked in the seventeenth century by a range to provide more room. Formerly known as Ruthven Castle, it was here that the Raid of Ruthven took place in 1582, when the 16-year-old James VI, at the request of William, Fourth Earl of Ruthven, came to the castle only to be held captive by a group of conspirators demanding the dismissal of favoured royal advisers. The plot failed, and the young James was released ten months later. Today the castle's chief attractions are its splendid sixteenth-century painted ceilings in the east tower's main hall.

Stanley Mills

Stanley village, 8 miles north of Perth on the A9 • Daily April–Sept 9.30am–5.30pm; Oct 10am–4pm • Charge • HES • Ⓦ historicenvironment.scot • Catch bus No. 34 from Mill St to Stanley

An unexpectedly grand complex of eighteenth-century red brick and pink sandstone buildings, **Stanley Mills** is dramatically backed by the wide Tay. Built to produce textiles, the complex has partly been converted into housing, but the museum section gives a vivid sense of the sights – and deafening sounds – of the working mill.

ARRIVAL AND DEPARTURE

PERTH AND AROUND

By train Perth connects with the main train lines north from Edinburgh and Glasgow; trains pull in at the station west of the centre, where Kings Place runs into Leonard St.
Destinations Aberdeen (hourly; 1hr 30min–1hr 50min); Blair Atholl (3–8 daily; 40min); Dundee (hourly; 25min); Dunkeld (5–8 daily; 20min); Edinburgh (every 1–2hr; 1hr 20min); Glasgow Queen Street (at least hourly; 1hr); Inverness (7–11 daily; 2hr); Pitlochry (7–11 daily; 30min); Stirling (roughly hourly; 30min).

By bus Perth is well connected by bus; the main bus station is just north of the railway station on the opposite side of Leonard St.
Destinations Aberfeldy (hourly; 1hr 25min); Crieff (hourly; 40min); Dundee (every 30min; 1hr 10min); Dunkeld (hourly; 30min); Edinburgh (hourly; 1hr 40min); Glasgow (hourly; 1hr 35min); Gleneagles (hourly; 25min); Inverness (every 2hr; 2hr 45min); Pitlochry (every 2hr; 45min); Stirling (hourly; 50min).

INFORMATION

Tourist office 45 High St (April–July & Sept–Oct Mon–Sat 9.30am–5pm, Sun 10.30am–3.30pm; Aug Mon–Sat 9.30am–6pm, Sun 10am–4.30pm; Nov–March Mon–Sat 9.30am–4.30pm; Ⓦ perthshire.co.uk).

ACCOMMODATION

SEE MAP PAGE 312

Kirkland B&B Manse Road ☎ 01738 636147, Ⓦ kirklandperth.co.uk. Two spacious and elegant doubles in a handsome Victorian manse building with a large garden. Welcoming, well-located near the centre and spotlessly clean. **££**

Parklands Hotel 2 St Leonards Bank Ⓦ thepark landshotel.com. Of the numerous central hotels in Perth, aim for this award-winning place close to the train station,

which has a touch of contemporary styling with flat-screen TVs and wi-fi in all rooms. It also has a good restaurant and bistro. **££**

★ **The Townhouse** 17 Marshall Place Ⓦ thetown houseperth.co.uk. Enjoying a leafy location on the South Inch Park, this lofty Georgian townhouse offers a pleasant peek at the genteel side of the city. Plush furnishings, all mod cons, home-made biscuits and helpful hosts. **££**

9

EATING

SEE MAP PAGE 213

63 Tay Street 63 Tay St ⊚ 63taystreet.com. At the top end of Perth's dining scene is this classy restaurant, serving modern Scottish food like chicken roulade with haggis, neep and honey mustard pomme puree. The '4 for £24' lunchtime deal is an absolute steal. **£££**

Café Tabou 4 St John's Place ⊚ cafetabou.co.uk. For moderately priced food try this buzzy café, with its menu of French classics (cordon bleu tartiflette) shellfish – and pleasant street-side seating. **£££**

Deans 77–79 Kinnoull St ⊚ letseatperth.co.uk. Serves indulgent dishes like collops of tender beef fillet, in a relaxed and stylish space, with a focus on Scottish ingredients. **£££**

Hinterland 10 St John's Place, ⊚ hinterlandcoffee. co.uk. A great little seasonal and independent café with plate glass windows for watching the world go by. They dish up 'super soup' and thick sandwiches crammed with salmon, topside beef and the like. They roast their own coffee, making this the best place in town for a caffeine fix. **££**

DRINKING

SEE MAP PAGE 312

Old Ship Inn 31 High St ⊚ oldshipinnperth.co.uk. The seventeenth-century *Old Ship Inn* serves real ale and basic pub grub.

Twa Tams 79 Scott St ⊚ thetwatamsperth.com. Has a good beer garden, regular live music (blues, jazz country and rock) and also serves a range of cheap meals.

ENTERTAINMENT

Perth Concert Hall 79 Scott St ⊚ horsecross.co.uk/venues/perth-concert-hall. Modern glassy concert hall, hosting touring orchestras, opera and recitals as well as more mainstream fare.

SHOPPING

SEE MAP PAGE 312

Farmers' Market King Edward St ⊚ perthfarmers market.co.uk. This market takes place on the first Saturday of every month (except Jan), with around forty stalls selling local produce from home-baked cakes to freshly butchered venison.

Provender Brown 23 George St ⊚ provenderbrown. co.uk. Perth's best deli, where you can buy everything from Isle of Mull cheeses and posh Scotch eggs to Scottish craft beers.

Strathearn

STRATHEARN – the valley of the River Earn – stretches west of Perth for some forty miles to **Loch Earn**, a popular water sports spot located just to the north of the Trossachs. The Roman general Agricola was here around two thousand years ago, trying to establish a foothold in the Highlands; later the area was frequented by Bonnie Prince Charlie and Rob Roy, both bound up in the north–south struggle between Highlands and Lowlands. Today, the main settlement in the valley is the well-heeled town of **Crieff**, which, despite its prosperous air, has some hints of the wilder Highland countryside close by, notably around the popular **Glenturret Distillery**.

Blackford

The village of **BLACKFORD**, just west of Gleneagles, is famous for its high-quality spring water. This, coupled with an abundance of locally produced barley, made Blackford the perfect place to brew beer, and in 1488 James IV demanded that ale made from the village's water be served at his coronation. These days the water is bottled and sold under the Highland Spring brand around the UK.

St Serf's

Dunning, 5 miles east of Auchterarder on the B8062 • April–Sept daily 9.30am–5.30pm; Oct–March access by arrangement • Free • ☎ 01764 684497

In the quiet village of Dunning is **St Serf's**, a rugged church with a Norman tower and arch, which houses the magnificent **Dupplin Cross**, reckoned to be the finest surviving carved Pictish stone. Dating from the early ninth century, it was made in honour of Constantine, the first king of the Picts, who also reigned over the Scots of Dalriada (Argyll). The combination of Pictish and Christian imagery – intricately carved Celtic-knot patterns, depictions of animals and warriors – illustrates the developing relationship between king and the Church.

Crieff and around

At the heart of Strathearn sits the old spa town of **CRIEFF**, in a lovely position on a south-facing slope of the Grampian foothills. Cattle drovers used to come to a market, or 'tryst', here in the eighteenth century, but Crieff really came into its own with the arrival of the railway in 1856. Shortly after that, Morrison's Academy, a local private school, took in its first pupils, and in 1868 the grand *Crieff Hydro*, then known as the *Strathearn Hydropathic*, opened its doors to Victorian visitors seeking water-therapy cures. These days, Crieff values its respectability and has an array of fine Edwardian and Victorian houses, with a busy little centre that retains something of the atmosphere of the former spa town.

The Glenturret Distillery

1 mile north of Crieff, just off the A85 to Comrie • April–Oct daily 10am–6pm; Nov–March Tues–Sun 10am–5pm • Charge • ⓦ theglenturret.com • Catch any bus going to Crieff, Comrie or St Fillans and ask the driver to drop you at the bottom of the Glenturret Distillery road, from where it's a 5min walk

From Crieff, it's a short drive or a twenty-minute walk north to the venerable **Glenturret Distillery**. Glenturret is Scotland's **oldest distillery**, established in 1775, and still one of the more attractive, with whitewashed buildings and pagoda roofs situated beside a gurgling stream. As well as the tours and tastings, you can take part in a Whisky Maker's Tour (£100).

Innerpeffray Library

4 miles southeast of Crieff on the B8062 road to Auchterarder • March–Oct Wed–Sat 10am–12.45pm & 2–4.45pm, Sun 2–4pm; Nov–Feb phone for appointment • Charge • ⓦ innerpeffraylibrary.co.uk

Little known but well worth a visit is the delightfully hidden **Innerpeffray Library**, situated in an attractive eighteenth-century building right by the River Earn. Beside an old stone chapel and schoolhouse, this serene and studious public library, founded in 1680, is the oldest in Scotland. It's a must for bibliophiles, its shelves containing some four thousand cloth and leather-bound books, mainly on theological and classical subjects, but also witchcraft and medicine. Among the rare Scottish books, there's a first edition of Samuel Johnson's *Journey to the Western Isles* (1775).

Drummond Castle Gardens

Near Muthill, 2 miles south of Crieff on the A822 • Easter weekend 11am–5pm; May Mon–Fri 1–5pm, Sat & Sun 11am–5pm; June–Sept daily 11am–5pm; Oct daily 11am–4pm; last entry 1hr before closing • Charge • ⓦ drummondcastlegardens.co.uk • Take bus Nos 47 or 18 from Crieff towards Muthill, then walk 1.5 miles up the castle drive

Of all the attractions around Crieff, most impressive are the magnificent **Drummond Castle Gardens**. The approach, up a splendid avenue of beech trees, is pretty enough, but by crossing the courtyard of the castle to the grand terrace you can view the garden in all its symmetrical glory. It was begun as early as 1630 (the date of the tall central sundial), though the design of the French/Italianate parterre is Victorian: it depicts a St Andrew's cross and incorporates other images associated with the Drummonds, including two crowns and the wavy motif found on the family crest. Italian marble statues punctuate the long lines of the cross, and the overall effect is of exceptional harmony and grace. The castle itself is closed to visitors.

9

ARRIVAL AND INFORMATION

By bus Buses from/to Stirling (7 daily; 55min) stop on the high street, near the junction with Hill St.

Tourist office In the town hall on High St (April–June Mon–Sat 10am–4pm, Sun 10.30am–3.30pm; July & Aug Mon–Sat 10am–5pm, Sun 10.30am–3.30pm; Sept–March

Mon–Sat 10.30am–3.30/4pm; ✆ 01764 652578).

Visitor centre At the bottom of the hill, on Muthill Rd (daily 9am–4.30pm; ⓦ crieff.co.uk). Incorporates a garden centre, an exhibition about cattle drovers and the Caithness Glass visitor centre and factory, which you can tour for free.

ACCOMMODATION

★ **Barley Bree** 6 Willoughby St, Muthill ⓦ barleybree. com. The obvious choice if you decide to stay in Muthill, a handsome eighteenth-century village with an ancient church. The rooms are chic and bright, and the French/ Scottish cooking has a well-deserved reputation for quality. $\overline{\underline{££}}$

★ **Comrie Croft** 4 miles west of Crieff, just off the A85 ⓦ comriecroft.com. Largish bunkhouse/activity centre set on a farm halfway between Crieff and Comrie, with its own private fishing loch, mountain-bike rental and a network of paths and walks; you can also camp here in the woodland, either in your own tent or in a Nordic kata, which are sturdy and beautiful tepee-style tents. They have an excellent tea garden serving homemade cakes and a farm shop. Kata (two-night minimum stay) $\overline{\underline{££}}$; Dorms $\overline{\underline{£}}$; doubles $\overline{\underline{££}}$; camping per person $\overline{\underline{£}}$

Crieff Hydro North of the centre near Crieff Golf

Course ⓦ crieffhydro.com. The imposing *Crieff Hydro* is still the grandest place in town, despite the institutional atmosphere. It has good leisure facilities including a pool, spa, zipline, mountain bikes, stables and a golf course. $\overline{\underline{££££}}$

Galvelmore House 5 Galvelmore St ⓦ galvelmore. co.uk. A friendly B&B close to the main drag, with a lovely oak-panelled lounge that has a selection of board games; they have doubles, triples and family rooms. $\overline{\underline{££}}$

★ **Gleneagles Hotel** Just west of Auchterarder, at the southern edge of Strathearn ⓦ gleneagles.com. Iconic Gleneagles is famously home to three championship golf courses and enclosed in more than eight hundred acres of countryside. The resort has welcomed leaders and celebrities from every corner of the globe, and their list of country pursuits includes archery, fishing, riding, wildlife photography and much more. It is, of course, astronomical. $\overline{\underline{££££}}$

EATING AND DRINKING

★ **Andrew Fairlie** Gleneagles Hotel, just west of Auchterarder, at the southern edge of Strathearn ⓦ andrewfairlie.co.uk. If staying the night at the hotel is beyond your means, consider eating at the main restaurant, the refreshingly unstuffy *Andrew Fairlie*, named after the chef who died in 2019. His wonderful legacy lives on courtesy of two Michelin stars and is perhaps the finest restaurant in all of Scotland, with dynamic dishes like roast fillet of brill with seaweed butter, and Borders roe deer with game bon bons and sauce poivrade. Three-course a la carte

menu £115, and a tasting menu £155. $\overline{\underline{££££}}$

★ **Delivino** 6 King St ⓦ delivino.co.uk. Just downhill from the tourist office, this swish Italian café serves antipasti, tapas, good pizzas, coffee and cakes. It also has a small but selective wine list. $\overline{\underline{££}}$

Yann's at Glenearn Glenearn House, Perth Rd ⓦ yannsatglenearnhouse.com. A good bet locally for fine food, with French Alpine dishes (mains £14–22) from Yann's home province served in a bistro-style setting. There are four attractive rooms here too (££). $\overline{\underline{£££}}$

SHOPPING

Crieff Food Co 3 High St, James Square ⓦ thecriefffoodco. co.uk. An outstanding and elegant food hall, piled with fine cheeses, fresh produce, deli goods, fresh fish and more. Their café is also a winner, serving breakfast and lunch as well as scrumptious tarts, eclairs and meringues.

Harrison's Fine Wines 1A Galvelmore St

ⓦ harrisonsfinewines.com. This independent shop stocks everything from Veuve Clicquot to vegan-friendly reds.

Strathearn Gallery 32 West High St ⓦ strathearn-gallery.com. This small commercial gallery on the corner of Galvelmore St regularly hosts exhibitions that include ceramics, jewellery and landscape paintings.

Loch Earn

At the western edge of Strathearn lies **Loch Earn**, a gently lapping Highland loch dramatically edged by rippling mountains. The A85 runs north along the loch shore from the village of **St Fillans**, at the eastern tip, to a slightly larger settlement, **Lochearnhead**, at the western end of the loch, where it meets the A84 linking the Trossachs to Crianlarich (see page 285). The wide tranquil expanse of Loch Earn is popular for **watersports**, particularly engine-based pursuits like water-skiing, powerboating and jet skiing.

ACCOMMODATION AND EATING **LOCH EARN**

Four Seasons Hotel St Fillans, at the eastern end of the loch ⓦ thefourseasonshotel.co.uk. A superb waterside location makes this hotel the area's best place to stay, and there are also half a dozen chalets (sleeping two to four) tucked behind the main building; it's a great place to organize loch-bound activities. The smart Seasons View restaurant does afternoon tea for £19.50 and a menu featuring the likes of Loch Etive trout and Highland Wagyu beef. Chalets **£££**; doubles **££**

Lochearnhead Hotel Lochside, Lochearnhead ⓦ lochearnhead-hotel.com. Cheerful hotel set back from the A85, with ten fresh-feeling en-suite bedrooms, some of which have views over the loch. There's also a bar selling evening meals. **££**

Strath Tay and around

Heading due north from Perth, both the railway and main A9 trunk road carry much of the traffic heading into the Highlands, often speeding straight through some of Perthshire's most attractive countryside in its eagerness to get to the bleaker country to the north. Perthshire has been dubbed 'Big Tree Country' by the tourist board in recognition of some magnificent woodland in the area, including a number of individual trees that rank among Europe's oldest and tallest specimens.

Many of these trees are found around the valley of the River Tay, which flows east towards the sea from attractive Loch Tay and is known as STRATH TAY. The loch is set among the high Breadalbane Mountains which include the striking peak of **Ben Lawers**, Perthshire's highest, and the hills that enclose the long, enchanting **Glen Lyon**. Studded around Loch Tay are the remains of crannogs – ancient dwellings built on man-made islands. Not far downriver is the prosperous small town of **Aberfeldy**; from here the Tay drifts southeast between the unspoilt twin villages of **Dunkeld** and **Birnam** before meandering its way past Perth.

Dunkeld

DUNKELD, twelve miles north of Perth on the A9, was proclaimed Scotland's ecclesiastical capital by Kenneth MacAlpine in 850. Its position at the southern boundary of the Grampian Mountains made it a favoured meeting place for Highland and Lowland cultures, and the town is one of the area's most pleasant communities, with handsome whitewashed houses, appealing arts and crafts shops and a charming cathedral. Dunkeld sits just across the River Tay from its sister village, Birnam. The town is a great starting point for signposted river and forest walks, including a half-hour stroll to the **Hermitage**, a cluster of Georgian follies on the River Braan.

Dunkeld Cathedral

Cathedral St • Daily April–Sept 10am–5.30pm; Oct–March 10am–4pm • Free • ⓦ dunkeldcathedral.org.uk

Dunkeld's partly ruined **cathedral** is on the northern side of town, in an idyllic setting amid lawns and trees on the east bank of the Tay. As early as 570, missionaries from Iona built a wattle monastery here; construction on the current building began in the early twelfth century and continued throughout the next two hundred years, but it was more or less ruined at the time of the Reformation. The present structure consists of the fourteenth-century choir and the fifteenth-century nave; the choir, restored in 1600 (and several times since), now serves as the parish church, while the nave remains roofless apart from the clock tower. Inside, look out for the effigy of the **Wolf of Badenoch**, Robert II's son, who was born in 1343. The Wolf acquired his name and notoriety when, after being excommunicated for leaving his wife, he took his revenge by burning the towns of Forres and Elgin and sacking the latter's cathedral.

By train The nearest train station is in nearby Birnam (see below).

By bus Buses travelling to and from Perth (every 30min; 40min) and Inverness (5 daily; 2hr 30min) stop opposite the *Royal Dunkeld Hotel* on Atholl St, Dunkeld.

ACCOMMODATION, EATING AND DRINKING

The Scottish Deli 1 Atholl St ⓦscottish-deli.com. Fill up on gourmet delights including artisan breads at this well-stocked deli, which, in the evening, morphs into a restaurant-cum-wine bar serving delicious Scottish tapas dishes such as Dunkeld smoked salmon with oatcakes and dill mayonnaise, as well as a selection of cheese and meat boards. ££

★ **The Taybank** Tay Terrace ⓦthetaybankdunkeld. com. A handsome riverside pub with a selection of smartly renovated rooms. It's also a good place to eat, with simple but delicious mains such as sautéed rope-grown Scottish mussels, and there are live music sessions in the convivial bar on Wednesday evenings. A wonderful beer garden too. ££

Birnam

Dunkeld is linked to its sister community, **BIRNAM**, by Thomas Telford's seven-arched bridge of 1809. This little village has a place in history thanks to Shakespeare, for it was on Dunsinane Hill, to the southeast of the village, that Macbeth declared: 'I will not be afraid of death and bane, / Till Birnam Forest come to Dunsinane'. The **Birnam Oak**, a gnarly old character propped up by crutches, which can be seen on the waymarked riverside walk, is inevitably claimed to be a survivor of the infamous mobile forest.

Birnam Arts

Station Rd • Wed–Sun 10am–4pm • Charge • ⓦbirnamarts.com

Just like Shakespeare, children's author Beatrix Potter drew inspiration from the Birnam area, recalling her childhood holidays here when penning the Peter Rabbit stories. A Potter-themed exhibition and garden can be found in the impressive **Birnam Arts**, a lively theatre, café and arts and community centre.

ARRIVAL AND DEPARTURE   **BIRNAM**

By train The Dunkeld and Birnam train station, just south of the A9 in Birnam, is a stop on services to Inverness (8 daily; 1hr 50min) and Perth (10 daily; 20min).

By bus Direct bus services to Inverness (5 daily; 2hr 30min) and Perth (every 30min; 40min) leave from opposite the *Birnam Hotel* on Perth Rd.

ACCOMMODATION

The Merryburn Hotel Station Rd ⓦmerryburn.co.uk. This old ironmonger's shop, whose many original Victorian features are still intact, has been converted into a small and inviting guesthouse, just across from Birnam Arts. Its five beautifully appointed rooms are complemented by a warming lounge bar. ££

Aberfeldy and around

From Dunkeld the A9 runs north alongside the Tay for eight miles to Ballinluig, a tiny village marking the turn-off along the A827 to **ABERFELDY**, a prosperous settlement of large stone houses that acts as a service centre for the wider Loch Tay area. Aberfeldy sits at the point where the Urlar Burn – lined by the silver birch trees celebrated by Robert Burns in his poem '*The Birks of Aberfeldy*' – flows into the River Tay.

Wade's Bridge

In Aberfeldy the Tay is spanned by the humpbacked, four-arch **Wade's Bridge**, built by General Wade in 1733 during his efforts to control the unrest in the Highlands, and one of the general's more impressive pieces of work. Overlooking the bridge from the south end is the **Black Watch Monument**, depicting a pensive, kilted soldier; it was erected in 1887 to commemorate the first muster of the Highland regiment gathered as a peacekeeping force by Wade in 1740.

Dewar's World of Whisky

Half a mile east of Aberfeldy, just off the A827 • April–Oct Mon–Sat 10am–6pm, Sun noon–4pm; Nov–March Mon–Sat 10am–4pm • Tours and tastings • Charge • ⓦ dewars.com/gl/en/aberfeldydistillery

The main set-piece attraction in Aberfeldy is **Dewar's World of Whisky**, at the Aberfeldy Distillery, which puts on an impressive show of describing the process of making whisky. A **Connoisseur Tour** is available for real aficionados, giving a more in-depth look around the distillery and a chance to taste (or 'nose') the whisky at different stages in its life. Tour tickets also include entry to the Heritage Museum, which relays the history of the Dewar family and the distillery, which began production in 1898.

Castle Menzies

1 mile west of Aberfeldy, across Wade's Bridge • Easter to late Oct Mon–Sat 10.30am–4.30pm, Sun 2–4.30pm • Charge • ⓦ castlemenzies.org

A mile west of Aberfeldy, **Castle Menzies** is an imposing, Z-shaped, sixteenth-century tower house, which until the middle of the last century was the chief seat of the Clan Menzies (pronounced 'Ming-iss'). With the demise of the family line, the castle was taken over by the Menzies Clan Society, which since 1971 has been involved in the ongoing process of restoring the building. Today, much of the interior is on view and most of it is refreshingly free of fixtures and fittings, displaying an austerity that is much truer to medieval life than the more ostentatiously opulent castles that you will find elsewhere in the country.

ARRIVAL AND INFORMATION

ABERFELDY

By bus Buses stop on Chapel St in Aberfeldy, near the junction with Dunkeld St (the A827), with regular services to Perth (up to 12 daily; 1hr 25min).

Tourist information There's a small info hub in The Locus Centre on the Square in the town centre (Mon–Fri 10am–2pm; ⓦ visitaberfeldy.co.uk), which has some good for advice on local accommodation and details of nearby walking trails.

ACTIVITIES

Land Rover trips A couple of miles west of Castle Menzies, near the hamlet with the unfortunate name of Dull (twinned with Boring, Oregon, USA), off the B846, Highland Safaris (ⓦ highlandsafaris.net) arranges Land Rover trips into the heather-clad hills nearby in search of eagles, red deer and grouse. Safaris range from a ninety-minute Forest Safari (£35) to a two and a half-hour Mountain Safari Trek (£47), while you can learn more about, and feed, red deer in the paddock at the Red Deer Centre by reception. At the lodge you can try your hand at gold and mineral panning (from £5).

Outdoor activities and bike rental Beyond Adventure (ⓦ beyondadventure.co.uk), located on the riverside just east of Aberfeldy, offers kayaking, rafting, gorge walking and other activities, plus bike rental (£35/day).

ACCOMMODATION

Balnearn Guest House Crieff Rd ⓦ balnearnhouse.co.uk. Stylish and unpretentious rooms close to the middle of town, with the added bonuses of a drying room for your outdoor gear, a guest lounge with log fire and homemade crepes for breakfast. ££

The Bunkhouse Glassie Farm, 3 miles from Aberfeldy along the winding track that starts near the footbridge ⓦ thebunkhouse.co.uk. The closest bunkhouse to Aberfeldy has two houses – one with four rooms sleeping twenty and another with three rooms sleeping fourteen – plus two self-catering kitchens and a communal area with magnificent views over the town. Dorms £

EATING AND DRINKING

Ailean Chraggan Across Wade's Bridge in Weem ⓦ chraggs.co.uk. The long, regularly updated lunch and dinner menu at this hotel-restaurant includes the likes of venison haunch with black pudding and dark chocolate and raspberry jus, as well as plenty of fishy mains. £££

★ **The Watermill** Mill St ⓦ aberfeldywatermill.com.

9

Aberfeldy isn't short on cafés, but the best bet for a good cup of coffee, a bowl of lunchtime soup or afternoon tea is this relaxed, superbly restored early nineteenth-century mill, with a pretty riverside garden. There's also an inspiring bookshop, gallery and crafts for sale. £

Loch Tay and around

Aberfeldy grew up around a crossing point on the River Tay, which leaves it six miles adrift of **Loch Tay**, a fourteen-mile-long stretch of fresh water connecting the western and eastern Highlands. Rising steeply above the loch's northern edge is Ben Lawers, the tenth-highest peak in Scotland, whose mineral-rich slopes support plant life more commonly seen in the Alps or Arctic.

Scottish Crannog Centre

Around half a mile from Kenmore, along the southern shore of the loch • April–Oct daily 10am–5.30pm • Charge • ⟨w⟩ crannog.co.uk

The main attraction around Loch Tay is the **Scottish Crannog Centre**, albeit one that has suffered a recent disaster. In June 2021, a fire (cause unknown) completely destroyed what had been a superbly reconstructed crannog in the loch, which was reached by a long wooden gangway – this thatched wooden dwelling had been furnished with sheepskin rugs, wooden bowls and other evidence to show how life was lived 2,500 years ago. Crannogs are Iron Age loch dwellings built on stilts over the water, with a gangway to the shore that could be lifted up to defy a hostile intruder, whether animal or human. Plans are now afoot to reconstruct three crannogs in the water on the opposite side of the loch, alongside a replica Iron Age village. In the meantime, you can try a range of activities, from spinning yarn to making flour and starting fires.

Glen Lyon

North of Loch Tay, the mountains tumble down into **Glen Lyon** – at 34 miles long, the longest enclosed glen in Scotland – where, legend has it, the Celtic warrior Fingal built twelve castles. The narrow single-track road through the glen starts at **Keltneyburn**, near Kenmore, at the northern end of the loch, although a road does struggle over the hills to **Bridge of Balgie**, halfway down the glen. Either way, it's a long, winding journey.

Fortingall

A few miles on from Keltneyburn, the village of **FORTINGALL** is little more than a handful of pretty thatched cottages, though locals make much of their 5000-year-old yew tree – believed (by them at least) to be the oldest living thing in Europe. The venerable tree can be found in the churchyard, with a timeline nearby listing some of the events the yew has lived through. One of these, bizarrely, is the birth of Pontius Pilate, reputedly the son of a Roman officer stationed near Fortingall.

Ben Lawers

Dominating the northern side of Loch Tay is moody **Ben Lawers** (3984ft), Perthshire's highest mountain; from the top there are incredible views towards both the Atlantic and the North Sea. The ascent – which shouldn't be tackled unless you're properly equipped for Scottish hillwalking – takes around three hours from the NTS car park, which you can reach by following a winding, hilly road off the A827.

Killin

The mountains of **Breadalbane** (pronounced 'bred-albin', from the Gaelic braghaid Albin meaning 'high country of Scotland') loom over the southern end of Loch Tay. Glens Lochay and Dochart curve north and south respectively from the small town of **Killin**, right in the centre of which the River Dochart comes rushing down over the frothy **Falls of Dochart** before disgorging into Loch Tay. A short distance west of Killin the A827 meets the A85, linking the Trossachs with Crianlarich (see page 285), an important waypoint on the roads to Oban, Fort William and the west coast.

There's little to do in Killin itself, but it makes a convenient base for some of the area's best walks.

INFORMATION AND ACTIVITIES
KILLIN

Tourist office On the ground floor of the old watermill by the falls (April–Oct daily 10am–4pm; ☎ 01567 820527).
Outdoor activities The helpful and enthusiastic Killin Outdoor Centre and Mountain Shop on Main St (April–Oct daily 8.45am–5.45pm; ⓦ killinoutdoor.co.uk) rents out mountain bikes, canoes and kayaks.

ACCOMMODATION AND EATING

The House at Bridge of Lochay Aberfeldy Rd ⓦ bridgeoflochay.co.uk. Traditional old whitewashed inn serving above-average food including steak and ale pies and venison steak. The twelve rooms are modern with a tweedy twist. **££**

The Old Smiddy Main St ☎ 01567 820619, ⓦ theoldsmiddykillin.co.uk. Offers three neat B&B rooms near the centre of the town, two of which have views of the river. The bistro-style café downstairs is a popular spot for cakes and ice creams. **£**

Highland Perthshire

North of the Tay Valley, **Highland Perthshire** doesn't discard its lush richness immediately, but there are clear indications of the more rugged, barren influences of the Highlands proper here. The principal settlements of **Pitlochry** and **Blair Atholl**, both just off the A9, are separated by the narrow gorge of Killiecrankie. Though there are reasons to stop in both places, inevitably the greater rewards are to be found further afield, most notably in the winding westward road along the shores of **Loch Tummel** and **Loch Rannoch** past the distinctive peak of **Schiehallion**, which eventually leads to the remote wilderness of **Rannoch Moor**.

Pitlochry

PITLOCHRY is undoubtedly a useful place to find somewhere to stay or eat en route to or from the Highlands. However, there's little charm to be found on its main street, with its crawling traffic and endless shops selling cut-price woollens and knobbly walking sticks to tourists, who use the town as a starting point for scenic hikes (see page 322). Far more appealing is the area south of the river, which is home to a renowned theatre and a serene botanical garden.

Edradour Distillery
2.5 miles east of Pitlochry on the A924 • Mid-April to Oct Mon–Sat 10am–5pm • Charge • ⓦ edradour.com

The **Edradour Distillery** – Scotland's smallest – has an idyllic position, tucked into the hills east of Pitlochry. Although the tour of the distillery itself isn't out of the ordinary, the lack of industrialization and the fact that the whole traditional process is done on site give Edradour more personality than many of its rivals.

Explorers: the Scottish Plant Hunters' Garden
Across the river from the town centre, near the theatre • April–Oct daily 10am–5pm • Charge• ⓦ explorersgarden.com

If you want to escape the bustle of Pitlochry's main drag, it's worth having a wander around **Explorers: the Scottish Plant Hunters' Garden**, a garden and forest area that pays tribute to Scottish botanists and collectors who roamed the world in the eighteenth and nineteenth centuries in search of new plant species. An open-air amphitheatre in the grounds is sometimes used for outdoor performances.

9

WALKS AROUND PITLOCHRY

BEN VRACKIE

Pitlochry is surrounded by good walking country. The biggest lure has to be **Ben Vrackie** (2733ft; OS Explorer map 386), which provides a stunning backdrop for the town, and deserves better than a straight up-and-down walk. However, the climb should only be attempted in settled weather conditions and if you're properly prepared.

The direct route up the hill follows the course of the Moulin burn past the inn of the same name. Alternatively, a longer but much more rewarding circular route heads northwest out of Pitlochry, along the edge of Loch Faskally, then up the River Garry to go through the **Pass of Killiecrankie**. This is looked after by the NTS, which has a visitor centre (see page 322) providing background on the famous battle here. From the NTS centre follow the route past Old Faskally to meet the main track at Loch a'Choire. Alternatively, you can turn back here and loop around Loch Faskally instead.

BLACK SPOUT

A lovely short hill walk from the south end of Pitlochry follows a path through oak forests along the banks of the **Black Spout** burn; when you emerge from the woods it's just a few hundred yards further uphill to the lovely Edradour Distillery (see page 321).

Pitlochry Power Station and Dam

Armoury Rd · Visitor Centre daily 9.30am–4pm · Free · ⓦ pitlochrydam.com

A short stroll upstream to the west of the theatre is the **Pitlochry Power Station and Dam**, a massive concrete wall that harnesses the water of artificial Loch Faskally, just north of the town, for hydroelectric power. Near the base of the dam there's a small observation cabin where you can take a peek at the underwater workings of Pitlochry's **salmon ladder**, a staircase of murky glass boxes through which you might see some nonplussed fish making their way upstream past the dam. An electronic counter shows how many of them have successfully completed the climb. You can learn more about the workings of the dam – one of nine built in the 1940s and 1950s as part of the Tummel Valley Scheme – and the lifecycle of the salmon, in the excellent **visitor centre**, which also possesses a smart little café.

With parking available at the theatre, nearby, the dam makes a good starting point for a complete loop of the loch (around nine miles to the Pass of Killiecrankie and back).

ARRIVAL AND DEPARTURE
PITLOCHRY

By train Pitlochry is on the main train line to Inverness (every 1–2hr; 1hr 35min); trains stop at Perth en route (30min).

By bus Buses from/to Perth (every 1–2hr; 40min) and Inverness (7 daily; 2hr 10min) stop near the train station.

INFORMATION AND ACTIVITIES

Tourist office 22 Atholl Rd (April–June & Sept–Oct Mon–Sat 9.30am–5.30pm, Sun 10am–4pm; July & Aug Mon–Sat 9.30am–6.30pm, Sun 9.30am–5.30pm; Nov–March Mon–Sat 10am–4pm; ☎ 01796 472215). Can sell you a guide to walks in the surrounding area and also offers an accommodation booking service.

Bike rental For bike rental (£24/day), advice on local cycling routes, as well as general outdoor gear, try Escape Route, 3 Atholl Rd (daily 9am–5.30pm; ⓦ escape-route. co.uk).

ACCOMMODATION

★ **Craigatin House and Courtyard** 165 Atholl Rd ⓦ craigatinhouse.co.uk. On the northern section of the main road through town, this is an attractive, contemporary B&B with large beds, soothing decor, superb breakfasts and a pretty garden. ££

Fonab Castle Hotel Foss Rd, south of the river

ⓦfonabcastlehotel.com. Once the headquarters of a power company, this turreted, waterside landmark has now been transformed into a luxury hotel with a spa and panoramic fine-dining restaurant. The interiors, with sparkly Swarovski wall coverings, may be a little bling for some tastes. **££££**

Moulin Hotel 11 Kirkmichael Rd, Moulin, on the outskirts of Pitlochry ⓦmoulinhotel.co.uk. Pleasant old travellers' inn with fifteen rooms swathed in different coloured tartan, including some with four-poster beds; there's also a great bar and restaurant (see below). **££**

Pitlochry Backpackers Hotel 134 Atholl Rd ⓦpitlochrybackpackershotel.com. Right in the centre of town, this hostel is based in a former hotel, and offers dorms, twin and double rooms, self-catering kitchen and a communal lounge; bike storage and drying room too. Breakfast costs extra. Dorms **£**; twin **££**

EATING AND DRINKING

Escape Route Café 3a Atholl Rd ⓦescape-route.co.uk. Super-popular café in a bike shop, dishing up fried breakfasts, toasties, soups, sandwiches and outstanding carrot cake in a snug wood-lined interior. The Fairtrade coffee is excellent. **£**

Moulin Inn 11 Kirkmichael Rd, Moulin, on the outskirts of Pitlochry ⓦmoulinhotel.co.uk. Joined to the hotel of the same name, this restaurant serves kitsch pub grub such as venison Braveheart in a cosy, country setting at the foot of Ben Vrackie; its beers, meanwhile, are brewed just a few paces away in its own brewery. **££**

ENTERTAINMENT

Pitlochry Festival Theatre Port na Craig, south side of the river ⓦpitlochryfestivaltheatre.com. On the southern edge of Pitlochry, just across the river, lies Scotland's renowned 'Theatre in the Hills'. A variety of productions – mostly mainstream theatre from the resident repertoire company, along with regular music events – are staged in the summer season and on ad hoc dates the rest of the year.

Blair Atholl

Three miles north of Killiecrankie, the village of **BLAIR ATHOLL** is a much quieter and more idiosyncratic stop than Pitlochry. Extravagant Blair Castle makes the place understandably popular with day-trippers, but if you decide to stick around there are plenty of walks and bike rides to enjoy in the surrounding countryside.

Blair Castle

Just off the B8079, midway between the train station and the bridge over the River Tilt • Easter–Oct daily 9.30am–5.30pm; last entry 1hr before closing; Nov–March occasional weekends only (see website for details) • Charge • ⓦblair-castle.co.uk

Seat of the Atholl dukedom, whitewashed, turreted **Blair Castle**, surrounded by parkland and dating from 1269, presents an impressive sight as you approach it up the drive. On a self-guided tour, you get to see thirty or so rooms displaying a selection of paintings, tapestries, antique furniture and plasterwork that is sumptuous in the extreme. It begins inside the soaring **entrance hall**, with every spare inch of wood panelling covered in targes (shields) and muskets. There are some lesser heralded gems here too, such as an exquisite collection of items hewn from bone made by French POWs at Edinburgh Castle, and several items belonging to Queen Victoria, among them a mourning pendant for Prince Albert and a wreath of oak leaves she wore during a three-week stay at the castle in 1844. The tour ends inside the vast **ballroom**, with its timber roof, antlers and mixture of portraits.

On the hour, a piper, one of the Atholl Highlanders, plays in front of the castle; this select group was retained by the duke as his private army – a unique privilege afforded to him by Queen Victoria, who stayed here in 1844.

Blair Atholl Watermill

Ford Rd • May–Oct Wed–Mon 9.30am–3.30pm; milling takes place Wed–Fri • Free • ⓦblairathollwatermill.co.uk

Close to the River Tilt is Blair Atholl's **Watermill**, which dates back to the 1590s. During the summertime you can wander around and witness the mill in action. Better still is a trip to the pleasant timber-beamed tearoom (see below), where you can enjoy home-baked scones and light lunches (many items are made with the mill's own flour).

Atholl Estates Information Centre Close to the bridge over the River Tilt, a 5min walk east of the train station (April–Oct daily 9am–4.45pm; ⓦatholl-estates.co.uk). Modern ranger station, where you can get details of the extensive network of local walks and bike rides, as well as information on surrounding flora and fauna.

ACCOMMODATION AND EATING

Atholl Arms Hotel On the main road, near the train station ⓦathollarms.co.uk. Grand but reasonably priced hotel with, predictably, lots of tartan amidst its thirty or so tastefully decorated rooms, some of which are pet-friendly. It's also the best place in town for a drink or a bar meal; the Atholl Highlander meat platter costs £14.95. <u>£££</u>

★ **Blair Atholl Watermill** Ford Rd ⓦblairathollwatermill.co.uk. Blair Atholl's top spot for tea, tray bakes, toasties and bagels in a charming (and still functioning) old watermill. <u>£</u>

Blair Castle Caravan Park In the grounds of Blair Castle ⓦblair-castle.co.uk. Busy but attractive campsite with laundry facilities, a games room and a shop selling the estate's own sausages; guests receive a discount to visit the castle. Two-night minimum stay July & Aug. Per pitch <u>£</u>

Loch Tummel

West of Pitlochry, the B8019/B846 makes a memorably scenic, if tortuous, traverse of the shores of **Loch Tummel** and then Loch Rannoch. These two lochs and their adjoining rivers were much changed by the massive hydroelectric schemes built in the 1940s and 1950s, yet this is still a spectacular stretch of countryside and one that deserves leisurely exploration. **Queen's View** at the eastern end of Loch Tummel is an obvious vantage point, looking down the loch to the misty peak of **Schiehallion**; the name comes from the Gaelic meaning 'Fairy Mountain'.

Schiehallion

Rising cone-like to a peak of 3553ft, **Schiehallion** is a popular, fairly easy and inspiring mountain to climb (3–4hr round trip), with views on a good day to the massed ranks of Highland peaks. The path starts up at Braes of Foss, just off the B846 that links Aberfeldy with Kinloch Rannoch. You'll get a good view of the mountain from the cosy *Loch Tummel Inn*, about halfway along Loch Tummel.

Loch Rannoch and around

Beyond Loch Tummel, marking the eastern end of **Loch Rannoch**, the small community of **Kinloch Rannoch** doesn't see a lot of passing trade – fishermen and hillwalkers are the most common visitors. Otherwise, the only real destination here is Rannoch railway station, a lonely outpost on the Glasgow–Fort William West Highland train line, sixteen miles further on: the road goes no further. Here you can contemplate the bleakness of **Rannoch Moor**, a wide expanse of bog, heather and wind-blown pine trees that stretches right across to the imposing entrance of Glen Coe (see page 388).

ARRIVAL AND DEPARTURE

LOCH RANNOCH AND AROUND

By train The West Highland Railway stops at Rannoch and, a little to the north, Corrour station, which has no road access at all.

Destinations (from Rannoch station) Corrour (3–4 daily; 12min); Fort William (3–4 daily; 1hr); Glasgow Queen Street (3–4 daily; 2hr 50min); London Euston (sleeper service Mon–Fri & Sun daily; 11hr–12hr 40min).

By bus A local bus service (Broons Bus No. 85) from Kinloch Rannoch provides connections with Rannoch railway station, sixteen miles to the west (up to 4 daily; 40min).

ACCOMMODATION AND EATING

LOCH RANNOCH

Loch Rannoch Hotel Half a mile west of Kinloch Rannoch along the B846 ⓦlochrannochhotel.com. Newly owned and freshly refurbished, this large, lochside hotel has supremely accomplished rooms, furnished in either traditional or contemporary fashion; the views from

RANNOCH MOOR

Rannoch Moor occupies roughly 150 square miles of uninhabited and uninhabitable peat bogs, lochs, heather hillocks, strewn lumps of granite and gnarled Caledonian pines, all of it over one thousand feet above sea level. Perhaps the most striking thing about the moor is its inaccessibility: one road, between Crianlarich and Glen Coe, skirts its western side, while another struggles west from Pitlochry to reach its eastern edge at Rannoch train station. The only regular form of transport here is the **West Highland Railway**, which stops at **Rannoch** and, a little to the north, Corrour, which has no road access at all – though it does have a great café (see below). **Corrour** stole an unlikely scene in the film *Trainspotting* when the four central characters headed here for a taste of the great outdoors; a wooden SYHA hostel is located a mile away on the shores of **Loch Ossian** and is only accessible on foot, making the area a great place for hikers seeking somewhere genuinely off the beaten track. From Rannoch train station, beside which is the isolated *Moor of Rannoch* hotel, it's possible to catch the train to Corrour and walk the nine miles back; it's a longer slog west to the eastern end of Glen Coe, the dramatic peaks of which poke up above the moor's western horizon. Determined hillwalkers will find a clutch of Munros around Corrour, including remote Ben Alder (3765ft), high above the forbidding shores of Loch Ericht.

most are fabulous. Guests have access to a leisure complex with an indoor pool, spa and gym. £££

RANNOCH MOOR

★ **Corrour Station House** Corrour Station ⓦ corrour. co.uk. Fantastically remote restaurant with rooms, only reachable by train or on a 20-mile hike. Soups, sandwiches and fine home baking, plus venison burgers, fish and chips and the like for dinner. £££

★ **Moor of Rannoch Hotel** Rannoch Station ⓦ moorofrannoch.co.uk. If it's isolation you want, this is the place to stay; there's no internet access, radio or TV but instead open fires, board games and a big whisky selection. The five comfy en-suite rooms look out over the boggy moorland. Off-road bikes to rent (£18). ££££

LOCH OSSIAN

Loch Ossian Youth Hostel A 1-mile walk northeast from Corrour's train station, on the shores of Loch Ossian ⓦ hostellingscotland.org.uk. Only accessible on foot, this is an excellent option for hikers seeking somewhere genuinely off the beaten track. There's a wood-lined self-catering kitchen for making basic meals, but no fridge. Dorms £

Northeast Scotland

PENNAN, ABERDEENSHIRE

Northeast Scotland

A large triangle of land thrusting into the North Sea, northeast Scotland consists of the area east of a line drawn roughly from Perth north to the fringe of the Moray Firth at Forres. The region takes in the county of Angus and the city of Dundee to the south and, beyond the Grampian Mountains, the counties of Aberdeenshire and Moray, and the city of Aberdeen. Geographically diverse, the south of the region is comprised predominantly of undulating farmland. However, as you travel further north this gives way to wooded glens, mountains and increasingly rugged terrain, fringed by a dramatic coastline of high cliffs and long sandy beaches.

10

The long-depressed city of **Dundee** is valiantly trying to shed its post-industrial image with a reinvigorated cultural scene and an impressive waterfront development based around **Discovery**, the ship of Captain Scott ('of the Antarctic') and a new outpost of the V&A. A little way up the Angus coast are the historically important towns of **Arbroath** and **Montrose**, which are linked by an especially inviting stretch of coastline, featuring scarlet cliffs and sweeping bays. Further south towards Dundee, these are replaced by gentler dunes and long sandy beaches, while inland the long fingers of the **Angus glens** – heather-covered hills tumbling down to rushing rivers – are overlooked by the southern peaks of the Grampian Mountains. **Glen Clova** is one of the most popular, along with **Glen Shee**, which attracts many visitors to its ski slopes. Handsome if uneventful market towns such as **Brechin**, **Kirriemuir** and **Blairgowrie** are good bases for touring the area, and extravagant **Glamis Castle** is well worth a visit.

The northeast was the southern kingdom of the **Picts**, reminders of whom are scattered throughout the region in the form of beautifully carved stones found in fields, churchyards and museums, such as the one at **Meigle**. Remote, self-contained and cut off from the centres of major power in the south, the area never grew particularly prosperous, and a handful of feuding and intermarrying families grew to wield a disproportionate influence, building many of the region's **castles** and religious buildings, and developing and planning its towns.

Aberdeenshire and **Moray** cover a large chunk of the northeast, some 3500 square miles, much of it open and varied country dotted with historic and archeological sites, from eerie prehistoric rings of standing stones to quiet kirkyards and a rash of dramatic castles. Geographically, the counties break down into two distinct areas: the **hinterland**, once barren and now a patchwork of fertile farms, rising towards high mountains, sparkling rivers and gentle valleys; and the **coast**, a classic stretch of rocky cliffs, remote fishing villages and long, sandy beaches.

Many of the most appealing settlements in these counties are along the coast, but while the fishing industry is but a fondly held memory in many parts, a number of the northeast's ports were transformed by the discovery of **oil** in the North Sea in the 1960s – particularly **Aberdeen**, Scotland's third-largest city. It's the region's obvious focal point, with bold architecture, attractive museums and a lively social scene, and continues to ride a diminishing wave of oil-based prosperity. The city's transport connections make it an undeniably handy base; there's an international **airport**, and **trains** connect the centre with Inverness and major points further south.

From Aberdeen, it's a short hop west to **Deeside**, a fertile yet ruggedly attractive area made famous by the royal family, who have favoured the estate at **Balmoral** as a summer holiday retreat ever since Queen Victoria fell in love with it back in the 1840s. Close by, the villages of **Ballater** and **Braemar** act as a gateway to the spectacular mountain scenery of the **Cairngorms National Park**. To the north lies the meandering

DUNNOTTAR CASTLE

Highlights

1 V&A Dundee Scotland's first design museum, this northern outpost of the Victoria & Albert is housed in a striking ship-like contemporary building. See page 334

2 Arbroath smokies A true Scottish delicacy: succulent haddock best eaten when it's still warm from the oak smoker. See page 338

3 Pictish stones Fascinating carved relics of a lost culture, standing alone in fields or protected from the elements in museums such as that at Meigle. See page 339

4 Aberdeen This northeastern city features a gorgeous cityscape carved out of granite, and a dramatic harbour. See page 349

5 Dunnottar Castle Scotland's moodiest clifftop ruin, with centuries of bloody tales to tell and views across the swirling North Sea. See page 359

6 Pennan and Gardenstown Tiny one-street fishing villages on the Aberdeenshire coast: there's no room for any more between the cliff and the sea. See page 367

7 Findhorn This intentional community by the sea has been spreading a gentle message about communality and eco living since the 1950s, and warmly welcomes visitors. See page 372

HIGHLIGHTS ARE MARKED ON THE MAP ON PAGE 330

NORTHEAST SCOTLAND

HIGHLIGHTS
1. V&A Dundee
2. Arbroath smokies
3. Pictish stones
4. Aberdeen
5. Dunnottar Castle
6. Pennan and Gardenstown
7. Findhorn

Orkney & Shetland

N O R T H   S E A

Don Valley, a quiet area notable for **castles** such as Kildrummy and Corgarff, both of which are appealingly remote. Further north still, the dramatic **coastline** is punctuated by picturesque fishing villages, and there is a handful of engaging sights including **Duff House**, an outpost of the National Galleries of Scotland, and the New Age community at **Findhorn**.

GETTING AROUND

10

By train Trains from Edinburgh and Glasgow connect with Dundee, Aberdeen and other coastal towns, while an inland line from Aberdeen heads northwest to Elgin and on to Inverness.

By bus The region has a reasonably comprehensive scheduled bus service; only in the most remote and

mountainous parts does public transport disappear altogether.

By car Northeast Scotland is well served by an extensive road network, with fast links between Dundee and Aberdeen, while the area north and west of Aberdeen is also dissected by a series of efficient routes.

Dundee

At first sight, **DUNDEE** can seem a grim place. In the nineteenth century, it was Britain's main processor of jute, the world's most important vegetable fibre after cotton, which earned the city the tag 'Juteopolis'. The decline of manufacturing wasn't kind to Dundee, and the city's population of 145,000 are still living with its effects. But regeneration is today's big buzzword, with some commentators drawing comparisons with Glasgow's reinvention as a city of culture in the 1980s and 1990s. A major star of the revived city is the V&A Dundee, a handsome new design museum housed in a ship-like modern building on the waterfront. Less apparent is the city's international reputation as a centre of biotechnology, computer game technology and cancer research.

Brief history

Even prior to its Victorian heyday, Dundee was a town of considerable importance. It was here, in 1309, that **Robert the Bruce** was proclaimed the lawful King of Scots, and during the Reformation it earned itself a reputation for tolerance, sheltering leading figures such as **George Wishart** and **John Knox**. During the Civil War, the town was destroyed by the Royalists and Cromwell's army. Later, prior to the Battle of Killiecrankie, it was razed to the ground once more by Jacobite **Viscount Dundee**, known in song and folklore as 'Bonnie Dundee', who had been granted the place for his services to the Crown by James II.

Dundee picked itself up in the 1800s, its train and harbour links making it a major centre for shipbuilding, whaling and the manufacture of **jute**. This, along with jam and journalism – the three 'Js' which famously defined the city – has all but disappeared, with only local publishing giant D.C. Thomson, publisher of the timelessly popular *Beano* and *Dandy* (among other comics and newspapers), still playing a meaningful role in the city. Look out for the statues of Dundee heroes **Desperate Dan** and **Minnie the Minx**, both from the old *Dandy* comic, given pride of place at the junction of Reform Street and City Square.

The Tay bridges

The best approach to Dundee is across the modern mile-and-a-half-long **Tay Road Bridge** from Fife. Running parallel a mile upstream is the **Tay Rail Bridge**, opened in 1887 to replace the spindly structure which collapsed in a storm in December 1879 only eighteen months after it was built, killing the crew and 75 passengers on a train passing over the bridge at the time. While the Tay bridges aren't nearly as spectacular as the bridges over the Forth near Edinburgh, they do offer a magnificent panorama of the city on the northern bank of the firth; look out for seals bobbing in the water.

DUNDEE

DRINKING & NIGHTLIFE
Beer Kitchen	4
Fisherman's Tavern	2
Ship Inn	1
Trades House Bar	3

● **EATING**
Agacan	1
Castlehill	2
Flame Tree Café	3
Metro Brasserie	4

■ **ACCOMMODATION**
Apex City Quay Hotel	3
Dundee Backpackers Hostel	2
Fisherman's Tavern	1
Malmaison	4
Premier Inn Dundee Centre	5

10

St Paul's Episcopal Cathedral

High St, close to the junction with Commercial St • Mon–Fri 9am–4pm, Sat 2–4pm, Sun for services • Free • ⓦ saintpaulscathedral.net

Midway between the Wellgate and Overgate shopping centres is the mottled spire of **St Paul's Episcopal Cathedral**, a rather gaudy Gothic Revival structure designed by George Gilbert Scott, notable for its vivid if sentimental stained glass and floridly gilded high altar. Immediately in front of the cathedral is a statue to one of the city's heroes, **Admiral Duncan of Camperdown**, who defeated a Dutch fleet not far offshore from Dundee during the Napoleonic Wars.

10

McManus Art Galleries and Museum

Albert Square • Mon–Sat 10am–5pm, Sun 12.30–4.30pm; last entry 15min before closing • Free • ⓦ www.mcmanus.co.uk

The **McManus Art Galleries and Museum**, Dundee's most impressive Victorian structure, is an unmissable stop for art lovers. The **ground-floor rooms** explore the nature of museums, the surrounding natural landscape and the making of modern Dundee, while upstairs there's the splendid **Victoria gallery**, its curved red walls densely hung with an impressive collection of works by masters including Rossetti and Henry Raeburn. The rest of this floor is equally engrossing: Dundee and the World shows an eclectic ethnographic collection; the **20th Century Gallery** showcases work by the Scottish Colourists and others; the **Long Gallery** is lined with historic and modern ceramics; while **Here and Now** displays fine art acquisitions, including contemporary photography. The museum's bright and attractive **café** is also a good pit stop, especially on a sunny day when you can sit on the stone terrace outside.

Verdant Works

West Henderson's Wynd, Blackness • April–Oct Mon–Sat 10am–6pm, Sun 11am–6pm; Nov–March Wed–Sat 10.30am–4.30pm, Sun 11am–4.30pm • Charge; joint ticket with Discovery Point available • ⓦ verdantworks.co.uk

An award-winning museum, **Verdant Works** tells the story of **jute**, from its harvesting in India to its arrival in Dundee on clipper ships. The museum, set in an old jute mill, makes a lively attempt to re-create the turn-of-the-twentieth-century factory floor, the highlight being the chance to watch jute being processed on fully operational quarter-size machines originally used for training workers. The excellent guides include one of the last mill workers.

DCA

152 Nethergate • Daily 10am–midnight • Free • ⓦ dca.org.uk

Principal among the city's many arts venues is the hip and exciting **DCA**, or Dundee Contemporary Arts, a stunning five-floor complex that incorporates galleries, a print studio, a classy design shop selling some of the prints made in-house, and an airy café-bar. It's worth visiting for the stimulating temporary and touring exhibitions of contemporary art, as well as an eclectic programme of art-house films and cult classics (see page 338).

V&A Dundee

River Esplanade • Wed–Mon 10am–5pm • Free; charge for some exhibitions • ⓦ vam.ac.uk/dundee

The undisputed star of Dundee's waterfront development is this bold new design museum, created by Japanese architect Kengo Kuma as a homage to the city's shipping heritage and to the rugged rocks of the nearby coastline. The building's two upended pyramids, wrapped in tiers of stone cladding, are uncompromisingly modern, and provide an interesting foil to the lofty masts of the neighbouring Discovery vessel. The museum hosts temporary exhibitions throughout the year, but the main attraction is the (free) Scottish Design Galleries, whose highlight is a brilliant reconstruction of Charles Rennie Mackintosh's Ingram Street Tearooms, which had been kept in storage since the 1970s. Other exhibits celebrate the country's technical prowess, architectural heritage and its painters, fashionistas and illustrators, including the creator of Dundee's own cartoon hero Dennis the Menace. Look out too for an ornate panel fragment from the Titanic, a winged Cartier headdress studded with diamonds and Natalie Portman's medieval/futurist Star Wars costume.

Discovery Point

Discovery Quay • April–Oct Mon–Sat 10am–6pm, Sun 11am–6pm; Nov–March Mon–Sat 10am–5pm, Sun 11am–5pm; last entry 1hr before closing • Charge; joint ticket with Verdant Works available • ⓦ rrsdiscovery.co.uk

10

Just south of the city centre on the waterfront, domed **Discovery Point** is an impressive development centring on the Royal Research Ship *Discovery*, which sits dramatically alongside in a dry dock. Something of an icon for Dundee's renaissance, *Discovery* is a three-mast steam-assisted vessel built in Dundee in 1901 to take **Captain Robert Falcon Scott** on his polar expeditions. A combination of brute strength and elegance, it has been beautifully restored, with polished wood panels and brass trimmings giving scant indication of the privations suffered by the crew. In the Antarctic, temperatures on board would plummet to -28°C and turns at having a bath came round every 47 days. Before you step aboard there is a series of interactive displays about the construction of the ship and Scott's journeys, including the chill-inducing 'Polarama' about life in Antarctica. Another highlight is Herbert Ponting's classic images of the ship and crew.

Unicorn

Victoria Dock • April–Oct Tues–Sun 10am–4pm; Nov–March Thurs–Sun 10am–4pm • Charge • ⓦ frigateunicorn.org

An endearingly simple wooden frigate built in 1824, **Unicorn** is the oldest British warship still afloat and was in active service up until 1968. Although the interior is sparse, the cannons, the splendid figureheads and the wonderful model of the ship in its fully rigged glory (the real thing would have featured over 23 miles of rope) are fascinating. The ship is moored across from *Discovery* on the other side of the road bridge near the multimillion-pound redevelopment of Victoria Dock (a footpath connects the two ships).

Dundee Law

A 30min walk north of the city centre, or take bus No. 22 from Commercial St

A mile or so north of town, **Dundee Law** is the plug of an extinct volcano and, at 571ft, the city's highest point. Once the site of a seventh-century defensive hillfort, it's now an impressive **lookout point**, with great views across the whole city and the Tay. The steep (and often windy) climb to the top, which is marked by a monument commemorating both world wars, takes around half an hour from the centre.

Mills Observatory

Balgay Hill, 2 miles west of the centre • April–Sept Tues–Fri 11am–5pm, Sat & Sun 12.30–4pm; Oct–March Mon–Fri 4–10pm, Sat & Sun 12.30–4pm; • Free • **P**lanetarium shows Oct–March every other Fri; see website for details • Charge • ⓦ leisureandculturedundee.com • Buses Nos 17 and 26 from Nethergate stop on Ancrum Rd, on the edge of Lochee Park

Balgay Hill, Dundee's smaller volcanic outcrop, sits a mile to the west of Dundee Law and is skirted by wooded **Lochee Park**. On its summit sits the **Mills Observatory**, Britain's only full-time public observatory with a resident astronomer. The best time to visit is after dark on winter nights; in summer there's little to be seen through the telescope, but well-explained, quirky exhibits and displays chart the history of space exploration and astronomy, and on sunny days you can play at being a human sundial and take in the fantastic views over the city through little telescopes. From October to March the **planetarium** runs a fortnightly show, while the observatory also has special opening times to coincide with eclipses and other astronomical events.

10

Broughty Ferry and around

ⓦ broughtyferry.co.uk • Connected to the city by a 20min bus ride; use National Express bus Nos 5 or 17, or Stagecoach Strathtay's Nos 73 and 73a; all leave from either High St or Seagate in the town centre

Four miles east of Dundee's city centre lies the seaside settlement of **BROUGHTY FERRY**, now engulfed by the city as a reluctant suburb. The ferry referred to in the name was a railway ferry, which transported carriages travelling between Edinburgh and Aberdeen; it was inevitably closed following the building of the first ill-fated Tay Rail Bridge. Comprising an eclectic mix of big villas built by jute barons up on the hillside and small fishermen's cottages along the shoreline, 'The Ferry', as it's known, has experienced a resurgence in popularity. It's now a pleasant and relaxing spot with some good restaurants and pubs, and both the beach and the castle's 'green' (or grounds) are popular run-around spots for kids.

Broughty Castle and Museum

Castle Approach • April–Sept Mon–Sat 10am–4pm, Sun 12.30–4pm; Oct–March Tues–Sat 10am–4pm, Sun 12.30am–4pm • Free • ☎ 01382 436916

The striking **Broughty Castle and Museum**, right by the seashore, is worth a look, if only to admire its location at the mouth of the River Tay. Constructed in 1496 to protect the estuary, and rebuilt in the nineteenth century, its four floors now house local history and military exhibits and cover the story of Broughty Ferry from 400 million years ago to its development as a fishing village.

Claypotts Castle

Just off the A92 at Claypotts Junction • Limited opening hours • Free • HES • ⓦ historicenvironment.scot

Just north of Broughty Ferry, at the junction of the A92 and B978, the chunky bricks of **Claypotts Castle** constitute one of Scotland's most complete Z-shaped tower houses. Built between 1569 and 1588, its two round towers have stepped defensive projections which support extra rooms, a sixteenth-century architectural practice that makes Claypotts look like it's about to topple over. Note that you can only view the castle from outside.

ARRIVAL AND DEPARTURE   DUNDEE

BY PLANE

Dundee's airport (ⓦ hial.co.uk) is two miles west of the city centre. There are no buses into the centre so expect to fork out around £10 for a taxi; alternatively, it's a 2-minute walk along the waterfront.

Destinations London City (Mon–Fri 2 daily, 1 on Sun; 1hr 25min).

BY TRAIN

Trains arrive at and depart from the station on Riverside Drive, about 300yd south of the city centre, near the river.

Destinations Aberdeen (every 30min; 1hr 15min); Arbroath (every 30min; 20min); Edinburgh (every 30min; 1hr 30min); Glasgow (hourly; 1hr 30min); Montrose (1–2 hourly; 30min).

BY BUS

Long-distance buses operated by Stagecoach Strathtay (☎ 01382 313700) arrive at the Seagate bus station, a couple of hundred yards east of the centre. For timetables and information contact Traveline Scotland (ⓦ travelinescotland.com).

Destinations Aberdeen (hourly; 2hr 20min); Arbroath (every 30min; 30–50min); Blairgowrie (every 30min–1hr; 50min–1hr); Forfar (every 30min; 30min); Glamis (2–5 daily; 35min); Kirriemuir (hourly; 55min); Meigle (hourly; 40min); Montrose (hourly; 1hr).

BY CAR

Car rental Arnold Clark, East Dock St (ⓦ arnoldclark.com); Enterprise, 131 Seagate (ⓦ enterprise.co.uk); Hertz, 25 Kings Cross Rd (ⓦ hertz.co.uk).

GETTING AROUND

By bus Local buses leave from the high street or from nearby Union St. Dundee Travel Shop at 92 Commercial St (ⓦ nxbus.co.uk/Dundee) sells Daysaver tickets, which provide unlimited bus travel for a day (£3.80), and hands out information on local bus routes.
By taxi There are taxi ranks on Nethergate, or try Dundee Private Hire (☎ 01382 203020).

INFORMATION

Tourist office Inside the V&A (April–Sept Mon–Sat 10am–5pm, Sun 10am–4pm; Oct–March Thurs–Mon 10am–5pm; ⓦdundee.com).

ACTIVITIES

Bike rental Spokes, at 272 Perth Rd (ⓦspokescycles. net), is the most central option for cycle rental, with bikes for £20/day.

Cycle routes/walking trails At the tourist office you can get route maps for Maritime and Heritage Walking Trails (1–2hr duration; free), which depart from the DCA. There's also a map of a citywide cycle route.

Indoor climbing Avertical World, at 7 Blinshall St (Mon–Wed 11am–10pm, Thurs & Fri 8.30am–10pm, Sat & Sun 10am–7pm; June & Aug Sat & Sunday until 5pm; ⓦaverticalworld.co.uk), offers roped climbing and bouldering in an old church west of the centre; 1hr taster sessions cost £20.

Football The city has two leading football clubs, Dundee (ⓦdundeefc.co.uk) and Dundee United (ⓦdundeeunitedfc. co.uk), whose stadiums face each other across Tannadice St in the north of the city.

Monifeith Golf Club 8 Princes St, Monifieth (ⓦmonifiethgolf.co.uk) Offers two challenging 18-hole courses east of Broughty Ferry.

10

ACCOMMODATION

SEE MAP PAGE 333

Apex City Quay Hotel 1 West Victoria Dock Rd ⓦapexhotels.co.uk. Large, sleek and modern hotel that stands out among the new developments of the dockland area, incorporating a spa, swimming pool and restaurant. ££

Dundee Backpackers Hostel 57 High St ⓦwww. hoppo.com. Dundee's only backpackers' hostel, with dorms and swish en-suite private rooms in a warren-like former merchant's house constructed in 1560. Dorms £; doubles/ twins ££

Fisherman's Tavern 10–16 Fort St, Broughty Ferry ⓦfishermanstavern-broughtyferry.co.uk. Neat

contemporary rooms – mostly en suite, and one with facilities for disabled guests – above a cosy, popular traditional pub with a roaring fire and good real ales. ££

Malmaison 44 Whitehall Crescent ⓦmalmaison.com. Part of a flash boutique chain and with gorgeous Victorian features, including a wrought-iron staircase and a grand dome. Handy for the city sights and waterfront. ££

Premier Inn Dundee Centre Riverside Drive ⓦpremierinn.com. Bland hotel that's part of a nationwide chain, but there's no denying it's well positioned beside Discovery Point and the train station. ££

EATING

SEE MAP PAGE 333

The **west end** of Dundee, around the main university campus and Perth Rd, is the best area for eating and drinking; the **city centre** has a few good pubs and one or two decent restaurants tucked away near the Repertory Theatre. **Broughty Ferry** is a pleasant alternative, with a good selection of pubs and restaurants that get particularly busy on summer evenings.

Agacan 113 Perth Rd ⓦagacan.co.uk. Tiny, moderately priced Turkish restaurant with an unmistakeable colourful exterior, and rough-hewn walls inside; they serve up decent kebabs (lamb doner) and stuffed pittas, and also do takeaways. ££

Castlehill 22 Exchange Stⓦcastlehillrestaurant. co.uk. Probably the most reliable spot for well-sourced,

confidently cooked fine Scottish food in the city. Half a dozen set menus including a three-course lunch menu and a six-course vegetarian menu, with dishes including spelt grain risotto with mushroom duxelle and truffle. ££££

Flame Tree Café 20a Exchange St ☎01382 204200. An unexpected apparition: this is an Australian café in Dundee, dishing up super fresh salads and sandwiches, and some of the best coffee in town, as well as rainbow-coloured and vegan doughnuts. £

Quayside Bar & Grill At the Apex City Quay Hotel, 1 West Victoria Dock Rd ⓦapexhotels.co.uk. A style-led, but still pleasant, restaurant space, on the ground floor of the dockland's sleekest hotel, serving imaginative Scottish cuisine like Ayrshire pork with an apple purée and black pudding. £££

DRINKING AND NIGHTLIFE

SEE MAP PAGE 333

Beer Kitchen 10 South Tay St ⓦinnisandgun.com. Run by the Innis & Gun brewery, this is a hipster pub with a great range of beers – especially cask matured beers – and fine food on the side, including an excellent weekend lunch. Try the squash tikka masala.

Fisherman's Tavern 10–16 Fort St, Broughty Ferry ⓦbelhavenpubs.co.uk/pubs/angus/fishermans-tavern. Just off the shore in a busy traditional cottage, this pub

serves a variety of real ales. There's a small garden for when the sun is shining; good place to watch sports on the big screen too.

Ship Inn 121 Fisher St, Broughty Ferry ⓦtheshipinn-broughtyferry.co.uk. A narrow pub with a warm atmosphere and nautical feel, right on the waterfront with good views over the Tay. Does good seafood dishes (crab salad) and a fine selection of beers.

10

Trades House Bar 40 Nethergate ⓦbelhavenpubs. co.uk/pubs/angus/trades-house. A converted bank fronted with stained-glass windows, which provides a friendly atmosphere for boozing in the heart of the city. Also does a decent selection of pub meals.

ENTERTAINMENT

Caird Hall City Square ⓦleisureandculturedundee. com/culture/caird-hall. The city's best venue for classical music, including visits by the Royal Scottish National Orchestra and other bigwigs; its bulky frontage dominates City Square.

Cineworld Camperdown Leisure Park ⓦcineworld. co.uk/cinemas/dundee. Nine-screen cinema a fair way out of the centre, which shows mostly blockbuster movies. Take bus No. 4 from Commercial St to get here.

DCA 152 Nethergate ⓦdca.org.uk. DCA has two comfy auditoria showing an appealing range of foreign and art-house movies alongside some of the more highbrow Hollywood releases.

Dundee Repertory Theatre Tay Square ⓦdundeerep. co.uk. This prodigious venue sits right at the heart of the Cultural Quarter, north of Nethergate. It's an excellent place for indigenously produced contemporary theatre and the home of the only permanent repertory company in Scotland.

DIRECTORY

Medical facilities Ninewells Hospital (☎01382 660111) is in the west of the city and has an Accident and Emergency department; Dundee Dental Hospital (☎01382 425791); Boots pharmacy, 49–53 High St (☎01382 221756).

Police Scotland's Tayside division is based at West Bell St (☎01382 223200 or ☎101).
Post office 4 Meadowside (Mon–Fri 9am–5.30pm, Sat 9am–12.30pm).

The Angus coast

The predominantly agricultural county of **ANGUS**, east of the A9 and north of the Firth of Tay, holds some of the northeast's greatest scenery and is relatively free of tourists. The coast from **Montrose** to **Arbroath** is especially inviting, with scarlet cliffs and sweeping bays, then, further south towards Dundee, gentler dunes and long sandy beaches.

GETTING AROUND

THE ANGUS COAST

By car Two roads link Dundee to Aberdeen and the northeast coast of Scotland. By far the more pleasant option is the slightly longer A92 coast road, which joins the inland A90 at Stonehaven, just south of Aberdeen.
By bus Intercity buses from Dundee to Aberdeen tend to use the A90, passing Forfar on the way.
By train The coast-hugging train line running north from Dundee is one of the most picturesque in Scotland, passing attractive beaches and impressive cliffs, and stopping in the old seaports of Arbroath and Montrose.

Arbroath and around

Since it was settled in the twelfth century, local fishermen have been landing their catches at **ARBROATH**, situated on the Angus coast where it starts to curve in from the North Sea towards the Firth of Tay, about fifteen miles northeast of Dundee. The name of the town stems from Aber Brothock, the burn which runs into the sea here, and although it has a great location, with long sandy beaches and stunning sandstone cliffs on either side of town, as well as an attractive old working harbour, Arbroath – like Dundee – has suffered from car-focused development.

The town's most famous product is the **Arbroath smokie** – line-caught haddock, smoke-cured over smouldering oak chips, and still made here in a number of family-run smokehouses tucked in around the harbour.

Signal House Museum

Ladyloan, just west of the dock • Thurs–Sat 10am–5pm • Free • ☎01241 435329

Down by the harbour, the elegant Regency **Signal House Museum** still stands sentinel, as it has since 1813 when it was built as the shore station for the Bell Rock lighthouse, improbably erected on a reef eleven miles offshore by Robert Stevenson. Bell Rock is

THE DECLARATION OF ARBROATH

Arbroath Abbey was the scene of one of the most significant events in Scotland's history when, on 6 April, 1320, a group of Scottish barons drew up the **Declaration of Arbroath**, asking the pope to reverse his excommunication of Robert the Bruce and recognize him as king of a Scottish nation independent from England. The wonderfully resonant language of the document still makes for stirring reading: 'For so long as one hundred of us remain alive, we will never in any degree be subject to the dominion of the English, since it is not for glory, riches or honour that we do fight, but for freedom alone, which no honest man loses but with his life'. It was duly dispatched to Pope John XXII in Avignon, who in 1324 agreed to Robert's claim.

10

the oldest remaining offshore lighthouse in the world. The interior of the house is now given over to some excellent local history displays: a schoolroom, fisherman's cottage and lighthouse kitchen have all been carefully re-created.

Arbroath Abbey

Abbey St, half a mile north of the dock • Daily April–Sept 9.30am–5.30pm; Oct–March 10am–4pm • Charge • HES • ⓦ www.historicenvironment.scot

By the late eighteenth century, chiefly due to its harbour, Arbroath had become a trading and manufacturing centre, famed for boot-making and sail-making (the *Cutty Sark*'s sails were made here). The town's real glory days, however, came much earlier in the thirteenth century with the completion in 1233 of **Arbroath Abbey**, whose rose-pink sandstone ruins, described by Dr Johnson as 'fragments of magnificence', stand on Abbey Street. The abbey was dissolved during the Reformation, and until the nineteenth century, when the first steps were taken to protect the abbey, it was little more than a source of red sandstone for local houses.

However, there's enough left to get a good idea of how vast the place must have been: the semi-circular **west doorway** is more or less intact, complete with medieval mouldings, and the **south transept** has a beautiful round window, once lit with a beacon to guide ships. In the early 1950s, the **Stone of Destiny** had a brief sojourn here when it was stolen from London by a group of Scottish nationalists and appeared, wrapped in a Scottish flag, at the High Altar. It was duly returned to Westminster Abbey, where it stayed until its relatively recent move to Edinburgh Castle (see page 61).

St Vigeans

Although now little more than a northwestern dormitory of Arbroath, the pristine and peaceful hamlet of **ST VIGEANS** is a fine example of a Pictish site colonized by Christians: the church is set defiantly on a pre-Christian mound at the centre of the village. Many **Pictish stones** and fragments, dating back to AD 842, are housed in the wonderful little museum, including the Drosten Stone, presumed to be a memorial. One side depicts a hunt, laced with an abundance of Pictish symbolism, while the other side bears an intricate Celtic cross.

Auchmithie

Four miles north of Arbroath by road or coastal footpath, the clifftop village of **AUCHMITHIE** is the true home of the Arbroath smokie. However, the village didn't have a proper harbour until the nineteenth century – local fishermen, apparently, were carried to their boats by their wives to avoid getting wet feet – so Arbroath became the more important port and laid claim to the delicacy.

ARRIVAL AND DEPARTURE

ARBROATH AND AROUND

By train Trains arrive at the station on Keptie St, less than a 10min walk from the seafront.

Destinations Aberdeen (every 30min; 1hr); Dundee (every 30min; 20min); Montrose (roughly every 30min; 15min).

By bus The bus station is on Catherine St, close to the railway station and within easy walking distance of the tourist information office.

Destinations Aberdeen (hourly; 1hr 45min); Dundee (hourly; 30min); Forfar (hourly; 45min); Montrose (every 30min; 25min).

ACCOMMODATION

★ **Brucefield B&B** Cliffburn Rd ⓦ brucefieldbandb. com. Rooms at this renovated 1920s manor house are as good as those in the region's best hotels, with high-end bathrooms and plush beds. Downstairs there's a sitting room with a free minibar, and outside there are seats overlooking a croquet lawn. **£££**

EATING AND DRINKING

But'n'Ben In Auchmithie, 4 miles east of Arbroath ⓦ thebutnben.com. One of the best restaurants along this stretch of coast, specializing in delicious, moderately priced seafood. The flavoursome platter of local smoked fish and shellfish is the choice meal here. Closed Tues. **£££**

M&M Spink 10 Marketgate ⓦ mmspink.co.uk. This tiny whitewashed shop is one of the most approachable and atmospheric places to try the famous Arbroath smokie (£8/

kg); chef and cookery writer Rick Stein described the fish here, still warm from the smoke, as 'a world-class delicacy'.
The Old Brewhouse 1 High St, by the harbour wall ⓦ oldbrewhousearbroath.co.uk. A convivial and moderately priced restaurant-cum-pub, where you can sit down and tuck into Arbroath smokies smothered in melted butter and lemon. **££**

Montrose and around

MONTROSE, a seaport and market town since the thirteenth century, can sometimes smell a little rich, mostly because of its position on the edge of a virtually landlocked two-mile-square lagoon of mud known as the **Basin**. But with the wind in the right direction, the ancient royal burgh of Montrose is a great town to visit, with a pleasant old centre and an interesting museum. The Basin, too, is of interest: flooded and emptied twice daily by the tides, it's a nature reserve for the host of geese, swans and wading birds that frequent the ooze.

If you have time to spare, be sure to check out the town's fabulous golden **seashore**. The beach road, Marine Avenue, across from the town museum, heads down through sand dunes and golf links to car parks fringing the fine, wide beach, which is overlooked by a slender white lighthouse.

Montrose Museum and Art Gallery

Panmure Place, on the western side of Mid Links Park • Thurs–Sun 10am–3pm • Free • ⓦ visitangus.com

Two blocks behind the soaring kirk steeple at the lower end of High Street, the **Montrose Museum and Art Gallery** is one of Scotland's oldest museums, dating from 1842. In the local history section look out for Pictish stones, and the mechanical paper sculpture of the town, with a green train running along the top and yachts sailing by. Outside the museum entrance stands a winsome study of a boy by local sculptor William Lamb.

William Lamb Memorial Studio

24 Market St • Times vary so check website • Free • ⓦ friendswilliamlambstudio.uk

Scottish sculptor William Lamb (1893–1951) was a superbly talented but largely unheralded artist. His career is all the more impressive because he taught himself to sculpt with his left hand, having suffered a war wound in his right. Much of his work can be seen in the moving **William Lamb Memorial Studio**, including bronze heads of the Queen, Princess Margaret and the Queen Mother. There's another Lamb sculpture, *Whisper*, outside the library on the high street.

Montrose Basin Wildlife Centre

Around a mile west of Montrose on the A92 • March–Oct daily 10.30am–5pm; Nov–Feb Fri–Mon 10.30am–4pm • Charge • ⓦ montrosebasin.org.uk

On the south side of the Basin, a mile or so out of town, the **Montrose Basin Wildlife Centre** has binoculars, high-powered telescopes and remote-control video cameras available for visitors who want to catch a glimpse of wading birds and kingfishers. Family-friendly guided walks also depart from the wildlife centre (see the website for a schedule).

The House of Dun

4 miles west of Montrose off the A935 • **Garden** and **estate** year-round dawn–dusk • Free • **House guided tour only** mid-Jan & Feb Sat & Sun; March Fri–Mon; April–early Sept daily; mid-Sept–mid Oct Thurs–Mon; late Oct daily; Nov & Dec Fri–Mon; 10.45am, 11.30am, 12.15pm, 1pm, 1.45pm, 2.30pm & 3.15pm • Charge • NTS • ⓦ nts.org.uk/visit/places/house-of-dun • Accessible on the hourly Montrose–Brechin bus service (No. 30); ask the driver to let you off outside

Across the Basin, four miles west of Montrose, is the Palladian **House of Dun**. Built in 1730 for David Erskine, Laird of Dun, to designs by William Adam, the house was opened to the public in 1989 after extensive restoration, and is crammed full of period furniture and *objets d'art*. Inside, the ornate relief plasterwork is the most impressive feature, extravagantly emblazoned with Jacobite symbolism. The buildings in the courtyard – a hen house, gamekeeper's workshop and potting shed – have all been renovated, and include a tearoom and a craft shop. There's a Victorian walled garden to explore, as well as formal planting and parkland.

ARRIVAL AND DEPARTURE

By train The town's train station is by the Basin's edge, a block back from the high street on Western Rd.

Destinations Aberdeen (every 30min–1hr; 45min); Arbroath (every 30min; 15min); Dundee (every 30min; 30min); Stonehaven (every 30min–1hr; 25min).

MONTROSE AND AROUND

By bus Most buses stop on the high street, close to Lloyds Pharmacy, or at the railway station.

Destinations Aberdeen (hourly; 1hr 20min); Brechin (for the House of Dun; hourly; 20min); Dundee (every 30min; 25min); Stonehaven (every 30min; 50min).

ACCOMMODATION AND EATING

36 The Mall The Mall, in the north of town ⓦ 36themall. co.uk. Attractive B&B accommodation with en-suite facilities in every room (twin, double and family). The breakfast menu includes fish smoked in nearby Arbroath. ££

Roo's Leap 2 Trail Drive, by the golf club ⓦ roosleap. com. The liveliest (though hardly cosiest) place in Montrose is this sports bar and restaurant offering burgers, steaks and sandwiches. Breakfasts served too. ££

Strathmore and the Angus glens

Immediately north of Dundee, the low-lying Sidlaw Hills divide the city from the rich agricultural region of **STRATHMORE**, whose string of tidy market towns lies on a fertile strip along the southernmost edge of the heather-covered lower slopes of the Grampian Mountains. These towns act as gateways to the tranquil **ANGUS GLENS**, offering some of the most rugged and majestic landscapes in northeast Scotland. **Glen Clova** in particular is well and truly on the tourist circuit, with the rolling hills and dales attracting hikers, bird-watchers and botanists in the summer, grouse shooters and deer-hunters in autumn, and winter skiers who pray for a bountiful snowfall.

GETTING AROUND

STRATHMORE AND THE ANGUS GLENS

By car The most useful road through the glens is the A93, which cuts through Glen Shee, linking Blairgowrie to Braemar on Deeside (see page 363). It's pretty dramatic

stuff, threading its way over Britain's highest main road, the Cairnwell Pass (2199ft). Public transport in the region is extremely limited.

Brechin

Eight miles west of Montrose, **BRECHIN** is an attractive town whose red-sandstone buildings give it a warm, welcoming feel. The chief attraction is the old **cathedral**, a building that's emboldened some (including the local football team) to proudly describe Brechin – in line with the historic definition – as a fully-fledged city.

The Cathedral

Bishop's Close, off the high street • Daily summer 9.30 am–5pm; winter until 4pm • Free • ⓦ brechincathedral.org.uk

There's been a religious building of sorts here since the arrival of evangelizing Irish missionaries in AD 900, and the red sandstone structure of the **cathedral** has become something of a hotchpotch of architectural styles. What you see today dates chiefly from an extensive rebuilding in 1900, with the oldest surviving part of the cathedral being the 106ft high round tower, one of only two in Scotland. The cathedral's doorway, built 6ft above the ground for protection against Viking raids, has some notable carvings, while inside you can see various Pictish stones, illuminated by the jewel-coloured stained-glass windows.

ARRIVAL AND DEPARTURE

BRECHIN

By bus Brechin is easy to get to and from; bus No. 30 runs   at least once an hour to Montrose, nine miles to the east.

TOURS

Caledonian Railway tours Brechin station ⓦ caledonianrailway.com. Trains operate every weekend from June to August, travelling along four miles of track   from Brechin to the Bridge of Dun. Diesel trains run on Saturdays, steam trains run on Sundays.

ACCOMMODATION

Gramarcy House 6 Airlie St ☎ 01356 622240. Bright, spacious and tastefully furnished rooms in a house set back from the main road. There's also a self-catering kitchen area   and the sunny breakfast room with bay windows gets the day off to a good start. Agnes, the owner, is friendly and helpful. <u>££</u>

Edzell and around

Travelling around Angus, you can hardly fail to notice the difference between organic settlements and planned towns that were built by landowners who forcibly rehoused local people in order to keep them under control, especially after the Jacobite uprisings. One of the better examples of the latter, **EDZELL**, five miles north of Brechin on the B966, was cleared and rebuilt with Victorian rectitude a mile to the west of its original site in the 1840s. Through the Dalhousie Arch at the entrance to the village the long, wide and ruler-straight main street is lined with prim nineteenth-century buildings, which now do a roaring trade as genteel teashops and antiques emporia.

The original village (identifiable from the cemetery and surrounding grassy mounds) lay immediately to the west of the wonderfully explorable red sandstone ruins of Edzell Castle, itself a mile west of the planned village.

Edzell Castle

A mile west of Edzell • April–Sept daily 9.30am–5.30pm • Charge; HES • ⓦ historicenvironment.scot

The main part of **Edzell Castle** is a good example of a comfortable tower house, where luxurious living rather than defence became a priority. However, it's the **pleasance garden** overlooked by the castle tower that makes a visit essential, especially in late spring and early to mid-summer. The garden was built by Sir David Lindsay in 1604, at the height of the optimistic Renaissance, and its refinement and extravagance are evident. The walls contain sculpted images of erudition: the Planetary Deities on the east side, the Liberal Arts on the south and, under floods of lobelia, the Cardinal Virtues on the west wall. In the centre of the garden, low-cut box hedges spell out the family mottoes and enclose voluminous beds of roses; in one corner sits a gabled summer house.

The Caterthuns

Four miles southwest of Edzell, lying either side of the lane to Bridgend (which can be reached either by carrying on along the road past the castle or by taking the narrow road at the southern end of Edzell village), are the **Caterthuns**, twin Iron Age hillforts that were probably occupied at different times. The surviving ramparts on the White Caterthun (978ft) – easily reached from the small car park below – are the most impressive; this is thought to be the later fort, occupied by the Picts in the first few centuries AD.

ARRIVAL AND DEPARTURE　　　　　　　　　　　　　　　　EDZELL AND AROUND　　10

By bus Edzell is five miles north of Brechin on the B966, and　linked to it by buses Nos 21, 29 and 30.

ACCOMMODATION AND EATING

Alexandra Lodge Inveriscandye Rd ⓦ alexandralodge. co.uk. Just a short walk east of the high street, this is a friendly B&B located on a quiet street in a little Edwardian lodge built in 1907. **££**

Glenesk Hotel High St ⓦ gleneskhotel.com. A thirty-room Victorian hotel with sweeping gardens, a golf course and full-size snooker table, plus a pool and spa. The bar has seven hundred whiskies. **£££**

Tuck Inn 44 High St ⓦ tuckinnedzell.co.uk. This old-school red-painted restaurant/café dishes up filling fodder such as scampi, fish and chips and treacle pudding. Eat in or take away. **££**

Glen Esk

Just north of Edzell, a fifteen-mile road climbs alongside the River North Esk to form **Glen Esk**, the most easterly of the Angus glen, which, like the others, is sparsely populated. Further up the glen there are some excellent **hiking** routes, including one to Queen Victoria's Well in Glen Mark and another up Mount Keen, Scotland's most easterly Munro. For information on hiking routes around Glen Esk, see ⓦ visitcairngorms.com.

Glenesk Folk Museum

Tarfside, 10 miles northwest of Edzell • Easter to Nov Mon–Fri 10am–5pm, Sat & Sun 10am–6pm • Free • ⓦ gleneskfolkmuseum.org

Ten miles along Glen Esk, the excellent **Glenesk Folk Museum** brings together records, costumes, photographs, maps and tools from the Angus glens, depicting the often-harsh way of life for their inhabitants. Housed adjacent to a former shooting lodge known as The Retreat, built by a retired sea captain in the 1840s, it's run independently and enthusiastically by the local community. The museum's main attraction is its collection of agricultural tools, some of which date from the eighteenth century. There's also a great little café with fine home baking.

ACCOMMODATION　　　　　　　　　　　　　　　　　　　　　　　　GLEN ESK

Glenesk Caravan Park Burn Estate ☎ 01356 648565. 1.5 miles north of the village, you can camp at this small,　child-friendly site. Per pitch **£**

Forfar and around

Around fifteen miles north of Dundee on the A90 lies **FORFAR**, Angus's county town and the ancient capital of the Picts. The town's wide high street is framed by some impressive Victorian architecture and small old-fashioned shops. If you stop here it's worth popping into the quaint bakeries that proudly stock the famous **Forfar bridie**, a semi-circular folded pastry-case of mince, onion and seasonings.

Just west of town, a series of glacial lochs peters out at **Forfar Loch**, now surrounded by a pleasant country park with a visitor centre and three-mile nature trail. Further west still is **Glamis Castle** (see page 344), whose ostentatious interiors, carefully sculpted gardens and château-like turrets make it one of Scotland's most fantastical fortresses.

Meffan Museum and Art Gallery

20 West High St • Thurs–Sat 10am–3pm • Free • ⓦ angusalive.scot

Midway along Forfar's high street, the **Meffan Museum and Art Gallery** exhibits Neolithic, Pictish and Celtic remains and a thoroughly enjoyable collection of replica historical shops and street scenes; the most disturbing examines the town's seventeenth-century passion for witch-hunting, with a taped re-enactment of locals baying for blood.

Restenneth Priory and around

A couple of miles east of Forfar in the middle of farmland are the remains of **Restenneth Priory**, approached along a side road off the B9113 (go beyond the Angus Archives to reach the car park). King Nechtan of the Picts was thought to have established a place of worship here in the eighth century, although the oldest parts of the present structure are from an Augustinian priory erected on the spot around 1100.

A little way south of this, off the B9128, a cairn in the village of **Dunnichen** commemorates a battle at nearby Nechtansmere in 685 in which the Picts unexpectedly defeated a Northumbrian army, thus preventing the Angles from extending their kingdom northwards.

EATING AND DRINKING   FORFAR AND AROUND

Cashleys 1 Castle St ⓦ cashleysrestaurant.com. Bringing a welcome dose of culinary sophistication to Forfar, this fine restaurant offers well thought out dishes like beetroot and whisky salmon, and Gochujang cauliflower. Wednesday's seven-course Tartan Tapas menu (£22) is great fun. **£££**

Tiffins 12 West High St ☎ 01307 461152. The carpet's seen better days and the wallpaper's old-fashioned, but the friendly staff make this tearoom a pleasant spot for a vanilla slice and a cup of tea. They also do good sandwiches. **£**

Glamis Castle

Dundee Rd, about 6 miles west of Forfar • mid-March–Oct daily 10am–6pm; last tour 4.30pm • Charge • ⓦ glamis-castle.co.uk • Take Stagecoach bus No. 20C from West High St in Forfar or Commercial St in Dundee

Pink-sandstone **Glamis Castle**, located a mile north of the picturesque village of **GLAMIS** (pronounced 'glahms'), is a wondrously over-the-top, L-shaped five-storey pile set in an extensive landscaped park. It's also one of Scotland's most famous castles: Shakespeare chose it as a central location in *Macbeth*, and its **royal connections** (as the childhood home of the late Queen Mother and birthplace of the late Princess Margaret) make it one of the essential stops on every coach tour of Scotland.

The bulk of the current castle dates from the fifteenth century, although many of the later additions give it its startling Disneyesque appearance. Glamis began life as a comparatively humble **hunting lodge**, used in the eleventh century by the kings of Scotland. In 1372, King Robert II gave the property to his son-in-law, Sir John Lyon, who built the core of the present building. His descendants, the earls of Kinghorne and Strathmore, have lived here ever since.

As you approach the castle down the long main drive, a riot of turrets, towers and conical roofs appears fantastically at the end of the sweeping avenue of trees, framed by the Grampian Mountains. Obligatory guided **tours** (50min) take in the fifteenth-century **crypt**, where the 12ft thick walls enclose a haunted 'lost' room, reputed to have been sealed with the red-bearded Lord of Glamis and Crawford inside, after he dared to play cards with the Devil one Sabbath. Artist Jacob de Wet was commissioned to produce the frescoes in the family **chapel**, completed in 1688, and his depictions of Christ wearing a hat and St Peter in a pair of glasses have raised eyebrows ever since. **Duncan's Hall**, a fifteenth-century guardroom, is the traditional – but inaccurate – setting for Duncan's murder by Macbeth (it actually took place near Elgin).

Kirriemuir and around

The sandstone town of **KIRRIEMUIR**, known locally as Kirrie, is set on a hill six miles northwest of Forfar on the cusp of glens Clova and Prosen. Despite the influx of hunters up for the 'season', it's still a pretty special place, a haphazard confection of narrow closes, twisting wynds and steep braes. The main cluster of streets has all the appeal of an old film set, with its old-fashioned bars, tiled butcher's shop, tartan outlets and haberdasheries, but somehow manages to avoid being contrived and quaint.

10

Barrie's birthplace

9 Brechin Rd • April–Oct Fri–Mon 10.30am–4.30pm • Charge • NTS • ☎ 01575 572646

Kirrie was the birthplace of **J.M. Barrie** (1860–1937). A local handloom-weaver's son, Barrie first came to notice with his series of novels about 'Thrums' – a village based on his hometown – and in particular *A Window in Thrums* and his third novel, *The Little Minister*. The story of **Peter Pan**, the little boy who never grew up, was penned by Barrie in 1904 – some say as a response to a strange upbringing dominated by the memory of his older brother, who died in a skating accident at the age of 13. **Barrie's birthplace**, a plain little whitewashed cottage which housed the family's ten children, has a series of small rooms decorated as they would have been during Barrie's childhood, as well as displays about his life and works.

Camera obscura

In the old cricket pavilion above town, just off West Hill Rd • April to mid-Oct Sat–Mon 11am–4pm • Donation • Ⓦ kirriemuircameraobscura.com

One of just three **camera obscuras** still functioning in Scotland, this unexpected treasure is run by the local community, along with a small café. It was donated to the town in 1930 by J.M. Barrie, and offers splendid views of Strathmore and the glens: on a clear day it's possible to see as far as Ben Ledi, almost sixty miles to the west. Note that when it's raining the Camera Obscura does not operate.

ARRIVAL AND DEPARTURE   KIRRIEMUIR AND AROUND

By bus The hourly No. 20 bus runs from Kirriemuir's high street to Forfar (15min) and Dundee (50min).

ACCOMMODATION AND EATING

Muirhouses Farm 2 miles north of town on the way to Cortachy Ⓦ muirhousesfarm.co.uk. Offering a proper taste of the countryside hereabouts, this is a working cattle farm one, two-bed cottage sleeping four people; weekend stays, midweek breaks and longer stays available. ££
Thrums Hotel Bank St Ⓦ thrumshotel.co.uk. Small, family-run hotel offering nine en-suite rooms (the larger premium rooms are just £5 more) as well as unfussy lunch and evening meals; the menu includes the likes of haggis balls with mustard mayo, and steak pie with chips and veg. ££

SHOPPING

Star Rock Shop 25 The Roods Ⓦ starrockshop.com. Pretty, old-style shop specializing in Scottish confectionery, which first opened in 1833, making it the oldest trading sweet shop in the country. This is a nice place to try the hard, sweet and milky Scottish candy known as tablet (£2/bag).

Glen Clova and around

With its stunning cliffs, heather slopes and valley meadows, **Glen Clova** – which in the north becomes **Glen Doll** – is one of the loveliest of the Angus glens. Although it can get unpleasantly congested in peak season, the area is still remote enough to enable you to leave the crowds with little effort. Wildlife is abundant, with deer on the mountains, wild hares, and even grouse and the occasional buzzard. The meadow flowers on the valley floor and arctic plants (including great splashes of white and purple saxifrage) on the rocks make it a botanist's paradise.

10

WALKS FROM GLEN DOLL

Ordnance Survey Explorer maps 388 & 387

These **walks** are some of the main routes across the Grampians from the Angus glens to Deeside, many of which follow well-established old drovers' roads. All three either fringe or cross the royal estate of Balmoral, and Prince Charles's favourite mountain – **Lochnagar** – can be seen from all angles. The walks all begin from the car park at the end of the tarred road where Glen Clova meets Glen Doll; all routes should always be approached with care, and you should follow the usual safety precautions.

CAPEL MOUNTH TO BALLATER

15 miles; 7hr

Initially, the path zigzags its way up fierce slopes before levelling out to a moorland plateau, leading to the eastern end of Loch Muick. It then follows the River Muick to Ballater.

CAPEL MOUNTH ROUND-TRIP

15 miles; 8hr

Follows the above route to Loch Muick, doubling back along the loch's southern shore. The dramatic Streak of Lightning path that follows Corrie Chash leads to a ruined stable below Sandy Hillock; the descent passes the waterfall by the bridge at Bachnagairn, where a gentle burn-side track leads back to Glen Doll car park.

JOCK'S ROAD TO BRAEMAR

14 miles; 7hr

A signposted path leads below Cairn Lunkard and along a wide ridge towards the summit of Crow Craigies (3018ft). From here, the path bumps down to Loch Callater then follows the Callater Burn, eventually hitting the A93 two miles short of Braemar.

Clova

The B955 from Dykehead and Kirriemuir divides at the Gella Bridge over the swift-coursing River South Esk. Around six miles north of Gella, the two branches of the road join up once more at the hamlet of **CLOVA**, home to little more than the hearty *Glen Clova Hotel*. An excellent, if fairly strenuous, four-hour walk from behind the old school at the back of the hotel leads up into the mountains and around the lip of **Loch Brandy**.

North from Clova village, the road turns into a rabbit-infested lane coursing along the riverside for four miles to a car park, which makes a useful starting point for numerous superb **walks**. There are no other facilities beyond the village.

ACCOMMODATION AND EATING   GLEN CLOVA AND AROUND

Glen Clova Hotel Clova, 15 miles north of Kirriemuir, along the B955 ⓦ clova.com. Inviting country hotel, which also has a selection of luxury lodges sleeping two to six people, and a private fishing loch. The restaurant serves up traditional Scottish food with a twist, such as timbale of haggis, neeps and tatties. Lodges **£££**; doubles **£££**

Glen Prosen

Five miles north of Kirriemuir, the low-key hamlet of **Dykehead** marks the point where **Glen Prosen** and Glen Clova divide. A mile or so up Glen Prosen, you'll find the house where Captain Scott and fellow explorer Doctor Wilson planned their ill-fated trip to Antarctica in 1910–11, with a roadside **stone cairn** commemorating the expedition.

From here on, Glen Prosen remains essentially a quiet wooded backwater, with all the wild and rugged splendour of the other glens but without the crowds. To explore the area thoroughly you need to go on foot, but a good road circuit can be made by crossing the river at the tiny village of **Glenprosen** and returning to Kirriemuir along the western side of the glen via Pearsie. Alternatively, the reasonably easy four-mile **Minister's Path** links Glen Prosen with Clova; it is clearly marked and leaves from near the church in the village.

Meigle Museum

Dundee Rd, Meigle • April–Sept daily 9.30am–5.30pm • Charge • HES • ⓦ historicenvironment.scot • Hourly bus No. 57 from Dundee to Perth passes through Meigle

Fifteen miles north of Dundee on the B954 lies the tiny settlement of **Meigle**, home to Scotland's most important collection of early Christian and Pictish **inscribed stones**. Housed in a modest former schoolhouse, the wonderful little **Meigle Museum** displays 26 pieces dating from the seventh to the tenth centuries, all found in and around the nearby churchyard. The majority are either gravestones that would have lain flat, or cross slabs inscribed with the sign of the cross, which were usually standing. Most impressive is the 7ft tall great cross slab, said to be the gravestone of Guinevere, wife of King Arthur. The exact purpose of the stones and their enigmatic symbols is obscure, as is the reason why so many of them were found at Meigle. The most likely theory suggests that Meigle was once an important ecclesiastical centre that attracted secular burials of prominent Picts.

Glen Isla and around

Three and a half miles north of Meigle is **Alyth**, near which, legend has it, Guinevere was held captive by Mordred. It's a sleepy village at the south end of **Glen Isla**, which runs parallel to Glen Shee, and is linked to it by the A926. If you decide to stay in the area, your best options for accommodation are in and around **Kirkton of Glenisla**, a small hamlet ten miles north of Alyth.

Reekie Linn

Close to the Bridge of Craigisla, which is a ten-minute drive north of Alyth along the B954, the River Isla narrows and then plunges some 60ft into a deep gorge to produce the classically pretty waterfall of **Reekie Linn**, or 'smoking fall', so-called because of the water mist produced when the fall hits a ledge and bounces a further 20ft into a deep pool known as the Black Dub. There's a car park beside the bridge, and the waterfall is a short walk away along the river's edge.

ARRIVAL AND DEPARTURE	**GLEN ISLA AND AROUND**
By bus Transport connections into the glen are limited. Alyth is on the main bus routes linking Blairgowrie with	Dundee.

ACCOMMODATION	
Glenisla Hotel Kirkton of Glenisla ⓦ glenisla-hotel. com. Cosy whitewashed hotel, which doubles as a good place for classy home-made bar food and convivial drinking.	They do a full Scottish breakfast for guests, and mains such as deep-fried scampi and rump steak. **££**

Glen Shee and around

The upper reaches of **Glen Shee**, the most dramatic and best known of the Angus glens, are dominated by its **ski fields**, ranged over four mountains above the Cairnwell mountain pass. The resorts here may not amount to much more than gentle training slopes in comparison with those of the Alps or North America, but they all make for a fun day out for everyone from beginners to experienced skiers. During the season (Dec–March), ski lifts and tows give access to gentle beginners' slopes, while experienced skiers can try the more intimidating Tiger run. In summer it's all a bit sad, although there are some excellent hiking and mountain-biking routes. Active types

10

SKIING IN GLEN SHEE

For information on skiing in Glen Shee contact **Ski Glenshee** (w ski-glenshee.co.uk), which also offers ski rental and lessons, as does the **Gulabin Lodge Outdoor Centre** (see below), at the Spittal of Glenshee. For the latest snow and weather conditions, phone Ski Glenshee or check out **VisitScotland's page**: w visitscotland.com/see-do/active/skiing-snowsports.

---

tend to overnight in Spittal of Glenshee, or twenty miles further south along the A93 in Blairgowrie (see below), a small town at the southern end of the glen.

Spittal of Glenshee

The small settlement of **SPITTAL OF GLENSHEE** (the name derives from the same root as 'hospital', indicating a refuge), though ideally situated for skiing, has little else to commend it other than the busy Gulabin Lodge Outdoor Centre. From Spittal the road climbs another five miles or so to the ski centre at the crest of the Cairnwell Pass. One of the loveliest walks (or cycle rides) hereabouts is a trek into the heart of Glenshee towards Glen Taitneach, which begins at the car park just beyond the humped back bridge near the outdoor centre. Although not a circular route (so you can go as far as you want), it's mostly flat, hence ideal for families, and becomes increasingly dramatic the further up the glen you go; there's a good chance of spotting Golden Eagles here too.

ACCOMMODATION AND ACTIVITIES SPITTAL OF GLENSHEE

Glenshee Camping Blacklunans w glensheecamping. co.uk. A fabulous, isolated retreat eight miles south of the Spittal of Glenshee offering a selection of cosy pods, shepherds huts and wagons, each sleeping between two- and four-people and with their own fire pit. Guests are free to avail themselves of the bothy, which has all the necessary amenities for cooking and a log fire. **££**

Dalmunzie Castle Blairgowrie w dalmunzie.com. A lovely Highland retreat in a magnificent turreted mansion, with first-class dining and over sixty malt whiskies to enjoy

by the fireside. The entrance is just south of Gulabin Lodge Outdoor Centre, across the bridge. **£££**

Gulabin Lodge Outdoor Centre Just off the A93 immediately north of Spittal of Glenshee w gulabinoutdoors.co.uk. Snow sports are the big draw here in winter, of course, but staff can also arrange summer activities like archery and rock climbing; mountain bike hire too. Pre-booking advised. There is also clean, basic accommodation in a nineteenth-century manse, with singles, doubles and family rooms all available. **££**

Blairgowrie

Travelling to Glen Shee from the south, you'll pass through the well-heeled little town of **BLAIRGOWRIE**, set among raspberry fields on the glen's southernmost tip, and a good place to pick up information and plan your activities. Strictly two communities – Blairgowrie and **Rattray**, set on either side of the River Ericht – the town's modest claim to fame is that St Ninian once camped at Wellmeadow, a pleasant grassy triangle in the town centre.

Cateran Trail

The **Cateran Trail** (w pkct.org) is an ambitious, long-distance footpath that starts in Blairgowrie then heads off on a long loop into the glens to the north following some of the drove roads used by caterans, or cattle thieves. It takes four to five days to tramp the 64-mile route, though of course it's possible to walk shorter sections of the way.

ARRIVAL AND DEPARTURE BLAIRGOWRIE

By bus Blairgowrie is well linked by hourly bus No. 57 to both Perth (50min) and Dundee (1hr).

ACCOMMODATION AND EATING

Bridge of Cally Hotel 6 miles north of town on the A93 w inspiredhotels.co.uk. Attractive medium-sized hotel right on the Cateran Trail with nicely presented rooms, some

with river views, and a welcoming restaurant/bar serving intriguing dishes like peppered duck with vanilla mashed potato, and venison casserole. **££**

Lands of Loyal Hotel Loyal Road ⓦlandsofloyal. com. Seventeen lush bedrooms in a converted shooting lodge just north of Alyth. Extravagant chateau-style decor, and fire-lit dining spaces where they serve game. Wood panelling and ornate stucco ceilings complete the country-house picture. **££££**

Little's 1 Riverside Rd ⓦlittlesrestaurant.com. Lovely little restaurant specializing in prettily presented fresh local fish, which might be marinated squid with olives or lemon sole fillet with mango chutney and straw chips. **££**

Aberdeen

10

The third-largest city in Scotland, **ABERDEEN**, commonly known as the 'Granite City', lies 120 miles northeast of Edinburgh on the banks of the rivers Dee and Don, smack in the middle of the northeast coast.

Since the 1970s, **oil** has made Aberdeen a wealthy and self-confident place, though heavily dependent on the vagaries of oil prices. The city can sometimes seem to exist only as a departure point for the transient population of some ten to fifteen thousand who live on the 130 oil platforms out at sea. But its **architecture** is stunning – a granite cityscape created in the nineteenth century by three fine architects: Archibald Simpson and John Smith in the early years of the century and, later, A. Marshall Mackenzie. Classical inspiration and Gothic Revival styles predominate, giving grace to a material once thought of as only good enough for tombs and paving stones. In addition, the urban **parks** are some of the most beautiful in Britain.

Getting your bearings is easy enough, as Aberdeen divides neatly into five main areas. The **city centre**, roughly bounded by Broad Street, Union Street, Schoolhill and Union Terrace, features the opulent Marischal College, the colonnaded Art Gallery with its fine collection, the burgeoning nightlife of Belmont Street, and homes that pre-date Aberdeen's nineteenth-century town planning and have been preserved as museums. Union Street leads west to the twin diversions of gentrified shopping and raucous nightlife that defines the **West End**. To the south, the **harbour** still heaves with boats serving the fishing and oil industries, while north of the centre lies attractive **Old Aberdeen**, a village neighbourhood presided over by King's College, St Machar's Cathedral and a stunning modern university library. The long sandy **beach** marks Aberdeen's eastern border, just a mile or so from the heart of the city.

Brief history

In the twelfth century, Alexander I noted 'Aberdon' as one of his principal towns, and by the thirteenth century it had become a centre for **trade** and fishing, a jumble of timber and wattle houses perched on three small hills, with the castle to the east and St Nicholas Kirk outside the gates to the west.

It was here that **Robert the Bruce** sought refuge during the Scottish Wars of Independence, leading to the garrison of the castle by Edward I and Balliol's supporters. In a night-time raid in 1306, the townspeople attacked the garrison and killed them all, an event commemorated by the city's motto 'Bon Accord', the watchword for the night. The victory was not to last, however, and in 1337 Edward III stormed the city, forcing its rebuilding on a grander scale. A century later Bishop Elphinstone founded the Catholic university in the area north of town known today as **Old Aberdeen**, while the rest of the city developed as a mercantile centre and important port.

Industrial and economic expansion led to the Aberdeen New Streets Act in 1800, setting off a hectic half-century of development that almost led to financial disaster. Luckily, the city was rescued by a boom in trade: in the **shipyards** the construction of Aberdeen clippers revolutionized sea transport, giving Britain supremacy in the China tea trade, and in 1882 a group of local businessmen acquired a **steam** tugboat for trawl fishing. Sail gave way to steam, and fisher families flooded in.

By the mid-twentieth century, Aberdeen's traditional industries were in decline, but the discovery of **oil** in the North Sea transformed the place from a depressed port into a boom town. This oil-borne prosperity may have served to mask the thinness of the region's other wealth creators, but it has nonetheless allowed Aberdeen to hold its own as a cultural and academic centre, and as a focus of the northeast's identity.

Union Street

10

The centre of Aberdeen is dominated by mile-long **Union Street** – still the grandest and most ambitious single thoroughfare in Scotland. The challenge for the early nineteenth-century city planners who conceived the street was the building of the ambitious **Union Street bridge**, spanning two hills and the Denburn gorge. The first attempt, a triple-span design by Glasgow architect David Hamilton, bankrupted the city and collapsed during construction. The famous civil engineer Thomas Telford then proposed the single-arch structure that became an engineering wonder of its age. Since completion in 1805 the bridge has been widened twice, the second time, in 1963, adding a row of shops to the southern side that obscures the dramatic impact of the structure.

ABERDEEN

● EATING		■ ACCOMMODATION	
Bonobo Café	4	Aberdeen Youth Hostel	5
Books and Beans	6	Allan Guest House	12
The Breadmaker	3	Butler's Guest House	8
Café 52	11	Carmelite	4
Fusion	7	Crombie Johnston Halls	1
Kilau Coffee	1	Dutch Mill	7
Moon Fish Café	5	Ferryhill House	11
Ninety-Nine Bar & Kitchen	9	Globe Inn	3
Poldino's	8	Malmaison	6
Sand Dollar Café	2	Marcliffe	10
Silver Darling	10	Skene House	2
		Roselea House	9

Castlegate

Any exploration of the **city centre** should begin at the open, cobbled **Castlegate**, where Aberdeen's long-gone castle once stood. At its centre is the late seventeenth-century **Mercat Cross**, carved with a unique gallery of Stewart sovereigns and topped with a unicorn. Castlegate was once the focus of city life but nowadays seems rather lifeless unless you dart along the easily missed lane to **Peacock Visual Arts** at 21 Castle St (Tues–Fri 9.30am–5.30pm; free; ⓦpeacock.studio), a hub for the northeast's contemporary art scene with a focus on printmaking; they also run live music events.

10

The Tolbooth Museum

Castle St • July–Sept Tues–Sat 10am–4pm, Sun 12.30–3.30pm • Free • ⓦ aberdeencity.gov.uk

As Union Street begins you have to crane your neck to see the towering, turreted spire of the **Town House**, though the steely grey nineteenth-century exterior is in fact a facade behind which lurks the early seventeenth-century **Tolbooth**, one of the city's oldest buildings. A jail for centuries, The Tolbooth now houses **The Tolbooth Museum** of crime and imprisonment, featuring winding narrow stairs leading to cramped cells. The prime grisly exhibit is the blade of the city's seventeenth-century guillotine.

St Andrew's Episcopal Cathedral

King St • May–mid-Sept Tues–Fri 11am–4pm, Sat 10.30am–1pm, Sun for services • Free • ⓦ standrewsaberdeen.org.

The sandstone **St Andrew's Episcopal Cathedral**, where Samuel Seabury, America's first bishop, was ordained in 1784, contrasts with the uniform granite of central Aberdeen. Inside, spartan whiteness is broken by florid gold ceiling bosses representing the (then) 48 states of the USA and 48 local families who remained loyal to the Episcopal Church during the eighteenth-century Penal Laws.

10

Provost Skene's House

45 Guestrow • Mon–Sat 10am–5pm, Sun 11am–4pm • Free • ⓦ aberdeencity.gov.uk

Tucked away between Broad Street and Flourmill Lane, **Provost Skene's House** is Aberdeen's oldest-surviving private house, dating from 1545. The house is now an excellent, recently refurbished museum, the highlight of which is the Hall of Heroes, featuring prominent people that are from, or who have had some association with, the city or area, for example Sir Alex Ferguson. There's also a costume gallery, archeological exhibits, period rooms and the Painted Gallery, where a cycle of beautiful religious tempera paintings from the mid-seventeenth century shows scenes from the life of Christ.

Marischal College

On Broad Street stands Aberdeen's most imposing edifice, and the world's second-largest granite building after the Escorial in Madrid – exuberant **Marischal College**, whose tall, steel-grey pinnacled neo-Gothic facade is in absolute contrast to the hideously utilitarian concrete office blocks opposite. This spectacular building, with all its soaring, surging lines, has been painted and sketched more than any other in Aberdeen, though it's not to everyone's taste – it was once described by an art historian as 'a wedding cake covered in indigestible grey icing'.

The college was founded in 1593 by the fourth Earl Marischal and coexisted as a separate Protestant university from Catholic King's, just up the road, for over two centuries. It was long Aberdeen's boast to have as many universities as the whole of England, and it wasn't until 1860 that the two were united as the University of Aberdeen. In 1893, the central tower was more than doubled in height by A. Marshall Mackenzie and the profusion of spirelets added, though the facade, which fronts an earlier quadrangle designed by Archibald Simpson in 1837–41, was not completed until 1906.

St Nicholas Kirk

Just north of Union St • May–Sept Mon–Fri noon–4pm; Oct–April contact church office • Free • ☏ 01224 643494

Between Upperkirkgate and Union Street stands **St Nicholas Kirk**. It's actually two churches in one, with a solid, central bell tower, from where the 48-bell carillon, the largest in Britain, regularly chimes. There's been a church here since 1157 or thereabouts, but as the largest kirk in Scotland it was severely damaged during the Reformation and divided into the West and the East Church, separated today by the transepts and crossing; only the north transept, known as Collinson's aisle, survives from the twelfth century.

The Renaissance-style **West Church**, formerly the nave of St Nicholas, was designed in the mid-eighteenth century by James Gibbs, architect of St Martin in the Fields in London. The **East Church** was rebuilt over the groin-vaulted crypt of the restored fifteenth-century St Mary's Chapel (entered from Correction Wynd), which in the 1600s was a place to imprison witches: you can still see the iron rings to which they were chained.

Aberdeen Art Gallery

Schoolhill • Mon–Sat 10am–5pm, Sun 11am–4pm • Free • Ⓦ aberdeencity.gov.uk

The first-rate **Aberdeen Art Gallery** was purpose-built in 1884 to a Neoclassical design by Scottish architect Alexander Marshall Mackenzie. You enter via the airy **Centre Court**, dominated by Barbara Hepworth's central fountain and thick pillars running down from the upper balcony, each hewn from a different local marble. The walls highlight the policy of acquiring contemporary art, with British work to the fore. The **Side Court** contains *Jungled*, a garish, erotic spin on stained-glass windows by Gilbert and George, and works gifted by the Saatchi collection. The **Memorial Court**, a calming, white-walled circular room under a skylit dome, serves as the city's principal war memorial. It also houses the Lord Provost's book of condolence for the 167 people who died in the 1988 Piper Alpha oil rig disaster. The **upstairs** rooms house the main body of the gallery's painting collection.

10

Belmont and Little Belmont streets

Opposite the Aberdeen Art Gallery is the city's answer to a Bohemian quarter: cobbled **Belmont** and **Little Belmont** streets feature a number of the city's more interesting bars, shops and restaurants, and **farmers' markets** take place on the last Saturday of each month (9am–3pm).

Union Terrace Gardens and around

West of Belmont Street and Denburn Road, the sunken **Union Terrace Gardens** are a welcome relief from the hubbub of Union Street. From here there are views across to the three domes of the Central Library, St Mark's Church and His Majesty's Theatre, traditionally referred to as 'Education, Salvation and Damnation'. Outside the theatre itself stands a grandiose gesturing statue of William 'Braveheart' Wallace, erected in 1888. The once derelict red-brick spire at the other end of the viaduct tops **Triple Kirks**, which is now at the centre of a student housing development. Built in 1843 and one of Archibald Simpson's most famous creations, it was Scotland's only example of a single building hosting three churches for three denominations.

The West End

The **West End**, the area around the westernmost part of Union Street, begins more or less at the great granite columns of the city's **Music Hall**, and looks better than ever after a major restoration. A block north is **Golden Square** – a misnomer as the trim houses, pubs and restaurants surrounding the statue of the Duke of Gordon are uniformly grey. The city has invested much in gentrifying the area north of Union Street, resulting in neat cobbles, old-fashioned lamps, a growing restaurant scene and a string of somewhat stuffy designer boutiques around Thistle Street.

Bon Accord Square

To the south of Union Street, wedged between Bon Accord Street and Bon Accord Terrace, **Bon Accord Square** is a typically elegant Aberdeen streetscape. A grassy centre surrounds a huge solid block of granite commemorating **Archibald Simpson**, architect of much of nineteenth-century Aberdeen.

The harbour

Aberdeen's **harbour**, at the mouth of the River Dee, is one of the busiest ports in the country. From the eastern end of Union Street, cobbled Shiprow winds downhill, passing the Maritime Museum on the right-hand side. The cobbles stop on **Market**

10

Street, which runs the length of the harbour with its brightly painted oil-supply vessels, sleek cruise ships and peeling fishing boats.

The Maritime Museum and Provost Ross's House

Shiprow • Mon–Sat 10am–5pm, Sun 11am–5pm • Free • Ⓦ aberdeencity.gov.uk

On Shiprow, peering towards the harbour through a striking glass facade, is the **Maritime Museum**, which combines a modern, airy museum with the aged labyrinthine corridors of Provost Ross's House. The museum is a thoroughly engrossing, imaginative tribute to Aberdeen's maritime traditions. Just inside the front entrance you'll see a blackboard updated every day with the price of a barrel of crude oil. Suspended above the foyer and visible from five different levels is a spectacular 27ft high model of an oil rig, which, along with terrific views over the bustling harbour, serves as a constant reminder that Aberdeen's maritime links remain very much alive.

The older industries of herring fishing, whaling, shipbuilding and lighthouse-keeping plus the exploration of the northwest passage also have their place, with well-designed displays and audio-visual presentations, many drawing heavily on personal reminiscences. Passages lead into **Provost Ross's House**, where intricate ships' models and a variety of nautical paintings and drawings are on display.

Footdee

An easy 20min walk from Market St or bus #15 from Union St (near St Nicholas Kirk)

At the north end of Market Street, Trinity Quay runs past industrial yards and down York Street towards **Footdee**, or Fittie, a quaint nineteenth-century fishermen's village of higgledy-piggledy cottages backing onto the sea. Their windows and doors face inwards for protection from storms but also, so they say, to stop the devil sneaking in the back door.

Duthie Park

Polmuir Rd • 24hr year-round; **David Welch** Winter Gardens daily March–Oct 9.30am–5.30pm; Nov–Feb 9.30am–4.30pm • Free • A 20min walk or 10min bus ride from the centre (Nos 17 or 18 from Union St)

From Market Street it's a short hop to **Duthie Park**, on the banks of the Dee at the end of Polmuir Road. The rose garden here, known as Rose Mountain due to its profusion of blooms, can be stunning in summer, but the real treat is the **Winter Gardens**, a steamy paradise of enormous cacti and exotic plants. By the obelisk, a parterre garden has been installed and outdoor concerts are occasionally held at the restored vintage bandstand. From the northwestern corner of Duthie Park a great cycle and walkway, the **Old Deeside Railway Line**, heads west out of the city past numerous long-gone train stations.

Old Aberdeen

A 10min ride north of the city centre on bus No, 20 from Littlejohn St

North of the modern centre and an independent burgh until 1891, tranquil **Old Aberdeen** has maintained a village-like identity. Dominated by King's College and St Machar's Cathedral, its medieval cobbled streets, wynds and little lanes are beautifully preserved, and the gleaming cube of the **university library** adds contemporary interest.

King's College Chapel

King's Campus, University of Aberdeen • Mon–Fri 10am–3.30pm • Free • Ⓦ abdn.ac.uk

The southern half of cobbled High Street is overlooked by **King's College Chapel**, the first and finest of the city's college buildings, completed in 1495 with a chunky Renaissance spire. Named in honour of James IV, the chapel's west door is flanked by his coat of arms and that of his queen. It stands on the quadrangle, whose gracious buildings retain a medieval plan but were built much later; those immediately north were designed by Alexander Marshall Mackenzie early in the last century, with the exception of Cromwell Tower at the northeast corner, completed in 1658. The highlights of the interior, which, unusually, has no central aisle, are the ribbed arched wooden ceiling, and the rare and beautiful examples of medieval Scottish woodcarving in the screen and the stalls. A carved wooden pulpit from nearby St Machar's is also here, while outside sits the flamboyant 1911 bronze and marble tomb of Bishop Elphinstone.

St Machar's Cathedral

The Chanonry • Mon–Sat 10am–4pm, Sun 2–5pm • Free • ⓦ stmachar.com

From King's College, High Street leads a short way north to **St Machar's Cathedral** on the leafy Chanonry, overlooking Seaton Park and the River Don. The site was reputedly founded in AD 580 by Machar, a follower of Columba, when he was sent by the latter to find a grassy platform near the sea, overlooking a river shaped like the crook on a bishop's crozier. This setting fitted the bill perfectly, and the cathedral, a huge fifteenth-century fortified building, became one of the city's first great granite edifices. Inside, the stained-glass windows are a dazzling blaze of colour, and the heraldic oak ceiling above the nave dates from 1520 and shows nearly fifty different coats of arms from Europe's royal houses and Scotland's bishops and nobles.

Seaton Park

A wander through Seaton Park, immediately to the north of St Machar's Cathedral, brings you to the thirteenth-century **Brig o' Balgownie**, which gracefully spans the River Don nearly a mile north of the cathedral. The bridge is best visited at sunset; Byron, who spent much of his childhood in Aberdeen, remembered it as a favourite place.

The beach

To reach the beach, take bus No. 15 from Union St; to reach the golf links take buses Nos 9 and 13

Aberdeen can surely claim to have the best sandy **beach** of all Britain's large cities. Less than a mile east of Union Street is a great two-mile sweep of clean sand, broken by groynes and lined all along with an esplanade. Further north, most of the beach's hinterland is devoted to golf links.

ARRIVAL AND DEPARTURE ABERDEEN

BY PLANE

Aberdeen Airport (ⓦ aberdeenairport.com), seven miles northwest of town, is served by flights from more than fifty UK and European destinations. Stagecoach bus No. 727 (£4 single) runs to the city centre from the airport; a taxi costs around £22.

Destinations Belfast (1 daily, 1hr 10min); Birmingham (Mon–Fri 3 daily, Sat & Sun 1–2 daily; 1hr 30min); Bristol (Mon–Fri & Sun 1–2 daily; 1hr 25min); East Midlands (Mon–Fri 2–3 daily; 1hr 25min); Kirkwall, Orkney (Mon–Fri 3 daily, Sat 2 daily; 50min); London Gatwick (Mon–Fri 2 daily, 1 on Sat; 1hr 40min); London Heathrow (Mon–Sat up to 12 daily; 1hr 30min); London Luton (Mon–Sat 1 daily; 1hr 25min); Manchester (Mon–Fri up to 8 daily, Sat 2 daily; 1hr 20min); Newcastle (Mon–Fri up to 6 daily, Sun 1 daily; 55min); Norwich (Mon–Fri 5 daily, Sat & Sun 1–2 daily; 55min); Stornoway (Mon–Fri 1 daily, 55min); Wick (Mon–Fri 2–3 daily; 35min).

BY TRAIN

The main train station is on Guild St, in the centre of the city.

There are lockers here for left luggage, which cost £2–4 for 24hr.

Destinations Arbroath (every 30min; 1hr); Dundee (every 30min; 1hr 15min); Edinburgh (roughly hourly; 2hr 25min); Elgin (up to 11 daily; 1hr 30min); Forres (up to 11 daily; 1hr 45min); Glasgow (hourly; 2hr 35min); Inverness (up to 11 daily; 2hr 20min); Inverurie (roughly hourly; 25min); London (3 daily, 1 nightly sleeper service; 7hr, sleeper service 10hr); Montrose (every 30min; 40min); Nairn (up to 11 daily; 1hr 50min); Stonehaven (every 30min; 15min).

BY BUS

The bus terminal is right beside the train station. For information on local and intercity bus times, visit ⓦ travelinescotland.com.

Destinations Ballater (hourly; 1hr 45min); Banchory (every 20min–1hr; 55min); Banff (every 30min; 1hr 55min); Braemar (roughly every 2hr; 2hr 5min); Crathie, for Balmoral (roughly every 2hr; 1hr 55min); Cullen (hourly; 2hr 30min); Dundee (hourly; 2hr 20min); Elgin (hourly; 2hr 25min); Forres (hourly; 2hr 55min); Fraserburgh (hourly;

10

10

1hr 30min); Inverurie (every 10min; 50min–1hr 20min); Macduff (hourly; 1hr 50min); Peterhead (every 30min; 1hr 15min); Stonehaven (every 15–30min; 35min).

BY CAR

Driving into Aberdeen is easy enough, but as many spaces are designated for local permit-holders it can be tricky (and expensive) to find somewhere central to park.
Car rental Arnold Clark, Canal Rd (ⓦ arnoldclarkrental. com); Budget, at the airport (ⓦ budget.co.uk); Europcar,

at the airport (ⓦ europcar.co.uk); Hertz, at the airport (ⓦ hertz.co.uk).

BY FERRY

Aberdeen has ferry links to Lerwick in Shetland and Kirkwall in Orkney, with frequent NorthLink services (ⓦ northlinkferries.co.uk) departing from Jamieson's Quay in the harbour.
Destinations Kirkwall, Orkney (Thurs, Sat & Sun, plus Tues in summer; 6hr); Lerwick, Shetland (daily; 10–12hr overnight).

GETTING AROUND

Aberdeen's centre is best explored **on foot**, but you might also need to use **buses** – most of which pass along Union St – to reach some sights.

BY BUS

Information and routes Most buses are operated by First (ⓦ firstbus.co.uk/Aberdeen); the bus station is on Guild St. Useful routes from the centre include the No. 15 bus to the beach esplanade, and the No. 20 bus to Old Aberdeen.
Tickets and passes All-day tickets covering city routes aboard any First bus cost £4.20; weekly passes are £17. If you plan to use the buses a lot, you can buy a First TravelCard (in £10 or £20 denominations) from the depot at 395 King

St, or the travel centre at 47 Union St, which also hands out transport maps; each time you travel the fare is deducted from the card.
Night buses Late-night services on Friday and Saturday – the last leaving at around 3.15am – cost a flat £3.20, and head to seven separate destinations on the city's outskirts.

BY TAXI

Taxis operate from ranks throughout the city centre, all of which attract long queues after the pubs and clubs empty at the weekend. If you don't manage to hail one, try Rainbow City Taxis (ⓦ rainbowcitytaxis.com) or ComCab Aberdeen (ⓦ comcab.co.uk).

INFORMATION

Tourist office 23 Union St, near the junction with Broad St (April–June & Sep Mon–Sat 9.30am–5pm, Sun 11am–4pm; July & Aug Mon–Sat 9am–6.30pm, Sun 10am–4pm; Oct–March Mon–Sat 9.30am–5pm; ⓦ visitabdn.com). The tourist office can also provide you with excellent leaflets detailing themed heritage trails around the city, each with a different focus, from maritime history and sculpture to the

city's use of granite.
Listings magazine/website Keep your eyes peeled for the free *What's On* programme published by Aberdeen Performing Arts, which lists upcoming events, art exhibitions and theatre productions. For details of local gigs, try ⓦ aberdeen-music.com.

ACTIVITIES

Football The local football team, Aberdeen, struggles to live up to its golden era of the 1980s when then-manager Alex Ferguson brought home league titles and European trophies. Home fixtures take place at Pittodrie Stadium

(ⓦ afc.co.uk), between King St and the beach.
Golf There are good options for golfing around Aberdeen; the municipal Kings Links (ⓦ sportaberdeen.co.uk) has a driving range and an artificial putting area near the beach.

ACCOMMODATION
SEE MAP PAGE 350

The emphasis on business trade means **weekday rates** can be considerably more expensive than weekends. Even in **low season** the whole city is frequently booked up, so it pays to arrange accommodation a week or more ahead of your arrival.

HOTELS

Carmelite Stirling St ⓦ carmelitehotels.com. Handily located near the Union Square mall, fusing tradition and modern style in a revamped 1820s hotel; they've also got a selection of cheaper 'cosy' rooms. The kitchen serves up a surprisingly modestly priced taste of Scotland. **££**

Ferryhill House 169 Bon Accord St ⓦ ferryhillhousehotel.co.uk. This mansion is set in its own grounds within walking distance of Union St. As well as nine very accomplished en-suite rooms, it offers good-value lunches and a great Malt Room for guests to sample real ales and whisky by a roaring fire. **££**
Malmaison 49–53 Queen's Rd ⓦ malmaison.com. Part of the stylish Malmaison chain, with striking contemporary decor and all the latest in hi-tech features, plus a day-spa and a brasserie decorated with Scottish art. **££**
★ **Marcliffe** North Deeside Rd, Pitfodels ⓦ marcliffe. com. Four miles west of the city centre, this 39-room hotel

in its own grounds is by far the most luxurious and tasteful option in the Aberdeen area. There's a spa, and a fine restaurant with suitably special dishes. **££££**

Skene House 95 Rosemount Viaduct ⓦskene-house. co.uk. Swish modern serviced one-, two and three-bedroom apartments in the cultural quarter with a great hotel-style breakfast served. Rooms are spacious and quiet with plain furnishings, and there are self-catering facilities. **££**

GUESTHOUSES AND B&BS

★ **Allan Guest House** 56 Polmuir Rd ⓦallanguesthouse.co.uk. Traditional-style guesthouse in a Victorian granite terrace not far from Duthie Park and just 5min from the city centre on bus No. 17. A good mix of eight well prepared single, twin and double rooms plus a DVD library and good breakfasts. **££**

Butler's Guest House 122 Crown St ⓦbutlersguesthouse.com. Central but dated rooms (some with shared shower facilities) that attract a mix of business travellers and holidaymakers, though it is fairly priced. A light (not cooked) breakfast is included in the rate. **££**

Dutch Mill 7 Queen's Rd ⓦdutchmill.co.uk. Has a range of comfortable if business-like rooms a mile west of the city centre. They're all above a bar and restaurant that serves the usual pub staples, from prawn cocktails to gammon steaks. **££**

Globe Inn 13–15 North Silver St ⓦthe-globe-inn.com. Easy-going city-centre inn with seven en-suite rooms above a bar that hosts live jazz and blues on Friday and Saturday. The rate includes a continental breakfast; cooked breakfast costs extra. **££**

Roselea House 12 Springbank Terrace ⓦroseleahouse. co.uk. Welcoming, and very cheap, guesthouse in a little stone bungalow near the bus station with accommodation suitable for people with restricted mobility. Floral decor and a friendly welcome. Cooked breakfast included. **£**

HOSTEL AND CAMPUS ACCOMMODATION

Aberdeen Youth Hostel 8 Queen's Rd ⓦhostellingscotland.org.uk/hostels/aberdeen. Hostel in a grand stone mansion a mile from the train station, with clean but rather dated dorms and private rooms. A good option for budget-conscious travellers. To get there take bus No. 11 or No. 17 from Union St. **£**

Crombie Johnston Halls College Bounds, Old Aberdeen ⓦabdn.ac.uk/accommodation. These private rooms in the city's best student halls are also in one of the most interesting parts of town. Rooms are available from early July to Sept, though there's also some year-round accommodation. Singles **£**; twins **££**

EATING

SEE MAP PAGE 350

CAFÉS

★ **Bonobo Café** 73–75 Skene St ⓦbonobotribe.co.uk. The city's first vegan establishment who are also a workers' cooperative. Psychedelic colours bedeck the front window, and the food is correspondingly colourful, with beetroot and coconut soup, green wraps with edamame, kale, mint and peas, and carrot bagels. The baking is first rate, with gluten free options, and on sunny days you can eat in the terrace garden. **££**

Books and Beans 22 Belmont St ⓦbooksandbeans. co.uk. As the name suggests, second-hand books go hand in hand here with decent lattes, pancake stacks, fresh soups and sandwiches. **£**

The Breadmaker 50–52 Rosemount Viaduct ⓦthebreadmaker.org.uk. Enjoy a coffee, sandwiches and fresh baking in this friendly place that gives people with learning difficulties training and meaningful employment. **£**

Kilau Coffee 57 High St ⓦkilaucoffee.wordpress.com. Quirky coffee specialists in Old Aberdeen who also serve salads such as squash, pine nut and halloumi, plus focaccia and so on, as well as excellent cakes. **£**

Sand Dollar Café 2 Esplanade ⓦsanddollarcafe.com. The cheery interior, decorated with seashells and model lighthouses, makes this the most attractive of the cafés along the beach esplanade. Great for breakfast or brunch, and look out for their jazz nights. **££**

RESTAURANTS

Café 52 52 The Green ⓦcafe52onthegreen.co.uk. Cosy, bohemian hangout by day that turns into a hip restaurant by night, with seafood, game and vegetarian meals among the tasty, reasonably priced options. **£££**

★ **Fusion** 10 North Silver St ⓦfusionbarbistro.com. A chic bistro done out in acid colours, where seasonal local produce is the highlight and fish and game feature heavily. Two courses for £29.95. Closed Sun & Mon. **£££**

★ **Moon Fish Café** 9 Correction Wynd ⓦmoonfishcafe. co.uk. Tucked away in the medieval Merchant's Quarter, Moon Fish serves artfully presented modern British food, cooked with local and seasonal produce. Two courses cost £30, three £38 and four £46. Changing exhibitions decorate the walls, and you look out at St Nicholas Kirk. Closed Sun & Mon. **££££**

Ninety-Nine Bar & Kitchen 1 Back Wynd ⓦ99aberdeen.com. Lounge-like bar/restaurant where, instead of the usual pub food, punters can order variously filled Bao buns with an assortment of sides like bang bang fried cauliflower. Also does great cocktails. **££**

Poldino's 7 Little Belmont St ⓦpoldinos.co.uk. An

10

10

Aberdonian Italian institution, combining fine flavours and quality with convivial dining. Classic Italian dishes like spaghetti vongole and penne zucchini; great pizzas too. £££
Silver Darling Pocra Quay, North Pier Ⓦ thesilverdarling.co.uk. Attractively located at the harbour in Footdee, beside the lighthouse, this classy French place specializes in fresh seafood, but there's also a terrific land-based menu. £££

DRINKING

SEE MAP PAGE 350

Brewdog Aberdeen 17 Gallowgate Ⓦ brewdog.com. The home of Brewdog, this hipster-friendly bar sets itself apart from the crowd, with exposed brickwork, dangly lightbulbs and a cracking selection of Scottish ales (most bottles £4.50).

The Grill 213 Union St Ⓦ thegrillaberdeen.co.uk. One of the city's older pubs, with a distinctive old-world charm and the finest range of malts in the city. Also sells real ales on tap and hot stovies.

Prince of Wales 7 St Nicholas Lane Ⓦ belhavenpubs. co.uk. Opened in 1850, the quintessential Aberdeen pub has a 20ft long bar and a flagstone floor. With fine pub grub, renowned real ales and a Sunday evening folk session, it's little wonder that it's often crowded.

St Machar Bar 97 High St, Old Aberdeen Ⓣ 01224 483079. The medieval quarter's only pub, a poky, old-fashioned bar attracting an intriguing mix of King's College students and workers.

Slains Castle 14–18 Belmont St Ⓦ eerie-pubs.co.uk. An old church is the perfect setting for this Gothic-themed bar, whose cocktail list includes potions named after the seven deadly sins. Live bands every Friday.

NIGHTLIFE

SEE MAP PAGE 350

Aberdeen's nightlife is at its liveliest during termtime.
The Blue Lamp 121 Gallowgate Ⓦ jazzatthebluelamp. com. A spacious bar featuring live jazz, usually at weekends, and a Monday folk session; there's also a much smaller snug for relative peace and quiet. Most acts start at 8pm.

Krakatoa 2 Trinity Quay Ⓦ krakatoa.bar. An exuberantly decorated tiki/pirate/live music bar with a capacity of 200. They do some great live music, jam sessions and karaoke, as well as mixing killer cocktails and serving a range of beers on tap. Check out the tropical fish tank in the ladies' toilet.

The Tunnels Carnegies Brae Ⓣ 01224 619930. One of the city's most popular live music venues, established within graffitied old tunnels under Union St. Live bands play a different musical genre every evening including reggae, hip-hop, ska and Northern Soul.

ENTERTAINMENT

You can buy tickets for most events at the city's theatres and concert halls from the **box office** beside the Music Hall on Union St (Mon–Sat 9.30am–6pm; Ⓣ 01224 641122).

CONCERT HALLS

Cowdray Hall Schoolhill Ⓦ aberdeencity.gov.uk. Classical music venue at the Aberdeen Art Gallery, often with visiting orchestras playing; occasionally it hosts free lunchtime concerts.

Music Hall Union St Ⓦ aberdeenperformingarts.com/ music-hall. A beautifully restored Neoclassical venue, generally featuring big-name comedy and music acts.

P&J Live East Burn Rd Ⓦ pandjlive.com. Huge hall with a mainstream vibe, hosting the biggest touring rock and pop acts as well as family-friendly shows.

THEATRES

ACT Aberdeen 33 King St Ⓦ aberdeenartscentre. com. Hosts a variety of theatrical productions, lectures, exhibitions and drama classes. They stage amateur dramatics and music events, as well as a long-established summer arts carnival.

His Majesty's Theatre Rosemount Viaduct Ⓦ aberdeenperformingarts.com. The city's main theatre resides in a beautiful Edwardian building, and its extensive programme ranges from highbrow drama and opera to pantomime.

Lemon Tree 5 West North St Ⓦ aberdeenperformingarts. com. The fulcrum of the city's arts scene, with live music, performance art, club nights, spoken word and comedy. The emphasis is on experimental and alternative events.

CINEMAS

Belmont Filmhouse 9 Belmont St Ⓦ belmontfilm house.com. Art-house cinema (with a comfortable café-bar) showing the more cerebral new releases alongside classic, cult and foreign-language films.

Cineworld Queen's Links Leisure Park, Links Rd Ⓦ cineworld.co.uk. Huge multiplex cinema close to the beachfront that shows all the mainstream releases.

SHOPPING

SEE MAP PAGE 350

Books and Beans 22 Belmont St Ⓦ booksandbeans. co.uk. This popular café (see page 357) has shelves packed with paperbacks and quiet spaces for reading.

La Gourmandise 63 Thistle St Ⓦ lagourmandise. co.uk. Well-run French patisserie shop that stocks gorgeous croissants, macaroons, tartlets and iced cakes, as well as freshly baked baguettes.

The Old Aberdeen Bookshop 140 Spital ⓦ oldaberdeen bookshop.co.uk. The city's best bet for second-hand and antiquarian books, specialises in academic titles, classics

and Scottish literature.

Tiso 1 John St ⓦ tiso.com. Well-stocked outdoor shop with separate sections for footwear, watersports, mountain sports and camping.

DIRECTORY

Medical facilities The Royal Infirmary, on Foresterhill, northeast of the town centre, has a 24hr casualty department (ⓣ 0345 4566000). Boots pharmacy is in the Bon Accord Centre on George St (ⓣ 01224 626080).

Police The main police station is on Queen St (ⓣ 08456

005700), including the lost property office.

Post office The central office is upstairs in the St Nicholas Centre, between Union St and Upperkirkgate, with other branches at 371 George St and 489 Union St.

10

Stonehaven and around

A pretty, pebble-dashed harbour town linked to Aberdeen by the A90, **STONEHAVEN** is a popular summer getaway. Its location along the sheltered Kincardine coastline certainly adds to the appeal, as does the respected **Stonehaven Folk Festival**, which takes place annually in early July. Less auspiciously, the *Carron Fish Bar* on Allardice St was the birthplace of a notorious Scottish snack – the deep-fried Mars Bar – in 1995.

The town itself is split into two parts, the picturesque working **harbour area** being most likely to detain you. The old high street, lined with some fine townhouses and civic buildings, connects the harbour and its surrounding **old town** with the late eighteenth-century planned centre on the other side of the River Carron. On New Year's Eve, High Street is the location for the ancient ceremony of **Fireballs**, when locals parade its length swinging metal cages full of burning debris around their heads to ward off evil spirits for the coming year. The **new town** focuses on the market square, overlooked by the dusky-pink granite market hall with its impressive steeple.

Another reason to base yourself in Stonehaven is **Dunnottar Castle**, a stunningly moody ruin perched on jagged cliffs two miles south. The area south and west of this is known as the **Mearns**, an agricultural district of scattered population and gathering hills famous for its links to Scots author Lewis Grassic Gibbon. Unfortunately, public transport into the Mearns is virtually non-existent.

Tolbooth Museum

Old Quay, down by the harbour • April–Sept daily except Tues 1.30–4.30pm • Free • ⓦ stonehaventolbooth.co.uk

On one side of the harbour, the sixteenth-century **Tolbooth** is Stonehaven's oldest building. Originally built as a storehouse during the construction of Dunnottar Castle (see below), it is now a **museum** of local history and fishing. Above it, rather fittingly, there's a top-notch seafood restaurant (see page 360).

Dunnottar Castle

2 miles south of Stonehaven along the coast • Daily April–Sept 9am–6pm; Oct 10am–5pm; Nov–Jan 10am–3pm; Feb 10am–4pm; last entry 1hr before closing • Charge • ⓦ dunnottarcastle.co.uk

Stonehaven's tourist office hands out free walking guides for the scenic amble to **Dunnottar Castle**, one of Scotland's finest ruined castles. This huge ninth-century fortress is set on a three-sided sheer cliff jutting into the sea – a setting striking enough to be chosen as the backdrop for Zeffirelli's film version of *Hamlet*. Once the principal fortress of the northeast, the mainly fifteenth- and sixteenth-century ruins are worth a good root around, and there are many dramatic views out to the crashing sea.

Siege and bloodstained drama splatter the castle's past: in 1297, the whole English Plantagenet garrison was burnt alive here by **William Wallace**, while one of the more gruesome tales from the castle's history tells of the imprisonment and torture of 122 men and 45 women Covenanters in 1685 – an event, as it says on the Covenanters' Stone in the churchyard, 'whose dark shadow is for evermore flung athwart the Castled Rock'.

Arbuthnott

Some five miles inland and south of Dunnottar Castle is the straggling village of **ARBUTHNOTT**, the home of prolific local author **Lewis Grassic Gibbon** (1901–35), whose romanticized realism perfectly encapsulates the spirit of the agricultural Mearns area. *Sunset Song*, his most famous work, is an essential read for those travelling in this area. He is buried (under his real name of James Leslie Mitchell) in the corner of the little village graveyard, overlooking the forested banks of the Bervie Water off the main road.

Grassic Gibbon Centre

Half a mile northwest of the church, along the B967 • Daily mid-Feb–March 10am–3pm; April–Oct 10am–4.30pm • Charge • Ⓦ grassicgibbon.com

The community-run **Grassic Gibbon Centre** and café is a great introduction to the fascinating and self-assured author who died sadly young of peritonitis. In the small exhibition beyond the café you'll find some of his personal effects housed in glass cabinets, plus snippets of information on local history.

ARRIVAL AND DEPARTURE

STONEHAVEN AND AROUND

By train Rail services from Aberdeen (every 30min; 25min) and Montrose (every 30min; 20min) pull in at Stonehaven station, just off Arduthie Rd.

By bus Buses from Aberdeen (several hourly; 35–50min) and Montrose (every 30min; 40min) stop at the southern end of Barclay St, near the junction with Cameron St.

ACCOMMODATION

★ **Arduthie House** Ann St, close to the junction with Margaret St Ⓦ arduthiehouse.scot. Attractive, arty five-bedroom B&B that has a small gallery/tearoom serving excellent cakes including treacle scones. It's located in a fine stone Georgian villa, with stuccoed fireplaces and stained glass. **££**

Marine Hotel 9–10 Shorehead Ⓦ marinehotel stonehaven.co.uk. Smart if rather monochrome en-suite rooms equipped with coffee machines and flat-screen TVs, right by the harbour. The bar has a decent selection of Belgian beers and whisky, including single malts from the local area. **£££**

EATING AND DRINKING

Carron to Mumbai 20 Cameron St Ⓦ carrontomumbaistonehaven.co.uk. The clue is in the title of this fabulous Indian restaurant housed inside a gorgeous Art Deco building; all the classics though the all-day Sunday buffet is a good bet. **££**

Creel Inn Catterline, 4 miles south of Dunnottar Castle, Ⓦ thecreelinn.co.uk. In Catterline, a clifftop hamlet typical of those along this stretch of coast, the whitewashed *Creel Inn* serves a fantastic selection of seafood and game. **£££**

The Stack Restaurant & Bar Dunnyfell Rd, Muchalls Ⓦ thestackrestaurant.com. Located in the coastal village of Muchalls, and named for the sea stacks that rise from the surrounding waters. The Stack has a smart modern interior and serves mains such as ale-battered haddock and roast loin of venison as well as some decent vegan options. **£££**

Tolbooth Restaurant Above the Tolbooth museum by the harbour Ⓦ tolbooth-restaurant.co.uk. Moderately expensive but beautifully sited restaurant, serving fresh Scottish seafood such as hand-dived west coast scallops with pea purée. **££££**

Deeside

More commonly known as **ROYAL DEESIDE**, the land stretching west from Aberdeen along the River Dee revels in its connections with the royal family, who have regularly holidayed here, at **Balmoral**, since Queen Victoria bought the estate. Eighty thousand Scots turned out to welcome her on her first visit in 1848. Victoria adored the place and the woods were said to remind Prince Albert of Thuringia, his homeland.

Deeside is undoubtedly handsome in a fierce, craggy, Scottish way, and the royal presence has helped keep a lid on any unattractive mass development. The villages strung along the A93, the main route through the area, are well heeled and have something of an old-fashioned air. Facilities for visitors hereabouts are first class, with a number of bunkhouses and hostels, some decent hotels, and plenty of castles and grounds to snoop around. It's also an excellent area for **outdoor activities**, with hiking routes into both the Grampian and Cairngorm mountains, alongside good mountain biking, horse riding and skiing.

By bus Stagecoach buses Nos 201, 202 and 203 from Aberdeen regularly chug along the A93, serving most of the towns on the way to Braemar. Bus No. 201 from Aberdeen runs to Crathes (45min), Banchory (50min), Ballater (1hr 45min) and Braemar (2hr 10min), while Nos 202 and 203 stop at Lumphanan and Banchory respectively.

Drum Castle

Near Drumoak, 10 miles west of Aberbeen off the A93 • **Castle** Jan–March & Oct–Dec Sat & Sun 10.30am-3pm; April–May & Sept Thurs–Mon 10.30am–4pm; June–Aug daily 10.30am–4pm • Charge • Garden of Historic Roses April–Oct daily 11am–4.15pm • Charge • NTS • ☎ 01330 700334

Squat **Drum Castle** stands in a clearing in the ancient woods of Drum, made up of the splendid pines and oaks that covered this whole area before the shipbuilding industry precipitated mass forest clearance. The castle itself combines a 1619 Jacobean mansion with Victorian extensions and the original, huge thirteenth-century keep, which has been restored and reopened. Given by Robert the Bruce to his armour-bearer, William de Irvine, in 1323 for services rendered at Bannockburn, the castle remained in Irvine hands for 24 generations until the NTS took over in 1976.

The main part of the house is Victorian in character, with grand, antique-filled rooms and lots of family portraits. The finest room is the **library**, within the ancient tower; you'll get an even better sense of the medieval origins of the place by climbing up to the upper levels of the tower, where the battlements offer views out over the forest.

Crathes Castle

Crathes, 2 miles east of Banchory • **Castle** Jan–March, Nov & Dec Sat & Sun 11am–4pm; April–Oct daily 10.30am–4.45pm; last entry 1hr before closing • Charge, includes access to the gardens • NTS • ☎ 01330 844525

Four miles west of Drum Castle and around two miles east of **Banchory** (a small town that acts as a gateway into rural Deeside), **Crathes Castle** is a splendid sixteenth-century granite tower house adorned with flourishes such as overhanging turrets, gargoyles and conical roofs. Its thick walls, narrow windows and tiny rooms loaded with heavy old furniture make Crathes rather claustrophobic, but it's enlivened by some wonderful ceilings painted with lively figures of musicians strumming their instruments; the earliest dates from 1602. The extensive grounds include a Go Ape climbing centre (see below).

ARRIVAL AND DEPARTURE | CRATHES CASTLE

By bus Stagecoach buses Nos 201, 202 and 203 from Aberdeen bus station stop at the entrance to Crathes Estate, as well as at nearby Banchory.

INFORMATION AND ACTIVITIES

Tourist office You can pick up local tourist information from the town library on Bridge St (Mon–Wed & Fri 10am–7pm, Thurs 10am–2.30pm, Sat 10am–3pm; ☎ 01330 700441)

Go Ape Zip wires, Tarzan swings, rope ladders and skateboard zip take you through the trees in the grounds of Crathes Castle (ⓦ goape.co.uk).

ACCOMMODATION AND EATING

Milton Brasserie Near the entrance to Crathes Castle ⓦ miltonbrasserie.com. Smart daytime brasserie just across from Crathes Castle, serving moderately priced a la carte meals such as beer-battered haddock with garden peas. ££

Raemoir House Just over 2 miles north of Banchory ⓦraemoir.com. Glamorous country-house hotel set in spacious parkland, with decadent, individually designed rooms in either the late seventeenth-century Ha'Hoose or the main Georgian mansion, and several, grand public areas. The best rooms have four-poster beds. **££££**

Tor-Na-Coille Hotel Inchmarlo Rd, Banchory ⓦtornacoille.com. Once a retreat for Charlie Chaplin and his family, *Tor-Na-Coille* has a scenic location on the town's southern edge. Some of the smart, largely tartan-decorated rooms overlook Banchory Golf Club's rolling fairways. **£££**

10 Ballater

Attractively hemmed in by the River Dee, the neat and ordered town of **BALLATER** was dragged from obscurity in the nineteenth century when it was discovered that waters from the local Pannanich Wells might be useful in curing scrofula. Deeside water is now back in fashion, though these days it's bottled and sold far and wide as a natural mineral water.

It was in Ballater that Queen Victoria first arrived in Deeside by train from Aberdeen back in 1848; she wouldn't allow a station to be built any closer to Balmoral, eight miles further west. Although the line has long been closed, the town's rather self-important royalism is much in evidence at the restored **train station** in the centre. The local shops that supply Balmoral with groceries and household basics also flaunt their connections, with oversized 'By Appointment' crests.

If you prefer to discover the fresh air and natural beauty that Victoria came to love so much, you'll find Ballater an excellent base for local **walks and outdoor activities**. There are numerous hikes from Loch Muick (pronounced 'mick'), nine miles southwest of town, including the Capel Mounth drovers' route over the mountains to Glen Doll (see page 346), and a well-worn but strenuous all-day trek up and around Lochnagar (3789ft), the mountain much painted and written about by the current Prince of Wales.

ARRIVAL AND DEPARTURE
BALLATER

By bus Buses stop at the northern end of Golf Rd, near the A93.

Destinations Aboyne (hourly; 20min); Banchory (hourly; 40min); Braemar (9 daily; 35min).

INFORMATION AND ACTIVITIES

Tourist office In the renovated former train station on Station Square (daily July & Aug 10am–6pm; Sept–June 10am–5pm; ⓦvisitballater.com).
Bike rental Good-quality bikes, including mountain

bikes and tandems, can be rented from Cycle Highlands (ⓦcyclehighlands.com, daily 9am–5pm) from £35/day at The Pavilion, Victoria Rd.

ACCOMMODATION

Auld Kirk ⓦtheauldkirk.com. As the name suggests, this pleasingly unorthodox B&B is based in a renovated church, which features an unmissable rocket-like spire. All of the rooms are upstairs, leaving the ground floor free for a licensed coffee lounge area. **£££**
Ballater Caravan Park South of Anderson Rd, close to the River Dee ⓦballatercaravanpark.com. Large campsite down by the water that mostly attracts touring caravans – tents are welcome too, though, and there are laundry and shower facilities. Per pitch **£**
★ **Ballater Hostel** Bridge Square ⓦballater-hostel.

com. Excellent, friendly and well-equipped hostel tucked away off the main road. Choose between a bunk bed with its own locker, or one of the private rooms. Facilities include kitchen, communal room with wood-burning stove, bike storage and drying room. Dorms **£**; doubles **££**
No 45 45 Braemar Rd ⓦno45.co.uk. Welcoming nineteenth-century house with eight good-sized doubles and twins, all of which are en suite. The bar downstairs is stacked full of whisky and bottled ales, and there's also a restaurant in the large conservatory out the back. **£££**

EATING AND DRINKING

Barrel Lounge 6 Church Square ☎01339 755488. If you fancy a wee dram with the locals, pop into this pub on the

main green. There's an open fire and the TV's usually on in the corner.

Courie Courie Bakery and Café Cambus O' May, 2 miles east of Ballater ⓦrcouriecourie.co.uk. Lovey artisan bakery and café doling out superb coffee and cakes; the sourdough is particularly worth sampling. **££**

Lochnagar Indian Brasserie 2 Church Square ⓦlochnagarindian.co.uk. A great location on the green, a warm welcome and excellent aromatic cooking, such as garlic chilli masala, and Goan lamb shank; book ahead. **££**

Balmoral Castle and around

8 miles west of Ballater, off the A93 • April–July daily 10am–5pm • Charge; includes audio tour • ⓦ balmoralcastle.com

10

Originally a sixteenth-century tower house built for the powerful Gordon family, **Balmoral Castle** has been a royal residence since 1852, when it was converted to the Scottish Baronial mansion that stands today. The royal family traditionally spend their summer holidays here each August, but despite its fame it can be something of a disappointment even for a dedicated royalist. For the three months when the doors are nudged open, the general riffraff are permitted to view only the ballroom, an exhibition room and the grounds. With so little of the castle on view, it's worth making the most of the **grounds** and larger estate by following some of the country walks, or allowing the free audio tour to guide you around.

Opposite the castle's gates on the main road, the otherwise dull granite church of **Crathie**, built in 1895 with the proceeds of a bazaar held at Balmoral, is the royals' local church.

INFORMATION	BALMORAL CASTLE AND AROUND

Tourist office In the car park by the church on the main road (April–Oct daily 10am–5pm; Nov–March Mon–Fri 10am–noon; ☎ 01339 742414).

Braemar and around

West of Balmoral, the road rises to 1100ft above sea level in the upper part of Deeside at the village of **BRAEMAR**, situated where three passes meet and overlooked by an unremarkable **castle**. It's an invigorating, outdoor kind of place, well patronized by committed hikers, but probably best known for its Highland Games, the annual **Braemar Gathering** (see page 364), on the first Saturday of September.

Linn of Dee

A pleasant diversion from Braemar is to head six miles west to the end of the road and the **Linn of Dee**, where the river plummets savagely through a narrow rock gorge. From here there are countless walks into the surrounding countryside or up into the heart of the Cairngorms (see page 405), including the awesome Lairig Ghru pass which cuts all the way through to Strathspey.

ARRIVAL AND DEPARTURE	BRAEMAR AND AROUND

By bus Buses from and to Ballater (9 daily; 35min) stop on Auchendryne Square, while long-distance coaches drop package tourists in the car park opposite the *Fife Arms Hotel*.

INFORMATION AND ACTIVITIES

Tourist office In the absence of a tourist office, there's good information at ⓦ braemarscotland.co.uk.
Outdoor activities Advice on outdoor activities, as well as ski, mountain bike and climbing equipment rental, is available from Braemar Mountain Sports at 5 Invercauld Rd (daily 9am–6pm; ⓦ braemarmountainsports.com).

ACCOMMODATION

Braemar Caravan Park Half a mile south of the village, off Glenshee Rd ⓦ braemarcaravanpark.co.uk. Year-round caravan site which also has thirty camping pitches and half a dozen heated camping pods sleeping four. Can get busy in the summer, so book ahead. Per pitch **£**; pods **££**
Braemar Youth Hostel Corrie Feragie, 21 Glenshee Rd

10

DEESIDE AND DONSIDE HIGHLAND GAMES

Royal Deeside is the home of the modern **Highland Games**, which claims descent from gatherings organized by eleventh-century Scottish king Malcolm Canmore to help him recruit the strongest and fittest clansmen for his army. The most famous of the local games is undoubtedly the **Braemar Gathering**, held on the first Saturday in September, which can see crowds of fifteen thousand. Since Queen Victoria's day, successive generations of royals have attended the event, which has become something of an overcrowded, overblown affair. You're not guaranteed to get in if you just turn up; the website (Ⓦ braemargathering.org) has details of how to book **tickets** in advance.

Vying for celebrity status in recent years has been the **Lonach Gathering** in nearby Strathdon on Donside, held the weekend before Braemar, where local laird Billy Connolly dispenses drams of whisky to marching village men and has been known to invite some Hollywood chums along – Steve Martin has appeared dressed in kilt and jacket, while in 2010 Robin Williams competed in the punishing hill race.

For a true flavour of the spirit of Highland gatherings, however, try to get to one of the events that take place in other local towns and villages at weekends throughout **July** and **August**, where locals outnumber tourists and the competitions are guaranteed to be hard-fought and entertaining. Local tourist offices should be able to tell you what's happening where.

Ⓦ hostellingscotland.org.uk. This handsome hostel sits a short stroll from the centre in a former shooting lodge with bike storage facilities and a big communal kitchen. £

★ **Ivy Cottage Guest House** Cluniebank Rd Ⓦ ivycottagebraemar.co.uk. A lovely Victorian home with trim and comfortable rooms, and a view of red squirrels and birds as you eat your breakfast. They also have two self-catering options, both with wood-burning stoves: a cottage and a bothy/studio (three nights from £195). ££

EATING AND DRINKING

Taste Beside the Mar Rd roundabout Ⓦ taste-braemar. co.uk. Reliably good coffee shop and moderately priced contemporary restaurant doing home-made, gluten-free soups (served with local bread) and a scrummy selection of cakes. £

The Don Valley

The quiet countryside around the **DON VALLEY**, once renowned for its illegal whisky distilleries and smugglers, lies at the heart of Aberdeenshire's prosperous agricultural region. From Aberdeen, the River Don winds northwest through **Inverurie**, where it takes a sharp turn west to **Alford**, then continues past ruined castles through the **Upper Don valley** and the heather moorlands of the eastern Highlands. This remote and under-visited area is positively littered with ruined castles, Pictish sites, stones and hillforts.

GETTING AROUND
THE DON VALLEY

By car Although public transport connects Aberdeen with Inverurie and Alford, getting any further than this without a car is all but impossible.

Alford and around

ALFORD (pronounced 'aa-ford'), 25 miles west of Aberdeen, only exists at all because it was chosen, in 1859, as the terminus for the Great North Scotland Railway. A fairly grey little town now firmly within the Aberdeen commuter belt, it's still well worth making the trip here for the **Grampian Transport Museum**.

Grampian Transport Museum
Main St · Daily: April–Sept 10am–5pm; Oct 10am–4pm · Charge · ⓦ gtm.org.uk

The **Grampian Transport Museum** is home to a diverse display of transport through the ages, from old tramcars and pushbikes to modern, eco-friendly cars. Notable exhibits include the Craigievar Express, a strange, three-wheeled steam-driven vehicle developed by the local postman for his rounds, and that famous monument to British eccentricity and ingenuity, the Sinclair C5 motorized tricycle. Many of the vehicles are taken from private collections so do vary from year to year.

10

Craigievar Castle
6 miles south of Alford on the A980 · Castle April–May & Sept Fri–Mon 10.30am–4pm; June-Aug daily 10.30am–4pm; Grounds daily 11am–5.30pm · Charge · NTS · ☏ 08444 932174

South of Alford, **Craigievar Castle** is a Disneyesque pink confection of turrets, gables, balustrades and cupolas bubbling over from its top three storeys. It was built in 1626 by a Baltic trader known as Willy the Merchant, who evidently allowed his whimsy to run riot here. Entertainingly-led guided tours (in necessarily small groups owing to the narrow corridors and small areas) take in a number of rooms, where you can admire Jacobean woodwork and original plaster ceilings, while the grounds hold a Victorian kitchen garden and a Scottish glen garden. With a bit more time on your hands, there are a couple of lovely waymarked trails too.

ARRIVAL AND INFORMATION
ALFORD AND AROUND

By bus Stagecoach buses Nos 218 and 220 link Aberdeen with Alford (1hr 10min).

Tourist office The Grampian Transport Museum (see above) stocks loads of tourist information.

The Upper Don Valley
Travelling west from Alford, settlements become noticeably more scattered and remote as the countryside takes on a more open, familiarly Highland appearance. The **Lecht Road**, crossing the area of bleak but wonderfully empty high country to the remote mountain village of Tomintoul (see page 411), passes the Lecht ski centre (see page 413) at 2090ft above sea level, but is frequently impassable in winter due to snow.

Kildrummy Castle and Gardens
Kildrummy, 10 miles west of Alford off the A97 · **Castle** April–Sept daily 10am–4pm · Charge · **Gardens** April–Oct daily noon–5pm · Charge · HES · ⓦ historicenvironment.scot

Ten miles from Alford stand the impressive ruins of the thirteenth-century **Kildrummy Castle**, where Robert the Bruce sent his wife and children during the Wars of Independence. The castle blacksmith, bribed with as much gold as he could carry, set fire to the place and it fell into English hands. Bruce's immediate family survived, but his brother was executed, and the entire garrison hanged, drawn and quartered. Meanwhile, the duplicitous blacksmith was rewarded for his help by having molten gold poured down his throat. The Sixth Earl of Mar used the castle as the headquarters of the ill-fated Jacobite risings in 1715, but after that Kildrummy became redundant and it fell into disrepair. Beside the ruins, the separate **Kildrummy Castle Gardens** are quite a draw, boasting everything from swathes of azaleas in spring to Himalayan poppies in summer.

Lost Gallery
4 miles north of Strathdon · Wed–Mon 11am–5pm · Free · ⓦ lostgallery.co.uk

Ten miles west of Kildrummy Castle, the A944 sweeps round into the parish of **Strathdon**, little more than a few buildings scattered along the roadside.

Four miles north of here, up a rough track leading into Glen Nochty, lies the unexpected **Lost Gallery**, which shows work by some of Scotland's leading modern artists in a wonderfully remote and tranquil setting; as well as paintings, there are indoor and outdoor sculptures.

Corgarff Castle

Corgarff, 10 miles southwest of Strathdon • April–Sept daily 9.30am–5.30pm • Charge • HES • ⓦ historicenvironment.scot

In Corgarff, just off the A939, lies **Corgarff Castle**, an austere and isolated tower house with an unusual star-shaped curtain wall and an eventful history. Built in 1537, it was turned into a barracks by the Hanoverian government in 1748, in the aftermath of Culloden, in order to track down local Jacobite rebels; a century later, English redcoats were stationed here with the unpopular task of trying to control whisky smuggling. Today the place has been restored to resemble its days as a barracks, with stark rooms and rows of hard, uncomfortable beds – authentic touches which also extend to graffiti on the walls and peat smoke permeating the building from a fire on the upper floor.

The northeast coast

The **NORTHEAST COAST** of Scotland from Aberdeen to Inverness has a rugged, sometimes bleak fringe with pleasant if undramatic farmland rolling inland. Still, if the weather is good, it's well worth spending a couple of days meandering through the various little fishing villages and along the miles of deserted, unspoilt beaches. The largest coastal towns are **Peterhead** and **Fraserburgh**, both dominated by sizeable fishing fleets; while neither has much to make a long stay worthwhile, the latter's Museum of Scottish Lighthouses is one of the most attractive small museums in Scotland. More appealing to most visitors are the quieter spots along the **Moray coast**, including the charming villages of **Pennan**, **Gardenstown**, **Portsoy** and **Cullen**.

GETTING AROUND   **THE NORTHEAST COAST**

By train Trains are a faster but less frequent option than taking the bus, running every 1–2hr from Aberdeen to Elgin (1hr 30min), Forres (1hr 45min) and Nairn (2hr).

By bus The main towns and villages along this stretch of coast are well served by buses, with hourly services from Aberdeen to Elgin (2hr 30min), Forres (2hr 50min) and Nairn (3hr 15min).

Forvie National Nature Reserve

3 miles north of Newburgh • Visitor centre April–Sept daily 9am–5pm; contact for winter hours • Free • ⓦ nature.scot

Fifteen miles north of Aberdeen and three miles north of Newburgh, a turning (signposted to Collieston) leads off the main A90 coast road to **Forvie National Nature Reserve**. This area incorporates the Sands of Forvie, one of Britain's largest and least disturbed **dune systems**, which is home to Britain's largest colony of breeding eider duck. There's a small but informative **visitor centre**, from which a network of **trails** winds along the coast and through the dunes, with one leading to the site of a fifteenth-century village buried by the shifting sands.

Cruden Bay

Superb sandy beaches can be found eight miles north of Forvie at **Cruden Bay**, from where a pleasant fifteen-minute walk leads to the huge pink-granite ruin of **Slains Castle**. The ruin itself is not especially interesting – it was over-modernized in the nineteenth century – though its stark clifftop beauty is striking, and it claims notoriety as the place that inspired Bram Stoker to write *Dracula*. The best approach is to pull into the Meikle Partans car park on the A975 north of the village and follow the obvious path until you begin to see the ruins.

Bullers of Buchan

Reached by driving one and a half miles north from Cruden Bay along the A975 or walking three precarious miles north from Slains Castle along the cliffs, the **Bullers of Buchan** is a splendid 245ft-deep **sea chasm**, where the ocean gushes in through a natural archway eroded by the sea. This is some of the finest cliff scenery in the country and attracts a huge number of (smelly) nesting seabirds.

Fraserburgh

10

Just west of a swooping, sandy bay, **FRASERBURGH** is a large and fairly severe-looking place, edged by warehouse-like superstores and farmland. The intriguing **Museum of Scottish Lighthouses** makes a short visit worthwhile, and you'll find good, seafront hotel rooms nearby in the sleepy fishing village of **St Combs**.

Museum of Scottish Lighthouses

Stevenson Rd • April–Oct Mon & Wed–Sun 10am–5pm, Tues noon–5pm • Charge • ⓦ lighthousemuseum.org.uk

At the northern tip of the town, an eighteenth-century lighthouse protrudes from the top of sixteenth-century **Fraserburgh Castle**. The lighthouse was one of the first to be built in Scotland and is now part of the excellent **Museum of Scottish Lighthouses**, where you can see a collection of huge lenses and prisms gathered from decommissioned lighthouses, and a display on various members of the famous 'Lighthouse' Stevenson family. The highlight of the museum is the tour of Kinnaird Head lighthouse itself, preserved as it was when the last keeper left in 1991, with its century-old equipment still in perfect working order. The **tearoom** features sea views and home baking.

ARRIVAL AND INFORMATION
FRASERBURGH

By bus Fraserburgh bus station is located on Hanover St. Destinations Aberdeen (every 30min; 1hr 30min); Banff (3 daily; 1hr); Macduff (3 daily; 55min).

Tourist office The visitor centre is housed inside the Museum of Scottish Lighthouses (ⓦ visitfraserburgh.com).

ACCOMMODATION

Coral Haven Guest House 53 Saltoun Rd ⓦ guesthousefraserburgh.co.uk. Inviting, rather old-fashioned family-run guesthouse with five simple rooms, though only one is en suite. A generous breakfast is included to see you on your way. **££**

Fraserburgh to Gardenstown

The coast road between **Fraserburgh** and **Gardenstown**, fifteen miles to the west, is particularly attractive: inland there are villages with pretty churches and cottages, while countless paths lead off it to ruined castles, clifftop walks and lonely beaches.

Pennan

PENNAN is a tiny fishing hamlet that lies just off the B9031 down a steep and hazardous hill. Consisting of little more than a single row of whitewashed stone cottages tucked between a cliff and the sea, the village leapt into the limelight when the British movie *Local Hero* was filmed here in 1982; you can stay at one of the identifiable landmarks from the film, the *Pennan Inn* (see page 368).

Crovie

Locals in the tiny but appealing village of **CROVIE** (pronounced 'crivie'), on the other side of Troup Head from Pennan, frequently have their doorsteps washed by the sea. The Head itself supports over 1,500 gannet nests. Wedged in against the steep cliffs, Crovie is so narrow that its residents have to park their cars at one end of the village and continue to their houses on foot.

10

Pennan Inn By the waterfront ⓦ thepennaninn.co.uk. Crovie's most recognizable landmark is the handsome whitewashed *Pennan Inn*, a key location in *Local Hero*. The three en-suite rooms are brightly painted and cosy. You can also grab a drink or something to eat in the bar, perhaps a Thai curry. **£££**

Gardenstown

GARDENSTOWN, a short way west of Crovie, is one of the more attractive villages along this stretch of coast, with stone cottages huddled around a wave-gnawed bay. It's considerably larger than Crovie and supports a small gallery and teashop down by the harbour.

Macduff

Heading west along the B9031 from Pennan brings you, after ten miles, to **MACDUFF**, a famous spa town during the nineteenth century that now has a thriving and pleasant harbour. Macduff and its neighbour Banff are separated by little more than the beautiful seven-arch bridge over the River Deveron.

By bus Buses from towns and villages along the northeast coast stop on Union Rd or Shore St, both near the harbour.

Destinations Banff (at least hourly; 5min); Cullen via Portsoy (hourly; 40min); Fraserburgh (1–2 daily; 55min).

ACCOMMODATION AND EATING

Mansfield House B&B 113 Duff St ☎01261 833557. Elegant B&B with soothing decor: the white room with its modern four-poster is especially attractive. Sea views, great service and a tasty breakfast. **££**

Seafront Café and Takeaway 33 Shore St ☎01261 831017. Cute and jaunty café serving soup, sandwiches, bacon butties, excellent fish and chips and huge cakes and scones. **£**

Banff and around

Roughly the same size as its neighbour, Macduff, **BANFF** has a mix of characterful old buildings and boarded-up shops, which give little clue to the extravagance of Duff House, the town's main attraction. Look out for the historic tollbooth building, and the town's pre-Reformation market cross.

Duff House

Half a mile south of Banff's high street • April–Sept daily 11am–5pm; Oct–March Fri–Sun 11am–4pm • Charge • HES • ⓦ historicenvironment.scot

Built to a design by William Adam in the 1730s, **Duff House** is an elegant four-floor Georgian Baroque house that was originally intended for one of the northeast's richest men, William Braco, who became Earl of Fife in 1759. It was clearly built to impress, and could have been even more splendid had Adam been allowed to build curving colonnades either side; Braco's refusal to pay for carved Corinthian columns to be shipped in from Queensferry caused such bitter arguments that the laird never came to live here, and even shut his coach curtains whenever he passed by. Since then, the house has been used variously as a hotel, family home and sanatorium. Today, it's home to a **tearoom** and a **gallery**, with an impressive collection of fine art provided by the National Galleries of Scotland.

By bus Local buses arrive at and depart from High St, or Low St, which runs parallel.

Destinations Macduff (at least hourly; 5min); Cullen via Portsoy (hourly; 35min); Fraserburgh (1–2 daily; 1hr).

TOURS

Boat trips From the harbour, Guide Charters & Cruises (ⓦ guidechartercruises.co.uk) offers wildlife-spotting, fishing and sightseeing trips along the coast. Trips (3hr) cost £30.

ACCOMMODATION AND EATING

Banff Links Caravan Park 1.5 miles west of Banff ⓦ banfflinkscaravanpark.co.uk. Well-equipped campsite close to the beach, located about halfway between Banff and Whitehills. Has a handy on-site shop and laundry facilities. Per pitch £

County Hotel 32 High St ⓦ thecountyhotel.com. The French bistro in the grand *County Hotel* does high-end food, with grilled scallops and the like costing £28 for two courses. The en-suite rooms here are pleasant enough, if a little bit too old fashioned. ££

Seafield Arms 5 Chapel St, Whitehills, 3 miles west of Banff ⓦ seafieldarms.co.uk. This 200-year-old inn in the nearby village of Whitehills has surprisingly twenty-

first-century rooms (plus a two-bedroom apartment) with Sky TV, wi-fi and gleaming bathrooms. Downstairs, high-quality pub food is served both in the bar and the popular restaurant that adjoins it – the menu includes plenty of local shellfish and seafood options; good value three-course evening meal for £20. ££

Trinity Manse Guest House 21 Castle St ⓦ trinitymanseguesthouse.com. This crystal-clean and welcoming guesthouse with friendly owners features excellent value, up-to-date rooms, including one that is suitable for families. The location bang in the centre of town is very convenient too. ££

Cullen and around

Twelve miles west of Banff is **CULLEN**. Strikingly situated beneath a superb series of arched viaducts, which were built because the Earl and Countess of Seafield refused to allow the railway to pass through the grounds of Cullen House, the town is made up of two sections: **Seatown**, by the harbour, and the **new town** on the hillside. There's a lovely stretch of sheltered sand by Seatown, where the colourful houses – confusingly numbered according to the order in which they were built – huddle end-on to the sea. The town is perhaps best known as the home of **Cullen skink** – a thick soup made from milk (or cream), potato and smoked haddock.

Six miles east of Cullen is the quiet village of **PORTSOY**, renowned for its green marble (once shipped to Versailles), and its annual traditional boat festival in early July.

ARRIVAL AND DEPARTURE   CULLEN

By bus Hourly bus No. 35A connects Cullen with Aberdeen (2hr 35min), arriving at and departing from The Square in the new town.

INFORMATION

Tourist office You can pick up leaflets about local walks at the town's independent tourist office on the main square of the new town (generally June–Aug daily 11am–5pm; ⓦ discovercullen.com), but as it's run by volunteers the opening hours can be sporadic.

ACCOMMODATION

Cullen Bay Hotel Cullen Bay ⓦ cullenbayhotel.com. Smart seafront hotel with fourteen very accomplished en-suite rooms (some with bath, some with shower) either with water or hill view, plus an excellent restaurant looking out to the beach – well worth eating at even if you're not staying here. £££

Buckie and Spey Bay

West of Cullen, the scruffy fishing town of **BUCKIE** marks one end of the **Speyside Way** long-distance footpath (see page 410). This follows the coast west for five miles to windy **Spey Bay**, at the mouth of the river of the same name, which can also be reached by a small coastal road from Buckie. It's a remote spot bounded by sea, river and sky. It is sometimes possible to see dolphins feeding if you wander along the long pebbly spit by the mouth of the Spey; this is also a good spot to see otters and birds, including ospreys.

Scottish Dolphin Centre

Spey Bay • April–Oct daily 10.30am–5pm • Free • ⓦ dolphincentre.whales.org

The main mission of the **Scottish Dolphin Centre** is researching the Moray Firth dolphin population (see page 401). The centre, run by the Whale and Dolphin Conservation Society, houses an exhibition and a café; alongside, the **Tugnet ice house**, a partially subterranean, thick-walled house with a turf roof used by fishermen in the days before electric refrigeration to store their ice and catches, makes for an atmospheric auditorium in which films of the underwater world are shown.

ACCOMMODATION

BUCKIE AND SPEY BAY

10

Rosemount B&B 63 East Church St, Buckie ☎ 01542 833434. Large B&B in a Victorian townhouse, with a cosy TV room to relax in. Rooms at the front of the house have views across the Firth. **££**

Elgin

The lively market town of **ELGIN**, a fifteen-mile drive from Buckie, grew up around the River Lossie in the thirteenth century. The centre has mostly kept its medieval street plan, and while the busy main street is choked with chain stores, it does open out onto an old cobbled marketplace with a tangle of wynds and pends on either side.

Elgin Cathedral

King St • Daily 10am–4pm • Charge; joint ticket with Spynie Palace (see page 371) available • HES • Ⓦ historicenvironment.scot

On King Street, a few blocks from the tourist office and clearly signposted, is the lovely ruin of **Elgin Cathedral**. Once considered Scotland's most beautiful cathedral, rivalling St Andrews in importance, it's little more than a shell today, though it does retain its original facade. Founded in 1224, the three-towered building was extensively rebuilt after a fire in 1270, and stood as the region's highest religious house until 1390 when the Wolf of Badenoch (illegitimate son of Robert II) burned the place down, along with the rest of the town, in retaliation for having been excommunicated by the Bishop of Moray when he left his wife; the notorious Wolf's tomb is in Dunkeld (see page 317). The cathedral suffered further during the post-Reformation period, when all its valuables were stripped, and the building was reduced to a common quarry for the locals. Unusual features include the Pictish cross slab in the middle of the ruins and the cracked gravestones with their memento mori of skulls and crossbones.

Elgin Museum

King St • April–Oct Mon–Fri 10am–5pm, Sat 11am–4pm; Nov–March open on request or if staff are in the building • Free • Ⓦ elginmuseum.org.uk

At the very top of High Street is one of Britain's oldest museums, the **Elgin Museum**, which has been housed here since 1843. Following a major refurbishment, it has plenty of modern touches, with displays on local history and some weird anthropological artefacts including a shrunken head from Ecuador. In addition, you can see an excellent collection of fossils, some well-explained Pictish relics and a display on the important Birnie hoard of silver Roman dinarii from 197 AD, found nearby.

Glen Moray

Bruceland Rd • Mon–Sat 9am–5pm (Oct–April closed Sat) • Charge • Ⓦ glenmoray.com

Elgin is on the edge of whisky country, with its attractive local distillery, **Glen Moray** part of the official Malt Whisky Trail (see page 412). Tours here are distinctive in that your guide is quite likely to be the stillman, mashman or one of the other workers from the distillery floor.

ARRIVAL AND INFORMATION

ELGIN

By train The train station, served by the Aberdeen–Inverness line, is slightly detached from the city centre on the south side of town. All services below run 5–11 times a day.

Destinations Aberdeen (1hr 30min); Forres (15min); Inverness (50min); Nairn (25min).

By bus The bus station is on Alexandra Rd, right in the town centre.
Destinations Aberdeen (hourly; 2hr 20min); Burghead (hourly; 30min); Duffus (hourly; 15min); Forres (every 30min; 25min); Inverurie (hourly; 1hr 40min); Lossiemouth (every 30min; 20min); Nairn (every 30min; 45min).
Tourist information Elgin Library, Cooper Park (Mon–Fri 10am–8pm, Sat 10am–4pm; ☎ 01343 562608).

ACCOMMODATION, EATING AND DRINKING

Ada 29 South St ⓦ adaturkishelgin.com. Ottoman-era Turkish cuisine, with mezze starters, falafel wraps and delicious chicken shish. Great service and an appealing lamp-hung interior. ££

Moraydale Guest House 276 High St ⓦ moraydaleguesthouse.com. Grand Victorian B&B with off-road parking and seven top-class rooms, some of which are on the ground floor. There's a sunny conservatory to eat your breakfast in. ££

Scribbles 154 High St ☎ 01343 542835, ⓦ facebook. com/scribbles.elgin. Rather try-hard interior design, but you'll find very good fruit smoothies, plus reasonable coffees, main meals and pizzas. Good for families with kids (crayons provided). ££

SHOPPING

Gordon & MacPhail 58 South St ⓦ gordonandmacphail. com. You can pick up some great picnic foods at this old-fashioned Aladdin's cave of delicacies; they claim to have the largest selection of whiskies in the world.

Pluscarden Abbey

6 miles southwest of Elgin • Daily 4.30am–8.30pm • Free • ⓦ pluscardenabbey.org

Set in an attractive, verdant valley southwest of Elgin, **Pluscarden Abbey**, looms impressively large in a peaceful clearing off an unmarked road. One of only two abbeys in Scotland with a permanent community of monks, it was founded in 1230 for a French order and, in 1390, became another of the properties burnt by the Wolf of Badenoch (see page 317); recovering from this, it became a priory of the Benedictine Abbey of Dunfermline in 1454 and continued as such until monastic life was suppressed in Scotland in 1560. The abbey's revival began in 1897 when the Catholic antiquarian, John, Third Marquess of Bute, started to repair the building. In 1948, his son donated it to a small group of Benedictine monks from Gloucester who established the present community. It is possible to **stay** here on retreat for a few days, taking part in the routines of monastic life; see the website for details.

Lossiemouth

Five miles north of Elgin across the flat land of the Laich of Moray, Elgin's nearest seaside town, **LOSSIEMOUTH** (generally known as Lossie), is a cheery golf-oriented seaside town blessed with lovely sandy beaches; the glorious duney spit of the **East Beach** is reached over a footbridge across the River Lossie from the town park. The town's only blight is the frequent sky-tearing noise of military aircraft from the nearby RAF base.

Spynie Palace

4 miles south of Lossiemouth off the A941 • April–Sept daily 9.30am–5.30pm; Oct–March Sat & Sun 9.30am–4.30pm • Charge; joint ticket with Elgin Cathedral available • HES • ⓦ historicenvironment.scot

Lossiemouth's development as a port came when the nearby waterways of **SPYNIE**, three miles inland, silted up and became useless to the traders of Elgin. Little remains of the settlement except hulking **Spynie Palace**, home of the bishops of Moray from 1107 until 1686. The enormous rectangular David's Tower – visible for miles around – offers stunning views from the top over the Moray Firth and the Spynie Canal.

Burghead

Another of this coastline's tightly packed, stone-built fishing villages, windswept **BURGHEAD**, nine miles northwest of Elgin, was once the site of an important Iron Age

10

fort and the ancient Pictish capital of Moray. Between 1805 and 1809 a fishing village was built on the promontory where the ancient fort had stood, in the course of which some unique Pictish stone carvings known as the **Burghead Bulls** were discovered. One is on display in the **Burghead Visitor Centre** (April–Sept daily noon–4pm; entry by donation; ⦿burghead.com), built into the round white lookout tower at the tip of the promontory; others can be seen in the Elgin Museum, the National Museum in Edinburgh and the British Museum in London. The tower offers great views of the Moray Firth, while inside are displays about Pictish times and the dramatic annual fire ceremony known as the **Burning of the Clavie**, one of only a few that still take place in Scotland. A burning tar barrel is carried around the town on January 11 to mark the old calendar's new year, before being rolled into the sea, sparks and embers flying.

ARRIVAL AND DEPARTURE   **BURGHEAD**

By bus Burghead is served by hourly bus No. 32 from Elgin (30min).

Findhorn

A wide sweep of sandy beach stretches five miles around Burghead Bay to **FINDHORN**, a tidy village with some neat fishermen's cottages, a delightful harbour dotted with moored yachts, a small **Heritage Centre** (May & Sept Sat & Sun 2–5pm; June–Aug daily 2–5pm; free; ⦿findhorn-heritage.co.uk) in the village's former salmon-net sheds and grass-roofed ice house, and a couple of good pubs. Like Lossiemouth, however, it's hard to escape the military presence in the area, with **RAF Kinloss**, one of the UK's most important front-line airfields, right on its doorstep.

The Findhorn Foundation

Findhorn is best known for the communal **Findhorn Foundation**, based beside the town's caravan park. Visitors are free to turn up and explore the rambling streets of the foundation, but it's worth trying to take a more informed look by means of a **guided tour** (see opposite). While you're here, don't miss the **Moray Art Centre** (Tues–Fri

---

FOUNDING FINDHORN

In 1962, with little money and no employment, Eileen and Peter Caddy, their three children and friend Dorothy Maclean, settled on a **caravan site** at Findhorn. Dorothy believed that she had a special relationship with what she called the 'devas … the archetypal formative forces of light or energy that underlie all forms in nature – plants, trees, rivers', and from the uncompromising sandy soil they built a remarkable **garden** filled with plants and vegetables, far larger than had ever been seen in the area.

A few of those who came to see the phenomenon stayed to help out and tune into the **spiritual aspect** of daily life at the nascent community. With its emphasis on inner discovery and development, but unattached to any particular doctrine or creed, the **Findhorn Foundation** has today blossomed into a **permanent community** of several hundred people, with a well-developed series of courses and retreats on subjects ranging from astro-shamanic healing to primal painting to organic gardening, drawing another eight thousand or so visitors each year. The original caravan still stands, surrounded by a whole host of newer timber buildings and eco-homes employing solar power and earth roofs.

The community has been acclaimed by the UN for their near-zero carbon footprint and, having been shunned locally for their perceived eccentricity, its approach to the environment and intentional communal living now seems visionary. Part of the collective ethos, though nothing is enforced or directed by the community, is to spread the word about existing in harmony with nature, and visitors are emphatically welcomed to join residential 'experience weeks' to find out more.

10am–5pm, Sat 10am–4pm; free; ⓦmorayartcentre.org), on the edge of the Findhorn Foundation but not officially a part of it. The centre, located in a terracotta-hued ecofriendly building, hosts eclectic and imaginative temporary exhibitions and regular (often free) art classes including woodworking and nature photography.

ARRIVAL AND DEPARTURE

THE FINDHORN FOUNDATION

By bus You can get here on Stagecoach bus No. 31 (every 1–2hr) from Forres High St (15min) and Elgin (30min).

INFORMATION AND TOURS

Visitor centre The visitor centre is near the foundation's main entrance (May–Sept Mon–Fri 10am–5pm, Sat & Sun 1–4pm; Oct–April Mon–Fri 10am–5pm; ⓦfindhorn.org).

Tours Guided tours (April, Oct & Nov Mon, Wed & Fri 2pm;

additional tours May–Sept at 2pm on Sat & Sun) cost £5; you can also guide yourself via a booklet (£5) available at the shop or visitor centre.

ACCOMMODATION

The visitor centre can provide you with information on staying within the community, either as part of an introductory **Experience Week** (cost based on your income), or simply overnighting. There are a number of **eco-houses** within the area around the Moray Art Centre offering good-value B&B accommodation.

Findhorn Bay Holiday Park At the entrance to the foundation, ⓦfindhornbayholidaypark.com. Despite enormous growth, the foundation is still situated on the same land as this caravan and camping park, which has

pitches (April–Oct only), stationary caravans (Dec–Oct), small wooden camping cabins and unusual eco-chalets (year-round). Per pitch £; eco cabin £; caravan £££; chalet per week ££££

Rainbow Lodge Ecovillage ⓦrainbowlodgefindhorn. com. A gorgeous green-painted eco home, where you can choose from a double, twin or single rooms or the self-catering studio. Rooms are sparely but attractively furnished, and visitors can use the sun-filled lounge and dining area.

EATING AND DRINKING

Bakehouse 91–92 Findhorn Rd ⓦbakehousecafe. co.uk. In Findhorn village, this moderately priced café sells food freshly prepared on site, from organic local cheeses to divine chocolate brownies. There are picnic benches for alfresco dining. Fri & Sat is pizza night. ££

★ **Phoenix Café** At the entrance to the Universal Hall ⓦphoenixshop.co.uk. Be sure to stop off at the community's excellent wholefood café, which serves healthy soups, organic pasties, herbal teas and irresistible organic cakes. £

ENTERTAINMENT

Universal Hall Arts Centre A short walk north of the visitor centre ⓦuniversalhall.co.uk. Connected to the *Phoenix café* is the strikingly beautiful Universal Hall Arts

Centre, a venue for stand-up comedy, drama, and good touring folk and jazz bands. Most events begin at 7.30/8pm.

10

The Great Glen and River Spey

GLEN COE

The Great Glen and River Spey

The Great Glen, a major geological fault line cutting diagonally across the Highlands from Fort William to Inverness, is the defining geographic feature of the north of Scotland. A huge rift valley was formed when the northwestern and southeastern sides of the fault slid in opposite directions for more than sixty miles, while the present landscape was shaped by glaciers that only retreated around 8000 BC. The glen is impressive more for its sheer scale than its beauty, but the imposing barrier of loch and mountain means that no one can travel into the northern Highlands without passing through it. With the two major service centres of the Highlands at either end, it makes an obvious and rewarding route between the west and east coasts.

11

Of the **Great Glen**'s four elongated lochs, the most famous is **Loch Ness**, home to the mythical monster; lochs **Oich**, **Lochy** and **Linnhe** (the last of these a sea loch) are less renowned, though no less attractive; all four are linked by the **Caledonian Canal**. The southwestern end of the Great Glen is dominated by the town of **Fort William**, the self-proclaimed 'Outdoor Capital of the UK'. Situated at the heart of the Lochaber area, it is a utilitarian base, with plenty of places to stay and excellent access to a host of adventure sports. While the town itself is charmless, the surrounding countryside is a magnificent blend of rugged mountain terrain and tranquil sea loch. Dominating the scene to the south is **Ben Nevis**, Britain's highest peak, best approached from scenic Glen Nevis. The most famous and dramatic glen of all, **Glen Coe**, lies on the main A82 road half an hour's drive south of Fort William, the two separated by the coastal inlet of **Loch Leven**. Nowadays, the whole area is unashamedly given over to tourism, with Fort William swamped by bus tours throughout the summer, but take a short drive from town and solitude is easy to find.

At the northeastern end of the Great Glen is the capital of the Highlands, **Inverness**, a sprawling city that hugs the northern end of the River Ness, close to the Beauly Firth; it's most often used as a springboard to more remote areas further north. Inevitably, most transport links to the northern Highlands, including Ullapool, Thurso and the Orkney and Shetland islands, pass through Inverness.

Rising high in the heather-clad hills above remote Loch Laggan, forty miles due south of Inverness, the **River Spey**, Scotland's second-longest river, drains northeast towards the Moray Firth through one of the Highlands' most spellbinding valleys. Famous for its ancient forests, salmon fishing and ospreys, the area around the upper section of the river known as **Strathspey** is just as spectacular as the Great Glen to the west. Strathspey is dominated by the **Cairngorms**, Britain's most extensive mountain massif, unique in supporting subarctic tundra on its high plateau.

BLOODY TALES BEYOND THE BEAUTY

Although best known for its windswept slopes and glassy lochs, the Great Glen has a turbulent and bloody **history**. Founded in 1655 and named in honour of William III, the town of Fort William was successfully held by government troops during both of the **Jacobite risings**. The country to the southwest, meanwhile, is inextricably associated with Bonnie Prince Charlie's flight after **Culloden** (see page 400). **Glen Coe** is another historic site with a violent past, renowned as much for the infamous massacre of 1692 as for its magnificent scenery.

DOLPHINS OF THE MORAY FIRTH

Highlights

❶ West Highland Museum Featuring loot from the Spanish Armada, relics from the Jacobite uprising and the rifle used in the Appin Murder, this little museum in Fort William provides a heady introduction to Highland history. See page 380

❷ Glen Coe Spectacular, moody, poignant and full of history – a glorious spot for hiking or simply absorbing the atmosphere. See page 388

❸ Glen Affric Head for the hills amid some of Scotland's best-hidden scenery, with ancient Caledonian forests, high peaks and gushing rivers. See page 394

❹ Culloden The visitor centre on the site of the last battle on British soil gives a stirring

and unsettling account of the fight, and the subsequent massacre of survivors and civilians. See page 400

❺ Dolphins of the Moray Firth Europe's most northerly school of bottlenose dolphins can be seen from the shore or on a boat trip. See page 401

❻ The Cairngorms Scotland's grandest mountain massif, located within Britain's largest national park, where rare plants, wild animals, inspiring vistas and challenging outdoor activities abound. See page 405

❼ Whisky nosing Take a tutored 'nosing' (tasting) on the very premises where the stuff is made and matured. See page 412

HIGHLIGHTS ARE MARKED ON THE MAP ON PAGE 378

A string of villages along the river provides useful bases for setting out into the wilder country, principal among them **Aviemore**, a rather ugly straggle of housing and hotel developments which nevertheless has a lively, youthful feel to it. A little way north, **Grantown-on-Spey** is more attractive, with solid Victorian mansions but much less vitality, while smaller settlements such as **Boat of Garten** are quieter.

Downriver, Strathspey gives way to the area known as **Speyside**, famous as the heart of Scotland's malt whisky industry. In addition to the Malt Whisky Trail that leads round a number of well-known distilleries in the vicinity of places such as **Dufftown**, the lesser-known **Speyside Way**, another of Scotland's long-distance footpaths, offers the chance to enjoy the scenery of the region, as well as its whiskies, on foot.

GETTING AROUND   THE GREAT GLEN AND RIVER SPEY

By bus The Great Glen is reasonably well served by buses, with several daily services between Inverness and Fort William. There are also frequent buses connecting Inverness with Aviemore and Grantown-on-Spey. Further north in malt whisky country, services are extremely limited.

By car The main A82 road runs the length of the Great Glen, although relatively high traffic levels mean that it's not a fast or particularly easy route to drive. The A9 and A95 allow for quick hops between towns on the western side of the Cairngorms, but elsewhere within the national park roads are necessarily narrower (and slower).

By boat The traditional and most rewarding way to travel through the Great Glen is by boat: a flotilla of kayaks, small yachts and pleasure vessels takes advantage of the Caledonian Canal and its old wooden locks during the summer.

By bike Well-marked routes make it possible to cycle all the way from Fort William to Inverness. Mountain bikers especially are drawn to the Cairngorms, where there are excellent trails for beginners and experts.

On foot The 79-mile Great Glen Way links Fort William with Inverness, and takes five to six days to walk in full (see page 383).

Fort William

With its stunning position on Loch Linnhe, tucked in below the snow-streaked bulk of Ben Nevis, **FORT WILLIAM** (known by the many walkers and climbers who come here as 'Fort Bill') should be a gem. Sadly, the anticlimactic end point of the West Highland Way (see page 384) has had its waterfront wrecked by ribbon bungalow development and an ill-advised dual carriageway. The main street and the little squares off it are more appealing, though occupied by some decidedly tacky tourist gift shops. Other than its excellent **museum**, the town is short on must-sees, but it's undeniably a convenient base for **outdoor activities** – most notably walking. Several cruises leave from the town pier every day, offering the chance to spot the marine life of Loch Linnhe, which includes seals and seabirds. Shops rent out kayaks and mountain bikes for independent exploration of the surrounding area, and local guides run mountaineering courses (in summer and winter) on the slopes of nearby Munros. Some of the best views of these peaks can be had from **Corpach**, a small village opposite Fort William on the other side of Loch Linnhe, which also has a number of places to stay and several outdoor activities operators.

West Highland Museum

Cameron Square, just off the high street • Mon–Fri 10am–4pm • Free • ⓦ westhighlandmuseum.org.uk

Collections at the splendid and idiosyncratic **West Highland Museum** cover virtually every aspect of Highland life and the presentation is traditional, but very well done, making a refreshing change from the state-of-the-art heritage centres popping up across Scotland. You'll find treasures from the Spanish Armada, quasi-religious relics associated with Bonnie Prince Charlie and the Jacobite uprising, and the long Spanish rifle used in the Appin Murder (an event which inspired Robert Louis Stevenson's *Kidnapped*). There's even a 550kg slab of aluminium, the stuff that's processed into silver foil just five miles north of town (you'll see the huge pipes running down the mountainside), and a section on the World War II commandos, who received their famously tough training in nearby Lochaber.

The Jacobite Steam Train

At the train station on Station Square • Fort William–Mallaig April–Oct 10.15am; return 2.10pm; May–Sept Sun–Fri 12.45pm; return 4.45pm; Sat 2.40pm; return 6.40pm • Charge • Ⓦ westcoastrailways.co.uk

Excursions from Fort William include the 84-mile return trip to Mallaig (see page 425) on the **West Highland Railway Line** aboard the **Jacobite Steam Train**. Heading along the shore of Loch Eil to the west coast via historic Glenfinnan (see page 423) and a sinuous Victorian viaduct, the train has stunning views of the water and distant mountains, though these days it's as popular for its role in the *Harry Potter* films. The locomotives used are black and barrel-shaped machines from the 1920s and 1930s tugging younger British Rail carriages from the 1960s.

ARRIVAL AND DEPARTURE   FORT WILLIAM

By train Fort William is one of the stops on the scenic West   Highland Railway from Glasgow. The train station is just

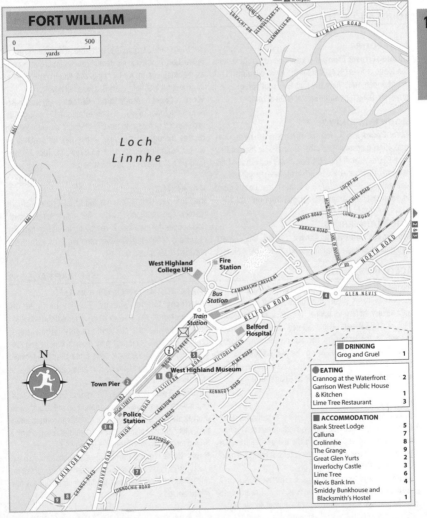

FORT WILLIAM

0 — 500 yards

11

Loch Linnhe

West Highland College UHI
Fire Station
Bus Station
Train Station
Belford Hospital
West Highland Museum
Town Pier
Police Station

◼ DRINKING	
Grog and Gruel	1

◼ EATING	
Crannog at the Waterfront	2
Garrison West Public House & Kitchen	1
Lime Tree Restaurant	3

◼ ACCOMMODATION	
Bank Street Lodge	5
Calluna	7
Crolinnhe	8
The Grange	9
Great Glen Yurts	2
Inverlochy Castle	3
Lime Tree	6
Nevis Bank Inn	4
Smiddy Bunkhouse and Blacksmith's Hostel	1

across the A82 dual carriageway from the north end of the high street.

Destinations Crianlarich (Mon–Sat 4 daily, Sun 3 daily; 1hr 50min); Glasgow Queen Street (Mon–Sat 3 daily, Sun 2 daily; 3hr 50min); London (1 nightly; 12hr); Mallaig (Mon–Sat 4 daily, Sun 3 daily; 1hr 20min).

By bus Intercity coaches from Glasgow and Inverness stop outside the train station on MacFarlane Way.

Destinations Drumnadrochit (9 daily; 1hr 25min); Edinburgh (1 daily; 4hr); Fort Augustus (9 daily; 50min); Glasgow (8 daily; 3hr); Inverness (Mon–Sat 9 daily, 6 on Sun; 2hr); Mallaig (Mon–Fri 3 daily; 1hr 20min); Oban (Mon–Sat 3 daily; 1hr 30min); Portree, Skye (4 daily; 3hr).

GETTING AROUND AND INFORMATION

By bus Fort William itself is small enough to get around on foot, but several accommodation options and activities operators listed below are based in Corpach, three miles along the Mallaig road – it's served by regular bus No. 45 (every 30min; 20min) from Middle St in Fort William.

Tourist office 15 High St (Mon, Tues & Thurs–Sat 9am–5pm, Wed 10am–5pm, Sun 10am–4pm; ⓦ visitfortwilliam. co.uk). Busy and very helpful tourist office, which stocks an excellent selection of maps and guidebooks on exploring the Great Glen.

TOURS AND ACTIVITIES

BOAT TOURS

Crannog Cruises Town pier (ⓦ crannog.net/cruises). Runs 1hr 30min cruises (£17.50) from the town pier down Loch Linnhe, where you'll have the chance to spot porpoises and grey seals. Daily trips April–Sept at noon & 2pm.

MOUNTAIN BIKING

Nevis Cycles Lochy Crescent, Inverlochy (ⓦ neviscycles. com). High-spec mountain bikes are available for rent here (from £35/day). Staff know the best routes and can also issue free maps. There's a second branch at the Nevis Range gondola base station (see page 387) – a location that boasts forest rides and a world-championship standard downhill track.

MOUNTAINEERING

Snowgoose Mountain Centre Station Rd, Corpach (ⓦ highland-mountain-guides.co.uk). Set beside *Smiddy*

Bunkhouse and *Blacksmith's Hostel*, this activity centre offers instruction, rental and residential courses for activities such as mountaineering, ice climbing and dinghy sailing. Sea-kayaking, for example, costs £60 for a full day.

West Coast Mountain Guides (ⓦ westcoast-mountainguides.co.uk). Long-established group of experienced guides who run climbing and mountaineering courses throughout the year. A five-day introduction to winter mountaineering costs £525/person. Trips to Skye (and even Norway) can also be arranged.

KAYAKING

Rockhopper Unit 17, Annat Industrial Estate, Corpach (ⓦ rockhopperscotland.co.uk). Get in touch with Rockhopper for sea-kayak coaching, including half-day excursions (£60) and two-day camping trips with meals provided (£260/person).

ACCOMMODATION

SEE MAP PAGE 381

The town itself isn't the most exciting place to base yourself, but Fort William's plentiful accommodation ranges from large luxury hotels to budget hostels and bunkhouses. Numerous **B&Bs** are also scattered across town, many of them in the suburb of Corpach on the other side of Loch Linnhe, three miles along the Mallaig road (served by regular buses), where you'll also find a couple of good **hostels**; try also nearby Banavie (see page 386).

HOTELS AND B&BS

★ **Crolinnhe** 37 Grange Rd ⓦ crolinnhe.com. Beautifully appointed guesthouse overlooking Loch Linnhe, with elegant French furniture in the rooms and attractive landscaped gardens outside. Their lakefront terrace is more Amalfi Coast than Scotland. ££££

★ **The Grange** Grange Rd ⓦ grangefortwilliam.com. A striking old stone house, with log fires, views towards Loch Linnhe and two luxurious suites; two, four or six night stay only; breakfast is brought to your room. ££££

Inverlochy Castle Torlundy, 3 miles north of the town centre on the A82 ⓦ inverlochycastlehotel.co.uk. Built on the site of a thirteenth-century fortress, this is one of Scotland's grandest and most luxurious country-house hotels with fantastic (and fantastically expensive) accommodation and Michelin-star food courtesy of fabled chef Michel Roux. ££££

★ **Lime Tree** Achintore Rd ⓦ limetreefortwilliam. co.uk. A stylish and relaxing option in an old manse, with a great modern restaurant and an excellent contemporary art gallery; they've also got the practicalities covered with a drying room, map room and bike storage. ££

Nevis Bank Inn Belford Rd ⓦ nevisbankinn.co.uk. Classy little hotel with a comprehensive range of rooms (including cosy doubles and double doubles) plus a fine restaurant. £££

THE GREAT GLEN WAY AND CYCLE PATH

Ordnance Survey Landranger maps 26, 34 and 41

The enormous cleft of the Great Glen is the most obvious – and by far the flattest – way of traversing northern Scotland from coast to coast. Stretching 79 miles, the **Great Glen Way** long-distance footpath is a relatively undemanding five-to-six-day hike that uses a combination of canal towpath and forest- and hill-tracks between Fort William and Inverness. Accommodation is readily available all the way along the route in campsites, hostels, bunkhouses and B&Bs, though in high season you should book ahead, and if you know you're going to arrive late somewhere it's worth checking that you can still get a meal either where you're staying or somewhere nearby.

There are various **guidebooks** that describe the route, including *The Great Glen Way*, published by Rucksack Readers (£13.99). For the best selection of guides, plus the relevant Ordnance Survey Landranger maps (£8.99 each) head to the tourist office in Fort William. Note, however, that forestry work can see the route diverted at short notice, so it's wise to check ⓦ highland.gov.uk/greatglenway before setting off.

Cyclists with mountain bikes or hybrids can also use the Great Glen Way, which offers a tranquil alternative to the hazardous A82 (currently the only option for those with road bikes). The route is well signposted and can be pedalled in one long day or two easier days, though of course you can tackle shorter sections. Bikes can be rented at Fort William, Banavie, Drumnadrochit and Inverness.

Whether you're cycling or walking, the suggested **direction** for following the route is from west to east, to take advantage of the prevailing southwesterly wind.

11

HOSTELS AND CAMPSITES

Bank Street Lodge Bank St ⓦ bankstreetlodge.co.uk. A bright and clean if functional 43-bed hostel, handy for transport options and the town centre. Choose between dorm accommodation and a good range of en-suite rooms. Dorms **£**; singles **£**; doubles **£££**

Calluna Connochie Rd ⓦ fortwilliamholiday.co.uk. Well-run self-catering and hostel accommodation a 10min walk from the centre of town, configured for individual, family and group stays. Also has laundry facilities, drying and kit rooms, plus kit for hire. The owners can also organize mountaineering trips. Three-night minimum stay. Dorms **£**; doubles **££**

★ **Great Glen Yurts** 3 miles northeast of Fort William off A82 (signposted from Torlundy) ⓦ greatglenyurts. com. Rotund and spacious, these luxury yurts occupy a magnificently peaceful setting with views of Ben Nevis. There's also a shepherd's hut and wooden cabins, and an open-sided kitchen is great for sociable evening meals. **££**

Smiddy Bunkhouse and Blacksmith's Hostel Snowgoose Mountain Centre, Station Rd, Corpach ⓦ highland-mountain-guides.co.uk. Alpine hostel and bunkhouse (one room for four and one room for six) on the site of an old blacksmith's workshop. It's 4 miles from Ben Nevis at the southwestern end of the Caledonian Canal. Dorms **£**

EATING   SEE MAP PAGE 381

Crannog at the Waterfront Town pier, just off the bypass on entering Fort William ⓦ crannog.net. Red-roofed restaurant with lochside views and fresh seafood, including Mallaig langoustine, plus a reasonable wine list. Good lunchtime deals. The neighbouring shack sells Cullen skink and oysters. **££**

Garrison West Public House & Kitchen Cameron Square ⓦ garrisonwest.co.uk. Located in an old stone building in the centre of town, this is a modern but unpretentious pub serving brunch, lunch, pub dinners –

they have a special 'bairn's menu' for kids. There are small snacks such as stovie scones and a helping of haggis with oatcakes as well as meaty burgers and veg alternatives including cauliflower and apple curry. Cask ales and live music sessions. **£££**

Lime Tree Restaurant The Old Manse, Achintore Rd ⓦ limetreefortwilliam.co.uk/the-restaurant. Serves an excellent selection of contemporary Scottish food, especially seafood dishes like razor clams and Loch Etive Sea Trout. **£££**

DRINKING   SEE MAP PAGE 381

Grog and Gruel 66 High St ⓦ grogandgruel.co.uk. Loud and friendly, the downstairs alehouse at *Grog and Gruel* is a good bet for Scottish beer. The upstairs restaurant is more

relaxed, doing mostly Mexican mains, including a spicy 'hog's breath chilli'.

Around Fort William

Any disappointment you harbour about Fort William town should be offset by the wealth of scenery and activities in its immediate vicinity. Most obvious – on a clear day, at least – is **Ben Nevis** (see page 386), the most popular, though hardly the most rewarding, of Scotland's high peaks. The path up leaves from beautiful **Glen Nevis**, also a starting point for some other excellent walks of various lengths and elevations. The mountain abutting Ben Nevis is **Aonach Mòr**, home of Scotland's most modern

11

THE WEST HIGHLAND WAY

OS Explorer maps 342, 347, 348, 364, 377, 384, 385 & 392

Opened in 1980, the spectacular **West Highland Way** was Scotland's first long-distance footpath, stretching some 96 miles from Milngavie (pronounced 'mill-guy'), six miles north of central Glasgow, to Fort William, where it reaches the foot of Ben Nevis, Britain's highest mountain. Today, it is by far the most popular such footpath in Scotland, and while for many the range of scenery, relative ease of walking and nearby facilities make it a classic route, others find it a little too busy in high season, particularly in comparison with the isolation of many other parts of the Highlands.

THE ROUTE

The route follows a combination of ancient **drove roads**, along which Highlanders herded their cattle and sheep to market in the Lowlands, military roads, built by troops to control the Jacobite insurgency in the eighteenth century, old coaching roads and disused railway lines. In addition to the stunning scenery, which is increasingly dramatic as the path heads north, walkers may see some of Scotland's rarer **wildlife**, including red deer, feral goats and, soaring over the highest peaks, golden eagles.

Passing through the Lowlands north of Glasgow, the route runs along the eastern shores of Loch Lomond, over the Highland Boundary Fault Line, then round Crianlarich, crossing open heather moorland across the **Rannoch Moor** wilderness area. It then passes close to **Glen Coe** (see page 388) before reaching **Fort William** (see page 380). Apart from a stretch between Loch Lomond and Bridge of Orchy, when the path is within earshot of the main road, this is wild, remote country: north of Rowardennan on Loch Lomond, the landscape is increasingly exposed, and you should be well prepared for changeable weather.

TACKLING THE ROUTE

Though this is emphatically not the most strenuous of Britain's long-distance walks – it passes between lofty mountain peaks, rather than over them – a moderate degree of **fitness** is required as there are some steep ascents. If you're looking for an added challenge, you could work a climb of **Ben Lomond** or **Ben Nevis** into your schedule. You might choose to walk individual sections of the Way (the eight-mile climb from Glen Coe up the Devil's Staircase is particularly spectacular), but to tackle the whole thing you need to set aside at least **seven days**; avoid a Saturday start from Milngavie and you're less likely to be walking with hordes of people, and there'll be less pressure on accommodation. Most walkers tackle the route from south to north, and manage between ten and fourteen miles a day, staying at hotels, B&Bs and bunkhouses en route. **Camping** is permitted at recognized sites.

INFORMATION

West Highland Way ⓦ westhighlandway.org. The route's official website includes details about the Way and an accommodation list. The site also has links to tour companies and transport providers, who can take your luggage from one stopping point to the next.

The West Highland Way Official Guide Includes a foldout map as well as descriptions of the route, with detailed cultural, historical, archeological and wildlife information. It costs £16.99 and is widely available locally.

ski resort and an internationally renowned honeypot for downhill mountain-bike enthusiasts.

The main road travelling up the Great Glen from Fort William towards Inverness is the A82, ten miles along which is the small settlement of **Spean Bridge**, a good waypoint for getting to various remote and attractive walking areas with several backpacker hostels – in glens **Spean** and **Roy** – found along the A86 trunk road, which links across the central Highlands to the A9 and the Speyside region.

Glen Nevis

A ten-minute drive south of Fort William, **GLEN NEVIS** is among the Highlands' most impressive glens: a classic U-shaped glacial valley hemmed in by steep bracken-covered slopes and swathes of blue-grey scree. With the forbidding mass of Ben Nevis rising steeply to the north, it's not surprising that the valley has served as a location in the films *Rob Roy* and *Braveheart*. Apart from its natural beauty, Glen Nevis is also the starting point for the ascent of **Ben Nevis** (see page 386).

A great **low-level walk** (six miles return) runs from the end of the road at the top of Glen Nevis. The good but very rocky path leads through a dramatic gorge with impressive falls and rapids, then opens out into a secret hanging valley, carpeted with wildflowers, with a high waterfall at the far end. If you're really energetic (and properly equipped) you can walk the full twelve miles on over **Rannoch Moor** to **Corrour Station** (see page 325), where you can pick up one of four daily trains to take you back to Fort William (50min).

11

ARRIVAL AND INFORMATION
GLEN NEVIS

By bus Bus No. 42 runs from the high street in Fort William, past the Glen Nevis Visitor Centre, campsite and SYHA hostel to the Lower Falls car park (3 daily; 25min) almost five miles up the Glen Nevis road.

Ben Nevis Visitor Centre 1.5 miles southeast of Fort William along the Glen Nevis road (daily 8.30am–6pm; ⓦ bennevis.co.uk); take bus No. 41 (summer only) from Fort William. Staff here can give good advice on climbing the mountain. It's also worth asking for a copy of the useful leaflet *Ben Nevis: safety information for walking the mountain track*.

ACCOMMODATION AND EATING

Note that the *Achintee Farm Guest House* and *Ben Nevis Inn* are on the opposite side of the river from the main **Glen Nevis road** from Fort William – drivers should get to these places via the Achintee road from Fort William; coming by bus (see page 380), get off at the Glen Nevis Visitor Centre and take the footbridge over the river.

Achintee Farm Guest House Achintee, across the river from the visitor centre ⓦ achinteefarm.com. Friendly B&B with adjoining self-catering rooms and apartments and a rugged little stone cottage, right by the *Ben Nevis Inn* at the start of the Ben Nevis footpath. Also has drying rooms. Doubles and apartments **££**; cottage **£££**

★ **Ben Nevis Inn** Achintee, across the river from the visitor centre ⓦ ben-nevis-inn.co.uk. A basic and cosy bunkhouse (booking advised) in the basement of a lively 250-year-old pub at the start of the Ben Nevis footpath; three separate rooms with own kitchenette, shower facilities and drying room. The pub has a terrific atmosphere, and the menu – such as ale-battered North Sea haddock – is especially tempting after a day on the mountain. **££**

Glen Nevis Caravan and Camping Park Half a mile past the visitor centre along the Glen Nevis road ⓦ glen-nevis.co.uk. Offers a range of lodges, caravans and pods (sleeping two or three) as well as camping pitches. Gorgeous views, and facilities include hot showers, a shop and restaurant, and wheelchair-accessible bathrooms. Per pitch **£**; pods **££**

Glen Nevis Hostel 1 mile past the visitor centre along the Glen Nevis road ⓦ hostellingscotland.org.uk/ hostels/glen-nevis. This friendly, year-round hostel is an excellent base for walkers and has full catering, as well as a decent kitchen. As you'd expect, it gets very busy in summer, so book ahead. Dorms **£**; doubles **£**

The Nevis Range

Situated seven miles northeast of Fort William by the A82, on the slopes of **Aonach Mòr**, one of the high mountains abutting Ben Nevis, the **Nevis Range** is Scotland's

11

ASCENT OF BEN NEVIS

Harvey's Ben Nevis Superwalker map (£13.50) is available from Fort William's tourist office and most local bookshops and outdoor stores.

Of all the walks in and around Glen Nevis, the **ascent of Ben Nevis** (4411ft), Britain's highest summit, inevitably attracts the most attention. In high summer the trail teems with hikers – around a hundred thousand trek up to the summit each year. However, this doesn't mean that the mountain should be treated casually. It can snow at the summit any day of the year and people die on the slopes, so make sure that you take the necessary precautions; in winter, of course, the mountain should be left to the experts. The most obvious **route**, a Victorian pony-path up the whaleback south side of the mountain, built to service the observatory that once stood on the top, starts from the helpful **Glen Nevis Visitor Centre** (see page 385). This also sells mountain equipment and last-minute supplies and is located a mile and a half southeast of Fort William along the Glen Nevis road. Return via the main route or, if the weather is settled and you're confident enough, make a side trip from the wide saddle into the **Allt a'Mhuilinn glen** for spectacular views of the great cliffs on Ben Nevis's north face. Allow a full day (8hr) for the climb and check the weather forecast before setting out (⊕ bennevisweather.co.uk is useful).

highest ski area. The fifteen-minute **gondola trip** (daily Easter–June, Sept & Oct 10am–5pm; July & Aug 9.30am–6pm; early Nov & late Dec–Easter 9am–4pm; £12.50; ⊕ nevisrange.co.uk/mountain-gondola) to get here, rising 2000ft, gives an easy approach to some high-level walking as well as spectacular views from the terrace of the self-service restaurant at the top station. There's also a **discovery centre** here, providing insights into the mountain's geology and wildlife. The **base station** area in Torlundy, just east of Fort William, also has a café, and there's a high-wire adventure course and nature trail nearby.

ARRIVAL AND INFORMATION
THE NEVIS RANGE

By bus Bus No. 42 runs year-round from Fort William to the gondola's base station (4 daily Mon–Sat, 2 daily on Sun; 20min).

Tourist information In the Mountain Discovery Centre, located at the top gondola station (June–Aug 9.30am–6pm; Sept & Oct 10am–4pm; ⊕ nevisrange.co.uk).

Neptune's Staircase

In the suburb of **Banavie**, three miles north of the centre of Fort William along the A830 to Mallaig, the Caledonian Canal (see page 397) climbs 64ft in less than half a mile via a punishing but picturesque series of eight locks known as **Neptune's Staircase**. There are stunning views from here of Ben Nevis and its neighbours, and it's a popular point from which to walk or cycle along the canal towpath.

ARRIVAL AND GETTING AROUND
NEPTUNE'S STAIRCASE

By bus Stagecoach bus No. 45A runs from Middle St in Fort William to Banavie (every 15–30min; 10min).

ACCOMMODATION AND EATING

Chase the Wild Goose Hostel Locheil Crescent, Banavie ⊕ chasethewildgoosehostel.com. A small, comfortable hostel with four-to eight-bed rooms close to Neptune's Staircase and also handy for the Great Glen Way. Self-catering kitchen, lounge and barbecue area for use in summer. Dorms £

Eagle Barge Inn Laggan Locks, at the northern end of Loch Lochy ⊕ eaglebargeinn.weebly.com. If you do

choose to cycle along the Caledonian Canal, look out for this unusual pub, where mains like peat-smoked salmon and real ale are offered aboard a wonderful 1920s Dutch barge. ££

Moorings Hotel Beside the Staircase in Banavie ⊕ moorings-fortwilliam.co.uk. This mid-sized hotel near the canal serves curries and other pub staples in its bar, as well as classy and beautifully presented Scottish dinners in the main restaurant. £££

★ **Treetops** Badabrie, Banavie ⓦ treetopsfortwilliam. co.uk. This modern chalet offers incomparable Ben Nevis

and Loch Linnhe views and soothingly cosy rooms. Superb breakfasts (veggie haggis is an option) and warmly welcoming and helpful hosts. ££

Spean Bridge and around

Ten miles northeast of Fort William, the village of **SPEAN BRIDGE** marks the junction of the A82 with the A86 from Dalwhinnie and Kingussie (see page 408). If you're here, it's well worth heading a mile out of the village on the A82 towards Inverness to the **Commando Memorial**, a bronze statue depicting a group of soldiers which commemorates the men who trained in the area during World War II. Their story is told in depth at the West Highland Museum in Fort William (see page 384). The statue looks out on an awesome sweep of moor and mountain that takes in the wider Lochaber area and the Ben Nevis massif.

Glen Roy

Three miles east of Spean Bridge, a minor road turns north off the A86 and up **Glen Roy**. Drive a couple of miles along the glen and you'll see the so-called 'parallel roads': not roads at all, but ancient beaches at various levels along the valley sides, which mark the shorelines of a loch confined here by a glacial dam in the last Ice Age.

Tulloch and around

East of Roy Bridge along the A86, just before **Tulloch**, the train line and the main road part company. From Tulloch's small railway station, accessible only by a single-track road and served by Caledonian sleeper services from London, trains swing south to pass Loch Treig and cross Rannoch Moor (see page 325).

Beyond the turn-off at the Tulloch station, the A86 runs alongside the artificial **Loch Laggan** with the picturesque Ardverikie Castle on its southern shore and the attractive walking area of Creag Meagaidh National Nature Reserve to the north.

ARRIVAL AND DEPARTURE   **SPEAN BRIDGE AND AROUND**

By bus Buses bound for Spean Bridge depart from Fort William's bus station a couple of times per hour, taking

15–30min to arrive in the centre of the village.

ACCOMMODATION AND EATING

Àite Cruinnichidh 3.5 miles west of Tulloch railway station, just south of A86 ⓦ highland-hostel.co.uk. A comfortable wood-lined bunkhouse in a beautiful setting, with good facilities including family rooms and a sauna, as well as local advice for walkers and cyclists. Two-night minimum stay other than for cyclists or those walking the

East Highland Way. Dorms £; private rooms ££
Old Pines Hotel and Restaurant A few hundred yards northwest of the Commando Memorial, on the B8004 to Gairlochy ⓦ oldpines.co.uk. A welcoming, if very overpriced, hotel, but the restaurant is well worth pursuing for its delicious home-made cooking and locally sourced

---

DOWNHILL MOUNTAIN BIKING ON THE NEVIS RANGE

From the top of the Nevis Range gondola station, you can experience a white-knuckle ride down Britain's only World Cup standard **downhill mountain-bike course**, a hair-raising 3km route that's not for the faint-hearted. There are also over 25 miles of waymarked off-road bike routes, known as the Witch's Trails, on the mountainside and in the Leanachan Forest, ranging from gentle paths to cross-country scrambles. At the entrance to the lower gondola station, **Nevis Cycles** (ⓦ neviscycles.com) rents general mountain bikes (from £15) as well as full-suspension ones for the downhill course. The **Nevis Bike School** (ⓦ nevisrange. co.uk/activities/bike) runs training courses (2hr 30min; £37/person, minimum three people). Depending on the trail you choose, you may also need to buy a **gondola pass** (from £11).

11

game and shellfish as well as home baking, pasta and ice cream. £££

Station Lodge At Tulloch Station ⓦ stationlodge.co.uk. The station building at Tulloch is now a friendly and well-equipped hostel that can provide cooked breakfasts, packed lunches and two-course dinners with advance notice. Dorms £

Glen Coe and around

Breathtakingly beautiful **GLEN COE** (literally 'Valley of Weeping'), sixteen miles south of Fort William on the A82, is a spectacular mountain valley between velvety green conical peaks, their tops often wreathed in cloud, and their flanks streaked by cascades of rock and scree.

Arriving from the south across the desolate reaches of Rannoch Moor, you're likely to find the start of the glen – with **Buachaille Etive Mòr** to the south and **Beinn a'Chrùlaiste** to the north – little short of forbidding. By the time you've reached the heart of the glen, with the huge rock buttresses known as the **Three Sisters** on one side and the Aonach Eagach ridge on the other combining to close up the sky, you'll almost certainly want to stop. Added to the compelling emotional mix is the story of the **massacre of Glen Coe** in 1692, the bloody nadir of the long-standing enmity between the clans MacDonald and Campbell.

Beyond the small village of **GLENCOE** at the western end of the glen, the glen itself (a property of the NTS since the 1930s) is virtually uninhabited and provides outstanding climbing and walking. From **Loch Leven** the main road goes west and over the bridge at Ballachulish en route to Fort William, while at the eastern end of the loch is the slowly reviving settlement of **Kinlochleven**, site of the world's largest indoor ice-climbing centre and a waypoint on the West Highland Way long-distance footpath (see page 384).

Brief history

In 1692, Glen Coe was the site of a notorious **massacre**, in which the MacDonald clan were victims of an abiding government desire to suppress the clans. Fed up with what they regarded as unacceptable lawlessness, and a groundswell of Jacobitism and Catholicism, the government offered a general pardon to all those who signed an oath of allegiance to William III by 1 January 1692. When clan chief **Alastair MacDonald** missed the deadline, a plot was hatched to make an example of 'that damnable sept', and **Campbell of Glenlyon** was ordered to billet his soldiers in the homes of the MacDonalds, who for ten days entertained them with traditional Highland hospitality. In the early morning of 13 February, the soldiers turned on their hosts, slaying around forty people and causing more than three hundred to flee in a blizzard.

Glencoe Mountain Resort

Half a mile south of the A82 at the foot of the mountain • Jan–Oct Mon–Thurs & Sun 9am–8.30pm, Fri & Sat 9am–10.30pm; Nov & Dec daily 9am–4.30pm • Chairlift; full-day ski/snowboard pass • Charge • ⓦ glencoemountain.co.uk

From the **Glencoe Mountain Resort** a chairlift climbs 2400ft to Meall a Bhùiridh, giving fine views over Rannoch Moor and to Ben Nevis. At the base station, there's a simple but pleasant café. Skiing, snowboarding and mountain biking sessions can all be arranged at this spectacularly located resort too.

Glencoe Village

Tucked between steep mountains, Loch Leven and the grassy banks of the River Coe, **Glencoe Village** is an attractive place to spend a couple of days. There's a good choice of accommodation in the area, and if you fancy a break from walking, the village museum and nearby visitor centre make for pleasant distractions.

WALKS AROUND GLEN COE

Ordnance Survey Explorer map 384

Flanked by sheer-sided Munros, **Glen Coe** offers some of the Highlands' most challenging **hiking** routes, with long steep ascents over rough trails and notoriously unpredictable weather conditions that claim lives every year. The walks outlined below number among the glen's less ambitious routes, but still require a map. It's essential that you take the proper precautions, and stick to the paths, both for your own safety and the sake of the landscape, which has become badly eroded in places. For a broader selection of walks, get hold of the Ordnance Survey *Pathfinder Guide: Fort William and Glen Coe Walks* (£11.99).

DEVIL'S STAIRCASE

A good introduction to the splendours of Glen Coe is the half-day hike over the **Devil's Staircase**, which follows part of the old military road that once ran between Fort William and Stirling. The trail, part of the West Highland Way (see page 384), starts at the village of **Kinlochleven** and is marked by thistle signs, which lead uphill to the 1804ft pass and down the other side into Glen Coe.

ALLT COIRE GABHAIL

Set right in the heart of the glen, the half-day **Allt Coire Gabhail** hike starts at the car park opposite the distinctive Three Sisters massif on the main A82. This explores the so-called 'Lost Valley' where the Clan MacDonald fled and hid their cattle when attacked. Once in the valley, there are superb views of the upper slopes of Bidean nam Bian, Gearr Aonach and Beinn Fhada, which improve as you continue on to its head, another twenty- to thirty-minute walk.

BUACHAILLE ETIVE BEAG

Undoubtedly one of the finest walks in the Glen Coe area that doesn't entail the ascent of a Munro is the **Buachaille Etive Beag** circuit, which follows the textbook glacial valleys of Lairig Eilde and Lairig Gartain, ascending 1968ft in only nine miles of rough trail. Park near the waterfall at **The Study** – the gorge part of the A82 through Glen Coe – and walk up the road until you see a sign pointing south to 'Loch Etiveside'.

11

Glencoe Folk Museum

Main St • Easter–Aug Wed–Sun 11am–3pm (last admission 2.30pm) • Charge • ⓦ glencoemuseum.com

If you have an hour to spare in Glencoe Village, it's worth paying a visit to the delightful heather-roofed **Glencoe Folk Museum**. Various games and activities for kids can be enjoyed within this cosy 1720 croft where items include a chair that reputedly once belonged to Bonnie Prince Charlie. Look out for their special storytelling events and workshops.

Glencoe Visitor Centre

1 mile east of Glencoe Village on the A82 • **Visitor centre** April–Oct 9am–4pm; Nov–Feb 10am–4pm • Free • **G**uided walks Easter & June–Sept; pre-book • Charge • Car park; charge • NTS • ⓦ nts.org.uk/visit/places/glencoe

The attractive and ecofriendly timber **Glencoe Visitor Centre** sits in woodland a mile south of Glencoe Village. It has a good exhibition, screenings of The Glen Revealed short film, plus information about the area's natural history and conservation issues, and some entertaining material on rock- and hill-climbing through the years. There's a decent café called The Highland Coo and a gift shop, and you may be able to join a ranger-led **guided walk** of the surrounding area.

ARRIVAL AND ACTIVITIES

GLEN COE AND AROUND

By bus To get to the NTS visitor centre or chairlift station from Fort William's bus station, hop on one of the Glasgow-

bound Scottish Citylink coaches (up to 8 daily; 30–45min). Bus No. 44 from Fort William also stops at least 10 times a day (3 on Sun) at Glencoe village en route to Kinlochleven.

ACCOMMODATION AND EATING

★ **Clachaig Inn** 2.5 miles south of Glencoe Village on the minor road off the A82 ⓦ clachaig.com. The liveliest, best-known hotel in the area is a great place to reward your exertions with cask-conditioned ales and heaped platefuls of food (such as Highland game pie); they also have 23 comfy en-suite rooms. £££

Glencoe Hostel Adjacent to the Glencoe Independent Hostel ⓦ hostellingscotland.org.uk/hostels/glencoe. A basic but decent wood-tiled hostel with a dining area, cosy lounge and well-equipped kitchen. Dorms £

Glencoe Independent Hostel North of the river, ⓦ glencoehostel.co.uk. Cheap and excellent independent hostel and bunkhouse in rustic whitewashed buildings, that also has two self-contained bothies sleeping five and six. Bike storage, drying room and laundry. Hostel £, bunkhouse £, bothies ££

Red Squirrel 150m south of the turn-off to Glencoe Independent Hostel ⓦ redsquirrelcampsite.co.uk. Sylvan year-round campsite, just south of the hostel on the road to *Clachaig Inn*. Campfires and pets permitted. Per pitch £

Scorrybreac On the north side of the river ⓦ scorrybreacglencoe.com. Secluded and friendly, a short walk from the centre of Glencoe village, *Scorrybreac* has four affordable en-suite rooms, the best of which have views over the mountains. ££

Kinlochleven

At the easternmost end of Loch Leven, the settlement of **KINLOCHLEVEN** is, thanks to its location on the West Highland Way, steadily reviving its fortunes. For many years it was a tourism backwater best known as the site of a huge, unsightly aluminium smelter built in 1904. The tale of the area's industrial past is told in **The Aluminium Story** (same hours as tourist information centre; free), a small series of displays in the same corrugated metal building as the post office and tourist information centre. As well as being close to Glen Coe, Kinlochleven stands at the foot of the Mamore hills, popular with Munro-baggers; Fort William is a day's walk away.

The Ice Factor

Leven Rd • Mon–Wed & Fri–Sun 9am–7pm, Thurs 9am–10pm • Charge •, ⓦ ice-factor.co.uk

Kinlochleven's disused aluminium smelter is now the home of an innovative indoor mountaineering centre called **The Ice Factor**. The facility includes the world's largest artificial ice-climbing wall (13.5m) as well as a range of more traditional climbing walls, plus equipment rental, a steam room and sauna. As well as climbing passes for experienced climbers, there are one-hour taster sessions (£29) and beginner climbing lessons (£30). There's a bar upstairs and food is available too.

ARRIVAL AND DEPARTURE   KINLOCHLEVEN

By bus The hourly No. 44 bus from Fort William runs to the centre of Kinlochleven (50min), passing Glencoe (35min) en route.

ACCOMMODATION AND EATING

Blackwater Hostel Beside the river on Lab Rd ⓦ blackwaterhostel.co.uk. A decidedly upmarket hostel, with en-suite dorms sleeping between two and eight and hobbit-sized wooden glamping pods available for rent. You can also camp here. Dorms £; glamping pod ££; camping per person £

Edencoille Guest House Garbhein Rd ⓦ kinlochlevenbedandbreakfast.co.uk. There's fine hospitality at this Edwardian-built house offering six rooms (including a quad), with notice, they can organize packed lunches, evening meals and guided walking trips. ££

Lochleven Seafood Café 5 miles west of Kinlochleven on the B836 (north side of the loch) ⓦ lochlevenseafoodcafe.co.uk. The best place to eat near Kinlochleven, this is a relaxed restaurant with an attractive outdoor terrace overlooking the loch. Specializes in local shellfish such as whole brown crab cooked in seawater. £££

MacDonald Hotel Fort William Rd ⓦ macdonaldhotel. co.uk. This central hotel has ten decent en-suite bedrooms as well as cabins and a campsite, but is best visited for its Bothy Bar, where you can join fellow walkers for fish and chips and other pub meals. Doubles ££; 4-person cabins £; camping per person £

Loch Ness and around

Twenty-three miles long, unfathomably deep, cold and often moody, **LOCH NESS** is bound by rugged heather-clad mountains rising steeply from a wooded shoreline, with attractive glens opening up on either side. Its fame, however, is based overwhelmingly on its legendary inhabitant, Nessie, the 'Loch Ness monster' (see page 391), who encourages a steady flow of hopeful visitors to the settlements dotted along the loch, in particular **Drumnadrochit**. Nearby, the impressive ruins of **Castle Urquhart** – a favourite monster-spotting location – perch atop a rock on the lochside and attract a deluge of bus parties during the summer. Almost as busy in high season is the village of **Fort Augustus**, at the more scenic southwest tip of Loch Ness, where you can watch queues of boats tackling one of the Caledonian Canal's longest flights of locks. You'll need your own **car** to complete the whole loop around the loch, a journey that includes an impressive stretch between Fort Augustus and the high, hidden Loch Mhòr, overlooked by the imposing Monadhliath range to the south.

Away from the lochside, and seeing a fraction of Loch Ness's visitor numbers, the remote glens of **Urquhart** and **Affric** make an appealing contrast, with Affric in particular boasting narrow, winding roads, gushing streams and hillsides dotted with ancient Caledonian pine forests. The busiest of these glens to the north is the often bleak high country of Glen Moriston, a little to the southeast of Glen Affric, through which the main road between Inverness and Skye passes.

11

GETTING AROUND **LOCH NESS AND AROUND**

By bus Using the A82, which runs along the western shore of Loch Ness, buses can travel the entire length of the loch, from Inverness to Fort Augustus. On the eastern side, however, regular bus services are limited to the stretch

---

NESSIE

The world-famous **Loch Ness monster**, affectionately known as **Nessie** (and by serious aficionados as *Nessiteras rhombopteryx*), has been a local celebrity for some time. The first mention of a mystery creature crops up in St Adamnan's seventh-century biography of **St Columba**, who allegedly calmed an aquatic animal that had attacked one of his monks. Present-day interest, however, is probably greater outside Scotland than within the country, and dates from the building of the road along the loch's western shore in the early 1930s. In 1934, the *Daily Mail* published London surgeon **R.K. Wilson**'s sensational photograph of the head and neck of the monster peering up out of the loch, and the hype has hardly diminished since. Recent encounters range from glimpses of ripples by anglers to the famous occasion in 1961 when thirty hotel guests saw a pair of humps break the water's surface and cruise for about half a mile before submerging.

Photographic evidence is showcased in two separate exhibitions located at **Drumnadrochit**, but the most impressive of these exhibits – including the renowned black-and-white movie footage of Nessie's humps moving across the water, and Wilson's original head-and-shoulders shot – have now been exposed as **fakes**. Indeed, in few other places on earth has watching a rather lifeless and often grey expanse of water seemed so compelling, or have floating logs, otters and boat wakes been photographed so often and with such excitement.

Yet while even high-tech sonar surveys carried out over the past two decades have failed to come up with conclusive evidence, it's hard to dismiss Nessie as pure myth. After all, no one yet knows where the unknown layers of silt and mud at the bottom of the loch begin and end: best estimates say the loch is over **750ft deep**, deeper than much of the North Sea, while others point to the possibilities of underwater caves and undiscovered channels connected to the sea. What scientists have found in the cold, murky depths, including pure white eels and rare arctic char, offers fertile grounds for speculation, with different theories declaring Nessie to be a remnant from the dinosaur age, a giant newt or a huge visiting Baltic sturgeon.

between Inverness and Foyers.

By car Although most visitors drive along the tree-lined A82 road on the western side of the loch, the sinuous, single-track B862/B852 (originally a military road built to link Fort Augustus and Fort George) that skirts the eastern shore is quieter and affords far more spectacular views.

Fort Augustus

FORT AUGUSTUS, a tiny, busy village at the scenic southwestern tip of Loch Ness, was named after George II's son, the chubby lad who later became the 'Butcher Cumberland' of Culloden fame; it was built as a barracks after the 1715 Jacobite rebellion. Today, it's dominated by comings and goings along the **Caledonian Canal**, which leaves Loch Ness here, and by its large former **Benedictine abbey**, a campus of grey Victorian buildings founded on the site of the original fort in 1876. The abbey has been converted into luxury flats. There are some good cycling routes locally, notably along the Great Glen cycle route.

ARRIVAL AND DEPARTURE
FORT AUGUSTUS

By bus Frequent buses ply the A82, linking Fort Augustus with Drumnadrochit (35min) and Inverness (1hr) to the north, and Fort William, 30 miles south (1hr).

INFORMATION

Tourist office In the car park north of the canal (April & May Mon–Sat 9.30am–5pm, Sun 10am–4pm; June Mon–Sat 9am–5pm, Sun 10am–4pm; July & Aug Mon–Sat 9am–6pm, Sun 10am–4pm; Sept & Oct Mon–Sat 9.30am–5pm, Sun 10am–3pm; Nov–March daily 10am–3pm; ☎ 01320 366779). Fort Augustus's very helpful tourist office hands out useful free walking leaflets and stocks maps of the Great Glen Way (see page 383).

Caledonian Canal Visitor Centre Ardchattan House, Canalside, by the locks (daily April–Oct 9am–5pm; Nov–March 9.30am–3.30pm; ⓦ scottishcanals.co.uk/destinations/fort-augustus/caledonian-canal-centre). Excellent visitor centre with information on the locale and the canal, a shop selling local produce, a café and good accommodation.

TOURS AND ACTIVITIES

Boat tours From its berth by the Clansman Centre, near the swing bridge, Cruise Loch Ness sails five miles up Loch Ness (2–4 daily; 50min £18; ⓦ cruiselochness.com), using sonar technology to provide passengers with impressive live 3D imagery of the deep where underwater cave systems,

salmon, cannibalistic trout (and, some would speculate, Nessie) are to be found.

Fishing The tourist office can advise you on how to obtain permits to fish the loch or nearby river.

ACCOMMODATION

Lovat Arms Hotel On the A82 in the centre of town ⓦ thelovat.com. Expensive hotel refurbished along ecofriendly principles and built on the site of the 1718 Kilwhimen Barracks. The brasserie serves inventive (and costly) dishes with a local focus. **££££**

★ **Lock Chambers** Ardchattan House, Canalside, ⓦ scottishcanals.co.uk/destinations/fort-augustus/airbnb-caledonian-canal-centre. The visitor centre offers seven lovely en-suite rooms, bookable on Airbnb: there are doubles, a bunk room sleeping four and a family room with a double and bunks. Some rooms have canal-facing

terraces, and all are tastefully and soothingly decorated. You can breakfast in the café downstairs. Doubles **££**; bunk room **££** family room **££**

Morag's Lodge Bunoich Brae, on the Loch Ness side of town ⓦ moragslodge.com. The atmosphere at this pleasant and well-equipped hostel, with four-and six-bed dorms, doubles, twins and family rooms liven up with the daily arrival of backpackers' minibus tours. They do bike hire (£20 per day including helmets and maps) and have a bothy bar for guests. Dorms **£**; doubles **££**

EATING AND DRINKING

Caledonian Canal Visitor Centre Café Ardchattan House, Canalside, by the locks ⓦ scottishcanals.co.uk/destinations/fort-augustus/caledonian-canal-centre. The best place for snacks – try the Loch Ness Chowder – home baking and coffee, plus local artisan ice cream. **£**

The Lock Inn Canalside, opposite the Caledonian Canal Visitor Centre ⓦ the-lockinn.co.uk. With attractive wood-panelled interiors and a wider selection of pub meals (such as chicken curry), *The Lock* is a slightly better choice than its neighbour, *The Bothy*. **££**

The east side of Loch Ness

The tranquil and scenic **east side** of Loch Ness is skirted by General Wade's old military highway, now the B862/B852. From Fort Augustus, the narrow single-track road swings up, away from the lochside through the near-deserted **Stratherrick** valley, which is dotted with tiny lochans. To the east of Fort Augustus you'll pass the massive earth workings of the Glendoe Hydro Development. From here, the road drops down to rejoin the shores of Loch Ness at **FOYERS**, where there are numerous marked forest trails and an impressive waterfall.

Past **Inverfarigaig** – where a road up a beautiful, steep-sided river valley leads east over to Loch Mhor – is the sleepy village of **DORES**, nestled at the northeastern end of Loch Ness, where the whitewashed *Dores Inn* provides a pleasant pit stop.

ARRIVAL AND DEPARTURE	THE EAST SIDE OF LOCH NESS

By bus Local buses run up and down the northeast side of the loch, shuttling visitors from Inverness south to Foyers (Mon–Fri up to 5 daily; 2 on Sat; 45min).

ACCOMMODATION AND EATING

DORES

Dores Inn North of the village centre, by the loch ⓦ thedoresinn.co.uk. Only 9 miles southwest of Inverness (and 11 miles north of Foyers), this old lochside pub is popular with Invernessians, who trickle out here on summer evenings for a stroll along the grey pebble beach and some monster-spotting; try the seabass with king prawns. **££**

FOYERS

Foyers House In Upper Foyers, up the track next to Waterfall Café ⓦ foyershouse-lochness.com. Out of the way, adults-only B&B with fabulous views of the loch from its terrace. The onsite Wee Dram restaurant and bar is top draw, offering sublime food and a terrific selection of malts. **££**

Waterfall Café In Upper Foyers, opposite the footpath to the waterfall ☏ 01456 486233. This friendly teashop still runs a live webcam of red squirrels nesting across the road – and does delicious breakfasts, lunches and baking to boot.

Drumnadrochit and around

Situated above a verdant, sheltered bay of Loch Ness fifteen miles southwest of Inverness, **DRUMNADROCHIT** is the southern gateway to remote Glen Affric and the epicentre of Nessie-hype, complete with a rash of tacky souvenir shops and two rival monster exhibitions whose head-to-head scramble for punters has occasionally erupted into acrimonious exchanges, detailed with relish by the local press.

Loch Ness Centre & Exhibition

On the main A82 • Daily Easter–June & Sept–Oct 10am–5pm; July & Aug 10am–6pm; Nov–Easter 10am–3.30pm; last entry 45mins before closing • Charge • ⓦ lochness.com

Of the two major monster hubs in Drumnadrochit, the **Loch Ness Centre & Exhibition** is the better bet, offering an in-depth rundown of eyewitness accounts and information on various Nessie research projects. It does a good job, mixing 'evidence' of the monster's existence with frank appraisals of pictures and sightings that turned out to be hoaxes.

Nessieland

Just west of the Loch Ness Centre & Exhibition on the A831 • Daily July & Aug 9am–7pm; Sept–June 9am–5pm • Charge • ⓦ nessieland.co.uk

Aimed mainly at families, the rather feeble **Nessieland** has an exhibition on monster sightings, a plastic model of Nessie for kids to clamber on, plus its own adventure playground. The wood-panelled and heavily tartanized interior of the adjacent *Loch Ness Lodge Hotel* is said to harbour a resident ghost.

11

Castle Urquhart

Beside Loch Ness, 2 miles southeast of Drumnadrochit and just off the A82 • Daily April–Sept 9.30am–6pm; Oct 9.30am–5pm; Nov–March 9.30am–4.30pm • Charge • HES • ⓦ historicenvironment.scot

The thirteenth-century ruined lochside **Castle Urquhart** was built as a strategic base to guard the Great Glen. The castle was taken by Edward I of England and later held by Robert the Bruce against Edward III, only to be blown up in 1692 to prevent it from falling to the Jacobites. Today, it's one of Scotland's classic picture-postcard ruins, particularly splendid at night when it's floodlit and the crowds have gone. In the small visitor centre, a short film highlights the turbulent history of the castle.

ARRIVAL AND DEPARTURE   DRUMNADROCHIT AND AROUND

By bus Drumnadrochit is served by frequent buses from Inverness (at least hourly; 30min), Fort William (up to 9 daily; 1hr 30min) and Fort Augustus (up to 10 daily; 35min). Buses stop near the post office, on the A82.

TOURS

Boat tours The sonar-equipped *Nessie Hunter* (ⓦ lochness-cruises.com) runs hourly trips (£16) on the loch from 10am to 5pm, from April to October (9am–6pm June–Aug).

ACCOMMODATION

Benleva Kilmore Rd, Kilmore ⓦ benleva.co.uk. Small, basic hotel in Kilmore, a 15min walk from the monster centres of Drumnadrochit. The eleven newly refurbished en-suite rooms have thick carpets and tartan furnishings, and there's a cracking breakfast to boot. **£££**

Borlum Farm A mile southeast of central Drumnadrochit, off the A82 ⓦ borlum.com. Attractive campsite overlooking the village, with space for caravans and tents. The site is part of a popular riding school offering lessons, rides and treks (from £20/hr). they also rent out two lovely croft cottages, one with a piano. Per pitch $\overline{£}$; cottages weekly **££££**

Glenkirk1 B&B 300m west of Nessieland Monster Centre along the A831 ⓦ lochnessbandb.com. Bright, friendly B&B in a former church located just a few minutes' walk from the centre, with three simple yet smartly decorated bedrooms up on the second floor. **££**

Loch Ness Backpackers Lodge Coiltie Farmhouse, Lewiston, 1 mile south of the centre of Drumnadrochit ⓦ lochness-backpackers.com. For a cheap bed for the night, head for this immaculate and friendly hostel, which has six- and seven-bed dorms, private rooms and family rooms, plus good facilities including a bar and two lounges. Coming from Drumnadrochit, follow the signs to the left. Dorms $\overline{£}$; doubles **££**

EATING AND DRINKING

Benleva Kilmore Rd, Kilmore ⓦ benleva.co.uk. One of many hotels doing bar food, *Benleva* sets itself apart by using local beer in some of its dishes, including the steak and ale pie with chips and seasonal veg. **££**

Fiddlers' Just south of the village green on the A82 ⓦ fiddledrum.co.uk. Busy, friendly bar with plenty of outside seating and, it's claimed, more than five hundred single malt whiskies. The mostly meaty menu has a couple of veggie options too, including a veggie and brie burger. **££**

Glen Affric

Due west of Drumnadrochit lies a vast area of high peaks, remote glens and few roads. The reason most people head this way is to explore the picturesque native forests and grand mountains of **Glen Affric**, heaven for walkers, climbers and mountain bikers. Munro-baggers (see page 10) are normally much in evidence, and it's possible to tramp 25 miles all the way through Glen Affric to Shiel Bridge, on the west coast near Kyle of Lochalsh.

Cannich and Loch Affric

The main approach to Glen Affric is through the small settlement of **CANNICH**, thirteen miles west of Drumnadrochit on the A831. Cannich is a quiet and uninspiring village, but it has an excellent campsite where mountain bikes can be rented. From the car park at the head of the single-track road along the glen, ten miles southwest of Cannich, there's a selection of **walks**: the trip around **Loch Affric** will take you a good five hours but allows you to appreciate the glen and its wildlife.

ARRIVAL AND DEPARTURE

GLEN AFFRIC

By bus From July to September, Ross's Minibuses (☎01463 761250, ⓦ ross-minibuses.co.uk) runs scheduled services to the car park at Glen Affric from Cannich (4 on Mon, Wed & Fri; 30min); Drumnadrochit (3 on Mon, Wed & Fri; 1hr 35min) and Inverness (2 on Mon, Wed & Fri; 2hr 10min). Its vehicles will also carry bikes if given advance notice.

INFORMATION AND ACTIVITIES

Tourist information Notice boards are dotted around the glen; the Forestry Commission website (ⓦ forestryandland. gov.scot/visit/glen-affric) includes an interactive map showing where they're located.

Volunteering For details of volunteer work in Glen Affric helping with restoration of the woodland, get in touch with the wonderful Trees for Life charity (ⓦ treesforlife.org.uk).

ACCOMMODATION AND EATING

Cannich Camping & Caravan Park In the centre of Cannich ⓦ highlandcamping.co.uk. Pretty, shaded campsite which also has a few basically furnished but well insulated pods sleeping three adults (or two adults and two children); facilities include lounge, laundry, play park and there's mountain bike hire (£20). Per person £; pod ££
Glen Affric Youth Hostel Allt Beithe, 20 miles southwest of Cannich ⓦ hostellingscotland.org.uk/ hostels/glen-affric. Utterly remote, this hostel near the head of Glen Affric makes a convenient if rudimentary stopover on the 25-mile hike through Glen Affric to Shiel Bridge. A wind turbine and solar panels provide the hostel with electricity but note that you'll need to bring all your own food. Dorms ££; twins ££

Inverness

Straddling a nexus of major road and rail routes, **INVERNESS** is the busy hub of the Highlands, and an inevitable port of call if you're exploring the region by public transport. Over a hundred miles from any other major settlement yet with a population rapidly approaching 100,000, Inverness is the only city in the Highlands. Crowned by a pink crenellated **castle** and lavishly decorated with flowers, the city centre still has some hints of its medieval street layout, though unsightly concrete blocks do an efficient job of masking it. Within walking distance of the centre are peaceful spots along by the Ness, leafy parks and friendly B&Bs located in prosperous-looking stone houses.

Brief history

The sheltered harbour and proximity to the open sea made Inverness an important entrepôt and shipbuilding centre during medieval times. **David I**, who first imposed a feudal system on Scotland, erected a castle on the banks of the Ness to oversee maritime trade in the early twelfth century, promoting it to royal burgh status soon after. Bolstered by receipts from the lucrative export of leather, salmon and timber, the town grew to become the kingdom's most prosperous northern outpost, and an obvious target for the marauding Highlanders who plagued this remote border area. A second wave of growth occurred during the eighteenth century as the Highland cattle trade flourished. The arrival of the **Caledonian Canal** and **rail links** with the east and south brought further prosperity, heralding a tourist boom that reached a fashionable zenith in the Victorian era, fostered by the royal family's enthusiasm for all things Scottish.

Inverness Castle

Mon & Thurs–Sun 10am–5pm • Charge • ⓦ highlifehighland.com
Looming above the city and dominating the horizon is **Inverness Castle**, a predominantly nineteenth-century red-sandstone building perched above the river. The original castle formed the core of the ancient town, which had rapidly developed as a port trading with Europe after its conversion to Christianity by St Columba in the sixth century. Robert the Bruce wrested the castle back from the English during the

Wars of Independence, destroying much of the structure in the process, and while held by the Jacobites in both the 1715 and the 1745 rebellions, it was blown up by them to prevent it falling into government hands. Today's edifice houses the **Sheriff Court** hence most of the castle is off limits. However, a new viewing point has opened up, offering unrivalled views of the city, and it's possible to wander the grounds, where a small plinth marking the start of the 73-mile Great Glen Way.

INVERNESS

■ EATING

Café 1	5
Café Artysans	1
Contrast	6
No 27	3
Rendezvous Café	2
Rocpool Restaurant	4

■ ACCOMMODATION

Bazpackers	4
Bught Caravan and Camping Site	10
Furan Guest House	9
Glenmoriston Town House Hotel	6
Heathmount Hotel	3
Inverglen Guesthouse	2
Loch Ness Country House Hotel	7
Moyness House	5
Rocpool Reserve	8
SYHA Inverness	1

■ NIGHTLIFE
The Ironworks | 1

■ DRINKING
Hootananny's | 2

Inverness Museum and Art Gallery

Castle Wynd • April–Oct Tues–Sat 10am–5pm; Nov–March Tues–Thurs noon–4pm, Fri & Sat 11am–4pm • Free • ⓦ highlifehighland.com

Below the castle, the revamped **Inverness Museum and Art Gallery** on Castle Wynd offers an insight into the social history of the Highlands, with treasures from the times of the Picts and Vikings, taxidermy exhibits such as 'Felicity' the puma, caught in Cannich in 1980, and interactive features including an introduction to the Gaelic language. It also houses the Highland Photographic archive and has impressive temporary art exhibitions.

Old High Church

Church St, next to Leakey's bookshop • Grounds open to public • Free • Church Sun services 11.15am • Free • ☎ 01463 250802

The **Old High Church**, founded in 1171 and rebuilt on several occasions since, stands just back from the east bank of the river on Church Street, hemmed in by a walled graveyard. Those Jacobites who survived the massacre of Culloden were brought here and incarcerated prior to their execution in the cemetery. If you look carefully you may see the bullet holes left on gravestones by the firing squads.

11

Scottish Kiltmaker Visitor Centre

In the Highland House of Fraser shop at 4–9 Huntly St, on the river's west bank • Mon–Sat 9.30am–5.30pm • Charge • ⓦ highlandhouseoffraser.com

Entered through the factory shop, the **Scottish Kiltmaker Visitor Centre** is an imaginative small attraction, complete with the outfits worn by actors for the *Braveheart* and *Rob Roy* films, which sets out everything you ever wanted to know about tartan. There's an interesting seven-minute film shown on the hour, and on weekdays you can watch various tartan products being made in the workshop. The finished products are, of course, on sale in the showroom downstairs, along with all manner of Highland knitwear, woven woollies and classy Harris tweed.

Ness Islands

From **St Andrews Episcopal Cathedral**, on the west bank of the river, you can wander a mile or so upriver to the peaceful **Ness Islands**, an attractive, informal public park reached and linked by footbridges. Laid out with mature trees and shrubs, the islands are the favourite haunt of local anglers.

Caledonian Canal

Half a mile upstream from the Ness Islands park, the River Ness runs close to the **Caledonian Canal**, which was designed by Thomas Telford in the early nineteenth century as a link between the east and west coasts, joining lochs Ness, Oich, Lochy and Linnhe. Today its main use is recreational, and there are cruises through part of it to Loch Ness (see page 391), while the towpath provides relaxing walks with good views.

ARRIVAL AND DEPARTURE INVERNESS

Train station **left-luggage** lockers cost £3–5 for 24hr, depending on size (Mon–Sat 6.40am–7.50pm, Sun 10.40am–6.20pm); the left-luggage room in the bus station costs £4/item/day (Mon–Sat 8.30am–5.30pm, Sun 9am–5.30pm).

By plane Inverness airport (ⓦ hial.co.uk) is at Dalcross, seven miles east of the city; from here, bus No. 11 (every 30min, 5.10am–8.35pm, 25min; £4.55; ⓦ stagecoachbus.

com) goes into town, while a taxi with Inverness Taxis (ⓦ inverness-taxis.com) costs around £15.

Destinations Belfast (6 weekly; 1hr 5min); Birmingham (Mon–Fri & Sun 1 daily; 1hr 30min); Bristol (1–2 daily; 1hr 5min); Kirkwall (Mon–Sat 1–2 daily; 45min); London Gatwick (4–5 daily; 1hr 50min); Luton (1 daily; 1hr 20min); Manchester (Mon–Fri 2 daily, Sat & Sun 1 daily; 1hr 30min); Stornoway (Mon–Fri 3–4 daily, Sat & Sun 1 daily; 40min).

By train The train station is on Station Square, just off Academy St, to the northeast of the centre.

Destinations Aberdeen (Mon–Sat 11 daily; 5 on Sun; 2hr 15min); Aviemore (Mon–Sat 11 daily, 7 on Sun; 40min); Edinburgh (Mon–Sat 8 daily, 5 on Sun; 3hr 30min); Glasgow Queen Street (3–4 daily; 3hr 20min); Kyle of Lochalsh (Mon–Sat 4 daily, 2 on Sun; 2hr 30min); London King's Cross (Mon–Fri & Sun 2 daily, 1 on Sat; 8hr–12hr 45min); Thurso (Mon–Sat 2 daily, 1 on Sun; 3hr 45min); Wick (Mon–Sat 4 daily, 1 on Sun; 4hr 20min).

By bus The main bus hub is just north of the train station, close to the public library.

Destinations Aberdeen (hourly; 3hr 50min); Aviemore (every 30min; 45min); Drumnadrochit (at least hourly; 30min); Fort Augustus (up to 9 daily; 1hr); Fort William (up to 9 daily; 2hr); Glasgow (5 daily; 3hr 25min–4hr); Kyle of Lochalsh (3 daily; 2hr); Nairn (every 20–30min; 45min); Perth (7 daily; 2hr 50min); Portree (3 daily; 3hr 15min); Thurso (Mon–Sat 5 daily, 3 on Sun; 3hr); Ullapool (2–4 daily; 1hr 25min).

GETTING AROUND

Car rental Budget, at the airport (ⓦ budget.co.uk).
Bike rental Ticket to Ride at The Pavilion, Bellfield Park

(ⓦ tickettoridehighlands.co.uk), rents out decent hybrid bikes for £35/day.

INFORMATION AND ACTIVITIES

Tourist office The tourist office is in an unsightly 1960s block at 36 High St, a 5min walk from the train station (April & May Mon–Sat 9am–5pm, Sun 10am–5pm; June Mon–Sat 9.30am–5pm, Sun 9.30am–5pm; July & Aug Mon–Sat 9am–6.30pm, Sun 9.30am–6pm; Sept & Oct Mon–Sat 9am–5pm, Sun 10am–4pm; Nov–March Mon–Sat 9am–5pm, Sun 10am–3pm). It stocks a wide range of literature, including free maps of the city and its environs,

and the staff can book local accommodation for a £4 fee. There's also a CalMac ferry booking office in the building (ⓦ calmac.co.uk).

Outdoor equipment Tiso Outdoor Experience at 2 Henderson Rd, on the Longman Estate (Mon–Sat 9am–6pm, Sun 10am–5pm; ⓦ tiso.com), has a large range of outdoor gear to rent or buy. There's also an indoor climbing wall and a path for testing walking boots before you buy.

TOURS

Inverness bus station is the departure point for a range of **day-tours** and **cruises** to nearby attractions, including Loch Ness, Skye, Orkney and the Moray Firth, where there's a chance to spot dolphins (see page 401). Inverness is also one of the few places where transport connections allow you to embark on a major **grand tour** of the Highlands.

The Highlands and Skye For exploring the northwest, ScotRail (ⓦ scotrail.co.uk) sells a Highland Rover pass (£95), offering four days of unlimited travel over eight consecutive days, with many train, ferry and coach routes included. Buy tickets at the train station or online.

Loch Ness Loch Ness cruises typically incorporate a visit to a monster exhibition at Drumnadrochit and Urquhart Castle. Jacobite Cruises, on Dochgarroch Lock at the northern point of the loch (ⓦ jacobite.co.uk), runs a 3hr coach trip (£37) to Loch Ness, including a 30min cruise and admission to Urquhart Castle (see page 391).

Orkney From June to August, John O' Groats Ferries (ⓦ jogferry.co.uk) runs day-trips to Orkney (£78), including visits to Kirkwall, Scapa Flow and the Ring of Brodgar. Departures leave daily from Inverness at 7.15am.

ACCOMMODATION

SEE MAP PAGE 396

HOTELS

Glenmoriston Town House Hotel 20 Ness Bank ⓦ glenmoristontownhouse.com. A smart contemporary hotel by the riverside just a few minutes' walk from the town centre, with muted decor and a good dining experience on offer at the *Contrast* brasserie (see page 399). ££££
Heathmount Hotel Kingsmill Rd ⓦ heathmounthotel. com. Reasonably central boutique hotel with blingy but comfortable rooms, some of which have four-poster beds; all come with Sky TV and an iPod dock. ££££
Loch Ness Country House Hotel Off the A82 Fort William Rd ⓦ lochnesscountryhouse.cobbshotels.com. Luxurious country-house hotel, three miles southwest of central Inverness. Offers modern Scottish food, fine

wines and more than two hundred malts, as well as very comfortable and spacious rooms. ££££
Rocpool Reserve Culduthel Rd ⓦ rocpool.com. Only a 10min walk south of the castle, this acclaimed hotel and restaurant has minimal but luxurious rooms (white cotton bedsheets, subtle splashes of colour and jacuzzis in the high-end rooms) – which are among the most expensive in Scotland – plus a swanky, French-inspired restaurant. ££££

B&BS

Furan Guest House 100 Old Edinburgh Rd ⓦ furan. co.uk. Good-value B&B a mile south of the centre, run by former hoteliers. Has a good choice of spotlessly clean rooms and a friendly resident cat. Laundry service available. ££

★ **Inverglen Guest House** 7 Abertarff Rd ⓦinverglenguesthouse.co.uk. Five supremely cosy and colourful rooms In a handsome villa. Smoked Scottish salmon is on the breakfast menu, and they run single-day or two-day photography workshops, with trips to nearby glens and castles. ££££

★ **Moyness House** 6 Bruce Gardens ⓦmoyness.co.uk. Warm, welcoming, upmarket B&B on the west side of Inverness, with original Victorian features (it was built in 1880) and a nice walled garden. ££££

HOSTELS

Bazpackers 4 Culduthel Rd ⓦbazpackershostel.co.uk. The cosiest and relaxed of the city's hostels, with more than thirty beds, including two dorms each with six 'pod' beds. female only dorms, and private twins and doubles Good location in an 1826 townhouse, great views and a garden, which is used for barbecues. Dorms £̄; twins/doubles ££

SYHA Inverness Victoria Drive, off Millburn Rd ⓦhostellingscotland.org.uk/hostels/inverness. Big SYHA hostel with large kitchens and communal areas, plus six-bed family rooms and cheap singles in addition to the usual dorms. However, it's almost a mile from the centre, and the building is devoid of character. Dorms £̄; twins ££

CAMPSITE

Bught Caravan and Camping Site Bught Park, a mile south of the centre, ⓦinvernesscaravanpark.com. Inverness's main campsite on the west bank of the river near the sports centre. Has good facilities, but it can get very crowded at the height of the season. Per person £̄

11

EATING

SEE MAP PAGE 396

Café 1 75 Castle St ⓦcafe1.net. You'll find contemporary Scottish cooking – like pan-seared venison with oven-roasted fig – in a bistro-style setting here. The restaurant's beef, lamb and pork is reared on a croft 8 miles north of Inverness. ££££

Café Artysans 7 Strothers Lane ⓦcafeartysans.org.uk. An attractive social enterprise café near the bus and train stations which helps train young people in the area. It's a good bet for breakfast (granola with fruit and yogurt), or a lunchtime sandwich served on farmhouse bread. £̄

Contrast 20 Ness Bank ⓦglenmoristontownhouse. com. This classy restaurant wlthln the *Glenmoriston Town House Hotel* (see page 398) serves brasserie fare like pork belly adobo and char sui monkfish; excellent set menus, including three-course early-bird for £24.95. ££££

No 27 27 Castle St ⓦnumber27inverness.uk. Top draw kitchen/bar serving the likes of Cajun spiced salmon fillet, superb washed down with a glass of wine or a draught American ale; there's a new guest ale every Sunday. ££

Rendezvous Café 14a Church St ⓦrendezvous-cafe. co.uk. Good coffee and big breakfasts are served inside and out at this modern corner café, which is one of the more relaxed places for coffee and a snack in the city centre. £̄

Rocpool Restaurant 1 Ness Walk ⓦrocpoolrestaurant. com. Another of the city's excellent, smart dining options, with a contemporary setting, attentive staff and deliciously rich food, like coriander and chilli monkfish stir-fry. ££££

DRINKING AND NIGHTLIFE

SEE MAP PAGE 396

Hootananny 67 Church St ⓦhootananninverness. co.uk. Lively watering hole with live music events, plus on Saturday afternoons there are ceilidhs from 2.30–4.30pm. Good, homely food too, like haggis neeps and tatties.

The Ironworks 122b Academy St ⓦironworksvenue. com. Large live music venue with space for a thousand music fans. The place to come for touring bands, stand-up comedy and the occasional club night.

DIRECTORY

Internet Inverness Library (Mon–Wed & Fri 9am–6.30pm, Thurs 9am–7pm, Sat 9am–5pm), on Farraline Park near the bus station, offers free internet access (ID required).

Medical facilities The Raigmore Hospital (☎01463 704000) is at Old Perth Rd on the southeastern outskirts of town, close to the A9.

Police 6 Burnett Rd ☎ 01463 228411

Post office 14–16 Queensgate (Mon & Wed–Sat 9am–5.30pm, Tues 9.30am–5.30pm).

Around Inverness

A string of worthwhile sights punctuates the approach to Inverness along the main route from Aberdeen. The low-key resort of **Nairn**, with its long white-sand beaches and championship golf course, stands within striking distance of several monuments, including whimsical **Cawdor Castle**, best known for its role in Shakespeare's *Macbeth*, and **Fort George**, one of several impressive Hanoverian bastions erected in the wake of the Jacobite rebellion. The infamous battle and ensuing massacre that ended Bonnie Prince Charlie's uprising took place on the outskirts of Inverness at **Culloden**, where a visitor centre and memorial stones beside a heather-clad moor recall the gruesome events of 1746.

Northeast of Inverness is the **Moray Firth**, one of the UK's best locations for spotting dolphins (see page 401). Closer to the city, where this inlet merges with the River Ness, is the start of the Beauly Firth, a sheltered sea loch bounded by the Black Isle in the north and the wooded hills of the Aird to the south.

GETTING AROUND

AROUND INVERNESS

By bus The region's main towns are well served by public transport, but to access Cawdor Castle and Fort George outside of the peak summer season (when special tourist routes are briefly opened) you will first need to travel to Nairn and then transfer to a taxi or the local Dial-a-Bus service (☎ 01667 456066).

By car The overloaded A96 links Inverness with Nairn, sixteen miles northeast, with quieter minor roads leading off it to Fort George, Cawdor Castle and Culloden. Heading northwest from Inverness, most traffic uses Kessock Bridge (the A9) to cross the Moray Firth; the A862, which skirts the shoreline and the mud flats, offers a slower, more scenic alternative.

Culloden

6 miles east of Inverness off the B9006 • Visitor centre Jan–April & Oct–Dec Wed–Sun 10am–4pm; May daily 10am–4pm; June–Sept daily 9am–4pm • Charge; includes audio-guide • NTS • ⓦ nts.org.uk/culloden • Hourly Stagecoach buses run from Falcon Square near Inverness train station to the visitor centre (35min)

The windswept moorland of **CULLODEN** witnessed the last-ever battle on British soil when, on 16 April 1746, the Jacobite cause was finally subdued – a turning point in the history of the Scottish nation. Today, this historic site attracts more than 200,000 visitors annually. Your first stop should be the superb **visitor centre**, which hosts costumed actors and state-of-the-art audio-visual and interactive technology, all employed to tell the tragedy of Culloden through the words, songs and poetic verse of locals and soldiers who experienced it. The *pièce de résistance* is the powerful 'battle immersion theatre' where visitors are surrounded by lifelike cinematography and the sounds of the raging, bloody fight.

Every April, on the Saturday closest to the date of the battle, there's a small commemorative service at Culloden. The visitor centre has a reference library and will check for you if you think you have an ancestor who died here.

Brief history

The second Jacobite rebellion began on 19 August 1745, with the raising of the Stuarts' standard at **Glenfinnan** on the west coast (see page 423). Shortly after, Edinburgh fell into Jacobite hands, and Bonnie Prince Charlie began his march on London. The ruling Hanoverians had appointed the ambitious young Duke of Cumberland to command their forces, which included troops from the Lowlands and Highlands. The duke's pursuit, together with bad weather and lack of funds, eventually forced the Jacobite forces – mostly comprised of Highlanders – to retreat north. They ended up at **Culloden**, where, ill fed and exhausted after a pointless night march, they were hopelessly outnumbered by the government forces. The open, flat ground of Culloden Moor was totally unsuitable for the Highlanders' style of courageous but undisciplined fighting, which needed steep hills and lots of cover to provide the element of surprise, and they were routed.

The end of the clan system

After the battle, in which 1,500 Highlanders were slaughtered (many of them as they lay wounded on the battlefield), **Bonnie Prince Charlie** fled west to the hills and islands, where fiercely loyal Highlanders sheltered and protected him. He eventually escaped to France, leaving his supporters to their fate – and, in effect, ushering in the end of the **clan system**. The clans were disarmed, the wearing of tartan and playing of bagpipes forbidden, and the chiefs became landlords greedy for higher and higher rents. The battle also unleashed violent reprisals on Scotland, as unruly government troops raped and pillaged their way across the region; within a century, the Highland way of life had changed beyond recognition.

The battlefield

Flags mark out the positions of the two armies while simple headstones mark the **clan graves**. The **Field of the English**, for many years unmarked, is a mass grave for the fifty or so government soldiers who died (though as this government force also included Scottish infantry regiments, the term 'English' is a pseudo patriotic misnomer).

Half a mile east of the battlefield, just beyond the crossroads on the main road, is the **Cumberland Stone**, thought for many years to have been the point from where the duke watched the battle. It is more likely, however, that he was much further forward and simply used the stone for shelter. Elsewhere, the restored **Leanach cottage** marks the spot where thirty injured Jacobites were burnt alive.

11

Cawdor Castle

14 miles northeast of Inverness off the A96 • May–Oct daily 10am–5.30pm • Charge • ⓦ cawdorcastle.com • To get here, take a train or bus from Inverness to Nairn (several per hour; 20–45min), then pick up a taxi for the final 6 miles (around £15) – book ahead with Taxi 24/7 Nairn (ⓣ 01667 459595) and a driver will meet you at the bus station; a cheaper but less reliable option is Nairn's Dial-a-Bus service (ⓣ 01667 456066), which must be booked by 6pm the day before you wish to travel

The pretty village of **CAWDOR**, eight miles east of Culloden, is the site of **Cawdor Castle**, a setting intimately linked to Shakespeare's *Macbeth*: the fulfilment of the witches'

THE DOLPHINS OF THE MORAY FIRTH

The **Moray Firth**, a great wedge-shaped bay forming the eastern coastline of the Highlands, is one of only three areas of UK waters that support a resident population of **dolphins**. Around two hundred of these beautiful, intelligent marine mammals live in the estuary, the most northerly breeding ground in Europe for this particular species – the bottlenose dolphin (*Tursiops truncatus*) – and you stand a good chance of spotting a few, either from the shore or a boat.

One of the best places in Scotland, if not in Europe, to look for them is **Chanonry Point**, on the Black Isle – a spit of sand protruding into a narrow, deep channel, where converging currents bring fish close to the surface, and thus the dolphins close to shore; a rising tide is the most likely time to see them.

Several companies run dolphin-spotting **boat trips** around the Moray Firth. However, researchers claim that the increased traffic is causing the dolphins unnecessary stress, particularly during the all-important breeding period when passing vessels are thought to force calves underwater for uncomfortably long periods. So, if you decide to go on a cruise to see the dolphins, which also sometimes provides the chance of spotting minke whales, porpoises, seals and otters, make sure that the operator is a member of the Dolphin Space Programme's accreditation scheme (ⓦ dolphinspace.org).

BOAT TOURS

Trips with these **accredited operators**, most of which operate between April and October, are especially popular in July and August, so be sure to book them well in advance. To get from Inverness to Avoch (20min) or Cromarty (50min) with public transport, take Stagecoach bus No. 26 from the bus station (at least hourly); note that not all services run as far as Cromarty, so check before boarding.

Dolphin Trips Avoch On the northern side of the firth in Avoch (ⓦ dolphintripsavoch.co.uk). Hourly sailings from Avoch's harbour, at the eastern end of the village, with trips lasting an hour (£25).

Ecoventures Victoria Place, Cromarty (ⓦ ecoventures. co.uk). Based on the Black Isle, on the northern side of the firth, Ecoventures runs 2hr wildlife cruises (£42) with the chance to spot dolphins, harbour porpoises and grey seals.

Phoenix Sea Adventures Nairn Marina (ⓦ phoenix-nairn.co.uk). Runs a range of trips from Nairn Marina (from £30).

prediction that Macbeth was to become thane of Cawdor sets off his tragic desire to be king. Though visitors arrive here in their droves each summer because of the site's dramatic associations, the castle, which dates from the early fourteenth century, could not possibly have witnessed the grisly eleventh-century events on which the Bard's drama was based. However, the immaculately restored monument – a fairy-tale affair of towers, turrets, hidden passageways, dungeons, gargoyles and crenellations whimsically shooting off from the original keep – is still well worth a visit. Outside is a 1620 walled kitchen garden, a formal flower garden and a rambling 1960s wild garden.

Fort George

13 miles northeast of Inverness, near Ardersier • Daily April–Sept 10am–4.30pm; Oct–March 10am–4pm • Charge • HES • ⓦ historicenvironment.scot • There are no scheduled bus services to Fort George – as with Cawdor Castle, the best bet is to take a bus or train from Inverness to Nairn, where you can pick up a taxi or local Dial-a-Bus service for the final stretch

Eight miles of undulating coastal farmland separate Cawdor Castle from **Fort George**, an old Hanoverian bastion with walls a mile long, considered by military architectural historians to be one of the finest fortifications in Europe. Crowning a sandy spit that juts into the middle of the Moray Firth, it was built between 1747 and 1769 as a base for George II's army, in case the Highlanders should attempt to rekindle the Jacobite flame. By the time of its completion, however, the uprising had been firmly quashed and the fort has been used ever since as barracks; note the armed sentries at the main entrance and the periodic crack of live gunfire from the nearby firing ranges. The dog cemetery commemorates regimental hounds, and there's a small café.

Walking on the northern, grass-covered casemates, which look out into the estuary, you may be lucky enough to see a school of bottlenose **dolphins** (see page 401) swimming in with the tide. This is also a good spot for birdwatching: a colony of kittiwakes occupies the fort's slate rooftops.

Nairn

One of the driest and sunniest places in the whole of Scotland, **NAIRN**, sixteen miles east of Inverness, began its days as a peaceful community of fishermen and farmers. The former spoke Gaelic, the latter English, allowing James VI to boast that a town in his kingdom was so large that people at one end of the main street could not understand those at the other end. Nairn became popular in Victorian times, when the train line offered a convenient link to its revitalizing sea air and mild climate, and today the 11,000-strong population still relies on tourism, with all the ingredients for a traditional seaside holiday – sandy beach, ice-cream shops and fish-and-chip stalls. The town has two championship golf courses, and Thomas Telford's **harbour** is filled with leisure craft rather than fishing boats.

Nairn Museum

Viewfield House, King St • April–Oct Mon–Fri 10am–4.30pm, Sat 10am–1pm; last admission 30min before closing • Charge • ⓦ nairnmuseum.co.uk

The **Nairn Museum** provides a general insight into the history and prehistory of the area: the **Fishertown Room** illustrates the parsimonious and puritanical life of the fishing families, while the weapon-filled **Military Room** includes information on the battles of Culloden and Auldearn.

ARRIVAL AND DEPARTURE

NAIRN

By train Nairn's railway station is just south of the centre, where Chattan Drive meets Cawdor St. Services run every 1–2hr from/to Aberdeen (2hr), Elgin (25min), Forres (10min) and Inverness (20min).

By bus Buses arrive at and depart from a car park on King St, just south of the police station.

Destinations Aberdeen (hourly; 3hr 15min); Elgin (every 30min; 45min); Forres (every 30min; 25min); Inverness (every 20min; 45min).

ACCOMMODATION AND EATING

Boath House Auldearn, 2 miles east of Nairn ⓦ boathouse.com. The most luxurious place to stay in the area, this is a fine Georgian country house set in magnificent gardens. Immaculate rooms are complemented by a fine restaurant that draws upon organic produce and regional dairy, fish and meat suppliers. <u>££££</u>

★ **Cawdor House** 7 Cawdor St ⓦ cawdorhousenairn. co.uk. A bright and attractive B&B set in a fine 1850s villa, conveniently located between the train station and the main shopping street. Good choice of breakfasts, with vegetarians well catered for. <u>££</u>

The Classroom 1 Cawdor St ⓦ theclassroombistro.com. Nairn's most popular bar/restaurant, serving tasty light bites, lunches and dinners. Try the house salad with sun-blushed tomatoes and chargrilled chicken. <u>£££</u>

Strathspey

The richly forested area around the River Spey's upper reaches – **STRATHSPEY** – is a magnet for outdoor enthusiasts. Of Strathspey's scattered settlements, **Aviemore** absorbs the largest number of visitors, particularly in midwinter when it metamorphoses into the UK's busiest ski resort. The village struggles to reflect the charm of its surrounding area, but it's a good first stop for information, to sort out somewhere to stay or to find out about nearby outdoor activities, which are likely to seem very enticing after a glimpse of the soaring Cairngorms mountain range or the Glenmore Forest Park, a protected area that's home to one of Scotland's last remaining tracts of ancient Caledonian pinewood.

For summer visitors who'd rather avoid Aviemore, the planned Georgian town of **Grantown-on-Spey** makes a good alternative base. Further upriver, the sedate villages of **Newtonmore** and **Kingussie** are older-established holiday centres, more popular with anglers and grouse hunters than canoeists and climbers. The whole area boasts a wide choice of good-quality accommodation, particularly in the budget market, with various easy-going hostels run by and for outdoor enthusiasts.

Aviemore and around

The once-sleepy village of **AVIEMORE** was first developed as a ski and tourism resort in the mid-1960s and, over the years, fell victim to profiteering developers with scant regard for the needs of the local community. Despite recent attempts to turn things around, it remains a soulless hotchpotch of retail outlets, café-bars and characterless housing developments. That said, Aviemore is undeniably well equipped with services and facilities and is the most convenient base for the Cairngorms.

In summer, the main activities around Aviemore are **walking** (see page 404) and **watersports**, and there are great opportunities for pony trekking and fly-fishing (for the latter, the Aviemore tourist office provides a brochure outlining which permits you'll need). For both the adventurous and novice cyclist, the entire region is great for mountain biking; the **Rothiemurchus Estate** has several excellent (and non-technical) way-marked trails running through its extensive lands. Sailing, windsurfing and canoeing are also popular, with a specialist centre at **Loch Insh** providing lessons and loaning out equipment. Wintertime sees the tourist focus switch away from the lochs and rivers and up towards the surrounding slopes, home to a well-established **ski resort**.

Strathspey Steam Railway

Aviemore Station, Dalfaber Rd • July & Aug Tues–Sun three times daily; reduced service at other times • Charge • ⓦ strathspeyrailway.co.uk

The main attractions of Aviemore are its outdoor pursuits, though train enthusiasts are also drawn to the restored **Strathspey Steam Railway**, which chugs the short distance between Aviemore and Broomhill, just beyond Boat of Garten village. Originally part of the Inverness & Perth Junction Railway (later the Highland Railway), which opened in 1863, the line was axed in the 1960s as a result of the infamous Beeching cuts.

11

However, by 1978, services had been restored between Aviemore and Boat of Garten, which were then extended to Broomhill in 2002. The return journey takes an hour and a half, with glimpses of the Cairngorm Mountains visible through the trees; for the best views sit on the right-hand side leaving Aviemore.

Cairngorm Ski Area

9 miles southeast of Aviemore · Ski season Dec–April, but varies depending on snowfall · ⓦ cairngormmountain.co.uk · Buses from Aviemore wind past Inverdruie, stopping at the Coire Cas car park, near the funicular railway's base station

By Continental European and North American standards it's all on a tiny scale, but occasionally snow and sun coincide at the **Cairngorm Ski Area** to offer beginner and expert alike a great day on the pistes. High above Loch Morlich in Glenmore Forest Park, the ski area is well served by public transport. From the car park at Coire Cas (2150ft), the year-round **funicular railway** is the principal means of getting to the top of the ski slopes.

Funicular Base Station

11

Accessed via the Coire Cas car park · Daily 9am–5pm · Free; charge for exhibition

At the Cairngorm Ski Area **funicular base station**, there's a new exhibition, The Cairngorm Story, which relays the history of the mountains, its climate, flora and fauna and so on. Here, too you can find out about various trails, check the latest weather report and – on Thursdays between May and October – join guided walks (£10) out to the Corries. There are a couple of excellent cafés here too.

Cairngorm Mountain Railway

Leaves from the funicular base station · currently closed, check website for details · Charge · ⓦ cairngormmountain.co.uk

The Cairngorm Ski Area base station is the departure point for the **Cairngorm Mountain Railway**, a two-car funicular system that runs to the top of the ski area. A highly controversial £15 million scheme that was bitterly opposed by conservationists,

---

WALKS AROUND AVIEMORE

Ordnance Survey Explorer maps 402 & 403

Walking of all grades is a highlight of the Aviemore area, though you should heed the usual safety guidelines (see page 45). These are particularly important if you want to venture into the subarctic climatic zone of the **Cairngorms**. However, as well as the high mountain trails, there are some lovely and well-signposted low-level walks in the area.

LOCH AN EILEAN

It takes an hour or so to complete the gentle circular walk around pretty Loch an Eilean (with its ruined castle) in the **Rothiemurchus Estate**, beginning at the end of the back road that turns east off the B970 a mile south of Inverdruie. The helpful estate visitor centres at the lochside and by the roadside at Inverdruie provide more information on other woodland trails.

RYVOAN PASS

Another good, shortish (half-day) walk leads along a well-surfaced forestry track from *Glenmore Lodge* (see page 406) up towards the **Ryvoan Pass**, taking in An Lochan Uaine, known as the 'Green Loch' and living up to its name, with amazing colours that range from turquoise to slate grey depending on the weather.

MEALL A' BHUACHAILLE

The **Glenmore Forest Park Visitor Centre** (daily 9am–5pm; ⓦ forestryandland.gov.scot) by the roadside at the turn-off to *Glenmore Lodge* is the starting point for the three-hour return climb of Meall a' Bhuachaille (2654ft), which offers excellent views and is usually accessible year-round. The centre has information on other trails in this section of the forest too.

CAIRNGORMS NATIONAL PARK

The **Cairngorms National Park** (Ⓦcairngorms.co.uk) covers almost 1750 square miles and incorporates the Cairngorms massif, the largest mountainscape in the UK and the only sizeable plateau in the country over 2500ft. It's the biggest national park in Britain, and while Aviemore and the surrounding area are regarded as the main point of entry, particularly for those planning outdoor activities, it's also possible to access the park from Perthshire as well as Deeside and Donside in **Aberdeenshire**. Crossing the range is a significant challenge: by road the only connection is the A939 from Tomintoul to Cock Bridge, frequently impassable in winter due to snow, while on foot the only way to avoid the high peaks is to follow the old cattle drovers' route called the **Lairig Ghru**, a very long day's walk between Inverdruie at the edge of Rothiemurchus and the Linn of Dee, near Inverey.

The name Cairngorm comes from the Gaelic An Carn Gorm, meaning 'the blue hill' after the blueish-tinged stones found in the area. The park is home to a quarter of Scotland's native woodland and a quarter of the UK's threatened wildlife species; the tracts of ancient **Caledonian forest** at Rothiemurchus (see page 403) are even home to red squirrels.

11

the railway has been closed since 2018 owing to structural problems, though it is likely to reopen again in 2023. The railway whisks skiers in winter, and tourists throughout the year, along a mile and a half of track to the top station at an altitude of 3600ft, not far from the summit of Cairn Gorm mountain (4085ft). The top station incorporates an exhibition/interpretation area and a café-restaurant from which spectacular views can be had on clear days. Note that there is no access beyond the confines of the top station and its open-air viewing terrace, so unless you're embarking on a winter skiing trip or a guided walk, you'll have to trudge up from the car park at the bottom.

ARRIVAL AND DEPARTURE

By train Aviemore's train station is on Grampian Rd, just south of the tourist office.
Destinations Edinburgh (Mon–Sat 12 daily, Sun 6 daily; 3hr); Glasgow (11 daily, Sun 6 daily; 2hr 50min); Inverness (Mon–Sat 11 daily, Sun 7 daily; 40min).

AVIEMORE AND AROUND

By bus Buses depart from outside the train station.
Destinations Cairngorm ski area (hourly; 30min); Edinburgh (6 daily; 3–4hr); Glasgow (5 daily; 2hr 40min–3hr 20min); Grantown-on-Spey (Mon–Sat every 30min–1hr, Sun 4 daily; 30min); Inverness (at least 11 daily; 45min).

GETTING AROUND AND INFORMATION

By bus The most useful local bus route is the No. 31, which runs hourly from Aviemore to the Cairn Gorm Mountain Railway (see page 404) via Rothiemurchus and Loch Morlich. The No. 34 service is also handy, running regularly to Grantown (roughly hourly; 40min) via Boat of Garten.
Tourist office 7 The Parade, Grampian Rd (April & May

Mon–Sat 9am–5pm, Sun 10am–5pm; June Mon–Sat 9am–6pm, Sun 9.30am–5pm; July & Aug Mon–Sat 9.30am–6.30pm, Sun 9.30am–6pm; Sept–March Mon, Tue & Thu–Sat 9am–5pm, Wed 10am–5pm, Sun 10am–4pm; Ⓦvisitaviemore.com). Offers an accommodation booking service and reams of leaflets on local attractions.

ACTIVITIES

FISHING
Rothiemurchus Estate Inverdruie (Ⓦrothiemurchus. net). Has a stocked rainbow trout-fishing loch, where success is virtually guaranteed. There are various permutations for fishing here including catch and release (£27/day) and a ninety-minute lesson followed by ninety-minute's fishing (£65).

HORSE RIDING
Alvie Stables 5 miles south of Aviemore, near Kincraig

(Ⓦalvie-estate.co.uk). Family-friendly riding centre set in superb countryside a short drive from Aviemore, offering 30min lessons and longer guided rides (£25/hr).

OUTDOOR TRAINING
National Outdoor Training Centre Glenmore Lodge, 8 miles east of Aviemore (Ⓦglenmorelodge.org.uk). For a crash course in surviving Scottish winters, you could do worse than try a week at the National Outdoor Training Centre, at the east end of Loch Morlich. This superbly

equipped and organized centre (complete with cosy apres-ski bar) offers winter and summer courses in hillwalking, mountaineering, alpine ski-mountaineering, avalanche awareness and much more.

SKIING

G2 Outdoor Plot 10, Dalfaber Industrial Estate, Aviemore (ⓦ g2outdoor.co.uk). The experts at G2 Outdoor will provide one-to-one tuition in the art of telemarking (£240/2hr for three people) and back-country skiing. In summer, they also run white water rafting and canyoning trips.

School of Snowsports Coylumbridge Hotel (ⓦ schoolofsnowsports.co.uk). A good bet for ski/board rental and lessons, with friendly and professional staff. Courses run mid-Dec to early April.

WATERSPORTS

See also G2 Outdoor in 'Skiing', above.

Loch Insh Outdoor Centre 6 miles up-valley near Kincraig (ⓦ lochinsh.com). Offers a whole host of land and water-based activities, in the form of courses and trips as well as equipment hire; for example kayaks (£15/90min, £25/3hr). To save visitors travelling back and forth from Aviemore, the centre also offers accommodation, and there's also a restaurant here.

ACCOMMODATION

HOTELS AND B&BS

Glenmore Lodge 8 miles east of Aviemore ⓦ glenmorelodge.org.uk. Specialist outdoor pursuits centre with excellent accommodation in en-suite twin rooms and self-catered lodges – guests can make use of the superb facilities, which include a pool, weights room, sauna and indoor climbing wall. Twins £̲£̲

Ravenscraig Guest House 141 Grampian Rd ⓦ ravenscraighouse.co.uk. This welcoming, family-friendly B&B has a handy central location. Single, double and family rooms available, plus a wide choice of breakfast options, including sausages bought from a local butcher. £̲£̲

bathroom, plus private rooms. Dorms £̲; doubles £̲£̲

Aviemore Youth Hostel 25 Grampian Rd ⓦ hostellingscotland.org.uk/hostels/aviemore. Aviemore's large SYHA hostel, with its own bike store and drying room, has rather plain rooms but is within easy walking distance of the town centre. Dorms £̲; singles £̲£̲; twins £̲£̲

Cairngorm Lodge Youth Hostel 6.5 miles east of Aviemore, by Loch Morlich ⓦ hostellingscotland.org. uk/hostels/cairngorm-lodge. This hostel towards the Cairngorms at Loch Morlich is located in an old shooting lodge. Dorms £̲; twins £̲£̲

HOSTELS AND BUNKHOUSES

Aviemore Bunkhouse Dalfaber Rd, next to the Old Bridge Inn ⓦ aviemore-bunkhouse.com. A large modern place beside a cosy pub and walking distance from the station, with six- and eight-bed dorms, all with their own

CAMPING

Rothiemurchus Caravan Park 2 miles southeast of Aviemore in Coylumbridge ⓦ rothiemurchus.net. Relaxed site for tents and caravans, nestled among tall pine trees at Coylumbridge, on the way to Loch Morlich. Per person £̲

EATING AND DRINKING

Old Bridge Inn Dalfaber Rd, next to Aviemore Bunkhouse ⓦ oldbridgeinn.co.uk. Fire-warmed pub that hosts regular live music sessions and serves up decent dinners; the menu includes pan-fried seabass with hot smoked salmon. £̲£̲£̲

The Winking Owl 123 Grampian Rd ⓦ thewinkingowl. co. Lively brewery pub serving draught ales and beers from the nearby Cairngorm Brewery alongside classy Mediterranean/Scottish food. First-rate programme of live music too in the adjoining Bothy Bar. £̲£̲

Carrbridge

Worth considering as an alternative to Aviemore – particularly as a skiing base – **CARRBRIDGE** is a pleasant, quiet village about seven miles to the north. Look out for the spindly Bridge of Carr at the northern end of the village, built in 1717 and still making a graceful stone arch over the River Dulnain.

Landmark Forest Adventure Park

Just off the B9153 at the southern end of the village • Daily April to mid-July & Sept–Oct 10am–5/6pm; mid-July to Aug 10am–7pm; Nov–March 10am–4pm • Charge • ⓦ landmarkpark.co.uk

The main attraction in Carrbridge is the **Landmark Forest Adventure Park**, which offers families a host of excellent outdoor and indoor activities the best of which are treetop trails, a climbing wall, and a new dinosaur kingdom complete with sound effects; elsewhere there's the Lost Labyrinth maze, Bamboozeleum (magical and illusory effects), and a couple of theme park type rides. Note that whilst the park is open year-round, some of the attractions are closed during the winter period, hence a reduced admission fee.

ARRIVAL AND DEPARTURE
CARRBRIDGE

By train The train station is around half a mile west of the village centre, served by trains from Aviemore (5–6 daily; 10min) and Inverness (4–5 daily; 30min).

By bus Frequent buses (every 1–2hr; 15min) from/to Aviemore stop at the car park 200m south of the river on the B9153.

ACCOMMODATION

MellonPatch Station Rd, roughly halfway between the train station and the Bridge of Carr ⓦ mellonpatch. com. Rambling house with good, large colour-themed rooms and friendly owners. The rates, including a full Scottish breakfast, are low for this area – and look out for woodpeckers and red squirrels in the garden. **££**

Boat of Garten

Seven miles northeast of Aviemore, close to the River Spey, sits the attractive village of **BOAT OF GARTEN**, which has a number of good accommodation options. A short drive or pleasant walk away on the other side of the river is the northeastern shore of **Loch Garten**, famous as the nesting site of the osprey, one of Britain's rarest birds.

Abernethy Forest RSPB Reserve

2.5 miles east of Boat of Garten, on the northeastern edge of Loch Garten • Reserve year-round • Visitor centre April–Aug daily 10am–6pm • Charge • **Guided walks** late May–early Aug Wed 9.30am; 3hr • Charge • ⓦ rspb.org.uk • To get here from the village, cross the Spey then take the Grantown road; the reserve is signposted to the right

The **Abernethy Forest RSPB Reserve** on the shore of **Loch Garten**, a short drive from the attractive village of Boat of Garten and seven miles northeast of Aviemore, is famous as the nesting site of one of Britain's rarest birds. A little over fifty years ago, the **osprey**, known in North America as the fish hawk, had completely disappeared from the British Isles. Then, in 1954, a single pair of these exquisite white-and-brown raptors mysteriously reappeared and built a nest in a tree half a mile or so from the loch. One year's eggs fell victim to thieves, and thereafter the area became the centre of an effective high-security operation. There are now believed to be up to three hundred pairs nesting across the UK.

The best time to visit is between April and August, when the ospreys return from West Africa and the RSPB opens a **visitor centre**, complete with powerful telescopes and CCTV monitoring of the nest.

ARRIVAL AND DEPARTURE
BOAT OF GARTEN

By train Strathspey Steam Railway trains (July & Aug daily, less frequent at other times) stop at the attractive old station in the centre of Boat of Garten and run to Aviemore (3 daily; 15min) and Broomhill (3 daily; 25min).

By bus Buses from Aviemore run hourly to Boat of Garten (12min), stopping outside the post office on Deshar Rd.

ACCOMMODATION AND EATING

Anderson's Deshar Rd, 300m west of the train station ⓦ andersonsrestaurant.co.uk. Attractive place for lunch or dinner, serving creative dishes based on local ingredients, like wild mushroom, spinach and chestnut pasta. **£££**

Boat Hotel Just across from the train station ⓦ boathotel.co.uk. The most elegant place to stay in the village, with fresh, airy bedrooms, some of which look down the garden to the heritage railway. The hotel also has a bistro serving its own interpretations of Scottish favourites – from Cullen skink to chicken tikka masala. **££**

★ **Fraoch Lodge** 15 Deshar Rd ⓦ scotmountainholidays.com. Excellent hostel providing high-quality home-cooked meals along with good facilities such as a purpose-built drying room, bike wash and bike shed. Enthusiastically run by experienced mountaineers, who also offer guided walking holidays. Minimum stay of two nights when booking in advance. Singles **£**; twins **££**

Old Ferryman's House Just east of the village, across

the Spey ☎ 01479 831370. A wonderfully simple and homely B&B, with an old-school approach: a wood-burning stove, no TVs, lots of books and delicious evening meals and breakfasts. **££**

Grantown-on-Spey

Around fifteen miles northeast of Aviemore, the pretty town of **GRANTOWN-ON-SPEY** makes a good alternative base for exploring the Strathspey area. Local life is concentrated around the central square, with its attractive Georgian architecture, but there are plenty of opportunities for hiking and biking in the immediate area.

ARRIVAL AND DEPARTURE
GRANTOWN-ON-SPEY

By bus Buses from Aviemore (roughly hourly; 35min) and Inverness (at least 2 per day Mon–Sat; 1hr 10min) stop on Grantown-on-Spey's high street.

GETTING AROUND AND INFORMATION

Bike rental You'll find good bikes and decent coffee at BaseCamp Bikes (Mon 10am–5pm, Tues–Sat 9.30am–5.30pm; ⓦ basecampmtb.com; £25/day), next door to the Co-op convenience store on the town's main square; they also offer a delivery service.

Tourist office Inside the town museum on Burnfield Avenue (April–Oct Mon–Sat 9.30am–5pm, ⓦ visitgrantown.co.uk), Grantown's seasonal tourist office has leaflets on local attractions, as well as maps of the area.

ACCOMMODATION

★ **Dunallan House** Woodside Avenue ⓦ dunallan.com. Large house with big double rooms – all en suite with private facilities – and comfy, welcoming lounges to relax in. The room on the top floor, with a freestanding bathtub across the landing, is the pick of the bunch. **££**
Garth Hotel Castle Rd, at the north end of the town square ⓦ garthhotel.com. If you're after some reasonably swish accommodation head for the large seventeenth-century *Garth Hotel*, where the restaurant serves

respectable, traditional meat-based dinners. **£££**
★ **Lazy Duck Hostel** Nethy Bridge, 6 miles south of town ☎ 01479 821642, ⓦ lazyduck.co.uk. A peaceful and comfortable retreat featuring a range of quirky accommodation possibilities, for example a four-bed hostel, woodman's hut and waterside lodge (both sleeping two), plus woodland camping (May–Oct). Great moorland walking on its doorstep too. Camping per pitch **£**, hostel **££**, hut and lodge **££££**

EATING AND DRINKING

★ **Craig Bar** Woodside Avenue ⓦ thecraigbar.co.uk. Snug pub full of military aviation memorabilia, from pictures of fighter planes to dangling model aircraft. Warm yourself by the fire with a pint of real ale while you choose some food. The choice is made easy; the jovial landlord only sells pies, made with free-range meat (though there are veggie versions), though there are chips too of course. **££**
★ **KJ's Bothy Bakery** Unit 9/2 Achnagonalin Industrial

Estate ⓦ mountaincafe-aviemore.co.uk. The team behind the now closed Mountain Cafe in Aviemore relocated here but are still their serving ace sandwiches, sausage rolls and soups, alongside 'kick-ass coffee' and cakes. **£**
The High Street Merchants 74 High St ☎ 01479 872246. An attractive wood-lined café and gallery on the high street serving organic, fair trade and local food; burgers and pizzas also available. **££**

Kingussie

Twelve miles southwest of Aviemore at the head of the Strathspey Valley, **KINGUSSIE** (pronounced 'king-yoos-ee') is a pleasant village best known for the free-to-access ruins of **Ruthven Barracks**, which stand east across the river on a hillock. The best-preserved garrison built to pacify the Highlands after the 1715 rebellion, it makes for great exploring by day and is impressively floodlit at night.

ARRIVAL AND DEPARTURE
KINGUSSIE

By train Kingussie's train station is on Station Rd, just south of the A86.
Destinations Edinburgh (Mon–Sat 7 daily, 5 on Sun; 2hr 40min); Glasgow (Mon–Sat 4 daily, 2 on Sun; 2hr 30min); Inverness (Mon–Sat 12 daily, 7 on Sun; 55min); Newtonmore (Mon–Sat 5 daily, 3 on Sun; 5min).

By bus Buses arrive at and depart from near the *Duke of Gordon Hotel*, on the high street.
Destinations Edinburgh (5 daily; 3hr 30min); Inverness (Mon–Sat 8 daily, 5 on Sun; 1hr); Newtonmore (roughly hourly; 5min).

ACCOMMODATION AND EATING

★**The Cross** North of the centre off Ardbroilach Rd ⓦ thecross.co.uk. One of the most appealing places to stay in the whole of Speyside, this relaxed but stylish restaurant with rooms is located in a converted tweed mill on the River Gynack. The restaurant is the most ambitious (and costly) in the area, where a three-course meal carefully crafted from fresh Scottish ingredients like Shetland lobster and Perthshire lamb costs £60. **££**

The Tipsy Laird 68 High St ⓦ thetipsylaird.co.uk. No-frills pub on the high street, which hosts occasional jam sessions and karaoke nights. They have a good selection of malt whiskies and offer simple bar food.

Newtonmore

Kingussie's closest neighbour, **NEWTONMORE**, is also its biggest rival. The two villages, separated by a couple of miles of farmland, both have long-established shinty teams that battle for dominance in the game – a fierce indigenous sport from which ice hockey and golf evolved. Newtonmore itself is notable for its top-notch **folk museum**, and there are plenty of mountain-biking routes in the forests to the south.

Highland Folk Museum

Kingussie Rd • Daily April–Aug 10.30am–5.30pm; Sept & Oct 11am–4.30pm • Free; donation requested • ⓦ highlandfolk.com

Newtonmore's chief attraction is the fantastically evocative **Highland Folk Museum**, one of Scotland's most rewarding outdoor sites. Split between a 1700s Township, the Middle Village, and a working croft, you could quite easily spend half a day here wandering around the thirty odd structures, many of which have been moved from their original location. Among the highlights is the Knockbain School from Kirkhill near Inverness dating from 1925; complete with a cast-iron range and rows of ink-drenched desks, you can try your hand at writing with a fountain pen under the watchful eye of a suitably stern Victorian teacher – she'll even mark it for you. Elsewhere there's the Black house from the Isle of Lewis, thickly thatched and encircled by a high stone wall so as to withstand the ferocious Atlantic weather, and Kirk's Store, where you can indulge all your sweet-toothed fantasies.

Laggan Wolftrax

8 miles southwest of Newtonmore on the A86, just beyond the junction with the A889 from Dalwhinnie • Free; car parking charge • ⓦ forestryandland.gov.scot; ⓦ lagganforest.com

Laggan Wolftrax is a superb, free facility with more than twenty miles of marked **mountain biking trails** to suit all abilities. The three-mile-long green route is the best place for those starting out, but expert riders might prefer the gruelling four-mile black route, which traverses a steep and rocky staircase made up of uneven slabs. The Laggan Wolftrax Centre itself has toilets, coin-operated showers and a superb café serving breakfasts and hot lunches.

ARRIVAL AND INFORMATION

NEWTONMORE

By train The train station is south of the centre on Station Rd.
Destinations Edinburgh (Mon–Sat 3 daily, 2 on Sun; 2hr 30min); Glasgow (Mon–Sat 2 daily, 1 on Sun; 2hr 20min); Inverness (Mon–Sat 5 daily, 3 on Sun; 55min); Kingussie (Mon–Sat 5 daily, 3 on Sun; 5min).
By bus Buses for Edinburgh and Inverness arrive at and depart from Main St.
Destinations Edinburgh (Mon–Fri 5 daily; 3hr 25min);

Inverness (Mon–Sat 8 daily, 5 on Sun; 1hr 10min); Kingussie (roughly hourly; 5min).
Tourist information The volunteer-run Wildcat Centre on Main St (June–Aug Mon–Thurs 10am–4pm, Fri & Sat 10am–1pm; Sept–May Mon–Sat 10am–1pm; ⓦ wildcatcentre.org) has loads of info on the town and surrounding areas. They also run the hugely popular Wildcat Experience, which entails tracking down 132 colourfully painted model wildcats scattered around town; a wildcat

11

trackpack, which includes brochure, map and pen, costs £10. There's also the Wildcat Trail, a 10km waymarked orbital walk around Newtonmore.

ACCOMMODATION

★**Coig Na Shee** Laggan Rd, a 10min walk west of Main St ⓦcoignashee.co.uk. A soothingly decorated B&B in an old Edwardian hunting lodge with five bright and immaculate rooms fitted out in different colours; good value, though there is a two-night minimum stay between May and September. ££

Newtonmore Hostel Craigellachie House, Main Street ⓦnewtonmorehostel.co.uk. Purpose built at the rear of the oldest house in the village, this wee wood-fronted hostel is a simple but pleasant place to stay. There's only space for twelve people, in three rooms, so book ahead. Dorms ££

Speyside

11

Strictly speaking, the term **SPEYSIDE** refers to the entire region surrounding the River Spey, but to most people the name is synonymous with the **whisky triangle**, stretching from just north of Craigellachie, down towards Tomintoul in the south and east to Huntly. Indeed, there are more whisky distilleries and famous brands concentrated in this small area than in any other part of the country.

At the centre of Speyside is the quiet market town of **Dufftown**, full of solid, stone-built workers' houses and dotted with no fewer than nine whisky distilleries. It's one of the best bases for a tour of whisky country, whether you're on the official Malt Whisky Trail or more independent explorations. Fewer visitors take the chance to discover the more remote glens, such as Glenlivet, which push higher up towards the Cairngorm massif, nestled into which is Britain's highest village, **Tomintoul**, situated on the edge of both whisky country and a large expanse of wild uplands. Though not surrounded by distilleries, the market town of **Huntly** has an impressive ruined castle and serves as a useful point of entry if you're coming into the region from the Aberdeenshire side.

GETTING AROUND

SPEYSIDE

By train The only mainline railway stops in the area are at Keith, twelve miles northeast of Dufftown, and Huntly.

By bus Transport connections are poor through the area, with irregular buses connecting the main villages.

Dufftown

The cheery community of **DUFFTOWN**, founded in 1817 by James Duff, fourth Earl of Fife, proudly proclaims itself 'Malt Whisky Capital of the World' for the reason that it produces more of the stuff than any other town in Britain. A more telling statistic, perhaps, is that as a result Dufftown also reportedly raises more capital for

---

THE SPEYSIDE WAY

The **Speyside Way** (ⓦspeysideway.org), with its beguiling blend of mountain, river, wildlife and whisky, is fast establishing itself as an appealing and less taxing alternative to the popular West Highland and Southern Upland long-distance footpaths. Starting at **Buckie** on the Moray Firth coast (see page 369), it follows the fast-flowing River Spey from its mouth at Spey Bay south to **Aviemore**, with branches linking it to **Dufftown**, Scotland's malt whisky capital, and **Tomintoul** on the remote edge of the Cairngorm mountains. Some 65 miles long without taking on the branch routes, the whole thing is a five- to seven-day expedition, but its proximity to main roads and small villages means that it is excellent for shorter walks or even cycling trips, especially in the heart of **distillery** country between Craigellachie and Glenlivet; the Glenfiddich, Glenlivet, Macallan and Cardhu distilleries, as well as the Speyside Cooperage, lie directly on or a short distance off the route.

the exchequer per head of population than anywhere else in the country. There are seven active distilleries around Dufftown, as well as a cooperage, and an extended stroll around the outskirts of the town gives a good idea of the density of whisky distilling going on, with glimpses of giant warehouses and whiffs of fermenting barley or peat smoke lingering on the breeze. On the edge of town along the A941 is the town's largest working distillery, **Glenfiddich** (see page 412).

There isn't a great deal to do in the town itself, but it's a useful starting point for orienting yourself towards the whisky trail. Dufftown's four major streets converge on its main square, scene of a lively annual party at Hogmanay when free drams are handed out to revellers.

Whisky Museum

24 Fife St • Mon–Fri 1–4pm • Free • ⓦ whisky.dufftown.co.uk

The tiny volunteer-run **Whisky Museum** has a slightly disorganized collection of illicit distilling equipment, most of which has been donated by local distilleries. There are also plenty of old books and photographs to help to give visitors a flavour for the industry's humble beginnings.

Keith & Dufftown Railway

Station Rd • April, May & Oct Sat & Sun 3 trips daily (June–Sept also on Fri) • Charge • ⓦ keith-dufftown-railway.co.uk

Restored by enthusiasts, the old Dufftown train station is now the departure point for the **Keith & Dufftown Railway**, which uses various restored diesel locomotives to chug forty minutes through whisky country to Keith, home of the Strathisla distillery (see page 412). The Keith & Dufftown Railway originally opened in 1862 before being absorbed into the Great North of Scotland Railway in 1866; the last passenger services were withdrawn in 1968.

ARRIVAL AND DEPARTURE
DUFFTOWN

By bus Buses from/to Aberlour (Mon–Sat hourly; 10–15min) and Elgin (Mon–Sat hourly; 50min) stop outside the railway station.

ACCOMMODATION, EATING AND DRINKING

★ **Dufftown Glassworks** 16 Conval St ⓦ dufftownglassworks.com. This combined café and gallery is a smart place to sit with a coffee and plan your trip around whisky country. The rocky road slices are scrumptious.

Morven On the main square ⓦ morvendufftown.co.uk. Simple, inexpensive B&B that's conveniently located near the tourist office and the Whisky Museum in the middle of town. The owners offer a small reduction for longer stays. **££**

Tannochbrae Guest House 22 Fife St ⓦ tannochbrae. co.uk. Pleasant and enthusiastically run former provost's house near the main square, with six comfortable en-suite rooms, a lovely restaurant, drawing room and a well-stocked whisky bar-cum-lounge. **££**

SHOPPING

The Whisky Shop 1 Fife St ⓦ whiskyshopdufftown. com. A mind-bogglingly well-stocked shop with over six hundred malts and umpteen beers, produced not just on Speyside but all over Scotland.

Tomintoul

Deep into the foothills of the Cairngorms, **TOMINTOUL** (pronounced '*tom*-in-towel') is, at 1150ft, the highest village in the Scottish Highlands, and the northern gateway to the **Lecht Ski Area** (see page 413). Its long, thin layout is reminiscent of a Wild West frontier town; Queen Victoria wrote that it was 'the most tumble-down, poor looking place I ever saw'. A spur of the Speyside Way connects Ballindalloch through Glenlivet to Tomintoul, and there are plenty of other terrific walking opportunities in the area, as well as some great routes for mountain biking.

11

TOURING MALT WHISKY COUNTRY

Speyside is the heart of Scotland's **whisky** industry, and the presence of more than fifty **distilleries** is testimony to a unique combination of clear, clean water, benign climate and gentle upland terrain. Yet for all the advertising-influenced visions of timeless traditions, whisky is a multimillion-pound business dominated by huge corporations, and to many working distilleries visitors are an afterthought, if not a downright nuisance. That said, plenty are located in attractive historic buildings that now go to some lengths to provide an engaging experience for visitors. Mostly this involves a tour around the essential stages in the whisky-making process, though a number of distilleries now offer pricier connoisseur tours with a tutored tasting (or **nosing**, as it's properly called) and in-depth studies of the distiller's art. Some tours have restrictions on children; typically, those under the age of 8 not allowed on tours.

There are nine distilleries on the official **Malt Whisky Trail** (ⓦ maltwhiskytrail.com), a clearly signposted seventy-mile meander around the region. These are Benromach, Cardhu, Dallas Dhu Historic Distillery, Glenfiddich, Glen Grant, Glenlivet, Glen Moray and Strathisla and the Speyside Cooperage. Unless you're seriously interested in whisky, it's best to just pick out a couple that appeal. All offer a guided tour. You could cycle or walk parts of the route, using the Speyside Way (see page 410). The following is a list of selected highlights from the area (not all are on the official trail).

Glen Grant Rothes ⓦ glengrant.com. Makes a well-known, floral whisky aggressively marketed to the younger customer. The highlight here is the attractive Victorian gardens, a mix of well-tended lawns and mixed, mature trees, a tumbling waterfall and a hidden whisky safe. Tours £10 including voucher. April–Oct 9.30am–5pm; Nov–March Mon–Sat 9.30am–5pm, Sun noon–5pm.

Glendronach 8 miles northeast of Huntly ⓦ glendronachdistillery.co.uk. Off the official trail, this isolated distillery makes much of the fact that, uniquely, its stills are heated in the traditional method by coal fires. Tours from £10. May–Sept daily 10am–4.30pm; Oct–April Mon–Fri 10am–4.30pm.

Glenfiddich On the A941 just north of Dufftown ⓦ glenfiddich.com. The biggest and slickest of all the Speyside distilleries, despite the fact that it's still owned by the same Grant family who founded it in 1887. It's a light, sweet whisky packaged in triangular bottles – unusually, the bottling is still done on the premises and is part of the £10 tours (offered in various languages). April–Oct daily 9.30am–4.30pm; Nov–March daily 11am–3pm.

Glenlivet On the B9008 to Tomintoul ⓦ theglenlivet. com. A famous name in a lonely hillside setting.

This was the first licensed distillery in the Highlands, following the 1823 act that aimed to reduce illicit distilling and smuggling. The Glenlivet 12-year-old malt is a floral, fragrant, medium-bodied whisky. Tours cost £12.50. Easter to mid–Nov Mon–Sat 9.30am–4pm, Sun noon–4pm.

Macallan Near Craigellachie ⓦ themacallan.com. Small tours, and a classy whisky aged in sherry casks to give it a rich colour and flavour. Tours £15. Easter–Sept Mon–Sat 9.30am–6pm; Oct–Easter Mon–Fri 9.30am–5pm.

Strathisla Keith ⓦ maltwhiskydistilleries.com. A small, old-fashioned distillery claiming to be Scotland's oldest (1786); it's certainly one of the most attractive, with the River Isla rushing by. Inside there's an old-fashioned mash tun and brass-bound spirit safes. You can arrive here on one of the restored trains of the Keith & Dufftown Railway. Tours from £15. April–Oct Mon–Sat 9.30am–5pm, Sun noon–5pm.

Speyside Cooperage Craigellachie ⓦ speyside cooperage.co.uk. This cooperage – which produces and repairs the casks used in whisky-making – is the only stop on the official trail that isn't a distillery and offers fascinating glimpses of a highly skilled and vital part of the industry. Tours £4. Mon–Fri 9.30am–5pm.

Glenlivet Crown Estate

Visitor Centre Main St • Mon–Fri 9am–5pm • ⓦ glenlivetestate.co.uk

If you've come this far it's worth exploring the **Glenlivet Crown Estate**, an extensive tract of carefully managed land abutting Tomintoul. A hugely popular recreation spot, the estate maintains a number of extensive walking and mountain bike trails and there are plenty of opportunities to spot wildlife, including reindeer; information about the estate's wildlife and useful maps of paths and bike trails are available from the tourist office or the estate **visitor centre** at the southern end of the long main street.

ARRIVAL AND INFORMATION

By car The only reliable way to reach Tomintoul is by car; from Grantown-on-Spey the A939 snakes east, passing Tomintoul on the way to Ballater.

Tourist office On the central square, the helpful tourist office (April–Oct Mon–Sat 10am–5pm; ☎ 01309 696261) also acts as the local museum, with mock-ups of an old farm kitchen and a smithy.

ACCOMMODATION

As well as the options listed below, it's possible to **camp** beside the Glenlivet Estate ranger's office for free, though there are no facilities here whatsoever.

★ **Argyll Guest House** 7 Main St ⓦ argyletomintoul. co.uk. Six spacious and comfy rooms, and a great breakfast choice including home-made bread and porridge. The hosts give expert advice on local hiking and biking. <u>££</u>

Smuggler's Hostel Main St ⓦ thesmugglershostel. co.uk. Billed as the highest hostel in the Highlands and run by the community, with six- and seven-bed dorms plus doubles and family rooms; good facilities including drying sheds, a well-equipped kitchen and spacious communal areas. Dorms <u>£</u>; doubles <u>££</u>

Lecht Ski Area

7 miles southeast of Tomintoul along the A939 • Year-round • Full-day pass £32; ski rental costs £20/day from the ski school at the base station • For information on skiing and road conditions, check ⓦ lecht.co.uk

The **Lecht** is the smallest and most remote of Scotland's five ski areas, but it works hard to make itself appealing with a range of winter and summer activities. While its runs include some gentle beginners' slopes, there's little really challenging for experienced skiers other than a **Snowboard Fun Park**, with specially built jumps and ramps. Snow-making equipment helps extend the snow season beyond January and February, while downhill bike tracks open in the summer (there's no bike rental on site, though).

Huntly

The ancient burgh of **HUNTLY**, ten miles east of Dufftown, has one of the smallest and prettiest, albeit rather skeletal, castles in the area. The town also makes a good base for salmon fishing on the Deveron River, which flows right past the castle, and it is just on the fringe of whisky country, with the isolated **Glendronach Distillery** (see page 412) the nearest to town.

Huntly Castle

Half a mile north of town near the river • April–Sept daily 9.30am–5.30pm; Oct–Nov Mon–Wed, Sat & Sun 9.30am–4.30pm • Charge • HES • ⓦ historicenvironment.scot

Huntly Castle, power centre of the Gordon family, sits in a peaceful clearing on the banks of the Deveron River, a ten-minute walk from the town centre down Castle Street. Built over a period of five centuries, it became the headquarters of the Counter-Reformation in Scotland in 1562.

ARRIVAL AND DEPARTURE

By train Huntly is on the main train route from Aberdeen to Inverness; services run up to 11 times a day from/to Aberdeen (55min), Elgin (35min) and Inverness (1hr 25min). The station is on the east side of town, across the River Bogie.

By bus Hourly buses from/to Aberdeen (1hr 20min), Elgin (1hr) and Inverness (2hr 30min) arrive at and depart from Gordon St in the town centre.

ACCOMMODATION

Castle Hotel Marquis Drive ⓦ castlehotel.uk.com. The former home of the duke of Gordon is now a classy hotel that stands at the end of a long driveway behind the castle ruins. The best rooms here have four-poster beds and fireplaces, and the on-site restaurant serves indulgent mains like baked guinea fowl. <u>£££</u>

Coynachie Guesthouse Gartly, about 5 miles south of Huntly ⓦ coynachieguesthouse.com. Handsome, family-run B&B in the countryside south of Huntly, with three good-sized bedrooms and a cosy breakfast room. <u>££</u>

11

The north and northwest Highlands

GLENFINNAN VIADUCT RAILWAY

The north and northwest Highlands

As you drive along a single-track road, with bagpipes blaring on Gaelic radio and only sheep, stags and moody Highland cattle for company, the bleak yet beautiful north and northwest Highlands feels like nowhere else in Britain. Here, the weather is as changeable as the scenery: a combination of bare mountains, remote glens, dark lochs and tumbling rivers surrounded on three sides by a magnificent coastline. Although the landscape, along with its tranquillity and space, is the main attraction, so too is the enduring sense of remoteness. The vast peat bogs in the north are among the most extensive and unspoilt wilderness areas in Europe and some of the west-coast crofting villages can still be reached only by boat.

Different weather conditions and cultural histories give each of the three coastlines a distinct character. For many visitors, the Highlands' **west coast** is the reason to visit Scotland. The Vikings, who ruled the region in the ninth century, called it the 'South Land', from which the modern district of Sutherland takes its name. After Culloden, the Clearances emptied most of the inland glens of the far north, and left the population clinging to the coastline, which is the main reason to come. Cut by fjord-like **sea lochs**, it is scalloped by white-sand **beaches** or **waterfalls** in high, shattered cliffs, with **mountains** sweeping up from the shoreline. Weather fronts roll over rapidly, but when the sun shines, the sparkle of the sea, the rich colours in the clear light and the clarity of the views to the Hebrides are pure magic. With exhilarating scenery everywhere you look, this isolated region has historically seen far fewer visitors than the rest of Scotland, but the wiggling single-track roads are slowly getting busier as touring visitors from around the world flock to complete the **North Coast 500** road trip. The north and northwest Highlands also provide some of the best **cycling**, **walking** and **sea-kayaking** in Britain, superlative trout and salmon **fishing**, and wildlife by the ton. In fact the only issues are the west coast's predictably unpredictable **weather**, and **midges** that drive even the locals to distraction from June to August.

The most visited part of the west coast is the stretch between Kyle of Lochalsh and Ullapool. This is **Wester Ross**, with quintessentially west-coast scenes of beautiful coast set against some of Scotland's most impressive mountains and Skye and the Western Isles on the horizon. The obvious highlights are the mountain landscape of **Torridon**, **Gairloch**'s sandy beaches, the botanic gardens at **Inverewe**, and **Ullapool** itself, a bustling fishing town and launch pad for the Outer Hebrides. However, press on north or south and you get a truer sense of the isolation that makes this coast so special. Traversed by few roads, the remote northwest is wild and bleak. Villages in the southwest tend to be more sheltered, but they are separated by some of the most extensive wilderness areas in Britain – lonely peninsulas like **Ardnamurchan**, **Glenelg** or **Knoydart**, a magnificently untamed expanse with no road access and the remotest pub in mainland Britain.

The other coasts receive fewer visitors, and of the two the **north coast** is more popular. Stretching from **Cape Wrath** at the very northwest tip of the mainland to **John O'Groats**, it is even more rugged than the west, its sheer cliffs and white-sand bays bearing the brunt of frequently fierce Atlantic storms. The only town here is the surfing hub of **Thurso**, jumping-off point for the main ferry service to Orkney.

All of this makes the fertile **east coast** of the Highlands such a surprise. Stretching north from Inverness to the old herring port of **Wick**, it is a place of rolling moors, green fields and woodlands that run down to the sandy beaches of the **Black Isle** and **Cromarty** and **Dornoch firths**. If the west coast is about raw nature, the east is one of

12

Highlights

❶ **North Coast 500** Scotland's answer to Route 66 loops around the entire north and northwest Highlands; an unforgettable road trip. See page 420

❷ **The West Highland Railway** Ride the rails of Britain's most scenic train journey from Glasgow to Mallaig via Fort William for scenery that's more spectacular by the mile. See page 424

❸ **Knoydart** It can only be reached by boat or a two-day hike, but thrilling remoteness is not the only reason to visit Britain's last wilderness – there's also its most isolated pub, *The Old Forge*. See page 426

❹ **Foodie Lochinver** The Highlands' foodie capital offers everything from slap-up pies to Michelin-starred cuisine, with some Scottish tapas thrown in for good measure. See page 441

❺ **Suilven** A glimpse of the fantastical sugarloaf outline of this iconic mountain is reason enough to travel to Assynt. See page 441

❻ **Dunnet Head** Come to the true tip of mainland Britain, all remote red cliffs and empty seascapes to Orkney. See page 449

❼ **Cromarty** A lovely mix-and-match of handsome Georgian townhouses and cute cottages all packaged up in a friendly small town on the coast. See page 452

HIGHLIGHTS ARE MARKED ON THE MAP ON PAGE 419

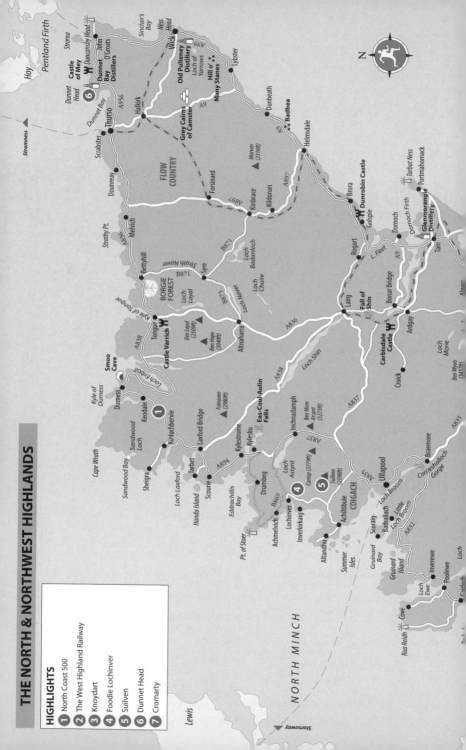

THE NORTH & NORTHWEST HIGHLANDS

HIGHLIGHTS

1. North Coast 500
2. The West Highland Railway
3. Knoydart
4. Foodie Lochinver
5. Suilven
6. Dunnet Head
7. Cromarty

THE NORTH COAST 500

Unveiled in 2014 as 'Scotland's answer to Route 66', the **North Coast 500** was created to tempt visitors up to this most remote corner of mainland Scotland, and it seems to be working. While driving or cycling in the north Highlands, you'll be asked, 'Are you doing the North Coast 500?' on a daily basis, and you probably are doing at least a stretch of the touring route, even if you didn't know. There are few alternative ways of getting around this part of Scotland, and certainly none more impressive than this route hugging the coastal fringes of the north Highlands.

With Inverness, Applecross, Durness and John O'Groats forming the four cardinal points of the route, pretty much everything in this chapter is covered by the North Coast 500. If you are on a mission to tour the full five hundred miles, try to incorporate **Plockton** and **Cromarty** – and, if time permits, **Skye** – into your itinerary; all short detours from the designated route but highlights of the region. See ⓦ northcoast500.com for more information on the official route.

human history: **Golspie**'s Sutherland Monument and castle, **Dornoch**'s fourteenth-century sandstone cathedral, relics of the **Picts** and several sites linked to the **Clearances**.

GETTING AROUND

THE HIGHLANDS

Getting around the **Highlands**, particularly the remoter parts, can be tricky without your own transport. **Bus services** are sporadic and often cease entirely on Sunday. Most sizeable villages have a petrol station or 24-hour fuel supply (typically card payment only), although these are few and far between in the west and north, so fill up early and be prepared for higher prices. Bear in mind, too, that the Highlands' single-track roads are far from fast; remember to pull in to let drivers behind overtake.

Morvern to Knoydart: the Rough Bounds

Its Gaelic name *Garbh-Chrìochan* translates as the **Rough Bounds**, implying a region geographically and spiritually apart, and the southwest corner of the Highlands is indeed remote and sparsely populated. From the empty district of **Morvern** to the isolated **Knoydart** peninsula are lonely mountains and moors, a rocky, indented coast studded with white beaches, and wonderful views to Mull, Skye and other islands. It's scenery that begs you to spend time exploring on foot.

Morvern

Bounded on three sides by sea lochs and in the north by desolate Glen Tarbet, the mountainous **Morvern peninsula** lies at the southwest corner of the Rough Bounds. Many inhabitants of St Kilda were settled here when the island was abandoned (see page 491), and the landscape can seem bleak until the coast reveals views to Mull.

Lochaline

Most visitors only travel through the Morvern peninsula to get to **LOCHALINE** (pronounced 'loch-*aa*lin') on the **Sound of Mull**, little more than a scattering of houses around a small pier built as a work-for-food scheme during famine in 1846. From here, a small ferry chugs to **Fishnish** – the shortest crossing to Mull from the mainland and cheaper than the Oban–Craignure crossing with a car. The town is also the departure point for excellent wreck-diving and snorkelling excursions in the Sound of Mull.

ARRIVAL AND DEPARTURE

MORVERN

By bus Shiel Buses (ⓦ shielbuses.co.uk) runs a service (No. 506) between Kilchoan and Fort William Mon–Sat (2hr 30min), plus another service (No. 507) between Fort William and Drimnin via Lochaline (Mon–Fri in termtime,

Tue & Thurs outside termtime).

By ferry To save the long journey around Loch Eil into the peninsula, a ferry nips across to Ardgour from Corran Ferry (ⓦ highland.gov.uk/corranferry), nine miles south of Fort William, every 20–30min (Mon–Sat 6.30am–9.30pm,

Sun 8.45am–9.30pm; 10min; £9 car, bikes and passengers free). In addition, CalMac operate a car ferry between Lochaline and Fishnish on Mull (Mon–Sat 7am–5.45pm, Sun 8.45am–4.45pm; 15min; ⓦ calmac.co.uk).

ACTIVITIES

Lochaline Dive Centre Lochaline ⓦ lochaline divecentre.co.uk. Based in the village centre, this outfit specializes in underwater archaeology on local wrecks, and provides drift, shallow, scenic and shore dives, and snorkelling excursions. Also offers air filling and cylinder rental, plus a lodge and the *O2 Café*.

EATING

★ Whitehouse Restaurant Lochaline ⓦ thewhite houserestaurant.co.uk. Arguably the best reason to visit Morvern, this is one of the Highlands' finest restaurants. Simple style belies outstanding modern European cooking that showcases local meat and seafood like smoked mussels and hand-dived scallops. Two-course lunch menu for £32, with dinner menus starting from £56 for four courses. Booking essential. **££££**

The Ardnamurchan peninsula

The **Ardnamurchan peninsula** is the most westerly point on the British mainland. Once ruled by Norse invaders, the peninsula lost most inhabitants during the Clearances and only a handful of crofting settlements cling to the coastline, making this one of the west coast's backwaters. Yet with its empty beaches and sea vistas, Ardnamurchan is an inspiring place.

A single-track road threads down its length, a superb route with a real sense of transition from ancient mossy oak forest to salt-sprayed moorland as you approach the sea. It's not fast, but this is slow travel at its best, with a huge variety of wildlife and scenery to make **walking** a pleasure; pick up a locally produced guide from tourist offices and most shops.

12

Strontian and Salen

Actually part of the near-roadless regions of **Sunart** and **Ardgour**, **STRONTIAN** serves as a gateway base for the peninsula. The village's moment of fame came in 1722, when local lead mines yielded the first-ever traces of **strontium**, which was named after the village.

The hamlet of **SALEN**, spread around another sheltered notch on the loch's shore, marks the turn-off for Ardnamurchan Point: from here it's 25 miles of scenic driving beside Loch Sunart – slow and all the better for it. The turf-roofed **Garbh Eilean Wildlife Hide** (free access) five miles west of Strontian is an opportunity to peer for seals, seabirds and the occasional eagle; on Mondays between Easter and October you'll find a knowledgeable ranger on-hand to help spot wildlife.

Ardnamurchan Natural History Visitor Centre

2 miles west of Glenborrodale • Easter–Oct Mon–Sat 8.30am–5pm, Sun 9am–5pm • Charge • ⓦ ardnamurchannaturalhistorycentre.com

The **Ardnamurchan Natural History Visitor Centre**, a small, child-friendly natural history centre, introduces the flora, fauna and geology of Ardnamurchan. The centre is in a timber 'Living Building' designed to allow in wildlife – pine martens nest within the walls, long-eared bats occasionally hang from the rafters and a glass wall descends into a wildlife pond. Otherwise there are the usual wildlife displays, a beautifully shot film, plus cameras trained on whatever's most interesting – the pine martens, perhaps, or a heronry opposite.

Kilchoan and Ardnamurchan Lighthouse

Lighthouse exhibition April–Oct daily 10am–5pm • **Lighthouse tour** April–Oct daily 11am–4pm • Charge; including entrance to the exhibition • ⓦ ardnamurchanlighthouse.com

KILCHOAN is Ardnamurchan's main village – a modest crofting settlement which straggles along the Sound of Mull. From here, the road continues to **Ardnamurchan Point**, the most westerly point in mainland Britain, marked by a 118ft-high **lighthouse**. The lighthouse buildings house a small café and an **exhibition** on local history, while tours go up the tower to see the lighting mechanism. Three miles northeast of the lighthouse, **Sanna Bay** is a white-sand beach with unforgettable views of the Small Isles.

ARRIVAL AND DEPARTURE

THE ARDNAMURCHAN PENINSULA

By bus A single service (Mon–Sat; ☎ 01967 431272) that begins at Fort William (currently 1.50pm) goes via Corran Ferry to reach Strontian (50min) before continuing to Kilchoan (2hr 40min); the bus from Kilchoan to Fort William currently departs at 7.50am.

By ferry A CalMac (ⓦ calmac.co.uk) car ferry operates

between Tobermory (Mull) and Kilchoan (April–Aug Mon–Sat 7 daily, Sun 5 daily; 35min; reduced service in winter).

By car The single-track road from Salen to Ardnamurchan Point is 25 miles long; allow just over an hour in each direction.

INFORMATION AND ACTIVITIES

Kilchoan tourist office In the community centre on Pier Road down towards the ferry slip (Mon–Sat 9am–5pm; Nov–March Mon–Fri 10am–4pm; ⓦ ardnamurchan.com).

Strontian tourist office The Oakwood Tourism and Craft Centre on the village green (May–Oct daily 10am–4pm; oakwoodtourismandcrafts.co.uk) has some good local

information.

Ardnamurchan Charters ⓦ www.west-scotland-marine.com. Operates wildlife-watching trips from Laga Bay, near Acharacle, to observe dolphins, seals, basking sharks, whales and possibly sea eagles. Also run trips around the Isle of Carna (ⓦ carnaconservation.org).

ACCOMMODATION AND EATING

STRONTIAN

Ariundle Centre 1 mile north of Strontian ⓦ ariundlecentre.co.uk. This tearoom and bunkhouse is a godsend for walkers and cyclists. Expect inexpensive fresh lunches and dinner such as steak in peppercorn sauce, and local ales and spirits in the licensed bar. Modern bunkhouse has dorms, family rooms and twins, most with en suite; it's set among woods a mile from the centre – turn right across Strontian bridge. Breakfast available for extra cost. Dorms $\overline{£}$; twins and family $\underline{££}$

SALEN

Salen Hotel Salen ⓦ salenhotel.co.uk. Less a small hotel than a restaurant with three smart rooms above – tastefully furnished where modern flair meets antiques – and family, self-catering accommodation in the cottage. The restaurant offers a Scottish gastropub menu for example haggis and whisky cream pot with salad and oatcakes, and a Scottish fish platter with hot and cold salmon and herring. Breakfast by prior arrangement. $\underline{££}$

GLENBORRODALE

Lochview Tearoom Ardnamurchan Natural History Visitor Centre ⓦ ardnamurchannaturalhistorycentre. com. The simple tearoom attached to the visitor centre rustles up excellent breakfast, home-made soups, scones and cakes.

KILCHOAN

★ **Ardnamurchan Campsite** Ormsaigbeg ⓦ ardnamurchanstudycentre.co.uk. Cracking views, plus campfires on the beach of a laudably back-to-basics campsite behind the loch – pure magic at sunset and usually spared summer midges by a breeze. Find it past the Ferry Stores. Camping per person $\overline{£}$

Puffin Café Kilchoan Community Centre, Pier Rd ⓦ ardpuffincoffee.co.uk. Colourful, artfully-decorated café (the owner is a silversmith) which takes its coffee pretty seriously and so should you – it's delicious, as are the home-baked cakes and scones; toasties and pizza too. $\overline{£}$

Acharacle and Glenuig

At the eastern end of Ardnamurchan, just north-west of Salen where the A861 heads north towards the district of Moidart, the main settlement is **ACHARACLE**, a nondescript crofting village set back from **Loch Shiel**. The reason to swing through is **Castle Tioram** (pronounced 'cheerum'), one of Scotland's most atmospheric monuments. Perched on a promontory above **Loch Moidart** and accessed via a sandy causeway (its Gaelic name means 'dry land'), the thirteenth-century fortress was the

12

seat of the MacDonalds of Clanranald until it was destroyed by their chief in 1715 to prevent it falling into Hanoverian hands. There's no entry into the castle, but for a slice of picture-postcard romantic Scotland, it's hard to beat. It's located three miles north of Acharacle via a side road off the A861.

Keep going north on the A861 and you'll roll through woods to arrive at **GLENUIG**, gathered on a picturesque inlet on the Sound of Arisaig. Barely a hamlet, it makes a fine base for walking, sea-kayaking – or partying, when the community centre hosts gigs every other Saturday (listings on ⓦ glenuig.org.uk).

ARRIVAL AND ACTIVITIES ACHARACLE AND GLENUIG

By bus Buses go from Fort William (Mon–Sat 1–2 daily) to Acharacle (1hr 20min) and Glenuig (1hr 10min).

By boat Loch Shiel Cruises runs trips to Acharacle from Glenfinnan at the head of Loch Shiel (April to Oct Wed & Sat;

£30; ⓦ highlandcruises.co.uk).

Sea-kayaking The owner of the *Glenuig Inn* runs half- and full-day trips in the Sound of Arisaig from £65.

ACCOMMODATION AND EATING

Glenuig Inn Glenuig ⓦ glenuig.com. A refurbished inn that ticks all boxes: an excellent hostel with single beds, not bunks; smarter en-suite rooms in an annexe; and

local beers plus well-priced bar food – lamb kofta kebabs, root vegetable curries and home-made burgers. Dorms $\overline{£}$; doubles $\overline{££}$

The Road to the Isles

The **Road to the Isles** from Fort William to Mallaig, followed by the West Highland Railway and the winding A830, traverses the mountains and glens of the Rough Bounds before breaking out near **Arisaig** onto a spectacular coast of sheltered inlets, white-sand beaches and wonderful views to the islands of Rùm, Eigg, Muck and Skye. This is a country commonly associated with **Bonnie Prince Charlie**, whose adventures of 1745–46 began on this stretch of coast with his gathering of the clans at **Glenfinnan** and ended here too at Loch nan Uamh when he embarked on a French frigate and fled into exile.

12

Glenfinnan

This sleepy village may be spectacularly sited at the head of Loch Shiel, but it's the local history that draws most visitors to **GLENFINNAN**, since it was here that Bonnie Prince Charlie raised his standard and rallied forces before the ill-fated march on London. That said, nowadays just as many visitors come to see the imposing arched viaduct, famously crossed by the *Hogwarts Express* in the *Harry Potter* films.

Glenfinnan Monument and Visitor Centre

Centre of the village • Daily March–Oct 9am–5.30pm; Nov–Feb 10am–4pm • Charge • NTS • ⓦ nts.org.uk

The spot where the Young Pretender raised his battle standard on August 19, 1745, is marked by one of Scotland's most iconic structures, **Glenfinnan Monument**, a 60ft column crowned with a Highland clansman in full battle dress, erected as a tribute by Alexander Macdonald of Glenaladale in 1815. It's a beautiful, brooding spot at the head of the loch that's best appreciated from a viewpoint behind the **Visitor Centre**. After admiring the view, pop inside for an account of the 1745 uprising through to the rout at Culloden (see page 400).

ARRIVAL AND DEPARTURE GLENFINNAN

By train A direct service links Fort William to Glenfinnan (Mon–Sat 4 daily, Sun 1 daily; 35min).

INFORMATION AND TOURS

Tourist information The Glenfinnan Visitor Centre is a good source of local information, as is the website

ⓦ roadtotheisles.com.

Loch Shiel Cruises ⓦ highlandcruises.co.uk. Runs

boat trips to view the superb scenery between April and October. Cruises embark from a jetty near *Glenfinnan House*

Hotel, signposted off the main road half a mile west of the monument.

ACCOMMODATION AND EATING

Prince's House Centre of the village, on the A830 ⓦglenfinnan.co.uk. This seventeenth-century former coaching inn offers homely rooms – the best at the front nod to Highlands tradition – and a warm welcome to match. The fine restaurant offers a seasonal, fresh menu or there's gastropub grub in the Stage House bistro and bar; expect West Coast salmon, lamb and venison. **£££**

Sleeping Car Glenfinnan station ⓦglenfinnan stationmuseum.co.uk. A 1958 camping coach is now a (very) mini-bunkhouse with two twin compartments (bunk beds), a family compartment for four, plus a kitchen, lounge and bathroom – a memorable if rather cosy place to stay. Linen costs extra. The adjacent *Dining Car* is open for light lunches from April to Oct (phone ahead for evening meals). The owners also run the neighbouring Station Museum. Twin **£**

Arisaig

The little coastal village of **ARISAIG** (meaning 'the Safe Place' in Gaelic) is an appealingly drowsy place scattered around a sandy bay. The only specific attraction in the village is the **Land, Sea and Islands Centre** (April–Oct Mon–Sat 10am–6pm, Sun 11am–5pm, Nov–March Mon 10am–1pm, Sat 10am–4pm, Sun 11am–4pm; donations; ⓦarisaiginfo.org.uk), a volunteer-run community project has some wonderful displays pertaining to crofting life, local characters and the area's role as a base for Special Operations during World War II. There's also a small research library of wildlife and walks – swot up before walking to a seal colony at nearby **Rhumach**, reached via a single-track lane heading west out of Arisaig.

Stretching for eight miles or so north of Arisaig along the road signposted 'Alternative Coastal Route' is a string of stunning white-sand, azure-water **beaches**: summer holiday favourites backed by flowery machair and with views out to Eigg and Rùm. Pretty **Traigh** beach is your spot to collect cowrie shells, but larger and more celebrated is **Camusdarach Beach** a mile or so north, where the beach scenes of the films *Local Hero* and *Highlander* were shot. If it's busy, two intimate beaches lie over the headlands on either side.

ARRIVAL AND INFORMATION   ARISAIG

By train Direct services run from Fort William to Arisaig (Mon–Sat 4 daily, Sun 1 daily; 1hr 5min).

By boat Arisaig Marine (ⓦarisaig.co.uk) sails from Arisaig

marina to Eigg, Rùm and Muck at 11am daily, from late April to late Sept.

Tourist information Inside the Land, Sea and Islands

THE WEST HIGHLAND RAILWAY

A fixture in lists of the world's most scenic train journeys, the brilliantly engineered **West Highland Railway** runs from Glasgow to Mallaig via Fort William. The line is in two sections: the southern part travels from **Glasgow** Queen Street station, up the banks of Loch Lomond to **Crianlarich**, then around Beinn Odhar on a horseshoe of viaducts to cross **Rannoch Moor**, where the track had to be laid on a mattress of tree roots, brushwood and thousands of tons of earth and ashes. You're out in the wilds here, the line long having diverged from the road. The route then swings into Glen Roy, passing through the **Monessie Gorge** to enter **Fort William**.

Leg two, from Fort William to Mallaig, is even more spectacular. Shortly after leaving Fort William the railway crosses the Caledonian Canal beside Neptune's Staircase at **Banavie**, before travelling along Locheil and crossing the 21-arch viaduct at **Glenfinnan**, where passengers get to live out *Harry Potter* fantasies. Then it's on to the coast, with views of the Small Isles and Skye before journey's end at **Mallaig**. You can book tickets through ⓦscotrail. co.uk. Between mid-April and Oct, this leg of the route is also served by the **Jacobite Steam Train** (ⓦwestcoastrailways.co.uk).

Centre (April–Oct Mon–Sat 10am–6pm, Sun 11am–5pm; Nov–March Fri–Mon 10am–4pm; ⓦ arisaiginfo.org.uk has some excellent local information.

ACTIVITIES

Arisaig Sea Kayak Centre ⓦ arisaigseakayakcentre. co.uk. Based at the *Arisaig Hotel*, this operator offers trips every day in season for all levels (guided day trips £95), as well as longer wild-camp adventures.

ACCOMMODATION AND EATING

★ **Camusdarach Campsite** Camusdarach ⓦ camusdarach.co.uk. By far the loveliest campsite in the area, its neat fields a pleasing balance of eco-emptiness and modern facilities, all spread behind sands so white they've featured in films. Glamping pods available for those who would rather not brave the elements. Decent takeaway pizzas and proper coffees available. Per pitch ͞£, pod ͞£͞£

Old Library Lodge and Restaurant Arisaig ⓦ oldlibrary.co.uk. This old stone building, formerly the stables for the Arisaig estate's horses, is not much to look at from the outside but its six rooms here are perfectly agreeable; the best ones overlook the bay. The popular dining room offers Scottish dishes: cullen skink or delicious crab sandwiches for lunch, loin of venison or a superb butter-poached hake for dinner. Doubles ͞£͞£͞£

Mallaig

The fate of **MALLAIG**, 47 miles west of Fort William, is to be seen as somewhere to go through, not to. Before the railway arrived in 1901 it consisted of a few cottages. Now in season it's full of visitors as the main embarkation point for ferries to Skye, the Small Isles and Knoydart. Even if not especially pretty, it is a solid town given a workaday honesty by its local **fishing** industry – it once had one of Europe's busiest herring ports and the harbour remains the source of the village's wealth.

Mallaig Heritage Centre

Beside the train station • April–June daily 11am–4pm; July–Sept daily 11am–6pm; Oct Mon–Sat 11am–4pm • Charge • ⓦ mallaigheritage.org.uk

Apart from the hubbub of the harbour, the town's only sight is **Mallaig Heritage Centre** – nothing to quicken the pulse but worth a browse for displays on the area's past and information about lifeboats, fishing and the highland galleys that once plied the waters of the Inner Hebrides and descend directly from Viking longships.

ARRIVAL AND DEPARTURE

MALLAIG

BY TRAIN
A direct service arrives from Fort William (Mon–Sat 4 daily, Sun 3 daily; 1hr 25min) and Glasgow (Mon–Sat 3 daily, Sun 1 daily; 5hr 30min), via Glenfinnan and Arisaig.

BY BUS
There are regular buses from Fort William to Mallaig via Glenfinnan and Arisaig (Mon–Fri 4 daily, Sat & Sun 1 daily; 1hr 10min).

BY FERRY
The CalMac ticket office (ⓦ calmac.co.uk) is at the main ferry terminal.

To/from Skye Regular services shuttle between Mallaig and Armadale (Mon–Sat 9 daily; mid-May–mid-Sept Sun 6 daily; 30min). Car reservations are essential in peak season.
To/from the Small Isles There are services between Mallaig and Eigg (Mon, Thurs, Sat & Sun 1 daily; 1hr 15min); Rùm (Fri–Mon & Wed 1 daily; 1hr 20min); Muck (Tues & Thurs–Sun 1 daily; 1hr 40min–2hr); and Canna (Fri–Mon & Wed 1 daily; 2hr 30min). Note, sailing days can change in winter so check timetable.
To/from Knoydart Western Isles Cruises (ⓦ westernislescruises.co.uk) sails from Mallaig to Inverie (Apr–Oct Mon–Sat 4 daily, Sun 3 daily; Nov–March Mon–Fri 5 daily, Sat & Sun 2 daily; 25min).

ACCOMMODATION

Mallaig Backpackers Main St ⓦ mallaigbackpackers. co.uk. 100yd south of the train station, this relaxed, independent modern hostel has two mixed dorms, a small kitchen and a lounge. 'Reception' is in the *Tea Garden* restaurant opposite the harbour. Dorms ͞£

Seaview Main St ⓦ seaviewguesthousemallaig.com.

12

Snug dimensions and surprisingly smart decor – tasteful shades of taupe and grey with a leaning towards modest boutique – set the tone in this central B&B with harbour views from five of the six rooms. Doubles **££**

EATING

The Bakehouse Old Quay ⓦoldquaybakehouse.com. For a coffee and croissant hit before boarding the ferry, look no further than this fantastic bakery, which also doles out a variety of breads (including sourdough and focaccia) and truly scrumptious handmade pizza. **££**

Cornerstone Main St ⓦseafoodrestaurantmallaig. com. A simple first-floor restaurant that's the locals' choice for classic seafood – expect a daily soup and a menu of fresh fish, simply but excellently prepared and well-priced. **££**

Tea Garden Main St ⓦmallaigbackpackers.co.uk. As central as it gets, with a terrace to watch the world go by and a relaxed dining room with a traditional bistro menu of Mallaig kippers, pints of prawns or home-made scones; fully licensed too. **££**

The Knoydart peninsula

Touted as 'Britain's last great wilderness', the very thought of the **Knoydart peninsula** stirs the imagination. The fact that it is inaccessible by car is part of the allure – to reach the heart of the peninsula, you either catch a **boat** from Mallaig or **hike** across rugged moorland, sleeping in stone bothies (marked on OS maps). The scenery is superb, flanked by **Loch Nevis** ('Loch of Heaven') and the fjord-like **Loch Hourn** ('Loch of Hell') and three Munros sweeping straight up from the sea. Unsurprisingly, the peninsula has long attracted walkers, but with increasingly comfortable accommodation, it is also gaining a cachet among holiday-makers in search of escapism: a place to slow down for a few days' self-imposed exile from modernity.

Brief history

At the end of the eighteenth century, around a thousand people eked out a living from this inhospitable terrain through crofting and fishing. **Evictions** in 1853 began a dramatic decrease in the population, which continued to dwindle through the twentieth century as a succession of landowners ran the estate as a hunting and shooting playground, prompting a famous land raid in 1948 by a group of crofters known as the '**Seven Men of Knoydart**', who claimed ownership of portions of the estate. Although their bid failed, their cause was invoked when the crofters of Knoydart finally achieved a **community buyout** in 1999. An offer to provide the money from theatre impresario Cameron Mackintosh was rejected because locals were wary of giving up control.

Inverie

Most of the peninsula's hundred or so occupants live in the sleepy hamlet of **INVERIE**. Spread along Loch Nevis, it has a pint-sized post office and shop (with wi-fi), a ranger

---

WALKING INTO KNOYDART

Ordnance Survey Explorer maps nos. 413 and 398

There are two main **hiking routes** into Knoydart. The trailhead for the first is **Kinloch Hourn** at the far east end of Loch Hourn (turn south off the A87 six miles west of Invergarry). From Kinloch Hourn, a well-marked path winds around the coast on the south side of Loch Hourn to Barrisdale, where there's bed and breakfast accommodation at Lochhournhead Farm (ⓦbarisdale.com), before continuing ten miles to Inverie; expect 18–20 hours' walk, in total. The second path into Knoydart starts from the west end of **Loch Arkaig**, approaching the peninsula via Glen Dessary. Hardened walkers reckon on knocking off the eighteen-mile journey in one long summer's day. The rest of us should set aside two. Either way, take wet-weather gear, a good map, plenty of food, warm clothes and a good sleeping bag, and leave your name and expected time of arrival with someone when you set off.

post with tips on local walks and wildlife, a pleasant tearoom and mainland Britain's most remote pub, *The Old Forge*. You're here for the Tolkienesque scenery, for walks and for the thrill of dropping off the radar.

ARRIVAL AND DEPARTURE
THE KNOYDART PENINSULA

By boat Western Isles Cruises (ⓦwesternislescruises. co.uk) sails from Mallaig to Inverie (May–Sept Mon–Fri 5 daily, Sat 4 daily, Sun 3 daily; April & Oct Mon–Fri 4 daily, Sat 4 daily, Sun 3 daily; Nov–March Mon–Fri 4 daily, Sat 2 daily, Sun 2 daily; 25min).

On foot It's a two-day hike into Knoydart; our box (see page 426) gives details.

INFORMATION AND ACTIVITIES

Tourist information A ranger post (ⓣ01687 462242) beside *The Old Forge* has information on the Knoydart Foundation, and on local history and wildlife. The adjoining shop (with wi-fi) sells walking leaflets plus local goods, from wild venison to woolly blankets.

Mountain biking Two mountain-bike trails – a 1.5-mile red-grade route and a 500yd blue-grade route– loop around Inverie. Knoydart Carbon Cycle rents bikes from the village centre (ⓣ01687 462242, ⓔamie@knoydart.org; £12).

ACCOMMODATION

Most beds are in Inverie, with a growing number of self-catering options (see ⓦknoydart.org). You can **camp** on Long Beach, east of Inverie centre, for £10 per person – pay the ranger or leave it in an honesty box at the campsite. The turf-roofed compost toilet, mountain water supply and cabin shelter make for a comfortable enough stay. Firewood (£4.50) for use in the fire-pits is available at the campsite, and visitors may be able to use the showers in the *Knoydart Bunkhouse* for a small charge.

★ **Doune Knoydart** 6 miles northwest of Inverie (owners collect guests by boat from Mallaig) ⓦdoune-knoydart.co.uk. This may be the ultimate Highland getaway, with en-suite doubles in restored pine-clad crofts behind a bay. As well as isolation and views, its lovely owners provide superb cooking (also available for non-

guests; call ahead). Minimum three nights. Full board. Doubles **££££**

The Gathering Inverie ⓦthegatheringknoydart. co.uk. Relaxed sophistication in a modern, ecofriendly B&B just west of the wharf that feels like self-contained accommodation (the owner lives opposite); each room sleeps four. Superb views and sensational breakfasts. Bring swimming gear to enjoy the hot tub with a view. Doubles **££**

Knoydart Foundation Bunkhouse Half a mile east of the pier, Inverie ⓦknoydart.org. The community hostel is on an old farm near Long Beach. Dorms are large, facilities include a kitchen and laundry, and there's internet access in a comfy lounge with a wood burner. Dorms **£**

EATING AND DRINKING

Knoydart Pottery & Tearoom Inverie ⓣ01687 460191. A lovely spot to lose a few hours (or a long, wet day): choose from sofas, a long communal table or the outdoor decking with the best loch view in Knoydart. Isla and Rhona serve up breakfast rolls, home-made soups and gluten-free home-baking. **£**

★ **The Old Forge** Inverie ⓦtheoldforge.co.uk. Britain's most isolated pub remains one of Scotland's finer boozers, fuelled by a convivial atmosphere and wonderful sense of remoteness. Generous bar meals feature local seafood – starters such as Loch Nevis mussels steamed in white wine and garlic, and for a main perhaps Scottish beef fillet in a whisky flambé – and terrific loch views. Regular live music sessions add to the conviviality here. **£££**

Kyle of Lochalsh and around

Prior to the construction of the Skye Bridge in 1995, the **Kyle of Lochalsh** was Skye's main ferry port, but these days it's mainly used as a terminus for the train route from Inverness. Nearby, the photogenic **Eilean Donan Castle** sits on the glassy shores of **Loch Duich**. Both are fixtures on the tourist trail, which makes the remote **Glenelg** peninsula to the south side of Loch Duich all the more inspiring. A few miles north of Kyle of Lochalsh, the village of **Plockton** is a lovely spot, with a superb setting on **Loch Carron**, a long inlet which acts as a dividing line between Kyle of Lochalsh and the splendours of Wester Ross to the north.

12

Kyle of Lochalsh

Truth be told, traffic has little reason to stop in **KYLE OF LOCHALSH**, especially since Skye or Plockton nearby offer more appealing accommodation. One good reason to pause here is the *Seaprobe Atlantis*, the UK's only semi-submersible **glass-bottom boat** (see below).

ARRIVAL AND ACTIVITIES
KYLE OF LOCHALSH

By train It's a glorious journey from Inverness to Kyle of Lochalsh (Mon–Sat 4 daily, Sun 1 daily; 2hr 35min); trains stop at Plockton (15min from Kyle) en route.

By bus Reservations are recommended for all services (w citylink.co.uk). Buses stop on the waterfront at the old slipway.

Destinations Fort William (7 daily; 1hr 55min); Glasgow (5

daily; 5hr 15min); Inverness (8 daily; 2hr); Kyleakin, Skye (6 daily; 5min).

Boat tours The glass-bottom *Seaprobe Atlantis* (w seaprobeatlantis.com) leads summer trips to protected seal and bird colonies on Seal Island (1hr; £20) or over the World War II wreck of HMS *Port Napier* (2hr; £32).

Loch Duich

Skirted on its northern shore by the A87, **Loch Duich** features prominently on the tourist trail: coach tours from all over the world thunder down from **SHIEL BRIDGE** en route to Skye and one of Scotland's most iconic castles, Eilean Donan. Not that it's just the happy hordes who visit: at the end of the loch is Glen Shiel, flanked by the **Five Sisters of Kintail** – a classic tough trek that ticks off three Munros (see page 10).

Eilean Donan Castle

Beside A87 near the village of Dornie • Daily March & Oct–mid-Dec 10am–4pm, April–June 10am–6pm, July & Aug 9am–6pm, Sept 9.30am–6pm • Charge • w eileandonancastle.com

After Edinburgh's fortress, **Eilean Donan Castle** has to be the most photographed monument in Scotland. Located on the A87, guarding the confluence of lochs Alsh, Long and Duich, its tower rises on an islet, joined to the shore by a stone bridge and set against a backdrop of mountains. Small wonder it has featured in *Highlander* and the James Bond adventure *The World is Not Enough*. The castle was established in 1230 by Alexander II to protect the area from the Vikings but was destroyed during the Jacobite uprising of 1719. It was rebuilt between 1912 and 1932 by a British army officer, John Macrae-Gilstrap, because of the Macrae clan's ancestral links to the area. Hence its three floors, including the banqueting hall, the bedrooms and the troops' quarters, are re-creations rather than originals, though the Jacobite and clan relics on display are all original; this includes a toddy ladle belonging to Bonnie Prince Charlie, as well as a lock of his hair, displayed in cabinets in the impressive-looking Billeting Room, which manifests a superb barrel-vaulted ceiling. Hand held audio guides (included in the entrance fee) do an excellent job of making sense of it all.

ARRIVAL AND DEPARTURE

By bus Citylink bus No. 917 (2 daily) stops at Eilean Donan Castle, about halfway between Inverness (1hr 50min) and Portree (1hr 20min).

ACCOMMODATION AND EATING
LOCH DUICH

Glenshiel Campsite Off the A87, just south of Shiel Bridge w glenshielcampsite.co.uk. This site's superb location at the west end of Glen Shiel beneath the Five Sisters makes it a great spot to bed down for the night; reception is in the (handy) little shop just before the site proper. Per person £

Kintail Lodge Hotel Off the A87, just north of Invershiel w kintaillodgehotel.co.uk. Lovingly converted from a former shooting lodge and standing at the foot of the Five Sisters of Kintail, the hotel is right on the shores of Loch Duich. Tastefully decorated, the nine en-suite rooms all have splendid views of the loch or the mountains. The restaurant specialises in the best of local produce, and a wide selection of ales, wines and malts is offered in either the resident's bar

or the traditional pub. Doubles **£££**
Ratagan Youth Hostel Ratagan, 2 miles south of Shiel Bridge ⓦhostellingscotland.org.uk. Superbly sited on

the loch, with views across to the Five Sisters. Traditional in public areas but dorms are more IKEAesque. Dorms **£**; doubles **££**

The Glenelg peninsula

Even though summer traffic trickles through for the Kylerhea ferry to Skye, sleepy **Glenelg peninsula** remains a quiet backwater jutting into the Sound of Sleat – one benefit of being on a road to nowhere. Indeed, the peninsula has probably changed little since Gavin Maxwell wrote about it in his otter novel *Ring of Bright Water* and he disguised its pristine coast by calling it 'Camusfeàrna'. The landward approach is equally impressive on a road that switchbacks over the Mam Ratagan Pass (1115ft), rewarding drivers with spectacular views over the **Five Sisters** massif. The main village, **GLENELG**, is an appealingly soporific spot – a row of whitewashed houses, surrounded by trees, that shows little indication of its time as a strategic centre in the 1700s, when a large barracks kept clans in check. The ruins of Bernera Barracks are on the left as you approach the ferry.

Glenelg Brochs

Nearly two miles south of Glenelg, a left turn up Glen Beag leads to the **Glenelg Brochs**, one of the best-preserved Iron Age monuments in Scotland. Its spectacular circular towers – Dun Telve and Dun Troddan – in a sheltered valley are thought to have been erected around two thousand years ago to protect surrounding settlements from raiders.

12

Arnsdale

A lonely backroad beyond Glenelg village snakes southeast through a scattering of old crofting hamlets, timber forests and views of Skye and Eigg that grow more spectacular at each bend. Eventually you drop down to the shore of Loch Hourn at **ARNISDALE**, actually two hamlets in the bosom of the mountains: **Camusbane**, a traditional crofting settlement ranged behind a pebble beach; and **Corran** a mile further, a minuscule, whitewashed fishing hamlet huddled around a river mouth. Display boards in the latter's **Ceilidh House and Heritage Centre** (always open; donation) relate local history, including that of Mansion House between the hamlets, built by Valentine Fleming, father of James Bond author Ian Fleming.

ARRIVAL AND DEPARTURE | THE GLENELG PENINSULA

By bus MacRae Kintail bus service (Mon, Tues & Fri 1 daily; ⓦmacraekintailbus.co.uk) operates from Kyle of Lochalsh to Glenelg (50min; request on boarding) and Arnisdale (1hr 40min; advance booking required) via Shiel Bridge.

By ferry The six-car Glenelg–Kylerhea turntable ferry (daily April–Oct 10am–6pm; June–Aug until 7pm; ⓦskyeferry.co.uk) shuttles to and from Skye every 20min; 5min.

ACCOMMODATION AND EATING

The Glenelg Inn Glenelg ⓦglenelg-inn.com. Snug, eclectic, with a fire in the grate and a spectacular lochside setting to boot. Comfortable rooms and a decent gastropub menu that showcases local seafood – fish, crab cakes, scallops – confirm this is a class act. Occasional live music. Doubles **£££**

Sheena's Tea Hut End of the road, Corran ☏01599 522336. Probably Britain's most remote cuppa, and well worth the journey. This charmingly ramshackle corrugated hut, now run by local legend Sheena's daughter, Lorraine, serves up cockle-warming soups, toasties and cakes, plus fish and chips. A true one-off. **££**

Plockton

With its picture-postcard cottages curved behind a tiny harbour and views across Loch Carron to mountains, **PLOCKTON** is one of the most picturesque settlements on the west coast. Until the end of the eighteenth century, Am Ploc, as the settlement was then known, was just another crofting hamlet. Then a local laird transformed it with a prosperous fishery, funding a planned village that was renamed 'Plockton'. It's packed in high season with yachties – a popular regatta fills the bay over a fortnight from late July – artsy second-home owners with easels in tow, and visiting families squelching over the seabed at low tide to take a turn around the small island. It may look familiar to first-time visitors – its flower- and palm-filled seafront featured in cult horror film *The Wicker Man*.

ARRIVAL AND DEPARTURE

PLOCKTON

By train Trains from Inverness stop in Plockton (Mon–Sat 4 daily, Sun 1 daily; 2hr 20min) before continuing on to Kyle of Lochalsh (15min).

INFORMATION AND ACTIVITIES

Tourist information In the absence of a tourist office, try Ⓦ visitplockton.com.

Calum's Seal Trips Ⓦ calums-sealtrips.com. Between Easter and October, this long-running outfit runs seal-watching trips – expect 'better views than the QE2' aboard this pretty, traditional cruiser. Perhaps true if you like seals (1hr; £15 or free if no seals).

ACCOMMODATION

An Caladh 25 Harbour St Ⓦ plockton.uk.com. Anna and Bob's whitewashed fisherman's cottage is one of the best of Plockton's many B&Bs, with sea views from front rooms – some en suites. Doubles **££**

Duncraig Castle Turn-off midway between Duirnish and Plockton Ⓦ duncraigcastle.com. On the opposite side of the bay from Plockton village in a truly stunning setting, this grand Baronial pile has undergone a top-to-bottom renovation. The impressive suite of individually designed rooms come with sumptuous beds and Egyptian cotton, and freestanding baths and underfloor heating in the bathrooms. Doubles **££££**

Plockton Hotel 41 Harbour St Ⓦ plocktonhotel.co.uk. This friendly, small hotel provides cosy, contemporary-cottage decor in rooms, the best rooms come with a view at the front. A four-room annexe on the harbour appeals for its shared kitchen as much as its cheaper rates that still include breakfast. Well-stocked pub downstairs, with a grassy beer garden overlooking the bay. Annexe **££**; doubles **£££**

EATING AND DRINKING

Plockton Inn Innes St Ⓦ plocktoninn.co.uk. The locals' choice offers excellent lunches like soup of the day or smoked mackerel pâté, then a fine evening menu including haggis and clapshot and their famous Plockton prawns. Good vegetarian options and live music on Tuesdays and Thursdays evenings during summer. **£££**

Plockton Shores 30 Harbour St ☎ 01599 544263. Metropolitan-styled café-restaurant that starts the day as a relaxed coffee and lunch stop, then shifts up a gear for modern Scottish dishes like scallops in lemon and honey glaze. Rotating exhibition of local artwork adorns the walls. **£££**

Loch Carron

North of Plockton are the twin sea lochs of **Loch Kishorn**, so deep it was once used as an oil-rig construction site, and **Loch Carron**, which cuts far inland to **STRATHCARRON**, a useful rail link between Kyle of Lochalsh and Torridon, but little else.

Attadale Gardens

2.5 miles south of Strathcarron • April–Oct daily 10am–5pm • Charge • Ⓦ attadalegardens.com

Made up of twenty artistically landscaped acres, **Attadale Gardens** are ranked among Scotland's finest by horticultural aficionados, yet they remain little visited compared to the country's larger National Trust properties. They are, though, utterly charming, the highlights being a stunning fernery – complete with Victorian drain – the nearby Rhododendron Dell, with trees perched precariously on rock ledges, a cleverly conceived sunken garden and an abundant kitchen garden. For kids (adults too), there's a delightful sculpture trail (mostly bronze animals), while, for a pause in proceedings, pop your head into the honesty café where you can grab a hot drink and a cake or an ice cream.

Lochcarron

With supermarkets, cafés, a bank and fuel set along a long, whitewashed seafront, **LOCHCARRON** represents a considerable hub hereabouts. While it's of more use than interest, two crafty sights warrant a pause. A mile north of town on the main road, the **Smithy Community Hub** (March–Sept Mon–Sat 11am–4pm), a nineteenth-century smithy and forge, is open erratically in season but has become a focus for local **crafts collectives** selling their wares. More celebrated are the tartans of **Lochcarron Weavers** (Easter–Oct Mon–Sat 9am–5pm; Nov–Easter Mon–Fri 10am–4pm◫ ◉lochcarron.co.uk), five miles south of the Community Hub towards Strome Castle, where you can see weaving demonstrations and buy fabrics and clothing.

ARRIVAL AND INFORMATION   LOCHCARRON

By rail Strathcarron is on the splendid Kyle of Lochalsh– Inverness line (Mon–Sat 4 daily, Sun 1 daily): trains run from/to Inverness (1hr 50min) and Kyle (40min).

By bus Timetables are coordinated so that buses meet train arrivals at Strathcarron. Services run to Lochcarron from

Shieldaig (Mon–Sat 1 daily; 35min) and Torridon (Mon–Sat 1 daily; 1hr; call ☎01520 722682 to request).

Tourist information Tourist information desk in the Smithy Community Hub (March–Sept Mon–Sat 11am– 4pm, ☎01520 722952).

ACCOMMODATION AND EATING

★ **Kishorn Seafood Bar** Kishorn, 6 miles northwest of Lochcarron ◉ kishornseafoodbar.co.uk. A baby blue, lodge-like café often named in the top-ten British seafood restaurants for local and fresh seafood, and it's not difficult to see why with dishes like peppered mackerel fillet, smoke roasted salmon with dill sauce, and scallops with garlic and wakame seaweed on the menu. Outdoor seating available. **£££**

Old Manse Church St, Lochcarron ◉theoldmanse lochcarron.com. Floral fabrics, pine furniture and wrought-iron beds – country style rules in the five spacious en-suite rooms of the *Old Manse*, on the road to Strome Castle. Perhaps its real appeal is the location before the loch – £10 extra buys you a room with a view. Doubles **££**

Wester Ross

The western seaboard of the old county of Ross-shire, **Wester Ross** is where the west coast ups the ante. Here, all the classic elements of Scotland's **coastal scenery** – craggy mountains, sandy beaches, whitewashed crofting cottages and shimmering island views – come together. Settlements such as **Applecross** and the peninsulas north and south of **Gairloch** maintain a simplicity and sense of isolation outside of peak season. There is some tough but wonderful **hiking** in the mountains around **Torridon** and **Coigach**, while **boat trips** and the prolific marine life and birdlife draw nature-lovers. The hub of activity is **Ullapool**, a proper fishing town and ferry port whose modest size ranks as a metropolis in these parts.

The Applecross peninsula

The **Applecross peninsula** sounds bucolic; the English-sounding name is a corruption of the Gaelic *Apor Crosan*, meaning 'estuary'. Yet the approach from the south – up a glacial U-shaped valley and over the **Bealach na Bà** (Pass of the Cattle) at 2054ft – is one of the classic drives and cycle pistes of the Highlands. With a sticker-strewn sign at the base warning off large vehicles and learner drivers (heed the advice), this former drovers' road provides the greatest road ascent in the UK, with a 1:5 gradient and switchbacks worthy of the Alps. Views across the Minch to Raasay and Skye more than compensate – assuming the

12

weather plays ball. The other way in from the north is a beautiful coast road that meanders from Shieldaig on Loch Torridon, past scattered crofting villages and with gorgeous seascapes.

Applecross

The sheltered, fertile coast around **APPLECROSS** village, where an Irish missionary Maelrhuba founded a monastery in AD 673, is a surprise after experiencing the wilds that surround it. Though popular in peak season, it feels exhilaratingly remote, with little to do but visit the excellent pub, potter along lanes exploring the craft shops, paddle a kayak or build sandcastles on the beautiful sandy beach. A small **Heritage Centre** (Easter–Oct Mon–Sat noon–4pm; ⓦ applecrossheritage. org.uk) near the site of St Maelrhuba's monastery, and beside Clachan church, showcases local history from the Mesolithic period to present day. There are several **waymarked trails** along the shore for all fitness levels that are great for walking off lunch. Come towards the end of July for the barnstorming annual Applecross Highland Games.

ARRIVAL AND DEPARTURE
APPLECROSS

By bus A service operated by Lochcarron Garage (☏ 01520 722205) takes passengers from Applecross to Inverness, with stop-offs in Lochcarron, Shieldaig and Kishorn.

INFORMATION AND ACTIVITIES

Tourist information Village websites are ⓦ visitapplecross.com and ⓦ applecross.uk.com. **Mountain & Sea Guides** ⓦ applecross.uk.com/ msg. Located by the fuel pumps, this company organizes mountain walking and climbing adventures, plus sea-kayaking, from half-day tasters to overnight wild-camping trips.

ACCOMMODATION AND EATING

Applecross Campsite East of the centre ⓦ visitapplecross.com. A popular, well-run two-field site above the village – the furthest field is the quietest – that also provides basic cabins sleeping four, with electricity and heating. The Flower Tunnel common area is a splendid spot to while away an afternoon. No fires allowed. Camping per person £; cabins ££

★ **Applecross Inn** On the waterfront ⓦ applecrossinn. co.uk. The heart of the community provides pretty, cottagey en suites in the eaves, all with sea views. In the lively bar downstairs are Highland ales and freshly prepared classic pasta dishes plus divine seafood like Applecross Bay prawns and king scallops. Outside, the *Applecross Inn-Side Out* food cart serves up quality fish and chips and ice cream from spring to autumn. Reservations recommended in season. Doubles £££

The Walled Garden Signposted northeast of the bay ⓦ applecrossgarden.co.uk. Head here to enjoy delicious food in the laidback atmosphere of a walled Victorian garden. Decent full Scottish breakfast, generous slices of divine home-made cake, with dishes like bouillabaisse stew and chickpea, feta and spinach parcels available in the evening. ££

Loch Torridon

Loch Torridon marks the northern boundary of the Applecross peninsula and a transition into some awe-inspiring scenery. From the water rise the mountains of **Liathach** and **Beinn Eighe**, shapely hulks of reddish, 750-million-year-old white quartzite. Around fifteen thousand acres of the massif are under the protection of the National Trust for Scotland, which makes this superb walking country, with a trio of Munros to bag.

Shieldaig

Smuggled off the main road on the shore of Loch Torridon, pretty **SHIELDAIG** (Herring Bay) is a gentle spot – until the Shieldaig Fete and Rowing Regatta liven things up with some wacky boat races over the first weekend in August. A track winding north up the peninsula from the village makes for an enjoyable stroll. Otherwise, simply enjoy the view to **Shieldaig Island**, managed by the National Trust for Scotland; in 2009 a pair of sea eagles pitched up on the island and have remained here ever since – stay patient and you may catch a glimpse of these magnificent birds.

Torridon

TORRIDON village, at the east end of the loch, marks where the road heads inland through spectacular Glen Torridon to Kinlochewe (see page 434). The village itself – thirty or so houses and a shop – straggles along the loch beneath the mountains, making it a fine launchpad for hikes. A **Countryside Centre** (April–Sept Sun–Fri 10am–5pm; free; ⓦnts.org.uk/visit/places/torridon) at the turning into the village provides advice on mountain walks plus information on geology, flora and fauna. In a large paddock a short walk from the centre are thirty or so red deer, which you can feed (food is available from the centre), and there's also a small museum (same hours) nearby which has information on the history and management of the animal, which are abundant in the region.

ARRIVAL AND ACTIVITIES   LOCH TORRIDON

By bus DMK Motors (☎01520 722682) from Strathcarron calls at Shieldaig and Torridon (Mon–Fri 1 daily).
Torridon Outdoors 1 mile south of turn-off into village ⓦthetorridon.com/torridon-outdoors. An operator based at the *Torridon Hotel* provides the full range of local fun: guided walks, gorge scrambling, coasteering and

climbing, plus kayaking and even clay pigeon shooting.
Shieldaig Outdoor Adventures ⓦshieldaig adventures.com. Based in Shieldaig, a range of activities on land and water, including sea kayaking, canoeing, mountain walking and archery, reveal the superb scenery and wildlife in the area: half- and full-day excursions available.

ACCOMMODATION AND EATING

SHIELDAIG

★ **Shieldaig Camping and Cabins** Temperance Brae ⓦshieldaigcampingandcabins.co.uk. In a wonderful, elevated position near the primary school at the village's north end, this pristine new campsite has nicely spaced pitches, in addition to a couple of cabins, plus a modern shower/toilet block; the views (from most pitches at least) are fabulous. Per pitch **£**; cabins **£**
★ **Tigh-an-Eilean** On the waterfront ⓦtighaneilean. co.uk. Faultless service and utter relaxation in a lovely small hotel on the waterfront with classy country accommodation plus a sensational restaurant (albeit for residents only); expect the likes of west coast sea bream with a Provençal tomato confit on innovative daily menus. Non-residents, though, can eat in the attached *Shieldaig Bar and Coastal Kitchen* which rustles up top-notch bistro dishes like bangers, mash and peas and wood-fired pizzas. Doubles **£££**

TORRIDON

Camping A wild camp is located beside the turning into the village next to the youth hostel. Dishwashing and a shower is in an adjacent public toilet. Beware the midges in summer, though.

Torridon Youth Hostel Start of village, 100yd from turn-off ⓦhostellingscotland.org.uk. Though the Seventies-vintage municipal building is no looker, this hostel is spacious and a popular choice with hikers and bikers thanks to a location beneath the peaks. Provides the usual kitchen, laundry and drying room, plus very cheap meals daily. Dorms **£**; doubles **££**
★ **Torridon Hotel** 1.5 miles southwest of turn-off into village ⓦthetorridon.com. This Victorian hunting lodge is one of the west coast's grandest stays. Sympathetically styled where boutique meets Baronial in public areas and master rooms; Classics are more up to date. The elegant 1867 restaurant offers a six-course tasting menu (£80) and a three-course table d'hôte menu (£62.50), within which you can expect gems such as Loch Torridon oyster velouté or Scrabster landed monkfish cheek with samphire; the whisky bar, meanwhile, has 350-plus malts a delight (tasting session £30). Doubles **££££**
Torridon Inn Next to the Torridon Hotel ⓦthetorridon. com. More cyclist- and walker-friendly than the neighbouring *Torridon Hotel* (same owners), with neat, modern en suites. Bar-bistro serves regional ales and good gastropub cooking – veggie moussaka, fish and chips or beef and venison pie. **£££**

12

Loch Maree

About eight miles north of Loch Torridon, **Loch Maree**, dotted with Caledonian-pine-covered islands, is one of the area's scenic highlights, best viewed from the A832 road that drops down to its southeastern tip through Glen Docherty; try to time your journey here with early dawn or dusk, when red deer take over the land. At the southeastern end of the loch, the A896 from Torridon meets the A832 from Achnasheen at small **KINLOCHEWE**, a good base if you're heading into the hills.

Beinn Eighe Nature Reserve

The A832 skirts the southern shore of Loch Maree, passing the **Beinn Eighe Nature Reserve**, Britain's oldest national nature reserve, set up in 1951. Parts of the reserve are forested with Caledonian pine, which once covered the whole country, and it is home to pine martens, wildcats, buzzards and golden eagles. A mile north of Kinlochewe, the **Beinn Eighe Visitor Centre** (May–Oct daily 10am–5pm; ⓦ nature.scot), on the A832, has an excellent exhibition on the reserve courtesy of wall-bound panoramic displays, as well as free leaflets covering local walks. Two **walks** start from the Coille na Glas-Leitir Trails car park just over a mile north of the visitor centre: a mile-long trail into ancient pine woodland and a 3.5-mile track into the mountains.

ACCOMMODATION AND EATING

LOCH MAREE

Kinlochewe Hotel On A832, centre of village ⓦ kinlochewehotel.co.uk. A traditional hotel dating back to 1850 with a warm welcome where rooms are comfy enough, though a couple share bathroom facilities. An annexe holds a very basic twelve-bed self-catering bunkhouse, with triple-deck bunks in one room (bedding not included). The bar does a fantastic line in regional ales and the restaurant, excels in good-value soups and casseroles. Doubles £̲£̲; dorm £̲

Loch Maree Hotel On A832, 9 miles north of Kinlochewe ⓦ lochmareehotel.com. Standing beside the loch in breath-taking scenery, this hotel is particularly popular with anglers. A cosy bar with wood burning stove, residents' lounge and a dining room with views over the loch are all big draws. Spacious guest rooms have a traditional Scottish feel with tartan soft furnishings, and some have four poster beds and loch views. £̲£̲

Gorse Bush Torrisdale Rd ⓦ thegorsebush.com. This brightly decorated, refurbed old village hall is always a good stop before or after the hills, serving filled rolls for lunch (grilled scallops, slow roasted pork) and superb dinners, perhaps sweet onion tart with wild mushrooms or steamed sea trout with crab bisque. A well-placed log-burner guarantees to warm the cockles. £̲£̲£̲

Gairloch and around

Cheerful and unpretentious, **GAIRLOCH** thrives as a low-key holiday resort, with several sandy beaches for the bucket-and-spade brigade, some good coastal walks within easy reach and an abundance of wildlife cruise operators that pray for passing minke whales. The township is divided into distinct areas spread along Loch Gairloch: to the south, in **Flowerdale Bay**, is Charlestown with the harbour; west, at the turn-off to Melvaig, **Achtercairn** is the centre of Gairloch; and along the north side of the bay is the crofting area of **Strath**. Near the *Old Inn* in Charlestown, the **Sòlas Gallery** (May–Oct Tues–Fri 1–5pm; ⓦ solasgallery. co.uk) is worth a stop for its ceramics and watercolours inspired by the Highlands landscapes. A 1.5-mile walk (round trip) tracks the Flowerdale River through a woodland glen to a waterfall.

Gairloch Museum

In the centre of Gairloch • April–Oct Mon–Fri 10am–5pm, Sat 11am–3pm; Nov–March Thurs–Sat 11am–4pm • Charge • ⓦ gairlochmuseum.org

Occupying a former nuclear bunker – hence the chilly grey concrete walls – the superb **Gairloch Museum** houses eclectic displays of traditional Highland life, from a mock-up croft house to one of the largest Fresnel lenses ever constructed, from the nearby Rua Reidh Lighthouse. The museum's most prestigious display, however, is the so-called

Poolewe Hoard, discovered by crofter Hector Maciver in 1877 and comprising a rich collection of Bronze Age items (axe heads, rings and ornamental objects) thought to date from around 570 BC.

Big Sand and Melvaig
The area's real attraction is its **coastline**. There's a **beach** just north of the harbour in Charlestown, a crescent of pure sand, or a more impressive stretch a few miles around the north side of the bay at **Big Sand** – it's cleaner, quieter and a mite pebblier. The B8021 terminates at the crofting hamlet of **Melvaig**.

Rua Reidh and around
From Melvaig, a private track heads three miles to **Rua Reidh** (pronounced 'roo-a-ray'), where a fully operational lighthouse houses a hostel in its keepers' quarters (see page 436). Around the headland lies beautiful **Camas Mòr** beach, from where a marked footpath tracks inland (southeast) beneath a sheer scarp slope, past a string of lochans and ruined crofts to **MIDTOWN** on the east side of the peninsula, four miles north of Poolewe on the B8057. Allow half a day, though be aware that few buses travel back from Poolewe (check times on ☎01445 712255).

Badachro
On the south side of Loch Gairloch, a single-track lane (built with the Destitution Funds raised during the nineteenth-century potato famine) winds past wooded coves and inlets along the loch to **BADACHRO**, a secluded, former fishing village with a wonderful pub (see page 436). Five miles on, Redpoint has beautiful peach-coloured beaches and marks the trailhead for the wonderful coastal walk to Lower Diabaig.

12

ARRIVAL AND INFORMATION   GAIRLOCH AND AROUND

By bus Public transport is minimal and requires careful planning. Bus stops for all services are at the *Old Inn*, Charlestown, as well as Achtercairn and Strath.
Destinations Inverness (Mon–Sat 1 daily; 2hr 20min); Poolewe (Mon–Sat 1 daily; 15min); Ullapool (Tues–Sat 1 daily; 1hr 25min).

Tourist information The superb community-run Gale Centre in Achtercairn (Mon–Sat 10am–5.30pm, Sun 11am–5pm; extended hours Easter–Oct ⓦgaleactionforum.co.uk).

ACTIVITIES

BOAT TRIPS
Gairloch prides itself on wildlife cruises from its harbour. Orcas and minke whales migrate past from late spring to late summer; porpoise and dolphins are common year-round, and seal-spotting is near enough guaranteed. All operators are located on the harbour at Charlestown and run trips between April and October.
Gairloch Marine Life Centre & Cruises Charlestown ⓦporpoise-gairloch.co.uk. The bay's largest operator runs three different trips a day (2hr/£35 and 4hr/£70), aboard two vessels, which deploys a mini-sub for underwater pictures and a hydrophone to pick up audio. Its visitor centre (Easter–Oct Mon–Fri 10am–3pm, Sat & Sun until 4pm) has

displays of local sea life.
Hebridean Whale Cruises Charlestown ⓦhebridean-whale-cruises.co.uk. As well as in-shore cruises, the longest-established operator runs trips in a high-speed RIB that allows it to reach further offshore into the North Minch out to the Shiant Isles off Lewis.

PONY TREKKING
Gairloch Trekking Centre Croft 3, Red Point ⓦgairlochtrekkingcentre.co.uk. Lead-rein rides for young or inexperienced riders, plus longer hacks (1hr £25; 2hr £50) along the beach and through pretty Highland scenery, between Easter and Oct.

ACCOMMODATION

GAIRLOCH
Old Inn Signposted off A832, Charlestown ⓦtheoldinn. net. Country character abounds in the rooms of this former

coaching inn set off the main road beside the Flowerdale River. Expect pretty patchwork-style quilts or tartan headboards in cosy en-suite rooms. **£££**

BIG SAND

Gairloch Sands Youth Hostel On B8021, 2.5 miles west of Gairloch ⓦ hostellingscotland.org.uk. This former hunting lodge is spectacularly sited above the foreshore, with vast views to Skye from its lounge. It dates back to 1880 and rather shows its age. Dorms £̄; doubles £̄£̄

Sands Caravan and Camping On B8021, 3.5 miles west of Gairloch ⓦ sandscaravanandcamping.co.uk. The best of the area's campsites, with pitches behind the dunes for sea views. Also rents 'wigwams' – actually Scandi-style cabins for up to five with electricity, heating and a fire-pit. Laundry facilities and play area, plus kayak and bike rental.

There's a well-stocked shop, while the cosy on-site *Barn Café* serves evening meals (reserve ahead) and there's a terrific pizza truck for takeaways. Per pitch £̄; wigwams for two £̄£̄

RUA REIDH

Rua Reidh Lighthouse Rua Reidh ⓦ stayatalighthouse. co.uk. Epic seascapes to the Hebrides in the only lighthouse hostel on Britain's west coast (see page 435), with four rooms (one room sleeps four) manifesting homely decorative touches and private bathrooms. Breakfasts, packed lunches and a buffet supper available. £̄£̄

EATING AND DRINKING

GAIRLOCH

Mountain Coffee Company Achtercairn ☎01445 712316. Here's an unusual find for a small Highlands town – a relaxed café with a global backpacker vibe. Coffees, mammoth-sized scones and toasted bagels with fresh fillings, plus a good bookshop on-site and rooms upstairs. **Old Inn** Signposted off A832, Charlestown ⓦ theoldinn. net. Flagstone floors and stone walls provide character in a modernized coaching inn. Posh-pub specials such as game casserole, plus beers of the on-site microbrewery, provide

the sustenance. £̄£̄£̄

BADACHRO

★ **Badachro Inn** ⓦ badachroinn.com. Settle onto the terrace with home-made chicken and leek pie or creel-caught langoustine and this pub by the old harbour is as fine a place as you'll find for a sunny afternoon. Inside are real ales, excellent malts and a fire for chill evenings. Look out for otters at dawn and dusk. £̄£̄£̄

Poolewe

It's a short hop over the headland from Gairloch to the sleepy village of **POOLEWE** at the sheltered southern end of Loch Ewe. During World War II, the Arctic convoy embarked from here and the deep-water loch remains one of only three berths for nuclear submarines. One of the area's best **walks** begins nearby, signposted from the lay-by viewpoint on the A832, a mile south. It takes a couple of hours to follow the easy trail across open moorland to the shores of **Loch Maree** (see page 434), then the car park at Slattadale, seven miles southeast of Gairloch. Double-check timetables (☎01445 712255), but you should be able to continue along the loch shore to catch the Wester bus from Inverness back to Poolewe from the *Loch Maree Hotel* just after 7pm (Tues, Thurs & Fri only).

Inverewe Gardens

Half a mile north of Poolewe on A832 • **Gardens** April–June Tues–Sat 9.45am–4pm; July & Aug 9.45am–5pm; Sept & Oct Wed–Sun 9.45am–4pm • **Restaurant** mid-April–Oct 11am–4pm • Charge • NTS • ⓦ nts.org.uk

Most visitors arrive in Poolewe for **Inverewe Gardens**, a subtropical-style oasis of foliage and riotously colourful compared to the wild coast. A network of paths and walkways wanders through more than a dozen gardens featuring exotic plant collections from as far afield as Chile, China, Tasmania and the Himalayas. You'll quite likely see plenty of wildlife too, including otters and seals, and herons nesting in the trees down by Camas Bay. Between April and September there are free guided walks at 1.30pm Monday to Saturday, and the self-service restaurant offers up soups and sandwiches. Visitors can also explore the opulent **Inverewe House**, which, with its original furnishings, feel happily lived in

ARRIVAL AND DEPARTURE

POOLEWE

By bus There's a bus to Poolewe from Gairloch (15min; Mon–Sat 7.45pm).

12

ACCOMMODATION AND EATING

Bridge Cottage Café In the centre of Poolewe ❶ 01445 781335. Ideal pit stop for a cup of tea or coffee, excellent light lunches or home-baked cakes. Owned by a Galician couple who endeavour to source local ingredients. There's also a tiny gallery upstairs.

Inverewe Gardens Camping & Caravanning of Poolewe on A832 ⓦ campingandcaravanningclub. co.uk. As trim a site as usual from a member of the Camping & Caravanning Club and largely occupied by motorhomes. Facilities are well maintained and a few pitches in a shady corner allow campers to wake up to loch views. Per pitch £̄

★**Pool House Hotel** Centre of Poolewe on A832 ⓦ pool-house.co.uk. Once the residence of Inverewe Gardens' Osgood MacKenzie, the Harrison family home remains one of the Highlands' most elegantly opulent small hotels – think rich fabrics, family antiques and art, loch views and a serene sense of calm. Don't be surprised if you struggle to leave the lounge. Minimum two-night stay. £̄£̄£̄£̄

Poolewe to Ullapool

At **LAIDE**, nine miles north of Poolewe, the road skirts the shores of **Gruinard Bay**. It's a great drive, offering fabulous views and, at the inner end of the bay, some excellent sandy beaches before you swing east, tracking high above Little Loch Broom, with gorgeous views to mountains opposite – **Badrallach**, seven miles from a left-turn at the head of the loch, is a magical spot to drop off the radar.

Inland, the route joins the A835 at **Braemore Junction**, above the head of Loch Broom. Easily accessible from a lay-by on the A835, the spectacular 160ft **Falls of Measach** plunge through the mile-long **Corrieshalloch Gorge**, formed by glacial meltwaters. After walking for five minutes you'll reach a Victorian suspension bridge that spans the chasm, offering a vertiginous view of the falls and gorge, whose 197ft vertical sides are draped in wych-elm, goat willow and bird cherry.

12

ACCOMMODATION AND EATING   POOLEWE TO ULLAPOOL

★**Badrallach** Croft 9, Badrallach ⓦ badrallach.com. Views, space and pure escapism literally at the end of the road. Alongside the campsite are beds in a snug bothy and B&B in a sweet two-bedroom cottage (3-night minimum). Excellent eco-friendly facilities. With fishing rod and kayak rental, too, this deserves a few days. Camping per person £̄; bothy £̄; cottage per night £̄£̄

Ullapool

ULLAPOOL, the northwest's principal town, is an appealing place spread across a sheltered arm of land in Loch Broom – a perfect base for exploring the northwest Highlands. Here you'll find all the cultural life of the only town worth the title in the region, with a penchant for barnstorming live music nights and a few excellent restaurants. Founded by the British Fisheries Society at the height of the herring boom in 1788, the grid-plan town remains an important fishing centre, which gives it a salty authenticity despite the hundreds of visitors who pass through in high season, bound north or to catch the **ferry** to Stornoway on Lewis (see page 485).

Ullapool Museum

7–8 West Argyle St • April–Oct Mon–Sat 10am–5pm • Charge • ⓦ ullapoolmuseum.co.uk

The only conventional attraction in town is the small but engaging **Ullapool Museum**, which occupies the old, Thomas Telford commissioned parish church, as

---

FESTIVALS IN ULLAPOOL

The town's annual highlight is the **Ullapool Book Festival** (ⓦ ullapoolbookfestival.co.uk) in May; the Highlands' answer to Hay-on-Wye.

evidenced by the pulpit, pews and gallery in situ. By way of artefacts, photographs and audio-visual displays it offers a marvellous insight into crofting, fishing and the sea, local weather and emigration. During the Clearances, Ullapool was one of the ports through which evicted crofters left to start new lives abroad – it also has some genealogy resources.

Isle Martin

ⓦ islemartin.org

Three miles northwest of Ullapool in Loch Broom, **Isle Martin** was inhabited on and off for a few thousand years – they say it was named after a follower of St Columba, who may be under a fifth-century gravestone in the old graveyard – until the last crofting families called it a day in 1949. Gifted to the RSPB in 1999, the four-hundred-acre island is a romantic spot to be a temporary castaway, with beaches, walks and views to the cliffs of Beinn Mor Coigach and the Summer Isles. Bothy-style accommodation is available in the *Croft House* (£60 per night) or bunk rooms in the *Mill House* (£20 per person). It's now possible to visit the island courtesy of a community-run passenger boat, which currently operates on Fridays, Saturdays and Sundays in July and August (£10). Otherwise, you can visit with your own boat (a donation is required) or via a RIB trip with Seascape Expeditions (£15; see page 439).

ULLAPOOL

0 — 250
yards

■ DRINKING
Ferry Boat Inn — 1

Loch Broom FM

Library

P

Tesco

Ullapool Clock ⓘ

Museum

Ullapool River

MOSS ROAD

A835 NORTH ROAD

RIVERSIDE TERRACE

CASTLE TERRACE

LADYSMITH STREET

MILL STREET

QUAY STREET

WEST TERRACE

MARKET STREET

PULTENEY STREET

SEAFORTH ROAD

ARGYLE STREET

GARVE ROAD

WEST ARGYLE STREET

SHORE STREET

Pier

CalMac Ticket Office

Cruise Booking Office

CalMac Terminal

Pier

Loch Broom

WEST SHORE STREET

N

● EATING
The Arch Inn — 4
The Ceilidh Place — 2
The Seafood Shack — 3
West Coast Delicatessen — 1

■ ACCOMMODATION
Broomfield Holiday Park — 5
The Ceilidh Place — 4
The Royal Hotel — 1
Tanglewood House — 2
Ullapool Youth Hostel — 3

Stornoway

CEILIDHS

The **ceilidh** is essentially an informal, homespun kind of entertainment, the word being Gaelic for a 'visit'. In remote Highland communities, talents and resources were pooled, people gathering to play music, sing, recite poems and dance. The dances themselves are thought to be ancient in origin; the Romans wrote that the Caledonians danced with abandon round swords stuck in the ground, a practice echoed in today's traditional sword dance, where the weapons are crossed on the floor and a quick-stepping dancer skips over and around them.

Highland ceilidhs, fuelled by whisky and largely extemporized, must have been an intoxicating, riotous means of fending off winter gloom. Like much of clan culture, however, the traditions died or were forced underground after the defeat of the Highlanders at **Culloden** and the passing of the 1747 Act of Proscription, which forbade the wearing of the plaid and other expressions of Highland identity.

Ceilidhs were enthusiastically revived in the reign of tartan-fetishist **Queen Victoria**, and in the twentieth century became the preserve of the village hall and hotel ballroom, buoyed to some extent by the popularity of jaunty 1950s TV programmes. More recently, though, the ceilidh has thrown off its dated associations, with places such as *The Ceilidh Place* in Ullapool (see below) and the *Taybank Hotel* in Dunkeld (see page 318) restoring some of its spontaneous, infectious fun to a night of Scottish music and dancing.

Whether performed by skilled traditional musicians or in more rollicking form by younger players, ceilidh music is irresistible, and it's common to find all generations gathering. Ceilidh dances look complex. Actually, most are reasonably simple and are explained or 'called' beforehand by the bandleader. We find a whisky or two earlier on helps.

12

Summer Isles

During summer, the *MV Shearwater* steamer (May–early Sept Mon–Sat 10am & 1pm; £40; ⓦsummerqueen.co.uk) and the RIB-safari operator Seascape Expeditions (£30; see below), run wildlife cruises and trips to the **Summer Isles**, twelve miles west of Ullapool, to view seabird colonies, grey seals, dolphins, porpoises and the occasional whale. Whether slow and stately or fast and full-on in caves, it's a trip worth taking (weather permitting).

ARRIVAL AND INFORMATION

ULLAPOOL

By bus Buses stop at the pier, near the ferry dock.
Destinations Durness (Durness Bus, ⓦthedurnessbus.com, July–Sept Mon–Sat 1 daily; 3hr); Inverness (Citylink, ⓦcitylink.co.uk, Mon–Sat 3 daily; 1hr 30min).
By ferry CalMac (ⓦcalmac.co.uk) sails to Stornoway, Lewis (Mon–Sat 2 daily, Sun 1 daily; 2hr 30min); two extra sailings run on Sun in peak season. Seascape Expeditions (ⓦsea-scape.co.uk) run trips to Isle Martin and Summer Isles during the summer.

Tourist office Argyle St (Mon–Sat 9.30am–5pm, Sun 10am–3pm; June–Aug Mon–Sat 9am–6pm, Sun 9.30am–4.30pm; Oct Mon–Sat 9.30am–4.30pm, Sun 10am–3pm; Nov–March Thurs–Mon 10am–3pm; ⓦullapool.com). This friendly, well-run tourist office also offers an accommodation booking service and you can also book CalMac ferry tickets here.

ACCOMMODATION

SEE MAP PAGE 438

Ullapool is busy from Easter through until September – **booking in advance** is essential.

HOTELS, GUESTHOUSES AND B&BS

★**The Ceilidh Place** 14 West Argyle St ⓦtheceilidhplace.com. Antique bed frames, old books on vintage cabinets and Roberts Radios add character to rooms of this lovely small hotel, where the mantra is 'no TVs, and proud'. Some are pepped up with stylish wallpaper, otherwise modern-rustic rules. The lounge and library, with honesty bar, offers sophisticated relaxation. The cheapest rooms share bathrooms. The owners also manages a bunkhouse directly opposite. **£££**

The Royal Hotel Garve Rd ⓦroyalhotel-ullapool.co.uk. Situated on the seafront of Loch Broom, the 55 stylish balcony rooms here offer spectacular views across the loch. There is a choice of bars and restaurants that offer a good selection of food, from pasta and pizzas to a full dinner service. **£££**

★**Tanglewood House** 1 mile south off A835

ⓦtanglewoodhouse.co.uk. Charm and character in an extraordinary, curved house full of art and antiques. Rooms are individually furnished; the Green Room, with a terrace to enjoy the position above Loch Broom, is worth its extra £16. Factor in a rocky beach beneath for a dip and this is a truly memorable stay. Doubles £̲£̲

HOSTELS AND CAMPSITES
Broomfield Holiday Park West Shore St ⓦbroomfieldhp.com. Hurrah: a campsite in the centre of town with loch views and space galore at the tip of Ullapool, plus standard facilities and all a short walk to the heart of Ullapool. Per pitch £̲

Ullapool Youth Hostel Shore St, ⓦhostellingscotland. org.uk. Busy hostel bang on the seafront, where prints and murals of seaside scenes help add a cheerful holiday atmosphere. There are dorms of various sizes, doubles, twins, two lounges, internet access and laundry plus lots of good information about local walks. Dorms £̲; doubles £̲£̲

EATING
SEE MAP PAGE 438

The Arch Inn 10–11 West Shore St ⓦthearchinn.co.uk. Ullapool's liveliest pub divides between a popular bar and informal restaurant with Scottish-European cooking: starters like sautéed scallops with pickled apple or Cullen skink, then sirloin steak alongside the usual fish and chips. £̲£̲

The Ceilidh Place 14 West Argyle St ⓦtheceilidhplace. com. This barn-like venue remains one of the best in town. After breakfasts, it shifts to a bistro menu – with the likes of home-made burgers and haddock and chips, then after 5pm the menu steps up a notch to include wild venison – and its bar hosts regular live music. Fantastic bookshop attached. £̲£̲£̲

The Seafood Shack West Argyle St, Ullapool ⓦseafoodshack.co.uk. This award-winning takeaway, with outside seating, has a reputation that draws people far and wide. Seafood fresh from local waters is cooked in a way that respects the quality, the daily changing menu might include hot garlic crab claws with salad and bread or salt and pepper squid with garlic mayonnaise. £̲

West Coast Delicatessen 5 Argyle St ⓦwestcoastdeli. co.uk. Fine food deli serves up proper coffees, home-made humous and fresh salads, tarts and cakes, plus unmissable 'pakora Fridays'. For a proper fry-up, the *Tea Store* (ⓦtheteastore.co.uk) over the road will do the job. £̲£̲

DRINKING
SEE MAP PAGE 438

Ullapool has no shortage of decent boozers. The liveliest pub around, the *Arch Inn*, hosts live bands, and live Scottish **folk music** is a feature at *The Ceilidh Place*.
Ferry Boat Inn 26–27 Shore St ⓦfbiullapool.com. Popular with locals with their dogs, the *FBI* remains a choice spot to swig a pint of ale at the lochside (midges permitting) and watch the boats. Live music on Saturdays, and also at sister pub *The Argyle* around the corner.

Assynt

If the landscape before Ullapool was impressive, the **Assynt** region just north has an epic, almost cinematic, quality. Marking the transition from Wester Ross into Sutherland, this region is one of the least populated areas in Europe and its landscape consists not of mountain ranges but of extraordinary peaks which rise individually from the moorland. See a mountain like **Suilven** and you understand why the name is said to derive from 'A-ssynt', meaning seen from afar, or 'ass' – Old Norse for rocky. Certainly, Assynt boasts some of the world's oldest rock formations, and roadside signs highlight the region's geological importance as the **Northwest Highlands Geopark** (ⓦnwhgeopark.com).

Coigach

Coigach is the peninsula immediately north of Loch Broom, accessible via a road off the A835. It's a beautiful drive, squeezing between the northern shore of Loch Lurgainn and mountains like mammoths, including **Cul Beag** (2523ft), craggy **Stac Pollaidh** (2012ft) and the awesome bulk of **Ben Mór Coigach** (2439ft), southeast, which presides over the area. There's some spectacular coastal scenery too. It's a place to unwind, with gorgeous views of the Summer Isles scattered offshore and signposted trails along coastal moors and mountains. If the steep Ben Mór Coigach–Sgùrr an Fhidhleir horseshoe (7 miles; 7hr) seems too tough, the Culnacraig circuit (5 miles; 2hr) between Achduart and Culnacraig also offers great views. Coigach's main settlement is **ACHILTIBUIE**, a crofting village spread above beaches and rocks. Sunsets here can be astonishing.

ARRIVAL AND INFORMATION
COIGACH

By bus The KSM Motors service from Ullapool to Achiltibuie (Mon–Fri 2 daily; 1hr 15min) doubles as the school bus, so services are scheduled around the start and end of the

school day.

Tourist information A useful website is ⊕ visitcoigach. com.

ACCOMMODATION AND EATING

Am Fuaran Bar Altandhu ⊕ amfuaran.co.uk. A lovely pub whatever the exterior suggests, as cosy as a cabin inside – log burner and all – and with a fine menu of steak pies, chickpea tagine, and scallops in sweet chilli. **££**

★ **Port A Bhaigh Campsite** Altandhu ⊕ portabhaigh. co.uk. Spread behind the beach with mesmerizing sea views to the Summer Isles and excellent facilities that include a laundry, this is as fine a campsite as you'll find in the Highlands. Midges can be horrendous but the *Am*

Fuaran Bar is literally over the road. Per pitch **£**

Summer Isles Hotel Achiltibuie ⊕ summerisleshotel. com. A stylish hideaway with a superb setting, fresh modern-country decor and lovely simple rooms, most in adjoining annexes. Its restaurant features seasonal modern British menus that dazzle with plates such as scallops or langoustine. The attached former crofters' pub serves up regional ales and a less glitzy bar menu during the day, plus occasional music in the evenings. **£££**

Lochinver and around

It's hard to think of a more beautiful route than the single-track road that wriggles north from Coigach towards Inverkirkaig. Unremittingly spectacular, the journey is the Highlands in miniature, threading through stunted beech woods, heaving valleys, open moorland and bare rock, past the startling shapes of Cul Beag (2523ft), Cul Mor (2785ft) and the distinctive sugar-loaf **Suilven** (2398ft) until it slaloms along the sea shore to Inverkirkaig, the start of two fantastic walks (see below). **LOCHINVER**, another two miles north, marks the return to civilization. One of the busier fishing harbours in Scotland, the small town (oversized village, really) has a pleasingly down-to-earth atmosphere. Factor in excellent budget and high-end accommodation and an established reputation for food, and it makes a natural base for the area.

Inverkirkaig Falls and Suilven

A car park at the south end of Inverkirkaig, three miles south of Lochinver, marks the start of a **walk** upriver to **Falls of Kirkaig**, itself the start of a long but gentle walk to the base of **Suilven** – its huge sandstone dome is as much of a landmark today as it was for Viking sailors. Serious hikers use the path as an approach to scale the peak (10–12hr), but you can also follow it for an easy five-mile, three-hour (return) ramble, taking in a waterfall and a secluded loch.

ARRIVAL AND INFORMATION
LOCHINVER AND AROUND

By bus Lochinver may be large by local standards, but connections are not great.

Destinations Ullapool during (termtime only; 1hr).

Tourist information A useful website is discoverassynt.

co.uk. The *An Cala Café & Bunkhouse* (see page 442) has displays on geology, wildlife and history and other information. Achins Bookshop in Lochinver sells the booklet *Assynt Walking Network* (£2).

ACTIVITIES

Cam-Mac Lochinver harbour ⊕ cam-mac-boat-trips. co.uk. Runs 2-hour cruises around Lochinver's coastline

between April and October.

ACCOMMODATION AND EATING

Some of the local accommodation is in a conjoined village, **Baddidarach**, on the north side of the loch; from

Lochinver, cross the bridge and turn left.

The Albannach Baddidarach ⓦ thealbannach.co.uk. This grand Victorian house provides a stay of exquisite taste and astonishing views over the walled garden to the sea loch and Suilven beyond. Individually decorated rooms vary from romantic to hip, with great bathrooms. ££££

An Cala Café & Bunkhouse Lochinver harbour ⓦ cadaleah.co.uk. The former seamen's mission by the harbour houses a cosy hostel and great café serving the likes of battered monkfish scampi or tandoori veggie masala. It has fourteen beds in three modern dorms – spotless if a bit tight for space in the six-bed – plus a good kitchen and laundry facilities. Dorms and doubles £

Inver Lodge Signed off Main St, Lochinver ⓦ inverlodge.

com. Refurbishment of a hillside hotel has created a (very expensive) five-star stay, featuring relaxed contemporary decor with a nod to Highlands country style and loch views. The latter are at their best from the restaurant, an outpost of *Chez Roux*, with fresh seafood plus rich French country dishes like confit duck leg. Doubles ££££

Lochinver Larder Main St, near bridge ⓦ lochinverlarder.co.uk. Sensational home-made pies, including exotics like venison and pork chorizo, have made it famous, but this fine bistro prepares other food too: think smoked fish tagliatelle, home-made fishcakes or breast of Grampian chicken in whisky cream sauce. Takeaway available. £££

North of Lochinver

There are two routes **north** from Lochinver: the fast A837 along the shore of Loch Assynt (see page 440) to join the A894, or the scenic B869 coast road. Hugging the indented shoreline, the latter offers coastal views, superb **beaches** and high cliff walks. The first village worth a detour is **ACHMELVICH**, four miles northwest of Lochinver, where a tiny bay cradles a white-sand beach lapped by azure water. It's popular (relatively speaking), but there are equally seductive beaches up the coast, including a tiny, hidden cove, **Port Alltan na Bradhan**, a mile north, plus a beautiful strand at **CLACHTOLL** a couple of miles beyond.

Old Man of Stoer

A side road that branches north off the B869 between **STOER** and **CLASHNESSIE** ends abruptly by a lighthouse at **Raffin**. The reason to come is a two-mile stroll along a boggy track to reach the **Old Man of Stoer**, a 197ft rock stack just off the Point of Stoer, the headland's tip, surrounded by sheer cliffs is occasionally scaled by climbers. It's worth a circuit around the south side of the headland to return with a vast view of the mountains of Assynt, after which you'll deserve a cuppa in the tea van at the car park (April–Sept Mon–Fri & Sun 11am–5pm, except in high winds and heavy rain).

ACCOMMODATION AND EATING   **NORTH OF LOCHINVER**

Achmelvich Beach Youth Hostel Achmelvich ⓦ hostellingscotland.org.uk. Although the open-plan lounge-kitchen of this 20-bed hostel in a former school and cottage struggles when full, most people are outside anyway – just 100yd away are the white sands of the beach. Dorms, a family room and private twins are available. Dorms £; twins ££

Clachtoll Beach Campsite Clachtoll ⓦ clachtollbeachcampsite.co.uk. This simple, neat site at the heart of the crofting village is all about its location right behind one of the most appealing stretches of powder white sand on the west coast. Per pitch £

Kylesku and around

Until a road bridge swept over the mouth of lochs Glencoul and Glendhu, **KYLESKU**, 33 miles north of Ullapool, was the embarkation point for a ferry that was the only link from the west Highlands to north Scotland. Off the main road since the bridge's construction in 1984, it's now a beautiful, soporific spot, where interlocking slopes plunge into the deep waters. Marking a last hurrah before the Assynt's sharp sandstone gives way to rounded quartzite, Kylesku is popular with walkers due to its proximity to **Quinag** (2651ft), less a single peak than several peaks reached by a **ridge walk**. The easiest ascent is from a car park on the A894 a few miles south of Kylesku. Also in

12

the area is Britain's highest waterfall, **Eas a Chùal Aluinn** (650ft), at the head of Loch Glencoul. It's five miles return east of a car park two miles south of Kylesku or a full day on a track around the north side of both lochs. Alternatively, boat tours run from the wharf.

ARRIVAL AND INFORMATION
KYLESKU AND AROUND

By bus There is no bus directly to Kylesku. A service runs from Durness to Kylestrome from where it is a 30-minute walk (45min).

Tourist information The North West Highlands Geopark visitor centre and café, *The Rock Stop* (April–Oct daily 10am–4.30pm; ⓦ nwhgeopark.com), is based in the old Unapool School Building; as well as loads of great

information, there's an exhibition on the region's geology and a super little café with stunning views from its big windows.

Tours Run by the Hotel Kylesku, Kylesku Boat Tours offers gentle cruises into lochs Glendhu and Glencoul (April, May & Sept 1 daily, June–Aug 2 daily; round trip 1hr 45min; £30; ⓦ kyleskuboattours.com).

ACCOMMODATION AND EATING

Kylesku Hotel Kylesku ⓦ kyleskuhotel.co.uk. A small hotel of crisp, modern style beside the loch with rooms in the main building and a handful more in a newer wing called 'Willy's Hoose', some of which have a private balcony and loch views. It provides by far the best food in the area,

all sourced locally – from the vegetables to the shellfish. Expect the likes of Kylesku seafood platter or Indian-style vegetable and lentil curry. Some of the smart rooms have a private balcony and loch views. **£££**

The far northwest coast

12

The **far northwest coast**, in Sutherland, is too far for some, but those who make the journey will find this captures the stark, elemental beauty of the Highlands like nowhere else. Here, as the geology shifts into ice-scoured pinkish quartzite barely covered by a thin skin of moorland, peaks become more widely spaced and settlements smaller and fewer, linked by twisting roads and shoreside footpaths. Up here, life feels exhilaratingly on the edge of civilization. The flip side is that accommodation and food are sparse; be prepared that places get booked up fast in season and the options are thin on the ground during the winter.

Scourie and around

Ten miles north of Kylesku, **SCOURIE** lies among a landscape marbled with lochs and lochans. This is prime Scottish **fly-fishing** territory; permits (£5–20) are available from the Fishing Tackle Shop in the garage (ⓦ scouriefillingstation.uk). There's also some terrific **walking** hereabouts up mountains like Ben Stack (2359ft) – locals yarn that its pyramidal peak inspired a visiting Hollywood executive to create the logo for Paramount Pictures – and a beautiful beach makes it a good choice for families.

Handa Island

Managed by the Scottish Wildlife Trust (ⓦ scottishwildlifetrust.org.uk) • No charge to visit, but donations encouraged • Ferries operate April–Sept Mon–Sat 9.30am–2pm, the last ferry back to the mainland is at 4.45pm • Charge

Reason enough to come through Scourie is **Handa Island**, the huge chunk of red Torridon sandstone just offshore. Carpeted with machair and purple heather, the island is maintained as a **wildlife reserve** by the Scottish Wildlife Trust and supports one of the largest seabird colonies in northwest Europe – razorbills and Britain's largest breeding colony of guillemots on ragged sandstone cliffs during summer, and puffins in clifftop burrows from late May to mid-July.

Ferries shuttle regularly in summer from **Tarbet**, a six-mile drive north of Scourie. When you arrive on Handa Island you will be greeted by a volunteer, who offers an introductory talk on the history and ecology of the island. Allow three hours at least to follow a **footpath** around the island – an easy and enjoyable walk taking in Great Stack, a 361ft rock pillar on the north shore, and fine views across the Minch.

ARRIVAL AND DEPARTURE
SCOURIE AND AROUND

By bus Scourie is on the Lairg to Durness service run by Durness Bus (☎01971 511223; Mon–Sat). This service has a capacity to carry bikes but must be booked in advance. Lairg connects with a train to Inverness.

Destinations Durness (Mon–Sat 1 daily; 1hr); Lochinver (Mon–Sat in school hols; 50min); Ullapool (same times; 1hr 10min)

ACCOMMODATION AND EATING

Scourie Caravan and Camping Park Scourie ⓦscouriecampsitesutherland.com. Spread behind the beach, this well-maintained site provides sea views to go with its flat pitches and tidy amenities block. On-site café-bar, The Anchorage, rustles up food and drinks and has a lounge area in case of bad weather. Per person £̄

Scourie Hotel Scourie ⓦscouriehotel.com. A traditional, family-run coaching inn whose fishing obsession only adds character. There are taxidermized trout in the wood-panelled cocktail bar, real ales in the public bar, and enormous maps of Scotland in the entrance hall.

Themed Highlands headboards are a nice touch in the simple, elegant rooms. Seasonal four-course dining menu for £35, or bar meals like fish and chips. A memorable stay. April–Sept. £̄£̄£̄£̄

★**Shorehouse** Tarbet wharf ⓦshorehousetarbet. co.uk. With its views of pristine shore, Handa and the Man of Stoer beyond, this feels like the restaurant at the end of the world. Nautical and airy inside, serving home-made soups and sandwiches, plus mains of salmon, hot mackerel and seafood platters. Couldn't be much fresher – they catch their own shellfish. £̄£̄£̄

Kinlochbervie

North of Scourie, the road sweeps through the Highlands at its starkest – rocks piled on rocks, bog and water, and a bare, stony coastline that looks increasingly inhospitable. For some that's a call to adventure: sailor and adventurer John Ridgway established an outdoor school on an isolated sea loch off **Loch Laxford** in the 1960s. The largest settlement here, reached on the B801, is **KINLOCHBERVIE**, where a huge fish market and harbour reveal this as the premier fishing port in the area, reduced in stature since its heyday in the late 1980s, but still serviced by trucks from all over Europe. Otherwise it's a scruffy, utilitarian place, usually visited only as a launchpad for Sandwood Bay (see below).

ARRIVAL AND DEPARTURE
KINLOCHBERVIE

By bus Kinlochbervie is on the Durness to Lairg service of Durness Bus (☎01971 511223; Mon–Sat 1 daily), which at Lairg connects with the train to Inverness.

Destinations Durness (40min); Scourie (30min); Ullapool (1hr 50min).

ACCOMMODATION AND EATING

Old School Restaurant and Rooms Inshegra, 1 mile before Kinlochbervie on B801 ⓦoldschoolhotel.co.uk. By far the most comfortable accommodation option in the area, with a handful of rather smart rooms including a

cute separate en-suite single. Guests are treated to good-value evening meals of home cooking: expect trio of black pudding or Cullen skink for starter and venison pie or veggie chilli for mains. £̄£̄

Sandwood Bay

A single-track road continues northwest of Kinlochbervie through **OLDSHOREMORE**, an isolated crofters' village above a stunning white-sand beach (a magic spot to wild camp), then on to **BLAIRMORE**, start of the four-mile walk to **Sandwood Bay**. The shell-white **beach** beyond the peat moors is one of the most beautiful in Scotland, flanked by rolling dunes and lashed by gales for much of the year. Vikings beached their longships here over a millennium ago – the name is a corruption of 'sand' and 'vatn', meaning sand and water. Good luck with them both if you decide to wild camp here.

It's possible to trek overland from Sandwood Bay north to Cape Wrath (see page 446), the northwestern tip of mainland Britain, a full day's walk away. If you're planning to meet the Cape Wrath minibus to Durness (see below), contact them first since it won't run if the weather turns bad.

The north coast

For years, very few visitors would travel the length of Scotland's isolated, wild north coast. Those who did get this far would most likely head for John O'Groats, take a photo, have a cuppa then head back. But these days the north coast has become a destination in its own right. The soaring popularity of the North Coast 500 route (see page 420) has brought an influx of tourers – cyclists, drivers, caravans and all – to Scotland's rugged northern shore, and few go home disappointed. This gorgeous stretch of road is backed by steep mountains in the west and by lochs and open rolling grasslands in the east, while between them is mile upon mile of crumbling cliffs, sheer rocky headlands and perfect white beaches that are nearly always deserted except for intrepid surfers who come for the best waves in Scotland. Visit between January and March and there's a chance you might witness the Northern Lights, too.

Wee **Durness** is a good jumping-off point for **Cape Wrath**, the windswept promontory at Scotland's tip which has retained an end-of-the-world mystique lost long ago by John O'Groats. Continuing east, **Tongue** enjoys an attractive setting and a Munro to climb nearby, while **Thurso**, the largest town on the north coast, is acclaimed by surfers. For everyone else it's a gateway to some of Scotland's most populous seabird colonies around **Dunnet Head** and **Duncansby Head**.

12

Durness and around

Scattered over sheltered sandy coves and grassy clifftops, **DURNESS** is the most northwesterly village on the British mainland, straddling the point where the road swings from peat bogs to the fertile limestone machair of the north coast. The village sits above Sango Sands bay, whose fine beach has made it a modest resort. Beatle **John Lennon** came here as a teenager on family holidays to stay with his Auntie Lizzie (Elizabeth Parkes) – his memories later went into the song '*In My Life*' and he revisited in 1969 with Yoko. Parkes is buried in the graveyard at Balnakeil, and there is a slightly bizarre memorial to Lennon at the Durness Village Hall which still attracts a trickle of die-hard Beatles fans throughout the year.

Smoo Cave

1 mile east of Durness • Year-round • Free • Tours daily Apr, May, Sep & Oct 11am–4pm; Jun–Aug 10am–5pm • Charge • ⓦ smoocavetours. com

A mile east of the village is **Smoo Cave**, a gaping hole in a limestone cliff created by the sea and a small burn. Tucked at the end of a narrow sea cove, the main chamber is accessible via steps from the car park. The hyped-up rock formations are quite impressive and if you wish to see more, then between April and October you can join twenty-minute tours into two further caverns led by a member of the Scottish Caving Association; note that advance bookings are not possible and if it has been raining, tours may not be run so do call in advance.

Balnakeil

A mile northwest of Durness, the white sands of **Balnakeil Bay** are stunning in any weather, but especially spectacular when sunny days turn the sea a brilliant Mediterranean turquoise. A path winds north through the dunes behind to reach

Faraid Head – fine views east to the mouth of Loch Eriboll and west to Cape Wrath make this circuit (3–4hr) the best in the area. While here, drop by the Balnakeil Craft Village, a hippie commune borne out of a disused 1970s military camp.

Cape Wrath

Closer to Iceland than London, the headland takes its name not from stormy seas but from the Norse word *hvarf* (circle), a throwback to the days when Viking warships passed en route to raid the Scottish coast. **Cape Wrath** exudes a powerful sense of nature in the raw. The British mainland's most northwesterly point – and one of only two capes in the country – is tipped by a Stevenson lighthouse and stands above **Clo Mor cliffs**, the highest sea cliffs in Britain and a prime breeding site for seabirds. On a clear day you'll gaze out to Orkney and the Outer Hebrides.

The surprise is that Cape Wrath is so easily reached on a day-trip from Durness. The journey begins two miles southwest at **Keoldale**. A foot-passenger **ferry** crosses the Kyle of Durness estuary to link with a **minibus** for the fourteen-mile run to Cape Wrath and the *Ozone* café at the lighthouse (open daily year-round; ☎01971 511314). With two to three days to spare, you could catch the ferry then walk a circuit to Sandwood Bay, catching a bus back to Durness from Kinlochbervie. There's a basic free bothy at Kearvaig. Note that the Ministry of Defence maintains Garvie Island (An Garbh-eilean) as an air bombing range and so occasionally closes the road to Cape Wrath.

ARRIVAL AND DEPARTURE

DURNESS AND AROUND

12

DURNESS

By bus Public transport is sparse; the key service is the Durness–Lairg service run by Durness Bus (☎01971 511223; Mon–Sat 1 daily) via Ullapool and Scourie, which has a cycle carrier (book ahead); at Lairg there are connections with the train to Inverness.

CAPE WRATH

By ferry and minibus The foot-passenger ferry from Keoldale runs from April to Sept (daily, first ferry at 9am, thereafter times vary and will be confirmed by the ferryman; £7.50 return; ☎07719 544207); call to confirm tides and Ministry of Defence schedules. It drops you on the opposite bank of the kyle to connect with a minibus to Cape Wrath (£13 return; ☎07742 670196).

INFORMATION AND ACTIVITIES

Tourist information Useful websites for Durness and Cape Wrath are ⓦ durness.org and ⓦ visitcapewrath.com.
Golf Durness golf course (ⓦ durnessgolfclub.org), the most northwesterly course on mainland Britain, is a nine-hole

with two tee-off options per hole to create 18 holes (£30). Closed to visitors Sun morning; equipment rental available too.

ACCOMMODATION AND EATING

DURNESS

Lazy Crofter Bunkhouse ⓦ visitdurness.com/ bunkhouse. Run by *Mackay's* next door, this is the finest bunkhouse on the north coast. It has a snug cabin atmosphere and gets extra marks for individual reading lights in two compact twins and two dorms. The terrace has sea views. Well-equipped kitchen, bike storage and drying room. Dorms £̲
★ **Mackay's** ⓦ visitdurness.com/rooms. Hand-made and vintage furniture, luxury linen, natural colours and genuine hospitality make this one of the best stays on the north coast. It also manages weekly self-catering options: from a sweet cabin to carbon-negative Croft 103's eco-

chic. No dinners, but they compensate for it with superb breakfasts, plus nibbles and wine in the evenings. £̲£̲£̲
Sango Sands Oasis ⓦ sangosands.com. This flat, spacious site spreads over cliffs above the turquoise waters of its namesake offering the most spectacular views; try and bag a cliff edge pitch if you can. The adjoining pub is now the only place in Durness serving dinner, with hearty bar standards. Out of season stay possible (and free), though with reduced facilities. Per person £̲
Smoo Lodge Durness ⓦ smoolodge.co.uk. Set beside the sea in vast grounds enclosed by dry-stone walls, this former sporting lodge dates from 1790. Refurbished to a high standard, the lodge offers a variety of stylish en-suite

rooms. Art by local artists adorn a comfortable lounge that enjoys delightful views and gives off homely warmth from the wood-burning stove. ££££

BALNAKEIL

Cocoa Mountain Balnakeil Craft Village ⓦ cocoamountain.co.uk. 'The Best Hot Chocolate', a rich bitter-sweet hot chocolate topped off by white chocolate, is the speciality in the bright modern café of this chocolatier. Sells snacks plus its chocolates and truffles. A treat after time in the wilds.

CAPE WRATH

Daill Camping Pods Daill Beach, ⓔ james. mather5038@btinternet.com. Cape Wrath's first non-bothy accommodation offering. A couple of basic camping pods (both doubles) with outdoor kennels for hardy companions. £5 extra for bedding, cooking equipment and crockery. Pod £

Tongue to Thurso

Vast and empty, the landscape between Tongue and Thurso has considerable drama. It's a bleak moorland intercut with sandy sea lochs and with few inhabitants: tiny **Tongue** is pleasant enough, as is **Bettyhill**, further east. But the real reason to venture this far is the landscape: a dead-end **coast road** west of Tongue; **Ben Hope** (3040ft), the most northerly Munro; or the blanket bog of the **Flow Country** inland.

Tongue and around

Having taken a slow circuitous route around Loch Eriboll and east over the moors of A'Mhoine, you roll finally into the pretty crofting township of **TONGUE**. Dominated from a hillside spur by the ruins of **Castle Varrich** (Caisteal Bharraich), a medieval stronghold of the Mackays (three-mile return walk), the village is strewn above the east shore of the **Kyle of Tongue**, which you can cross either via a causeway or by a longer and more scenic single-track road around its southern side. When the tide recedes, this shallow estuary becomes a mass of golden sand flats, superb on sunny days, with the sharp profiles of **Ben Hope** (3040ft) and **Ben Loyal** (2509ft) looming like twin sentinels to the south, and the Rabbit Islands a short way out to sea. A dead-end road offers views of the islands, plus superb seascapes and scenery as it threads through Talmine towards a beach at **Strathan**; take the left turn to Melness before Tongue causeway.

12

ACCOMMODATION AND EATING   **TONGUE AND AROUND**

Ben Loyal Hotel Tongue ⓦ benloyal.co.uk. Some of the tastefully decorated en-suite rooms have views over the Kyle of Tongue. Seafood fresh off the owner's boat is served in a relaxed atmosphere along with favourites such as lamb shank or home-made burgers. With decent prices and regular live music, this is the choice of many locals. ££

THE FLOW COUNTRY

A detour inland on the A897 east of Bettyhill towards Helmsdale heads south into the **Flow Country** tundra. The name (pronounced to rhyme with 'now') derives from *flói*, an Old Norse word meaning 'marshy ground', and this 1544-square-mile expanse of blanket bog – the largest in the world, says UNESCO, which has it filed under 'possible' on its World Heritage status – is both a valuable carbon sink and a home to a wide variety of birdlife. The RSPB's **Forsinard Flows Visitor Centre** (Easter–Oct daily 9am–5pm; free; ⓦ rspb.org.uk/forsinard), at the train station in **FORSINARD**, is the gateway to the so-called Forsinard Flows. Pick up a leaflet then follow the mile-long **Dubh Lochan Trail**. Follow the boardwalk to the Flows Lookout Tower before walking over flagstones to learn about its blanket bog. En route, you get to see bog asphodel, bogbean, and insect-trapping sundew and butterwort; you've also got a good chance of spotting greenshanks, golden plovers and hen harriers. During the summer, the visitor centre runs **guided walks** through the area to explain the wonders of peat; wellies or walking boots are recommended.

Kyle of Tongue Hostel & Holiday Park East of Kyle of Tongue Bridge ⓦtonguehostelandholidaypark.co.uk. The Duke of Sutherland's old shooting lodge has been repurposed as a large, well-equipped hostel with spacious dorms and family rooms, plus great mountain views. Hostelling Scotland affiliated. Dorms £; doubles ££

Tongue Hotel Tongue ⓦtonguehotel.co.uk. This nineteen-bedroom small hotel marries relaxed modern taste with the architectural heritage of a former ducal hunting lodge. There are antiques in the best rooms, even the odd marble washstand, and spacious proportions throughout. The Superior rooms are worth the extra £30. £££

Bettyhill and around

Twelve miles east of Tongue, **BETTYHILL** is a major crofting village, set among rocky green hills. In Gaelic it was known as *Am Blàran Odhar* ('Little Dun-coloured Field'). The origins of the English name are unknown but it was definitely not named after Elizabeth, Countess of Sutherland, who presided over the Strathnaver Clearances whose sorry tale is told in the Strathnaver Museum. The village is also surrounded on either side by beautiful beaches: **Farr beach**, a splendid crescent of white sand, is behind the museum, while the unbroken arc of **Torrisdale Bay** sweeps west of the town beyond the Naver River. Both receive good surf. For more cerebral stuff, the 24-mile **Strathnaver Trail** runs south along the B873 to Altnaharra, past historical sites from the Neolithic, Bronze and Iron Age periods, as well as the remains of crofting villages cleared in the early 1800s.

Strathnaver Museum

In the old Farr church, east of the main village • April–Oct Mon–Sat 10am–5pm • Charge • ⓦ strathnavermuseum.org.uk

The volunteer-run **Strathnaver Museum** houses exhibits of ethnological and archaeological interest – crofting items including a bizarre fishing buoy made from a dogskin, Pictish stones and a 3800-year-old early Bronze Age beaker – and also narrates the Sutherland Clearances through a short film. Its most famous item is free to view – the **Farr stone**, a ninth-century engraved Pictish gravestone, is in the west end of the graveyard.

12

ACCOMMODATION AND EATING   **BETTYHILL AND AROUND**

Bettyhill Hotel Main road ⓦbettyhillhotel.com. Two-hundred-year-old coaching inn sporting twenty contemporaneously furnished, individually-designed rooms plus the excellent *Eilean Neave restaurant*, which serves up Scottish dishes like Highland chicken in a whiskey cream sauce; you can also get more pub-style grub in the convivial bar which also hosts live, folksy music. ££

The Store Café Bettyhill Off the main road, north of the village ⓦstorecafe.co.uk. A great find in a village with very little options, this unassuming store front hides a lovely friendly atmosphere. A stove, around which tables, chairs and settees are arranged keeps the room cosy. Good cakes, fresh sandwiches, hot lunch options and great coffee – what more do you need? £

Thurso

THURSO feels like a metropolis after the wild west. In reality it's a modest administrative service centre, most of whose visitors only pause before catching the ferry to Orkney from its port, **Scrabster**. Yet it makes a good base for the area, and is a hive of lovely traditional shops, cafés, bars and restaurants. The town is legendary among British **surfers**, drawn to a wave which barrels off a reef just east of the harbour, and hosts surfing championships, including two World Championships for kayak surfing. One of the most powerful waves in Europe, 'Thurso East' is not a break for beginners.

The town's name derives from the Norse word *Thorsa*, literally 'River of the God Thor', and in Viking times this was a major gateway to the mainland. Later, ships set sail for the Baltic and Scandinavian ports loaded with meal, beef, hides and fish. Much of the town, however, dates from the 1790s, when Sir John Sinclair built a large new extension to the old fishing port. Consequently, Thurso's grid-plan streets have some rather handsome

Victorian architecture in local, greyish sandstone, not least the **Thurso Library**, opened in 1862 as the Miller Institute and complete with clocktower and a pillared facade. There's little sign of the town's older roots except **Old St Peter's Church** up the High Street, a substantial ruin with origins in the thirteenth century, and the small circular well house with a conical roof on Manson's Lane; built around 1823, it was once the main water supply for the town. Also, check out the Swanson Gallery on Davidson's Lane, which hosts year-round exhibitions of fine artwork, and Glass Creations on Riverside Road, where artist Ian Pearson forms and shapes his magical pieces.

ARRIVAL AND DEPARTURE   THURSO

By train Trains to Thurso leave from Inverness and go up the east coast via Lairg (Mon–Sat 3–4 daily, Sun 1 daily). Destinations Inverness (3hr 50min); Lairg (2hr 5min); Wick (30min).

By bus Buses depart from the train station, Olrig St and Sir George's St.
Destinations Inverness (4–5 daily; 3hr); John O'Groats

(Mon–Fri 6–10 daily, Sat 5 daily; 1hr); Wick (Mon–Fri 8–10 daily; 35min).

By ferry NorthLink ferries (ⓦ northlinkferries.co.uk) operate ferries to Stromness, Orkney (2–3 daily; 90 mins), from Scrabster, a mile west of town, linked by buses from the train station.

ACTIVITIES

North Coast Watersports Dunnet Campsite ⓦ northcoastwatersports.com. Offers equipment rental, including boards (£20/day), wetsuits (£20/day), and boots

and gloves (£5/day), as well as lessons in both surfing and stand-up paddleboarding.

ACCOMMODATION

12

Forss House Hotel 5 miles west of Thurso on A836 ⓦ forsshousehotel.co.uk. Built in 1810 as a hunting lodge, this fourteen-bedroom hotel offers an upmarket stay, with a choice of traditional accommodation in the main house or more modern rooms in annexes. The Forss River, which wends through the grounds, offers fine salmon fishing. **££££**
Pennyland House B&B West of Town on A9, ⓦ pennylandhouse.co.uk. One of Thurso's best B&Bs, its six rooms are named after golf courses and each has its own character, whether it be a sea view or an eighteenth-century fireplace. King-size beds, excellent breakfast and en

suites seal the deal. **££**
Sandra's Backpackers Hostel 24–26 Princes St ⓦ sandras-backpackers.co.uk. The only hostel in town is a clean enough, zero-frills but well-run place with four-bed dorms, triples and en-suite doubles. Kitchen, lounge and laundry facility Dorms **£**; doubles **££**
Thurso Bay Camping & Caravan Park Scrabster Terrace ⓦ thursobaycamping.co.uk. Large, trim site a 5min walk west from the town centre. As well as views to Dunnet Head and Orkney, it has an on-site coffee shop/diner and a laundry. Per pitch **£**

EATING

Bydand 2 Traill St ⓦ bydand.co.uk. Family-run, this tiny restaurant serves locally-sourced meat and fish dishes with great flavour and nicely presented: Cullen skink, beef cheeks. **££**
Caffe Cardosi 1 Traill Street ☎ 01847 896212. This busy and friendly corner café is in a central location, ideal to pop in for a lunchtime sandwich or delicious slice of butterscotch shortbread washed down with a cappuccino. **££**
★ **Captain's Galley** Harbour, Scrabster ⓦ captains

galley.co.uk. Fish fresh off the boat is the speciality – unfussy dishes like roast hake with borlotti broth and mussels – on three-course menus that win awards for sustainability as much as flavour. Also offers takeaway fish and chips of whatever's freshest. Reservations essential. **£££**
Y Not Bar and Grill Meadow Lane ⓦ theinnynot. co.uk. Rock 'n' roll memorabilia, sizzling steaks and stacked burgers in this split-level diner and live-music venue (gigs weekends only). **££**

Dunnet and around

Despite the publicity given to John O'Groats, the most northerly point of mainland Britain is actually **Dunnet Head**, four miles north of the sleepy village of **DUNNET**. There's not a great deal to do beyond popping into Britain's most northerly micro-distillery, the Dunnet Bay Distillers (ⓦ dunnetbaydistillers.co.uk) – who are to thank for the fantastic Rock Rose gin and Holy Grass vodka – but Dunnet Head is an evocative spot, covered in heather and bog, the plummeting red cliffs at the headland are marked by a Stevenson lighthouse, and the whole north coast spreads out before you from Cape Wrath to Duncansby Head on a clear day.

Dunnet Bay

Just south of Dunnet lies **Dunnet Bay**, a vast, golden beach backed by huge dunes. Surfers come for a smattering of reef breaks plus a beach break that offers shelter for beginners depending on whereabouts on the bay you tuck in. At the northeast end of the bay, the **Seadrift Visitor and Ranger Centre** (May–June & Sept Mon, Tues, Thurs, Fri & Sun 2–5pm; July–Aug from 10.30am; free; ☏01847 821531) holds an exhibition about the fauna of the northwest coast and ecology of its sand dunes. It also stocks information leaflets on local history and nature walks.

Mary-Ann's Cottage

South end of Dunnet • June–Sept daily 2–4.30pm • Charge • ☏ 01847 851765

Signposted off the through road in Dunnet, **Mary-Ann's Cottage** is a farming croft vacated in 1990 by the then 93-year-old Mary-Ann Calder. Her grandfather built the cottage and today it is maintained as she left it, full of mementoes of the three generations who lived and worked there over 150 years. With its antique rocking chair before a blackened hearth, still with its old metal teapot, and family photos, it's a very intimate portrait of a recent past that already feels distant.

Castle of Mey

5 miles east of Dunnet • May–Sept Wed–Sun 10.20am–4pm; closed late July–early Aug • House tours every 30min from 11am • Charge • Gardens & grounds only • Charge • ⓦ castleofmey.org.uk

The handful of houses that make up the village of Mey whizz past in a moment – yet it was here that the late Queen Mother had her Scottish home. The original **Castle of Mey** was a sixteenth-century Z-plan affair, owned by the earls of Caithness until 1889, and bought in a state of disrepair in 1952, the year the Queen Mother's husband, George VI, died. She spent her summer holidays here each August, which may help explain why it's a modest wee place, unstuffy inside despite the facade that bristles with turrets. The walls are hung with works by local amateur artists and watercolours by Prince Charles (who still visits in late July, when it's closed for two weeks), and personal mementoes of the Queen Mum remain on show – guides are more than happy to explain their significance. The **gardens** outside are a lovely spot for an amble on a sunny day, not least for their views across the Pentland Firth.

ARRIVAL AND DEPARTURE
DUNNET AND AROUND

By bus Bus No. 80 between Thurso (stops at train station and Olrig St) and John O'Groats passes through Dunnet and Mey (Mon–Fri 7 daily, Sat 5 daily).

ACCOMMODATION AND EATING

Castle Arms Hotel Mey ⓦcastlearmshotel.co.uk. A simple but comfortable stay almost opposite the castle entrance whose seven en-suite rooms – including a family suite and a room for people with disabilities – represent very good value. The restaurant prepares good pub grub such as local steak and fish and chips plus daily specials and decent vegetarian options. **£̲£̲**

Dunnet Bay Caravan Club Dunnet Bay ⓦcaravanclub. co.uk. On the plus side excellent location behind the dunes – a surfer's paradise when waves are firing – and immaculate facilities. The bad news is it's geared to motorhomes and is expensive due to a £12 surcharge for non-Caravan Club members. Per pitch **£̲**

John O'Groats and around

Snap-happy tourists, windswept pilgrims and knackered cyclists convene at **JOHN O'GROATS**, the most northeasterly settlement on mainland Britain. Consisting of a car park, a souvenir village and not much else, the place has never quite lived up to its folkloric name, although a regeneration project has brought some new life to the place with the opening of a seafront hotel and a sparkly new café. There are plenty of prettier places to see the sea in north Scotland, but as one end of the Land's End to John O'Groats tour, there's always a happy flow of people either beginning or ending a life-affirming journey here.

Duncansby Head

Marked by a lonely square-towered lighthouse and spectacular cliffs, **Duncansby Head** is the actual northeastern point of mainland Britain and offers the edge-of-the-world experience that you might have hoped for at John O'Groats, two miles west. The birdlife here is prolific – fulmars, razorbills, puffins, guillemots and kittiwakes in their thousands – and south of the headland lie spectacular 200ft high cliffs, cut by sheer-sided clefts known locally as *geos*, and several impressive sea stacks. Ask nicely at the tourist office and somebody might be able to take you on a free guided tour.

ARRIVAL AND INFORMATION   JOHN O'GROATS AND AROUND

By bus John O'Groats has regular bus services from Thurso (Mon–Fri 7 daily, Sat 5 daily; 1hr) and Wick (Mon–Fri 7 daily, Sat 5 daily; 50min).

By ferry The John O'Groats passenger ferry (ⓦjogferry. co.uk/ferry.aspx) sails to Burwick, Orkney (May–Sept 2 daily; 45min). It also offers afternoon cruises around the seabird colonies and stacks of Duncansby Head or the Atlantic grey seal colonies of Stroma (May–Aug daily 2.30pm; 1hr 30min; £20).

Tourist office Beside the main car park (Easter–Oct daily 9am–5pm; ⓦvisitjohnogroats.com).

ACCOMMODATION AND EATING

The Inn at John O'Groats ⓦtogethertravel.co.uk/ destinations/scotland/john-ogroats/accommodation. A multi-million-pound regeneration has brought a tired old seafront hotel back to life as *The Inn*, with neat self-catering apartments and a brightly coloured, Scandi-style extension to boot. All part of the same Natural Retreats development, there are also 23 high-spec wooden lodges facing out to sea. The *Storehouse Café* offers sandwiches, pizzas and the best coffee for miles, or champagne for those with something to celebrate. **£££**

12

The Black Isle and around

The **east coast** of the Highlands is nowhere near as spectacular as the west, and feels more lowland than highland. Heading north from Inverness, you're soon into the **Black Isle** – not an island at all, but a peninsula whose rolling hills, prosperous farms and deciduous woodland make it more reminiscent of Dorset or Sussex than the Highlands. It probably gained its name because of its mild climate: there's rarely frost, which leaves the fields 'black' all winter. Another explanation is that the name derives from the Gaelic word for black, *dubh* – a possible corruption of St Duthus (see page 454).

The Black Isle is littered with **prehistoric sites**, but the main incentive to detour east off the A9 is **Cromarty**, a picturesque fishermen's town that is arguably the highlight of the entire Highlands' east coast. If you're heading this way with your own transport, a string of villages along the south coast are worth a stop en route for a modest cultural fix, while **Chanonry Point** is among the best **dolphin-spotting** sites in Europe. In a lay-by just across the Kessock Bridge from Inverness, the small **Scottish Dolphin Centre** (March–Oct Thurs–Mon 10.30am–3.30pm; free; ⓦdolphincentre.whales.org) provides the chance to observe (and listen to) the creatures, and you can get out into the water with Dolphin Trips Avoch a few miles west (£20; ⓦdolphintripsavoch.co.uk).

Fortrose and Rosemarkie

FORTROSE, ten miles northeast of Inverness, is a quietly elegant village dominated by the beautiful ruins of a once huge, early thirteenth-century **cathedral** (open access) founded by King David I. It languishes on a pretty green bordered by red-sandstone and colour-washed houses. **ROSEMARKIE** a mile on is equally appealing, with its neat high street of stone houses. On sunny days local families descend on the sandy beach, where a cheap-and-cheerful café has picnic benches looking out to sea. If you're lucky, you might spot a dolphin in the bay.

Groam House Museum

High St, Rosemarkie • April–Oct Mon–Fri 11am–4.30pm, Sat & Sun 2–4.30pm; Nov–early Dec Sat 1.30–4.15pm • Free • ⓦ groamhouse. org.uk

At the lower end of Rosemarkie's high street, **Groam House Museum** displays fifteen intricately carved **Pictish standing stones** (among them the famous Rosemarkie Cross Slab) dating from as early as the eighth century. It also screens a video that highlights other sites in a region that was a stronghold of Pictish culture – a primer to tempt any history buff into a visit to Portmahomack (see page 455). There's also a harp to pluck, and kids can 'build their own' digital Rosemarkie Stone and print it out.

ARRIVAL AND DEPARTURE

FORTROSE AND ROSEMARKIE

By bus Stagecoach bus No. 26 from Inverness to Cromarty stops at both Fortrose and Rosemarkie (Mon–Sat every 30min, Sun 5 daily; 30–35min).

ACCOMMODATION

★ **Fortrose Bay Campsite** Wester Greengates ⓦ fortrosebaycampsite.co.uk. This superbly-run campsite has neat grassy pitches, somewhat unusually, positioned either side of a (not very busy) through road, and while this doesn't detract from its appeal, you'd do well to try and bag a waterfront spot. Facilities are excellent, and the hospitable owners are a font of local knowledge. Per pitch £̄

Cromarty

An appealing jumble of handsome Georgian townhouses and pretty workers' cottages knitted together by a cat's-cradle of lanes, **CROMARTY**, the Black Isle's main settlement, is simply a joy to wander around. An ancient ferry crossing on the pilgrimage trail to Tain, it became a prominent port in 1772, fuelling a period of prosperity that gave Cromarty some of the Highlands' finest Georgian houses. The railways poached that trade in the nineteenth century – a branch line to the town was begun but never completed – but the flip side of stagnation is preservation. Out of town, there's a fine four-mile circular coastal **walk**: leave town to the east on Miller Road and turn right when the lane becomes 'The Causeway'. For a simpler shoreline walk, turn left here, following the path to the water.

Cromarty Courthouse

Church St • April–mid-Oct Tues–Thurs, Sat & Sun noon–4pm • Free • ⓦ cromarty-courthouse.org.uk

The streets are gorgeous, but to help bring Cromarty's past alive try this child-friendly **museum** in the old **Courthouse**, which tells the history of the courthouse and town using audio-visuals and slightly haunting 'talking' mannequins in period costume. You are also issued with an audio handset and a map for an excellent **walking tour** around the town.

Hugh Miller's Birthplace Cottage and Museum

Church St • April–Sept daily 1–5pm; Oct Mon, Thurs & Sun 1–5pm • Charge • NTS • ⓦ nts.org.uk

Cromarty's most celebrated son is **Hugh Miller**, a nineteenth-century stonemason turned author, geologist, folklorist and Free Church campaigner. His thatched cottage **birthplace** has been restored to give an idea of what Cromarty must have been like in his day, with decor that swings between cosy rustic and rather formal Victoriana, and displays that highlight his efforts as a social reformer. The building now housing the **museum** was built by his father, though Miller only lived here for three years. On display are a handful of personal effects, including his desk, mallet and shepherd's plaid (he was a prolific walker), as well as a mourning brooch containing a lock of his hair. Friendly staff and a pretty garden add to the appeal.

ARRIVAL AND DEPARTURE   CROMARTY

By bus Stagecoach bus No. 26 runs from Inverness main   bus station (Mon–Sat every 30min, Sun 5 daily; 1hr).

ACTIVITIES

EcoVentures Off Bank St, next to Sutor Creek   the Moray Firth to see the resident bottlenose dolphins and
ⓦ ecoventures.co.uk. Between April and October sails from   other wildlife up to three times daily (2hr; £42).
the harbour in a powerful RIB out through the Sutor stacks to

ACCOMMODATION AND EATING

Royal Hotel Marine Terrace ⓦ royalhotel-cromarty.   dinners like sea trout with vegetable ratatouille. The same
co.uk. On the seafront just behind the harbour, this   ethos carries into wood-fired pizzas, best washed down
traditional inn provides fairly bland but perfectly acceptable   with Cromarty Brewery beers. **£££**
rooms which overlook the Firth. Superiors provide the most   **Sydney House** High St ⓦ sydneyhouse.co.uk. Antique
character through a mix and match of antique furnishings   wood or wrought-iron beds and pretty dressing tables are
and more modern decor. There is a good restaurant serving   typical of the furnishings picked up over the years by the
Scottish cuisine. **£££**   owners to lend character to the three en suites in their smart
★ **Sutor Creek** 21 Bank St ⓦ sutorcreek.co.uk. A lovely   redbrick house just off High St. The best rooms look out over
café-restaurant full of laidback seaside charm. It focuses on   the rear gardens. **££**
local and seasonal food, whether light lunches or excellent

Strathpeffer

Visitors first came to this leafy Victorian spa town to take the waters. In the 1970s and 1980s they arrived with coach tours to wallow in its faded glamour. Now **STRATHPEFFER** is restyling itself again as a place for activities in the surrounding hills, with a focus – ironically – on 'wellbeing' that sees it return to its origins as a renowned European **health resort**. All manner of guests disembarked from the *Strathpeffer Spa Express* train: George Bernard Shaw, Emmeline Pankhurst (who caused a scandal with a lecture on women's rights) and Franklin and Eleanor Roosevelt on honeymoon.

Renovation has transformed the town's Victorian grand pavilion into an arts centre and upgraded the adjacent **Upper Pump Room** (April–Sept Mon–Sat 10am–5pm, Sun 1–5pm; donation), where displays narrate the spa town's fascinating history and you can shop in a traditional sweet shop. The Highland Museum of Childhood (April–Oct Tues–Sat 11am–4pm, Sun noon–4pm; charge; highlandmuseumofchildhood.org. uk), located in the old railway station, features a collection of children's toys, games, costume, books, photographs and much more.

For all the appeal of the town's faded grandeur, it's the hills that will make you stay. Within striking distance is **Ben Wyvis**, an approachable Munro usually scaled without complication from **GARBAT**, six miles west of Strathpeffer, in five hours. Another excellent hike in the area is up Cnoc Mor hill, where the Iron Age hillfort of **Knock Farril** affords superb panoramic views to the Cromarty Firth and surrounding mountains.

ARRIVAL AND DEPARTURE   STRATHPEFFER

By bus Stagecoach bus No. 27 from Inverness drops
passengers in the town square (Mon–Sat 12 daily; 45min).

12

ACCOMMODATION AND EATING

Craigvar The Square ⓦ craigvar.com. As central as it gets, this B&B provides two beautifully furnished rooms and a suite, all with great outlooks and some thoughtful touches like fresh fruit and decanters of sherry. Good breakfasts set you up for a day in the hills and a relaxing atmosphere to settle into afterwards. ££

Museum Café Old Victorian Station ☎ 07759 690459. Located just down from the Museum of Childhood, this attractive café is set in a lovely old station building, where you can eat alfresco on the platform rather than in the main tearoom itself. The menu ranges from hot food and snacks to sandwiches and splendid cakes. £

Red Poppy Main St ⓦ redpoppyrestaurant.co.uk. Bright, modern bistro serving up well-manicured dishes like lamb cutlets on colcannon with minted hollandaise, and hand dived scallops on a cauliflower risotto and pea puree. Good value lunch, High Tea, and early evening (5–6pm) menus too. ££

The Dornoch Firth and around

For centuries, visitors on the pilgrim trail to the **Fearn peninsula** came from the south by ferry from Cromarty. Nowadays the area north of **Dornoch Firth** is linked by the A9, skirting past the quiet town of **Tain**, best known as the home of Glenmorangie whisky, and the neat town of **Dornoch** itself, an unexpected pleasure known for its cathedral and golf courses.

Tain

There's a sense of having arrived somewhere as you swing through the handsome buildings of central **TAIN**. Reputedly Scotland's oldest royal burgh, it was the birthplace of **St Duthus**, an eleventh-century missionary. Many a medieval pilgrim came to venerate his miracle-working relics enshrined first in a sanctuary then in fourteenth-century **St Duthus Collegiate Church**. James IV visited annually, usually fresh from the arms of his mistress, Janet Kennedy, whom he had installed in nearby Moray.

Tain Through Time

Tower St • April–Oct Mon–Fri 10am–5pm, June–Aug also Sat 10am–5pm • Charge • ⓦ tainmuseum.org.uk

Installed in three buildings of St Duthus church and graveyard, the town museum, **Tain Through Time**, is a good place to gen up on the Fearn peninsula's Pictish past and Tain's pilgrimage history, the latter taking in King James's guilty conscience. The dressing-up box is handy if you have kiddies to entertain, and the ticket price includes an audio **walking tour** of the town (set aside twenty minutes). The same ticket gets you into a neighbouring **museum** with a dry display of Tain silver, alongside clan memorabilia.

Glenmorangie Distillery

On the A9, 1 mile northwest of Tain • Tours June–Aug daily 10am–4pm; every 30min, April–May & Sept–Oct Mon–Sat 10am–3pm; hourly; pre-booking recommended; Nov–March 10am or 2pm by appointment • Charge • Shop Mon–Fri 10am–5pm, April–Oct also Sat 10am–4pm, June–Aug also Sun noon–4pm • ⓦ glenmorangie.com

Whatever the history, Tain's most popular attraction is the **Glenmorangie Distillery**. Tours of the whisky distillery and warehouses explain the alchemic process that ferments mashed malt, distils the liquid in Scotland's tallest stills then matures it in oak casks to create a delicate, vanilla-y malt. There's a dram or two to finish, naturally. Die-hard whisky aficionados should consider the more comprehensive tasting session on the Innovator Tour.

ARRIVAL AND DEPARTURE
TAIN

By train Tain is on the Inverness–Thurso Far North Line (6 daily; Inverness, 1hr 10min; 4 daily Thurso 2hr 35min).
By bus Stagecoach east coast buses from Inverness to Thurso (No. X99) stop in Tain (Mon–Sat 3 daily; Sun 2 daily; Inverness 50min; Thurso 2hr 15min).

ACCOMMODATION

Golf View House 13 Knockbreck Rd ⓦbedand
breakfasttain.co.uk. Just south of the centre, this former
manse offers a lovely B&B stay in its five rooms. Decor is
relaxed contemporary Scottish with a touch of romance and
en-suite bathrooms are excellent. Factor in fine views to the
Dornoch Firth and full Scottish breakfasts. **££**

Portmahomack and around

The fishing village of **PORTMAHOMACK**, strung out around a curving sandy beach, is
a surprise after the rolling fields of the **Fearn peninsula** east of Tain. Though all but
empty nowadays, this was a heartland of eighth-century Picts before Viking raids
became too much.

Tarbat Discovery Centre

Tarbatness Rd • April Mon–Sat 2–5pm; May Mon–Sat 10am–5pm; June–Sept Mon–Sat 10am–5pm, Sun 2–5pm; Oct daily 2–5pm •
Charge • ⓦtarbat-discovery.co.uk

Archaeological digs in the church at the edge of the village have unearthed sculpted
artefacts, including some fine gravestones decorated with Celtic animals or mythical
beasts, all well presented in the church as the **Tarbat Discovery Centre**. It marks the
first stop on a trail of other Pictish sites south on the peninsula – pick up their handy
leaflet to locate other standing stones on the peninsula, including those at Hilton and
Shandwick.

Tarbat Ness

North of Portmahomack lies **Tarbat Ness**, a gorse-covered point with one of the
tallest lighthouses in Britain at its tip. Come for sea views and a seven-mile stroll
(2–3hr round trip). The **walk** heads south from Tarbat Ness for three miles, following
a narrow passage between the cliffs and foreshore, to the hamlet of Rockfield. A
road leads past fishermen's cottages to Portmahomack to rejoin the road back to the
lighthouse.

12

ARRIVAL AND DEPARTURE　　　　　　　　　　　　**PORTMAHOMACK AND AROUND**

By bus Buses from Tain, Lamington St, go east to
Portmahomack (Mon–Fri 4 daily; 20min), and to
Shandwick, Hill and Fearn (Mon–Sat 4–5 daily).

ACCOMMODATION AND EATING

Caledonian House Main St, Portmahomack
ⓦcaledonian-house.co.uk. Located in the centre of
Portmahomack, Caledonian House has three en-suite
rooms that have enormous beds. There are great sea views
over the breakfast table where a full plate of Highland
delights are served. **££**

Oystercatcher Main St, Portmahomack ⓦthe-
oystercatcher.co.uk. This pretty place in a harbour-side
cottage prepares bistro lunches, then dinner menus
specializing in seafood, including a cheeky house Bloody
Mary – crab with spiced tomato frappé with a zing of vodka.
Reservations recommended. **££££**

Dornoch

DORNOCH, a genteel, villagey town eight miles north of Tain, lies on a headland
overlooking the **Dornoch Firth**. Blessed with good looks and a sunny climate (by
Scottish standards) and surrounded by sand dunes, it has morphed into a modest
upmarket resort: all antiques shops and fine accommodation in the historic sandstone
centre, a championship **golf course** plus miles of sandy beaches just outside.

The Cathedral

Castle St • Mid-May to mid-Sept Mon–Fri 10am–4pm; Sun services 11am • Free • ⓦdornoch-cathedral.com

Dating from the twelfth century, Dornoch became a royal burgh in 1628. Pride
of place among its oldest buildings grouped around the square is the imposing

Cathedral, founded in 1224 and built of local sandstone. The original was horribly damaged by marauding Mackays in 1570, and much of what you see today was restored by the Countess of Sutherland in 1835, though the worst of her Victorian excesses were removed in the twentieth century, when the interior stonework was returned to its original state. The stained-glass windows in the north wall were later additions. The counterpart to the cathedral is the fortified sixteenth-century **Bishop's Palace** opposite, now refurbished as a hotel (see below).

Historylinks

The Meadows • March–Oct daily 10am–4pm • Charge • ⓦ historylinks.org.uk

A block behind the Bishop's Palace on the high street, **Historylinks** is a small museum which tells the story of Dornoch, from local saints and the last witch burning in Scotland, which occurred here in 1727, to the history of the local Royal Dornoch golf course; look out for a beautiful cast iron illuminated clock that once graced the tower of the clubhouse. Around the village, the signposted Historylinks Trail takes you on a tour around Dornoch's historic sights.

ARRIVAL AND DEPARTURE
DORNOCH

By bus Stagecoach's Inverness–Scrabster service (via Thurso) stops at Dornoch.

Destinations Inverness (6 daily; 1hr 10min); Thurso (Mon–Sat 5 daily, Sun 2 daily; 1hr 45min).

INFORMATION AND ACTIVITIES

Tourist office Located in the Dornoch Hub building on Argyll Street (Mon–Fri 9am–6pm, plus Sat June–Aug and Sun July & Aug; ⓦ visitdornoch.com), this is one of few tourist offices in the region, and accordingly has loads of info.

Royal Dornoch Golf Club Golf Rd ⓦ royaldornoch. com. Opened over four hundred years ago, this golf club maintains a par 70 Championship links course (£210 single round) rated among the world's best by many golf media, and the easier par 71 Struie course (£50 single round). Booking is essential to play. Note that it has a dress code of no T-shirts (except polo shirts).

ACCOMMODATION AND EATING

2 Quail Castle St ⓦ 2quail.com. What it lacks in size this three-room B&B makes up in traditional country character and charm. Decor is beautiful, featuring tartan fabrics and paint shades of mossy green and soft mustard, old pine furnishings and oil paintings by local artists. The owner is a chef, so breakfasts are excellent; two- or three-course dinners are available on request. £££

Dornoch Castle Hotel Castle St ⓦ dornochcastlehotel. com. For a splurge, choose the fabulous historic Deluxe rooms in the turreted tower of the Bishop's Palace. Elsewhere this smart hotel is more modern – spacious Superiors with pillow chocolates and whisky miniatures or comfy but bland garden-facing rooms. The well-stocked bar is particularly good for whisky fans, while modern British cuisine like Highland venison is available in *Grant MacNicol at the Castle* restaurant. They even have a whisky micro-distillery housed in the old fire station within the grounds. ££££

Luigi's Castle St ⓦ luigidornoch.com. A modern metropolitan-styled bistro focuses on soups, ciabattas and pizzas during the day and seafood like crab cakes with sweet chilli jam in the evenings. £££

North to Wick

North of Dornoch, the A9 hugs the coast for most of the sixty miles to **Wick**, the principal settlement in the far north of the mainland. The most telling landmark in the stretch is the **Sutherland Monument** near Golspie, erected to the first duke of Sutherland, the landowner who oversaw the eviction of thousands of tenants during the Clearances. That bitter memory haunts the small towns and villages of this stretch, including **Brora**, **Dunbeath**, **Lybster** and pretty **Helmsdale**. Nonetheless, many of these settlements went on to flourish through a thriving fishing trade, none more so than Wick, which was once the busiest herring port in the whole of Europe.

Golspie and around

Ten miles north of Dornoch the A9 rolls through the red-sandstone town of
GOLSPIE. It's a pleasantly bustling if fairly forgettable place, and for most visitors
serves only as a gateway to good mountain bike trails or the grandest castle of this
coastline.

Dunrobin Castle

A9, 1 mile north of Golspie • Daily May–Sept 10am–5pm; Oct 10.30am–4.30pm; • Charge • ⓦ dunrobincastle.co.uk

Mountain-biking aside, the reason to stop in Golspie is to tour the largest house
in the Highlands, **Dunrobin Castle**, north of the centre. Modelled on a Loire
chateau by Sir Charles Barry, the architect behind London's Houses of Parliament,
it is the seat of the Sutherland family, once Europe's biggest landowners with
a staggering 1.3 million acres. They were also the driving force behind the
Clearances here – it's worth remembering that such extravagance was paid for by
evicting thousands of crofters.

Only a tenth of the 189 furnished rooms are visited on tours of the **interior**,
as opulent as you'd expect with their fine furniture, paintings (including works
by Landseer, Allan Ramsay and Sir Joshua Reynolds), tapestries and objets d'art.
Alongside, providing a venue for falconry displays (daily 11.30am & 2.30pm),
the attractive **gardens** are pleasant to wander en route to Dunrobin's **museum**,
housed in the former summerhouse and the repository of the Sutherlands' vulgar
hunting trophies – heads and horns on the walls plus displays of everything from
elephants' toes to rhinos' tails – and ethnographic holiday souvenirs from Africa.

The last extravagance is that the castle has its own **train** station (summer only) on the
Inverness–Wick line; no surprise, considering the duke built the railway.

The Sutherland Monument

Approaching Golspie, you can't miss the **monument** to the first duke of Sutherland
on the summit of **Beinn a'Bhragaidh** (Ben Bhraggie). The stiff **climb** to the
monument (round trip 1hr 30min) provides vast coast views but the steep path is
tough going and there's little view until the top. Head up Fountain Road and pass
(or park at) Rhives Farm, then pick up signs for the Beinn a'Bhragaidh footpath
(BBFP).

ARRIVAL AND DEPARTURE

GOLSPIE AND AROUND

By bus Stagecoach's Inverness–Thurso service stops at
Golspie.
Destinations Inverness (Mon–Sat 4–7 daily, Sun 2 daily;
1hr 25min); Thurso (Mon–Sat 4–6 daily, Sun 2 daily; 1hr

35min).
By train Dunrobin Castle is a summer stop on the
Inverness–Thurso line (April–Oct Mon–Sat 3 daily; 2hr
15min from Inverness, 1hr 35min from Thurso).

ACTIVITIES

Highland Wildcat Trails (ⓦ highlandwildcat.com) have
information on the area's black- red- and blue-graded
mountain biking trails, including a huge single-track

descent from the summit of Ben Bhraggie to sea level. All
trails are accessed from the end of Fountain Rd.

ACCOMMODATION AND EATING

Coffee Bothy Fountain Rd ☎ 01408 633022. A cabin-
style café popular with bikers and walkers. Fill up on all-
day breakfasts, fresh soups and ciabattas beforehand and
reward yourself with home baking afterwards. £̲
Invicta House B&B 10 Ferry Rd ⓦ invictahouse.co.uk.
Expect country charm at this welcoming B&B, which
comprises a double and a twin with en suites and a single
with shared bathroom. There's a small patchwork and

quilting shop on the premises. £̲£̲
Sleeperzzz Rogart, 8 miles west of Golspie
ⓦ sleeperzzz.com. Sleep in the quirkiest accommodation
for miles around: a first-class railway carriage parked in
a siding beside the Inverness–Thurso line; there's also a
1950s goods van (sleeping two) and a B&B (sleeping three)
occupying the old waiting room. Per person £̲; B&B £̲£̲

12

Helmsdale

HELMSDALE is one of the largest villages between Golspie and Wick. It's certainly the most picturesque: a tight little grid of streets set above a river-mouth harbour. Romantic novelist Barbara Cartland was a frequent visitor and must have looked as exotic as a flamingo in its grey stone streets. For all its charm, it's a newcomer, founded in the nineteenth century to house the evicted inhabitants of Strath Kildonan, which lies behind it, and which subsequently flourished as a herring port.

Timespan Heritage Centre

Dunrobin St • Mid-March–Oct Mon–Sun 10am–5pm; Nov–mid-March Tues noon–4pm, Sat & Sun 10am–3pm • Charge • ⓦ timespan.org.uk

Good looks and sleepy ambience aside, the appeal of Helmsdale is the **Timespan Heritage Centre** beside the river. An ambitious venture for a place this size, the modern museum tells the story of Viking raids, crofting in re-created houses, the Kildonan Gold Rush, the Clearances, and fishing through high-tech displays, a movement sensor to navigate animations of local yarns, and audio-tours. It also has an art gallery, and a café serving up soups and cakes, with lovely views out to the river.

ARRIVAL AND INFORMATION

HELMSDALE

By train On the Inverness–Thurso line (4 daily; 2hr 35min from Inverness, 1hr 10min from Thurso).
Tourist information Strath Ullie Crafts on the harbour

doubles as a source of tourist information (Mon–Sat 10am–5.30pm; ⓦ helmsdale.org).

ACCOMMODATION AND EATING

Helmsdale Hostel Stafford St, ⓦ helmsdalehostel. co.uk. Superbly renovated hostel in the old school gymnasium offering six en-suite rooms each sleeping four people (two bunks); self-catering kitchen, lounge, cycle shed and drying facilities. Dorms per person £̄; doubles £̄£̄
La Mirage Dunrobin St ⓦ lamirage.co.uk. Not quite

'The North's Premier Restaurant' as it claims, but possibly the most bizarre due to the tastes in decor of a former proprietor who styled herself after Barbara Cartland. The menu, although as dated as Babs herself, is solid: fish or seafood platters and steaks. £̄£̄

Lybster and around

Another neat planned village, **LYBSTER** (pronounced 'libe-ster') was established at the height of the nineteenth-century herring boom. Two hundred boats once worked out of its picturesque small harbour, a story told in the **Waterlines** heritage centre here (May–Oct daily 11am–5pm; charge; ☎01593 721520) – there are modern displays about the 'silver darlings' and the fishermen who pursued them, plus a smokehouse and a café.

Seven miles north of Lybster, the **Grey Cairns of Camster** are the most impressive of the prehistoric burial sites that litter this stretch of coast. Surrounded by moorland, these two enormous reconstructed burial chambers were originally built five thousand years ago with corbelled dry-stone roofs in their hidden chambers. A few miles further north on the A99, the 365 uneven **Whaligoe Steps** lead steeply down to a natural harbour surrounded by high cliffs.

Wick

Since it was founded by Vikings as *Vik* (meaning 'bay'), **WICK** has lived by the sea. It's actually two towns: Wick proper and, south across the river, **Pulteneytown**, created by the British Fisheries Society in 1806 to encourage evicted crofters to take up fishing. By the mid-nineteenth century, Wick was the busiest herring port in Europe, with a fleet of more than 1,100 boats, exporting fish to Russia, Scandinavia and the West Indian slave plantations. Robert Louis Stevenson (who wrote *Treasure Island* here) described it as 'the meanest of man's towns, and situate certainly on the baldest of God's bays'.

The demise of its fishing trade has left Wick down at heel, reduced to a mere transport hub. Yet the huge harbour in Pulteneytown and a walk around the surrounding area – scruffy rows of fishermen's cottages, derelict net-mending sheds and stores – gives an insight into the scale of the former fishing trade.

Wick Heritage Centre

Bank Row, Pulteneytown • Easter–Oct Mon–Sat 10am–5pm, last entry 3.45pm • Charge • ⓦ wickheritage.org

The volunteer-maintained **Wick Heritage Centre** is the best place to evoke the heyday of the fishing boom. Deceptively labyrinthine, it contains a fascinating array of artefacts from the old days, including fully rigged boats, boat models and reconstructed period rooms, plus a superb archive of photographs from the Johnstone Collection captured by three generations of a local family between 1863 and 1975.

Old Pulteney Distillery

Huddart St • May–Sept Mon–Fri 10am–5pm, Sat until 4pm, Oct–April Mon–Fri 10am–4pm • Tours 11am & 2pm or by arrangement • Charge • ⓦ oldpulteney.com

Until city fathers declared Wick dry in the 1920s, fishermen consumed three hundred gallons of whisky a day. The last distillery in town – and second most northerly in Scotland – distils more refined malts nowadays; most are light or medium-bodied, with a hint of sea salt. The tours give a close-up glimpse of a functioning distillery, which is less polished than some of the others in the Highlands and more charming for it. Needless to say, it ends with a dram or full tastings.

ARRIVAL AND DEPARTURE · WICK · 12

By plane Wick John O'Groats Airport (ⓦ hial.co.uk) has flights to and from Aberdeen (Mon–Fri 2 daily; 35min) with Eastern Airways.

By train The train station is immediately south and west of the central bridge. Trains from Inverness (Mon–Sat 3 daily, 4hr 20min) make a long but scenic journey via Lairg, Helmsdale, then the Flow Country inland.

By bus Local buses depart just south and west of the central bridge. They run to John O'Groats then Thurso; long-distance routes to and from Inverness involve a coordinated change at Dunbeath.

Destinations Inverness (Mon–Sat 6 daily, Sun 4 daily; 3hr); John O'Groats (Mon–Fri 7 daily, Sat 5 daily; 35min); Thurso (Mon–Sat 5 daily; 30–35min).

ACTIVITIES

Caithness Sea Coast ⓦ caithness-seacoast.co.uk. Between April and October, they offer ninety-minute coastal cruises (£36) as well as longer trips to Lybster (3hr; £60) and one-way trips in either direction (£36).

ACCOMMODATION AND EATING

Bord de l'Eau Market St ☎ 01955 604400. Riverside bistro offers a slice of France. Changing menu of Gaelic and seafood dishes, plus some French classics. The best seats are in the airy conservatory.

Mackays Union St ⓦ mackayshotel.co.uk. Oversized headboards, streamlined oak furnishings and iPod docks make this Wick's prime accommodation option. First- and second-floor rooms are our pick. The acclaimed *No.1 Bistro* serves the likes of lemon-and-garlic roast chicken with Moroccan spices, plus superb fish and chips. **£££**

Skye and the Small Isles

FAIRY POOLS, SKYE

13 Skye and the Small Isles

For many visitors the Isle of Skye (An t-Eilean Sgiathanach) is the Highlands in miniature. With its shapely summits and shifting seascapes, its superb hiking routes, wildlife and crofting villages, it crams much of the region's appeal into one manageable island. It even has classic Highlands weather. According to one theory, Skye is named after the Old Norse for 'cloud' (*skuy*), earning itself the Gaelic moniker *Eilean a' Cheò* (Island of Mist). Despite unpredictable weather, tourism has been an important part of the economy since the railway reached Kyle of Lochalsh in 1897. The Edwardian bourgeoisie swarmed to its mountains, whose beauty had been proclaimed by the Victorians ever since Sir Walter Scott visited in 1814, arguably the most successful tourism PR campaign in Scottish history. People still come in droves, yet Skye is deceptively large. You'll get the most out of it – and escape the worst crowds – if you explore the remoter parts of the island, and visit outside of the tourist season, which enters full-throttle between June and August.

The Clearances saw an estimated thirty thousand indigenous *Sgiathanachs* (pronounced 'ski-anaks') emigrate in the mid-nineteenth century; today, the population is just over nine thousand. Tourism is by far the island's biggest earner and has attracted hundreds of incomers from the rest of Britain over the last couple of decades, including an increasing quota of artists and first-time B&B owners. Nevertheless, Skye remains the most important centre for **Gaelic culture** and language outside the Western Isles. Over a third of the population is fluent in Gaelic, the Gaelic college on Sleat is the most important in Scotland, and the Free Church maintains a strong presence.

In contrast to the crowds on Skye, the so-called **Small Isles** – the improbably named Rùm, Eigg, Muck and Canna – to the south only receive a trickle of visitors. Each with a population of fewer than a hundred and with its own identity, they are easily accessible by ferry from Mallaig and Arisaig, though limited accommodation means an overnight visit requires planning.

Skye

Skye ranks among Scotland's most visited destinations, with all the summer coach tours that suggests. Yet Scotland's second-largest island also has twenty Munros to bag, and year-round hikers and climbers pay homage to the **Cuillin** Ridge, whose peaks dominate the island; you'll need experience and determination to explore them. For years, the hiking-and-heather view of Skye was all you'd get, but over the last decade a new generation of islanders, including an influx of younger settlers, has introduced a vibrant arts and crafts scene and revolutionized the food and accommodation on offer. Nowadays, Skye holds its own against anywhere in Scotland. In fact, so sophisticated is some of the relaxation on offer that the island is no longer the preserve of hikers and coach tours. The former congregate around Cuillin or the impressive rock formations of the **Trotternish** peninsula, the latter **Dunvegan** and its castle or **Portree**, the island's capital, with modest charm and amenities. And if the summer crush really gets too much, there's always the peaceful **Isle of Raasay** off the east coast.

OLD MAN OF STORR

Highlights

❶ The Cuillin Countless lochans, twelve
Munros, one challenging eight-mile ridge trail
– and the mountains are almost as impressive
seen on the road to Glenbrittle as up on the trail.
See page 467

❷ Loch Coruisk Few sights in Scotland prepare
you for the drama of this glacial loch in the
Cuillin – the boat ride there from Elgol just adds
to the fun. See page 468

❸ Trotternish Take a walk into the bizarre,
Tolkienesque landscapes of the Quiraing or
say hello to the 'Old Man'; this peninsula has
some of Skye's most distinctive scenery. See
page 472

❹ Fine dining Whether you opt for silver
service at *Kinloch Lodge*, French influenced
cuisine at Michelin-starred *Loch Bay* or cosy
seafront dining at *The Ferry Inn*, you'll be in for
a foodie treat on Skye. See pages 466, 471
and 473

❺ Isle of Raasay A glimpse of what Skye might
have been like before the tourists arrived. Hike
to the flat top of Dun Caan and survey the epic
surrounds. See page 474

❻ Isle of Eigg Sample off-grid island living
in the most compelling of the Small Isles,
with sandy beaches, an easy climb and peace
everywhere. See page 476

HIGHLIGHTS ARE MARKED ON THE MAP ON PAGE 464

13

ARRIVAL AND DEPARTURE

By car The Skye Bridge sweeps across from Kyle of Lochalsh and is toll-free. If driving, don't underestimate the size of Skye. Fuel is available 24hr at Broadford, as well as at Portree, Armadale, Dunvegan and Uig.

By ferry From Mallaig, CalMac (☎0800 0665000; ⓦcalmac.co.uk) operates regular car ferries across to

Armadale on the Sleat peninsula (Mon–Sat 9 daily in summer, 3 daily in winter, Sun 6 daily in summer, 1 daily in winter; 35min). In addition, a tiny community-run car ferry, the Glenachulish (☎01599 522313; ⓦskyeferry. co.uk) hops across to Kylerhea from Glenelg, south of Kyle of Lochalsh (daily April–mid-Oct daily 10am–6pm; June–

SKYE & THE SMALL ISLES

N

HIGHLIGHTS

1. The Cuillin
2. Loch Coruisk
3. Trotternish
4. Fine dining
5. Isle of Raasay
6. Isle of Eigg

0 — 10
miles

SKYE CRAFTS

Skye has a growing number of independent craft traders, each offering a great opportunity to pick up some unique, high-quality locally produced crafts. Some give free tours without prior arrangement, but most have limited hours in winter. Check out Ⓦ art-skye.co.uk for a wider selection, but here are a few of our favourites:

Skyeskyns Stein Ⓦ skyeskyns.co.uk. The friendly folk at Scotland's only functioning tannery offer informative, witty tours explaining the whole process of leather making. Upstairs, you can browse the final products, from surprisingly affordable woolly rugs right up to tailored gilets pushing the £1000 mark.

Skye Weavers Signposted off the B884, 1 mile east of Glendale Ⓦ skyeweavers.co.uk. Stop by Skye Weavers and you may well catch Roger or Andrea pedalling on their extraordinary bicycle-powered loom. They'll happily talk you through the weaving process, and you can browse their exquisite shawls, scarves and other items in the small shop next door.

Uig Pottery Uig pier Ⓦ uigpottery.co.uk. Hand thrown ceramics at this friendly pottery with harbour views. As well as tableware, they have a range of handmade Celtic knotwork. If you can't get to Uig, call in at *Crocks and Rocks*, their shop in Portree.

Aug until 7pm; every 20min; 5min). In bad weather CalMac and Glenachulish often cancel services, so check before you travel.

By train Mallaig is served by direct trains from Fort William (3–4 daily; 1hr 20min) and Glasgow Queen St (Mon–Sat 3 daily, Sun 2 daily; 5hr 10min). There are also trains from Inverness to Kyle of Lochalsh (Mon–Sat 3–4 daily, Sun 1–2 daily; 2hr 40min).

By bus Stagecoach operate summer-only services from Kyle of Lochalsh to Portree (No. 917; Mon–Fri 4 daily) or Armadale (Nos 50 & 51; Mon–Fri 8 daily). These services both stop at Kyleakin and Broadford. There are also Citylink connections in summer from Glasgow via Fort William to Portree and Uig.

Moving on to the Western Isles CalMac ferries leave from Uig on the Trotternish peninsula to Tarbert on Harris (2 daily Mon, Tues, Thurs & Sat; 1 daily Wed, Fri & Sun) and Lochmaddy on North Uist (2 daily Mon, Wed & Fri 1 daily Tues, Thurs, Sat & Sun). Reduced service in winter.

GETTING AROUND

By bus Bus services peter out in more remote areas and don't run on Sundays. Skye DayRider tickets for unlimited one-day travel cost £9.50 (Ⓦ stagecoachbus.com).

INFORMATION AND ACTIVITIES

Tourist information VisitScotland operates an iCentre in Portree and Ⓦ isleofskye.com is a useful resource for information about the island.

Sea Kayak Skye A one-woman company running sea-kayaking trips and qualification courses for all abilities. Skye day-trips, as well as longer jaunts to Orkney, St Kilda or the Small Isles available (Ⓦ seakayakskye.org).

The Sleat peninsula

Thanks to the CalMac ferry from Mallaig to **ARMADALE**, many people's introduction to Skye is the **Sleat** (pronounced 'Slate') **peninsula** at the southern tip of the island. The irony is that it's unlike almost anywhere else hereabouts – an uncharacteristically fertile area branded 'The Garden of Skye'. The main attraction is the **Armadale Castle** estate which, along with the Torabhaig Distillery just up the road, makes for an entertaining few hours.

Armadale Castle

On A851, 0.5 mile north of Armadale • Gardens April–Oct Wed–Sun 9.30am 5.30pm; with exceptions; last entry 30min before closing • Charge • Ⓦ armadalecastle.com

Armadale Castle, a mile north of the ferry terminal, is the shell of the neo-Gothic seat of the MacDonald clan – the laird moved into the gardeners' cottage when the kelp fertilizer market collapsed in the 1920s. Intended as an account of the clan, its modern **Museum of the Isles** is actually more interesting for its

13

perspectives on Highland history, with sections on the Jacobite period and its aftermath, featuring Bonnie Prince Charlie keepsakes such as the shoe buckles he wore at the Battle of Culloden, his snuff mull, and a set of three firing glasses he once owned. Elsewhere, there are a couple of cannonballs fired at the castle by HMS *Dartmouth*, sent by William III. Just as appealing is the castle's forty-acre wooded **garden**, where you can try your hand at archery and clay-pigeon shooting. At the time of writing, the museum and café were closed for ongoing works.

Torabhaig Distillery

On A851, four miles north of Armadale Castle • Mon–Fri 10am–5pm, Sat & Sun 10am–4pm • Tours • Charge • ⓦ torabhaig.com

Converted from a 200-year old farmstead, **Torabhaig distillery** became only the second ever licensed distillery on Skye upon its opening in 2017, hence its first single malt – a medium-peated version – only came into production in 2020. An old Viking name meaning 'Bay of God', Torabhaig was the brainchild of Sir Iain Noble, founder of Noble Grossart (Scotland's first modern merchant bank) and prominent Gaelic language activist, but following his death in 2010 it was left to his wife Lucilla to press ahead with plans for its completion. Given the early stages of the distillery's development, there's relatively little to see here on a standard tour, though that doesn't make it any less enjoyable; what you will get to see are the eight Douglas fir washbacks and the two magnificent copper stills, named after Sir Iain and his wife – and of course you get to try a dram at the end. Should you wish to hang around, the café here is very good.

Isleornsay

Having retired as Skye's main fishing port, **ISLEORNSAY** (Eilean Iarmain), six miles north of Armadale, is a pretty, secluded village. Come for the views: out across the bay to a necklace of seaweed-encrusted rocks and the tidal **Isle of Ornsay**, and behind it all a dramatic panorama of peaks on the mainland.

ARRIVAL AND GETTING AROUND   SLEAT PENINSULA

By ferry Reservations are recommended in peak season (ⓦ calmac.co.uk) for the Mallaig–Armadale crossing (Mon–Sat 9–11 daily, Sun 6–8 daily; 35min).
By bus All bus services from/to Armadale are via Broadford.

Destinations Broadford (Mon–Fri 5 daily, Sat 2 daily; 30min); Portree (Mon–Fri 2 daily; 1hr 20min); Sligachan (Mon–Fri 2 daily; 1hr).

ACCOMMODATION AND EATING

Bar Am Praban Near Isleornsay. This homey bar rendered almost entirely in wood enjoys a good location on the Sleat peninsula coast. There's a good selection of whiskies and locally-brewed Skye beers. Make the most of good weather with a drink in the beer garden overlooking the water. *Bar Am Praban* also does excellent, rich food, including steaks, lobster, fish and chips, and a good cheese board. **££**

The Inn @ Àird a' Bhàsair Ardvasar, 0.5 miles south of Armadale ⓦ the-inn-at-aird-a-bhasair.co.uk. This pretty little inn – one of the oldest on Skye – has benefited from refurbishment to create comfortable, contemporary accommodation as well as the smart Linne restaurant, which specializes in local seafood – scallops and crab, plus Speyside beef. **££££**

★ **Eilean Iarmain** Isleornsay ⓦ eileaniarmain.co.uk. This small hotel in a whitewashed hamlet is a charmer,

romantically furnished in cosy country style: antiques, pretty fabrics, awesome views and not a TV in sight. The restaurant serves fine-dining dishes such as venison with garlic and white truffle mash (two courses £25), or there's informal eating in the delightful bar. Regular folk music nights often run into the wee hours. **££££**

★ **Kinloch Lodge** 1 mile north of Isleornsay ⓦ kinloch-lodge.co.uk. The island's smartest hotel remains the home of Lord and Lady Macdonald of Macdonald, and as such is furnished with antiques and clan mementos. As famous is the food of Marcello Tully; molecular tasting menu or succinct lunch menus showcase super-fresh island ingredients. Expect silver service, and up-to-the-nines clientele. There's also an on-site spa offering massages. Dinner, bed and breakfast **££££**

Kyleakin

The **Skye Bridge** that rendered the ferry crossing redundant in 1995 has been a mixed blessing for the old port of **KYLEAKIN** (pronounced 'kyle-*a*kin', with the stress on the second syllable). On the one hand, it's now bypassed; on the other, that leaves its neat centre that bit quieter, even in high season. Bizarrely, it's also evolved into something of a backpackers' hangout.

The bridge has been less kind to **Eilean Bàn**, an island from which the bridge leapfrogs to cross Loch Alsh. From 1968 to 1969, its lighthouse keeper's cottage was briefly the home of Gavin Maxwell, author of *Ring of Bright Water*. The island now serves as a nature reserve and can be visited on tours booked through the Bright Water Visitor Centre (see below) in Kyleakin.

ARRIVAL AND INFORMATION

KYLEAKIN

By bus There are buses from and to Kyle of Lochalsh (Mon–Fri 4 daily; 5min) and Portree via Broadford (2 daily; 55min).

Tourist information Available in the Bright Water Visitor Centre, The Pier (Easter–Sept, regular hours 10am–4pm; phone to confirm times; ☎01599 530040; ⓦeileanban.org).

ACCOMMODATION AND EATING

Skye Backpackers Kyleakin ⓦskyebackpackers.com. The quirkier and better-equipped of Kyleakin's two hostels. Dorms, doubles, and a couple of stationary hippie caravans out the back offer a basic night's sleep. The Groove Lounge has a log burner and board games. Doubles **££**; dorms **£**; caravan dorm **£**

Broadford

Skye's second-largest village, **BROADFORD** (An t-Àth Leathann), strung out along the main road, has a traffic problem and a charm bypass. It is indeed handy for its full quota of facilities – not least a large supermarket and 24-hour fuel – but you won't want to hang around here for too long. Fill the tank, load up the boot with supplies and go explore the island.

ARRIVAL AND DEPARTURE

BROADFORD

By bus Broadford is served by local buses from and to Kyle of Lochalsh (2 daily; 25min), Kyleakin (Mon–Fri 5 daily, Sat & Sun 2 daily; 15min) and Portree (Mon–Fri 5 daily; Sat & Sun 2 daily; 40min).

ACCOMMODATION AND EATING

Café Sia On the A87, Broadford ⓦcafesia.co.uk. The best pizzas on Skye, wood-fired to perfection, and probably one of the best coffees too. Also serves breakfast, and the outdoor deck has views out to the Red Cuillin.

★ **Tigh an Dochais** 13 Harrapool ⓦskyebedbreakfast. co.uk. Jaw-dropping views down Broadford Bay through walls of glass are the draw at this striking B&B, although streamlined contemporary style and a calm, grown-up vibe are just as good reasons to check in. **£££**

The Cuillin and Red Hills

They have razor-edge ridges, the slopes plummet in scree fields and the lonely lochs are imbued with an almost tangible magic. Small wonder that, for many people, the spectacular **Cuillin** range is the sole reason to visit Skye. When the clouds disperse, these spectacular peaks dominate the island. There are three **approaches**: from the south, by foot or by boat from Elgol; from *Sligachan Hotel* to the north; or from Glenbrittle to the west of the mountains. Glen Sligachan is one of the most popular routes as it divides the granite of the round-topped **Red Hills** (aka the Red Cuillin) to the east from the Cuillin themselves (aka the **Black Cuillin;** on account of the colour of their coarse-grained jagged gabbro. With twenty Munros between them, these are mountains to take seriously. There are around five fatalities a year here and many routes are for experienced climbers only. If you're unsure, hire a guide.

13

Elgol, Loch Coruisk and Glen Sligachan

The road to **ELGOL** (Ealaghol) at the tip of the Strathaird peninsula is one of the most impressive on Skye, swooping into the heart of the Red Hills to culminate in beautiful views of the Small Isles above Elgol pier.

The chief reason for visiting Elgol is to take a boat, whether a wildlife cruise or a trip across Loch Scavaig to visit **Loch Coruisk**. This isolated, glacial loch lies beneath the highest peaks of the Cuillin and is a superb trip, about an hour by boat and then up to a half-day ashore. **Walkers** use the boat simply to begin hikes in the Red Hills or over the pass into **Glen Sligachan**. Alternatively, you can walk round the coast to the bay of **Camasunary**, over two miles to the east – a difficult walk that involves a tricky river crossing and negotiating 'The Bad Step', an overhanging rock with a 30ft drop to the sea – and head north to Glen Sligachan. Conversely, a time-honoured approach into Glen Sligachan is from the north via the *Sligachan Hotel* (see page 469), a popular hikers' base.

Glenbrittle

Yet another route into the peaks is from **Glenbrittle** on the west side. The valley edges the most spectacular peaks of the **Cuillin**, a semicircle of mountains which ring Loch Coruisk, before it runs to a beach at Loch Brittle. One of the least demanding walks is a five-mile round trip (3hr) from Glenbrittle campsite (see page 469) up Coire Làgan to a lochan squeezed among stern rock faces. An equally good reason to come is the **Fairy Pools**, one of Britain's most celebrated wild swimming destinations. The scenery

---

WALKING IN THE CUILLIN

Ordnance Survey Explorer map 411

For many walkers and climbers, there's nowhere in Britain to beat **the Cuillin**. The main ridge is just eight miles long, but with its immediate neighbours it is made up of over thirty peaks, twelve of them Munros. Those intent on doing a complete traverse of the Cuillin ridge usually start at **Gars-bheinn**, at the southeastern tip, and finish off at **Sgùrr nan Gillean** (3167ft), descending on the famous *Sligachan Hotel* for a well-earned pint. The entire journey takes a minimum of sixteen hours, which either means a very long day or two days and a bivouac. A period of settled weather is pretty much essential, and only experienced walkers and climbers should attempt it. Take note of all the usual safety precautions and be aware that **compasses** are unreliable in the Cuillin, due to the magnetic nature of the rocks.

If you're based in Glenbrittle, one of the more straightforward walks is the five-mile round trip from the campsite up **Coire Làgan**, to a crystal-cold lochan squeezed in among the sternest of rockfaces. If you simply want to bag one or two of the peaks, several corries provide relatively straightforward approaches to the central Munros. From the *Glenbrittle Youth* Hostel, a path heads west along the southern bank of the stream that tumbles down from the **Coire a' Ghreadaidh**. From the corrie, you can climb up to An Dorus, the obvious gap in the ridge, then ascend **Sgùrr a' Mhadaidh** (3012ft) or **Sgùrr a' Ghreadaidh** (3192ft) to the south. Alternatively, before Coire a'Ghreadaidh, you can head south to the Coir' an Eich, from which you can easily climb **Sgùrr na Banachdaich** (3166ft) via its western ridge. To the south of the youth hostel, the road crosses another stream, with another path along its southern banks. This path heads west past the impressive **Eas Mòr** (Great Waterfall), before heading up to the **Coire na Banachdaich**. The pass above the corrie is the main one over to Loch Coruisk, but also gives access to Sgùrr Dearg, best known for its great view of the **Inaccessible Pinnacle** or 'In-Pin' (3235ft) – it doesn't actually live up to the name, but Scotland's most difficult Munro requires good rock-climbing skills. Back at Eas Mòr, paths head off for Coire Làgan, by far the most popular corrie thanks to its steep sides and tiny lochan. If you're unsure about any hike or want help, hire a guide: try Skye Guides (🌐 skyeguides.co.uk).

is superb as the river tumbles beneath peaks – the downside is water temperature of 8–10°C at best, and its popularity is such that in summer months tailbacks of cars have been known to extend for miles along the single-track road. The pools are signposted from Glumagan Na Sithichean car park, five miles from the Glenbrittle turn.

ARRIVAL AND ACTIVITIES

THE CUILLIN AND RED HILLS

By bus Elgol is accessed most easily from Broadford (Mon–Fri 4 daily; 40min). Sligachan is a stop on the Portree–Broadford route (Mon–Sat 6–7 daily; Broadford 30min, Portree 15min).

Boat trips Two operators offer superb trips from Elgol to Loch Coruisk (Easter–Oct): the *Misty Isle* (Mon–Sat;

£20 single, £28 return; ⓦ mistyisleboattrips.co.uk) and the *Bella Jane* (daily; £18 single, £32 return; ⓦ bellajane. co.uk). Standard return trips take 3hr: 45min each way, 1hr 30min ashore. The owner of *Bella Jane* also runs wildlife-watching and walking trips to the Small Isles in a fast RIB as Aquaxplore (Easter–Oct daily; from £20).

ACCOMMODATION AND EATING

★ **Coruisk House** Elgol ⓦ coruiskhouse.com. A taste of Skye with simple super-fresh menus – fillet of cod with Orbost Iron Age pork belly, or roast loin of venison with port and juniper sauce – with a set four courses for £65. Above are two beautiful cottage rooms of understated luxury, plus they have an upper and lower suite; no children under 14. Expect dinner, a relaxing night and an awesome breakfast. Reservations essential. **££££**

Glenbrittle Campsite End of road, Glenbrittle ⓦ dunvegancastle.com/glenbrittle/campsite. With sea views and the beach in front, and mountains behind, this spacious, remote site is the best of both worlds. The bad news is midges. Thousands of them, though they vanish with a breeze. The on-site shop and café sells camping essentials and proper coffee. Closed mid-Oct to March. Per person **£**

Glenbrittle Youth Hostel Glenbrittle ☎ 01478 640278, ⓦ hostellingscotland.org.uk. Mountain chalet vibe in this modern hostel popular with climbers and whose excellent

facilities include laundry, drying room, bike storage and an open lounge arrangement. Its old wood panelling and leather sofas combine into a sort of rugged Scandi chic. Offers frozen prepared meals. Closed Oct–March. Dorms **£**; twin **££**

Sligachan Bunkhouse On A87 ⓦ sligachanselfcatering. com. There are peaks just beyond the back door from this modern, clean, no-frills bunkhouse adjacent to the *Sligachan Hotel*. Within are four dorms sleeping four or six plus a laundry, a spacious kitchen and a small lounge with a fireplace. Closed Nov–Feb. Dorms **£**

Sligachan Hotel and Campsite On A87 ⓦ sligachan. co.uk. This long-standing launchpad for hikers is almost embraced beneath Cuillin's peaks. Alongside comfy freshly decorated en-suite rooms, it maintains the barn-like *Seumas' Bar* which serves dishes like venison stew or rib of beef with haggis, and is stocked with over 400 whiskies and serves beer from the on-site Cuillin Brewery. **£££**.

Minginish

If the Cuillin has disappeared into the mist for the day and you have your own transport, you can while away a happy afternoon exploring the nearby **Minginish** peninsula, north of Glen Brittle.

Talisker whisky distillery

By Loch Harport, Carbost • Daily March–Oct 10am–5pm; Nov–Feb 10am–4pm • **Tours**; adults only • Charge • ⓦ malts.com

One ideal wet-weather activity is a guided tour of the **Talisker whisky distillery**, which produces a sweet full-bodied single malt with a whiff of smoke and peat. Skye's oldest distillery is situated on the shores of Loch Harport at **CARBOST**, not at the village of Talisker itself, which lies on the west coast of Minginish. Proper whisky fanatics will splash out for the excellent Talisker Tasting Tour.

ACCOMMODATION AND EATING

MINGINISH

Old Inn and Waterfront Bunkhouse Carbost ⓦ theoldinnskye.co.uk. A chalet-style building and lochside location lend this bunkhouse a cheerful holiday atmosphere. It has five well-appointed B&B rooms and a family chalet. It's managed by the historic *Old Inn* next door,

which provides good bar meals – fresh local seafood plus cheaper staples like haggis, neeps and tatties in a whisky cream sauce. Dorms **£**, doubles **££**

★ **The Oyster Shed** Carbost ⓦ facebook.com/ oystershedskye. This artisanal farm shop serves the

13

freshest, best-value seafood you'll find anywhere on Skye. They now even smoke their own salmon, oysters and shellfish. Lobster tail in garlic butter and chips or hot smoked trout and chips. Take away or eat on the picnic benches overlooking Loch Harport. **££**

Dunvegan

DUNVEGAN (Dùn Bheagain) is something of a letdown after the route there, skirting the bony sea cliffs and stacks of the west coast. Yet it has one of Skye's most famous traditional sights, plus two of the island's more interesting peninsulas, Duirinish and Waternish, in its backyard.

Dunvegan Castle

1 mile north of Dunvegan • April–mid-Oct daily 10am–5.30pm; last entry 30min before closing • Charge • ⓦ dunvegancastle.com

Just north of the village, **Dunvegan Castle** sprawls over a rocky outcrop, sandwiched between the sea and several acres of attractive **gardens**. It's been the seat of the Clan MacLeod since the thirteenth century – and the chief still lives here with his family today – but the present facade is a product of Victorian romanticism. Older architecture remains inside, where you get the usual furniture and oil paintings alongside some more noteworthy items, with tour guides on-hand to bring the history to life. The most intriguing display is the remnants of the **Fairy Flag**, carried back to Skye, they say, by the Gaelic boatmen of King Harald Hardrada after the Battle of Stamford Bridge in 1066. MacLeod tradition states that the flag was the gift of a fairy to protect the clan – as late as World War II, MacLeod pilots carried pictures of it for luck. Seal-spotting boat trips are available from the grounds during the summer.

ARRIVAL AND DEPARTURE
DUNVEGAN

By bus Dunvegan is served by buses that loop around northern Skye from Portree (Mon–Fri 4–6 daily, Sat 3 daily; 45min); half of them stop at the castle.

ACCOMMODATION AND EATING

Jann's Cakes Dunvegan ☎01470 521730. This tiny place on the high street is a Skye legend for its high-quality cakes and home-made chocolates, and also prepares fresh sandwiches and soups, plus hot organic meals like tagine and curries. **£**

Kinloch Campsite Loch Dunvegan ⓦ kinloch-campsite. co.uk. The campsite spreads across the head of Loch Dunvegan just as its name (literally 'loch head') suggests, although motorhomes and caravans claim the prime waterfront – campers pitch at the sides and on a low hill. Per person **£**

The Old School Dunvegan ⓦ oldschoolrestaurant.

co.uk. Offers traditional Scottish dishes such as venison haunch with whisky and honey sauce or hake with langoustine bisque. Raw stone walls add character to a lofty and rather smart dining room. Live traditional music every other Saturday. **£££**

Roskhill House Roskhill, 3 miles south of Dunvegan ⓦ roskhillhouse.co.uk. Stone walls, crafts and home-made cakes bring charm to this old croft house, whose modern oak furnishings and bed throws over crisp white linen lend understated style to your stay. Great breakfasts too. **££**

The Duirinish peninsula

Much of the **Duirinish peninsula**, west of Dunvegan, is inaccessible to all except walkers prepared to scale or skirt the area's twin flat-topped basalt peaks: Healabhal Bheag (1600ft) and Healabhal Mhor (1538ft). The mountains are better known as **MacLeod's Tables** – the story goes that the MacLeod chief held a royal feast on the lower of the two for James V.

Colbost Croft Museum

Colbost village • Closed at time of writing due to storm damage • Charge • ⓦ dunveganmuseums.co.uk

Local history plus information about nineteenth-century crofting is told through news cuttings in this restored black house, four miles up the road from Dunvegan. A guide is usually on hand to answer questions, and the peat fire is often lit.

ARRIVAL AND INFORMATION

By bus Buses go to Colbost from Portree via Dunvegan (Mon–Fri 4 daily; 1hr 10min; termtime only).

Tourist information A useful website on the area is ⓦ glendaleskye.com.

ACCOMMODATION AND EATING

Carter's Rest 8/9 Upper Milovaig, 4 miles west of Colbost ⓦ cartersrestskye.co.uk. Little touches like a digital radio impress almost as much as furnishings such as super king beds in this luxury four-star B&B with astonishing coast views. Two-night minimum stay. £££

★ **Chidakasha Skye** Holmisdale, 3 miles west of Colbost ⓦ chidakashaskye.co.uk. An incarnation of the old Red Roof Gallery, this cosy veggie/vegan café has a loyal fan base for its superb lunches of soups and salads, plus home-baking with a huge range of teas and infusions.

Occasionally holds intimate live music nights.

★ **Three Chimneys** Colbost ⓦ threechimneys.co.uk. An intimate, gourmet restaurant at the vanguard of Skye's foodie revolution. Seven courses of Skye menus (£98) offer exquisite seafood plus unfussy mains like blackface lamb with rosemary maize. Shorter, cheaper menus also available, as well as a vegetarian option. Reservations essential. Six sumptuous guest rooms are available across the courtyard. Doubles ££££

Waternish

Waternish is a backwater by Skye's standards. Though not as spectacular as Duirinish or Trotternish, it provides equally good views over to the Western Isles, and, with fewer visitors, feels appealingly remote. To reach the peninsula, you cross the **Fairy Bridge** (Beul-Ath nan Tri Allt or 'Ford of the Three Burns'), at the junction of B886. Legend has it that the fourth MacLeod clan chief was forced to say farewell to his fairy wife here when she had to return to her kind – her parting gift was the Fairy Flag (see page 470). At the end of the road that continues north from Stein is the medieval shell of **Trumpan Church**.

Stein

STEIN, looking out over Loch Bay to the Western Isles, is Waternish's prettiest village, a row of whitewashed cottages built in 1787 by the British Fisheries Society. The place never really took off and was more or less abandoned within a couple of generations. Today, it's a little livelier, thanks to a world-class restaurant and historic pub – there are few nicer places on Skye for a pint on a sunny summer evening.

ACCOMMODATION AND EATING

★ **Loch Bay Seafood Restaurant** Stein ⓦ lochbay-restaurant.co.uk. With Michelin-starred chef Michael Smith at the helm, this tiny, romantic restaurant continues to set the standard for this part of Scotland; one menu only with the focus mainly on fresh seafood (turbot and oyster with velvet crab sauce), but there's much more besides, for example Highland wood pigeon with neep remoulade and

wild garlic. Reservations advised. ££££

Stein Inn Stein ⓦ thesteininn.co.uk. This eighteenth-century waterfront inn – the oldest on Skye – is as traditional as you would hope. Come for local ales, an impressive array of malts and uncomplicated dishes like beer-battered Mallaig haddock and chips. Above are five cheerful en-suite rooms with sea views. £££

Portree

With a population of around 2500, **PORTREE** is something of a metropolis by Skye's standards. That said, the town still has a small-village feel and is one of the most attractive ports in northwest Scotland, its deep, cliff-edged harbour filled with fishing boats and circled by multicoloured houses. Originally known as Kiltaraglen, it takes its current name – some say – from Port Rìgh (Port of the

13

King), after the state visit James V made in 1540 to assert his authority over the chieftains of Skye.

The focus of activity for many visitors is the **harbour**, with an attractive wharf that dates from the early nineteenth century and a fishing fleet that still lands a modest catch. Looming behind is **The Lump**, a steep and stumpy peninsula on which public hangings once attracted crowds of up to five thousand. The tidy town centre spreads around **Somerled Square**, built in the late eighteenth century as the island's administrative and commercial centre. Rather sadly, it now serves as Portree's bus station and car park.

ARRIVAL AND INFORMATION

PORTREE

By bus Portree is the hub of all transport on the island and has mainland connections from Glasgow with Citylink. Destinations Broadford via Sligachan (2–6 daily; 50min); Dunvegan (Mon–Sat 3–6 daily; 45min); Glasgow (3–4 daily; 6hr 15min); Glenbrittle (Mon–Sat 2 daily; 50min); Trotternish circuit via Old Man of Storr, Staffin and Uig (Mon–Sat 6 daily; 2hr total circuit).

Tourist office Just off Bridge St is the Portree iCentre (July & Aug Mon–Sat 9am–6pm, Sun 9am–5pm; April, May, Sep & Oct Mon–Sat 9am–5pm, Sun 10am–4pm; Nov–March Mon–Sat 9.30am–4.30pm; ⓦ visitscotland.com), this is now the island's sole tourist office, hence has loads of information and can book accommodation.

ACCOMMODATION

Cuillin Hills Hotel Turn left at end of Bosville Terrace ⓦ cuillinhills-hotel-skye.co.uk. Lord MacDonald's old hunting lodge, secluded in fifteen acres, is the smartest formal hotel in Portree, and with views over the Sound of Raasay makes a luxurious country stay with town facilities to hand. Accommodation is spacious and comfortable, refurbished into a sort of Highlands chic. **££££**

Portree Youth Hostel Centre of town, on Bridge Rd ⓦ hostellingscotland.org.uk. This sparkling hostel is one of the best equipped on the island, with some 55 beds

across bunk dorms and private doubles with en suites; lounge, kitchen and laundry facilities too. Dorms **££**, doubles **££**

★ **Viewfield House** Signposted off A87 ⓦ viewfieldhouse.com. The last word in Scots Baronial–style is this pile on the southern edge of town. It's almost eccentric in its Victorian grandeur, all fabulous floral wallpaper, hunting trophies, stuffed polecats and antiques. Rooms are individually furnished; some tranquil, some gloriously over the top. **££££**

EATING AND DRINKING

Café Arriba Quay Brae ⓦ cafearriba.co.uk. This local institution packs in the punters, who come for a gossip over coffee or tea served in large china pots as much as the globe-trotting lunch menu of home-made soups, wraps, pastas or creative fast food like wild-boar hot dogs. Good veggie options available. **£**

Dulse and Brose Bosville Hotel ⓦ perlehotels.com. The name translates as 'seaweed and oatmeal' and the menu is as varied as this suggests; everything from home-smoked chicken to Moroccan fishcakes, all served in sophisticated,

chic surroundings. The neighbouring *Merchant Bar* is the best boozer in town, serving Skye beers and a wealth of whiskies in an understated, cool space. **£££**

★ **Scorrybreac** Bosville Terrace ⓦ scorrybreac.com. Just eight tables in what could be somebody's living room; this is in fact one of Skye's best restaurants. Chef Calum Munro serves the likes of coffee-seared venison or smoked haddock with curried egg in charmingly intimate quarters. No surprise it got a nod from Michelin just months after opening. Tasting menus £45 & £85.

Trotternish

Protruding twenty miles north of Portree, the **Trotternish peninsula** has some of the island's most bizarre scenery, particularly on the east coast, where volcanic basalt has pressed down on softer sandstone and limestone, causing massive landslides. These, in turn, have created sheer cliffs, peppered with outcrops of hard, wizened basalt – pinnacles and pillars that are at their most eccentric in the **Quiraing**, above Staffin Bay, a long arc of beach just north of Staffin village.

Old Man of Storr

6 miles north of Portree along the A855

The most celebrated column of rock on Skye, the **Old Man of Storr** is all that is left after one massive landslip. Huge blocks of stone still occasionally break off the cliff of the Storr (2358ft) above. A half-hour trek from the car park ascends to the pillar, but don't expect to have it to yourself – this is one of the island's signature sights, and will be busy whatever the weather.

Quiraing

Just past Staffin Bay, a single-track road cuts east across the peninsula into the **Quiraing**, a spectacular area of rock pinnacles, sheer cliffs and strange rock formations produced by rock slips. From the busy main car park on the saddle, it's a long but gentle traverse to the rocks. Once you're among them, you can make out 'The Prison' to your right, and the 131ft 'Needle' to your left. 'The Table', a sunken platform where locals used to play shinty, lies a further fifteen-minute scramble up the rocks.

Skye Museum of Island Life

On the A855, 2 miles southwest of Duntulm • Easter–Sept Mon–Sat 9.30am–5pm; last entry 30min before closing • Charge • ⓦ skyemuseum.co.uk

It's a short trip from Duntulm to the best of the island's folk museums. Run by a local family, the **Skye Museum of Island Life** – an impressive collection of eight thatched black houses decorated with home furnishings and farming tools – provides an insight into a way of life commonplace only a century ago. Behind the museum are the graves of **Flora MacDonald**, heroine during Bonnie Prince Charlie's flight, and her husband. Such was her fame that the original mausoleum fell victim to souvenir hunters and had to be replaced. The Celtic cross headstone is inscribed with a tribute by Dr Johnson, who visited her in 1773: 'A name that will be mentioned in history, and, if courage and fidelity be virtues, mentioned with honour'.

Uig

Skye's chief ferry port for the Western Isles is **UIG** (Uige; pronounced 'oo-ig'), which curves its way round a dramatic, horseshoe bay. In the past, most people would just pass through here, but with a clutch of excellent places to stay and eat now, as well as the chance to pop into the Skye Brewery or Uig Pottery by the pier – this is becoming a destination in its own right. Don't miss the lovely, gentle **walk** up Glen Uig, better known as the **Faerie Glen**, a hobbity landscape of miniature hills at the east end of the bay.

ARRIVAL AND GETTING AROUND   TROTTERNISH

By ferry CalMac (ⓦ calmac.co.uk) operates from Uig. Destinations Tarbert on the Isle of Harris (1–2 daily; 1hr 40min); Lochmaddy on North Uist (1–2 daily; 1hr 45min).

By bus A circular bus route (service Nos 57A and 57C) loops around the peninsula from Portree via the Old Man of Storr, Staffin and Uig (Mon–Sat 6 daily; 2hr total circuit).

ACCOMMODATION AND EATING

★ **Cowshed Bunkhouse** Just south of Uig, off the A87 ⓦ skyecowshed.co.uk. Skye's first 'boutique bunkhouse', with underfloor heating and all, is far closer to chic hotel than banged-up bothy. The relaxed, open-plan living and dining area is kitted out with a log-burner and Space Invaders gaming table, and offers panoramic views of Uig harbour. Sophisticated dorms and luxury pods for up to three adults. Dorm **£**, pod **££**

★ **The Ferry Inn** On the A87, Uig ⓦ theferryinnskye. com. This luxury inn has three en-suite doubles, with either bay or woodland views, above a fabulous local pub and sophisticated restaurant. The long, impressive bar was made from elm wood salvaged from the Clan Donald estate, and the cask Isle of Skye Brewing Co ales are brewed just a few hundred yards away (see page 474). Food is local produce, lovingly presented. Reservations for a table are essential. Two-night minimum stay and no under 18s in the hotel. **££££**

Glenview B&B 3 miles south of Staffin ⓦ glenviewskye. co.uk. Three spacious, king-sized rooms decorated in quirky, vintage style. Owners Kirsty and Simon also run Earth and Skye Yoga and Shilasdair Yarns on the same premises, so you can join a yoga and meditation class or browse the natural dye yarn shop. **££**

SHOPPING

Isle of Skye Brewing Co Uig pier ⓦ skyeale.com. In 1992, a few Skye locals joked that the only solution to the island's poor standard of beers would be to brew their own. Three years later, those same locals set up their own brewery and these days any self-respecting Skye pub has their ales on tap. You can pop into their brewery in Uig to have a taster and pick up a bottle or two.

Uig Pottery Uig harbour ⓦ uigpottery.co.uk. When you're based on an island with more than its fair share of natural beauty, it's little surprise to discover that most of the island's arts and crafts are in some way inspired by those surrounds. Both sea and landscape influence the work that goes on in this working pottery, with the resulting ceramics on sale in their on-site shop. You can drop in to shop for tableware and other homeware, or simply to watch the creative process in action.

Isle of Raasay

The hilly, fourteen-mile island of **Raasay** (Ratharsair) sees few visitors and is home to only around 170 people. Yet in many ways it's the ultimate Skye escape, with plenty of walks – intimate strolls compared to the wide spaces of Skye – and rich flora and fauna, including golden eagles, snipe, orchids and the unique Raasay vole, not to mention the castaway thrill of a small island. Most visitors come on foot – if you come by car, be aware there's no petrol (filling) station. The ferry docks in Churchton Bay, near **INVERARISH**, the island's tiny village set within thick woods on the southwest coast. The chief – indeed only – attraction here is the **Isle of Raasay Distillery** (ⓦ raasaydistillery. com), a state-of-the-art facility which began distilling in 2017. Its first single malt, a lightly-peated version, rolled off the production line in 2020; you can partake in one of three different tours; the views from here are fantastic too.

Dun Caan

Most visitors come to walk into the island's interior – a rugged terrain of sandstone in the south and gneiss in the north. The obvious destination is the flat-top volcanic plug of **Dun Caan** (1456ft) where James Boswell danced a Highland jig when he visited with Dr Johnson in 1773. The five-mile trail to the top is easy to follow; a splendid trek along the burn through forest behind Inverarish, culminating in epic 360-degree views of Skye and the mainland from the top. The quickest return is down the northwest slope, but you can also get back to the ferry along the path by the southeast shore, passing the abandoned crofters' village of Hallaig. Keep your eyes peeled for roaming eagles overhead and the odd scuttling grouse.

ARRIVAL AND INFORMATION   ISLE OF RAASAY

By ferry The CalMac ferry (Mon–Sat 8–10 daily, Sun 2 daily; 25min; ⓦ calmac.co.uk) to Raasay departs from Sconser, 3 miles northeast of *Sligachan Hotel*.

Tourist information ⓦ raasay.com.

ACTIVITIES

Raasay House. Activities on offer (Easter–Oct, weather-dependent other months) are guided walks and canyoning, boat trips (round Raasay; approx. 3hr; £55), coasteering, sailing and sea or loch kayaking. Bike rental available for £40/day.

ACCOMMODATION AND EATING

Raasay House Short walk from ferry pier ⓦ raasay-house.co.uk. The MacLeods' rebuilt manor offers everything from four-star deluxe rooms with balconies and views to the Cuillins to modern bunkrooms. This is also the only place to eat out on the island, in the convivial bar/restaurant. Dorms £; doubles ££££

The Small Isles

Seen from southern Skye or the west coast of the Highlands, the **Small Isles** – Rùm, **Eigg**, **Muck** and tiny **Canna** – lie scattered in a silver-grey sea like a siren call to

13

adventure. After centuries of being passed between owners, most islands have stabilized into tight-knit communities of crofters. While Muck is still privately owned, Eigg was bought out by its islanders in 1997, ending more than 150 years of property speculation, and other islands have been bequeathed to national agencies. Rùm, by far the largest and most visited of the group, passed to the Nature Conservancy Council (now Scottish Natural Heritage) in 1957; and Canna has been in the hands of the National Trust for Scotland since 1981.

Many people come on a day-trip from Mallaig, but the Small Isles deserve longer. They are an opportunity to experience some off-grid island life while walking, bird-watching or simply admiring seascapes. Accommodation requires **forward planning** and public transport on the islands is nonexistent. But regular ferries mean you're not as cut off as the atmosphere suggests. Better still, services link all islands for a happy week of island-hopping.

ARRIVAL AND DEPARTURE

THE SMALL ISLES

Be aware that boats are frequently cancelled by bad weather, so check forecasts.

By ferry CalMac (ⓦ calmac.co.uk) sails from Mallaig (late March to mid-Oct daily, otherwise Mon–Sat), however, it doesn't sail to all of the islands each day. Long day-trips

are possible on Sat. Sheerwater (ⓦ arisaig.co.uk) sails return trips daily from Arisaig (see page 424) to Eigg, plus Rùm or Muck from April to October. The ride doubles as a wildlife cruise, so, while enjoyable, is more expensive than travelling with CalMac.

Rùm

After almost a century as the 'Forbidden Isle' – the exclusive sporting estate of self-made Lancastrian industrialists the Bulloughs – **Rùm** has opened up. Indeed, since it passed to Scottish Natural Heritage (SNH) in 1957, visitors are positively encouraged. Many come to hike the eight-mile **Rùm Cuillin Ridge Walk**, tracking a crown of peaks that are modest by Skye's standards – the summit of Askival is only 2663ft – but every bit as impressive in looks. And in recent years, crofting land has been released as SNH tries to encourage a community. Most of the island's twenty or so inhabitants live around **KINLOCH** on the east coast, and many are employed by SNH, which runs the island as a National Nature Reserve. SNH have reintroduced native woodland and **white-tailed eagles (aka sea eagles)**, most of which promptly

---

HIKING IN THE RÙM CUILLIN

Ordnance Survey Explorer map 397

Rùm's **Cuillin** may not be as famous as Skye's, but in fine weather offers equally exhilarating **hiking** possibilities. Whatever route you choose, be sure to take all the usual safety precautions (see page 45).

The most popular walk is to traverse most or part of the **Cuillin Ridge**, roughly a twelve-hour round trip from Kinloch. The most frequent route is via Coire Dubh, then on to the saddle of Bealach Bairc-mheall. From here, you can either climb Barkeval to the west, or go for **Hallival** (2372ft) southeast, which looks daunting but is only a mild scramble. South of Hallival, the ridge is grassy, but the north ridge of **Askival** (2663ft) needs to be taken carefully, sticking to the east side. Askival is the highest mountain on Rùm, and if you're thinking of heading back, or the weather's closing in, Glen Dibidil provides an easy descent.

To continue along the ridge, head west to the double peak of **Trollaval** (or Trallval). The descent to Bealach an Fhuarain is steep, after which it's another scramble to reach the top of **Ainshval** (2562ft). Depending on the time and weather, you can continue along the ridge to **Sgùrr nan Gillean**, descend via Glen Dibidil and take the coastal path back to Kinloch, or skip the Sgùrr and go straight on to the last peak of the ridge, **Ruinsival**.

13

flew to neighbouring islands. The island is renowned for its **Manx shearwaters**, which nest in burrows on high peaks. You can learn more about the flora and fauna in an unmanned **visitor centre** halfway between the wharf and castle.

The best **beach** is **Kilmory** in the north of the island, a flattish walk on tracks through Kinloch then Kilmory glens (ten miles, five-hour return from Kinloch). Bear in mind that Rùm is the wettest of the Small Isles, and is notorious for midges (see page 43) – come prepared.

Kinloch Castle
Kinloch, signposted 20min walk from ferry

Most day-trippers to Rùm head straight for **Kinloch Castle**, a squat, red-sandstone edifice. Built at huge expense in 1900 – the red sandstone was shipped in from Dumfriesshire and the soil for the gardens from Ayrshire – its interior is sheer Edwardian decadence. It's also appealingly bonkers. From the galleried hall, with its tiger rugs, stags' heads and giant Japanese incense burners, to the Soho snooker table in the Billiard Room, the interior is packed with technical gizmos accumulated by **Sir George Bullough** (1870–1939), the spendthrift son of self-made millionaire, Sir John Bullough, who bought the island as a sporting estate in 1888.

At the time of writing, a buyer was still being sought for the castle, but this has been ongoing for years. Tours of the downstairs area have been run intermittently in recent years. For information on tours contact the Reserve Office, Native Scot (☎0131 3144181).

ARRIVAL AND INFORMATION RÙM

By ferry The longest day-trip possibilities from Mallaig are on Sat (just under 11hr). Note that overnight visitors cannot bring dogs, but day-trippers can. Summer timetables are: Arisaig–Rùm (Tues & Thurs 1 daily; 2hr 15min–2hr 30min); Canna–Rùm (Mon, Wed, Fri & Sat 1 daily; 1hr); Eigg–Rùm (Mon, Tues & Thurs 1 daily; 1hr–1hr 10min); Mallaig–Rùm (Mon, Wed, Fri, Sat & Sun 1 daily; 1hr 20min–2hr 30min).

Tourist information There is an unmanned visitor centre on the way from the ferry to Kinloch Castle. Another good source of information is ⓦ isleofrum.com.

ACCOMMODATION AND EATING

Visitors are permitted to **wild camp** and there are two simple **bothies** (three nights maximum) in Dibidil, on the southeast coast, and Guirdil, on the northwest coast. You'll find a shop/post office/off-licence in Kinloch, beside the community hall, which serves **teas** and **snacks** (summer 10am–noon on ferry days, 5–7pm most evenings).

Ivy Cottage Kinloch ⓦ ivycottageisleofrum.com. Delivers loch views from two pleasant en-suite rooms (one of which can be used as a family room) and the conservatory where you have breakfast and (vegetarian/vegan) dinner, both of which are included in the price. They also have a self-catering shepherds hut on-site. Bikes to rent, and a craft shop next door. £££

Kim's Kitchen Kinloch. Located in the Rùm village hall beside the general store and post office, Kim's Kitchen has a range of fresh food and drinks, although the highlight is the Friday Fish Supper, which is fried in Prosecco batter to eat in or take away. Sending an email in advance of your visit is advisable as ingredients are ordered based on anticipated demand. £

Kinloch Village Campsite ☎01687 460328. A community-run campsite with an appealing location spread along the shore on the south side of Kinloch Bay. On-site are two tiny, insulated camping cabins with four beds each. Camping per person £; cabins for two £

Rum Bunkhouse Kinloch ⓦ rumbunkhouse.co.uk. This impressive bunkhouse is the most comfortable option on the island for walking groups who don't want to brave the bothies. Twenty beds (one twin, three four-beds and a six-bed dorm), plus a large living area with sofas and a wood-burning stove. There are also two-four berth cabins and space for camping. Dorm £; twin ££, cabins £££

Eigg

Eigg – which measures just five miles by three – does little to conceal its volcanic origins. It is made of a basalt plateau, and a great stump of pitchstone lava, known as An Sgùrr, rises in the south. Geology aside, Eigg has an appealingly strong sense of community among its hundred-odd residents. This was given an enormous boost in 1997 when they (alongside the Scottish Wildlife Trust) pulled off the first **buyout** of a Highlands estate, thereby ending Eigg's unhappy history of private ownership. The anniversary is celebrated with an all-night **ceilidh** on the weekend nearest 12 June. Its other world-first is that its electricity grid is powered entirely by renewable sources.

Galmisdale

Ferries arrive into **Galmisdale Bay**, in the southeast corner of the island. Head up through woods for superb sea views, or track the shore south to see crofting ruins before the Sgùrr cliffs – the remains of Upper and Lower Grulin settlements. If the tide is low you can scramble along the shore into Cathedral Cave or Massacre Cave (**Uamh Fhraing**), where all but one of Eigg's 396 inhabitants died in 1577, suffocated by the MacLeods of Skye, who lit a fire in the cave mouth. Bring a torch and prepare to feel spooked.

An Sgùrr

The largest piece of pitchstone in the UK, **An Sgùrr** (1289ft) is the obvious destination for a hike. Actually, the route up is not as daunting as the cliffs suggest; the path is signposted left from the main road, crossing boggy moor to approach the summit from the north via a saddle (3–4hr return). The rewards are wonderful views to Muck and Rùm.

Cleadale

For an easy stroll, strike out to **CLEADALE**, the main crofting settlement in north Eigg. It's spectacularly sited beneath the island's basalt ridge, **Beinn Bhuidhe**, and above a beach known as Camas Sgiotaig, or the **Singing Sands**, because the quartz grains squeak underfoot. The views from here to Rùm, its peaks often cloaked by clouds, are unforgettable.

ARRIVAL AND DEPARTURE   EIGG

By ferry Summer timetables are: Canna–Eigg (Mon & Sat 1 daily; 2hr 20min); Mallaig–Eigg (Mon, Thurs, Sat & Sun 1hr 15min); Muck–Eigg (Sat 1 daily; 35min); Rùm–Eigg (Mon, Tues & Thurs 1 daily; 1hr–1hr 45min).

INFORMATION AND ACTIVITIES

By minibus or bike A minibus is scheduled around ferries (☎01687 482494; £2). Bike rental is available from Eigg Adventures (⊚eiggadventures.co.uk; £20/day), based at the harbour, as is kayak rental (£20/2hr).

Tourist information The friendly locals at the pier centre – An Laimhrig – will give you all the information you need (there's a craft shop and well-stocked mini-supermarket here, too). Alternatively, visit ⊚isleofeigg.org.

ACCOMMODATION AND EATING

Galmisdale Café and Bar An Laimhrig ⊚galmisdale-bay.com. Island ingredients go into home-made soups, quiche, pizza, lamb or venison burgers and blackboard specials such as fishcakes. Evening meals available during peak months. **£**

Glebe Barn Galmisdale ⊚glebebarn.co.uk. Eigg's hostel on the hill above the harbour has a spacious lounge with awesome coast views and pleasant wee dorm rooms. Better still is the self-contained cottagey *Glebe Apartment* – a superb stay for up to five people. Dorms **£**; twins **£**; annexe **££**

Kildonan House Down a long, unmarked road, north side of Galmisdale Bay ⊚kildonanhouseeigg.co.uk. A traditional stay in an eighteenth-century farmhouse. Warm and welcoming host Marie offers three pleasingly simple pine-panelled rooms, one with an en-suite shower, all with sea views and dinners (usually the catch-of-the-day) included. **£££**

★ **Lageorna** Cleadale ⊚lageorna.com. Beautiful, modern rooms full of contemporary crafts – think rustic wooden beds (built on Rùm) and knitted throws – and with astonishing views, plus a lovely vintage cottage that sleeps six. The owner also prepares superb three-course set menus for just £30, which may include dishes such as venison on a bed of spicy puy lentils; reservations recommended. Doubles **££**; cottage **££££**

13

Sue Holland's Croft Cleadale Ⓦ eiggorganics.co.uk. On an organic croft, this is the only designated campsite and it's a belter, with views and sunsets to inspire poetry. The old cowshed is now a basic bothy for up to four, or for more comfort choose a yurt. Sue also runs crofting tours and courses on growing vegetables. Camping per person £; bothy and yurt ££

Muck

Barely two miles long, tiny **Muck** is the smallest and most southerly of the Small Isles. Low-lying and almost treeless, it is extremely fertile, so has more in common with Coll and Tiree than its neighbours. Its name derives from *muc*, the Gaelic for 'pig' (or possibly *muc mara*, 'sea pig' or porpoise, which are plentiful), and has long caused embarrassment to lairds – they preferred to call it the 'Isle of Monk' because it briefly belonged to the medieval church.

PORT MÓR is the hub of all activity, where visitors arrive and just about all of the thirty or so residents live – a tenth of the 320 of the early 1800s. A mile-long road connects Port Mór with the island's main farm, **Gallanach**, which overlooks rocky skerries on the north side. The nicest sandy **beach** is Camas na Cairidh, to the east of Gallanach. For a stiffer challenge, **Beinn Airein** (2hr return), in the southwest corner of the island, is worth climbing, despite being only 450ft above sea level, for a 360-degree panorama of surrounding islands from its summit.

ARRIVAL AND INFORMATION   MUCK

By ferry Summer timetables are: Canna–Muck (Sat 1 daily; 1hr 35min); Eigg–Muck (Thurs, Sat & Sun 1 daily; 45min); Mallaig–Muck (Tues & Thurs–Sun 1 daily; 1hr 30min–2hr).

Tourist information The Craft Shop & Tea Room (see below) doubles as an information point. See also Ⓦ isleofmuck.com.

ACCOMMODATION AND EATING

To **wild camp** on the island, check in at The Craft Shop & Tea Room to find out about any areas currently off-limits.

The Craft Shop & Tea Room Port Mór ☎ 0790 8956822. The only shop on the island prepares daily soups and sandwiches made from fresh home-baked bread, plus afternoon teas and dinners of fresh shellfish prepared on request.

Gallanach Lodge Gallanach Bay Ⓦ gallanachlodge. co.uk. A purpose-built luxury lodge that takes full advantage of a superb position above the beach to provide fantastic views to Rùm. The style is island boutique – rustic, handmade beds in rooms with hotel-style mod cons. Full board only. ££££

Isle of Muck Bunkhouse Port Mór ☎ 01687 462042. Three bunkrooms and two doubles in the island's simple wee hostel, sited near the port. Life revolves around the Raeburn stove in the simple living room and the kitchen. Hardly luxurious but full of character. Extra charge for bedding. Per person £

Canna

Measuring a mere five miles by one, **Canna** is managed as a **bird sanctuary** by the National Trust for Scotland (NTS). There are no roads, just open moorland stretched over a basalt ridge, and few people now that the population has dwindled to eight. While Canna doesn't receive many visitors by ferry, plenty come by yacht for the best harbour in the Small Isles, a sheltered bay off Canna's main hamlet, **A' Chill**. Notwithstanding walks (see below), you come to Canna for birdlife; this has been a sanctuary since 1938, and 157 species have been recorded, including golden and white-tailed eagles, and Manx shearwaters, razorbills and puffins on cliffs at the western end.

Although less obviously scenic than other Small Isles, the flattish terrain makes for enjoyable **walks**. You can circuit the entire island on a long day (10hr; twelve miles), or from the dock it's about a mile across a grassy plateau to the cliffs on the north shore and Compass Hill, named because its high iron content distorts compasses. A mile west is Carn a' Ghaill, Canna's summit at a heady 688ft.

ARRIVAL AND INFORMATION

By ferry Summer timetable: Eigg–Canna (Mon & Sat; 1 daily; 2hr 20min); Mallaig–Canna (Mon, Wed, Fri & Sun 1 daily, Sat 2 daily; 2hr 30min–3hr 45min); Muck–Canna (Sat 1 daily; 1hr 35min); Rùm–Canna (Mon, Wed & Fri–Sun 1 daily; 1hr 5min).

Tourist information ⓦ theisleofcanna.com.

ACCOMMODATION AND EATING

With permission from the NTS, you may **wild camp** on Canna, though bring supplies.

Canna Café West Bothy ⓦ cafecanna.co.uk. Cute little licensed café on the shore. Main dishes include line caught mackerel fillets and home-made venison and ale pies, but be sure to pre-order lobster, crab and seafood platters. **£££**

Tighard ⓦ tighard.scot. The Sanday room is the pick – spacious, traditional and with sweeping sea views – in the only B&B on Canna. Its other two smaller and simpler twins also enjoy sea views. Friendly hosts Colin and David also offer packed lunch and dinner with prior arrangement. **££**

The Western Isles

GEARRANNAN, LEWIS

The Western Isles

Beyond Skye, across the unpredictable waters of the Minch, lie the wild and windy Outer Hebrides, officially known as the Western Isles. A 130-mile-long archipelago stretching from Lewis and Harris in the north to the Uists and Barra in the south, the islands appear as an unbroken chain when viewed from across the Minch, hence their nickname, the Long Isle. In reality there are more than two hundred islands, although only a handful are inhabited, with the total population around 28,000. This is truly a land on the edge, where the turbulent seas of the Atlantic smash up against a geologically complex terrain whose coastline is interrupted by a thousand sheltered bays and sweeping sandy beaches. The islands' interiors are equally dramatic, veering between flat, boggy, treeless peat moor and bare mountaintops soaring high above a host of tiny lakes, or lochans.

The major difference between the Western Isles and much of the Hebrides is that the islands' fragile economy is still mainly concentrated around crofting, fishing and weaving, and the percentage of incomers is low. In fact, the Outer Hebrides remain the heartland of **Gaelic** culture, with the language spoken by the majority of islanders. Its survival is partly thanks to the efforts of the Western Islands Council, the Scottish Parliament and the influence of the Church in the region: the Free Church and its various offshoots in Lewis, Harris and North Uist, and the Catholic Church in South Uist and Barra.

Lewis and Harris form two parts of the same island. The interior of the northernmost, **Lewis**, is mostly peat moor, a barren and marshy tract that gives way to the bare peaks of **North Harris**. Across a narrow isthmus lies **South Harris**, with wide beaches of golden sand trimming the Atlantic in full view of the rough boulder-strewn mountains to the east. Across the Sound of Harris, to the south, a string of tiny, flatter isles linked by causeways – **North Uist**, **Benbecula**, **South Uist** – offers breezy beaches, whose fine sands front a narrow band of boggy farmland, which, in turn, is bordered by a lower range of hills to the east. Finally, tiny **Barra** contains all the above landscapes in one small Hebridean package and is connected by causeway to even tinier **Vatersay**.

In contrast to their wonderful surroundings, villages in the Western Isles are seldom picturesque in themselves, and are usually made up of scattered, relatively modern croft houses dotted about the elementary road system. The Outer Hebrides' only sizeable settlement is Stornoway, a town which retains a modicum of charm thanks to what's left of its old harbour frontage and traditional and Victorian buildings in the near vicinity. Many visitors, walkers and nature-watchers forsake the main settlements altogether and retreat to secluded cottages, simple hostels and B&Bs.

ARRIVAL AND DEPARTURE

By plane There are scheduled flights from Glasgow, Edinburgh, Inverness and Aberdeen to Stornoway on Lewis, and from Glasgow to Barra and Benbecula. Be warned: weather conditions are notoriously changeable, making flights prone to delay and even cancellation. On Barra, the plane lands on the beach, so the timetable is adjusted with the tides.

By ferry CalMac car ferries run two services daily from Ullapool to Stornoway; one or two daily from Uig, on Skye, to Tarbert and Lochmaddy; and operate daily from Oban to Barra and Mallaig to South Uist. The timetables quoted in the text are summer frequencies – check ⓦ calmac.co.uk for the latest and always book ahead.

CALLANISH STANDING STONES

Highlights

❶ Cycling the Hebridean Way Usually tackled south–north to make use of the prevailing wind, the scenic 185-mile Hebridean Way crosses ten islands from Vatersay to the Butt of Lewis. See page 487

❷ Garenin, Lewis An abandoned crofting village whose black houses have been beautifully restored. Some are now self-catering cottages, one is a café, and a couple have been left as they were when they were last inhabited. See page 490

❸ Callanish standing stones, Lewis Scotland's finest standing stones have a serene lochside setting on the west coast of the Isle of Lewis. See page 491

❹ Boat trip to St Kilda Permanently inhabited until 1930, now a UNESCO World Heritage Site; getting to this tiny, remote island chain forty miles north-west of North Uist is an adventure in itself. See page 491

❺ St Clement's Church, Harris Rodel's pre-Reformation church, at the southernmost tip of Harris, boasts the most ornate sculptural decoration in the Outer Hebrides. See page 495

❻ Barra and Vatersay beaches Barra and its tiny neighbour, Vatersay, are dotted with stunning, deserted golden-sand beaches backed by flower-cloaked machair. See page 503

HIGHLIGHTS ARE MARKED ON THE MAP ON PAGE 484

THE WESTERN ISLES

0 _____ 25
miles

HIGHLIGHTS

1 Cycling the Hebridean Way
2 Garenin, Lewis
3 Callanish standing stones, Lewis
4 Boat trip to St Kilda
5 St Clement's Church, Harris
6 Barra and Vatersay beaches

N

Sula Sgeir
Butt of Lewis   Port of Ness

A857

Barvas

Garenin   2   A858
Carloway
3
Callanish
Standing
Stones

A857

Stornoway

A858

A866

Arid Uig   *Bernera*

Bernera

L e w i s

A859

Scarp

An Cliseam
(2619ft)

A859

Tarbert

Taransay

Scalpay

Shiant
Isles

H a r r i s

A859

Leverburgh
5   St Clement's
Church

Berneray

North Uist

A867   Lochmaddy

Monach
Islands

Benbecula

A865

South
Uist

1

Beinn Mhor
(2034ft)

Lochboisdale

Eriskay

Barra

Castlebay

Vatersay   6

Sandray

Pabbay

Mingulay
Barra Head

W E S T E R N   I S L E S

4   St Kilda

T h e   M i n c h

Ullapool

T h e   L i t t l e   M i n c h

Neist
Point

Uig

Portree   *Raasay*

S k y e

A87
Broadford

S M A L L   I S L E S

Canna

Hyskeir   *Rùm*

Armadale

Eigg

Mallaig

Muck

Arisaig

Tiree   Oban

GAELIC IN THE WESTERN ISLES

All Ordnance Survey maps and many **road signs** are exclusively in **Gaelic**, a difficult language to the English-speaker's eye, with complex pronunciation (see page 578), though the English names sometimes provide a rough guide. If you're driving, it's a good idea to pick up a bilingual Western Isles **map**, available at most tourist offices. We've put the English equivalent first in the text, with the Gaelic in parentheses.

14

GETTING AROUND

By car and by ferry A series of causeways makes it possible to drive from one end of the Western Isles to the other with just two interruptions – the ferry from Harris to Berneray, and from Eriskay to Barra. If you're going to take the ferry, it's advisable to book in advance. Note that petrol stations can be a long distance apart (and might be closed on Sundays).

By bus The islands have a decent bus service, though there are no buses on Sundays.

By bike The wind makes cycling something of a challenge – head from south to north to catch the prevailing wind. It's free to take bikes on all ferry services, or if you prefer to rent there are rental outlets in Barra and Stornoway.

Lewis (Leodhas)

Shaped rather like the top of an ice-cream cone, **Lewis** is the largest and most populous of the Western Isles. Nearly half of the island's inhabitants live in the crofting and fishing villages strung out along the northwest coast, between **Callanish** (Calanais) and **Port of Ness** (Port Nis), in one of the country's most densely populated rural areas. On this coast you'll also find the best-preserved **prehistoric remains** – Dun Carloway (Dùn Charlabhaigh) and the Callanish standing stones. The landscape is mostly peat bog – hence the island's Gaelic name, from *leogach* (marshy) – but the shoreline is more dramatic, especially around the Butt of Lewis, the island's northernmost tip. The rest of the island's population live in **Stornoway**, on the east coast, the only real town in the Western Isles. To the south, where Lewis is physically joined with Harris, the land rises to over 1800ft, providing an exhilarating backdrop for the excellent beaches that pepper the isolated western coastline around **Uig**.

Stornoway (Steòrnabhagh)

In these parts, **STORNOWAY** is a buzzing metropolis, with around eight thousand inhabitants, a one-way system, a pedestrian precinct and all the trappings of a large town. It's a centre for employment, a social hub for the island and home to the Western Isles Council (**Comhairle nan Eilean Siar**), set up in 1974, which has done so much to promote Gaelic language and culture. Aesthetics are not its strong point, however, and the urban pleasures on offer are limited, but in July Stornoway hosts the **Hebridean Celtic Festival** (ⓦhebceltfest.com), a Celtic music festival held in Lews Castle grounds, and at An Lanntair arts centre.

For centuries, life in Stornoway has focused on its **harbour**, whose quayside was once filled with barrels of pickled herring, and whose deep and sheltered waters were thronged with coastal steamers and fishing boats in its nineteenth-century heyday, when over a thousand boats were based at the port. Today, most of the catch is landed on the mainland, and, despite the daily comings and goings of the CalMac ferry from Ullapool, the harbour is a shadow of its former commercial self – the nicest section is Cromwell Street Quay, by the tourist office, where the remaining fishing fleet ties up for the night.

Stornoway's commercial centre, to the east, is little more than a string of unprepossessing shops and bars. The one exception is the old **Town Hall** on South

Beach, a splendid Scots Baronial–style building from 1905, its rooftop peppered with conical towers, above which a central clocktower rises. One block east along South Beach, and looking rather like a modern church, you'll find **An Lanntair** (Gaelic for 'lantern'), Stornoway's modern cultural centre.

Museum nan Eilean (Lews Castle)

Across the bay from the town centre • Grounds 24hr • Free • Museum April–Sept Tues–Sat 10am–5pm, Oct–March Tues–Sat 1–4pm • Free • ⓦ lews-castle.co.uk

14

The castellated pomposity of **Lews Castle** was built by Sir James Matheson in 1863 after resettling the crofters who used to live here. As the former laird's pad, it has long been seen by many as a symbol of old oppression: it was here, in the house's now-defunct conservatory, that Lady Matheson famously gave tea to the Bernera protesters, when they marched on Stornoway prior to rioting; when the eccentric

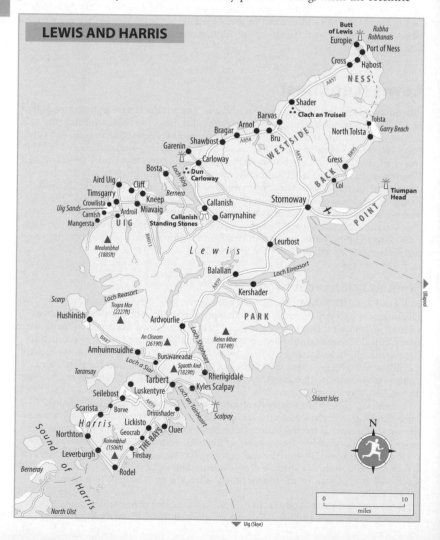

THE HEBRIDEAN WAY

A dual aspect long-distance route has traversed the Western Isles archipelago since 2017. The 156-mile **walking trail** and 186-mile **cycle trail** (National Cycling Route 780) cover different ground but each stretches from Vatersay in the south to Lewis in the north (the walk ends in Stornoway and the cycle at the Butt of Lewis). The Hebridean Way is astonishingly varied and flower-strewn machair, white-sand beaches, craggy mountains and lochs zip by, as golden and even white-tailed eagles fly overhead. You'll need to know the ferry schedules – passengers can take bikes aboard for free – and although it's remote, there are places to rest and pick up supplies. For a stress-free trip, allow four to six days for cycling and ten to twelve days for walking (see ⓦvisitouterbebrides.co.uk for details).

14

Lord Leverhulme took up residence, he had unglazed bedroom windows which allowed the wind and rain to enter, and gutters in the asphalt floor to carry off the residue.

The building was closed for over 25 years before undergoing a £14 million makeover that included a new extension to house a state-of-the-art bilingual museum, telling the story of the islands' geology, Gaelic culture and struggles of the nineteenth century. The museum has long-term loan of six Lewis Chessmen, twelfth-century Viking chess-pieces, which were carved from walrus ivory and whale teeth. Lews Castle's external attraction is its mature wooded **grounds**, a unique sight on the Western Isles, for which Matheson imported thousands of tons of soil. Hidden among the trees is the **Woodland Centre**, which has a straightforward exhibition on the history of the castle and the island, and a decent café serving soup, salads and cakes.

ARRIVAL AND GETTING AROUND   STORNOWAY

By plane Stornoway Airport (ⓦhial.co.uk) is 4 miles east of the town centre: there are five buses (Mon–Sat only) which take 15mins, or it's a £5 taxi ride into town.

By ferry Ferries between Stornoway and Ullapool (Mon–Sat 2–3 daily, Sun 1 daily; 2hr 30min; ☏0800 0665000) run from the octagonal CalMac ferry terminal on South Beach, near the bus station.

By bus The bus station (☏01851 704327) is on South Beach in the town centre.

Destinations Arnol (Mon–Sat 4–7 daily; 30min); Barvas (Mon–Sat 4–7 daily; 20min); Callanish (Mon–Sat 3–6 daily; 32min); Carloway (Mon–Sat 2–6 daily; 45min); Garenin (Mon–Sat 3–4 daily; 1hr); Great Bernera (Mon–Sat 4 daily; 1hr); Leverburgh (Mon–Sat 4–5 daily; 2hr); Port of Ness (Mon–Sat 6–8 daily; 1hr); Shawbost (Mon–Sat 6–9 daily; 45min); Tarbert (Mon–Sat 5 daily; 1hr); Tolsta (Mon–Sat hourly; 40min); Uig (Mon–Sat 4 daily; 1hr–1hr 30min).

By car Car rental is available from Mackinnon Self-Drive, 18 Inaclete Rd (ⓦmackinnonselfdrive.co.uk) from around £25/day – they're based in Stornoway and local deliveries are free (but let them know if you're taking the car off Lewis and Harris).

INFORMATION AND ACTIVITIES

Tourist office 26 Cromwell St (April to mid-Sept Mon–Sat 9am–5.45pm; mid-Sept to Oct Mon–Sat 9am–4.45pm; Nov–March Mon–Fri 9am–5pm; ⓦvisitouterhebrides. co.uk).

Bike hire Bike Hebrides, 6 Sand St (ⓦbikehebrides.com; closed Sun), offers bike rental from £27.50/day; usefully they also do repairs.

Surfing Surf Lewis at 10 East St, Sandwick (ⓦsurflewis. com) offers beginner lessons (£45/2hr 30min) and equipment hire (board £15, wetsuit £10/day).

ACCOMMODATION   SEE MAP PAGE 488

Cabarfeidh Hotel Manor Park ⓦcabarfeidh-hotel. co.uk. Large, reasonably upmarket hotel near Lews Castle with an excellent choice of cooked breakfasts including kippers, pancakes with syrup and the full Scottish fry-up. **£££**

Heb Hostel 25 Kenneth St ⓦhebhostel.co.uk. A clean, centrally located terrace house in salmon pink, converted into a simple hostel, with dorms, a family room and private doubles; free breakfast, laundry and kitchen facilities. Run by a friendly resident warden. Dorms **£**; shepherd's hut **££**

14

Hebridean Guest House 61 Bayhead St ⓦ hebridean-guest-house.co.uk. Whitewashed property, a 5min walk from the harbour and within easy reach of Lews Castle with a large range of en suite and tastefully decorated rooms. **£££**

Jannel 5 Stewart Drive ⓦ jannel-stornoway.co.uk. A short walk from the town centre, this B&B is run by a delightful landlady and boasts five immaculate en-suite

rooms. **££**

Laxdale Holiday Park Laxdale Lane ⓦ laxdale holidaypark.com. The well-equipped campsite has caravans, a self-catering lodge (week-long stays only), a wigwam for groups and a purpose-built bunkhouse, as well as a sheltered spot for tents. It lies a mile or so along the road to Barvas. Bunkhouse per person **£**; wigwam **££**; camping per pitch **£**

EATING

SEE MAP PAGE 488

An Lanntair Kenneth St ⓦ lanntair.com. Arts venue with a stylish, modern café-bar-restaurant that serves food all day. Light lunches include soup and bread, or for more substantial eating, they do burgers, fish and chips and

pastas. **££**

★ **Digby Chick** 5 Bank St ⓦ digbychick.co.uk. Smart, modern, buzzy little bistro with a real emphasis on using local produce, such as the famous Stornoway black pudding.

STORNOWAY

■ ACCOMMODATION	
Cabarfeidh Hotel	1
Heb Hostel	5
Hebridean Guest House	4
Jannel	2
Laxdale Holiday Park	3

■ DRINKING	
The Criterion Bar	1

● EATING	
An Lanntair	4
Digby Chick	3
Thai Café	1
The Good Food Boutique	2

There are some interesting options on offer here like their Indian-French fusion of salmon with curried bisque, tandoori onions and coconut bonbons, or ordinary battered fish 'n' chips if curry's not your thing. Closed Sun. £££

Thai Café 27 Church St ☎01851 701811. Despite the name, this is actually a restaurant, serving authentic no frills Thai food. The lunchtime pad Thai is particularly good value, while evening mains like the spicy Jungle Curry – stir-fried beef and peppers in a spicy coconut gravy, are delicious. No licence, so bring your own bottle (£1 corkage). Closed Sun. ££

The Good Food Boutique 59 Cromwell St ⓦthegood foodboutique.co.uk. Deli counter and storeroom with quality international and local produce. Takeaway sandwiches and salad boxes are available (think *porcetta* with apple and chilli chutney) or there's everything you need for a picnic or barbecue (cheese, olives, meat, marinades, bread, wine). Closed Sun. £̄

14

DRINKING

SEE MAP PAGE 488

The Criterion Bar 32 Point St ☎01851 701990. A tiny, authentic no-frills Stornoway pub, where they have regular informal (music) sessions – if nothing's going down, try nearby *MacNeill's*.

The road to Ness (Nis)

The A857 crosses the vast, barren **peat** bog that characterizes the interior of Lewis, an empty, undulating wilderness riddled with stretch marks formed by peat cuttings and pockmarked with freshwater lochans. The whole area was once covered by forests, but these disappeared long ago, leaving a deposit of peat that continues to serve as a valuable energy resource, with each crofter being assigned a slice of the bog.

Twelve miles across the peat bog the road approaches the west coast of Lewis and divides, heading southwest towards Callanish, or northeast through **BARVAS** (Barabhas), which has a handy shop and petrol station. Just beyond Barvas, a signpost points to the pleasant **Morven Gallery** (Easter–Sept Mon–Sat 10.30am–5pm; free; ⓦmorvengallery.com), which hosts exhibitions by local artists and photographers and has a handy café too, serving great coffee, where you can hole up during bad weather. Three miles further up the road, you pass the 20ft monolith of **Clach an Truiseil**, the first of a series of prehistoric sights between the crofting and weaving settlements of **Ballantrushal** (Baile an Truiseil) and **Shader** (Siadar).

Ness (Nis)

At the northern tip of Lewis, **NESS** (Nis) is made up of a string of densely populated, fervently Presbyterian villages. Ness has the highest percentage of Gaelic-speakers in the country (75 percent), but the locals are perhaps best known for their annual culling of young gannets on **Sula Sgeir**. These scattered settlements have none of the photogenic qualities of Skye's whitewashed villages: the churches are plain and unadorned; the crofters' houses relatively modern and smothered in grey pebbledash or harling; the stone cottages and enclosures of their forebears often lie half-abandoned in the front garden: a rusting assortment of discarded cars and vans store peat bags and the like. The road terminates at the fishing village of **PORT OF NESS** (Port Nis), with a tiny harbour and lovely golden beach. It's worth noting that there are few shops (other than mobile ones) in these parts, so it's as well to stock up in Stornoway before you set out.

Shortly before you reach Port of Ness, a minor road heads two miles northwest to the hamlet of **EUROPIE** (Eoropaidh) – pronounced 'Yor-erpee'. By the road junction that leads to the Butt of Lewis stands the simple stone structure of **St Moluag's Church** (Teampull Mholuaidh), amid the runrig fields, now acting as sheep runs. Thought to date from the twelfth century, when the islands were still under Norse rule, but restored in 1912 (and now used once a month by the Scottish Episcopal Church for sung Communion), the church features a strange south chapel with only a squint window connecting it to the nave. In the late seventeenth century, the traveller Martin Martin noted: 'They all went to church … and then standing silent for a little time, one of them gave a signal … and immediately all of them went into the fields, where they fell a-drinking their ale, and spent the remainder of the night in dancing and singing'. Church services aren't what they used to be.

ARRIVAL AND DEPARTURE NESS

By bus There's a regular bus service between Stornoway and Port of Ness (Mon–Sat 6–9 daily; 50min).

ACCOMMODATION

Galson Farm South Galson (Gabhsann Bho), eight miles north east of Barvas ⓦ galsonfarm.co.uk. An attractive converted eighteenth-century farmhouse with four beautifully appointed room, two sitting rooms, and, on four evenings a week, a two-course set meal for £27. **££**

Westside (An Toabh Siar)

Heading south-west from the crossroads near Barvas (see page 489) brings you to the **Westside**. The main road lies a mile or so inland from the coast, but several villages meander down towards the sea. At **Arnol** and **Garenin** (Gearrannan) there are beautifully preserved black houses to explore, and, at **Callanish** (Calanais), the islands' justifiably popular standing stones.

Arnol Blackhouse

42 Arnol • April–Sept Mon–Sat 9.30am–5.30pm; Oct–March Mon–Tues & Thurs–Sat 10am–4pm • Charge • HES • ⓦ historicenvironment.scot

In Arnol, the remains of numerous black houses lie abandoned by the roadside. One, however, has been very carefully preserved to show exactly how a true black house, or *taigh dubh*, would have been. The dark interior is lit and heated by a small peat fire, kept alight in the central hearth of bare earth; smoke drifts up through the thatch, helping to keep out the midges and turn the heathery sods and oat-straw thatch itself into next year's fertilizer. The animals would have slept in the byre, separated only by a low partition, while potatoes and grain were stored in the adjacent barn. The elderly woman who lived here moved out very reluctantly in 1964, only after the council agreed to build a house with a byre for her animals (the building now houses the ticket office). Across the road is a ruined black house, abandoned in 1920 when the family moved into No. 39, the white house, or *taigh geal*, next door. A little beyond the black house, a path leads down to **Loch na Muilne**, where you've a good chance of spotting the very rare red-necked phalarope (May–Aug).

Garenin (Gearrannan)

Garenin • May–Sept Mon–Sat 9.30am–5.30pm • Charge • ⓦ gearrannan.com

In the parish of Carloway (Carlabhagh), with its croft houses, boulders and hillocks rising out of the peat moor, a mile-long road leads off north to the beautifully remote coastal settlement of **GARENIN** (Gearrannan). Here, rather than re-create a single museum-piece black house as at Arnol, a whole cluster of nine thatched crofters' houses – the last of which was abandoned in 1974 – has been restored and put to use as accommodation for holiday-makers and a museum. As an ensemble, they give a great impression of what a **Baile Tughaidh**, or black house village, must have been like. The first house you come to houses the ticket office and **café**. The second house has been restored to its condition at the time of abandonment, so there's electric light but no running water, lino flooring, but a peat fire and box beds – and a weaving machine in the byre. The third house has interpretive panels and a touch-screen computer telling the history of the village and the folk who lived there.

ST KILDA (HIORT)

Britain's westernmost island chain is the **St Kilda** (ⓦ nts.org.uk) archipelago, forty miles from North Uist. Dominated by Britain's highest cliffs and sea stacks, Hirta, the main island, was occupied until 1930 when the last 36 Gaelic-speaking inhabitants were evacuated at their own request. The island was then bought by the Marquess of Bute, to protect the island's millions of nesting seabirds. In 1957, having agreed to allow the army to build a missile-tracking radar station here linked to South Uist, he bequeathed the island to the NTS. St Kilda is one of only two dozen **UNESCO World Heritage Sites** with a dual status reflecting its natural and cultural significance. Despite its inaccessibility, several thousand visitors make it out here each year. Between mid-May and mid-August, the NTS organizes volunteer **work parties**, which either restore and maintain the old buildings or take part in archaeological digs – for more information, contact the NTS (ⓦ nts.org.uk). For the armchair traveller, the best general book on St Kilda is Tom Steel's *The Life and Death of St Kilda*, or else there's the classic 1937 film *The Edge of the World* by Michael Powell (which was actually shot on Foula in Shetland). Several companies offer **boat day-trips** for around £190 per person plus £5 landing fee. The sea journey (8hr return) is not for the faint-hearted and there's no guarantee that you'll be able to land.

14

Next door, there are toilets, while the rest have been converted into **self-catering cottages** and a **hostel** (see page 492).

Dun Carloway (Dùn Charlabhaigh)
Signposted off the A858 • Open 24hr • ☎ 01851 710395

Just south of Carloway village, **Dun Carloway** (Dùn Charlabhaigh) perches on top of a conspicuous rocky outcrop overlooking the sea. One of Scotland's best-preserved **brochs**, or fortified towers, its dry-stone circular walls reach a height of more than 30ft on one side. The broch consists of two concentric walls, the inner one perpendicular, the outer one slanting inwards, the two originally fastened together by roughly hewn flagstones, which also served as lookout galleries reached via a narrow stairwell. The only entrance to the roofless inner yard is through a low doorway set beside a crude and cramped guard cell. As at Callanish, there have been all sorts of theories about the purpose of the brochs, which date from between 100 BC and 100; the most likely explanation is that they were built to provide protection from Roman slave traders.

Callanish (Calanais) standing stones
Loch Roag • **Stones** 24hr year-round • Free • **Callanish Visitor Centre** April, May, Sept & Oct Mon–Sat 10am–6pm; June–Aug Mon–Sat 9.30am–8pm; Oct–March Wed–Sat 10am–3pm • Charge • ⓦ calanais.org

Overlooking the sheltered, islet-studded waters of Loch Roag (Loch Ròg) on the west coast, are the islands' most dramatic prehistoric ruins, the **Callanish standing stones**. These monoliths – nearly fifty slabs of gnarled and finely grained gneiss up to 15ft high – were transported here between 3000 BC and 1500 BC, but their exact function remains a mystery. No one knows for certain why the ground plan resembles a colossal Celtic cross, nor why there's a central burial chamber. It's likely that such a massive endeavour was prompted by the desire to predict the seasonal cycle upon which these early farmers were entirely dependent, and indeed many of the stones are aligned with the positions of the sun and the stars. Whatever the reason for their existence, there's certainly no denying the powerful primeval presence, not to mention sheer beauty, of the stones.

You can visit the stones at any time, but if you need shelter or some simple sustenance, head to the nearby **Callanish Visitor Centre**, which has a small museum that explores the theories about the stones. If you want to commune with standing stones in solitude, head for the smaller circles in more natural surroundings a mile or two southeast of Callanish, around Garynahine (Gearraidh na h-Aibhne).

ARRIVAL AND DEPARTURE

WESTSIDE

By bus A circular bus service connects Callanish, Carloway and Garenin to Stornoway (Mon–Sat 3–6 daily; Callanish 32min, Carloway 45min, Garenin 1hr).

ACCOMMODATION

Eilean Fraoich Campsite Shawbost (Siabost) ⓦeileanfraoich.co.uk. Located behind the old village church, this pristine, flat, grassy campsite is in complete contrast with the surrounding undulating landscape. The site offers a kitchen with the usual appliances, a dining room attached, and laundry facilities and quoted price includes a car and two adults. Closed Nov–March. Per pitch £̲

The Gearrannan Hostel/Taigh Dhonnchaidh 7a Callanish (Calanais) ☎01851 643416, ⓦgearrannan. com/hostel. Taigh Dhonnchaidh or 'Duncan's House' is a converted thatched black house that's part of a sort of living museum (with an actual museum in the village, too). The hostel has one room with ten bunks, plus a family room for three. It's cosy and warm, and walk-ins are accepted if they have space. Dorms £̲, Triple £̲£̲

Uig (Uuige)

It's a long drive along the B8011 to the remote district of **UIG**, which suffered badly from the Clearances. The landscape here is hillier and more dramatic than elsewhere, a combination of myriad islets, wild cliff scenery and patches of pristine golden sand.

Timsgarry (Timsgearraidh)

The main road takes you through the narrow canyon of Glen Valtos (Glèann Bhaltois) to **TIMSGARRY** (Timsgearraidh), overlooking **Uig Sands** (Tràigh Uuige), the largest and most prized of all Lewis's golden strands, where the sea goes out for miles at low tide; the best access point is from the cemetery car park in Ardroil (Eadar Dha Fhadhail), a couple of miles south of Timsgarry.

Comunn Eachdraidh Uig

Timsgarry, just off the B8011 at the Aird Uig turn-off • April–Oct Mon–Sat noon–5pm • Charge • ⓦceuig.co.uk

A giant wooden statue of one of the **Lewis Chessmen**, which were found in a local sandbank in 1831, heralds the **Comunn Eachdraidh Uig** in Timsgarry. Inside, you can see some replicas of the twelfth-century Viking chess-pieces, six of which now reside in Museum nan Eilean (Lewis Museum). As well as putting on some excellent temporary exhibitions, the museum has bits and bobs from black houses and is staffed by locals, who are happy to answer any queries you have; there's also a welcome **tearoom** attached.

ARRIVAL AND DEPARTURE

UIG

By bus There are regular buses from Stornoway to Uig (Mon–Sat 4 daily; 1hr–1hr 30min).

ACCOMMODATION AND EATING

Ardroil campsite Ardroil (Eadar Dha Fhadhail) ☎01851 672248. The location, by one of the most remote and incredible sandy beaches in the Western Isles, is unbeatable. There's a small utilities block with showers and sinks for washing dishes plus a very handy electric socket. Nearest shop is a 10min walk. Per person £̲

Baile na Cille Timsgarry (Timsgearraidh) ☎01851 672242, ⓦbailenacille.co.uk. A chaotic kind of place, run by an eccentric couple who are very welcoming to families and dogs and dish up wonderful set-menu dinners for £30 a head. Closed mid-Sept to mid-April. £̲£̲£̲

Kneep campsite Kneep (Cnip) ⓦkneepcampsite.co.uk. Small campsite beside the wonderful sandy Reef Beach (Tràigh na Beirghe) and an ideal place to take a kayak (if you have one) to explore the tiny islands nearby. The site is run by the local community and the only facilities are a small unisex toilet block with coin-operated showers (£1 a shower). Per person £̄

Suainaval 3 Crowlista (Cradhlastadh) ⓦ suainaval.com. The best B&B in the whole area, run by a truly welcoming couple; rooms have pine floors and furnishings, Harris Tweed chairs and fabulous views over the golden sands of Uig. ££

Harris (Na Hearadh)

14

Harris, whose name derives from the Old Norse for 'high land', is much hillier, more dramatic and much more immediately appealing than Lewis, its boulder-strewn slopes descending to aquamarine bays of dazzling white sand. The shift from Lewis to Harris is almost imperceptible, as the two are, in fact, one island, the 'division' between them embedded in a historical split in the MacLeod clan, lost in the mists of time. The border was also, somewhat crazily, a county boundary until 1975, with Harris lying in Inverness-shire, and Lewis belonging to Ross and Cromarty. Nowadays, the dividing line is rarely marked even on maps; for the record, it comprises Loch Reasort in the west, Loch Seaforth (Loch Shìphoirt) in the east, and the six miles in between. Harris itself is more clearly divided by a minuscule isthmus, into the wild, inhospitable mountains of **North Harris** and the gentler landscape and sandy shores of **South Harris**.

Tarbert (An Tairbeart)

Sheltered in a green valley on the narrow isthmus, **TARBERT** (An Tairbeart) is the largest settlement on Harris and a wonderful place to arrive by boat. The port's mountainous backdrop is impressive, and the town is attractively laid out on steep terraces sloping up from the dock.

Isle of Harris Distillery

Tarbert • Year-round Mon–Fri 10am–5pm, plus March–Oct Sat; tours March–Oct (1hr 15min; see online for times) • charge for tours • ⓦ harrisdistillery.com

Islanders are justifiably proud of the award-winning **Isle of Harris Distillery** gin, which is infused with hand-harvested local sugar kelp (you'll see the distinct rippled bottles everywhere you go in the Outer Hebrides). They are also a whisky distillery, and tastings of their single malt is available during tours. The distillery has a community feel and a relaxed canteen perfect for tea and cake.

ARRIVAL AND INFORMATION
TARBERT

By ferry There are CalMac car ferries to and from Uig on Skye (Mon–Sat 1–2 daily; 1hr 45min).

By bus Tarbert is served by six different bus routes and is reachable from Stornoway and all the nearby coastal settlements.

Destinations Hushinish (schooldays Mon–Fri 2–3 daily; school holidays Tues & Fri 3 daily; 40min); Leverburgh (Mon–Sat 6–8 daily; 45min–1hr); Leverburgh via the Bays (Mon–Sat 2–4 daily; 1hr); Rhenigdale (by request ☎ 07769 159218; Mon–Sat 2–3 daily; 30min); Scalpay (Mon–Sat 4–6 daily; 20min).

Tourist information There's a welcome point at the Essence of Harris retail shop at the pier (Mon–Sat 9am–5pm; ☎ 01859 502011).

ACCOMMODATION

Coel na Mara 7 Direcleit ⓦ ceolnamara.com. With your own transport, this secluded B&B, just south of Tarbert, is a good choice. Nicely furnished throughout, with great views over East Loch Tarbert, there are four rooms, the smallest and cheapest of which doesn't have en-suite facilities. ££

Harris Hotel Scott Rd ⓦ harrishotel.com. Just a 5min walk from the harbour, this is Tarbert's longest-established and largest hotel. The twenty-three en-suite rooms are tastefully furnished, and some have sea views. The hotel is also open to the public for food – even on a Sunday – with a lunch menu that includes a generous portion of venison burger. £££

No. 5 hostel 5 Drinishader (Drinisiadar) ⓦ 5drinishader. co.uk. A converted cottage, three miles south of Tarbert, offering bed linen and laundry service along with canoes, kayaks (£18/half day) and canoes (£25/day) for rent. The hostel has twin rooms, plus one four-bed dorm; there's also a five-bed croft house that can be booked as one unit. Dorms £̲

EATING AND DRINKING

Pierhouse Restaurant Hotel Hebrides, Pier Rd ⓦ hotelhebrides.com. There aren't many options in Tarbert, but this smart hotel restaurant is just around the corner from the ferry terminal. Local produce with an emphasis on sustainability (Isle of Lewis lamb with colcannon, red wine and mint jus) and attentive service. £££

14

North Harris (Ceann a Tuath na Hearadh)

Mountainous **North Harris** was run like some minor feudal fiefdom until 2003, when the locals managed to buy the land for a knock-down £2 million. If you're coming from Stornoway on the A859, it's a spectacular introduction to Harris, its bulging, pyramidal mountains of ancient gneiss looming over the dramatic fjord-like **Loch Seaforth** (Loch Shìphoirt). From **ARDVOURLIE** (Aird a' Mhulaidh) , you weave your way over a boulder-strewn saddle between mighty **Sgaoth Aird** (1829ft) and An Cliseam or the **Clisham** (2619ft), the highest peak in the Western Isles. This bitter terrain, littered with debris left behind by retreating glaciers, offers but the barest of vegetation, with an occasional cluster of crofters' houses sitting in the shadow of a host of pointed peaks, anywhere between 1000ft and 2500ft high.

ACCOMMODATION   NORTH HARRIS

Rhenigidale (Reinigeadal) Hostel 4 miles off the A859 ⓦ gatliff.org.uk. A member of the Gatliff Hebridean Hostels Trust, this well-equipped twelve-bed hostel also has camping space for three small tents outside. It's situated in an isolated coastal community – there's a (request-only: call ☎ 07769 159218 by 8pm the day before) bus connection or else it's a magnificent six-mile (3hr) hike over the rocky landscape from Tarbert: ask at the tourist office for directions. No advance booking and no phone. Dorms £̲, camping £̲

South Harris (Ceann a Deas na Hearadh)

The mountains of **South Harris** are less dramatic than in the north, but the scenery is no less attractive. There's a choice of routes from Tarbert to the ferry port of **Leverburgh**, which connects with North Uist: the east coast, known as **The Bays** (Na Baigh), is rugged and seemingly inhospitable, while the **west coast** is endowed with some of the finest stretches of golden sand in the whole of the archipelago, buffeted by the Atlantic winds.

The west coast

The main road from Tarbert into South Harris snakes its way west for ten miles across the boulder-strewn interior to reach the coast. Once there, you get a view of the most stunning **beach**, the vast golden strand of **Luskentyre** (Tràigh Losgaintir). The road continues to ride above a chain of sweeping sands, backed by rich **machair**, that stretches for nine miles along the Atlantic coast. In good weather the scenery is particularly impressive, foaming breakers rolling along the golden sands set against the rounded peaks of the mountains to the north and the islet-studded turquoise sea to the west – and even on the dullest day the sand manages to glow beneath the waves. A short distance out to sea is the island of **Taransay** (Tarasaigh), which once held a population of nearly a hundred, but was abandoned as recently as 1974. South of Luskentyre lies **Scarista** (Sgarasta), where one of the first of the Hebridean Clearances took place in 1828, when thirty families were evicted, and their homes burnt.

Seallam!

Northton (Taobh Tuath) • Summer Mon–Fri 10am–5pm, winter Wed–Fri 10am–5pm • Charge • ⓦ hebridespeople.com

HARRIS TWEED

Far from being a picturesque cottage industry, as it's sometimes presented, the production of **Harris Tweed** is vital to the local economy, with a well-organized and unionized workforce. Traditionally the tweed was made by women, from the wool of their own sheep, to provide clothing for their families, using a 2500-year-old process. Each woman was responsible for plucking the wool by hand, washing and scouring it, dyeing it with lichen, heather flowers or ragwort, carding (smoothing and straightening the wool, often adding butter to grease it), spinning and weaving. Finally, the cloth was dipped in stale urine and 'waulked' by a group of women, who beat the cloth on a table to soften and shrink it while singing Gaelic waulking songs. Harris Tweed was originally made all over the islands and was known simply as *clò mór* (big cloth).

In the mid-nineteenth century, Catherine Murray, **Countess of Dunmore**, who owned a large part of Harris, started to sell surplus cloth to her aristocratic friends; she then sent two sisters from Strond (Srannda) to Paisley to learn the trade. On their return, they formed the genesis of the modern industry, which continues to serve as a vital source of employment, though demand (and therefore employment levels) can fluctuate wildly as fashions change. To earn the official **Harris Tweed Authority (HTA)** trademark of the Orb and the Maltese Cross – taken from Lady Dunmore's coat of arms – the fabric has to be hand-woven on the Outer Hebrides from 100 percent pure new Scottish wool, while the other parts of the manufacturing process must take place only in the local mills.

The main **mills** are actually in Carloway and Shawbost, in Lewis, where the wool is dyed, carded and spun. In the last few decades, there has been a revival of traditional tweed-making techniques, with several small producers following old methods, using indigenous plants and bushes to **dye** the cloth: yellow comes from rocket and broom; green from heather; grey and black from iris and oak; and, most popular of all, reddish brown from crotal, a flat grey lichen scraped off rocks.

There's loads of information on local history, geology, flora and fauna at **Seallam!** a purpose-built heritage centre close to the village of **Northton** (Taobh Tuath), overlooked by the round-topped hill of Chaipabhal at the westernmost tip of South Harris. As well as detailing the area's history of emigration, it's a useful centre for ancestor-hunters, and there's a good section on St Kilda (see page 491).

Leverburgh (An t-Ob)

From Northton the road veers to the southeast to trim the island's south shore, eventually reaching the sprawling settlement of **LEVERBURGH** (An t-Ob). Named after Lord Leverhulme, who planned to turn the place into the largest fishing port on the west coast of Scotland, it's the terminal for the CalMac **car ferry** service to Berneray and the Uists. The hour-long journey across the skerry-strewn Sound of Harris is one of Scotland's most tortuous ferry routes, with the ship taking part in a virtual slalom-race to avoid numerous hidden rocks – it's also a great crossing from which to spot seabirds and sea mammals.

Rodel (Roghadal)

A mile or so from Renish Point (Rubha Reanais), the southern tip of Harris, is the old port of **RODEL** (Roghadal), where a smattering of picturesque ancient stone houses lies among the hillocks. Down by the old harbour where the ferry from Skye used to arrive, you'll find the former *Rodel Hotel*, a solid, stone-built hotel originally erected in 1781 and slated for redevelopment by the owners of the Harris Distillery.

St Clement's Church (Tur Chliamainn)

Rodel • Daily April–Sept 9.30am–5.30pm, Oct–March 10am–4pm • Free • HES • ⓦ historicenvironment.scot

14

On top of one of the grassy humps, with sheep grazing in the graveyard, is **St Clement's Church** (Tur Chliamainn), burial place of the MacLeods of Harris and Dunvegan in Skye. Dating from the 1520s – in other words pre-Reformation, hence the big castellated tower (which you can climb) – the church was saved from ruination in the eighteenth century, and fully restored in 1873 by the Countess of Dunmore. The bare interior is distinguished by its wall tombs, notably that of the founder, Alasdair Crotach (also known as Alexander MacLeod), whose heavily weathered effigy lies beneath an intriguing backdrop and canopy of sculpted reliefs depicting vernacular and religious scenes – elemental representations of, among others, a stag hunt, the Holy Trinity, St Michael and the devil, and an angel weighing the souls of the dead. Look out, too, for the *sheila-na-gig* halfway up the south side of the church tower; unusually, she has a brother displaying his genitalia, below a carving of St Clement on the west face.

ARRIVAL AND INFORMATION
SOUTH HARRIS

By ferry There's a daily ferry between Leverburgh and Berneray, North Uist (1–2 daily in winter, 3–4 daily in summer; 1hr).

By bus There's a regular bus service along the west coast

between Leverburgh and Tarbert (Mon–Sat 6–8 daily; 45min–1hr), and a less frequent one via The Bays on the east coast (Mon–Sat 2–4 daily; 1hr).

ACCOMMODATION AND EATING

THE BAYS

★ **Lickisto Blackhouse Camping** Lickisto (Liceasto) ⓦ lickistoblackhousecamping.co.uk. Beautiful campsite by a rocky bay with a restored black house for the campers' use. A couple of renovated thatched byres house basic washing facilities, while the black house is the place to cook, eat and congregate with other campers by the peat fire. A Bedouin tent and yurts, sleeping two-to four people, also available. Closed Nov–Feb. Yurts $\overline{££}$; Bedouin tent $\overline{££}$; camping per pitch $\overline{£}$

Old School House Finsbay (Fionnsbhagh) ⓦ theoldschoolhousefinsbay.com. Attractive Victorian former village schoolhouse with two en-suite twin rooms. It's run by a very friendly couple who provide good home cooking and generous portions for dinner and breakfast. $\overline{££}$

Skoon 4 Geocrab ⓦ skoon.com. There aren't too many places to stop and have a bite to eat, so *Skoon Gallery and Studio* is something of a boon. There's always soup and bread, both home-made, or from time to time they do a full afternoon tea. $\overline{££}$

THE WEST COAST

Beul-na-Mara Seilebost ⓦ beulnamara.co.uk. This is a perfectly decent B&B run by an excellent host, but what makes it particularly special is the stunning location, overlooking the golden sands of Luskentyre Bay (Tràigh Losgaintir). $\overline{£££}$

Pairc an t-Srath Borve (Na Buirgh) ⓦ paircant-srath. co.uk. A working croft house, tastefully furnished with antiques and Harris tweeds that has a superb view from the dining room, particularly at sunset. Guests can recover from a hard day's hiking in the in-house sauna. Book into the dining room for dinner (open to a limited number of non-residents), where three beautifully prepared courses are served for £38. $\overline{££}$

★ **Temple Café** Northton (Taobh Tuath) ⓦ templeharris.com. Great waterside café in a unique stone and timber building resembling a hobbit house. They offer tasty deep-filled pies and quiches that come with a crunchy salad as well as a good selection of tray bakes and scones. $\overline{£}$

LEVERBURGH

★ **Am Bothan** Ferry Rd ⓦ ambothan.com. Quirky, bright-red timber-clad bunkhouse that makes for a pretty luxurious, very welcoming hostel close to the ferry. Lovely big kitchen/living room, plus laundry and drying facilities too. Closed Nov–March. Dorms $\overline{£}$

The Anchorage Ferry Terminal ⓦ anchoragerestaurant. co.uk. Lots of locally sourced seafood on offer in this lively bar/restaurant by the ferry slipway. Considerably more expensive than your average Hebridean eatery, but there are cheaper options like roast vegetable fregola. Reservations essential during summer. Closed Sun. $\overline{£££}$

North Uist (Uibhist a Tuath)

Compared to the mountainous scenery of Harris, **North Uist** – seventeen miles long and thirteen miles wide – is much flatter and for some comes as something of an anti-climax. Over half the surface area is covered by water, creating a distinctive peaty-brown lochan-studded 'drowned landscape'. Most visitors come here for the trout- and salmon-fishing and the deerstalking, all of which (along with poaching) are critical to the survival of the island's economy. Others come for the smattering of prehistoric sites, the birds, the otters, or the sheer peace of this windy isle and the solitude of North Uist's vast sandy beaches, which extend – almost without interruption – along the north and west coasts.

14

Lochmaddy (Loch nam Madadh) and around

Despite being situated on the east coast, some distance away from any beach, the ferry port of **LOCHMADDY** – 'Loch of the Dogs' – makes a good base for exploring the island. Occupying a narrow, bumpy promontory, overlooked by the brooding mountains of North Lee (Lì a Tuath) and South Lee (Lì a Deas) to the southeast, it's difficult to believe that this sleepy settlement was a large herring port as far back as the seventeenth century. While there's not much to see in Lochmaddy itself, there are several prehistoric sites in the surrounding area.

Taigh Chearsabhagh
Mon–Sat 10am–5pm (4pm in winter) • Charge • ⓦ taigh-chearsabhagh.org

The only thing to keep you in Lochmaddy is **Taigh Chearsabhagh**, a converted eighteenth-century merchant's house, now home to a community arts centre, with a simple airy café, post office, shop and excellent museum, which puts on some worthwhile exhibitions. Taigh Chearsabhagh was one of the prime movers behind the commissioning of a series of seven sculptures dotted about the Uists. Ask at the arts centre for directions to the ones in and around Lochmaddy, the most interesting of which is the **Both nam Faileas** (Hut of the Shadow), half a mile or so north of the town. The hut is an ingenious dry-stone, turf-roofed camera obscura built by sculptor Chris Drury that projects the nearby land, sea and skyscape onto its back wall – take time to allow your eyes to adjust to the light. On the way back, keep a lookout for otters, which love the tidal rapids hereabouts.

ARRIVAL AND DEPARTURE	LOCHMADDY AND AROUND
By ferry There's a daily ferry from and to Uig, Skye (1–2 daily; 1hr 40min).	**Destinations** Balivanich (Mon–Sat 6–8 daily; 30–45min); Balranald (Mon–Sat 3 daily; 50min); Eriskay (Mon–Sat 3 daily; 2hr 20min); Lochboisdale (Mon–Sat 5–6 daily; 1hr 30min).
By bus A regular bus service runs down the backbone of the Uists to Lochboisdale and Eriskay.	

ACCOMMODATION

Hamersay House Lochmaddy ⓦ hamersayhouse.co.uk. One of the region's more upmarket hotels; stylish and modern inside and out. The in-house brasserie has lots of pricey seafood options like langoustines for £20 while the vegetarian option is usually more economically palatable. **£££**

Berneray (Bhearnaraigh)

The ferry connection with Harris leaves from the very southeastern point of **Berneray**, a low-lying island immediately to the north of North Uist and connected to the latter via a causeway. Two miles by three, with a population of around 140, the island has a superb three-mile-long sandy beach on the west and north coast, backed by rabbit-free dunes and machair. The **Nurse's Cottage** (June–Aug Mon–Fri 11am–3pm; free), just past the harbour, has a small historical display on the island.

ARRIVAL AND INFORMATION	BERNERAY
By ferry The ferry from Leverburgh on Harris arrives at the very southern tip of Berneray (1–2 daily in winter, 3–4 daily	in summer; 1hr).
	By bus There's a decent bus connection with Lochmaddy

14

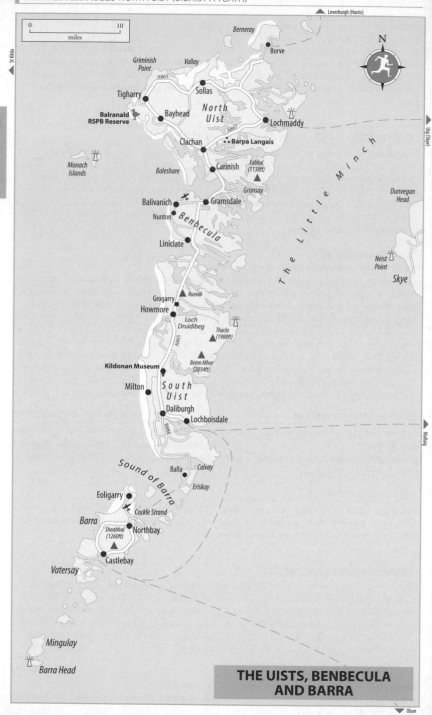

Leverburgh (Harris)

N

St Kilda

Ug (Skye)

Berneray

Borve

Griminish
Point

Vallay

A865

Tigharry

Sollas

*North
Uist*

Lochmaddy

Balranald
RSPB Reserve

Bayhead

A867

Clachan

Barpa Langais

Monach
Islands

Baleshare

Carinish

*Eabhal
(1138ft)*

The Little Minch

Dunvegan
Head

Balivanich

Grimsay

Gramsdale

Nunton

Benbecula

Neist
Point

Liniclate

Skye

Grogarry

Rueval

Howmore

Loch
Druidibeg

*Thacla
(1988ft)*

A865

Kildonan Museum

*Beinn Mhor
(2034ft)*

Milton

*South
Uist*

Daliburgh

Lochboisdale

Mallaig

B888

Sound of Barra

Balla

Calvay

Eriskay

Eoligarry

Cockle Strand

Barra

*Sheabhal
(1260ft)*

Northbay

Castlebay

Vatersay

Mingulay

Barra Head

THE UISTS, BENBECULA
AND BARRA

0   10
miles

(Mon–Sat 5–6 daily; 20min).
Tourist information The community website

ⓦ isleofberneray.com is a useful source of information.

ACCOMMODATION AND EATING

Berneray Hostel 2 miles north of the ferry port ⓦ gatliff.org.uk. The island has a wonderful Gatliff Trust hostel, which occupies a pair of thatched black houses in a lovely spot by a beach, beyond the main village. Twenty-one beds in three shared dorms along with common room and self-catering kitchen; there are also plenty of tourist pamphlets and even some binoculars if you fancy doing a

spot of whale watching. No advance booking. Dorms $\overline{£}$

Bistro on Berneray ⓦ bernerayshopandbistro. co.uk. Bright blue licensed bistro and local shop a few minutes from the north Uist causeway. The menu includes sandwiches and grilled wraps, plus fresh Berneray crab and langoustines (when available). $\underline{££}$

14

Balranald

Seven miles northwest of Clachan is the **Balranald RSPB Reserve**, best known for its **corncrakes**, once common throughout Britain but now among the country's rarest birds. They're good at hiding, so you're unlikely to see one; however, the males' loud 'craking' can be heard from May to July throughout the Uists and Barra: one or two usually make a loud noise right outside the RSPB **visitor centre**, from which you can pick up a leaflet outlining a two-hour **walk** along the headland, marked by posts. A wonderful carpet of flowers covers the machair in summer, and there are usually corn buntings and arctic terns inland, and gannets, Manx shearwaters and skuas out to sea. On a clear day you can see the unmistakeable shape of St Kilda (see page 491).

ACCOMMODATION BALRANALD

Balranald Hebridean Holidays Balranald ⓦ balranaldhebrideanholidays.com. Lovely campsite by the RSPB reserve, surrounded by fields of wildflowers and close to a sandy beach – they've also got a Corncrake pod

sleeping two as well as a washing machine and tumble drier, while the office sells basic provisions. Closed Oct–March. Per pitch $\overline{£}$; pod $\underline{££}$

Clachan (Clachan na Luib) and around

CLACHAN (Clachan na Luib), centred on the main crossroads of the A865 and the A867 from Lochmaddy, has a post office and general store. Offshore, to the southwest, lie two flat, tidal, dune and machair islands, the largest of which is **Baleshare** (Baile Sear), with its fantastic three-mile-long beach, connected by causeway to North Uist. In Gaelic the island's name means 'east village', its twin 'west village' having disappeared under the sea during a freak storm in the fifteenth or sixteenth century. The storm also isolated the **Monach Islands** (also known by their old Norse name of Heisker or Heisgeir in Gaelic), once joined to North Uist at low tide, now eight miles out to sea. The islands were inhabited until the 1930s, when the last remaining families moved to Sollas.

ACCOMMODATION CLACHAN AND AROUND

★ **Bagh Alluin** 21 Baleshare (Baile Sear) ⓦ baghalluin. co.uk. A secluded, beautifully designed modern B&B with large rooms and fantastic views. Run by a friendly Dutch artist, who can point you in the right direction to see the best of the island's wildlife. $\underline{££}$

Langass Lodge Loch Eport, just off the A867 ⓦ langasslodge.co.uk. A former hunting lodge beside a small wood (a very rare sight in the Uists). It has reasonably tasteful, spacious rooms, a bar and restaurant that serves excellent local seafood, as well as meat and veggie dishes;

£35 for a two-course meal. $\underline{£££}$

★ **Moorcroft Holidays** 17 Carinish (Cairinis) ⓦ moorcroftholidays.co.uk. An exposed but flat and very well-equipped campsite, with sea views; the bunkhouse is pretty luxurious with three twin rooms, lovely wooden floors and furnishings, a modern kitchen and a homely living/dining room. If you prefer some privacy, they also rent out pods for up to three people that have a fridge, sink and cooking facilities. Closed Nov–March. Bunkhouse per person $\overline{£}$; camping per person $\overline{£}$; pods $\underline{££}$

EATING AND DRINKING

Claddach Kirkibost Centre Claddach Kirkibost (Cladach Chireoist) ⓦ claddach-kirkibost.org. Community-centre café in a conservatory with sea views. Soups, sandwiches and simple dishes, even the occasional curry or Tex-Mex dish, mostly made from local produce. Closed Sun. **££**

Westford Inn Claddach Kirkibost (Cladach Chireoist) ⓦ westfordinn.com. North Uist's only pub – luckily it's a good one – is housed in the eighteenth-century factor's house. There's a wood-panelled bar plus several smaller rooms with real fires in bad weather, Isle of Skye Brewing Company ales on tap and pub food until 9pm. **£££**

Benbecula (Beinn na Faoghla)

Blink and you could miss the pancake-flat island of **Benbecula** (put the stress on the second syllable), sandwiched between Protestant North Uist and Catholic South Uist. Most visitors simply trundle along the main road that cuts across the middle of the island in less than five miles – not such a bad idea, since the island is scarred from the postwar presence of the Royal Artillery, who once made up half the local population. The only reason to come to **BALIVANICH** (Baile a Mhanaich), Benbecula's grim, grey capital, is if you're flying into or out of **Benbecula Airport**, or you need an ATM or a supermarket.

Museum nan Eilean

Liniclate School (Sgoil Lionacleit) • Termtime Tues–Sat 10am–1pm & 2–5pm • ☎ 01870 603692

The only secondary school (and public swimming pool) on the Uists and Benbecula is in Liniclate (Lionacleit), in the south of the island. The school is home to the small **Museum nan Eilean**, which puts on temporary exhibitions on the history of the islands, as well as occasional live music and other events.

ARRIVAL AND DEPARTURE

BENBECULA

By plane Benbecula Airport (ⓦ hial.co.uk/benbecula-airport) is just a 10–15min walk north of Balivanich. The airport serves Glasgow, Inverness and Stornoway and there's a small café inside the terminal building.

By bus Buses en route to and from South or North Uist stop outside Balivanich's airport.

Destinations Berneray (Mon–Sat 5–7 daily; 1hr 10min); Eriskay (Mon–Sat 5–7 daily; 1hr 30min); Lochboisdale (Mon–Sat 7–8 daily; 1hr); Lochmaddy (Mon–Sat 6–7 daily; 30min).

ACCOMMODATION AND EATING

Nunton House Hostel Nunton ⓦ nuntonhousehostel.com. Four small dorm rooms (each sleeping four) in the eighteenth-century former clan chief's house, where Bonnie Prince Charlie dressed up in Flora MacDonald's maid's clothing before his escape over the sea to Skye. Sadly, the prince wouldn't recognize the place these days as all the charm has been modernized out of it, save for the delightful hearth. Dorms **£**

Otter's Edge Liniclate (Lionacleit) ⓦ ottersedge-holidays.co.uk. Flat, wind-buffeted, grassy field right next to the main school (and museum) on Benbecula – facilities are quite good (including laundry and hot showers), though it's not the most romantic of spots. Closed Oct–March. Per pitch **£**

Stepping Stone Balivanich (Baile a Mhanaich) ☎ 01870 603377. A modern café-restaurant that serves cheap sandwiches and soups at lunchtime and more varied dishes in the evening, such as chicken supreme with a whisky sauce. **££**

South Uist (Uibhist a Deas)

South Uist is the largest and most varied of the southern chain of islands. The west coast boasts some of the region's finest machair and beaches – a necklace of gold and grey sand strung twenty miles from one end to the other – while the east coast features a ridge of high mountains rising to 2034ft at Beinn Mhòr. There are few places to stop for food and drink, until you get to the south of the island.

The Reformation never took a hold in South Uist (or Barra), and the island remains Roman Catholic, as is evident from the various roadside shrines. The only blot on South Uist's landscape is the Royal Artillery missile range, which dominates the northwest corner of the island. Whatever you do, however, don't make the mistake of simply driving down the main A865 road, which runs down the centre of the island.

The north

14

The northern half of the island contains the best **mountains** and **beaches**. To climb the mountains, you need a detailed 1:25,000 map, to negotiate the island's maze of lochans; to reach the beaches (or even see them), you have to get off the main road and pass through the old crofters' villages that straggle along the west coast.

One of the best places to reach the sandy shoreline is at **HOWMORE** (Tobha Mòr), a pretty little crofting settlement with a number of restored houses, many still thatched, including one distinctively roofed in brown heather. It's an easy walk from the village church across the flower-strewn machair to the gorgeous beach. In among the crofts are the shattered, lichen-encrusted remains of no fewer than four medieval churches and chapels, and a burial ground now harbouring just a few scattered graves. The sixteenth-century **Clanranald Stone**, carved with the arms of the clan who ruled over South Uist from 1370 until 1839, used to lie here, but is now displayed in the nearby Kildonan Museum (see below).

ACCOMMODATION
THE NORTH

Howmore (Tobha Mòr) hostel Howmore (Tobha Mòr) ⓦ gatliff.org.uk. Simple Gatliff Trust hostel occupying a lovely cosy thatched croft house near the village church, and just a short walk from the beach. Fully equipped kitchen. No advance bookings and bring provisions, as the nearest shop is seven miles away. Dorms **£**

Kinloch Grogarry (Groigearraidh) ⓦ kinlochuist.com. A fine, modern B&B with three rooms sheltered by a little patch of woodland and overlooking freshwater Loch Druidibeg – run by a very keen angler, who will do three-course evening meals for £27.50 or packed lunches for £12. Two-night minimum stay. **££**

Orasay Inn Lochcarnan (Loch a' Charnain) ⓦ orasayinn. co.uk. A modern purpose-built hotel and restaurant (evening meals only) off the main road with well-kept rooms, some of which have a private decked area. **££**

Lochboisdale (Loch Baghasdail) and around

LOCHBOISDALE occupies a narrow, bumpy promontory on the east coast, but, despite being South Uist's chief settlement and ferry port, has only very limited facilities (there's a bank here, but the nearest supermarket is three miles west in Dalabrog).

Kildonan Museum (Taigh-tasgaidh Chill Donnain)
5 miles south of Howmore • April–Oct daily 10am–5pm • Charge • ⓦ kildonanmuseum.co.uk

Reasonably large museum featuring mock-ups of Hebridean kitchens through the ages, two lovely box beds and an impressive selection of old photos, accompanied by an unsentimental yet poetic text on crofting life in the last two centuries. Pride of place goes to the sixteenth-century **Clanranald Stone**, carved with the arms of the clan who ruled over South Uist from 1370 to 1839. The museum café serves sandwiches and home-made cakes and has a choice of historical videos for those really wet and windy days.

ARRIVAL AND INFORMATION
LOCHBOISDALE AND AROUND

By ferry One ferry connects Mallaig to Lochboisdale (winter one on Tues & Sat; summer one daily; 3hr 30min).
By bus There's a regular bus service along the spine road (as they call it) to North Uist (Mon–Sat only).

Destinations Balivanich (Mon–Sat 2–5 daily; 1hr); Berneray (Mon–Sat 1 daily; 2hr 50min); Eriskay (Mon–Sat

4–6 daily; 40min); Lochmaddy (Mon–Sat 1–2 daily; 1hr 30min).

Tourist office Pier Rd (Easter–Oct Mon–Sat 9am–5pm; also open for an hour to meet the ferry; ☎ 01878 700286).

ACCOMMODATION AND EATING

Heron Point Lochboisdale ⊛ heronpoint.co.uk. Homely B&B just a mile up the road from the ferry terminal with four en-suite bedrooms. Efficiently run by a very friendly host who cooks up a wonderful breakfast of smoked salmon and poached eggs. ££

Kilbride Café & Campsite West Kilbride ☎ 07751 251522, ⊛ kilbride-campsite.business.site. Tea, coffee, juices and milkshakes, along with home-baking and a basic hot menu of tasty burgers, fish and chips and all-day-breakfasts. The café benefits from the same beautiful views of the Sound of Barra as the adjacent campsite, which has thirty hard pitches and loads of green space for tents. Camping £

Lochboisdale Hotel Lochboisdale ⊛ lochboisdale.com. The town's long-established hotel is a convenient place to shelter if you're waiting for a ferry, and it does fish and chips and other typical bar meals. If you are staying over, the accommodation is a bit dated but the rooms are spacious, comfortable and have great views over the harbour. £££

Polochar Inn Polochar (Poll a' Charra) ⊛ polocharinn. com. One of the best places to hole up in, right on the south coast overlooking the Sound of Barra, it has its own sandy beach close by; all the rooms have sea views, and on the ground floor there is a good pub with an attached restaurant which dishes up the likes of creamy pesto gnocchi or scallops and black pudding. ££

Eriskay (Eiriosgaigh)

Famous for its patterned jerseys and a peculiar breed of pony, originally used for carrying peat and seaweed, barren, hilly **Eriskay** has been connected by a causeway to the south of South Uist since 2001. The pretty island, which measures just over two miles by one, and shelters a small fishing community of about 150, makes an easy day-trip from South Uist.

For a small island, Eriskay has had more than its fair share of historical headlines. The island's main beach on the west coast, Coilleag a Phrionnsa (Prince's Cockle Strand), was where **Bonnie Prince Charlie** landed on Scottish soil on 23 July 1745 – the sea bindweed that grows here to this day is said to have sprung from the seeds Charles brought with him from France. The prince, as yet unaccustomed to hardship, spent his first night in a local black house and ate a couple of flounders, though he apparently couldn't take the peat smoke and chose to sleep sitting up rather than endure the damp bed.

ARRIVAL AND DEPARTURE

ERISKAY

By ferry CalMac run a small car ferry between Eriskay and Ardmhor on Barra (5 daily except Sun in winter when there's 2; 40min).

By bus There's a regular bus service between Eriskay and Lochboisdale (Mon–Sat 4–6 daily; 40min).

ACCOMMODATION AND EATING

Am Politician Rubha Ban ☎ 01878 720246. The island's purpose-built pub named after the SS *Politician* (see below) is unlikely to win any design awards around. However, it offers great views out to sea from its conservatory where

---

SS POLITICIAN

Eriskay's greatest claim to fame came in 1941 when the **SS Politician**, or 'Polly' as she's fondly known, sank on her way from Liverpool to Jamaica, along with her cargo of bicycle parts, £3 million in Jamaican currency and 264,000 bottles of whisky, inspiring *Whisky Galore*, Compton MacKenzie's book, and the Ealing comedy (filmed on Barra in 1948 and released as *Tight Little Island* in the US). The real story was somewhat less romantic, especially for the 36 islanders who were charged with illegal possession by the Customs and Excise officers. Nineteen of the islanders were found guilty and imprisoned in Inverness. The ship's stern used to be seen at low tide northwest of Calvay Island in the Sound of Eriskay until the sea finally swallowed it up. One of the original bottles (and other memorabilia) can be viewed at *Am Politician* (see above).

you can dine on scallops with black pudding as well as the usual pub grub options. ££
Oir na Mara ☎01878 720216. This plain, modern bungalow B&B is kept by a true perfectionist; the rooms are spotlessly clean and the bedding is high quality. Tea and home-made cakes are offered to guests on arrival, and Eriskay's pub is conveniently nearby for mealtimes. ££

Barra (Barraigh)

14

Four miles wide and eight miles long, **Barra** is the Western Isles in miniature: sandy beaches backed by machair, mountains of Lewisian gneiss – the oldest rock in Britain – prehistoric ruins, Gaelic culture and a laidback, welcoming population of around 1200. A kind of feudal island state, it was ruled over for centuries, with relative benevolence, by the MacNeils. Unfortunately, the family sold the island in 1838 to Colonel Gordon of Cluny, who had also bought Benbecula, South Uist and Eriskay. The colonel deemed the starving crofters 'redundant' and offered to turn Barra into a state penal colony. The government declined, so the colonel called in the police and proceeded with some of the cruellest forced Clearances in the Hebrides. In 1937, the 45th chief of the MacNeil clan bought back most of the island, and in 2003 the estate was gifted to the Scottish government.

Castlebay (Bàgh a Chaisteil)

The only settlement of any size is **CASTLEBAY** (Bàgh a Chaisteil), which curves around the barren rocky hills of a wide bay on the south side of the island. It's difficult to imagine, but Castlebay was a herring port of some significance back in the nineteenth century, with hundreds of boats in the harbour and curing and packing factories ashore. Barra's religious allegiance is immediately announced by the large Catholic church, Our Lady, Star of the Sea, which overlooks the bay; to underline the point, there's a Madonna and Child on the slopes of **Sheabhal** (Heaval; 1260ft), the largest peak on Barra and a fairly short hike from Castlebay – although there's no marked path and the ground is steep and can be boggy.

Kisimul Castle

April–Sept daily 9.30am–5.30pm • Charge • HES • ⓦ historicenvironment.scot • Access by ferry from Castle Slip Landing, Castlebay (call for sailing times), weather permitting

As its name suggests, Castlebay has a castle in its bay, the picturesque medieval islet-fortress of Caisteal Chiosmuil, or **Kisimul Castle**, ancestral home of the MacNeil clan. The castle burnt down in the eighteenth century, but when the 45th MacNeil chief – conveniently enough, a wealthy American and trained architect – bought the island back in 1937, he set about restoring the castle. There's nothing much to see inside, but the whole experience is fun – head down to the slipway at the bottom of Main Street, where the ferryman will take you over.

Dualchas

The Square • April–Sept Mon, Tues & Wed 10am–1pm • Charge • ☎01871 810413

The Barra Heritage Centre, known as **Dualchas** (Gaelic for Heritage), is on the road that leads west out of town. It's an unpretentious little museum, housing the odd treasure like the monstrance from St Barr's Church in Northbay. There are lots of old newspapers, photo archives and local memoirs to trawl through; the museum also has a handy **café** serving soup, toasties and cakes.

The north

If you head to the north end of the island from Castlebay, you have a choice of taking the west- or the east-coast road. The west-coast road takes you past the island's finest

14

sandy beaches, particularly those at **Halaman Bay** and near the village of Allasdale (Allathasdal). The east-coast road wends its way in and out of various rocky bays, one of which, **Northbay** (Bàgh a Tuath), shelters a small fishing fleet and a little island sporting a statue of St Barr, better known as Finbarr, the island's Irish patron saint.

At the north end of the island, Barra is squeezed between two sandy bays: the dune-backed white sand west side takes the full force of the Atlantic breakers and is a wonderful hidden spot for a stroll, while the east side boasts the crunchy shell sands of Tràigh Mhòr, better known as **Cockle Strand**. The beach is also used as the island's **airport**, with planes landing and taking off according to the tides, since at high tide the beach (and therefore the runway) is covered in water. As its name suggests, the strand is also famous for its cockles and cockleshells, the latter being used to make harling (the rendering used on most Scottish houses).

To the north of the airport is the scattered settlement of **EOLIGARRY** (Eòlaigearraidh), which boasts several sheltered sandy bays. Here, too, is **St Barr's Church** (Cille-Bharra), burial ground of the MacNeils (and the author Compton MacKenzie). The ground lies beside the ruins of a medieval church and two chapels, one of which has been reroofed to provide shelter for several carved medieval gravestones and a replica of an eleventh-century rune-inscribed cross, the original of which is in the National Museum of Scotland in Edinburgh.

ARRIVAL AND GETTING AROUND   BARRA

By plane Barra Airport (ⓦ hial.co.uk) has direct flights from and to Glasgow, timetables depend on tide times.

By ferry The main ferry terminal on Barra is in Castlebay where the ferry from Oban arrives: from Eriskay, you arrive at Ardmhor, an uninhabited spot on the northeast of the island.

Destinations Coll (Wed; 4hr); Eriskay (5 daily, 2 in winter on Sun; 40min); Oban (summer daily, winter Wed & Fri–Mon; 5hr); Tiree (Wed; 2hr 45min).

By bus There's a fairly decent bus service out of Castlebay,

which does the rounds of the island daily except Sunday. Book in advance for the Vatersay bus.

Destinations Airport (Mon–Sat 4–7 daily; 30min); Eriskay ferry (Mon–Sat 2–5 daily to coincide with ferry timetable; 25min); Eoligarry (Mon–Sat 3–6 daily; 35min); Vatersay (Mon–Sat 2–3 daily; 20min).

By car or bike Barra Car Hire (ⓣ 01871 890313) will deliver cars to either ferry terminal or the airport, and Barra Bike Hire (ⓦ barrabikehire.co.uk) will do the same with bikes (from £18/day).

ACCOMMODATION

Castlebay Hotel Castlebay ⓦ castlebayhotel.co.uk. The *Castlebay* is the more welcoming of the town's two hotels – a grey Victorian pile, with spectacular views over the bay from the restaurant and some of the rooms. The six rooms vary in price considerably but are united by their desperate need of modernisation. **££**

★ **Dunard Hostel** Castlebay ⓦ dunardhostel.co.uk. A relaxed, family-run place just west of the ferry terminal in Castlebay, that has twins, dorm beds and a family room. There's a well-equipped kitchen, a long dining table and a cosy living room with resident cats snoozing by the fire. They've also got a couple of garden camping pods, a double and a twin. Dorms **£**; twins **££**; pods **££**

Heathbank Hotel Northbay (Bagh a Tuath) ⓦ barrahotel.co.uk. Converted mission church, now home to a comfortable six-room hotel and unpretentious local watering hole and upmarket restaurant. **£££**

Tigh-na-Mara Castlebay ⓦ tighnamara-barra.co.uk.

For value and location – just a few minutes from the pier in Castlebay – you can't beat this simple Victorian guesthouse overlooking the sea, which also has three single rooms. Closed Nov–March. **££**

CAMPING

Croft 183 Balnabodach (Buaile nam Bodach) ⓦ croft183.com. A well-equipped campsite on the rocky eastern side of the island, with kitchen and laundry facilities, plus a hostel building with twin-bed hostel rooms, private doubles and family rooms. Dorms **£**; doubles **£**; family room **££**; camping per pitch **£**

★ **Scurrival campsite** 3 Eoligarry (Eòlaigearraidh) ⓣ 01871 890292. This is a lovely, simple site with showers and toilet facilities, overlooking the sea and close to the wide sandy beach of Scurrival (Tràigh Sgurabhal) in the north of the island. Closed Nov–March. Dorms **£**

EATING AND DRINKING

Barra Airport Café Tràigh Mhòr ⓦ facebook.com/ | barraairportcafe/. Wonderful little café with views of the planes landing and taking off from the beach airport. Coffee, cake and specials including soup of the day and falafel wrap. Open for fish suppers on Friday and Saturday nights in summer (5–7pm).

★ **Café Kisimul Castlebay** ⓦ cafekisimul.co.uk. As well as offering Italian comfort food and great music, the *Kisimul* also cooks up the best curry in northwest Scotland – try the unique scallop pakora starter. **££**

ENTERTAINMENT AND SPORT

Films are occasionally shown on Saturday evenings at the **local school** – look out for the posters – where there is also a **swimming pool** (Tues–Sun), **library** and **sports centre**, all of which are open to the general public. A mobile 'screen machine' also rolls into Castlebay from time to time (ⓦ screenmachine.co.uk).

14

Orkney

ST MAGNUS CATHEDRAL, KIRKWALL

Orkney

Orkney is a captivating and fiercely independent archipelago of seventy or so mostly low-lying islands, with a population of around twenty-two thousand. The locals tend to refer to themselves as Orcadians, regarding Scotland as a separate entity, and proudly flying their own flag. For an Orcadian, 'the Mainland' invariably means the largest island in Orkney rather than the rest of Scotland, and throughout their distinctive history the islands have been linked to lands much further afield, principally Scandinavia.

Orkney has excellent coastal walking, abundant birdlife and beautiful white-sand beaches. It has two chief settlements: **Stromness**, an attractive old fishing town on the far southwestern shore, and the capital, **Kirkwall**, at the dividing point between East and West Mainland. Relatively heavily populated and farmed throughout, the Mainland is joined by causeways to a string of southern islands, the largest of which is **South Ronaldsay**. The island of **Hoy**, the second largest in the archipelago, south of Mainland, presents a superbly dramatic landscape, with some of the highest sea cliffs in the country. Hoy, however, is atypical: Orkney's smaller, much quieter **northern islands** are low-lying, fertile outcrops of rock and sand, scattered across the ocean.

ARRIVAL AND DEPARTURE ORKNEY

By plane Loganair (ⓦ loganair.co.uk) operates direct flights to Inverness, Aberdeen, Edinburgh, Glasgow and Sumburgh in Shetland. Be warned: weather conditions are notoriously changeable, making flights prone to delay and even cancellation.

By ferry NorthLink Ferries run regular passenger and vehicle ferry services daily from Scrabster (with a shuttle bus from Thurso) to Stromness and less frequently from Aberdeen and Lerwick (in Shetland) to Kirkwall; Pentland Ferries run daily car ferries from Gills Bay (near John O'Groats) to St Margaret's Hope; and John O'Groats Ferries run a small passenger ferry to Burwick. The timetables in the text are summer frequencies – check online for the latest sailing schedule and always book ahead.

GETTING AROUND AND TOURS

By plane Loganair (ⓦ loganair.co.uk) run flights from Kirkwall to most of the outer isles, using an eight-seater plane, with discounted fares to North Ronaldsay and Papa Westray and between the islands if you stay over.

By ferry Getting to the other islands by ferry from the Mainland isn't difficult but travel between individual islands isn't straightforward. Contact Orkney Ferries (ⓦ orkneyferries.co.uk) about additional Sunday sailings in summer, which often make useful inter-island connections. Tickets are expensive. Book ahead if you're taking a vehicle.

By bus The bus service on Orkney Mainland is pretty good overall. Except in Stromness and Kirkwall, there are no scheduled bus stops so just stand at a safe, visible spot and flag the bus down. On the smaller islands, a minibus usually meets the ferry and will take you to your destination. Check ⓦ orkney.gov.uk for bus timetables.

By bike Cycling is an option if the weather holds, since there are few steep hills and distances are modest, though the wind can make it hard going. For Orkney Cycle Hire in Stromness, see page 511; for Cycle Orkney in Kirkwall, see page 518.

Stromness

STROMNESS is an enchanting port at which to arrive by boat, its picturesque waterfront a procession of tiny sandstone jetties and slate roofs nestling below the green hill of Brinkies Brae. It makes a great introduction to Orkney and is an excellent base too. Its natural sheltered harbour (known as Hamnavoe) has been used since Viking times, but the town itself only really took off in the eighteenth century when the Hudson's Bay Company made Stromness its main base from which to make the journey across the

15

SKARA BRAE

Highlights

❶ Maeshowe Orkney's – and Europe's – finest Neolithic chambered tomb, built nearly 5,000 years ago. See page 513

❷ Skara Brae Older than Stonehenge or the Great Pyramids, Skara Brae is a mesmerizing Neolithic settlement, crammed with domestic detail. See page 514

❸ St Magnus Cathedral, Kirkwall Beautiful red sandstone Romanesque cathedral in miniature, built by the Vikings in the twelfth century. See page 516

❹ Scapa Flow Visitor Centre, Hoy Learn about the wartime history of Orkney's great natural harbour – once Britain's chief naval base and site of the scuttling of the German High Seas Fleet in 1919. See page 519

❺ Old Man of Hoy One of Orkney's most iconic geographical features, this 450ft-high stack is popular with climbers from all over the world; be warned though, it's not an easy ascent. See page 522

❻ Westray Thriving Orkney island with seabird colonies, sandy beaches, a sixteenth-century ruined castle and a figurine that's one of the earliest representations of the human form found in the UK. See page 526

❼ North Ronaldsay Orkney's northernmost island features a world-renowned bird observatory, seaweed-eating sheep and Britain's tallest land-based lighthouse. See page 532

HIGHLIGHTS ARE MARKED ON THE MAP ON PAGE 510

North Atlantic. Today, Stromness remains a key fishing port and ferry terminal and is the focus of the popular four-day **Orkney Folk Festival**, held in May.

Unlike Kirkwall, the old town of Stromness still hugs the shoreline, its one and only street, a narrow winding affair still paved with great flagstones and fed by a tight network of alleyways or closes. The central section, which begins at the imposing sandstone *Stromness Hotel*, is known as **Victoria Street**, though in fact it takes on several other names as it threads its way southwards. On the east side of the street the houses are gable-end-on to the waterfront, and originally each one would have had its own pier, from which merchants would trade with passing ships.

ORKNEY

0   10
miles

N

Mull Head
Papa Westray
North Ronaldsay **7**
Noup Head
Pierowall
Westray **6**
Rapness
Start Point
Sanday
Kettletoft
Rousay
Eday
Egilsay
Brough Head
Birsay
Evie
Wyre
Whitehall
Tingwall
Stronsay
Skara Brae **2**
Dounby
Mainland
Lamb Head
Balfour
Shapinsay
Auskerry
Wide Firth
1
Finstown
Maeshowe
Kirkwall **3**
Stromness
Mull Head
Graemsay
Hoy
Houton
Orphir
Copinsay
St Mary's
Scapa Flow
Churchill Barriers
5
Ward Hill (1577ft)
Old Man of Hoy
Rackwick
Hoy
Lyness
Flotta
Burray
St Margaret's Hope
4
South Ronaldsay
Longhope
Swona
Burwick
Tomb of the Eagles
Brough Ness
Pentland Firth
Dunnet Head
Stroma
Pentland Skerries
Thurso
Gill's Bay
John O'Groats
Duncansby Head
Wick
Aberdeen

Lerwick
Scrabster

HIGHLIGHTS

1. Maeshowe
2. Skara Brae
3. St Magnus Cathedral, Kirkwall
4. Scapa Flow Visitor Centre, Hoy
5. Old Man of Hoy
6. Westray
7. North Ronaldsay

ORKNEY FESTIVALS

The **Orkney Folk Festival** (ⓦ orkneyfolkfestival.com) is a four-day music festival, held at the end of May and centred on Stromness but with gigs all over the Mainland – it's very popular with locals and visitors alike, so expect tickets to sell out fast. The biggest cultural event, by far, however, is the week-long **St Magnus Festival** (ⓦ stmagnusfestival.com), a superb arts festival held during June, with events held all over the Mainland and the outer islands. July is peppered with several island regattas and agricultural shows, culminating in the agricultural **County Show** held in Kirkwall on the second Saturday of August.

To find out **what's on** (and the weather forecast), tune in at 7.30am to *Around Orkney* (Mon–Fri) on Radio Orkney (93.7FM), and buy yourself a copy of *The Orcadian*, which comes out on Thursdays (ⓦ orcadian.co.uk).

Pier Arts Centre

Victoria St • Tues–Sat 10.30am–5pm • Free • ⓦ pierartscentre.com

A warehouse on one of the old jetties on Victoria Street now forms half of the **Pier Arts Centre**; the other half is a modern glass-and-steel structure framing views of the harbour. The gallery has a remarkable permanent collection of twentieth-century British art, including work by Scottish sculptor Eduardo Paolozzi, and, most notably, by members of the Cornish group such as Barbara Hepworth, Ben Nicholson, Terry Frost, Patrick Heron and the self-taught Alfred Wallis. The collection is constantly being added to, with contemporary works by the likes of Anish Kapoor enhancing the original bequest.

15

Stromness Museum

52 Alfred St • April–Sept daily 11am–5pm; Oct–March Mon–Sat 11am–1pm & 1.45pm–3.30pm • Charge • ⓦ stromnessmuseum.co.uk

At the junction of Alfred Street and South End stands the **Stromness Museum**, built in 1858. Highlights include an early inflatable boat like the one used by John Rae, the Stromness-born Arctic explorer, and some barnacle-encrusted crockery from the German High Seas Fleet that was sunk in Scapa Flow in 1919 (see page 519).

ARRIVAL AND DEPARTURE   STROMNESS

By ferry Car ferries operated by NorthLink (ⓦ northlinkferries.co.uk) arrive in the centre of Stromness from Scrabster (2–3 daily; 1hr 30min), which is connected to nearby Thurso by shuttle bus. The tiny passenger ferry to Moaness Pier on Hoy (via Graemsay), run by Orkney Ferries (ⓦ orkneyferries.co.uk), departs from the old harbour in Stromness (Mon–Fri 4–5 daily, Sat & Sun 2 daily; 25min).

By bus Buses depart from Stromness Ferry Terminal. Check ⓦ stagecoachbus.com for timetables.
Destinations Houton (Mon–Fri 2 daily; 15min); Kirkwall (Mon–Sat 2 hourly, Sun every 2hr; 30min); Skara Brae (Mon, Thurs & Sat 1 daily; 20min, also hop-on, hop-off bus 1 daily April–Oct); St Margaret's Hope (Mon–Sat hourly; 1hr 5min).

INFORMATION AND GETTING AROUND

Tourist information Local information can be found in various venues throughout the town including the Pier Arts Centre and Stromness Museum, ⓦ orkney.com).

By bike Orkney Cycle Hire, 54 Dundas St (ⓦ orkneycyclehire. co.uk), rent bikes from £10 a day.

ACCOMMODATION   SEE MAP PAGE 512

Brinkies Guest House Innertown ☎ 01856 851881. A substantial double-bay fronted Victorian guesthouse located a 10min walk up from the town. Rooms enjoy fantastic views and the residents' lounge has loads of reading matter. £̲£̲
Brown's 47 Victoria St ⓦ brownsorkney.co.uk. A

family-run place overseen by the very friendly Mrs Brown and situated right in the centre of town. There are twins, doubles, triples and quads as well as regular bunk beds in very small dorms. Single £̲; dorms £̲; doubles £̲£̲
Burnside Farm 1 mile north of Stromness on A965 ⓦ burnside-farm.com. A cracking B&B run by a local

couple on a working farm. The views are great, and the furnishings and facilities are truly top-notch: en-suite wet-rooms, plus bere bannocks for breakfast. **££**

Hamnavoe Hostel 10a North End Rd ⓦhamnavoehostel.co.uk. A good 10min walk from the ferry terminal and no beauty from the outside, but inside it's all spotlessly clean, welcoming and well equipped. There's a choice of small dorms or singles, some en suite, some not.

Dorms and singles **£**

Point of Ness Campsite A mile south of the ferry terminal at Point of Ness ☎01856 873535. Busy council-run campsite in a superb (though extremely exposed) setting, with great views over to Hoy; facilities include a TV lounge and a washing machine. Per pitch for large tent/caravan with electricity **£**

EATING

SEE MAP PAGE 512

Hamnavoe Restaurant 35 Graham Place ☎01856 850606. Friendly little front-room restaurant, with a real fire burning. The menu concentrates on nicely presented local produce – try the tusk or hake straight off the boats. Booking is essential. **£££**

Julia's Café and Bistro 20 Ferry Rd ⓦjuliascafe.co.uk. Daytime café right opposite the ferry terminal, with a sunny conservatory and tables outside if the weather's good enough. It's comfort food for the most part, including a decent home-made fish pie. **££**

DRINKING

SEE MAP PAGE 512

Ferry Inn 10 John St ⓦferryinn.com. Situated opposite the ferry terminal, this is the most popular and welcoming

pub in town, serving up classic pub grub as well as local Orkney beer on draught.
scallops, Orkney steak and ale pie, washed down with

West Mainland

The great bulk of the **West Mainland** – west of Kirkwall, that is – is fertile
farmland, fenced off into a patchwork of fields used either to produce crops or
for cattle-grazing. Fringed by a spectacular western coastline, West Mainland is
littered with some of the island's most impressive prehistoric sites, such as the
village of **Skara Brae**, the standing **Stones of Stenness**, the chambered tomb of
Maeshowe and the **Broch of Gurness**, as well as one of Orkney's best-preserved
medieval castles at **Birsay**. Despite the intensive farming, some areas are too barren
to cultivate, and the high ground and wild coastline include several interesting
wildlife reserves.

15

Stenness

The parish of **Stenness**, northeast of Stromness along the main road to Kirkwall, slopes
down from Ward Hill (881ft) to the lochs of Stenness and Harray: the first is tidal, the
second is a freshwater trout loch. The two lochs are joined by a short causeway that
may well have been a narrow isthmus around 3000 BC, when it stood at the heart
of Orkney's most important Neolithic ceremonial complex, centred on the burial
chamber of **Maeshowe**.

Stones of Stenness

Guided tours June–Aug Mon, Wed & Fri 10am; Sept & May Wed 10am • Free • HES • Ⓦ historicenvironment.scot

The most visible part of the complex between lochs Stenness and Harray is the **Stones
of Stenness**, originally a circle of twelve rock slabs, now just four, the tallest of which is
a real monster at over 16ft, and remarkably slender. A broken tabletop lies within the
circle, surrounded by a much-diminished henge (a circular bank of earth and a ditch)
with a couple of entrances.

Ring of Brodgar

Guided tours June–Aug daily 1pm; Sept & May Thurs 1pm • Free • HES • Ⓦ historicenvironment.scot

Less than a mile to the northwest of the Stones of Stenness, past the huge **Watch Stone**
which stands beside the road at over 18ft in height, you reach another stone circle, the
Ring of Brodgar, a much wider circle dramatically sited on raised ground. Here there
were originally sixty stones, 27 of which now stand, all wonderfully misshapen, about
8–10ft high; of the henge, only the ditch survives.

Maeshowe

Guided tours daily April–Sept 10am–5pm; Oct–March 10am–4pm • Charge; book in advance • HES • Ⓦ historicenvironment.scot • If
arriving in your own vehicle, you'll need to book a car park space several days in advance

Maeshowe, one of Europe's most impressive Neolithic burial chambers, lies less than
a mile northeast of the Stones of Stenness. Dating from 3000 BC, its excellent state
of preservation is partly due to its construction from massive slabs of sandstone
weighing up to thirty tons. The tours (lasting in total around 55 minutes) start on
the hour at Stenness visitor centre, where a shuttle bus takes visitors to the tomb
and back.

You enter the central chamber down a low, long passage, one wall of which is
comprised of a single immense stone. The entrance is narrow and not suitable for those
who suffer from claustrophobia. Inside, you can stand upright and admire the superb
masonry of the lofty corbelled roof. Remarkably, the tomb is aligned so that the rays of

the winter solstice sun hit the top of the Barnhouse Stone, half a mile away, and reach right down the passage of Maeshowe to the ledge of one of the three cells in the walls of the tomb. When Maeshowe was opened in 1861, it was virtually empty, thanks to the work of generations of grave-robbers, who had left behind only a handful of human bones. The Vikings, however, left copious runic graffiti, cut into the walls of the main chamber, including phrases such as 'many a beautiful woman has stooped in here, however pompous she might be' and the more prosaic 'Thor and I bedded Helga'.

ARRIVAL AND DEPARTURE
STENNESS

By bus Buses from Stromness to Kirkwall (Mon–Sat hourly, Sun every 2hr; 15min) to Stenness Visitor Centre, with a shuttle bus to Maeshowe. The hop-on, hop-off open-top bus runs daily April–Oct (Stromness to Kirkwall) and visits all the sites.

ACCOMMODATION AND EATING

Merkister Hotel Harray Loch ⓦ merkister.com. Substantial hotel on the northeastern shore of the Loch of Harray, popular with the locals and visiting anglers. The bar's lively and does reliable, locally sourced dishes such as fish and chips or steak, but there's a restaurant too, offering a wider range of local seafood. **££**

Mill of Eyrland 4 miles southwest of Maeshowe on A964 to Orphir ⓦ millofeyrland.co.uk. Carefully converted former mill by a little stream; it's filled to the brim with wonderful antiques and old machinery, as well as all mod cons; and enormous breakfasts at the communal dining table. **££**

Standing Stones Hotel ⓦ thestandingstones.co.uk. This welcoming hotel and hostelry with great views over Stenness Loch has seventeen en-suite rooms. Food is served in a comfortable lounge and features dishes highlighting Orkney produce such as steak and Orkney ale pie. **£££**

Skara Brae

Daily April–Sept 10am–5pm; Oct–March 10am–4pm • Charge • HES • ⓦ historicenvironment.scot

The extensive remains of a small Neolithic fishing and farming village, dating from 3000 BC, were discovered at **Skara Brae** in 1850, after a fierce storm ripped off the dunes covering them. The village is amazingly well preserved, its houses huddled together and connected by narrow passages, which would originally have been covered over with turf. The houses themselves comprise a single, spacious living room, filled with domestic detail, including dressers, fireplaces, built-in cupboards, beds and boxes, all ingeniously constructed from slabs of stone.

The **visitor centre** houses an excellent **café/restaurant** and an introductory **exhibition**, with a few replica finds, and some hands-on stuff for kids. Beyond is a full-scale replica of House 7 (the best-preserved house), complete with a fake wood and skin roof. It's all a tad neat and tidy, with fetching uplighting – rather than dark, smoky and smelly – but it gives you the general idea, and makes up for the fact that, at the site itself, you can only look down on the houses from the outer walls.

In the summer months, your ticket to Skara Brae also covers entry to nearby **Skaill House**, (April–Oct) built for Bishop George Graham in the 1620s, but much extended since. The house's prize possession is Captain Cook's dinner service from the *Resolution*; it was delivered after Cook's death when the *Resolution* and the *Discovery* sailed into Stromness in 1780.

ARRIVAL AND DEPARTURE
SKARA BRAE

By bus Services are limited (Mon, Thurs & Sat only; also hop-on hop-off bus 1 daily April–Oct). Alternatively, since it's only 7 miles from Stromness, you could just rent a bike (see page 511).

EATING AND DRINKING

★ **Orkney Brewery** Quoyloo ⓦ orkneybrewery. co.uk. The old schoolhouse in Quoyloo has been tastefully converted into a state-of-the-art microbrewery, with tasting tours (£7.50) and also a great café where local produce is very much to the fore – try the home-made bere bannock burgers. **£**

Birsay and around

Occupying the northwest corner of the Mainland, the parish of **BIRSAY** was the centre of Norse power in Orkney for several centuries before Kirkwall got its cathedral.

Earl's Palace

Birsay is dominated by the imposing sixteenth-century sandstone ruins of the **Earl's Palace**, built by Robert Stewart, Earl of Orkney, using the forced labour of the islanders, who weren't even given food and drink for their work. By all accounts, it was a 'sumptuous and stately dwelling', built in four wings around a central courtyard, its upper rooms decorated with painted ceilings and rich furnishings; surrounding the palace were flower and herb gardens, a bowling green and archery butts. The palace lasted barely a century before falling into rack and ruin; the crumbling walls and turrets retain much of their grandeur, although inside there is little remaining domestic detail.

Brough of Birsay

Accessible 2hr either side of low tide • Mid-June to Sept daily 9.30am–5.30pm; tide times available at Kirkwall tourist offices and on Radio Orkney (93.7FM; Mon–Fri 7.30–8am) • Charge • HES • ⓦ historicenvironment.scot

Over half a mile northwest of Birsay village is the **Brough of Birsay**, a substantial Pictish settlement on a small tidal island. Here there's a small ticket office, where you can see a few artefacts gathered from the site, including an antler pin and a game made from whalebone. The focus of the village was, and still is, the sandstone-built twelfth-century **St Peter's Church** (mid-June–Sept daily 9.30am–5.30pm; charge; HES), which is thought to have stood at the centre of a monastic complex; the foundations of a courtyard and outer buildings can be made out to the west. Close by is a large complex of Viking-era buildings, including several houses, a sauna and some sophisticated stone drains.

ARRIVAL AND DEPARTURE   BIRSAY AND AROUND

By bus Bus services from Kirkwall (Mon–Sat 2 daily; 30–40min) will get you to Birsay.

ACCOMMODATION AND EATING

Barony Hotel 1 mile east of Birsay ⓦ baronyhotel.com. Stark hotel overlooking the Loch of Boardhouse. The hotel bar is the only watering hole around – decor in the rooms is a bit dated, but it's clean and comfy enough and the trout from the loch is worth sampling. ££

Birsay Bay Tearoom 500yd south of the Earl's Palace ⓦ birsaybaytearoom.co.uk. For light snacks and home-made cake, head for the modern tearoom, at the southern edge of the village, which boasts superb views of the Brough (binoculars provided). £

Birsay Outdoor Centre 1 mile southeast of Birsay at junction of A967 and B9056 ⓦ orkney.gov.uk. A large council-run hostel with a fully equipped kitchen and a drying room; there's also a campsite alongside. Dorms £; per pitch for large tent/caravan with electricity £

Broch of Gurness

Evie • April–Sept daily 9.30am–5.30pm • Charge • HES • ⓦ historicenvironment.scot

The best-preserved broch on Orkney is the **Broch of Gurness**, on the north coast, still surrounded by a remarkable complex of later buildings. As at Birsay, the sea has eaten away half the site, but the broch itself, from around 100 BC, still stands, its walls reaching 12ft in places and its inner cells intact. Clustered around the broch, the compact group of homes has survived amazingly well, complete with their original stone shelving and fireplaces. The best view of the site is from the east, where you can make out the 'main street' leading towards the broch.

ARRIVAL AND DEPARTURE   BROCH OF GURNESS

By bus Bus services from Kirkwall get you to Evie (Mon–Sat 5 daily; 30min), from which it's a 30min walk to the broch.

15

ACCOMMODATION

Howe Bothy Evie ☎01856 751449. Comprises a tiny four-bunk bothy (groups only) in an old cart shed or a little en-suite double with a kitchen in the old cow byre – both beautifully converted by local artist, John Vincent. Use of a boat if you fancy some trout fishing. Two-night minimum stay. Bothy ££ for up to four; double £

Kirkwall

Initial impressions of **KIRKWALL**, Orkney's capital, are not always favourable. It has nothing to match the picturesque harbour of Stromness, and its residential sprawl is far less appealing. However, it does have one great redeeming feature – its sandstone **cathedral**, without doubt the finest medieval building in the north of Scotland. In any case, if you're staying any length of time in Orkney you're more or less bound to find yourself in Kirkwall at some point, as the town is home to the islands' better-stocked shops, and it is the ferry terminal for most of Orkney's northern isles.

St Magnus Cathedral

Broad St • April–Sept Mon–Sat 9am–6pm, Sun 1–6pm; Oct–March Mon–Sat 9am–1pm & 2–5pm • Free • Guided upper-level tours Thurs & Sat 11am & 2pm • Charge • ⓦ stmagnus.org

Standing at the very heart of Kirkwall, **St Magnus Cathedral** is the town's most compelling sight. This beautiful red-sandstone building was begun in 1137 by the Orkney Earl Rögnvald (aka St Ronald), spurred on by the growing cult surrounding the figure of his uncle Magnus, killed by his cousin Håkon in 1117 (see page 525). When Magnus's body was buried in Birsay, a heavenly light was said to have shone overhead, and his grave soon drew pilgrims. When Rögnvald took over the earldom, he moved the centre of religious and secular power from Birsay to Kirkwall, before he himself was murdered.

Today much of the detail in the soft sandstone has worn away – the capitals around the main doors are reduced to artistically gnarled stumps – but it's still an immensely impressive building. Inside, the atmosphere is surprisingly intimate, the bulky sandstone columns drawing your eye up to the exposed brickwork arches, while around the walls is a series of mostly seventeenth-century tombstones, many carved with skull and crossbones and other emblems of mortality, alongside chilling inscriptions calling on the reader to 'remember death waits us all, the hour none knows'. In the square pillars on either side of the high altar, the bones of Magnus and Rögnvald are buried.

In the southeastern corner of the cathedral lies the tomb of the Stromness-born Arctic explorer John Rae, who tried to find Sir John Franklin's expedition; he is depicted asleep, dressed in moleskins and furs, his rifle and bible by his side. Beside Rae's tomb is Orkney's own Poets' Corner, with memorials to, among others, George Mackay Brown, Eric Linklater and Edwin Muir.

Bishop's and Earl's Palaces

Palace Rd • April–Aug Tues–Sat 10am–4pm; Sept Tues–Thurs 10am–4pm • Charge • HES • ⓦ historicenvironment.scot

South of the cathedral are the ruins of the **Bishop's Palace**, residence of the Bishop of Orkney from the twelfth century. It was here that King Håkon died in 1263 on his return from defeat at the Battle of Largs. Most of what you see, however, dates from the time of Bishop Robert Reid, founder of Edinburgh University, in the mid-sixteenth century. The walls still stand, as does the tall round tower in which the bishop had his private chambers; a narrow spiral staircase takes you to the top for a good view over Kirkwall.

The ticket for the Bishop's Palace covers entry to the neighbouring **Earl's Palace** – better preserved and a lot more fun to explore – built by the infamous earl, Patrick Stewart

KIRKWALL

0 — 100
yards

Hatston Ferry Terminal & Stromness

AYRE ROAD
AYRE ROAD
HARBOUR STREET
Orkney Ferries
SHORE STREET
ST CATHERINE'S PLACE
CROMWELL ROAD

Orkney Wireless Museum

BURNMOUTH ROAD
BURGH ROAD
MOUNTHOOLIE LANE
BRIDGE STREET
GARDEN ST

Model Yacht Lake

Peedie Sea

Bus Station & Kirkwall Travel Centre
JUNCTION ROAD
WEST CASTLE ST
LAING STREET
QUEEN STREET
MILL STREET

N

Library
JUNCTION ROAD
CASTLE STREET
ALBERT STREET
THE STRYND
KING STREET
SCHOOL PLACE

Town Hall
Orkney Museum
TANKERNESS LANE
BROAD STREET
St Magnus Cathedral
St Magnus Centre
PALACE ROAD

Pickaquoy Centre &

Earl's Palace
Bishop's Palace
WATERGATE
DUNDAS CRESCENT

PICKAQUOY ROAD
JUNCTION ROAD
WALLS CLOSE
FRASER'S CLOSE
WATERGATE

Orkney Arts Theatre

WARRENS WALK
VICTORIA ROAD
VICTORIA STREET
VICTORIA LANE
BUTTQUOY PLACE
BUTTQUOY CRESCENT

UNION STREET
MAIN STREET
JUNCTION ROAD

◉ EATING
Helgi's	1
Lucano	4
Real Food Café	3
Trenabies Bistro	2

■ ACCOMMODATION
Avalon House	1
Kirkwall Youth Hostel	5
Lynnfield Hotel	6
Orkney Caravan Park	3
Peedie Hostel	2
West End Hotel	4

Scapa Bay &

Highland Park Distillery, Airport &

15

around 1600 using forced labour. With its grand entrance, fancy oriel windows, dank dungeons, massive fireplaces and magnificent central hall, it has a confident solidity, and is a fine example of Scottish Renaissance architecture. The roof may be missing, but many domestic details remain, including a set of toilets and the stone shelves used by the clerk for his filing. The earl enjoyed his palace for only a short time before he was imprisoned and charged with treason. The earl might have been acquitted, but he foolishly ordered his son, Robert, to organize an insurrection. Robert held out for four days in the palace against the Earl of Caithness, before being captured, sent to Edinburgh and hanged there, and his father was beheaded at the same place five weeks later.

Orkney Museum

Broad St • Mon–Sat 10.30am–12.30pm & 1.30–5pm • Free • ☎ 01856 873535

Opposite the cathedral stands the sixteenth-century **Tankerness House**, a former home for the clergy, and now home to the **Orkney Museum**. A couple of rooms have been

15

restored as they would have been in 1820, when it was the Baikie family's private home. The rest houses some of the islands' most treasured finds, among the more unusual of which are a witch's spell box and a lovely whalebone plaque from a Viking boat grave discovered on Sanday.

ARRIVAL AND INFORMATION KIRKWALL

By plane Kirkwall Airport (⬩hial.co.uk) is 3 miles southeast of town on the A960; take the half-hourly bus (15min), or a taxi (£10).

Destinations within Orkney Eday (Mon & Wed 1–2 daily; 10–30min); North Ronaldsay (Mon–Sat 3 daily, 2 on Sun; 20–30min); Papa Westray (Mon–Fri 3 daily, Sat & Sun 2 daily; 15–35min); Sanday (Mon–Fri 2 daily, Sat & Sun 1 daily; 15min); Stronsay (Mon–Fri 2 daily, Sat & Sun 1 daily; 10–25min); Westray (Mon–Fri 2 daily, Sat & Sun 1 daily; 15–25min).

By ferry NorthLink Ferries (⬩northlinkferries.co.uk) run services from Shetland (3 weekly; 5hr 30min) and Aberdeen (3–4 weekly; 6hr), and all cruise ships dock at the Hatston terminal, a mile northwest of town; a shuttle bus takes you into Kirkwall (or Stromness if you prefer). Ferries for Orkney's northern isles leave from the town pier in Kirkwall. Destinations within Orkney (⬩orkneyferries.co.uk) Eday (2–3 daily; 1hr 15min–2hr 25min); North Ronaldsay (Tues & Fri; 2hr 40min); Papa Westray (Tues & Fri; 2hr 15min);

Sanday (2 daily; 1hr 25min); Shapinsay (3–5 daily; 45min); Stronsay (1–3 daily; 1hr 40min–2hr); Westray (2–3 daily; 1hr 25min).

By bus The bus station is behind the Kirkwall Travel Centre, West Castle St ⬩stagecoachbus.com).

Destinations Birsay (Mon–Sat 2 daily; 30–40min); Burwick (2–3 daily; 40min); Evie (Mon–Sat 4–5 daily; 30min); Houton (5–6 daily; 25min); Kirkwall Airport (Mon–Sat every 30min, 10 on Sun; 15min); Skara Brae (Mon, Thurs & Sat only; 50min, also hop-on hop-off bus1 daily April–Oct); St Margaret's Hope (Mon–Sat hourly; 35min); Stromness (Mon–Sat 2 hourly, Sun every 2hr; 30min); Tingwall (Mon–Sat 3–5 daily; 25min).

Tourist office Kirkwall Travel Centre, West Castle St, houses the tourist office (daily 9am–5pm; ⬩orkney.com).

Bike rental Cycle Orkney, Tankerness Lane (⬩cycleorkney. com), rents bikes from £25/day – children's bikes (£10) and some electrics (£35) available.

ACCOMMODATION SEE MAP PAGE 517

HOTELS AND B&BS

Avalon House Carness Rd ⬩avalon-house.co.uk. Don't judge a B&B by its drab, modern exterior; this is a comfortable, purpose-built guesthouse run efficiently by a very welcoming couple, and situated a pleasant 20min coastal walk from the town centre. £̲£̲

Lynnfield Hotel Holm Rd ⬩lynnfield.co.uk. Small ten-room hotel in a quiet spot a mile or so out of town near the distillery – the dark wood furnishings make the place seem really quite grand in style and the food is excellent – try the North Ronaldsay mutton, which comes from the island's famous seaweed-eating flock. £̲£̲£̲

West End Hotel 14 Main St ⬩westendkirkwall.co.uk. Orkney's first hospital is now a good old-fashioned hotel located in a quiet street, just a few minutes' walk south of the centre. £̲£̲

HOSTELS AND CAMPSITES

Kirkwall Youth Hostel Old Scapa Rd ⬩hostellingscotland.org.uk. A good 10min walk out of the centre on the road to Orphir – the welcome at this former WWII military base is friendly enough, but it's no beauty outside or in. Dorms £̲; twins £̲£̲

Orkney Caravan Park Peerie Sea Loan ⬩orkneycaravanpark.co.uk. Central and well equipped, since it is behind (and run by) the local leisure centre, but not exactly picturesque; a couple of pods sleeping five and six respectively. Per pitch £̲; pods £̲£̲

Peedie Hostel 1 Ayre Houses ⬩stayinkirkwall.co.uk/ peedie-hostel. Centrally located overlooking the old harbour and out to sea, this is a clean and comfortable hostel with a good mix of singles, twins and four-bed (or family) dorms. Well-equipped kitchens, washing machine and tumble dryer available. Dorms £̲; twin £̲

EATING SEE MAP PAGE 517

Helgi's 14 Harbour St ⬩helgis.co.uk. Popular modern pub on the harbourfront serving nicely presented bar food, from burger/fish and chips to fajitas. £̲£̲

Lucano 31 Victoria St ⬩lucanokirkwall.co.uk. Busy, bright, modern, authentic Italian – the family hail from Basilicata – offering 10-inch pizzas, fresh pasta and risotto with an Orcadian angle. It's popular so book ahead.

Breakfast available, too. £̲£̲

Real Food Café 25 Broad St ⬩www.judithglue.com. Cheery cream and sky-blue wood-panelling decor at this small café at the back of Judith Glue's gift shop, opposite the cathedral. Try the Westray crab as a starter or main course salad and beer bannocks. Judith also owns the excellent Storehouse Restaurant with Rooms in Bridge Street. £̲£̲

Trenabies Bistro Albert St ☎01856 874336. This cosy, old-fashioned café with booths is a classic Kirkwall institution – order Cajun fries and a panino.

ENTERTAINMENT

New Phoenix Cinema Pickaquoy Centre ⓦpickaquoy. co.uk. The 'Picky' is a modern leisure centre, but its 1600-seat hall also serves as the town's main large-scale venue for a whole variety of events – it also houses the 250-seat New Phoenix cinema.

Lamb Holm, Burray and South Ronaldsay

Southeast from Kirkwall, the narrow spur of the **East Mainland** juts out into the North Sea and is joined to several smaller islands – the largest of which are **Burray** and **South Ronaldsay** – thanks to the remarkable Churchill Barriers, causeways built as part of the Scapa Flow defences in World War II. As with the West Mainland, the land here is heavily farmed, but it contains fewer of Orkney's famous sights.

15

Lamb Holm: the Italian Chapel

June–Aug daily 9am–5.30pm; May & Sept 9am–5pm; April & Oct 10am–4pm; Nov–March 10am–1pm • Charge

Special camps were built on the uninhabited island of **Lamb Holm** to accommodate the 1700 men involved in building the Churchill Barriers, 1,200 of whom were Italian POWs. The camps have long since disappeared, but the Italians left behind the extraordinary **Italian Chapel**, by the main road (A961). This, the so-called 'Miracle of Camp 60', must be one of the greatest adaptations ever, made from two Nissen huts, concrete, barbed wire and parts of a rusting blockship. It has a great false facade, and colourful trompe l'oeil decor, lovingly restored by the chapel's original architect, Domenico Chiocchetti, in 1960.

Burray

The largest of the little islands between the Mainland and South Ronaldsay, **Burray** has a population of around 400. The main village expanded in the nineteenth century

---

SCAPA FLOW

Apart from a few oil tankers, there's very little activity in the great natural harbour of **Scapa Flow**, yet for the first half of the twentieth century, the Flow served as the main base of the Royal Navy, with more than a hundred warships anchored here at any one time. The coastal defences required to make Scapa Flow safe to use as the country's chief naval headquarters were considerable, and many are still visible all over Orkney, ranging from half-sunk blockships to the causeways known as the Churchill Barriers and the gun batteries that pepper the coastline.

Scapa Flow's most celebrated moment in naval history, however, was when the entire **German High Seas Fleet** was interned here immediately after World War I and then scuttled on the orders of the commanding officer, Admiral von Reuter, on Midsummer's Day 1919 – the greatest loss of shipping in a single day in history. To find out more about Scapa Flow's wartime role, visit the museum on Hoy (see page 521).

Scapa Flow is one of the world's greatest **wreck dive sites**, and although there is currently no one offering dives, Scapa Scuba (ⓦscapascuba.co.uk), based in Stromness, do have dive gear for hire. The land-based Wartime Orkney Explorer private tour (ⓦorkneyuncovered.co.uk) gives expert insight into the history of Scapa Flow and beyond, showing what life was like for civilians and military personnel guarding Orkney's shores during two world wars (see website for details and other tour options; 7hr; £380 for two).

during the boom years of the herring industry, but was badly affected by the sinking of the blockships during World War I. The two-storey warehouse, built in 1860 in order to cure and pack the herring, has since been converted into the *Sands Hotel* (see below).

Orkney Fossil and Heritage Centre

April–Sept daily 10am–5pm • Charge • Ⓦ orkneyfossilcentre.co.uk

Burray's chief attraction is the **Orkney Fossil and Heritage Centre**, housed in a converted farm on the island's main road. The UV 'glow room', where the rocks reveal their iridescent colours, is a particular favourite with kids, though be sure to show them the coprolite (fossilized poo) among the main displays, too. Upstairs, there's a lot of wartime memorabilia and a whole section on the Churchill Barriers – kids can practise building their own – while the ground floor has a community-run café.

ARRIVAL AND DEPARTURE   BURRAY

By bus Buses from Kirkwall to St Margaret's Hope call in at   Burray village shop (Mon–Sat hourly; 30min).

ACCOMMODATION AND EATING

Sands Hotel 14 Main St Ⓦ thesandshotel.co.uk. An   few original features. The bar menu dishes include herring
imposing former fish warehouse overlooking Burray   in oatmeal, and mince and tatties; the restaurant serves up
harbour – now a hotel with simple pine furnishings and a   local scallops and black pudding. **£££**

South Ronaldsay

Low-lying **South Ronaldsay** is the largest of the islands linked to the Mainland by the Churchill Barriers. It was traditionally the chief crossing point to the Scottish mainland, as it's only six miles across the Pentland Firth from Caithness. Today, car **ferries** arrive at St Margaret's Hope, and there's a passenger ferry between John O'Groats and Burwick, on the island's southernmost tip.

St Margaret's Hope

South Ronaldsay's main settlement is **ST MARGARET'S HOPE**, which local tradition says is named after Margaret, Maid of Norway, daughter of the Norwegian king, who is thought to have died here aged eight in 1290. As the granddaughter of Alexander III, Margaret had already been proclaimed queen of Scotland and was en route to marry the future Edward II of England, thereby unifying the two countries. Today, St Margaret's Hope – or 'The Hope', as it's known locally – is a quiet, pleasing little gathering of stone-built houses overlooking a sheltered bay.

Smiddy Museum

Cromarty Square • April–Aug daily 2–4.30pm • Free • ☎ 01856 831331

The village smithy on Cromarty Square has been turned into a **Smiddy Museum**, which is particularly fun for kids, who enjoy getting hands-on with the old tools, drills and giant bellows. There's also a small exhibition on the annual **Boys' Ploughing Match**, in which local boys compete with miniature hand-held ploughs.

ARRIVAL AND DEPARTURE   SOUTH RONALDSAY

By ferry Pentland Ferries (Ⓦ pentlandferries.co.uk)   there's also a free shuttle service from Thurso train station
operates car catamarans from Gill's Bay (3–4 daily; 1hr),   for certain sailings.
near John O'Groats (linked by bus to Wick and Thurso).   **By bus** There is a regular bus service from Kirkwall to St
John O'Groats Ferries (Ⓦ jogferry.co.uk) runs a passenger   Margaret's Hope (Mon–Sat hourly; 30min), and a summer-
ferry from John O'Groats to Burwick on South Ronaldsay   only one to Burwick, which connects with the John O'Groats
(May–Sept 2–3 daily; 40min). Its departure is timed to   ferry (May–Sept 2–3 daily; 40min).
connect with the arrival of the Orkney Bus from Inverness;

15

ACCOMMODATION AND EATING

ST MARGARET'S HOPE

Bankburn House 0.5 miles south of the Hope on A961 Ⓦ bankburnhouse.co.uk. Solid Victorian sea captain's house, just outside the Hope, with a variety of rooms, some en suite, some with shared facilities, all with high ceilings and period features. £̲£̲

Murray Arms Hotel Back Rd Ⓦ themurrayarmshotel. com. Located in the centre of village this popular eatery and watering hole has six en-suite rooms, some with garden views. Substantial breakfasts and meals showcasing local seafood are available in the bar. £̲£̲

St Margaret's Cottage Church Rd ☎ 01856 831637. Handsome sandstone house on the edge of The Hope, run by a genuine Orcadian couple, with three rooms available – very handy for the Pentland ferry. £̲£̲

Wheems 2 miles southeast of the Hope Ⓦ wheemsorganic.co.uk. Rambling old croft house and organic farm with a host of different accommodation, including a yurt (three people), bell tents (three people), pods (four people) and a sloping field for camping, with all the usual facilities. Yurts, bell tents and pods £̲£̲; per pitch £̲

BURWICK

Sea View Cottage on B9041 just five minutes' drive from Burwick Ⓦ banksoforkney.co.uk. This charming self-catering 100-year old stone cottage for three overlooking the Pentland Firth has a fully modernised interior. Also available is Banks Barn which sleeps five people. Per week £̲£̲£̲£̲

Skerries Bistro Banks Ⓦ skerriesbistro.co.uk. Ultra-modern bistro, with its own chambered cairn nearby, overlooking the Pentland Firth, offering local fish and king scallops as big as steaks, plus delicious home-made puddings and cakes. £̲£̲£̲

Hoy

Hoy, Orkney's second-largest island, rises sharply out of the sea to the southwest of the Mainland. The least typical of the islands, but the most dramatic, its north and west sides are made up of great glacial valleys and mountainous moorland rising to over 1500ft, dropping into the sea off the red-sandstone cliffs of St John's Head, and, to the south, forming the landmark sea stack known as the **Old Man of Hoy**, best accessed from the wild and lonely village of **Rackwick**. Most of Hoy's four hundred residents live on the gentle, fertile land in the southeast, around **Lyness** and **Longhope**. This part of the island is littered with buildings dating from the two world wars, when Scapa Flow was the Royal Navy's main base.

North Hoy

Much of **North Hoy**'s magnificent landscape is made up of rough grasses and heather, which harbour a cluster of arctic plants (a lot of midges) and a healthy population of mountain hares and birdlife. Facilities are minimal, however, with the nearest shop in Longhope (see page 523), and both the villages – Hoy and Rackwick – are absolutely tiny, with very little in the way of transport. If you're walking to Rackwick from Hoy, take the footpath that goes past Sandy Loch and along the large open valley of **Berriedale** (1hr 30min).

Dwarfie Stane

Halfway along the road from Hoy to Rackwick, duckboards head across the heather to the **Dwarfie Stane**, Orkney's most unusual chambered tomb, cut from a solid block of sandstone and dating back to 3000 BC. Among the copious Victorian graffiti is an inscription on the northern exterior, where Major Mouncey, a former British spy in Persia and a confirmed eccentric who dressed in Persian garb, carved his name backwards in Latin and also carved in Persian the words 'I have sat two nights and so learnt patience'. Since 2015, however, most of the visitors descending on the Dwarfie Stane car park are here to see a young pair of **sea eagles** – the first to nest on Orkney for 142 years – who have chosen a nearby site to attempt to breed. In 2018, two chicks were successfully hatched for the first time in 140 years, with further successes in 2019 and 2020.

Rackwick

RACKWICK is an old crofting and fishing village squeezed between towering sandstone cliffs on the west coast. These days only a few of Rackwick's houses are inhabited all year round. A building beside the hostel has a tiny **museum** with a brief rundown of Rackwick's rough history, but for a deeper insight into how folk used to live in these parts, head over to the **Craa Nest**, the oldest croft house in the village, just up the path to the Old Man; last occupied in 1940, the place still has its box-beds, barn and kiln intact.

The Old Man of Hoy

Despite its isolation, Rackwick has a steady stream of walkers and climbers passing through en route to the **Old Man of Hoy**, a great sandstone stack, 450ft high, perched on an old lava flow that protects it from the erosive power of the sea. It is a popular challenge for rock climbers, and a 1966 ascent, led by Chris Bonington, was the first televised climb in Britain. The well-trodden footpath from Rackwick is an easy three-mile walk (3hr round-trip) – although the great skuas will dive-bomb you during the nesting season (May–Aug), when the surrounding cliffs provide ideal rocky ledges for thousands of nesting seabirds, including puffins.

15

ARRIVAL AND GETTING AROUND

NORTH HOY

By ferry The passenger ferry from Stromness to Moaness Pier, by Hoy village (Mon–Fri 4–6 daily, Sat & Sun 2 daily; 25min; ☎ 01856 872044) also serves the island of Graemsay en route.

By bus A Hoy Community bus operates a hail and ride service on two routes, Longhope to Lyness and Moaness Pier to Longhope (limited service check online for details; ⓦ hoyorkney.com).

ACCOMMODATION AND EATING

Beneth'ill Café Hoy ⓦ benethillcafe.co.uk. Friendly, simple café, a short walk from Moaness Pier, offering sandwiches, paninis and salads along with home-made puddings, proper coffee, teas, hot chocolate, juices and alcoholic drinks. £

Hoy Centre 1 mile west of Moaness Pier ☎ 01856 873535 ext 2417. A council-run, SYHA-affiliated hostel in an old school. Situated in Hoy village, this place is large and

modern, with a well-equipped kitchen, washing and drying facilities and all rooms en suite. Dorms £; Family room ££

Rackwick Outdoor Centre Signposted at entrance to village, 0.5 miles north of the beach ☎ 01856 873535 ext 2901. Housed in Rackwick's tiny little former schoolhouse, this simple hostel has just eight beds in two rooms and a small kitchen. The central location in Rackwick village is great. Camping permitted. Dorms £

Lyness

Along the sheltered eastern shore of Hoy, high moorland gives way to a gentler environment. Hoy defines the western boundary of Scapa Flow, and **LYNESS** played a major role for the Royal Navy during both world wars. Many of the old wartime buildings have been cleared away over the last few decades, but the harbour and hills around Lyness are still scarred with the scattered remains of concrete structures that once served as hangars and storehouses during World War II, and are now used as barns and cowsheds. Lyness also has a large **naval cemetery**, where many of the victims of the various disasters that have occurred in the Flow now lie, alongside a handful of German graves.

Scapa Flow Visitor Centre and Museum

March, April & Oct Mon–Sat 10am–4pm; May–Sept daily 10am–4pm • Free • ⓦ orkney.com

The old oil pump house, standing opposite Lyness ferry terminal, has been turned into the **Scapa Flow Visitor Centre**, giving a fascinating insight into wartime Orkney – even the **café** has an old NAAFI feel about it. As well as the usual old photos, torpedoes, flags, guns and propellers, there's a paratrooper's folding bicycle, and a whole section devoted to the 1919 scuttling of the German High Seas Fleet and the 1939 sinking of the *Royal Oak*. The pump house also retains much of its old equipment used to pump oil off tankers into sixteen tanks, and into underground reservoirs cut into the neighbouring hillside. From April to October there are regular guided walks around the former naval base.

ARRIVAL AND DEPARTURE

LYNESS

By ferry The roll-on/roll-off car ferry to/from Houton on the Mainland (Mon–Fri 6 daily, Sat & Sun 2–5 daily; 35min–1hr; ☎01856 811397) sometimes calls in at the oil terminal island of Flotta, and begins and ends its daily schedule at Longhope – if you're taking a vehicle over, you should book in advance.

ENTERTAINMENT

Gable End Theatre 1.5 miles south of Lyness Pier ⓦ orkneycommunities.co.uk/iohdt. Established in the old North Walls school buildings, this community-run theatre (with its own wind turbine) shows regular films and puts on the occasional theatre piece and gig – check their Facebook page for the latest information.

Longhope

A causeway was built during World War II connecting Hoy with **South Walls** (pronounced 'Waas'), a fertile tidal island more densely populated with farms and homes than Hoy. Along the north coast is the main settlement of **Longhope**, an important safe anchorage even today.

Hackness Martello Tower

April–Sept daily 9.30am–5.30pm • Charge • ⓦ historicenvironment.scot

Longhope's strategic importance during the Napoleonic Wars is evident at the Point of Hackness, where the **Hackness Martello Tower** stands guard over the entrance to the bay, with a matching tower on the opposite promontory of Crockness. Built in 1815, these two circular sandstone Martello towers are the northernmost in Britain, and protected merchant ships from American and French privateers. You enter Hackness Tower via a steep ladder connected to the upper floor, where nine men and one officer shared the circular room.

ARRIVAL AND DEPARTURE

LONGHOPE

By ferry The roll-on/roll-off car ferry from Houton on the Mainland to Lyness begins and ends each day at Longhope – book ahead if you're taking a vehicle over (1 daily, 1hr 20min; ☎01856 811397).

ACCOMMODATION

Cantick Head Lighthouse Cottage 3.5 miles west of Longhope ⓦ cantickhead.com. In a stunning location by the lighthouse at the southwestern tip of Hoy, this cottage offers comfortable accommodation for up to five guests in two rooms. There's a welcome pack to greet guests at this truly magical location. Cottage (minimum stay 3 nights) **£££**

Old Hall Cottage 2 miles southeast of Longhope ⓦ oldhallcottage.co.uk. Lovely 200-year-old converted byre sleeps six at a squeeze and is let out on a nightly basis or as B&B; lovely sheltered garden overlooking Scapa Flow. **££**

Stromabank Hotel 1.5 miles southeast of Longhope ⓦ stromabank.co.uk. This small, unpretentious hotel is housed in the old schoolhouse on the hill above Longhope, with views over the Pentland Firth – there are four en-suite rooms available and the bar serves as the local pub. Bar food available in the evening. **££**

Shapinsay

Just a few miles northeast of Kirkwall, **Shapinsay** is the most accessible of Orkney's northern isles. A gently undulating grid-plan patchwork of rich farmland, it's a bit like an island suburb of Kirkwall, which is clearly visible across the bay.

Balfour

Shapinsay's only village is **BALFOUR**, named after the family who owned the island, reformed the island's agricultural system and rebuilt the village – previously known as Shoreside – to house their estate workers. The family's grandiose efforts in estate management have left some appealingly eccentric relics around the village. Melodramatic fortifications around the harbour include the huge and ornate **gatehouse**. There's also a stone-built coal-fired **gasometer**, which once supplied castle and harbour with electricity and, southwest of the pier, the castellated **Douche** or Dishan Tower, a seventeenth-century doocot converted into a Victorian saltwater toilet and shower.

The old smithy, halfway along Balfour's main street, houses the volunteer-run **Shapinsay Heritage Centre** (May–Sept daily noon–4pm), where there is information about the island, and a series of workshops held during the summer, plus a range of arts and crafts for sale. Tea and cakes are also available.

Balfour Castle

Shapinsay's chief landmark is **Balfour Castle**, an imposing baronial pile visible as you approach on the ferry and a short walk from the village. Designed by David Bryce, it was completed in 1848 by the Balfour family of Westray, who had made a small fortune in India the previous century. The Balfours died out in 1960 and for the last few years the castle had been used as an exclusive-use holiday or dining retreat. The house is now privately owned and not open to the public.

ARRIVAL AND DEPARTURE   SHAPINSAY

By ferry Shapinsay is an easy day-trip from Kirkwall (3–5 daily; 30min; ☎ 01856 872044).

ACCOMMODATION AND EATING

★ **Iona Cottage** a few minutes east of Balfour on B9059 @ islandselfcatering.co.uk. This self-catering cottage for up to six people has three en-suite bedrooms and features a spacious sun porch with views across Elwick Bay to Kirkwall. Green energy is supplied via a wind turbine and local produce is available from a village shop. Per week **££££**

Rousay, Egilsay and Wyre

The hilly island of **Rousay** is one of the more accessible northern isles as well as being home to a number of intriguing prehistoric sites. The group of a dozen or so houses above the ferry terminal is the only settlement of any size, but a single road runs around the edge of the island, connecting a string of farms that make use of the more cultivable coastal fringes. Many visitors come on a day-trip, as it's easy enough to reach the main points of archeological interest on the south coast by foot from the ferry terminal.

Rousay's diminutive neighbours, **Egilsay** and **Wyre**, contain a few medieval attractions of their own, which can be visited on a day-trip from Rousay itself, or from the Mainland.

Rousay

Rousay was one of the few parts of Orkney to suffer Highland-style clearances. One laird, Lieutenant General Traill-Burroughs, built a wall to force crofters onto a narrow coastal strip and eventually provoked so much distress and anger that a gunboat had to be sent to restore order. You can learn about the history and wildlife of the island from the well-laid-out display room of the **Rousay Heritage Centre** housed in the back of the ferry waiting room.

Trumland House

Gardens May–Oct daily 10am–5pm • Charge • ☎ 01856 821322

The island's laird, Lieutenant General Traill-Burroughs, built **Trumland House**, the forbidding Jacobean-style pile designed by David Bryce, in the 1870s, hidden in the trees half a mile northwest of the ferry terminal. The house is undergoing much-needed restoration, as are the landscaped **gardens**, though these can still be visited; the rhododendrons have been pushed back and there are now lovely wooded walks and a walled garden.

The three cairns

The road west from Trumland House runs past a trio of intriguing prehistoric cairns, starting with **Taversoe Tuick**. Dating back to 3500 BC, it's remarkable in that it exploits its sloping site by having two storeys, one entered from the upper side and one from the lower.

A little further west is the **Blackhammar Cairn**, which is entered through the roof via a ladder; the long interior is divided into 'stalls' by large flagstones.

Finally, there's the **Knowe of Yarso**, another stalled cairn dating from the same period. It's worth the stiff climb up the hill from the road, if only for the magnificent view. The remains of 29 individuals were found inside, with the skulls neatly arranged around the walls.

Midhowe Cairn

The southwestern side of Rousay is home to the island's most significant and impressive archeological remains. Approached from the east, **Midhowe Cairn** comes as something of a surprise, due to its immense size – it's known as 'the great ship of death' and measures nearly 100ft in length – and because it's housed within a stone-walled barn with a corrugated roof. You can't explore the roofless communal burial chamber, dating back to 3500 BC, only look down from the overhead walkway. The central corridor, 25yd long, is partitioned with slabs of rock, with twelve compartments on each side, where the remains of 25 people were discovered in a crouched position with their backs to the wall.

Midhowe Broch

A hundred yards beyond Midhowe Cairn is Rousay's finest archeological site, **Midhowe Broch**, whose compact layout suggests that it was originally built as a sort of fortified family house, surrounded by ditches and ramparts. The interior of the broch, entered through an impressive doorway, is divided into two separate rooms, each with its own hearth, water tank and quernstone, all of which date from the final phase of occupation around AD 150.

Egilsay

Egilsay, the largest of the low-lying islands close to the eastern shore of Rousay, makes for an easy day-trip. The island is dominated by the ruined twelfth-century **St Magnus Church**, with its distinctive round tower. It's possible that it was built as a shrine to Earl (later St) Magnus, who arranged to meet his cousin Håkon here in 1117, only to be treacherously killed on Håkon's orders by his cook, Lifolf. If the weather's fine, walk due east from the ferry terminal to the coast, where there's a beautiful sandy bay overlooking Eday.

Wyre

Wyre, southwest of Egilsay, opposite Rousay's ferry terminal, is another possible day-trip. It's best known for **Cubbie Roo's Castle**, the 'fine stone fort' and 'really solid stronghold' mentioned in the *Orkneyinga Saga*, and built around 1150 by local farmer Kolbein Hruga. The outer defences have survived on three sides of the castle, which has a central keep, up to 6ft high, with its central water tank still intact. Close by stands the roofless twelfth-century **St Mary's Chapel**. To learn more about Cubbie Roo or any other aspect of Wyre's history, pop into the **Wyre Heritage Centre** near the chapel.

ARRIVAL AND DEPARTURE
ROUSAY, EGILSAY AND WYRE

By ferry Rousay makes a good day-trip from the Mainland, with car ferries from Tingwall (5–6 daily; 30min), linked to Kirkwall by bus (5 daily; 30min–1hr). Most of the Rousay ferries call in at Egilsay and Wyre, but some are request journeys and must be booked the day before (☎01856

751360).

By bus A bus runs every Thursday (7am–7pm; book ahead on ☎01856 821360, ⓦaroundrousay.co.uk/bus). Minibus tours are available on demand (☎01856 821234; £35; 5–7hr) from the ferry terminal on Rousay.

ACCOMMODATION AND EATING

ROUSAY
Accommodation and eating options on Rousay are very limited. If you're coming for the day or self-catering, bring your own provisions, as Rousay Stores, the island's main general store, is in the northeastern corner of the island.
The Space The Old Kirk On the B9604 2 miles east of the ferry terminal, ⊜info@thespaceorkney.com. Sleeping up to eight people, this fantastic conversion of an old chapel is stunningly set in a secluded spot on the hillside above the sea. Popular with musicians and artists (it has its own recording studio) it is also available for families or

friends. Minimum stay four days £££
The Taversoe 3 miles west of ferry terminal ⓦtaversoehotel.co.uk. Unpretentious accommodation in four rooms (all with sea views). Serves classic pub meals – fish and chips, scampi or burgers. ££
Trumland Farm 0.5 miles west of ferry terminal ☎01856 821252. This working organic farm has two apartments (sleeping five) and a studio (sleeping two) – you can also camp here, and they offer bike rental (£8/day). Per week ££££

Westray

Although exposed to the full force of the Atlantic weather in the far northwest of Orkney, **Westray** shelters one of the most tightly knit, prosperous and independent island communities, with a population of six hundred. Fishing, farming and tourism are the mainstays of the economy. The landscape is very varied, with sea cliffs and a trio of hills in the west, and rich low-lying pastureland and sandy bays elsewhere. However, Westray repays a longer stay, especially as there's lots of good accommodation and the locals are extremely welcoming.

Pierowall

The main village and harbour is **PIEROWALL**, set around a wide bay in the north of the island, eight miles from Rapness ferry terminal on the island's southernmost tip. Pierowall is a place of some considerable size, relatively speaking, with a school, several shops and a bakery (Orkney's only one off the Mainland).

Westray Heritage Centre
May–Sept Mon 11.30am–5pm, Tues–Sat 9am–noon & 2–5pm, Sun 1.30–5pm; Oct–April by appointment, open most Wed 2–4pm • Charge • ⓦwestrayheritage.co.uk

The village's **Westray Heritage Centre** is a very welcoming wet-weather retreat, and a great place to gen up on (and with any luck catch a glimpse of) the Westray Wife or **Orkney Venus** – the first and finest of a series of remarkable, miniature Neolithic figurines found in the last decade in the dunes to the northwest of Pierowall.

Noltland Castle
Daily April–Sept 9.30am–5.30pm; Oct–March 10am–4pm • Free • HES • ☎0131 668 8600

The island's most impressive ruin is the colossal sandstone hulk of **Noltland Castle**, which stands above the village. This Z-plan castle, pockmarked with over seventy gun loops, was begun around 1560 by Gilbert Balfour, a shady character from Fife, who was Master of the Household to Mary, Queen of Scots, and was implicated in the murder of her husband Lord Darnley in 1567. Balfour was eventually forced to flee to Sweden, where he was found guilty of plotting to murder the Swedish king and executed in 1576.

Noup Head

The northwestern tip of Westray rises up sharply, culminating in the dramatic sea cliffs of **Noup Head**, particularly spectacular when a westerly swell is up. During the summer months the guano-covered rock ledges are packed with over 100,000 nesting guillemots, razorbills, kittiwakes, fulmars and puffins: a heady sensation of sight, sound and smell. The open ground above the cliffs, grazed by sheep, is superb maritime heath and grassland, carpeted with yellow, white and purple flowers, and a favourite breeding ground for arctic tern and arctic skua.

Castle o'Burrian

The sea cliffs in the southeast of the island around **Stanger Head** are not that spectacular, but it's here that you'll find **Castle o'Burrian**, a sea stack that is the best place on Westray at which to see **puffins** nesting (mid-May to Aug) – there's even a signpost from the main road.

ARRIVAL AND GETTING AROUND WESTRAY

By plane You can fly from Kirkwall (Mon–Fri 2 daily, Sat & Sun 1 daily; 15min) and go on the world's shortest scheduled flight between Westray and Papa Westray (Mon–Sat 1 daily; 2min).

By ferry Westray is served by car ferry from Kirkwall (2–3 daily; 1hr 25min; ☎ 01856 872044), and there's a passenger ferry between Pierowall (Westray) and Papa Westray (3–6 daily; 25min; ☎ 01856 872044).

By bus A minibus (May–Sept; at other times phone; ⓦ westraybusservice.co.uk) meets the ferry and connects with the Papa Westray ferry at Gill Pier in Pierowall; book a seat for the bus on the ferry.

INFORMATION AND TOURS

Tourist information ⓦ westraypapawestray.co.uk.
Tours Guided tours of the island – including puffin tours between April and mid-July – by minibus can be arranged with Westraak (ⓦ westraak.co.uk), who will meet you at the ferry.

ACCOMMODATION AND EATING

★ **Chalmersquoy** ⓦ chalmersquoywestray.co.uk. The barn is a converted farm hostel at the southern edge of Pierowall; it's luxurious inside, with family rooms and twin bunks available, has a small campsite, *Chalmersquoy*, adjacent to it – run by a genuinely friendly Westerly family. Bed and breakfast and self-catering is also available. Dorms £; doubles ££; camping per pitch £

No. 1 Broughton Pierowall ⓦ no1broughton.co.uk. ££ Top-notch, good-value B&B in a renovated mid-nineteenth-century house with views across the bay, with three en-suite rooms, a lovely conservatory and even a small sauna. ££

Pierowall Hotel Pierowall ⓦ pierowallhotel.co.uk. The social hub of Pierowall itself is unpretentious and very welcoming – the cheaper rooms have shared facilities. The popular bar has excellent fish and chips, fresh off the boats.

Papa Westray

Across Papa Sound from Westray is the island of **Papa Westray**, known locally as 'Papay'. With a population of around ninety, Papay has fought hard to keep itself viable over the last couple of decades, helped by a hefty influx of outsiders. With one of Orkney's best-preserved Neolithic settlements, and a large nesting seabird population, Papay is worth an overnight stay or a day-trip from its big neighbour. The northern tip of the island around **North Hill** (157ft) is an RSPB reserve, and during the breeding season you're asked to keep to the coastal fringe, where razorbill, guillemot, fulmar, kittiwake and puffin nest, particularly around Fowl Craig on the east coast, where you can also view the rare Scottish primrose, which flowers in May and from July to late September. Papay holds the ØY Festival in mid-November (Ⓦpapawestray.co.uk), a three-day celebration of the island and its magnetism, and its inspiration to writers, artists, musicians and thinkers, plus the more prosaic Papay Fun Weekend in mid-July.

Holland House

Central point of the island • Farm buildings open year-round • Free

Papay's visual focus is **Holland House**, occupying the high central point of the island and once seat of the local lairds, the Traill family. Visitors can explore the old farm buildings, including a kiln, a doocot and a horse-powered threshing mill. An old bothy for single male servants has even been restored and made into a small **museum**, filled with bygone bits and bobs, from a wooden flea trap to a box-bed.

15

Knap of Howar

From Holland House, it's around half a mile to the western shore, where Papay's prime prehistoric site, the **Knap of Howar**, stands overlooking Westray. Dating from around 3500 BC, this Neolithic farm building makes a fair claim to being the oldest standing house in Europe. It's made up of two roofless buildings, linked by a little passageway; one has a hearth and copious stone shelves, and is thought to have been some kind of storehouse.

The Kelp Store Heritage & Arts Centre

0.5 miles east of the Papay Co-op • Contact Papay Ranger for opening times • Ⓦ thekelpstore-papawestray.com

This stone building down by the old pier was once used for storing kelp, but these days it is home to the **Kelp Store Heritage Centre**, a great wet-weather retreat and place to learn about the history of the island. As well as acting as the island's heritage centre, the place also puts on various events from musical evenings to whisky-tasting sessions.

Holm of Papay

Boat trips by arrangement • ☎ 07931 235213 • Charge

Papay's Ranger can take **visitors** by boat to the **Holm of Papay**, the little island off the east coast, in order to explore an impressive Neolithic chambered cairn. Visitors enter via a trapdoor in the modern roof to witness the mysterious ancient carvings.

ARRIVAL AND DEPARTURE
PAPA WESTRAY

By plane You can fly direct from Kirkwall to Papa Westray (Mon–Fri 3 daily, Sat & Sun 2 daily; 25min) for around £15 return if you stay overnight. Papay is also connected to Westray by the world's shortest scheduled flight (Mon–Sat 1 daily) – 2min or less with a following wind; this is very popular and with only ten seats (including that of the pilot) gets booked up very quickly.

By ferry The passenger ferry from Gill Pier in Pierowall (3–6 daily; 25min; ☎ 01856 677216) also takes bicycles.

Car ferries On Tuesdays, the car ferry goes from Kirkwall to Papa Westray via North Ronaldsay, taking over four hours; on Fridays, the car ferry from Kirkwall to Westray continues to Papa Westray; at other times, you must catch a bus to connect with the Papa Westray ferry from Pierowall. The bus should be booked ahead, while on the Westray ferry (☎ 01857 677758); it accepts a limited number of bicycles.

GETTING AROUND AND INFORMATION

Guided tours The Papay Ranger offers Papay Peedie Tours by minibus (☎ 07931 235213) – full-days with lunch (May–Aug Wed, Thurs & Sat; £60, children £30) – you can even do it from Kirkwall as a 12hr day-trip. The tour takes you through history from Neolithic times to Celtic origins and Christian influence. Then after a three-course lunch at the Heritage centre you take a walk around the RSPB reserve. At other times, you can arrange bespoke tours with the Ranger. **Tourist information** Ⓦ papawestray.co.uk

ACCOMMODATION AND EATING

Beltane House East side of the island ⓦ papawestray.co.uk. The Papay Community Co-op offers six private single, double, twin and family rooms (*Papa Westray Hostel*), a place to camp, and a shop, all within the old estate workers' cottages at Beltane, east of Holland House. They've also got some attractive wooden camping bothies resembling upturned wooden boat shelters. *Beltane House* runs a self-service café for all island visitors to use and also opens its 'bar cupboard' every Saturday night from 8pm, with bar meals available. Private rooms **££**; shared rooms **£**; camping per person **£**; camping bothies **££**

Eday

A long, thin island, **Eday** shares more characteristics with Rousay and Hoy than with its immediate neighbours, dominated as it is by heather-covered upland, with farmland confined to a narrow strip of coastal ground. However, Eday's hills have proved useful in their own way, providing huge quantities of peat that has been exported to the other peatless northern isles for fuel, and was even, for a time, exported to various whisky distillers. Sparsely inhabited, Eday has no main village as such. The ferry terminal is at the south end of the island, whereas the sights (and most of the amenities) are all in the northern half, about four miles away. The island post office, petrol pump and community shop all cluster in Hammarhill.

Eday Heritage Centre and HMS Otter

May–Sept daily 10am–4pm; Nov–March by appointment • Free; donation requested • Heritage Centre ☎ 01857 622331; North School ☎ 01857 622225

Eday Heritage Centre, in an old Baptist chapel a mile north of the island's airport, has historical displays on Eday, with information on the island's tidal energy testing centre in the Fall of Warness. Perhaps the most unusual attraction, however, is in the nearby former North School, opposite the island shop, where several internal sections of the Cold War-era **submarine** HMS *Otter* have been reassembled in the old school hall – a truly eerie experience.

Eday Heritage Walk: Mill Loch to Red Head

The clearly marked **Eday Heritage Walk** (4hr 30min return) begins at Mill Loch, which is breeding ground of several pairs of **red-throated divers** where a bird hide overlooks the loch. Clearly visible over the road is the 15ft **Stone of Setter**, Orkney's most distinctive standing stone, weathered into three thick, lichen-encrusted fingers. From here, passing the less spectacular Braeside and Huntersquoy chambered cairns en route, you can climb the hill to reach Eday's finest, the **Vinquoy Chambered Cairn**, which has a similar structure to that of Maeshowe. You can crawl into the tomb through the narrow entrance: a skylight inside lets light into the main, beehive chamber but not into the four side cells. From the cairn, you can continue north to the viewpoint on the summit of **Vinquoy Hill** (248ft), and to the very northernmost tip of the island, where lie the dramatic red-sandstone sea cliffs of **Red Head**, where numerous seabirds nest in summer.

Carrick House

Mid-June to mid-Sept Sun 2pm, other times by appointment • Charge • ☎ 01857 622260

The grandest home on Eday is Carrick House, on the northeast coast. First built by the laird of Eday in 1633, it's best known for its associations with the pirate **John Gow** – on whom Sir Walter Scott's novel *The Pirate* is based – whose ship *The Revenge* ran aground on the Calf of Eday in 1725. He asked for help from the local laird but was taken prisoner in Carrick House, before eventually being sent off to London where he was tortured and executed. The highlight of the tour – if it can be called as such – is the bloodstain on the floor of the living room, where John Gow was detained and stabbed while trying to escape.

ARRIVAL AND INFORMATION   EDAY

By plane You can make a day-trip by plane from Kirkwall to Eday on Wednesdays (1 on Wed; 10min).
By ferry Eday is served by regular car ferry from Kirkwall (2–3 daily; 1hr 15min–2hr; ☎01856 872044). The ferry terminal is at Backaland pier in the south, although you should be able to get a lift to the north of the island with someone off the ferry if you ask around.
Tourist information ⓦ visiteday.wordpress.com.

GETTING AROUND AND TOURS

By minibus Eday's minibus (May to mid-Sept Mon, Wed & Fri or by appointment; 2hr; £15; ☎01857 622206) will collect you from the ferry, take you on a tour of the island and deposit you wherever you want; every Thursday it will simply take you wherever you wish to go (without the tour). Eday also has a Ranger service, offering weekly guided walks – check Eday Scarfs Facebook page (ⓦfacebook.com/edayscarfs/).

ACCOMMODATION AND EATING

Eday Community Hostel London Bay, Just south of the airport ⓦ hostellingscotland.org.uk. An SYHA-affiliated, community-run hostel, situated in an exposed spot; phone ahead as there's no resident warden. Washing machine and dryer, bike rental and wi-fi, and guided walks can be arranged. Small area for camping too. Dorms £̲£̲

Stronsay

A low-lying island, **Stronsay** is strongly agricultural, its interior an almost uninterrupted collage of green pastures. The island features few real sights, but the coastline has enormous appeal: a beguiling combination of sandstone cliffs, interspersed with wide white sands and (in fine weather) turquoise bays. Stronsay (population 350) in the nineteenth century became one of the main Scottish centres for curing herring, until stocks were depleted in the 1930s, and the industry began a long decline.

Whitehall

WHITEHALL, in the north of the island, is the only real village, made up of rows of stone-built fishermen's cottages set between two large piers. Wandering along the tranquil, rather forlorn harbourfront today, it's hard to believe that the village once supported a small army of gutters, coopers, coal merchants, butchers, bakers, several Italian ice-cream parlours and a cinema. It was said that, on a Sunday, you could walk across the decks of the boats to **Papa Stronsay**, the tiny island that shelters Whitehall from the north. The old Fish Mart by Whitehall pier houses a small **museum** (ask at the adjacent café for access), with a few photos and artefacts from the herring days.

Papa Stronsay

Ferry The island's monks take visitors to the island by boat, by prior arrangement • ⓦ papastronsay.com

Clearly visible from the harbour front at Whitehall is the island of **Papa Stronsay**, which is thought originally to have been a **monastic retreat** and later, during the herring boom, was home to no fewer than five fish-curing stations. In 2000, the island was bought by **Transalpine Redemptorist monks**, who had broken with the Vatican over celebrating Mass in Latin. They built themselves the Golgotha Monastery, complete with its own creamery; they have since been accepted back into the Roman Catholic Church and renamed the **Sons of the Most Holy Redeemer.**

The island features in the *Orkneyinga* Saga as the place where Earl Rognvald Brusason was murdered by Earl Thorfinn Sigurdsson.

Vat of Kirbuster to Burgh Head

Signposts show the way to Orkney's biggest and most dramatic natural arch, the **Vat of Kirbuster**. Before you reach the arch there's a seaweedy, shallow pool in a natural sandstone amphitheatre, where the water is warmed by the sun and kids and adults can safely wallow: close by is a rocky inlet for those who prefer colder, more adventurous swimming. You'll find progressively more nesting seabirds, including a few puffins (mid-May to Aug), as you approach **Burgh Head**, further along the coast.

ARRIVAL AND GETTING AROUND   STRONSAY

By plane Flights from Kirkwall (Mon–Fri 2 daily, Sat 1 daily; 25min) and from Sanday (Mon–Sat 1 daily; 6min). **By ferry** Stronsay is served by a regular car ferry service from Kirkwall to Whitehall (1–3 daily; 1hr 40min–2hr; 01856 872044). **By taxi/car** There's no bus service, but Don Peace (01857 616335) operates taxis and offers car rental.

ACCOMMODATION AND EATING

Storehouse Whitehall 01857 616263. A good alternative to the *Stronsay Hotel*, this welcoming little B&B in Whitehall offers en-suite rooms, a guest lounge and full board on request. **££**

Stronsay Fish Mart Whitehall stronsaycafehostel. weebly.com. The old fish market, by the ferry terminal, has been refurbished as a hostel (three twins and a family room, all en suite), a heritage centre and a cheap and cheerful daytime café serving tea, sandwiches and delicious home-made cakes. Dorms **££**

Stronsay Hotel Whitehall 01857 616213. Stronsay's only hotel, right by the ferry terminal, has four modern en-suite rooms, while the hotel bar serves up generous portions of cheap and cheerful pub food. **££**

15

Sanday

Despite being the largest of the northern isles, **Sanday** is the least substantial, a great low-lying, drifting dune strung out between several rocky points. The island's sweeping aquamarine bays and vast stretches of clean white sand are the finest in Orkney, and in dry, clear weather it's a superb place to spend a day or two. The sandy soil is very fertile, and the island remains predominantly agricultural even today, holding its own agricultural show each year in early August. The coastline offers superb walks, with particularly spectacular sand dunes to the south of the vast, shallow, tidal bay of **Cata Sand**.

Start Point Lighthouse

Accessible only during low tide • nlb.org.uk

The island has a long history as a shipping hazard, with many wrecks smashed against its shores, although the construction of the **Start Point Lighthouse** in 1802 on Sanday's exposed eastern tip reduced the risk for seafarers. Shipwrecks were not an unwelcome sight as the island has no peat, and driftwood was the only source of fuel other than cow dung – it's even said that the locals used to pray for shipwrecks in church. The 82ft high Stevenson lighthouse, from 1870, sports very natty and unusual vertical black and white stripes and stands on a tidal island, accessible either side of low tide (it takes an hour to walk there and back).

Quoyness Chambered Cairn

Sanday is rich in archaeology, with hundreds of sites, the most impressive of which is **Quoyness Chambered Cairn**, on the fertile peninsula of Els Ness. The tomb, dating from before 2000 BC, has been partially reconstructed, and rises to a height of around 13ft. The imposing, narrow entrance, flanked by high dry-stone walls, would originally have been roofed for the whole of the way into the 13ft long main chamber, where bones and skulls were discovered in the six small side cells.

ARRIVAL AND DEPARTURE
SANDAY

By plane The airfield is in the centre of the island and there are regular flights to Kirkwall (Mon–Fri 2 daily, Sat 1 daily; 10min) some flights to Stronsay (ⓦ loganair.co.uk; 6min).
By ferry Ferries from Kirkwall to Sanday (2 daily; 1hr

25min) arrive at Loth Pier, at the southern tip of the island.
By bus All sailings are met by the on-demand Sanday Bus (ⓣ 07513 084777), which will take you to most points on Sanday, but advance reservation is recommended.

INFORMATION AND TOURS

Tourist information ⓦ sanday.co.uk.
Tours On Wednesdays between May and September there's the Sanday Experience, a three-hour guided bus tour of the

island, including a visit to the heritage centre (£40; ⓣ 07513 084777).

ACCOMMODATION AND EATING

Ayre's Rock 6 miles northeast of the ferry terminal ⓦ ayres-rock-hostel-orkney.com. If you're on a budget, this is a great place to stay: a well-equipped hostel, a couple of caravans and a small campsite (with several wooden camping pods for hire) overlooking the bay, with washing and laundry facilities and bike rental. All facilities £̄
Belsair Hotel Kettletoft ⓣ 01857 600206. The Belsair is one of two pubs in Kettletoft, Sanday's original fishing port.

Decent pub food is on offer (fish and chips, burgers and the like) on a daily basis. Accommodation also available. £̄
Braeswick 2 miles north of the ferry terminal ⓦ braeswick.co.uk. Despite the rather plain exterior, this B&B is a good choice, with three very pleasantly decorated rooms and a breakfast room with lovely views over the bay and an excellent base for bird-watching. £̄£̄

North Ronaldsay

North Ronaldsay – or 'North Ron' as it's fondly known – is Orkney's most northerly island, with a population of around fifty. Separated from Sanday by some treacherous waters, it has an outpost atmosphere, brought about by its extreme isolation. Measuring just three miles by one, and rising only 66ft above sea level, the only features to interrupt the flat horizon are **Holland House** – built by the Traill family, who bought the island in 1727 – and the two lighthouses at **Dennis Head**. North Ronaldsay has been inhabited for centuries, and continues to be heavily farmed, with **seaweed** playing an important role in the local economy.

Bird Observatory

ⓦ nrbo.org.uk

The island's most frequent visitors are ornithologists, who come to clock the rare migrants that land here briefly on their spring and autumn migrations. The peak times of year for migrants are from late March to early June, and from mid-August to early November. However, many breeding species spend the spring and summer here, including gulls, terns, waders, black guillemots, cormorants and even the odd corncrake – the permanent **Bird Observatory**, in the island's southwest corner, can give advice on recent bird sightings.

> ### NORTH RONALDSAY SHEEP
>
> The island's **sheep** are a unique, tough, goat-like breed, who feed mostly on seaweed, giving their flesh a dark tone and a rich, gamey taste, and making their thick wool highly prized. A high **dry-stone dyke**, running the thirteen miles around the edge of the island, keeps them off the farmland, except during lambing season. North Ronaldsay sheep are also unusual in that they refuse to be rounded up by sheepdogs like ordinary sheep, but scatter far and wide at some considerable speed. Instead, once a year the islanders herd the sheep communally into a series of **dry-stone punds** near Dennis Head, for clipping and dipping, in what is one of the last acts of communal farming practised in Orkney.

15

The Lighthouses and the Wool Mill

Exhibition May–Aug daily 10am–5pm • Free • Lighthouse Tours; by appointment ☎ 07703 112224 • Charge • Wool Mill Tours; by appointment ☎ 07526 629654 • Charge • ⓦ northronaldsay.co.uk

The attractive, stone-built **Old Beacon** was first lit in 1789, but the lantern was replaced by the current huge bauble of masonry in 1809. The **New Lighthouse**, designed by Alan Stevenson in 1854 just to the north, is Britain's tallest land-based lighthouse, at over 100ft. There's an exhibition on the lighthouse in one of the keepers' cottages, as well as an exhibition on the history of life on the island and a café. You can also climb the 176 steps to the top of the lighthouse and admire the view – on a clear day you can see Fair Isle, and even Shetland. This can be combined with a tour of the island's **Wool Mill** where they turn the North Ron fleeces into yarn and felt (ⓦ northronaldsayyarn.co.uk).

ARRIVAL

NORTH RONALDSAY

By plane Your best bet is to catch a flight from Kirkwall (Mon–Sat 3 daily, 2 on Sun; 15min): if you stay the night on the island, you're eligible for a bargain £21 return fare.

By ferry The ferry direct from Kirkwall to North Ronaldsay runs just once a week (Fri; 2hr 40min), though there are also summer sailings via Papa Westray (Tues; 3hr 10min; ☎ 01856 872044).

GETTING AROUND

By minibus A minibus usually meets the ferries and planes (☎ 01857 633244) and will take you off to the lighthouse, but phone ahead to make sure.

Bike rental Bikes can be hired at the Lighthouse Visitor Centre and dropped off at the airport or ferry terminal, or at your holiday accommodation (ⓦ northronaldsay.co.uk; £10/day).

ACCOMMODATION AND EATING

Bird Observatory ⓦ nrbo.co.uk. You can stay at the ecofriendly bird observatory, either in an en-suite guest room or in a hostel bunk bed (two four-bed dorms and a twin), or you can camp. The *Obscafé* serves decent evening meals (££ for two courses) – try the mutton, washed down with Dark Island beer. Doubles ££; dorms £; camping per person £

The Lighthouse ⓦ northronaldsay.co.uk. Great little café in the old lighthouse keepers' cottages serving snacks and affordable evening meals (by arrangement) – sample one of their North Ronaldsay mutton pies. Closed Mon. ££

Shetland

FAIR ISLE

Shetland

Shetland is a striking contrast from neighbouring Orkney. While the latter is within sight of the Scottish mainland, the archipelago of Shetland lies beyond the horizon, closer to Bergen in Norway than Edinburgh, and to the Arctic Circle than Manchester. With little fertile ground, Shetlanders have traditionally been crofters, often looking to the sea for an uncertain living in fishing and whaling or the naval and merchant services. The 23,000 islanders tend to refer to themselves as Shetlanders first, and, with the Shetland flag widely displayed, they regard Scotland as a separate entity. As in Orkney, the Mainland is the one in their own archipelago, not the Scottish mainland.

The islands' capital, **Lerwick**, is a busy little port and the only town of any size; many parts of Mainland can be reached from here on a day-trip. **South Mainland**, a narrow finger of land that runs 25 miles from Lerwick to **Sumburgh Head**, is an area rich in archaeological remains, including the offshore Iron Age **Mousa Broch** and the ancient settlement of **Jarlshof**. A further 25 miles south of Sumburgh Head is the remote but thriving **Fair Isle**, synonymous with knitwear and exceptional birdlife. The **Westside** of Mainland is sunnier but also more sparsely inhabited, as is **North Mainland**. A mile off the west coast, **Papa Stour** boasts some spectacular caves and stacks; much further out are the distinctive peaks and precipitous cliffs of the remote island of **Foula**. Shetland's three **North Isles** bring Britain to a dramatic, windswept end: **Yell** has the largest population of otters in Scotland; **Fetlar** is home to the rare red-necked phalarope; north of **Unst**, there's nothing until you reach the North Pole.

Weather has a serious influence in these parts. In winter, gales are routine, and even in the summer months it'll often be windy and rainy. The wind-chill factor is not to be taken lightly, and there's often a dampness in the air, even when it's not actually raining. While there are some good spells of dry, sunny weather (often bringing in sea mist) from May to September, it's the **simmer dim**, the twilight which lingers through the small hours at this latitude, which makes Shetland summers so memorable.

ARRIVAL AND DEPARTURE SHETLAND

By plane Loganair (ⓦloganair.co.uk) operate direct flights to Sumburgh Airport (ⓦhial.co.uk), 25 miles south of Lerwick, from Inverness, Aberdeen, Edinburgh, Glasgow, Manchester and Kirkwall in Orkney, plus summer flights from Bergen in Norway.

By ferry NorthLink (ⓦnorthlinkferries.co.uk) runs an overnight car ferry daily from Aberdeen to Lerwick (12hr 30min), calling in at Kirkwall in Orkney on Mondays, Wednesdays and Fridays (14hr 30min).

GETTING AROUND AND TOURS

By plane Airtask (ⓦairtask.com/shetland-islands-inter-island-service/shetland) runs flights from Tingwall Airport, 5 miles west of Lerwick, to the more remote islands. To reach Tingwall Airport, either take the bus from Lerwick bus station (Mon–Fri 10 daily, 2 on Sat; 15min), or there's a dial-a-ride taxi service, which must be booked a day in advance (ⓣ01595 745745).

By ferry The council-run inter-island ferries (ⓦwww.shetland.gov.uk/ferries) are excellent and fares are very low.

By bus The bus network (ⓦzettrans.org.uk) is pretty good in Shetland, with buses from Lerwick to every corner of

Mainland, and even via ferries across to Yell and Unst.

Car rental It's worth considering car rental once on the islands. Bolts Car Hire (ⓦboltscarhire.co.uk) and Star Rent-a-Car (ⓦstarrentacar.co.uk) have vehicles available at Sumburgh Airport and in Lerwick.

Tours There's a range of escorted tours and boat trips around the Mainland, great for those without a vehicle. Specific tours are mentioned throughout the text, but Shetland Wildlife (ⓦshetlandwildlife.co.uk) offer a variety of tours and holidays, while the more adventurous might consider Sea Kayak Shetland (ⓦseakayakshetland.co.uk).

16

BROCH OF MOUSA

Highlights

① Shetland Museum Beautifully designed modern waterside museum, with imaginative displays telling the story of Shetland, and a great café too. See page 539

② Traditional music Catch some local music at the regular informal sessions in Lerwick, or at the annual Shetland Folk Festival. See page 542

③ Isle of Noss Traffic-free island nature reserve where you're guaranteed to see seals, guillemots, gannets and puffins. See page 542

④ Mousa Take a short boat trip to this remote islet, which boasts Scotland's finest 2000-year-old broch and nesting storm petrels. See page 544

⑤ Jarlshof Crowd-free archeological site mingling Iron Age, Bronze Age, Pictish, Viking and medieval settlements. See page 545

⑥ Sumburgh Head Explore Shetland Mainland's southernmost lighthouse, and then enjoy the spectacular view out to Fair Isle from the lighthouse café. See page 545

⑦ Fair Isle Magical little island halfway between Shetland and Orkney, with a lighthouse at each end and a world-famous bird observatory in the middle. See page 546

⑧ Hermaness Run the gauntlet of the dive-bombing 'bonxies' for spectacular views of nesting seabirds and Muckle Flugga, Britain's most northerly point. See page 556

HIGHLIGHTS ARE MARKED ON THE MAP ON PAGE 538

Lerwick

The focus of Shetland's commercial life, **LERWICK** is home to a third of the islands' total population. Its sheltered **harbour** is busy with ferries and fishing boats, and oil-rig supply vessels. In summer, the quayside comes alive with visiting yachts, cruise liners, historic vessels such as the *Swan* and the occasional tall ship. Behind the old harbour is the compact town centre, made up of one long main street,

SHETLAND

HIGHLIGHTS

1. Shetland Museum
2. Traditional music
3. Isle of Noss
4. Mousa
5. Jarlshof
6. Sumburgh Head
7. Fair Isle
8. Hermaness

SHETLAND PONIES

Shetland is famous for its diminutive **ponies**, but it's still a surprise to find so many of them on the islands. A local ninth-century carving shows a hooded priest riding a very small pony, but traditionally they were used as pack animals, and their tails were essential for making fishing nets. During the Industrial Revolution, Shetland ponies were exported to work in the mines in England, being the only animals small enough to cope with the low galleries. Shetlands then became the playthings of the English upper classes (the Queen Mother was patron of the Shetland Pony Stud-Book Society) and they still enjoy the limelight at the Horse of the Year show.

Commercial Street; from here, narrow lanes, known as **closses**, rise westwards to the late Victorian new town.

Leir Vik ('muddy bay') was established for the **Dutch** herring fleet in the seventeenth century. Later, it became a year-round **fishing** centre, and whalers called to pick up crews en route to the northern hunting grounds. Business was conducted from the jetties of buildings known as **lodberries**, several of which survive beyond the *Queens Hotel*. Lerwick expanded in the Victorian era, and the large houses and grand public buildings established then still dominate, notably the **Town Hall**. Another period of rapid growth began during the oil boom of the 1970s, when the farmland to the southwest disappeared under a suburban sprawl and the town's northern approaches became an industrial estate.

16

Commercial Street

Lerwick's attractive shopping hub is the narrow, winding, flagstone-clad **Commercial Street**, set back one block from the Esplanade. Although the closses that connect the Street to Hillhead are now desirable, it was not so long ago that they were regarded as slum-like dens of iniquity, from which the better-off escaped to the Victorian new town laid out on a grid plan to the west.

Fort Charlotte

Commercial St • Daily April–Sept 9.30am–5.30pm; Oct–March 10am–4pm • Free • HES • ⓦ historicenvironment.scot

Commercial Street's northern end is marked by the towering walls of **Fort Charlotte**, which once stood directly above the beach. Begun for Charles II in 1665, the fort was attacked and burnt down by the Dutch in August 1673. In the 1780s, it was repaired and named in honour of George III's queen. Since then, it's served as a prison and a Royal Navy training centre; it's now open to the public, except when used by the Territorial Army.

Shetland Museum

Hay's Dock • Tues–Sat 10am–4pm, Sun noon–5pm • Free • ⓦ shetlandmuseumandarchives.org.uk

Lerwick's chief tourist sight is the **Shetland Museum**, housed in a stylishly modern waterfront building off Commercial Road, half a mile north of the town centre. The permanent exhibition begins in the Lower Gallery, where you'll find replicas of the hoard of Pictish silver found at St Ninian's Isle (see page 544), the Monks Stone, thought to show the arrival of Christianity in Shetland, and a block of butter, tax payment for the king of Norway, found preserved in a peat bog. Kids can try grinding flour with a quernstone and visit a dark 'trowie knowe'. Among the boats, artistically suspended in the Boat Hall, is a sixareen, once used as a Foula mailboat. The Upper Gallery concentrates on the islands' social history, from knitting and whaling to the oil industry. The museum also hosts temporary art exhibitions, puts on events and demonstrations, and shows archive films.

Böd of Gremista and Shetland Textile Museum

May–Sept Tues–Sat 11am–4pm • Charge • ⓦ shetlandtextilemuseum.com

Just beyond Lerwick's main ferry terminal, a mile and a half north of the town centre, stands the **Böd of Gremista**, the birthplace of **Arthur Anderson** (1792–1868), naval seaman, philanthropist, Shetland's first native MP and founder of Shetland's first newspaper, the *Shetland Journal*. The building has been completely restored and now houses the **Shetland Textile Museum**, which puts on special exhibitions on the heritage of the islands' knitting culture.

ARRIVAL AND DEPARTURE

LERWICK

By plane Flights from outside Shetland land at Sumburgh Airport, 25 miles to the south. Flights within Shetland depart from Tingwall Airport.

Destinations within Shetland Fair Isle (Mon, Wed & Thurs 2–3 daily, 1 on Tues, Fri, Sat; 25min); Foula (Mon 1 daily, Tues, Wed & Fri 2 daily; 15min); Out Skerries, calling at Whalsay on request (Mon & Wed 1 daily, Thurs 2 daily; 20min); Papa Stour (Tues 2 daily; 10min). Weather conditions can affect the schedule, which is reduced in winter.

By ferry NorthLink ferries (ⓦ northlinkferries.co.uk) from Aberdeen (daily; 12hr 30min) and Orkney (2–3 weekly; 6hr) arrive at Lerwick's ferry terminal, about a mile north of the town centre. Ferries to other islands within Shetland leave

BÖDS

With only one Hostelling Scotland hostel in Shetland, it's worth knowing about the islands' unique network of **camping böds** (March–Oct). Traditionally, a böd was a small building beside the shore, where fishermen stored their gear and occasionally slept; the word was also applied to trading posts established by Hanseatic merchants. Today, the tourist board uses the term pretty loosely: the places they run range from stone-built cottages to weatherboarded sail lofts. To stay at a böd, you must **book in advance** with the Shetland Amenity Trust (Wcamping-bods.com), as there are no live-in wardens. The more basic böds have no cooking facilities or electricity, but all have a solid fuel stove, cold water, toilets and bunk beds with mattresses – those with electricity have a meter, for which you need £1 coins. If you're camping, they're a great way to escape the wind and rain.

from the town harbour.

Destinations Bressay (approximately every 30min–1hr daily; 7min); Fair Isle (alternate Thurs; 5hr); Skerries (Wed; 2hr 30min).

By bus Buses stop on the Esplanade, close to the old harbour, or at the Viking Bus Station on Commercial Rd, north of the town centre (Wzettrans.org.uk).

Destinations Brae (Mon–Sat 8 daily; 45min); Hamnavoe (2–3 daily; 30min); Hillswick (Mon–Sat 3 daily; 1hr 40min); Laxo (Mon–Sat 2 daily; 40min); Levenwick (Mon–Sat 6–8 daily, 5 on Sun; 30min); Scalloway (Mon–Sat hourly, 4 on Sun; 20min); Sumburgh Airport (Mon–Sat 6–7 daily, 5 on Sun; 45min); Tingwall (Mon–Fri 7 daily, Sat 4 daily; 10min); Toft (Mon–Sat 5–6 daily; 50min); Vidlin (Mon–Sat 3 daily; 45min); Voe (Mon–Fri 5 daily, 3 on Sat; 35min); Walls (Mon–Sat 6 daily; 50min).

16

INFORMATION

Tourist office The tourist office is at the Market Cross, Commercial St (April–Sept Mon–Sat 9am–5pm, Sun 10am–4pm; Oct–March Mon–Sat 10am–4pm; Wshetland. org).

Accommodation Check out Wshetlandvisitor.com

Website/newspaper For what's on, consult the *Shetland Times* on Fridays (Wshetlandtimes.co.uk).

ACCOMMODATION   SEE MAP PAGE 540

Fort Charlotte Guest House 1 Charlotte St Wfortcharlotte.co.uk. Small guesthouse with great central location (on the south side of the fort), five spacious en-suite rooms and a welcoming host. **££**

Islesburgh House Hostel King Harald St Whostellingscotland.org.uk. Hostelling Scotland-affiliated, spacious Victorian hostel offering well-worn but comfortable accommodation, family rooms, a café, free wi-fi and laundry facilities. Dorms **£**; Doubles **££**

Queens Hotel 24 Commercial Street Wkqghotels. co.uk. In existence since the early 1860s, The Queens has an old-fashioned charm. Situated in Lerwick's conservation area, it offers comfortable rooms with most overlooking the picturesque harbour and easy access to town centre amenities. Doubles **££**

Rockvilla Guest House 88 St Olaf St Wrockvillaguesthouse.com. This super guesthouse, in one of the handsome Victorian houses in the upper part of town, is run by a very hospitable couple, who keep the place spotless and serve up top-notch breakfasts – fast, free wi-fi throughout the building. Doubles **££**

Woosung 43 St Olaf St Wwoosung-bb.com. Family-run B&B, up on the hill above the harbour, run by a very friendly local landlady. The whole place is kept spotlessly clean, and all rooms are en suite with fridge and microwave. Doubles **££**

EATING   SEE MAP PAGE 540

Fjarå Sea Rd Wfjaracoffee.com. Unlikely location (by the big Tesco), 15min walk from town, this modern, buzzy café has been a big hit with the locals – it's right by the shoreline so the views are great and sandwiches and salads are imaginative. Booking advised for the evening when the menu gets more adventurous. **££**

Fort Café 2 Commercial St ☎01595 693125. Lerwick's best fish-and-chip shop, situated below Fort Charlotte: takeaway or eat inside in the small café. **£**

Peerie Shop Café Esplanade Wpeerieshop.co.uk. Designer shop/gallery/café in an old lodberry (see page 539), with a good range of cakes, soup and sandwiches, a great breakfast and what is probably Britain's northernmost latte. Closed Mon. **£**

LERWICK'S FESTIVALS

On the last Tuesday in January, Lerwick plays host to **Up Helly-Aa** (ⓦuphellyaa.org), the largest of the winter fire festivals held in Shetland. In late April/early May, the **Shetland Folk Festival** (ⓦshetlandfolkfestival.com) features four days of musical mayhem, spread across the archipelago, with everything from local groups to international folk bands; book early as gigs sell out. Held over a week at Mareel, Lerwick, in July, **Fiddle Frenzy** (ⓦshetlandarts.org) shows how fiddling is central to Shetland's musical culture. It's curated by different musicians each year and includes classes for budding fiddlers. The **Shetland Accordion and Fiddle Festival** (ⓦshetlandaccordionandfiddle.com) is organized by the local accordion and fiddle club over a long weekend in early to mid-October. Threatening to eclipse even the Shetland Folk Festival is **Shetland Wool Week** (ⓦshetlandwoolweek.com), a week-long celebration of all things knitty in late September/early October.

DRINKING AND ENTERTAINMENT

The Lounge 4 Mounthooly St ☎01595 692231. Lerwick's friendliest pub, where local musicians often gather for a session in the upstairs room. Thursday night is quiz night.

Mareel North Ness ⓦshetlandarts.org/venues/mareel. Lerwick's modern cultural complex is the place to come for films and gigs – and also to sink into one of the leather sofas and enjoy views over the north bay, while tucking into burger and chips, ciabatta sandwiches and salads or nachos and other bar snacks.

16

Bressay and Noss

Shielding Lerwick from the full force of the North Sea is the island of **Bressay**, dominated at its southern end by the conical Ward Hill (744ft) – 'da Wart' – and accessible on a regular car and passenger ferry from Lerwick (takes about 7min). The chief reason for visiting Bressay is the tiny but spectacular island of **Noss**, off the east coast, whose high cliffs support a huge seabird colony in breeding season. If you've time to kill before the ferry back, pop into the **Bressay Heritage Centre** (May–Sept Tues, Wed, Fri & Sat 10am–4pm; ⓦbressay.org) by the ferry terminal.

Noss

Appropriately enough for an island that slopes gently into the sea at its western end, and plunges vertically 500ft at its eastern end, **Noss** has the dramatic and distinctive outline of a half-sunk ocean liner, while its name means 'a point of rock'. Inhabited until World War II, it's now a nature reserve and sheep farm, managed by Scottish Natural Heritage, who operate a RIB **ferry** from Bressay.

On the island, the old farmhouse contains a small visitor centre, where the warden will give you a quick briefing and a free map. Nearby is a sandy beach, while behind the 'haa' (laird's house) is a **Pony Pund**, a square stone enclosure built for the breeding of Shetland ponies. The most memorable feature of Noss is its eastern **sea cliffs**, rising to a peak at the massive Noup (500ft), from which can be seen vast colonies of cliff-nesting gannets, puffins, guillemots, shags, razorbills and fulmars: one of the highlights of Shetland. As Noss is only a mile or so wide, it's easy enough to walk to the sea cliffs and back (allow 4hr), but make sure you keep close to the coast, since otherwise the great skuas (locally known as 'bonxies') may well dive-bomb you.

ARRIVAL AND GETTING AROUND   BRESSAY AND NOSS

By ferry The car ferry to Bressay departs from the town harbour in Lerwick (every 30min–1hr; 7min; ☎01595 743974) and arrives in Maryfield on the west coast. The RIB ferry to Noss (May–Aug Tues, Wed & Fri–Sun; £3 return; ☎nature.scot) leaves from the east coast, 3 miles from Maryfield – an easy walk or short journey by bike, bus or car.

By bus No direct buses cross Bressay to the Noss ferry, but the bus that meets the Monday, Wednesday and Friday ferry at 1pm from Lerwick will take you part of the way.

Boat trips Shetland Seabird Tours run a 3hr sightseeing boat from Lerwick (April–Oct daily 9.45am & 12.45pm; £50; ⓦ shetlandseabirdtours.com), allowing you a sea view of the vast bird colonies.

Scalloway

As you approach **SCALLOWAY** from the east, there's a dramatic view over the town and the islands beyond. Once the capital of Shetland, Scalloway's importance waned during the eighteenth century as Lerwick, just six miles to the east, grew in trading success and status. Nowadays, Scalloway is fairly sleepy, though its harbour remains busy enough, with a small fishing fleet and the North Atlantic Fisheries College (NAFC) on the far side.

Scalloway Castle

If the door is locked, collect key from Scalloway Museum or Scalloway Hotel • Free • HES • ⓦ historicenvironment.scot

In spite of modern developments nearby, Scalloway is dominated by the imposing shell of **Scalloway Castle**, a classic fortified tower house built with forced labour in 1600 by the infamous earl, Patrick Stewart, and thus seen as a powerful symbol of oppression. Stewart, who'd succeeded to the Lordship of Shetland in 1592, held court here, reputedly increasing his power and wealth by using harsh justice to confiscate assets. He was eventually arrested and imprisoned in 1609 for his aggression toward his fellow landowners; his son, Robert, attempted an insurrection and both were executed in Edinburgh in 1615. The castle fell into disrepair in the following century; what remains is fun to explore.

16

Scalloway Museum

Castle Street • May–Sept Mon–Sat 11am–4pm, Sun 2–4pm • Charge • ⓦ scallowaymuseum.org

The **Scalloway Museum** occupies the old knitwear outlet next to the castle, and has a café overlooking the ruin. The displays range from Neolithic finds to the impact of modern aquaculture, and there's a replica wheelhouse and a longship for the kids to play with, but the most interesting section tells the story of the **Shetland Bus** (see page 544). There are models of some of the fishing boats that made the trip across the North Sea, a replica of the Lewis guns that were hidden in oil drums aboard the ships and a miniature radio receiver supplied to the Norwegian Resistance.

ARRIVAL AND DEPARTURE | SCALLOWAY

By bus There are regular buses to Scalloway from Lerwick (Mon–Sat hourly, 4 on Sun; 20min) and a less frequent service from Scalloway to Trondra and Burra (Mon–Sat 4 daily; 20min).

ACCOMMODATION AND EATING

The Cornerstone ⓦ thecornerstonebandb.com. Bright, modern café and B&B on the corner of the main street, with five modern rooms. Café serves breakfast fry-ups until 11.30am, comfort food until 2pm, then scones and cakes after that. Doubles ££

Da Haaf ☎ 01595 772480. Unpretentious restaurant in the NAFC with views over Scalloway harbour. Simple, super-fresh grilled fish dishes, high-quality fish and chips and tasty home-made puddings. ££

South Mainland

Shetland's **South Mainland** is a long, thin finger of land, only three or four miles wide but 25 miles long, ending in the cliffs of **Sumburgh Head** and **Fitful Head**. It's a beautiful area with wild undulating landscapes, lots of good green farmland, fabulous views out to sea and the mother of all brochs on the island of **Mousa**, just off the east coast. The most concentrated points of interest are at the southern end of the peninsula, where you'll find a crofting museum, **Jarlshof**, Shetland's most impressive archaeological treasure, and the superb new lighthouse visitor centre at Sumburgh Head itself.

Mousa Broch

Day-trip April–Sept Sun–Fri 11.30am; 3hr • Charge • **Storm petrel trip** late-May–mid-July Mon, Wed & Sat 10.30pm; 2hr 30min • Charge; advance booking required • ⓦ www.mousa.co.uk

Accessible by boat from Sandwick, the island of **Mousa** boasts the most amazingly well-preserved broch in the whole of Scotland. Rising to more than 40ft and looking rather like a Stone Age cooling tower, **Mousa Broch** has a remarkable presence and features in both *Egil's Saga* and the *Orkneyinga Saga*, contemporary chronicles of Norse exploration and settlement. To get to the broch, simply head south from the jetty along the western coastline for about half a mile. The low entrance passage leads through two concentric walls to a central courtyard, divided into separate beehive chambers. Between the walls, a rough (very dark) staircase leads to the top parapet; a torch is provided for visitors.

Thousands of **storm petrels** breed around the broch, only returning to the nests after dark. The ferry runs special late-night trips, setting off in the 'simmer dim' (twilight). Even if you've no interest in the storm petrels, which appear like bats as they flit about in the half-light, the chance to explore the broch at midnight is worth it alone.

St Ninian's Isle

Halfway down South Mainland, a road leads to **Bigton**, on the west coast. From the village, a signposted track heads down to a spectacular sandy causeway, or **tombolo**, connecting **St Ninian's Isle**. The tombolo – a concave strip of shell sand with Atlantic breakers crashing on either side – is usually exposed so you can walk over to the island, where you'll find the ruins of a medieval church.

THE SHETLAND BUS

The story of the **Shetland Bus** – the link between Shetland and Norway that helped to sustain the Norwegian Resistance through the years of Nazi occupation – is extraordinary. Under threat of enemy attack, small Norwegian fishing boats ran arms and resistance workers from Shetland into lonely fjords. The trip took 24 hours and on the return journey boats brought back Norwegians wanted by the Gestapo, or volunteers for Norwegian forces fighting with the Allies. For three years, through careful planning, the operation was remarkably successful: cryptic instructions to boats were broadcast by the BBC. Local people knew what was going on, but the secret was well kept. In total, 350 refugees were evacuated, and more than 400 tons of arms, large amounts of explosives and 60 radio transmitters were landed in Norway.

Originally established at **Lunna** in the northeast of the Mainland, the service moved to **Scalloway** in 1942, partly because the village offered good marine engineering facilities at Moore's Shipyard on Main Street, where a plaque records the morale-boosting visit of the Norwegian Crown Prince Olav. Explosives and weapons were stored in the castle, and **Kergord House** in Weisdale was used as a safe house and training centre for intelligence personnel and saboteurs. The hazards, tragedies and elations of the exercise are brilliantly described in David Howarth's book, *The Shetland Bus*; their legacy today is a heartfelt closeness between Shetland and Norway.

Crofthouse Museum

May–Sept daily 10am–1pm & 2–5pm • Free • ⓦ shetlandheritageassociation.com

Housed in a well-to-do thatched croft in Southvoe, built around 1870, the **Crofthouse Museum** re-creates the feel of crofting life, with a peat fire, traditional box beds and so forth. Adjacent to the living quarters is the byre for the cows and tatties, and the kiln for drying the grain. Crofting was mostly done by women in Shetland, while the men went out haaf-net fishing for the laird. Down by the nearby burn, there's also a restored thatched horizontal mill.

Old Scatness Broch and Iron Age Village

Mid-May to Aug Fri 10.15am–4.30pm; check ahead • Charge • ⓦ shetlandamenity.org

Extending the airport revealed a vast Iron Age archaeological site known as **Old Scatness Broch and Iron Age Village**. At the centre of the site are the remains of an Iron Age broch, surrounded by a settlement of interlocking wheelhouses – so-called because of their circular ground plan – two of which have been either partially or wholly reconstructed.

Jarlshof

Daily April–Sept 9.30am–5.30pm; Oct –March restricted hours; check ahead • Charge • HES • ⓦ historicenvironment.scot

Of all the archaeological sites in Shetland, **Jarlshof** is the largest and most impressive. What makes Jarlshof so amazing is the fact that you can walk right into a house built 1600 years ago, which is still intact to above head height. The site is big and confusing, scattered with the ruins of buildings dating from the Bronze Age to the early seventeenth century. The name – misleading, as it is not primarily a Viking site – was coined by Sir Walter Scott, who used the ruins of the Old House in his novel *The Pirate*. However, it was only at the end of the nineteenth century that the Bronze Age, Iron Age and Viking settlements you see now were discovered, after a violent storm ripped off the top layer of turf.

The Bronze Age smithy and Iron Age dwellings nearest the entrance are nothing compared with the cells which cluster around the **broch**, close to the sea. Only half of the original broch survives, and its courtyard is now an Iron Age aisled roundhouse, with stone piers. However, it's difficult to distinguish the broch from the later Pictish **wheelhouses** which now surround it. Still, it's all great fun to explore, as you're free to roam around the cells, checking out the in-built stone shelving, water tanks, beds and so on. Inland lies the maze of grass-topped foundations marking out the **Viking longhouses**, from the ninth century AD. Towering over the whole complex are the ruins of the laird's house, built by Robert Stewart, Earl of Orkney and Lord of Shetland, in the late sixteenth century, and the **Old House of Sumburgh**, built by his son, Patrick.

Sumburgh Head Lighthouse

Daily April–Sept 11am–5.30pm • Charge • ⓦ sumburghhead.com

The Mainland comes to a dramatic end at **Sumburgh Head** (262ft), which rises sharply out of the land only to drop vertically into the sea. The road up to it is the perfect site for watching nesting seabirds such as kittiwakes, fulmars, shags, razorbills and guillemots, as well as gannets diving for fish. This is also the easiest place in Shetland to get close to **puffins**: during the nesting season (May to early Aug), you simply need to look over the western wall, just before you enter the lighthouse complex, to see them arriving at their burrows a few yards below with beaks full of sand eels.

You can visit the clifftop lighthouse, built by Robert Stevenson in 1821, and explore some of the outbuildings, including the reconstructed WWII secret radar

16

hut which helped protect the Royal Navy anchored in Scapa Flow. As well as a visitor centre with an exhibition on the history of the lighthouse, there's a **Marine Life Centre**, with hard-hitting displays on the worrying recent decline in seabird numbers. After roaming the complex, you can settle down and enjoy the sea views from the lighthouse's **café**.

ARRIVAL AND DEPARTURE
SOUTH MAINLAND

By plane Sumburgh Airport, at the southernmost tip of South Mainland, is Shetland's main airport. There's a bus service to Lerwick (Mon–Sat 6–7 daily, 5 on Sun; 45min) or else it's a £44 taxi ride (☎ 01950 460560).

By bus There are regular buses from Lerwick to Levenwick (Mon–Sat 7–8 daily, 5 on Sun; 30min); Sandwick (Mon–Sat 8–10 daily, 5 on Sun; 25min); Sumburgh (Mon–Sat 6–7 daily, 5 on Sun; 45min).

ACCOMMODATION AND EATING

Betty Mouat's Cottage Scatness ⓦ camping-bods. com. Next to an excavated broch and not far from the airport, this stone-built cottage is a camping *böd* with two bedrooms (one sleeping six, another four), hot water, a solid-fuel stove and an electricity meter (£1 coins needed). Dorms £

Levenwick Campsite Levenwick ⓦ levenwick. shetland.co.uk. Small, terraced campsite run by the local community with hot showers and laundry facilities and a superb view over the east coast. Per pitch £

★ **Mucklehus** Levenwick ⓦ mucklehus.co.uk. A lovely B&B run by a local artist in a former Master Mariner's house built in 1890 near the sandy beach in Levenwick, 18 miles south of Lerwick; the rooms are small, but stylish. Sitting

room for guests too. Doubles ££

Solbrekke B&B Park Rd, Sandwick ☎ 01950 431410. Surrounded by lovely gardens overlooking the island of Mousa Broch, this two double-bedroom property is in an ideal spot from which to explore South Mainland's attractions. Doubles ££

The Spiggie Dunrossness ⓦ spiggie.co.uk. Guesthouse with six en-suite rooms and two self-catering apartments. The restaurant has great views out to Foula and, if you're lucky, incredible sunsets. Bar meals are reasonably priced, or you can have well-presented dishes such as lobster or whatever the local catch is, a la carte in the restaurant. Doubles £££

Fair Isle

Marooned in the sea halfway between Shetland and Orkney, **Fair Isle** is very different from both. The weather reflects its isolated position: you can almost guarantee that it'll be windy, though if you're lucky your visit might coincide with fine weather – what the islanders call 'a given day'. Fair Isle's population had tumbled from 400 to 44 by the 1950s, at which point evacuation was seriously considered. The laird, **George Waterston**, who'd set up a bird observatory in 1948, passed it into the care of the NTS in 1954 and rejuvenation began. Today, Fair Isle supports a community of around sixty.

The north end of the island rises like a wall, while the Sheep Rock, a sculpted stack of rock and grass on the east side, is another dramatic feature. The croft land and the island's scattered white houses are concentrated in the south. Fair Isle has two **lighthouses**, one at either end of the island, both designed by the Stevenson family and erected in 1892 – the South Lighthouse can be visited by appointment (✉ info@ southlightfairisle.scot; charge).

Fair Isle Bird Observatory

ⓦ fairislebirdobs.co.uk

In 2019, a devastating fire destroyed the Fair Isle Bird Observatory (FIBO), however, a complete rebuild is underway and the observatory is scheduled to reopen in the spring of 2023 – check the website for updates. Standing just above the sandy bay of North Haven where the ferry from Shetland arrives, it housed an exhibition on the island past and present and served as one of the major European centres for ornithology. As a result, the island is a haven for twitchers, who descend on the island whenever a major rarity is spotted; for more casual birders, however, there's also plenty of summer resident birdlife to enjoy. The high-pitched screeching that fills the sky above the airstrip comes from hundreds of arctic terns, and arctic skuas can also be seen here. Those in search of puffins should head for the cliffs around Furse, and to find gannets, aim for the spectacular Stacks of Scroo.

George Waterston Museum

May–Oct Mon 2–4pm, Wed 10.30am–noon, Fri 2–3.30pm • Free • Ⓦ shetland.org

Fair Isle is known for its **knitting** patterns, still produced with great skill by the local knitwear cooperative. There are samples on display at the **George Waterston Museum**, next to the Methodist Chapel. Particularly memorable are stories of shipwrecks; in 1868, the islanders undertook a heroic rescue of all 465 German emigrants aboard the *Lessing*. More famously, *El Gran Grifon*, part of the retreating Spanish Armada, was lost here in 1588 and three hundred Spanish seamen were washed up on the island. Food was in such short supply that fifty died of starvation before help could be summoned from Shetland.

ARRIVAL AND DEPARTURE   FAIR ISLE

By plane Airtask (Ⓦ airtask.com) flies from Tingwall to Fair Isle (April–Oct Mon–Sat 1–3 daily) for around £90 return.
By ferry The passenger ferry connects Fair Isle with either Lerwick (alternate Thurs; 4–5hr) or Grutness in Sumburgh (Tues, alternate Thurs & Sat; 3hr); since the boat only takes a limited number of passengers, it's advisable to book in advance (Ⓣ 01595 760363). The crossing can be rough.

ACCOMMODATION AND EATING

If you're staying over, book accommodation in advance; note that camping is not permitted. There are separate dining options, hence all accommodation is booked on a full-board basis. There is a shop/post office, Stackhoull Stores, in the south of the island (closed Tues & Sat afternoon, and all-day Thurs & Sun).

Auld Haa Guesthouse Close to the Museum Ⓣ 01595 760349. The accommodation may not be fancy but the warm-hearted, easy-going host offers tasty nutritious food and great local knowledge. Excellent views from the garden include the chance to see gannets plunging into the shimmering sea. Doubles **£££**

Fair Isle Guest House Upper Leogh, 1.5 miles south of the airport Ⓦ kathycoull.com. You'll be well looked after at this whitewashed B&B by spinning and weaving expert, Kathy Coull, who also runs textile courses. Double **££**

South Light House 2 miles south of the airport Ⓦ southlightfairisle.scot. B&B at the southernmost tip of the island, not literally in the lighthouse, but in the adjacent keepers' cottages – note bathrooms are not en suite. Doubles **£££**

The Westside

The western Mainland of Shetland – known as the **Westside** – stretches west from Weisdale and Voe to Sandness. Although there are some important archeological remains and wildlife here, the area's greatest appeal lies in its outstanding **coastal scenery** and walks. Cut by several deep voes, the coastline is very varied; aside from dramatic cliffs, there are intimate coves and some fine beaches, as well as the stunning island of **Papa Stour**.

Walls and around

Once an important fishing port, **WALLS** (pronounced '*waas*'), appealingly set round its harbour, is now a quiet village which comes alive once a year in the middle of August for the Walls Agricultural Show, the biggest farming bash on the island. If you're just passing by, you might like to stop by the **bakery and tearoom**, but Walls also has several good **accommodation** options.

Stanydale Temple

Three miles east of Walls lies the finest Neolithic structure in the Westside, dubbed the **Stanydale Temple** by the archaeologist who excavated it because it resembled a temple on Malta. Whatever its true function, it was twice as large as the surrounding oval-shaped houses (now in ruins) and was certainly of great importance, perhaps as some kind of community centre. To reach it, follow the black-and-white poles across the moorland for half a mile from the road.

ARRIVAL AND DEPARTURE   THE WESTSIDE

By bus There's an infrequent bus service between Lerwick and Skeld (Mon–Sat 1–3 daily; 1hr), and between Lerwick and Walls (Mon–Sat 5–6 daily; 45min), with a feeder service from Sandness (Mon–Sat 2–3 daily; 45min) – some journeys are dial-a-ride and need to be booked in advance (☎01595 745745).

ACCOMMODATION AND EATING

Bo's B&B 1.5 miles southwest of Walls ⓦbosimmons. wix.com/bosbandb. One double room for B&B in a newly built ecofriendly house, a glamping-style bothy and a wooden camping pod for the hardy, situated on the road from Walls to Burrastow. B&B £££; bothy £; pods £

★ **Burrastow House** 3 miles southwest of Walls ⓦburrastowhouse.co.uk. Beautifully situated off the beaten track southwest of Walls, parts of the house date back to 1759 and have real character; others are more modern. The cooking is superb and evening meals are available for non-residents, too. Doubles £££

Skeld böd Skeld ⓦcamping-bods.com. Sitting right above the marina close to the sea, this is the most recent addition to Shetland's network of böds, converted from the local shop, and sleeping six. You need £1 coins to operate the electricity. Dorms £

Voe House Walls ⓦcamping-bods.com. This five-bedroom camping böd is Shetland's largest, with its own peat fire. Note that *Voe House*, confusingly, is not in Voe but in Walls. Dorms £

Papa Stour

Formed of volcanic lava and ash, the rocky island of **Papa Stour** has been eroded into some of the most impressive coastal scenery in Shetland. In good weather, it makes for a perfect day-trip, but in foul weather or a sea mist it can appear pretty bleak. Its name, meaning 'big island of the priests', derives from its early Celtic Christian connections. The land is very fertile, and once supported three hundred inhabitants, but in the early 1970s the population crisis was such that the island had to advertise for incomers – today, the population is around a dozen. There is no accommodation, but you can wild camp and there are toilets by the ferry terminal.

ARRIVAL AND DEPARTURE   PAPA STOUR

By plane Airtask (ⓦairtask.com) flies from Tingwall twice every Tuesday, so a day-trip is feasible (around £75 return).

WALKING ON PAPA STOUR

Ordnance Survey Explorer map 467

To reach the best of Papa Stour's coastal scenery, head for the west of the island. From **Virda Field** (285ft), the highest point, you can see the treacherous rocks of **Ve Skerries**, where a lighthouse was erected as recently as 1979. The coastline from here southeast to Hamna Voe has some of the island's best stacks, blowholes and natural arches. The most spectacular is **Kirstan's Hole**, a group of partly roofed cleft, extending far inland, where shags nest on precipitous ledges. Look out, too, for red-throated divers, which regularly breed on inland lochs such as Gorda Water.

16

By ferry The ferry runs from West Burrafirth, five miles north of Walls, to Papa Stour (Wed, Fri & Sat 2 daily, Sun 1 daily; 40min; ☎01955 745804) – book in advance, and reconfirm the day before departure.

Foula

At 'the edge of the world', **Foula** is the most isolated inhabited island in the British Isles, separated from the nearest point on Shetland by about fourteen miles of often turbulent ocean. Seen from the Mainland, its distinctive mountainous outline is unforgettable. Its western **cliffs**, the second highest in Britain after those of St Kilda, rise to 1220ft at **The Kame**; a clear day offers a panorama stretching from Unst to Fair Isle. On a bad day, the exposure is complete and the cliffs generate turbulent blasts of wind known as 'flans', which rip through the hills with tremendous force.

Arriving on Foula, you can't help but be amazed by the sheer size of the island's immense, bare mountains, whose summits are often hidden in cloud, known as 'Foula's hat'. The gentler eastern slopes provide good crofting land, and plentiful peat, around which the island's population of around forty is scattered. The only road, running along the island's eastern side, is used by Foula's remarkable fleet of clapped-out vehicles.

Foula's name is derived from the Old Norse for 'bird island', and its home to a quarter of a million **birds**. Arctic terns wheel overhead at the airstrip, red-throated divers can usually be seen on the island's smaller lochs, while fulmars, guillemots, razorbills, puffins and gannets cling to the rock ledges. However, it's the island's colony of **great skuas** or 'bonxies' that you can't fail to notice, with an estimated 3,000 pairs on Foula, making it the largest colony in the world. During the nesting season (May–Aug), they attack anyone who comes near; the best advice is to hold a stick above your head or stick to the road and the coast.

16

ARRIVAL AND DEPARTURE   FOULA

By plane Airtask (⊛airtask.com) flies from Tingwall (Mon 1 daily, Tues, Wed & Fri 2 daily, 15min); tickets cost around £86 return.

By ferry Be sure to book and reconfirm your journey by ferry (⊛bkmarine.org), which departs from Walls (Tues & Thurs, additional sailings in summer subject to weather conditions; 2hr. The ferry arrives at Ham, in the middle of Foula's east coast.

INFORMATION AND TOURS

Tourist information Foula has its own resident part-time Ranger, who usually greets new arrivals and offers local advice (mid-April to Oct). It's also possible to arrange for guided walks with a Ranger (Wed & Fri; ⊛foulaheritage. com), or you can download self-guided walk leaflets from the website. There's no shop on the island, so bring your own supplies.

Boat trips Day-trips are not possible on the regular ferry, but The Swan Trust (⊛swantrust.com) do boat trips on Wednesdays from Walls.

ACCOMMODATION

Leraback Foula ☎01595 753226. Other than self-catering, the only accommodation on Foula is at this B&B near Ham. It's a simple but very welcoming place to stay; full board only and they'll collect you from the airstrip or pier. Double **££**

North Mainland

The **North Mainland**, stretching over thirty miles from the central belt around Lerwick, is wilder than much of Shetland, with relentlessly bleak moorland and some rugged and dramatic coastal scenery. It's all but split in two by the isthmus of **Mavis Grind**: to the south lies **Sullom Voe**, Shetland's oil terminal, and **Brae**, the area's largest town; to the north is the remote region of **Northmavine**, boasting some of Shetland's most scenic cliffs.

Voe

If you're travelling north, you'll pass by **VOE**, at the main crossroads of the North Mainland. If you stay on the main road, it's easy to miss the picturesque little port, a tight huddle of homes and workshops down below the road around the pier (and signposted Lower Voe). Set at the head of a deep, sheltered sea loch, Voe has a Scandinavian appearance, helped by the presence of the **Sail Loft**, now a **camping böd**.

ACCOMMODATION   VOE

Sail Loft By the harbour ⓦ camping-bods.com. Originally a giant storeroom, this enormous böd is situated right by the loch and has hot showers, a kitchen and a solid- fuel fire in the smaller of the two rooms. Bring £1 coins for the electricity meter. Dorms $\overline{\underline{£}}$

Lunnasting

Lunnasting is the area to the northeast of Voe, on the east coast. The main town is **VIDLIN**, departure point for the Out Skerries (see page 553), three miles east of Laxo, which is the ferry terminal for Whalsay (see page 552).

The Cabin Museum

Tues, Thurs, Sat & Sun 1–5pm • Free • ⓦ shetland.org

Halfway between Laxo and Vidlin, the B9071 passes **The Cabin Museum**, a modern barn packed to the rafters with wartime memorabilia collected by the late Andy Robertson. You can try on some of the uniforms and caps or pore over the many personal accounts of the war written by locals.

Lunna

The long thin peninsula of Lunna Ness is pinched in the middle at the tiny remote settlement of **LUNNA**, a couple of miles northeast of Vidlin. It was here, at **Lunna House**, originally built in 1660, that the Shetland Bus made its headquarters during World War II (see page 544). Nearby lies the whitewashed **Lunna Kirk**, built in 1753, which has a simple tiny interior including a carved hexagonal pulpit. In the graveyard, several unidentified Norwegian sailors, torpedoed by the Nazis, are buried.

Brae

BRAE is a sprawling settlement that still has the feel of a frontier town, having expanded hastily in the 1970s to accommodate the workforce for the nearby **Sullom Voe Oil Terminal**, the largest of its kind in Europe. During World War II, Sullom Voe was home to the Norwegian Air Force and a base for RAF seaplanes.

ACCOMMODATION AND EATING   BRAE

★ **Busta House**, ⓦ bustahouse.com. A laird's house with stepped gables that sits across the bay from Brae. Even if you're not staying the night it's worth coming for lunch in the Long Room, for a stroll around the wooded grounds, or for the excellent set-menu meal (£35) in the *Pitcairn* *Restaurant*. Double $\overline{\underline{£££}}$

Frankie's ⓦ frankiesfishandchips.com. Popular fish and chip café with great views over Busta Voe. As well as fish straight off the boats, you can get king scallops, smoked haddock and mussels. Takeaways too. $\overline{\underline{££}}$

Northmavine

Northmavine, the northwest peninsula of North Mainland, is unquestionably one of the most picturesque areas of Shetland, with its often-rugged scenery, magnificent coastline and wide-open spaces. The peninsula begins a mile west of Brae at **Mavis Grind**, a narrow isthmus at which it's said you can throw a stone from the Atlantic to the North Sea, or at least to Sullom Voe.

Hillswick

HILLSWICK was once a centre for deep-sea or haaf fishing, and later a herring station. In 1900, the North of Scotland, Orkney & Shetland Steam Navigation Company built the **St Magnus Hotel** to house their customers, importing it in the form of a timber kit from Norway. It still stands overlooking St Magnus Bay, rather magnificently clad in mustard and black timber.

Down by the ancient harbour is **Da Böd**, which was founded by a Hanseatic merchant in 1684, later became Shetland's oldest pub, and is now the Hillswick Wildlife sanctuary (ⓦ hillswickwildlifesanctuary.org), where visitors are welcome to visit from May to September after 2pm. The sanctuary is embarking on a major project to upgrade the facilities that will provide its visitor centre with some art, crafts, photos and literature on an environmental and wildlife theme, which is due to open by 2023. The stony beach by the harbour is very sheltered, but the nicest sandiest **beach** is on the west side of the Hillswick isthmus, overlooking Dore Holm, a short walk across the fields from the hotel.

Esha Ness

Just outside Hillswick, a road leads west to the exposed headland of **Esha Ness**, celebrated for its splendid coastline views. Spectacular red-granite **cliffs**, eaten away to form fantastic shapes by the elements, spread out before you as the road climbs away from Hillswick: to the south, out at sea, are the stacks known as **The Drongs**, while in the distance the Westside and Papa Stour are visible. After three miles, you reach Braewick café and campsite, with a great view over the wide bay of Brae Wick, from which several small dead-end roads lead off to the coast.

Tangwick Haa Museum

Easter–Sept daily 11am–5pm • Free • ⓦ tangwickhaa.org.uk

One small dead-end road, off the main road, leads south to the **Tangwick Haa Museum**, housed in a seventeenth-century building, which tells the often-moving story of this remote corner of Shetland and its role in the dangerous trade of deep-sea fishing and whaling.

Esha Ness Lighthouse

West of Braewick, where the road divides, the northernmost branch ends at **Esha Ness Lighthouse**, a great place to view the red-sandstone cliffs, stacks and blowholes. Beware of the latter, some of which are hidden far inland. The best example is the **Holes of Scraada**, a partly roofed cleft, half a mile north of the lighthouse, where the sea suddenly appears 300 yards inland from the cliff line. The incredible power of the sea can be seen in the various giant boulder fields above the cliffs: these **storm beaches** are formed by rocks torn from the cliffs in storms and deposited inland.

16

ACCOMMODATION AND EATING   **NORTHMAVINE**

HILLSWICK AND AROUND
Almara Urafirth ⓦ www.almara.shetland.co.uk. This modern B&B – up on a hill overlooking Ura Firth – serves

up a friendly family welcome, big breakfasts and excellent views. **££**
St Magnus Bay Hotel Hillswick ⓦ stmagnusbayhotel.

co.uk. Large, distinctive mustard and black hotel with large, high-ceilinged public rooms and rooms ranging from the spacious to the cosy. The restaurant serves generous and filling portions – the Sunday carvery is particularly popular. £££

ESHA NESS

Braewick café and campsite Braewick, 4 miles northwest of Hillswick ☎ 01806 503345. Café with great views of the Drongs, serving soup, sandwiches and toasties, plus home-made cakes and scones. The campsite is pretty exposed but you can always book one of the four wooden wigwams if the wind gets too much. Wigwams ££; camping per pitch £

Johnnie Notions Böd Hamnavoe, 1.5 miles north of Braewick ⓦ camping-bods.com. One of the few places to stay in Esha Ness, this tiny four-bed böd – the birthplace of a pioneer in smallpox inoculation – is in a remote hamlet of Hamnavoe, north of Braewick. There's no electricity and cold water only, but there is a solid-fuel stove. Dorms £

Whalsay

The island of **Whalsay** (population around 1,000) is in a world of its own, with a dialect even other Shetlanders struggle to fathom. The islands' fishing crews operate a very successful pelagic fleet of immense super-trawlers which can fish far afield in all weathers, catching a wide range of species. The island is extremely fertile, but crofting takes second place to fishing here.

Symbister

16

The island's chief town is **SYMBISTER**, whose harbour is usually dominated by the presence of several of the island's sophisticated, multi-million-pound purse-netters, some over 180ft long; you'll also see smaller fishing boats and probably a few 'fourareens', which the locals race regularly in the summer months.

Pier House

Mon–Sat 9am–1pm & 2–5pm, Sun 2–4pm • Free

Alongside the busy harbour is the tiny grey-granite **Pier House**, the key for which resides in the shop opposite. This picturesque little building, with a hoist built into one side, is thought to have been a Hanseatic merchants' store, and contains displays on how the Germans traded salt, tobacco, spirits and cloth for Whalsay's salted, dried fish from medieval times until the eighteenth century.

Whalsay Heritage Centre

May–Sept Wed & Fri–Sun 2–5pm • Charge • ⓦ whalsayheritage.co.uk

Overlooking the town is the imposing Georgian mansion of **Symbister House**, built in grey granite and boasting a Neoclassical portico. It was built in the 1830s at great expense by the laird Robert Bruce, reputedly not because he wanted to live on Whalsay but because he wanted to deprive his heirs of his fortune. It's now part of the local school, though you can still see the old doocot behind the house, and various outbuildings in the Midden Court, one of which houses a **heritage centre** on the history of the island.

ARRIVAL AND DEPARTURE WHALSAY

By ferry Car ferries run regularly to Whalsay from Laxo on the Mainland (☎ 01595 743973; 30min) – book ahead to take a car. In bad weather, especially southeasterly gales, the service operates from Vidlin instead. Laxo–Symbister (roughly every 45min; 30min).

ACCOMMODATION AND EATING

Oot Ower Lounge and Campsite Huxter ☎ 01806 566658. A family-run pub overlooking the Loch of Huxter – this is pretty much the only place to eat and drink on the island (phone ahead to check they're open and serving food), with the likes of fish and chips, and somewhere to camp. Per pitch £

SHOPPING

Shoard Brough, 2 miles northeast of Symbister. The country's remotest charity and recycling shop is in Brough. It has limited opening hours but is a must if you're in the area.

Out Skerries

Lying four miles out to sea, off the northeast tip of Whalsay, the **Out Skerries** consist of three low-lying rocky islands, Housay, Bruray and Grunay, the first two linked by a bridge (population around seventy). That people live here at all is remarkable, and that it's one of Shetland's more robust communities is astonishing, its affluence based on fishing and on salmon farming in a nearby inlet. There are a few prehistoric remains, but the majority of visitors are divers exploring the wreck-strewn coastline, and ornithologists hoping to glimpse rare migrants.

The Skerries' jetty and airstrip are both on the middle island of **Bruray**, which boasts the Skerries' highest point, Bruray Wart (173ft), an easy climb, and home to the islands' ingenious spiral-channel collection system for rainwater, which can become scarce in summer. The easternmost island, **Grunay**, is now uninhabited, though the abandoned lighthouse keepers' cottages on the island's chief hill remain; despite appearances, the Stevenson-designed lighthouse itself sits on the outlying islet of Bound Skerry. The largest of the Skerries, **Housay**, has the most indented and intriguing coastline, to which you should head if the weather's fine.

16

ARRIVAL AND DEPARTURE   OUT SKERRIES

By ferry Ferries to and from Skerries leave from Vidlin on the Mainland (Mon & Fri–Sun; 1hr 30min) and Lerwick (Wed; 2hr 30min), but day trips are only possible from Vidlin (Fri & Sun). Make sure you book your journey by 5pm the previous evening (☎01595 745804), or the ferry might not run. You can take your car over, but, with less than a mile of road to drive along, it's not necessary.

ACCOMMODATION

Camping is allowed, with permission. There is a shop, and a shower/toilet block by the pier.
Rocklea ☜ rockleaok.co.uk. The only B&B on the islands is a modern croft house on Bruray run by the very welcoming Johnsons, who offer optional full board. Doubles **££**

The North Isles

Many visitors never make it out to Shetland's trio of **North Isles**, thinking that they are too remote. This is a shame, as the ferry links are in fact frequent and inexpensive, and the roads fast. Much of the scenery is the familiar Shetland landscape of undulating peat moorland, dramatic coastal cliffs and silent glacial voes. However, the spirit of independence and self-sufficiency in the North Isles is much more keenly felt. **Yell** is best known for its vast otter population but is otherwise often overlooked. **Fetlar**, the smallest, is home to the rare red-necked phalarope, while **Unst** has the widest appeal, as the most northerly land mass in the British Isles, and for its nesting seabird population.

Yell

If you keep to the main road, which cuts across the island of Yell, you'll pass a lot of fairly uninspiring peat moorland. Get onto the minor roads, though, and you'll begin to appreciate the island and have more chance of spotting one of Yell's numerous **otters**.

16

Burravoe

At **BURRAVOE**, in the southeastern corner of Yell, a whitewashed laird's house dating from 1672 houses the **Old Haa Museum** (April–Sept Mon–Thurs & Sat 11am–4pm, Sun 2–5pm; free; ⊚oldhaa.com). Stuffed with artefacts, the museum has lots of material on the history of the local herring and whaling industry and there's a pleasant wood-panelled café on the ground floor. From May to August, you'll find thousands of **seabirds** (including puffins) nesting in the cliffs above Ladies Hole, less than a mile northeast of the village.

Mid Yell and around

The island's largest village, **MID YELL**, has a small marina, a couple of shops and a leisure centre with a swimming pool. A mile northwest of the village, on a hill above the main road, stands the spooky, abandoned eighteenth-century **Windhouse**; skeletons were found under the floor and in its wood-panelled walls, and the house is now believed by many to be haunted (its ghost-free lodge is a camping böd; see page 541).

ARRIVAL AND TOURS
YELL

By ferry Ferries to Ulsta (Yell) from Toft on the Mainland are very frequent (every 30min–1hr; 20min), as are ferries from Gutcher across the Bluemull Sound to Belmont (Unst) and Hamar's Ness (Fetlar) – note its cash or cheque only on the ferries (⊚www.shetland.gov.uk).

By bus An integrated bus and ferry service from Lerwick goes all the way to Gutcher (Mon–Sat 1 daily; 2hr 10min). On Yell, buses from Ulsta run to Gutcher (Mon–Sat 3–4 daily; 30min).

Guided tours Local otter spotter John Campbell (⊚shetlandnature.scot) takes groups of two or three in search of otters (£120 per person) – book in advance.

ACCOMMODATION AND EATING

Quam West Sandwick ⊚quambandbyellshetland. co.uk. Large, kit-built Scandinavian-style working croft with sheep, ducks, hens and Shetland ponies on site. There are wonderful sea views across Yell Sound, and dinner is available for an extra £15 a head. Doubles **££**

Tearoom Old Haa Museum ☎01957 722339. Enjoy home-baked cakes and a welcome cup of tea or coffee beside a lovely old fireplace adorned with fire irons.

Windhouse Lodge camping böd Mid Yell ⊚camping-bods.com. The Windhouse gatehouse, on the main road near Mid Yell, has a wood- and peat-fired heater and hot showers. Bring £1 coins for the electricity meter. Dorms **££**

Fetlar

Fetlar is the most fertile of the North Isles, much of it grassy moorland and lush green meadows with masses of summer flowers. It's known as 'the garden of Shetland', though that's pushing it a bit, as it's still an unforgiving, treeless landscape. **Sir Arthur Nicolson** cleared much of the island's population at forty days' notice to make room for sheep. Today, Fetlar's population of around sixty lives on the southern and eastern sides of the island.

Houbie and around

At the tiny, main settlement, **HOUBIE**, in the centre of the island, there's the **Fetlar Interpretive Centre** (May–Sept Mon–Sat 11am–4pm, Sun 12.30–4pm; charge; ⊚fetlar. org), a welcoming museum with information on Fetlar's outstanding birdlife and the archaeological excavations that took place near Houbie. For a sandy bay in which to relax, the **Sand of Tresta** is less than a mile to the west.

Loch of Funzie

Fetlar is one of very few places in Britain where you'll see the graceful **red-necked phalarope** (late May–early Aug): the birds are unusual in that the female does the courting and then leaves the male in charge of incubation. A hide has been provided overlooking the marshes (or mires) to the east of the **Loch of Funzie** (pronounced

'Finny'); the loch itself is also a good place at which to spot the phalaropes, and is a regular haunt of red-throated divers.

ARRIVAL AND GETTING AROUND
FETLAR

By ferry Ferries to Fetlar (Mon–Sat 6–9 daily, Sun 5 daily; 25–40min) depart regularly from both Gutcher (Yell) and Belmont (Unst), and dock at Hamar's Ness, three miles northwest of Houbie.

By bus There's a Funzie to Hamar's Ness service (Mon–Sat 4 daily), which is a dial-a-ride electric minibus service – to use it you must book your journey the day before (☎01595 745745).

By car If you do have your own vehicle, bear in mind that there's no petrol station on Fetlar, so fill up before you come across.

ACCOMMODATION AND EATING

Aithbank Böd Aith ⊛ camping-bods.com. A cosy wood-panelled cottage, a mile east of Houbie, with two rooms, sleeping a total of seven. Hot water, kitchen including cooker with grill and hotplates. Dorms £

Fetlar Café Houbie ☎01957 733227. The island's only café lives inside the island shop/post office in Houbie. Cooked breakfasts, soup, sandwiches, toasties or an omelette all on offer. £

Gord Houbie ☎01957 733227, ⊜gord@fetlarshetland. co.uk. The modern house attached to the island shop in Houbie is also a B&B with great sea views from all the rooms. All guests are full board only, and they do meals for non-residents by arrangement. Doubles ££££

Unst

While much of **Unst** is rolling grassland, the coast is more dramatic: a fringe of cliffs relieved by some beautiful sandy beaches. As Britain's most northerly inhabited island, there is a surfeit of 'most northerly' sights. Most visitors head straight for Hermaness to see the seabirds and look out over Muckle Flugga and the northernmost tip of Britain, to the North Pole beyond.

Muness Castle

On the south coast of the island, not far from **UYEASOUND**, lie the ruins of **Muness Castle**, a diminutive defensive structure, with matching bulging bastions and corbelled turrets at opposite corners. The castle was built in 1598 by the Scots incomer, Laurence Bruce, stepbrother and chief bullyboy of the infamous earl, Robert Stewart. The inscription above the entrance asks visitors 'not to hurt this wark aluayis', but the castle was sacked by Danish pirates in 1627 and never really re-roofed.

Baltasound

Unst's main settlement is **BALTASOUND**, five miles north of Uyeasound; its herring industry used to boost the local population to around 10,000 during the fishing season. As you leave Baltasound, heading north, take a look at **Bobby's bus shelter**, an eccentric, fully furnished, award-winning Shetland bus shelter on the edge of the town.

Keen of Hamar

The **Keen of Hamar**, east of Baltasound and clearly signposted from the main road, is one of the largest expanses of serpentine debris in Europe and home to an extraordinary array of plant life. It's worth taking a walk on this barren, exposed, almost lunar landscape that's thought to resemble what most of northern Europe looked like at the end of the last ice age. Armed with a Scottish Natural Heritage leaflet (kept in a box by the stile or download it from ⊛nature.scot), you can identify some of the area's numerous rare and minuscule plants, including Norwegian sandwort, frog orchid, moonwort and the mouse-eared Edmondston's chickweed, which flowers in June and July and is found nowhere else in the world.

16

Haroldswick

Near the shore, at **HAROLDSWICK**, you'll find the **Unst Boat Haven** (May–Sept Mon–Sat 11am–4pm, Sun 2–4pm; charge; ⓦunstheritage.com), displaying a beautifully presented collection of historic boats along with many tools of the trade and information on fishing. If you want to learn about other aspects of Unst's history, head for the nearby **Unst Heritage Centre** (same details as the Boat Haven), housed in the old school building by the main crossroads, where they also put on have-a-go activities such as spinning, knitting and potting.

Saxa Vord RAF base

Just north of Haroldswick is **SAXA VORD** (also, confusingly, the name of the nearby hill), home to the eyesore former **RAF base**, containing self-catering accommodation, a restaurant, bar and hostel, where there's also a basic café and an **exhibition** on the history of the RAF on Unst (ⓦsaxavord.com). The former base is also home to **Shetland Reel**, Britain's most northerly gin distillery, offering guided tours (May–Sept Mon–Sat noon; Oct–March by appointment only; ⓦshetlandreel.com).

Hermaness Nature Reserve

The road that heads off northwest from Haroldswick leads eventually to the bleak headland of **Hermaness**, home to more than 100,000 nesting seabirds (May–Aug). There's an excellent **visitor centre** (ⓦnature.scot) in the former lighthouse keepers' shore station, where you can pick up a leaflet showing the marked routes across the reserve. Whatever you do, stick to the path so as to avoid annoying the vast numbers of nesting great skuas. From Hermaness Hill, you can look down over the jagged rocks of the wonderfully named Vesta Skerry, Rumblings, Tipta Skerry and **Muckle Flugga**. There are few more dramatic settings for a lighthouse than Muckle Flugga, and few sites could ever have presented as great a challenge to the builders, who erected it in 1858. Beyond the lighthouse is **Out Stack**, the most northerly bit of Britain. The views from here are marvellous, as is the birdlife; there's a huge gannetry on one of the stacks, and puffins burrow all along the clifftops.

ARRIVAL AND INFORMATION   UNST

By ferry Ferries (☎ 01595 745804) shuttle regularly across Bluemull Sound from Gutcher on Yell over to Belmont on Unst (every 30min–1hr; 10min).

By bus An integrated bus and ferry service goes from Lerwick to Baltasound on Unst (Mon–Sat 1–2 daily; 2hr 40min). From Belmont, Unst's ferry terminal, buses run to Baltasound (Mon–Sat 3–4 daily; 15min), Haroldswick (Mon–Sat 3–4 daily; 30min) and Uyeasound (Mon–Sat 3–4 daily; 10min).

Tourist Information ⓦ visit-unst.com.

ACCOMMODATION

Bordanoost Lodge Haroldswick ⓦbordanoostlodge. co.uk. Delightful guesthouse offering three en-suite double rooms with quality furnishings and extra special touches have views over either the cliffs or beach and gardens. Doubles **££**

Gardiesfauld Uyeasound ☎01957 755279. A large, clean, modern hostel near Uyeasound pier which allows camping, and offers bike rental. Dorms **£**; camping per person **£**

EATING AND DRINKING

Baltasound Hotel Baltasound ⓦbaltasoundhotel. co.uk. A range of rooms both in the hotel itself and in log cabins. Wherever you stay, it's a good idea to book yourself in for dinner or self-cater – the only other option is the bar food at the *Baltasound Hotel*. **£**

Saxa Vord Restaurant ☎01957 711711. Delicious and homely meals incorporate only the best local produce: mains might include Shetland lamb shank or Highland chicken breast stuffed with haggis. A hearty carvery is served on Sundays. **££**

Skibhoul Café & Stores Baltasound ⓦ skibhoulbakery. com. The island's main shop is attached to the local bakery (founded in 1885). As well as freshly made bread and cakes, the speciality pizzas and quiche are popular – there's also a self-service café and reading corner in the store. £

Victoria's Vintage Tea Room Haroldswick ⓦ victoriasvintagetearooms.co.uk. Bone china, patterned bunting and checked tablecloths for a surreal 'high tea' experience in this cheerful tearoom close to Unst Boat Haven, with views across the bay.

16

KILDALTON CROSS, ISLAY

Contexts

History

Scotland's colourful and compelling history looms large, not just for visitors to the country, but for its inhabitants too. Often the nation's history has been defined either by fierce internecine conflict or epic struggles with England, yet from earliest times the influences of Ireland, Scandinavia and Continental Europe have been as important, particularly in aspects of Scotland's creative and cultural development. This has nurtured a sophistication and ambition in Scots that few associate with the land of warring clans and burning castles, peppering the country's story not just with tragic yet romantic heroes, but also notable fighters, innovators and politicians.

Prehistoric Scotland

Scotland was settled by successive waves of peoples arriving from the east. These first inhabitants were **hunter-gatherers**, whose heaps of animal bones and shells have been excavated, among other places, in the caves along the coast near East Wemyss in Fife. Around 4500 BC, **Neolithic farming peoples** from the European mainland began moving into Scotland. To provide themselves with land for their cereal crops and grazing for their livestock, they cleared large areas of upland forest, usually by fire, and in the process created the characteristic moorland landscapes of much of modern Scotland. These early farmers established permanent settlements, some of which, like **Skara Brae** on Orkney, were near the sea, enabling them to supplement their diet by fishing and develop their skills as boatbuilders.

Settlement spurred the development of more complex forms of religious belief. Neolithic people built large chambered burial mounds or **cairns**, such as **Maeshowe** in Orkney. This reverence for human remains suggests a belief in some form of afterlife, a concept that the next wave of settlers, the **Beaker people**, certainly believed in. They placed pottery beakers filled with drink in the tombs of their dead to assist the passage of the deceased on their journey to, or their stay in, the next world. They also built the mysterious **stone circles**, thirty of which have been discovered in Scotland, including that of **Callanish** (Calanais) on the Isle of Lewis. The exact function of the circles is still unknown, but many of the stones are aligned with the sun at certain points in its annual cycle, suggesting that the monuments are related to the changing of the seasons.

The Beaker people also brought the **Bronze Age** to Scotland. Bronze, an alloy of copper and tin, was stronger and more flexible than flint, which had long been used for axe-heads and knives. Agricultural needs plus new weaponry resulted in a state of endemic warfare as villagers raided their neighbours to steal livestock and grain. Bronze Age people responded to the danger by developing a range of defences, among them spectacular **hillforts** and **crannogs**, and smaller settlements built on artificial islands.

4500 BC	3000 BC	2000 BC	100 BC–AD 100
Neolithic people move into Scotland.	Neolithic township of Skara Brae built.	Callanish standing stones erected on Lewis in the Western Isles.	Fortified Iron Age brochs built across Scotland.

The Picts

Conflict in Scotland intensified in the first millennium BC as successive waves of settlers, arriving from the south and using iron, competed for land. These fractious times witnessed the construction of hundreds of **brochs** or fortified towers. Concentrated along the Atlantic coast and in the northern and western isles, the brochs were dry-stone fortifications often over 40ft in height; the best-preserved can be found on the Shetland island of **Mousa**.

At the end of the prehistoric period, immediately before the arrival of the Romans, Scotland was divided among a number of warring Iron Age tribes, who, apart from raiding, were preoccupied with wresting a living from the land, growing barley and oats, rearing sheep, hunting deer and fishing for salmon. The Romans gave them their collective name Picti, or **Picts**, meaning painted people, after their body tattoos.

The Romans

The **Roman conquest** of Britain began in AD 43. By AD 80 the Roman governor, Agricola, felt secure enough in the south of Britannia (Britain) to begin an invasion of **Caledonia** (Scotland), building a string of forts across the Clyde–Forth line and defeating the Caledonian tribes at the **Battle of Mons Graupius**. The long-term effect of his campaign, however, was slight. Work on a major fort – to be the base for 5,000 soldiers – at Inchtuthil, on the Tay, was abandoned and the legions withdrew. In AD 123, the Roman e**mperor Hadrian** sealed the frontier against the northern tribes and built **Hadrian's Wall**, which stretched from the Solway Firth to the Tyne and was the first formal division of the island of Britain. Twenty years later, the Romans again ventured north and built the **Antonine Wall** between the Clyde and the Forth. This was manned for about forty years, but the Romans largely gave up their attempt to subjugate the north and instead adopted a policy of containment.

The Romans produced the first **written** accounts of Scotland. Dio Cassius, writing in AD 197, captures the common Roman contempt of their Pictish neighbours:

They dwell in tents, naked and unshod, possess their women in common, and in common rear all their offspring. Their form of rule is democratic for the most part, and they are very fond of plundering;

They can endure hunger and cold and any kind of hardship; for they plunge into the swamps and exist there for many days with only their heads above water, and in the forest they support themselves on barks and roots (Roman History, LXXVII).

The Dark Ages

Following the departure of the Romans, traditionally put at AD 410, the population of Scotland changed considerably. By AD 500, the **Picts** occupied the northern isles, and the north and the east as far south as Fife. Today, their settlements can be identified by place names with a 'Pit' prefix, such as Pitlochry, and by the existence of carved symbol stones, like those found at Aberlemno in Angus. To the west, between Dumbarton and Carlisle, was a population of **Britons**. Many of the Briton leaders had Roman

AD 43	83	142	162
The Roman conquest of Britain begins.	The Romans defeat the British tribes at the Battle of Mons Graupius in northeast Scotland.	The Romans build the Antonine Wall between the Firth of Forth and the Firth of Clyde.	The Romans withdraw from the Antonine Wall and retreat behind Hadrian's Wall.

THE NORTHERN ISLES

With their sophisticated ships and navigational skills, the **Vikings**, beginning their expansion in the eighth century, soon gained supremacy over the Pictish peoples in Shetland, Orkney, the extreme northeast corner of the mainland and the Western Isles. For the next six centuries the Northern Isles were distinct from the rest of what is now called Scotland, becoming a base for raiding and colonization in Britain and Ireland, and forming links with the Faroes, Iceland, Greenland and, more tenuously, North America. Norse culture flourished, and buildings such as St Magnus Cathedral in Kirkwall, Orkney, give some idea of its energy. However, there were bouts of unrest, and finally Shetland was brought under direct rule from Norway at the end of the twelfth century.

When Norway united with Sweden under the Danish Crown in the fourteenth century, **Norse power** began to wane and Scottish influence increased. In 1469, a marriage was arranged between Margaret, daughter of Christian I, king of Denmark, and the future King James III of Scotland. Short of cash for Margaret's dowry, Christian mortgaged Orkney to Scotland in 1468, followed by Shetland in 1469; neither mortgage was redeemed and both were annexed in 1472. The laws, religion and administration of the Northern Isles became Scottish, though their Norse heritage is still very evident in place names, dialect and culture.

names, suggesting that they were a Romanized people, possibly a combination of tribes maintained by the Romans as a buffer between Hadrian's Wall and the northern tribes, and peoples pushed west by the Germanic Anglo-Saxon invaders, who landed on the east coast and settled around Dunbar in East Lothian.

On the west coast, to the north and west of the Britons, lived the so-called **Scotti (the Roman catch-all for the Gaels who raided Britannia)**, who eventually gave their Latin name to the whole country. The first 'Scotti' arrived in the fourth century AD, and about a century later their king, Fergus Mór, moved his base from Antrim to Dunadd, near Lochgilphead, where he founded the kingdom of Dalriada. The Britons and the Picts spoke variations of P-Celtic, from which Welsh, Cornish and Breton developed, but these new settlers spoke Q-Celtic, the precursor of modern Gaelic.

The final addition to the ethnic mix was Scandinavian; from around 800, **Norse** invaders began to arrive, settling mainly in the Northern Isles and the northeast of the mainland.

Many of the Britons had been **Christians** since Roman times and it was a Briton, St Ninian, who conducted the first missionary work among the Picts at the end of the fourth century. Attempts to convert the Picts resumed in the sixth century with the arrival of **St Columba from Ireland, he** established the island of **Iona** as a centre of Christian culture, opening the way for peaceable contacts between the Picts and Gaels and intermarriage became commonplace. The king of Dalriada, **Kenneth MacAlpine**, the son of a Pictish princess, claimed the kingdom of the Picts and united the two kingdoms, creating the kingdom of Alba (later known as Scotia) in AD 843. Kenneth and his successors gradually expanded their kingdom and by 1034, almost all of what we now call Scotland was under their rule.

397	563	843	1286
St Ninian establishes the first Christian church north of Hadrian's Wall.	St Columba founds a monastery on Iona and begins to convert the Picts.	Kenneth MacAlpine becomes the first king of the Scots and the Picts.	Death of Alexander III sparks the Wars of Scottish Independence.

The Middle Ages

The succession of **Malcolm III**, known as Canmore ('Big head' or 'great chief'), in 1057 marked the beginning of a period of fundamental change in Scottish society. Having spent seventeen years at the English court, Malcolm sought to apply to Scotland a range of ideas he had brought back with him. He and his heirs established a secure dynasty based on succession through the male line (as opposed to the female succession practised by the Picts) and introduced **feudalism** into Scotland, a system that was diametrically opposed to the Gaelic system – the followers of a Gaelic king were his kindred, whereas the followers of a feudal king were vassals bought with land.

The Canmores, independent of the local nobility, who remained a military threat, also began to reform the **Church**. This development started with **Margaret**, Malcolm III's English wife, who brought Scottish religious practices into line with those of the rest of Europe. **David I** continued the process by importing monks to found a series of monasteries, principally along the border at Kelso, Melrose, Jedburgh and Dryburgh. Similarly, the dynasty founded a series of **royal burghs**, towns such as Edinburgh, Stirling and Berwick, recognized as centres of trade. Their charters usually granted a measure of self-government, and the monarchy hoped this liberality would both encourage loyalty and increase the prosperity of the kingdom. Scotland's Gaelic-speaking clans had little influence within the burghs, and gradually Scots – a northern version of Anglo-Saxon – became the main **language** throughout the Lowlands.

The Wars of Scottish Independence

In 1286, Alexander III died, and a hotly disputed succession gave **Edward I**, king of England, an opportunity to subjugate Scotland. In 1291, Edward presided over a conference where the rival claimants to the Scottish throne presented their cases. Edward chose **John Balliol** over **Robert the Bruce**, his main rival; he obliged Balliol to pay him homage, thus turning Scotland into a vassal kingdom. Bruce refused to accept the decision and in 1295 Balliol renounced his allegiance to Edward and sided with France – beginning what is known as the '**Auld Alliance**'. In the ensuing conflict, the Bruce family sided with the English, Balliol was defeated and imprisoned, and Edward seized control of almost all of Scotland.

Edward had shown little mercy during his conquest of Scotland – he had most of the population of Berwick massacred – and his cruelty provoked a truly national resistance. This focused on **William Wallace**, a man of relatively lowly origins who raised an army of peasants, lesser knights and townsmen that was fundamentally different to the armies raised by the nobility. Figures like Balliol, holding lands in England, France and Scotland, were part of an international aristocracy for whom warfare was the means by which they struggled for power. Wallace, by contrast, led proto-nationalist forces determined to expel the English from their country. Probably for that very reason Wallace never received the support of the nobility and, after a bitter ten-year campaign during which he notched up a couple of notable victories over English armies, he was betrayed and executed in London in 1305.

In 1306, Robert the Bruce defied Edward and had himself crowned king of Scotland. Edward died the following year, but the unrest dragged on until 1314, when Bruce decisively defeated a large English army under Edward II at the **Battle of**

1296	1314	1320
Edward I of England invades Scotland.	Under Robert the Bruce, the Scots defeat the English at the Battle of Bannockburn.	The Declaration of Arbroath, asserting Scottish independence, is sent to the pope.

FLODDEN FIELD

In 1513, possibly the largest Scots army ever to invade England was decimated at **Flodden Field**, just south of the border. The English king Henry VIII had invaded France, and the Scots, under James IV, opted to stand by the 'Auld Alliance' with France and invade England. The Scots army, numbering around 30,000, took several English strongholds before being confronted near Branxton, three miles southeast of Coldstream.

The English artillery was lighter and more manoeuvrable and forced the Scots to come down off their advantageous position on **Branxton Hill**. The heavily armoured Scottish noblemen got stuck in the mud, and their over-long **pikes** and lances proved no match for the English **bills** (like a hooked halberd). English losses were heavy, but the Scots lost as many as 10,000, including the king himself, his son (an archbishop), nine earls, fourteen lords and numerous Highland clan chiefs, all of whom fought at the head of their troops. After the battle, James's blood-stained surcoat was sent to Henry, but his body was denied burial and no one knows what became of it.

If Bannockburn was Scotland's greatest victory over the English, and Bonnie Prince Charlie's last stand at Culloden their most noble defeat, Flodden was simply an unmitigated disaster. It became the subject of numerous songs and ballads and remains a painful memory for Scots even today. The English, meanwhile, have forgotten all about it.

Bannockburn. At last Bruce was firmly in control of his kingdom, and in 1320 the Scots asserted their right to independence in a successful petition to the pope, now known as the **Declaration of Arbroath**.

The Stewart dynasty

Following Bruce's death in 1329, the Scottish monarchy gradually declined in influence. The last of the Bruce dynasty died in 1371, to be succeeded by the 'Stewards', hence **Stewarts**, but thereafter a succession of Scottish rulers, culminating with James VI in 1567, came to the throne when still children. The power vacuum was filled by the nobility, whose key members exercised control as Scotland's regents. The more vigorous monarchs of the period, notably **James I**, did their best to curb the power of such families, but their efforts were usually nullified at the next regency. **James IV** might have restored the authority of the Crown, but his invasion of England ended in a terrible defeat for the Scots – and his own death – at the **Battle of Flodden Field**.

The reign of **Mary, Queen of Scots** (1542–67), typified the problems of the Scottish monarchy. Mary came to the throne when just one week old, and immediately the English king, Henry VIII, sought to marry her to his 5-year-old son, Edward. Beginning in 1544, the English launched a series of devastating attacks on Scotland, an episode Sir Walter Scott later called the 'Rough Wooing', until, in the face of another English invasion in 1548, the Scots – or at least those not supporting Henry – turned to the 'Auld Alliance'. The French king proposed marriage between Mary and Dauphin Francis, promising military assistance against the English. The 6-year-old queen sailed for France in 1548, leaving her loyal nobles and their French allies in control. When she returned thirteen years later, following the death of Francis, she had to pick her way

1371	**1413**	**1468**
Robert II becomes the first of the Stewart (Stuart) kings to rule Scotland.	University of St Andrews is founded.	James III marries Margaret of Denmark and receives Orkney and Shetland as part of her dowry.

through the rival ambitions of her nobility and deal with something entirely new – the religious Reformation.

The Reformation

The **Reformation** in Scotland was a complex social process, whose threads are often hard to unravel. Nevertheless, it is quite clear that, by the end of the sixteenth century, the established Church was held in general contempt. Many of the higher clergy regarded their relationship with the Church purely in economic terms, and forty percent of known illegitimate births were the product of the 'celibate' clergy's liaisons.

Another spur to the Scottish Reformation was the identification of Protestantism with anti-French feeling. In 1554, **Mary of Guise**, the French mother of the absent Queen Mary, had become regent, and her habit of appointing Frenchmen to high office was seen as an attempt to subordinate Scotland's interests to those of France. There was considerable resentment, and in 1560, with English military backing, Protestant nobles succeeded in deposing the French regent. When the Scottish Parliament assembled, it asserted the primacy of Protestantism by forbidding the celebration of Mass and abolishing the authority of the pope. The nobility proceeded to confiscate two-thirds of Church lands, a huge prize that did much to bolster their new beliefs.

The return of Mary, Queen of Scots

Even without the economic incentives, Protestantism was a highly charged political doctrine. **Luther** had argued that each individual's conscience was capable of discerning God's will. This meant that a hierarchical priesthood, existing to interpret God's will, was unnecessary. This point was made very clearly to Queen Mary by the Protestant reformer **John Knox** at their first meeting on her return in 1561. Subjects, he told her, were not bound to obey an ungodly monarch.

Mary ducked and weaved, trying to avoid an open breach with her Protestant subjects. At the same time, she was engaged in a balancing act between the factions of the Scottish nobility. Her difficulties were exacerbated by her disastrous second marriage to **Lord Darnley**, a cruel and politically inept character, whose jealousy led to his involvement in the murder of Mary's favourite, David Rizzio, who was dragged from the queen's supper room at Holyrood and stabbed 56 times. The incident disturbed the Scottish Protestants, but they were entirely scandalized in 1567 when Darnley himself was murdered and Mary promptly married the **Earl of Bothwell**, widely believed to be the murderer. The Scots rose in rebellion, driving Mary into exile in England at the age of just 25. The queen's illegitimate half-brother, the Earl of Moray, became regent, and her son, the infant James, was left behind to be raised a Protestant prince. Mary, meanwhile, became perceived as such a threat to the English throne that Queen Elizabeth I had her executed in 1587.

Knox could now concentrate on the organization of the reformed Church, or **Kirk**, which he envisaged as a body with power over the daily lives of the people. **Andrew Melville**, another leading reformer, wished to push this theocratic vision further. He proposed the abolition of all traces of the rule of bishops in the

1482	1513	1560
Berwick-upon-Tweed captured by the English.	The Scots are defeated by the English at the Battle of Flodden Field.	The Scottish Church breaks with the Roman Catholic Church.

Church and that the Kirk should adopt a **Presbyterian** structure, administered by a hierarchy of assemblies, part-elected and part-appointed.

The religious wars

James VI disliked Presbyterianism because its quasi-democratic structure appeared to threaten his authority. He was, however, unable to resist the reformers until, strengthened by his installation as James I of England after Elizabeth's death in 1603, he restored the Scottish bishops in 1610. Raised in Episcopalian England, James's son **Charles I** had little understanding of Scottish reformism. His belief in the divine right of kings was entirely counter to Protestant thought. In 1637, Charles attempted to impose a new prayer book on the Kirk, laying down forms of worship in line with the High Anglican Church. The reformers denounced these changes as 'popery' and organized the **National Covenant**, a religious pledge 'to recover the purity and liberty of the gospel as it had been professed and established'.

Charles declared all the **Covenanters** to be rebels, but when he called a General Assembly of the Kirk, it promptly abolished the episcopacy. Charles pronounced the proceedings illegal, but lack of finance stopped him from mounting an effective military campaign – whereas the Covenanters, well financed by the Kirk, assembled a proficient army under Alexander Leslie. In desperation, Charles summoned the English Parliament, the first for eleven years, hoping it would pay for an army. However, Parliament was much keener to criticize his policies than to raise taxes. In response, Charles declared war on Parliament in 1642.

Until 1650, Scotland was ruled by the Covenanters, and the power of the Presbyterian Kirk grew considerably. Laws were passed establishing schools in every parish and, less usefully, banning trade with Catholic countries. The only effective opposition to the theocratic state came from the **Marquis of Montrose**, who had initially supported the Covenant but lined up with the king when war broke out. His army was drawn from the Highlands and Islands, where the Kirk's influence was weakest. Montrose won several notable victories against the Covenanters, but the reluctance of his troops to stay south of the Highland Line made it impossible to capitalize on these successes, and he was eventually captured and executed in 1650.

The Civil War and the Restoration

Montrose's campaigns, however, were a side show to the **civil war** being waged further south. Here, the Covenanters and the English Parliamentarians faced the same royal enemy and in 1643 formed an uneasy alliance. There was, however, friction between the allies. Many Parliamentarians, including Cromwell, favoured a looser form of doctrinal control within the state Church than the Presbyterians did. They also suspected the Scots of hankering after the return of the monarchy, a suspicion confirmed when, at the invitation of the earl of Argyll, the future Charles II came back to Scotland in 1650. To regain his Scottish kingdom, Charles was obliged to renounce his father and sign the Covenant, two bitter pills taken to impress the population. In the event, the 'Presbyterian restoration' was short-lived. Cromwell invaded,

1587	1592	1603
Mary, Queen of Scots, is executed on the orders of Queen Elizabeth I.	Presbyterianism becomes the established religion.	James VI of Scotland becomes James I of England.

THE HIGHLANDS

The country that was united with England in 1707 contained three distinct cultures: in south and east Scotland, they spoke **Scots**; the local dialect in Shetland, Orkney and the far northeast, though Scots-based, contained elements of **Norn** (Old Norse); while the language of the rest of north and west Scotland, including the Hebrides, was **Gaelic**. These linguistic differences were paralleled by different forms of social organization and customs. The people of north and west Scotland were mostly **pastoralists**, moving their sheep and cattle to Highland pastures in the summer and returning to the glens in the winter. They lived in single-room dwellings, heated by a central peat fire and sometimes shared with livestock, and in hard times they subsisted on cakes made from the blood of their live cattle mixed with oatmeal. **Highlanders** supplemented their meagre income by raiding their clan neighbours and the prosperous Lowlands, whose inhabitants regarded their northern compatriots with a mixture of fear and contempt.

However, the institutions of this society had not existed from time immemorial. This is especially true of the **clan**, a term that only appears in its modern usage in the sixteenth century. In theory, the clan bound together blood relatives who shared a common ancestor, a concept clearly derived from the ancient Gaelic notion of kinship. But in practice many of the clans were of non-Gaelic origin – such as the Frasers, Sinclairs and Stewarts, all of Anglo-Norman descent – and it was the mythology of a common ancestor, rather than the actuality, that cemented the clans together. Furthermore, clans were often made up of people with a variety of surnames, and there is evidence of individuals changing their names when they swapped allegiances.

It was not until the late seventeenth century that certain **tartans** became associated with particular clans. Previously, Highlanders wore a simple belted plaid wrapped around the body. The detailed codification of the tartan was produced by the Victorians, whose romantic vision of Highland life originated with George IV's visit to Scotland in 1822, when he appeared in an elaborate version of Highland dress, complete with flesh-coloured tights.

defeated the Scots at Dunbar and forced Charles into exile. Until the Restoration of 1660, Scotland was united with England and governed by seven commissioners.

Although the restoration of **Charles II** brought bishops back to the Kirk, they were integrated into an essentially Presbyterian structure of Kirk sessions and presbyteries, and the General Assembly, which had been abolished by Cromwell, was not re-established. More than three hundred clergymen, a third of the Scottish ministry, refused to accept the reinstatement of the bishops and were edged out of the Church and forced to hold open-air services, called **Conventicles**, which Charles attempted to suppress.

Charles II was succeeded by his brother **James VII** (James II of England), whose ardent Catholicism caused a Protestant backlash in England. In 1689, he was forced into exile in France and the throne passed to **Mary**, his Protestant daughter, and her Dutch husband, **William of Orange**. In Scotland there was a brief flurry of opposition to William when **Graham of Claverhouse**, known as 'Bonnie Dundee', united the Jacobite clans against the government army at the **Battle of Killiecrankie**, just north of Pitlochry. However, the inspirational Claverhouse was killed on the point of victory, the clans

1638	1650	1689
National Covenant proclaimed by Scottish Presbyterians.	The Scots Royalist army are defeated at the Battle of Dunbar by the English under Oliver Cromwell.	Unsuccessful Jacobite uprising against William of Orange.

dispersed, and the threat passed. In Scotland, William and Mary restored the full Presbyterian structure and abolished bishops, though they chose not to restore the political and legal functions of the Kirk, which remained subject to parliamentary control.

The Union

From 1689 to 1697, William was at war with France, a war partly financed by Scottish taxes and partly fought by Scottish soldiers. Yet many Scots, mindful of the Auld Alliance, disapproved of the war and others suffered financially from the disruption to trade with France. There were other economic irritants too, principally the legally sanctioned monopoly that English merchants had over trade with the English colonies. This monopoly inspired the **Darien Scheme**, a plan to establish a Scottish colony in Panama. The colonists set off in 1698, but the scheme proved a miserable failure. The colony collapsed with the loss of £200,000 – an amount equal to half the value of the entire coinage in Scotland – and an angry Scottish Parliament threatened to refuse the king taxes as rioting broke out in the cities.

The situation in Scotland was further complicated by the question of the succession. Mary died without leaving an heir and, on William's death in 1702, the crown passed to her sister **Anne**, who was also childless. The English Parliament secured the Protestant succession by passing the Act of Settlement, naming the Electress Sophia of Hanover as the next in line to the throne. The Act did not, however, apply in Scotland, and the English feared that the Scots would invite James Edward Stewart back from France to be their king. Consequently, Parliament appointed commissioners charged with the consideration of 'proper methods towards attaining a union with Scotland'. In response the Scottish Parliament passed the **Act of Security** in 1703, stating that Scotland would not accept a Hanoverian monarch unless they had first received guarantees protecting their religion and their trade.

Nevertheless, the Scottish Parliament unexpectedly passed the **Act of Union** by 110 votes to 69 in January 1707. Some historians have explained the vote in terms of bribery and corruption. This certainly played a part (the Duke of Hamilton, for example, switched sides at a key moment and was rewarded with an English dukedom), but there were other factors. Scottish politicians were divided between the Cavaliers – Jacobites (supporters of the Stewarts) and Episcopalians – and the Country party, whose Presbyterian members dreaded the return of the Stewarts more than they disliked the Hanoverians. There were commercial considerations too. In 1705, the English Parliament had passed the Alien Act, which threatened to impose severe penalties on cross-border trade, whereas the Union gave merchants of both countries free access to each other's markets. The Act of Union also guaranteed the Scottish legal system and the Presbyterian Kirk, and offered compensation to those who had lost money in the Darien Scheme.

Under the terms of the Act, both parliaments were to be replaced by a new British Parliament based in London, with the Scots apportioned 45 MPs and 16 peers. There were riots when the terms became known, but no sustained opposition.

1692	1695	1698
Glencoe massacre: 38 members of the MacDonald clan are murdered by anti-Jacobite Campbells.	Bank of Scotland is established.	The Darien Scheme: 1,200 Scots leave in order to establish a colony in Panama.

BONNIE PRINCE CHARLIE

Prince Charles Edward Stewart – better known as **Bonnie Prince Charlie** or 'The Young Pretender' – was born in 1720 in Rome, where his father, 'The Old Pretender', claimant to the British throne (as the son of James VII), was living in exile with his Polish wife. At the age of 25, with no knowledge of Gaelic, an imperfect grasp of English and a strong Catholic faith, the prince set out in disguise for Scotland with two French ships. He arrived on the Hebridean island of **Eriskay** (see page 502) on 23 July, 1745, with just seven companions, and was immediately implored to return to France by the clan chiefs, who were singularly unimpressed by his lack of army. Charles was unmoved and went on to raise the royal standard at **Glenfinnan** (see page 423), thus signalling the beginning of the **Jacobite uprising**. He only attracted fewer than half of the potential 20,000 clansmen who could have marched with him and promises of support from the French and English Jacobites failed to materialize. Nevertheless, after a decisive victory over government forces at the **Battle of Prestonpans**, near Edinburgh, Charles made a spectacular advance into England, getting as far as Derby. London was in a state of panic: its shops were closed and the Bank of England, fearing a run on sterling, slowed withdrawals by paying out in sixpences. But Derby was as far as Charles got. On December 6, threatened by superior forces, the Jacobites decided to retreat to Scotland, against Charles's wishes. Pursued back to Scotland by the Duke of Cumberland, he won one last victory, at Falkirk, before the final disaster at **Culloden** (see page 400) in April 1746.

The prince spent the following five months in hiding, with a price of £30,000 on his head, and literally thousands of government troops searching for him. He certainly endured his fair share of cold and hunger while on the run, but the real price was paid by the Highlanders themselves, who risked their lives (and often paid for it with them) by aiding and abetting the prince. The most famous of these was 23-year-old **Flora MacDonald**, whom Charles first met on South Uist in June 1746. Flora was persuaded to convey Charles 'over the sea to Skye', disguised as an Irish servant girl by the name of Betty Burke. She was arrested just seven days after parting with the prince in Portree, and held in the Tower of London until July 1747.

Charles boarded a ship back to France in September 1746, but, despite his promises – 'for all that has happened, I hope, Madam, we shall meet in St James's yet' – never returned to Scotland, nor did he ever see Flora again. After a string of mistresses, he eventually got married at the age of 52 to the 19-year-old **Princess Louise of Stolberg-Gedern** in an effort to produce a Stewart heir. They had no children, and she fled from his violent drunkenness; in 1788, Prince Charles died in the arms of his illegitimate daughter in Rome. Bonnie Prince Charlie became a romantic legend but the real consequence of 1745 was the virtual annihilation of the Highland way of life.

The Jacobite risings

When James VII (II) was deposed he fled to France, where he planned the reconquest of his kingdom with the support of the French king. In 1702, James's successor, William, died, and the hopes of the Stewarts passed to James, the 'Old Pretender' ('Pretender' in the sense of having pretensions to the throne; 'Old' to distinguish him from his son Charles, the 'Young Pretender'). James's followers became known as **Jacobites**, derived from Jacobus, the Latin equivalent of James. The accession to the British throne of George I, son of Sophia, Electress of Hanover, sparked the **Jacobite**

1707	1715	1746
The Act of Union unites the kingdoms of Scotland and England.	Jacobite uprising against the accession of Hanoverian King George I.	Bonnie Prince Charlie's Jacobite army is defeated at the Battle of Culloden.

uprising of 1715. Its timing appeared perfect. Scottish opinion was moving against the Union, which had failed to bring Scotland any tangible economic benefits. The English had also been accused of bad faith when, contrary to their pledges, they attempted to impose their legal practices on the Scots. There were also many in England who toasted the 'king across the water' and showed no enthusiasm for the new Hanoverian ruler. In September 1715, the fiercely Jacobite John Erskine, Earl of Mar, raised the Stewart standard at Braemar Castle. Eight days later, he captured Perth, where he gathered an army of more than ten thousand men, drawn mostly from the Episcopalians of northeast Scotland and from the Highlands. Mar's rebellion took the government by surprise. They had only four thousand soldiers in Scotland, under the command of the Duke of Argyll, but Mar dithered and lost the military advantage. The **Battle of Sheriffmuir** in November was indecisive, however, by the time the Old Pretender arrived the following month six thousand veteran Dutch troops had reinforced Argyll. The rebellion disintegrated and James retreated to exile in France in February 1716.

The **Jacobite uprising of 1745**, led by James's dashing son, Charles Edward Stewart (known as **Bonnie Prince Charlie**), had little chance of success. The Hanoverians had consolidated their hold on the English throne and Lowland society was uniformly loyalist. Despite early successes which allowed him to march as far south as Derby, Charles was ultimately forced to retreat and finally met his match at the **Battle of Culloden**, near Inverness, in April 1746, the last set-piece battle on British soil. Outnumbered and outgunned, the Jacobites were swept from the field, with more than a thousand men killed or wounded compared to the Duke of Cumberland's three hundred or so. After the battle, many of the wounded Jacobites were slaughtered, an atrocity that earned Cumberland the nickname 'Butcher'.

In the aftermath of the uprising, the wearing of tartan, the bearing of arms and the playing of bagpipes were all banned. Rebel chiefs lost their land and the Highlands were placed under military occupation. Most significantly, the government prohibited the private armies of the chiefs, thereby effectively destroying the clan system.

The Highland Clearances

Once the clan chief was forbidden his own army, he had no need of the large tenantry that had previously been a vital military asset. Conversely, the second half of the eighteenth century saw the Highland population increase dramatically after the introduction of the easy-to-grow and nutritious **potato**. Between 1745 and 1811, the population of the Outer Hebrides, for example, rose from 13,000 to 24,500. The clan chiefs adopted different policies to deal with this. Some encouraged emigration, and as many as six thousand Highlanders left for the Americas between 1800 and 1803. Others developed alternative forms of employment for their tenantry, mainly fishing and gathering kelp (seaweed), while some developed **sheep runs** on the Highland pastures, introducing hardy breeds. But extensive sheep farming proved incompatible with a high peasant population and many landowners decided to clear their estates of tenants, some of whom were forcibly moved to tiny plots of marginal land, where they were to farm as **crofters**.

The pace of these **Highland Clearances** accelerated after the end of the Napoleonic Wars in 1815, when the market price for kelp, fish and cattle declined, leaving

1759	1762	1843
Scotland's national poet, Rabbie Burns, is born in Alloway.	Beginning of the Highland Clearances.	The Great Disruption: a third of the Church of Scotland leave to form the Free Church of Scotland.

sheep as the only profitable Highland product. The most notorious Clearances took place on the estates of the countess of Sutherland, who owned a million acres in northern Scotland. Between 1807 and 1821, around 15,000 people were thrown off her land, often with considerable brutality. As the dispossessed Highlanders scratched a living from the acid soils of tiny crofts, they learnt through bitter experience the limitations of the clan. Famine forced large-scale emigration to America and Canada, leaving the huge uninhabited areas found in the region today.

However, not all landowners acted cruelly or insensitively and many settlements around Scotland, from Inveraray in the west to Portsoy in the northeast, owe their existence to so-called 'improving landlords', who invested in infrastructure such as fishing harbours, decent housing and communities of sustainable size. They brought economic prosperity to previously disadvantaged areas. Those left crofting, however, still led a precarious existence, often taking seasonal employment away from home. In 1886, in response to the social unrest, Gladstone's Liberal government passed the **Crofters' Holdings Act**, granting three of the crofters' demands: security of tenure, fair rents to be decided independently and the right to pass on crofts by inheritance. But Gladstone did not increase the amount of land available for crofting and shortage of land remained a major problem until the **Land Settlement Act** 1919 made provision for the creation of new crofts. Nevertheless, the population of the Highlands has continued to decline since then, with many of the region's young people finding life in the city more appealing, and work opportunities there much greater.

Industrialization

Glasgow was the powerhouse of Scotland's **Industrial Revolution**. The passage from Glasgow to the Americas was much shorter than that from rival English ports and a lucrative transatlantic trade in tobacco had developed as early as the seventeenth century. This stimulated Scottish manufacturing, since, under the terms of the Navigation Acts, Americans were not allowed to trade manufactured goods. Scottish-produced linen, paper and wrought iron were exchanged for Virginia tobacco and, when the American War of Independence disrupted trade in the 1770s and 1780s, the Scots successfully turned to trade with the West Indies and, most important of all, to the production of cotton. In 1787, Scotland had only nineteen textile mills; by 1840 there were nearly two hundred.

The growth of the textile industry spurred the development of other industries. In the mid-eighteenth century, the **Carron Ironworks** was founded near Falkirk, producing mainly military munitions. By 1800, it was the largest ironworks in Europe. Scotland's **shipbuilding** industry began as early as 1802, when the steam vessel *Charlotte Dundas* was launched on the Forth and Clyde Canal. The growth of the iron and shipbuilding industries, plus extensive use of steam power, created a massive demand for coal from the coalfields of southern Scotland.

Industrialization led to a concentration of Scotland's **population** in the central Lowlands. In 1840, one-third of the country's industrial workers lived in Lanarkshire, and Glasgow's population grew from 17,000 in the 1740s to more than 200,000 a century later. Such sudden growth created urban overcrowding on a massive scale and, as late as 1861, 64 percent of the entire Scottish population lived in one- or two-room

1846	1886	1890
Highland potato famine: 1.7 million Scots emigrate.	Crofters' Holdings Act grants security of tenure in the Highlands and Islands.	Forth Rail Bridge opens, spanning the Firth of Forth.

houses. For most Clydesiders, 'house' meant a couple of small rooms in a grim tenement building, where many of the poorest families were displaced Highlanders and Irish immigrants; the Irish arrived in Glasgow at the rate of a thousand a week during the potato famine of the 1840s.

By the late nineteenth century, a measure of prosperity had emerged from industrialization and the well-paid Clydeside engineers went to their forges wearing bowler hats and starched collars. They were confident but their optimism was misplaced. Scotland's industries were very much geared to the export market, and after **World War I** conditions were much changed. During the war, when exports had been curtailed by a combination of U-boat activity and war production, new industries had developed in India and Japan, and the eastern market for Scottish goods never recovered. The postwar world also witnessed a contraction of world trade, which hit the shipbuilding industry very hard and, in turn, damaged the steel and coal industries.

These difficulties were compounded by the financial collapse of the early 1930s, and by 1932 28 percent of the Scottish workforce was unemployed. Some 400,000 Scots emigrated between 1921 and 1931, and those who stayed endured some of the worst social conditions in the British Isles. By the late 1930s, Scotland had the highest infant mortality rate in Europe. There was a partial economic recovery in the mid-1930s, but high unemployment remained until the start of **World War II**.

The Labour movement

In the late eighteenth century, conditions for the labouring population varied enormously. Handloom weavers were well paid, whereas the coal miners remained serfs, bought and sold with the pits they worked in. The **Scottish Reform Act 1832** extended the franchise to include a large proportion of the middle class, and thereafter political radicalism assumed a more distinctive working-class character. During the next thirty years, as Scotland's economy prospered, skilled workers organized themselves into **craft unions**, such as the Amalgamated Society of Engineers, to negotiate improvements for their members within the status quo. Politically, the trade unions gave their allegiance to the Liberal Party, but in 1888 **Keir Hardie** left the Liberals to form the Scottish Socialist Party, later merged with the Independent Labour Party (ILP), founded in Bradford in 1893. Scottish socialism as represented by the ILP was ethical rather than Marxist in orientation, owing a great deal to the kirk background of many of its members. But electoral progress was slow, partly because the Roman Catholic priesthood consistently preached against socialism.

Red Clydeside

In the early years of the twentieth century, two small Marxist groups established themselves on what became known as **Red Clydeside**: the **Socialist Labour Party (SLP)**, which concentrated on workplace militancy, and the party-political **British Socialist Party (BSP)**. During World War I, local organizers of the SLP gained considerable influence by playing on the fears of the skilled workers, who felt their status was undermined by the employment of unskilled workers. After the war, the influence of the shop stewards culminated in a massive campaign for the forty-hour working week. The strikes and demonstrations of the campaign, including one with 100,000

1914–18	1928	1939	1939–45
100,000 Scots lose their lives in World War I.	The National Party of Scotland is formed.	The population of Scotland reaches five million.	34,000 Scottish soldiers lose their lives in World War II; 6,000 civilians die in air raids.

people (and the Red Flag flying) in St George's Square, Glasgow, panicked the government into sending in troops and tanks. The rank and file had little interest in revolution, however, though many of the activists did go on to become leaders within the newly formed **Communist Party of Great Britain**.

The rise of the Labour Party

The ILP, by then an affiliated part of the socialist **Labour Party**, made its electoral breakthrough in 1922, sending 29 Scottish MPs to Westminster. Their high hopes of social progress and reform were dashed, like trade union militancy, by the 1930s Depression. At the 1945 general election, Labour won forty seats in Scotland and up until 2015 the party dominated Scottish politics. In 1955, the Conservatives had 36 Scottish MPs; by 1997 none at all, though they returned one MP in the 2005 general election and have over a dozen MSPs in the Scottish Parliament.

The ILP MPs of the 1920s combined their socialism with a brand of Scottish nationalism. The Labour Party maintained an official policy of self-government for Scotland, endorsing home rule in 1945 and 1947, but these endorsements were made with less and less enthusiasm. In 1958, Labour abandoned the commitment altogether, adopting a unionist vision of Scotland, much to the chagrin of many Scottish activists.

Towards devolution

The **National Party of Scotland** was formed in 1928, its membership mostly drawn from the non-industrial parts of the country. A mixture of practical politicians and left-leaning eccentrics, such as the poet Hugh MacDiarmid, in 1934, it merged with the right-wing Scottish Party to create the **Scottish National Party**. The SNP achieved its electoral breakthrough in 1967 when Winnie Ewing won Hamilton from Labour in a by-election. The following year the SNP won 34 percent of the vote in local government elections, and both the Labour and Conservative parties, wishing to head off the nationalists, began to work on schemes to give Scotland a measure of self-government, the term **devolution** becoming common currency.

The Scottish referendum

The situation took a dynamic turn in 1974, when Labour were returned to power with a wafer-thin majority. The SNP held seven seats, which gave them considerable political leverage, and meant that devolution was firmly on the agenda. The SNP had also run an excellent election campaign, concentrating on North Sea oil, now being piped ashore in significant quantities. Their two most popular slogans, 'England expects ... Scotland's oil' and 'Rich Scots or Poor Britons?', seemed to have caught the mood of Scotland.

In 1979, the Labour government, struggling to hold onto office, put its devolution proposals before the Scottish people in a **referendum**. The 'yes' vote gained 33 percent, the 'no' vote 31 percent – but the required forty percent threshold wasn't reached, Scottish opinion had shifted away from home rule; the reluctance to embrace it was based on uncertainty about the consequences, concerns about multi-layered

1979	**1996**	**1999**	**2009**
Scottish referendum for devolution fails to gain required forty percent.	The Stone of Scone is returned to Scotland.	Labour win the most seats in Scotland's first-ever general election.	Carol Ann Duffy becomes the first Scottish poet laureate of Britain.

government and, in some areas, a fear that the assembly might be dominated by the Clydeside Conurbation.

Scotland under Thatcher

The incoming Conservative government of **Margaret Thatcher** set its face against any form of devolution. It argued that the majority of Scots had voted for parties committed to the Union – Labour, the Liberals and themselves – and that only a minority supported the separation advocated by the SNP. At the same time, the government asserted that any form of devolution would lead inevitably to the break-up of the United Kingdom and that the devolution solutions put forward by other parties would result inescapably in separation.

As the Thatcher years rolled on, growing evidence suggested that few Scottish voters accepted either this reasoning or the implication that Scots did not know what was good for them. The Conservatives' support in Scotland was further eroded by their introduction of the deeply unpopular **Poll Tax**, a form of local taxation that took little account of income. The fact that it was imposed in Scotland a year earlier than in England and Wales was the source of further resentment.

Scotland after Devolution

Scotland's first-ever **general election** took place in 1999, using proportional representation (PR) rather than the first-past-the-post system employed in Westminster elections. This meant that, despite winning 39 percent of the vote, Labour had to enter into a coalition with the Liberal Democrats in the 129-seat assembly. The SNP were the second-largest party, with just under thirty percent of the vote. Over the course of two parliamentary terms, the coalition introduced policies to the left of the New Labour programme in Westminster, abolishing tuition fees for Scottish university students and granting state support for the elderly in care.

However, under the commanding leadership of **Alex Salmond**, the nationalists took advantage of voter disenchantment with Labour in both Holyrood and Westminster, becoming the largest party in 2007 (by one seat) and forming a minority administration. Four years later, the SNP won an outright parliamentary majority and immediately called a referendum on independence, to be held in 2014. The referendum had an incredible energizing effect on the political scene in Scotland – the debate politicized a whole new generation, and as the campaign went on, the impossible – Scottish independence – began to look possible. Opinion polls in the final weeks before the vote gave the Yes vote a slim majority, but in the end, predictions of economic chaos tipped the balance and the No vote won 55 to 45 – the turnout (85 percent) was a UK record for any election.

Having lost the argument for independence, some predicted the demise of the SNP. Yet, despite the resignation of Alex Salmond, the SNP went from strength to strength, with **Nicola Sturgeon**, the extremely popular new leader, leading the party to victory in all but one of the Scottish Westminster constituencies in the 2015 general election – a record never before achieved by any party.

The 2016 Holyrood elections saw Scotland's political landscape change again, leaving SNP just shy of an outright majority, the Conservatives in second place and women

2011	2013	2014
The Scottish National Party win a majority in the Scottish Parliament.	Andy Murray becomes the first Scot to win Wimbledon men's singles title since 1896.	Scotland votes against independence in a referendum.

leading all three of the country's major political parties. That same year saw the **Brexit** referendum, in which 52 percent of UK voters opted to leave the EU, though in Scotland 62 percent voted to remain in the EU, prompting many within the SNP to call for another independence referendum; recent polls suggest that decided voters are evenly split on the issue of Scottish independence.

Following the failure of the UK parliament to approve a withdrawal agreement by the end of the proposed leaving date (31 October 2019), an extension was granted by the EU, and the UK officially exited the EU on 31 January 2020.

The Scottish economy

Scotland has benefited from the economic prosperity enjoyed in the UK as a whole, but the decline of heavy industry has been all but total, and **unemployment** has produced profound social problems in parts of Glasgow, Edinburgh and smaller towns. Meanwhile, in Orkney, Shetland and in northeast Scotland, particularly around Aberdeen, the **oil industry** – although well past its boom – continues to underpin an economy which might otherwise have struggled to cope with the uncertainties of agriculture and, especially, **fishing**. In spite of encouraging signs of recent progress, the Highlands and Islands remain an economically fragile area that needs special measures, distance from markets being a fundamental problem. Increasingly, the local environment is seen as a major asset, and the establishment of a system of **National Parks** has gone some way to creating a firm framework in which tourism can develop alongside local communities and the interests of the natural world. That said, this has also led to some recent, and very well documented, problems, not least the phenomenal success of the North Coast 500 (see page 420), which, due to the sheer volume of people now undertaking this route, has placed enormous strain on much of the local infrastructure.

The Scottish economy, like the rest of the world, was hit hard by the Covid-19 pandemic. At the time of writing, there had been around 1.94 million cases and over 12,000 deaths. Due to a successful vaccination program, Scotland is recovering and is welcoming travellers once again.

2016	**2020**	**2022**
Scotland votes to remain within the EU, but the UK as a whole votes to leave.	The UK officially leaves the EU on 31 January.	Scotland slowly comes out of the Covid-19 pandemic and eases restrictions. The Scottish National Party wins the election.

Books

Scottish writing is alive and well and so prolific that it can be difficult to keep up with it. This selection covers both classic and modern, and titles marked with ★ are particularly recommended.

FICTION

★ **Iain Banks** *The Bridge, The Crow Road, Espedair Street, A Song of Stone, The Wasp Factory, Dead Air, The Steep Approach to Garbadale*. Just a few titles by this astonishingly prolific author, who also wrote sci-fi as Iain M. Banks. His work can be funny, pacey, thought-provoking, imaginative and downright disgusting, but it is never dull. His final novel, *The Quarry*, was published posthumously in 2013.

Christopher Brookmyre *One Fine Day in the Middle of the Night, The Sacred Art of Stealing, A Tale Etched in Blood and Hard Black Pencil* and *Bedlam*. All very funny, inventive novels that refuse to be categorized – you'll probably find them in the crime section, but they're as much politico-satirical.

John Buchan *The Complete Richard Hannay*. This single volume includes *The 39 Steps, Greenmantle, Mr Standfast, The Three Hostages*, and *The Island of Sheep*. Good gung-ho stories with a great feel for the Scottish landscape. Less well known, but better, are Buchan's historical romances such as *Midwinter*, a Jacobite thriller, and *Witch Wood*, a tale of religious strife in the seventeenth century.

Anne Donovan *Hieroglyphics*, her first collection of short stories, and *Budda Da*, her hilarious first novel, were both nominated for major prizes, and rightly so. Her novel *Being Emily* is about growing up in Glasgow.

★ **Lewis Grassic Gibbon** *A Scots Quair*. A landmark trilogy set in northeast Scotland during and after World War I, the events seen through the eyes of Chris Guthrie, torn between her love for the land and her desire to escape a peasant culture.

Alasdair Gray *Lanark: A Life in Four Books*. A postmodern blend of social realism and labyrinthine fantasy. Gray's extraordinary debut as a novelist, featuring his own allegorical illustrations, takes invention and comprehension to their limits.

★ **Neil M. Gunn** *The Silver Darlings*. Probably Gunn's most representative and best-known book, evocatively set on the northeast coast and telling the story of herring fishermen during the great years of the industry.

James Hogg *The Private Memoirs and Confessions of a Justified Sinner*. Complex, dark mid-nineteenth-century novel dealing with possession, myth and folklore, looking at the confession of an Edinburgh murderer from three different points of view.

Jackie Kay *Trumpet*. The protagonist is dead before the novel begins. He was a Black Scottish jazz trumpeter, who

left a wife in mourning and a son in deep shock when the posthumous medical report revealed him to be a woman. *Red Dust Road* is a warm and moving memoir of growing up Black, gay and adopted in 1960s Glasgow. Kay is also a well-regarded poet (see page 576).

James Kelman *Busconductor Hines*. The wildly funny story of a young Glasgow bus conductor with an intensely boring job and a limitless imagination. *How Late it Was, How Late* is Kelman's Booker Prize–winning and disturbing look at life as seen through the eyes of a foul-mouthed, blind Glaswegian drunk.

★ **A.L. Kennedy** *Looking for the Possible Dance*. This talented writer dissects the difficulties of human relationships on a personal and wider social level. More recent novels *Original Bliss* and *Paradise* have the same deft touch, as do her collections of short stories, *Indelible Acts* and *What Becomes*.

Alexander McCall Smith *44 Scotland Street* and *The Sunday Philosophy Club* series. Prolific author of feel-good novels set in middle-class Edinburgh: the *44 Scotland Street* series centres on the occupants of the address and *The Sunday Philosophy Club* novels are gentle detective yarns with a female amateur sleuth.

Naomi Mitchison *The Bull Calves* is set in 1747 and comments on the terrible aftermath of the Jacobite uprising. *Lobster on the Agenda*, written in 1952, closely mirrors contemporary life in Kintyre where Mitchison lived.

★ **Ian Rankin** *The Hanging Garden, The Falls* and *Fleshmarket Close*. Superbly plotted dark stories featuring Rebus, the famous maverick police detective who haunts the bars of Edinburgh. Made into a TV series and the subject of a guided tour in the city. Rebus retired in *Exit Music*, but returned in *Standing in Another Man's Grave*.

Sir Walter Scott *The Waverley Novels*. The books that did much to create the romanticized version of Scottish life and history.

Muriel Spark *The Prime of Miss Jean Brodie*. Wonderful evocation of middle-class Edinburgh life and aspirations.

Robert Louis Stevenson *Dr Jekyll and Mr Hyde, The Master of Ballantrae, Weir of Hermiston*. Nineteenth-century tales of intrigue and adventure.

★ **Alan Warner** *Morvern Callar*. Bleakly humorous story of a supermarket shelf-packer from Oban who finds her boyfriend has committed suicide in her kitchen. It'll grip you. *The Sopranos* is the story of five teenage convent choir girls who go to Edinburgh for a competition, full of an explosive mixture of adolescent sexuality and naivety. Its sequel, *The Stars in the Bright Sky*, sees them off on holiday. *The Dead Man's Pedal* is a teenage boy's rite of passage in small-town Scotland in the 1970s.

★ **Irvine Welsh** *Irvine Welsh Omnibus*. A compendium including *Trainspotting*, *The Acid House* and *Marabou Stork Nightmares*, all of which can also be found as separate titles.

Welsh trawls through the horrors of drug addiction, sexual fantasy, urban decay and hopeless youth but, thankfully, his unflinching attention is not without humour. *Skagboys*, is a prequel to *Trainspotting*; while *A Decent Ride* is set in the same dark underworld. His latest effort, *The Blade Artist*, revisits the life and times of Begbie, one of the central characters in *Trainspotting*.

POETRY

Robert Burns *Selected Poems*. Scotland's most famous bard (see page 161). Immensely popular all over the world, his best-known works are his earlier ones, including '*Auld Lang Syne*' and '*A Red, Red Rose*'.

Douglas Dunn *New Selected Poems 1964–2000*. A writer of delicately wrought poetry, ranging from the intensely private to poems involved with Scottish issues.

Kathleen Jamie *The Queen of Sheba, Jizzen and The Tree House*. Although often set in Scotland, her work has a wider significance; its tone is strong, almost angry, and its themes both personal and universal. *Findings* is a prose journal of her travels around her native Scotland. In her latest, *The Bonniest Companie*, Jamie set out to write a poem a week during the independence referendum year of 2014. Jamie was appointed Makar in 2021.

Jackie Kay *The Adoption Papers, Other Lovers* and *Life Mask*. Kay explores being Black, Scottish and gay and deals with personal relationships in an accessibly intimate way. *Fiere* is the poetic counterpoint to her memoir *Red Dust Road*.

★ **Liz Lochhead** *Bagpipe Muzak*. In a strong straightforward style, coupled with shrewd observations, Lochhead speaks with immediacy on personal relationships. Some of her best work is in *The Colour of Black & White: Poems (1984–2003)*. *Fugitive Colours* was written during her time as Makar (2011–16).

★ **Norman MacCaig** *Selected Poems*. Justly celebrated for its keen observation of the natural world, MacCaig's work remains intellectually challenging without being arid. His poetry, rooted in the Highlands, uses detail to explore a universal landscape.

Hugh MacDiarmid *Selected Poems*. Immensely influential, not least for his nationalist views and use of Scots, MacDiarmid's poetry is richly challenging. His poem

'*A Drunk Man Looks at a Thistle*' is acknowledged as a masterpiece of Scottish literature.

★ **George Mackay Brown** *Collected Poems*. Brown's work is as haunting, beautiful and gritty as the Orkney islands that inspire it. *Travellers*, published posthumously, features work either previously unpublished or which had appeared only in newspapers and periodicals.

Sorley Maclean (Somhairle MacGill-Eain) *From Wood to Ridge: Collected Poems*. Written in Gaelic, his poems have been translated in bilingual editions all over the world, and deal with the sorrows of poverty, war and love.

McMillan and Byrne (eds) *Modern Scottish Women Poets*. The work of more than a hundred women writers of the twentieth century, some of whom have sunk into undeserved obscurity.

Edwin Morgan *New Selected Poems*. A love of words and their sounds is evident in Morgan's poems, which are refreshingly varied and often experimental, he commented on the Scottish scene with shrewdness and humour.

Edwin Muir *Collected Poems*. Muir's idyllic childhood on Orkney at the turn of the twentieth century remained with him as a dream of paradise in contrast to his later life in inhospitable Glasgow. His poems are passionately concerned with Scotland.

Don Paterson *God's Gift to Women, Landing Light, Nil Nil, and 40 Sonnets*. The only poet to have won the T.S. Eliot Prize twice, he is deservedly much respected.

Iain Crichton Smith *Collected Poems*. Born on the Isle of Lewis, Crichton Smith wrote with feeling and sometimes bitterness, in both Gaelic and English, of the life of the rural communities, the iniquities of the Free Church, the need to revive Gaelic culture and the glory of the Scottish landscape.

HISTORY, POLITICS AND CULTURE

★ **Neal Ascherson** *Stone Voices*. Intelligent, thought-provoking ponderings on the nature of Scotland and the road to devolution, interspersed with personal anecdotes.

Bella Bathurst *The Lighthouse Stevensons*. Straightforward account of the fascinating lives and amazing achievements of Robert Louis Stevenson's family, who built many of the island lighthouses round Scotland.

Colin Bell *Scotland's Century – An Autobiography of the Nation*. Richly illustrated and readable account of the social

history of Scotland, based on radio interviews with people from all walks of life.

Tom Devine *The Scottish Nation 1700–2000*. The best post-Union history, from the last Scottish Parliament to the new one.

Rosemary Goring *Scotland: The Autobiography: 2000 Years of Scottish History by Those Who Saw it Happen*. Fascinating first-hand accounts from the likes of Tacitus, Mary, Queen of Scots, Oliver Cromwell, Adam Smith, Billy

Connolly, as well as ordinary people.

★ **David Howarth** *The Shetland Bus*. Wonderfully detailed story of the espionage and resistance operations carried out from Shetland by British and Norwegian servicemen, written by someone who was directly involved.

Fitzroy Maclean *Bonnie Prince Charlie*. Very readable and more or less definitive biography of Scotland's most romanticized historical figure, written by the 'real' James Bond.

Alistair Moffat *Border Reivers*. A vivid account of nearly three hundred years of savage raiding and mayhem which makes us look at the now peaceful area with different eyes.

T.C. Smout *A History of the Scottish People 1560–1830* and *A Century of the Scottish People 1830–1950*. Widely acclaimed books, of particular interest to those keen on social history. Smout combines enormous learning with a clear and entertaining style.

ART, ARCHITECTURE AND HISTORIC SITES

Jude Burkhauser *Glasgow Girls: Women in Art and Design 1880–1920*. The lively contribution of women to the development of the Glaswegian Art Nouveau movement is recognized in this authoritative account.

Alan Crawford *Charles Rennie Mackintosh*. Part of the World of Art series, describing the major contribution of Scotland's premier architect and designer.

Philip Long and Elizabeth Cumming *The Scottish Colourists 1900–30*. A recognition of the importance of the

work of this group of artists; lavishly illustrated.

★ **Duncan MacMillan** *Scottish Art 1460–1990*. Overview of Scottish painting with good sections on landscape, portraiture and the Glasgow Boys. *Scottish Art in the 20th Century 1890–2001* offers a detailed look at modern art.

Steven Parissien *Adam Style*. A well-illustrated account of the birth of the Neoclassical style, named after the Scottish Adam brothers, Robert and James.

MEMOIRS AND TRAVELOGUES

Patrick Baker *The Cairngorms: A Secret History*. Compelling account of this spellbinding, yet still relatively little known about, mountain range, incorporating nuggets like the search for the elusive wildcat to the discovery of aircraft wreckage. A terrific companion if you're planning to spend any time in the area.

Patrick Barkham *Islander*. In this wonderful book, the acclaimed natural history writer embarks upon an enlightening trawl around some of Britain's smaller islands, including, in Scotland, Barra, Eigg and Orkney – and you'll want to visit them too after reading this.

★ **Madeleine Bunting** *Love of Country: A Hebridean Journey*. The author's journey through the islands of Scotland's northwest coast, undertaken over a six-year period, is a luminous portrayal of the region's myriad different landscapes, as well as its complex history.

★ **Elizabeth Grant of Rothiemurchus** *Memoirs of a Highland Lady*. Hugely readable recollections written with wit and perception at the turn of the eighteenth century, charting social changes in Edinburgh, London and Speyside.

Hamish Haswell-Smith *The Scottish Islands*. An exhaustive and impressive gazetteer with maps and absorbing information on all the Scottish islands. Filled with attractive sketches and paintings, the book is breathtaking in its thoroughness and lovingly gathered detail.

★ **Samuel Johnson and James Boswell** *A Journey to the Western Isles of Scotland* and *The Journal of a Tour to the Hebrides*. Lively accounts of a famous journey around the islands taken by the great lexicographer Dr Samuel Johnson and his biographer and friend James Boswell.

John Lister-Kaye *Song of the Rolling Earth*. The author tells what led him to become a passionate naturalist and turn a derelict Highland estate into a field study centre where he encourages others to live in harmony with the natural environment. An inspiring story.

George Mackay Brown *Letters from Hamnavoe*. A selection of writings from a weekly column in *The Orcadian*, chronicling everyday life in Orkney during the early 1970s. Gentle and perceptive.

Alasdair MacLean *Night Falls on Ardnamurchan*. A classic story of the life and death of the Highland crofting community in which the author grew up.

Alastair McIntosh *Poacher's Pilgrimage: An Island Journey*. The author, who grew up on Lewis, undertakes a return pilgrimage to the island, as well as to Harris to the south, in what is a warm, poetic, and occasionally very funny, book.

★ **Alistair Moffat** *The Hidden Ways*. In this eminently readable book, the insatiable historian sheds fascinating light on some of Scotland's lesser known drove roads, walking a dozen or so of them from the Borders to the Highlands; by turns informative and engaging.

Robert Louis Stevenson *Edinburgh: Picturesque Notes*. First published in 1879, this is a charming evocation of Stevenson's birthplace – its moods, curiosities and influences on his work.

Betsy Whyte *The Yellow on the Broom*. A fascinating glimpse of childhood in a traveller family between the wars, both on the road and in council housing for part of the year to comply with school attendance. *Red Rowans* and *Wild Honey* continue the story.

Language

Language is a thorny, complex and often highly political issue in Scotland. If you're not from Scotland yourself, you're most likely to be addressed in a variety of English, spoken in a Scottish accent. Even then, you're likely to hear phrases and words that are part of what is known as Scots, now officially recognized as a distinct language in its own right. To a lesser extent, Gaelic, too, remains a living language, particularly in the *Gàidhealtachd* or Gaelic-speaking areas of the northwest Highlands, Western Isles, parts of Skye and a few scattered Hebridean islands. In Orkney and Shetland, the local dialect of Scots contains many words carried over from Norn, the Old Norse language spoken in the Northern Isles from the time of the Vikings until the eighteenth century.

Scots

Scots began life as a northern branch of Anglo-Saxon, emerging as a distinct language in the Middle Ages. From the 1370s until the Union in 1707, it was the country's main literary and documentary language. Since the eighteenth century, however, it has been systematically repressed to give preference to English.

Robert 'Rabbie' Burns is the most obvious literary exponent of the Scots language, but there was a revival in the last century led by poets such as Hugh MacDiarmid. Only recently has Scots enjoyed something of a renaissance, getting itself on the Scottish school curriculum in 1996, and achieving official recognition as a distinct language in 1998. Despite these enormous political achievements, many people (rightly or wrongly) still regard Scots as a dialect of English. For more on the Scots language, visit Ⓦ sco.wikipedia.org.

Gaelic

Scottish **Gaelic**, (*Gàidhlig*, pronounced 'gallic') is one of the four Celtic languages to survive into the modern age (Welsh, Breton and Irish Gaelic are the other three). Manx, the old language of the Isle of Man, died out early last century, while Cornish was finished as a community language in the eighteenth century. Scottish Gaelic is most closely related to Irish Gaelic and Manx – hardly surprising since Gaelic was introduced to Scotland from Ireland around the third century BC. Some still argue that Scottish Gaelic is merely a dialect of its parent language, Irish Gaelic, and indeed the two languages remain more or less mutually intelligible. From the fifth to the twelfth centuries, Gaelic enjoyed an expansionist phase, thanks partly to the backing of the Celtic Church in Iona.

Since then, Gaelic has been in steady decline. Even before the Union with England, power, religious ideology and wealth gradually passed into non-Gaelic hands. The royal court was transferred to Edinburgh and an Anglo-Norman legal system was put in place. The Celtic Church was Romanized by the introduction of foreign clergy, and, most important of all, English and Flemish merchants colonized the new trading towns of the east coast. In addition, the pro-English attitudes held by the Covenanters led to strong anti-Gaelic feeling within the Church of Scotland from its inception.

The two abortive Jacobite rebellions of 1715 and 1745 furthered the language's decline, as did the Clearances that took place in the Gaelic-speaking Highlands from the 1770s to the 1850s, which forced thousands to migrate to central Scotland's new industrial belt or emigrate to North America. Although efforts were made to halt the decline in the first half of the nineteenth century, the 1872 Education Act gave no official recognition to Gaelic, and children were severely punished if they were caught speaking the language in school.

The 2011 census put the number of Gaelic-speakers at under 60,000 (just over one percent of the population), the majority of whom live in the **Gàidhealtachd**, though there is thought to be an extended Gaelic community of perhaps 250,000 who have some understanding of the language. Since the 1980s, great efforts have been made to try and save the language, including the introduction of bilingual primary and nursery schools, and a huge increase in the amount of broadcasting time given to Gaelic-language and Gaelic music programmes, and the establishment of highly successful Gaelic colleges such as Sabhal Mòr Ostaig (ⓦsmo.uhi.ac.uk).

Gaelic grammar and pronunciation

Gaelic is a highly complex tongue, with a fiendish, antiquated **grammar** and, with only eighteen letters, an intimidating system of spelling. **Pronunciation** is easier than it appears at first glance; one general rule to remember is that the stress always falls on the first syllable of a word. The general rule of syntax is that the verb starts the sentence whether it's a question or not, followed by the subject and then the object; adjectives generally follow the word they are describing.

SHORT AND LONG VOWELS

Gaelic has both short and long vowels, the latter being denoted by an acute or grave accent.

a as in cat; before nn and ll, as in cow
à as in bar
e as in pet
é like rain
i as in sight

í like free
o as in pot
ò like enthral
ó like cow
u like scoot
ù like loo

VOWEL COMBINATIONS

Gaelic is littered with diphthongs, which, rather like in English, can be pronounced in several different ways depending on the individual word.

ai like cat, or pet; before dh or gh, like street
ao like the sound in the middle of colonel
ea like pet, or cat, and sometimes like mate; before ll or nn like cow

èa as in hear
ei like mate
eu like train, or fear
ia like fear
io like fear, or shorter than street
ua like wooer

CONSONANTS

The consonants listed below are those that differ substantially from the English.

b at the beginning of a word like the **b** in big; in the middle/end of a word like the **p** in pair
bh at the beginning of a word like the **v** in van; elsewhere it is silent
c as in cat; after a vowel it has aspiration before it
ch always as in loch, never as in church
cn like the **cr** in crowd
d like the **d** in dog, but with the tongue pressed against the back of the upper teeth; at the beginning of a word or before e or i, like the **j** in jam; in the middle

or at the end of a word like the **t** in cat; after i like the **ch** in church
dh before and after a, o or u is an aspirated **g**, rather like a gargle; before e or i like the **y** in yes; elsewhere silent
fh usually silent; sometimes like the **h** in house
g at the beginning of a word as in get; before e like the **y** in yes; in the middle or end of a word like the **ck** in sock; after i like the **ch** in loch
gh at the beginning of a word as in get; before or after a, o or u rather like a gargle; after i sometimes like the **y** in gay, but often silent

l after i and sometimes before e like the **l** in lot; elsewhere a peculiarly Gaelic sound, produced by flattening the front of the tongue against the palate

mh like the **v** in van

p at the beginning of a word as in pet; elsewhere it has aspiration before it

rt pronounced as **sht**

s before e or i like the **sh** in ship; otherwise as in English

sh before a, o or u like the **h** in house; before e like the **ch** in loch

t before e or i like the **ch** in church; in the middle or at the end of a word it has - aspiration before it; otherwise as in English

th at the beginning of a word, like the **h** in house; elsewhere, and in the word *thu* (you), silent

GAELIC PHRASES, VOCABULARY AND COURSES

One of the best introductory **teach-yourself Gaelic** courses is *Speaking Our Language* by Richard Cox, based on the TV series, much of which you can watch on YouTube. If you just want to get better at pronouncing Gaelic words, try *Blas na Gàidhlig* by Michael Bauer, or for a phrasebook, your best bet is *Everyday Gaelic* by Morag MacNeill. You can also do some self-learning on the Gaelic section of the BBC website ⓦ bbc.co.uk.

GREETINGS AND BASIC WORDS

yes tha
no chan eil
hello hallo
how are you? ciamar a tha thu?
fine tha gu math
thank you tapadh leat
welcome fàilte
come in thig a-staigh
good day latha math
goodbye mar sin leat
goodnight oidhche mhath

cheers slàinte
yesterday an-dé
today an-diugh
tomorrow maireach
hotel taigh-òsda
house taigh
story sgeul
song òran
music ceòl
book leabhar
bread aran
water uisge
whisky uisge beatha
post office post oifis
Edinburgh Dun Eideann
Glasgow Glaschu
America Ameireaga
Ireland Éire
England Sasainn
London Lunnain

GAELIC GEOGRAPHICAL AND PLACE-NAME TERMS

The purpose of this list is to help with place-name derivations from Gaelic and with more detailed map reading.

abhainn river
ach or auch, from achadh field
ail, aileach rock
Alba Scotland
aonach ridge
ard, ardan or arden, from àird a point of land or height
aros dwelling
ault, from allt stream
bad brake or clump of trees
bagh bay
bal or bally, from baile town, village
balloch, from bealach mountain pass
ban white or fair
bàrr summit
beg, from beag small
ben, from beinn mountain
blair, from blàr field or battlefield

cairn, from càrn pile of stones
camas bay or harbour
cnoc hill
coll or colly, from coille wood or forest
corran a spit or point jutting into the sea
corrie, from coire round hollow in mountainside or whirlpool
craig, from creag rock or crag
cruach bold hill
drum, from druim ridge
dubh black
dun or dum, from dùn fort
eilean island
ess, from eas waterfall
fin, from fionn white
gair or gare, from geàrr short
garv, from garbh rough
geodha cove
glen, from gleann valley
gower or gour, from gabhar goat
inch, from innis meadow or island

inver, from inbhir river mouth
ken or kin, from ceann head
knock, from cnoc hill
kyle, from caolas narrow strait
lag hollow
larach site of an old ruin
liath grey
loch lake
meall round hill
mon, from monadh hill
more, from mór large, great
rannoch, from raineach bracken
ross, from ros promontory

rubha promontory
sgeir sea rock
sgurr sharp point
sron nose, prow or promontory
strath, from srath broad valley
tarbet, from tairbeart isthmus
tigh house
tir or tyre, from tìr land
torr hill, castle
tràigh shore
uig shelter
uisge water

Norn and Norse terms

Between the tenth and seventeenth centuries, the chief language of Orkney and Shetland was Norn, a Scandinavian tongue close to modern Faroese and Icelandic. After the end of Norse rule, and with the transformation of the Church, the law, commerce and education, Norn gradually lost out to Scots and English, eventually petering out completely in the eighteenth century. Today, Orkney and Shetland have their own **dialects**, and individual islands and communities within each group have local variations. The dialects have a Scots base, with some Old Norse words; however, they don't sound strongly Scottish, with the Orkney accent – which has been likened to the Welsh one – especially distinctive. Listed below are some of the words you're most likely to hear, plus some terms that appear in place names, not just in Orkney and Shetland, but also in parts of the Hebrides.

NORN PHRASES AND VOCABULARY

ayre beach
bister farm
böd fisherman's store
bruck rubbish
burra heath rush
crö sheepfold
eela rod-fishing from small boats
ferrylouper incomer (Orkney)
fourareen four-oared boat
foy party or festival
geo coastal inlet
haa laird's house
hap hand-knitted shawl
howe mound
kame ridge of hills
kishie basket
mool headland

moorit brown
mootie tiny
muckle large
noost hollow place where a boat is drawn up
noup steep headland
peerie/peedie small
plantiecrub/plantiecrö small dry-stone enclosure for growing cabbages
quoy enclosed, cultivated common land
roost tide race
scattald common grazing land
scord gap or pass in a ridge of hills
setter farm
shaela dark grey
sixern/sixareen six-oared boat
soothmoother incomer (Shetland)
voe sea inlet

Glossary

Auld Old

Bairn Baby

Ben Hill or mountain

Black house Thick-walled traditional dwelling

Bonnie Pretty

Bothy Primitive cottage, hut or mountain shelter

Brae Slope or hill

Brig Bridge

Broch Circular prehistoric stone fort

Burn Small stream or brook

Byre Shelter for cattle; cottage

Cairn Mound of stones

CalMac Caledonian MacBrayne ferry company

Ceilidh (pronounced 'kay-lee') Social gathering involving dancing, drinking, singing and storytelling

Central belt Central Scotland between the Forth and Clyde including Edinburgh and Glasgow

Clan Extended family

Clearances Evictions from the Highlands

Corbett A mountain between 2500ft and 3000ft high

Covenanters Supporters of the Presbyterian Church in the seventeenth century

Crannog Celtic lake or bog dwelling

Croft Small plot of farmland with house, common in the Highlands

Dirk A long dagger

Dolmen Grave chamber

Dram Literally, one-sixteenth of a fluid ounce, usually refers to any small measure of whisky

Dun Fortified mound

Firth A wide sea inlet or estuary

Gàidhealtachd Gaeldom, Highlands or Gaelic-speaking area

Gillie Personal guide used on hunting or fishing trips

Glen Deep, narrow mountain valley

Harling Limestone and gravel mix used to cover buildings

Hogmanay New Year's Eve

Howff Meeting place; pub

HES Historic Environment Scotland, a government-funded heritage organization

Jacobite Supporter of the Stewart claim to the throne, most famously Bonnie Prince Charlie

Kilt Knee-length tartan skirt worn by Highland men

Kirk Church

Laird Landowner

Law Rounded hill

Links Grassy coastal land; coastal golf course

Loch Lake

Lochan Little loch

Mac/Mc These prefixes in Scottish surnames derive from the Gaelic, meaning 'son of'. In Scots 'Mac' is used for both sexes. In Gaelic 'Nic' is used for women: Donnchadh Mac Aoidh is Duncan MacKay, Iseabail Nic Aoidh is Isabel MacKay

Machair Sandy, grassy, lime-rich coastal land, generally used for grazing

Manse Official home of a Presbyterian minister

Mercat Cross lit. Market Cross

Munro A mountain over 3000ft high

Munro-bagging The sport of trying to climb as many Munros as possible

NTS The National Trust for Scotland, a heritage organization

Peel Fortified tower, built to withstand Border raids

Pend Archway or vaulted passage

Presbyterian The form of Church government used in the official (Protestant) Church of Scotland, established by John Knox during the Reformation

RIB Rigid inflatable boat

Runrig A common form of farming in which separate ridges are cultivated by different occupiers under joint agreement

Sassenach Derives from the Gaelic **Sasunnach**, meaning literally 'Saxon'; used by Scots to describe the English

Scottish Baronial Style of architecture favoured by the Scottish land-owning class featuring stepped gables and round turrets

Sheila na gig Female fertility symbol, usually a naked woman displaying her vulva

Shinty Stick and ball game played in the Highlands, with similarities to hockey

Smiddy Smithy

SNH Scottish Natural Heritage, a government-funded conservation body

SNP Scottish National Party

Sporran Leather purse worn in front of, or at the side of, a kilt

Tartan Check-patterned woollen cloth

Thane A landowner of high rank; the chief of a clan

Trews Tartan trousers

Wee Small

Wee Frees Followers of the Free Presbyterian or Free Church of Scotland

Wynd Narrow lane

Yett Gate or door

Small print and index

A ROUGH GUIDE TO ROUGH GUIDES

Published in 1982, the first Rough Guide – to Greece – was a student scheme that became a publishing phenomenon. Mark Ellingham, a recent graduate in English from Bristol University, had been travelling in Greece the previous summer and couldn't find the right guidebook. With a small group of friends he wrote his own guide, combining a contemporary, journalistic style with a thoroughly practical approach to travellers' needs.

The immediate success of the book spawned a series that rapidly covered dozens of destinations. And, in addition to impecunious backpackers, Rough Guides soon acquired a much broader readership that relished the guides' wit and inquisitiveness as much as their enthusiastic, critical approach and value-for-money ethos. These days, Rough Guides include recommendations from budget to luxury and cover more than 120 destinations around the globe, from Amsterdam to Zanzibar, all regularly updated by our team of roaming writers.

Browse all our latest guides, read inspirational features and book your trip at **roughguides.com**.

Rough Guide credits

Editors: Zara Sekhavati, Philippa MacKenzie
Cartography: Carte
Picture editor: Piotr Kala

Layout: Pradeep Thapliyal
Head of DTP and Pre-Press: Katie Bennett
Head of Publishing: Kate Drynan

Publishing information

Thirteenth edition 2022

Distribution

UK, Ireland and Europe
Apa Publications (UK) Ltd; sales@roughguides.com
United States and Canada
Ingram Publisher Services; ips@ingramcontent.com
Australia and New Zealand
Booktopia; retailer@ booktopia.com.au
Worldwide
Apa Publications (UK) Ltd; sales@roughguides.com

Special Sales, Content Licensing and CoPublishing
Rough Guides can be purchased in bulk quantities
at discounted prices. We can create special editions,
personalised jackets and corporate imprints tailored to
your needs. sales@roughguides.com.
roughguides.com

Printed in Spain

Help us update

We've gone to a lot of effort to ensure that this edition of
The Rough Guide to Scotland is accurate and up-to-date.
However, things change – places get "discovered", opening
hours are notoriously fickle, restaurants and rooms raise
prices or lower standards. If you feel we've got it wrong
or left something out, we'd like to know, and if you can
remember the address, the price, the hours, the phone
number, so much the better.

Please send your comments with the subject
line **"Rough Guide Scotland Update"** to mail@
uk.roughguides.com. We'll credit all contributions and
send a copy of the next edition (or any other Rough Guide
if you prefer) for the very best emails.

ABOUT THE AUTHORS

Norm Longley has spent most of his working life in central/eastern Europe – he is the author
of the Rough Guides to Slovenia and Romania – but more recently has turned his hand to
home shores, contributing to Scotland, Wales and Ireland guides. He lives in Somerset and can
occasionally be seen erecting marquees on the Rec in Bath.

Rachel Mills is a freelance writer and editor based by the sea in Kent. She is a co-author for
Rough Guides to New Zealand, India, Canada, Ireland and Great Britain; a regular contributor
to Telegraph Travel and loveEXPLORING.com; and an expert in sustainable, responsible
tourism. Follow her @rachmillstravel.

Olivia Rawes is a freelance travel writer and photographer. As well as *The Rough Guide to
Scotland*, she's a co-author for Rough Guides to Yorkshire and Europe on a Budget. She also
writes about travel for various publications including *SUITCASE*, *The Telegraph*, loveEXPLORING.
com and SheerLuxe.

Helena Smith grew up near the Trossach Mountains in Scotland and under Zomba Plateau
in Malawi, two beautiful places which inspired her love of the outdoors. She is a writer,
photographer and co-founder of Wilder, a social enterprise doing wildlife planting in urban
spaces.

Jackie Staddon and **Hilary West** are experienced travel writers, updaters and editors and
have combined their skills over the last 20 years or so to produce a host of guidebooks on
various destinations from around the world. Scotland is one that holds a special place in their
hearts.

Photo credits

(Key: T-top; C-centre; B-bottom; L-left; R-right)

All images **iStock** and **Shutterstock** except:

Dreamstime 14, 19BR, 22B, 290/291

Helena Smith/Rough Guides 52/53, 113, 155, 293, 480/481, 506/507

The Three Chimneys 23T

Cover: Stag in the highlands **Andy Morehouse/Shutterstock**

Index

Map symbols

The symbols below are used on maps throughout the book

International boundary	International airport	Gardens	Battlefield
County boundary	Domestic airport	Whisky distillery	Lighthouse
Chapter boundary	Tourist office	Skiing	Observatory
Motorway	Post office	Golf course	Zoo
Major road	Hospital	Swimming Pool	Nature reserve
Minor road	Internet access	Viewpoint	Abbey
Pedestrian road	Bus stop	Waterfall	Monastery
Steps	Parking	Peak	Chapel
Footpath	Statue	Cave	Building
Railway	Train station	Rocks	Church
Tram line	Point of interest	Cairn(s)	Cemetery
Ferry route	Stately home	Stone circle	Park
Canal	Castle	Standing stone	Forest
Wall	Museum	Ruins/archeological site	Beach

Listings key

- Accommodation
- Eating
- Drinking/nightlife
- Shopping